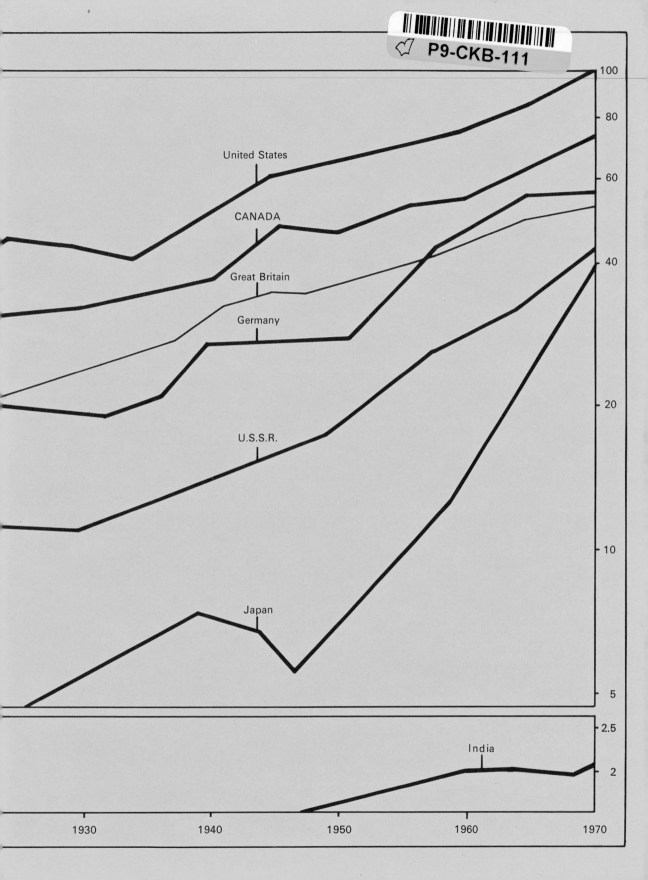

ECONOMICS

ECONOMICS

THIRD CANADIAN EDITION

PAUL A. SAMUELSON
INSTITUTE PROFESSOR
MASSACHUSETTS INSTITUTE OF TECHNOLOGY

ANTHONY SCOTT
PROFESSOR OF ECONOMICS
UNIVERSITY OF BRITISH COLUMBIA

McGRAW-HILL COMPANY OF CANADA LIMITED
TORONTO/MONTREAL/NEW YORK/LONDON/SYDNEY/JOHANNESBURG/MEXICO
PANAMA/DÜSSELDORF/SINGAPORE/RIO DE JANEIRO/KUALA LUMPUR/NEW DELHI

ECONOMICS

THIRD CANADIAN EDITION

Copyright © 1966, 1968, 1971 by McGraw-Hill
Company of Canada Limited. All Rights Reserved.

Adapted from ECONOMICS written by Paul A. Samuelson.
Copyright © 1955, 1958, 1961, 1964, 1967, 1970 by
McGraw-Hill, Inc. All Rights Reserved.
Copyright 1948, 1951 by McGraw-Hill, Inc. All
Rights Reserved.

Library of Congress Catalog Card Number 74-167726.

ISBN 0-07-092863-0

1234567890 BP-71 987654321

Printed and bound in Canada.

PREFACE

This book is an introduction to economics. It is written for a half-year or full-year beginning course and for students who may or may not go on to further study of economics. This edition is an unusually thorough revision of earlier editions.

Economics is an important subject. And experience shows it can also be an exciting one. It deals with inflation and unemployment, with how some people enjoy great wealth and even more live in deadening poverty. A subject is at its liveliest when it faces challenging problems to be solved; so in a sense—now that our cities are blighted, our environment polluted, inflation melts the value of our cash—political economy takes on a cardinal importance in every person's education. Particularly in this edition, I have tried to use the touchstone of "relevance" for my exclusions and inclusions, knowing from experience that this is also the key to reader motivation and interest.

A RIGOROUS INTRODUCTION   Why does a scholar interested in the frontier of research write a textbook? In my case, for two reasons: I sensed that there was coming to be a widening *gap* between the technicalities of advanced economics and what the intelligent nonprofessional has to know about the subject if he is to be a good citizen, a competent statesman, an effective businessman, or a cogent critic or defender of the modern mixed economy. And like economists here and abroad, I lamented the fact that in our generation we did not have any great introductory treatise like those which have become classics in other subjects—*The Principles of Psychology* by William James, *Differential and Integral Calculus* by Richard Courant or *Pure Mathematics* by G. H. Hardy, and in the present age *Lectures on Physics* by the Nobel laureate Richard Feynman.

Eschewing encyclopedic coverage, I have taken their motto for my motto: Nothing unnecessarily hard, but nothing essential being omitted as beyond the grasp of the serious student; and above all, nothing that later will have to be unlearned as wrong.

The reception of the book seems to have been favorable. But a book is like a child, taking on a life of its own. Our knowledge grows, times and problems change, so that no one can embalm and preserve in amber the corpus of a dynamic science.

REVISIONS IN THIS NEW EDITION   Although the most obvious change has been the addition of two new chapters—Chapter 38, "Economic Inequality: Poverty, Affluence, and the Quality of Life," and Chapter 39, "Economic Problems of Cities and Regions, and the Polluted Environment"–all of the book has been thoroughly revised, with no single page going unscathed. And some basic rearrangements of chapter groupings and topics have been introduced in both the macroeconomics and the microeconomics. (E.g., experience suggested that the simple multiplier be brought into Chapter 12's introduction to income determination rather than be left in the following chapter's applications to fiscal policy; and the important Phillips-curve tradeoff between inflation and unemployment has been removed from appendixes and introduced into the main text. Or again, partly through the counsel of various colleagues at MIT and elsewhere, I have drastically changed the chapter groupings of the microeconomic treatment of costs, competitive and otherwise.)

But the biggest change has been a change in the spirit of the book. I have tried to go over every paragraph with a glass to root out complacency and smugness. True, the New Economics has had some great triumphs in scientific content and in successful applications. *But why get rid of one kind of orthodoxy just to replace it by the deadening rule of a new establishment economics?* John Kenneth Galbraith proposes new viewpoints for the new industrial state. Radical economists are knocking at the door, to insist that every facet of our society be subjected to unsparing criticism. Libertarian economists, like Milton Friedman of the University of Chicago, are challenging the consensus of post-Keynesian analysis—not by the naked force of plutocratic intimidation of teachers characteristic of the Joseph McCarthy period—but by deployment of data and the use of logical reasoning. All of these views deserve a dispassionate hearing, and in this edition I try to evaluate cogent criticisms. Equally important, I have hoped to render unto the realm of value judgment that which "neutral, *wertfrei*" scholarship cannot cope with. While it has been toil to update the book and to change its design so that hard things could be made easier, it has been a release and a joy to breathe this new spirit into the work.

TO THE READER   Experience proves that anyone can learn economics from this book—not to become a professional scholar in the field but to gain genuine basic *literacy* in the subject. Experience also shows that an economics text has to be read with care. Each chapter is carefully planned. Each has a comprehensive summary. The diagrams and tables are defined so that each also tells its own story.

No author can tell you how best to read a textbook. Obviously, this is not like a novel or detective story, hammock reading for a drowsy day. The first time you read a chapter, turn its pages for perspective. Then read and underline, not stopping to overcome every difficulty. You will be pleasantly surprised to find that the final summaries and checklists of key concepts will help synthesize your understanding. And on review and rereading—giving independent attention to the self-contained story of the figures and tables—your understanding will deepen. (I should call to your attention the *Study Guide and Workbook*, which has been prepared to go along with this edition. Even if your instructor does not assign it, you may find it a great time-saver in the end.)

You will discover that harder or less important material—they are not always the same!—has been put in appendixes, or often in footnotes. And in this edition I have introduced the innovation of giving some final "Questions For Discussion" that are marked as "extra-credit problems" which enable the highly trained student to pursue on his own some of the fascinating further developments of the subject. If you are in a fast, brief course, don't be put off by this carefully planned layering of more difficult material: experience has proved that this gives the more intensive course meat to bite into, without really inconveniencing those who work with the severest time limitations. And to the bright honors student, may I say: Don't be put off by the attempt to state matters plainly. This book is as challenging as you may care to make it. (Not a few who are now professors have written me to say that they used parts of it in their final review for their Ph.D. oral exams.)

Finally, I've tried to look ahead to what you might still want to know about in 1980. Praise is always sweet to the ears of an author, and it has been pleasant when readers have written to say some kind word about the book. But I must confess that I would have to consider it the highest praise of all if—when the elections of the 1980s come around and the issues of tariffs, the public debt, and the environment are under debate—some of you should pull your old economics textbook down from the shelf for a rethinking of the issues. That would be any author's dream of glory!

TO THE INSTRUCTOR   Some teachers who use this book prefer to teach microeconomics before macroeconomics. A good case can be made for either ordering, and experimental programs show each to have advantages. This text has been carefully designed for either program. The instructor who wishes to deal first with microeconomics can skip from Part One to Part Three, knowing that the exposition and cross references have been tailored with his needs in mind. Because college courses in economics are taught by large-lecture and small-section methods, we have used MIT classrooms as a laboratory, one year trying out lecturing to a large group and another year confining classes to 25 students. A good text must be prepared with both needs in mind.

I have not hesitated to segregate some of the material into appendixes. Often this involves slightly more difficult topics, with which briefer courses can easily dispense. Sometimes, as in the case of the discussion of the stock market in Chapter 4's Appendix or the presentation of cases on supply and demand in Chapter 19's Appendix, the material is not more difficult, but is such as can be conveniently skipped. Occasionally a teacher has written me questioning the advisability of this use of the appendixes. My answer is a pragmatic one based on experimentation: because courses differ in their time span and emphasis, it is incumbent upon an author to give signals as to which sections are organically necessary and which are dispensable. For example, in this edition I have added a brief treatment of von Neumann game theory. The fact that it is put at the end of Chapter 24's Appendix will not inconvenience the reader eager for a terse account of this important subject; but this arrangement will be deemed a blessing by those instructors who lack the time for such a topic.

In this edition, I have particularly emphasized the welfare-economics aspects of competitive and other pricing, putting great stress on "externalities," public goods, and interpersonal-equity considerations. (A term like "Pareto optimality" is named in but one appendix footnote, but the issue of economic efficiency is emphasized as never before.)

A textbook should be dedicated to one's children—of whom I have my share—but they will forgive me for naming my longest-time collaborator, Marion.

Paul A. Samuelson
Cambridge, Massachusetts.
February, 1970

PREFACE
TO THE THIRD
CANADIAN EDITION

The demands of students, different from those of teachers, have been widely consulted in making this new revision of Professor Samuelson's leading text-book. In the first revision the task was broad but simple: to analyze economic events and policies against a background of Canadian data and institutional practices. To this was added some revision of the balance of the book, to reflect the Canadian economist's special concerns: international trade and foreign economic policy, regionalism and federalism, and raw-material production. These revisions did satisfactorily guide several successive groups of readers to the application of non-national principles of analysis to "our" economy, and they did save them from uncertainty about whether statements made in other works about the United States, or Great Britain, applied with equal force in Canada.

Although my revisions have been extensive, the majority of the topics and the purely analytical sections remain much as they are in Professor Samuelson's eighth edition. For these, he is overwhelmingly the senior author. I have tried to make available to Canadian readers an up-to-date, readable introduction to the methods of economics, firmly embedded in a familiar domestic context. Accordingly, I have had to describe a large number of Canadian institutions, often discussing how their functions are performed in other places, especially in the United States. In addition, I have changed the emphasis in many chapters by frequent references to the open nature of the Canadian economy, which makes Canada particularly susceptible to the influence of goods and factors moving from abroad; and I have indicated the impact of this openness on our economic structure and policy.

I was prepared to make many alterations to stress the regional nature of our economy, as opposed to what I had always assumed to be an American emphasis on geographical unity. On close reading, this "difference" turned out to be very much a matter of degree: the American economist is in fact aware of regional differences and the problems they create for national policy. And so, although I added considerable material on this subject, I avoided overemphasizing "regionalism."

Other differences between the two economies (For example, Canada has two official languages, and there is more public ownership, and a higher rate of immigration in Canada than in the United States.) were pointed out where relevant. But the original perception in the revision was paramount: the Canadian economy is part of a worldwide economy, and the Canadian economy works much as others do in this system of linkages and flows.

In this third edition, however, it has become possible to cater much more to the interests of students in their own country's problems. Both supply and demand are responsible. There has been a veritable landslide of sophisticated Canadian studies of the working and performance of our economy, on which revisions of this text can be directly or indirectly based. Contrasted with the shortage of information he faced ten or fifteen years ago, the Canadian economist has, at last, ample material at his disposal which enables him to speak with some authority on a wide spectrum of Canadian issues.

Demand is also responsible. Perhaps because analysis seems much more relevant to Canadian questions, students today show an increased interest not only in the economics of taxation, banking, and the tariff, but also in the economic analyses applicable to separatism, urban issues, foreign ownership, and rural poverty. Canadian readers also are interested in China, socialism, and racial prejudice, but for different reasons than those which apply elsewhere.

These considerations have led to the wholesale revision of chapters or appendices on the Eastern European economy, regionalism, the city, foreign ownership, racial prejudice and language discrimination, and resource policy that should take the interested reader some steps further in his own inquiry into these current questions.

Like its American counterpart, this edition presents the most recent data available and refers to events and studies of current importance. For assistance with this attempt to present a completely accurate picture of the Canadian economic structure, I am greatly indebted to many people. Among my helpers, I should mention Elayne Van Snellenberg, Clive Southey, Mrs. Helen Moore, Mrs. E. V. New, Mrs. Sandy Pearce, Darcy McDowall, Jim Phelps, Peter Victor, and especially Floyd Sully. Among professional colleagues, I would thank Professors Ronald Bodkin, David Bond, John Boyd, D. R. Campbell, Ralph Huenemann, Peter Lusztig, Gordon Munro, R. Pendergast, Gideon Rosenbluth, Ronald Shearer, Russell Uhler, Robert Will, J. H. Young, and an equal number of economists who corresponded helpfully on particular points. Mr. W. A. Beckett and Professor J. E. Latourrette have generously made special statistical compilations available for this edition. As in the previous edition, Dr. Elizabeth Bond deserves the reader's gratitude for her assistance on matters both economic and editorial. The index was prepared by my wife, Barbara. The editors of McGraw-Hill have contributed constructively to the planning and preparation of this edition.

For the student who would like to have additional assistance, a *Study Guide and Workbook* is available. Written by Professor Romney Robinson of the University of Toronto and rewritten for Canadian readers by Professor Gordon Munro of the University of British Columbia, this book has been carefully designed to provide the serious student with a ready means of testing his comprehension of the subject matter.

My greatest debt is to Professor Paul Samuelson who has turned me loose on this project; I must accept all responsibility for the alterations and additions to his earlier editions. My respect and admiration for his work is most clearly demonstrated by my increasing unwillingness to tamper with the analytical portions of his text, which have already served so many Canadian students. The need, in preparing these Canadian editions, to closely scrutinize the structure and wording of his book has impressed me with its breadth and unity. Hence, the disclaimer made at the outset in this Preface: my aim has not been to produce a new work but to bring to Canadians the advantages long afforded American readers by the availability of this book. In this edition, too, I join other Canadian economists in saluting Paul Samuelson on his receiving, in 1970, the Nobel Prize for economics.

Anthony Scott
Vancouver, British Columbia.
June, 1971

CONTENTS

Part 2   Determination of National Income and its Fluctuations

Part 6   Current Economic Problems

PART 1
BASIC
ECONOMIC
CONCEPTS
AND NATIONAL
INCOME

1
INTRODUCTION

The Age of Chivalry is gone; that of sophisters, economists, and calculators has succeeded. EDMUND BURKE

As a scholarly discipline, economics is not yet two centuries old. Adam Smith wrote his path-breaking book, *The Wealth of Nations* in 1776, about seventeen years after the fall of Montcalm, and about thirteen years before George Washington's inauguration as the first president of the United States. And the nearness of timing is no coincidence: political freedom from the tyranny of monarchy was perhaps related to the emancipation of free-market pricing from the interfering hand of state regulation.

Adam Smith, of course, represented only a beginning. In more than the century and a half that elapsed from the publication of *The Wealth of Nations* to the publication of John Maynard Keynes' *General Theory of Employment, Interest and Money* (1936), economics—or political economy, as it used to be called—went through many stages of development. At almost the halfway point, there appeared the massive critique of capitalism by Karl Marx: *Das Kapital* (1867, followed by two posthumous volumes). A billion people, one-third of the world's population, blindly regard *Das Kapital* as economic gospel. And yet, without the disciplined study of economic science, how can anyone form a reasoned opinion about the merits or lack of merits in the classical, traditional economics? Or about the achievements of the "New Economics" that has evolved since 1929? Or about the problems unsolved?

■ FOR WHOM THE BELL TOLLS

Few study economics merely to judge the merits in the grand debates concerning historic capitalism, the modern mixed economy, or the collectivist economic systems of the East. One studies economics to answer many and diverse questions. Here are some of the more common ones.

> Is old-fashioned poverty from niggardliness of nature extinct? And what about "poverty midst plenty" as in the post-1929 Great Depression when factories lay idle and people couldn't find jobs? Has this given way to the modern pockets of poverty in various parts of Canada?

POVERTY, DEVELOPMENT, AND AFFLUENCE We grow more prosperous each year, and our present affluence is an outgrowth of the lower standard of productivity prevailing in past generations. In recent years all over the world, men have become preoccupied with economic development.

> How can preindustrial economies, teeming with masses of people and poorly endowed with natural resources, break through the vicious circle of poverty and backwardness? How can policies be formulated and programs be promulgated that will speed the pace of *economic growth and development?*

Look at the front flyleaf: Contrast the Western world's affluence with the poverty of India, whose growth curve barely shows on the chart; and note the success story of Japan within its century of contact with the modern world.

Undoubtedly this new interest in development and growth has made economics an exciting and vital subject both in the capitals of the world and in isolated regions.

PERSONAL STAKE IN ECONOMICS An even more immediate reason for studying economics is that it deals with many of the matters that will concern us most:

> What kinds of jobs are available? What do they pay? How much in goods will a dollar of wages buy now, and how much in a time of galloping inflation? What are the chances of "bad times" when a man cannot find work? Will there always be buyers for the crops of farmers and the yields of fishermen? Are the black days of the depressed 1930s likely to return? Will automation and scientific discovery make man obsolete? How can one make a killing in the stock market? Or best run a business?

ECONOMICS FOR THE CITIZEN Beyond personal family matters, economics also deals with political decisions in which each citizen must participate. Here are a dozen vital problems:

> Will the government add to my taxes to help unemployed miners, or are there other things it can do to help mitigate the problem of unemployment? Should I vote to build a new school and road now, or vote to put this aside until business slackens and cement prices come down and jobs are needed? Should I vote to keep married women out of public employment, so there will be more jobs for men? What about combines legislation that purports to fight monopolies?
> If you are a humanitarian, deeply concerned to improve the lot of the poor, the disadvantaged immigrant, and the aged, will legislating a good, stiff, high minimum wage serve to help or hinder the good cause for which you fight?
> Why not "fair-share" rationing?
> What consequences will follow if the federal budget is not balanced in every year? Is it true that the prosperity of the Western world is dependent on military expenditures? Need peace, or the "threat of peace," cause unemployment in our factories and our mines? Should our government wash its hands of this problem, relying on individual entrepreneurship and private demand to replace spontaneously our wartime export markets?

ECONOMICS AND NATIONAL SECURITY As even Adam Smith said, security is even more important for a nation than opulence. Survival itself can depend on economics. Canadian nationalism today indicates a new determination to survive as a separate entity. How much should be spent on developing an independent military strength? Can economic modes of calculation indicate an optimum defense policy somewhere between the extremes of economically ruinous military expenditures and total dependence on the United States for national security? What determines how much a country can afford to spend on armed forces? Is it worthwhile running the risk of inflation in order to spend more?

Another aspect of security and defense demands the attention of economists. Much of the "cold war," and the struggle in Southeast Asia, has consisted of conflicts between different types of economic systems. Which system promises the highest level of national wealth at the earliest possible time? Will such a system lead to economic dominance for the country which adopts it? Is it necessary for the achievement of military power, or of national independence? If, for example, the United States falls behind the Soviet Union economically, would the world be prey to the latter country militarily?

An introduction can serve as a preview. Figure 1-1 shows in one graphic

Will the gap narrow?

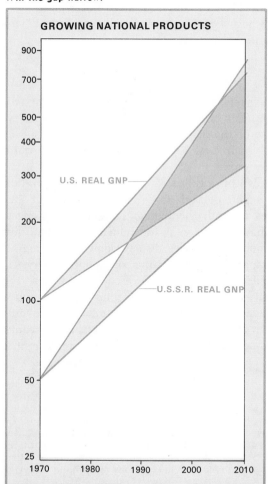

FIG. 1-1. The range of estimates shown here can make no claim to accuracy, but they do portray the nature of the Soviet challenge to the United States. (Note: All indexes are based upon United States real GNP for 1970 = 100 and U.S.S.R. real GNP for 1970 = 50.) In the decade preceding 1970, the United States grew toward the top of the projected range of growth rates. The U.S.S.R., because of bad weather and crops and shortening of the workweek, seems to have moved lower down on its projected range of growth rates.

picture the economic-growth prospects for the United States and the Soviet Union. As the principal exponents of two different economic systems, these nations are competitors for world economic leadership. We shall learn that the economist has not the clairvoyance of the astronomer, who can tell you exactly where all the planets will be in the year 2000 A.D. The economist may give no more than the calculated prudent odds. Even if he is substantially correct, however, his projections merely open up further questions: Should the smaller nations adopt the same economic system as the competitor who wins this race for leadership? Can they affect by their own choices which competitor will emerge as leader?

National defense; nationalism, both economic and political; and the choice of an economic system are three more issues that require economic understanding before any progress can be made with them. A person who has never made a systematic study of economics is handicapped in even thinking about national issues; he is like a deaf man trying to appreciate a symphony: give him a hearing aid, and he may still lack talent, but at least he has a fighting chance of sensing what music really is. The head of state[1] must be constantly making vital decisions that involve economics. But of course he need not *himself* be a professional student of economics; he need only be an intelligent "consumer" of the (often conflicting) economic information given him.

■ LIGHT AND FRUIT

Of course most students do not expect to specialize in economics. Most will study it for only a term or two, and this book is intended to give an overview of the whole subject. As in the case of the man who wrote that he had "never gotten over learning long division," your view of the world can never be quite the same after even one course in economics.

C. P. Snow, scientist and novelist, once called for an end of the separation of "the two cultures." Economics is part of both these cultures, a subject that can combine the attractive features of both the humanities and the sciences. For two centuries, educated men have found in it the human interest of life itself, while at the same time, economic principles display some of the logical beauty of Euclid's geometry. To appreciate the charms of quantum physics, sophisticated mathematical techniques must first be mastered; but to sense the aesthetic structure of economic analysis requires only a feeling for logic and a capacity for wonderment that such mental constructs really do have a life-and-death significance for billions of men all over the world. Of course, mere beauty is not enough. We do not study economics for its own sake, but for the light it sheds.

---

[1] As an example, Winston Churchill was a great man—a leader without peer, an orator, a gifted writer, and a shrewd judge of the Hitlerian threat while most around him slept. Yet all his life, Churchill was a babe in the woods when it came to economics. In 1925, as Chancellor of the Exchequer, he put England back on the gold standard at the pre-1914 parity of $4.87 for the British pound. (Chapter 32 will explain what this means). Experts at the time warned against such folly, and history has recorded that England has never quite recovered from her stagnation of the late 1920s.

■ WHAT ECONOMICS IS

Beginners used to want a short definition of economics; and in response to this demand, there was no shortage of supply. Here are a few such definitions:

1. Economics is the study of those activities which, with or without money, involve exchange transactions among people.

2. Economics is the study of how men choose to use scarce or limited productive resources (land, labor, capital goods such as machinery, technical knowledge) to produce various commodities (such as wheat, beef, overcoats; concerts, roads, bombers, yachts) and to distribute them to various members of society for their consumption.

3. Economics is the study of men in their ordinary business of life, earning and enjoying a living.

4. Economics is the study of how mankind goes about the business of organizing its consumption and production activities.

5. Economics is the study of wealth.

The list is a good one. Yet a scholar can extend it many times over. It is always hard to compress into a few lines an exact description of a subject, one that will differentiate its boundaries from those of other disciplines and convey to the beginner all the things it is. Economics certainly does involve all the elements stressed in these various definitions—and all those implied in the larger list that could be compiled.

Economists today agree on a general definition something like the following:

Economics is the study of how men and society end up choosing, with or without the use of money, to employ scarce productive resources, which could have alternative uses, to produce various commodities over time and distribute them for consumption, now and in the future, among various people and groups in society.

■ THE QUEEN OF THE SOCIAL SCIENCES

Economics borders on other important academic disciplines. *Political science, sociology, psychology,* and *anthropology* are all social sciences whose studies overlap those of economics. Some universities still have joint departments of "political economy" in recognition of this lack of clear limits between the subjects. Here is just one example of how they complement one another.

In impoverished India cows are sacred animals and, numbering millions, are allowed to walk through the streets foraging for food. While a naïve economist might regard these herds as a prime source for protein supplement to an already inadequate diet, the more profound scholar will take the psychology of custom into account when analyzing Indian economic development.

Economics also draws heavily on the study of *history.* Was it a coincidence that prices rose for centuries in Spain and Europe after Columbus discovered America with all its gold? Why did the age of the steamship and railroad help the prairie farmer, hurt the farmers of Vermont and Oxfordshire, and help the slum dwellers of London? The interpretation of recorded history must be approached with *analytical* tools for facts will never "tell their own story"; yet this need for theorizing does not deny the old Chinese proverb "One peek is worth a thousand finesses." Facts count.

Among the numerous other subjects relating to economics, the study of *statistics* is of special importance. Governments and businesses issue vast amounts of numerical information. Most of what we know about the actual shapes of the various curves to be seen in turning over the pages of this book has to come from a careful statistical analysis of recorded information. The mathematical methods of probability and statistics find many of their most important applications in the realm of economics.

Although every introductory textbook must contain geometrical diagrams, knowledge of *mathematics* itself is needed only for the higher reaches of economic theory. Logical reasoning is the key to success in the mastery of basic economic principles, and shrewd weighing of empirical evidence is the key to success in mastery of economic applications.

NOBEL PRIZE IN ECONOMICS   Since the turn of the century Nobel prizes have been given annually in physics, chemistry, medicine and physiology, literature, and peace. As if to commemorate the coming of age of economics as a science, a new Nobel prize in economics was instituted in 1969.

The first award went jointly to Professors Ragnar Frisch of Norway and Jan Tinbergen of the Netherlands. Both men have been pioneers in the statistical, theoretical, and mathematical advances of the modern generation. Yet each has also been passionately concerned with economic policy, both within his own country and for the world at large. (The second award went to Professor Paul Samuelson of MIT, senior author of this text.) The recognition of these men symbolizes the recognition of the many-sided nature of economic scholarship.

ECONOMIC DESCRIPTION AND ANALYSIS

It is the first task of modern economic science to *describe*, to *analyze*, to *explain*, and to *correlate* the behavior of production, unemployment, prices, and similar phenomena. To be significant, descriptions must be more than a series of disconnected narratives. They must be fitted into a systematic pattern—i.e., constitute true analysis.

Because of the complexity of human and social behavior, we cannot hope to attain the precision of the physical sciences. Economists cannot perform the controlled experiments of the chemist or biologist. Like the astronomer, we must be content largely to "observe." But economic events and statistical data observed are, alas, not as well behaved and orderly as the paths of heavenly satellites. Fortunately, our answers need not be accurate to several decimal places; on the contrary, if the right general *direction* of cause and effect can be determined, we shall have made a tremendous step forward.

ECONOMIC POLICY AND REFORM

This brings us to the important problems of economic policy. Ultimately, understanding should aid in *control and improvement*. How can the vagaries of the business cycle be diminished? How can economic progress and efficiency be furthered? How can adequate standards of living be made more widely available?

At every point of our analysis we shall seek to shed light on these policy problems. To succeed in this, we must all try to cultivate an objective and detached ability to see things as they *are*, regardless of our likes or dislikes. The fact must be faced that economic issues are close to everybody emotionally. Blood pressures rise and voices become shrill whenever deep-seated beliefs and prejudices are involved, and some of these prejudices are thinly veiled rationalizations of special economic interests.

We know that a doctor passionately interested in stamping out disease must first train himself to observe things as they are. His bacteriology cannot be different from that of a mad scientist out to destroy mankind by plague. Wishful thinking is bad thinking and leads to little wish fulfillment. "Where it is a duty to worship the sun, the laws of heat will be poorly understood."

"Beauty is in the eye of the beholder" is an aphorism reminding us that judgments of better or worse involve *subjective* valuations. But this does not deny that one girl's nose may be *objectively* shorter than another's. Similarly, there are elements of valid reality in a given economic situation, however hard it may be to recognize and isolate them. There is not one theory of economics for the Right Wing and one for the Left Wing, one for workers and one for employers, one for the Russians and one for the Chinese. On the basic economic principles concerning prices and employment, most economists are in fairly close agreement.

This statement does not mean that economists always agree in the *policy* field. Economist A may be for full employment at any cost. Economist B may not rank it of primary importance. Basic questions concerning right and wrong goals to be pursued cannot be settled by science as such. They belong in the realm of ethics and "value judgments." The citizenry must ultimately decide such issues. What the expert can do is point out the feasible alternatives and the true costs that may be involved in the different decisions. But still the mind must render to the heart that which is the heart's domain.

And peculiarly in the social sciences we must realize that we are subjects —even victims—of our preconceptions, prejudices, sentiments, and sordid interests.[2]

■ METHODOLOGY OF ECONOMICS: BRIEF PREVIEW

No one can understand a complicated subject such as chemistry without long and careful study. This is an advantage and a disadvantage. The man on the street or behind a newspaper desk cannot possibly consider himself a final authority on such a subject—which is all to the good. On the other hand, the new student of chemistry must become familiar with all the basic concepts for the first time, which takes a good deal of effort.

---

[2] Which questions we ask, and from what perspective we photograph the "objective reality"—these are themselves at bottom subjective in nature.

From childhood days on, everyone knows *something* about economics. This acquaintance is both helpful and deceptive: helpful, because much knowledge can be taken for granted; deceptive, because it is natural and human to accept superficially plausible views. A little knowledge may be dangerous. On close examination common sense may prove to be really nonsense.

A union leader who has successfully negotiated several labor contracts may feel that he is an expert on the economics of wages. A businessman who has "met a payroll" may feel that his views on price control are final. A banker who can balance his books may conclude that he knows all there is to know about the creation of money.

Each individual naturally tends to judge an economic event only by its immediate effects upon himself. A worker thrown out of employment in the buggy industry cannot be expected to reflect that new jobs may have been created in the automobile industry; but we must be prepared to investigate whether this is so.

In an introductory survey, the economist is interested in the workings of the economy *as a whole* rather than in the viewpoint of any one group. Social and national policies rather than individual policy are his goals. Too often, "everybody's business is nobody's business." It is just as well, therefore, to reiterate at the beginning that an elementary course in economics does not pretend to teach one how to run a business or bank, how to spend money wisely, or how to get rich quick from the stock market. But it is to be hoped that general economics will provide a useful background for many such activities.

Certainly, the economist must know a good deal about how businessmen, consumers, and investors behave and think. This does not mean that those individuals must use the *same language and methods* in approaching their decisions as economists find useful in describing their behavior—any more than the planets need know that they are following the elliptical paths traced by the astronomer. Just as many of us have been "speaking prose" all our lives without knowing it, so too would many businessmen be surprised to learn that their behavior is capable of systematic economic analysis. This lack of awareness is not necessarily to be deprecated. It does not help a baseball pitcher to know the laws of aerodynamics; and if we become self-conscious about how to button our shirts, we may find it harder to do.

THEORY VERSUS PRACTICE   The economic world is extremely complicated. As we noted, it is usually not possible to make economic observations under the controlled experimental conditions characteristic of scientific laboratories. A physiologist who wishes to determine the effects of penicillin on pneumonia may be able to "hold other things equal" by using two test groups that differ only in the fact that they do and do not get penicillin injections. The economist is less fortunately situated. If he wishes to determine the effect of a gasoline tax on fuel consumption, he may be vexed by the fact that, in the same year when the tax was imposed, pipelines were first introduced. Nevertheless, he must try—if only mentally—to isolate the effects of the tax, "other things being equal." Otherwise, he will understand the economic effects neither of taxation nor of transportation improvements, nor of both together.

The difficulty of analyzing causes when controlled experimentation is impossible is well illustrated by the confusion of the savage medicine man who thinks that both witchcraft and a little arsenic are necessary to kill his enemy, or that only after he has put on a green robe in spring will the trees do the same.[3] As a result of this limitation and many others, our quantitative economic knowledge is far from complete. This does not mean that we do not have great amounts of accurate statistical knowledge available. We do. Reams of census data, market information, and financial statistics have been collected by governments, trade associations, and business concerns.

Even if we had more and better data, it would still be necessary—as in every science—to *simplify*, to *abstract* from the infinite mass of detail. No mind can apprehend a bundle of unrelated facts. All analysis involves abstraction. It is always necessary to *idealize*, to omit detail, to set up simple hypotheses and patterns by which the facts can be related, to set up the right questions before going out to look at the world as it is. Every theory, whether in the physical or biological or social sciences, distorts reality in that it oversimplifies. But if it is good theory, what is omitted is outweighed by the beam of illumination and understanding that is known over the diverse empirical data.

Properly understood, therefore, theory and observation, deduction and induction, cannot be in conflict. The test of a theory's validity is its usefulness in illuminating observed reality. Its logical elegance and finespun beauty are irrelevant. Consequently, when a student says, "That's all right in theory but not in practice," he really means, "That's not right in the relevant theory," or else he is talking nonsense.

THE TYRANNY OF WORDS   Particularly in the social sciences, we must watch out for the "tyranny of words." The world is complicated enough without introducing further confusions and ambiguities as (1) two different names are unknowingly being used for the same thing or (2) the same one word is being applied to two quite different phenomena.

Jones may call Robinson a liar for holding that the cause of depression is oversaving, saying, "Underconsumption is really the cause." Schwartz may enter the argument, asserting, "You are both wrong. The real trouble is underinvestment." They may go on arguing; but, if they really stopped to analyze their language, they might find that there were no differences in their opinions about the facts and that only a verbal confusion was involved.

Similarly, words may be treacherous because we do not react in a neutral manner to them. Thus a man who approves of a government program to speed growth will call it a program of "sensible planning," while an unsympathetic opponent will describe the same activity as "totalitarian bureaucratic regimentation." Who can object to the former, and who would condone the latter? Yet they refer to the same thing. One does not have to be an expert in *semantics*—the study of language and its meaning—to realize that scientific discussion requires us to avoid such emotional terminology wherever possible.

---

[3] In logic this is sometimes called the *post hoc, ergo propter hoc* fallacy (after this, therefore necessarily because of this).

SOCIAL VERSUS PHYSICAL SCIENCE?   Some distortions of thinking that result from emotion and prejudice are so blatant as to be clearly recognizable. But at a deeper level, one can ask:

> Since economics deals with man and not with inanimate objects, and since the scientist is himself necessarily a man, can there be any hope of an *objective* science of economics? Can the methods of the physical sciences—observation and quantitative measurements, mathematical model building—ever work in the study of human affairs?

No simple answer can be given to this profound question. In a sense, precisely because we are ourselves men, we have an advantage over the natural scientist. He cannot usefully say, "Suppose I were an H_2O molecule; what might I do in such a situation?" The social scientist often, knowingly or unknowingly, employs such introspective acts of *empathy*.

Still a problem remains. Perhaps most experienced scholars would put it this way:

> Slavish imitation of the physical sciences is a mistake in the study of humans and society. Yet there is no substitute for patient *attendance to the empirical facts* of life, and no substitute for *systematic reasoning* about them. As in the case of modern biology, great advances have resulted from mathematical scientific methods, despite the earlier warnings against imitating the physical sciences. Let experience tell the final story.

EXACTITUDE AND SUBJECTIVITY   But note this important point. Even in the so-called exact physical sciences, how we *perceive* the observed facts depends on the theoretical spectacles we wear. The light that hits a newborn baby's eyes forms no pattern: the baby sees but it does not perceive. Modern historians of science have learned the same lesson from gestalt psychology: post-Newtonians perceived the "same facts" differently from pre-Newtonians. To a degree we are all prisoners of our theoretical preconceptions. It is not so much discordant fact that kills off an old false theory as the final emergence of a new theory.

That is why science belongs to the young. The old know too many things that are just not so. To illustrate this we do not have to consider a soft science like economics, in which it is taken for granted that your uncles will believe that what was good enough for Arthur Meighen ought to be good enough for you. Let us listen to Nobel laureate Max Planck, the physicist renowned for his discovery of the revolutionary quantum theory. In his *Scientific Autobiography*, Planck reports what he observed in the development of physics:

> This experience gave me also an opportunity to learn a fact—a remarkable one in my opinion: A new scientific truth does not triumph by convincing its opponents and making them see the light, but rather because its opponents eventually die, and a new generation grows up that is familiar with it.

Just as Galileo, Newton, and Einstein revolutionized perceptions in physics, so did Smith, Marshall, Keynes—indeed all the names that appear on the family tree of economics shown on the back flyleaf of this book—transform economic

Facts tell different story to scientists wearing different theoretical spectacles:

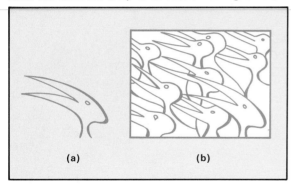

(a)   (b)

FIG. 1-2. If you look at problems of depression unemployment through pre-Keynesian glasses, you may think little of it is due to forces that government tax and expenditure policies can change. In (a) is this a picture of a leftward-looking bird? Or is it a rightward-looking antelope (or rabbit)? In the presence of (b)'s field of birds, most people think it a bird. But next to the footnote's field of antelopes, most will see it as an antelope. (Source: N. R. Hanson, *Patterns of Discovery*, London: Cambridge University Press, 1961.)

understanding. Figure 1-2, taken from a philosophic study of physics, illustrates the irreducible subjective element in *any* science. Does the picture show a bird looking to the left? Or an antelope (or rabbit) looking to the right? It is not an optical illusion to say it is one rather than the other. Each is admissible.[4]

So it is with many scientific facts and theories. When you adopt a new systematic model of economic principles, you comprehend reality in a new and different way. We do not have to be students of physics or gestalt psychology to realize how literally these words apply to the contrasts between new and old economics, or between free-world and iron-curtain economics. So let us be forewarned.

PROBABILITY OF ERRORS: NORMAL OR NOT   There is another important difference between an exact science like physics and a less exact science like economics. Our laws may hold only "on the average," with considerable dispersion of exceptions around that average. Figure 1-3 gives a preview of a vital statistical relationship whereby consumption spending by families can be related to the dollar incomes people have. Note that the observation points do not fall exactly on the line, as they might in chemistry or astronomy. Still, we do see a pattern that is stable in a probability sense—the same sense in which a life-insurance company can *count on* a stable proportion of deaths in a sample of 100,000

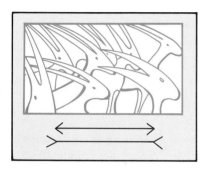

[4] Contrast your gestalt perception of Fig. 1-2's image with its appearance when placed next to this field of antelopes. The bird-antelope ambiguity cannot be dismissed as an optical "illusion"; it is unlike the accompanying two lines, which are really the same length even though most people wrongly infer the lower line to be the longer. What Fig. 1-2 portrays is an objectively reproducible shape that looks subjectively different depending on the context in which it appears. But once we see the forelegs of the beast, we are right to perceive it as an antelope.

Economic laws are probability laws, not exact relationships:

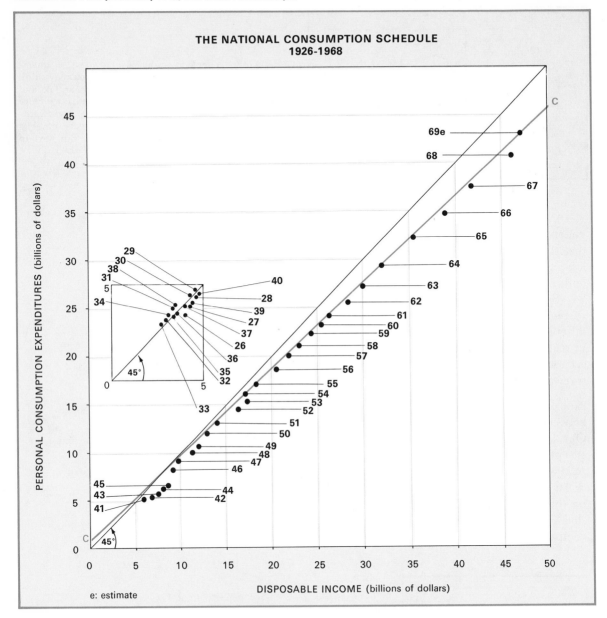

FIG. 1-3. Observed points of consumption spending fail to fall exactly on the line. But clustering of the data around the line does confirm the regularity of the relationship between dollar incomes and spending. (Source: Fig. 11-5, which shows that 92½ per cent of income spent on consumption and 7½ per cent going towards saving is about par for the course.)

policy holders of a given age (even though any one man's living or dying cannot be foretold). And note a further important point: the chance deviations around

Abnormal as well as normal probability patterns of errors occur in economics:

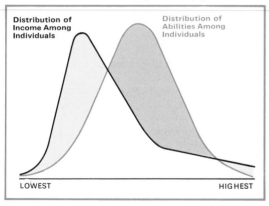

FIG. 1-4. Although behavior on the average is predictable in economics, there are exceptions and deviations around the average. The brown curve depicts the well-behaved case in which the deviations follow the symmetric bell-shaped "normal curve of error." The black curve of abnormal error, which is skewed off to the right, has relatively more extreme deviations than does the normal curve. Where this occurs in the social sciences, we cannot guarantee laws of average behavior with quite so much accuracy. (Source: Fig. 6-5, where normal distribution of abilities is contrasted with asymmetric distribution of dollar incomes and great spread among them.)

the expected values will form an especially simple frequency pattern called the "normal curve of error." The normal curve is symmetric and bell-shaped; this is because the addition of *many independent* errors tends to give a resultant error which (through probable cancellation) is more likely to be small than large. When this normal distribution appears in economics, it resembles distributions from gambling dice, genetics, or surveying instruments.[5]

In economics, "normality" may not always prevail. Figure 1-4 here reproduces a later diagram, Fig. 6-5, page 156, depicting how abnormally spread out people's incomes are in comparison with the allegedly "normal" distribution of their abilities (IQ's, verbal or mathematical aptitudes, etc.). The curve of distribution of incomes is asymmetric: unlike the symmetric normal curve, it has a long tail skewed to the right. This reflects the fact that while there are a few multimillionaires with incomes equal to hundreds of times the average income, no one can be that many dollars below the average. Such asymmetric super-extended distributions, alas, appear often in economics. One says "alas" because such abnormal probability laws do not lead to the same *precision of average behavior* that the natural sciences can often count on.

Despite the approximate character of economic laws, it is a field blessed with many important regularities and valid principles.

---

[5] Gambling houses in Nevada and Monte Carlo know very well from experience that repeated coin tossing (or dice throwing) will generate a sequence with the following two properties: (*a*) If we write down 1 for heads and 0 for tails, a random series of tossing will give sequences—such as 0, 1, 0, 1, 1, 0, 1, 0, 0, 0, 1, 0—which eventually average out close to ½ by the famous "law of large numbers." (*b*) For a long enough sequence of random tosses of a symmetric coin, the fraction of heads appearing will approach a normal-error dispersion around the expected value of ½. This "central limit law" (of approach to a normal distribution) enabled mathematicians like de Moivre, Laplace, and Gauss to predict with great accuracy how often deviations will tend to occur, the expected size of the absolute errors halving when the sequence quadruples in length. Economic distributions, like that of income, may have tails too dispersed to be subject to this normal distribution.

■ THE WHOLE AND THE PART: THE "FALLACY OF COMPOSITION"

A good final warning in economics is this: things are often not what at first they seem to be. The following true statements provide examples:

1. If all farmers work hard and nature cooperates in producing a bumper crop, total farm income may *fall*, and probably will.

2. *One* man may solve his own unemployment problem by great ingenuity in hunting a job or by a willingness to work for less; but *all* cannot necessarily solve their problems in this way.

3. Higher prices *for one industry* may benefit its firms; but if the prices of *everything* bought and sold increased in the same proportion, no one would be better off.

4. It may pay Canada to reduce tariffs charged on goods imported, even if *other* countries refuse to do likewise.

5. It may pay a firm to take on some business at much *less than full costs*.

6. *Attempts* of individuals to save more in depression *may lessen the total* of the community's savings.

7. What is prudent behavior for an *individual* may at times be folly for a *nation* or a *province*.

Let us emphasize: Each of the above statements is true; but each is outwardly paradoxical. In the course of this book, the seeming paradoxes will be resolved. There are no magic formulas or hidden tricks. It is typical of economics that anything which is really correct must seem perfectly reasonable once the argument is carefully developed.

At this point it is just as well to note that many of the above paradoxes hinge upon a single confusion or fallacy, called by logicians the "fallacy of composition." In books on logic, this is defined as follows:

Fallacy of composition: a fallacy in which what is true of a part is, on that account alone, alleged to be also necessarily true of the whole.

Very definitely, in the field of economics, it turns out that what seems to be true for individuals is not always true for society as a whole; and conversely, what seems to be true for all may be quite false for any one individual. For everybody to stand on tiptoe to watch a parade does no good, even though a single person may gain a better view in so doing. Countless similar examples can be given in the field of economics. You might amuse yourself by checking over the previous seven examples to see which are probably related to the fallacy of composition. Or better still find some new ones.

We have come to the end of our introductory survey. Perhaps the best answer to the question, "Why study economics?" is the famous one given by Lord Keynes in the final lines of his 1936 classic, *The General Theory of Employment, Interest and Money*:

"The ideas of economists and political philosophers, both when they are right and when they are wrong, are more powerful than is commonly understood. Indeed the world is ruled by little else. Practical men, who believe themselves to be quite exempt from any intellectual influences, are usually the slaves of some defunct economist. Madmen in authority, who hear voices in the air, are distilling their frenzy from some academic scribbler of a few years back. I am sure that the power of vested interests is vastly exaggerated compared with the gradual encroachment of ideas."

SUMMARY

■ 1 Economics, both a science and an art, is studied for a variety of reasons; to understand problems facing the citizen and family; to help governments in both underdeveloped and advanced nations promote vigorous growth, while avoiding depression and inflation; to analyze fascinating patterns of social behavior.

■ 2 Among many definitions, the leading one today defines economics thus: How we choose to use scarce productive sources with alternative uses, to meet prescribed ends—what goods to produce, how, and for whom, now or later.

■ 3 Overlapping with other social or behavioral sciences—psychology, sociology, history—economics uses the deductive methods of logic and geometry, and inductive methods of statistical and empirical inference. Because it cannot employ controlled experiments of the physicist, it raises basic problems of methodology: subjective elements of introspection and value judgment; semantic issues of ambiguous and emotional meanings; probability laws of large numbers, both of normal-error-distribution and abnormally skewed type.

QUESTIONS FOR DISCUSSION

1. Would a major depression like that of the 1930s, or a peacetime inflation, affect you (a) seriously, (b) moderately, or (c) not at all?

2. Discuss the emotional content of the following words: regimentation, planning, usury, socialist, monopolist, gambling, speculation, "made in Canada," American way of life, free enterprise, cartels, thrift, hoarding.

3. Give examples of the fallacy of composition and of the *post hoc, ergo propter hoc* fallacy. Is the former involved in the debate over cigarettes and longevity? Is the latter involved in this debate?

4. Can you fit into the brief definition of economics many of this chapter's problems?

5. In Fig. 1-3, is income the cause and consumption the effect? Or vice versa? To answer this, economic study is needed. Similarly, does the fact that smoking and cancer are related prove that smoking causes cancer? Is low IQ among the poor genetically caused?

6. "As every insurance company knows, single events may be unpredictable at the same time that large number of events average out to virtual certainty." Show how this same statistical fact can be helpful in economics, as for example in the case where we study how thousands of families choose to spend their incomes on consumption as against saving.

7. "Facts by themselves are dumb; before they will tell us anything we have to arrange them, and the arrangement is a theory." Elucidate.

8. Review your understanding of the following concepts:

economics as distinct from other disciplines	subjectivity and theorizing
analysis and policy	valuation and so-called "facts"
practice and theory	tyranny of words
wishful thinking, semantics	controlled experiment
exactitude and probability	fallacy of composition
normal and skewed errors	*post hoc* fallacy
	definition of economics

A PREVIEW

Here in Part One we deal with the fundamental tools needed to analyze the basic facts and institutions of modern economic life, culminating this survey in the unifying concept of national income.

In Part Two we analyze the causes of prosperity and depression: how the processes of saving and investment interact to determine the level of prices, income, and employment; and how public monetary and fiscal policies can stabilize business activity at a healthy level of progressive growth.

Part Three is concerned with the forces of competition and monopoly, which act through supply and demand to help determine—efficiently or inefficiently—the composition of the national income, in terms of both goods and services to be produced and their prices. (Unlike Part Two's "macroeconomics," this is "microeconomics.")

Part Four treats distribution of income: wages, rent, interest, and profits.

Part Five discusses international trade in both its monetary and real aspects.

The last chapter of Part Five and all of Part Six deal with some of our most vital current economic problems: development of backward countries; promotion of economic growth and control of inflation; poverty, inequality, and the quality of economic life; economics of discrimination and problems of environmental blight.

2

CENTRAL
PROBLEMS OF EVERY
ECONOMIC SOCIETY

To get land's fruit in quantity
Takes jolts of labor ever more,
Hence food will grow like one, two, three . . .
While numbers grow like one, two, four . . .

Song of Malthus: A Ballad on Diminishing Returns   ANONYMOUS

At the foundations of any community there will always be found a few universal economic conditions. Certain background problems are as crucial today as they were in the days of Homer and Caesar, and they will continue to be relevant in the brave new world of the future.

In Section A of this chapter we see that every society must meet a certain trio of *basic problems of economic organization.* Section B shows that technological *knowledge,* together with limited amounts of *land, labor,* and *capital,* defines the available choices between goods and services open to a community and that these *production possibilities* are subject to change and to the law of diminishing returns. Section C develops the point that the basis of any economy' is its *population,* or *human element.*

We shall leave to Chapter 3 those important special economic features characteristic of our own mixed economy—a system of private and public enterprise intertwined.

A.   PROBLEMS OF ECONOMIC ORGANIZATION

Any society, whether it consists of a totally collectivized communistic state, a tribe of South Sea Islanders, a capitalistic industrial nation, a Swiss Family Robinson, a Robinson Crusoe—or, one might almost add, a colony of bees—

must somehow confront three fundamental and interdependent economic problems.

1. WHAT commodities shall be produced and in what quantities? That is, how much and which of alternative goods and services shall be produced? Food or clothing? Much food and little clothing, or vice versa? Bread and butter today, or bread and grape plantings today with bread, butter, and jam next year?

2. How shall goods be produced? That is, by whom and with what resources and in what technological manner are they to be produced? Who hunts, who fishes? Electricity from steam or from waterfall or from atoms? Large- or small-scale production?

3. For WHOM shall goods be produced? That is, who is to enjoy and get the benefit of the goods and services provided? Or, to put the same thing in another way, how is the total of national product to be *distributed*[1] among different individuals and families? A few rich and many poor? Or most people in modest comfort?

These three questions are fundamental and common to all economies, but different economic systems try to solve them differently. In a primitive civilization, custom may rule every facet of behavior. WHAT, How, and For WHOM may be decided by reference to traditional ways of doing things. To members of another culture, the practices followed may seem bizarre and unreasonable; the members of the tribe or clan may themselves be so familiar with existing practices as to be surprised, and perhaps offended, if asked the reason for their behavior. Thus Kwakiutl Indians of high rank considered it meritorious to accumulate wealth and then give it away in the *potlatch*—a roisterous celebration. Such deviations from our own modes of distributing wealth will not surprise anthropologists; from their studies they know what is correct behavior in one culture is often the greatest crime in another.

In the bee colony, all such problems, even those involving an elaborate cooperative division of labor, are solved automatically by means of so-called "biological instincts." (Fair enough as a description, but not much of an "explanation.")

At the other extreme we can imagine an omnipotent benevolent or malevolent dictator who by arbitrary decree decides WHAT, How, and For WHOM. Or we might imagine economic organization by decree, but with decrees drawn up by democratic vote or by selected legislative authorities.

As Chapter 3 develops at length, the WHAT, How, and FOR WHOM questions in a so-called "capitalist free enterprise economy" are determined primarily[2] by a system of prices (of markets, or profits and losses).

---

[1] WARNING: Usually, when an economist is talking about "distribution," he means the distribution of incomes—the principles which determine labor's wage, land's rent, capital's interest, and the whole FOR WHOM process. The man on the street usually means, by distribution, wholesaling and retailing—how goods once produced get into the hands of the consumer. Avoid this last confusing usage.

[2] There has never been a 100 per cent purely automatic enterprise system, although Victorian England came close. Certainly in our system, the government has an important role in modifying the workings of the price system. We live in what may be called a "mixed economy."

■ THE LAW OF SCARCITY

WHAT to produce, HOW, and FOR WHOM would not be problems if resources were *unlimited*: if an *infinite* amount of every good could be produced, or if human wants were fully satisfied, it would not then matter if too much of any particular good were produced. Nor would it then matter if labor and materials were combined unwisely. Since everyone could have as much as he pleased, it would not matter how goods and incomes were distributed among different individuals and families.

There would then be no *economic goods*; i.e., no goods that are relatively *scarce*; and there would hardly be any need for a study of economics or "economizing." All goods would be *free goods*, like air. (Even air is no longer a truly free good in our society.)

In the world as it is, even children learn in growing up that "both" is not an admissible answer to a choice of "Which one?" Compared with backward nations or previous centuries, modern industrial societies seem very wealthy indeed. But higher production levels seem to bring in their train higher consumption standards. People feel that they want and "need" central heating, indoor plumbing, refrigerators, education, movies, radios, television, books, autos, travel, music, chic clothes, and so forth. The biological scientist may tell them that they can be well nourished on a thin porridge for a few cents a day,[3] but that possibility leaves them as cold as the information that the chemicals in their bodies are worth only a couple of dollars. Anyone who has kept a family budget knows that the necessities of life—the absolute musts—have little to do with the minimum *physiological* needs of food, clothing, and shelter.

In *The Affluent Society*, J. Kenneth Galbraith[4] has eloquently pointed out that Americans today have for the most part gone beyond the level of physiological necessity; that often the consumer flits from one purchase to another in response to pressures of fashion and advertising. Without challenging Galbraith's thesis that the time has come to spend more on public needs and less on private needs, one may properly point out that our total product would have to become many times higher than its present level if everyone were to become able to live at the level of a moderately well-off doctor, lawyer, professor, or advertising man—to say nothing of the living standards of the really well-to-do.

Whether or not people would be "genuinely" happier spending twice as much as now, observation suggests that people in the suburbs now act *as if* they want more income to spend: they take on extra work; they resist tax increases;

[3] A study suggests that in North America modern standards of adult nutrition could be bought (in 1970) for less than $110 per year. But what a diet this implies: kidneys, cabbage, wheat flour, and not much else! George J. Stigler, "The Cost of Subsistence," *Journal of Farm Economics*, May, 1945, pp. 303-314. This paper achieved fame as a forerunner of an important mathematical technique of economics and national defense called "linear planning." Victor E. Smith of Michigan State University in the same journal (May, 1959, pp. 272-283) reported that a family of three could get a "palatable diet" for about 50 cents per person per day, perhaps 65 cents in the 1970s.

[4] John Kenneth Galbraith, *The Affluent Society* (Houghton Mifflin, Boston, 1958).

they end up saving much the same fraction of their incomes as in 1900; and middle-class mothers seem to work harder than their mothers did. Even if the national income were divided up equally between every man, woman, and child —an extreme case—there would be only about $53 per week to go around.

Therefore, while it recognizes the important germ of truth in the notion that ours has become an affluent society, economics must still contend with *scarcity* as a basic fact of life.

B.   THE TECHNOLOGICAL CHOICES OPEN TO ANY SOCIETY

■ SOCIETY'S PRODUCTION-POSSIBILITY CURVE

We have discussed the basic economic fact that *limitation* of the total resources capable of producing different commodities necessitates a choice between relatively scarce commodities. This can be illustrated quantitatively by simple arithmetic examples and geometrical diagrams. Diagrams and graphs are indispensable visual aids in many aspects of economics. A little care at the beginning in understanding them will be rewarded manyfold later on.

Consider an economy with only so many people, only so much technical knowledge, only so many factories and tools, and only so much land, water power, and natural resources. In deciding WHAT shall be produced and How, the economy must really decide just how these resources are to be allocated among the thousands of different possible commodities. How much land should go into wheat cultivation? Or into pasturage? How many factories are to produce hairpins? How much skilled labor should go into machine shops?

These problems are complicated even to discuss, much less solve. Therefore we must simplify. So let us assume there are to be produced only two economic goods (or classes of economic goods). For dramatic purposes, we can choose the pair Adolf Hitler ranted about—guns and butter. These two commodities are commonly used to illustrate the problem of choosing between civilian and war goods, but the same analysis applies to *any* choice of goods. Thus the more

Full employment of scarce resources means society must choose between more guns or more butter:

1st, This can be shown by a table:

ALTERNATIVE POSSIBILITIES IN THE PRODUCTION OF BUTTER AND GUNS		
POSSIBILITIES	BUTTER (millions of lbs.)	GUNS (thousands)
A	0	15
B	1	14
C	2	12
D	3	9
E	4	5
F	5	0

TABLE 2-1. Economic resources can be shifted from butter production to gun production, in effect enabling us to transform butter into guns. The cost of getting extra guns can be reckoned as the extra butter we are forced to sacrifice.

resources the government uses to build public roads, the less will be left to produce private houses; the more the public chooses to consume of food, the less it can consume of clothing; the more society decides to consume today, the less can be its production of machines and capital goods to turn out more consumption goods for the next year or decade.

But let us stick to the example of guns and butter. Now, suppose that *all* resources are thrown into the production of civilian goods (butter). There will still be a *maximum* amount of butter that can be produced per year. (The exact amount depends upon the quantitative and qualitative resources of the economy in question and the technological efficiency with which they are used.) Suppose 5 million pounds of butter is the maximum amount that can be produced with the existing technology and resources.

At the other extreme, imagine that 100 per cent of society's resources had been devoted instead to the production of guns. Only some maximum number of guns could then be produced: 15 thousand guns of a certain description can perhaps be produced if we are really willing to produce no butter.

These are two extreme possibilities; in between there are still others. If we are willing to give up *some* butter, we can have *some* guns; if we are willing to give up still more butter, we can have still more guns. A schedule of a number of possibilities is given in Table 2-1, *F* being the extreme where all butter and no guns are produced, and *A* being the opposite extreme where all resources go into guns. In between, at *E*, *D*, *C*, and *B*, butter is being given up increasingly in return for more guns. Butter is "transformed" into guns, not physically, but by diverting resources from one use to the other.

It is even more illuminating to represent this same production-possibility or

2d, Or be shown graphically by plotting the points on a grid:

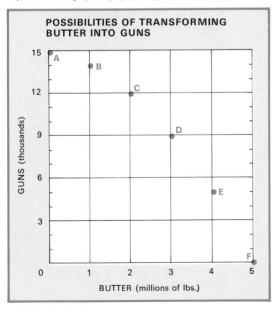

FIG. 2-1. Each marked point is a careful plot of each gun-and-butter numerical combination from Table 2-1. (Guess where the point midway between B and C might approximately fall. Read off its guns-butter numbers, and pencil them into Table 2-1 at about the right place.)

production-transformation schedule by measuring butter along the horizontal axis and guns along the vertical, as in Fig. 2-1.

The reader should now be able to go directly from the numerical table to the diagram: for *F*, by counting over 5 butter units to the right and going up 0 gun units; for *E*, by going 4 butter units to the right and going up 5 gun units; and finally, for *A*, by going over 0 butter units and up 15 gun units.

We may fill in all intermediate positions, even those involving fractions of a million pounds or of a thousand guns, as in the so-called "production-possibility curve" shown in Fig. 2-2.

The curve that we now have represents this fundamental fact:

> *A full-employment economy must always in producing one good be giving up something of another.* This assumes, of course, that at least some resources can be transferred from one good to another; e.g., steel is used for guns and also for butter via farm machinery.
>
> *Substitution* is the law of life in a full-employment economy. The *production-possibility frontier* depicts society's menu of choices.

■ UNEMPLOYMENT AND INEFFICIENCY

But what if there had been widespread unemployment of resources: idle men, idle land, and idle factories? We have already warned that our economic laws may then be quite different. This is one such instance.

With unemployment, we are not on the production-possibility frontier at all, but somewhere *inside* it, say, at *U* in Fig. 2-2, producing only 2 million pounds of butter and 6 thousand guns. If resources are idle, by putting them to

3rd, Or we can picture production possibilities by drawing a smooth curve:

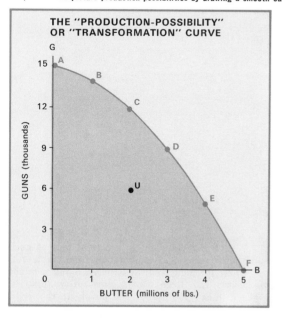

THE "PRODUCTION-POSSIBILITY" OR "TRANSFORMATION" CURVE

FIG. 2-2. This shows how society can choose to substitute guns for butter, assuming a given state of technology and a given total of resources. Any point *inside* the curve, such as *U*, indicates that resources are not being fully employed in the best-known way. (Source: Table 2-1. A smooth curve has been passed through the points of the previous chart.)

work we can have more butter *and* more guns. We can move from *U* to *D* and *E* and thereby get *more* butter *and more* guns.

This throws important light on the different experiences in World War II of three countries: Canada, Germany, and Russia. After 1939, how was Canada able to arm for war and to enjoy civilian living standards higher than ever before? Largely by taking up the slack of unemployment and creating a sizeable war material industry. On the other hand, Hitler's war effort began in 1933, long before any formal declaration. It stemmed from a period of unemployment acute enough to win him the votes to get into power peacefully. Almost all the extra output made possible by utilizing previously unemployed workers and plants was siphoned into German war goods rather than into higher civilian consumption. Still a third case is that of the Soviet Union in World War II. The Russians had little unemployment before the war and were already on their rather low production-possibility curve. They had no choice but to substitute war for civilian goods—with consequent privation.

Business-cycle unemployment is not the only way of being inside the *p-p frontier*. If an economy is inefficiently organized, it may also be well short of the frontier—as in China of 1960, when the ideological drive for a "great leap forward" resulted in ousting of experts and an abortive attempt to make steel in backyard furnaces, or as in an economy riddled with monopoly and subject to arbitrary decrees by corrupt and incompetent bureaucrats. (We shall analyze monopoly in Part Three. For China, see the Appendix to this chapter and Chapter 3.)

■ SOME USES OF THE PRODUCTION-POSSIBILITY CONCEPT

This concept, represented as a simple curve, can help introduce many of the most basic concepts in economics. For example, Fig. 2-2 illustrates the basic definition of economics given in Chapter 1, namely, the problem of *choosing* among *scarce* or limited resources ("means" capable of *alternative* uses), in order to achieve best *goals* ("ends"). Land, labor, and capital can be used to produce guns or butter along the frontier curve in Fig. 2-2. Where does the society choose to end up? Southeastward in the diagram, with much of civilian goods? Or northwestward, with much of defense goods? Economics is a *quantitative* subject: choice is not a qualitative matter of "either-or," but rather of how many of each good and just where we draw the line of final decision.

The production-possibility frontier also permits us to give a rigorous definition of scarcity.

> *Definition*: "Economic scarcity" refers to the basic fact of life that there exists only a finite amount of human and nonhuman resources, which the best technical knowledge is capable of using to produce only a *limited* maximum amount of each and every good, as shown by the *p-p frontier*. And thus far, nowhere on the globe is the supply of goods so plentiful or the tastes so limited that the average man can have more than enough of everything he might fancy.

The production-possibility schedule can also help make clear the three basic problems of economic life: WHAT, HOW, and FOR WHOM.

WHAT goods are produced and consumed can be depicted by the point which we choose on the *p-p frontier.*

How goods are to be produced involves an efficient choice of methods and proper assignment of different amounts and kinds of limited resources to the various industries. What would happen if the men well fitted for machine-tooling of guns ended up on the farms? We should be *inside* the *p-p frontier,* not on it. Or what if government regulations made the land most suitable for corn be used for wheat production, and the land most suitable for wheat be used for corn? We should end up with less of both corn and wheat, inside the production-possibility frontier on a diagram whose axes were labeled C and W. Being inside the frontier is a crime of *economic* inefficiency; but it need not involve any *engineering* inefficiency, since, on the wrongly allocated land, production might still be following the latest methods known to science.[5]

FOR WHOM goods are to be produced cannot be discerned from the *p-p* diagram alone. Sometimes, though, you can make a guess from it: if you find a society on its *p-p* curve with many yachts and few compact cars, you are justified in suspecting that it enjoys considerable inequality of income and wealth among persons.

■ PICTURES IN AN EXHIBITION

The graphs of Figures 2-3 to 2-7 are meant to be self-explanatory. They show that the production-possibility curve can illustrate many familiar, but basic,

Production-possibility curves illustrate many economic cases:

1st, Choice between luxuries and necessities:

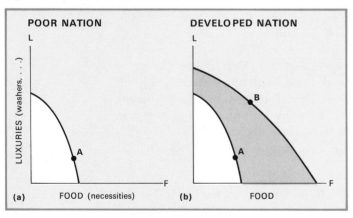

FIG. 2-3(a). Before development, the nation is so poor it must devote almost all its resources to food, enjoying few comforts.

FIG. 2-3(b). After development, it goes from A to B, expanding its food consumption very little compared with its increased consumption of nonnecessities.

---

[5] More difficult is the notion that the economy should often prefer scientifically *less* efficient methods over methods that are allegedly technically more efficient. EXAMPLE: Physics texts teach that converting heat to motion at 2,500°F is intrinsically more efficient than converting it at 1,200°. Yet if metals that can stand the higher temperature are scarce and dear, it is *economically* better for the engineer and businessman to use the thermodynamically less efficient method!

2d, Choice between public and private goods:

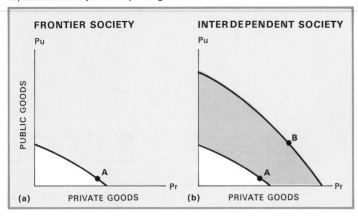

FIG. 2-4(a). The economy is poor and dispersed as in pre-Confederation days: the proportion of resources going to government is low.

FIG. 2-4(b). The economy is more prosperous and chooses to spend more of its higher income on governmental services (roads, defense, research, education); in dense urban life, it has no choice but to spend on traffic lights, police, and city planning.

economic processes. Later chapters will deal with each of these in depth, and it is necessary here only to comprehend the common-sense ideas involved.

Figure 2-3 illustrates how a society consumes much food when it is poor but shifts toward comforts and luxuries as it develops, a topic to be met in Chapter 11.

Figure 2-4 illustrates how the electorate must choose between private goods bought at a price and public goods paid for largely by taxes, a topic to be met in Chapter 8.

Figure 2-5 illustrates how an economy chooses between (1) current consumption goods and (2) capital goods (machines, etc.), which makes possible more of *both* goods in the future. Much of Parts Two, Four, and Six will deal with this basic investment problem.

3d, Choice between more consumption today and capital goods to enhance tomorrow's possibilities:

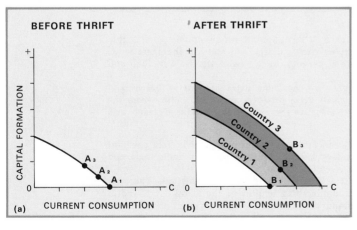

FIG. 2-5(a). Three countries start out even, but Country 1 does no saving for the future at A_1 (merely replacing used-up machines). Country 2 abstains modestly from consumption at A_2. Country 3, by democratic vote or private sacrifice, is at A_3, investing much in new machines and sacrificing much of current consumption.

FIG. 2-5(b). In the next years, Country 3 has forged ahead of Country 2, which has moved ahead of nonprogressing Country 1. Possessing more machines for labor to work with, Country 3 now can have more of *both* goods than can Country 2. Country 1 remains where it started.

4th, Case where technical advance outstrips thrift alone:

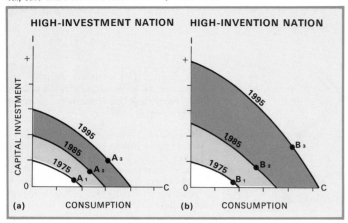

FIG. 2-6(a). Country A, on the left, is thrifty and advances by accumulating capital goods.

FIG. 2-6(b). Country B advances even more from 1975 to 1985 because it spends more on science and technical research. From 1985 to 1995 it grows faster still by using both methods: technical progress and much capital formation.

5th, How output on fixed land will not keep pace with population:

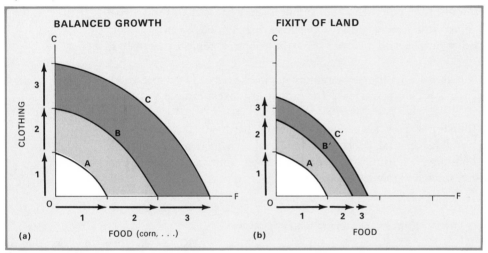

FIG. 2-7(a). We begin initially at the lower curve *A*. But population now doubles and is able to spread over double the previous land, leaving each country and state in the same land-labor balance as before. Hence the new curve *B* permits exactly twice the scale of food and clothing production.

Finally, let labor and land both rise again by the same extra amount as between *A* and *B*. We end up at *C*, gaining fully as much of extra products as we did before from the same balanced additions of labor and land. Note that the arrows 1, 2, and 3 on each axis show no diminishing length.

FIG. 2-7(b). We begin at the same *A* curve as in Fig. 2-7(a). But now land is held constant while population doubles. Each laborer has less land to work with than under balanced growth. Hence, the *B'* curve is below the *B* curve of Fig. 2-7(a).

Finally, add another equal increment of labor, still holding land constant. The new extra product is even lower, as shown by the diminishing lengths of the arrows 1, 2, and 3, which depict extra output. We shall understand the reasons for all this after the "law of diminishing returns" has been mastered.

Figure 2-6 shows how Economy B, blessed by unusual scientific and engineering discoveries, might surpass A which was undergoing more thrift and investing for the future, but with less progressive technology. Growth discussions, in Part Six, will develop this theme.

Finally, Fig. 2-7 prepares us for the next topic, the law of diminishing returns.

■ THE LAW OF DIMINISHING RETURNS

The fixity of land in Figure 2-7 introduces us to a famous economic relationship, the so-called "law of diminishing returns." This law states the relation, *not* between two goods (such as guns and butter), but rather between an *input* of a factor of production (such as labor) and the resulting output of a good it helps produce (such as butter or, in the traditional examples, corn).

> More specifically, the law of diminishing returns refers to the amount of *extra output* that we get when we successively add *extra* units of a *varying factor input* to a *fixed* amount of some *other factor input*. (Note the emphasized words.)

Here is an example to illustrate the law of diminishing returns. We make the following controlled experiment: Given a fixed amount of land, say, 100 acres, we shall first add no labor at all. We note that there is then no corn output, and so we record zero output in Table 2-2.

Now we make a second related experiment. We add 1 extra unit of labor to the same fixed amount of land. How much output do we now get? Pure reason cannot tell us: we must look to the facts of the experiment. When we do this we observe, let us say, that we now have produced positive output of corn

Diminishing returns is a fundamental law of economics and technology:

MAN-YEARS OF LABOR	TOTAL PRODUCT, BUSHELS	EXTRA OUTPUT ADDED BY ADDITIONAL UNIT OF LABOR
0	0	
		2,000
1	2,000	
		1,000
2	3,000	
		500
3	3,500	
		—
4	3,800	
		100
5	3,900	

RETURNS OF CORN WHEN EQUAL UNITS OF LABOR ARE ADDED TO FIXED LAND

TABLE 2-2. Law of diminishing returns refers to successively lower extra outputs (e.g. of corn) gained from adding equal increments of a variable factor input (e.g. labor) to a constant amount of a fixed factor input (e.g. land). (Pencil in the extra output of the fourth laborer).

exactly equal to 2,000 units (bushels or whatever units you choose to measure corn in). We now summarize the result of this second experiment: Adding 1 extra unit of labor to fixed land gives us extra output of 2,000 units.

To observe the law of diminishing returns, we must make a third controlled experiment. We still hold land fixed. Once more we vary the labor input and make sure to add again exactly the same extra unit of labor as before; i.e., we now go from 1 unit of labor to 2 units of labor. We breathlessly await the outcome of the experiment in terms of extra corn produced. Shall we now have a total of 4,000 units of corn, which would again represent exactly 2,000 extra units of output produced by the extra unit of the varying labor? Or shall we find *diminishing* returns, with the new extra unit of factor input adding less than the 2,000 extra units of output which was previously added?

If the law of diminishing returns does in fact hold, our experiment can have but one result: the second extra labor unit will add *less extra output* than did the first. Adding a third extra unit of labor will, if diminishing returns holds, result in *still lower* extra output. And so forth. Table 2-2 gives numerical values to illustrate exactly what diminishing returns means.

The law of diminishing returns is an important, often-observed, economic and technical regularity; but it is not universally valid. Often it will hold only *after* you have added a considerable number of equal doses of the varying factor. Beyond that point, we say the law of diminishing returns has set in. (Before such a point the varying factors might be yielding increasing extra returns, since until then we find that adding extra varying factor inputs to a fixed factor input leads to increasing rather than diminishing extra outputs.[6])

Why is the law of diminishing returns plausible? Frequently we feel that by adding land and labor together—no factor input being fixed and all being varied in the same proportion so that the whole *scale* of operations is getting larger— output should also increase proportionately and extra outputs need not diminish. For why should the extra outputs diminish if each of the factor inputs always has as much of the other inputs to work with?

In short, *balanced* scale changes may often be expected to leave factor inputs and outputs in the same ratios. [Reexamine Fig. 2-7(a).]

On the other hand, when we do hold one factor input or group of factor inputs constant and vary the remaining factor inputs, we see that the varying factor inputs have *less and less of the fixed factor inputs to work with.* Consequently, we are not too surprised that such extra varying factor inputs begin to add less and less extra product. In effect, the fixed factor of production (land) is decreasing in proportion to the variable factor input (labor). As we crowd the land more and more, we may still get some extra corn by intensive cultivation of the soil; but the amount of extra corn per unit of extra labor will become less and less. We shall see in Part Four that the real wage paid to workers depends

---

[6] If one were to change Table 2-2, replacing 2,000 by 900, he would find that the law of diminishing returns becomes valid only after the second row; at first there would actually be increasing extra returns to each equal additional unit of labor.

upon the extra output a last man adds for his employer. Diminishing returns reveals that living standards in crowded China or India are low because of this basic technical truth, and not *merely* because land happens to be owned by the state or by private landlords.

In conclusion, we may summarize as follows:

> *The law of diminishing returns*: An increase in some factor inputs relative to other fixed factor inputs will, in a given state of technology, cause total output to increase; *but after a point the extra output resulting from the same additions of extra factor inputs is likely to become less and less.* This falling off of extra returns is a consequence of the fact that the new "doses" of the varying factor inputs have less and less of the fixed resources or factors to work with.

■ ECONOMIES OF SCALE AND MASS PRODUCTION: A DIGRESSION

Before leaving this section we ought to take note of a phenomenon that is different from our controlled variation of one thing at a time.

> Suppose we merely increase "*scale* of operations," i.e., increase all the factors at the same time in the same degree. In many industrial processes, when you double *all* factor inputs, you may find that your output is more than doubled; this phenomenon is called "*increasing* returns to *scale*."
>
> Our previous law of diminishing returns always refers to cases where *some* factors were varied while some remained fixed. Hence, this case of increasing returns to scale is not a direct refutation of the law of diminishing returns.
>
> Increasing returns to scale, or so-called "economies of mass production," are often associated with one of the following advances: (1) the use of nonhuman and nonanimal power sources (water and wind power, steam, electricity, turbines and internal-combustion engines, internal nuclear energy); (2) the use of automatic self-adjusting mechanisms (lathes, jigs, servomechanisms); (3) the use of standardized interchangeable parts; (4) the breakdown of complex processes into simple repetitive operations; (5) the specialization of function and division of labor; and many other technological factors as well. The automobile-production assembly line and the historical development of modern textile spinning and weaving are examples typifying these diverse factors.
>
> Upon thought, it will be evident that *each of these economies or savings comes into full play only if a large enough number of units is being produced to make it worth while to set up a fairly elaborate productive organization.* If only a few guns are to be produced, they might just as well be produced by hand; but if resources are available to produce many thousands, it will pay to make certain elaborate initial preparations that need not be repeated when still more units are to be produced. In such cases, where mere scale matters much, the tendency for land fixity to force diminishing extra returns to labor could be thwarted for a long time by an increase in the total labor scale involved.[7]

---

[7] Accordingly, it might come about that, unlike our earlier simplified picture, we should have to pay two butter units for our first gun unit; but to get still another gun unit we should have to pay only one butter unit because of the efficiency of mass production. This would be a case of decreasing rather than increasing extra-costs-for-one-good-in-terms-of-another. When strong increasing returns to scale predominate, advanced treatises show that you have to redraw Fig. 2-2 to be "bowed in" (convex from below) rather than "bowed out" (concave from below), at least near each axis.

Economies of scale are very important in explaining why so many of the goods we buy are produced by large companies. We shall see that they are important in helping explain "the division of labor" and pattern of "specialization." They raise questions to which we shall return again and again in later chapters—as, for example, monopoly.

■ LAW OF INCREASING (RELATIVE) COSTS

We are now in a position to explain why the *production-possibility frontier* has been drawn in a bowed-out or concave curve in all our diagrams. If the *p-p frontier* were a straight line, the relative costs of getting some extra guns in terms of sacrificed butter would always be the same. Economists would term this a case of "constant (relative) costs." But actually it is more common in life to meet the law of increasing (relative) costs.

> *Definition*: The "law of increasing (relative) costs" prevails when in order to get *equal* extra amounts of one good, society must sacrifice ever-increasing amounts of the other good.

A bowed-out or concave curvature of the *production-possibility frontier* depicts the law of increasing (relative) costs—as shown by the fact that when we want more farm goods (e.g. butter), their (relative) cost in terms of sacri-

Land scarcity for food, plus diminishing returns, entails increasing (relative) costs:

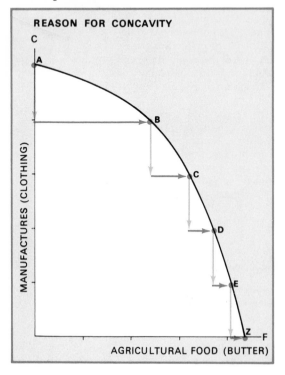

FIG. 2-8. In going from *A* to *B*, *B* to *C*, *C* to *D*, *D* to *E*, and *E* to *Z*, we have to give up equal amounts of Manufactures as we transfer equal labor amounts out of the manufacturing industry. Note the equal vertical arrows below *A*, below *B*, . . . , etc. But, as equal units of varying labor are added to fixed agricultural land, diminishing returns yield less and less of extra food—as measured by the shorter and shorter horizontal arrows. This accounts for the curve's bending, or for the law of increasing relative costs.

ficed manufactures (e.g. guns) rises, as seen in Fig. 2-8, by the steeper absolute slope at *C* than at *B*.

Why is this reasonable? We shall see that the law of increasing (relative) costs is related to, but definitely not the same thing as, the law of diminishing returns. We shall see that, along with the law of diminishing returns, economists must be able to assume that manufactures and food use the factors of production, such as labor and land, in different proportions or intensities to deduce this law of (increasing) relative costs.

To derive the law of increasing (relative) costs, let us use an oversimplified example. In Fig. 2-8, suppose that Manufactures (clothing) require *labor alone* and negligible land. But suppose that Agricultural Food (butter) requires, along with labor, fertile *land that has grown scarce enough to have become private property*. Now we have the two ingredients to explain the law of increasing (relative) costs shown in the *p-p frontier*: The two industries use land and labor in different proportions; so transferring varying amounts of labor onto fixed Agricultural land will turn out to bring into play the law of diminishing returns. Let us see exactly how.

> Begin by using all labor to produce Manufactures, at *A* in Fig. 2-8. Now sacrifice equal amounts of Manufactures to get more Agriculture, going to *B* and *C*. How is this transformation accomplished? By transferring *equal amounts of labor* away from Manufactures. But note that these equal amounts of transferred labor are applied to a fixed total of Agricultural land. As equal amounts of varying labor are applied to a fixed land factor, each has less and less acres to work with and hence adds less and less of extra Agriculture product. We see then why each new Agriculture is procured at higher and higher costs in terms of Manufactures.[8]

■ THE LABOR THEORY OF VALUE: A DIGRESSION [9]

On reflection, one sees that the law of increasing (relative) costs serves as a rebuttal to the so-called "labor theory of value," which was adopted by Karl Marx (1818-1883) from the earlier classical writers Adam Smith (1723-1790) and David Ricardo (1772-1823). According to it, goods should exchange at prices dependent upon their labor requirements alone.

> Thus, if the production of food requires 2 labor hours while the production of manufactures requires 6 labor hours, manufactures should have a value of 3 (or %)

---

[8] The common sense of this law of increasing (relative) costs does not depend upon one of the goods using labor alone. It depends only on having the two goods—call them clothing and butter—differing in the proportions of factors they require. Thus, note that the first few clothes can be produced in part with the kind of resources that are no good for butter anyway. If more clothing is wanted, we must use resources that are valuable for butter production; and if we insist upon having all clothing, we must be prepared to take farmers and farmlands, which are very efficient in the production of butter, and transform them to the production of clothing even though they can produce only very little in this sphere. Thus, increasing (relative) costs are to be expected in such a case. Even if resources could be divided into two uniform classes, such as homogeneous land and homogeneous labor, increasing costs would still result from the fact that clothing and butter do not require the same proportion of these resources—butter taking more land, and clothing requiring relatively more labor. (An extra-credit problem, for geometry-inclined students, returns to this problem at the end of Chapter 26's Appendix.)

[9] This section can be skipped in brief courses.

times that of food. Marx argued that only "exploitation" keeps this from actually happening under capitalism.

What are the merits of this doctrine? As Smith pointed out: "In that early and rude state of society which precedes the accumulation of stock [i.e., capital] and the appropriation of land, . . . the quantities of labour . . . seem to be the only circumstance which can afford any rule for exchanging them for one another. . . ."

But Smith, and Ricardo too, recognized that as soon as land and capital are scarce, goods whose production require land and capital in especially heavy proportions will, even if their labor hours are the same, have to be valued higher. Marx saw this too in the third (posthumous) volume of his *Das Kapital* (1894); but, particularly in his first, 1867, volume, he thought the disparity from labor value was somehow "exploitative" and would lead to "contradictions" that would cause capitalism to break down.

In later chapters, we shall deal repeatedly with causes of unemployment and of business cycles, and with efficient pricing under both communism and capitalism. A fair-minded reader of 1970—whether in Moscow, Idaho, or Moscow, Russia—will then be in a position to judge whether the "labor theory of value" is of more than historical interest in the twentieth and twenty-first centuries.

Figure 2-8, which is as applicable under capitalism as under communism, under anarchism as under fascism, illustrates that the labor cost to get an extra unit of food, relative to the labor cost to produce a unit of manufactures, is not something that is a constant. If society wants much food—as near Z—limited land (a fact in China, Russia, India, Switzerland, the United States, and Canada) will invoke the law of diminishing returns and require that food be valued at a high price relative to manufactures. Why this rise in food price attributable to land scarcity and labor? To benefit idle landlords? Of course not. In China and Russia, the State owns the land; there is no wealthy landlord class. Still, even in those societies, as Chapter 31 will elucidate, adhering to the labor theory alone will result in inefficient production inside the *p-p frontier*; aside from distorted answers to the question of How, there will result distorted answers to the WHAT problem, as too much is produced of some goods and too little of others in terms of what the State and the consumers really desire and what technology determines could be available to them to choose from.[10]

In leaving this digression, one may note that abandonment of the labor theory of value to ancient history need not affect one way or the other the passion for social reform or conservation of the status quo.

C. THE UNDERLYING POPULATION BASIS OF ANY ECONOMY: PAST AND FUTURE POPULATION TRENDS

■ THE MALTHUS THEORY OF POPULATION

The law of diminishing returns has an important and interesting application in the field of population. Around 1800, Thomas Robert Malthus, a young English

---

[10] If all goods used land and every other input in the same proportions as labor, Fig. 2-7's frontier would become a straight line. In this case prices *proportional* to labor hours would involve none of the above distortions.

clergyman, used to argue at breakfast against his father's perfectionist view that the human race was getting ever better. Finally the younger Malthus became so agitated that he wrote a book. His *Essay on the Principle of Population* (1798) was an instantaneous best-seller. It went through several editions and for a century influenced the thinking of people all over the world (including Charles Darwin, the expositor of the famous doctrine of biological evolution). It is still a living influence today. Malthus' views depend directly on the law of diminishing returns, and continue to have relevance.

Malthus first took the observation of Benjamin Franklin that, in the American colonies where resources were abundant, population tended to double every 25 years or so. Malthus postulated, therefore, *a universal tendency for population—unless checked by food supply—to grow at a geometric progression*. Now, anyone with imagination knows how fast geometric progressions grow—how soon 1, 2, 4, 8, 16, 32, 64, 128, 256, 512, 1,024, . . . , becomes so large that there is no space in the world for all the people to stand.[11]

All this left members of the perfectionist school, such as the elder Malthus and William Godwin, unimpressed. So at this point Malthus in effect unleashed the devil of the law of diminishing returns.

> As population doubles and redoubles, it is exactly as if the globe were halving in size, until finally it has shrunk so much that food and subsistence fall below that necessary for life. Because of the law of diminishing returns, food tends *not* to keep up with the geometric-progression rate of growth of population.

Mind you, Malthus did not say that population *would* increase at these rates. This was only its *tendency* if unchecked. He considered it an important part of his argument to show that, in all places in all times, checks do operate to hold population down. In his first edition he put emphasis on *positive* checks that act to increase the death rate: pestilence, famine, and war. Later he backed down from this gloomy doctrine and held out hope for the human race through *preventive* checks operating on the birth rate. Although the birth-control movement is called neo-Malthusianism, Malthus, himself an early-nineteenth-century clergyman, advocated only *moral restraint* with prudential postponement of early marriages until a family could be supported. In fact, he preached that the struggle for existence was an illustration of the wisdom of Nature, keeping poor people from getting soft and lazy.

This important application of diminishing returns illustrates the profound effects a simple theory can have. Malthus' ideas had widespread repercussions. His book was used to support a stern revision of the English poor laws, whereby destitution was considered a result of laziness and unemployment a state to be

---

[11] At 6 per cent compound interest, money doubles in value every 12 years. It has been estimated that the $24 received by the Indians for Manhattan island would, if deposited at compound interest, be today worth at least as much as all real property on the island. At 6 per cent, Sir Francis Drake's plunder of Spanish gold would today equal Britain's wealth.

World population has more than quadrupled since 1800:

POPULATION OF THE WORLD (in millions)			
	1800	1940	1970
Europe (including all of USSR)	188	572	700
North, South, and Central America	29	277	510
Asia, Africa, and Oceania	702	1,396	2,400
World	919	2,245	3,620

TABLE 2-3. (Sources: W. S. Thompson, *Plenty of People,* **Ronald, New York, 1944; United Nations** *Statistical Year Book.***)**

made as uncomfortable as possible. His opinions also bolstered the argument that trade-unions could not improve the welfare of workers, since any increase in their wages would only cause them to reproduce until there was again barely subsistence enough for all.

Despite the statistics covering many countries incorporated in his later editions, it is today recognized that his views were oversimplifications. In his discussion of diminishing returns, Malthus never fully anticipated the miracles of the Industrial Revolution. In the next century technological innovation *shifted* production-possibility curves rapidly *outward* and made possible better stand-ards of living for more people, even though at the same time medical advances were prolonging human life and further lessening the positive checks to popula-tion. Nor did he anticipate that after 1870 in most Western nations family *fertility* as measured by actual number of children would begin to fall far short of family *fecundity*, or biological reproductive capacity.

Nevertheless, the germs of truth in his doctrines are still important for understanding the population behavior of India, Haiti, China, and other parts of the globe where the balance of numbers and food supply is a vital factor.

Table 2-3 shows how much world population has increased. This increase was made possible mainly through the declining death rate, resulting from scientific advances in medicine and from the improved living standards made possible by the Industrial Revolution. Life expectancy of a Western baby has doubled since 1800 to over 70 years at present, and standards of living far exceed those of any previous century.

Even more dramatic has been the reduction in death rates in low-income regions. Ceylon offers the dramatic case where control of mosquitoes by DDT greatly reduced malaria, cutting the death rate by 34 per cent in a single year.[12] In India alone, one of the fruits of modern science has been a great increase in average life expectancy. In the last 20 years India's population grew by at least

---

[12] The side-effects or long-run repercussions of DDT usage are now being felt. However, it *did* reduce Ceylon's death rate by substantially eliminating malaria. Chapter 39 will discuss such matters of environmental pollution.

120 million, an amount greater than the combined populations of France and England.

Professor Kingsley Davis of California, an expert on population, has warned against the facile belief that it is primarily hunger (or even malnutrition) which makes life so short in poor societies. The role of disease is important as an independent factor: if inexpensive science greatly lengthens life without greatly increasing productivity and greatly changing preindustrial attitudes, the fears of Malthus take on a new relevance.

■ CONTROLLING POPULATION GROWTH

As we shall see in Part Six, much of the world is in a state of underdevelopment and poverty. If the birth rate were to continue at the high levels typical of the past—when you had to have six or more children in order to ensure that there would be a surviving child to carry on your line—population numbers would explode, and the law of diminishing returns would vitiate the gains from technical progress. Little wonder then that, wherever religious and ethical attitudes permit, there is beginning to be an active birth-control movement.

Education is, of course, basic. But nevertheless the new chemical means appropriate to the advanced Western nations—the so-called "pill"—are often inordinately expensive in poorer lands. The required couple of dollars a month may seem little in our economy; but in Java or El Salvador you could raise a family on that much. International and national foreign-aid programs have made some impact in persuading some nations to promote family planning. No doubt changes in ethical attitudes will alter the receptivity of other nations, while chemical research and technical changes will vastly alter costs in this as in other areas.

All that needs stressing here is the fact that there is this important relationship between population density and average standards and amenities of life.

■ DO WESTERN NATIONS FACE DEPOPULATION?

At the end of World War I men still feared the Malthusian curse of overpopulation. However within a generation the pendulum had swung to the other extreme; for Western Europe and most of North America were undergoing a profound revolution in population, and best sellers carried such flashy titles as *The Twilight of Parenthood* and *England Without People.*

After 1870—earlier in France—birth rates began to drop in most countries of Western European civilization. After World War I, and especially after the Great Depression of the 1930s, the drop became precipitous.

The crisis in births, however, was hidden for a time. Observations that there was an excess of births over deaths gave a misleading feeling of security, because they ignored the fact that North America and Western Europe temporarily had an unusually large number of women in the childbearing age groups. Why this excess in these age groups? Because people in 1900 had larger families than people in 1935 were having. With so many women of the age to be mothers,

Net reproduction rates make correction for changing age distribution:

NET REPRODUCTION RATES FOR VARIOUS COUNTRIES

Canada	1.28	1930-35	Germany			
	1.16	1935-39	Total	0.71	1933	
	1.23	1967	West	1.18	1966	
United States			Belgium	0.90	1939	
Total	0.98	1930-40		1.13	1967	
	1.72	1960	Netherlands	1.15	1935-39	
	1.21	1967		1.28	1968	
White	0.96	1935-40	Australia	0.98	1935-39	
	1.66	1960		1.35	1966	
	1.16	1967	Palestine			
Nonwhite	1.14	1935-40	Moslems	2.17	1940	
	2.04	1960	Jews	1.61	1945	
	1.56	1967	Israel			
United Kingdom	0.78	1935-39	Jews	1.73	1966	
	1.29	1966	Japan	1.49	1935-39	
France	0.87	1935-37		0.74	1966	
	1.25	1967	India	1.25	1931	
Sweden	0.78	1935-39		1.31	1941	
	1.09	1967	Soviet Union	1.72	1926	
				1.54	1938	
				1.14	1965	

TABLE 2-4. An NRR (net reproduction rate) permanently greater than 1 means ultimate population growth. An NRR less than 1 means ultimate population decline. The NRR for Canada is now substantially above 1. (Source: *Population Index,* **April, 1969,** Office of Population Research, Princeton, N.J.)

prewar birth *totals* temporarily held up; and yet the number of births *per mother* was low—so low that if the same prewar rates had continued, the future growth of the population would have eventually ended and turned into a decline.

Thus before World War II there was every good reason for the population expert to despair for the future of the population of Western nations. Indeed, in 1943 one member of parliament remarked that the case for the new family allowances rested on the fact "that we already are within sight of the beginning of a decline in our population." The following year, the Family Allowance Act was passed granting to mothers a monthly average allowance of $6.04 per child.[13]

---

[13] Most authorities believe birth rates are to be explained by social rather than biological factors. Thus, the French Canadians, who long had high birth rates, once came from just those rural regions of France with the lowest rates. Second-generation Italian and Jewish city dwellers show greatly reduced rates. Ironically, the highest rates of all are to be found among—of all peoples—the North American Indians, suggesting that we may yet give the country back to the Indians. Their rate of natural increase—like their net reproduction rate— is twice that of whites; about one-half of all Canadian Indians are under sixteen, compared to less than one-third for other Canadians.

■ OUR AMAZING POPULATION UPSURGE

Just then something remarkable happened to jar the expert. Nobody yet knows quite how to explain it. During and after World War II the pattern of fertility began steadily to climb, reaching new heights. Every year now brings more than 360,000 babies.

Some of the reasons are, of course, obvious. With the war came prosperity, and the backlog of depression-deferred marriages began to melt. The desire to avoid wartime conscription, and postwar arrival of unmarried immigrants, also had something to do with the increase in marriages. The number of bachelors and spinsters shrank; and the age of (first) marriage fell sharply, so that more than half the girls were married by the time they were twenty-one, and half the men by the age of twenty-two!

With many more recent marriages, it was only natural to expect the birth rate to leap upward. But more than that, people stepped up the rate at which they had children. In the 1950s third and fourth children became fashionable among the middle classes, a dramatic reversal from the prewar situation.

A glance at a college faculty—young, old, and middle-aged—will show the changing trends in this regard: the associate professors have already had more children than retired professors, and the final score is not yet in. Paradoxically, poorer nations such as Japan and Italy, which used to have high birth rates, now restrict family size more than do the rich nations.

Table 2-4 shows that the richer countries of Western Europe had prewar net reproduction rates[14] far below unity and now have rates above the critical level of unity. Canada has come to have a net reproduction rate that is one of the highest in the world or in recent history, and only recently has begun to show a change in trend.

■ ANOTHER TURN OF THE TIDE?

The North American birth rate, constant since about 1945, began to fall about 1956. This rate, calculated as the number of births per thousand people, was affected in part by a temporary drop in the percentage of women who were of child-bearing age. More significant for the longer run trend is the fact that the fertility and net reproduction rates have also been falling. It is true that national surveys of the number of children that American women say they *want* still average 3.1, but the *actual* number they have has been slowly declining. *Even the total number of Canadian births declined each year from 1958 to 1968.*

---

[14] Demographers define the net reproduction rate (NRR) as "the *average* number of girl babies that will be born to a representative newly born girl in her lifetime." Thus, if 1,000 girls born in 1970 will, by 2015 A.D., have produced 1,600 girl babies, the NRR = 1,600/1,000 = 1.6; and were such a fertility rate to be maintained indefinitely, population would ultimately be growing at the rate of 60 per cent per "generation," i.e., about every 25 years, the average age of a mother when giving birth. (Explain exactly what NRR = 0.7 or = 1.0 means, showing why 1.0 is the watershed between decay and positive growth.)

Finally, in 1969, the rise in the number of new families reversed the birth decline.

No doubt economic factors are involved here. Professor Richard Easterlin of the University of Pennsylvania has put forward an interesting hypothesis. He speculates that a young married couple will be less eager to have many children if their current income is falling far below that which their own families had a few years earlier. He points out that in the 1950s, when young people were scarce and their incomes relatively high, they hastened to have many children. In the early 1970s, when the vast crop of war babies has been coming into the labor market and bidding down incomes, the comparison is less favorable. In Easterlin's view, this helps to explain the decline in NRR.

Whatever the explanation of the turn of the tide in North America, let us be clear on four things: (a) the Canadian birth rate is a little higher than the American, but tends to rise and fall at the same times; (b) both rates are high compared to those in other advanced nations; (c) even if fertility rates continue to fall, total Canadian births will rise in this decade because of family formation among members of the post-war baby boom; (d) birth rates in North America and Europe are as little as one-half of those in Africa and Latin America.

When birth rates fall, migration becomes a strong force shaping national populations.

■ MIGRATION

Canada's is an open economy—immigrants and their families add to the population and emigrants reduce it. Three great periods of immigration (1880-1890, 1900-1930, and 1950-1960) brought almost two-thirds of the nine million settlers and workers who have come to Canada. Most of these new arrivals have been between 20 and 44 years of age, and have tended to distort the age-structure pattern shown in Fig. 2-9. In some decades, however, emigration from Canada (mostly to the United States) has exceeded the inflow (mostly from Europe); and, over the past 120 years, emigration is believed to have offset more than three-quarters of immigration. (See Table 2-5.) This musical chairs game was formerly regarded as a "displacement" of resident Canadians by foreigners, and gave support to the political theory that Canada was not able to absorb large numbers of new workers and dependents. But recent data suggest that it is largely the immigrants themselves who move on to the United States or back to their country of birth, a certain percentage remaining permanently in Canada. Thus, of the 460,000 persons leaving Canada (and not returning) between 1951 and 1961, almost 360,000 were immigrants who had arrived in Canada between the same two dates! The remaining 100,000 were evenly split between native-born and "older" foreign-born Canadians.

Thus, emigration can no longer be regarded as a continual leakage of the Canadian population, though some recent estimates do suggest that Canada is unable or unwilling to hold as large a fraction of the more highly trained graduates of its schools and universities as it does of workers and tradesmen. Instead,

SOURCES OF POPULATION GROWTH IN CANADA, 1851-1969 (millions of persons)

INTER-CENSAL DECADE	(1) TOTAL POPULA-TION AT START	(2) TOTAL POPULA-TION AT END	(3) TOTAL INCREASE (2 — 1, or 6 + 9)	(4) BIRTHS	(5) DEATHS*	(6) NET NATURAL INCREASE (4 — 5, WITH ADJUSTMENTS)	(7) IMMIGRA-TION	(8) EMIGRA-TION AND RESIDUAL DISAP-PEARANCE	(9) NET MIGRATION (7 — 8, or 3 — 6)
1851-61	2.44	3.23	.79	1.28	− .61	.67	.21	− .09	.12
1861-71	3.23	3.69	.46	1.37	− .72	.65	.18	− .37	− .19
1871-81	3.69	4.32	.63	1.48	− .75	.72	.35	− .44	− .09
1881-91	4.32	4.83	.51	1.54	− .82	.72	.90	−1.11	− .21
1891-1901	4.83	5.37	.54	1.55	− .83	.72	.33	− .51	− .18
1901-11	5.37	7.21	1.84	1.93	− .81	1.12	1.76	−1.04	.72
1911-21	7.21	8.79	1.58	2.34	− .87*	1.35	1.61	−1.38	.23
1921-31	8.79	10.38	1.59	2.42	− 1.06	1.36	1.20	− .97	.23
1931-41	10.38	11.51	1.13	2.29	− 1.07	1.22	.15	− .24	− .09
1941-51	11.51	14.01	2.50	3.19	− 1.17*	1.97	.55	− .38	.17
1951-61	14.01	18.09	4.08	4.47	− 1.32	3.15	1.54	− .61	.93
1961-65	18.09	19.86	1.77	2.28	− .72	1.56	.50	− .29	.21
1965-69	19.86	20.94	1.08	1.50	− .61	.89	.76	− .57	.19
Total Period	2.44	20.94	18.50	27.65	−11.36	16.29	10.04	−8.00	2.04

*Adjusted for war deaths.

TABLE 2-5. (Source: Camu, Weeks, and Sametz, *Economic Geography of Canada*, Toronto: The Macmillan Co. of Canada Ltd., 1964; and Bank of Canada *Statistical Summary*.)

statisticians and demographers look to figures of "net immigration"–immigrants minus emigrants—in making their population forecasts. This figure ran at almost 100,000 per year in the booming 1950s, but averaged out to about 40,000 during the following decade. Thus, although net immigration provided almost one-third of all additions to the Canadian population in the 1950s, the likely current contribution to growth from abroad is expected to be less than one-sixth.

■ ECONOMIC EFFECTS OF POPULATION GROWTH

The economic impact of population changes is already very noticeable. Our suburbs teem with children; our schools are overcrowded. The bulge of postwar births has already hit colleges: by 1980 college enrolment will triple that of 1968, but the number of pupils attending elementary school will actually fall.

Figure 2-9 shows that the number of dependents—in school, or in retirement—in proportion to those of working age (between 15 and 64 years) has recently hit levels unparalleled since the nineteenth century. Will workers have to support *more* nonworkers? The proportion of dependents at school should be levelling off in the 1970s, but the proportion of people who have retired may continue to increase.

From the military manpower viewpoint, time may be working against the countries of Western Europe. Table 2-6 shows estimates of future populations for certain countries. Note the high estimate for the Soviet Union, where only

The burden of the dependent age-groups is falling:

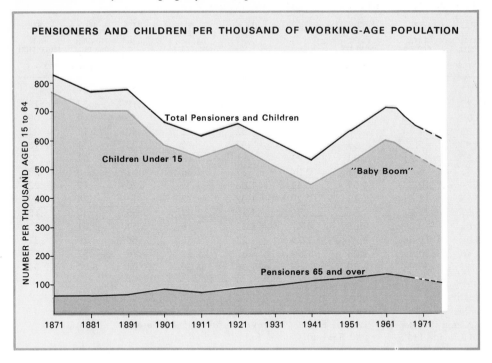

PENSIONERS AND CHILDREN PER THOUSAND OF WORKING-AGE POPULATION

FIG. 2-9. In spite of a boom from 1941 to 1961, falling family size over 100 years has steadily reduced the number of dependent children per 1,000 in the productive ages. The steep downward swing will continue at least until the mid-1970s. Innovations in care for the aged have failed to increase their number relatively to younger people, and have made little impact on the total curve. Immigration has been an important source of the productive-age group. (Source: Urquhart & Buckley, *Historical Statistics of Canada*, **Cambridge University Press, 1965, and Canada Census Data.**)

recently have net reproduction rates been low; and note the rather low figures for Sweden and the United Kingdom.

Is our population upsurge a good thing? Economics alone cannot answer such a general question. The joys and aches of family life are not to be measured in mere dollars and cents. Yet we can study certain economic aspects of population growth; and when we come to do so in later chapters, we shall find that the answers are rarely simple.

On the one hand, *growing* population makes for high money spending, as homes and factories are being replicated in like numbers. Therefore it may act against unemployment, and by the same reasoning, it could also aggravate inflationary threats. On the other hand, a considerably higher *level* of population threatens us with the law of diminishing returns. It fills our cars with people and fills our roads with cars; it pollutes the air with smog, it pollutes our

Canadian, U.S., and Soviet populations gain relative to rest of Europe:

ESTIMATED FUTURE POPULATION OF DIFFERENT COUNTRIES IN 1980 (in millions)				
	ANNUAL GROWTH (% per year)	1966	1975	1980
Canada	1.5	20	23.2	25.2
United States	1.3	197	221	236
United Kingdom	0.7	55	58.6	60.6
France	1.1	49	55	57
Soviet Union	1.2	233	260	275
Sweden	0.9	7.8	8.4	8.8
Italy	0.9	52	56	59
Japan	1.0	99	108	114

TABLE 2-6. Note the different rates of growth (1963-1966 average) in the first column, showing Canada, the United States and the Soviet Union growing fastest and the United Kingdom, Sweden, and Italy slowest. (Source: United Nations *Statistical Year Book* and DBS.)

water with filth; it spoils the countryside and ruins privacy. (Chapter 39 will deal with urban and environmental problems.)

SUMMARY

A. PROBLEMS OF ECONOMIC ORGANIZATION

■ 1 Every economy must somehow solve the three fundamental economic problems: WHAT kinds and quantities shall be produced of all possible goods and services; How economic resources shall be used in producing these goods; and FOR WHOM the goods shall be produced, i.e., the distribution of income among different individuals and classes.

■ 2 Societies meet these problems in different ways—by custom, instinct, fiat and decree, and in our mixed economy, largely by a system of price and markets.

■ 3 The basic problems are important because of the fundamental fact of all economic life: with limited resources and technology, standards of living are limited. Economic goods are *scarce* rather than free; society must choose among them, because not all needs and desires can be fulfilled.

B. TECHNOLOGICAL CHOICES OPEN TO ANY SOCIETY

■ 4 With given resources and technology, the production choices open to a nation between two such goods as butter and guns can be summarized in the *production-possibility curve*, or *frontier*. This indicates the way in which one good can be transformed into another by transferring resources from its production to that of the other.

■ 5 Production-possibility curves can illustrate many basic economic processes: how we use relatively *less* of our resources for food *necessities* as we develop; how we choose between *private* market goods and *public* governmental goods; between *current consumption* and *capital goods* that enhance *future* capacity to produce. The *p-p frontier* can illustrate *technical progress* and pave the way for diminishing returns.

■ 6 *The law of diminishing returns* asserts that, after a point, as we add more and more of a variable factor input (such as labor) to a fixed factor input (such as land), the amount of extra product will fall off. This law is really a matter of proportions: the varying factor input has less and less of the fixed factor input to work with.

■ 7 *Economies of mass production or of scale* are often described as "increasing returns *to scale.*" The word "scale" is a warning that *all* factor inputs are being varied simultaneously, with none held fixed as in the law of diminishing returns. Many modern processes do pass through an initial stage of increasing returns to scale.

■ 8 *The labor theory of value* can validly predict the price in terms of labor hours alone only in a hypothetical time when land and other nonlabor factors of production are abundant enough to be freely available.

■ 9 Once such factors as land became scarce, market price ratios depend on the whole mix of labor-wage, land-rent, and capital-interest costs. The *p-p frontier* ceases to be a straight line and becomes a curve which is concave (from below); it depicts the law of increasing (relative) costs. To get equal amounts of one good requires society to sacrifice more and more of the other. All this results when goods use factors of production in different proportions, and hence unbalanced transfers of productive factors bring the law of diminishing returns into play.

C. UNDERLYING POPULATION BASIS OF ANY ECONOMY: PAST AND FUTURE POPULATION TRENDS

■ 10 Malthus' theory of population rests on the law of diminishing returns. He thought that a population, if unchecked, would tend to grow in geometric rate, doubling every generation or so. But each member of the growing population would have less natural resources and land to work with. Therefore, because of diminishing returns, income would have a tendency to fall so low as to lead to a stable population at a level of starvation and pestilence.

■ 11 For a century and a half after Malthus, populations grew by leaps and bounds everywhere. Numbers grew primarily because death rates fell sharply as a result of improved medical and public health technology; yet technological progress in industry more than offset the law of diminishing returns.

■ 12 After 1870 birth rates began to fall. Prior to World War II, advanced nations had net reproduction rates below 1 and faced depopulation. Since 1939 the middle classes have swung back toward a larger-family pattern, a trend predicted by few and with momentous future consequences. Only recently has the tide been slowly turning.

■ 13 Immigration is an important but declining influence on Canadian population. The emigration of skilled and educated persons now attracts more attention than the migration of workers and their families.

QUESTIONS FOR DISCUSSION

1. Without looking at the next chapter, can you anticipate how a price system through supply and demand solves the three problems of economic organization?

2. Explain what economists mean by "*scarcity*," by *free goods*, by *inefficiency*.

3. Draw society's *p-p frontier* if scientific inventions increased the productivity of given resources in butter production only, and not in guns.

4. If land were increased in a number of steps and labor were held constant, would the law of diminishing returns hold? Illustrate and tell why this would indeed happen.

5. Describe and contrast (a) the law of diminishing returns; (b) the law of increasing (relative) costs; (c) the phenomenon of increasing returns to scale.

6. How many were there in your great-grandparents' family? In your parents' family? How many do you think there will be in your own family?

7. "Population pressure doesn't cause war, as is commonly believed. Careful study suggests cause and effect are just the reverse. Nations that want to expand try to persuade their citizens to grow in numbers so the nation will be militarily strong and will have a pretext for expansion." Discuss.

8. *Extra-credit problem* for those mathematically inclined: We can illustrate the "linear programming" technique referred to in footnote 3 on Stigler's least-cost-diet problem. Suppose each unit of milk, beans, and meat has respectively (1, 8, 2) calories and (4, 2, 1) vitamins. Suppose each unit of the 3 goods costs ($1, $2, $3) respectively. Suppose you must buy at least 120 calorie units per month and 180 vitamin units. Can you show by experiment that the least monthly cost is $60 per month, with meat not being bought at all, and with milk at 40 and beans at 10 units? Mathematically the linear programmer writes this as

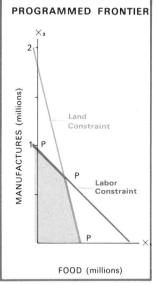

PROGRAMMED FRONTIER

Minimize $Z = \$1X_1 + \$2X_2 + \$3X_3$, subject to
$$1X_1 + 8X_2 + 2X_3 \geqq 120$$
$$4X_1 + 2X_2 + 1X_3 \geqq 180$$
$$X_1 \geqq 0, X_2 \geqq 0, X_3 \geqq 0$$

A similar linear programming problem will define a *p-p frontier* like that shown here. Suppose food (such as butter) and manufactures (such as clothing) each take 1 unit of labor. But food being land intensive takes 4 acres of land, while manufactures take only 1 acre. If society has 1 (million) men and 2 (million) acres, the frontier is defined by

$$1X_1 + 1X_2 \leqq 1$$
$$4X_1 + 1X_2 \leqq 2$$

the first giving the heavy dark brown part and the second the heavy light brown part.

9. Review your understanding of the following concepts:

economic and free goods	increasing returns to scale
substitution and law of scarcity	law of increasing (relative) costs
production-possibility frontier	labor theory of value
law of diminishing returns	Malthusian population theory
total versus extra product	age distribution of population
productive factors or inputs	net reproduction rate (NRR)

Appendix: Alternative Economic Organizations

■ THE CHOICE

Surprisingly many ways of organizing the economy are in use: tribal custom, feudalism, religious sanctions, and so forth. In the more developed societies, however, the range of choice among types of organization is narrowed. The requirements become demanding. A workable industrialized system must be able to answer the WHAT, HOW, and FOR WHOM questions satisfactorily to a large sophisticated population, while adapting to changing tastes for new products and the advancing techniques for making them. Indeed most people would say that the choice had, after the last 100 years, narrowed to two: capitalism versus the various forms of collectivism. This Appendix is concerned mainly about the forms that socialist, and communist, economic organization may take.

Of course, historians will rightly object to the idea of "choice" of economic system. Few peoples have had the opportunity to pick their next system from a menu; and revolution has, like indigestion, often been required to correct their choices. Rather, most societies have, while developing, simply adapted the systems used by their neighbors or imposed by their conquerors. Thus in 1867 the Fathers of Confederation felt neither the desire nor the power to devise a new scheme for organizing the Canadian division of labor, trade, specialization. Instead they carried on the individualist system then in use in Britain and the United States, already familiar to farmers and businessmen in Quebec and the other provinces.

This Appendix is also designed to correct the impression that the alternative systems are definite and uniform. Our own system, for example, is a changing compromise. It is often called "capitalist" in that most productive capital goods are the private property of persons and firms, who thus tend to steer our economy's production differently from how it would be steered if capital were collective, or state, property. But in this book we see again and again that decisions about the use and price of capital are to some degree influenced or even made by the state. The state also influences choices and decisions about work, families, saving, and so forth. So "capitalism," like the "enterprise system," "price system," and "market system," is simply a description of part of what is called hereafter the *mixed economy*.

Pure capitalism, undiluted *laissez-faire*, died before Queen Victoria did. The rest of this book will be about the mixed economy. So let us turn briefly to the systems.

■ THE CRISIS OF CAPITALISM

Marx wrote *Das Kapital*, subtitled "an analysis of capitalist production," in 1867. He dwelt mainly on the historical development and stability of the European economy's stages, culminating in the industrialization of the 19th century, as perceived alike by him, his utopian-socialist contemporaries, and the classical political economists Adam Smith and David Ricardo. Arguing that the capitalist system could no longer perform the complicated tasks assigned to it, he foretold repeated and deepening "crises" of shortage, hunger, unemployment, and revolt until a new power appeared capable of sweeping way the old and creating the new system.

World War I appeared to many to be this final crisis of the old system, and in Russia a Marxist revolt did sweep away much of the old. But elsewhere new governments of new states were established on non-revolutionary lines, and the future of the capitalistic way of life seemed, for a decade, serene.

Then it was assailed by the rise of the dictatorships, the Great Depression, and the next war. By 1950 the war-weakened world economy was divided into great blocs. Russia and her European satellites stood within the Iron Curtain in uneasy partnership with China. On the other side was "the West," a non-homogeneous collection of mixed economies ranging from right-wing Switzerland and America to left-wing Norway and New Zealand. And a little aside stood a third bloc, the watchful new nations and the old less-developed nations, committed to neither economic system represented by the other two blocs.

Little wonder then that profound social philosophers, like Harvard's Joseph Schumpeter, thought in 1945 that they could foresee the end of capitalism in the next few years. Rejecting the Marxist predictions, they nevertheless feared that the staggering problems of development and post-war recurring cycles of inflation and unemployment would lead the West to massive state interventions that would, in themselves, amount to the end of capitalism.

In this they were apparently wrong. The modern mixed economy, using the "new economics" of monetary and fiscal policy,[1] has been able to perform well against cyclical instability. The war-destroyed European nations recovered by a mixture of private initiative and state planning. Japan, Israel, and other less-developed societies all sprinted ahead. Rates of productivity growth increased everywhere. The Marxian historical timetable—savagery to feudalism, feudalism to capitalism, capitalism to socialism and on to communism—has for the moment been shown not to be inevitable. Is it a fairy tale?

This question, of the inevitability of final capitalist crisis and the resurgence of peoples in new economic systems, is itself a sufficient reason to survey the alternative systems, not all of which are Marxist.[2] The systems are also of interest as part of the intellectual history of the human race, and of the social history of protest. But most of all, they are of interest in disabusing our minds of the tyranny of certain facile generalizations which, like most facile generalizations, simply will not stand up to the hard facts of actual experience.

Thus, is it true that without free markets for goods and services, democratic freedoms and political civil rights cannot prevail? Many economic libertarians argue that *personal liberties* and *property liberties* are one and are inseparable. But are they right? At the other extreme, many advocates of socialism argue that "political democracy" is but a sham if the state does not get rid of "production for profit" and replace it by "production for use" and guarantee "fair shares" all around. But are they right?

And in particular, is the argument correct in the learned and persuasive book, *The Road to Serfdom* (1945), by Friedrich Hayek (of Austria, Britain, the United States, and Germany), that each step away from the market system and toward the social reforms of the welfare state, is *inevitably* a journey that must end in a totalitarian state with neither efficiency nor liberty? The opposing view is that gradual evolutionary reforms are the only way to prevent a cataclysmic descent through revolution into communist dictatorship. If the evolutionists are

right, Hayek is quite wrong. Let us review the troops.

■ A BOUQUET OF ISMS

Men have always had visions of a more perfect society: Plato's Republic, Sir Thomas More's Utopia, Marx's Dictatorship of the Proletariat, and so on without number. It is only too easy to look at concrete present-day imperfections and then to contrast them with the ideal features of a vaguely defined utopia. Beyond agreeing that the present order has faults, different schools of reform have little in common.

At the one extreme are the anarchists, who believe in no government at all; at the other, the apologists for an all-powerful collectivized, totalitarian, communistic social order, where the first person singular is all but replaced by the first person plural. Within the field of socialism itself, we find subdivisions: Christian socialism, state and Marxian socialism, guild socialism, Fabian (evolutionary) socialism, and many others.

In the minds of some Canadians, socialists are still bearded characters who meet in a candle-lit cellar to plot sabotage and bloody revolution. Worse, such people use the term "socialist" as a disparaging stereotype to discredit anyone who believes in pensions, medical services, progressive taxation, monopoly regulation, a tax on capital gains, free love, or even the encouragement of student protest.

Some Canadians are so suspicious that they support some welfare and socialization policies in order to "forestall the socialists." These are attitudes they share with most Americans. At the other extreme are people who have brought with them various brands of socialism or Marxism from their European birthplaces, agrarian radicals, home-made revolutionaries, and a very large group whose ideas stem from their trade union affiliations, ranging from Gompers-type laborism and Catholic socialism to west-coast syndicalism and communism. (The reader should turn to Chapter 7 for a description of these threads in our labor organization.) Many persons at the "left" of this wide and disparate spectrum of theories adhere to the New Democratic Party (NDP, based on the former CCF) or to the Communist Party (whether or not they actually carry membership cards). But political loyalties aside, some "socialist" ideas will be found in the platforms or the

---

[1] As outlined in Chapters 13 to 16 later in this book.
[2] See the Appendix to the next chapter, page 72.

minds of members of all parties: Quebec Liberals and separatists, prairie Conservatives, and British Columbian Social Crediters.

Looking abroad, we see that while the United States has managed to sustain two huge parties both of which are free to advocate the free-enterprise system while experimenting with elements from other "isms," elsewhere politics are generally divided among anywhere from three to twelve or more parties. Almost all have the words "liberal," "radical," "progressive," or "socialist" in their titles, and we must be careful in interpreting their viewpoints. First, bear in mind that European parties often represent a *class* of persons: farmers, pensioners, small retail traders, landholders, industrialists, workers, or other distinct groups. The name matters less than the representation. Second, "liberalism" in Europe was a nineteenth-century revulsion from church, nobility, and government toward individual self-determination; "radicalism" was an extreme form of this individualism. Thus radicals often oppose what we now think of as left-wing objectives. Third, "progressives" stand for different things in different places. In Canada and the United States in the 1920s and 1930s they were western-farm-based and stood for easy money in financial policy and for a mixture of individualism and collectivism in other economic matters. But elsewhere the word is associated with socialist aims. Fourth, "socialism" does not mean much in a European party title: France has a party paradoxically called Radical Socialist, which is radical (individualist) and conservative. Even Hitler's party was called "national socialist" (Nazi).

One important distinction most "socialist" parties do wish to maintain is the difference between the *means* each advocates on the route to socialism. Some espouse violence, revolution, and the seizure of property and the reins of power. Others, like Britain's Labour Party and the ruling parties in most of Scandinavia pursue a gradual, nonrevolutionary extension of socialism by peaceful and democratic means. Although they differ from the European social democrats in important details, Canada's socialists in the NDP party would wish to be classified with them when a broad survey of all the "isms" is being made.

It is clear, therefore, that we do not have to master all the thousand and one different "isms" in order to understand the world today. It is enough to understand something of (1) relative *laissez-faire*, or mixed-economy private enterprise, (2) socialism, (3) communism, and (4) fascism. There is no hard and fast boundary between these; it is a matter of degree. Moreover, we cannot even range these along a line, with fascism at the extreme right wing and communism at the extreme left wing. In some ways —although neither would admit it—communism and fascism have much in common.

■ FASCISM

This is easier to characterize politically than economically. Be it in Hitler's Germany, Mussolini's Italy, Franco's Spain, Salazar's Portugal, or Perón's Argentina, fascism is usually characterized by a one-man dictatorship, by one political party with all others abolished, by the disappearance of civil liberties of the type granted in our Bill of Rights. Fascistic movements are always highly nationalistic, often with emphasis placed on a vaguely defined "master race" which exploits minority groups. In the words of Mussolini, fascists are urged to "live dangerously"—to value war and national power as ends in themselves. The individual is to be secondary to the state.

On the economic side, Mussolini's fascism happened to toy with the notion of a "syndicalist," or "corporate," state; each industry and group of workers was organized in a syndicate, and these were to meet and bargain and plan how the economy should be run. However, this syndicalism has never come to much and has not been especially characteristic of other fascist regimes. Almost all of them are against free and militant trade-unionism; almost all give the central government great regulatory power over every sphere of economic life. Some work hand in glove with religious authorities; others are anti-church. Often capitalists and the lower middle classes contribute to the initial strength of fascist movements; but later, when the fascist movement begins to take on—as they sometimes do—revolutionary aspects, the capitalists may regret the Frankenstein's monster that they helped to create.

Their only consolation lies in the fact that one of the earmarks of a fascist regime is opposition to communism; often it sails into power by exaggerating the immediate likelihood of a Bolshevik revolution, and after it has come into power, the threat of communism is used as an excuse for the suppression of democratic processes.

■ SOCIALISM

In defining fascism we were able to point to Nazi Germany or fascist Italy. Socialism cannot be so easily described. Of course, we can describe the Swedish socialist government or the British Labour Party's program, but these do not present dramatic contrasts with our system. In many ways they are very similar to the mixed systems produced by our NDP governments in Saskatchewan and Manitoba and even by the eclectic governments in Ontario and Quebec. They certainly fall far short of the central direction of Eastern Europe, Russia, or China.

A few common elements seem to characterize socialist philosophy:

1. *Government ownership of productive resources.* The role of private property is gradually to be lessened as key industries such as railroads, coal, and even steel are gradually nationalized. Unearned profits from increases in land value are also limited. (In West Germany and the United Kingdom, enthusiasm for nationalization seems to be ebbing.)

2. *Planning.* Instead of permitting the free play of profit motives in a *laissez-faire* market economy, coordinated planning is to be introduced. Sometimes the program of "production for use rather than profit" is advocated; advertising expenditure on gadgets is to be reduced; workers and professional people are to develop instincts of craftsmanship and social service so that they will be guided by other motives than those of our "acquisitive society."

3. *Redistribution of income.* Through government taxing powers, inherited wealth and swollen incomes are to be reduced. Social security benefits and cradle-to-grave welfare services provided by the collective purse are to increase the well-being of the less privileged classes.

4. *Peaceful and democratic revolution.* As distinct from communism, socialism often advocates the peaceful and gradual extension of government controls—revolution by ballot rather than by bullet. This strategy is more than a means; rather, it is a deep philosophical tenet of faith.

BRITISH SOCIALISM   A brief look at British socialism will point out the modern issues. Just when Adam Smith's classical "liberal" economics had won the day from its mercantilistic and feudal predecessors, English intellectual opinion began to move beyond *laissez-faire* and toward socialism. A key example is John Stuart Mill, who was brought up by an eight-

eenth-century exponent of utilitarian individualism, but who had by the last half of the nineteenth century turned to a kind of socialism. And in the twentieth century, university and night-school intellectuals were won to the Fabian doctrines of the inevitability of gradual socialism; and the socialist views of Bernard Shaw and Beatrice and Sidney Webb had also become the views of the trade-union movement.

All this was hidden until World War I. After that war, the Liberal party was ground away between the millstones of the Conservative and Labour parties. And after World War II, Labour really came into power. Its early goals included (1) vast extension of welfare services by the state—in which Conservative governments in large degree have acquiesced; (2) heavy redistributive income and estates taxation—in which to a degree the Conservatives also acquiesce; (3) extensive centralized planning, including stringent regulation of industrial location and of local land use and zoning; and finally (4) initially a fairly sweeping program of nationalization, beginning with coal, power, and railroads and, in the doctrines of the left wing of the party, reaching beyond steel to many branches of wholesaling and distribution, engineering, and ordnance.

Today, the Labour Party finds itself quite divided on how far to carry traditional socialism. This shows itself in debates over the extent to which nationalization should be pressed and the degree to which reliance should be placed on market mechanisms. At the intellectual level, now that so many of the goals set up years ago in *Fabian Essays* have been realized, there is much soul searching going on; and challenging new Fabian essays are hard to write. Is "redistribution of income and wealth among individuals and welfarism designed to make capitalism work well" adequate? And can the mixed economy command the idealistic enthusiasms that more sweeping reforms are able to fire? Has the improvement of living standards pushed the militant poor up into the contented middle classes? Has making society more fluid tended to drain off the bright son of poor parents to Oxford and the Establishment, alienating him from the radical trade-union tradition?

Nor is this quandary unique to Britain. In Sweden, Norway, Denmark, Australia, and New Zealand, the so-called "middle way" of moderate labor socialism has now been in or near power for a third of a century. Yet every one of these economies begins to look more and more like what we ourselves have become since the institution of Ontario Hydro, workmen's compensation, family allowances, hospital insurance, and Quebec steel.

FRENCH "INDICATIVE PLANNING"   Ideologically rather removed from traditional socialism is the remarkable development in France of planning by the state. Even before De Gaulle, many important industries were owned and run by the French government: railroads, electricity, and mines, for example. The tools of economics—marginal-cost pricing of power, benefit-cost analysis of the worthwhile program of investments in these state industries—deserve much of the credit for the remarkable rate of real growth in France during the last two decades. But that is not all.

Even private industry is brought into a comprehensive national plan. There is, however, one important difference from the traditional planning of socialist societies. In the French mixed economy, participation in *Le Plan* is mostly voluntary. (But, as everywhere these days, what business firm dares get the authorities too angry at it—particularly when permission to go to the capital markets is controlled by government?)

Representatives of different industries sit down together in committees, presided over by the civil servants who serve the plan. Businessmen are given quantitative information on national goals for the years just ahead; and they respond with information on what these goals will mean for their own industries. In turn, these replies are made the basis for a recalculation of the aggregates and the details of the plan.

> In the end, each industry learns that it can count on an expanding market. And as business firms in those industries proceed to meet these indicated goals, they do generate the production, income, and demand called for by the plan.

How has it all worked out? Apparently, remarkably well if we can judge by results. Almost too well to be credible, when one considers the informality of the arrangements and their quasi-voluntary nature. In the late 1960s, many an English reformer would have traded some of the "pie in the sky" of traditional socialism for some pragmatic fruits of indicative planning. A National Economic Develop-

ment Council ("NEDDY") was set up to imitate the French methods; and Harold Wilson's Labour government set up a Ministry of Economic Affairs to promote such programs.

Similarity must not conceal diversity. In Egypt and many countries recently released from colonialism, there has been widespread nationalization of industry; in the repeated examples of this process during the last decades, there have as yet been few cases where the result has been a rapid rate of real economic growth. Similarly, the economy of Argentina, despite resources and technology that many a poor country would envy, stagnated under state controls introduced by Dictator Perón. What has been the relation between the particular brand of socialism of Sukarno's Indonesia, Castro's Cuba, and Nkrumah's Ghana and their respective GNPs?

◼ MARXIAN COMMUNISM AND SOVIET RUSSIA: HISTORY

Marxian communism represents a departure both from earlier utopian socialist movements and also from evolutionistic socialist movements of the last century. Karl Marx (1818-1883), who began as a student of Hegelian philosophy but ended up as the messiah of a new doctrine of "scientific socialism," worked in exile with his friend and financial sponsor Friedrich Engels to establish a whole new theory of economics and history. For three-quarters of a century after Karl Marx and Friedrich Engels issued their 1848 Communist Manifesto, numerous international socialist conferences were held; yet outside the British Museum, not much seemed to be accomplished.

In 1917, the big moment came. Czarist Russia was knocked out of the war by the Germans. Lenin, a follower of Marx, was transported in a sealed railroad car across Germany and into Russia. Aided by Trotsky, a one-time New Yorker, Lenin's Bolsheviks snatched power from the moderate Kerenski regime that had overthrown the monarchy. Preaching peace and promising land for the peasants and a dictatorship of the proletariat, the followers of the Red hammer and sickle gained adherents in the navy and army and forcibly took power.

There followed the "ten days that shook the world." The meeting of the democratic Constituent Assembly, only few of whose elected representatives were pro-Bolshevik, was forbidden. An army was organized and trained by Trotsky, and successive towns were won over to the revolutionary forces—often by strategic capture of the water and power supply alone. Then followed a great civil war between the Red and White armies, the latter aided by Poland and Western powers. In the end, the officers of the White army ended up chiefly in Paris, driving taxicabs and drinking vodka to the memory of Czar Nicholas.

THE REVOLUTION ACHIEVED   The world expected a Russian collapse; but the communist regime persisted—not without experiencing horrible famines, in which literally millions perished. Aristocrats and bourgeoisie were ruthlessly "purged" and "liquidated"—new words for age-old processes brought to a new perfection. The Communist party was the only political party permitted; only a few per cent of the population could belong to this elite group; it elected the members of local "soviets" of factories and farms. These elected representatives to still higher soviets, until, at the very top, over all the federated Union Republics, stood the Council of People's Commissars of the Supreme Soviet of the U.S.S.R. (Union of Soviet Socialist Republics).

The Soviet leaders had no blueprints to guide them. Marx had confined himself largely to the faults of capitalism and had revealed very little about what the promised land was to be like. It was not even on the timetable that backward Russia, which had hardly emerged from feudalism into capitalism, should experience its revolution before the downfall of the top-heavy industrialized nations. During the 1920s, Lenin compromised with capitalistic enterprise in the NEP (New Economic Policy). But in 1928-1929, the first Five-Year Plan for industrialization of manufacturing and collectivization of agriculture was introduced. This was followed by a second Five-Year Plan.

Because of the rapid pace of capital formation, war preparedness, and the state of Russian technology, consumption was severely rationed throughout these years. Workers had ration cards that were honored at specific stores, but money continued to be used. Excess money income could be spent only upon special goods at higher prices than the basic ration. Real and money wages differed among occupations, with piece rates and incentive pay for high productivity becoming ever more dominant.

Stalin, one of Lenin's many lieutenants, finally won out in the struggle for power after Lenin's death in the early 1920s. Trotsky and other old-line revolutionaries were accused of plotting with foreign powers against the Soviet Union, and in the middle 1930s a tremendous purge of generals and officials culminated in the sensational Moscow trials—sensational because all the defendants vied with each other in avowing their own guilt. After the Chamberlain-Hitler appeasement pact, Nazi Germany and Soviet Russia in 1939 signed a nonaggression pact, which lasted until Hitler—flushed with his victory over Poland and France and lusting for the farmlands of the Ukraine—attacked Russia.

With fanatical patriotism and aided by the Western allies, the Russians traded their blood for the Germans' until few Germans were left in the Russian homeland. After the defeat of the Axis, the short-lived comradeship with the West flickered out, and the world stood in the shadow of the hydrogen bomb, with Russia trying to spread her influence over Europe and Asia and with the Atlantic nations, the United States, and ourselves bent on stopping her on the one hand, and China threatening her on the other.

In the postwar period, Stalin's one-man rule became more and more paranoid, and his death in 1953 brought in the inevitable revulsion toward his regime. What seemed to be a thaw set in under the committee rule of Khrushchev, and sprigs of criticism began to push up their sprouts. But the Poles, Hungarians, and Leningrad students learned the hard way that winter was not quite over. Peaceful coexistence became the new official line, and was continued after Khrushchev's replacement by the committee rule of Brezhnev. Faced by the rivalry of China, Russia was in no mood to tolerate a free press and electorate in Czechoslovakia, much less dissident intellectuals at home.

The actual operation of the Soviet Union's economy will be reviewed in the Appendix to Chapter 3 following. There is found the answer to the question of how the Soviet Union decided the three basic problems: WHAT is to be produced, How, and FOR WHOM?

SUMMARY TO APPENDIX

■ 1   A variety of economic systems have evolved which seek to answer the WHAT, How, and FOR WHOM questions of the population and economy. In the course of evolution, the systems themselves are ever changing. The stereotype *laissez-faire* system no longer exists. Nevertheless different systems have certain identifiable economic features.

■ 2   Marx wrote of the imminent demise of the capitalist system due to inherent weaknesses of capitalism itself. The modern mixed economy has replaced capitalism in many countries and has on the whole performed well, but the rise of the modern mixed economy did not follow the Marxian timetable. A principal reason for surveying alternative systems is to gain some measure of insight into various systems and to rid ourselves of facile generalizations about various systems.

■ 3   Fascism is more a political than an economic entity, usually involving strong nationalism, a dictatorship, and the disappearance of civil liberties. The government is given strong regulatory power over the economy.

■ 4   Socialism, despite the widespread use of the label, is a difficult system to describe and define. Common elements in a socialist system are: (1) Government ownership of productive resources; (2) Centralized or governmental planning; (3) Redistribution of income; and (4) Introduction of socialism by peaceful and democratic "revolution."

■ 5   British Socialism has its roots in intellectual history, but it became functional after World War II when the Labour Party came into power. Its original goals were extension of state welfare services, heavy redistributive income and estate taxes, extensive centralized planning, and large-scale nationalization. Today many of the original goals have been realized, and the British Labour Party finds itself divided on how far to carry traditional socialism and the means of implementation.

■ 6   French "indicative planning" provides an interesting example of state economic planning wherein private planning participates "voluntarily" in the plan.

■ 7   Marxian Communism was implemented in Soviet Russia after the 1917 revolution—not without setbacks and both economic and human cost. Moreover, because Marx had never provided a blueprint for the communist society, the government had to feel its way through a variety of policies and five-year plans. Consumption was sacrificed to investment in industrial and military capital formation. Stalin's regime became increasingly repressive, while Khrushchev and his successors have chosen peaceful coexistence.

QUESTIONS FOR DISCUSSION

1. Make a list of a number of "isms," describing each and its history.
2. Describe your own vision of Utopia. Does it differ from the present?
3. Compare and contrast fascism and communism. What is the relation of socialism and capitalism to each other? To *laissez-faire* and the mixed economy?
4. "The Russians claim that they have 'industrial democracy.' This is clearly a different commodity from political democracy as we know it. Even defenders of the Soviet Union will admit that expressions of opinion against the government or the Communist party will not be tolerated. Free press—in our sense—is forbidden. Even if a majority of the Russian people were to prefer their form of government, no one should blind himself to its great differences from our own concepts of democracy and freedom." Discuss this as objectively as you can.
5. Review your understanding of the following concepts:
laissez-faire, mixed economy
anarchism; fascism, socialism, communism
nationalization of industry
indicative planning, French style

3

PRICE FUNCTIONING
OF A "MIXED ECONOMY"

Every individual endeavours to employ his capital so that its produce may be of greatest
value. He generally neither intends to promote the public interest, nor knows how much he
is promoting it. He intends only his own security, only his own gain. And he is in this
led by an invisible hand *to promote an end which was no part of his intention. By pursuing*
his own interest he frequently promotes that of society more effectually than when he
really intends to promote it. ADAM SMITH, The Wealth of Nations (1776)

■ THE MIXED ECONOMY

Most of our attention will be devoted to the special features of economic life
found in twentieth-century industrial nations (with the exception of the Communist nations surveyed in the Appendix to this chapter). In most of these countries
there was a trend in the past few centuries toward less and less direct governmental control of economic activity; gradually feudal and preindustrial conditions were replaced by greater emphasis on what is loosely called "free private
enterprise," or "competitive capitalism."

Long before this trend had approached a condition of full *laissez-faire* (i.e.,
of complete governmental noninterference with business), the tide began to turn
the other way. Since late in the nineteenth century, in almost all the countries
under consideration there has been a steady increase in the economic functions
of government.

Ours is a "mixed economy" in which both public and private institutions
exercise economic control.

Section A of this chapter shows how our mixed economy tackles the three
problems of economic organization that must be met by any society. Section B
describes some fundamental characteristics of the present economic order.

A.   HOW A FREE ENTERPRISE SYSTEM SOLVES THE BASIC ECONOMIC PROBLEMS

In a system of free private enterprise, no individual or organization is *consciously* concerned with the triad of economic problems set forth in Chapter 2: WHAT, HOW, and FOR WHOM. This fact is really remarkable.

To paraphrase a famous economic example, let us consider such a city as Toronto, or Montreal. Without a constant flow of goods in and out of the city, it would be on the verge of starvation within a week. A variety of the right kinds and amounts of food is involved. From the surrounding counties, from the ten provinces, and from the far corners of the world, goods have been traveling for days and months with Central Canada as their destination.

How is it that more than 2 million people are able to sleep easily at night without living in mortal terror of a breakdown in the elaborate economic processes upon which the city's existence depends? For all this is undertaken *without coercion or centralized direction* by any conscious body!

Everyone notices how much the government does to control economic activity—tariff legislation, pure-food laws, utility and railroad regulations, minimum-wage regulations, fair-labor-practice acts, social security, price ceilings and floors, price and incomes policies, public works, national defense, national and local taxation, police protection and judicial redress, zoning ordinances, municipal water or gas works, and so forth. What goes unnoted is how much of economic life proceeds *without* direct government intervention.

Hundreds of thousands of commodities are produced by millions of people more or less of their own volition and without central direction or master plan.

■ NOT CHAOS BUT ECONOMIC ORDER

This functioning alone is convincing proof that a competitive system of markets and prices—whatever else it may be, however imperfectly it may function—is not a system of chaos and anarchy. There is in it a certain order and orderliness. It works.

A competitive system is an elaborate mechanism for unconscious coordination through a system of prices and markets, a communication device for pooling the knowledge and actions of millions of diverse individuals. Without a central intelligence it solves one of the most complex problems imaginable, involving thousands of unknown variables and relations. Nobody designed it. It just evolved, and like human nature, it is changing; but it does meet the first test of any social organization—it can survive.

A dramatic example of the importance of a pricing system is Germany after World War II. In 1946-1947 production and consumption had dropped to a low level. Neither bombing damage nor postwar reparation payments could account for this breakdown. *Paralysis of the price mechanism* was clearly to blame: Money was worthless; factories closed down for lack of materials; trains could not run for lack of coal; coal could not be mined because miners were hungry; miners were hungry because peasants would not sell food for money and no industrial goods were available to give them in return. Prices were legally fixed, but little could be bought at such prices; a black market characterized by barter or fantastically high prices existed. Then in 1948 a "miracle" happened. A thoroughgoing currency reform set the price mechanism back into effective operation. Immediately production and consumption soared; again the WHAT, HOW, and FOR WHOM were being resolved by markets and prices.

The fact to emphasize is that such so-called miracles are going on all around us all the time—if only we look around and alert ourselves to the everyday functioning of the market. A revolutionist out to destroy the capitalist system could ask nothing better than a great inflation or deflation that would paralyze the price mechanism.[1]

■ THE INVISIBLE HAND AND "PERFECT COMPETITION"

Students of economics have to avoid the error of thinking that a price mechanism must work chaotically if it is not controlled by somebody. Having learned this lesson, they must not go to the other extreme and become enamored of the beauty of a pricing mechanism, regarding it as perfection itself, the essence of providential harmony and beyond the touch of human hands.

Adam Smith, whose *Wealth of Nations* (1776) is the germinal book of modern economics or political economy, was thrilled by the recognition of an order in the economic system. Smith proclaimed the principle of the "Invisible Hand"; every individual, in pursuing only his own selfish good, was led, as if by an invisible hand, to achieve the best good for all, so that any interference with free competition by government was almost certain to be injurious. (See this chapter's initial quotation.) While Smith did recognize some of the realistic limitations on this doctrine, it was not until later that economists discovered this truth: The virtues claimed for free enterprise are fully realized only when the complete checks and balances of "perfect competition" are present.

> *Perfect competition* is defined by the economist as a technical term: "Perfect competition" exists only in the case where no farmer, businessman, or laborer is a big enough part of a large total market to have any personal influence on market price; on the other hand, when his grain, merchandise, or labor is large enough in size to produce depressing or elevating effects on market prices, some degree of monopolistic *imperfect competition* has set in, and the virtues of the Invisible Hand must be that much discounted.

Actually, some of the praise of perfect competition is beside the point. As discussed earlier, ours is a mixed system of government and private enterprise; as will be discussed later, it is also *a mixed system of monopoly and competition.* A cynic might say of perfect competition what Bernard Shaw said of Christianity: The only trouble with it is that it has never been tried.

---

[1] In the 1970s governments in the Soviet Union and Eastern European countries are rediscovering some virtues of a pricing system. Imitation is the sincerest form of flattery.

Historians quarrel over whether there ever was a golden age of free competition. And certainly, competition is not now perfect in the economist's sense. We do not even know whether, because of the fundamental nature of large scale production and technology, consumers' tastes, and business organization, competition is becoming less or more intense. The statistics suggest at least a slight weakening of monopolistic concentration of power as giant conglomerates coexist in diverse industries.

In any case, society need not accept as inevitable any trend toward big business, mergers, trusts, and cartels such as began to swell in the 1890s. The challenge is to work out laws and customs that help to improve the working of our less-than-perfect competitive system. The polar cases—*laissez-faire* and totalitarian dictatorship of production—dramatize economic principles. Yet the relevant choice for policy today is not a decision between these extremes, but rather the degree to which public policy should do *less* or *more* in modifying the operation of particular private economic activities.

■ THE PRICE SYSTEM

Just how does the unconscious automatic price mechanism operate? The bare outlines of a *competitive* profit-and-loss system are simple to describe.

Everything has a price—each commodity and each service. Even the different kinds of human labor have prices, usually called "wage rates." Everybody receives money for what he sells, and uses this money to buy what he wishes.

If more is wanted of any one good—say, shoes—a flood of new orders will be given for it. This will cause its price to rise and more to be produced.

Similarly, if more of a commodity such as tea becomes available than people want to buy at the last-quoted market price, its price will be marked down by competition. At the lower price people will drink more tea, and producers will no longer produce quite so much. Thus equilibrium of supply and demand will be restored (as the next chapter and Part Three will show).

What is true of the markets for consumers' goods is also true of markets for *factors of production* such as labor, land, and capital inputs. If welders rather than glass blowers are needed, job opportunities will be more favorable in the welding field. The price of welders, their hourly wage, will tend to rise, while that of glass blowers will tend to fall. Other things being equal, this will cause a shift into the desired occupation. Likewise, an acre of land will go into sugar cultivation if sugar producers bid the most for its use. In the same way, machine-tool production will be determined by supply and demand.

THE GENERAL-EQUILIBRIUM SYSTEM   In other words, we have a vast system of trial and error, of successive approximation to an *equilibrium system of prices and production*. We shall see later that the matching of supply and demand and of prices and costs helps solve our three problems simultaneously. Here are the bare outlines:

1. WHAT things will be produced is determined by the *dollar votes* of consumers—not periodically at the polls, but every day in their decisions to purchase this item and not that. Of course, the money that they pay into business

cash-registers ultimately provides the payrolls, rents, and dividends that consumers receive in weekly income. Thus the circle is a complete one.

2. How things are produced is determined by the competition of different producers. The method that is cheapest at any one time, because of both physical efficiency and cost efficiency, will displace a more costly method.

The only way for producers to meet price competition and maximize profits is to keep costs at a minimum by adopting the most efficient methods. For example, synthetic rubber will be made from oil rather than alcohol if the price of the one is in a certain relation to the price of the other; or electric power will be generated by steam rather than atomic power if the price of coal is below some critical level. The large tractor-operated farm will displace the family-size farm if this leads to lower costs of production.

> *International example:* Bob Jones farms *extensively*, with much Canadian land relative to each hour of labor; Pierre Reny farms *intensively*, using much labor to each hectare of French land. Who orders these sensible How decisions, which properly adjust to the fact that France is more densely populated than Canada? Parliament? The Chamber of Deputies? The UN? Of course not. The price system is society's signaling device. Like a master who gives carrots and kicks to coax his donkey forward, the pricing system deals out profits and losses, to get WHAT, How, and FOR WHOM decided.

3. FOR WHOM things are produced is determined by supply and demand in the markets for productive services: by wage rates, land rents, interest rates, and profits, all of which go to make up everybody's income—relative to everyone else and relative to the whole. (Of course, the character of the resulting distribution of income is highly dependent upon the *initial* distribution of property ownership, upon acquired or inherited abilities, educational opportunities and presence or absence of discriminations against women or particular races.)

Note this: Consumer votes do not by themselves determine WHAT goods are produced. Demand has to meet with a supply of goods; so business cost and supply decisions, along with consumer demand, help to determine WHAT. Just as a broker may help arrange a match between buyer and seller, the auctioneer in the commodity market acts as the go-between who reconciles the consumer votes and business supplies that impinge on the market. (The next chapter explains how.) The profit seeker is society's agent to determine How, seeking least factor-costs for producing each good and being punished by ruthless competition if he fails to use best methods.

■ A PICTURE OF PRICES AND MARKETS

To amplify this highly simplified explanation, turn to Fig. 3-1. It gives a bird's-eye view of the way market pricing reconciles public demand and supply with business supply and demand. Note that markets serve as the connecting device between the public and business. Twenty minutes of poring over this diagram may be worth hours of disconnected musing about economic pricing. (In Chapters 10 and 31, similar circular-flow diagrams will appear.)

A competitive system is impersonal but not completely so. The consuming families face business enterprises on two fronts, with only prices in between.

The competitive price system uses supply-demand markets to solve the basic economic problems—What, How and For Whom:

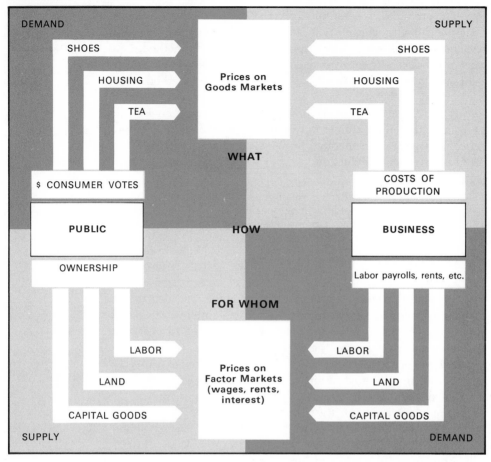

FIG. 3-1. All demand relations are shown in the dark brown areas; all the supply relations in the light-brown areas. See how consumer dollar votes of demand interact in the upper goods markets with business cost-supply decisions, thus helping determine What is produced. And how business demand for inputs or productive factors meets the public's supply of labor and other inputs in the lower factor markets to help determine wage, rent, and interest income— i.e., For Whom goods are produced. Business competition to buy factor inputs and sell goods most cheaply determines How goods are to be produced. (Warning: All parts of the diagram interact together. What depends on the lower part, just as For Whom depends on the upper part—carpenter wages depend on housing demand, and demand for yachts depends on oil-land royalties.)

One front is the widely dispersed one, the retail market on which consumers buy thousands of small items from a score of different retail establishments; grocery, drug, and department stores; movie theaters; gasoline stations; and from electric-power companies, government post offices, landlords, railroad lines, and insurance companies.

On the other front—the market for labor and other productive services—relations are not always so peaceful. To the family breadwinner his wage is not simply another price; it is the difference between luxury and comfort, between comfort and privation. The laborer may feel inferior to the large corporation in bargaining power, and he may turn to collective bargaining by means of trade-unions. By doing this, he may at times be helping to restore competition, while at other times he may be causing conditions to deviate still further from perfect competition.

■ ETHICAL ASPECTS OF INCOME DISTRIBUTION

The above picture of competition tending toward ideal efficiency, toward being on the production-possibility frontier and not inside it, is a highly over-simplified one. But even if the system worked perfectly as described above—which everybody knows not to be the case—many would not consider it ideal. In the first place, goods go where there are the most votes or dollars. A rich man's dog may receive the milk that a poor child needs to avoid rickets. Why? Because supply and demand are working badly? No. Because auction markets are doing what they are designed to do—putting goods in the hands of those who can pay the most, who have the most money votes. Defenders and critics of the price mechanism should recognize this fact.[2]

Or suppose the invention of automatic machines should cause the competitive price of labor to fall, thereby reducing incomes of the poor. Would all ethical observers regard that as necessarily right or ideal?

Should the fact that a man inherited 500 square miles of range land, for which oil companies offer a million dollars per year, necessarily justify so large an income?

These questions are discussed widely and repeatedly. Whether incomes should be completely determined by a competitive struggle—the survival of the survivors—is an ethical question that goes beyond the mechanics of economics. In the modern mixed economy, the electorate insists on providing minimum standards when the market fails to do so. Economics teaches how interventions can be accomplished at least costs in terms of inefficiency.

■ IMPERFECTIONS OF COMPETITION

As we said earlier, one drawback to the picture of the price system as described above is the fact that, in the real world, competition is nowhere near "perfect." Firms do not know when consumer tastes will change; therefore they may overproduce in one field and underproduce in another. By the time they are ready to learn from experience, the situation may have changed again. Also, in a competi-

---

[2] Cecil Woodham-Smith, *The Great Hunger: Ireland 1845-9* (Hamish Hamilton, London, 1962), relates the unbelievable details of how a *laissez-faire* Victorian government let millions of Irish children, women, and men literally starve when a fungus destroyed the potato crop. Gilbert Tucker, *The Canadian Commercial Revolution, 1845-51* (Carleton Library, Toronto, 1964) recounts the same government's cold attitude to the attempts of Canadian organizations to relieve cholera-ridden Irish immigrants.

tive system many producers simply do not know the methods of other producers, and costs do not fall to a minimum. In the competitive struggle one can sometimes succeed as much by *keeping knowledge scarce* as by keeping production high.

The most serious deviation from perfect competition comes from *monopoly elements*. These—as we shall see later on—may result in wrong pricing, incorrect and wasteful resource allocation, and monopoly profits. We shall be reminded again and again how strict is the economist's definition of a "perfect competitor"; the mere presence of vigorous rivalry is not enough for perfect competition.

MONOPOLY ELEMENTS   The economic definition of "imperfect competitor" is *anyone who buys or sells a good in large enough quantities to be able to affect the price of that good*. To some degree that means almost all businessmen, except possibly the millions of farmers who individually produce a negligible fraction of the total crop. All economic life is a blend of competitive and monopoly elements. Imperfect (monopolistic) competition is the prevailing mode, not perfect competition. A good approximation of perfect competition may be the most society can strive for.

Of course, as we shall later see, a businessman cannot set his prices completely as he pleases and still make profits. He must take into account the prices of goods that are substitutes for his own. Even if he produces a trademarked coal with unique properties, he must reckon with the prices charged for other coals, for oil and gas, and for house insulation.

Businessmen, farmers, and workers both like and dislike competition. We all like it when it enables us to expand our market, but we label it as "chiseling," "unfair," or "ruinous" when the knife cuts the other way. The worker whose livelihood depends on how the market prices his labor may be the first to howl when competition threatens to depress wages. Farm groups, aware of what competition can do to agricultural prices, constantly bring pressure to bear on the government to restrict production and thereby raise prices.

In the idealized model of an efficiently acting competitive market mechanism, consumers are supposed to be well informed. They recognize low quality and avoid it; they never buy drugs that turn out to be poisonous or ineffective. Most important, their "desires" are supposed to represent genuine "wants" and "needs" and "tastes." But in actual life, as critics like Galbraith never tire of repeating, business firms spent much money on advertising to *shape*—and, some insist, *distort*—consumer demands. We are terrorized into buying deodorants; from childhood on, we are conditioned to desire what business wants to sell. The sequence "consumer demand → corporate price and production" is often inverted to become "corporate advertising → consumer demand → high price and profit."

Some of the basic factors responsible for monopoly-creating bigness in business may be *inherent in the economies of large-scale production*. This is especially true in a dynamic world of technological change. Competition by numerous producers would simply not be efficient in many fields and could not last. Trademarks, patents, and advertising are often responsible for still other market imperfections. It would be humanly impossible, therefore, to attempt to create *perfect* competition by law. The problem is one of achieving reasonably effective "workable competition."

We shall proceed later to a more microscopic examination of supply and demand. After that discussion we shall be in a position to appraise the workings of the price system more judiciously. A competitive price system is one way of organizing an economy, but not the only way. Admiration should not inhibit reform. Still it is of interest that some socialist nations are making increasing use of the price mechanism in their "command" societies. (See Appendix.) A price system is not perfect, but neither are its alternatives.

■ ECONOMIC ROLE OF GOVERNMENT

It was said earlier that ours is not a pure price economy but a *mixed economy* in which elements of government control are intermingled with market elements in organizing production and consumption. The economic role of government is now so important that two chapters in Part One are devoted to it. An outline of its influence can be briefly indicated here.

WELFARE MINIMA   Democracies are not satisfied with the answers to WHAT, HOW, and FOR WHOM given by a perfectly unrestrained market system. Such a system might dictate that certain people starve from lack of income while others receive inadequate or excessive incomes.

Therefore the citizenry through their government step in with expenditure to supplement the real or money incomes of some individuals. Thus, governments may provide hospital beds for citizens or may present the needy with monthly allowances in times of unemployment or old age. Minimum standards of life are widespread modern goals.

PUBLIC SERVICES AND TAXES   More than this, government provides certain indispensable "public goods" without which community life would be unthinkable and which by their nature cannot appropriately be left to private enterprises. Government came into existence once people realized, "Everybody's business is nobody's business." Obvious examples of public goods are the maintenance of national defence and of internal law and order, and the administration of justice and of contracts.[3]

By and large, in its expenditure of money, government is behaving exactly like any other large spender. By casting sufficient votes in the form of dollar bids in certain directions, it causes resources to flow there. The price system then takes over and performs much as if these were private rather than public needs.

---

[3] Here is a later example of a government service: lighthouses. These "public goods" save lives and cargoes; but lighthouse keepers cannot reach out to collect fees from skippers. So we have here a divergence between *private* and *social* advantage. Philosophers and statesmen have always recognized the necessary role of government in such cases of "external-economy divergence between private and social advantage." Much more on public goods will come later in Chapters 8, and 23, and elsewhere.

Actually, most government expenditure is paid for out of taxes collected. It is here that an important element of *coercion* enters. It is true that the citizenry as a whole imposes the tax burden upon itself; also, each citizen is sharing in the collective benefits of government. But there is not the same close connection between benefits and tax payments as holds when the individual citizen puts a nickel into a gum machine or makes an ordinary purchase. I need not smoke Buckinghams or buy nylon stockings or choose fried eggs, but I must pay my share of the taxes used to finance the various activities of government.

LAWS AND FIATS   Moreover, a second important form of coercion is involved in the universal custom of passing governmental laws: thou shall not sell false weight, thou shalt not employ child labor, thou shalt not burn houses, thou shalt not pour out smoke from thy factory chimney, thou shalt not sell or smoke opium, thou shalt not charge more than the ceiling price for food, and so forth. This set of rules gives the framework within which private enterprise functions; it also modifies the direction of that functioning. Together with government expenditure and taxation, *the decrees of government* supplement the price system in determining the economic fate of the nation.

It would be fruitless to debate whether public enterprise or private enterprise is the more important—as fruitless as to debate heredity versus environment. Without either, our economic world would be an entirely different one.

Finally, as we shall see in Parts Two and Six, it is part of the government's function to help stabilize acute and chronic cycles of unemployment and inflation and to help achieve and maintain healthy economic growth.

B.   CAPITAL, DIVISION OF LABOR, AND MONEY

There are three further important features of modern economic society:

1. Modern advanced industrial technology rests upon the use of vast amounts of *capital*: elaborate machinery, large-scale factories and plants, and stores and stocks of finished and unfinished materials. "Capitalism" got its name because this capital, or "wealth," is primarily the private property of somebody—the capitalist.

2. The present-day economic system is characterized by an almost incredibly elaborate degree of *specialization* and intricate *division of labor*.

3. Ours is a system that makes extensive use of *money*. The flow of money is the lifeblood of our system. It also provides the measuring rod of values.

All these features are interrelated, each with the other and all with the price mechanism described in Section A of this chapter.

Thus we shall see that, without the great facility for trade and exchange which money provides, an elaborate division of labor would be impossible. Money and capital become related through credit activities of the banking system and through the organized financial markets upon which securities can be transformed into money by sale or vice versa. Of course, the relationship between the price mechanism and money is immediate and obvious.

■ CAPITAL AND TIME

No one has trouble seeing that production of economic goods can result from use of such inputs as labor and land (including in the latter term natural resources generally). These are often called *"primary* factors of production," for the reason that neither land nor (these days) labor is regarded as a result of the economic process, but instead exists by virtue of physical and biological rather than economic factors.[4]

Capital, which is the word often used to refer to capital goods generally, is a different kind of production factor. A capital good differs from the primary factors in that it is *an input which is itself the output of the economy.*

> Capital goods, then, represent *produced* goods that can be used as factor inputs for further production, whereas labor and land are primary factor inputs not usefully thought of as being themselves produced by the economic system.

Part Four will show that, just as wages and rent are the factor-prices of primary labor and land, the 6 or 10 or 15 per cent interest rate per annum can in a more subtle way be usefully regarded as the factor-price that rewards and rations society's scarce supply of various capital goods and investment projects.

Because an interest rate is a percentage per unit of time (per month or year or decade), it calls our attention to another way of looking at capital—a way that stresses its special relationship with time. Let us survey this important economic role of capital. If men had to work with their hands on barren soil, productivity and consumption would be very low indeed. Thus, when an anthropologist asked of mourning tribesmen, "Who died?" they replied, "What is death? We have lost the needle!" Over a long time our own economy has amassed a vast stock of equipment, factories and housing, inventories, and drained land.

Men learned very early that the simple, direct methods of production can be improved upon by using *time-consuming indirect methods.* We who are inside the economic system are not conscious of *how roundabout* productive processes have become. An outside observer would be struck with the fact that almost no one in our system seems to be producing *finished goods.* Almost everyone is seen to do work of a preparatory nature; with final consumption a distant future goal. The farmer spends his time in fattening hogs, the truck driver in carrying them toward market, and the packer in advancing them

---

[4] Some qualifications will be evident. Land can sometimes be made by drainage or filling in; this has been accomplished with much of the Tantramar marshes and with Toronto's lake shore. Natural resources such as minerals are laid down by nature, but it may take much economic effort to locate, use, and process them. Therefore they come to have some of the properties of capital goods. Even if one abandons in the Western world a Malthusian theory of population, whereby people seem to be given a cost of production not unlike that of machines, one realizes that the process of education consists of investing in people, thereby making them more productive factors of production. When you see a medical-school graduate, you are in a certain sense looking at a chunk of capital or at an economic production factor that is partially capital.

further toward the last stage of consumption. A steel worker prepares pig iron, part of which will become a hammer to build a house; another bit will become part of a pig-iron furnace; which in turn will prepare pig iron to be used in making further hammers and more pig-iron furnaces; and so forth.

■ THE NEED TO FORGO PRESENT CONSUMPTION

The fact that it takes time to get things started and synchronized is important. It explains why society does not automatically replace all direct processes by more productive indirect ones, and all indirect processes by still more indirect processes. The advantage in doing so is balanced by the initial disadvantage of having to *forgo present consumption goods* by diverting resources from current production to uses that will bear fruit only after some time.

To the extent that people are willing to save—to abstain from present consumption and wait for further consumption—to that extent society can devote resources to new capital formation.[5] And to the extent that people are unconcerned about the future, they may at any time try to "dissave"—to snatch present pleasures at the expense of the future. How? By diverting resources away from the endless task of *replacing and maintaining* capital and to the job of producing extra present-day consumption goods. (Turn back to Fig. 2-5 of Chapter 2, page 27, to review the process of forgoing current consumption in favor of capital formation which adds to future production possibilities.)

We may summarize as follows: Economic activity is future-oriented. By the same token, current economic consumption is largely the consequence of past efforts. Current productive efforts, so to speak, produce for the future, in order to repay the past for present consumption. Also, in progressive societies some fraction of current consumption is sacrificed to new production of net capital formation, which will increase future production.

■ CAPITAL AND PRIVATE PROPERTY

Physical capital goods are important in any economy because they help to increase productivity. This is as true of Soviet communism as it is of our own system. But there is one important difference. By and large, private individuals own the tools of production in a mixed economy.

What is the exception in our system—government ownership of the means of production—is the rule in a socialized state where productive property is collectively owned. The returns from such real capital goods accrue to the government, not to individuals directly. The government then decides how such income is to be distributed among individuals. The communist government also decides how rapidly resources are to be invested in new capital formation: the government decides by how much *present* consumption should be curtailed in

---

[5] We shall later see that, *sometimes* in our modern monetary economy, the more people try to save, the less capital goods are produced; and paradoxically, that the more people spend on consumption, the greater the incentive for businessmen to build new factories and equipment.

order to add to the total of factories, equipment, and productive stocks of goods that are necessary if *future* output is to rise.

Individual capitalists earn interest, dividends and profits, or rents and royalties on the capital goods that they supply. Every patch of land and every bit of equipment has a deed, or "title of ownership" that belongs to somebody directly—or if it belongs to a corporation, then indirectly it belongs to the individual stockholders who own the corporation. Moreover, each kind of capital good has a money market value; hence each claim or title to ownership of a capital good also has a market value. A share of common stock of Canadian Pacific is quoted at a certain price, a Massey-Ferguson bond at its price; a mortgage on a house is valued at some amount; the deed to a house and lot is appraised by the real-estate market at some price; and so forth.

It should be pointed out that our mixed-economy governments do own a good deal of the national real capital, e.g., Canadian National Railways as well as provincial hydro and gas companies. In addition, their agencies, such as the Central Mortgage and Housing Corporation, the Industrial Development Bank, and the Quebec Société Générale de Financement are important sources of capital loans for homeowners and business. But none is large enough to permit government to control, through it, the *total* rate of capital formation.

Also, we note that the *legal property rights of an individual are relative and limited*. Society determines how much of his property a man may bequeath to his heirs and how much must go in inheritance and estate taxes to the government. Society determines how much the owners of public-utility companies— such as electric and gas firms or telephone companies—can earn and how they must run their business.

Even a man's home is not his castle. He must obey zoning laws and, if necessary, make way for a railroad or slum-clearance project. Interestingly enough, most of society's economic income *cannot* be capitalized into private property. Since slavery was abolished, human earning power is forbidden by law to be capitalized. A man is not even free to sell himself: he must rent himself at a wage.

SPECIALIZATION, EXCHANGE, AND DIVISION OF LABOR

Turn now to the second characteristic feature of the present-day economy. The economies of mass production upon which modern standards of living are based would not be possible if production took place in self-sufficient farm households or regions. *Specialization* of function permits each person and region to use to best advantage any peculiar differences in skill and resources. Even in a primitive economy men learn that, rather than have everyone do everything in a mediocre way, it is better to institute a *division of labor*—better for fat men to do the fishing, lean men to do the hunting, and smart men to make the medicine, with each exchanging his products for the goods he needs.

Besides resting upon any interpersonal differences in ability, specialization accentuates and creates differences. Hunting makes a man thin and good at stalking prey; a region with no resources especially adapted to weaving may nevertheless develop skills which give it advantages in this. (Specialization may involve some costs, breeding half men—anemic clerks and brutish stokers—and producing social alienation.)

Finally, specialization may pay, even with no natural or acquired differences in skills: often in this way alone can a large enough volume of activity be reached to realize all the economies of large-scale production mentioned in the preceding chapter. Two *identical* Indian twins might find it better for one to make all bows and the other all arrows—even if they had to draw lots to see which would make which—because only in this way could each be making enough of each item to warrant introducing improved techniques.

> To illustrate the increased productivity of specialization, Adam Smith provided the classical example of pinmaking. One man could at best make a few dozen imperfect pins per day. But when a small group of men are subdivided with respect to function so that each performs simple repetitive operations, they can turn out hundreds of thousands of perfect pins per day.[6]

Moreover, the simplification of function made possible by specialization lends itself to mechanization and the use of labor-saving capital. At the same time it avoids the wasteful duplication of tools that would be necessary if every man had to be a Jack-of-all-trades; and it also saves time lost in going from one job to another. The modern conveyor system of automobile assembly illustrates the efficiency of specialization. Today automation is the watchword.

■ SPECIALIZATION AND INTERDEPENDENCE

Clearly, however, specialization and division of labor involve one serious problem—that of *interdependence*. A single-celled low form of life such as the

---

[6] Smith recognized that specialization and division of labor were limited by the extent of the market, i.e., by the volume that can be sold. Smith would have approved of the European Common Market, which aims to lower the internal tariff barriers to trade and create a market big enough to support fruitful mass production and specialization.

The following passage describing the extent of specialization in meat slaughtering is often quoted: "It would be difficult to find another industry where division of labor has been so ingeniously and microscopically worked out. The animal has been surveyed and laid off like a map; and the men have been classified in over thirty specialties and twenty rates of pay, from 16 cents to 50 cents an hour. The 50-cent man is restricted to using the knife on the most delicate parts of the hide (floorman) or to using the ax in splitting the backbone (splitter); and, wherever a less skilled man can be slipped in at 18 cents, 18½ cents, 20 cents, 21 cents, 22½ cents, 24 cents, and so on, a place is made for him, and an occupation mapped out. In working on the hide alone there are nine positions, at eight different rates of pay. A 20-cent man pulls off the tail, a 22½-cent man pounds off another part where good leather is not found, and the knife of the 40-cent man cuts a different texture and has a different 'feel' from that of the 50-cent man. Skill has become specialized to fit the anatomy. . . .

"The division of labor grew with the industry, following the introduction of the refrigerator car and the marketing of dressed beef, in the decade of the seventies. Before the market was widened by these revolutionizing inventions, the killing gangs were small, since only the local demands were supplied. But when the number of cattle to be killed each day increased to a thousand or more, an increasing gang or crew of men was put together; and the best men were kept at the most exacting work." From J. R. Commons, *Quarterly Journal of Economics*, vol. XIX, 1904, pp. 3, 6.

amoeba or paramecium may not be particularly good at doing anything complicated, but it can live alone and like it. In higher animals such as man, every cell
will die if once the heart cells fail. When all goes well, the extreme specialization
of cells is very efficient—but at the cost of extreme interdependence.

In modern economic society this process is carried to the *n*th degree. No
one man makes the smallest fraction of the commodities that he consumes. In
medieval times the artisan made one article and exchanged it for many others.
Today a worker produces not even a single good; he may make only shoe
tongues or simply turn bolt 999 on the Ford assembly line. Such may be his
whole life work. In exchange for doing this he will receive an income adequate
to buy goods from all over the world.

Thus, specialization involves complete mutual dependence. A bank in
Austria fails, and the natives of Fiji, who carry water in empty Standard Oil
cans and clothe their infants in Pillsbury flour bags, lose their livelihood—yes,
and may even starve. In the backwash of a strike or war, a breakdown in transportation and the economic fabric of exchange reveals how perilously modern
economic life depends upon exchange. Would we, if we could, turn the clock
back to a simpler and poorer life? Or can we keep the advantages of division of
labor by finding policies that will prevent breakdown?

■ BARTER VERSUS THE USE OF MONEY

Along with capital and specialization, money is a third aspect of modern economic life. Without the use of money our present division of labor and exchange
would be impossible. To be sure, we could imagine a state of *barter*, where one
kind of merchandise is traded directly for another. In primitive cultures it is not
uncommon for food to be traded for weapons, or aid in the building of a house
exchanged for aid in clearing a field. Even in the most advanced industrial
economies, if we strip exchange down to its barest essentials and peel off the
obscuring layer of money, we find that trade between individuals or nations
largely boils down to barter—transforming one good into another by exchange
rather than by physical transmutation.

Barter represents a great improvement over a state of affairs in which
every man had to be a Jack-of-all-trades and master of none. A great debt of
gratitude is owed to the first two ape men who suddenly perceived that each
could be made better off by giving up some of one good in exchange for some
of another. Nevertheless, simple barter operates under grave disadvantages. An
elaborate division of labor would be unthinkable without the introduction of a
great new improvement—the use of money.

In all but the most primitive cultures men do not directly exchange one
good for another. Instead they sell one good for money, and then use money to
buy the goods they wish. At first glance this seems to complicate rather than
simplify matters, to replace a single transaction by two transactions. Thus, if I
have apples and want nuts, would it not be simpler to trade one for the other
rather than to sell the apples for money and then use the money to buy nuts?

Actually, the reverse is the case: the two transactions are simpler than one.

Ordinarily there are always people ready to buy apples and always some willing to sell—at a price—nuts; but it would be an unusual *coincidence* to find a person with tastes exactly opposite to my own, with an eagerness to sell nuts and buy apples. Such a coincidence would be as unlikely as the chance of flipping a dozen "tails" in a row. (Even if the unusual should happen—as occasionally it must—there is no guarantee that the desires of the two parties with respect to the exact *quantities* and terms of the exchange would coincide.)

To use a classical economic phrase: Instead of there being a double coincidence of wants, there is likely to be a want of coincidence; so that, unless a hungry tailor happens to find a farmer who has both food and a desire for a pair of pants, neither can make a trade.

Money does simplify economic life. But do not for a moment forget that, for society as a whole, a mere increase in the total of money will not enable people to consume more than the real products technically producible with the economy's existent totals of labor, land, and capital. And money can cause financial crisis.

∎HISTORICAL STAGES OF MONEY

If we were to reconstruct history along hypothetical, logical lines, we should naturally follow the age of barter by the age of commodity money.

COMMODITY MONEY   Historically a great variety of commodities has served at one time or another as a medium of exchange: cattle (from which comes the Latin stem of "pecuniary" and also the words "capital" and "chattel"), tobacco, leather and hides, furs, olive oil, beer or spirits, slaves or wives, copper, iron, gold, silver, rings, diamonds, wampum beads or shells, huge rocks and landmarks, and cigarette butts.

Each of the above has some advantages and disadvantages. Cattle are not divisible into small change; but while it is being hoarded, such "money" is likely to increase by reproduction, giving the lie to the doctrine of Aristotle that "money is barren." Beer does not improve with keeping, although wine may. Olive oil provides a nice liquid currency that is as minutely divisible as one wishes. Iron will rust and is of so little value that one would need a cart instead of a pocketbook. The value of a diamond is not proportional to weight but varies with its square; therefore, if cut up into pieces it loses value.

The yearly additions to (by mining) or subtractions from (by use in teeth or jewelry) the accumulated stock of *precious metals* are small in percentage terms; so the total amounts and value of these substances do not fluctuate wildly. Silver has luster but will tarnish in air. Gold keeps its attractive sheen but, unless mixed with an alloy, is soft. Gold's high specific gravity makes detection of counterfeiting and admixture easy; but through most of historical time, gold's scarcity value has been so great per ounce as to require inordinately minute coins for ordinary purchases.

Most kinds of money tended once to be of some value or use for their own sake. Thus, playing-card money could be used in gaming, wampum had decorative uses, and paper money began as warehouse or mint receipts for so much metal. But the intrinsic usefulness of the money medium is now the least important thing about it.

PAPER MONEY   The age of commodity money gives way to the age of paper money. The essence of money, its intrinsic nature, is typified by paper currency. *Money, as money rather than a commodity, is wanted not for its own sake but for the things it will buy!* We do not wish to use up money directly, but rather to use it by getting rid of it; even when we choose to use it by holding it, its value comes from the fact that we can spend it *later on.*

Money is an artificial, social convention. If for any reason a substance begins to be used as money, all people will begin to value it, even if they happen to be teetotalers or vegetarians or disbelievers in its intrinsic usefulness. As long as things can be bought and sold for a given substance, people will be content to sell and buy with it. Paradox: money is accepted because it is accepted!

The use of paper currency (dollar bills, fives, tens, . . .) has become widespread because it has many conveniences as a medium of exchange. Currency is easily carried and stored away. By the printing of more or fewer zeros on the face value of the bill, a great or small amount of value can be embodied in a light, transportable medium of little bulk. By the use of decimal points it can be made as divisible as we wish. By careful engraving, the value of the money can be made easily recognizable and can be protected from counterfeiting and adulteration. The fact that private individuals cannot create it at will in unlimited amounts keeps it scarce, i.e., an economic rather than a free good.

> Given this limitation in supply, modern currencies have value, i.e., can buy things, independently of any gold, silver, or government backing. The public neither knows nor cares—and need not know or care—whether its currency is in the form of Bank of Canada notes, or in copper or nickel coin. So long as each form of money can be converted into any other at fixed terms, the best is as good as the worst.[7]

BANK MONEY   Finally, along with the age of paper money, there is the age of bank money, or bank deposits. Today at least nine-tenths of all transactions, by value if not in number, take place by cheque. A professor will have his salary paid directly into his bank account, after income taxes have already been deducted at the souce by his employer. His rent or dentist bills will be paid by cheque; his gasoline and hotel bills, by a credit card. Except for petty cash for lunches and carfare, he needs and usually carries little cash.

This completes the discussion of the way in which money performs its essential functions. In Part Two, we shall examine in detail the monetary and credit operations of banks and the government to see how they bear on fluctuations in prices, production, and employment.

---

[7] In Canada, a century ago, it was the exception rather than the rule for notes and coins to exchange for each other at par. Each had different prices which varied from day to day, so that it was necessary for storekeepers to weigh metal coins and keep daily lists of values; and it became a profession in itself to change money, buying and selling it at a profit.

SUMMARY

A. PRICING AND MIXED ENTERPRISE

■ 1 In our mixed private enterprise system, the price mechanism, working through supply and demand in competitive markets, operates to answer the three fundamental problems of economic organization. The system is not perfect, but it works to solve the WHAT, HOW, and FOR WHOM.

■ 2 The dollar votes of people affect prices of goods; these prices serve as guides for the amounts of the different goods to be produced. When people demand more of a good, a competitive businessman can make a profit by expanding production of that good. Under perfect competition, he must find the cheapest method of production, using labor, land, and other factors that are relatively cheap and economizing on the use of relatively expensive factors; otherwise, he will incur losses and be eliminated.

At the same time that the WHAT and HOW problems are being resolved by prices, so is the problem of FOR WHOM. The distribution of income is determined by competitive bidding up or down of factor-prices—wages of each kind of labor, rents of land, royalties of books, and various returns to capital. Anyone possessing fertile well-located land or widely admired crooning ability will be supplied with many dollar votes for his use in the markets for consumer goods. Anyone without property or education and with skills that the market cares little about will receive a low annual income; the price system doesn't try for equality.

■ 3 Our economy is mixed in two senses: Governments modify private initiative and participate alongside of it; monopolistic elements condition the working of perfect competition.

B. CAPITAL, DIVISION OF LABOR, AND MONEY

■ 4 Capital goods—produced inputs such as machinery, housing, and inventories of goods in process—add tremendously to a nation's output. *Roundabout*, time-consuming methods take time to get started: hence, adding to the stock of capital goods requires a temporary sacrifice of present consumption. The interest rate serves to ration and to coax.

■ 5 Under the mixed economy, capital goods are largely owned as private property; the incomes they produce go to their owners and to taxes. Under communism, the state owns capital goods. In no system are private-property rights unlimited.

■ 6 Specialization and division of labor characterize modern economies. This raises productivity, but at the cost of interdependence.

■ 7 Without exchange, division of labor could not be highly developed. Simple barter is inefficient and tends to be superseded by the use of money. Commodity money is in turn superseded by paper money and bank money.

Unlike other economic goods, money is valued because of social convention; we value it indirectly for what it buys rather than for its direct utility. Its misbehavior—in producing depression or inflation—governments can no longer tolerate.

QUESTIONS FOR DISCUSSION

1. During World War II did we let consumers' dollar demand determine their sugar consumption? Why not? Why recourse to rationing?

2. Could supply and demand for labor work out to give salesmen with a "gift of gab" five times the income of skilled surgeons? At other times could it operate to give surgeons twice the income of accountants?

3. Do you think that an "instinct of craftsmanship" and a "sense of social responsibility" could ever replace the "profit motive"? Read the chapter head's Invisible Hand quotation aloud. What do you think Smith is trying to say there? And here: "I have never known much good done by those who affected to trade for the public good."

4. List a number of cases where the government modifies the working of an automatic price system. For example: pure food and drug laws; minimum wages; interest ceilings.

5. List cases where monopoly elements intervene. How can business by advertising shape, as well as respond to, consumer demands and wants?

6. Assuming it cannot borrow abroad, what must China do if it wishes to become an efficient industrialized nation in the next few generations?

7. "Lincoln freed the slaves. With one pen stroke he destroyed much of the capital the Southern United States had been able accumulate over the years." Comment.

8. Would ice cubes make a good unit of money? Radium? What would?

9. What are some of the advantages of using cheques on bank deposits rather than paper currency or metal coins? List any disadvantages.

10. *Extra-credit problem*: Anticipating Chapter 14's discussion of the so-called quantity theory of money and prices, suppose when we woke up tomorrow each dollar bill became two dollars. Would we all be *twice* as well off? Would we be *any* better off if the change caused all prices (including wage rates) to double? Refer to Chapter 1's "fallacy of composition" to demonstrate that one man's increase in money might make him better off, but that it is dangerous to extrapolate to all of society.

11. Review your understanding of the following concepts:

mixed economy	abstinence and waiting, forgoing
demand-and-supply markets for goods and for factors of production	dissaving by failure to maintain and replace capital goods
profit seeking, cost minimizing	specialization, interdependence
price "rationing"	division of labor, exchange
perfect and imperfect competition	barter versus money pricing
roundaboutness of production	commodity, paper, and bank-deposit money

Appendix: What, How and For Whom in the Soviet Union, Yugoslavia, and Maoist China

How does the Soviet Union today get the three basic problems decided: WHAT shall be produced, How, and FOR WHOM?

In broad outline,[1] the picture is this: The state owns almost all factors of production: factories, mines, and land. Workers generally earn their living by wages; they do have considerable choice of occupation, but a Soviet citizen does not have unlimited right to seek employment in any region and industry that happens to capture his fancy.

WHAT   A political decision is made that defense and capital formation are to be pushed hard; what is left over is permitted to go to consumers' goods. While a Russian can indicate his preferences among different goods by the way he spends his income, any resulting shortages or gluts have only recently been permitted to result in the bidding up or down of consumer-goods prices, thereby automatically producing the positive or negative returns that serve to rechannel resources. So long as goods were very scarce, central planners could decide that people would want so much of food, so much of shoes, and so much of various other necessities of life. Any and all of these were eagerly bought as they became available: if the local store or commissary had shoes not exactly your size, you were glad to take them a little large rather than do without.

Now that some of the comforts—and even luxuries—of life are beginning to become available, it is no longer enough to think of giving people what they need, and centralized planning has become a little more difficult. These days certain goods will not get bought at all, and the planners have come to learn that they must cut back on them. Even advertising and selling have reared their heads in Russia! It is harder to learn what people do want than what they do not want, and marketing surveys are still in their infancy. The Soviet commissars are not so skilled in determining what people would want most if they had the choice; but they do find it useful to watch what Americans and others abroad like to consume and then belatedly introduce such products: thus that rare comrade who gets a car will find it resembling our cars of the past; and experts tell us this imitative pattern, which is not at all irrational since it assumes that what one human being will like will also be sought by another, is becoming more common.

With respect to capital goods and military expenditure, *direct state decisions* are made. Industrialization is pushed hard: electrification, transportation, mining development, a big push in chemicals and fertilizers, collectivization of agriculture and crop patterns—*such matters are broadly determined by conscious political decision.*

HOW   Private enterprise is negligible in importance. Instead, the typical Soviet factory will be a state-owned *enterprise*: just as the president of General Motors owns little of its total stock, the manager or head of this state-owned enterprise has no ownership of its capital; but he does get better-than-average pay for his work, plus various travel expenses, auto transport, and other special privileges. He may even get bonuses, and his chance of promotion to a bigger enterprise will depend upon how well his enterprise meets its quota.

It used to be true that the managerial bonus was tied to total output alone, disregarding the quality of the goods or the efficiency with which they were produced. This system resulted in the hoarding of production materials which might have been well used by other enterprises, or in devious schemes to have the manager's quota set unrealistically low so that, on paper, the manager would appear highly productive. Stories have even been told of a transport enterprise which moved carloads of water back and forth in order to claim it had met a target of so many ton-miles. Similarly sewing machines and tractors were manufactured "efficiently" without a model change long after the demand for them had been saturated.

In recent years, however, such meaningless physical quotas are beginning to be replaced by "profitability" criteria of performance that do involve

---

[1] F. D. Holzman's *Readings in the Soviet Economy* (Chicago: Rand McNally, 1962), is a useful reference. See also, in P. A. Samuelson's *Readings in Economics*, 6th Edition (New York: McGraw-Hill, 1970), articles by Harvard's expert Abram Bergson.

economic valuations (in terms of the scarcity of resources) of diverse goods. Today the success of many enterprises producing consumer goods, as well as the success of a few other enterprises, is judged on the basis of a profit rate that includes a charge on capital used by the enterprise. In order to make a profit at all, the goods or services of the enterprise must be sold, and that means they must be of acceptable quality. In this way, particularly in the field of consumer goods, a higher degree of efficiency is encouraged. Although the enterprise still operates on the plan handed to it from above, the profitability criterion is a step in the direction of rational pricing methods. (But it is worth noting that under this new decentralization of management, Russia has the same grave difficulty as the West in persuading industries to stop polluting rivers and the air! In both economies, no price is set on the exploitation of the environment.)

The decision of how to combine various productive factors—land and labor, degree of mechanization—appears to depend on a mixture of purely technical considerations and adaptations to the scarcities of various economic resources. A continual process of trial and error goes on. The observer finds operations curiously uneven: on the one hand, he may see a military ballistic plant which has achieved a precision of ball bearings and gyroscopes rivaling the best in the world; on the other hand, he may find things being done in an almost unbelievably primitive way, with the quality of output practically worthless. (Example: A Soviet farmwoman may be assigned one cow to take care of; on an Ontario dairy farm, a man and wife may take care of 50 cows, in addition to performing countless other daily chores.)

All Soviet economic life is a pyramid tapering upward. Above the individual enterprises in an industry and region will be a regional economic council. Above the regional councils will be a council of ministers; alongside the ministries will be the planners of the Gosplan. Experts tell us it is quite misleading to concentrate on the organizational charts of the process, for *there is a constantly changing mixture of centralization and decentralization*; fiat, delegated responsibility, and initiative; carrots of reward and kicks or imprisonments as penalties.

Some things are very much the same everywhere. The head of an enterprise will, almost certainly, be a member of the Communist party. A successful bureaucrat there is something like a successful "organization man" here: he must be obedient but resourceful, both obsequious and arrogant, energetic and nonsentimental. The point is not that the worst types get ahead. Rather the point is that ability does count on the average; but mere technical ability without the skill of getting along with people will not usually be enough either in Hamilton or in Volgograd.

Experts also tell us that it is quite naïve to think that there is an elaborate formalized structure of planning, so that one could write a treatise on pure communistic economics that would equal in length a treatise on the general equilibrium of purely competitive market systems, which is long indeed.

FOR WHOM To a considerable degree the Russian economy works for the security of the state and for the future. How much the present generation of Russians consume of private goods is not primarily determined by their day-to-day spending and working decisions. True, they do earn wages (and a small amount of interest or lottery winnings on government bonds is also permitted). Moreover, wages are by no means equal, and certainly not higher for the needy and handicapped than for the energetic and skilled. Skilled workers get much more than unskilled. Free trade-unions as we know them do not exist, but woe to the manager who gets all the workers against him. Piece rates and incentive systems are frequently used, and there is much exhortation toward working hard for the fatherland and for the "brotherhood of man." (Soviet novels often had for their plots the tale of how a good boy and girl foil the malingering of antisocial culprits and by use of a virtuous tractor overcome the recalcitrance of the stubborn soil. Boy meets girl here as everywhere, but the durable goods are much in evidence.)

Social classes as Marx and Engels knew them in 1848 may not exist in the Soviet Union, but there is a definite pattern of social and political stratification. A poor boy who is bright may become a physicist and live well. It is important for him to rank high in the exams that select the few who can go to college. (His way at the university is completely paid for, just as the comrade who puts the shot in the Olympics is paid to pursue that occupation.) After graduation he hopes to score well enough to be able to pursue the study of physics in Moscow, rather than be sent out as a technician and engineer to the

Ural Mountains or some other distant post. As a well-paid professor he can look down on all but the top bureaucrats: he may have a car, a cottage in the country, and finely equipped laboratories. Of course, he cannot take it with him, but he can at least hope to give his son a good start in the stiff educational competition.

There are various economic devices by which the system ensures that it gets the FOR WHOM it desires —heavy emphasis on industrialization and military security.

For one thing, goods at every stage of production are subject to heavy taxation (the so-called "turnover tax," which is assessed on the *total* value of an item at each successive stage of production rather than on the true value *added*). The resulting elevation of prices in relation to wages paid out ensures that the public will be able to consume only a part of all that they can produce, in quite the same way as our economy uses taxes to siphon resources away from private and into public channels. Over-all anti-inflationary policy is needed there as here!

Another device is to set a much higher mark-up over production costs for consumers' goods, ensuring that they generally are priced much higher (and hence their consumption is discouraged) than are military and capital goods. As a third device, certain consumers' goods, such as comfortable housing, are just not purchasable at any price for any but the few lucky persons of peculiar economic and political advantage.

By all such methods the Soviet authorities fight the battle against the price inflation that would burst out as workers try to spend their incomes on the limited supply of consumers' goods. To one who has studied modern economics, it is evident that these are devices by which their society determines FOR WHOM goods will be produced in accordance with *social* decision making.

■ NEW TRENDS IN IRON CURTAIN ECONOMICS?

Soviet economics is in a state of flux. In recent years intense debates have broken out concerning the use of some kind of supply-and-demand pricing, coupled with profitability criteria that look a little like the analytical tools of Western economics. Marxian concepts seem to be reserved for training of the young, especially for alleged explanation and denouncement of capitalistic economies. Among the high-level planners themselves, few words are

squandered on Marxist interpretation. Instead, as in the much-debated writings of E. Liberman, there are attempts to get away from setting of crude quantitative goals expressed in physical units. There is to be emphasis on quality and on weighting items by their importance, setting for the plant manager the goal of maximizing something very like a profitability magnitude. The hope is to get him to try new products and methods and economize on input requirements, rather than concentrate on establishing a low output quota for his plant. Since 1967, the Soviet Union, and the satellites, notably Czechoslovakia, have experimented with various partially-free markets.

Mathematical methods, such as the input-output analysis associated with W. W. Leontief of Harvard, have been released from Stalin's ban, and are debated as a possible tool for helping the planners allocate their available resources. More advanced methods, known in the West as linear and more general mathematical programming, have been developed by eminent Soviet mathematicians (Kantorowich, Pontryagin, . . .); rates of discount, rather like the interest rates used in mixed economies to screen out less important capital or investment projects, have been proposed in considerable variety. Although it cannot yet be said that they rely on the socialist game of a pricing system as will be described in the Appendix of Chapter 31, there seems increasingly to be a pragmatic mixture of physical accounting, and economic planning. And the pendulum oscillates between epochs of decentralization and of centralization.[2] Moreover, in the Satellite

---

[2] Agricultural performance, as in the case of China, still seems to be remarkably bad on the Russian collective and state farms. These appear to be much too large for efficiency, averaging 7,000 and 22,000 acres of sown land, in contrast to the 400-acre average of our efficient commercial farms. Private farming is permitted in only minute degree, but the product of these private efforts seems to be many times higher per unit of input than on the collective and state farms. Uniform rules, ill informed and subject to swings of fad and fashion, get imposed on everybody in a region. Supplies of tractor equipment, spare parts, fertilizers, and fungicides are quite limited, and optimal use is not made of them by the rural populace, who have little incentive to be efficient. Despite unfavorable weather, much improved efficiency would seem technically feasible and is being sought after in each of the communist bloc economies by different methods, each closer to the price mechanism of the capitalist or free market economy.

countries—Poland, Hungary, Czechoslovakia, . . .—the issues of pricing and/or planning are hotly debated.

This is not the place to describe the differences between Marxian and Western economics, nor the developments of either. But the back flyleaf of this book does give a sketch of the family tree of economic doctrines and ideas. Perhaps the widening gulf between the ideology of the Russians and the Chinese, despite the fact that both claim legitimate descent from Marx via Lenin, suggests that the Soviet is moving a small step toward reconciliation with the economic tools of modern analysis. This is not meant to suggest in the least that the Russians are turning to capitalistic enterprise systems or that mixed economies are veering down the road to serfdom and totalitarianism. Rather, the notions of scarcity of production resources, production, costs, substitution, and resource allocation (the pattern of distribution of resources among the many alternative uses) have to be objectively regarded as fundamental in almost any economic system. While methods of resource allocation may differ as between nations, to the individual consumer wishing to purchase a pound of tea, the various systems have approximately the same end result. The consumer purchases the tea when he finds it available on the retail shelves and he pays for the tea with cash from his pocket, be it in Canada, the Soviet Union, or Maoist China.

All in all, it is a mistake to think that most people are miserable in the Marxist countries. While it is undoubtedly true that few citizens of the West would trade their degree of economic comfort and political freedom for life in the Soviet Union, it is also true that a Soviet citizen thinks that he is living in a paradise in comparison with life in Communist China, where industry is very much more primitive and comfort and living standards much lower. Remember, too, that life under the czars was no bed of roses for most classes; and to the eye of the traveler from impoverished Asia and Africa, the rising degree of Russian affluence must seem impressive.

As already mentioned, the family tree of Marxian economics shows a branching out in the middle 1960s. China and Russia cannot agree on the true apostolic succession of Lenin and Marx. These ideological splits would be merely ironical, were it not that the future existence of the whole human race is at stake in this age of the nuclear bomb.

■ DIVERSITY ON THE LEFT

In the last part of the twentieth century the communist world no longer presents a monolithic front. The dominance of the Soviet Union is challenged by China, Yugoslavia, Rumania, and Albania. Hungary and Czechoslovakia, in the absence of Russian intervention, showed signs of divergence from the Moscow pattern. The two most interesting variants of communist development are, from the viewpoint of economics, the Yugoslav and Chinese alternatives.

YUGOSLAV DECENTRALIZATION The communist resistance movement came to power under Tito after World War II. From 1945 to 1950 a program of planned development along conventional Stalinist lines worked out badly—both in terms of planning goals and in comparison with post-World War I similar years. Following the political break with the eastern European socialist economies in 1948, Yugoslavia undertook a new "separate path to socialism" involving "decentralization and popular participation." The experiment has excited much interest abroad, both for its own sake and as a successful retreat from Soviet dominance.

In essence, Titoism involves a return to greater dependence on market pricing, on profitability criteria and incentives. It does not mean abandonment of socialism and one-party control, nor of central planning of macroeconomic goals. But it does mean that a factory may be run by its own workers in many sectors of the economy. Here is a sample case.

Twenty to one hundred workers in a factory form a workers' council. Nominally they elect their own managers. (They may even advertise for a trained executive!) They "borrow" their capital from the central pool. (Sometimes capital is "auctioned" off to the highest bidder.) *The firm can decide to produce what it thinks will sell.* It may import raw materials from abroad, sometimes even on foreign credit. It can cut costs in the hope that, after it has paid its income and land taxes, what is left over can go to the workers as bonus income or be plowed back into the enterprise.

How have things worked out? From 1950 to 1970 progress has been uneven, and there have been oscillations between centralization and decentralization. But the system has been viable, and growth under it has surpassed that of the earlier Stalinist period. Even if the cynicism expressed by insiders concerning the amount of power the workers themselves exercise is justified, this system of syndicalist structure presumably offers some countervailing influence to the power of the bureaucrats, those whom Milovan Djilas has called "the new class."

MAOIST CHINA   China is as far to the left of the U.S.S.R. as Yugoslavia is to the right. But by any common-sense definition, China is under-developed: a huge population wresting a living from limited resources. For centuries, population pressure and uncertain crops have kept millions of her people on the brink of starvation.

Even by the calculations of unfriendly Western economists—such as T. C. Liu of Cornell—China's growth rate of national output from 1952 to 1957, about 6½ per cent per year, was better than in the preceding Nationalist regime, in the 'twenties and 'thirties. It was achieved while Mao's strategy was to put all his eggs in one basket: he put all his investment funds into manufacturing. In this strategy he relied on the "collectivization" of peasant farming to make up for his depriving agriculture of investment funds.

This collectivization process, in 1958, was transformed into Mao's "Great Leap Forward." Enterprises as large as whole counties, "communes," took over from the family and the village as a way of life and from the farm and the collective as the unit for economic planning and production. Furthermore, industry itself was in large part to be decentralized and meshed with the rural commune.

The excesses of this frenzied reorganization (e.g., the attempts to make iron and steel in backyard furnaces), and set-backs in farm output led to a strong political reaction, and Mao lost much of his nominal power. The Liu Shao-ch'i group reinstated but modified the old priorities, finding some funds for investment in agriculture and light industry. But some of the economic costs of the Great Leap had still to be paid: in the communes the peasant incentives were impaired, and in industry the help received from Russia was abruptly terminated.

These problems were aggravated by several years of bad crop weather, beginning in 1959. During this period much food was imported, especially grain from Canada.

Yet, although the policies of the Great Leap clearly failed, it is not so clear that they were all irrational. Thus, although the backyard steel furnaces produced little steel, the quest for an "intermediate technology" (that is, production processes suited to countries that are rich in labor but poor in capital) does make sense. And the agricultural communes, for all their problems, were intended to increase agricultural output, not merely to increase the state's share of a fixed level of crops. (In fact, Mao has written sharply of Stalin's agricultural procurement as "draining the pond to catch the fish.")

Since 1959 there has been an almost complete blackout of economic data, in the domestic Chinese press as well as in Peking's foreign-language publications. Yet we do have a few bits and snatches of information. For example, a delegation of Pakistani officials visiting China in 1965 asked for and received a set of official figures for grain output. According to these figures, the 1957 level of grain output was restored by 1961. Of course, population had grown in the meantime, so that the 1957 *per capita* figure was not reached again until about 1963. (The Chinese have launched vigorous birth-control campaigns, but population growth remains above 2 per cent a year.) If these Chinese grain statistics are reliable, they indicate a substantially more rapid recovery from the "bad years" after the Great Leap than outside observers had previously guessed.

Beginning in 1966, Chairman Mao (or those around him) began to reassert control over economic policies, through the mechanism of the Great Proletarian Cultural Revolution. Published attacks on economic reforms of the Yugoslav type, on Western technical knowledge, and on Liu Shao-ch'i himself became very strident. (Liu was called a "renegade, hidden traitor, and scab.") But what effect this has had on the organizing or the functioning of the economy is still a matter for conjecture. In 1969, Professors Liu and Galenson of Cornell argued as follows:

"The national product fell by roughly 15 per cent from 1958 to 1961 . . . Only by 1965 did the economy finally regain the 1958 level . . . . The Great Proletarian Cultural Revolution . . . led to a loss of 400,000 specialists who would have completed their training during 1967-68 had the schools not been closed. . . . . Economism — i.e., efficiency, became one of the worst epithets. . . . Revolutionary mass enthusiasm replaced trained management. . . . Essenti-

Gradual economic reform need not lead to serfdom.

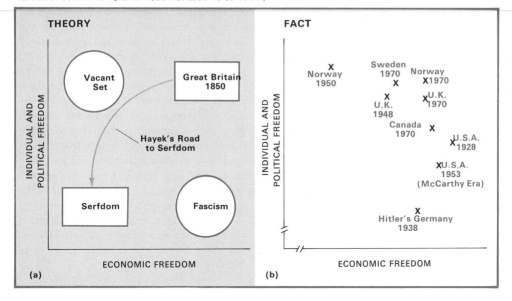

FIG. 3-2. In contrast to the libertarian view of Hayek, in (a), that government modification of market *laissez-faire* leads to political serfdom, observe the facts of history in (b). In Scandinavia or Britain, loss of business and property control has involved no concomitant loss in personal liberties and no approach to the totalitarian pattern in which the individual enjoys neither form of freedom.

ally, there has been no significant economic growth for the decade 1958-68."[3]

But Cambridge's Joan Robinson expressed a more optimistic view:

> "Whatever disturbances there may have been in the course of the Cultural Revolution, economic development seems to have been running on. The harvest for 1968 is reported to be good once more; in some industries there have been setbacks due to disturbances, but in many there are claims of new technical advances, increased production, savings in costs and improvements in quality due to the simplified organization and high morale that the Cultural Revolution brought into the factories."[4]

■ A NONECONOMIC VIEW

There is a temptation for those living in the most prosperous part of the world to succumb to com-

placency, both about themselves and about their mixed economy. And indeed the Western world has made tremendous progress since even so recent a date as 1929.

But at the same time, we find that many features of economic life, which we are about to study in detail, are ethically troublesome, especially to the younger generation. We see economic change and improvement over the last century, yet we are still faced with many seemingly unanswerable questions. For example, how fast must a mixed economy ideally change over time? You cannot expect a hungry mother in Nova Scotia to give the same answer as a debutante from Havergal.

Thus we are faced with value judgments above and beyond the scope of the "neutral science" of economics. We must remember that these same value-judgment questions lie in the background of our purely economic discussions of the remaining text. Beyond the internal questions of technical economics, there emerge basic political questions concerning the possible combinations of (1) *individual* freedom—civil liberties and personal rights—

---

[3] Letter to *New York Times*, 17 June, 1969, by Professors Walter Galenson and Ta-Chung Liu.

[4] Joan Robinson, *The Cultural Revolution in China* (London: Penguin Books Ltd., 1969), p. 149.

(2) *economic* freedoms—not only in WHAT and How to produce (by personal choice versus central control and plan), but also FOR WHOM to produce (decisions by private resource owners versus the state). The possible combinations are usually unheeded. At one extreme, almost always those who wish to reform the workings of the system wish to turn to government for new programs and measures. But those concerned to conserve what they regard as valuable in our society counter them with the arguments: "In seeking *a better division* of the pie, you will *reduce the size* of the pie by creating distorting inefficiencies. But more important, *personal and property freedoms are one and inseparable.* Only in the Herbert Spencer *laissez-faire* society, that you find so repellant, will men be free to speak their minds and choose their rulers."

Let us momentarily and cautiously relax the rigor of analysis and speculate about what has not yet been capable of scientific agreement.

What are the presumed relationships, suggested by experience and plausible reflection, between the state of individual freedoms and the interventions by government in the mixed economy?

Figure 3-2 suggests an eclectic alternative to the despairing extreme of a Hayek who says, Economic reform is the road to serfdom; and to the extreme of those who, like Sidney and Beatrice Webb, argued: Political democracy is nothing without the economic democracy that comes only with collective ownership of the means of production.

Then perhaps one may read in the face of history the more optimistic message: One can have the best of both worlds—programmed improvement of the workings of the market economy along with those best things of life that aren't measured in monetary terms—freedom to do one's own thing, freedom to criticize, and freedom to change.

SUMMARY TO APPENDIX

1 State ownership of the factors of production is basic to the Soviet system. Workers earn wages and have a degree of choice of occupation.

2 The WHAT question in the Soviet Union is largely answered by state planners. The division between defense and capital formation and consumer goods is purely a state decision, although the consumer exerts some influence over the assortment of consumer goods to be produced.

3 The How decision is made partly by the central planners and partly by the manager of a state enterprise in response to bonus criteria. Economic valuations in terms of resource scarcity are becoming more prevalent in determining How than they were in earlier years.

4 The FOR WHOM decision is largely made by the state, although income will determine which individuals receive consumer goods—provided the goods are available. The state turnover tax and a much higher mark-up over production costs for consumer goods assure that monetary command over resources is diverted to the state so that the emphasis on industrialization and military security may continue—at the expense of consumption.

5 New trends behind the Iron Curtain include the adoption and adaptation of certain Western tools such as profitability criteria and the use of discount rates which resemble interest rates. Similarly, experiments with partially free markets have occurred in several Soviet bloc countries as the pendulum oscillates between centralization and decentralization. In satellite countries the issues of pricing and/or planning are being debated.

6 Yugoslavia has experimented with decentralization and with popular participation which involves greater dependence on market pricing, profitability criteria, and cooperative organization; though central planning of macroeconomic goals remains an important part of the system.

7 Maoist China is at the other extreme of the communist spectrum. After uneven spurts and changes in policies. China may be moving ahead economically, although the data available after 1959 is sketchy at best.

■ 8 One must be careful in comparing the "success" of different systems because the starting conditions, the goals, and the means of measurement vary among systems. Value judgments which are beyond the scope of the "neutral science" of Economics are involved.

QUESTIONS FOR DISCUSSION

1. Outline WHAT, HOW, and FOR WHOM in the Soviet Union.

2. What economic aspects of the Western world have predisposed developing countries like Ghana, Egypt, and Indonesia to experiment with the Soviet path to development?

3. Review your understanding of the following concepts:
centralized planning, Soviet style
Yugoslavian hybrid
Maoist communes and decentralization
new U.S.S.R. pricing and profitability trends
economic freedoms, individual freedoms

4

SUPPLY AND DEMAND: THE BARE ELEMENTS

You can make even a parrot into a learned political economist—all he must learn are the two words "supply" and "demand." ANONYMOUS

Every short statement about economics is misleading (with the possible exception of my present one). ALFRED MARSHALL

Chapters 2 and 3 introduced the three basic problems every economy must face. (1) WHAT shall be produced of the great variety of possible goods and services, and in precisely what quantities? (2) How shall society combine its different productive factors—land, labor, and so forth—to produce each good? (3) FOR WHOM shall goods be produced—which is the problem of how the national product is to be distributed among the different members of the populace with their different labor skills and ownerships of land and capital goods?

Chapter 2 showed that a variety of systems could be thought of to solve these three problems. WHAT, HOW, and FOR WHOM might be determined by custom, instinct, or even by centralized, collective fiats. But Chapter 3 indicated that the modern mixed economy relies primarily on none of these to solve its basic problems. Instead it relies on a system of markets and prices.

The consumer, so it is said, is the king. Or rather, with every man a king, each is a voter who uses his money as votes to get the thing done that he wants done. His votes must compete with other men's votes; and the people with the most votes end up with the most influence on what gets produced and on where those goods go.

Now our task is to see just how this spending of money votes—this system of "consumer sovereignty"—takes place.

■ THE MARKET MECHANISM

Let us take an example. You wake up this morning with an urge for a new pair of shoes. You would not think of saying, "I'll go down to the city hall and vote for the mayor most likely to give me a new pair of shoes. Of course, I mean a new pair of size 9, soft-leather, dark-brown shoes."

Or, to take an actual case from history, suppose men begin to get prosperous enough to afford meat every day and do not have to fill up on potatoes. How does their desire to substitute meat for potatoes get translated into action? What politician do they tell? What orders does he in turn give to farmers to move from New Brunswick to Alberta? How much extra rent does he decide will be needed to bribe landlords to transfer land from potato production to cattle grazing? And how does he make sure that people get what they want of pork and lamb as well as of beef? And who is to get the choice cuts?

Why belabor the obvious? Everyone knows it never worked itself out that way at all. What happened was this. Consumers began to buy fewer potatoes and more meat. That raised the price of meat and cut the price of potatoes. So there resulted losses to the potato growers and gains to the ranchers. Ranch labor found it could hold out for higher wages, and many a potato digger quit his job for a better-paying job elsewhere. In time, the higher meat prices brought larger productions of beef, pork, and lamb. And the different parts of the cow— its horn, hide, liver, kidneys, choice tenderloin, and tough ribs—got auctioned off for what each part would bring.

To show that it is not some important government official or businessman who sets relative prices, see what actually happened when science discovered that liver was good for anemia. Kidneys, mysteriously, were previously dearer than liver. In fact, according to the records, you could hardly give liver away before this discovery. Now go to the butcher shop: price liver; and, if you can find any, also price kidneys. A veritable revolution has taken place; the price of liver has risen greatly relative to the price of kidneys, so as to *ration* the limited supply of liver among the eager demanders for it—all through the *impersonal* workings of supply and demand.

Similar revolutions are taking place in the economic market place all the time. As people's desires and needs change, as engineering methods change, as supplies of natural resources and other productive factors change, the market place registers changes in the prices and the quantities sold of commodities and productive services—of tea, sugar, and beef; of land, labor, and machines. There exists a *system of prices*, a concept that is far from obvious.

The purpose of this chapter is to show how supply and demand work themselves out in the competitive market *for one particular good*. We shall define a demand curve and then a supply curve. Finally, we shall see how the market price reaches its competitive equilibrium, where these two curves intersect— where the forces of demand and supply are just in balance.

■ THE DEMAND SCHEDULE

Let us start with demand. It is commonly observed: The quantity of a good that people will buy at any one time depends on price; the higher the price charged for an article, the less the quantity of it people will be willing to buy; and, other

A demand schedule relates quantity demanded to price:

DEMAND SCHEDULE FOR WHEAT

	(1) PRICE ($ PER BU.) P	(2) QUANTITY DEMANDED, MILLION BU. PER MONTH Q
A	$5	9
B	4	10
C	3	12
D	2	15
E	1	20

TABLE 4-1. At each market price, there will at any time be a definite quantity of wheat that people will want to demand.

At a lower price, the quantity demanded will go up —as more people substitute it for other goods and feel they can afford to gratify their less important wants for wheat.

things being equal, the lower its market price, the more units of it will be demanded.

> Thus there exists at any one time a definite relation between the market price of a good (such as wheat) and the quantity demanded of that good. The relationship between price and quantity bought is called the "demand schedule," or "demand curve."

Table 4-1 gives an example of a hypothetical demand schedule. At any price, such as $5 per bushel, there is a definite quantity of wheat that will be demanded by all the consumers in the market—in this case 9 (million) bushels per month. At a lower price, such as $4, the quantity bought is even greater, being 10 (million) units. From Table 4-1 we can determine the *quantity demanded at any price,* by comparing Column (2) with Column (1).

■ THE DEMAND CURVE

The numerical data of Table 4-1 can be given a graphic interpretation also. The vertical scale in Fig. 4-1 represents the various alternative prices of wheat, measured in dollars per bushel. The horizontal scale measures the quantity of wheat (in terms of bushels) that will be demanded per month.

A city corner is located as soon as we know its street and avenue; a ship's position is located as soon as we know its latitude and longitude. Similarly, to plot a point on this diagram, we must have two coordinate numbers: a price and a quantity. For our first point A, corresponding to $5 and 9 million bushels, we move upward 5 units and then over to the right 9 units. A dot marks the spot *A*. To get the next dot, at *B*, we go up only 4 units and over to the right 10 units. The last dot is shown by *E*. Through the dots we draw a smooth dark brown curve, marked *dd*.

This picturization of the demand schedule is called the "demand curve." Note that quantity and price are inversely related, *Q* going up when *P* goes down. The curve slopes downward, going from northwest to southeast. This important property is given a name: the *law of downward-sloping demand*. This

A downward-sloping curve depicts demand:

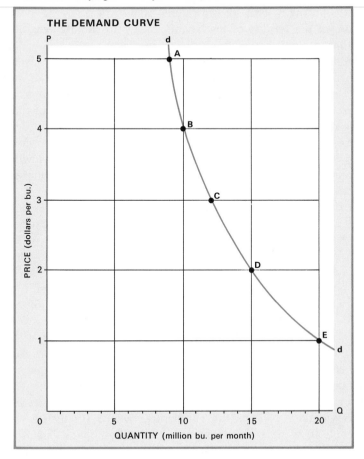

THE DEMAND CURVE

PRICE (dollars per bu.)

QUANTITY (million bu. per month)

FIG. 4-1. Prices are measured on the vertical axis, and quantities demanded on the horizontal axis. Each pair of Q, P numbers from Table 4-1 is plotted here as a point, and a smooth curve passed through the points gives us the dark brown demand curve.

The fact that dd goes downward and to the right illustrates the very important "law of downward-sloping demand."

law is true of practically all commodities: wheat, electric razors, cotton, ethyl gasoline, cornflakes, and theater tickets.

> *The law of downward-sloping demand*: When the price of a good is raised (at the same time that all other things are held constant), less of it will be demanded. Or, what is the same thing: If a greater quantity of a good is thrown on the market, then—other things being equal—it can be sold only at a lower price.

■ REASONS FOR LAW OF DOWNWARD-SLOPING DEMAND

This law is in accordance with common sense and has been known in at least a vague way since the beginning of recorded history. The reasons for it are not hard to identify. When the price of wheat is sky high, only rich men will be able to afford it; the poor will have to make do with rye bread, just as they still must do in poorer lands. When the price is still high but not quite so high as before, persons of moderate means who also happen to have an especially great liking for white bread will now be coaxed into buying some wheat.

Thus a first reason for the validity of the law of downward-sloping demand comes from the fact that *lowering prices brings in new buyers.*

Not quite so obvious is a second, equally important, reason for the law's validity; namely, each reduction of price may coax out some *extra purchases by each of the good's consumers;* and—what is the same thing—a rise in price may cause any one of us to buy less. Why does my quantity demanded tend to fall as price rises? For two main reasons. When the price of a good rises, I naturally try to *substitute* other goods for it (rye for wheat or tea for coffee, for example). Also, when a price goes up, I find myself really poorer than I was; and I will naturally cut down on my consumption of most normal goods when I feel poorer and have less real *income.*

Here are further examples of cases where I buy more of a good as it becomes more plentiful and its price drops. When water is very dear, I demand only enough of it to drink. Then when its price drops, I buy some to wash with. At still lower prices, I resort to still other uses; finally, when it is really very cheap, I water flowers and use it lavishly for any possible purpose. (Note once again that someone poorer than I will probably begin to use water to wash his car only at a lower price than that at which I buy water for that purpose. Since market demand is the sum of all different people's demands, what does this mean? It means that even after *my* demand stops expanding very much with price decreases, the *total* bought in the market may still expand as new uses for *new people* come into effect.)

To confirm your understanding of the demand concept, imagine there is an increase in demand for wheat brought about by a boom in people's incomes or by a great rise in the market price of the competing rye, or simply by an increased desire of people to spend their money on wheat. Show that this *shifts* the whole demand curve in Fig. 4-1 rightward, and hence upward; pencil in such a new curve and label it *d'd'* to distinguish it from the old *dd* curve. Note that such an increase in demand means that more will now be bought at each price—as can be verified by carefully reading off points from the new curve and filling in a new Q column for Table 4-1.

■ THE SUPPLY SCHEDULE

Let us now turn from demand to supply. The demand schedule related market prices and the amounts *consumers* wish to buy. How is the supply schedule defined?

> By the *supply schedule, or curve,* is meant the relation between market prices and the amounts of the good that *producers* are willing to supply.

Table 4-2 illustrates the supply schedule for wheat, and Fig. 4-2 plots it as a supply curve. Unlike the demand curve, the supply curve for wheat normally rises upward and to the right, from southwest to northeast.

The supply schedule, relating price to quantity produced, can also be plotted as a curve:

SUPPLY SCHEDULE FOR WHEAT

P/Q	POSSIBLE PRICES ($ PER BU.) P	QUANTITY SELLERS WILL SUPPLY, MILLION BU. PER MONTH Q
A	$5	18
B	4	16
C	3	12
D	2	7
E	1	0

TABLE 4-2. At each P, there is listed the Q that producers will want to bring to market.

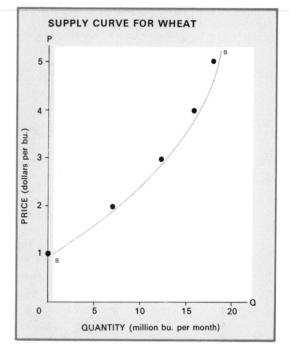

FIG. 4-2. Each Q, P pair of numbers in Table 4-2 is
here plotted as a point. A smooth light brown curve
passed through them gives the upward-sloping supply
curve ss.

At a higher price of wheat, farmers will take acres out of corn cultivation
and put them into wheat. In addition, each can now afford the cost of more
fertilizer, more labor, more machinery, and can even afford to grow extra wheat
on poorer land. All this tends to increase output at the higher prices offered.

As will be seen in Part Three, our old friend the law of diminishing returns
provides one strong reason why the supply curve would slope upward. If society
wants more wine, more and more labor will have to be added to the same limited
hill sites suitable for producing wine grapes. Even if this industry is too small to
affect the general wage rate for labor, each new man will—according to the law
of diminishing returns—be adding less and less extra product; and hence the
necessary cost to coax out additional product will have to rise. (Cost and returns
are opposite sides of the same coin, as will be shown later.[1])

How shall we depict an increase in supply? An increase in supply means an

---

[1] While the exceptions to the law of the downward-sloping demand are few enough to
be unimportant in practice, we shall encounter in Part Three some interesting exceptions to
the upward-sloping supply curve. Thus, suppose that a family farmer produces wheat and its
price rises so much as to give him a much higher income. With wheat so lucrative, he is at
first tempted to *substitute* some of his leisure time to produce more of it. But might there
not reasonably come a time when he feels comfortable enough at his higher *income* to be
able to afford to take things a little easier and supply less than before?

Equilibrium market price is at the point where the amounts supplied and demanded match:

SUPPLY AND DEMAND SCHEDULES FOR WHEAT				
	(1) POSSIBLE PRICES ($ PER BU.)	(2) QUANTITY DEMANDED, MILLION BU. PER MONTH	(3) QUANTITY SUPPLIED MILLION BU. PER MONTH	(4) PRESSURE ON PRICE
A	$5	9	18	Falling
B	4	10	16	↓ Falling
C	3	12	12	Neutral
D	2	15	7	↑ Rising
E	1	20	0	Rising

TABLE 4-3. Only at the equilibrium price of $3 will quantity demanded by consumers equal quantity supplied by producers. At any lower price, amount demanded would exceed amount supplied; at any higher price, amount supplied would exceed amount demanded.

increase in the amounts that will be supplied at each different price. Now if you pencil the new supply curve into Fig. 4-2, you will see that it has shifted *rightward*; but for an upward-sloping supply curve, this change means the new *s's'* curve will have been shifted rightward and *downward* (not rightward and upward as in the case of a shifted downward-sloping demand curve). To verify that *s's'* does depict an increase in supply, fill in a new column in Table 4-2 by reading off points from the new diagram carefully.

■ EQUILIBRIUM OF SUPPLY AND DEMAND

Let us now combine our analysis of demand and supply to see how competitive market price is determined. This combining is done in Table 4-3. Thus far we have been considering all prices as possible. We have said, "If price is so and so, sales (Q) will be so and so; if price is such and such, sales will be such and such; and so forth." But to which level will price *actually* go? And how much will then be produced and consumed? The supply schedule alone cannot tell us. Neither can the demand schedule alone.

Let us do what an auctioneer would do, i.e., proceed by trial and error. Can situation *A* in Table 4-3, with wheat selling for $5 per bushel, prevail for any period of time? The answer is a clear No. At $5, the producers will be supplying 18 (million) bushels to the market every month [Column (3)]. But the amount demanded by consumers will be only 9 (million) bushels per month [Column (2)]. As stocks of wheat pile up, competitive sellers will cut the price a little. Thus, as Column (4) shows, price will tend to fall; but it will not fall indefinitely to zero.

To understand this better, let us try the point *E* with price equal to only $1 per bushel. Can that price persist? Again, obviously not, for a comparison of Columns (2) and (3) shows that consumption will exceed production *at that price*. Storehouses will begin to be emptied; disappointed demanders who cannot get wheat will tend to bid the price up. This upward pressure on price is shown by Column (4)'s rising arrow.

We could go on to try other prices, but by now the answer is obvious.

> The equilibrium price, i.e., the only price that can last, is that at which the amount *willingly* supplied and the amount *willingly* demanded are equal. Competitive equilibrium must be at the intersection point of supply and demand curves.

Only at C, with a price of $3, will the amount demanded by consumers, 12 (million) bushels per month, exactly equal the amount supplied by producers, 12 (million). Price is at equilibrium, just as an olive at the bottom of a cocktail glass is at equilibrium, because there is no tendency for it to rise or fall. (Of course, this stationary price may not be reached at once. There may have to be an initial period of trial and error, of oscillation around the right level, before price finally settles down and the amount supplied balances the amount demanded.

Figure 4-3 shows the same equilibrium in pictorial form. The supply and demand curves, superimposed on the same diagram, cross at only one intersection point. This point C represents the equilibrium price and quantity.

At a higher price, the black bar shows the *excess* of amount supplied over amount demanded. The arrows point downward to show the direction in which price will move because of the competition of *sellers*. At a price lower than the

The equilibrium market price is where demand and supply curves intersect:

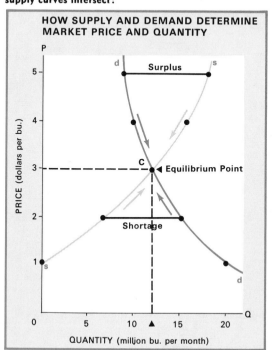

FIG. 4-3. At the C equilibrium intersection, the amount supplied just matches the amount demanded.

At any lower P, the excess amount demanded will force P back up; and at any P higher than the equilibrium, the amount supplied will be excessive and P will be forced back down to the equilibrium level.

$3 equilibrium price, the black bar shows that the amount demanded exceeds the amount supplied. Consequently, the eager bidding of *buyers* requires us to point the arrow indicators upward to show the pressure that they are exerting on price. Only at the point *C* will there be a balancing of forces and a stationary maintainable price.

Such is the essence of the doctrine of supply and demand.

■ EFFECT OF A SHIFT IN SUPPLY AND DEMAND

Now we can put the supply and demand apparatus to work. Gregory King, an English writer of the seventeenth century, noticed that when the harvest was bad, food rose in price; and when it was plentiful, farmers got a lower price. Let us try to explain what happens by our diagrams.

Figure 4-4(a) shows how a spell of bad weather *reduces* the amount that farmers will supply at each and every market price and thereby displaces the equilibrium point *E*. The *ss* curve has shifted to the left and has become *s's'*. The demand curve has not changed. Where does the new supply curve *s's'* intersect *dd*? Plainly at *E'*, the new equilibrium price where the amount demanded and the new reduced amount supplied have again come into balance. Naturally, *P* has risen. And because of the law of downward-sloping demand, *Q* has gone down.

Diagrams show effects on price of demand and supply shifts:

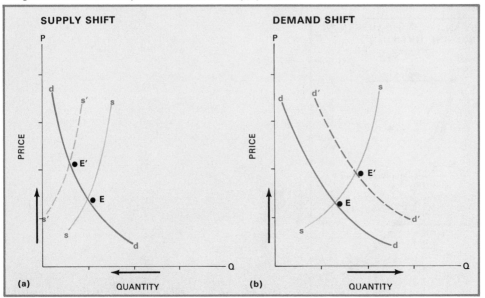

FIG. 4-4(a). If supply shifts leftward for any reason, the equilibrium-price intersection will travel up the demand curve, giving higher *P* and lower *Q*.

FIG. 4-4(b). If demand shifts rightward, the equilibrium will travel up the supply curve.

Suppose the supply curve, because of good weather and fertilizers, had ~~increased~~ instead. ~~Draw in a new equilibrium E'' with lower P and higher Q.~~

Our apparatus will also help us analyze the effect of an increase in demand. Suppose that rising family incomes make everyone want more wheat. Then at each unchanged P, greater Q will now be demanded. The demand curve will shift rightward to $d'd'$. Figure 4-4(b) shows the resulting travel up the supply curve as enhanced demand competitively raises equilibrium price.

■ A VOLUNTARY OR A CONSCRIPTED ARMY?

Reliance on supply and demand i.e. on market pricing can be a viable substitute for explicit governmental directions and control. An excellent example is military recruitment. A nation can choose to utilize a compulsory draft where all able-bodied young men may be compelled to serve in the armed forces. Such a system was adopted by Canada during World War II although specific exemptions were granted to individuals who could be of more benefit to the nation outside of the military or who were for some reason unable to serve. But such exemptions were rare. Another form of compulsory service which may be used in periods of less than all-out war is a lottery which selects without bias that subset of young men called into the armed forces.

Another way to recruit a peacetime army of limited size is the simple price or market mechanism employed by Canada today. *The wages of the armed services are simply raised to whatever level is necessary to coax out an adequate supply of volunteers.* Figure 4-5, on the next page, contrasts the case of reliance on the price mechanism (supply and demand) to the case of a compulsory draft (conscription). In Fig. 4-5(a) the conscription or command intersection F, comes at an arbitrary low wage at which an additional number of young men are compelled through a draft to serve in the armed forces. In Fig. 4-5(b), the peacetime army is recruited by raising the wage to that of the intersection E where the number of men supplied balances out the number of men demanded. This second system results in a different composition as well as a different number serving in the armed forces. Just as the rich have more yachts and filet mignon than the poor, so too do their sons better manage to avoid the tedium and danger that national defense necessitates. Minority groups and individuals who face less lucrative alternative occupations in civilian life generally bulk larger in a volunteer army, such as Canada's, than they might in an equitably-run draft, such as that of the United States. Moreover, those less eager to serve will, under a voluntary system, generally be the last to volunteer at each wage.

As Fig. 4-5(c) indicates, during a shooting war of many casualties, perhaps no wage however high would tempt the requisite number of men to volunteer. But even then, raising military pay could somewhat lower the tax that the rest of the community is, in effect, levying on those males who happen to be of prime military age when war breaks out.

The present discussion warns that one must take care in speaking of *dollar* costs when there may well be very important costs which cannot be directly measured in dollars and cents. In the draft case the government was seen to pay out much less in military wages than it did in the volunteer-army case. But there are other "real" costs to the community or nation which military wages do not reflect and these additional costs may outweigh the savings in wages. This is because there is a cost attached to the careers which were interrupted and that is the civilian goods which were not produced because the manpower was drained off into the military forces. (Actually, since the volunteers are probably used more effectively in uniform and probably represent youths with less productive civilian alternatives and with greater tolerance for risk and military discipline, the "real" or additional costs may be a bit less with a volunteer army than with a drafted one.) How then did the true or real costs get hidden in the compulsory-army case? In effect, a *non-money* tax was being put on young, healthy males, and particularly on those whose number happened to be drawn. In the volunteer-army case, part of this cost-burden is shifted to older people and women and to those who get deferred, and it is only this *explicit* tax on them (needed to pay the higher military wages), that shows up in money terms. Yet the economic burden is there in any case.

■ TWO STUMBLING BLOCKS

It is well to pause here to consider two minor sources of possible confusion concerning supply and demand. These have puzzled students of economics in all generations. The first point deals with the important fact that in drawing up a

In peace, market pricing might handle army recruitment:

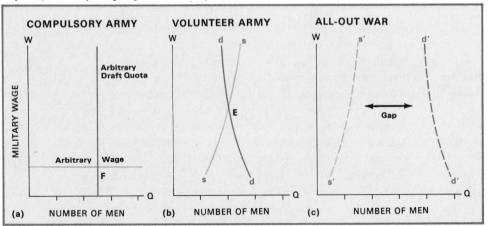

FIG. 4-5(a). By command, wage is set low at *F* and those unlucky enough to be conscripted serve at that low wage.

FIG. 4-5(b). Here raising military pay (and improving conditions!) coaxes out the needed supply at the *E* intersection. Those serve who least dislike military life, who have least attractive civilian alternatives, and whose families are least affluent. (Defense forces are of lesser size along *dd* as the authorities use men less wastefully and rely more on nonuniformed civilian employees.)

FIG. 4-5(c). If risk of death rises in shooting war so that no sufficient number of volunteers are forthcoming to meet expanded defense needs, supply-and-demand fail and must be supplemented by some more direct form of coercion.

demand schedule or curve, one always insists that "other things must be equal." The second deals with the exact sense in which demand and supply are equal in equilibrium.

"OTHER THINGS EQUAL"   To draw up a demand schedule for wheat, we vary the price of wheat and observe what would happen to its quantity bought *at any one period of time in which no other factors are allowed to change so as to becloud our experiment.* Specifically, this means that, as we change wheat's P, we must not at the same time change family income or the price of a competing product such as rye or anything else that would tend to *shift* the demand schedule for wheat. Why? Because, like any scientist who wants to isolate the effects of one causal factor, we must try to vary only one thing at a time. True enough, in economics we cannot perform controlled experiments in a laboratory, and we can rarely hold other things constant in making statistical observations of economic magnitudes. This limitation on our ability to experiment empirically in economics makes it all the more important *to be clear in our logical thinking,* so that we may hope to recognize and evaluate important tendencies—such as the effect of P on Q demanded—when other tendencies are likely to be impinging on the situation at the same time.

The case of demand shift in Fig. 4-4(b), on page 88, can illustrate this common fallacy based upon a failure to respect the rule that other things must be held equal in defining a demand curve. Suppose that the supply curve shifts little or not at all. But suppose the demand curve shifts up to $d'd'$ in good times when jobs are plentiful and people have the incomes to buy more wheat; and suppose in the more depressed phase of the business cycle demand always shifts down to dd. Now take a piece of graph paper and plot what would actually be recorded in the statistics of the wheat market.

In good times you would record the equilibrium point E', and in bad times the equilibrium point E. Take a ruler and join the points E and E'. The fallacy to be avoided like the plague is expressed as follows: "I have disproved the law of downward-sloping demand; for note that when P was high, so too was Q—as shown by E'. And when P was lowered, instead of that change increasing Q, it actually lowered Q—as shown by E. My straight line joining E and E' represents an upward-sloping, not a downward-sloping, demand curve; so I have refuted a basic economic law."

Being alerted beforehand, one detects the fallacy of this argument. For at the same time that P went up, other things were *not* held constant; rather, income was also raised. The tendency for a rise in P to choke off purchases was more than masked by the countertendency of rising income to raise purchases. Instead of testing our economic law by moving *along* the demand curve, the beginner has measured changes that result from the *shift* of the demand curve.

Why is this bad scientific method? Because it leads to absurd results such as the following: "On the basis of my revolutionary refutation of the law of downward-sloping demand, I confidently predict that, in the years when the harvest is especially large, wheat will sell for a higher rather than a lower price." Not only will such reasoning lead to absurd predictions that would lose fortunes for a speculator or a miller, but it also leads to a failure to recognize other important economic relationships, such as the fact that, when family incomes go up, demand curves for goods such as wheat tend to shift rightward.

MEANING OF EQUILIBRIUM   The second stumbling block is a more subtle one, less likely to arise but not so easy to dispel. It is suggested by the following:

"How can you say that the equality of supply and demand determines a particular equilibrium price? For, after all, *the amount one man sells is precisely what another man buys.* The quantity bought must always equal the quantity sold, no matter what the price; for that matter, whether or not the market is in equilibrium, a statistician who records the Q bought and the Q sold will always find these necessarily identical, each being a different aspect of exactly the same thing."

The answer to this must be phrased something like this:

You are quite right that measured Q bought and measured Q sold must be identical as recorded by a statistician. But the important question is this: At which P will the amount that consumers are *willing to go on buying* be just matched by the amount that producers are *willing to go on selling?* At such a price, where there is equality between the *scheduled* amounts that suppliers and demanders want to go on buying and selling, and only at such an equilibrium P, will there be no tendency for price to rise or fall.

At any other price, such as the case where P is above the intersection of supply and demand, it is a trivial fact that whatever goods change hands will show a statistical identity of measured amount bought and sold. But this measured identity does not in the least deny that suppliers are eager at so high a price to sell more than demanders will continue to buy; and that this excess of scheduled supply over scheduled demand will put downward pressure on price until it has finally reached the equilibrium level where the two curves intersect.

At this equilibrium intersection, and there alone, will everybody be happy: the auctioneer, the suppliers, the demanders—as well as the patient statistician, who always reports an identity between the measured amounts bought and sold.[2]

■ WHAT SUPPLY AND DEMAND ACCOMPLISHED: GENERAL EQUILIBRIUM

Having seen how supply and demand work, let us take stock of what has been accomplished. The scarce goods of society have been rationed out among the possible users of them. Who did the rationing: a board? a committee? No. The auctioneering mechanism of competitive price did the rationing. It was a case of "rationing by the purse."

FOR WHOM goods are destined was *partially* determined by who was willing to pay for them. If you had the money votes, you got the wheat. If you did not, you went without. Or if you had the money votes, but preferred not to spend them on wheat, you did without. The most important needs or desires for goods —if backed by cash!—got fulfilled.

The WHAT question was being *partially* answered at the same time. The rise

---

[2] A similar question of measured identity versus scheduled intersection could arise in the discussion of income determination in Chapter 12.

in market price was the signal to coax out a higher supply of wheat. It was the signal for men and other scarce resources to move into the wheat-production industry from alternative uses.

Even the How question was being *partially* decided in the background. For with wheat prices now high, farmers could afford expensive tractors and fertilizers and could bring poorer soils into use.

Why the word "partially" in this description of how the competitive market helped solve the three problems? Because this wheat market is but one market of many. What is happening in the corn and rye markets also counts; and what is happening in the market for fertilizer, men, and tractors obviously matters much.

We must note that the pricing problem is one that involves *interdependent markets*, not just the "partial equilibrium" of a single market.[3]

There are, so to speak, auctioneers operating simultaneously in the many different markets—wheat, corn, fertilizer, and land; labor, wool, cotton, mutton, and rayon; bond, stock, and personal loans. Each ends up at the equilibrium intersection point of his supply and demand schedules—wheat, corn, fertilizer prices, and land rent; labor wage, wool, cotton, mutton, and rayon prices; bond price and its interest yield, stock prices and dividend yield, interest charges on personal loans.

No market is an island unto itself: when wool P rises (because, say, of sheep disease abroad), it pulls up the P's of domestic labor, fertilizer, and land needed for expanded wool output; and it raises the P's of rival goods like cotton that some demanders will now turn to; it might well lower the P of wool spinners and of suit-company stock shares, since the latter must now pay more for their raw materials and may bid less eagerly for spinning labor.

The new "general-equilibrium set of interdependent prices" adjusts to the new situation. The price system meets the problem posed by the basic definition of economics: the study of (1) how *scarce means with alternative uses*—limited land and labor that can be switched from one industry to another—are allocated, and (2) how to *achieve ends or goals*—as prescribed by the tastes for wool, nylon, food, and housing of sovereign consumers, possessed of factors of production that give them money-income votes for the market place. Each separate

---

[3] The alert reader will not have to be reminded that the competitive market gives goods to those with money votes and does so efficiently. But the distribution of the money votes depends on for how much you can sell your labor and property in competitive and imperfectly competitive factor markets, and it is affected in an important way by (1) how lucky you are, (2) how lucky your parents and in-laws were, and (3) the advantages and disadvantages of your genetic and acquired skills and aptitudes. If a student writes on a final exam, "For Whom is decided (in part) by how people decide to use their money votes," he is not wrong. Indeed, he gets possibly 50 per cent credit. However, he will not get the other 50 per cent unless he adds, "The basic problem of For Whom is the process by which the money votes *themselves* get determined, which is primarily not by supply and demand in a single good's market, but by supply and demand in the labor, land, and other interdependent factor markets of Part Four. And factor supplies depend much on distribution of ownership, and hence on the inheritance of wealth."

market, with its supply and demand curves, is doing its bit toward creating the general-equilibrium set of prices, which in our society resolves the basic economic problems of WHAT, HOW, and FOR WHOM.

■ PERFECTION AND IMPERFECTIONS OF COMPETITION

Our curves of supply and demand strictly apply only to a *perfectly competitive* market where some kind of *standardized* commodity such as wheat is being auctioned by an organized exchange that registers transactions of *numerous* buyers and sellers. The metal exchange in London and the grain exchange in Winnipeg are two such examples. Stock exchanges, such as those in New York, London, Toronto, and Montreal, do not auction goods and commodities or productive services rendered by factors of production; but they do provide a market where shares of common stocks such as those of General Motors and Imperial Oil are auctioned at each moment of the working day. Many corporate bonds are also bought and sold in the bond division of these exchanges.

The economists' curves of supply and demand are important ways of idealizing the behavior of such markets. They do not pretend to give an accurate microscopic description of what is going on during each changing moment in such a market place, as men from the various brokerage houses are milling around on the trading floor while frantically giving hand and voice signals to the specialist who serves as auctioneer for each grain or company stock. Nonetheless, the tools of supply and demand do summarize the important average relationships resulting over a period of time from such organized trading.

As far as these fundamental tools of supply and demand are concerned, it matters little what kind of exchange the goods are traded on: whether hand signals, slips of paper or modern computers are used; whether the auction is of the familiar kind, where the auctioneer calls out a *minimum* starting price and accepts higher and higher bids until only one high bid is left to get the Renoir painting in question; whether there is a "Dutch auction," where the price starts high instead of low and moves downward at stated time intervals until an eager buyer, fearing that someone else will get in the bid first, finally gives the first bid and gets the merchandise; or whether the auctioner asks for written bids and offers in order to be able to make up a table or chart like those of Table 4-3 and Fig. 4-3 and find the equilibrium intersection at one fell swoop.

Indeed, the market need not have a single auctioneer: all the bidding may well take place by telephone calls and personal contact as in the case of the market for Canadian government bonds, which is a much more perfect one than the corporate bond market on the floor of the Toronto or Montreal Stock Exchange. The same can be true of stocks listed on the so-called "over-the-counter market," a market which is conducted throughout the country completely by telephone and by daily mailing of price-quotation lists by different brokers; for example, an important stock such as Pine Point, which was listed originally on this market, may actually behave more nearly like our competitive model than does some stock *inactively* traded on the floor of the Toronto Stock Exchange.

Needless to say, the requirements for absolutely perfect competition are as hard to meet as the requirements for a perfectly frictionless pendulum in physics. We can approach closer and closer to perfection but never quite reach it; yet this fact need not do serious damage to the usefulness of our employing the idealized concept. Actually, it matters little to the economic scientist that different grades of wheat will call for slight variations from the quoted market prices. It matters little, too, that dealers in foreign exchange, whose bids and offers determine whether the price of an American dollar (or an English pound) will be $1.01 rather than $1.00 (or $2.43 rather than $2.45), use the telephone and cable rather than a trading floor with auctioneer or specialist dealer presiding. Nor does it matter in the case of standardized cotton goods, so-called "gray goods," that they are sold and bought in an informal way by many competing firms: so long as there are *numerous* buyers and sellers on each side, *well-informed* about quality and about each others' prices and having no reason to discriminate in favor of one merchant rather than another and no reason to expect that variations in their *own* bids and offers will have an *appreciable effect* upon the prevailing market price—so long as all this is true, the behavior of price and quantity can be expected to be much like that predicted by the curves of supply and demand.

Supply and demand tools have many applications:

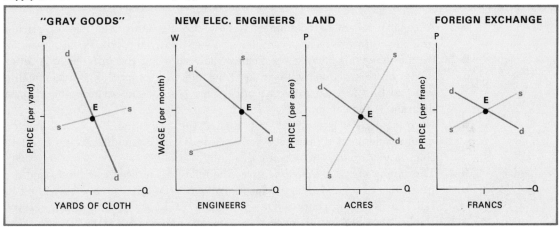

FIG. 4-6. Here are a few examples of the many uses of supply and demand. Note that these diagrams have straight lines rather than the curved lines of previous figures: in connection with supply and demand and many other diagrams, the economist often makes such simplified drawings merely because the eye takes them in rapidly; usually, this is a tolerably good approximation to the true empirical curves, but when this is not so, it is easy to modify the straight lines. (Example: The supply of graduating electrical engineers is a relatively fixed number, and this is depicted in the vertical supply line in the second diagram; however, it is an exaggeration in view of the fact that, as the wage gets low enough, some graduates will take jobs in other fields and some will go to graduate school—which is the reason why the *ss* curve bends to the southwest at low wages.) Can you interpret the four cases?

The various diagrams in Fig. 4-6 illustrate how the tools of supply and demand might be used to give a good approximate description of various economic situations other than that of a staple commodity such as wheat: there is pictured a competitive market for cotton gray goods (unbleached cotton bolts); for a factor of production such as newly graduating electrical engineers, whose price is represented by a wage per month; for a capital asset such as a corner lot of land or a bond; and finally, as will be explained later in the discussion of international trade in Part Five, a foreign exchange market in which the price in Canadian dollars of a German Deutschmark, an English pound, an American dollar, or a single unit of any other foreign currency is determined by the bids of those who need foreign currency and by the offers of those who want to sell such currencies to get Canadian dollars.[4]

To be sure, not all today's markets are anywhere near to being perfectly competitive in the economist's sense. We shall see later, in Part Three, that elements of monopoly power or of market imperfection many enter in, and these imperfections will require us to modify the competitive model. After we have learned how to handle such cases, we shall recognize that the world is a blend of competition and imperfections—which means that the competitive analysis, properly qualified, is still an indispensable tool for interpreting reality.

SUMMARY

■ 1   A basic problem of economics is how the mechanism of market pricing grapples with the triad of problems WHAT, HOW, and FOR WHOM.

■ 2   By the *demand schedule* we mean a table showing the different quantities of a good that people will—at any time and with other things held equal—want to buy at each different price. This relationship, when plotted on a diagram, is the *demand curve*.

■ 3   With negligible exceptions, the higher the price the lower will be the quantity demanded, and vice versa. Almost all commodities are subject to this "law of *downward*-sloping demand."

■ 4   The *supply curve or schedule* gives the relations between the prices and the quantities of a good that producers will—other things equal—be willing to sell. Usually supply curves *rise upward* and to the *right*: diminishing returns implies that higher P is needed to coax out higher-cost extra Q.

---

[4] Question 11 at the end of this chapter reproduces from a newspaper its financial reports for a single day, showing what might have been the market price quotations for grains, bonds, gold, common stocks, and foreign exchange. After studying economics, one is in a better position to understand the basic forces underlying these price quotations; but only experience and study can make one reasonably expert at the hazardous game of forecasting. The stock market is discussed in this Appendix; Chapter 20's Appendix discusses the economics of speculation in organized commodity markets.

■ 5 Market equilibrium can take place only at a price where the quantities supplied and demanded are *equal*. At any price higher than the equilibrium intersection of the supply and demand curves, the quantity producers will want to go on supplying will exceed the quantity consumers will go on demanding; downward pressure on price will result as some sellers undermine the going price. Similarly, the reader can show why a price lower than the equilibrium price will meet irresistible upward pressure.

■ 6 Competitive pricing rations out the limited supply of goods to those with desire or need backed by money votes. Along with helping to decide FOR WHOM, it signals changes in WHAT shall be produced and in HOW goods shall be produced. But any one market only "partially" helps solve the WHAT, HOW, and FOR WHOM because of its interdependence with other commodity and factor markets in setting "the general-equilibrium system of prices."

■ 7 To illustrate the allocation function of supply and demand, one can contrast the case of a compulsory draft for the military services with the case where service pay is raised high enough to coax out a voluntary army. Although money costs appear greater, the real cost to the nation may be less if re-enlistments cut out training needs and better use is made of service personnel.

■ 8 Organized trading markets exist for a number of staple commodities such as wheat; they may also exist for some common stocks, bonds, and other financial items. There are still other markets that behave much like an auction market, even if there is no formal auctioneering procedure: so long as there are numerous well-informed suppliers and demanders, each too unimportant to have *by himself* an appreciable effect upon the price of the standardized good in question—so long as such conditions prevail, the tools of supply and demand will give an adequate approximation of the behavior of such markets. Yet, as will be seen later, a good deal of modern economic reality departs from the strict competitive model of the economist, and he must find tools applicable to monopoly and imperfect competition.

QUESTIONS FOR DISCUSSION

1. Although we should all like to escape the hardship implied by higher market price, show that rising market prices may perform some useful functions in time of scarcity. Show how such hardships might work themselves out in some different kind of economy.

2. Define carefully what is meant by a demand schedule or curve. State the law of downward-sloping demand—that there is some kind of *inverse* relation between P and Q, the latter going down when the former goes up.

3. Define the concept of a supply schedule or curve. Show that an increase in supply means a rightward and downward *shift* of the supply curve. Contrast this with the rightward and upward shift implied by an increase in demand. Why the difference? Treat the cases of decreased supply and demand.

Industrial stocks

Range 1970/71 High $	Range 1970/71 Low $	Company	Indic. Div. Rate $	Week Ended Feb. 26 High $	Low $	Close or Latest $	Net Chge.	Sales 100s	Ind. Yld. %	P/E ratio latest 12 Mos.	Earnings per Share: 1970 or latest interim	$	Earnings per Share: 1969 or latest fiscal year	$
9.00	5.50	A-1 Steel and Iron A	0.60	LJan.22,1971		7.50	....	nil	8.0	2.4	'70 Feb	3.18	'69 Feb	1.87
10.00	3.00	Do. B	0.60	7.50	7.50	7.50	+0.50	1v	8.0	5.6	'70 Feb	1.33	'69 Feb	.60
9.87	3.65	A.G.F. Mgt. B pfd. ..	P0.30	7.75	7.00	7.50	—0.50	25T	4.0	20.8	Aug 9m	.22	'69 Nov	.63
6.12	2.25	Abel-Black Corp.	...	3.40	3.25	3.25	unch.	7T	..	10.5	'70 Mar	.31	'69 Mar	.28
13.00	6.75	Abitibi Paper	P0.19	7.50	7.12	7.37	unch.	1234M	2.6	30.7	'70 Dec	.21	'69 Dec	.64
53.50	48.25	Do. 7½% ser. A pf. .	3.75	51.50	51.12	51.50	+0.50	2T	7.3	..	Mar 3m	x12.13	'69 Dec	x16.19
11.25	4.00	Acklands Ltd.	P0.18	5.87	5.12	5.87	+0.62	62T	3.1	7.4	Aug 9m	.25	'69 Nov	1.12
21.50	18.00	Do. 6% pfd.	R1.125	18.00	18.00	18.00	unch.	1T	6.3	..	'69 Nov	x7.71	'68 Nov	x7.91
14.00	9.12	Do. 2 pf. ser. A 6% cv.	*0.96	10.00	9.25	9.62	—0.37	24T	10.0	..	'69 Nov	x7.71	'68 Nov	x7.91
22.00	5.87	Acres Ltd. .... stk.	...	9.37	8.62	9.00	+0.12	41T	..	..	*'70 Dec 14m	.32	'69 Oct	.92
38.75	28.87	Do. 7.20 pfd.	3.60	36.00	35.00	36.00	+1.00	28T	10.0	..	......	....	......	....
5.15	1.25	Do. warr.	...	2.40	2.05	2.35	+0.30	18T	..	..	......	....	......	....
....	....	Admiral Corporation .	...	LApr.18,1969		20.75	....	nil	..	66.9	69 Dec	U.29	'68 Dec	U.10

Government of Canada bonds

Feb. 26, 1971

	Bid	Ask	Yield
Sept.perp.	41.00	43.00	6.98
Apr 71	100.00	100.07	5.12
Apr 71	100.00	100.10	5.04
Jun 71	99.90	100.00	4.97
Jun 71	100.60	100.70	5.14
Oct 71	100.70	100.80	4.97
Oct 71	101.75	101.85	4.94
Dec 71	100.80	100.90	4.96
Apr 72	100.60	100.70	4.93
Apr 72	102.40	102.50	4.93
Sept 72	99.20	99.30	4.74
Dec 72	100.40	100.50	4.96
Feb 73	105.35	....	5.10
Feb 73	103.70	103.80	4.95
Apr 73	104.00	104.10	4.94
July 73	103.50	103.60	4.95
July 73	104.00	104.10	4.89
Oct 73	100.30	100.40	4.82
Dec. 73	103.30	103.40	4.93
Jun 74	105.50	106.00	5.02
Jun 74	102⅝	102⅞	5.05
Dec 74	100.00	....	...
Apr 74	105.75	106.25	5.07
Oct 74	108.50	109.00	5.24
Apr 75	105.50	106.00	5.61
July 75	105.50	106.00	5.69
Oct 75	100.00	100.25	5.44
Apr 75	103.00	104.00	5.41
Dec 75	107.50	108.00	5.35
Apr 76	100.00	100.25	5.44
Jun 74/76	89.00	90.00	5.43
Sept 77	106.50	107.00	5.71
July 78	108.50	109.00	6.45
Jan 75/78	86.50	87.50	5.98
Oct 79	80.00	81.00	6.11
Aug 80	93.00	94.00	6.35
Sept 83	82⅞	83⅛	6.48
Jun 88	80.50	81.50	6.84
Feb 89	99⅞	100⅛	6.73
May 90	83.00	84.00	6.75
Sept 92	86.50	87.50	6.87
Oct 95	95.00	96.00	6.84

Winnipeg cash

	High Feb. 26, 1971	Low Feb. 26, 1971	High Prev. week	Low Prev. week
$ per bushel				
Oats—				
2 Cw.	.83⅜	.82¾	.84¼	.83½
3 Cw.	.82⅜	.82	.83¼	.82½
Barley—				
1 Feed	1.27	1.25½	1.27⅞	1.27⅜
2 Feed	1.25¼	1.23½	1.26⅛	1.22⅞
1 Malt	1.28⅛	1.26¾	1.28⅞	1.28⅜
Rye—				
1 & 2 Cw. .	1.14⅜	1.11¼	1.15½	1.14⅞
3 Cw.	1.08¾	1.05¼	1.08⅞	1.08¼
Flax—				
1 Cw.	2.49⅜	2.48½	2.50⅞	2.49¾
2 Cw.	2.44¼	2.43½	2.45½	2.44¼
3 Cw.	2.19¾	2.18½	2.20½	2.19¼
Rapeseed—Vancouver				
#1 Cdn. ...	3.04½	2.94⅜	3.14¼	3.09⅛
#2 Cdn. ...	2.89⅝	2.79⅜	2.99¼	2.94

Daily US$ - UK£ rates

March 1, 1971

	U.S.$	U.K.£
Mon.	1.00 24/32	2.43 4/8
Fri.	1.00 22/32	2.43 2/8
Thurs.	1.00 21/31	2.43 7/8
Wed.	1.00 24/32	2.43 6/8
Tues.	1.00 11/32	2.43 6/8
Ave.	1.00 102/160	2.43 17/40

U.S. rate reported by Bank of Canada.

U.K. bid rate reported by Toronto-Dominion Bank.

Gold bars quoted

Rate Reported by Toronto Stock Exchange
Feb. 26

Canadian kilo bars of gold approximately 32 oz. each.

	Bid (per oz.)	Asked (per oz.)
Latest price	$38.85	$39.85
Previous week	$38.65	$39.65

Reprinted from The Financial Post, March 6, 1971.

4. What factors might increase the demand for wheat? The supply? What would cheap mechanical pickers do to cotton or blueberry prices? To farm wages?

5. Spell out arguments to show that competitive price must settle down at the equilibrium intersection of supply and demand. Use too-high or too-low P.

6. "An increase (or decrease) in supply will lower (or raise) price. An increase (decrease) in demand will generally raise (lower) price. While we can predict that an increase in demand accompanied by a decrease in supply will be followed by a rise in price, we cannot guess without further information what will happen if we *simultaneously increase* demand and *increase* supply." Verify. Puzzle out this use of parentheses, common in economics, for alternatives.

7. "A simultaneous increase of demand and decrease of supply, as in question 6 is statistically impossible. Demand and supply are identically the same thing." Comment in terms of the section "Two Stumbling Blocks."

8. Give the pros and cons of voluntary blood donations. Illustrate with one of the situations in Fig. 4-5.

9. "If there is only one seller or only a few very large sellers, monopoly and imperfect competition theory will need to be considered rather than the tools of competitive supply and demand. If products are far from being standardized, then each brand-name seller may well have a degree of control over his price not enjoyed by the perfect competitor as defined by the economist." Verify. Make a check list of conditions needed for "perfect competition."

10. *Extra-credit problem*, only for those who know some mathematics: The demand curve is a functional relation between Q and P, namely, $Q = f(P)$. Downward-sloping demand means Q falls as P rises, or in terms of calculus that $df(P)/dP < 0$. Other variables, such as income (X_1) or price of rye (X_2), are being held constant, etc.; hence $f(P)$ is short for $f(P; X_1, X_2, \ldots)$, and a change in any X_i shifts the demand curve. Similarly, denote the supply functional relationship between Q and P by $Q = s(P)$, with $ds(P)/dP > 0$. Then, equilibrium intersection price, P^*, is the root of the equation $f(P) = s(P)$.

11. Try to puzzle out what the newspaper reports on the opposite page mean.

12. Review your understanding of the following concepts:

demand schedule or curve	movements along a schedule
law of downward-sloping demand	how supply and demand in one market
supply schedule or curve	"partially" solve WHAT, HOW, and
diminishing returns	FOR WHOM
equilibrium intersection	general equilibrium prices
shifts of schedules	imperfectly competitive situations

Appendix: Stock Market Fluctuations

Wall Street means the New York Stock Exchange and the brokers' houses and financial firms that go with it. It dominates the world's exchanges. Every second, supply and demand bid up and bid down the prices of common stocks (equity shares). One year a man makes a fortune; another year he is ruined.

The New York Stock Exchange lists more than 1,000 securities, as do the Paris *Bourse* and the London stock exchange (and many other "exchanges" for the trading of inter-bank obligations, foreign currencies, metals, and farm products). Its origins were like a club's, with rules for membership. Rights to trade are still *memberships* dictated not by the government but by the other members. In order to trade directly on the New York Stock Exchange you must buy a seat. Some other exchanges, like New York's American Exchange, or Montreal's Canadian Exchange, began as "curb" exchanges: brokers literally met on the street curb to buy and sell, giving hand signals to clerks hanging out the windows to record transactions. The price of seats is lower than on the main exchanges.

Nowadays every advanced country where shares

are widely held has its exchange. Canada has Toronto and Montreal. In addition, there are important regional exchanges in Chicago, Boston, Vancouver, and Winnipeg, that deal in local or smaller industries' stocks not listed in New York or Toronto.[1] In fact the regional exchanges might cease to exist if the market for all "local" stocks broadened and if the larger exchanges were to permit trading by more than the limited number of select "seat-holders."[2]

PEOPLE'S CAPITALISM

The stock exchanges for many years tried to sell the notion of "people's capitalism," in which everyone owns stocks and therefore will vote to take account of the interests of property. Few would oppose the notion of a wider and more equal distribution of wealth, but it is a bit of a confidence trick to entice a union worker—or his wife—into owning a few shares so that at the polls they will go easy on corporate tax rates—when, in fact, their own well-being is trivially affected by what happens to the few shares they own compared to even a 1 per cent change in wage rates or pension benefits.[3]

In any case only about 800,000 out of approximately 20 million Canadians (and about 27 million out of over 200 million U.S. citizens) own any appreciable amount of stocks, and that is a generous estimate. Now that private and public pension funds are beginning to invest in common stocks, low-income people indirectly are beginning to acquire some protection of their savings against inflation, a privilege that until recently was enjoyed primarily by the affluent (apart from those poor who held "the widow's friend," a little real estate).

---

[1] Trading, valuing, and speculating in some shares of some industries, like mining and petroleum, are very specialised. Some "regional" exchanges are actually providing a location for specialists.

[2] In the 1965 *Windfall Report*, Mr. Justice Arthur Kelly said of the Toronto Stock Exchange members, "The view that the Exchange was a private gaming club seemed to have motivated them [i.e. the broker owners] in turning to their own advantage special privileges which were not available to the public." Since that time, stricter regulations on inside information and trading have been imposed by most exchanges and their governments.

[3] Note that many of these people are not directly concerned because "their" shares are either locked in a safety deposit box and rarely considered for disposal or managed by a pension or mutual fund.

THE GREAT CRASH

One traumatic event long kept the general populace fearful to venture into stock ownership—the memory of the 1929 panic and crash on Wall Street, which ushered in the long and painful depression of the 1930s.

During the fabulous stock market boom of the "roaring twenties," housewives, Pullman porters, college students between classes—all bought and sold stocks. Most purchases in this wild "bull" market were "on margin"; i.e., the buyer of $10,000 worth of stocks had to put up only $2,500 or less in cash and borrowed the difference, pledging his newly bought stocks. What matter that he had to pay his broker 6, 10 or 15 per cent per year on his borrowing when in one day Massey-Harris or Abitibi might jump 10 per cent in value!

The most wonderful thing about a bull market is that it fulfills its own hopes. If people buy because they think stocks will rise, their act of buying sends up the price of stocks. This causes them to buy still further, and sends the dizzy dance off on another round. And unlike a game of cards or dice, no one loses what the winners gain. Everybody gets a prize! Of course, the prizes are all on paper and would disappear if everyone tried to cash them in. But why should anyone wish to sell such lucrative securities?

When the whole world is mad, 'tis folly to be sane. Suppose one had been so wise or so naïve as to believe that the public-utilities holding companies were paper pyramids on cardboard foundations; or that certain dream real-estate developments were midway between pine thicket and swamp? What could such a social misfit have done? He would soon learn the first rule of property values: "A thing is worth what people *think* it is worth." Unfortunately, to be successful, this has to be applied in connection with the second rule, which is as hard to follow in practice as belling the cat or catching birds by putting salt on their tails: "Don't be the sucker left holding the bag."

When the black October crash of 1929 came, everyone was caught, the big-league professionals and the piddling amateurs—John D. Rockefeller, Sir James Dunn, Sir Harry Oakes, and the economics professor in Alberta. The bottom fell out of the market. Brokers had to sell out the "margin" accounts of investors who could no longer pony up extra funds to cover the depleted value of their collateral,[4] sending the market down still further. Even those who did not buy on margin lost one-third of their capital by the end of the year, and five-sixths by 1932!

The bull market was over. The bear market had taken its place. And as the former had lived on its dreams, so the latter was consumed by its own nightmares. Billions of dollars of security values were wiped out every month, taking with them not only the capital of gamblers out for speculative gains, but also the widow's mite supposedly invested for steady income. A "blue chip" stock like United States Steel fell from a 1929 high of 261 to a 1932 low of 21, while less respectable securities dropped off the board completely, becoming worthless. Even though U.S. President Hoover and his administration were friendly toward business, in vain did they try to restore confidence by predicting "prosperity is just around the corner" and "stocks are excellent buys at their present levels."

Finally, the stock market began to follow general business recovery. Figure 4-7, on pages 102 and 103, shows the movements of stock market values over the whole period. Although stocks were bullish in 1936-1937 and again during World War II, it was not until the mid-fifties that they returned to anything like the peak levels of 1929. The boom in glamor growth stocks, which ended in the mid-1962, mid-1966, and 1969 collapses, confirmed the fact that human nature never changes much.

In Figure 4-7, the index of Canadian share prices (on an *annual*, not daily basis) is superimposed over the Dow-Jones, New York, average. The day-to-day fluctuations (important to the speculator) are not shown. But it is clear that the two markets have moved together, as would be expected when investors in both countries can choose which market to invest in.

■ FAVORABLE ODDS

Actual historical experience has shown that, even in the face of the great crash, over a lifetime one would have done better in risky common stocks than in

---

[4] Frederick Lewis Allen's amusing and interesting chronicle of the 1920s, *Only Yesterday*, gives a detailed account of the role of the stock-market boom in American life. J. K. Galbraith's *The Great Crash, 1929* (Boston: Houghton Mifflin, 1955) is more recent and recounts vividly the events of 1928-1931.

safe gilt-edged bonds or savings accounts.

It was shown in the 1930s that equity holders did better than bondholders for most of the years between 1870 and World War I. A study at the University of Chicago in the 1960s found that this had become even more true in the 1925-1960 years.

In an age of inflationary price creep and growth of the mixed economy, you can throw a dart at the financial page to select your portfolio of stocks at *random* and, on the average, come out substantially ahead of your "prudent" brother who stays invested in government bonds and savings deposits!

Again, Fig. 4-7's charts of the 30 Dow-Jones "blue chip" industrial stocks and DBS's Index of Canadian common stock prices illustrate these facts.

■ THE CULT OF EQUITIES

People, of course, go from one extreme to another. After shunning the stock market for many years, by the 1970s they began to think that you couldn't lose in it. As a result they have bid up common-stock prices to the point where their dividend yields are scarcely 3 per cent, whereas good bonds in Canada yield 7 or more per cent. Why this inverted structure when bonds are allegedly safer? Obviously, investors—most of whom are in fairly high tax brackets—are shooting for low-tax capital gains rather than heavily taxed dividends. Capital gains, too may help more than bonds to keep investors' purchasing power ahead of inflationary erosion.

Experience with markets abroad shows that all good things eventually come to an end. When Canadian or U.S. stock prices get bid high enough, there will be plenty of room for steep declines, and investing in common stock will cease to be as much of a one-way street as it seemed to be between 1945 and 1970.

■ OUTGUESSING THE MARKET?

To the age-old question, "Does the market follow business activity or business activity follow the market?" no simple answer can be given. It is reasonably clear that business activity, national income, and corporate earnings determine stock prices and not vice versa; and also that the psychological effects of market movements no longer have primary importance. But still the market can occasionally *anticipate* changes in national income and total purchasing power. It then appears to be leading them

The only thing sure about stock prices is that they will fluctuate:

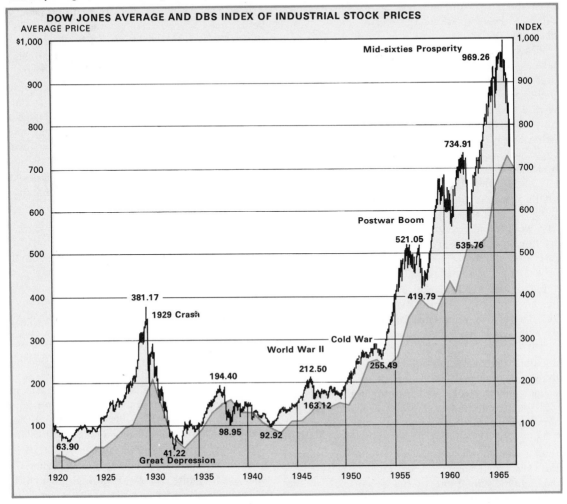

FIG. 4-7. As money national income rises, from real growth and price-level increases, the trend in common-stock prices is upward. But note the severe oscillations. The upper line represents the Dow Jones Average; the lower line traces the similar DBS Index of Canadian common-stock prices (1935 = 100). The graph for the years from 1965 to 1970 appears on the opposite page. (Source: Dow Jones and Co. Inc., and DBS 11-503, *Historical Monthly Statistics*; DBS 11-502, Canadian Statistical Review, *Historical Summary*; and Bank of Canada *Statistical Summary*.)

when really it is following what it thinks they will be doing later.

HOW TO INVEST There are no simply stated fool-proof rules for making money out of the stock market. Anyone who can accurately predict the future course of business activity will prosper; but

there is no such person. At least four main classes of investors and speculators can be distinguished.

1. The group who simply *buy and hold.* Because the national economy has a long-term upward trend, they fare reasonably well over the long run. They might do a little better if they followed the statistical advice of investment services as to how to switch to

FIG. 4-7 *continued*

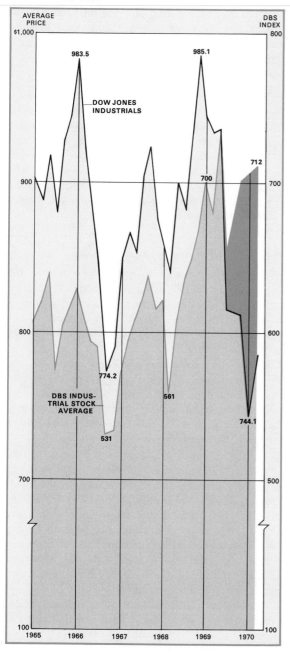

of 30 industrial stocks or of the similar DBS index of Canadian traded stocks.

The effect of this holding group is neither to stabilize nor to destabilize prices; to the extent that they freeze shares off the market and limit the number of tradings, they tend to make the market "thinner." In a thin market there are so few transactions that the attempt to buy a few hundred shares of a stock may send its price up a few points because of the absence of ready sellers around the ruling market price. An attempt to sell may depress the price a few points.

2. At the other extreme are the hour-to-hour, day-to-day ticker watchers, to be seen in every brokerage office. Generally speaking, they buy and sell, sell and buy. Usually, they make money only for their brokers.

The existence of this group has the effect of making the market less thin. Because of this group, any investor can expect to be able to liquidate his market holdings at any time at some price, although not at a price predictable in advance nor that he would like. Still, even this restricted "liquidity" enhances the attractiveness of securities traded on organized exchanges over and above the unlisted issues of smaller companies bought and sold by brokers over the counter.

3. In between are those speculators who play intermediate swings of many months or years. The least successful of these are the amateurs whose entrance into the market at the top when it is too late is supposed to be the signal for the "smart money" to leave. The most successful speculators are those who are able to avoid the extremes of enthusiasm of the mob and to discern underlying business conditions. This does not mean that they simply buy because a stock looks low and sell when it looks high. On the contrary, they buy when stocks look as if they will continue to rise. When a drop seems imminent, they sell short or, more conservatively, they simply go into cash or high-grade bonds. It takes cool nerves to sell short, because on the whole the market is overoptimistic. But if a single individual does it cleverly, he may achieve success in avoiding the losses of a bear market.

The behavior of such speculators is often destabilizing to prices. They "pile on" to a price rise and send it farther; they similarly *accentuate* a decline.

Thus, in the mid-1960s certain so-called "performance" or "venture" mutual investment funds

companies of more favorable growth prospects. Surprisingly, though, representative studies show that the best mutual funds and investment counselors rarely do much better than the Dow-Jones average became prominent. The funds would buy electronic or airline glamor stocks just before the latter stocks became glamorous. Then as people saw the funds buying, the public would be attracted to the same stocks. After the prices of the glamor stocks and hence of the funds' shares had been bid up, the performance funds would sell out to the public at a nice profit, moving on to new fields ripe for conquest. The evident perils in this are well illustrated by a modern Wall Street story.

A broker phones me, telling me to buy XYZ at $2.00 a share. I buy 100 shares. He phones me to say: "XYZ has risen to $3.00; better buy a couple of hundred more." I do. He calls again: "Better buy 300 XYZ at $5.00." Again I do, but when next he calls I finally refuse to buy and ask to sell. "What, sell XYZ," he says, "sell it *to whom?*" (*In joco veritas.*)

Despite these possible dangers, the popularity of venture mutual fund stocks has been growing rapidly in Canada. A report on Canadian Mutual Funds, published in 1969, stated ". . . competition between mutual funds has tended to accord more emphasis to comparisons of rate or return (performance) than is warranted even by the undoubted importance of that information."[5] The report went on to warn that many Canadian investors seemed momentarily to be forgetting that a high return carried with it a high degree of risk of loss. Any judgment based upon performance over a matter of months or a year is subject to doubt—5 years would be a minimum time period for adequate assessment. Nevertheless investors have moved rapidly into these performance funds. So rapidly in fact that by the end of 1968, 80 per cent of all new mutual fund shares sold were of the venture variety.[6]

4. Finally, there are individuals who study special situations. From public or inside sources, they learn in advance of changes in the fortunes of particular companies: of rumored bankruptcies; of special stock dividends, split-ups, or mergers; of likely earnings and dividend announcements. When combined with the successful characteristics of the third group, members of this group—such as the elder statesman of two wars, Bernard Baruch—make the largest

profit from the market. Since World War II some alert operators have been able to run $1,000 up to $10,000,000 or more—at the same time keeping profits in the form of less heavily taxed capital gains.

But the would-be investor must take to heart Baruch's caution:

> If you are ready to give up everything else—to study the whole history and background of the market and all the principal companies whose stocks are on the board as carefully as a medical student studies anatomy—if you can do all that, and, in addition, you have the cool nerves of a great gambler, the sixth sense of a kind of clairvoyant, and the courage of a lion, you have a ghost of a chance.

■ SCIENCE OF STOCKS

Buying common stocks is an art, not a science. No one can draw the line between risky speculation and safe investment. But an art or craft, being science in a still-primitive state, has its general rules of behavior. Here are a few gleaned from scientific study of this unscientific field.

1. You can't compile a good track record by *consulting the stars.* Don't laugh. Financial services have gotten rich—their clients haven't though—by selling astrological advice, and one man made a fortune purporting to interpret the signals being given in the comic strips!

2. Hunches work out to nothing in the long run.

3. *The best brains in Wall Street scarcely do as well as the averages* (Standard & Poor's, Dow Jones, DBS stock price index etc.). At first this seems surprising. They have all the money needed for any kind of research and digging. But remember, they are all competing with each other; and if there is a bargain for one man to see, it is also there for another; and hence it will already have been wiped out of existence by competitive bids.

4. Chartists claim to see in plots of stock prices "resistance levels," "gaps," "head-and-shoulder formations," "flags," "pennants," "channels"—all of which are supposed to improve your odds of guessing right. Experienced investors say: "The chartists generally end up with holes in their shoes. So forget it."

5. Are there then no good tricks? Alas, few indeed. Because inflation and growth push the country

---

[5] Canada: Committee on Mutual Funds and Investment Contracts, *Report* (Queen's Printer, Ottawa, 1969), p. 62.
[6] *Ibid.*, p. 63.

ahead, a random investment will probably show capital gains in the long run. Not much more can be said. Statisticians have demonstrated that the day-to-day changes in stock prices are very much like a "random-walk"—like the brownian motion you see in a microscope due to the chance impacts of invisible and unpredictable atoms on just-visible huge molecules or colloidal particles. Wall Street doesn't believe this random-walk theory, but the Ph.D.'s in the business schools laugh at their disbelief.

6. To have unusual performance, you must be able to predict increases in the per share earnings of companies *before* the market place in general is aware of them. *Afterward* is too late. For each stock tends to sell at a certain "price-earnings ratios,"—e.g., stagnant and cyclical C.P.R. at 12/1, glamorous IBM at 40/1. And if you are correct in foretelling an unanticipated rise in earnings, the market will probably mark up the stock price once those earnings become visible. (As a kicker, if you are early in recognizing an area of glamorous earnings growth, you may find the market multiplying your holdings by higher and higher price-earnings ratios—and after that has happened, it is a good time to get out.)

7. The above rule is easy to state but practically impossible to put into practice even if you have a vast research staff and inside management contacts. Hence, unless you like the fun of investing your own money—and are willing to pay something for that fun in the form of bad performance—most amateurs would be well advised to buy shares in some mutual fund. A mutual fund buys 30 to 100 stocks deemed best by professional money managers and gives you your prorated share in them. If the market goes up, your mutual fund shares will probably go up; but it works both ways. (WARNING: Most mutual funds are sold by salesmen who get a fat commission for doing so—usually an 8 per cent "load" skimmed off your principal. Through the mail or from some banks and trust companies you can buy no-load funds involving no sales commission at all, and which experience shows do about the same on the average as the heavy-load funds. How do the no-load funds manage this? Simply by paying the same management fees to money managers but cutting out the selling expenses—the equivalent in finance of the "discount retail store" that quotes low prices for cash-and-carry. You can recognize no-loads on the financial pages by *equality* of "bid" and "asked.")

FOR REVIEW

Review your understanding of the following concepts:

New York, Toronto, Montreal, and other exchanges
common stocks or equities
great crash
dividend versus bond yield
equities and inflation protection

price-earnings multiple
random-walk versus chartism
mutual funds:
 load and no-load
 performance or
  venture funds

5

BUSINESS
ORGANIZATION AND
INCOME

The able businessman generally finds that in the long run the capital at his command grows in proportion to his ability. ALFRED MARSHALL

To understand our business civilization, we must first understand the organization and functioning of business enterprise. The first part of this chapter leads up to the analysis of the modern corporation, primarily by an extensive case study; the last half deals with the financial structure of corporations, particularly the modern large-scale or "giant," corporation. The Appendix presents a brief introduction to the fundamentals of accounting. Without some comprehension of accounting, there can be no deep understanding of the economics of enterprise. The "new industrial state"—to use the name John Kenneth Galbraith has coined for the organization of our large corporate bureaucracy—is something new in the history of mankind.[1] If the corporate structure is not to control man, society must see that it stays subject to control.

■ BIG, SMALL, AND INFINITESIMAL BUSINESS

There are more than 8½ million business units in North America. All but a small portion of these enterprises are very small-scale units, owned by a single person. Most businesses are here today and gone tomorrow, the average life expectancy of a business being only six years. Some will terminate in bankruptcy; many more will be voluntarily brought to a close with sighs of regret

[1] John Kenneth Galbraith, *The New Industrial State* (Boston: Houghton Mifflin, 1967), p. 320.

for dashed hopes and an expensive lesson learned; still others will come to a joyous end when their "self-employed" owners finally land good, steady jobs.

Faster than old businesses die, new ones are born. The present population of business concerns grew up as a result of the cumulative excess of business births over business deaths during previous years. As an economy grows, we can expect a steady excess of business births over deaths.

By number the tiny, transient, self-owned "individual proprietorship" is overwhelmingly the dominant form of North American business. But in terms of dollar value, political and economic power, payrolls, and employment, only slightly more than one-hundred "giant corporations" occupy a strategically dominant position.

Let us glance briefly at the role in our economy of "infinitesimal businesses."

There are more than 430,000 farmers in Canada, with average net income (from all sources) of about $4,500; 25,000 grocery store owners, many of them over 65 years of age and earning less than the minimum taxable income; 18,700 service stations, or one for every 250 cars; and so it goes.

Some of these ventures are highly successful; but it is still true to say that most do not earn for their owners much more than they could get with less effort and risk by working for somebody else. Thus, chain stores do about 47 per cent of all the grocery business, the rest being divided among the independents. Most of these independents consist of the so-called "Ma and Pa" stores, doing less than $100 of business every day. These are often started by people who have only a few thousand dollars of initial capital—less than half the amount necessary for an adequate grocery store to do the $150-a-day business necessary if the owner is to earn even minimum wages for his effort. Such small-scale efforts are doomed from their very beginning. When the owner's initial capital is used up, they are finished. They illustrate why one-third to one-half of all North American retail businesses are discontinued within 3 years. (It is somewhat sobering to note that despite the brave and worthy discussions of "black capitalism," most U.S. Negro businesses are small and of low profitability, being confined chiefly to a protected market of service needs for blacks—as, for example, restaurants, undertaking, hairdressing and barber shops, dry cleaning, etc.)

Of course, business fields differ in the amount of capital required. To build a modern service station in Ontario recently cost between $70,000 and $100,000 (land included), but the average cost of renting a station is only $3,000-$6,000. Occupations with a high "rate of turnover of inventory"—such as vegetable stores—obviously require less initial capital than drugstores, hardware stores, or jewelry stores, where many items of stock will stay on the shelves for 3 to 5 years and where the average "turnover ratio" of annual sales to stock of inventory may be a great deal less than one.

Aside from the capital necessary to open a business, there is the tremendous amount of personal effort required. Self-employed farmers usually work from 55 to 60 hours per week during the peak summer months. Similarly, it has been estimated that the people who are their own bosses put in more hours per week than wage earners. Who, on his Sunday ride in the country, has not pitied some self-employed drudge, whose own efforts and those of all his family hardly suffice to cause him to break even?

Still, people will always want to start out on their own. *Theirs* may be the successful venture. Even if they never do succeed in earning more than a few thousand a year, there is something attractive about being able to make their own plans and do the variety of tasks that a small enterprise calls for.

■ THE SINGLE PROPRIETORSHIP

We gain insight into the principal forms of business organization—the single proprietorship, the partnership, and the corporation—by following the history of a particular business venture as it grows from a small beginning into a good-sized corporation. In the last part of this chapter, we shall turn to the subject of the giant corporation and its modern economic role.

Let us suppose you decide to start a business to produce toothpaste. You may have hit upon a good preparation in your chemistry class; or perhaps you simply looked up an old formula in the *Encyclopaedia Britannica*. To be a single proprietor you need not get anybody's permission; you simply wake up one morning and say, "Today, I am in business!" And you are.

You can hire as few or as many men as you wish, borrow whatever capital you can. At the end of the month whatever is left over as profits—after all costs have been met!—is yours to do with as you like. And there is nothing to stop you from going to the cash-register at any time, taking out $800 if you can find it there, and giving it to your wife to buy a fur jacket or a Chippendale chair. (Of course, as an individual, you must pay personal income taxes on all earnings.)

The losses of the business are all yours, too. If your sales fail to cover the costs you have incurred, your creditors can ask you to dig deeper into your personal assets: the bonds set aside for Junior's education, the old farmstead, and the rest. In legal terms, an individual proprietor has "unlimited liability" for all debts contracted by the business. All his property, with the exception of a small minimum, is legally attachable to meet those debts.

■ BUSINESS GROWTH AND THE NEED FOR SHORT-TERM CAPITAL

Suppose the business is prospering tremendously—perhaps because your low price has induced a chain of 5-and-10-cent stores to place a large order for tubes of paste to be marketed under its name. You are now making more money than you expected to; but you find yourself harder pressed for cash than ever before. Why? Because you are not *paid in advance* for your sales, whereas you must pay your workers and suppliers promptly on receipt of their services. For the moment you are putting out money and getting nothing for it, i.e., nothing except the certainty of future payment on the sales orders which you have booked, nothing but a miscellaneous batch of "goods in process"—unfinished toothpaste, empty tubing, and so forth.

To some extent, the stringency of cash can be relieved by your not paying for supplies until the end of the month or even longer. However, there is a limit to how far your suppliers will let you run up bills. Also, letting your so-called "accounts payable liabilities" pile up is an expensive way of raising capital, because goods are often billed at 2 per cent discount if paid within 30 days. When you do not take advantage of such discounts, you are, in effect, paying a very high interest rate—up to 24 per cent per year!

Where is such a single proprietor to borrow? A consumer loan company is allowed to charge about 2 per cent per month (almost 30 per cent per year) on loans under $1,500, and would probably charge you 3 per cent per month or 40 per cent per year for the $40,000 you need; and even it will prefer to lend to a man with a steady wage that can be "attached" or "garnisheed" in case of non-payment. If you own a home without a mortgage, a loan at 9 or 10 per cent might be raised upon it. To do so appears to risk your family's future well-being; but, as we'll see below, your personal wealth is in jeopardy whatever you do to finance your single proprietorship. So, if you have enough confidence, you may go ahead and mortgage.

Why can't you call on your bank for a commercial loan at 9 per cent? Ordinarily, a chartered bank will not provide "venture capital" for an unproven enterprise. The local manager looks at your chequing balance and finds it has always been near the vanishing point; this is natural, since as fast as payments have come in, you have had to write cheques to stave off the ever-insistent claims of your creditors. Ordinarily, the bank likes to establish "lines of credit" for its customers. These are idle part of the year, and fully-loaned during the busy season (prior to the harvest by farmers, and before Christmas by merchants). The loan is cancelled when the cash comes in. It is futile to pretend that 3 months from now your growing business will be more flooded with cash than now. At that time you will be applying for continuous renewal of the loan; you know it, and your banker knows it.

Sometimes bank managers are allowed to extend "term loans" of some years' duration, depending on general credit conditions and the state of the older bankers' prejudice against this kind of lending. But even if allowed, the bank manager could not conscientiously provide capital for a business like yours. No matter how certain and glorious the future of the business appears to you, to the banker you are only one of numerous would-be entrepreneurs; and most, he knows, are destined for failure even in the best of times, and almost all would be wiped out if a really big depression came along. For the bank actually to protect the sums entrusted to it by its depositors, it would have to charge you an extra risk premium of perhaps 10 per cent or more,[2] in addition to, say, 9 per cent interest. Otherwise, the gains from successful ventures would not offset the losses of the unsuccessful ones.

There are a few other possibilities. Your bank might give you a Small

---

[2] Another alternative has been used extensively in Germany but not in Canada, the United States, or Britain: German banks buy part ownership in business and share in the profits. Such participation in ownership inevitably leads to management responsibilities by the banks and often to monopoly control of business by banking interests. For this reason, and others, such activity is legally forbidden to our banks, which are rarely sources of venture capital.

Business Loan at 9 per cent for several years, but you would have to offer collateral and spend the loan on property and equipment. (The government, under the Small Business Loans Act, in effect insures the bank against your being wiped out.) Or you might turn to the federal Industrial Development Bank which has power to lend at longer term, perhaps on a ten-year mortgage at about 12 per cent. But it, too, would be helpful chiefly if you needed more building or machinery, not circulating assets. Finally, in some cities and provinces there are local lenders, sometimes publicly supported, who have limited funds to help bring a business to town or keep it there.

Despite your makeshift attempts to raise capital, the business is still suffering from growing pains. You have exhausted all possibilities of raising further loan capital. Perhaps the time has come to look for a partner.

■ THE PARTNERSHIP

Any two or more people can get together and form a partnership. Each agrees to provide some fraction of the work and capital, to share some percentage of the profits, and of course to share the losses or debts. A purely oral agreement will do; but it is more businesslike and makes for less misunderstanding if you have a lawyer draw up a formal partnership agreement.

In the case of the toothpaste business, suppose your brother-in-law is given a part ownership in the business in return for putting up $40,000 capital. Like you, he is to work for the company for, say, $8,000 per year as compared with your $12,000. You are to receive two-thirds of all profits or losses, computed after the partnership withdrawals are treated as costs; he gets one-third.

Your partner has put up $40,000 in cash. What have you brought into the venture? In the first place, you have, of course, some unfinished barrels of toothpaste to contribute, along with some uncollected accounts receivable for goods already delivered. This does not seem like much.

Actually, what you bring to the partnership is an intangible but valuable asset: the profitable sales orders and the know-how, or what is called "good will." In short, you are bringing with you a potential profit-earning power over all costs and drawings, of, say, $15,000 a year. You are letting your partner have a $8,000-a-year job—which we shall assume is perhaps equal to what he can get elsewhere—and, in addition, for $40,000 he is purchasing a one-third slice of $15,000 every year.

To get this much per year from bond investments would cost him much more than $40,000. He would have to buy $100,000 worth of 5 per cent government bonds to get such a return, or $83,333 worth of 6 per cent private bonds. Aside from the risk element, your partner is getting a good buy for his $40,000, since he will annually collect some 12½ per cent on his investment. So your two-thirds share is justified by the good will that you supply.[3]

---

[3] Good will and capitalized earning power are discussed in the accounting Appendix to this chapter.

And your business continues to prosper and grow. Each year, both partners agree to take out of the business only their stipulated drawings (which are like wages) and about a fifth of their share of profits, plowing the rest of the profits back into the business. Why do you decide to take any profits from the business at all? Because you need the cash to pay your personal income taxes, which are levied not only on your salaries but also *upon your respective shares of the partnership's earnings.*

Why does a business like this grow? Here are some possible reasons: (1) Your toothpaste sales have risen as a result of your trade name's becoming advertised and better known and as a result of your sending out more salesmen. (2) As more toothpaste is produced, economies of large-scale production are realized so that you are able to cut your price. (3) A new factor of growth results from "vertical integration." You decide to buy a chemical factory, to produce your own raw materials, and you also become your own wholesaler, thus operating three stages rather than only one "stage of production." (4) The company also grows by "horizontal integration": you take advantage of a profitable opportunity to buy out a number of competitors who produce similar toothpastes. (5) New "complementary products" such as soap and lipstick are added. You feel that bringing in the new lines under the same roof will help to spread the overhead expenses, and your salesmen feel that they might just as well get many orders as few when making a call. (6) You might even become an infant "conglomerate," growing by adding *unrelated* activities to your business (e.g., machine tools, car repairs, horoscopes). (7) Finally, your business may grow just because you are producing a better toothpaste.

■ NEW NEEDS AND SOURCES FOR CAPITAL

Once again, the enterprise finds itself in a paradox: the more successful it is and the faster it grows, the harder up it is for capital. The $40,000 of new "equity capital" brought into the business did not stay long in the form of cash. It was quickly transformed into circulating assets such as goods in process and office supplies. In part it went to pay off the most pressing liabilities.

The remainder was used as a down payment on a factory building and equipment. The difference between the down payment and the purchase price of the factory was secured by a mortgage loan on the property. The mortgage money was advanced by a life-insurance company and was to be amortized or paid off in installments over a period of 20 years, along with 9 per cent interest per year on the actual principal still unpaid at any time. In case the loan should not be paid, the holder of the mortgage of course has the right to foreclose the mortgage, i.e., to take over the ownership of the building and sell it for what it will bring. Since the down payment on the factory came to about one-third of its price, since this price was a bargain price to begin with, and since each year the insurance company will be getting back part of its principal, the risk taken by the company is not very great. The only way it could lose would be if there were a disastrous real-estate crash within the first few years.

Despite the continuous plowing of profits back into the business, growth still leaves you needing more capital. But now, having established your reputation, so to speak, new avenues of borrowing are open to you. Your banker will be glad to lend you money to tide you over the busy pre-Christmas period. An industrial finance company, such as the Traders' Finance Company, will lend you money on the basis of your safe, but as yet uncollected, "accounts receivable" (i.e., the sums owed to you for goods already sold).

Suppose, when all is said and done, you need still more capital than you can raise by any kind of borrowing. The painful necessity arises of getting more "equity" capital by letting some new people share in the profits (and losses) of the business. (As a matter of fact, even if you could still find some institutions to borrow from, it would be unwise to do so. You have already superimposed too many liabilities and fixed charges on a narrow equity base. As long as things go well, it would be nice to earn 12½ per cent profit on capital that costs you only 9 per cent. But if losses should occur, they will fall all the more heavily on you, the two partners, who are the residual owners.)

▣ DISADVANTAGES OF THE PARTNERSHIP FORM

One possibility of getting more ownership capital is to admit new partners. There is no limit to the number of partners that you can admit; there have been partnerships in the brokerage and banking fields involving more than 100 people. However, every time a new partner is admitted, or one dies or resigns, a whole new partnership must be formed.[4]

As the number of partners increases, there emerges a feature of both proprietorships and partnerships that has been soft-pedalled in our discussion up to now. A single proprietor is liable *without limit* to the full extent of his family's fortune for all the debts he contracts. In a partnership each partner is similarly liable, but now for all debts contracted by the partnership. If he owns 1 per cent of the partnership and the business fails, then he will be called upon to foot 1 per cent of the bills and the other partners will be assessed their 99 per cent. Suppose they cannot pay any part of their assessment. Then the 1 per cent partner may be called upon to pay *for all*, even if it means selling his fine etchings or auctioning his family home.

---

[4] More weighty is the real disadvantage stemming from the fact that a partnership can be dissolved whenever any party finds the existing arrangement unsatisfactory and wishes to withdraw. The law of partnerships also makes it impossible for any partner to sell his share to a new party without the consent of his partners; if agreement cannot be secured, a costly liquidation of the assets of the partnership may be inevitable.

The reader may recall that the novelist William Dean Howells has his famous title character Silas Lapham, a rising self-made paint tycoon, present his partner with the ultimatum: "You buy me out or I'll buy you out." Silas' two excuses, that his were the real brains and energy responsible for the success of the business and that the proffered price exceeded his partner's original investment, were cleverly seen through by Mrs. Lapham. She pointed out that, without the partner's money at the critical time, the business could never have succeeded and that Silas' offer to sell was premised upon the knowledge that his partner was not in a position to buy the whole of the business.

This feature of *unlimited liability* reveals why both single proprietorships and partnerships tend to be confined to small, personal enterprises (even apart from the difficulties of raising capital). Even when he controls everything, the single owner hesitates to get involved in unpredictable ventures that risk his home and personal assets. Likewise, the partner draws back from putting his capital into complex ventures promoted and guided by his partners, over whom he can exercise little control.[5]

This explains why agriculture and retail trade are the only sectors of our economy where more than half of the business done is done by single proprietors and partnerships. In the field of investment banking, concerns like J. P. Morgan & Company used to advertise proudly "not incorporated" so that their creditors could have the extra assurance. But even these concerns have converted themselves into corporate entities.

Comparatively recently did the giant brokerage concern Merrill Lynch, Pierce, Fenner & Smith incorporate. For a long time it had many major partners and scores of junior partners, illustrating that the barriers to running a large enterprise put up by the partnership form are not insuperable. Such giant partnerships now are rare.

Undoubtedly, unlimited liability and the red tape needed to ensure continuity are the main drawbacks to the partnership form.

■ THE CORPORATION

At this point, therefore—or even long before—you will probably decide to form a corporation rather than a partnership. Usually you will incorporate in the province in which you live and operate.

Centuries ago, corporation charters were awarded by governments very rarely and only by special acts of the king and legislature. In the seventeenth century, several joint stock companies were chartered for trade, such as the East India Company. Another, the Hudson's Bay Company, was very active in the development of North American resources and markets. Incorporation at this time was an expensive and complicated process: either a charter had to be applied for in England and obtained from the Crown; or a special bill had to be passed in the local House of Assembly and approved by the governor and in London. The early railroads here and abroad often had to spend as much money in getting a charter through the legislature as in preparing their roadbeds. Gradually, corporation laws were modified, and in the mid-nineteenth century it became possible to obtain a general charter without applying for an act of Parliament. Under the present Canadian system, a limited company may be incorporated under the federal Companies Act or under a provincial Companies or Corporation Act (although some corporations, such as railroads, banks, and

---

[5] Most provinces have enacted provisions for "limited partnerships," a compromise between the partnership and the corporation. The general partners usually control operations, as above. But a group of limited partners may contribute capital to a specified amount and have their liability limited to that amount.

insurance companies, can still obtain charters only by special acts of Parliament or the provincial legislature). Ordinary business corporations, however, are created by the following procedure: an application for a charter is made to the Secretary of State by a minimum of three persons intending to incorporate; a memorandum of agreement between the applicants is drawn up by a lawyer, wherein the proposed by-laws of the company are set out; a charter (known as letters patent) is then issued and the corporation is established.

Let us see how the incorporating procedure works in the case of your tooth-paste company. You decide to issue 20,000 shares of common stock in the corporation: 6,600 going to you; 3,300 to your partner; 100 to your wife; and the other 10,000 to be sold to outside interests. Although each share is to have an initial stated value of $10, your lawyer has advised you to make them no-par shares, since "par value" has no particular significance anyway.

The 10,000 shares to be sold to the public are to be marketed through the local office of an *investment dealer*. These firms are simply merchandisers of securities; and as with any merchant, their profit comes from the difference between their buying and selling prices. Because yours is such a small business, they must drive a hard bargain, especially since they can claim that the costs of selling the securities are likely to be high. Thus the investment brokers may offer you $10 per share and plan to resell at a price of $12.50 per share. Had you been a large company, you might have held out for as much as $12.25—or even in some cases $12.40—out of the $12.50 selling price, because of the threat that you might take your offering to another dealer or syndicate.

For a large company the investment dealer would probably have agreed to *underwrite* the new issue of 10,000 shares. This means that he would have guaranteed the purchase of the full 10,000 shares at a set price. If the market then refused to buy all these shares from the investment dealer at his announced price, he, not you, would have to absorb the loss. But he probably regards you as too small and untried a business to justify his assuming the risk of underwriting. So he takes your issue on a "best effort" basis; and if he cannot sell all the shares, you end up raising less capital. (Also, as a "sweetener," he may insist upon having being given warrants—which are options to buy stock later at today's low price.)

CORPORATION STRUCTURE   Fortunately, all goes well, and he pays you $100,000 in cash for the securities sold. Unlike the case of the partnership, you need not concern yourself with the people to whom he has sold the shares or with the fact that they may resell their shares. The names of the owners of the shares are registered with the company or its bank agent in case they get lost and so that you will know where to send the dividend cheques or the announcements of stockholders' meetings.

Ordinarily, each share gives its owner one vote. Shares in the corporate earnings are also in direct proportion to the number of shares owned. Those with 100 shares get 100 votes and correspondingly higher dividend cheques.

The outside owners of 10,000 shares have paid in $100,000 cash to the company. What have you and your partner paid in? Obviously not cash, but rather a sizable amount of earning assets: plant, equipment, goods in process, and perhaps good will, which is, as we have already seen, the capitalized value of the presumed "excess earning power" of the business, resulting from its trademarks, patents, know-how, and so forth.

Back in the old days before 1929, you and your investment dealer might have evaluated the good will as liberally as you wished, possibly giving yourself 20,000 rather than 10,000 shares. This practice has been called "watering the stock." Today, you would have to submit any public issue to the scrutiny of government officers and the Stock Exchange. They would have to satisfy themselves that there were no misleading claims in your prospectus before permitting the new flotation. However, they do not pretend to pass judgment on or attest to the value of the stock. *Caveat emptor*—let the buyer beware—still prevails as a doctrine!

■ ADVANTAGES AND DISADVANTAGES OF THE CORPORATE FORM

PRIVATE ADVANTAGE   The corporation has solved most of the problems that bothered you about the partnership. It is an almost perfect device for the raising of large sums of capital. Of first importance, every stockholder now has *limited liability*, indicated to your suppliers and creditors by the addition of the word "Limited" (Ltd.) to the company name. After paying $12.50 per share, the investor need not worry about his personal estate's being in jeopardy. If worse comes to worst and the business becomes bankrupt, the most that each shareholder could lose would be his original $12.50 per share. He cannot be assessed further.

Of secondary importance is the fact that the corporation is a fictitious legal person created by the state. It exists not by "natural right" but only at the pleasure of the state. The corporation, as distinct from its owners, can be sued in court and can sue. Any officer of the company, unlike any partner, is strictly limited in his legal ability to act as agent for the other owners and to commit them financially. Also, the corporation may have "perpetual succession" or existence, regardless of how many times the shares of stock change hands by sale or bequest and regardless of whether there are 10,000 different stockholders. No group of shareholders can force any other group to sell or retain their holdings, and only a majority vote rather than unanimity is needed to reach day-to-day business decisions. Normally, the stockholders will be too numerous to meet for every decision; they will prefer to elect a board of directors consisting of a dozen or so members to represent them between annual meetings, in much the same way that democratic electorates select legislative representatives to act for them. As we shall see, the problem of keeping large corporations "truly democratic" is a hard one.

You will face one disadvantage to incorporation that has become increasingly serious in recent years. *The government taxes corporate income.* Thus, during World War II, a profitable corporation might have had to pay as much as 80 per cent of its income to the government in excess-profit taxation. Most sizable corporations must pay almost half of each extra dollar of income. (This is *in addition* to the personal income tax that owners pay on dividends they get.)

The corporate tax is a rather high price for a small business to pay for limited liability and greater ease of raising capital. Yet there are also tax *advantages* offered by the corporate form. There is a loophole in our present law: *undistributed* corporate profits escape *personal* income taxes; only paid-out dividends are so taxed. A rich man who is taxed about 70 cents of every dollar of personal income can say, "Why pay such rates on partnership earnings? Let's incorporate, pay the lower corporate tax, and keep dividends low."[6]

Another loophole is used to avoid the disadvantages of double taxation under the corporate form when the owners of a closely held corporation vote most of its earnings to themselves and their relatives in the form of high salaries, pensions, and perquisites. The National Revenue Department tries to check up on avoidance of taxes by such padding of expenses; but it is always hard to know whether a given in-law is worth $25,000 a year and whether a trip to a Bermuda convention is truly a business rather than a personal expense.

SOCIAL ADVANTAGE   When Prime Minister Gladstone was shown electricity on a visit to Michael Faraday's laboratory, he asked, "What is the use of electricity?" Faraday gave the amusing reply, "I suppose some day, Sir, you may come to put a tax on it." Surely the advantage of the corporate force to society is not merely that the state can tax it.

> Large-scale production is technically efficient, and a large corporation is an advantageous way for investors to pool the irreducible risks of business life. Without limited liability and the corporation, society simply could not reap the benefit that comes when large supplies of capital can be attracted to competing corporations that produce a variety of complementary products, that pool risks, and that best utilize the economies of sizable research units and managerial know-how. That is why the privilege of the corporate form is legalized.

■ HOW A CORPORATION CAN RAISE CAPITAL

Let us suppose your corporation continues to grow as a result of vertical, horizontal, or conglomerate combinations, new products, economies of mass production, advertising promotion, and so forth. Besides borrowing on promissory notes or mortgages, buying on credit, and relying on earnings not paid out in dividends, what new forms of financing are available to you?

---

[6] To some extent he is only putting off the evil day, for his dividends later will be taxable when he receives them. But against their certainty must be weighed these factors: (a) the delay in paying tax is itself worth money to him; (b) tax rates may change favorably; (c) for certain cases the government allows the distribution of past profits at what amounts to a flat 15 per cent personal tax; (d) for some years Canada has reduced "double taxation" of dividends by allowing taxpayers to subtract 20 per cent of dividend income from their personal taxes; and (e) lawyers may be able to work out a way of having the accumulation of past profits come to the shareholder as a "capital gain" rather than as dividends—and tax collectors may be able to prevent them.

BONDS   First, you may issue bonds. In Canada, a typical bond is a "debenture," which is simply a promissory note, nicely printed on gilt paper, issued in $1,000 or other denominations so as to be readily marketable for resale. A bond is a security promising to pay a certain number of dollars every 6 months or so for a number of years until it matures. At that time the borrowing company promises to pay off the principal of the bond at its face value. (Often the company has the right to call in the bond a few years before its maturity date by paying the bondholders some previously agreed-upon price.) The dollar installments paid every 6 months, the interest earnings of the bond, are usually called the "coupon" payments, because the owner of most bonds cuts off a certain little corner of the bond each 6 months and then mails it in to receive his interest payment.[7]

Ordinarily, payments for the coupons and principal must be made on time, regardless of whether the company has been making earnings or not. Otherwise the company is in default of its obligations and can be taken to court like any debtor.[8] Of course, there is no particular reason why a partnership could not borrow by the use of bonds; but ordinarily it would not be well enough known to succeed in interesting a lender. For that matter, a small corporation can rarely raise capital by issuing bonds.

COMMON STOCKS   Issuing bonds and issuing common stocks are opposite methods of financing. The common stockholder is providing "equity" capital. He shares in profits and in control of business decisions, but he must also share in all losses. His is a more risky venture, because he can never receive any dividends until the fixed charges owed to the bondholder are paid off. The bondholder gets a limited but steadier income. Unless the corporation is bankrupt or in danger of being so, the bondholder ordinarily has no legal control over the decisions of the business; but a wise management will take care to stay on good terms with all sources of future capital.

PREFERRED SHARES   Between bonds and common stocks are so-called "preferred shares." These pay *at most* a stated dividend—say, a stipulated 6 per cent of the face value per share—no matter how profitable the business becomes. The preferred shareholder is more likely to get his dividend even when profit is small than is the common stockholder, because legally he stands next in line after the bondholder and before the common stockholder. The latter gets no dividends if the preferred share fails to receive its full dividend.

---

[7] A hybrid form of bond called a parity bond has been successfully used by the British Columbia Hydro Authority. These bonds, guaranteed by the provincial government, pay a specified rate of interest (6¾ per cent on a 1969 issue) but have an additional feature whereby the holder may, at any time, cash in the bond for the full purchase price. Normally the principal of a bond is not repaid until maturity.

[8] Such bonds are general claims against all the assets of a corporation. Mortgage bonds, secured by all or some pieces of property are not uncommon. Convertible bonds, which can be exchanged for a stated number of common shares, are a popular hybrid. There are even income bonds, whose interest is payable only if there are large enough earnings; but Canada's 20 per cent dividend tax credit (see footnote 6) makes these rare.

Usually "cumulative" preferred shares are issued. This means that, if for 5 years of hard times there has not been enough in the way of earnings to pay any of the 6 per cent dividends on the preferred shares, when good times come back again the "cumulated" $30.00 (= 5 × $6.00) of unpaid preferred stock dividends must be made good before the common stockholders can begin to receive any dividends. Often, too, preferred shares are "callable" and "convertible." The first term means that at some previously stated value, say, $103, the company can buy back its outstanding preferred shares. The second term refers to the right given the preferred shareholder of converting each share into shares of common stock at some stipulated ratio.[9]

HYBRID CONVERTIBLES   After decades of price inflation, investors have become wary of putting their funds in bonds which merely repay the principal in dollars that have deteriorated in purchasing power. To tempt them back into bonds, corporations have occasionally resorted to *convertible bonds* which, while paying a below normal interest rate (e.g. 5½ per cent), are convertible into a specified number of shares of common stock. The investor can, in a way, have his cake and eat it too. If prices remain steady, he has a safe bond. If inflation sends stock prices upward, the investor can convert and protect the real purchasing power of his principal. *Convertible preferred stock* (into common shares) similarly exists. Finally some companies issue *warrants*, which are options to purchase, during a specified period, shares of common stock at some stated exercise price. Thus in the period before the warrant expires, it may be bought or sold. Such warrants are often very volatile in comparison with the common stock. You may make a fortune on warrants if you are correct; you may also lose your shirt.

■ ADVANTAGES OF DIFFERENT SECURITIES

From the standpoint of the investor, bonds, preferred shares, and common stock form a sequence of increasing risk and decreasing security—balanced by an increasing chance of making high earnings or capital gains. Thus a risky, unsecured mining share will yield double or triple the percentage on a bond— if the mine pays at all! But a number of tax influences spoil this neat sequence. Because common stocks may rise in value and give untaxed capital gains, they now often have a spread of dividend yields that begins even lower than bonds: some "growth stocks" like IBM and Moore Corp. yield less than the safest government bond. (To test his understanding of these three forms of securities, the reader should make sure that he understands why common stocks tend to be better investments in time of inflation than the other two.) Another tax aspect is the attractiveness given to preferred and common stocks by the Canadian dividend tax credit—to reduce their personal income tax, holders are willing to buy stock even when its yield is out of the sequence suggested above.

---

[9] Some preferred shares are made more attractive by being made "participating." This means that, once profit exceeds some agreed-upon figure, they share with the common stock-holder in any further profits. But this form is rare.

In any case, bonds are far from being a perfectly safe investment. During the depression, many companies went bankrupt and defaulted on their bonds, paying off only a few cents on the dollar. The basic risk in all corporate investment is a possible loss of earning power, which will greatly reduce the value of its assets. Often a company will undergo reorganization in which the stockholders may be squeezed out completely (this is why many Canadian mining companies have the word "Consolidated" inserted into their titles). The courts may appoint a "receiver" or trustee to run the business, and the bondholders may be given bonds (or even stocks!) equal only to some fraction of their original investment. And of course, certain bondholders have prior claims over holders of other types of bonds.

Bonds are also more vulnerable than stocks and shares to changes in general credit conditions. The less easy it is to get credit, the higher are all rates of interest, including bond yields. And (as will be explained in detail in Chapter 29) this tends to push bond prices down. Thus the holders of bonds may suddenly find, when market rates of interest rise, that the value of their bonds has dropped without any change in the basic soundness of the corporation, or the coupon payments that it makes every 6 months. Common stock is least prone to this effect; preferred shares tend to react like bonds.

From the corporation's view, bond debt creates low but inflexible fixed charges. These may be embarrassing in bad times. (In the Great Depression, the bondholders of many of the largest Canadian firms were in the United States or Europe. This meant that Canada as a whole had to find a fixed amount of foreign currency to pay abroad every year, even when Canadian exports were bringing in only a fraction of their previous foreign-currency earnings. Economists then likened this to the plight of the corporations, calling it the "fixed overhead burden of the staple economy.") Preferred stock is slightly better with respect to flexibility; and equity capital is most flexible of all.

▪ COOPERATION

Few people who wanted to make and sell toothpaste would think of starting a co-op. But cooperative societies are an important alternative to the corporation, and they do sell a lot of toothpaste, not to mention apples, fish, maple syrup, and Eskimo carvings. Furthermore, they have played a major role in the development of the western provinces' economy and politics. They are on the whole more important in Canada than in the U.S., but are insignificant in both countries alongside the huge European organizations. St. Francis Xavier University in Nova Scotia is well known for its success in teaching the elements of organizing this kind of business to Maritimers, and recently to visitors from all over the world. The co-op movement is scarcely growing in Canada, but it is far from static in the newly developed countries.

> In a *marketing* co-op, farmers, fishermen, or other producers form a society to act as a collector, processor, and distributor of their goods. In place of a corporation's shareholders, each co-op member (who is also a user of the co-op) contri-

butes some capital and is entitled to just one vote.[10] Thus, the democratic nature of cooperation is stressed. Each year between seasons the "profit" after all costs (including a price paid to each member for the produce he has delivered) is distributed in proportion to patronage: a farmer who has delivered 4 per cent of the wheat to a pool will get, in addition to his price, 4 per cent of whatever amount the directors choose to distribute to the members. Such co-ops sell about one billion dollars worth of produce every year in Canada.

Often these same people, and city dwellers in Europe too, will form *consumers'* cooperatives, organizing wholesale buying units and running their own retail stores, service stations, medical clinics, and funeral centers. The same Rochdale principles apply. Usually the co-ops do not engage in keen price competition with other retailers, but instead sell at stable prices to their membership and distribute the equivalent of "bargains" in the patronage dividend every year. Consumer co-ops are one of the most important outlets for grocery products in Britain, though they are having a difficult time competing with the newer chain supermarkets. It appears that the very local and democratic structure of co-ops makes it hard for them to hire and to work with aggressive managers and staff without becoming a commercial business, which of course they wish to avoid.

Cooperatives usually hold evangelical attitudes toward this type of business organization, and work hard to bring about its growth.[11] But in Canada their success has in recent decades been greatest in a third type of business, having rather different historical roots: the credit union. This is a type of savings bank, organized internally on similar lines to producers' co-ops; members often have a common bond, such as belonging to the same parish or co-op, or working in the same factory. Their members deposit savings, and the problem of lending these savings safely (mostly to other members) is simplified by the common bond and the directors' personal knowledge of all their members. The Dominion Bureau of Statistics recently estimated that more than 10 per cent of all consumer credit flowed through credit unions.

■ PUBLIC OWNERSHIP

Canadian readers do not need to be told of the importance of public ownership and control. Served as they are by the CBC, CNR, Air Canada, and Atomic Energy of Canada Ltd., provincial hydro and telephone utilities, and liquor stores, and municipal theaters, garbage collection, libraries, and water utilities, it is clear that the role of government discussed earlier on page 61 has been extended and varied.

The minimum necessary role for government is surveyed in Chapter 8. Sometimes, as in the case of the CNR, the government has taken over ownership after the collapse of the previous private corporations. Sometimes, as in the case of the liquor board and the utilities, provincial governments have wished to get different pricing, availability of services, or investment policies than profit-seeking owners would provide. In particular, many Crown corporations have had as their purpose the *development* of a region, product, industry, or service,

---

[10] Usually, following the famous Rochdale (England) principles laid down by pioneer cooperatives in 1844, members receive a fixed rate of interest on their capital share.

[11] The tax laws appear to favor co-ops over corporations: co-ops are exempt from taxation for the first three years of operation, and pay no corporation tax on patronage dividends. This gesture may account for their survival and growth. In any case, it does lead to complaints that the cooperator is unfairly undertaxed compared to the shareholder in competing firms.

rather than profit in the direct sense. Usually they monopolize most of their market.

So diverse are their aims and characters that a "typical" public enterprise is hard to find. As an example consider Ontario Hydro. It is based not on a charter but on a particular act of the Ontario legislature. As there are no stockbrokers, the government appoints a board of six directors (two can be cabinet members), who are given a certain term of appointment but are basically responsible to the government, the owner. Their chief job is to plan and run a system of powerhouses and transmission lines that sell electrical energy to local utilities. To do this they have a cadre of managers, in most respects identical to that to be found in a large corporation. The separation of ownership and control, therefore, appears between the directors and managers on the one hand and the government and public of Ontario on the other. Hydro can raise money by issuing bonds (but not shares) and by retaining earnings.

Hydro, a near-independent body, is a prototype for many Crown corporations. At the other extreme are the Post Office[12] and the liquor boards, which are practically departments of the government itself, though providing services that might be privately controlled; and "agencies" of the government like the National Harbours Board, Canadian Arsenals Ltd., and the Bank of Canada which, though given a very independent status, have regulatory or service tasks that would otherwise have to be done inside the government.

The displacement of private by public enterprise (often said to be a CCF-NDP goal) has actually closely paralleled the growth of private corporate firms in Canada. Political parties of all complexions have encouraged public ownership: for example, the Conservatives and the CNR; Social Credit and B.C. Hydro. Consequently, Canadian debate about public ownership tends to center either on personalities or on claims for its efficiency in particular cases, rather than on its generic advantages. (For example, the debates regarding Quebec's Société Générale, B.C. Hydro, and, most recently, Ontario's membership in the Federal Medicare scheme have been concerned with their manner and their aims, and rarely with whether the government should be in business at all. This question arose in the discussions of Saskatchewan's program for compulsory prepaid medical care.)

■ THE GIANT CORPORATION

While we should not infer that all corporations go through three stages, we have now carried our toothpaste enterprise far enough up the ladder of success. The next sections will be devoted to the economic position and power of the very large modern corporation and the problems that it creates for the economy.

A list of the largest corporations reads like an honor roll of Canadian business, almost every name being familiar household words. Aluminum Ltd.

---

[12] The United Kingdom, the home of penny postage, has now, surprisingly, reconsidered the place of the Post Office in government. In 1969, Britain changed its Post Office from a government department to a public business corporation. A similar conversion of Canada's postal department to a Crown corporation is contemplated.

(Alcan), Imperial Oil (Esso), George Weston Ltd., International Nickel, Massey-Ferguson, Canadian Pacific (CPR), Bell Telephone, Steel Co. of Canada (Stelco), Canada Packers (York meats), Distillers Corporation-Seagrams, and T. Eaton Co. all have assets or sales in the top ten. But even the largest of these is a pygmy compared to the huge American corporations (with which many large Canadian firms are connected). In automobiles, General Motors, Ford, and Chrysler; in trade, The Great Atlantic and Pacific Tea Company (A & P), Sears, and F. W. Woolworth; in food, Kraft, Borden, and Swifts; in soaps and oils, Lever Brothers and Procter and Gamble—all dominate the scene in both countries. One of the largest of all is A. T. & T. to which the Canadian Bell system is linked.

The size of financial organizations can hardly be measured by sales or assets. But, judged by the funds that they manage or control, such chartered banks as the Bank of Montreal, The Royal Bank, and the Canadian Imperial Bank of Commerce, and insurance companies like the Sun Life and Manufacturers Life must be classed with the large industrial companies and compared to such giants abroad as the Bank of America, the Chase Manhattan Bank, National City Bank, Metropolitan Life and Prudential Life in the United States, or Barclay's Bank and the Prudential Assurance Co. of England.

Altogether there are now almost 200 U.S. companies with assets above the billion-dollar mark, and a dozen or so in other countries! (Outside the United States, many of the largest businesses are publicly owned, like the CNR and Ontario Hydro. But few of these, anywhere, would make the top 200.)

The tremendous concentration of economic power involved in giant corporations may be gauged from the following facts: In 1956, twenty-eight "giants" had about 29 per cent of the real assets of all Canadian manufacturing firms, and the top 100 industrial firms now account for two-thirds of the earnings of all Canadian industrial corporations. In the grocery trade, four chains accounted for 31 per cent of sales in 1958. The field of transportation and communication is highly concentrated. The government owned Canadian National Railways and the privately owned Canadian Pacific Railway together have 70 per cent of the operating revenue of all railways. The telephone industry is dominated by the privately owned Bell Telephone Company which accounts for 60 per cent of the operating revenue of the industry. The Canadian system of branch banking insures that the financial sector of the economy is highly concentrated. Furthermore, the Canadian assets of nine leading insurance companies constitute three-quarters of all Canadian life insurance assets. In the light of the evidence, it appears that about three-fifths of Canada's output (excluding government administration and defense) originates in sectors dominated by large corporations.[13]

Their power did not grow overnight. After 1900, their percentage importance steadily mounted. In the 1920s and 1930s gas, power, and transit utilities

---

[13] Gideon Rosenbluth, "Concentration and Monopoly in the Canadian Economy," in *Social Purpose for Canada*, edited by M. Oliver (Toronto: University of Toronto Press, 1961). Much of the above information is collected annually by the *Financial Post*.

were gathered together into regional networks—often with a gain in efficiency. Since World War II the largest corporations have, if anything, grown faster than the economy.

Most corporate growth involved continual plowing-back of profits and new stock and bond issues. But there is another way. Since World War II, more and more existing firms have been acquired in "horizontal" (potential competitors) or "vertical" (suppliers and customers) mergers. Even more recently there was a wave of "conglomerate mergers," bringing together scores of companies belonging to quite unrelated industries. The giants meet repeatedly on diverse battlefields: Bell, Molsons, Noranda, CPR, Southams, Imperial Oil, and CIL compete in the sale of dozens of products. Foreigners, however, have usually taken over firms in the same industry as the parent's; American, Japanese, and European firms tend to concentrate on acquiring subsidiaries in vertical and horizontal, not conglomerate, mergers.

Whether by their own financing or by merger, corporate growth breeds success—and success breeds further success.[14] But there are economic and political barriers to largeness, and firms do not grow indefinitely. The statistical evidence on profits suggests that profits increase with size but that the very biggest firms in an industry sometimes seem to show a slight dropping off of *percentage* profits compared with the next to the largest. Statistics also suggest that, relatively, the giants have probably lost a little ground since 70 years ago, when the "trust movement" had not yet run afoul of the amendments to the Canadian Criminal Code prohibiting conspiracy in restraint of trade (1889). And just as a hotel may be always full—but with different people—so do we find the list of biggest corporations to be a changing one; nevertheless the list changes at a very slow rate.

■ DIVORCE OF OWNERSHIP IN THE LARGE CORPORATION

Let us examine the internal workings of one of these giant corporations. *The most striking feature is the diversification of ownership among thousands and thousands of small stockholders.* In 1970 more than 34,000 people had preferred shares, and more than 244,000 had common shares in Bell Telephone of Canada, although most holdings were very small indeed (10 shares or less). The stock exchange has a goal of "people's capitalism," in which the masses have appreciable ownership of society's capital. Now over 18 per cent of urban households do own some publicly traded stock; and others own untraded securities. Yet it is highly probable that as few as 10 per cent receive an appreciable return.

In a path-breaking study,[15] Berle and Means pointed out that this wide

[14] A larger percentage of small firms than of large firms falls in the class of firms making losses.

[15] A. A. Berle, Jr., and Gardner C. Means, *The Modern Corporation and Private Property* (New York: Commerce Clearing House, 1932). See R. A. Gordon, *Business Leadership in the Large Corporation* (Washington: Brookings Institution, 1945), Chapter II. R. J. Larner in a 1966 *American Economic Review* study has shown that the Berle-Means Thesis on separation of ownership and control was even truer in the 1960s than in 1929: whereas 6 of the 200 largest U.S. corporations were privately owned (80 per cent or more of the stock) in 1929, in 1963 there were none; and 84.5 per cent of the firms had no group of stockholders owning as much as 10 per cent!

diversification of stockholding has resulted in a *separation of ownership and control*. Recent studies show that in the typical giant corporation in the United States, all management together—officers and directors—hold only about 3 per cent of the outstanding common stock. The largest single minority ownership groups typically hold only about a fifth of all voting stock. Such a small fraction has been deemed more than enough to maintain "working control".[16]

■ LEADERSHIP AND CONTROL OF THE LARGE CORPORATION

The problem of keeping a large corporation truly democratic is a difficult one. Until recent years, a dozen stockholders would turn up for the annual meeting. More recently, many hundreds have been attending a few U.S. meetings, but not Canadian meetings.

Decisions at the annual meeting are really settled by use of "proxies." Each stockholder is asked to mail in a proxy permitting the management to exercise his votes. Some do not reply; but enough usually do to establish a quorum and a comfortable plurality for management. The Securities and Exchange Commission has tried to improve the democratic structure of U.S. corporations by insisting that motions to be decided at the annual meeting be indicated on the proxy statement so that stockholders can indicate their preferences; also, rival groups must be permitted mailing access to the stockholders, and so forth. Such reforms remove protection from idle, incompetent, or unscrupulous managements.

Nevertheless, most corporation managements could be said to be self-perpetuating. Whether the corporation runs well or poorly, whether the managers work efficiently or not, the typical small stockholder can do little about it. He can rubber-stamp approval or relieve his feelings by not voting. In either case management goes undisturbed.

Recently, there has been a slight change. Thanks to government rules, some challenging minority groups have attempted—and successfully attempted!—to oust the in-group and put themselves in as new managers. Thus, an outsider may court the proxies of the individual shareholder, organizing a campaign and using all the devices of modern publicity to oust the incumbent officers.

In a sense, therefore, we can hope that democratic control of corporations by stock owners has increased. But competent observers still insist that, barring blatant incompetence, management can count on remaining in office; and often the proxy battle is fought merely to determine which minority group shall control.[17]

---

[16] You can even pyramid control by owning one-fifth of a million-dollar company, which owns one-fifth of a five-million-dollar company, and so forth. Such a pyramid of so-called "holding companies" can give control over billions to small ownership at the base.

[17] A dissatisfied stockholder can always sell his shares and buy into another company. If enough stockholders do so, the company will find it hard ever to raise capital by selling a new issue; the fall in its share prices may depress the value of "stock options" issued to company executives as an incentive bonus and could galvanize other stockholders into a proxy revolt.

■ A MANAGERIAL REVOLUTION

Who makes corporate decisions? Primarily, the increasingly important class of *professional managers*—what Galbraith calls the "technostructure." The old-time captain of industry, for all his creativeness and ability to calculate the risks necessary to build up a great enterprise, often had something of the buccaneer in his make-up and an irresponsible "the-public-be-damned" attitude. In company after company, the original founder has been replaced by a new type of executive, usually having a different surname. He is less likely to be a self-made man than a graduate of a well-known business school: he will probably have acquired special training and management skills. The new professional executive is more adept at public relations and in the handling of people. He is necessarily more the "bureaucrat," often interested as much in preserving the *status quo* as in taking extreme risks.

Typically, the dominant man will be the president of the corporation. As he begins to feel his years, he may be made chairman of the board of directors. The chairman of the board, together with a small executive or steering committee of the board of directors, gives advice and approval to the actions of the president and his many vice-presidents.

The exact role of the board of directors varies from company to company and from group to group. Some "outside" directors are simply well-known men selected to give prestige. Others are insiders with special knowledge who take an active part in determining policy; they may be vice-presidents or employees of the corporation. On the whole, it would be going too far to say that most boards of directors act simply as rubber stamps to approve the decisions already taken by the officers of the company. But it is true that, so long as management possesses the confidence of the board, that body will usually not actively intervene to dictate specific policies. This is the same administrative procedure usually followed by the board of governors of a university or charity, and is not too unlike the parliamentary system of ministerial responsibility.

Generally speaking, there will be no clash of goals between the management and stockholders. Both will be interested in maximizing the profits of the firm—to wit, the growth in earnings and market price per share. But in two important situations there may be a divergence of interests, not infrequently settled in favor of management. First, insiders may vote themselves and their friends or relatives large salaries, expense accounts, bonuses, retirement pensions, and stock options at the stockholders' expense.[18]

A second conflict of interest may arise in connection with undistributed profits. The managers of every organization have an understandable tendency

[18] Other conflicts can involve outright cheating; executives may take bribes, throw business to their own companies, or violate securities rules by using inside knowledge and spreading false rumors to make market profits on the company's stock. The management of Texas Gulf Sulfur and the Windfall mine came under fire in 1965 for just this behavior in connection with Northern Ontario mining discoveries. A recent president of Chrysler had to resign when it was discovered he had secret ownership in a supplying firm. Such cases are rare, but not rare enough.

to try to make it grow and perpetuate itself. The psychological reasons are subtle and by no means always selfish. In some cases, when profits are plowed back into a company, there is reason to suspect that the same capital could better be invested by the stockholders elsewhere or be spent upon consumption. Indeed, the case occasionally arises when a company would be well advised to wind itself up and pay back its capital. But a cynic might doubt that management is likely to vote itself out of existence and out of jobs.

■ THE NEW INDUSTRIAL STATE

Thorstein Veblen, at the turn of the century, looked forward to a time when engineers would run the price system. John Kenneth Galbraith has in our time become the philosopher of the new industrial state. In his words:

> ". . . the influence of the technostructure of the mature firm extends to *shaping the demand* for its particular product or range of products. . . . [emphasis added]
>
> "Paralleling these changes, partly as a result and partly as a cause, has been a profound shift in the locus of economic and political power. The financier and the union leader are dwindling influences in the society. They are honored more for their past eminence than for their present power. The technostructure exercises much less direct political power than did the antecedent entrepreneur. But that is because it has far more influence as an arm of the bureaucracy and in its influence on the larger climate of belief. The scientific, technical, organizational and planning needs of the technostructure have brought into being a large educational and scientific estate."[19]

■ FOREIGN OWNERSHIP AND THE MULTI-NATIONAL FIRM

The new role of the "technostructure" of modern management is seen most clearly when it goes international. Then the firm becomes a "legal person," apparently different from its founders and, even, from its native land.

As a first step, a firm may take over, or set up, a subsidiary. It will choose a country with markets made too expensive by transport or tariff barriers to serve from the home plants.

Many such subsidiaries have been found to be less profitable than branch plants back home. Then why were they set up? Seemingly, they were symptomatic of the main management's own determination to expand, even if shareholders could find better investments on their own. And once set up, their management makes the interests of the owners even more remote. Market and legal differences, of course, mean that foreign subsidiaries must be given more local discretion than would be given to a simple branch plant. Often, then, it becomes difficult to determine in whose interest it is being run. Little profit is being remitted; managers at home must delegate powers to managers abroad whose chief interest is survival—not even personal promotion, if the manager is a national of the new country.[20]

Furthermore, such foreign subsidiaries nowadays get a very mixed recep-

---

[19] John Kenneth Galbraith, *The New Industrial State* (Boston: Houghton Mifflin, 1967), p. 320.

[20] A good recent study of management and behavior is A. E. Safarian's *Performance of Foreign Owned Firms* (Montreal: Canadian American Committee, 1969).

tion. Governments, concerned by unemployment and rural stagnation, welcome new industries, especially those foreign-owned plants that promise good management, permanence, and prompt tax payments. But public response varies. In the former colonial countries, especially those on guard against Western "imperialism," distrust of foreign owners may be so great as to lead to their exclusion, or to compromise forms of joint ownership. Even in more industrialised societies, like Australia, not to mention western Europe, there is much-expressed alarm at *le défi américain*—the penetration of markets by American technology and managerial attitudes. Direct investment (in foreign plants instead of in foreign securities) becomes expensive and less profitable as parents must meet stiffening local conditions.

Canadian attitudes to U.S. (and European and Japanese) investment are, as Prime Minister Trudeau put it, those of one who must sleep with an elephant. The fear of being rolled on cannot be quieted by assurances of industrial growth, or employment. Even the majority that does not believe in a conspiracy or a takeover, worries about so many economic decisions being made outside the country. Will Safarian's finding that such managements have been statistically indistinguishable from those of domestic firms continue to be valid?

We can return to foreign ownership later (in Chapter 25 and the Appendix to Chapter 34). Here we ask further where the decisions *are* taken. Is local autonomy, reported a few paragraphs above to be inevitable, on the increase? No, say the reporters of the *multi-national corporation*. Sometimes it is not clear what the "nationality," if any, of such huge firms is. Some of their subsidiaries have flourished faster than the parents, and head offices may be moved where taxes are low or restrictions fewest. Their senior management may then become not only separated from ownership, but also from national allegiance. It is likely that in the next decade, quicker overseas communications will reduce the independence of subsidiaries. If so, much economic power may be wielded neither by local officers, nor by owners of shares and property, nor by governments in parent countries, but by the managerial structure of the multi-national firm itself, in some respects *independent* of national connections and responsibilities.[21]

■ THE EVIL OF MONOPOLY

In view of all the above facts, it is not surprising to find that most important North American industries are characterized by a few large corporations whose share of the output of that particular industry is vastly greater than their numerical importance would warrant. Figure 5-1 gives a list of some large

---

[21] "The relation between ownership and control in the large corporation is different when the corporation is a subsidiary. Ownership is not widely diffused among many stockholders, but rather concentrated, often to the point of the parent being the sole stockholder. In effect, ownership rights are exercised by the management of the parent corporation. The management of a subsidiary, wishing to exercise effective control over decisions, faces not a multitude of relatively powerless shareholders but the managers of its parent." (*Foreign Ownership and the Structure of Canadian Industry*, Report of the Task Force on the Structure of Canadian Industry, M. E. Watkins (Ottawa: Queen's Printer, 1968), pp. 32, 33. Reproduced with the permission of Information Canada.

Some industries are dominated by a very few sellers:

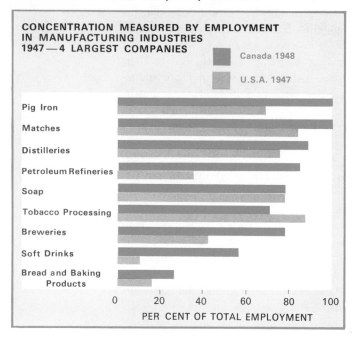

CONCENTRATION MEASURED BY EMPLOYMENT
IN MANUFACTURING INDUSTRIES
1947 — 4 LARGEST COMPANIES

Canada 1948

U.S.A. 1947

Pig Iron

Matches

Distilleries

Petroleum Refineries

Soap

Tobacco Processing

Breweries

Soft Drinks

Bread and Baking
Products

0   20   40   60   80   100

PER CENT OF TOTAL EMPLOYMENT

FIG. 5-1. In many industries, a few firms get most of the business. Rosenbluth reports that, in general, concentration is greater in Canada than in the United States, as most of these industrial comparisons show. MIT's expert M. A. Adelman suggests that concentration was even higher back in the 1900s. (Note too that these are manufacturing industries, excluding railways and airlines, banks and supermarkets.) (Source: Gideon Rosenbluth, *Concentration in Canadian Manufacturing Industries,* NBER, 1957.)

industries and depicts their degree of concentration by showing the relative proportion of total industry employment controlled by the first four dominant corporations in the late 1940s. New concentration data are under preparation, but the situation in these industries has not changed much.

In Part Three we shall analyze some of the problems raised by monopoly and imperfect competition. In the past century, particularly, in the United States, since the 1890 Sherman Antitrust Act, there has been great concern over the breaking down of free competitive markets under the encroachment of large-scale enterprise. In recent years, American officials of General Electric, Westinghouse, and other electric suppliers were even sent to jail for colluding on monopoly price setting. There have been a few successful prosecutions in Canada (see Chapter 25).

From an economic point of view it does not much matter which of the following monopolistic devices cause price to be too high: (1) mergers of competing firms, (2) cooperative "pools" or "cartel agreements," (3) so-called "trusts" (involving selected "trustees" who "coordinate" pricing policy), (4) interlocking directorates, (5) "holding-company" control, (6) tacit collusion and trade-association action, (7) government "resale price maintenance" legislation and government-sponsored "commodity agreements" (wheat, sugar, cotton, etc.).

Too high a price, wastage of resources, and creation of monopoly profits are economic evils, however brought about and whatever the legal technicalities of the matter. This we shall study in Part Three, but a brief preview has been presented here.

■ THE CURSE OF BIGNESS?

Is bigness itself a bad thing? Undoubtedly there is much popular hostility toward large corporations. Even if they could do so, General Motors or Stelco would be most reluctant to swallow up competitors until they accounted for, say, nine-tenths of their respective industries. They would fear the effect on public opinion. Is this antagonism toward big business directed toward bigness itself? Or against the alleged evils of monopoly that are often supposed to be associated with bigness? What should public policy be toward a "benevolent, well-behaving, efficient" giant corporation?

The so-called "A & P" case in the United States provides an example. This chain of food stores is noted for its low prices. Yet the Department of Justice prosecuted it under the antitrust acts. Leaving aside certain minor irregularities that the company may have engaged in, the basic issue was clearly posed: Shall it be a crime to grow large as a result of efficiency and continued maintenance of low competitive prices? The federal courts seemed to answer, Yes. Fortunately, this trend is abating.

Other examples show that policy problems are often complex. In the mid-fifties there was a rash of mergers: for example, in the auto industry Nash combined with Hudson to form American Motors, and Studebaker with Packard. Often there was a "tax angle" to the merger; but in some cases, firms merged in order to try to become more efficient, so as to be able to compete with General Motors and Ford. Do such mergers—even though they undoubtedly increase the size of the merged units—really *reduce* competition rather than increase it? In Canada the issue became even more urgent in the 1950s. The Director of Investigations and the Restrictive Trade Practices Commission both urged that the merging of a number of independent breweries into Canadian Breweries Ltd. (Dow, O'Keefe, Carlings, etc.) and the merging of the two dominant Western Canadian sugar companies reduced competition sufficiently to harm the public interest. But in interpreting the law, the courts held that these mergers were not shown to "virtually stifle competition" or have a complete monopoly.

A strong defence of big business is that it alone can undertake the research and development that lead to a rising standard of living. Time and again even government has handed its research problems over to the firms competent to see the project through, as with the development of a commercial atomic power plant by the Canadian General Electric Company for the federal Atomic Energy of Canada Ltd. In the words of Schumpeter, a world-famous economist who died in 1950:[22]

---

[22] J. A. Schumpeter, *Capitalism, Socialism, and Democracy* (New York: Harper, 1942). Whatever the merits of the Schumpeter thesis, it is still true that there have been great productivity changes in competitive agriculture; that many basic inventions come from independent persons or small companies; and that there is no evidence of an upswing in inventiveness during the 1890s, a decade of monopoly concentration.

Reference should be made to J. Kenneth Galbraith's doctrine of "countervailing power" in *American Capitalism* (Boston: Houghton Mifflin, 1952). It is there argued that big units do characterize American life, but that "big labor" checks big business, and vice versa; that big Sears and A & P check their big suppliers, and so a kind of tolerable equilibrium is achieved, albeit not one of a competitive type.

"The modern standard of life of the masses evolved during the period of relatively unfettered 'big business.' If we list the items that enter the modern workman's budget and from 1899 on observe the course of their prices not in terms of money but in terms of the hours of labor that will buy them—i.e., each year's money prices divided by each year's hourly wage rates, we cannot fail to be struck by the rate of the advance which, considering the spectacular improvement in qualities, seems to have been greater and not smaller than it ever was before. . . . Nor is this all. As soon as we go into details and inquire into the individual items in which progress was most conspicuous, the trail leads not to the doors of those firms that work under conditions of comparatively free competition but precisely to the doors of the large concerns—which, as in the case of agricultural machinery, also account for much of the progress in the competitive sector—and a shocking suspicion dawns upon us that big business may have had more to do with creating that standard of life than keeping it down."

But many studies fail to confirm Schumpeter's conviction that big business is essential for technical change. For example, research has shown that many crucial inventions have come from single persons or small firms. Furthermore, competitive agriculture, as Chapter 20 will show, is also capable of large productivity increases. When monopoly concentration boomed in the 1890s, inventions did not.

If Schumpeter *is* correct about our reliance on big business for technical progress, the future problem may not be one of choosing between large monopolistic corporations and small-scale competitors, but rather that of devising ways to improve the social and economic performance of large corporate aggregates. To keep the tremendously creative abilities of the modern large-scale corporation working toward the public good—that may have to be the goal for the years ahead. But if Schumpeter's belief is wrong, we may find ourselves turning to policies to aid the lonely researcher and the small firm.

SUMMARY

■ 1 The present population of businesses has grown up as a result of a cumulative excess of business births over business deaths. The great majority of businesses consist of infinitesimal single proprietorships, largely in retail and service establishments. Their turnover is rapid.

■ 2 One should understand how an enterprise grows, its needs and avenues for short-term or long-term capital, and the advantages and disadvantages of the corporate form over the single proprietorship and partnership.

■ 3 One should also be acquainted with the fundamental legal rights involved in the corporation and with the general features of bonds and of preferred and common stocks.

■ 4 Compared to the United States, Canadians are major users of government enterprise and cooperatives as effective alternatives to the modern corporation.

■ 5 The problems created by the separation of ownership and control and by the concentration of economic wealth and monopoly power in the modern giant corporation deserve serious study. (Part Three will discuss imperfect competition and combines policies.)

Accounting is a great help to the understanding of economics, and its fundamental principles are presented briefly in the Appendix to this chapter.

QUESTIONS FOR DISCUSSION

1. Imagine you are starting a business of your own. Write its case history.

2. Compare the advantages and disadvantages of (*a*) the single proprietorship, (*b*) the partnership, and (*c*) the corporate form of business organization.

3. List ways of raising capital for small, medium, and large businesses.

4. What are the advantages and disadvantages of different securities?

5. Discuss the structure of the large modern corporation.

6. What is meant by calling ours the age of the "Managerial or Bureaucratic Revolution?", of the "Multi-national Corporation?" Does this apply inside government?

7. Give examples of conflict of interest between stockholders and management. Of coincident interests. Of problems of democratic control.

8. Defend "bigness as such." Attack it. What evils might accompany it?

9. What are the economic evils of monopoly? Give examples.

10. What are the economic disadvantages of public ownership? Why is it so prevalent in Canada? Give examples of how local public enterprises obtain capital.

11. Review your understanding of the following concepts:

single proprietorship	bonds, common, preferred
partnership	stocks; hybrids
corporation	proxy, minority control
unlimited and limited liability	director, executive, technostructure
investment banking	forms of monopoly control
securities commissions, co-operatives, Crown corporations	conglomerate, merger, collusion
corporate, personal income tax	evils of monopoly
	possible dynamic advantages of bigness

Appendix: Elements of Accounting

In this "age of accounts" a little literacy in accounting has become a prime necessity.

■ THE BALANCE SHEET

We begin with the two fundamental accounting statements: the Balance Sheet and the Statement of Profit and Loss (or the so-called "Income Statement").

The Balance Sheet is presented in a report, usually annually. It represents an instantaneous "still picture" of the condition of the enterprise on some particular day, usually the last day of the year. Corresponding to the dollar value of every *asset*—tangible or intangible—there must necessarily be an exactly equal total amount of *claims* or *ownership*. The value of a $40,000 house is exactly matched by

**A Balance Sheet is a point-of-time showing that
Assets = Liabilities + Net Worth:**

BALANCE SHEET OF PEPTO-GLITTER, LTD.,
AS OF DECEMBER 31, 1975.

ASSETS		LIABILITIES AND NET WORTH	
		Liabilities	
Current Assets:		**Current Liabilities:**	
Cash	$ 20,000	Accounts payable	$ 20,000
Inventory	80,000	Notes payable	30,000
		Long-term Liabilities:	
Fixed Assets:		SBL note	50,000
Equipment	130,000	Bonds payable	50,000
Buildings	170,000		
		Net Worth	
		Capital:	
		Preferred stock	50,000
		Common stock	. . . .
Total	$400,000	Total	$400,000

TABLE 5-1.

somebody's claim to its ownership, say, of $25,000 owed to a creditor and $15,000 owned by its owner.

This is the fundamental identity underlying every Balance Sheet:

Value of Assets = value of total claims or ownership
            = value of liabilities (owed)
               + value of proprietorship (owed)
or   Assets = Liabilities + Net Worth

Let us illustrate this by considering a simple Balance Sheet, as shown in Table 5-1; this lists Assets on the left and on the right Liabilities and Net Worth for a new company whose operations have just begun.

A blank space has been deliberately left next to the Common Stock Net Worth item because you should realize that the only correct entry compatible with our fundamental Balance-Sheet truism is $200,-000. A Balance Sheet must always balance—because Net Worth, i.e., ownership of the "residual claimants," always adjusts itself to make a balance.

To illustrate this, suppose a thief steals all the cash, and a fire burns up one-half the inventory. The accountant will learn of this sad news without turning a hair. "Total Assets are down $60,000 all told; Liabilities remain unchanged. Very well, I must write down Net Worth by $60,000 to only $190,-000." Such is his way of keeping score.

A number of interesting facts are revealed by even this simple Balance Sheet. First, it is customary to divide up Assets according to whether they will be convertible into cash by normal operations within a year or not, the first category being called Current Assets and the second Fixed Assets. The Liabilities can also be subdivided into Current and Long-term Liabilities, depending upon whether they come due in less than a year.

Here is something to be emphasized about a Balance Sheet: Although its two sides must balance *in total*, yet no single item on one side is matched by an item on the other side. Thus, Bonds do not correspond in value to the Equipment or Buildings, nor do Capital items correspond to Cash. The only correct statement about a Balance Sheet is that creditors have a general claim of a definite value against the enterprise, and owners have a residual claim against the rest.

Most of the specific items listed are more or less self-explanatory. Cash consists of coins, currency, and money on deposit in the bank. Cash is the only asset whose value is exact rather than an estimate. All other valuations involve some guesswork, albeit careful guesswork. Moreover, all accounting valuations must be made relative to the actual intended purpose or use of the asset in question. If a business is a going concern and not in the process of liquidation, the accountant will be careful not to value doubtful assets at the low figure they would bring at a forced sale; he rather will value them at their worth to the company in its normal operation.

Inventory, consisting in the case of our toothpaste company of sugar, chemicals, tubing, raw materials, and other goods in process, can be valued in many different ways. Many conservative companies use original cost of the inventories or present market value, whichever is lower. Especially difficult problems arise when the prices of materials vary from month to month. Should we figure the chemical cost of the toothpaste at the original price of the ingredients actually used, which of course were bought some time ago when prices were different? Or should we figure, as our cost, the price that must *now* be paid for the chemicals to replace those being used up? An elementary discussion cannot go into these two possible methods of inventory valuation.[1] Obviously, the choice of one of the two methods will make a great difference in stated profits during a time of inflation or deflation. It will also make a difference in income taxes. Therefore the government is compelled to say, "Use whichever method you wish, but having made up your mind, stick to it." So much for inventories.

If we assume that the Equipment and Buildings items were bought just at the end of 1975, then their Balance-Sheet values will be listed equal to their purchase price. This follows a fundamental accounting rule or convention: "At time of purchase a thing is presumed worth what the enterprise pays for it." However, as we shall see in connection with the Income Statement and the next year's Balance Sheet, hard problems are involved in deciding how to evaluate exactly equipment and buildings that have depreciated through use and age.

On the Liabilities side, Accounts Payable are, as their name implies, the sums owed for goods bought and charged. Notes Payable are promissory notes owed to the banks or to a finance company. The SBL Note listed under the Long-term Liabilities is a 5-year loan guaranteed by the federal Small Business Loans Act. The Bonds Payable are a long-term loan, floated at a 7 per cent coupon rate, and not due for 15 years. (NOTE: What appears as a Liability to this company may show up as an Asset to some-

one else; thus the creditors who own these bonds will carry them as left-hand-side Assets, "Bonds Receivable.")

Turning now to Net Worth items, we find that 500 shares of $100, 4 per cent, cumulative (non-participating) preferred stock have been issued; and 20,000 shares of no-par common stock were issued at $10 each. (Fill this in under correct heading in Table 5-1.)

This completes our first glance at a simple Balance Sheet.

■ THE STATEMENT OF PROFIT AND LOSS, OR INCOME STATEMENT

Now let time march on. During the following months, the firm is profitably engaged in producing and selling toothpaste. To show its flow of income over the 12 months of the year, we must turn to its Income Statement, or—as many companies prefer—the Statement of Profit and Loss, Table 5-2.

This is a statement which reports the following: (1) Pepto-Glitter's revenues from sales in 1976, (2) the expenses to be charged against those sales, and (3) the profit remaining after expenses have been deducted. That is,

Total Profit = Total Revenue minus Total Costs

(the fundamental identity of the Income Statement).

You will understand it better if at first you disregard the figures in the Manufacturing Cost of Goods Sold section (the indented figures) and look only at those in the right-hand column. Sales were $240,-000; and the cost of manufacturing the goods sold came to $170,000. After deducting another $14,000 for Selling and Administrative Costs, $56,000 remained in Net Operating Profit. Out of this, a total of $6,000 + $17,500 in interest and taxes had to be paid, leaving $32,500 in Net Earnings after Taxes. Dividends of $2,000 on the preferred and $10,500 on the common were paid, leaving $20,000 of net profit (Addition to Surplus) retained in the business.

Now turn to the indented Manufacturing Cost of Goods Sold section, which lists the costs incurred in this part of the business. The firm's outlays for materials, labor, and miscellaneous expenses are listed, together with an item for Depreciation. (Depreciation is worth a section to itself, and we shall consider it soon.) The sum of these four items ($175,000) is the Total Manufacturing Cost. Then

---

[1] Accounting texts refer to them as "First-in-first-out" (FIFO) and "Last-in-first-out" (LIFO) and analyze them in detail.

The flow of income over the year is shown by the income statement:

INCOME STATEMENT OF PEPTO-GLITTER, LTD., FROM JANUARY 1, 1976, TO DECEMBER 31, 1976.		
Net Sales (after all discounts and rebates)		$240,000
Less: Manufacturing Cost of Goods Sold:		
Materials	$ 50,000	
Labor Cost	100,000	
Depreciation Charges	20,000	
Miscellaneous Operating Cost	5,000	
Total Manufacturing Cost	$175,000	
Add: Beginning Inventory	80,000	
	$255,000	
Deduct: Closing Inventory	85,000	
Equals:		
Manufacturing Cost of Goods Sold	$170,000	170,000
Gross Profit (or Gross Margin)		$ 70,000
Less: Selling and Administration Costs		14,000
Net Operating Profit		$ 56,000
Less: Fixed Charges and Local Taxes		6,000
Net Earnings before Income Taxes		$ 50,000
Less: Corporation Income Taxes		17,500
Net Earnings after Taxes		$ 32,500
Less: Dividends on Preferred Stocks		2,000
Net Profits of Common Stockholders		$ 30,500
Less: Dividends Paid on Common Stock		10,500
Addition to Surplus		$ 20,000

TABLE 5-2.

follows what may seem a puzzling adjustment. The value of the inventory on January 1 is added, and that of the year-end inventory is deducted. The result, which differs from Manufacturing Cost by $5,000, is the Manufacturing Cost *of Goods Sold.* What is the difference between these terms, and why this inventory adjustment?

Pepto-Glitter began the year with inventory of $80,000 in raw materials and finished goods. During the year, it built up inventories by an extra $5,000. In this case, it would be false to attribute all the manufacturing cost to *the goods actually sold.* Some of these costs are really attributable to goods to be sold *in the future.* To neglect this fact would be to overstate the Manufacturing Cost of Goods Sold in this year; it would be subtracting too much from this year's Net Sales and understating this year's Profits.

If there had been no change in the amount of inventory, then all would be simple: Manufacturing Cost and Manufacturing Cost of Goods Sold would be identical.

On the other hand, what if we had had less inventory on hand at the year's end than at the beginning? Clearly, we would be fooling ourselves if we did not recognize that the cost of the goods we have sold this year ought really to be *greater* than the money we have paid out to labor and to other firms. We would have neglected the cost element of used-up and unreplaced inventory.

Summary: To reach a valid figure for Manufacturing Cost of Goods Sold, we must adjust the Manufacturing Cost figure thus:

If the Closing Inventory shows an increase over the Beginning Inventory, deduct that increase; if the Closing Inventory has decreased, add that decrease.

Instead of subtracting $5,000 directly from the $175,000 total manufacturing expense, the accountant does it in two steps. Rather than working with the difference between the two, he first adds the total Beginning Inventory, then subtracts the Closing Inventory. This procedure has the advantage of being standardized; it is the same whether inventory is up or down, whereas a single change-in-inventory figure would in some cases be a subtraction, in others an addition. And the accountant's method also reveals the change in inventory relative to the size of the total inventory.

Note that the items in Table 5-2 differ from Table 5-1's Balance-Sheet items. Income items refer to *flows* over time: moving-picture action. Balance-Sheet items refer to *stocks* at an instant of time: still pictures.

■ DEPRECIATION (CAPITAL COST ALLOWANCE)

At first, one may wonder why any Depreciation Charges have been made for 1976. The buildings and equipment were newly bought at the beginning of the year, and surely they will not have been worn out already. (It will, of course, be necessary to spend money on men to maintain the equipment and keep the factories painted; but their wages are already included in Labor Cost or Miscellaneous Operating Cost and are not included in Depreciation Charges.)

Here is where the farseeing wisdom of the accountant comes to the fore. He points out that not a cent may have to be spent upon replacement of equipment for 10 years, at which time all the machines may *suddenly* have to be bought anew. It would be nonsense to charge nothing to depreciation for 9 years and fool yourself into thinking you are making a nice profit and then suddenly in the tenth year you have to charge off all the value of the machines at once and think you have incurred a great loss in that year.

Actually, he points out, the equipment is *being used up all the time*. A truer, undistorted picture of net income or profit will be reached if the costs of the capital equipment are spread more evenly over its lifetime. The value of equipment declines as a result of age and use; it depreciates from its price as new to its final scrap value. In recognition of this, the accountant depreciates the value of fixed capital items by some *gradual* formula. Of the various proposed methods, here are two widely used ones.

The first is called "straight-line depreciation."

Suppose that you have a truck whose cost new is $10,100 and whose economic life is 10 years; after this its physical life may continue but its economic life will be over, because of its unreliability and maintenance costs. Suppose that its scrap value at the end of 10 years is $100. According to the straight-line method, you will each year charge off to depreciation one-tenth of the lifetime decline in its total value, $10,000 (new price minus scrap value). Thus, $1,000 will be entered in Depreciation Charges every year.

A second method of more rapid early depreciation has become popular. In Canada, income tax regulations *require* all taxpayers (except farmers and fishermen) to use this method for tax purposes. Instead of writing off a new asset steadily by the straight-line method, firms must use the "declining-balance" method.

Disregarding scrap value as negligible, consider the 10-year $10,000 truck. Instead of taking one-tenth its value for depreciation in the first year, the tax law lets you charge off, under the declining-balance method, twice that amount, or 2×10 per cent = 20 per cent in its first year. So you get a much larger deduction for tax purposes. Evidently you cannot go on charging off that amount for each year of life, since that would leave you with zero value by the halfway point, at the end of 5 years. What the declining-balance method does is to let you take off 20 per cent of *remaining* value or balance each year. In the second year, then, you take off 20 per cent of the $8,000 of remaining value, or $1,600. In the third year you take off 20 per cent of what is left, namely, of $6,400. So the process goes. It can be calculated that by the time the asset has reached half the length of its useful life, you have been permitted to write off for tax purposes almost two-thirds its value—rather than one-half, as under the straight-line method. It is later in life that the declining-balance method begins to be less generous in order to compensate for its early generosity.[2]

----

[2] A quite different method, called the "service-unit method," or "unit-of-production method," can be mentioned only briefly here. According to this we should estimate the number of miles, loads, or service units that the truck will perform in its life. Thus, if the truck goes a million miles in 10 years and its loss of value during that time is $10,000, then each mile used up represents about 1 cent.

Although depreciation is usually figured by some apparently exact formula, every accountant knows that the allowances are really very rough, being subject to large and unpredictable errors and involving arbitrary corrections and assumptions. He comforts himself with two thoughts: (1) A rough method of depreciation, like an imperfect watch, is often better than none at all. (2) Mistakes in depreciation will ultimately "come out in the wash" anyway.

Let us see why a mistake in depreciation ultimately tends to correct itself. Suppose that the truck lasts 15 years rather than the predicted 10. We have then been overstating our depreciation *expenses* during the first 10 years. But in the eleventh and later years there will be no depreciation charged on the truck at all, since it has already been written down to its scrap value by the end of the tenth year. Our profits in these later years tend, therefore, to be overstated by about as much as they were understated in the earlier years. After 15 years, everything is pretty much the same after all. That is, except for taxes. Different methods of depreciation result in a different apparent distribution of earnings over time,

and therefore in a different pattern over time of corporation income taxes. Naturally, a businessman prefers a method of depreciation that will make his income average out more steadily over time, so as to keep his effective tax rate as low as possible and permit him to cancel off losses against profits; and he also likes a fast method (such as the declining balance) that enables him to put off the evil day of taxes as far as possible.

Governments often allow accelerated depreciation to encourage investment, especially if the new property is to be in a region the government is trying to build up. This may vary from 100 per cent write off in one year (i.e., taxable income reduced by the whole amount of new investment) to various straight-line depreciation rates over 3, 4, or 5 years. This approach reduces the harmful effect of taxation on "venture capital" by cutting actual taxes paid. The Kennedy administration, following a policy adopted by Sweden some years ago, introduced in the 1960s an "investment tax credit" that actually gave a subsidy to firms investing in new equipment. This tax credit could be turned off and on to stabilize

After the year's operations, we get a new Balance Sheet:

BALANCE SHEET OF PEPTO-GLITTER, LTD., AS OF DECEMBER 31, 1976

ASSETS			LIABILITIES AND NET WORTH		
			Liabilities		
Current Assets:			**Current Liabilities:**		
Cash		$ 17,000	Accounts payable	$ 10,000	
Inventory		85,000	Notes Payable	17,000	
Sinking Fund to Replace Equipment		5,000	Reserve for Taxes	21,000	
(Government bonds)					
Fixed Assets:			**Long-term Liabilities:**		
Equipment	$130,000		SBL Note	50,000	
Less: Allowance (or Reserve)			Bonds Payable	50,000	
for Depreciation	15,000				
		115,000			
Buildings	$170,000		*Net Worth*		
Less: Allowance (or Reserve)			**Capital Stock:**		
for Depreciation	5,000		Preferred Stock	50,000	
		165,000	Common Stock	200,000	
Intangible Assets:			**Surplus:**	20,000	
Patents		10,000			
Good Will		21,000			
Total		$418,000	Total	$418,000	

TABLE 5-3.

investment and was repealed by the Nixon Administration during the Vietnam inflation.

■ THE RELATION BETWEEN THE INCOME STATEMENT AND THE BALANCE SHEET

Now we must relate the description by the Income Statement of what has happened during the year to the Balance Sheets at the beginning and end of the year. Table 5-3 shows the Balance Sheet of our toothpaste corporation at the end of its first year of operation. It has prospered. Net Worth, the difference between Total Assets and Total Liabilities, has increased between the beginning and end of the accounting period by $20,000—from $250,000 to $270,000. The amount of this increase, as seen by comparing Balance Sheets, just equals the earnings or profits *available* to the common stockholders but not paid out to them in dividends, or as we saw at the bottom of the Income Statement, just equal to $30,500 minus $10,500, or $20,000 of undistributed profits.

Some Net Worth item must be written up by $20,000. It would clearly never do to increase the Preferred Stock Capital Account, because such stockholders are not the residual claimants to the profits of the corporation and no new stock has been sold. Conceivably, one could add the $20,000 to the Common Stock Capital Account. However, this is not done. Instead, the Common Stock Capital Account is left at its original par or issued value.

It is more informative to create a new account called Surplus—or sometimes Earned Surplus or Earnings Retained in the Business—to show how much of the increase in "book value" or Net Worth has resulted from accumulated undistributed earnings plowed back through the years.

In many ways Surplus is a misleading word. It sounds like something extra or unnecessary, or too often like a nice spare chunk of cash which the company's workers or stockholders might hope to stage a raid against. Actually, Surplus is distinctly not an Assets account, much less a pool of liquid cash. It simply indicates a part of the ownership—over and above Liabilities to creditors and original subscribed capital ownership—in the polyglot Assets of the corporation. A glance at Table 5-3 will convince us that the $20,000 of Surplus is not matched by an equivalent amount of cash on the Assets side.

We must again warn against trying to link *specific* items on the two sides of the Balance Sheet. Only the final *totals* correspond. It is not even possible to say exactly how the $20,000 plowed back into the business, or added to Surplus, was used. An addition to Surplus must be associated with an increase in Assets and/or a decrease in Liabilities—that is all we can say.

It would be an equal mistake to think that the profits of a corporation accrue in the form of cash, so that on the last day of the year, just before the board of directors decided upon its dividend rate, there was some $30,500 of cash on hand, available either for the stockholders or to be reinvested in the business. In the case of our toothpaste company, the very handsome profit earned was largely embodied in the form of new non-cash Assets and lowered Liabilities; not very much more than $10,500 could have been paid out as cash dividends without forcing serious changes in the financial decisions of the company—decisions such as to borrow more, to grow more slowly, to sell off some of the equipment and inventory at a loss, or to operate with a ludicrously low cash balance.

■ SUMMARY OF ELEMENTARY ACCOUNTING RELATIONS

Before taking a last look at the new complexities introduced in the 1976 Balance Sheet over that of the 1975, we may briefly summarize the relationship between Balance Sheets and Income Statements:

1. The Balance Sheet indicates an instantaneous financial picture: it is like a measure of the stock of water in a lake.

2. The Income Statement shows the flow of sales, cost, and revenue over the year or other accounting period: it measures the flow of water in and out of the lake.

3. The change in total Net Worth between the beginning and the end of the period—as shown by comparing the new and old Balance Sheets—is also to be understood from an examination of the changes in Surplus as appended at the end of Table 5-2's Income Statement: the change in the lake's level over the year we can relate to the flows during the year. (If new common stock is sold, that will be revealed by comparing the two Balance Sheets.)

There do remain, however, certain changes in the Balance-Sheet items from their previous levels in the earlier period to which the intervening Income Statement gives no clue. A closer look at the December 31, 1976, Balance Sheet will therefore prove instructive, although enough has been said already to introduce the reader to the fundamentals of accounting.

■ RESERVES AND FUNDS

The new Balance Sheet looks much like the old for the most part; but some new items are present for the first time. The last of these new items, Surplus, we have already explained. Among the Liabilities there is a new item called Reserve for Taxes of $21,000. It is not hard to understand. The taxes that the corporation will have to pay the government are as much short-term Liabilities as the Accounts Payable or Notes Payable.

Taxes Payable might have been a better title, since the word "Reserve" suggests a pool of cash, which it decidedly is not. Instead, the Reserve for Taxes is simply an earmarking of part of the Total Assets of the company for a special creditor—a reminder that the owners' Net Worth is less by the amount of owed taxes. We shall soon see there are three main kinds of "Reserves," and not one represents a pool of cash or liquid Assets.

Let us turn to the Assets side for new items.[3] The first stranger, entitled "Sinking Fund to Replace Equipment," is listed midway between the Current and Fixed Assets. It is an asset consisting of, say, 6 per cent government bonds which are to be held for the purpose of ultimately providing part of the money to buy new machines when the old ones are to be replaced. Although the corporation could change its mind and use the Sinking Fund bonds for some other purpose, it presumably will not choose to do so. The nature of this Sinking Fund is very understandable; it is simply a pool of liquid Assets set aside for a specific future purpose.

ALLOWANCE FOR DEPRECIATION Turning to the Fixed Assets, we find ourselves in for a surprise. From our previous discussion of the Depreciation Charges of the Income Statement, we should have expected the Buildings and Equipment items to total $280,-000. Why? Because at the beginning of the year they added up to $300,000, because no new equipment was bought during the year, and because the Income Statement told us that $20,000 of depreciation accrued during the period as part of the necessary costs of production.

Why, then, are these Fixed Assets carried on the

new Balance Sheet at the old $130,000 and $170,-000 figures? Looking more closely, we see that they really are not. From the $130,000 nominal Equipment valuation, there is subtracted a $15,000 Allowance (or Reserve) for Depreciation, so that really only $115,000 is carried for Equipment. Similarly, from the $170,000 original value of the Buildings, there is subtracted a $5,000 Allowance for Depreciation. Our faith in the accountant's sanity is restored; but we may still wonder why he goes through this roundabout procedure of stating "two" as "four minus two" instead of simply as "two."

Actually, he has his good reasons. An honest accountant knows his Depreciation estimate is only the roughest of guesses. Were he simply to guess and put down the final figure of $115,000 for Equipment, the public would not know how much reliance to place upon the figure. So he puts down $130,000 of original value, which is firmly rooted in the solid fact of original cost; and he then carefully isolates his own guessed-at Allowance for Depreciation. Then the public is in a better position to evaluate the reliability of the final $115,000 figure. The round-about procedure does no harm, and may do good.

Now we know the precise meaning of Allowances (or Reserves) for Depreciation. They are not sums of money; they are not sinking funds of liquid Assets that can be spent on replacement. They are simply *subtractions from overstated Assets figures.* Thus, the Allowance for Depreciation of Buildings of $5,000 is simply an explicit correction of the original value of the Buildings, which would be an overstatement of the value left in them. This correction must be made to keep Assets and Net Worth from both being artificially inflated.

It must be made regardless of whether at the same time any money is or is not being set aside into sinking funds to replace the Depreciation asset. Note that there is no Sinking Fund for Buildings and that the Sinking Fund to Replace Equipment is only one-third as large as the estimated Allowance for Depreciation of Equipment. As a matter of fact, businesses rarely set aside any considerable sums of money in replacement sinking funds. This is because liquid gilt-edge bonds earn at most only a few per cent interest, whereas capital invested in the firm's own activities usually brings in much more.[4]

---

[3] Neither this Balance Sheet nor the previous one contains a frequently met Current Assets item called Prepaid Expenses. Often an enterprise will pay its rent or buy some of its supplies a number of months in advance. Very properly, the enterprise is regarded as possessing on its Balance Sheet an equivalent asset.

[4] Where, then, will the money be coming from to replace any particular machine or building if no sinking

We have met two kinds of Reserves: (1) a Liability Reserve, like that for taxes, which is really simply a liability of fairly certain amount, and (2) an Asset Valuation Reserve like that for Depreciation (or allowance for estimated uncollectible bills), which is really simply a subtraction from an overstated asset. A third so-called "Surplus Reserve" (or, more properly, "Appreciation of Earned Surplus"), which is also not to be confused with a sum of money, may be mentioned: Sometimes a firm takes part of its Surplus and sets it aside under a different name so the stockholders will not be tempted to lobby for higher dividend payments. For example, our toothpaste company might earmark half of its $20,000 Surplus account into a Reserve for Research and Development. This $10,000 Reserve would no more consist of cash or liquid funds than does Surplus itself, or than does any other kind of Reserve. It should never be confused with a fund.[5]

This completes the *fundamentals* of accounting. The rest of the Appendix deals with some further developments.

■ INTANGIBLE ASSETS

Only one further new category of Assets can still be found on the December 31, 1976, Balance Sheet. To illustrate that an asset need not be a tangible commodity, a piece of equipment, or a sum of money, a patent has been introduced into the picture. Let us suppose that it is a patent on a profitable new chemical process, which gives us exclusive production rights for 17 years.

Such a patent is obviously worth money. Of course, as 5, 10, 12, and 16 years pass, the patent will be coming near to the end of its 17-year life and will be declining in value. Therefore, some

_____

funds have been set aside? Ordinarily, the equipment can be purchased with sales dollars earned by *other* equipment that is not currently calling for replacement expenditure. The selling price of the output of such other equipment contains an accounting allowance for depreciation expense, and a corresponding sum of money is available for investment elsewhere in the business. Speaking somewhat loosely, we may say that each asset not needing replacement lends its Depreciation Charges to those which need replacement, knowing that it too will be taken care of when the need arises.

[5] The problem of Reserves becomes even more complicated in connection with contingencies that may or may not occur. Thus Reserve for Depression Contingencies or for Renegotiation would fall halfway between true Liability and Surplus Reserves.

depreciation formula will be applied to it just as if it were a truck.

GOOD WILL AND MONOPOLY EARNING POWER   So much for Patents as an illustration of an intangible asset. Let us suppose that, at the same time we bought the patent, we also took over a rival toothpaste company. This horizontal combination will presumably add to our monopoly position and earning power. Therefore we were willing to buy the company for more than its trifling Assets—which happened to consist solely of a little inventory—were worth. Perhaps part of the purchase price went as profits to those who promoted this little monopolistic merger.

An example of the capitalization of earning power is J. P. Morgan's formation of the giant United States Steel Corporation at the turn of the century. He bought out the Andrew Carnegie steel plants and combined them with half a dozen other holdings. But in economics, as in atomic physics, the whole is equal to more than the sum of its parts.

After Morgan had put the pieces together, he found himself with some 130 million dollars of extra capital value!

Who was hurt by this transaction? Certainly not Carnegie or Morgan. Even the people who bought the stock had no right to complain that it had been "watered," since for many years they got more than a fair return on their investments. To have sold them the stock for its actual cost (without water) would be (1) To make them a free gift of the enlarged profits of the concern, and (2) to give them the privilege of reselling the stock at the higher price that its earning power could earn for it in a competitive stock market. (Of course the consumer was not given the full benefit in lower steel prices of the efficiencies achieved by the merger; but in terms of standards of the time, there was nothing illegal or unethical about this merger.)

Our practical-minded accountant, however, is not concerned with such matters of public policy and political economy as whether the consumer will or will not now pay higher prices. He will tell our toothpaste company or J. P. Morgan the same thing: "If you paid a certain sum of money for some assets, they must presumably be worth that much to you. If the assets don't exist, they must be created. 'Good Will' is their name." But since this term has come into bad repute in recent years, it is often lumped in with some other assets.

The intangible asset Good Will is thus the difference between what a company pays in buying out another company and what it gets in identifiable Assets.

■ ACCOUNTING ABUSES

In economics and finance nothing can be measured with the great accuracy of the physical sciences. But approximate measurement will suffice, so long as the method of measurement remains roughly the same over time.

Nowhere is this better illustrated than in accounting. When auditors certify that a company has prepared its accounting reports properly, they are not really able to swear that all measurements are 100 per cent accurate. But it is valuable for anyone who is contemplating buying the stock of the company to know that the usual methods of accounting have been adhered to. For example, when the company reports a rise of 10 per cent in earnings per share over the previous year, then even though there may be some uncertainty in the exact figures for each year, the direction of the improvement should be not at all in doubt.

Unfortunately, in the 1960s and 1970s certain abuses crept into the accounting used by some of the "conglomerates." Here are a few examples.

1. Manipulation of the way the assets taken over by the conglomerate are treated—good will adjustments and so forth—have been used to permit the conglomerate *to report rising per share earnings every year even though actual operating earnings have fallen.*

2. Conglomerates will issue many securities that are *convertible* into common stock—convertible bonds, convertible preferred stock, warrant options to buy new common stock at low prices, stock options for executives and underwriters. These really are potential common stock which, in many cases, are sure to become actual common stock. Hence, if we were to restate the earnings per share to allow for this *dilution*—and many accounting committees have recommended that this be done—what looks like a rising profile of earnings per share may actually be a dismally falling one.

3. Sometimes a small conglomerate will take over a larger corporation that is cash-rich, using in the end the money of the company swallowed to do so. Even where this is not illegal or unethical, it may be possible only because the old accounting reports of the giant carried its assets *concealed by under valuations.*

4. Sometimes conglomerates give the appearance of becoming more profitably efficient in their operations than their predecessor companies, when actually all the improvements in per share earnings have resulted merely from taking advantage of tax loopholes—such as changing convertible preferred stocks into convertible bonds so that their dividend return will now appear in the form of interest, which is deductible under the law from corporation income subject to taxes. There may be nothing illegal or even unethical about this razzle-dazzle, but the alert investor will have to learn how to discern that this is all that is taking place and that further improvement is not possible.

The accounting profession and government agencies are working to reform some of these abuses. But, alas, the old adage *caveat emptor*—let the buyer beware—must still prevail.

■ CONCLUSION

Finally, some interesting relations between economics and accounting can be briefly mentioned. (1) All Balance Sheets depend on valuation of Assets, which is one of the basic questions of the capital and interest theory discussed in Part Four. (2) National-income statistics depend on the accounting data of sales, cost, and so forth, as Chapter 10 shows. (3) As we shall see in a later discussion of how firms set price, accounting cost data play an important role in price determination.

The accountant deals with *money* magnitudes; the economist tries to probe deeper to the underlying *real* magnitudes. Especially in periods of great inflation or deflation, the accountant realizes that his ordinary methods may give strange results.

One example is the problem of changing price levels and depreciation. Suppose prices are rising sharply. If I sell my goods for enough to cover labor and other costs and also to cover depreciation, you might think I am breaking even. What would an accountant say who figures depreciation on the basis of the past low prices originally paid for my machines and building? He, too, would say I am breaking even. But in fact I can be said to have been selling my goods at a *real* loss; for when my machines and buildings have worn out, I shall not have enough money to *reproduce them* at the new higher price level. The same is true of a merchant who sells off his inventory at less than replacement cost.

So we must beware of fictitious money overstatements of real profits during rising prices and of fictitious understatements of profits during falling prices. (Later, in national-income statistics, you will note that profits are "adjusted" for inventory re-valuations.)

SUMMARY TO APPENDIX

Instead of a lengthy recapitulation, here is a check list of accounting concepts that you should under-stand:

■ 1 The fundamental Balance-Sheet relationship be-tween Assets, Liabilities, and Net Worth and the breakdown of each of these categories into Current and Fixed Assets, Current and Long-term Liabilities, Capital and Surplus.

■ 2 The character of the Income Statement (or Profit-and-Loss Statement) and the relationship between undistributed profit and Surplus changes on the new Balance Sheet.

■ 3 The whole problem of Depreciation, both in its income-statement aspect as a necessary ex-pense, which need not be an expenditure, and in its balance-sheet treatment as a deduction from a purposely overstated asset; also the logic of principal depreciation methods. Al-though any errors in calculating depreciation tend to cancel out eventually, recent tax con-cessions that allow rapid depreciation do im-prove the cash position of corporations.

■ 4 The difference between a Fund or a pool of liquid Assets and three kinds of so-called "Reserves"; also the meaning of intangible Assets like Patents and Good Will.

QUESTIONS FOR DISCUSSION

1. Describe the Balance Sheet's right-hand side. Its left-hand side. What items must match from the "fundamental identity"?

2. You are a banker deciding whether to lend money to the toothpaste company. Why be especi-ally interested in current items?

3. Write out a list of many different Assets, de-scribing the nature of each in a few lines. Do the same for Liabilities.

4. Is an Income Statement a "still picture" at an instant of time? Why not?

5. A company has 10 million dollars of net sales and 9 million dollars of costs of all kinds (includ-ing taxes, interest, etc.). It rents its equipment, its inventory does not change in the year, and it has no preferred stock. It pays no dividends. Draw up its simplified 1976 Income Statement.

6. The same company as in question 5 owes no money, having been completely equity-financed years ago. Fill in the year-end Balance Sheets below.

ASSETS			LIABILITIES AND NET WORTH		
	1975	1976		1975	1976
			Liabilities	0	0
			Net Worth	$50 million	....
Total	$50 million	....	Total	....	....

7. Redo problems 5 and 6, making the following changes: In addition to the other expenses, its build-ings depreciate by 2 million dollars; also its inven-tory has fallen off by 3 million dollars.

Draw up an Income Statement showing its loss for the year, and adjust its 1976 Balance Sheet accordingly.

8. Describe two methods of calculating Deprecia-tion, and explain tax advantages.

9. Differentiate between three different kinds of Reserves. Which, if any, are "Funds"? Which cash? Describe intangible Assets. Give examples of ac-counting abuses.

10. Guess how much you would pay for a business that is sure of yielding a net profit of $15,000 per year with little risk of principal. Suppose its Total Assets exclusive of Good Will were valued at $100,000. What would you guess for Good Will?

11. Review your understanding of the following concepts:

Balance-Sheet identity
Income-Statement identity
Assets, Liabilities, and Net Worth
Current versus Fixed Assets
Surplus, earnings, dividends
Manufacturing Cost of Goods Sold
Manufacturing Cost, inventory change
Depreciation (as expense and reserve)
Intangible Assets—Patents and Good Will
Assets and Liability Reserves versus
   Sinking Fund

6

AFFLUENCE AND POVERTY: INDIVIDUAL AND FAMILY INCOME

Such poverty as we have today in our great cities degrades the poor, and infects with its degradation the whole neighbourhood in which they live. And whatever can degrade a neighbourhood, can degrade a country and a continent and finally the whole civilized world, which is only a large neighbourhood. GEORGE BERNARD SHAW

Everyone realizes the importance of income. The expression "Clothes make the man" would be more nearly right if it were "Income makes the man." That is to say, if you can know but one fact about a man, knowledge of his income will probably reveal most about him. Then you can roughly guess his political opinions, his tastes, and education, his age, and even his life expectancy.

Furthermore, unless a family has a steady stream of money coming in every week, month, and year—even though it has saintly endurance—that family is sick. Not only its materialistic activities, but its nonmaterialistic activities—the things that convert existence into living—must suffer: education, travel, health, recreation, and charity, to say nothing of food, warmth, and shelter.

It is commonplace to state that the North American standard of living and level of family income are the highest in all the world. But few people realize how small the average Canadian or American income really is, or how great the range between the highest and the lowest incomes.

This chapter gives some basic facts about incomes and wealth, here and abroad. North America has been described by Harvard's J. Kenneth Galbraith as The Affluent Society. And the mixed economies of Western Europe are following hot on our heels.

Yet the Affluent skyscraper remains based on a foundation of poverty: and as we shall see, this kind of poverty is new in history and different from that found in most other parts of the earth.

■ THE DECLINE OF POVERTY

It is now well over a century since Karl Marx and Friedrich Engels in 1848 issued the Communist Manifesto containing the lines: "Workers of the world unite! You have nothing to lose but your chains." While some of Marx's predictions about the future of industrial capitalism were proved correct in the intervening years, one of his most famous has proved to be quite wrong. His assertion that *the rich will become richer and the poor will become poorer* cannot be sustained by careful historical and statistical research. In Europe and in North America there has definitely been a steady secular improvement in minimum standards of living, whether measured by food, clothing, housing, or length of life. This fact about capitalism is clear from statistics to be presented shortly.

It used to be fashionable for economic historians to dwell on the evils of the Industrial Revolution and the poverty-ridden condition of the masses in the disease-producing cities. In point of fact, no Dickens novel did full justice to the dismal conditions of child labor, length of the working day, and conditions of safety and sanitation in early nineteenth-century factories. A work week of 84 hours was the prevailing rule, with time out at the bench for breakfast and sometimes supper, as well as lunch. A good deal of work could be got out of a six-year-old child; and if a man lost two fingers in a machine, he still had eight left.

However true their lurid picture of industrial factory towns, the earlier historians erred in thinking that conditions were worse than in the preindustrial era. The earlier "putting-out," or domestic, system, in which wool or yarn was provided to workers for them to spin or weave in their homes, brought the worst conditions of the sweatshop into the home. The whole family, was figuratively, forced to run on the treadmill to keep alive.

Furthermore, poverty is never so obvious in the country as in the industrial cities, where it forces itself on the observer. The idyllic picture of the healthful, happy countryside peopled by stout yeomen and happy peasantry is a mirage in most parts of the world. Even the best known slum areas of Montreal or Halifax, not to mention Harlem and Chicago's black belt, present to their residents better conditions than the rural slums they have escaped: north-central New Brunswick and Newfoundland (where about 80 per cent of the "farms" produce for sale crops worth less than $2,500 per year); beautiful Gaspé (where three or four times as many children die in their first year as in Toronto or Montreal). Farther west people live in misery and squalor in Indian settlements, ghost mining towns, and isolated infertile farming communities.

Modern historians therefore emphasize that the living standards of the industrial present, inadequate as they may seem, are nevertheless great improvements over previous periods of commercial enterprise and agrarian feudalism.

Higher productivity gives us more product and more leisure.

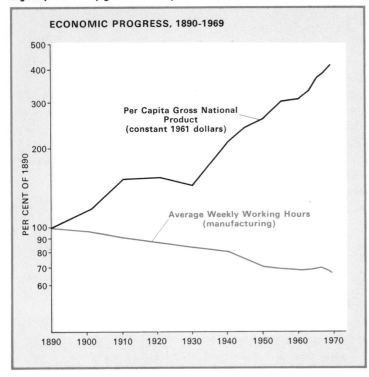

ECONOMIC PROGRESS, 1890-1969

FIG. 6-1. Technological improvements, better capital goods, and more highly skilled labor have raised production faster than the growth of population. Note: This is a "ratio," or "semilog," chart; the vertical scale is arranged so that equal vertical distances depict equal percentage rather than equal absolute changes. Example: 400 is as far above 200 as 200 is above 100. (Source: Urquhart & Buckley, *Canadian Historical Statistics*, **Cambridge University Press, 1965;** and O. J. Firestone, *Canada's Economic Development 1867-1953*, **London: Bowes & Bowes, Ltd., 1956.)**

■ TWO WORLDS?

Most of Asia and Africa are even today at lower levels of living than were the Western countries before the Industrial Revolution. Figure 6-1 shows how fortunate Canada's growth in output has been. A great economic statistician, Simon Kuznets of Harvard, has recently shown that the leading Western nations have for decades been averaging rapid rates of growth of output per head. Examine the front leaf chart to see how fast countries have grown.

What about the progress of the poorer countries? We lack data to give firm answers. Professor Kuznets has made shrewd guesses and inclines to the view that their productivity growth has been lagging behind. He makes the important observation:[1]

> ". . . the presently developed countries were already in advance of the 'rest of the world' when modern industrialization began—and the latter only increased the disparity."

[1] Simon Kuznets, "Quantitative Aspects of the Economic Growth of Nations: 1," *Economic Development and Cultural Change*, Vol. V (1956), p. 25. From 1956 to 1970 there have been some success stories: Thailand, Taiwan, Korea, and Mexico, for example, have made some remarkable progress.

Table 6-1 shows the wide international spreads of income per head. The same spreads can sometimes be found between the regions of one country, so that the over-all average for Canada or the United States conceals the persisting disparities. States such as Mississippi, for example, have scarcely attained per capita incomes equal to those reached in Pennsylvania and New York back in 1910 or those found in France today. The economist would expect these differences to disappear with time, and this faith is confirmed by the gradual convergence of the incomes of the American states. But the differences between the Canadian provinces are more worrying. Until 1961, the per capita levels had maintained their differences stubbornly for four decades: there was no apparent tendency for the Atlantic Provinces to converge on Quebec or Ontario. (Recent data led the Economic Council of Canada in 1969 to detect hopeful evidence for "some narrowing of regional income disparities and the elimination of poverty.")

◼ DISTRIBUTION OF INCOME IN CANADA

A poll of students will show that they are not very sure about what their own family incomes really are. Usually it turns out they have a slightly exaggerated notion of their father's earnings. And despite the recent (quite justified) claim of a prominent clubwoman that "women spend 70 per cent of the national income, and we soon hope to get hold of the rest," an astonishing number of wives have no conception of their husbands' paycheques. In addition, there are some people so inept at keeping records and with such variable earnings that they do not themselves know how much they make. Even where income is known within the family, there is a quite natural reticence to reveal it to outsiders; thus investigators who made a 1939 survey of the birth-control habits of native white Protestants of Indianapolis often found it harder to get financial data than intimate personal information.

In the absence of statistical knowledge, it is understandable that one should form an impression of the North American standard of living from the full-page magazine advertisements portraying a jolly family in an air-conditioned man-

Americans enjoy highest standard of living in world:

PER CAPITA GNPs, 1970			
United States	$4,900	Japan	$1,500
Canada	3,600	Italy	1,490
Sweden	3,300	USSR	1,300
Denmark	3,000	Poland	1,100
West Germany	2,800	Portugal	600
Norway	2,800	Turkey	320
France	2,750	China (Taiwan)	300
United Kingdom	2,400	UAR (Egypt)	190
Israel	1,900	Korea	115
Czechoslovakia	1,600	India	90

TABLE 6-1. All estimates have been converted into 1970 U.S. dollars at exchange rates designed to reflect actual purchasing powers; but all figures should be regarded as rough approximations, particularly in countries at drastically different stages of development. (Sources: Center for International Studies, MIT, and authors).

Few Canadian families reach income of $15,000:

FREQUENCY DISTRIBUTION OF INCOMES OF CANADIAN
FAMILIES AND UNATTACHED INDIVIDUALS, 1965

(1) INCOME CLASS	(2) Percentage of All Families and Individuals in This Class	(3) Percentage of Total Income Received by Families and Individuals in This Class	(4) Percentage of Families and Individuals in This Class and Lower Ones	(5) Percentage of Total Income Received by Families and Individuals in This Class and Lower Ones
Under $1,000	6.9	0.7	6.9	0.7
1,000 - 1,999	8.9	2.3	15.8	3.0
2,000 - 2,999	9.1	3.9	24.9	6.9
3,000 - 3,999	10.7	6.4	35.6	13.3
4,000 - 4,999	11.2	8.4	46.8	21.7
5,000 - 5,999	11.9	11.2	58.7	32.9
6,000 - 6,999	10.6	11.8	69.3	44.7
7,000 - 7,999	7.6	9.6	76.9	54.3
8,000 - 9,999	11.3	16.9	88.2	71.2
10,000 - 14,999	8.9	17.5	97.1	88.7
$15,000 and over	2.9	11.4	100.0	100.0

TABLE 6-2. Half of these families and unattached individuals are below the median income of $5,327. The average or arithmetic mean income (that each would have if total income were distributed equally) is about $6,049, or $116 per week. More families have incomes around the modal $5,250 level than around any other income. One quarter of all families received income of less than $3,095. The highest quartile in the income frequency distribution received incomes ranging upward from $7,820. (Source: Distribution of Income, DBS 13-528.)

sion, with a Mercedes, a station wagon, a motor launch, and all the other good things that go to make up comfortable living. Actually, of course, this sort of life is still beyond the grasp of 90 per cent of the public and even beyond most families from which the select group of college students comes.

THE SOBER TRUTH   In the early 1970s, after 10 years of prosperity, the average Canadian family gets about $120 per week. Such an average is derived by pretending that all families, and unattached persons, divide the total income equally. Of course, in real life, income is distributed far from equally; and there is no guarantee that an attempt to divide it equally would leave the total unchanged.

If the members of a classroom, or of the whole country, write down their family incomes on cards, these cards may be sorted into different income classes; i.e., some cards will go into the $0-to-$999 class, some into the $1,000-to-$1,999 class, and so forth. In this way we get the *statistical frequency distribution* of income. At one extreme will be the very poor, who have drawn a blank in life; at the other, the very rich. In between fall the vast majority.

Table 6-2 summarizes recent statistics on this subject. Column (1) gives the *income class interval.* Column (2) shows the percentage of families and individuals in each income class. Column (3) shows the percentage of the total of all income that goes to the people in the given income class. Columns (4) and (5) are computed from (2) and (3), respectively. Column (4) shows what percentage of the total number of families and individuals belongs to each income class *or below.* Column (5) shows what percentage of total income goes to the people who belong in the given income class or have still lower incomes.

This table shows it would be a great mistake to think that the poor and the rich are equally distributed around the middle. The Biblical statement, "For ye have the poor always with you," gives no inkling of their vast numbers. Abraham Lincoln pointed up this fact picturesquely in his statement, "The Lord prefers common people. . . . He made so many of them."

A glance at the income distribution in Canada shows how pointed is the income pyramid and how broad its base. "There's always room at the top" is certainly true; this is so because it is hard to get there, not because it is easy. If we made an income pyramid out of a child's blocks, with each layer portraying $1,000 of income, the peak would be far higher than the Eiffel Tower, but almost all of us would be within a yard of the ground.

The middle, or "median," income class (which divides the upper from the lower half of the people) corresponds to a modest income—only about $5,327 in the 1965 table. The median income falls short of the average (or "arithmetic mean") income of $6,049. This is primarily because the distribution of incomes is always a skewed one, with a long tail of incomes stretching out above the mean. The mode (or "modal income"), the size of income received by the largest number of families, is close to the median at $5,250.

■ POVERTY IN AN AFFLUENT CANADA

In the 1960s, inspired perhaps by President Kennedy's war on poverty, Canadian governments dropped their complacent acceptance of widespread poverty amidst affluence. Both Canada and the United States, and their provinces or states, and municipalities, launched or accelerated gigantic social programs. Prior to Chapter 38's extended discussion, here is a brief outline of the forces organized against poverty.

Aid was traditionally given by the provinces (and the municipalities) to those in need. Beginning in 1927, Ottawa began to offer social welfare directly or by sharing provincial assistance expenses 50-50. Nowadays the two levels of government spend almost 4 billion dollars on welfare, not to mention vast sums for old-age retirement and hospital and medical care. More constructively, the federal welfare program includes about 100 million dollars for manpower centers and placement; for relocation and mobility of workers; and for training programs. For depressed communities, especially backward rural areas, the Agricultural Rehabilitation and Development Act (ARDA) and other Regional Development schemes have studied, experimented, and innovated in the betterment of whole communities.

DEFINITION OF POVERTY   Economists have tried to come at the measurement of the low-income problem in two ways. The first is to postulate a minimum-decency (or minimum-subsistence) income, and investigate who are below it. This is the "poverty-line" approach. The second, on page 149, is to measure the spread of incomes between the rich and the poor: the degree of inequality.

Let us see how large the group is that is stuck below some adequate income level. Economists have two techniques for this. First, from social-service workers they have taken over carefully calculated budgets purporting to measure the cost of a barely-adequate living standard. To check and supplement such data, the Economic Council of Canada has used a second method. It is based on the finding[2] that poor families generally must and do spend most of their income on essentials, having little left over for drugs, medical care, education, recreation, travel, or savings. Conservatively, the ECC decided to classify as "low-income families" those that spend 70 per cent of their income entirely for food, clothing, and shelter. They then found which income levels showed this kind of spending. They found for example, that in 1970 a family of five, living on $5,200 per year or $100 per week, would on the average have to spend more than three-quarters of its income on essentials. Hence it was classified as falling below the poverty line as were single persons with incomes of $2,000 and couples with $3,300.[3]

Judged by these standards, the tables, such as Table 6-2, for the late 1960s would show at least 850,000 men, women, and children (maybe half-a-million families) below the minimum-decency line! And this is down from 1961—the ten years of prosperity have lifted 2 or 3 per cent of Canada's families above the poverty level.

Not surprisingly, such a decline in poverty always accompanies a period of prosperity; cycles in unemployment and poverty move together. If we ignore these cyclical swings, and look at the long trend, a gradual poverty decline shows up in the figures. This can be explained by a cheapening of the cost of living in relation to incomes over the years. (In Canada, for instance, average wages, measured in constant-dollar terms, have risen from an annual figure of $1,486 in 1931 to $3,679 in 1961; hence a typical wage now will buy roughly *twice* as much as in the period following World War I. But the *minimum-*decency notion, of how much a wage-earner *ought* to have, has also gone up; for *as the nation as a whole gets more prosperous, the definition of minimum standards is raised.*)

The decline is certainly visible. Goldberg and Podoluk[4] found that the lowest one-fifth of wage-and-salary earners received only 2 per cent of all such incomes in 1931, but almost 4 per cent by 1951. The 1961 census shows that this figure has risen even further.[5]

But at the same time, the *number* of impoverished persons is not decreasing rapidly even though their proportion of the total population may be decreasing. It is this alarming rise that motivated Kennedy and Johnson, and Diefenbaker and Pearson to launch their "War on Poverty."

Canada's anti-poverty policy has been aimed heavily at rural squalor and

---

[2] From "Engel curves"—see Chapter 11, footnote 2.

[3] These poverty incomes were raised 30 per cent from their 1961 levels to allow for the increase in the cost of living to 1970.

[4] Simon Goldberg and Jenny Podoluk, "Income Size Distribution Statistics in Canada—A Survey and Some Analysis," *Income and Wealth Series VI* (London: Bowes and Bowes, 1957), p. 159. They found that family wage incomes were more evenly distributed than individual incomes.

[5] Note that the council does not believe that two can live as cheaply as one. They put the cost as 3,300/2,000 or 165 per cent.

low incomes. There is much justification for this rural emphasis. For example, Poduluk found that in 1961 the average earnings of rural families were $4,200, while the average income of similar families in metropolitan areas was $6,500, or 50 per cent greater. Both of these statistics included some families in very serious poverty, but the rural situation was by far the worse.[6]

Table 6-2, Column (4), shows that 15.8 per cent of all families were below the $2,000 line in 1965. To raise them all above this low line would not, in fact, be expensive; it is easy to calculate that the sum required is about 3 per cent of personal income.

> Take a sample of 1,000 families. Their mean income is $5,500, and their total income therefore is 5.5 million dollars. The poorest 16 per cent of the families would require 0.32 million dollars in order to receive $2,000 each (160 families multiplied by $2,000 gives you 0.32 million dollars). This is about 6 per cent of total income; but these families already earn about 2½ per cent. Thus, a further transfer of about 3½ per cent of total income is needed to raise the income of these families to $2,000. (This calculation can easily be adopted to show the expense of other anti-poverty goals.) Moving from this sample of 1,000 families to the whole population, the required 3½ per cent of total family income is perhaps 2 per cent of GNP.

The trouble with such a transfer program to deal with poverty is that a minimum of 850,000 people would be literally dependent on government relief of various kinds. Of course, many are wholly dependent now: they include a disproportionate fraction of women (especially widows with children), old persons, young workers with children, unemployed persons of all ages, and members of such groups as Indians, Negroes, new immigrants, and (as we have seen) rural people, especially farm workers in Quebec and the Maritime provinces. However, most people believe that transfers, or a "guaranteed income," like the dole of the 19th century, are *not* the single answer to this problem. Rather, anti-poverty programs must distinguish between the situations of each kind of family in poverty in order to arrive at a permanent solution.

■ HOW TO MEASURE INEQUALITY AMONG INCOME CLASSES

Measuring inequality is the alternative to measuring the number in poverty. How great is the spread of incomes, and how shall we measure the degree of inequality of income distribution? From Table 6-2, we can estimate that roughly half of all Canadians fall in the middle-income range of $3,100 to $7,800. This means that one-fourth fall below $3,100 and an equal number have incomes above $7,800. Of course, the fact that there are the same number of individuals and families in the above-$7,800 group as in the below-$3,100 group does not

---

[6] What to do about slum poverty, when people are pouring into the cities, is a much more difficult problem for policy-makers. So far, the typical measure is to designate areas where unemployment is worse and longer-lasting than in most of the country, then to attempt to train the unemployed for jobs there or elsewhere, while at the same time subsidizing industries for expanding or moving into such low-income, unemployed, labor areas. Canada's ARDA and the United States' ARA and Appalachian programs are typical. The United Kingdom has been working on such designated development areas for over 30 years.

mean that they each receive the same percentage of the total income. Actually, the lowest fourth of the population receives less than one-third of the income received by the highest fourth (as Fig. 6-2 can confirm).

Incomes are distributed with neither absolute equality nor absolute inequality:

PERCENTAGE OF FAMILIES	PERCENTAGE OF INCOME		
	ABSOLUTE EQUALITY	ABSOLUTE INEQUALITY	ACTUAL 1965
0	0	0	0
20	20	0	6
40	40	0	16
60	60	0	30
80	80	0	56
95	95	0	80
100	100	100	100

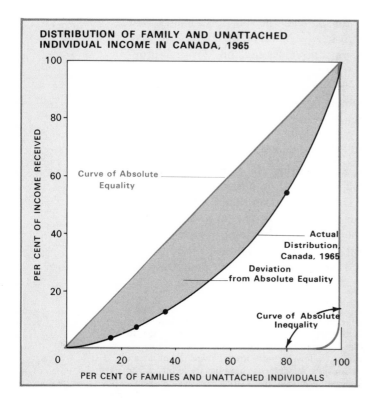

DISTRIBUTION OF FAMILY AND UNATTACHED INDIVIDUAL INCOME IN CANADA, 1965

Curve of Absolute Equality

Actual Distribution, Canada, 1965

Deviation from Absolute Equality

Curve of Absolute Inequality

PER CENT OF INCOME RECEIVED

PER CENT OF FAMILIES AND UNATTACHED INDIVIDUALS

FIG. 6-2. By plotting from the table above, we can see that the actual distribution-of-income curve lies between the two extremes of absolute equality and absolute inequality. **The shaded area of this Lorenz chart (as a percentage of half the square's area) measures relative inequality of income. (How would the curve have looked back in the roaring 1920s when inequality was greater? In a 1984 welfare state that narrows income differences?)**

This suggests how to go about the task of getting a numerical measure of the degree of inequality of income distribution. We can ask, What per cent of all income goes to the lowest 10 per cent of the population? What to the lowest 20 per cent? The lowest 50 per cent? The lowest 95 per cent? And so forth. Such data can be derived from Columns (4) and (5) of Table 6-2 on page 146.

If incomes were absolutely uniformly distributed, the lowest 20 per cent of the population (which in this case would mean *any* 20 per cent) would receive exactly 20 per cent of the total income; the lowest 80 per cent would receive 80 per cent of the income; and the highest 20 per cent would also get only 20 per cent of the income.

This is depicted by the so-called "Lorenz curve" in Fig. 6-2. It plots percentage of people, ranked from the poorest up, on the horizontal axis and percentage of total income they receive on the vertical axis.

The second column of the table in Fig. 6-2 gives data for the diagonal line in the hypothetical case of absolute equality.

At the other extreme, we have the equally hypothetical case of absolute *inequality*, where everybody (say, 99 out of 100 people) has no income, except for one person who has *all* the income. This is shown in the third column of the table. Why those numbers? Because the lowest, 0, 20, 80, and 99 people have no income at all. But the lowest 100 do include the last man; and all the people, of course, have all the income. The lowest curve on the Lorenz diagram—the dark, almost right-angled line represents this limiting case of absolute inequality.

Any actual income distribution, such as that of 1965, must fall between these extremes. Its Lorenz curve is given in Fig. 6-2 by the indicated intermediate curve, with the shaded area indicating the deviation from absolute equality, and hence giving us a measure of the degree of *inequality* of income distribution. (Since we shall meet Lorenz curves often, this figure deserves careful study.)[7]

■ TRENDS IN EQUALITY

What is happening to the degree of inequality of incomes in modern nations? Is it getting greater, as pessimists feared? By calculating Lorenz and other curves, scholars find that inequality is definitely less in Canada than it was in 1931, but slightly *more* than it was at the end of World War II. A glance at Fig. 6-3(b)

---

[7] M. O. Lorenz was a German statistician of the 1900s. Another way to measure income-inequality deserves mention here. The Italian-born Swiss professor of economics Vilfredo Pareto was often called, with somewhat questionable accuracy, the ideological precursor of fascism. By using a certain logarithmic chart called the "Pareto chart," he found that the "upper tail" of the income data of many different countries and many different times fell along straight lines of almost the same slopes. He came to believe this to be a fundamental natural law. According to Pareto's Law, there is an *inevitable tendency for income to be distributed in the same way—regardless of social and political institutions and regardless of taxation.* In the past 60 years, more careful studies have refuted the universality of Pareto's Law, as well as its inevitability. Thus, in Great Britain, in the period just following World War II, income taxation had gone so far as to leave only 70 people with incomes of more than $24,000 after taxes were paid! More on this in Chapter 38's discussion of inequality.

Inequality differs among nations and is different for income than for wealth:

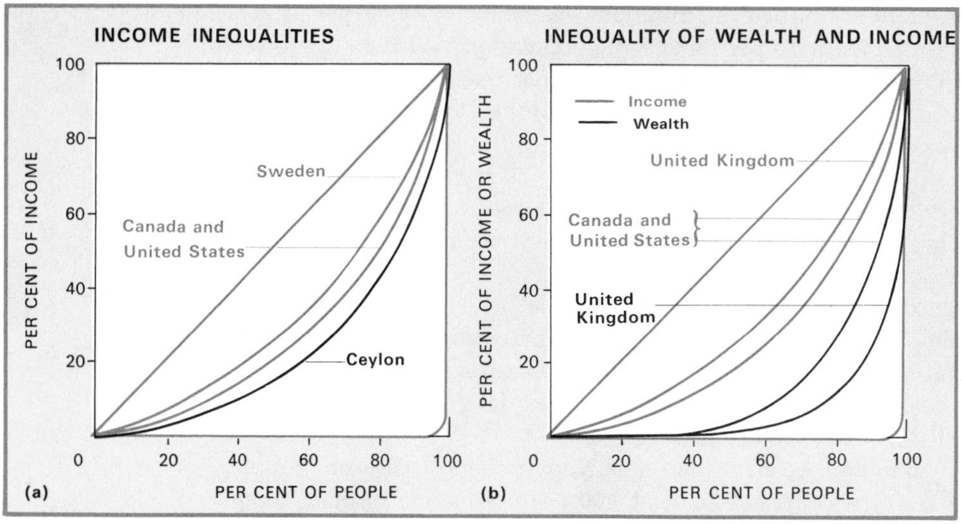

FIG. 6-3(a). Advanced economies show less inequality of income distribution than do pre-industrial economies—contrary to dire predictions of scientific socialists that the rich get richer and the poor get poorer under capitalism. The mixed economy shows greater equality.

FIG. 6-3(b). Holdings of wealth tend to be more concentrated than do incomes earned annually. The United States, Canada, and the United Kingdom have similar equality of incomes; but British wealth is much more concentrated than American or Canadian.

will show that the United Kingdom and North America have rather similar degrees of inequality of incomes, the major difference apparently not being attributable so much to differences in social philosophy as to the fact that there is a larger fraction of subsistence farmers and low-paid urban and Negro workers in the North American economy.

Which country today has the greatest equality? No one knows how to compare the inequality in the Soviet Union[8] or China with that in mixed economies. If we confine ourselves to the noncommunist world, it has been suggested that Israel may lead the list. Sweden and other mixed economies have low inequality, as the comparison in Fig. 6-3(a) shows.

Before industrialization, was there a golden age of greater equality of distribution? Fragmentary historical data suggest otherwise. Have developed societies generally greater inequality than underdeveloped nations? Casual tourist

---

[8] A very careful study of wage inequalities in Russia's communistic economy, Abram Bergson, *The Structure of Soviet Wages* (Cambridge, Mass.: Harvard University Press, 1944), showed inequalities and dispersions between the best-paid and the poorest-paid workers surprisingly like those of our own society. Shostakovich, other top Soviet musicians, and top scientists probably make more there than do similar persons in the West. The inequality of political privilege among Soviet bureaucrats, military officers, Communist party members, and the Soviet public at large is not susceptible to precise numerical measurement. Employment incomes in mixed economies like Australia and Sweden were found in a 1965 study to be slightly more equal than in Poland.

observation often suggests the reverse; the extremes of poverty and wealth *appear* greater in poor countries than in industrialized ones. The limited statistics available do confirm this view; thus, the Lorenz curve for a country like Ceylon in Fig. 6-3(a) will show greater inequality than will such a curve for Western countries, like Sweden or the United States. In general, as development proceeds, incomes within a nation are believed to become more equal.

■ DISTRIBUTION OF WEALTH

A Lorenz curve of distribution of *wealth* ownership shows considerably more inequality than does a curve of *income* distribution. Figure 6-3(b) shows how great is the difference between the wealth and income curves. Whereas the United Kingdom, and Canada and the United States have similar inequality of incomes, note that the United Kingdom has much greater inequality of wealth than do Canada and the United States. In part this is because certain peers and tycoons in Britain own tremendous concentrations of land and other property. But study of the data shows that much of the difference comes from the fact that many North Americans of quite modest incomes do have positive net worth (i.e., assets minus liabilities), whereas this is less common among lower-income Britons.[9]

Turn back to Fig. 3-1, on page 58. It shows that the For Whom problem is determined by (1) the price that people can get for the factors they supply—land, labor, machinery, and general capital goods, and (2) the amounts of these factors that they start out with. If labor could be ignored, then the distribution of incomes would be about that determined by the distribution of wealth: at the same interest return, twice the wealth will yield twice the income. Hence, property incomes show great Lorenz inequality.

The earnings from work—wages, salaries, earnings of unincorporated entrepreneurs—are evidently less unequally distributed. But of course they are not uniform, as the following sections show.

■ INCOME DIFFERENCES AMONG OCCUPATIONS

What single profession seems to make the most money? In recent years it has without question been the doctors. They have forged well ahead of lawyers. Medical doctors and surgeons have mean earnings close to $30,000, lawyers $8,000 less. Why the difference? Primarily because the costs of training doctors are so high and the capacities of our medical schools are so low. Although the demand has increased, North America as a whole does not train many more doctors than it did in 1910. Canadian training has expanded from a low pre-war level, but we depend surprisingly on immigrant doctors to keep ahead. This slowness of supply keeps incomes (the price of medical consultation) high; and

---

[9] Canadian data on the distribution of wealth are just now being developed. But data derived from a consumer-survey of net worths in seven Canadian cities suggest that the Canadian distribution of wealth is not unlike the American. (J. V. Poapst, *Consumer Survey*, Study for the Porter Commission, Appendix A, Table 90.)

medical societies are accused of helping to keep the doctors' incomes up by various devices, including the insistence on high standards of practice.

Architects and consulting engineers, lawyers and notaries, dentists, and accountants are estimated to have mean incomes of about $22,111, $22,014, $18,273, and $14,517 respectively. College teachers as a class have a mean salary of about $13,000. Full professors at the largest universities get over $20,000; older professors and professors of physics and engineering average higher incomes than do younger professors and professors of Greek and botany. Teachers' salaries have been improving recently, and now nurses are the lowest-paid of all professionals. Their median salary is still not much above $5,000. And even with special perquisites, the final figure is unbelievably low.

Do incomes increase with age? Not in the lowest-paid manual jobs. For such work, a man is at his best in his early twenties; after that he goes downhill. In the professions and in business executive jobs, earnings do increase with age. Professors at age 50 have salaries twice those of new lecturers; and some outside income too. Doctors and lawyers reach their prime around fifty; both can hope to work beyond the normal retirement ages. A junior executive with a B.A. or business degree will begin training at over $600 a month; if he is very successful, he may retire as chairman of the board, earning, say, $100,000 a year and with stock bonuses and retirement provisions.[10]

On the other hand, many corporations and institutions have been fixing inflexible retirement ages of sixty-five. With improvements in life expectancies, this poses a problem of long years of wasteful and unhappy retirement. The ultimate solution seems to be along these lines: Let each man taper off slowly rather than abruptly, other factors besides chronological age being decisive.

■ IS COLLEGE WORTH WHILE?

How do education and training affect lifetime income? Are they worth their cost? The evidence answers, Decidedly yes. Men who attend only 8 years of school have an average income of only $3,990. Those who attend college do almost twice as well. Unemployment among high-school dropouts exceeds that of graduates by a growing margin.

Even if you have to borrow at 6 per cent interest, put off years of gainful employment, live away from home, and pay for food and books, your lifetime earnings in the professions that are open only to college graduates will probably turn out to be more than compensatory. (Good grades help: in the United States, a *Time* study showed, in its own argot, that "greasy grinds" end up with slightly higher pay than do "big men on campus"; both outearn the anonymous face in the college crowd.)

Money is not everything—better to be uneducated, poor, and happy than to be well-off and miserable? The U.S. Governmental Commission on Mental

---

[10] Salaries of top officers do increase with the size of the firm, but by no means in strict proportion. U.S. statistics suggest that the head of Corporation A, twice the size of Company B, will *not* get twice the salary that the head of B gets, but only about 30 per cent more.

Doctors and consulting engineers show great income inequalities:

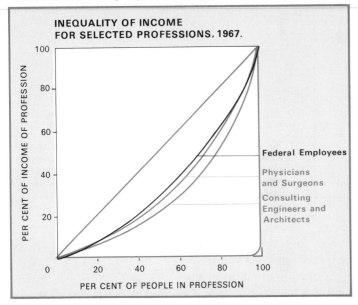

INEQUALITY OF INCOME
FOR SELECTED PROFESSIONS, 1967.

PER CENT OF INCOME OF PROFESSION

Federal Employees

Physicians
and Surgeons

Consulting
Engineers and
Architects

PER CENT OF PEOPLE IN PROFESSION

FIG. 6-4. Why should the curve for salaried federal employees fall closer to the absolute equality line than that shown for medical doctors and surgeons? Why would one expect the curve for dentists to be just above the curve for physicians and surgeons? How might the curves look for speculators in common stock or for military officers? (Source: Department of National Revenue, *Taxation Statistics*, **Part I, 1969**.)

Illness and Health reported a 1960 survey of how people with different education compared mentally. Were college graduates worried and depressed in comparison with those of little schooling? Surprisingly, the answer was, Definitely not. College graduates reported greater happiness and less mental illness. True, they were more introspective; but coupled with this went a greater sense of well-being and satisfaction. Their perspectives were broader and aspiration levels higher; and when they worried, their worries tended to be over genuine rather than imagined troubles.

Figure 6-4 shows how professions differ in inequality of earnings. Can you guess why the order of inequality is architect, . . . civil servant?

Education is one of society's most profitable investments. Human capital yields a return as great as or greater than capital in the form of tools and buildings. That is why economists urge developed and undeveloped countries to spend more on education and training, an undertaking now advocated strongly by the Economic Council of Canada.

■ DIFFERENCES IN ABILITY AND INCOMES

In Part Four we shall study in detail the economic principles underlying the distribution of income. Our common sense enables us to anticipate part of its analysis and suggests that one factor helping to explain differences in income must be *differences in people.*

These differences in people may be physical, mental, temperamental, or even moral. They may be associated with biological inheritance through the genetic cells or with social and economic environment. They may be permanent —like being blue-eyed—or acquired, like educational advantage or being blond.

Are abilities more normally distributed than market incomes?

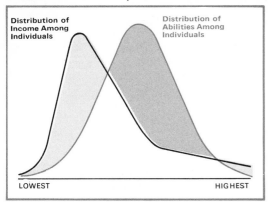

Distribution of
Income Among
Individuals

Distribution of
Abilities Among
Individuals

LOWEST   HIGHEST

FIG. 6-5. Heights, intelligence quotients, and many measured human traits seem to follow a so-called "normal" bell-shaped statistical distribution. Market incomes seem to be more skewed, highest incomes being more than a hundred times the lowest (as in the black curve).

These differences may even involve such conventionalities as the possession or nonpossession of a union card, and one's propensity to drop aitches in speaking or to acquire just the right mixture of bilingualism.

These differences provide us with only part of the answer to the puzzle of income distribution. Physical traits (such as height or hip girth) and measured mental traits (such as intelligence quotient or tone perception) appear to be *not* so different among people as are the differences in income distribution. Often, the scientist who measures individual traits finds that they are "normally" distributed, with most people in the middle and fewer people at each end, as represented by the bell-shaped curve of Fig. 6-5. (If their IQ scores depart from the normal distribution, psychologists often *rescale* them so as to force agreement!) Incomes—even those from work, but especially those from property ownership—are distributed *skewly*, as shown by the other curve with a very long tail off in the direction of the highest-paid individuals.

Actually, there is nothing particularly sacred about the so-called "normal curve." If *heights* of cubes (not people) are normally distributed, then their *volumes* will be skewed off to the right. Moreover, careful examination of census data on incomes suggests that *each kind of wage* income may tend to approximate roughly a bell-shaped distribution curve of modest symmetry. But when we add together the distributions of earnings for women as well as men, for property owners as well as workers, for lucky speculators, and other diverse groups, the great "skewness" of the whole distribution does emerge. Moreover, if we follow each wage earner over a period of years, a pattern of dispersion will emerge, one of the important factors causing differences among individuals being the different degrees of unemployment they suffer.

Perhaps a warning is in order at this point against jumping to the conclusion that there is something *necessary* and *inevitable* about this dispersion of income. Within the framework of the mixed economy, fundamental changes in education have already made significant changes in inequality. Moreover, as no one knows better than the man at the top, our system of progressive income

Anyone can climb the ladder of success, but it helps to start high:

CLASS ORIGINS OF 611 CANADIAN-BORN MEMBERS OF THE ECONOMIC ELITE	NUMBER	PER CENT
Father in economic elite	135	
Father in other elite groups (government, clergy, military, etc.)	13	
Wife from an elite family	41	50
Father in substantial business	42	
Attended private school	75	
Attended university and/or father in middle-class occupation	197	32
Probably lower than middle-class origins	108	18

TABLE 6-3. In Porter's sample, another 150 members of the elite were foreign-born. Many of them had scientific and engineering backgrounds; otherwise, their origins appeared to be much like those of the Canadian-born elite. (Source: John Porter, *The Vertical Mosaic*, Toronto: University of Toronto Press, 1965; and the *Canadian Journal of Economics and Political Science*, 1957, p. 390.)

taxation has already greatly changed the relative take-home and—what is more important—the "keep-at-home" pay of the high- and low-paid; and presumably this will continue to be an abiding feature of Canadian life, especially given recent tax revisions. However it is always subject to control by the electorate.

In particular, we must remember that the chief victims of our tolerance of inequality are members of minority groups, and "segregated" labor forces such as that of Quebec. The disabilities of these segments of our society are dealt with in Chapter 38.

ECONOMIC STRATIFICATION AND OPPORTUNITY

The New World has always been considered the land of opportunity, where anyone with ability might get ahead in the world. The success legend of Horatio Alger, Jr.'s, "poor but proud" hero who worked his way to the top and married the boss's daughter—or vice versa—has no doubt been overdrawn. But it did have elements of truth as compared with the former situation in European countries, where an aristocratic tradition lingered and where free schooling beyond the primary grades was established late in history.

For example, the "old school tie" and, more important, the correct accent were until recently almost indispensable to political and social advancement in Britain; even with the free scholarship system, few members of the lower or middle class could jump this hurdle. In this country, few people even recognize a "prep school" accent, and variations in speech are geographical rather than social. The secretary is almost indistinguishable in appearance from the blue-blood debutante.

Moreover, ours has been a rather more materialistic civilization in which success is interpreted in business terms. Because "money talks," it is easier for outsiders to break into the upper crust than it would be in a culture that puts greater emphasis upon tradition. The *nouveaux riches* of one generation may become the social arbiters of the next.

RECRUITMENT OF THE ELITE   Nevertheless, careful investigations of the social origins of the "business elite" have turned up some surprising facts. The *economic* elite of Canada was defined by John Porter to consist, in 1955, of nearly 1,000 businessmen who shared 1,300 of the 1,600 directorships of the 900 largest or most powerful corporations, and were, for the most part, managers or presidents themselves of one or more of the corporations. Typically, the member of this elite was not a poor immigrant or a farm boy, nor was he born in a slum; more likely his father was also in the elite of *his* day, was able to buy his son a good education and often to insert him directly into the family enterprise. Table 6-3, on page 157, summarizes one part of Porter's findings.

In the United States, similar studies on the "power elite" have been conducted by economists Taussig and Joslyn, by *Fortune* magazine, and by sociologist C. Wright Mills. It has been found that, of the successful American business leaders since 1928, between 60 and 70 per cent had a professional or businessman father. These general proportions have not changed radically since World War I.

Do these studies indicate that North American economic society is hardening along caste lines? Two diametrically opposite explanations of the statistics are possible:

(1) In the past there was high social mobility in Canada and the United States: all the cream rose to the top, leaving naturally less gifted people at the bottom. (2) There are strong, and perhaps growing, barriers to circulation between the economic classes.

Some economists incline to the first view, feeling that "you can't keep a good man down." Many sociologists would disagree. They would emphasize the thousand and one subtle psychological, social, economic, and educational disadvantages of the children of less fortunate families; that equal ability is not always able to give rise to equal achievement.[11]

---

[11] When the first edition of this book was written, the senior author inclined toward the view that it was becoming increasingly difficult to go from the bottom to the top. Now he is not so sure. Recent careful studies of the origins of business leaders back before 1900 suggest that the present may compare favorably with the good old days, which may not have been so good after all. Increasingly, as organizations become bigger, the elements of nepotism and personal favoritism seem to become less important, and the increasing emphasis upon civil-servant-like quasi-objective tests of performance suggests greater mobility among the elite. Perhaps we are becoming a "meritocracy."

The arithmetic of "transition probabilities" can be made to yield the following results. Divide society into two classes, so that I am either a U in the Upper class or a *non-U* in the Lower. If a child's chance to move out of his parents' class is as great as to stay in, then $\frac{1}{2}$ the children, grandchildren, great-grandchildren, and descendants generally of a U parent will be U's. But if there is social stratification so that a child has only $\frac{1}{4}$ chance of moving into a class different from his parents, $\frac{3}{4}$ $(= \frac{1}{2} + \frac{1}{4})$ of the children of U's will be U's. However, it can be deduced that only $\frac{5}{8}$ $(= \frac{1}{2} + \frac{1}{8})$ of grandchildren of U's will be U's; and only 9/16 $(= \frac{1}{2} + 1/16)$ of their great-grandchildren. Evidently, the chance of remote descendants of U's being also U's goes ultimately down to $\frac{1}{2}$, with 50 per cent of the excess above the $\frac{1}{2}$ equality level wiped out at each new generation. Hope for the *non-U*'s means despair for the U's only if a fair race is deemed a tragedy. For more on the arithmetic of transition probabilities, see W. Feller, *An Introduction to Probability* (New York: Wiley, 1957).

Whichever view is right, the implications for policy are the same. Human beings are a nation's most important form of social capital—high-yielding form, moreover, in which we have invested too little in the past. Talent, wherever it may be, is worth seeking out and nurturing. And, as it will be discussed in later chapters, equality of opportunity has not always been a feature of Canadian society. The position of minority groups in our country gives us particular cause for concern.

SUMMARY

■ 1 Incomes of the poorest today are higher than in earlier times. The belief that the poor are becoming poorer in modern industrial nations will not stand up under careful factual examination. Since the Industrial Revolution incomes and standards have been showing a definite rise.

■ 2 Incomes and standards of life in Western Europe and in North America are not only higher than in other continents, but are rising faster annually than in the underdeveloped nations.

■ 3 The median income, revealed in factual studies of the distribution of Canadian incomes, is lower than popularly believed. The differences in living standards are very great between professions and between regions.

■ 4 The Lorenz diagram is a convenient device for measuring the spreads or inequalities of income distribution. It shows what percentage of total income goes to the poorest 1 per cent of the population, to the poorest 10 per cent, to the poorest 95 per cent, and so forth. The modern distribution of Canadian income appears to be less unequal than in 1931 or than that in underdeveloped countries, but it still shows a considerable measure of inequality with little change in recent decades. An interesting question is to try to relate the skew distributions of income to the more "normal" differences in human mental and physical abilities.

■ 5 There is a strong positive correlation between income and social status of a person's parents and grandparents and his own, but the exact direction of causation is hard to establish.

■ 6 Within the affluent society the public war against poverty goes unceasingly on. As each rampart is conquered, higher standards of performance are set by society for itself. The vicious circle by which poverty is environmentally inherited has to be broken if the antipoverty war is to be won. The problems of poverty and disadvantaged minority groups will be discussed later in Chapters 38 and 39.

QUESTIONS FOR DISCUSSION

1. Let each member of the class write down on a slip of paper an estimate of his own family's income. From these, draw up a frequency table showing the distribution of incomes. What is the median income? The arithmetic mean or average income?

2. How much do you think it takes for a childless married couple to live comfortably in your community? How would the money be spent?

3. Were your parents better off than their parents? What does this suggest with respect to the advantages and disadvantages of capitalism and the modern mixed economy?

4. Formulate some of your own ethical beliefs concerning how unequal incomes should be for people of different abilities and needs. How do you justify these beliefs? Would a nineteenth-century Canadian agree? A Russian? A South Sea Islander? What would be the relevance of the U.S. Bureau of Labor Statistics report that those in the under-$1,000 income class give 3.3 per cent of their income to church and charity while those in the over-$10,000 class give 2.6 per cent?

5. Review your understanding of the following concepts:

income distribution	Lorenz curve of income and wealth
mean, median, and modal income	normal and skew distributions
per capita incomes	social stratification
minimum budget	war against poverty

7

LABOR
AND INDUSTRIAL
RELATIONS

Mr. Hennessey: *But these open-shop min say they're f'r unions.*
Mr. Dooley: *Shure, if properly conducted. No strikes, no rules, no contracts, no scales,*
hardly iny wages an' dam few mimbers. FINLEY PETER DUNNE

Almost everybody is at some time in the labor force. Half of our hours awake
are spent on the job. Earnings from work—wages, salaries, and unincorporated
earnings—constitute fully four-fifths of the total of national income. It is no
wonder that the late Sumner Slichter of Harvard said—with pardonable exaggeration— that ours is a *laboristic* rather than a capitalistic society.

This chapter surveys the important role of labor unions in Canadian life,
paving the way for the more detailed discussion of wage determination in Part
Four.

■ WHO BELONGS TO UNIONS?

About 2 million Canadians, comprising almost one-third of the nonagricultural
working force, belong to unions; most of these men are production workers.
Approximately half of the total union membership is in manufacturing, and
some of Canada's largest and most important industries are highly unionized
(for example, railroads, hauling operations, steel, automobiles, and construction).

Figure 7-1, on the next page, shows the growth of union membership since
1911: the steady advance up to World War I, the upsurge during that war and
immediately thereafter, and the rather sharp decline and levelling off during the
1920s. It shows the sudden acquisition of new members during the recovery
years following the Great Depression; the continued rapid growth during World
War II; and finally, the stagnation followed by growth of recent years.

Unionism rose slowly between the wars but accelerated in the forties and in periods of full employment:

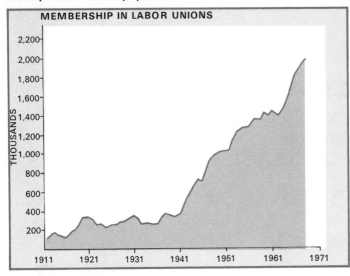

FIG. 7-1. Of nonagriculture paid workers, approximately 33 per cent belong to unions, as against 15 per cent in 1931. The recent trend has shown rapid increase in periods of high employment, in spite of forecasts of slow decline. "Automation" may retard future growth as difficult-to-organize white-collar workers supplant production workers. (Source: Department of Labour, *Labour Organization in Canada*, 1969.)

To what unions do workers belong? Here are the ten largest, with size of membership: the United Steelworkers of America (U.S.A.), 150,000; the Canadian Union of Public Employees (CUPE), 124,500; the United Automobile, Aerospace and Agricultural Implement Workers of America (UAW), 113,000; Public Service Alliance of Canada (PSAC), 96,200; the United Brotherhood of Carpenters and Joiners of America (CJA), 73,500; the International Brotherhood of Teamsters, Chauffeurs, Warehousemen and Helpers of America (TCWHA), 56,200; the International Brotherhood of Electrical Workers (IBEW), 56,000; the International Association of Machinists and Aerospace Workers (IAMAW), 52,700; the International Woodworkers of America (IWA), 49,300; and the Fédération nationale des services (Service Employees' Federation), 44,800.[1]

Most of these international unions belong to the merged American Federation of Labor-Congress of Industrial Organizations (AFL-CIO) in the United States and to the Canadian Labour Congress (CLC) in Canada. However, two of them, the Public Employees and the CBRT, are Canadian national groups (they have no American affiliation but belong only to the CLC federation); and another union, the Teamsters, following a row about corruption, became independent of both AFL-CIO and later from the CLC.

An additional 208,000 workers belong to the largely French-speaking Confederation of National Trade Unions (CNTU) which has a structure somewhat unlike that of the AFL-CIO group of unions.

---

[1] Canada Department of Labour, *Labour Organization in Canada* (Ottawa: Queen's Printer, 1969).

Statistics of memberships understate the influence of unions. Many non-union people are covered by union agreements on wages, hours, and working conditions. If you took a solemn oath never to join a union or work under a union agreement, you would have to give up all hope of being a worker in many sectors of manufacturing. You would have to give up a career in mining; in construction; in transportation. Where could you go? You could avoid unions on the farm, in domestic service, in finance, and in trade.

Besides outright trade unions, there are many organizations of professional people—like the Canadian Medical Association (CMA), to which 20,000 doctors belong, and the Canadian Association of University Teachers—which in fact are important forces lobbying for higher incomes and specified working conditions. You would be naïve to think that the CMA and similar associations are not important influences on the interplay of supply and demand, even though economic betterment is not primary in their official constitutions. Within government itself is the new frontier of unionization: policemen, postal workers, and clerks.

■ NATIONAL AND LOCAL UNIONS

There are three layers in the structure of North American unions: (1) the *local* union, (2) the *national* union (American unions with Canadian chapters are called *international* unions), and (3) the *federation* of national unions.

To a member, the *local* is the front line of unionism. He joins the local in his plant or town. He pays his dues to it. Usually, the local union signs the collective bargaining agreement determining his wages and work conditions.

But the local is only a single chapter or lodge of the national union. Thus, a linotypist in Toronto belongs to the local union located there, but this is one of hundreds of local chapters of the International Typographical Union, whose headquarters is in Colorado Springs. Part of the local dues—one-half or less, usually—goes to the national or international union; the bylaws and practice of the local cannot transcend the broad policies laid down at the national level. The president and other officers of the local are probably local workers; but the important office of business agent is a full-time job, the salary for which is often paid by the national union. The trend is increasing for the national unions to lend a hand in collective bargaining by the local.

Altogether there are about 160 national and international unions in Canada. We have seen that 10 of these have more than 40,000 members. The average national or international union has about 12,500 members; but, if we exclude the 18 largest, the average size is less than 7,000.

The number of local union chapters or lodges is no less than 8,900. Some have as few as a dozen men. A few giant locals cover thousands of men. In the United States, for example, the Ford local of the UAW in Detroit is the largest of all. It alone has 30,000 members! The vast majority of locals number from 50 to 1,000 workers, with an average membership of 200.

■ NATIONAL UNIONS AND THE FEDERATION

The AFL-CIO and the CLC are federations made up primarily of national and international unions. They are dependent upon these member national unions for financial support. Like the Big Five nations on the Security Council of the United Nations, the national unions have insisted upon their "sovereignty" and right of veto and their right to "exclusive jurisdiction" over workers in their area. Most of the headaches and fights come from such jurisdictional disputes.

The public thinks of the federation as being the most important part of the labor movement; but it is not. It acts as spokesman for labor; yet its own power is strictly limited. Thus I. W. Abel wields more real power in his capacity as head of the United Steel Workers than he does as vice-president of the AFL-CIO. Former Seafarers' boss, Hal Banks, had more to fear from government action than he did from criticisms of his union by the CLC.

As a federation the AFL-CIO strongly disapproves of union discrimination against Negroes, but has little power to act against those few U.S. member unions which still follow restrictive practices. When the Mine, Mill, and Smelter workers and other communist-dominated unions were expelled from the Canadian federation, this was considered a major step in establishing an independent role for the federation and a precedent-setting action.

Figure 7-2 gives an organization chart. Members belong to a local, which (a) belongs to a national or international union, or is a single entity directly chartered by the CLC; and (b) usually belongs to a city labor council and a provincial federation which support locals in difficult negotiations and act in labor's interest in city and provincial politics. Every international union belongs to the CLC and the AFL-CIO; Canadian national unions belong only to the CLC. These grand federations have contact with local membership largely through the nationals and internationals. (A bigger diagram would show some other boxes,

The international structure of federated unions:

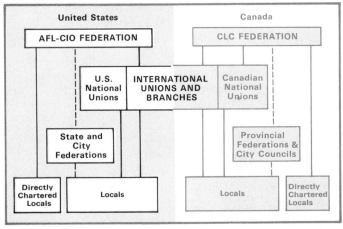

FIG. 7-2. Internationals and locals are the important units in the federations. Internationals belong to both the AFL-CIO and the CLC, and provide an essential link between them. French-Canadian members of the CNTU have no international links, but are acquiring a similar decentralized structure.

especially departments of the CLC that coordinate trades and crafts in the building industry.)

■ THE URGE TO UNIONIZE

What are the general functions of unions? They differ from the medieval guilds, which accommodated masters, craftsmen, and apprentices. Why were men tempted to form and join the new organizations?

WAGES AND WORKING CONDITIONS   In past centuries wages were low everywhere. Productivity was then low, so that no way of dividing the social pie could have given the average man an adequate slice. But workers often felt that they were at the particular mercy of the boss. They felt poor, uninformed, and helpless to hold out economically against the employer, with his greater staying power in any conflict. Shops were organized on dictatorial principles, and orders were passed down from on high; the worker was but a cog in the machine, a dehumanized robot. Such was the worker's image of the situation as revealed in historical records.

Men gradually discovered that in numbers there is strength. One hundred men acting in concert seemed to have more bargaining power than all had by acting separately. Workers began to meet in chapels and taverns. They formed fraternal societies for mutual contacts, entertainment, and discussion. Gradually such early unions began to offer mutual death benefits and various other forms of insurance, and promoted self-education. They also began to propose standard wage rates that members were to insist on getting paid.

Naturally, employers fought back. Their smaller number had always enabled them to act in concert in setting wages and working conditions, to the despair of the workers. Now they learned that strength came from formal cooperation. Each employer backed up the other and refused to hire men on the "black list" of known labor agitators. Singly and in concert they invoked the powers of the law against labor "conspiracies."[2]

We can use the supply and demand apparatus of Chapter 4 to illustrate this history. Figure 7-3, on the next page, while oversimplified, shows that workers who participate in concerted action to set standard wages must accept the consequences in changed numbers of jobs. Imagine the curves to refer to the supply and demand conditions in a particular local trade.

A strong bosses' association might refuse to pay more than $2 per hour, and a competitive supply of only 7 (thousand) workers would accept this wage. Had the market been freer, competition among masters for men and among men for jobs would have led to movement along the arrows to the equilibrium wage C, and work for 12 thousand. If instead a new union imposes a standard wage

[2] The chief weapons used by employers to fight unions were (1) discriminatory discharge of union members, (2) the blacklist, (3) the lockout, (4) the "yellow-dog" contract, (5) the labor spy, (6) the strikebreaker and armed guards, and (7) the "company union." More recently, employers have used the courts to fight against unions.

Workers and bosses set non-competitive wages:

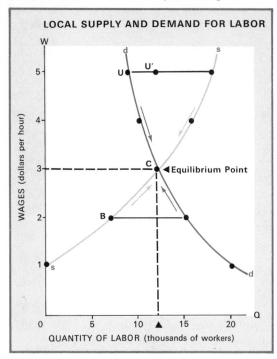

FIG. 7-3. At the C equilibrium wage, the amount of labor supplied just matches the amount demanded (jobs offered). At a lower wage B, organized bosses find only 7,000 willing workers. Alternatively, a strong union may hold the wage at $5 as long as excess unemployed workers don't offer to work for less. If they do, the union wage will collapse back to C. (A really tough union may even battle its way to U', if monopolistic bosses wish to avoid costly strikes.) (Source: Figure 4-3, with minor modifications, and Table 4-3.)

rate of $5 on unorganized employers, there would be a competitive demand for only 9 thousand members; another 9 thousand workers in excess supply at this wage would have to take jobs elsewhere, or remain unemployed.[3]

But organized workers or employers are bucking eager market forces. At $5 the excess supply of workers may lead to wage cutting back down toward C; even if the local labor force is limited, the supply curve reveals that new arrivals will be attracted by the high wage. Symmetrically, the bosses (without the union) would have difficulty holding the wage down to $2. An *excess demand* for 7 thousand men exists among employers at this bargain price, and they will each tend to shade their wage offers upward toward equilibrium C, in spite of their resolve to bargain together.

Most North American unions exist for *economic* betterment: to try to get not only higher wages, but also shorter hours, more vacations, fringe benefits such as pensions, and better working conditions. Such direct economic goals can, as in the diagram, be thought of as a form of wage, having a money cost to the employer and a money value to the worker. The formal analysis here, stemming

---

[3] A very tough union might even impose on a monopolistic group of employers an all-or-nothing bargain at U': 12 thousand jobs at $5, or shut down forever. This would probably put some weak employers out of business.

from Chapter 4 and developed fully in Chapter 28, indicates how industrial relations can be visualized. At least in part, the union attempts to operate on the employers' demand curve; the employers' association tries to work on the supply curve.

OTHER GOALS   While economic goals are the major preoccupation and reason for the existence of unions today, unions do also still perform purely social functions. Unions may back blood drives and charities, start cooperative stores, credit unions, and scholarship funds. Indeed unions may fill the lives of some members just as churches, lodges, and junior leagues occupy others. (This is not to deny that a co-worker down the line may never do more than pay his union dues; or that still another non-union worker, whose wage is nevertheless determined by collective bargaining, may detest the whole idea of organized labor.) Canadian unions, like many European and unlike most American unions, have from earlier days carried this habit of group action beyond the quest for direct benefits and self-help into politics. For example, instead of merely a neutral and dutiful interest in "civic betterment," a frequent committee activity of American unions, Canadian unions have often nominated "Labor" candidates in municipal and school-board elections. And in wider political arenas, some groupings of Canadian unions have backed various parties, just as Canadian farmers (between 1900 and 1939) backed "Progressive" and "United Farmers" parties in the provinces and at Ottawa. At an earlier stage, the unions were divided between support for the Liberal party and the radical parties of syndicalists and communists. Since the 1930s, however, there has been a trend toward increasing collective support for the participation in the CCF and its successor the NDP. But, unlike the British Trades Union Congress, the Canadian unions are apparently unable to "deliver" their members' votes effectively; the political tendencies of Canadian unionists, while stronger than those of their American brothers, have not yet shown the unanimity and devotion that carried the British Labour party and the Swedish Social-Democratic party into power.

■ ORIGIN AND GROWTH OF THE CANADIAN LABOR MOVEMENT

EARLY CRAFT UNIONS   Before Confederation, Canadian labor was organized only in a few highly skilled trades, of which type-setting was the most important. The form of organization was brought with them by British immigrant workers. Sometimes, especially in boom periods, other tradesmen (often in building— carpenters and masons—and in shoemaking) either formed similar groups or joined together in local all-trades unions.

In the 1870s this tendency was magnified by contacts with new American trade (skilled-workers) unions, and permanent affiliations were made with American "National" (usually later changed to "International") unions of iron molders, printers, and railway workers, and with one or two British building and iron-workers' societies. At the same time, as in the United States, the local branches formed interunion local committees, later known as "Trades and Labour Councils," in Toronto, Montreal, and other cities. The steady development of these craft unions continued for decades, with increasing help from and affiliation with American international bodies.

THE KNIGHTS OF LABOR   Just after Confederation, however, this development was disturbed by the rapid-spread formation of assemblies of the Noble Order of the Knights of Labor. This organization originated in the United States, where it emerged from the Populist revolt against big-business interests. Membership was open to all workers, skilled and unskilled. By 1886, the highwater mark, the Knights had some 700,000 members, more than 15,000 of them in Canada (in almost 260 locals). The Knights represented an attempt to form one great labor union to speak for all workers. This looseness spelled its death in the United States by the 1890s, but permitted its survival in Canada until almost 1910. Although the Knights sometimes toyed with the ideas of socialism, and were certainly active in political reform and agitation, their leaders were more concerned with "uplift" and further organization than with hard-headed bargaining or serious politics. Unable to make headway with industrial (all trades in one industry) bargaining, they gave way to new groups with narrower aims.

THE AFL AND THE TLC   The older craft unions, meanwhile, fighting off the Knights, built up their own memberships and began to seek forms for joint action among unions. The Trade and Labour Councils in 1886 formed what was to become the Trades and Labour Congress of Canada (TLC), just as the American craft unions (many of them parents or affiliates of the Canadian unions) were forming the American Federation of Labor (AFL). While there were many differences, the hard-core membership in both countries (printers, building trades, teamsters, and machinists) stuck to the line established by Samuel Gompers, who helped to found and dominated the AFL from 1886 till his death in 1924.

Gompers' main principles were simple:

1. He insisted on *"business unionism,"* i.e., unionism aiming at day-to-day higher wages and better working conditions, not engaging in the class struggle to alter the form of society. Labor was to get more and still more by evolution, not by violent revolution.

2. He committed the AFL to the principle of *federalism*, with each national union having autonomous sovereignty and "exclusive jurisdiction" over its craft specialty. This meant that the AFL would not tolerate "dual unionism"; two unions could not try to organize the same workers; and a group of workers could not break away from a recognized national union.

3. Finally, he insisted on *voluntarism*, with the government not to interfere in collective bargaining, either in favor of or against labor. In politics he favored rewarding labor's friends and punishing its enemies, but he would not commit labor to any one political party.

Thus, the TLC and the AFL were polar opposites of the Knights of Labor in almost every respect. As the Knights dwindled in importance, the TLC and AFL grew. Eventually the philosophy of Gompers and the AFL turned out to be the dominant philosophy of the American labor movement. But the TLC was to face not only the new ideas that further shaped the AFL, but also some of more purely Canadian foundation.

In retrospect, these Canadian influences seem to have had strong regional ties, though they often merged and clashed at the center. In the Maritime provinces, Nova Scotia's Provincial Workmen's Association was firmly based on the coal industry and up till 1917 welcomed workers from all industries while exerting a strong influence on Nova Scotia labor law. In Quebec, the clergy organized French-speaking Catholic *syndicats*, somewhat similar to the units of the Catholic labor unions then rising in France, Belgium, and Holland. The movement was intended to further the anti-individualist sentiments in Pope Leo XIII's encyclical *Rerum Novarum*. Preferring cooperation to strikes, the predominantly unskilled city workers of Montreal and Quebec and the rural primary workers set up in opposition to the older, English-speaking, Protestant craft unions. They did not form any central federation till after World War I. In view of the gentle philosophy of the *syndicats*, it is not surprising that the AFL-TLC unions whose jurisdictions they overlapped regarded them as company unions and strikebreakers.

In the West, some vigorous organizations appeared with strong syndicalist leanings. (Not to be confused with the French-Canadian *syndicats*, syndicalists were early cousins of Communists, with some anarchistic ancestors. They agreed on the need for the overthrow of capitalism, the management and ownership of each business by its workers, and, in milder form, "industrial" as opposed to "craft" unionism.) Study groups, speech-making, strikes, and violence were all parts of their program, and at their height such unions not only took over the important Vancouver and New Westminster Trades and Labour Council, but in 1919 inspired the formation of the One Big Union (OBU). This group swept the prairie provinces, captured the Winnipeg Trades and Labour Council from the TLC, and led the extraordinary Winnipeg General Strike of 1919. But by 1920 the TLC had regained most of its affiliates and the government had by strong measures enjoined, imprisoned, or exiled the more revolutionary leaders. The way was now open for the TLC to recommence its slow march towards craft recruitment, recognition as plant bargaining agent, and political action.

SLOW GROWTH IN THE TWENTIES   Whereas industrialization, full employment, urbanization, and the growth of evangelical unionism boosted the membership of unions before 1920, growth in the 1920s was very slow. Both radical and craft unions met determined opposition from employers, and the "open shop" reappeared in industries organized in the war and just after. Also, the 1920s were one of those rare periods when simultaneous high-employment and constant prices discouraged active unionism.

In the United States the craft affiliates of the AFL elected William Green to succeed Gompers, thus excluding John L. Lewis, head of the United Mine Workers, who favored the displacement of craft by industrial unions which would include all workers in a given plant or industry. This craft-versus-industrial debate was already relatively more important in Canada than in the United States, for Canada's dominant primary industries had already, under the *syndicats*, the Industrial Workers of the World (IWW), OBU, and the United Mine Workers itself, experienced the industrial approach. But this controversy was obscured in Canada by another about national versus international congresses; the 1920s and 1930s saw repeated attempts to form all-Canadian organizations, many of them around the giant Canadian Brotherhood of Railway Employees (based largely on CNR workers) which was excluded from the TLC unions because its jurisdiction clashed with the exclusive jurisdiction of an international AFL railway union. Numerous other all-Canadian alliances were tried, but by the mid-thirties all had withered, except for the CBRE-based congress. The TLC with its international craft union base stood supreme, though with depleted membership.

THE RISE OF INDUSTRIAL UNIONS   With the slow recovery period in the mid-thirties (more noticeable in the United States than in Canada) came a new era for unionism. The depression had soured the U.S. public on the slogans of the "open shop" and the "American way" (i.e., individualism rather than collective action) and had excited class antagonisms.

But within the AFL itself, the old insistence on the exclusive jurisdiction of national craft unions stood in the way of organization of the great mass-production industries. To this day the Carpenters' and Machinists' unions have never been able to settle some of their differences.

Astute observers in 1933 saw the handwriting on the wall: industrial unions were to play an important part in the future. John L. Lewis of the United Mine Workers, and other leaders formed in 1935 the Congress of Industrial Organizations (CIO). Helped by new government attitudes, legislation, and court decisions, a whirlwind campaign followed in which the important mass-production industries, such as automobiles, were organized, despite the bitter opposition of the principal companies in these industries.

In Canada, the TLC managed briefly to avoid this split, so that some old unions were associated both with the CIO in the United States and with the TLC in Canada. But the strain was too great, both for these international unions and for the TLC. In 1939-40 the CIO internationals and the CBRE (which by then had lost most of its Canadian allies) formed the Canadian Congress of Labour (CCL), a second national federation dominated by the "industrial" approach. By this time the AFL-TLC unions, too, had learned the important lesson of industrial unionism. They began to organize whole industries; but for them the craft principle remained dominant. With the exception of the Quebec federation of *syndicats*, interunion strife on the issues of craft-versus-industry and of Canadian nationalism was allowed to lapse. The war brought higher wages, full employment, and a new generation of potential members. The organizers in the two groups had their hands full keeping their members represented in bargaining.

COMMUNISM AND NATIONALISM IN UNIONS   We saw that, especially in the Canadian West, the industrial unions were much influenced by the radical leaders.

During the depressed 1930s, new-style Communists played a shifting role in union organization. For a while they attempted to set up their own labor federation, but the party line changed and organizers were told to "bore from within" the established federations. By the advent of World War II, Communist organizers had become experienced and relied-upon officers in many local and national offices; so that in 1942, with Canada and Russia now on the same side in the war, the two national federations spreading into war industries, and all of Canada (during the emergency) under the same set of labor laws, the Communists were able to field a team of experienced, self-sacrificing, able leaders.

But by the end of the war, the CCL was ready for a showdown. With the closing of the Iron Curtain in 1948-49, a change from collaboration to hostility appeared in world Communist tactics with the West. The CCL in Canada and the CIO in the United States almost simultaneously moved in on eight or nine Communist-led member unions, which were eventually expelled or reorganized under non-Communist leadership.

The TLC had a tougher time with its Communist officers and member unions. Finding them well-entrenched in its hierarchy, the AFL executive council pressed the Canadian federation to deal with the Communist-led Canadian Seamen's Union and urged that it be replaced by the Seafarers' International Union. TLC leadership saw this pressure more as a threat to the Canadian autonomy of the TLC than as a simple question of Communism. Finally, in 1949-50 the CSU was expelled, but the SIU was not welcomed; and some other Communist-led groups were cleared of Communists.

Not all expelled unions expired—some still hold scattered but important bargaining rights in various plants, though they are hard-pressed by the richer and larger internationals. Their leaders, at a time when their interests meshed well with those of the trade union movement, made a big contribution to the growth of unionism in Canada. But today, cut off from the larger federations and deprived of sympathetic American affiliates, their over-all economic influence is small and their impact on Canadian unionism almost negligible.

In the United States, public attitudes to large-scale unionism have been recently focussed more on gangsterism than on Communism. After the repeal of prohibition, corrupt gunmen worked their way into a few urban unions (e.g., the longshoremen around New York). Labor had some success in cleaning its own house; in cities with effective law enforcement, the evil of labor gangsterism is pretty well under control.

One trouble spot does remain: fraud and mismanagement of the sizable union funds are not yet completely at an end. Teamster Dave Beck got rich speculating with union funds, and other misuses of union welfare funds by Beck and later by "Jimmy" Hoffa have been turned up by congressional investigating committees. Because Teamster members believed "Jimmy delivers the goods for us," Hoffa remained in control even after the courts found him guilty.

Stirred by public revelations of graft, Congress overcame labor opposition and passed the Labor-Management Reporting and Disclosure (Landrum-Griffin) Act (1959). Among other things, this requires filing of union financial reports, limits union loans to officials to $2,000, and prohibits nonwage payments by employers to union representatives. The Act also provides a "Bill of Rights" for union members, which guards against rigged elections and summary disciplining of members by the union.[4]

UNIONISM IN THE 1970s   By the mid-1960s, Canadian unionism had been shaken up again. The slow and reluctant reunification of the AFL and CIO in the United States was matched in 1956 by a more eager joining of the TLC and the CCL into a grand federation now called the Canadian Labour Congress (CLC). It consists of 94 international unions, dominated by the 150,000-member United Steelworkers of America; 21 national unions, dominated by the Canadian Union of Public Employees with almost 124,500 members and the old CBRE (now the CBRT) with 34,800 members; and 143 directly chartered local unions with an average of about 110 members each. Unlike the united AFL-CIO in the United States, its federation constitution contains no ban on "dual" unionism; but the fact that 80 per cent of its membership is affiliated with international unions indicates that many jurisdictional overlaps will be straightened out in the United States before conflicts arise in Canada.

But this grand federation still has no connection with almost one-fifth of Canadian organized labor (CLC: 1.6 million members; all unions: 2.0 million). The largest "independent" is the Teamsters Union with its ubiquitous offshoots into milk-delivery and car-salesmanship. Altogether there are nearly 190,000 unaffiliated members of national and international groups, from the ultra-conservative railway brotherhood of conductors to the Communist-led west-coast fishermen and Mine, Mill, and Smelter workers.

Potentially more important is the Quebec federation of *syndicats*, now wholly reorganized and revitalized as the Confederation of National Trade Unions (CNTU). It now has 12 national unions, 50 one-shot locals, and about 201,000 members altogether; however, many (perhaps most) French-speaking Catholic workers belong to the CLC unions (including the CLC president, Claude Jodoin).

During the resurgence of Quebec in the 1950s, attention was directed to the much lower level of wages and working conditions in Quebec than in Ontario, to the militant and skillful tactics of the CCL-TLC organizers in Quebec industries, and to the tougher practice of Catholic unions in Europe. New aggressive leaders bargained and led bloody strikes (often with clergy support), and a format closer to that of the rest of the North American labor movement was adopted. In 1956 the CNTU came within an ace of joining the CLC. But, influenced by spreading Quebec nationalism, its members decided to go it alone as a second federation in Canada.

---

[4] There are few reported instances of gangsterism or fraud in Canada. Spokesman Eugene Forsey's explanation: ". . . our criminal law is national, so that the thief cannot play hop, skip, and jump from province to province . . . all our judges are appointed by the national government, . . . so that there is no chance of influencing them through local political machines. The thief has little to gain, and is almost certain to be caught, and promptly and severely punished." (Eugene Forsey, "U.S. Labour Organizations and Canadian Labour," reprinted in Watkins and Forster, eds., *Economics: Canada*, Toronto, McGraw-Hill, 1963, p. 266.)

By 1965, Communism in unions was seldom discussed in Canada, but Canadian nationalism was still a strong issue. Employers, strikebound by international unions, still pointed to the strike funds pouring into the local from American treasuries. The French-Canadian labor movement made much of both Canadian and Quebec nationalism. And in jurisdictional matters it has been claimed that national groups have no chance of survival against the powerful American groups.

Probably, though, the discussion of "foreign domination" serves mainly to obscure an urgent internal economic question. By having the scattered 2 million Canadian organized labor force grouped into 4,500 locals, most of them duplicates of locals in the United States, plus some 2,700 locals of Canadian groups, Canadian labor, like Canadian business, finds itself overorganized. There are not enough members (at an average of about 285 members per local) to undertake the leadership, bargaining, research, and political action required for the movement to flourish. Instead, hundreds of small meetings every month monopolize the time and funds of local leaders. Probably larger groups covering greater portions of industry and larger regions are indicated, but there are few signs that such regrouping is coming about. In the meantime the conservative bias of most unions, the vested interest of local officials in their positions, and the inability of the unions to adapt advantageously to technical change and automation are the result. (Canadian examples: the railway firemen's frantic efforts to prevent the abolition of their jobs in diesel locomotives, and the strikes, both in Canada and the United States, of typographers and longshoremen resisting the adoption of labor-saving techniques.)

After a long history of strike, the union movement in North America seems to have settled down, with only a few, though large, industrial sectors to be organized. Their success may be measured by the extent to which a new breed of man moves to the top. Back in the days when unions were being born and fighting for their lives, colorful men such as John L. Lewis were the leaders. The new men who are replacing them are often educated men with gifts as *administrators*. With millions of members and literally hundreds of millions of dollars in their welfare funds, North American unions are in need of men who can administer, who can deal persuasively with Parliament and Congress, with management, and with the public, and who can understand some of the larger issues involved. For the traditional union organizer, an important function still exists. Cesar Chavez' grape growers and the postal workers of Montreal bear witness to the need for organizing unions among the restless unskilled workers and among the civil servants and teachers.

■ HOW DEMOCRATIC ARE UNIONS?

Earlier we discussed the problems involved in democratic control by stockholders of corporation management. Similar problems arise in connection with unions. It is true that union officials are elected to office and all union members are given equal votes. But officers once elected often stay in power for a considerable time, and between annual conventions the union is usually run by a small executive board. Men such as Donald McDonald, Jean Marchand, and the late Walter Reuther have on the whole been popular with members; but if a member disagreed with the general policies laid down by such leaders he might not get very far.

The average union member does not participate very actively in policy formation. However, according to the late Sumner Slichter, who must still be regarded as one of the most astute students of the American labor movement:[5]

> "This does not mean the rank and file lack influence. Their influence is great, but influence is not participation. If democracy simply means strong rank and file influence, most unions are democratic. The typical situation in a union is similar to that found in most organizations, churches, and clubs of all sorts. There is a minority which is sufficiently interested in the affairs of the organization to attend business meetings and to participate actively in discussing problems. In the case of unions this minority usually asks the officers to press for stiff demands—stiffer than employers would be willing to grant without a long fight, stiff enough to force many employers out of business. In order to avoid trouble, the great majority of the union would settle for much less than the active minority demands.
>
> "Quite naturally the professional leader feels on the spot. If he disappoints the active minority too deeply, his leadership will be challenged. If he gets the inactive majority into too much trouble, he may provoke revolt also. He compromises, as, of course, he must. Usually he is more interested in placating the active minority that the inactive majority because he knows that the support or opposition of the active members is more important than the support or opposition of the inactive members. The record shows that union officials lose their jobs, not for being too radical for the majority, but for being too conservative for the minority."

■ HOW COLLECTIVE BARGAINING WORKS

Let us examine how collective bargaining is carried on.[6] Consider a production-line worker in a factory that has just been organized. A CLC union has petitioned its provincial Labour Relations Board for an election to determine the exclusive bargaining agent in this plant. The worker marks a secret ballot in favor of the union, and it wins more votes than an existing so-called "company union" which has no outside affiliations and which management prefers to deal with. The board then certifies the new union as the collective bargaining agent for the plant, limiting any other union from negotiating directly with management.[7]

A day is set for the new union representatives to meet representatives of management at the bargaining table. Seated at the table may be a vice-president in charge of industrial relations, and perhaps with him a lawyer who specializes in the labor field. On the union side will be the local business agent of the union and a small committee of union officers; and, sometimes, handling the negotia-

---

[5] S. H. Slichter, *The Challenge of Industrial Relations* (Ithaca, N.Y.: Cornell University Press, 1947), p. 111.

[6] Chapter 28 includes a more analytical discussion of the collective bargaining process.

[7] Actually about half-a-million workers come under federal, rather than provincial, arrangements.

tions will be an expert from international union headquarters. He may be neither a lawyer nor a professional economist, but the economic research staff of the union helps him prepare an extensive brief backing up the union's demands.

Hourly wage rates are not the only issue in bargaining. In addition, the union may ask for a dues "checkoff" (whereby union dues are automatically deducted from the payroll of union members). The union may bargain for a "union shop," requiring all employees to become union members within 30 days after employment. Pension and health-insurance demands may be discussed at the bargaining table. In many industries where piece rates prevail, the structure of rates is an important subject for negotiation; the exact work load—how many looms each man will attend, and similar matters—may be discussed, and the general problem of how rapidly technological improvements shall be adopted will enter into the final contract. The seniority rights of workers and a grievance procedure for handling cases of discharge—these and many other problems will come into collective bargaining.

Indeed, management has become worried over the inroads that organized labor has been trying to make into what it regards as its prerogatives. Many employers claim they can no longer run their businesses the way they feel is best. They find it hard to hire whom they will, fire for just cause, determine work methods, and decide on the order in which people will be laid off. They feel that every new decision occasions a meeting of a new committee; and time that could better be spent on production must be devoted to labor relations. They claim the worker acts as if he has a right to any job he has held for some time. Such critics complain that many unions oppose incentive wage schemes, insist upon rigid seniority, discourage efficient work methods, and seriously limit the autonomy of management. A recent casebook on collective bargaining devotes more space to issues arising from the workers' rights in jobs than to any other single subject.

But at last the agreement, covering many pages of fine print, is signed. Everything is set down in black and white, including provisions for grievances that arise during the life of the contract; usually, too, there are provisions for the *arbitration* of issues that arise under it, each side agreeing in advance to accept the decision of an impartial outside arbitrator. The usual life of an agreement is one or more years, no strikes being allowed, with provisions made for reopening negotiations for a new agreement under specified conditions.

Collective bargaining is a complicated business—a matter of give and take. And many businessmen recognize the grain of realism in the statement by Philip Murray, who headed the CIO.[8]

"Employers generally get the kind of labor relations they ask for. If the unions indulge in 'excesses,' then the employer as a rule has no one but himself to blame

[8] P. Murray and M. L. Cooke, *Organized Labor and Production* (New York: Harper, 1940), pp. 259-260.

for it. For instance, if he engages the services of labor espionage agencies such as the Railway Audit, Pinkerton's or others, if he stocks up his plant with tear gas, hand grenades, submachine guns, blackjacks, rifles, and other implements of war, if he hires high-priced Wall Street lawyers to harass the union before the Labor Board and in the courts, if he distributes to his foremen anti-union literature and lets it be known to them that any harm they can do to the union would be forgiven by him, if he contributes to anti-labor organizations such as the notorious Johnstown Citizens' Committee, if he quibbles over words, if he refuses to consent to an election or to sign a contract when he knows the union has a majority, if after a contract has been forced from him he delays and hampers the settlements of grievances, if he continues to discriminate against union members, then labor will answer in kind and nine out of ten businessmen, viewing it from afar, will say, 'Ah, another excess.' "

Murray's 1940 explanation of unrest as a reaction to employer unresponsiveness is today widely accepted. But there are other clues to the incidence of restlessness. Wherever workers must perform according to decisions made elsewhere, in narrow conditions of work which they cannot understand or choose, the results are wild-cat strikes and bad relations with the employer and within the union itself. In discussing this alienation and discontent of individual workers, the recent Task Force on Industrial Relations commented:

". . . The collective bargaining process may be compounding the situation by subjecting workers to a new but equally frustrating type of subordination. While improving the worker's status *vis-à-vis* his employer, collective bargaining has trapped him in a collective set of rules and regulations which can contain him even more. Individualism can be sacrificed as easily in a bilateral system of industrial government as in a unilateral one. Workers may thus come to rebel not only against their employer and their work, but also against the very agent and process which have been introduced to protect their interests."[9]

Under these circumstances, it is obvious that even well-intentioned managements may still be faced by unhappy workers and militant union officers acting as "managers of discontent." But most union-management situations, in the long run are more evenly balanced. Responsive employer behavior produces a responsible and flexible union leadership, and in most industries a successful pattern of fruitful cooperation. For the country as a whole, it is a rare year that strikes have wasted as much as one-quarter of one per cent of available working time—and many industries steadily do much better than this.[10]

This record does not mean that peace is maintained when the management or the union is soft. Hard bargaining on both sides is likely to accompany a good management-labor relationship; apathy on both sides or one-sided dominance postpones solutions and leads to breakdowns. In healthy cases, each side has a respect for the rights of the other. The two sides are not in love, but they are compatible.

---

[9] *Canadian Industrial Relations*, Report of the Task Force on Industrial Relations (Ottawa: Queen's Printer, 1969), p. 98. Reproduced with the permission of Information Canada.

[10] Canada, compared with other countries, tends to have fewer but longer strikes. This may reveal striking flaws in our systems of bargaining; irreconcilable differences about conditions and power; or just easy private and public adjustment to work stoppages.

■ ROLE OF GOVERNMENT IN COLLECTIVE BARGAINING

Although unions are relatively free in this country in comparison with their control in collectivist countries, government has played an important role in their historic development. Two hundred years ago, when labor first tried to organize in England and America, the common-law doctrines against conspiracy in restraint of trade were used against their members. Well into this century, unions and their members were convicted by courts, assessed for damages, and harrassed by various injunctive procedures.

Parliament initially adopted a similar antagonism to measures that would have improved working conditions for women and children and to reforms involving hours and wage rates. In the following paragraphs is recorded the development of government's role in collective *bargaining*. But it should be noted that, since the nineteenth century the provinces and Ottawa have been active in passing legislation on working conditions, or what labor economists call labor standards. By 1885 there were some "factory Acts" controlling women's and children's labor: boys under 14 and girls under 18 could not be employed more than 10 hours a day or 60 hours a week. From this unadventurous beginning there emerged laws regulating hours, safety, minimum-pay, Sunday-work, fresh-air, workmen's compensation, and apprentice protection, to comprise one of the most diverse systems in the world, though hardly as complete as the "laboristic" economies of Scandinavia, New Zealand, or the United Kingdom. In Canada most of these standards have followed prevailing industrial practice, making available to more workers the gains already won in union-organized sectors rather than preceding them. But these minimum standards have, of course, changed the environment in which each decade's negotiators have argued and bargained.

In the nineteenth century, the problem for unions was to obtain recognition from employers, so that they might bargain, without at the same time becoming either a "conspiracy in restraint of trade," vulnerable to criminal proceedings, or a legal entity like a corporation open to injunctions and civil suits for damages by outraged employers. After very slow development (far behind the United Kingdom) through the nineteenth century, in 1892 Canadian criminal law finally removed the obstacles to employees combining and making agreements (with employers) "in restraint of trade." The civil recognition of unions appeared slowly, and is still in the process of development. In Canada and the United States, a maze of "labor law" exists providing for union and management conduct at every stage of industrial relations, further complicated in Canada by the relatively minor role of the federal government (as compared with the provincial governments) in labor matters.

THE IDI ACT   In 1907, Mackenzie King, then Deputy-Minister of Labour in Ottawa, created the Industrial Disputes Investigation Act (IDI Act).[11] In the

---

[11] King had examples from which to work, of course. The provinces had attempted to set up *voluntary* conciliation machinery earlier. King and others had applied similar machinery to railway disputes in 1900. The whole idea, including elements of compulsion, stemmed from an early New South Wales statute.

next sixty years, Ottawa and the provinces were to make many experiments with labor law, but the IDI principles were everywhere clearly visible. In brief, this Act replaced informal or nonexistent labor relations with a compulsory sequence of meetings between union and management before a board. Until this sequence of investigation was completed, the right to strike was suspended. Compared with the previous situation, and the legal routes being followed by other countries, this Act is unique:

1. In compelling employers to meet the union before a board, it implied *recognition* of the union.
2. It carried out a general belief of King's that *investigation and publicity* would help remedy any wrong or dispute.
3. Contrary to U.K. and U.S. ideas of that time, it embodied the principle that strikes and lockouts were *against the public interest*, so that the public was justified in intervening in a "private" argument.

The IDI Act was a Dominion measure, and it applied only to industries (like railroads and shipping) not under provincial jurisdiction. But between its passage in 1907 and 1925, it broadened in coverage until most of the organized workers in Canada came directly under it. Following an adverse Ontario court decision in 1925, till 1939 most union negotiation was governed by a kaleidoscopic variety of provincial laws, all basically variants of the old Dominion 1907 IDI Act.

THE INFLUENCE OF THE WAGNER ACT   After their own experiments with railroad labor law, and with the abolition of the use of the injunction as an employer weapon against unions (1926 and 1932), the architects of the U.S. New Deal designed the National Labor Relations Act (Wagner Act), which was passed in 1935 and approved by the Supreme Court in 1937. Along with the compulsory negotiation philosophy of the old IDI Act, the Wagner Act was to become one of the two main influences in the shaping of Canadian law on labor matters. It stated bluntly: "Employees shall have the right to self-organization, to form, join, or assist labor organizations, to bargain collectively through representatives of their own choosing, and to engage in concerted activities, for the purpose of collective bargaining or other mutual aid or protection" (Sec. 7). Moreover, it set up the National Labor Relations Board (NLRB) to make sure that employers do not engage in "unfair labor practices" against labor.[12] The NLRB also goes into plants and holds elections to see what organization is to be regarded as the collective bargaining representative for all the workers. It can, and does, issue "cease and desist orders" against employers, enforceable by the courts after appeal; and it often makes employers reinstate with back pay employees unjustly discharged.

---

[12] The term "unfair labor practices" as used in the Wagner Act was a broad one referring to employers' activities that interfere with employees' rights to self-organization. Examples of such employer practices are (1) firing men for joining a union, (2) refusing to hire men sympathetic to unions, (3) threatening to close an establishment if employees join a union, (4) interfering with or dominating the administration of a union, or (5) refusing to bargain with the employees' designated representatives. NOTE: Workers had various rights to organize, but legislation of the 1930s explicitly encouraged and expanded those rights.

In 1937-39, various Canadian provinces began to put these Wagner principles into their labor acts. The British Columbia 1937 law, for example,

> "combined in one statute, for the first time in Canada, the new American policy on compulsory bargaining with the old Canadian policy on compulsory dispute settlement. The right of employers and employees to organize for any lawful purpose was recognized. Intimidation or loss of employment to prevent persons from joining an association or becoming an officer were prohibited, as was the 'yellow dog' contract which made it a condition of work that the employee would not join a union. Employers were required to negotiate with the representatives of employees. Added to this was a system of a compulsory conciliation patterned, with modifications, after the Dominion IDI Act."[13]

Between 1939 and 1947, the federal government, under its wartime emergency powers, resumed legal jurisdiction over labor matters. At first it resumed an IDI-type policy; but in 1944, under the famous PC 1003, it brought in for the whole country both compulsory recognition and bargaining, and compulsory conciliation meetings with government officers and in three-party boards. The strike was, as always in Canadian legislation, banned both during the period of a contract and during the period of negotiation and conciliation.

When the wartime emergency ended, in 1947, the provinces adapted the PC 1003 system to their various regions and problems. For the most part, the IDI-plus-Wagner mixture remains, but most of these have added their own ingredients. Some of these ingredients are from the U.S. Taft-Hartley Act of 1947 which reversed somewhat the favorable position of unions over employers in collective bargaining. Like it, some Canadian acts make unions liable to suits, forbid secondary boycotts and sympathetic strikes, and ban the "closed shop" —an arrangement where the employer must take new employees from among union members.

Most provinces and the Dominion now have labor relations boards, whose chief job is to certify groups as the union with whom an employer or group of employers must bargain. Thus they have to decide on sticky questions: should machinists at a mine be represented by a machinists' union, or by the industrial union that claims jurisdiction over the whole mine, including muckers, cooks, and truck drivers? Such boards also often take votes to ascertain the workers' wishes on a bargaining unit, and also to define their attitude to striking during bargaining. Provinces also have compulsory *conciliation*, sometimes superintended by the labor relations board. In nearly all provinces, striking is forbidden (1) during the life of an agreement,[14] and (2) until some mediation and concilia-

---

[13] H. D. Woods and Sylvia Ostry, *Labour Policy and Labour Economics in Canada* (Toronto: Macmillan, 1962), p. 59.

[14] This no-strike feature has long been a distinct part of Canadian labor law. Disagreements during the life of a contract are usually about the interpretation of the contract: seniority rules for promotion, firing and re-hiring after a close-down; unfair dismissal; whether a worker comes into one pay class or a higher one. They are invariably settled by an *arbitrator*, a mixture of investigator and judge, appointed jointly by the union and management, or sometimes by the government. In a few industries, arbitrators also take the place of conciliators, if the parties cannot agree on a new contract. But the essence of arbitration is that, unlike conciliation, both parties agree in advance to accept the arbitrator's ruling.

tion procedure has been followed. Now, though, IDI-type formal conciliation boards are no longer compulsory, and the parties can proceed to a strike vote or lockout.

> In Quebec a rather different system is followed. Briefly, it provides that wages and hours of work agreed upon by workers and employers in a region's industry are "extended." That is, the government "decrees" that these conditions shall be obligatory for similar firms in that district. In operation since 1934, this is actually a non-Parliamentary way of setting labor standards, since the decreed wage now amounts to a minimum wage, at least for that industry.

> Other minimum labor standards, for hours of work, minimum wages, safety in mines, factories and railways, statutory holidays, employment of women and children, workmen's compensation, and so forth, have both in Quebec and in the other provinces been gradually built up in laws since the first Factory Acts in the 1880s. These have replaced the "freedom" of employees to respect such conditions by quitting. They also replaced a rather feeble right of workers to sue employers for damages resulting from industrial injuries.

An unresolved problem for Canadians is the organization of civil servants and other public employees. These workers and the public long believed that it was against the public interest to allow strikes to interfere with the conduct of essential Crown functions, ranging from fighting in a war (where a strike is called mutiny) to putting out fires. But the extension of Crown functions to running railroads led to the organizing of some government employees, and the growth of urban functions led to the organizing of municipal workers. (So that the CUPE and the PSAC are composed chiefly of public employees.) Now teachers, postmen, and Ottawa's white-collar workers are organized, and the civil service commissions are beginning to act like management in collective bargaining. Indeed, *de facto* collective bargaining is proceeding everywhere among public workers, and only the legal form and the right to strike are in doubt. In this respect, Canada is like most European countries, but quite unlike the United States.

■ CURRENT BARGAINING PROBLEMS

The key issues facing Canada and other nations in the 1970s are these:

1. Organized labor tries to improve its money wage rates, in the hope that this will not induce a commensurate rise in prices leaving *real wages* little or no better off. Because the strike is labor's ultimate bargaining weapon, and the right to refuse a wage increase even though this brings on a strike is the employer's ultimate weapon, work stoppages provide the headlines in labor relations.

2. In an age of rapid technical change and much talk of "automation," union men are often more concerned about *job security* than about mere money wage gains. What good is a raise in pay for a job that no longer exists?

3. Modern mixed economies seem to be subject to a new disease—a tendency for anything like an approach to full employment to lead to "creeping inflation."

STRIKES   The power to strike is central to present-day collective bargaining. This power is exercised sparingly. Figure 7-4 shows that the loss of manhours as a

Work stoppages were most serious just after the war:

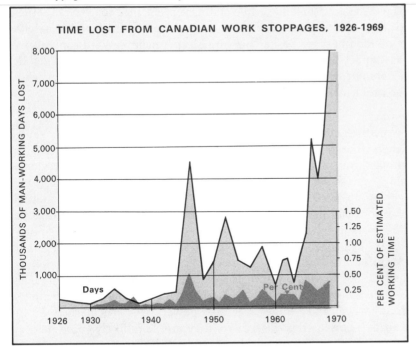

TIME LOST FROM CANADIAN WORK STOPPAGES, 1926-1969

FIG. 7-4. While time lost from strikes is measured in thousands of man-working days, as a per cent of total labor-days worked, it has reached over one-half of one per cent only once and has averaged .18 per cent for the period 1945-1966. (Source: Urquhart and Buckley, *Historical Statistics of Canada*, **Cambridge University Press, 1965;** *Monthly Review of Business Statistics*; **DBS No. 11-003,** *Canadian Statistical Review*; **and Canadian Department of Labour, Economics and Research Branch,** *Strikes and Lockouts in Canada, 1967.*)

result of strikes is growing at a rate smaller than the growth of the labor force. Indeed, the common cold causes more lost work than strikes do.

In Chapter 28 we shall see that, without the right to strike, a union's power to bargain would, for better or worse, be substantially altered. Although striking workers suffer heavy losses and demoralization, the strike or the power to call a strike can wring concessions from very tough employers. Yet many employers have been willing to risk the financial and trade losses of a shutdown, and have thus resisted union demands without a strike.

When strikes involve key industries (such as steel) or key functions (such as the railroads or shipping) or take place on a nation-wide scale in an important sector of the economy, the public interest becomes paramount. Two men are not free to engage in a fight if it does harm to other people. Just as the rights of private property and of personal freedoms are not absolute and must be reconciled when they come into conflict with the rights of others and of the public generally, so too must the rights of "free collective bargaining" be subject to limitation and coordination with social necessities.

These are not academic questions, as the Montreal Police strike of 1969 evidences. In fact, the governments, while stating a preference for private settlement, will not let a crippling strike persist beyond the point of public safety. British Columbia (and perhaps Saskatchewan) is experimenting with compulsory arbitration—at cabinet discretion. The unionization of public and quasi-public workers—teachers, air controllers, firefighters, police, and defense employees— accentuates the problem of avoiding pivotal work stoppages.

PRODUCTIVITY RESTRAINTS   Unions become especially concerned when new techniques or processes threaten the job security of their members. The word "sabotage" arose when laborers threw their wooden shoes (sabots) into the works of the new machines brought in by the Industrial Revolution to replace workers. "Featherbedding" refers to any rules imposed on employers merely for the purpose of keeping up the demand for workers: use of small shovels, limitation on number of bricks laid per day, requirement that use of music recordings be accompanied by a stand-by orchestra that does nothing but draw pay, requirement of a fireman (i.e., coal shoveler) on a diesel engine under the pretense that he is needed for safety reasons.

Entrenched unions have power to enforce uneconomical makeshifts. The railroads have been a flagrant example. As Chapter 28 will show, there are limits on how much unions can raise wages, but their powers are particularly great in connection with dying industries. Elsewhere, they are more likely to be helpful in the orderly introduction of improved production techniques.

WAGE-COST CREEPS   Repeatedly we shall be discussing the problems involved in inflation. Few modern countries have been able for long to enjoy simultaneously (1) reasonably full employment and (2) reasonably stable price levels. Part of the difficulty will be found to arise in the realm of monetary and fiscal policy. Part may come from a tendency for wage rates to be sticky against downward adjustments, but only too prone to rise in excess of productivity improvements even before full employment is approached.

Some of this wage pressure seems to be associated with our system of free collective bargaining. In good times workers ask for, and get, steady wage increases. Unsuccessful strikes only slow down the process. Under voluntary or compulsory arbitration the chances are not even that the rate will be raised or be cut; the rate is almost sure to be raised. It appears cheaper for all directly concerned to buy labor peace by granting wage awards which average more than is compatible with steady prices. In the words of the 1969 Report of the Task Force on Industrial Relations:

> "Collective bargaining is meant to serve the economic and related interests of those who choose to make use of it, and not necessarily those of society as a whole. Although these two sets of interests may at times coincide, they may also conflict. Unrealistic expectations about the relationship between collective bargaining and the attainment of society's economic objectives should be avoided."[15]

---

[15] *Canadian Industrial Relations*, Report of the Task Force on Industrial Relations Ottawa: Queen's Printer, 1969), p. 112. Reproduced with the permission of Information Canada.

SUMMARY

■ 1   Labor unions occupy an important but not expanding role in our economy, in terms both of membership and of influence. Their present structure is in three layers: (*a*) local unions, (*b*) national and international unions, and (*c*) federation of unions (CLC and CNTU), the first two being the most important.

■ 2   By the 1880s, the typical pattern of federated, gradualistic business unionism had been established. Since 1933, the CIO and finally the AFL have modified the pattern in the direction of *industrial* unionization of whole mass-production industries rather than relying solely upon *craft unionization* of skilled workers. Political activity has fluctuated.

■ 3   Union *economic goals* can be represented and analyzed in supply-and-demand terms.

■ 4   After a union has been recognized by a Labour Board as the exclusive bargaining agent, management and labor representatives meet together to negotiate a contract fixing wage rates, work conditions, productivity standards, degree of union recognition, seniority rights, and grievance procedures.

■ 5   In 1907 the IDI Act established the Canadian system of compulsory conciliation before the right to strike.

■ 6   Right up until the middle 1930s there was bitter opposition to unions. But finally, the pendulum of government swung to support of collective bargaining, and since the principles of the Wagner Act (1935) were woven into federal and provincial laws, most primary and manufacturing industries have become partly unionized. The result has been easier organization but still vigorous collective bargaining between the opposing groups. After 1947 the provinces felt the laws had become one-sided in favor of labor and gradually changed the balance. Strike threats in crucial industries always invoke governmental action.

■ 7   Aside from strikes and featherbedding, a major post-World War II problem has been the relation of wage increases to the price level. If patterns of "successive rounds of general wage increases" are established that go far beyond the 2 or 3 per cent yearly increase in productivity, then the price level is almost sure to rise in an inflationary manner and "cost-push" inflation will become a serious problem—as we shall see in Chapter 40.

QUESTIONS FOR DISCUSSION

1.   Describe the structure of organized labor. Describe the layers of the union movement. Which are the largest unions in your locality?

2.   Until the middle 1930s, American and Canadian unions followed the "craft" principles associated with Samuel Gompers. What are these? How have they been modified since the 1930s? What factors explain why Canadian labor has been more active in politics than American labor, but less active than European labor?

3. Give some contrasting examples of peaceful collective bargaining and of collective bargaining that was followed by *compulsory* arbitration. Also give some contrasting examples of collective bargaining that is (*a*) local, (*b*) nationwide, and (*c*) international.

4. Describe the swing of the pendulum in the attitude of legislatures and courts toward organized labor before and after the IDI Act.

5. Should policemen have the right to strike? Postmen? Milkmen? Anyone?

6. "Wage rates tend to be sticky as far as downward moves are concerned." Why might this be increasingly true? Interpret the phrase "inflationary wage-cost push."

7. Review your understanding of the following concepts:

national and local union	strike, lockout, work stoppage
CLC and CNTU federations	labor relations boards,
UAW, USA, CBRT	conciliation, arbitration
collective bargaining	IDI, Wagner Acts
business versus revolutionary	featherbedding
unionism	wage-cost push on prices
craft versus industrial unions	automation and occupational trends
excess supply and	
excess demand	

8

THE ECONOMIC ROLE OF GOVERNMENT: EXPENDITURE, REGULATION, AND FINANCE

Democracy is the recurrent suspicion that more than half the people are right more than half the time.   E. B. WHITE

Government plays an increasing role in the modern mixed economy. This is reflected in the quantitative growth of government expenditure, of redistribution of income by government, and of direct regulation of economic life. So in this chapter we survey government expenditure. In the next chapter we survey government taxation and provincial and local finance. In Part Six we analyze government's role in the fight against poverty and inequality and against environmental blight.

■ THE GROWTH OF GOVERNMENT EXPENDITURE

Before World War I, federal, provincial, and municipal government expenditure amounted to little more than one-tenth of our whole national income. During World War II, it became necessary for the government to consume about half of the nation's greatly expanded total output. Within half a century, the cost of all government in Canada rose from half a billion dollars spent in 1913 to more than 21 billion dollars per year in the early 1970s.

For more than a century, Canadian income and production have been rising. At the same time, in almost all countries and cultures, the trend of governmental expenditure has been rising even faster. Each period of emergency —each war, each depression—expands the activity of government. After each emergency is over, expenditures never seem to go back to previous levels.

Nor is the end in sight. Government expenditure receded from its wartime peak, but it was still far in excess of its prewar level of less than 800 million

Are government spending and debt growing faster than national output?

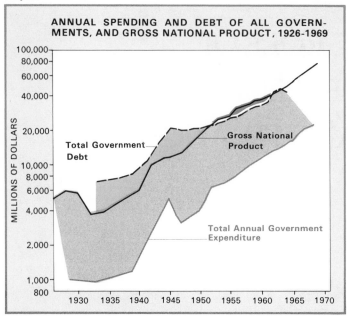

ANNUAL SPENDING AND DEBT OF ALL GOVERN-
MENTS, AND GROSS NATIONAL PRODUCT, 1926-1969

FIG. 8-1. Government expenditure and debt are those of the three levels of government combined (including school boards). Note the relative trends. This is a "ratio" or "semilog" chart, with vertical distances reflecting percentage changes. Thus steepness of slope measures percentage rate of increase. (Source: O. J. Firestone, *Canada's Economic Development 1867-1953*, **London: Bowes & Bowes, Ltd., 1956; DBS; Public Accounts.**)

dollars, which used to be considered alarmingly high. In the years ahead, regardless of which political party holds office, the upward trend seems likely to continue.

Figure 8-1 shows the historical trend of total government expenditure and combined government debts relative to the growth of gross national product. And Table 8-1 points up the fact that rich countries tend, relatively, to spend

Government share of national product is biggest in wealthy, developed countries:

GOVERNMENT RECEIPTS AS PERCENTAGES
OF GROSS NATIONAL PRODUCT, 1970

DEVELOPED COUNTRIES	RECENT AVERAGE TAX, PER CENT	LESS DEVELOPED COUNTRIES	RECENT AVERAGE TAX, PER CENT
Sweden	41	India	13
France	39	Spain	12
West Germany	35	Colombia	11
United Kingdom	33	Philippines	11
Canada	29	Mexico	10
United States	29	Jamaica	9
Switzerland	22	Nigeria	9
Japan	20	Afghanistan	6

TABLE 8-1. Governments of poor, underdeveloped countries show a persistent tendency to tax and spend less, relative to national product, than do those of more advanced countries. With higher income comes greater interdependence and less need to spend on private necessities. (Source: First National City Bank of New York; IMF; authors. Data include all tax and nontax receipts of all levels of government.)

more on government than do poor countries. (Also refer back to Fig. 2-4, page 27.)

These are the facts about public finance. Some may deplore them; some may approve of them—but there they are. They make clear the increasingly important economic role of government.

Note that mixed economies, such as Sweden, France, and (supposedly *laissez-faire*) Germany spend relatively more on government. And these happen to be the kinds of nations which have shown the greatest growth and progress in recent decades. Contrary to the "law" enunciated by Australia's Colin Clark —that taxing more than 25 per cent of GNP is a guarantee of quick disaster— the modern welfare state has been both humane and solvent.[1]

■ THE GROWTH OF GOVERNMENT CONTROLS AND REGULATION

The increase in collective expenditure is only part of the story. Besides larger direct participation by government in national production, there has been a vast expansion in its laws, regulations, and executive fiats governing economic affairs.

Perhaps the North American frontier in the nineteenth century came as close as any economy ever has to that state of *laissez-faire* which Carlyle called "anarchy plus the constable." The result was a century of rapid material progress and an invironment of individual freedom. There were also periodic business crises, wasteful exhaustion of irreplaceable natural resources, extremes of poverty and wealth, corruption of government by vested interest groups, and at times the supplanting of self-regulating competition by monopoly.

No longer does modern man seem to act as if he believed "That government governs best which governs least." Gradually, and in the face of continuing opposition, the powers of government were interpreted broadly and used to "secure the public interest" and to regulate the economic system. In the United States, after 1890 the Sherman Antitrust Act and other laws were invoked against monopolistic combinations in "restraint of trade." The U.S. federal government exercised national controls over railroads, food and drugs, banking, and high finance (through the Securities and Exchange Commission, or SEC, especially after the crash of 1929).

But in 1867, Canada had less to regulate than did the United States. Moreover, at this point, neither the authorities in Westminster (who still favored *laissez-faire* at home in England) nor the colonial voters in British North America were disposed to worry much when government regulation or incentive stepped out of the "liberal" (i.e., individualist and free-enterprise) formula. John A. Macdonald fastened on to the tariff as one instrument of government

[1] When account is taken of high Canadian per capita incomes, our government share is a modest one. Still we raise a larger fraction from personal income taxes than does a country like France. Studying the pattern among scores of countries reveals that the share of government tends to be least at low income per capita and where foreign trade—which is an easy object to tax in poor nations—is relatively unimportant. Exceptions remain, e.g., the low portion for the Caribbean countries compared with those of South America.

policy, raising it in his "National Policy" to encourage (not to regulate) the new manufacturing industries he thought the country needed. Similarly, he and his immediate successors began financing railroad building, especially of the CPR; just as his forerunners had backed canals and his descendants were to back airlines and pipelines. Thus the early intrusions of the Canadian government were "developmental" more than "regulatory."

With growth, Ottawa and the provinces were forced to think more about regulation. Since the early 1870s, the banking and insurance businesses had been inspected and regulated (though very loosely), by the Department of Finance. The amendment of the Criminal Code against combines in restraint of trade came almost simultaneously with the U.S. Sherman Antitrust Act in 1889. The Board of Transport Commissioners, to regulate rail rates, was set up in 1904. Other boards and commissions were appointed irregularly thereafter, at both the provincial and federal levels.

POLITICAL EVOLUTION   With the passage of time, the radical doctrines of one era became the accepted and even reactionary beliefs of a later era. Legislation was expanded to include minimum-wage laws; Workmen's Compensation laws (1910); unemployment insurance and old-age pensions; maximum-hour laws for children, women, and men; regulation of factory conditions, compulsory collective bargaining, and fair-labor-relations acts. And, as the authority of government expanded, so did the activities of its own departments (and Crown corporations). Not only the army and the post office, but also the CNR, a short-lived merchant fleet, the CBC, Air Canada, the Wheat Board, and Polymer Rubber were founded by the federal government; a large number of provincial and municipal undertakings were started, and new ones are initiated every year. Private property is never wholly private, individual enterprise rarely individual, and free enterprise not completely free.

To understand this trend toward all-pervasive government, one must acquire a certain historical perspective. Each new step generated strong political feelings on both sides. Thus much of the 1937 CCF (NDP) platform, which would today cause no fluttering of pulses, was once considered dangerously radical. Canada cannot, and would not if it could, return to the conditions of the nineteenth century, as recalled by reconstructed pioneer villages and the old Ontario school reader. Still, it would be wrong to think these historical processes inevitable. The role of government is never stable, and its importance fluctuates. The next decade may see a decline in government control of those services which people now feel must be regulated or provided by the state. Further, as with the post office, society may reverse its preferences for public ownership.

If the mixed economy is to work well, social institutions and beliefs must be capable of adjusting themselves to changes in taste, technology, or doctrine. The economic systems in the greatest peril of extinction are those which, however strong they may appear in the short run, lack the flexibility to accommodate themselves in an evolutionary manner to accumulating tensions and social changes. Without the realization that much historic change in the role of government is independent of dogmatic radicalism and last-ditch conservatism,

Transfer payments and municipal and provincial expenditures are the most rapidly growing expenditures:

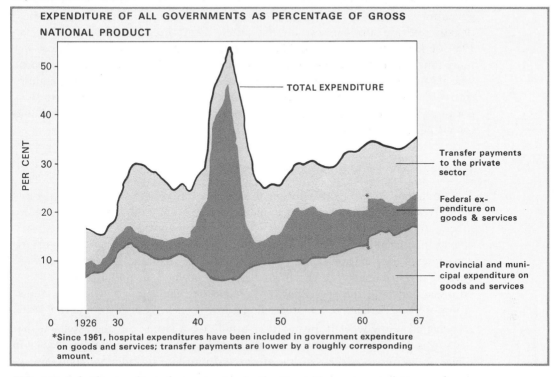

EXPENDITURE OF ALL GOVERNMENTS AS PERCENTAGE OF GROSS NATIONAL PRODUCT

*Since 1961, hospital expenditures have been included in government expenditure on goods and services; transfer payments are lower by a roughly corresponding amount.

FIG. 8-2. Federal expenditure began to rise in the Great Depression, and increased even more during the war. Defense spending has contracted during recent years and development and welfare spending of provinces, urbanization problems, and the increased decentralization of the whole federation have combined to make Ottawa's share less than half of total government expenditures. (Source: DBS and Economic Council of Canada, *Sixth Annual Review*.)

and simply technocratic and pragmatic in its origins, neither left-wing, nor right-wing, nor middle-of-the-road groups can effectively advance their own long-range interests.

■ FEDERAL, PROVINCIAL, AND MUNICIPAL FUNCTIONS

Although in 1867 it was expected that the provinces and municipalities would do most of the government spending, by 1870 Ottawa already did more than half. By the turn of the century, however, the municipalities and the provinces had developed more duties and more sources of revenue, and the federal share fell to 38 per cent. The federal government did little more than pay for national defense, meet pensions and interest on past wars, finance a few public works, and pay the salaries of judges, legislators, and other government officials. Almost all its tax collections came from liquor and tobacco excises and particularly from tariff duties levied on imports. Life was simple. Municipal governments performed many functions and depended primarily on property taxes.

Interrupted by World War I, the relative decline of federal spending continued till at least 1933. Figure 8-2 shows that in the late Depression the federal government began to spend more on goods and services. Transfer payments[2] (mostly welfare and interest on the public debt) bulged. The war costs of 1939-41 kept Ottawa ahead of the provinces and deflated transfers. But at the same time, the provinces began to grow in needs and power; so that today provincial and municipal spending on goods and services exceeds federal spending. (In most years since the 1920s, the municipalities have spent slightly more than the provinces, but the proportions have been close. Good data are not available for the period before the 1920s.)[3]

■ FEDERAL AND PROVINCIAL EXPENDITURE

The Canadian government is by far the biggest business in the country. It buys more typewriters and more steel, meets a bigger payroll, and handles more money than any other organization. The numbers involved are so large that they convey no meaning to the human mind. (When the detailed spending of the departments he controlled in the King and St. Laurent governments were queried in Parliament, C. D. Howe snapped, "What's a million?" His answer outraged MPs and the press, but they would be calmer today. The mere translation of such Parliamentary proceedings now costs well over a million a year.)

We all know what it means to be a mile from home, but the assertion that the sun is 93 million miles from the earth or that there are enough molecules in a glass of water to make a string of pearls from here to kingdom come always leaves us unimpressed. Perhaps public expenditure will have more meaning if we remember that each billion dollars amounts to about $50 per Canadian man, woman, and child. A current federal annual budget of about 10 billion dollars would be equivalent, then, to about $500 per capita—just over one month of the average annual income.

Figure 8-3 gives the percentage of the federal budget expenditures for different categories of national services in the fiscal years ended March 31, 1957, and 1970.

In the main, the cost of past and future wars accounted for the greatest percentage of expenditure in the past. In the fiscal year 1956-57, defense, veterans' services, and debt together amounted to half of all spending. Today, however, health and welfare (including old age pensions) require almost one-third of federal outlays. The other items are mostly self-explanatory. General payments to other levels of government have gone down because the provinces now collect their own direct taxes through the federal tax collector, instead of depending on their former grants, handed out by Ottawa. "Other," Item 6,

---

[2] Transfer payments are defined as those government expenditures or payments made outright to the recipient and not in return for current production of goods and services. They are discussed on pages 193-194 of this chapter.

[3] Somewhat similar trends are evident in American financial history, but the states have always been smaller spenders than the other two levels of government.

Welfare is taking over from military expenditures:

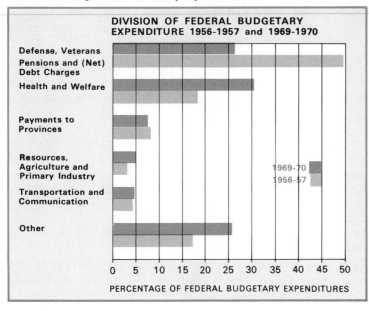

FIG. 8-3. Whereas defense, veterans' benefits, and public debt caused such "military" expenditures to absorb **49 per cent of the 1956-1957 budget, the military** share had fallen to **26 per cent in the 1969-70 budget**, and health and welfare had outstripped it easily. (Source: Canadian Tax Foundation, *The National Finances*, **1969-1970**.)

includes the traditional costs of running the federal government itself, and the provision of courts, clerks, and consular corps.

Figure 8-4 shows that education and health are the main areas of provincial spending, with roads not far behind. Education is also the chief responsibility

Education is the number one provincial and municipal expense:

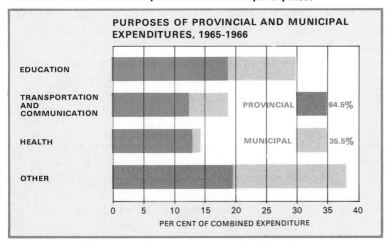

FIG. 8-4. The population outburst and move to the suburbs has put strain on provincial and local finance, especially for schools. At the same time, development and highways call for more borrowing, creating a burden of interest in "other." (Source: Canadian Tax Foundation, *Provincial Finances*, **1969**.)

of municipal governments and school boards. "Other" includes a hefty burden
of direct and guaranteed debt incurred for development and capital works.

■ THE CHANGING FUNCTIONS OF GOVERNMENT

The last quarter of a century has witnessed great political changes. How great
have been the economic changes? How great have been the departures from the
traditional capitalistic system? We can tackle these questions by considering
government activity under five headings:

DIRECT CONTROLS   As noted, there has been an increase in the amount of government *control*. Much of this regulation can hardly be dignified by the title of
"planning," and market prices still run most activities. Economic analysis of
government interference deserves detailed discussion and will be met in later
chapters.

SOCIAL CONSUMPTION OF PUBLIC GOODS   As we have also seen, the increase in
government expenditure means that as a nation we are consuming more of our
national product *socially* rather than individually through private money purchases. Rather than pay to ride on the public roads as we do to ride on railroads,
we pay for such valuable services by taxes.

Note that socially consumed goods and services are *largely produced by
private enterprise*. The government pays for a hospital or typewriter, but these
are produced by private enterprise. And so it is with most government expenditure on productive goods. This is not what the original socialists meant by
socialism—government ownership and operation of factories and land.[4]

STABILIZING FISCAL AND MONETARY POLICY   As will be seen in Parts Two and Six,
an important function performed by modern governments involves the control
of runaway price inflation and the prevention of chronic unemployment and
stagnant growth. Two principal weapons are used: monetary and fiscal policy.

A central bank—which is a bank for bankers and which is given the power
to issue currency—either is directly in the executive branch of government or,
more commonly, is set up as a public nonprofit organization ultimately responsible to the legislature. We shall study how our version of it, the Bank of
Canada, exercises *money and credit policies* in the interest of high production
and price stability.

Since the beginning of recorded history, governments have had constitutional authority over money. But only in the last 40 years has it become widely
recognized that *fiscal policy of government*—variations in expenditure and tax
totals, which create a surplus or deficit rather than a balanced budget—has profound effects on unemployment, total production, money and real incomes, and
on the level of prices. Bad fiscal policy can make the business cycle worse.
Stabilizing fiscal policy can moderate the ups and downs of business. Now that

---

[4] See the discussion of socialism, communism, and fascism in the Appendix to Chapter 2.

governments are large, claiming to have *no* fiscal policy is like claiming to be dead: left to themselves, budgets will definitely not balance; a policy of trying to balance the budget in every month, year, decade, or over the whole business cycle—these all involve deliberate social policy choice.

Chapters 13 and 16 will study monetary and fiscal policy in depth.

GOVERNMENT PRODUCTION   There has been continued expansion in this direction in recent decades. Historically, our government has performed certain direct productive operations, and not others. The post office has long been a function of government, while we have (since World War I) divided the management of railroads, telegraphs, airlines, and even pipelines between public and private corporations. Airports are usually publicly owned but bus terminals are private. The federal government provides most wharfs and harbors; provincial governments own many hydro and telephone systems; and municipalities run water utilities and street transport systems.

The reasons for drawing the line at one place rather than another are partly historical and are to some degree changing; but, economically, the distinction is not completely arbitrary, as we saw in connection with developmental enterprises. Again, the legislatures have decided that, in the special case of "public utilities affected with public interest," there is limited possibility of effective competition among many independent producers, and so they must be publicly regulated or owned; but one would not expect the production of soap to be a natural candidate for governmental operation.

In connection with this fourth category, which involves the use of human and other resources directly by the government, we should recognize that there has been a substantial rise of the federal payroll and in the number of government employees (although the latter was frozen in 1969 by Prime Minister Trudeau). Many of the latter are in the Ottawa and provincial offices, in regional laboratories, in the armed services, and so forth. Even if they are not directly producing private goods and services in competition with private industry, such resources are being directly used by the government; as we shall see, it behooves us all as citizens that they be used wisely and in the right amounts relative to the importance of our different national needs.

WELFARE PAYMENTS   Finally, we turn to an activity of government that has expanded tremendously since 1929 and that will continue to loom large in the decades ahead, namely, *government welfare payments*, which transfer purchasing power to the needy or worthy without regard to their providing a service in return. This category of transfer expenditures deserves further discussion. Because of their magnitude, our system is sometimes called the "welfare state."

■ TRANSFERS AND TAXES IN THE WELFARE STATE

Transfer payments are mostly made to veterans, old people, the handicapped, and unemployed people. It is important to understand that government cheques received by such people differ economically from those received by civil servants or government suppliers. In our later discussions of national-income accounting, the difference will show up again: the former are not counted as national income or output, but simply as "transfers." The latter are part of national income.

Government expenditures (a) do cover services rendered; (b) do use up resources and national production; and (c) do provide direct or indirect collective consumption to the Canadian community as a whole. However financed (by taxes, sale of postage stamps, or otherwise) the dollars are spent to provide services for public use. In this they are like dollars used by a large railroad to provide passenger services. Both flows of dollars are part of national income.

Transfer payments are something else again. Socially, they may be some of our most desirable expenditures, but nevertheless they are not part of national output or national income. Why? As an example, let us consider a blind widow's pension. (a) The widow does not render any concurrent services to the government or its citizens in exchange for the pension. (b) She does not provide any labor, land, or capital, or current national production in exchange for the pension. (c) Her pension is for her own enjoyment and not for the collective consumption of the public. It is true that the pension does increase her purchasing power, does permit her to live more adequately and to buy goods and services from other individuals. These goods and services *that she buys* are part of the national income and output; but they are *attributable* to (and have already been counted as the output of) the people and private factories that have produced them, not to her or the government.

Transfer expenditures have grown greatly in recent years. They grew partly as a result of the Depression, which made relief expenditures necessary, but they grew mostly because new minimum standards of health, nutrition, and security have been set up by the collective conscience of the Canadian people. Society now rules that children shall not have rickets because of the bad luck or weakness of their parents; that poor people shall not die young because of insufficient money for operations and needed care; that the old shall live out their years with some minimum of income. Current discussion of "guaranteed annual income" or a "negative income tax" reflect this view.

Do welfare payments expand the public sector of the economy? We shall later see that, "on the first round," these payments do not directly consume goods and services; but by swelling the purchasing power of their recipients, they do create orders and jobs for the business sector "on the second round." The thing to note is that *the production induced by this respending is probably both privately produced and privately consumed.*

Unless these payments are financed by new money creation or by bond borrowing, larger taxes will have to be levied on the public, and it is in recognition of this link between taxpayers and welfare recipients that they are called "transfer payments."

In connection with welfare programs of the government, mention should be made of the fact that various *redistributions* of income among citizens are also accomplished *by the form in which the government allocates the burden of the taxes it levies* on different groups and classes. The next chapter shows that there is a tendency in modern states for the well-to-do to be taxed absolutely and relatively more heavily than those below the median income level.

Thus, suppose there were no program of direct governmental transfers. But suppose the government made the very rich pay all the taxes for national defense and most of the taxes for civilian programs. Is it not evident, then, that it would be altering the distribution of the after-tax disposable incomes that different classes have to spend on bread, cars, and anything else?

> One must include in the activities of the modern welfare state both pro-grams of *transfer payments* to be spent by pensioners and those on assist-ance and *redistributions of income* brought about by arranging that the higher income classes will bear the bulk of the tax burden.

■ COMBINED EXPENDITURES OF ALL LEVELS OF GOVERNMENT

The division of spending on goods and services *plus* transfers of all levels of government is shown in Table 8-2 and emphasizes the trends which we have just discussed. Recall that Fig. 8-2 showed that the provinces have grown in

Education and social assistance are important expenditures of combined governments:

TRANSFERS AND GOODS AND SERVICES SPENDING BY ALL GOVERNMENTS								
	1933	1939	1945	1950	1955	1960	1965	1967
As Percentage of Total Expenditure								
Defence	1.6	9.9	44.3	14.7	24.6	14.1	9.9	8.7
Health	3.7	3.7	1.2	5.6	5.2	7.8	9.9	11.7
Social assistance (including veterans' benefits)	19.4	16.9	12.5	20.5	17.7	17.7	16.8	16.5
Education	11.3	10.1	3.3	10.7	11.4	14.6	16.4	20.9
Transportation and communications	9.4	12.8	3.0	11.4	11.8	13.3	12.8	11.7
Net debt charges	31.5	20.8	8.6	11.2	7.7	7.9	7.9	6.8
All other	23.1	25.8	27.1	25.9	21.6	24.6	26.3	23.7
Total functional expenditure	100.0	100.0	100.0	100.0	100.0	100.0	100.0	100.0
As Percentage of Gross National Product								
Defence	0.4	2.3	21.2	3.4	6.3	4.1	2.9	2.7
Health	1.0	0.8	0.6	1.3	1.3	2.2	2.9	3.7
Social assistance (including veterans' benefits)	5.3	3.9	6.0	4.8	4.6	5.1	4.9	5.2
Education	3.1	2.3	1.6	2.5	2.9	4.2	4.8	6.6
Transportation and communications	2.5	2.9	1.4	2.6	3.0	3.8	3.7	3.7
Net debt charges	8.6	4.7	4.1	2.6	2.0	2.3	2.3	2.1
All other	6.3	5.9	13.0	6.0	5.6	7.0	7.6	7.5
Total functional expenditure	27.2	22.7	47.9	23.1	25.6	28.7	29.0	31.4

TABLE 8-2. Like Fig. 8-2, this table shows both transfers and government services. Note how debt charges (the burden of the debt) have declined, how defense has risen and fallen, and how education and welfare have boomed. [Source: Economic Council of Canada, 6th *Annual Review* (September, 1969), Table 3-2, p. 29. Reproduced by permission of Information Canada.]

relative importance when the over-all picture is viewed. This is because the functions which happen to be the particular domain of the provincial governments rather than that of the federal government have become an increasing part of the whole.

Notice that many of the percentage items fluctuate *cyclically*, rising and falling with the work to be done: the percentage spent on defense was greatest during World War II; the percentage cost of education is reaching a peak in the 1970s, as the children born during the peak of the "Baby Boom," seen in Fig. 2-9 (page 42), start attending high school; social assistance was at its peak (though in primitive forms) in the Great Depression; and debt charges (the aftermath of heavy borrowing for defense, development, *and* social assistance) have fallen relatively even since the early 1930s.

There is also the following overall *trend*, but it is faint: as a percentage of GNP, all expenditures and transfers have risen from about 27 per cent to about 32 per cent. Relatively the cyclical redistribution of spending has been more important than its trend.

For the rest of this chapter we shall try to use the tools of economic analysis developed earlier to understand the nature of the various governmental programs already surveyed.

■ GRAPHICAL ANALYSIS OF GOVERNMENT ACTIVITY[5]

The production-possibility concept of Chapter 2, particularly Fig. 2-3 on page 26, gives insight into the nature of government activity. Figure 8-5(a) indicates further how society can choose between (a) *private goods* (bread, shoes, dictionaries), which families buy voluntarily out of their after-tax incomes at prices set by markets, and (b) *public goods* (destroyers, services of policemen and civil servants, weather forecasts, cleanup of Lake Erie), which we consume collectively and which involve government expenditure (financed by taxes, deficit borrowing, printing of money).

What determines the actual E_1 position, which represents about one-quarter of the total product devoted to *public goods* and three-quarters to *private*? It is legislative decision that puts E_1 where it is and also determines the exact composition of the social expenditure as divided between the three levels of government.

What about the composition of the private sector at the point E_1? On reflection, one realizes that it does indeed depend on governmental decision making, but only in the following respects: (1) Welfare transfers by government help to determine the distribution of spending incomes of people in the private community, money which they can spend voluntarily for different goods purchased in the market. (2) Tax legislation by our representatives decides how to allocate the tax burden among different individuals and classes; such decisions impinge in a similar way on the allocation, in the background, of E_1's *private goods* among persons.

---

[5] The next two sections are separable from the rest of the chapter.

Cutting out waste is not the same as cutting scope of government:

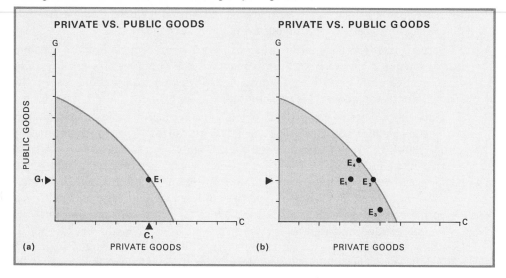

FIG. 8-5(a). Along society's production-possibility frontier giving choices between private and public expenditure on goods and services, we begin at a point such as E_1.

FIG. 8-5(b). Cutting out waste and increasing governmental efficiency take society from E_1, inside the *p-p frontier*, out to it. This permits the previous level of government to be reached at E_2 with less sacrifice of private goods. (Cutting down on scope without change in efficiency would mean, however, moving inside the frontier down to E_3.) At E_4 the populace has decided to allocate the new affluence that efficiency has brought among new extra goods of both private and governmental type.

Aside from transfer and tax influence, the private consumption of goods is determined by voluntary market decisions of individuals—as they decide to buy white rather than rye bread, beef rather than pork, boats rather than autos, and Scotties rather than Kleenex.

Suppose international tension ended, thereby permitting us to cut down greatly on government expenditure and on taxes so as to leave people with more money to spend individually. Provided the economic system were made to run smoothly without temporary or permanent unemployment, you should be able to show that the point E_1 would then move down the *p-p frontier* curve toward more private and less social spending.

Suppose the electorate agrees with Galbraith's *The Affluent Society*, and decides it would prefer to enjoy less private consumption of cars and other things and enjoy more social consumption of roads, parks, schools, and hospitals. You should be able to show the upward and leftward movement of E_1 as it climbs the production-possibility frontier.

■ WASTE IN GOVERNMENT AND SCOPE

Our diagram helps to disentangle a common confusion. Government expenditure can be reduced in two quite different ways: First, the people can succeed in making their public activities more *efficient.* They can abolish graft and waste and insist on better planning of programs and on more efficient administration. This is sometimes called "cutting out fat without cutting muscle."

Second, they can change the *scope* of government, reducing public expenditure by having the government drop many of the functions it performs. The government can build fewer roads, provide less weather information, cease to do research, or abandon conservation activities.

Figure 8-5(b) helps keep the problem of efficiency in government distinct from the problem of scope of government. Its move from E_1 out to E_2 on the *p-p frontier* shows the result of a successful program of increasing the *efficiency* of government activity: we can now get the same quantity of government goods and services for less sacrifice of resources from the private economy. If the electorate wants to leave the scope of government unchanged, E_2 the new point will be due right of old point E_1, with same G_1 level of social consumption but with private goods now increased as shown. (This came about in the background in something like the following way: the savings in efficiency resulted in tax reductions large enough to give people the extra income sufficient to use up all the resources released by government.)

As an alternative to the above case, suppose people succeed in reducing government expenditure solely by cutting down on the *scope* of government activity. Then there will have been no change in efficiency. Inside the frontier, the nation moves down and to the right of E_3.

Consider still another alternative. Suppose everyone favors efficiency and we do succeed in getting out to the *p-p frontier.* But now the electorate decides it will use its greater affluence for *both* private and additional social wants. If it decides to spend its extra income on something from both categories, then it will move up and to the right to the point marked E_4.[6] (Please reread Fig. 8-5.)

■ SOCIAL AND PRIVATE WANTS: EXTREME LAISSEZ-FAIRE

Let us return from graphs to the basic issues. *Why is governmental use of goods and services ever required at all?* What light can economic analysis throw on this?

[6] Recall the alleged law that no government can tax and spend more than 25 per cent of the national income without creating disaster; or that the increase of the public sector for defense, public works, education, and free hospital services has gone as far as our country can stand economically. If there were an absolute real limit, the transformation curves would have a corner at about E_1 and would move off horizontally to the left. There appears to be no evidence of any such discontinuity. The possibility that inflation might be the consequence of going northwest of some critical E point is a quite different argument; after study of Part Two, one can appraise such an allegation. (An advanced treatise would discuss the fact that as society taxes to transfer from private to social consumption, some distortions of incentives and efficiency are likely to result; in changing the division of the pie, you may *alter its size.* This constitutes one of the genuine costs of government, and sensible electorates will want to give it due weight in deciding whether this should lower or expand government's proper scope.)

In the first place, suppose all goods could be produced efficiently by perfectly competitive enterprise at any scale of operations. And suppose that all goods were like loaves of bread, the total of which can be definitely divided up into separate consumptions of different individuals, so that the more I consume out of the total, the less you consume. And suppose that there were neither altruism toward other people nor envy of them. And suppose that each person had equal initial access to human and natural resources, had equal opportunity in every sense, and could carry on his activities independently of others, much as in pioneer days.

If *all* these idealized conditions were met, would there be any need whatsoever for a mixed economy? Why should there be any government functions at all? Indeed, why speak of a society at all, since the world could then be regarded as an array of independent atoms with absolutely no organic connections among them? Clearly, such a case of zero government is at one extreme pole.

Yet even in this case, if there were to be a division of labor between people and regions, and if a pricing system such as that described in Chapters 3 and 4 and in Part Three were to work, the need would soon grow for government courts and policemen to ensure honesty, fulfillment of contract, nonfraudulent and nonviolent behavior, freedom from theft and from external aggression, and guarantee of the legislated rights of property. This would be *laissez-faire* with minimal government—and a very good system it might be if the ideal conditions presupposed for it were truly present.

◼ SOCIAL WANTS IN REAL LIFE

Each and every one of the idealized conditions enumerated above is lacking in some degree in real life as mankind has always known it. Abilities, opportunities, and ownership of property exhibit disparities, depending on biological and social history. It is a fact that many kinds of production can take place most efficiently only in units too large for "perfect competition" as defined exactly by the economist; and many other imperfections mar the simplicity of the scenario. All this forms the subject of analysis throughout this book—analysis designed to provide perspective for the important compromises that a free society must make. But here, in a chapter on public expenditure, we shall concentrate on the factors that call for governmental activity.

Let us consider national defense. Nothing is more vital to a threatened society than its security. But national defense, regarded as a commodity, differs completely from the case of a private commodity like bread. Ten loaves of bread can be divided up in many ways among individuals in a group; but national defense has to be provided more or less automatically for all. Most individuals will appreciate it, much as they appreciate quantities of bread; but even among them some would be more willing, if necessary, to give up more bread for a given level of defense than others would. Some, who are pacifists, may profess that defense expenditure does not interest them particularly; while still others may sincerely experience pain from this social good and would require much bread to bribe them into voluntarily voting for national defense.

Could market *laissez-faire*, with no political voting and coercion, give the group the national defense desired by the majority? Evidently not. If I knew that I was going to be protected anyway by the defense you had paid for, why should I come into the market place and exercise a dollar demand for it? Patriotism would of course motivate me; but it would show itself in the way that I and my neighbors *voted in elections* and in the way we acquiesced to the coercive fiats legislated by our responsive government, rather than *in our day-to-day private purchasing.*

To be sure, the example of national defense is a dramatic and extreme case. But when you think of the night policeman, the presiding judge, the appropriation for a park concert, or the damming of a river upstream to prevent floods downstream—indeed, when you think of government activities in general—you find the same common element:

> The benefits from a social good, unlike those from a purely private good, are seen to involve *external consumption effects on more than one individual.* If a good can be subdivided so that each part can be *competitively* sold separately to a different individual with no external effects on others in the group, it is not a likely candidate for governmental activity.

In Part Three more will be said about external effects: so-called "external diseconomies," such as the smoke from my factory chimney which contaminates the air for all; and "external economies," such as the advantage your fruit trees get from the straying bees I raise to help pollinate my own fruit trees. It is enough here to give examples of government activities justifiable because of external effects.

> Take our earlier case of a lighthouse to warn against rocks.[7] Its beam helps everyone in sight. A businessman could not build it for a profit, since he cannot claim a price from each user. This certainly is the kind of activity that government would naturally undertake. It would meet Abraham Lincoln's test: "The legitimate object of government is 'to do for the people what needs to be done, but which they can not, by individual effort, do at all, or do so well, for themselves.'"
>
> Or take the case of government provision of research on wheat farming. No one competitive farmer is large enough; and he also knows he cannot retain the monetary advantage of the research financed by him. Nevertheless, there is a great

---

[7] The analysis of this section owes much to the nineteenth-century analysis of Knut Wicksell and other economists and to the important treatise by Richard A. Musgrave, *The Theory of Public Finance* (McGraw-Hill, New York, 1959). In the lighthouse example, one thing should be noticed: the fact that the lighthouse operators cannot appropriate in the form of a purchase price a fee from those it benefits certainly helps to make it a suitable social or public good. But even if the operator were able—say, by radar reconnaissance—to claim a toll from every nearby user, that fact would not necessarily make it socially optimal for this service to be provided like a private good at a market-determined individual price. Why not? Because it costs society zero extra cost to let one extra ship use the service; hence any ships discouraged from those waters by the requirement to pay a positive price will represent a social economic loss—even if the price charged to all is no more than enough to pay the long-run expenses of the lighthouse. If the lighthouse is socially worth building and operating—and it need not be—a more advanced treatise can show how this social good is worth being made optimally available to all.

benefit to the group and to society from learning about and adopting any improvements that might be uncovered by research on farming. As a result of these considerations, because of a clear *externality* in the use of knowledge, no prudent private firm can be expected to invest its scarce dollars up to the point of best advantage to the group as a whole.[8] Therefore governmental activity in this area, whether in its own laboratories or by commissioning of private university research, may well be a desirable act of representative democracy. (Where a government project, like an atomic pile, involves external *dis*economies, policy makers will have to take them into account.)

This concludes our brief economic analysis of the nature of government activity. In Part Three the discussion will go beyond the questions of government finance and will develop the economic principles that determine when a government might prudently intervene in *laissez-faire* to restrain monopoly, regulate it where it is inevitable, and use tax or subsidies to offset distorting external diseconomies and economies. The next chapter will discuss public finance as it relates to the tax systems of the federal, provincial, and local governments and will discuss expenditures of the provinces and localities and their coordination with the federal government.

SUMMARY

■ 1 The economic role of government has been a generally expanding one. More and more activities in our complex, interdependent society have been coming under direct regulation and control.

■ 2 A larger fraction of the total output here and abroad has been going to collective consumption of *public* rather than *private* goods.

■ 3 An increasing part of the national income is being *transferred* by taxation and government welfare expenditure from the relatively rich to the relatively poor.

■ 4 There has been in Canada a trend towards state ownership of industry and society's means of production. Yet there has been little detailed government planning.

■ 5 After World War I, federal expenditure increased more rapidly than provincial and municipal expenditure. During the Depression of the 1930s, expenditures on relief, public works, and similar matters expanded the federal budget. But the postwar budget remained many times the size of the prewar levels because of increased defense and development outlays, interest on the public debt, and welfare payments. Provincial and municipal spending on goods and services now exceed that of the federal government.

■ 6 Provincial and municipal expenditures have been rising since the Second World War: the principal items are education, health, highways, public welfare, and the ordinary police and safety functions of government.

---

[8] Unless it can *patent*, and keep to itself, the rights to produce and sell a new seed or machine.

■ 7 The production-possibility frontier of Chapter 2 can help distinguish be-tween reducing government expenditure (*a*) by reducing government waste or (*b*) by reducing governmental scope of activity.

■ 8 Economic analysis of private goods consumable solely by individuals points up the contrast with social *public* goods which involve "external consump-tion effects" on more than one individual in the group. National defense, research, law enforcement, conservation, lighthouse operation, and similar activities must pass the test of involving such "external effects" if they are to be easily justifiable as government activities.

QUESTIONS FOR DISCUSSION

1. Name things which government does now that it did not do in the past.

2. Between now and 1980 how would you expect the government's share in the national income to develop? Why? What factors affect your answer?

3. How much does the increasing economic cost of government reflect decreasing efficiency? How would you go about making a scientific study of this?

4. "The radical doctrines of three decades ago are the conservative doctrines of today." Is this ever true? Always true? Give favorable cases and exceptions.

5. "Government expenditure on goods and services represents public goods, many of which are *produced* by market-operated private enterprise." Appraise.

6. "To bring back the federal budget to anywhere near the pre-World War II level, welfare programs and defense will have to be the main items cut." Discuss.

7. Define, giving examples, transfer payments and redistributive taxes. Are hospital insurance and medical insurance, respectively, transfers?

8. Review your understanding of the following concepts:

government spending	welfare state, socialism
public debt and budget	transfer expenditures
laissez-faire versus controls	private versus public goods
fiscal policy	efficiency and scope

9

THE ECONOMIC ROLE
OF GOVERNMENT: FEDERAL
TAXATION AND LOCAL FINANCE

The division of responsibilities and taxing powers is the essence of a federal state. ROYAL COMMISSION ON TAXATION, 1966

Discussion of public finance continues in this chapter with an analysis of taxation. Then follows a survey of the federal tax system, of taxation at the provincial and local (municipal) levels, and of the interrelations among the different branches of government. Finally comes the problem of tax incidence—upon whom does the burden of each tax ultimately fall? How does the tax burden on rich and poor compare with their respective benefits from government expenditures?

■ ECONOMIC NATURE OF TAXATION

FINANCING REAL EXPENDITURE   The state needs money to pay its bills. It gets the dollars to pay for its expenditures primarily from taxes. However, what the state really needs to build a bridge or run a lighthouse is not so much money as *real economic resources*: steel and watchmen—in short, the use of society's scarce supplies of labor, land, and capital goods.

> In deciding how to tax themselves, therefore, the people are really deciding how resources needed for social wants shall be taken from all the various families and from the enterprises they own and be made available for governmental goods and services.

ALTERING DISTRIBUTION OF INCOMES   The state also spends on *welfare transfers*, which go to particular individuals in the community for them to spend on their private needs and wants. Again, money is a veil that cloaks the *redistribution* of command over real goods and services which results from action by the state to tax some and give to others.

Recall also that, even if there were no direct welfare transfers, the state is altering the distribution of incomes that results from *laissez-faire*. In deciding who shall be made to pay for the resources spent on social goods and services, the electorate can vote taxes that will fall heavily on the rich rather than on the poor; on the energetic rather than the lethargic; on the owners of intangible resources such as land and property, rather than the owners of labor power.

Thus both taxation and transfers help determine the distribution of private incomes.

In the distant past, taxes were levied by those in power against those out of power purely in terms of expediency. A nobleman at the court of Louis XIV might get off scot-free, while a merchant in Marseilles or a peasant in Normandy was sorely burdened. When scholars tried to form more rational guides to taxation, what principles finally emerged?

BENEFIT VERSUS SACRIFICE PRINCIPLES   Of the many principles concerning optimal taxation, two major groups can be distinguished:

1. There is the general notion that different people should be taxed in proportion to the "benefit" they can be expected to receive from public activity.

2. There is the general principle that people should be taxed in such a way as to lead to a desirable pattern of "sacrifice"; or what is really the same thing, that taxation should be arranged to accomplish whatever the good society regards as the proper *redistribution* of market-determined incomes.[1]

Such general principles are important; but, although commanding wide support, they are too vague to discriminate clearly between acceptable and unacceptable taxes, or systems of tax.

To see why, consider benefit taxation. If you and I were *exactly* alike, then the benefit we received from public roads, national defense, and general government services would also be the same. Alternatively, take redistributional taxation. If we were exactly alike, then the amount of sacrifice we each ought to make would again be equal. Either way we obtain the same conclusion:

Dictum of horizontal equity: Those who are essentially equals should be taxed equally.

This notion of horizontal equity was important in the past and is still so. If Man A and Man B are alike in every respect except color of hair, there is presumably no reason to tax them differently—any more than, in a rule of law, the fact that A has a friend in the government should relieve him from taxation. (As we shall see, the existence of loopholes in tax laws shows how necessary it is not to forget this dictum.)

---

[1] Economists who think the utilities of different persons can be added together to form a total social utility speak of taxing to produce maximum total utility, or to produce some specified pattern of utility sacrifice. Thus, if each extra dollar brings less and less satisfaction to a man, and if the rich and poor are alike in their capacity to enjoy satisfaction, a dollar taxed away from a millionaire and given to a median-income person is supposed to add more to total utility than it subtracts. See Chapter 21 and also Fig. 20-7 for more on this.

However, people are rarely so nearly identical. To tax unlike people we must modify the dictum of horizontal equity as follows:

> If equals are to be taxed equally, there is a presumption that unequals are to be taxed unequally.

This corollary, dealing with *un*like taxpayers, raises questions about how to achieve *vertical*, instead of *horizontal*, equity. It brings back the old problems. Neither the benefit principle nor the optimal-sacrifice principle, used with this corollary, can by itself resolve society's tax-policy issues.

Imagine that Man *A* and Man *B* are alike in every respect, except that *B* is ten times richer in income and property. What does the benefit principle require? Should *B* pay the same *absolute* tax dollars for police protection as *A*? Or should he pay the same *percentage* of his income as tax to defray police expense? Or should he, his wealth requiring more police protection than *A*'s poverty, achieve fairness by paying a *larger percentage* of his income in taxes?

The general philosophy of optimal-sacrifice or redistributive taxation similarly leaves unanswered the question of the best tax formula. It is one thing to say that the rich have greater "ability" to pay taxes than the poor, that their "sacrifice" is less when they pay a dollar of taxes than when the poor pay a dollar. This still leaves open the question: *How much* differently should unequals in income be taxed? What do we mean by "vertical equity"?

The coordination of the two aims has exercised many philosophers of public finance.

■ PRAGMATIC COMPROMISES IN TAXATION

How have modern mixed societies tended to resolve these difficult philosophical questions? Democracies have generally adopted pragmatic solutions that will please neither the zealots in favor of benefit notions nor the zealots in favor of thoroughgoing redistributional-sacrifice notions. Modern tax systems are a compromise.

Where various public services at the local and national levels are peculiarly for the benefit of recognizable groups, and where those groups have no special claim for favorable or unfavorable treatment by virtue of their average incomes or other characteristics, modern governments generally rely on taxes of the benefit type. Thus, local roads are usually paid for by local residents; taxes collected on gasoline may on the whole be devoted more specifically to road construction than to schools or libraries.

PROGRESSIVE AND REGRESSIVE TAXATION   On the other hand, extensive reliance has been placed on *graduated income taxes*. A man with $20,000 of income is taxed more than a man with $10,000 of income—even if the former claims to benefit very little from government expenditures. Not only does the higher-income man pay larger income tax, but he in fact pays a progressively *higher fraction* of his income. This "progressive graduation" of the rate of tax is in contrast to a strictly "proportional tax" that makes each man always pay exactly the *same proportion* of his income, and in even greater contrast to a so-called "regressive" tax, which takes a larger fraction from low incomes than it does from high.

Definition: A tax is called *proportional, progressive,* or *regressive* depending upon whether it takes from high-income people the *same* fraction of income, a *larger* fraction of income, or a *smaller* fraction of income than it takes from low-income people.

The words "progressive" and "regressive" can be misleading. They are technical terms relating to proportions that taxes bear to different incomes. They have to be appraised on their merits, and it would be wrong to read into the word "progressive" emotional overtones of being up-to-date or particularly right-minded.

A personal income tax that is graduated to take more and more out of each extra dollar of income is progressive. While many taxes on sales of goods will be seen to be regressive, the reader should know that a tax on fine wine, which only the rich can afford, might well be progressive. Even a tax that is strictly proportional on estates left at death could be progressive, since the man with twice the income tends on the average to have and bequeath more than twice the wealth.

DIRECT AND INDIRECT TAXES   Aside from their degree of progressivity, taxes can also be classified under the headings *direct* or *indirect.*

"Indirect taxes" are usually defined as taxes that are levied *against goods and services* and thus only indirectly on people. Examples are: excises or sales taxes; cigarette stamp taxes; tariff duties on imports; turnover taxes, which, in contrast to retail excises, are levied every time a farmer sells wheat to a miller and a miller sells flour to a baker and on all transactions at any stage of production; value-added taxes, which tax only the costs added at each stage of production.

"Direct taxes" are levied directly on people (e.g., income, inheritance, real property, and poll taxes).

There are, of course, many borderline cases that do not fall neatly into one category or the other. We generally associate direct and progressive taxes together; indirect and regressive (or proportional) taxes together. But there are many exceptions to such a rule: a poll tax of $2 per head is a direct tax, but a highly regressive tax in that it takes a larger fraction of income from the poor than from the rich; as mentioned, an indirect tax on cameras or rare brandy might well be more progressive than many income taxes.[2]

---

[2] Throughout the world, economists today do not often use this indirect-direct distinction for analytical purposes. It was inherited from theorists of the Classical School, especially David Ricardo and John Stuart Mill (the influential nineteenth-century economist). But a clearer distinction (between income and sales tax, for example) will not do for today's political, legal, and constitutional discussions, because in some federations, nineteenth-century legal draftsmen (such as the Fathers of Confederation) assigned taxing rights between the central government and the provinces or states simply by stating that "the provinces may levy only direct taxes." Since 1867, finance ministers and judges have often debated John Stuart Mill's definition of "direct taxation." According to Mill, a direct tax is "one which is demanded from the very persons who, it is intended or desired, should pay it. Indirect taxes are those which are demanded from one person in the expectation and intention that he shall indemnify himself at the expense of another: such as the excise or customs."

Income and sales tax provide most of federal revenue:

TAXATION REVENUE RECEIPTS OF FEDERAL GOVERNMENT, 1969-1970	REVENUE	
	MILLIONS OF DOLLARS	PER CENT
Progressive		
Personal income tax	$ 4,500	36
Estate taxes (succession duties)	110	1
Intermediate		
Corporation income taxes	2,455	20
Old Age Security fund taxes	1,840	14
Regressive		
Manufacturers' sales tax	1,677	13
Customs duties	753	6
Other	1,790	10
Total Federal Budgetary		
Tax Revenue	$12,525	100

TABLE 9-1. The corporation income tax, important in the past, now produces less revenue than personal income tax. NOTE: Old Age Security taxes include small income, corporation, and sales taxes. (Source: *Budget Speech*, June 3, 1969.)

Modern tax systems are, to repeat, a compromise. They give some weight to benefit notions; some weight to sacrifice and redistribution notions; and, one may add, some weight to expediency and politics—and to the economic fact of life that increasing certain taxes, however favorable it looks to an ardent redistributionist, would at the same time be expected to harm people's incentives and the efficiency of society's use of resources.

■ FEDERAL TAXATION

The wide variety of present federal taxes[3] is indicated by Table 9-1. Of these, the first two, personal income taxes and estate taxes, bear down "progressively" more on people with higher incomes.

Sales taxes are relatively "regressive" in that they take a larger fraction of the poor man's income than they do of the rich man's.

The corporation tax is intermediate in its effects. In one way, it is progressive, since most dividend dollars do go to people of more than median income. (Although it is true that many poor widows and orphans own some shares of stock, still the total that they own is not a large fraction of all stock shares.) But to the extent that corporations can pass the tax on to the consumer in higher prices, a tax on business profits may end up being regressive or proportional.

A brief glance at the various taxes will be helpful.

[3] The "progressiveness" of each of these taxes is classified according to the *Report* of the Royal Commission on Taxation 1966-67 (chaired by Kenneth LeM. Carter), Vol. 2 (Ottawa, Queen's Printer).

SALES AND CUSTOMS TAXES   In order of regressiveness, these would probably come first, and there has long been controversy over them. Most federal regressive taxes are truly "indirect"; they are hidden among the costs of production and marketing and are completely unknown to consumers. Almost half of this revenue is raised by a general sales tax of 12 per cent at the manufacturers' level; but about one-quarter is levied as customs (import) duties and at least another quarter in special taxes on liquor, tobacco, and other "luxury" items. Prior to World War I Canada depended on the customs duty for its national revenue; even now it relies on it and other indirect taxes more than do the United States or the United Kingdom. However, economists believe the manufacturers' sales tax is not very regressive, because most foods and fuels (which make up much of the budget of low-income families) are exempt from it. The same cannot be claimed for liquor and tobacco taxes.

OLD AGE SECURITY   Most Canadians must make contributions to the schemes of pensions and assistance.

1. About one million persons in their late sixties or older receive a federal pension of $79.58 per month from the Old Age Security Fund (OASF). All taxpayers contribute to this fund on the "4-3-3" formula: 4 or 3 percentage points added to personal income, corporation, or manufacturers' sales tax. Thus one part of total contributions is progressive and another part is regressive. The maximum total personal income-tax contribution is $240, paid by all those with a taxable income of $6,000 or more; for such people, the OASF contribution is, essentially, a poll tax. Other old-age assistance, including the guaranteed monthly income of $31.83 to old age security recipients, is paid for out of other tax revenues. This assistance, when added to the OASF pension of $79.58, provides a total guaranteed monthly income of $111.41.

2. Since 1966, people have had additional pension coverage under the Canada Pension Plan (CPP) or the Quebec Pension Plan. Each employer and employee make contributions amounting to about 1.8 per cent of the latter's earnings, up to $82.80 each (not shown in Table 9-1). Thus a typical worker pays up to $322.80 a year to both OASF and CPP.

3. The Social Development Tax was introduced in 1969 and is set at 2 per cent of taxable income up to a maximum tax of $120. While the extremely general term "Social Development" was used by the government in order not to link the tax to a specific purpose, the reader may note that this tax was introduced at approximately the same time as the federal medicare scheme. If the Social Development tax is added to the OASF and the CPP taxes, an average worker must meet a combined tax payment of about $440 annually.

CORPORATION INCOME TAXES   After a corporation has paid all its expenses and reckoned its annual income, it must pay part of its income to the federal and provincial governments. In 1970, a corporation paid income tax at the rate of 23 cents on each dollar of net income below $35,000; and 52 cents on each dollar above $35,000. (These were the combined federal and provincial rates in Ontario and Quebec; they were one or two cents lower in other provinces.)[4]

Many people think the peacetime tax rate is too high, that corporations are discouraged from venturing on worthwhile (but risky!) job-making investment projects. They argue that a small corporation would be able to grow more rapidly if it could plow back into the business what the government takes in taxes. Proponents of these views also say it is unfair "double taxation" for the government to tax corporate earnings and also to make the stockholders pay personal income taxes on the dividends received from corporations. To meet this criticism, Canada has since 1949 toned down the "double taxation" of corporate income by permitting individual taxpayers to deduct from their personal income tax 20 per cent of their Canadian dividends. This "dividend tax credit"[5] has the effect, at least on paper, of assuring that owners of the shares of small corporations pay taxes on profits only once, and pay only about 30 per cent extra tax on the earnings of large corporations.

There are some who argue that corporations should be taxed heavily, with the bigger corporations taxed at progressively heavier rates. They believe that, if government must collect large sums of money and if further increases in the personal income tax are not feasible, then a tax on corporations is better than a sales or payroll tax. Moreover, they point out that corporations do not distribute all their earnings to stockholders but retain some to be plowed back into the business. The stockholder may avoid personal income tax on these corporate savings by capital-gains loopholes, as we shall see. According to these critics, a corporation tax will at least partially remedy the situation. The problem is too complex for a final evaluation here.

■ THE PROGRESSIVE PERSONAL INCOME TAX

Spring used to be an unhappy season, for people had to make a lump-sum payment for taxes on the previous year's income, which had often already been spent. Now things are better. All through the year employers automatically withhold from each paycheque most of what we shall have to pay to the government. This puts us on a pay-as-you-go basis: by the end of the year our taxes are more or less all paid up.

For some two million families, with earnings below $3,000 and no appreciable property income, that is all there is to it. They simply fill in a short form

---

[4] In wars, this and other countries have had an "excess-profits tax" on corporations and other firms in addition to the above ordinary income tax. Thus, during World War II, on all their profit they paid up to 70 per cent in taxes, some corporations being taxed 80 cents of extra dollars earned and keeping only 20 cents.

In recent years, critics of direct, progressive taxes have urged adoption of "value-added" taxes: these differ from "turnover" taxes that put a tax on every sale by business, in that value added is calculated after purchases of materials from other firms have been subtracted, as will be discussed in the next chapter. Aside from not pyramiding the tax burden through production stages, countries use value-added taxes to increase their foreign-trade advantages.

[5] A tax credit is a sum subtracted directly from one's tax bill whereas a tax exemption or deduction is a subtraction made to arrive at taxable income, on which the tax is then figured.

The income-tax schedule climbs progressively as income grows:

AMOUNTS AND PERCENTAGES OF FEDERAL AND PROVINCIAL INCOME TAX, 1970

		SINGLE TAXPAYER			MARRIED—TWO CHILDREN			
		Tax				Tax		
Net Income	Taxable Income	Amount	Average Rate	Marginal Rate	Taxable Income	Amount	Average Rate	Marginal Rate
(1)	(2)	(3)	(4)	(5)	(6)	(7)	(8)	(9)
$	$	$	%	%	$	$	%	%
1,500	400	59	3.9	3.9	—	—	—	—
2,500	1,400	230	9.2	17.1	—	—	—	—
3,500	2,400	446	12.7	21.6	800	118	3.4	3.4
5,000	3,900	817	16.3	24.7	2,300	422	8.4	20.2
6,500	5,400	1,244	19.1	28.4	3,800	791	12.2	24.6
8,000	6,900	1,657	20.7	27.5*	5,300	1,215	15.2	28.3
10,000	8,900	2,229	22.2	28.6	7,300	1,764	17.6	27.5*
12,000	10,900	2,825	23.5	29.8	9,300	2,353	19.6	29.5
15,000	13,900	4,073	27.1	41.6	12,300	3,414	22.8	35.3
25,000	23,900	8,651	34.6	45.7	22,300	7,910	31.6	45.0
40,000	38,900	16,320	40.8	51.1	37,300	15,496	38.7	50.6
70,000	68,900	33,716	48.1	57.9	67,300	32,728	46.8	57.4
100,000	98,900	52,715	52.7	63.3	97,300	51,643	51.6	63.1

*Note the accidental dip in marginal rates at about $7,000 *taxable* income.

TABLE 9-2. Most of the tax concessions to marriage are in the exemptions that push down taxable incomes as families grow. Tax percentages are of "Net Income," which includes all types of income taxpayers must report, before personal exemptions, medical expenses, and donations are subtracted, minus pension premiums and other compulsory payments and dues. (Source: National Revenue Department and Tax Foundation.)

showing what has been earned and what has already been deducted. The government refunds any excess they have paid.

Those with sizable incomes must fill out a complex form.

How much does a typical person have to pay at each income level? As an example, a bachelor may have been taxed as follows in the spring of 1970. First he subtracted a minimum $1,000 plus a standard *exemption* to cover contributions to charity, medical costs, union dues, etc.; total $1,100. The remainder was "taxable income" [Columns (2) and (6) of Table 9-2]. Total tax to Ottawa, his province, and old-age pensions is shown in Columns (3) and (7).

Columns (4) and (8) show how progressive the tax really is. For a single taxpayer ... no dependents, with taxable income of $3,900 (i.e., total earnings of $5,000) the total tax is $817 or 16.3 per cent. With twice that total earnings, $10,000, the average rate is 22.2 per cent. A magnate earning a salary of $100,000 per year pays more than one-half of this, in personal income tax, to all governments.[6]

---

[6] That is why magnates attempt not only to get much of their income in the form of dividends (which will bring in a "dividend tax credit"), but also to realize their gains as "capital gains," which may bear lower tax, or which may even go untaxed.

Note that it always pays to earn more income. Columns (4) and (5) show that as the taxpayer's income rises from $3,500 to $5,000 the *extra* thousand costs him an extra (817 — 446) = $371 in taxes. This 24.7 per cent of the marginal $1,500 income is called the "marginal tax rate"—it finally reaches about 63 per cent on a taxable income of $100,000. No matter how much tax must be paid, some part of every extra layer of income can be kept by the taxpayer: it is never worthwhile to earn less income to save income taxes.[7] The rate of provincial income tax amounts to about 24 per cent of the federal tax collections. Thus it too is progressive, especially if the wife works.

Taxpayers who have some dependents, or a disability, pay less tax than do single people without disabilities. This results from exempting part of their income before taxable income is determined (in Table 9-2). While such allowances do reduce tax rates on the poor (and put many persons below the income tax level altogether), they also reduce the taxes of the rich. Indeed, the current $1,600 exemption for a wife and two children means a saving of about $465 in taxes for a $10,000-a-year man, but saves nothing for a family in poverty with about $2,300 in earned income. This same exemption would save over $900 for an executive earning $50,000. Those who would help the taxable poor should urge tax credit, not income exemption. The very poor need transfers—a negative tax, perhaps.

The proportion of Canadian tax revenue that comes from personal income tax has risen from 8 per cent in 1939-40 to 27.6 per cent in 1967. This is not just because rates have gone up. It is because the average family is now so much better off that, even at *unchanged* rates, the total collections would have more than doubled.[8] This is best illustrated by the fact that while in 1939 7 per cent of the labor force paid taxes, today 70 per cent do.

At the same time, of course, rates have gone up (especially on the lowest incomes), and the population and number of earners have almost doubled. Thus, even with the same over-all structure of federal taxes, we may expect the proportion of revenue coming from personal income tax to increase steadily. This phenomenon of a large change in revenue, because of taxpayers moving into different tax brackets, is one aspect of *built-in-flexibility* in the total tax system, and will be referred to again later (sometimes as "fiscal drag").

---

[7] The combined Canadian personal income tax structure is progressive only up to a taxable income of $6,000. Then there is a "notch". At this level the OAS and the Social Development taxes are at their maximum amounts, and hence become, for higher incomes, lump-sum or regressive taxes. Their regressive nature is, however, sufficient to outweigh the progression of the income tax only up to $8,000. As an illustration of the actual combined income tax rate, a single person with a taxable income between $6,000 and $8,000 must pay 26.8 per cent at the margin. This rate is lower than the 28.7 per cent marginal tax in the $4,000-to-$6,000 bracket. The income-tax structure, at $6,000, has become regressive in the marginal (not the average) rates. The marginal tax structure becomes progressive again just above $8,000, at 30.9 per cent. The "notch" is slight; its significance lies in the capacity of the regressive tax, embedded in a generally progressive system, to reduce the steady increase of marginal rates—i.e., to reduce the rate of progression.

[8] An increase in personal exemptions, as proposed in the 1969-70 White Paper, would work the other way.

Progressive taxes tend to reduce inequality of income distribution.

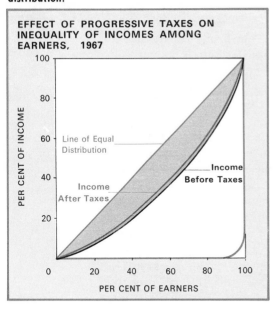

EFFECT OF PROGRESSIVE TAXES ON INEQUALITY OF INCOMES AMONG EARNERS, 1967

FIG. 9-1. The black line represents the unequal distribution of income before taxes. The curved brown line to the left of it shows how progressive (or "graduated") taxes result in a more equal distribution of "disposable" income after taxes. (Source: *Taxation Statistics*, 1969.)

TAXATION AND INEQUALITY   The progressiveness of income tax tends somewhat to reduce the inequality of disposable income. Note how the area of the inequality on the Lorenz diagram on Fig. 9-1 has been reduced; progressive taxation has shifted the curve a little nearer to the 45° line of equality.

LOOPHOLES AND EROSION OF THE TAX BASE   On paper our tax rates look progressive. But many items in the total income base escape taxation. First, there are exemptions of $1,000 per person. Second, real income in the form of owner-occupied homes avoids taxation. Third, there is also some illegal tax evasion—cheating by farmers, doctors, waiters, or salesmen with fake expense accounts, but this is said to be surprisingly small. Fourth, more important than evasion is legal tax *avoidance*, which is possible because Parliament has permitted so many tax "loopholes" that allow large amounts of income to go untaxed or to be taxed at lower levels. For example, certain industries, especially mining and petroleum, are given handsome tax exemptions.

If loopholes were closed and the erosion of the tax base corrected, rates on all income levels could be reduced without revenue loss.

Here are a few facts. Less than two-thirds of all true income is included in the tax base. Those with incomes of over 1 million dollars do not in fact pay an over-all rate of 70 or even 50 per cent. In 1967, 82 per cent of all Canadian income taxes came from the low-bracket rates of 20 per cent or less: It is not the rich who pay for the bulk of government; they are too few. It is the median income group, who, by their numbers, predominate. Critics often say, "The tax collector digs deep into high incomes, but with a sieve."

■ PROGRESSIVE TAXES, INVESTMENT, AND SPENDING

Often, doubts are raised as to whether high income taxes discourage effort and risk-taking. So far as effort is concerned, this is not an easy question to answer. For we shall later see that taxation will cause some people to work harder in order to make their million. Many doctors, scientists, artists, and businessmen who enjoy their jobs and the sense of power or accomplishment that they bring will work as hard for $30,000 as for $100,000; still others may prefer more leisure to more work as a result of progressive taxes. The net result is hard to evaluate. We shall return to this problem in Part Four.

The effects of progressive tax rates on risky investment could be quite adverse. In part, the government says to the taxpayer, "Heads I win, tails you lose." But recent reforms have improved the taxpayer's ability to carry forward or carry backward his losses, and also to spread out an extraordinarily high income by averaging it with the previous four years' income, thereby moderating greatly the penalty for erratic earnings from venturesome investment.

Careful studies at the Harvard Business School, cited in Part Four, confirm what has just been said—that there are in fact sufficient perfectly respectable "loopholes" open to wealthy people so that they may typically pay but 50 per cent tax rates, not the 70 per cent shown in tax tables. They take risks and try for less heavily taxed capital gains;[9] they invest in shares with tax credits; they drill for oil, grow trees, or feed beef cattle—all more lightly taxed.

Opposing any unfavorable effect of progressive taxes on investment, jobs, and national growth, there is an offsetting effect. To the extent that dollars are taken from frugal wealthy people who spend small fractions of their extra dollars rather than from poor ready spenders, progressive taxes may tend to keep spending power at a high level—at too high a level if inflation is threatening. But statistics on how people spend extra dollars, as we shall later see, suggest that this effect on total spending may not be so great.

Economic science can point out these various crosscurrents of progressive taxation. The 1967 (Carter) Royal Commission on Taxation clearly and daringly indicated possible improvements, especially in saying "a dollar is a dollar"—treating all types of incomes, whether it be dividends, profits, or capital gains, identically. The 1969 (Benson) White Paper picked up some of the Carter ideas. It promised greater integration of corporate and personal taxes (less "double taxation") and taxation of capital gains both on personal property—such as homes and antique furniture—and on financial securities and shares. But, in the

---

[9] When we remember the loopholes discussed in this study, which show how the well-to-do can hope to convert heavily taxed income into untaxed or less heavily taxed capital gains from risky ventures, we find that *high tax rates may encourage risk-taking by those who seek capital gains* and who know that the government finances up to 70 per cent of their deductible costs.

The real-estate property tax still dominates provincial and municipal finance:

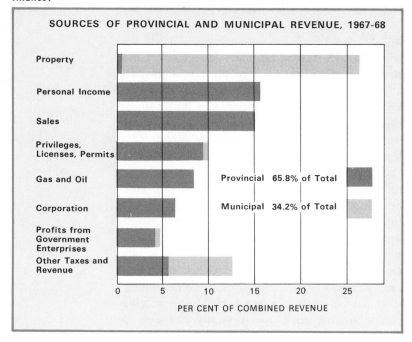

FIG. 9-2. Most local revenues stem from regressive taxes, not easy to expand as needs grow. But the provinces can get their shares of federal income and corporation tax collections and federal grants, which have a more progressive basis. (Grants are not shown here.) (Source: Table 9-3)

last analysis, each voter judges the costs and gains, and decides which combination of equality, fairness, and incentive to initiative he favors in our society.

■ PROVINCIAL AND MUNICIPAL REVENUES

To see the main sources of funds to finance such expenditure, refer to Fig. 9-2 and Table 9-3. Most of the traditional sources, the local property tax and the provincial sales tax, are "regressive" in the terms used in the previous discussion. But more and more the provinces depend on the income and corporation taxes "abated" from federal tax collections, and the municipalities, particularly the school boards, depend on the provinces. Therefore, the degree of reliance on "progressive" taxes is increasing.

PROPERTY TAX Note that the property tax still accounts for over twenty-five per cent of total revenues of provinces and municipalities. It is used more by municipalities and school boards than by the provinces.

The property tax is levied primarily on real estate, land, and buildings. Each locality sets an annual tax rate. In a large city $55 on each $1,000 of

Provinces and municipalities have different tax bases:

TAXES AND OTHER REVENUES OF PROVINCES
AND MUNICIPALITIES, 1967-1968 (millions of dollars)

SOURCE	PROVINCIAL	MUNICIPAL
Taxes:		
Income		
Individuals	1,470	—
Corporations	610	—
General and other sales	1,420	10
Motor fuel and fuel oil sales	800	—
Real and personal property and business	40	2,450
Estate tax and succession duties	120	—
Other	320	210
Total Taxes	4,780	2,670
Nontax Revenue:		
Privileges, licenses, and permits	900	60
Contributions from government enterprises	400	30
Sales and services	70	260
Other revenue	20	180
Total Nontax Revenue	1,390	530
Total Net General Revenue	6,170	3,200

TABLE 9-3. Excludes grants from other levels of government, which raised the total revenue of the provinces and municipalities by 50 per cent above that shown. (Source: *Local Government Finance* and *Provincial Government Finance, 1967-1968*, DBS.)

assessed valuation (5.5 per cent, or 55 mills) might be the rate. If my house has been assessed at $10,000, my tax is $550. However, in many places assessed valuations tend to be but a fraction of true market value. Houses like mine may have a market value of $20,000, but be assessed at half that. My true tax rate is less than 5.5 per cent.

The property tax is rather inflexible. Assessments and rates change slowly. In bad times, when real-estate values fall, the property tax is burdensome, giving rise to bankruptcy, mortgage foreclosures, and forced sales. In the zooming postwar economy, valuations and rates have been edging up.

In colonial times, a man's total income and wealth may have all been connected with real estate; if so, then the effect of a tax on such property would have been roughly the same as a proportional tax on income, and hence its classification as a direct tax. Today, when so much of wealth and income is divorced from real estate, the property tax may be regressive relative to income —especially since small properties tend to be assessed relatively higher than large.

HIGHWAY-USER TAXES   As the name suggests, these revenues come from two primary sources: from a tax on gasoline and from license fees on autos, trucks, and drivers. In Canada, they are not necessarily equal to the money spent on roads. All revenues are assigned to the "Consolidated General Fund" for schools or welfare, just as some colleges use profits from football games to buy fencing foils or even Greek manuscripts.

Nevertheless, highway taxes are usually justified on the ground that the taxpayer is simply paying for the *benefit* of using the roads in much the same way as he pays for a railroad ticket or for his use of water and electricity.

SALES TAXES   Provinces are getting more and more revenue from general retail sales taxes. Each purchase at the department, drug, and grocery store pays a percentage tax. (Usually, food and medicines are exempt.) Also, provinces usually add their own liquor and tobacco excises to the federal excises. Most people —including many cigarette smokers and moderate drinkers—feel vaguely that there is something immoral about tobacco and alcohol.[10] They somehow think two birds are being killed with one stone when these articles are taxed: the province gets revenue, and vice is made more expensive. (Note the element of self-contradiction here.)

The same moral attitude would hardly apply to a 5 per cent tax on everything a consumer buys: shoes, soap, a church candle. Rich and poor are taxed alike on each dollar spent: since the poor are forced to spend a larger portion of their total dollars, one sees that a sales tax on nonluxuries is a regressive tax, taking a larger fraction of low than high incomes.

PROVINCIAL INDIVIDUAL INCOME TAXES   The provinces have had the right to all "direct" taxes since 1867, and since 1962 have all returned to exercising this right on personal incomes. In general, Ottawa "abates" its collection by an announced percentage (28 per cent in 1969), and the provincial treasury either has this amount sent to it by Ottawa or undertakes to collect it itself. We have seen earlier that if the provincial tax is a fixed percentage of a progressive total income tax, then the provincial portion must also be progressive.

BUSINESS TAXES   Provinces and localities often charge license fees for the privilege of acting as a corporation, being an auctioneer, and so forth. Ontario and Quebec tax the net income of a corporation as well and collect miscellaneous other fees from business enterprises.

RESOURCE REVENUES   In addition, all provinces but Prince Edward Island collect special natural resource revenues. Some of these are actually landlord's income from the sale or rent of Crown land: Alberta gets royalties and bonuses from oil rights, and most provinces get a royalty or Crown due from miners' and loggers' privileges and licenses to exploit public lands. But other revenues are true specific taxes on the business exploitation of privately owned natural resources; there are various levies like property taxes, producing relatively little revenue, and important business income taxes on logging and mining, collected in Ontario and British Columbia. These fatter taxes apply to the harvest of public

---

[10] In a hearing of the 1969 British Columbia Royal Commission, a former head of the Provincial Liquor Commission testified that the Liquor Board's view was that consumption of alcohol was evil!

and private lands alike. The precise legal or political theory behind the imposition and acceptance of this patchwork of rents and taxes is obscure, but they produce considerable provincial revenue for six of the provinces.

DEATH TAXES   Death taxes in Canada have been changed in the last few years and are in a tangle. As in other countries, there are alternative basic systems: inheritance taxes on individuals who succeed to wealth upon the death of a relative or friend; and estate taxes, levied upon the dead giver's estate as a whole. Up to 1958, most Canadian estates were liable to *succession duties*, a hybrid in which a certain rate was levied progressively on the estate as a whole, and another (inheritance tax) rate to each beneficiary, the rate depending on the amount of the bequest and the relationship of the recipient to the dead giver. For example, widows paid the lowest inheritance rate. Quebec, Ontario, and British Columbia presently use the succession principle. The other provinces and Ottawa now levy straight taxes on estates, from which large exemptions for dependents are allowed. The rates are progressive, from 15 per cent on estates of about $50,000, to over 50 per cent on estates of $300,000 or over. Three-quarters of federal estate tax is "abated" to the provinces. A "gift tax" on donations between members of a family assures that taxes cannot be avoided by dispersing estates *before* death.

Thus death taxes are "progressive." The poor widow's inheritance usually pays no tax at all because of liberal exemptions, while the rich man's estate pays at a progressive rate. Social reformers attach great importance to death taxes for the purpose of preventing the development of a permanent moneyed caste, living not on its effort and intelligence, but on its property bequeathed from one generation to the next. Yet, as of the late 1960s, the right to "split income," to make gifts, and to set up complex "trusts" all these have reduced death-tax collections to a low level. (This is also happening in Great Britain.)

■ FEDERAL FINANCE AND INTERGOVERNMENTAL GRANTS

The federal government has access to more revenue sources than the other two levels of government: it *may* levy all the direct and all the indirect taxes. Furthermore, the progressiveness and built-in-flexibility of its pattern of taxes allows it to keep up with rising costs without having to legislate frequent new tax rates. Yet the spending responsibilities of provinces and municipalities are just as important, and have grown as fast as, or faster than, federal needs.

To overcome this deficit, Ottawa has made increasingly larger payments to the provinces, the legal and political nature of which varies widely. Indeed, the political history of federation is implied by the history of these payments. But only three kinds of payment belong in a quick survey of the period from 1960 to 1970.

CONDITIONAL GRANTS   Ottawa decides on the need for some social service, and provides the funds. But the provinces administer the service and put up some funds too. (EXAMPLE: In 1970 Ottawa granted over 800 million dollars to the provinces on the condition that (*a*) the money was used for hospital insurance and (*b*) the provinces matched this amount, roughly, dollar-for-dollar.)

UNCONDITIONAL GRANTS   Sometimes called block grants, these funds have no strings attached. Uncommon in the United States, they were until about 1962 the mainstay of our grant system. They were designed to help each province plug the gap between its needs and its revenue sources. Since 1963, however, they are limited to the poorer provinces, as their self-explanatory names suggest: Equalization Grants, and Atlantic Provinces Grants. Unconditional grants remedy a traditional objection to conditional grants: Ottawa's dictating the policies and activities of the provinces. But an unconditional grant runs into another objection: Ottawa has no control over vast sums it raises from its taxpayers, the spending of which is handed over to the provincial legislatures.

TAX ABATEMENT, OR SHARED TAXES   This system has largely replaced the pre-1962 unconditional grants to all provinces. Ottawa collects most direct taxes, but each province takes a share "abated" from the federal taxes collected in its territory. Provincial rates can be set at any level, but Ottawa will only abate an agreed percentage of its collections. (EXAMPLES: Saskatchewan and Manitoba, in connection with their medical plans set provincial income taxes at 33 per cent of federal collections, when Ottawa abated only 28 per cent. Thus their taxpayers pay 5 per cent more income tax than taxpayers in other provinces. Ontario also collects its own corporation tax. Quebec receives a hefty 50 per cent abatement of federal personal taxes because it has chosen to "contract" out of many federal-provincial programs, and it collects both its own income taxes and its own corporation taxes. But rates paid by taxpayers in Ontario and Quebec are very close to those paid in other provinces.)

Similarly, *within* the provinces there are both conditional and unconditional grants from the provincial treasuries to the municipalities, school boards, etc. The former are primarily for schools and welfare. The latter prevent a too-heavy dependence on the property tax, the only other important source open to most municipalities. Both help maintain, throughout each province, certain minimum standards of schooling and other public services. In this way, well-to-do suburbanites who have fled the city are made to share the burden, and richer regions can help backward areas.

Thus federal grants work toward narrowing the great regional differences between the eastern provinces and the rest. They also strengthen minimum standards within each province. But from east to west and from city to backwoods, there remain sizable differences. It still matters where one is born.

DOUBLE TAXATION OF PROVINCIAL INCOMES   Both in provincial corporation and personal income taxes, there are serious legal problems about the "residence," "domicile," or "locus" of taxpayers or of taxable incomes, especially when a person has several homes, or a business has branches and handles transactions in many provinces. Though this threat of double taxation is annoying, and the rulings are usually arbitrary, the present situation at its worst involves filling out two or more income tax returns and hiring lawyers to make sure that the highest taxes are avoided (whenever the taxpayer can, by his conduct, affect the jurisdiction in which he is taxable). It is a far better situation than that in the late 1930s. Today the income and corporation taxes are more or less coordinated, the provincial personal tax especially being an "abatement" of federal tax. Thus, as Table 9-2 shows, neither the average nor the marginal total tax paid to all governments approaches more than about 70 per cent. But in the 1930s, a tangle of separate income taxes, levied independently by Ottawa and the provinces, sometimes resulted in marginal rates, from two or more levels of taxes, greater than 100 per cent! After a certain income, it did *not* pay to earn any more. (Actually, it paid to leave certain provinces, or in the case of certain millionaires, to leave Canada altogether.)[11]

PROVINCIAL AND LOCAL DEBT   Even when these extra "senior-government sources" are counted in, it is still not true that the total of provincial and municipal expenditures equals the total of their revenues. The difference represents new borrowing or debt repayment. The war prosperity swelled provincial tax revenues. At the same time it became impossible to build new schools and highways. As a result, most provinces were then able to run a surplus and retire a part of their previously accumulated debt.

But since the war, provinces and municipalities have again been increasing their debts. Their costs have risen as new school and highway projects have been undertaken. In the 1970s it will be provinces and municipalities that are subjected to the greatest financial strains.

In the interwar period, most provincial and municipal borrowing tended to behave perversely, so as to accentuate rather than dampen the business cycle. In the 1920s, when the growth of the federal public debt slackened, municipalities, provinces, and provincial Crown corporations floated tremendous bond issues in order to build needed streets, schools, highways, and utilities at the high wages and prices then prevailing in the building industry. But when the Depression of the 1930s came, the value of real estate dropped, and the municipalities found that their property-tax revenues would scarcely cover the burden of their 1920 borrowings. (Many places went into "receivership" and were put under trustees by senior governments, from the then Dominion of Newfoundland to the suburban municipality of North Vancouver. Alberta defaulted on its payments to bondholders.) The provinces attempted to smooth out the cut in their revenues by borrowing even for current purposes, such as relief payments

---

[11] The famous Rowell-Sirois Report on Dominion-Provincial relations recommended methods of overcoming this type of double taxation (1940). During World War II the problem was solved by the provinces *renting* their rights to levy income taxes to Ottawa. Since then the system has gradually returned to the freedom of the provinces to levy whatever taxes they choose; but the federal government "abates" a proportion of its direct taxes and most provinces choose to levy this share of federal tax (in 1967: 28 per cent of personal income tax; 10 per cent of corporate tax; and 75 per cent of federal estate tax).

Note that "double taxation" may have two meanings: (a) corporate profits may be taxed by corporation and personal taxes; (b) any income may be taxed by two jurisdictions. In its second meaning, double taxation between countries is prevented by a series of tax treaties between Canada and her neighbors.

to the unemployed. But because the money market would not buy many such bonds, this way out of the "perversity" of borrowing and spending did not work.

Currently economists are giving thought to ways of coordinating the timing of municipal and provincial spending (and borrowing) so that along with federal spending they will counterbalance private spending spurts and stops over the business cycle. The new tax independence of the provinces makes such coordination administratively more difficult than it would have been over twenty years ago. But schemes are being devised to give provinces (and perhaps municipalities) financial incentives to delay capital borrowing and spending in boom periods, while making it easier for them to borrow during slumps. To do this, it will be necessary somehow to bring them, with the federal government, into closer contact with the money-creating Bank of Canada.

■ CONCLUSION: THE THORNY PROBLEM OF TAX INCIDENCE

In ending this survey of taxes and other revenues, let us note a few warnings. Even if the electorate has made up its mind about how the tax burden shall be borne by individuals, the following difficult problems remain:

Who ultimately pays a particular tax? Does its burden stay on the person against whom it is first levied? One cannot just assume that the person a legislature says a tax is levied on will end up paying that tax. He may be able to *shift* the tax: shift it "forward" on his customers, by raising his price as much as the tax; or shift it "backward" on his suppliers, who end up charging him less than they would have done had there been no tax.

Economists therefore say: We must study the final incidence of the tax— the way its burden ultimately gets borne, the totality of its effect on commodity prices, factor prices, resource allocations, efforts, composition of production and consumption, and the quantities of each commodity produced and each factor supplied. To locate a tax's final incidence therefore is so broad a problem as to require all the advanced tools of economics for its detection.

> EXAMPLE: Does a tax on wheat raise the price to the consumer by as much as itself, so that the incidence is on the consumer? Or does the tax raise the price by half itself or not at all, so that the incidence is partially on the producers? Does it change oat prices? And does the tax kill off all or much of wheat production, so that it is having incidence effects beyond those which show up in money prices and wages and even beyond the burdens that you can allocate among the different citizens?

However, we can get the feel of the problem by asking about the effects which are felt by either the buyer or the seller of a taxed commodity. Imagine, for example, that the government levies a tax of 10 cents a yard on the cotton gray goods mentioned earlier in Chapter 4, page 95, no matter what the price. In Figure 9-3, the demand curve *dd* shows the quantity Q bought at each price P. And, before the tax, *ss* shows the amounts sellers will be willing to offer at each P. E shows equilibrium price and quantity.

Now, the effect of a tax is to *shift ss*. In order to get sellers to offer a par-

A tax falls on both buyers and sellers:

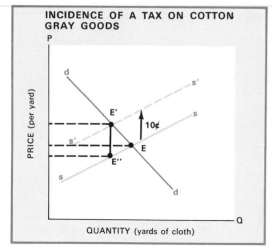

INCIDENCE OF A TAX ON COTTON GRAY GOODS

PRICE (per yard)

QUANTITY (yards of cloth)

FIG. 9-3. A ten-cent tax shifts the price upward by less than 10¢. Thus the incidence is partly on buyers and partly on sellers.

ticular Q, it is now necessary to pay them the old P plus the government's 10 cents. Hence, the supply curve shifts upward 10 cents, to the parallel position $s's'$. The amount consumers must pay rises, consequently, from E to E'. But have consumers paid the full tax? No. Because the distance from E' to E'' is equal to 10 cents, the rise in price must be less, only about 7 cents, while sellers take a 3-cent cut in the amount they receive. Their net amount—available for their own income, or for the wages of their workers—falls from E to E''. Unless dd is vertical, or ss horizontal, the incidence will always be divided between buyers and sellers. It is rarely on one party only. And because Q also falls, land and labor must be reallocated to other markets, where prices and wages will change, causing changes in demand for still other commodities ... until the "burden" of the tax is seen to extend far beyond the two parties to the cotton-goods market.

In Part Three, Chapter 19, this thorny problem is tackled further, with the help of the "elasticity" concept (see Fig. 19-6); and it is raised again in Part Four. The question of tax incidence is both relevant and current, although economists are not yet agreed on final results. Some think the corporate income tax falls mostly on the consumer; some argue it falls mostly on stockholders and capitalists.

Figure 9-4, on the next page, is a valiant attempt to determine statistically how progressive or regressive our over-all tax and expenditure structure was in 1961. Experts agree that the results of such a study can be only approximate, since no one knows just how a corporate tax or other tax gets shifted. Even an expert is not a magician capable of making a controlled experiment in which he (1) measures things without taxes, then (2) measures things with taxes, and finally (3) determines tax incidence as the difference between these situations.

Note the slow progression of tax around the median income level. The very affluent do get taxed to help the poor, but the man in the middle is something

Who pays the taxes and gets the benefits of spending?—an expert's estimate:

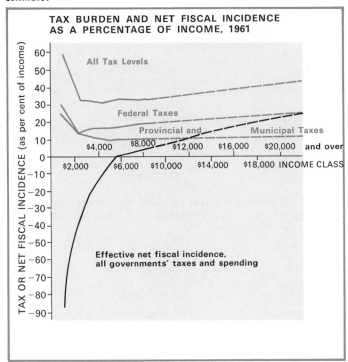

FIG. 9-4. The three upper curves show taxes as a percentage of income. Although the federal government depends heavily on the individual income tax, its other revenues tend to be regressive; so its total tax structure is not progressive under $4,000. However, even the regressive provincial and municipal tax structure is outweighed by the favorable impact of expenditures on the lower "net incidence" (of taxes and expenditures) curve, which has a definitely negative "burden" on low incomes. (Source: *The Incidence of Taxes and Public Expenditures in the Canadian Economy*, by **W. I. Gillespie, Study Number 2, Royal Commission on Taxation, 1966.)**

of a forgotten man when it comes to tax burden. But, as the curve in Fig. 9-4 shows, when we attempt to determine which classes benefit from government expenditure, the needy show a much more favorable "net incidence" than the affluent.

SUMMARY

■ 1 Taxes enable the government to pay for the *real* resources it needs for its public activities. Taxes also finance welfare transfer expenditures that change the distribution of income; and the over-all way taxes are levied affects the final distribution of incomes among people.

■ 2 Notions of "benefit" and of "proper sacrifice or redistribution" are the two principal theories of taxation. Justice implies taxing equals equally, unequals unequally. Direct and progressively graduated taxes on incomes are in contrast to indirect and regressive excises.

■ 3 Almost half of federal revenue comes from personal and corporation income taxes. The rest comes from "regressive taxes" on sales and imports. The personal income tax, except for loopholes and erosion of the tax base, is steeply progressive, tending to redistribute income from rich to poor.

■ 4 The property tax is the most important source of municipal revenue. Sales taxes and resource revenue are important for the province. In the postwar period, provinces and municipalities have been spending more than they tax, thereby increasing their debts.

■ 5 The federal government makes large tax payments to the provinces, as well as conditional and unconditional grants for highways and social welfare. The provinces help the municipalities in education, highways, and public assistance.

■ 6 The incidence of a tax is its ultimate division of burden, its total effect on prices and other economic magnitudes. Those upon whom a tax is levied may succeed in shifting part of its burden forward or backward. The economists' tools of Parts Three and Four will help in tackling this difficult problem. Progression in the benefits of public expenditure seems to offset the regressive curves of taxation.

QUESTIONS FOR DISCUSSION

1.   Make a list of different taxes in order of their progressiveness. What is the importance of each at the federal, provincial, and municipal level?

2.   How do you think different government functions should be allocated among the three levels of government? How about revenues and grants?

3.   Should a citizen in Ontario be taxed to help a citizen in Newfoundland? To help a citizen in Quebec? In Ontario? In Mexico or India?

4.   "Since people don't change their smoking habits as a result of taxation, and since the poor smoke, a tax on cigarettes is really no different from a tax on bread." Do you agree? If so, what ought to be done?

5.   Calculate from Table 9-2 the personal income tax paid by a typical doctor, lawyer, teacher, stenographer, mechanic, and carpenter.

6.   Who pays for education in Canada? Try to trace back the incidence, and suggest improvements.

7.   "More kids and cars mean municipal expenditure and debt." Evaluate.

8.   Is the property tax on a house a direct or an indirect tax? The tax on a developer building new houses for sale or rent? How does the Canadian constitution define property taxes?

9.   Review your understanding of the following concepts:

tax revenues and real resources	horizontal and vertical equity
benefit and sacrifice notions	conditional and unconditional grants
direct and indirect taxes	budget surpluses and deficits
progressive and regressive	tax incidence and shifting
exemptions versus credits	

10

NATIONAL PRODUCT AND INCOME

The time has come, the walrus said,
To speak of many things.
Of shoes, and ships, and sealing wax,
Of cabbages—and kings   LEWIS CARROLL

One of the most important concepts in all economics is the national income—or, technically, the gross national product (GNP). This measures the economic performance of the whole economy. Of course, man does not live by bread alone. Nor does our society live by GNP alone. But on our way to the state of affluence where material well-being will fall to the second level of significance, we do need a summary measure of aggregate economic performance.

This chapter's discussion of national income can serve as the unifying summary of Part One's introduction to the *basic economic processes and institutions* of modern mixed societies. Alternately, this analysis of national income, its anatomy and accounting structure, can be regarded as the introduction to the treatment of macroeconomics of Part Two—the study of the physiological forces that determine total employment, production, real income, and the price level. The concept of national income is indispensable preparation for tackling the great issues of unemployment, inflation, and growth.

■ THE YARDSTICK OF AN ECONOMY'S PERFORMANCE

What is national income? It is the loose name we give to the money measure of the over-all annual flow of goods and services in an economy. Often, instead of it, we use the almost equivalent, precise term "national product" or "net national

Net national product is measured as flow of output or as equal flow of costs:

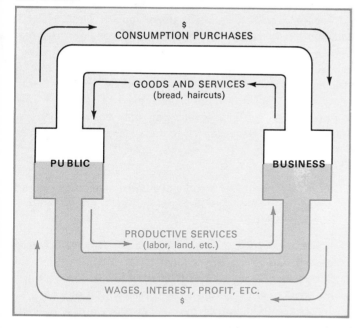

FIG. 10-1. In the upper loop, people spend their money on final goods; the total dollar flow of these per year is one measure of net national product, NNP.

The lower loop measures the annual flow of costs of output: the earnings that business pays out in wages, rent, interest, dividends, and accrued profits. With profit properly reckoned as a residual, the two measures of NNP must always be identical.

product" (NNP);[1] or perhaps more often the slightly different concept of "gross national product" (GNP).

If you asked an economic historian just what the Great Depression really meant, his best brief answer would be: "From a 1929 NNP of 5.5 billion dollars there was a drop to a 1933 NNP of 3.0 billion dollars. This halving of the money value of the flow of goods and services in the Canadian economy caused hardship, bankruptcy, riots, and political turmoil."

In brief, national income or product is the final figure you arrive at when you apply the measuring rod of money to the diverse apples, grain, and machines that any society produces with its land, labor, and capital resources.

■ TWO MEASURES OF NATIONAL PRODUCT: AS GOODS-FLOW
   OR AS EARNINGS-FLOW

How do we measure the net national product, NNP? The general idea is simple. Figure 10-1 shows the circular flow of dollar spending in an economy with no government and no accumulation of capital or net saving going on.

---

[1] We shall have occasion below to note the special and narrow use of the term "national income" by the Dominion Bureau of Statistics.

FLOW-OF-PRODUCT APPROACH   Each year the public consumes goods and services: goods such as apples, oranges, and bread; services such as haircuts. The public spends dollars for these consumer goods, as in the upper loop of Fig. 10-1. We add together all the consumption dollars spent for these final goods to arrive at the total of NNP.

Thus, in our simple economy, one can easily calculate national income or product as the sum of the annual flow of final goods and services: (price of bread × number of loaves) + (price of apples × number of apples) + ...

Why use market prices as weights in evaluating and summing diverse physical commodities and services? Because, as we shall see in Part Three, market prices are reflectors of the relative desirability of diverse goods and services.

The *net national product*, or "national income evaluated at market prices," as it is technically named, is definable as the total money value of the flow of final products of the community.[2]

EARNINGS OR INCOME APPROACH   There is a second, equivalent way to calculate NNP in so simple an economy. Go to the lower loop in Fig. 10-1: What is the total cost of output which business is paying out to the public? It is paying out wages, interest, rents, and profit. Why? Because these factor earnings of land, labor, and capital are the *costs* of production of the flow of product. (NOTE: Here the economist, unlike the accountant, does count profit as a cost or earning item.)

The statistician can measure the annual flow of such factor earnings or income in the lower loop.[3] In this way, he will *again* arrive at the NNP.

Net national product is also definable, from a second viewpoint, as the total of factor earnings (wages, interest, rents, and accruing profits) that are the costs of production of society's final goods.

Now we have calculated NNP by the upper-loop flow-of-product approach and by the lower-loop earnings-flow approach. Which is bigger? Answer: They must be *exactly* the same.

Here is the reason for this identity. Recall that we have included "profit" in the lower loop—along with wages, interest, and rents. What exactly is profit? Profit is what you have left over from the sale of product (your apples, bread, oranges, and manicures) *after* you have paid the other factor costs. *So profit automatically is the residual that takes on the size needed to make the lower-loop approach via earnings* exactly *match the upper-loop approach via flow of goods.*

This all reflects the useful device of double-entry which accountants use to keep the two sides of their books in perfect balance.

---

[2] In our first, simplest model, the only final product is private consumption expenditures. But in a moment we shall see that government expenditures on goods and services, private net investment, and net exports are also to be included.

[3] When we leave our simple model, taxes will have to be included here properly.

To sum up: NNP, or net national product, is measurable as the flow of product; but it is also convenient for the statistician to measure it via the earnings approach in the lower loop. With the proper definition of profit and its inclusion as an economic earning and cost, each approach will yield exactly the same NNP.

An example will show how to go from business accounts to national accounts in the simplest case, without government and investment, and where all final products are produced from land, labor, and capital in 10 million identical one-stage firms or farms.

INCOME STATEMENT OF TYPICAL FARM

OUTPUT ATTRIBUTABLE TO FARMING		EARNINGS	
Sales of goods		Costs of production	
(wheat, apples, etc.)	$1,000	Wages	$ 800
		Rents	100
		Interest	25
		Profit (residual)	75
Total	$1,000	Total	$1,000

Adding all the 10 million farms gives the NNP account easily in this trivial case.

NATIONAL PRODUCT ACCOUNT (in millions!)

UPPER-LOOP FLOW OF PRODUCT		LOWER-LOOP EARNINGS OR INCOMES	
Final output (10 × 1,000)	$10,000	Wages (10 × 800)	$ 8,000
		Rents (10 × 100)	1,000
		Interest (10 × 25)	250
		Profit (10 × 75)	750
NNP total	$10,000	NNP total	$10,000

Note that the definition of profit makes the firm's two sides balance; hence the two NNP approaches must still match after summation.

■ REAL VERSUS MONEY NATIONAL PRODUCT: USING A PRICE INDEX
   TO "DEFLATE"

We saw that NNP uses the measuring rod of money prices in the market to combine diverse apples, bread loaves, and other goods to a single total figure. But one would hardly choose to measure things with a rubber rather than a wooden yardstick—one that stretched in your hands from day to day.

This is one of the problems economists have to solve when they use money as their measuring rod. Everyone knows that inflations and deflations can send most prices up or down. Or, as the economist puts it, "The value of money does change between years like 1929 and 1933, or 1939 and 1971 or 1972."

What can be done about this? Economists can repair most of the damage due to the changeability of our measuring rod by using an *index number of*

We deflate by a price index to correct for our rubber money yardstick:

SAMPLE CALCULATION OF REAL NNP

DATE	(1) MONEY NNP, BILLIONS OF CURRENT DOLLARS	(2) INDEX NUMBER OF PRICES	(3) REAL NNP, IN BILLIONS OF 1929 DOLLARS $(3) = \frac{(1)}{(2)} \times 100$
1929	5.5	100	$\frac{5.5}{100} \times 100 = 5.5$
1933	3.0	75	$\frac{3.0}{75} \times 100 = 4.0$

TABLE 10-1. Using price index of Column (2), we deflate Column (1) to get real NNP, Column (3). (Riddle: Can you show that 1929's real NNP was 4.1 billion dollars in terms of 1933 prices? Hint: With 1933 as a base, 1929's price index is 133⅓.)

prices.[4] A 1929-1933 comparison will illustrate the process by which one uses a price index number to "deflate" a "current *money* NNP," converting it into a "*real* NNP in terms of dollars of unchanged 1929 purchasing power."

Table 10-1 gives the actual 1929 and 1933 NNP figures to the close approximations of 5.5 and 3.0 billion dollars. It shows a fall of money NNP to 55 per cent of its old level. But the government estimates that prices of goods and services dropped on the average about 25 per cent in the Depression. Using 1929 as a base of 100, this means the 1933 price index was about 75. So our 3.0 billion-dollar 1933 NNP was really worth more than 55 per cent of the 5.5 billion-dollar NNP of 1929.

How much more? Table 10-1 divides through by the price index number to "deflate" and shows that "*real NNP*" *fell only to three-quarters the 1929 level:* thus in terms of dollars of 1929 purchasing power, it fell down to 4.0 billion dollars. Hence, part of the fall shown by the money NNP was due to the optical illusion of the changing price yardstick.

Figure 10-2 shows the history of money NNP (expressed in the actual dollars and prices that were current in each historical year). Then, for comparison, the real NNP (expressed in 1969 dollars) is shown. Note that part of the increase in money NNP is spurious, being due merely to inflation of our money yardstick's price units in the last 30 years.

■ AVOIDING "DOUBLE COUNTING" OF INTERMEDIATE GOODS

Returning to current money figures, we can now show how to handle "inter-

---

[4] Computing a price index would be easy if all prices were to change by the same percentage. When all *P*'s triple, the index rises from 100 to 300; when all halve, it drops to 50. If *P*'s increase in different degrees, but all end up between double and triple their base, the index is certainly between 200 and 300. Just where? Evidently we need some kind of an *average* of the price changes, each being *weighted* in accordance with its approximate economic *importance*. The official indexes are good approximations, but some basic problems remain: getting an accurate sample of prices; allowing for quality improvements; deciding which average to use (arithmetic or geometric mean, median, etc.); defining relative-economic-importance weights, in a static and in a changing world.

mediate" goods (which are not truly *final* goods) and thus avoid counting anything two, three, or more times.

IGNORING INTERMEDIATE GOODS   We do want to count bread in NNP, but we must *avoid also counting in the dough that goes to make the bread.* That would indeed be double counting, since the only reason we want the dough is for the final bread. Turn back to the two-loop diagram in Fig. 10-1. You can see bread (and haircuts) there; but you do not see any dough, flour, or wheat. Where are they? These are so-called "intermediate products" that are produced during all the stages leading up to the final bread product, and they are hidden in the block marked "business." That is as it should be. We do not want such intermediate products to be double-counted along with the final product.

How rising prices spuriously inflated the growth of our net national product:

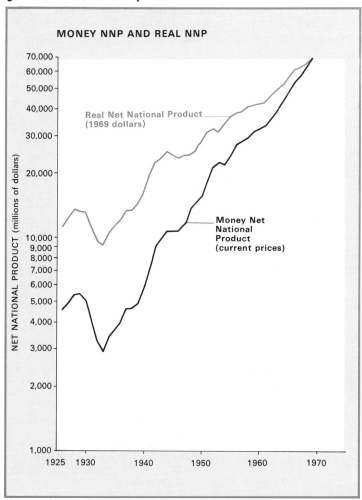

FIG. 10-2. The increase in money NNP since the Depression and World War II exaggerates the rise in real NNP; because the price index has generally been rising since then, we must use it to deflate the money NNP and arrive at the real NNP trends. Note that this is a "ratio" or "semilog" chart with vertical distances arranged to reflect percentage changes. A steeper slope depicts a greater percentage of increase. (Source: DBS)

USING "VALUE ADDED" TO AVOID DOUBLE COUNTING   A new statistician who is being trained to make NNP measurements might well be puzzled, saying:

> I can see that, if you are careful, your upper-loop approach to NNP will avoid including intermediate products. But I'm a little uncertain whether or not you might find yourself in some difficulty when you use the lower-loop approach. After all, doesn't the Dominion Bureau of Statistics gather income statements from the accounts of business firms? Won't it then be picking up what millers pay to farmers, what bakers pay to millers, and what grocers pay to bakers? Won't this result in double counting or even triple and quadruple counting of some items that go through several stages of production?

This is a legitimate question. Fortunately, we can give it a satisfactory answer. The statistician making lower-loop earnings or factor-cost measurements is always very careful to use what he calls the "value added" approach.

The value-added approach refuses to include *all* the expenses shown on each firm's business income statement in the lower-loop factor earnings. Which expenses are excluded? All purchases of materials and services from *other* business firms are excluded, because those dollars will get properly counted in NNP from the reports of such *other* firms.

EXAMPLE: Pepto-Glitter Co. buys electric power from the Ontario Hydro. This expense on the Pepto income statement is *not* included in value added. Why should it be? It is not a wage, interest, rent, or profit payment. In fact, it is not a payment to any Pepto-Glitter productive factor; hence it never shows up in the lower loop at all. It stays inside the business block, where it and all other such expenditures by a firm on intermediate goods are carefully subtracted from Pepto's receipts. What is left? Pepto's true value added—which is exactly the sum of *its* wages, interest, rent, and profit costs.

Mind you, the electric power was produced by the Hydro workers—and by the Hydro interest, rent, and profit receivers. So do not fear that this electrical activity will get overlooked by the NNP statistician. It will not. He will pick it up as the value added of the Ontario Hydro. This is as it should be: we want to count each thing once, not twice or three times.

NNP is the sum of value added of all the separate stages:

BREAD RECEIPTS, COSTS, AND VALUE ADDED
(in cents per loaf)

STAGE OF PRODUCTION	(1) SALES RECEIPTS		(2) COST OF INTERMEDIATE MATERIAL OR GOODS		(3) VALUE ADDED (WAGES, PROFIT, ETC.) (3) = (1) — (2)
Wheat	8	—	0	=	8
Flour	11	—	8	=	3
Baked dough	20	—	11	=	9
Delivered bread	30	—	20	=	10
	69	—	39	=	30 (sum of value added)

TABLE 10-2. To avoid double counting, we carefully calculate value added at each stage, subtracting all the costs of materials and intermediate products not produced in that stage but bought from other business firms. Note that every intermediate product appears both in Column (1) and with opposite sign in Column (2); hence it is canceled out.

Table 10-2 illustrates by means of the several stages of a loaf of bread how careful adherence to the value-added approach will enable us to subtract the intermediate expenses that show up in the income statements of farmers, millers, bakers, and grocers—ending up with the desired equality between (1) net value of final bread and (2) the lower-loop factor-costs embodying the sum of the value-added data of all stages. All this can be summarized as follows:

Value-added approach. To avoid double counting, we take care to include in net national product only final goods, and not the intermediate goods that go to make the final goods. By resolutely sticking to the *value added* at each stage, taking care to subtract expenditures on the intermediate goods bought from other firms, the lower-loop earnings approach properly avoids all double counting and records wages, interest, rent, and profit exactly one time.

Our earlier example with 10 million farmers can now have added to it 10 million second-stage manufacturers, who buy wheat and farm goods and add value to them by processing them into bread and other final products by the use of labor, land, and capital. Alongside the farmer's income statement we now have the manufacturer's income statement.

INCOME STATEMENT OF TYPICAL MANUFACTURER

OUTPUT ATTRIBUTABLE TO MANUFACTURING		EARNINGS	
Sales of goods	$5,000	Costs or "value added"	
Minus goods bought from		Wages	$3,500
other firms	−1,000	Rent	100
		Interest	100
		Profit (residual)	300
Total	$4,000	Total	$4,000

To get total NNP for society, we can add the left-hand sides of the 10 million farmers *and* 10 million bakers; or to get lower- rather than upper-loop NNP, we add the right-hand items for *all* these 20 million firms.

NATIONAL PRODUCT ACCOUNT (in millions)

UPPER-LOOP FLOW OF PRODUCT		LOWER-LOOP EARNINGS OR INCOMES	
Final output (finished bread, etc.)		Wages (8,000 + 35,000)	$43,000
[50,000 = 10,000 (on farms)		Rent (1,000 + 1,000)	2,000
+ (50,000 − 10,000) (in		Interest (250 + 1,000)	1,250
manufacturing)]	$50,000	Profit (750 + 3,000)	3,750
NNP total	$50,000	NNP total	$50,000

■ NET INVESTMENT, CAPITAL FORMATION

So far we have banished all capital growth from our discussion. We talked of people as wanting to currently consume bread, apples, oranges, and haircuts.[5]

---

[5] Indeed, the economic statistician counts in the NNP all consumption items that people want to spend *their* incomes on. He draws the line at illegal expenditures, e.g., opium consumption or prostitution. When black-market operations were important, he found it necessary to supplement his statistics with estimates of black-market money transactions.

In real life, however, people often want to devote part of their income to saving and investment. Instead of eating bread *now*, they may want to build new machines to help produce more bread for *future* consumption, or they may want to add to the inventory of bread in their deep-freeze compartments. In short, we must recognize that the final goals of people do include net investment or capital formation, not simple current consumption.

If people are using part of society's production possibilities for capital formation rather than consumption, the economic statistician recognizes that he must include such output in his upper-loop flow of NNP. So really, we must modify our original definition to read:

> Net national product is the sum of *all* final products, such as consumption goods and services, and including also *net* investment.

This net investment (or net capital formation) will include the net additions to our stock of (1) buildings, (2) equipment, and (3) inventories.

> WARNING: To economists, investment always means real capital formation—production of added goods in inventories, of new plants, houses, and tools. To the layman, investment means merely using money to buy an outstanding share of GM stock, to buy a corner lot, to open a savings account. It is important not to confuse these meanings: If I take $1,000 from my safe and now put it in the bank or buy common stock from a broker, the economist says that neither investment nor saving has gone up from this act alone. Only if some physical capital formation takes place is there investment; only if society consumes less than its income, devoting resources to capital formation, is there saving.

■ NET INVESTMENT EQUALS GROSS INVESTMENT MINUS DEPRECIATION

How does the economist get accurate figures on net investment?

First he has to make estimates of inventories and of their changes. Harder still is his task of estimating net investment in buildings and equipment.

To get net investment, subtract depreciation from gross investment:

GROSS AND NET INVESTMENT (millions of dollars)					
INVESTMENT COMPONENTS	1926	1932	1968	1969	1970
New construction—Residential	$205	$ 76	$ 3,294	$ 3,830	$ 3,537
—Non-residential	242	123	4,488	4,704	5,253
Machinery and equipment	261	108	5,049	5,483	5,919
Change in business inventories	135	−100	712	1,010	135
Business Gross Investment	$843	$207	$13,543	$15,027	$14,844
Allowance for capital consumption or depreciation (also = difference between GNP and NNP)	−512	−508	−7,423	−7,785	−9,898
Business net investment	$331	$−301	$ 6,120	$ 7,242	$ 4,946

TABLE 10-3. After subtracting capital depreciation from business *gross* investment, we get business *net* investment. Note that the final figure was negative in 1932, as can be seen also in Fig. 10-3. Can you explain this? (Source: DBS; and Bank of Canada *Statistical Summary*.)

Why can't he just jot down *all the* buildings built and *all* the machines produced, add them in with his calculated net inventory change, and let it go at that? He does indeed make such a calculation. But the resulting figure is too large —too gross. Recognizing this he gives a new name to the result, namely, "gross investment" rather than "net investment."

Why the word "gross"? The statistician uses this word to emphasize that he has not yet made any *allowances for the using up of capital*, i.e., no allowance for capital *depreciation*. (Recall the accounting appendix of Chapter 5.)

One would not think much of a statistician who estimated the change in human population by ignoring deaths. If he just added up gross births, without subtracting a good estimate for deaths, he would get an exaggerated notion of the net change in population. The same holds for economic equipment and buildings: net change is always gross births (of capital) minus deaths (or capital depreciation). This can be summed up in the definition:

> Net investment always equals gross investment minus depreciation.

Table 10-3 gives typical figures relating net and gross investment. They differ only by depreciation; and fortunately, this is a sluggish item that changes slowly over a period of a few years. That is why many forecasters, who really are interested in net investment, are satisfied to work with the gross investment figures, which are easier to find in the newspapers and official statistics.

■ GROSS NATIONAL PRODUCT VERSUS NET NATIONAL PRODUCT

Gross investment can be estimated fairly accurately, requiring no difficult depreciation estimate. For this reason governments and the United Nations sensibly decided to calculate a gross national product figure *first* rather than a net national product figure.

> Gross national product (GNP) is equal to the sum of final products such as consumption and gross investment (which is the sum of the increase in inventories plus gross births or production of buildings and equipment).

Table 10-3 suggests it will be easy enough to get NNP from GNP after we know what is the total depreciation figure that is to be subtracted from GNP.[6] This is important to know, for Canada's official statisticians at the Dominion Bureau of Statistics do not present NNP data. (American Department of Commerce statisticians do so, but less frequently than they publish GNP data.) They concentrate on GNP for the very good reason that depreciation figures cannot be quickly and accurately measured each quarter. Even if the economist likes to talk about NNP, he is quite content to work with GNP data, knowing that the two concepts do move together closely during any period of several years.

---

[6] Here is a convenient rule of thumb: NNP is usually about eleven-twelfths of GNP, depreciation nowadays being about one-twelfth of GNP.

We have seen that NNP calculated by the upper-loop purchases approach must be identical with the lower-loop earnings-flow NNP. Obviously if depreciation estimates are added to each calculation the two GNPs must also be identical. To distinguish the concepts from each other, Dominion Bureau of Statistics statisticians have given a special name to each: if the national total is calculated

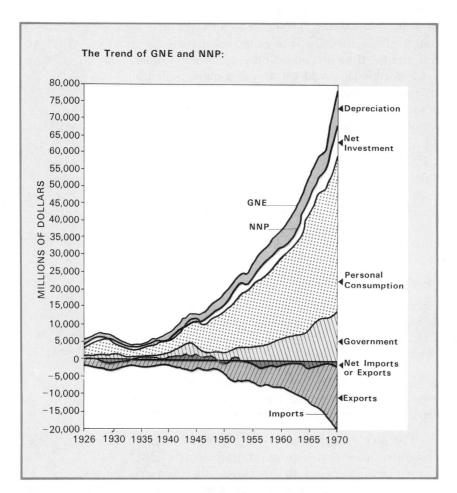

FIG. 10-3. The large mass in the middle is consumption, which dominates GNE. But note the World War II and postwar growth of government, near the bottom axis. NNP is the second line from the top; it has grown at the same rate as GNE. Net imports entered the GNE total negatively in the 1960s; and, as net exports, positively in World War II. [Imports are plotted downward from the zero axis, and exports are then plotted upward from imports, leaving a narrow band of net imports (minus) or net exports (plus). Government spending is measured upward from the wiggly net import line, minus or plus; and all other spending bands are added upward from government.] (Source: Urquhart and Buckley, *Historical Statistics of Canada*, Cambridge University Press, 1965; and Bank of Canada *Statistical Summary*.)

by the flow-of-product approach, it is called gross national expenditure (GNE); if it is reached by the earnings-flow approach, it is called GNP.

> Gross national expenditure (GNE) is identical in amount to gross national product (GNP). GNE is the sum of all final outputs. GNP is the sum of all factor earnings.[7]

These are the basic concepts of national-product accounting. But now we must include two real-world sectors we have ignored: the government and international trade. Both produce final outputs and factor earnings.

■ GOVERNMENT EXPENDITURE ON GOODS AND SERVICES

GNE must somehow take into account the billions of dollars of product that a nation collectively consumes. But how do we measure government consumption?

After some debate,[8] the income statisticians of Canada, the United States, and the United Nations decided to use the simplest method of all. To the flow of (1) consumption product and (2) investment product, they simply add (3) *all* government expenditure on goods and services. (Repeatedly in the next few chapters, you will see $C + I + G$, which stands for these three components.)

Here are examples. Along with bread consumption and gross investment, we introduce into GNE government expenditures on jet fighters. We include government expenditure on the services of jet pilots, judges, policemen, national-income statisticians, firemen, and agricultural chemists.

In short, all the government payroll expenditures on its employees plus the goods (typewriters, guns, and airplanes) it buys from private industry are included in this third great category of flow of product, labeled G and called "government expenditure on goods and services."

Figure 10-3 pictures GNE and its major components.

EXCLUSION OF TRANSFER PAYMENTS   Does this mean that every dollar the government pays out is included in GNP and GNE? Definitely not. If you get an old-age pension from the government, we call that a "transfer payment" and do not treat it as part of GNE. Why not? Because it is not a government expenditure on final goods and services of this year. Or if your aunt receives a widow's assistance payment, that welfare expenditure is also considered a transfer item. The same goes for pensions to the blind, veterans, and other welfare recipients. These transfers are not payments for *current* productive services.

Many other government transfer items[9] could be mentioned, but we can

---

[7] To be consistent, GNE minus depreciation ought to be named net national expenditure (NNE). But although this term has been used by some economists, NNP is commonly used for the net figure calculated by either method.

[8] Why is the valuation of government output a problem? Simply because so little of the goods and services which the government produces ever reach the market. They have no market price to serve as a value guide.

[9] The name "transfer payment," as used in Chapter 8 and here, is a little misleading. If you tax me to give a relief dole to my unemployed neighbor, that does sound like a "transfer." But suppose you print a new 20-dollar bill to give him, or borrow by selling bonds to make relief payments. He gets money that is not transferred from anybody else. Economists still call the relief payments transfers, regardless of how they are financed.

conclude with one large item: interest on the public debt. The interest paid on federal bonds was included years ago in GNP, but the fairly universal custom now is for countries to treat this as a transfer item. It is not now included in G, on the argument that it is not a payment for current goods and services.[10]

Do not think that the Minister of Finance's budget fails to take account of all government transfer payments. The budget back on page 191 did include these: the government surplus does equal taxes minus the sum of G *and* transfers. The official budget also includes some purely bookkeeping expenses. But do not confuse these budget accounts with national-income accounts, which are related but distinct.

TREATMENT OF TAXES   In using the flow-of-product approach to compute GNE as $C + I + G$, we need never worry about taxes or how government finances itself. Whether the government taxes, issues interest-bearing IOUs, or prints new noninterest IOU banknotes, the statistician computes G as the value of government expenditure on goods and services (evaluating these items at their actual costs to the government, wherever the money came from) and the private $C + I$ at actual market prices.

It is all very well to ignore taxes in the upper-loop flow-of-product approach. But what about in the lower-loop earnings or cost approach to GNP? In this lower loop, we do indeed have to take account of all taxes.

Consider wages, for example. Part of what my employer pays me in wages I have to give to the government in the form of personal income taxes. So these direct taxes do definitely get included in the wage component of the lower loop, and the same holds for direct taxes (personal or corporate) on interest, rent, and profit.

Or take the sales and other indirect taxes that manufacturers and retailers have to pay on a loaf of bread (or on the wheat, flour and dough stages). Suppose these indirect taxes total 5 cents; and suppose wages, profit, and other value-added items add up to 30 cents in cost to the bread industry. (We do not care how much of this 30 cents later goes to direct taxes.) What will the bread sell for in the upper loop? For 30 cents? Of course not. The bread will sell for 35 cents, equal to 30 cents of factor-costs plus 5 cents of indirect taxes.[11]

Hence we always find taxes included in the lower-loop cost approach to GNP and NNP.

---

[10] How to treat government items in GNE is still somewhat controversial. (1) Some experts argue that G should be broken down into government current consumption and government net investment (increase in its buildings, equipment, and inventories), just as private product is so broken down. And some nations do this. (2) Some experts say too, that part of G is really "intermediate" rather than "final" product—much like dough rather than bread—in that it merely contributes to final product already counted in (e.g., weather information for farmers who help give us our daily bread). But few nations make estimates of how much such double counting may be involved in the G figures.

[11] This is plainly so by definition of our residual profit and from the fact that residual profit is treated as a cost; but this result definitely says *nothing at all* about whether the tax is passed forward to the consumer or backward to the factors, whose wages and other returns might have been higher had there been no taxes. Chapter 19 analyzes such a "tax incidence" problem of the sort described in Chapter 9.

■ NET EXPORTS

Countries with "open" economies, like Canada, the United Kingdom, and Japan, cannot afford to ignore data on their exports and imports. In the United States, where exports and imports are a relatively small part of GNE, this sector is often buried in some other part of GNP; but by contrast, almost one quarter of Canada's output of goods and services goes abroad. How is it to be taken into account when it is clearly not shown in the closed circuit of loops in Figure 10-1?

First, Canadian GNP is understood to mean the income or product accruing to all "permanent residents" of Canada. Residents are not necesarily citizens and may live temporarily abroad. If Lord Thompson owns a newspaper in Canada and is permanently resident in Britain, his income therefrom is added into the *British* GNP, rather than the Canadian. Similarly, if a Canadian earns dividends from a British mine, this is part of the Canadian income and not the British, being treated as payment for a property service that we have exported.

It is obviously not easy to calculate international flows of income and expenditure. Fortunately, economists have been measuring the balance of payments for each country far longer than they have been calculating the national income. Details of the method will be discussed in Part Five. The bare logic, however, is as follows. Exports (E) are all goods and services for which residents of other countries pay Canada: items such as wheat, and services such as shipping, insurance, accommodation for American tourists, dividends and interest payments on Canadian capital abroad, and fees for Canadian engineers working in foreign countries. Imports (M) are similar goods and services bought by Canadians from foreign sellers and include interest and dividends paid for the use of foreign capital in Canada.

Although our exports such as wheat and ore are primary products, they are final output from the Canadian point of view as no further value will be added to them here. Hence, exports must be included with C, gross I, and G to comprise GNE. But the flow of imports shows that much of the final expenditure by Canadians must include foreign goods and services. Therefore imports must be subtracted from GNE. The usual method is to calculate "net exports" $(E - M)$, the surplus of exports over imports. In fact, this "surplus" may be a deficit, as has often been the case for Canada in recent years: the whole term $(E - M)$ can be positive or negative. $(E - M)$ is shown by the thin wiggle along the bottom axis of Figure 10-3.[12]

Now that the government and foreign trade have been brought into the picture, a final comprehensive definition can be given.

> GNE is definable as the sum of the four major components in the upper-loop flow of product: personal *consumption*, plus *government* expenditure on goods and services, plus *gross investment* in new machines and structures, plus *net exports* of goods and services. In defining NNP we simply adapt the above definition by altering gross investment to net investment.

---

[12] The Canadian balance was one of the first to be calculated in full (by Jacob Viner) and published regularly (by DBS).

Here are two ways of arriving at NNP in actual numbers:

GROSS NATIONAL EXPENDITURE, GROSS NATIONAL PRODUCT, AND NET NATIONAL
PRODUCT, 1969 (billions of dollars)

GNE, OR FLOW-OF-PRODUCT APPROACH		GNP, OR EARNINGS AND COST APPROACH	
C: Personal consumption expenditure on goods and services	$46.5	Wages, salaries, and supplements	$43.2
I: "Net" investment [Inventory accumulation and business capital spending *less* revaluations and capital consumption allowance (depreciation)]	6.1	Military pay and allowances	0.9
		Corporation profits before taxes	7.9
		Deduct: Dividends paid to non-residents	−0.8
G: Government Spending:	16.7	Interest and miscellaneous investment income	3.2
Expenditure on goods and services	13.8	Accrued net income of farm operators	1.7
Fixed capital and inventories	2.9	Net income of non-farm unincorporated business including rent	4.4
E - M: Current account balance	−0.8	Inventory valuation adjustment	−0.5
Exports of goods and services	18.5	Indirect taxes less subsidies	10.6
Imports of goods and services	−19.3	Residual error of estimate	−1.0
Residual error of estimate	1.0		
NNP: "Net" National Product	**$69.5**	**NNP: "Net" National Product**	**$69.5**
Depreciation or consumption allowance	9.0	Depreciation or consumption allowance	9.0
GNE: Gross National Expenditure	**$78.5**	**GNP: Gross National Product**	**$78.5**

TABLE 10-4. The left side measures flow of product and expenditure at market prices. The right side measures flow of costs (factor earnings and indirect taxes). GNE and GNP, which introduce depreciation, are also shown. Be sure you understand the main items. (Source: DBS and Bank of Canada *Statistical Summary*.)

GNP and NNP are each definable as a lower-loop total of costs: to factor-costs such as wages, interest, rents, and profit (always carefully excluding double counting of intermediate goods brought from other firms), there will have to be added all the indirect business taxes that do show up as an expense of producing the flow of products; and in the case of gross national product there will also be included depreciation expense, whereas the net national product will be less by the amount of this estimated expense.

The two loops yield identical magnitudes by definition (i.e., by careful adherence to the procedures of "double-entry" bookkeeping).[13]

[13] Statisticians must always work with incomplete reports and must fill in some gaps by estimation. As will be seen in a moment, approximate guesses can differ somewhat from GNP

■ CANADA'S GNE, GNP, AND NNP

Armed with an understanding of the concepts involved, we can turn to the actual data in the important Table 10-4, a table which merits lengthy study.

FLOW-OF-PRODUCT APPROACH   Look first at the left side of Table 10-4. This gives the upper-loop flow-of-product aproach to GNE. We have four components. Of these, C and G and their obvious classifications require little comment.

The final net-export item will be discussed further in Chapter 13. Remember that it may be positive *or* negative: in 1969 we had a deficit on current account, so that net exports were minus .8 billion dollars. In some GNE accounts net exports (being the extra exports not paid for by imports) are shown as our "net foreign investment" (exports we lend to foreigners at our expense), so that 1969 negative net exports would be negative net foreign investment. Net foreign investment can then be added to domestic business net investment to get total investment. But in Canada we usually keep them separate. In any case, along with C, G, and domestic I, net exports do represent a fourth component of the flow of product.

Adding up the four components on the left gives the important total NNP of 69.5 billion dollars. This is the harvest we have been working for: the money measure of the Canadian economy's over-all performance for 1969.

Finally, note that if we add depreciation back into the figures, we have the GNE of 78.5 billion dollars—which is higher because it contains gross rather than net investment in its measure of product.

LOWER-LOOP FLOW-OF-COST APPROACH   Now turn to the right-hand side of the table. Here we have all the value-added items plus taxes.

A few explanations are in order. Wages,[14] salaries, and supplementary incomes include all take-home pay and fringe benefits, and they also have in them the income tax deductions and other taxes that wage earners have to pay.

Interest is a similar item. (Note again, interest on government bonds is not included as part of G or NNP, being treated as a transfer.)

Rent income of persons requires only one explanation. It, of course, includes rents received by landlords. In addition, if you own your own home, you are treated as paying rent to yourself. This is a so-called "imputed" item and makes sense if we really want to measure the housing services the Canadian people are enjoying and do not want the estimate to be changed every time a tenant buys the house he has been renting. Admittedly, this imputed item has to be estimated, since no one reports rental receipts on his own home.

by what is officially reported as the "residual error of estimate" or, in the United States, as "statistical discrepancy." Along with the civil servants who are each heads of units called wages, interest, and so forth, there is actually a man with the title "head of statistical discrepancy." If data were perfect, he would be out of a job; but as real life is never so, his task of reconciliation is one of the hardest of all.

[14] The late Sir Arthur Bowley of the London School of Economics noted how remarkably constant over almost a century is wages' share of national income. No one is sure why this should be so. (The wages' share does rise at the expense of profit during recession; in recent decades the wage share has perhaps shown a slight upward creep, as seen in Chapter 36.)

Lastly, turn to profit. This should be the last kind of income dealt with because it is the residual—determined as what is left after all the other items have been taken into account. There are two kinds of profits: those of corporations and those of unincorporated business. Corporate profits of 7.9 billion dollars are shown, but we must deduct 0.8 billion dollars in dividends paid to foreigners; for remember that we are deriving the net *national* product. The remainder will be divided as follows: corporate taxes, 3.0 billion dollars; undistributed corporate profits "plowed back" into the company, 1.7 billion dollars; dividends, 2.4 billion dollars. Total: 7.1 billion dollars; but its disposition is not shown.

Unincorporated-enterprise profits arise on farms and from such proprietorships and partnerships as are found in running retail stores, law offices, and those few manufacturers that remain unincorporated (as "family firms"). The table calls these items "incomes," because they really comprise a mixture of returns on labor, land, and capital put into the business by their owners.

At the end, we tack on not only the residual error of estimate and inventory valuation adjustment,[15] but also business *indirect* taxes. The latter have to be included if the lower loop is to match the upper loop. Recall that business and personal direct taxes are already part wages, rents, interest, or profits.

Again, on the right side, the flow-of-cost approach gives us the same 69.5 billion dollars of NNP and the same GNP figure of 78.5 billion dollars, which was arrived at by adding back in the gross item of depreciation.

■ FOUR RELATED CONCEPTS: DISPOSABLE, PERSONAL, AND NATIONAL INCOMES, AND GROSS DOMESTIC PRODUCT

Table 10-4 summarized the fundamentals of national-income accounting. For purposes of broad economic understanding, our task is over. But a businessman, citizen, or statesman who wants to follow carefully just what is happening from month to month and quarter to quarter in the Canadian economy or abroad will benefit from a brief discussion of four other concepts that are measured and reported on by the Dominion Bureau of Statistics and similar official units elsewhere.

Disposable income, personal income, (narrowly defined) national income, and gross domestic product (GDP) are useful rearrangements of the above data.

Disposable income. How many dollars per year do private individuals and families have available to *them* to spend? The concept of disposable income tries to answer this question. Broadly speaking, to get disposable income, one sub-

---

[15] The statistician must trace the "inventory-valuation adjustment" throughout both accounts. On the GNE side, he shows investment in inventories as their physical change times the average price ruling *within* the year. Thus the profits of unincorporated and incorporated firms (especially farms holding stocks of grain) as shown above contain a markup (or markdown, if prices of grain, etc., fell within the year). To make the totals in the two loops match (i.e. to make GNP equal to GNE) he then subtracts this markup from the GNP side, as is reported in "inventory-valuation adjustment."

**The direct national-income aggregates tend
to move together:**

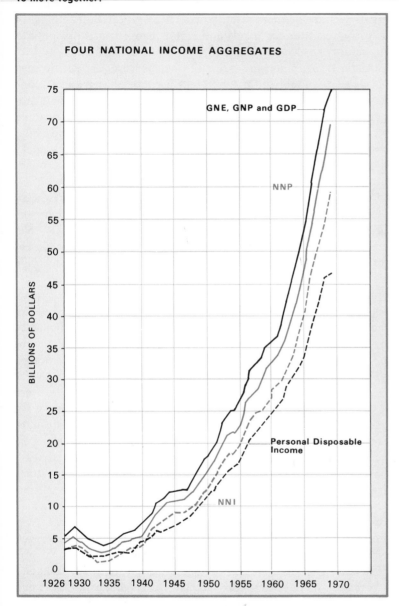

FOUR NATIONAL INCOME AGGREGATES

FIG. 10-4. NNP averages about eleven-twelfths of GNP, GNE, and
GDP. NNI subtracts indirect business taxes, capital consumption
allowances, etc., and the residual error of estimate from GNP and
GNE. Because of direct personal taxes and corporate saving, personal disposable income is about 92 per cent of NNI. GDP differs
somewhat from GNP in magnitude but the difference is within the
line.

tracts all taxes direct or indirect from NNP, subtracts all corporate earnings that were not paid out in dividends but retained as net corporate savings, and adds in transfer payments of welfare or interest-on-federal debt type. The result is, so to speak, what actually gets into our hands and is left there for us to dispose of as we please.

Disposable income is an important series of data because, as will be seen in Part Two, it is this sum (suitably adjusted to take account of interest on loans that the consumer must pay) that people divide between (1) consumption spending and (2) net personal saving. Thus, in recent years people have been spending about 94 per cent of disposable income on consumption and interest and about 6 per cent on net personal saving. It is this series that will be watched eagerly by a department-store head and a policy maker apprehensive over inflationary pressure or too little consumption spending.

Personal income. Unlike disposable income, personal income measures what persons receive, before they pay direct taxes. So disposable income plus personal direct taxes = personal income. This total can be calculated more quickly than disposable income, and in the United States it is available more frequently. For this reason it is often cited in both countries. But DI and PI tend to move closely together over time.

National income (NNI), narrowly defined. We have followed the common practice and used the term "national income" to refer generally to all the concepts of this chapter—GNE, GNP, NNP, and so forth. But mention should be made of a narrower sense in which the Dominion Bureau of Statistics defines the term. Indeed, for technical reasons, the Dominion Bureau of Statistics prefers this total to NNP. Its full name is Net National Income at Factor Cost (NNI), and, as Figure 10-4, on the previous page shows, it stands mid-way between NNP and DI. It is simply NNP without the indirect business taxes (hence the term "at factor cost" in its full name).[16] All direct taxes, personal and corporate, are left in, as are the undistributed earnings of corporations. All transfers are left out. Thus it might be called the full factor earnings of *productive* activity.

Thus we have two bits of national-accounts terminology: "factor cost" means that indirect taxes have been subtracted from the "market prices"; and "net" means that depreciation has been subtracted from "gross."

Gross domestic product. While GNP measures Canadians' income from production, wherever it is, GDP measures Canadian production, whoever gets paid for it. How many dollars' worth of products are made by factors of production *used* in Canada? The GNP does not answer this question; for Canadian work done by a commuting American autoworker or Swiss engineer is left out: the GNP regards their incomes as payments for "imports of work." The GNP

---

[16] Recall that NNP is a measure of the total values of all final goods and services sold. As Table 10-4 shows, each of these values contains, basically, two things: the cost of hiring factors (including a profit payment), and indirect taxes such as sales tax and excise. Thus NNP is the value of output "at market prices"—what people have to pay. But NNI is this value "at factor costs"—what people are paid. Indirect taxes are a wedge between factor costs and market prices.

also leaves out interest and dividends paid to foreign lenders and owners; but adds in interest, wages, and dividends paid to Canadians out of production abroad. GDP adjusts for these characteristics. It includes every factor payment made in Canada (even to foreigners, for imported factors) and excludes incomes of Canadians earned for factor services abroad. (Consequently, the GNP can be divided down totally by kinds of income, wages, interest, etc.; whereas the GDP can be divided down to show *all* total factor rewards in *each* industry. Not surprisingly, then, the GNP is often used for Canadian income studies, while the GDP is a background for industry studies. The Appendix to this chapter says something more about the GDP.)

Figure 10-4, on page 241, plots four of the important national-income concepts, GDP, NNP, NNI, and DI, and shows how much alike are their movements and how predictably slow are their drifts apart. That is why most people are content to watch NNP (or GNP) alone, occasionally supplementing it with data on disposable income.

This chapter has now given us the tools to chart the progress and health of an economy. It is a culmination of the introductory survey that is the task of Part One. It is a prelude to the subject of Part Two, the analysis of the macroeconomic forces that determine the level, trend, and cyclical fluctuations of the national income and general level of prices.

SUMMARY

■ 1 Net national product, NNP, is definable as a dollar flow of total product for a nation: the sum of consumption plus net investment (domestic and foreign) plus government expenditure on goods and services. $NNP = C + I + G$.

■ 2 By use of a price index, we can "deflate" NNP in current dollars to arrive at a more accurate measure of "real NNP, expressed in dollars of one base-year's purchasing power." Use of such an average price index (of consumer-goods, investment-goods, and government-goods prices) is an approximate way of allowing for the rubber yardstick implied by changing levels of prices.

■ 3 Because of the way we define residual profit, we can match the flow-of-product measurement of NNP by the lower-loop flow-of-cost measurement. This uses factor earnings, carefully computing *values added* to eliminate double counting of intermediate products. And after adding all (before-tax) wage, interest, rent, and profit income, it adds to this total all *indirect* tax costs to business. (NNP definitely does *not* include transfer items such as receipt of interest on government bonds, or receipt of welfare pensions, or consumer-loan interest).

■ 4 An "open" economy is one which relies heavily on trade with other nations, so that exports are large relative to NNP. Net exports = exports — imports, and may be positive (surplus) or negative (deficit). Positive net exports may be viewed as a loan to, or investment in, other nations.

■ 5 Net investment is positive when people are devoting part of society's resources to creating more buildings, equipment, and inventory than is currently being used up in the form of depreciation. Net investment equals
gross investment minus depreciation. As depreciation is hard to estimate,
the statisticians have more confidence in their measures of gross than of
net investment.

■ 6 For the foregoing reason, the official statistics put greatest stress on gross
national product rather than net. GNE = GNP = NNP + depreciation,
always. Since depreciation is sluggish, and rarely varies much from twelve
per cent of GNP (or fourteen per cent of NNP), we can generally use GNP
and NNP interchangeably.

■ 7 Disposable, personal, (narrowly defined) national income, and GDP are
four additional official measurements. GDP is GNP plus wages, interest,
and profits paid to foreigners less foreign factor incomes paid to Canadian
residents. NNI is simply NNP with indirect business taxes (gasoline, sales,
and other nonincome taxes) removed. Personal income (PI) is what factors
are paid for productive activity. Disposable income (DI) is what people
actually have left to spend on consumption or to save after all taxes, corporate saving of undistributed profits, and transfer adjustments have been
made.

More information about national-income accounting is given in the Appendix to this chapter. Also given are some selected figures on the nation's recent
economic history: the Dominion Bureau of Statistics' important production
index; and data on employment and unemployment. These vital aggregates chart
a nation's economic health.

QUESTIONS FOR DISCUSSION

1. Compare the two-loop flow of money in Fig. 10-1 with Fig. 3-1 on page 58 which
shows the way a pricing system solves society's WHAT, HOW, and FOR WHOM.

2. "You can't add apples and bread." Show that money lets us do this.

3. Convince a skeptic that services do count as well as material goods—that we want
most goods for the consumption services they provide us.

4. Making a guess how prices have risen since 1968, test your knowledge of the
deflating process by penciling in, on Fig. 10-2, recent money NNP and recent real NNP.
How might you deflate for population change? If the United Kingdom has 1970 NNP
of 40 billion pounds, and if £1 buys what $2.50 will buy, how would you express
United Kingdom NNP in Canadian 1970 dollars?

5. R. Crusoe produces upper-loop product of $1,000. He pays $750 in wages, $125 in
interest, and $75 in rent. What must his profit be? Calculate NNP in the upper-loop
and lower-loop way and show they must agree exactly.

6. From a recent *Bank of Canada Statistical Summary* or *Canadian Statistical Review*
(DBS), recalculate Table 10-4 for a later year than 1969. Explain the profit adjustments
and treatment of the corporation. Explain the inventory adjustment.

7. Distinguish between government transfer expenditure and the G that goes into $NNP = C + I + G + (E - M)$. To get disposable income, why remove all taxes from NNP and add in transfers? What about undistributed corporate profit?

8. Review your understanding of the following concepts:

NNP in two equivalent views

1970 money NNP in current dollars, and 1970 real NNP in 1966 dollars

intermediate goods, double counting, value added

gross investment $-$ depreciation $=$ net investment

depreciation $+$ NNP $=$ GNE $=$ GNP

$NNP = C + I + G + (E - M)$

government transfers, indirect and direct taxes

net exports of goods and services

dividends, undistributed profits

income of unincorporated enterprise

valuation and adjustment

GDP, NNI, PI, and DI

Appendix: The Official National Income Data

The main text of this chapter has expounded the basic principles of national income. Here some special points are elaborated.

■ A FEW BRAIN TEASERS

Readers often like to worry about fine points. Here are a few sample cases.

1. *Services of a housewife* never get counted in the NNP. So if a man marries his housekeeper, the NNP may go down! Or if a wife arranges with her neighbor for each to clean the other's house in return for $5,000 a year, then the NNP would go up by $10,000.

This item is not omitted for logical reasons, but rather because it would be hard to get accurate estimates of the money value of a wife's services. So long as the number of women working at home does not change much in relative importance, the ups and downs of NNP will be about the same whether or not we include this item or similar items such as home-grown vegetables and other do-it-yourself activities.

All this illustrates an important rule of approximate measurement in economics. *Often it does not matter which definition of measurement you use, so long as you stick to one definition consistently.*

2. For many items it is hard to know whether

to put them in the *intermediate* or *final* class. EXAMPLES: A carpenter's sand paper is certainly not to be charged as a final consumption item. Like bread dough, it is an intermediate expense item that has already been counted in as part of the fine homes and tables he builds.

What about his overalls? His carfare from one job to another? His carfare from home to work? The coffee he buys a prospective customer? The coffee he himself drinks? The football game he takes a prospective customer to, in his campaign for more business? Would you treat the last differently if he himself likes football?

Each of these items can raise an argument. Each has an element of intermediate business expense in it, and each an element of consumption. The tax collector and the national-income statistician do not always agree on the treatment of these, and we can raise questions about each one's decisions. (EXAMPLE: The tax collector will not let anyone deduct his commuting costs to work *in town*; but out of town he may be able to. The sandpaper is clearly deductible from taxable income and from NNP; but the overalls are not if it can be shown that wearing them saved an ordinary suit's wearing out. So it goes. Close decisions and arbitrary ones.)

3. *Gifts that are not disguised payments for work*

How to picture relations among official national-income data:

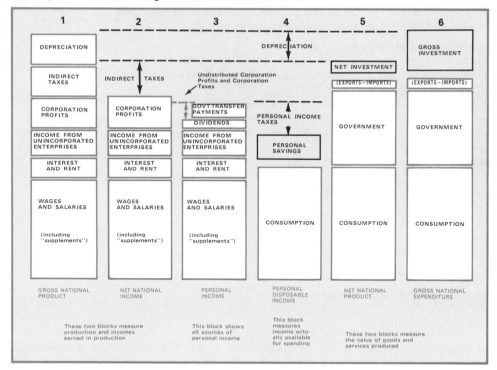

FIG. 10-5. This shows the operations in going from GNP flow-of-cost on the left to GNE flow-of-purchases on the right. In the middle is personal disposable income, DI, the smallest income aggregate.

done or for goods and services are not included in NNP. They are like government transfers that we have already discussed. The same goes for the allowance a father gives his son. But what about the fee he pays the son for mowing the lawn? In logic it should be in NNP, but it rarely is.

4. If I buy an old painting, a corner lot, or a used car from someone else, that transaction is not a final transaction to be put into NNP. He and I have just *exchanged assets*: money for picture. Nothing has been produced.[1] So this is more in the nature of a special kind of transfer.[2] It illustrates an important

---

[1] If a broker earns a fee for arranging the deal, that fee is counted as part of NNP. Just as some men produce satisfactions in the form of bread, brokers and salesmen produce satisfactions in the form of bringing transactors together.

[2] Do not confuse this kind of transfer with the government transfers we have talked about.

fact: the total dollar volume of all intermediate transactions greatly exceeds the volume of the final transactions that we call national income or product. The loops of Fig. 10-1 include only a minority of the transactions that are taking place within the business and public blocks of that diagram.

Note, too, that we try not to let *capital gains due to mere price changes* enter into NNP. If Wall Street bids up my Ford stocks, I may feel rich and spend more of my *DI*. But that windfall gain is not attributable to current economic activity, and the statistician tries to keep it out. For similar reasons he makes the inventory valuation adjustment in corporate profits.

5. One could go on giving borderline cases, but we conclude with only one more. In measuring GNE we are not interested in consumption and investment goods merely for their money value: *money is the measuring rod used to give some approximate figure to the underlying "satisfactions" or "benefits"*

How the official statistics of national income are interrelated:

RECONCILIATION OF NATIONAL INCOME CONCEPTS (billions of dollars)							
	1926	1936	1946	1956	1966	1969	1970
Gross National Product (GNP)	5.1	4.6	11.9	31.4	61.4	78.5	84.5
Less:							
Depreciation (Capital consumption allowance)	0.6	0.6	1.1	4.0	7.4	9.0	9.9
Indirect taxes minus subsidies	0.6	0.7	1.4	3.7	8.1	10.6	11.3
Residual error of estimate	−0.2	—	—	0.3	−0.1	−1.0	−0.5
Equals:							
Net National Income (NNI)	4.1	3.3	9.4	23.4	46.0	59.9	63.8
Less:							
Undistributed corporate profits	0.2	0.1	0.5	1.4	2.6	1.7	2.4
Corporate taxes	—	0.1	0.7	1.4	2.4	3.0	2.9
Plus:							
Net transfers (and adjustments)	0.2	0.5	1.7	2.2	4.7	6.1	7.6
Equals:							
Personal Income (PI)	4.1	3.6	9.9	22.8	45.7	61.3	66.1
Less:							
Personal Taxes*	0.1	0.1	0.9	2.2	6.2	10.8	11.5
Equals:							
Personal Disposable Income (DI)	4.0	3.5	9.0	20.6	39.5	50.5	54.6
Less:							
Personal net saving	0.5	−0.1	0.9	1.1	3.4	4.0	4.0
Equals:							
Consumption (C)	3.5	3.5	8.0	19.5	36.1	46.5	50.6
Plus:							
Government (G)	0.4	0.5	1.7	4.4	9.8	13.8	15.8
Net investment (I)	0.4	−0.1	0.8	5.0	9.2	9.0	7.6
Exports − Imports (E − M)	0.2	0.2	0.4	−1.3	−1.2	−0.8	1.1
Equals:							
Net National Product (NNP)	4.4	4.1	10.9	27.5	53.9	68.5	75.1
Plus:							
Depreciation	0.6	0.6	1.1	4.0	7.4	9.0	9.9
Residual error of estimate	0.1	—	−0.1	−0.1	0.1	1.0	−0.5
Equals:							
Gross National Expenditure (GNE)	5.1	4.7	11.9	31.4	61.4	78.5	84.5

*Income taxes, succession duties, estate taxes, employer and employee contributions to social insurance and government pension funds, and other.

TABLE 10-5. Each total corresponds to a block in Fig. 10-5—the reader should examine them together. Note that the NNP figure is not shown explicitly in the national accounts, and that detail may not add to the totals shown because of rounding. Also, note that Government (G) is, here, government *current* expenditure on goods and services only, in line with the new DBS definitional breakdown of National Income Accounts. It does not include government capital expenditures which, instead, are included in net business and government investment (I). Contrast this to the classification used in Table 10-4, which is useful for analyzing fiscal policy in a simple framework. (Source: DBS.)

or "*psychic income*" *that comes from goods.* Strictly speaking, then, each time I play a phonograph record, shouldn't that act get into the GNE at its fair market value? In principle, Yes. And if I have put a dime in a juke box, it may in fact get directly into the GNE; but playing it at home will not get it directly into the GNE.

Indirectly, this enjoyment of a psychic pleasure

does tend to get in the GNE to the extent that I wear out the record by playing it. Hence, as I replace my records, my consumption purchases at the store give a rough money measure of my enjoyments—but only a rough measure.

The statistician admits this, defending his practice by saying that a man's house is his castle and no accountant can enter his abode to measure his actual current consumptions; instead, he settles for treating a thing as consumed when it enters his abode. This all works well enough, except in one case.

More and more these days we spend our consumption dollar on durable consumers' goods. Actually, then, in the years that we are building up our home inventories of such durable goods, our true psychic consumption is being overstated by our retail purchases; and vice versa in the years when we run them down.

Some purists say, "In GNE, let's try to estimate actual home consumption of services or durables and put that in C, not in the mere retail purchases of the year." The Dominion Bureau of Statistics thinks this too hard a job to do, but for special purposes economists have tried to make (from gas and mileage records, for example) more accurate estimates of auto consumption than is provided by new car sales.[3]

Fortunately, in the long run, the two methods tend to come to the same thing, particularly if society is not growing too fast.

■ THE OFFICIAL STATISTICS

Figure 10-5, on page 246, summarizes the relations of the different Dominion Bureau of Statistics data on national income or product. Many find careful study of this summary and of Table 10-5 a great aid to understanding.

Table 10-6 along with national-income data, gives some other principal aggregates which businesses and public officials watch closely.

■ A THIRD APPROACH TO NATIONAL PRODUCT: GDP

In developing the flow-of-product approach, we eventually subtracted all payments for productive

activity except "factor costs" and "indirect taxes." We wound up with estimates of expenditure on *final output*, that are classified as C, G, gross I, or (E − M). This tells us nothing about the value added in each *industry* (such as agriculture, printing, baking, railways, etc.), because the output of most industries is the input of others, therefore it doesn't make up a part of *final* output, and it isn't reported in GNE or NNP accounts.

It is possible, however, for statisticians to find out how much value is added in each industry, and to add these amounts together. This has been done for years in such well-known, though partial, indexes as the Index of Industrial Production (and the U.S. Federal Reserve Board Index). The final index is an average of the indexes for each of the industries, each one measuring the growth or decline of value added ("deflated," as on page 227) in that industry. These indexes are extremely useful as a third, industry-by-industry, value-added measure of aggregate product.

Recently the Dominion Bureau of Statistics, here leading the world, has expanded the coverage of its total index from manufacturing and mining industries only to the whole economy. This expanded index is called the Gross Domestic Product at factor cost (GDP). It is called "Domestic" rather than "National" product because it concentrates on the *production or output* generated within Canada rather than the income of Canadian residents. Thus the chief difference in definition between GDP and GNP or GNE (apart from indirect taxes) is that if earnings arising from production go to a foreigner, they are left out of the GNP but remain in the GDP. For example, the wages of a Detroit resident working in Sarnia are included in GDP but not in GNP. Conversely if a Canadian gets dividends from foreign production, the dividends enter GNP but not GDP. In other countries, and sometimes in Canada, the GDP is called the real domestic product. It is useful because it tells us about the Canadian final output or production *per se* and because of its fine breakdown into industries. Furthermore the GDP measure provides a fairly independent check on the trends, long-run and quarterly, of the "deflated" GNP and GNE. Table 10-6 gives indexes since 1936.

■ THE IDENTITY OF MEASURED SAVING AND INVESTMENT

To pave the way for the discussion of intersecting

[3] It is interesting that in the case of a house, the most durable consumers' good of all, the officials do actually follow this principle: they do not take expenditures on a house as its C, but estimate the house use separately.

These aggregates chart the nation's economic health:

PRINCIPAL ECONOMIC AGGREGATES (all income data in millions of current dollars)

(1)	(2)	(3)	(4)	(5)	(6)	(7)	(8)	(9)	(10)
Year	Gross National Product $ Million	Net National Product $ Million	Net National Income (at Factor Cost) $ Million	Personal Disposable Income $ Million	Net Saving as Percentage of Disposable Income	Government Expenditure on Goods and Services as Percentage of GNE	Index of Gross (Real) Domestic Product (1949 = 100)	Civilian Labor Force (Thousands)	Unemployment as Percentage of Civilian Labor Force
1926	5,146	4,574	4,086	3,961	10.6	7.58	—	3,658	3.0
1928	6,050	5,374	4,678	4,495	4.0	6.80	—	3,861	1.9
1930	5,720	5,001	4,343	4,267	-2.4	8.78	—	4,060	9.1
1932	3,814	3,236	2,597	2,951	-8.2	12.38	—	4,211	17.6
1934	3,969	3,433	2,738	3,070	-3.6	10.53	—	4,338	14.5
1936	4,634	4,059	3,314	3,452	-2.8	9.71	52.4	4,466	12.8
1938	5,272	4,633	3,942	3,953	1.4	10.13	56.5	4,588	11.4
1940	6,713	5,927	4,985	4,775	6.0	15.61	69.2	4,607	9.2
1942	10,265	9,174	7,977	6,898	20.3	35.28	95.0	4,569	3.0
1944	11,848	10,771	9,453	8,027	21.8	41.60	103.0	4,548	1.4
1945	11,863	10,821	9,506	8,311	16.1	30.14	97.0	4,520	1.6
1946	11,885	10,814	9,363	8,923	10.0	13.93	89.8	4,862	3.4
1947	13,169	11,866	10,206	9,584	5.1	10.20	93.8	4,954	2.2
1948	15,127	13,623	11,834	11,079	9.0	9.61	97.1	5,035	2.3
1949	16,300	14,569	12,708	11,849	7.8	10.56	100.0	5,092	2.8
1950	17,955	15,995	13,888	12,688	5.2	10.74	106.4	5,198	3.6
1951	21,060	18,760	16,294	14,794	9.0	13.35	114.6	5,230	2.4
1952	24,042	21,505	18,504	16,072	8.0	15.06	122.7	5,344	2.9
1953	25,327	22,483	19,270	16,904	7.8	15.10	126.7	5,386	3.0
1954	25,233	22,087	18,979	16,984	4.8	15.16	123.9	5,476	4.6
1955	27,895	24,368	20,948	18,239	4.7	14.47	136.3	5,585	4.4
1956	31,374	27,354	23,432	20,153	6.5	14.11	147.7	5,738	3.4
1957	32,907	28,520	24,522	21,107	5.7	13.90	147.0	5,970	4.6
1958	34,094	29,713	25,458	22,646	7.1	14.24	148.9	6,120	7.1
1959	36,266	31,543	27,105	23,948	5.7	13.72	156.5	6,186	6.0
1960	37,775	32,739	28,147	25,075	6.1	13.98	158.5	6,391	7.0
1961	39,080	33,898	29,062	26,011	5.8	16.25	161.4	6,518	7.2
1962	42,353	36,759	31,649	28,243	8.2	15.98	171.4	6,608	6.0
1963	45,465	39,517	34,100	30,018	8.4	15.72	180.2	6,748	5.5
1964	49,783	43,455	37,198	31,725	6.5	15.43	192.9	6,933	4.7
1965	54,897	48,097	40,969	35,149	8.8	15.13	206.3	7,100	3.9
1966	61,421	54,007	46,032	38,579	9.7	15.99	218.7	7,420	3.6
1967	65,608	57,712	49,306	41,709	9.6	16.58	224.5	7,631	3.9
1968	71,454	63,005	53,871	44,964	9.0	16.90	234.7	7,919	4.8
1969	78,537	69,471	59,868	50,557	6.8	17.60	245.5	8,162	4.7
1970	84,468	74,570	63,770	53,595	7.4	18.70	252.3	8,374	5.9

TABLE 10-6. Forecasters like to use the GDP index because it moves sensitively. Statesmen worry about the unemployment figures. (Source: DBS.)

saving and investment schedules in Chapter 12, we can here show that the national-income statistician defines the saving he measures as exactly the same thing as the investment he measures. This equality of measured saving and measured investment is an identity of double-entry bookkeeping and holds by definition.

What is the measure of investment? Forgetting government and foreign trade, we know I is the output in the upper loop that is not C. What is the measure of saving S? Again forgetting government and corporate saving, we know that S is that part of the lower-loop disposable income, or NNP, that is not spent on C. To summarize:

$$I = \text{upper-loop NNP minus } C$$
$$S = \text{lower-loop NNP minus } C$$

But the two loops must give the same measure of NNP. So $I = S$: the identity between measured saving and investment.

Our task will be done once we bring the corporation and the government into the picture. Investment is just as before. But now saving S must be split into three different terms: (1) net personal saving, which people do out of their disposable incomes; (2) net corporate saving, that part of cor-

porate incomes which they fail to pay out as dividends; finally (3) net government surplus (or "saving"), which represents the algebraic excess of its tax revenues over its expenditure on goods and services *and* on transfers.

Our identity of measured S and I now has to be written in terms of the three components of total S.[4]

$$I \equiv NPS + NCS + NGS$$

---

[4] The eager reader can test his grasp of this fundamental identity (which must hold at all times whether or not an economy is in equilibrium or is galloping to or from an equilibrium) by going back to the discussion (page 240) of how disposable income is defined in terms of NNP — taxes — NCS + transfers, and how NPS = $DI - C$. These relations combined with the $C + I + G$ breakdown of NNP can be used to give an algebraic demonstration of our identity.

Thus, from the definition of DI,
$$NNP \equiv DI + NCS + T_x - T_r$$
Adding and subtracting G and splitting up DI gives
$$NNP \equiv C + [NPS + NCS + (T_x - T_r - G)] + G$$
$$\equiv C + [NPS + NCS + (NGS)] + G$$
But recall the upper-loop definition
$$NNP \equiv C + [I] + G$$
So we do indeed verify
$$[I] \equiv [NPS + NCS + NGS]$$

PART 2
DETERMINATION OF NATIONAL INCOME AND ITS FLUCTUATIONS

11

SAVING, CONSUMPTION, AND INVESTMENT

We are all Keynesians now. MILTON FRIEDMAN

In Part One the groundwork was laid for an understanding of the concept of national income. Now we can go beyond the anatomy of the problem to its physiology. What causes national income to rise? To fall? Why is NNP what it is at any time, rather than something larger or smaller? What causes too little total spending—recession and depression? What causes too much total spending—inflationary rises in the index of prices? Part Two analyzes these basic problems of 'macroeconomics' (which is the study of the aggregate performance of the whole GNP and of the general price level).

This chapter provides an introduction to what is called the "modern theory of income analysis." The principal stress is upon the *level of total spending as determined by the interplay of the monetary forces of saving and investment.*

Although much of this analysis is due to an English economist, John Maynard Keynes (later made Lord Keynes, before his death in 1946), today the broad fundamentals of the "new economics" are increasingly accepted by economists of all schools of thought, including, it is important to notice, many who do not share Keynes' particular policy views and who differ on technical details of analysis.[1]

---

[1] Keynes himself was a many-sided genius who won eminence in the fields of mathematics, philosophy, and literature. In addition, he found time to run a large insurance company, to advise the British Treasury, to help govern the Bank of England, to edit a world-famous economic journal, and to sponsor ballet and drama. He was also an economist who knew how to make money, both for himself and for King's College, Cambridge. His 1936 book, *The General Theory of Employment, Interest and Money*, created the greatest stir in economic thinking of the century and will live as a classic. Readers today will also enjoy his own *Essays in Persuasion and Biography*, and Robert Lekachman's *The Age of Keynes*.

The income analysis here described is itself neutral: it can be used as well to defend private enterprise as to limit it; as well to attack as to defend government fiscal intervention. When business organizations such as the Canadian Chamber of Commerce, the Private Planning Association of Canada, or the Bank of Montreal use the terminology of saving and investment, it is absurd to think that this implies that they are "Keynesian," in the sense of belonging to that narrow band of enthusiasts associated with some of the policy programs that Keynes himself espoused during the Great Depression. Even Marxian economists, who at first resented Keynesian economics literally as a "mere palliative" to the ills of capitalism, have come to recognize its explanatory powers.

In recent years 90 per cent of North American economists have stopped being "Keynesian economists" or "anti-Keynesian economists." Modern economists are "post-Keynesians," keen to render obsolete any theories that cannot meet the test of experience or applicability. Thus, in the 1970s, post-Keynesians accord an importance to the role of money in the process of income determination that would have surprised the first disciples of Keynes (but which would not at all have surprised that brilliant virtuoso of finance).

■ THE CLEAVAGE BETWEEN SAVING AND INVESTMENT MOTIVATIONS

The most important single fact about saving and investment activities is that in our industrial society they are generally done by *different people* and for *different reasons.*

This was not always so; even today, when a farmer devotes his time to draining a field instead of to planting and harvesting a crop, he is saving and at the same time investing. He is "saving" because he is abstaining from *present* consumption in order to provide for larger consumption in the *future*—the amount of his saving being measured by the difference between his net real income and his consumption. But he is also "investing"; i.e., he is undertaking net capital formation, improving the productive capacity of his farm. Not only are saving and investment the same things for a primitive farmer, but his reasons for undertaking them are the same. He abstains from present consumption (saves) only because he wants to drain the field (to invest). If there were no investment opportunity whatsoever, it would never occur to him to save; nor would there be any way to save for the future, should he be so foolish as to wish to.

In our modern economy, net capital formation or investment is carried on by business enterprises, especially corporations. When a corporation or a small business has great investment opportunities, its owners will be tempted to plow back much of its earnings into the business. To an important degree, therefore, some business saving does get motivated directly by business investment.

Nevertheless, saving is primarily done by an entirely different group: by individuals, by families, by households. An individual may wish to save for a great variety of reasons: because he wishes to provide for his old age or for a future expenditure (a vacation or an automobile). Or he may feel insecure and wish to guard against a rainy day. Or he may wish to leave an estate to his children or to his children's children. Or he may be an eighty-year-old miser with no heirs who enjoys the act of accumulating for its own sake. Or he may already have signed himself up to a savings program because an insurance salesman was persuasive. Or he may desire the power that greater wealth brings. Or thrift may simply be a habit, almost a conditional reflex whose origin he does not himself know.

> Whatever the individual's motivation to save, it has usually little to do with society's investment opportunities.

This truth is obscured by the fact that in everyday language "investment" does not always have the same meaning as in economics. We have defined "net investment", or capital formation, to be the net increase in the community's real capital (equipment, buildings, inventories). But the plain man speaks of "investing" when he buys a piece of land, an old security, or any title to property. For economists these are clearly *transfer* items. What one man is buying, someone else is selling. There is net investment only when *additional real capital* is created.

In short, even if there are no *real* investment opportunities that seem profitable, an individual may still *wish* to nonconsume—to save. He can always buy an existing security asset; he can accumulate, or *try* to accumulate, cash.

Thus we are left with our proposition:

> Saving and investing are often desired by different individuals and for independent reasons. While it is families who primarily decide to save, net capital formation takes place largely in business enterprise.

■ THE VARIABILITY OF INVESTMENT

The amount of investment is highly variable from year to year and decade to decade. This capricious, volatile behavior is understandable when we come to realize that profitable investment opportunities stem from *new* discoveries, *new* products, *new* territories and frontiers, *new* resources, *new* population, *higher* production and income. Note the emphasis on "new" and on "higher." Investment depends on the *dynamic* and relatively unpredictable elements of *growth* in the system and on elements outside the economic system itself: technology, politics, optimistic and pessimistic expectations, "confidence," governmental tax and expenditure, legislative policies, and much else.

> The extreme variability of investment is the next important fact to be emphasized.

The independence of forces operating upon saving and investment is like the independence of forces operating on Chapter 4's supply and demand schedules. While recognizing this independence, we should also recognize two qualifications: (1) often at the corporate level, decisions to invest are closely related to the funds that corporations are able to save out of their earnings and that need not be paid out in dividends; (2) at all times, but particularly in times of tight money and high interest rates, how much entrepreneurs can indulge their desire to invest in new profitable opportunities will depend on how much finance is made available to them by people's saving. Just as the independent forces operating on supply and demand are resolved by what happens to market prices, so we shall see that saving and investment decisions are resolved by what happens to the level of income and employment and to interest rates.

We shall see that an industrial system such as our own can do many wonderful things. It can mobilize men, tools, and know-how to respond to any given demand for goods. Over time it can improve upon its own response.

But there is one thing it cannot always do.

> Unless proper macroeconomic policies are pursued, a *laissez-faire* economy cannot guarantee that there will be exactly the required amount of investment to ensure full employment: not too little so as to cause unemployment, nor too much so as to cause inflation.
>
> As far as total investment or money-spending power is concerned, the *laissez-faire* system is without a good thermostat. For decades there might tend to be too little investment, leading to deflation, losses, excess capacity, unemployment, and destitution. For other years or decades, there might tend to be too much investment, leading to periods of chronic inflation— unless prudent and proper public policies in the fiscal (i.e., tax and expenditure) and monetary (i.e., Bank of Canada central bank) fields are followed.

Nor is there an Invisible Hand guaranteeing that the good years will by themselves equal the bad, or guaranteeing that scientists will discover just in the nick of time precisely enough new products and processes to keep the system on an even keel. From 1855 to 1875 railroads were built all over the world. Canada's CPR, belatedly completed in 1886, marked the end of this boom; till 1895, nothing quite took the place of this activity.

Canada had its own private upsurge until 1913; then wartime business investment sagged until the 1920s, when the automobile and hydro electric and public utilities produced another worldwide economic revolution. In the 1930s plastics and radio had no comparable effect on total net investment.

In the years following World War II, much of the time we were plagued by too much investment spending relative to the resources released by those acts of renouncing consumption which economists call "saving." Then, throughout the 1950s and until 1962, we experienced sluggish growth, with increasing unemployment. After this, high investment returned and by the late 1960s inflation problems were back.

Thus we see that the instabilities are not all on the downward side. Economic history is, alas, a history of inflations. Anyone who came of age in 1970 has seen prices almost double in his own brief lifetime. Unless proper policies are followed, he can look forward to gyrating prices for the rest of his life.

While a realist must recognize that an economy like ours in 1929 or in the 1970s will not *by itself* maintain stability of prices and full employment, critics should still recognize that there are certain elements in a pricing economy that can work toward stability if given a chance to operate and if helped by vigorous public stabilizing actions. As we shall see later, *the structure of interest rates—* which determines how costly and hard it is to get credit for investing activities —can be helped by central bank monetary policy to play a *stabilizing* role in moderating investment fluctuations, even those stimulated by events abroad. Also, to a considerable extent the frictions that keep various prices inflexible and sticky in a modern mixed economy can be offset by public fiscal actions. This, then is one of our most important economic lessons:

> Where the stimulus to investment is concerned, the system is somewhat in the lap of the gods. We may be lucky or unlucky; and one of the few things you can say about luck is, "It's going to change." Fortunately, things need not be left to luck. We shall see that perfectly sensible public and private policies can be followed that will greatly enhance the stability and productive growth of the mixed economy.

The next chapters will show how investment and saving determine the equilibrium level of national income. First, we must understand the important budgetary patterns, reflecting how people consume and save at different income levels.

■ BUDGETARY EXPENDITURE PATTERNS

No two families spend their money in exactly the same way. Yet statistics do show that there is predictable regularity—on the average—in the way people allocate their expenditures on food, clothing, and other major items. Literally thousands of budgetary investigations have been made of the ways that people at different levels of income spend their money; and there is remarkable agreement on the general, qualitative patterns of behavior.[2] What are they? Figure 11-1, on the next page, tells the story.

Poor families must, of course, spend their incomes largely on the necessities of life: food, shelter, and, in lesser degree, clothing. As income increases, expenditure on many food items goes up. People eat more and eat better. They shift away from cheap, bulky carbohydrates to more expensive meats and proteins—and to milk, fruit, vegetables, and labor-saving processed foods.

There are, however, limits to the amount of extra money that people will spend on food when their incomes rise. Consequently, the *percentage* importance of food expenditure declines as income increases. (Actually, there are a few cheap, but filling, items such as spaghetti whose consumption decreases absolutely with income increase. These are called "inferior goods" in Part Three.)

After you get out of the very poorest income class, your proportion of income spent on shelter is pretty constant for a wide range. This is expressed in

---

[2] Figure 11-1's relative behavior patterns are called "Engel's Laws", after the nineteenth-century Prussian statistician Ernst Engel (not to be confused with Marx's friend Friedrich Engels). These averages of consumption expenditure do vary fairly regularly with income; but averages do not tell all the story. Within each income class, there is a spread around the average.

Family expenditures show fairly regular income patterns:

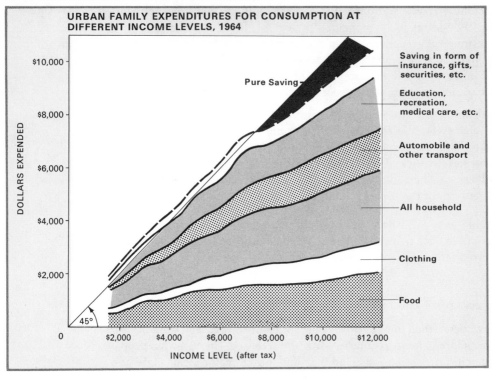

FIG. 11-1. Careful sampling of urban families verifies the importance of income as a determinant of consumption expenditure. Notice the drop in food as a percentage of higher incomes. Note also the rise in saving, from below zero at low incomes to substantial positive levels. (The waves in the curves are due to "sampling errors" in this 1964 survey. They can be smoothed out by advanced statistical methods. See Fig. 11-2.) (Source: DBS.)

a familiar rule of thumb: One week's salary should cover one month's expenditure on rent and house utilities. The other rule of thumb—that you should pay about 2 year's income for a house—has a hollow ring these days.

Expenditure on clothing, recreation, and automobiles increases more than proportionately to after-tax income, until high incomes are reached. Of course, luxury items, by definition, increase in greater proportion than income; and in many ways, as we shall see in a moment, saving is the greatest luxury of all, particularly at very high incomes.

■ THE PROPENSITY TO SAVE AND PROPENSITY TO CONSUME

An important use of after-tax income is saving for the future rather than consuming now. This aspect is what interests us most. It is a matter of common observation that rich men save more than poor men, not only in absolute amounts but also in percentage amounts. The very poor are unable to save at all. Instead they "dissave," i.e., spend more every year than they earn, the dif-

Most saving is done by families with incomes above the average:

PROPENSITY OF FAMILIES TO SAVE AND CONSUME		
(1) DISPOSABLE INCOME AFTER TAXES	(2) NET SAVINGS (+) NET DISSAVING (—)	(3) CONSUMPTION
$ 2,000	$—300	$2,300
3,000	—175	3,175
4,000	0	4,000
5,000	+200	4,800
6,000	+425	5,575
7,000	+675	6,325
8,000	+975	7,025
9,000	+1,325	7,675
10,000	+1,725	8,275

TABLE 11-1. The break-even point at which people cease to dissave and begin to do positive saving is here shown at $4,000. How much of each extra dollar do people around this income level devote to extra consumption? How much to extra saving?

ference being covered by going into debt or using up previously accumulated savings. Thus, income is a prime determinant of saving, as shown in Table 11-1.[3]

Table 11-1 gives data on saving and consumption indicative of family patterns in the 1970s, the so-called "propensity-to-save" and the "propensity-to-consume." Column (2) shows the net saving that accompanies each level of disposable income. The "break-even point," where the family neither saves nor dissaves, instead consuming all its income, falls at $4,000. Below this, as at $3,000 or $2,00), they actually consume more than their income; they dissave (see the –$175 and –$300 data). Above $4,000 they begin to do positive saving.

Column (3) shows the consumption pattern at each income level—the so-called "propensity to consume." Since each dollar of income is divided between the part consumed and the remaining part saved, Columns (3) and (2) are not independent: they must always exactly add up to Column (1). (Check that they do.)

Economic analysis is interested not simply in the total figures of saving and consumption, but in the *extra* saving and consumption that each *extra* dollar of income brings. Thus, as income goes from $4,000 to $5,000, the extra $1,000 of income is divided between $800 of extra consumption and $200 of extra saving —split up 80 and 20 per cent, so to speak. (Where did these numbers come from? You get them from $4,800 minus $4,000 and $200 minus $0. And verify that the division between consumption and saving of extra income dollars

[3] These data do not depict long-run behavior of each family when its income moves from a *permanent* low level to a *permanent* high level. Transitorily, saving rises much; but as people get accustomed to higher "perman nt income," consumption rises and saving becomes more moderate. Surprising as it may seem, statistics show that people with $12,000 of *permanent* income save about the same *fraction* of their income as do people with $6,000 of *permanent* income.

How we depict important consumption-income and saving-income patterns:

1st, A table presents the propensity-to-consume schedule:

PROPENSITY TO CONSUME AND PROPENSITY TO SAVE

	(1) DISPOSABLE INCOME (AFTER TAXES)	(2) CONSUMPTION EXPENDITURE	(3) MARGINAL PROPENSITY TO CONSUME (MPC)	(4) NET SAVING (4) = (1) — (2)	(5) MARGINAL PROPENSITY TO SAVE (MPS)
A	$ 2,000	$2,300		$— 300	
			$\frac{875}{1,000} = .875$		$\frac{125}{1,000} = .125$
B	3,000	3,175		— 175	
			$\frac{825}{1,000} = .825$		$\frac{175}{1,000} = .175$
C	4,000	4,000		0	
			$\frac{800}{1,000} = .800$		$\frac{200}{1,000} = .200$
D	5,000	4,800		+ 200	
			$\frac{775}{1,000} = .775$		$\frac{225}{1,000} = .225$
E	6,000	5,575		+ 425	
			$\frac{750}{1,000} = .750$		$\frac{250}{1,000} = .250$
F	7,000	6,325		+ 675	
			$\frac{700}{1,000} = .700$		$\frac{300}{1,000} = .300$
G	8,000	7,025		+ 975	
			$\frac{650}{1,000} = .650$		$\frac{350}{1,000} = .350$
H	9,000	7,675		+1,325	
			$\frac{600}{1,000} = .600$		$\frac{400}{1,000} = .400$
I	10,000	8,275		+1,725	

TABLE 11-2. Each dollar of income not consumed is saved. And each extra dollar of income goes into extra consumption or extra saving—giving us two important concepts we are to study: the MPC and MPS. (NOTE: $825 = 4,000 — 3,175. What about $800?)

beyond $5,000 is, respectively, 77.5 and 22.5 per cent, then 75.0 and 25.0 per cent. . . . Does it seem reasonable to you that richer people will consume a little less of each extra income dollar than will poorer?[4])

Family propensity-to-save and propensity-to-consume patterns have been

[4] Students at first find it hard to understand that, even when family income is below the break-even point and saving is negative, nonetheless each *extra* income dollar goes partly into positive extra saving and partly into positive extra consumption. To convince yourself, compare row 2 of Table 11-1 with row 1. Adding $1,000 to $2,000 of income gives $3,000. The extra income makes consumption go from $2,300 to $3,175, a gain of $875 with $125 of extra saving.

rather stable. (Workers, however, have generally seemed to save less than the self-employed.)

To understand how saving and investment determine the level of national income and employment, we must continue to study in detail (1) the propensity-to-save schedule, relating saving and income, and its twin brother (2) the propensity-to-consume schedule, relating consumption and income.

■ THE PROPENSITY-TO-CONSUME SCHEDULE IN DETAIL

Table 11-2 rearranges these same data in more convenient form. First, identify its similarity to Table 11-1. Then disregard its Columns (3) to (5), and notice how consumption expenditure goes up at each higher level of income.

This same consumption-income relation can be shown even more vividly in diagrammatic form. In Fig. 11-2 the total of consumption expenditure in Column (2) is plotted against family disposable income of Column (1); through the resulting circles A, B, C, D, E, F, G, and H, a smooth curve has been drawn.

> This relation between consumption and income is called the *consumption schedule*, or *propensity-to-consume schedule* or often simply the *propensity to consume*. It is a basic, important concept whose general properties we must study.

It will help you to understand its properties if, first, you look at the 45°

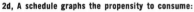
2d, A schedule graphs the propensity to consume:

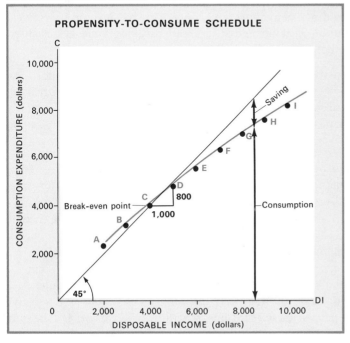

FIG. 11-2. The curve through A, B, . . . , H is the consumption schedule, or the propensity to consume. Its slope at any point, measured by forming a little triangle and relating altitude to base, is the MPC, the marginal propensity to consume. The 45° line helps locate the break-even point and helps our eye measure net saving. Can you see how? (Source: Tables 11-1 and 11-2.)

line also shown in Fig. 11-2. Inasmuch as the vertical axis of consumption has been drawn to the same scale as the horizontal axis of income, any point lying on the 45° helping line has the following simple property: Its indicated consumption expenditure—measured by the vertical distance of the point from the horizontal axis—is exactly equal to 100 per cent of its indicated level of disposable income—measured by the horizontal distance of the point from the vertical axis. (Use your eye to verify that any point *not* on the 45° line cannot possibly be equidistant from the two axes. Reread the description of the 45° line.)

THE "BREAK-EVEN" POINT   The 45° line will tell us right away, therefore, whether consumption spending is equal to, greater than, or less than the level of income. The point on the consumption schedule where it intersects the 45° line shows us the level of disposable income at which families just break even. This break-even point is at C; here, consumption expenditure is exactly equal to disposable income; the family is borrowing nothing and on balance saving nothing.

Similarly, *anywhere else* on the propensity-to-consume curve, the family cannot be just breaking even. To the right of point C, the curve lies below the 45° line; the arrows in Fig. 11-2 show that the vertical distance (consumption expenditure) is less than the horizontal distance (disposable income). If the family is not spending all its income, then it must be saving the remainder. The 45° line tells us more than that; it enables us to find *how much* the family is saving. Net saving is measured by the distance from the propensity-to-consume curve up to the 45° line, as shown by the appropriate saving arrow.

Similarly, to the left of point C, our 45° helping line tells us that the family is for the moment somehow spending more than the income it receives. The excess of consumption over income is its "net dissaving" and is measured by the vertical distance between the two curves. To review:

> When the propensity-to-consume schedule lies above the 45° line, the family is dissaving. Where the two curves meet, the family is just breaking even. Where the propensity to consume lies below the 45° line, the family is performing net positive saving. And the amount of dissaving or saving is always measured by the distance between the two curves.

THE "PROPENSITY-TO-SAVE SCHEDULE"   This means that we can easily derive from the consumption schedule in Fig. 11-2 a new schedule: the propensity to save, or as it is sometimes called, the "saving schedule."

Graphically, this is shown in Fig. 11-3. Again we show disposable income on the horizontal axis; vertically we now show what the family *does not* spend, i.e., we show its net saving, whether negative or positive in amount.

This propensity-to-save curve comes directly from Fig. 11-2. It is simply the distance between the 45° line and the propensity-to-consume schedule. At a point such as *A* in Fig. 11-2, the fact that the family's savings were negative was indicated by the propensity-to-consume schedule lying above the helping

3d, The saving schedule is the exact twin of the consumption schedule:

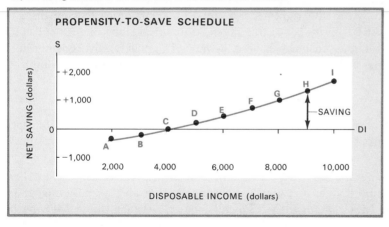

FIG. 11-3. This saving schedule comes from subtracting consumption from income. (Graphically, we vertically subtracted the consumption schedule from the 45° helping line.) Note that the break-even point C is at the same level as in Fig. 11-2. Why? Measure MPS by the curve's slope at any point. Does MPS + MPC = 1 everywhere? (It had better!)

line. Figure 11-3 shows this fact of negative saving directly, and similarly for the positive saving that begins when family income pushes past point C.

■ THE MARGINAL PROPENSITY TO CONSUME

In the next chapter, we shall be attaching much importance to the *extra* amount that people will want to spend on consumption if given an *extra* dollar of income. Economists are so interested in this concept that they have given it a special name, the "marginal propensity to consume," or MPC. (The word "marginal" is used by the economist to mean "extra"; thus, marginal cost will later be defined as extra cost of producing an extra unit of product; marginal utility as extra utility; marginal revenue as extra revenue; and so forth.)

Column (3) back in Table 11-2 shows how we compute the marginal propensity to consume. From C to D, income rises by $1,000, going from $4,000 to $5,000. By how much does consumption rise? Consumption grows from $4,000 to $4,800 or by $800. The extra consumption is therefore .80 of the extra income. Out of each extra dollar of income, 80 cents goes to consumption and 20 cents goes to saving. We therefore can say that the marginal propensity to consume is .80 between C and D, which agrees with Column (3) of Table 11-2.

You can easily compute MPC between other income levels. In Table 11-2, MPC begins at .875 for poor people and finally falls to .600 at higher incomes.

Now we know how to compute MPC numerically. What is its geometric meaning? It is a numerical measure of the steepness of slope of the consumption schedule.[5] Look again at Fig. 11-2. Below points *C* and *D* a little triangle is drawn. As we move to the right from *C* by $1,000, in order to stay on the schedule, we must go up by $800; this gives a numerical slope of $800/$1,000, or .80. NOTE: If higher incomes have a lower MPC, the family consumption schedule will look slightly bowed (convex from above, concave from below).

■ THE MARGINAL PROPENSITY TO SAVE

Along with the marginal propensity to consume goes a Siamese-twin concept, the "marginal propensity to save," or MPS. This is defined as *the fraction of each extra dollar that goes to saving instead of to consumption.*

Why are MPC and MPS related like Siamese twins? Since each extra dollar of income must be divided between extra consumption and extra saving, it is obvious that, if MPC is .75, then MPS must be .25. (What would MPS be if MPC were .6? Or .99?) A comparison of Columns (3) and (5) of Table 11-2 confirms our common-sense feeling that at any income level, MPC and MPS must always add up to exactly 1, no more and no less.[6]

■ BRIEF REVIEW OF DEFINITIONS

For the record, let us jot down the main definitions now learned:

1. The propensity-to-consume schedule (or consumption schedule) relates in a table or a curve the level of consumption to the level of income.

2. The propensity-to-save schedule (or saving schedule) relates saving to income. Since what is saved is the same as what is nonconsumed, saving and consumption schedules are Siamese twins in the sense that

Saving + consumption = disposable income

3. The "break-even point" is the income level where net saving is zero. Below it, there is dissaving, or negative saving; above it, positive net saving.

---

[5] By numerical slope of the *XY*, we always mean the numerical ratio of the length *ZY* to the length of *XZ*. Look at the drawing on this page. If *XY* were a curve, we could find the slope of any point on it (1) by placing a ruler tangent to it, and (2) applying the procedure of this triangle to that tangential line.

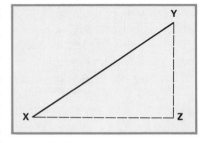

[6] You can also verify from Fig. 11-3 that the numerical steepness of slope of the propensity-to-save schedule is the geometric expression of MPS. This shows: The saving schedule will always have the opposite curvature to that of the consumption schedule; as MPC falls, MPS must rise. And since every extra dollar divides up between positive extra consumption and extra saving, it follows that neither the consumption nor the saving schedule *anywhere* has a slope as steep as the 45° line, which by definition has a slope of 1. Remember, we are here discussing marginal propensities. Thus, at point *A*, the family is spending more than its income; but that does not alter the fact that, at *A*, its *marginal* propensity to consume out of *extra* income is less than 1. (These family data show more exaggerated curvature than would seem realistic in the 1970s for *permanent* income levels.)

Graphically, the break-even point is where the 45° helping line intersects the consumption schedule, or where the saving schedule intersects the horizontal axis.

4. The marginal propensity to consume (MPC) is the amount of *extra* consumption generated by an *extra* dollar of income. Graphically, it is given by the slope of the consumption schedule—a steep slope meaning a high MPC and a flat one meaning a low MPC.

5. The marginal propensity to save (MPS) is the *extra* saving generated by an *extra* dollar of income, or the slope of the saving schedule. Because the part of each dollar that is not consumed is necessarily saved, MPS = 1 — MPC always. Hence, higher income that lowers MPC must raise MPS, implying a convex (from above) consumption schedule and a concave (from below) saving schedule.

■ THE COMMUNITY'S OVER-ALL CONSUMPTION SCHEDULE

So far we have been talking about the consumption patterns shown by families of different incomes. To study what determines a nation's income, we are interested in a propensity-to-consume schedule slightly different from the family-budget schedule. We are interested in the "national propensity-to-consume schedule," relating total consumption to total "disposable (after-tax) income." This is because we are interested in how the total of *all* consumption spending in Canada changes as the total of our spendable income rises.

While aggregate income is not the only factor determining aggregate consumption, common sense and statistical experience tell us that it is one of the most important factors. Note in Fig. 11-4 (on the next page) how closely consumption seems to follow yearly disposable income; the only exceptional period is that of World War II, when goods were scarce and rationed and people were urged to save.

Figure 11-5 (on page 267) shows this relationship between consumption and disposable income in the form of a "scatter diagram" for the years 1926 to 1968. Each dot marks the magnitude for each year. The resulting scatter of points shows no particular curvature, so that a straight-line consumption schedule was drawn in. The actual data fall near, but not exactly on, the "fitted" consumption schedule,[7] reminding us that economics is not, like physics, an exact science. A good rule of thumb is this: Out of each dollar of disposable income about 7 cents goes for saving, S, and 92 cents goes for consumption, C, (actually, a few fractional points go to paying interest on past loans, but this share of spending can be neglected).

---

[7] So that no reader may think there is great accuracy in this line, let it be mentioned that it was fitted by stretching a black thread from the lower corner through the peacetime data at what appeared a reasonable position. As in the case of supply and demand curves in Chapter 4 and Part Three, it will be convenient to go back and forth between drawing propensity-to-consume schedules as curved lines or more simply as straight lines when that does no gross violence to the actual facts.

4th, National consumption did move with national income:

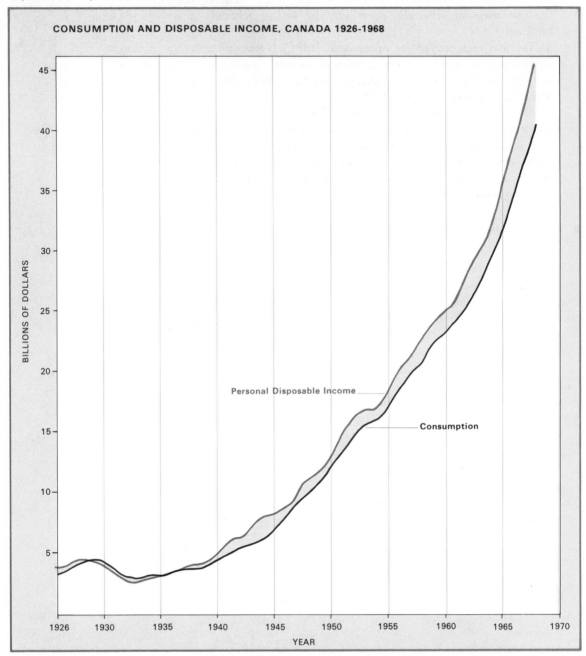

CONSUMPTION AND DISPOSABLE INCOME, CANADA 1926-1968

FIG. 11-4. Good forecasts of consumption come from income data. Can you see how great saving became during World War II's goods shortage and rationing? (Source: Urquhart and Buckley, *Historical Statistics of Canada* and Bank of Canada *Statistical Summary*.)

5th, The national consumption schedule in statistical form:

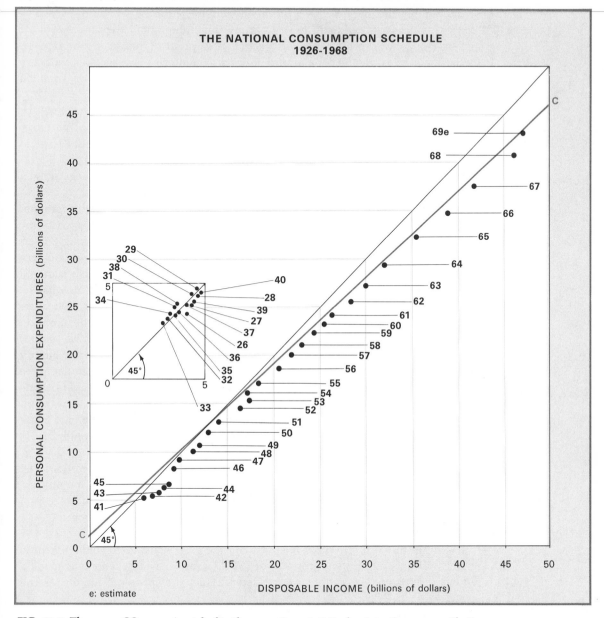

THE NATIONAL CONSUMPTION SCHEDULE
1926-1968

FIG. 11-5. The curve *CC* approximately fits the peacetime statistical points. Can you verify its slope of about .92? (Source: Urquhart and Buckley, *Historical Statistics of Canada*; and Bank of Canada *Statistical Summary*.)

■ QUALIFICATIONS

We are now prepared for the theory of income determination. We have introduced the crucially important concepts of consumption and saving schedules that will be used in the next chapter. But warnings are in order.

The national consumption schedule must be in some sense an aggregation of the family schedules. Yet even if we knew that the family schedules were perfectly reliable, we should still have to know something about the *distribution* of increased incomes before we could get the new point of total consumption on the national schedule. So long as the national-income rise is associated with the distribution of extra income that is typical for such a rise, then we shall be moving along on an unshifted national consumption schedule CC.

Aside from the distribution of income, there is a second factor that must be taken into account in any attempt to relate the family and national patterns. Suppose my income were to go from $6,000 to $40,000 a year. Would I spend and save my money in the same way that the budget studies showed $40,000-a-year people spend their money? Not necessarily. Especially at the beginning, I would be *nouveau riche* and have different patterns of behavior.[8]

A third reason why it is difficult to go from the family to the national consumption schedule is suggested by the expression "keeping up with the Joneses." Fifty years ago, if your family had $2,000 worth of purchasing power, you would have been quite well off and above the break-even point of zero saving. But today many people have incomes above that level. Because man is a social animal, what he regards as necessary comforts of life depends on what he sees others consuming. So today, with $2,000 of income, you would be desperately poor and unable to make ends meet. This fact that one man's consumption depends upon the incomes and consumption of others means that we cannot expect the final national pattern to be the simple sum of the separate family patterns. It also means that we must expect the consumption schedule to be shifting upward each decade as living standards rise. Hence, in Fig. 11-5, one would be foolish to push the line back to the income of 1900 or forward to 1999. It is a succinct description of history rather than necessarily the best guess of the consumption schedule a bank or government economist would use in estimating next year's consumption.

A number of other important qualifications will occur to the reader. The national consumption schedule will shift as prices change and total population grows. Statisticians sometimes try to allow for this by working with per capita consumption and per capita income, expressed in real terms by means of a deflating price index of the sort discussed in the last chapter.[9]

We can think of still other reasons why the propensity-to-consume schedule might shift around. Thus, at the end of World War II, many economists made a famous wrong prediction. They neglected the fact that people came out of the

---

[8] Modern theoretical and statistical researches by Professors Merritt Brown, James S. Duesenberry, Milton Friedman, and Franco Modigliani suggest strongly that if people were generally to get a prescribed percentage increase in their incomes that was permanent, they would probably add more to their consumption expenditure than would be indicated by budget studies recorded for a single year such as 1950 or 1970. This warning, which appeared in footnote 4, is worth repeating.

[9] Thus, instead of working with simple total dollar C, statisticians may correct it for Price and Population, by working with doubly deflated $C/(\text{Price} \times \text{Population})$; likewise, they may replace DI by its doubly deflated $DI/(Pr \times Po)$, to get *per capita real* income.

war hungry for goods and with greatly increased amounts of liquid assets (such as government bonds and bank deposits); for this and other reasons, the consumption schedule turned out to be at a higher level than many pessimistic predictions had indicated.

Again we are reminded that no social science can have great exactitude. We shall have to use tools such as the propensity-to-consume curve—or curves of supply and demand—which we know are subject to error and which tend to shift over time rather than remain stable.

The last chapter showed that the national income accounts *always measure* an identity between saving and investment. This chapter showed that the *motives* and *desires* behind saving and investment are generally quite distinct—which certainly raises the suspicion that the total flow of dollar spending is not guaranteed to proceed at exactly the same rate year in and year out. The hard facts of history confirm this suspicion: at times the economy experienced overexuberant demand and inflation; at times—and they were of considerable duration— it experienced considerable unemployment and excess capacity; in the absence of determined public programs of fiscal and monetary controls, only at rare times have economies enjoyed full employment and steady price levels.

The next two chapters investigate how the forces of saving and investment interact to produce an equilibrium level of national income, which can be at high or low employment and which can be conducive to price stability or to price inflation.

SUMMARY

■ 1　Motivations making people want to engage in saving and to engage in investing activities are different. History shows there is no automatic tendency for the same number of investment dollars to get spent always at the same rate. Hence, our modern mixed economy would be subject to inflationary and depression swings if proper public fiscal and monetary policies did not act to help stabilize the economy and reinforce its spontaneous internal mechanisms that strive to achieve stability.

■ 2　Consumption (food, clothing, and total) and saving, unlike investment, are not volatile and unpredictable. Income is one of their most important determinants. The propensity to consume is the schedule relating total consumption to total income. Because any dollar of income is either saved or consumed, the propensity-to-save schedule is the other side of the propensity-to-consume picture.

■ 3　The characteristics of family or national propensity-to-consume and propensity-to-save schedules are summarized in the brief review of definitions on page 264 and must be thoroughly understood prior to the analysis of income determination in the next chapter.

■ 4　We could aggregate the family consumption schedules to get the national propensity-to-consume schedule, (*a*) if we knew the distribution of income for each level of disposable income, (*b*) if families always stuck to the same consumption-income patterns in the short run and the long, (c) if we could forget the fact that one man's consumption is influenced by the income levels of his neighbors, and (d) if price levels, population, corporate saving, and taxes could be neglected.

The statistical data suggest that total consumption expenditure follows rather closely the changes in total disposable income. But in using the propensity-to-consume concept for the discussion of income determination in the next chapter, we must beware of forming an exaggerated notion of the accuracy and empirical stability of such a theoretical concept.

QUESTIONS FOR DISCUSSION

1. Summarize familiar budget patterns. Food, clothing, luxuries, saving.

2. What are some of the reasons why people save? What are some of the forms in which they keep their assets?

3. Exactly how were the MPC and MPS in Table 11-2 computed? Illustrate between *A* and *B*. Explain why it must always be true that MPC + MPS = 1.

4. I consume *all* my income. Draw my consumption and saving schedules.

5. Do you think the break-even point is the same in Toronto as in St. John's, Newfoundland? What do you think is the current break-even point in your community? List a number of ways a person can incur negative net saving for a while.

6. "Along the consumption schedule, income changes more than does consumption." Why? Show that this is even more true on the saving schedule.

7. What factors must be taken into consideration if we want to aggregate family budgetary propensity-to-consume schedules to arrive at a national propensity-to-consume schedule? What would happen to the amount consumed out of 45 billion dollars of disposable income if the degree of inequality of income were increased? To the amount saved? What if total taxes out of the 45 billion dollars were to increase? If people were to have more government bonds and bank deposits, how would that affect saving out of the 45 billion dollars?

8. Contrast the meaning of this chapter's beginning quotation with the following 1966 letter to the editor of *Time Magazine* by Professor Milton Friedman of the University of Chicago.

Sir: You quote me (Dec. 31, 1965) as saying: "We are all Keynesians now." The quotation is correct, but taken out of context. As best I can recall it, the context was: "In one sense, we are all Keynesians now; in another, nobody is any longer a Keynesian."

9. Review your understanding of the following concepts:

family motives for saving	after-tax, or disposable, income
business motives for investing	permanent versus transitory income
volatile investment decisions	national consumption schedule
consumption and saving schedules	versus family schedule
MPC and MPS: MPC + MPS = 1	shifts of *CC* with price, time,
break-even point and 45° line	and other changes

12

INCOME DETERMINATION: THE SIMPLE THEORY AND THE MULTIPLIER

Given the propensity to consume and the rate of new investment, there will be only one level of employment consistent with equilibrium. J. M. KEYNES (1936)

Economists are agreed that an important factor in causing income and employment to fluctuate is fluctuations in investment. Whether we are to face a situation of inflationary bidding up of prices or shall live in a frigid state of mass unemployment depends, as will be seen, upon the level of investment.

From 1953 to 1963, the Canadian economy suffered from a growth in unemployment and some insufficiency of total demand. Memories are short, and there is danger that we shall forget the tremendous costs that were associated with the mass unemployment of the prewar Great Depression. It is scarcely an exaggeration to say that the economic costs of that depression were of the same general magnitude as the costs of all the economic resources which had to be used up in World War II itself. Figure 12-1 reminds us that in past years the Canadian economy, because of failure to maintain full-employment growth, lost billions of dollars' worth of goods and services. But by the late 1960s, Canada had substantially eliminated unemployment and concern shifted to "overheating" of the economy or excessively high levels of demand in relation to the productive capacity of the nation, a situation which was accomplished by inflation with its own myriad problems.

Then in late 1969 it became apparent that in attempting to deal with inflation, we were encountering the rare and costly combination of continued high levels of price increase along with rising unemployment.

POVERTY Figure 12-1 might also serve to remind us that nations are actually subject to three kinds of poverty:

(1)   Ancient poverty due to famine and inadequate production potential;
(2)   Unnecessary poverty due only to bad purchasing-power behavior of the system;
(3)   Poverty due only to uneven and undesirable distribution of an opulent total NNP.

Long ago, for our advanced Western nations, overt poverty of the first type was conquered in the triumph of technology. This is illustrated by Fig. 2-3 (*a*) and (*b*), on page 26. But only with the development of modern income analysis has Type (2), "poverty midst plenty"—like that of 1929-39—been rendered obsolete. Here in Part Two we learn how and why. Then in Part Six we can grapple with the third kind of poverty, which does still remain to challenge us.

This chapter and the next one outline the modern theory of income determination. Because the problems are so important and because the analysis is so useful, Section A of the present chapter stresses the fundamentals—how saving and investment, or what is the same thing, how consumption and invest-

Cost of sluggish growth rivals that of war:

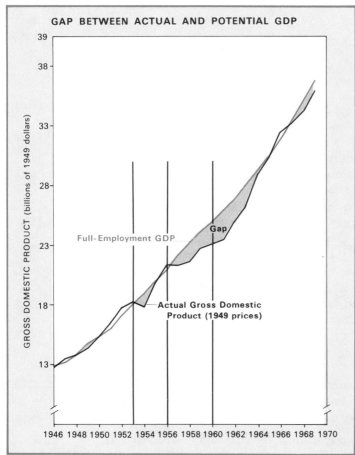

FIG. 12-1. The shaded area shows the gap between what we actually produced in recent years and what our economic system was capable of producing at reasonably high employment and capacity utilization. On a few occasions, such as in 1952, the economy overshoots "reasonable" achievements. The three vertical lines indicate the accepted dating of important business down-turns, in 1953, 1956, and 1960. Note that the gap beginning in 1956 was never removed before 1960 which made it worse. For dating, see Appendix to Chapter 13. GDP is an alternative measurement to GNP, explained in Chapter 10 (see page 242). (Sources: ECC and DBS.)

ment interact to determine the equilibrium level of national income at full employment, below full employment, or with over-full employment inflationary conditions. Then, in Section B, we turn to the interesting "multiplier" principle that shows how each dollar change in investment leads to more than a dollar— i.e. to a "multiplier"—change in NNP, and to an analysis of deflationary gaps and of price inflation.

Once the tools of this chapter are mastered, we are ready to understand next chapter's analysis of how government expenditure and government tax policy can alter the income equilibrium, and of the change in the analysis that is necessary when we formally admit exports and imports to our income theory.

A. USING THE CONSUMPTION AND SAVING SCHEDULES TO DETERMINE INCOME

The last chapter gave a simplified picture of the propensity-to-consume and the propensity-to-save schedules for the community. As discussed, they are drawn up on the basis of our knowledge of the thriftiness of different families, the distribution of incomes between families, and so forth. (At the beginning we shall make the further simplifying assumptions that there are no taxes, undistributed corporate profits, transfers, government expenditure, or foreign trade of any kind to worry about; hence, we do not have to concern ourselves for the moment with any distinction between net national product and disposable income, and we can use the word "income" to refer to either. Also, we shall initially neglect any changes in the price level.)

Figure 12-2 on the following page shows the nation's propensities to consume and to save. Each point on its consumption schedule shows how much the nation will *want to continue to consume* at that level of disposable income. Each point on the saving schedule shows how much it will want to continue to save at that income level. Recall that the two schedules are clearly related: since $C + S$ = income always, the CC and SS curves are Siamese twins that would add up always to the 45° line.

■ HOW INCOME IS DETERMINED AT THE LEVEL WHERE SAVING AND INVESTMENT SCHEDULES INTERSECT

We have seen that saving and investment are dependent on quite different factors: Saving tends to depend in a "passive" way upon income, while volatile investment often depends upon "autonomous" factors of dynamic growth.

For simplicity, first suppose investment opportunities are such that net investment would be exactly 6 billion dollars per year regardless of the level of NNP. This means that, if we now draw a schedule of investment against NNP, it will have to be a *horizontal* line—always the same distance above the horizontal axis. Turn to Fig. 12-3 on page 275, where this investment schedule is labeled *II* to distinguish it from the *SS* savings schedule. (*II* does *not* mean Roman numeral two.)

Society's national income determines its consumption and saving:

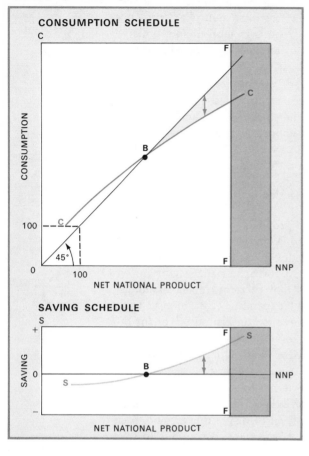

FIG. 12-2. *CC* is the propensity-to-consume and *SS* is the propensity-to-save schedule for the community.

Recall that these are closely related: the break-even point *B* is shown on the upper diagram where *CC* intersects the 45° line and on the lower diagram where *SS* intersects the horizontal axis. Can you explain why the vertically aligned arrows *must* be equal? (The curvature is slightly exaggerated here to help identify the two schedules. The two points marked 100 should help emphasize the important property of the 45° line: it depicts a vertical distance equal to exactly 100 per cent of the horizontal distance.)

The vertical black line *FF* depicts the full-employment NNP. Above this critical level *real* product cannot increase (and beyond it we could no longer adhere to our simplifying assumption of ignoring price-level changes).

The saving and investment schedules intersect at *E*, which corresponds to a level of NNP equal to the distance from *O* to *M*.

This intersection of the *saving and investment schedules is the equilibrium toward which national income will gravitate.* Under our assumed conditions, no other level of income can perpetuate itself.

The remaining pages of this chapter are devoted to the single task of explaining this important truth.

Let us see why the equilibrium income must eventually be at *E*, the point of intersection between the investment and saving schedules. We consider three cases.

The first case is that in which the system is *at E* itself, where the *II* schedule of what business firms *want* to invest and keep investing just intersects the *SS* schedule of what families *want* to save. Consequently, everyone will be content to go on doing just what he has been doing. Firms will not find inventories piling up on their shelves, nor will they find sales so brisk as to force them to produce more goods. So production, employment, and income spending will remain the same. NNP in the first case does truly stay at the point *E*; and we can rightly call that "equilibrium."

The second case is where the system is *first* at an NNP *higher* than at *E*, so that it begins east of *E*, at an income level where the *SS* schedule is higher than the *II* schedule. Why can't the system stay there indefinitely? Because at such an income level, families are saving—are refraining from spending on consumption — *more* than business firms will be *willing to go on investing*. Firms will thus find they have too few customers and that their inventories are piling up against their wishes, and they will not want to go on being forced into such undesired inventory investment. What can they do about it? They can certainly cut back production and lay off workers. This moves NNP gradually downward, which means westward in Fig. 12-3. Where does the system stop being in such disequilibrium? Only when it gets back to *E*, the equilibrium intersection point. There the longer-run tendency to change has disappeared.

The third case should be mastered by the reader. Show that if NNP were *below* its equilibrium level, strong forces would be set up to move it eastward back to *E*. (HINT: At any NNP level where families' *intended* saving falls short of business firms' *intended* investment, the result is consumption of more goods than are being currently produced. What does this mean? It means that business will find itself having to sell inventory off its shelves faster than its production line is producing such goods. Once businessmen notice that they are being forced into less investment, i.e., into more *involuntary* inventory *disinvestment*, than the *II* curve shows they want, what will they do? They will then expand production and hire new men. This will complete the demonstration that the system does move back eastward until it gets to *E*.)

We can show equilibrium determination of national income in the following equivalent ways:

1st, By intersection of saving and investment schedules:

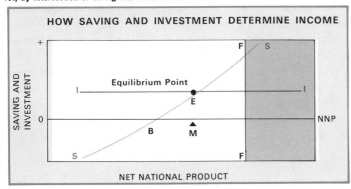

FIG. 12-3. *E* marks the spot where investment and saving curves intersect. Equilibrium is at the intersection of *SS* and *II* curves because at no other level of NNP could the desired saving of families continually match the desired investment of business.

All three cases then lead to the same summary:

The only equilibrium of national income is at E, where the saving and investment schedules intersect. At any other point, the *desired* saving of families will not match the *desired* investment of business, and this discrepancy will cause businessmen to change their production and employment levels in such a way as to return the system to the equilibrium intersection.

Before we go on, a warning is in order. An equilibrium level like E is a point where the system tends to stay. But there is nothing necessarily optimal about every equilibrium point. Note the vertical black line FF and the gray shaded area to the right of it in Fig. 12-3 that depict full-employment income. Note the fact that the E equilibrium shown is at a level of NNP lower than that corresponding to F's full employment.

During a great depression, a capitalistic system may be firmly stuck at a point of very great unemployment. It is then at the E given by its low II schedule. No one would make the mistake of thinking that such a deep-unemployment equilibrium point is in any sense a good thing. Instead, the government would intervene in the economic system to try to shift the curves until a new equilibrium point E' was attained at a desirable level (as in Fig. 12-7, on page 286).

■ INCOME DETERMINATION BY CONSUMPTION AND INVESTMENT

There is a second way of showing how income is determined, other than by the intersection of the saving and investment schedules. The final result is exactly the same, but our understanding and confidence in the theory of income determination will be increased if we work through this second approach.

This second approach is called the consumption-plus-investment rather than the saving-investment approach. The $C + I$ approach[1] takes advantage of the Siamese-twins property of the saving and consumption schedules. Thus it must always lead to exactly the same equilibrium income as does the saving-and-investment approach. This is shown by the fact that when you line up Fig. 12-4 vertically under Fig. 12-3, you always find that in both charts E marks exactly the same NNP equilibrium.

The $C + I$ approach has the advantage of concentrating on *total spending*: spending for consumption goods plus spending for investment goods. The $C + I$ approach vertically adds the II schedule of business' *desired* investment to the CC consumption schedule of families' *desired* consumption spending.

Only where the two *desired* amounts of spending add up to equality with the value of NNP being produced will there be equilibrium.

With what must the combined $C + I$ schedule intersect to depict this equilibrium? Figure 12-4 introduces a 45° line to provide our looked-for intersection point. The 45° line, we have seen, has the useful property that it lays

---

[1] When government is brought into the picture, $C + I$ will become $C + I + G$. Adding foreign trade will make it $C + I + G + (E - M)$.

2d, By intersection of $C + I$ schedule with 45° line:

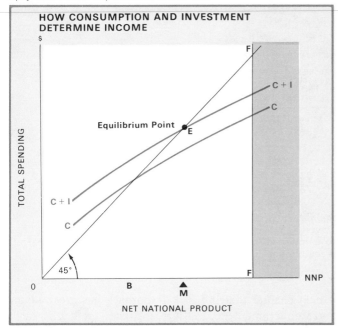

HOW CONSUMPTION AND INVESTMENT
DETERMINE INCOME

$

TOTAL SPENDING

Equilibrium Point

E

F

C + I

C

C + I

C

45°

0   B   M   F   NNP

NET NATIONAL PRODUCT

FIG. 12-4. Adding II to CC gives the $C + I$ curve of total spending. At E, where it intersects the 45° line, we get the same equilibrium as in the saving-and-investment diagram. (Note the similarities between this figure and Fig. 12-3: the investment added to CC is the same as II of Fig. 12-3; B and F each come at the same place on the two diagrams, and so must the E intersection.)

out in the vertical direction a distance always exactly equal to the income shown on the horizontal axis. So the 45° line is admirably designed to depict the expense that firms are incurring for the productive factors required to produce national output, and which they must be getting back if they are to feel safe to continue hiring the same number of men and producing the same level of NNP.[2]

We can summarize the $C + I$ method of income determination thus:

> The equilibrium level of national income is at the intersection of the $C + I$ schedule of desired total spending with the 45° line depicting value of total output.[3] This equilibrium E corresponds exactly to the saving-and-investment equilibrium because of the Siamese-twins relation between the consumption and the saving schedules.

[2] As the intermediate texts would put it: If the system is not at this intersection, there will be *unintended* inventory investment or disinvestment and/or *unforeseen windfall* profits or losses. As a result, there cannot be equilibrium; but rather a chain of new decisions will be set up to expand or contract output, and possibly to raise or lower prices. So the system will move in disequilibrium until it ends up at the intersection point of equilibrium. Those same intermediate texts point out that *measured S* and *measured I* stay identical even during the worst disequilibrium, by virtue of some people's experiencing unintended losses or gains and/or experiencing unintended investment or saving. (Remember, too, that economists include profit in total business expense.)

[3] Some writers like to call the $C + I$ curve an aggregate *demand* curve, and the 45°-line curve an aggregate *supply* curve. Then, using Chapter 4's language, they say: The equilibrium level of income is where the aggregate demand and supply curves intersect.

3d, The tendency toward equilibrium is shown by arithmetic table:

INCOME DETERMINATION BY SAVING AND INVESTMENT (in billions of dollars)

(1) LEVELS OF NNP AND DI	(2) SCHEDULED CONSUMPTION	(3) SCHEDULED OR PLANNED OR MAINTAINABLE SAVING (3) = (1) — (2)	(4) SCHEDULED OR PLANNED OR MAINTAINABLE INVESTMENT	(5) EXPENSE INCURRABLE BY BUSINESS TO PRODUCE NNP (5) = (1)		(6) SCHEDULED SPENDING THAT WOULD PERMANENTLY COME BACK TO BUSINESSES (6) = (2) + (4)	(7) RESULTING TENDENCY OF INCOME
$118	$106	$12	$6	$118	>	$112	Contraction
109	100	9	6	109	>	106	Contraction
100	94	6	6	100	=	100	Equilibrium
91	88	3	6	91	<	94	Expansion
82	82	0	6	82	<	88	Expansion
73	76	−3	6	73	<	82	Expansion

TABLE 12-1. The bold brown row depicts the equilibrium NNP, where the 6 billion dollars that businessmen will be willing to continue to invest is just matched by families' intended saving. (In higher rows, firms will be forced into unintended inventory investment and will respond by cutting production and NNP back to equilibrium. Interpret the lower rows.)

We shall see in the next chapter that the $C + I$ approach has great advantages in helping to analyze government expenditure and fiscal policy. It easily turns itself into an exactly similar $C + I + G$ approach.

■ ARITHMETIC DEMONSTRATION OF INCOME DETERMINATION: A DIGRESSION FOR A THIRD RESTATEMENT

A thoughtful reader may still want to know more about *why* the equilibrium level of income will have to be at the intersection of the saving and investment schedules. What forces push income to that level and no other?

An arithmetic example may help verify this important matter. Table 12-1 shows an especially simple pattern of the propensity to save against income. The break-even level of income where the nation is too poor to do any net saving on balance is assumed to be 82 billion dollars. Each change of income of 9 billion dollars is assumed to lead to a 3-billion-dollar change in saving and a 6-billion-dollar change in consumption; in other words, MPC is for simplicity here assumed to be constant and exactly equal to $2/3$ with MPS = $1/3$. For this reason, the saving-propensity schedule SS in Fig. 12-5 (page 281) takes on the especially simple form of a perfectly straight line.

What shall we assume about investment? For simplicity, let us suppose again that the only level of investment that can be voluntarily maintained indefinitely is exactly 6 billion dollars, as shown in Column (4) of Table 12-1.

Now, Columns (5) and (6) are the crucial ones. Column (5) shows how much total expense business firms undergo at each level of national production for wages, interest, rent, *and* profit. This is the NNP of Column (1) copied once again into Column (5), because our repeated discussions of Chapter 10 showed that upper- and lower-loop measurements must be the same.

Column (6), on the other hand, shows what business firms would in fact be *getting back* in the long run in the form of scheduled or voluntary consumption spending plus scheduled or voluntary investment. (It's really the $C + I$ schedule of Fig. 12-4.)

When business firms as a whole are temporarily producing a high total product, higher than the sum of what consumers will buy and what business as a whole wants to be investing in equipment and inventory accumulation, businesses will find themselves forced involuntarily to pile up inventories of unsalable goods. At the same time their total sales revenue will be so low as to be putting disagreeable downward pressure on their profit position. With scheduled *SS* above *II*, therefore, they will want to contract their operations, and NNP will tend to fall. (Contrariwise, when $II > SS$ and inventories are being involuntarily depleted and profit margins improving, they will increase their employment, and production and NNP will rise.)

When business firms as a whole are temporarily producing at an expense greater than what they can recover, they will want to contract their operations, and NNP tends to fall. When they are getting back more than their current expense for production, they increase their production and NNP rises.

> Only when the level of scheduled saving in Column (3) is exactly equal to that of scheduled investment in Column (4) will business firms stay continually in aggregative equilibrium. Their sales will then be just enough to justify continuing their current level of aggregate output. NNP will neither expand nor contract.

This same story is shown in Fig. 12-5. NNP can be read in either of two ways: on the horizontal axis or (from the nature of a 45° line) as the equivalent vertical distance from that axis up to the helping 45° line. The line *SS* represents the saving schedule; the line *II* represents the scheduled level of investments that can be maintained over time. Consumption can also be seen in the figure. Since income not saved is consumed, consumption is always the vertical distance from the saving schedule to the 45° line.

Now we can use Fig. 12-5 to confirm what has just been shown by the arithmetic of Table 12-1. No level of income can *long persist* if it is higher than the equilibrium level given by the *scheduled* saving and investment intersection at 100 billion dollars. To the right of the intersection point E, the expense incurred by businesses would exceed the *amount received back* by businesses in the form of maintainable consumption plus maintainable investment.

Graphically, this is shown by the following: The amount continuously paid out by business is the whole distance up to the 45° line, i.e., from Q to R; but the amount that would continuously be received back by business would be only the sum of voluntary investment QK and consumption JR. There is a gap of JK.

Businesses face a real dilemma. For a while they could keep their prices high and let unsold goods pile up on their shelves, but that would not represent an equilibrium situation and could not persist. Or for a while they could lower prices on their goods and sell below needed cost with less profit; but that, too, could not last.

Thus, it is completely clear that income cannot *permanently* be maintained higher than the equilibrium level—*the level where the amount of saving that people want to do is matched by the amount of investment businessmen are willing to maintain.* A persistent gap of the JK type must, through attempts to cut down losses and excessive inventories, result in a contraction of employment and net national product back toward the equilibrium point, where there is no gap. Therefore the arrow near Q points leftward back toward the equilibrium level.

A similar argument shows why income will tend to rise from any place to the left of the equilibrium-intersection level. Indicate on the diagram the relation between business expense and what business can permanently receive back. Show that there will be a favorable gap (as at J'K'): Business either will be selling so much as to be depleting inventories on their shelves or will be temporarily raising their prices and earning extra profits. In either case, they will be tempted to expand their employment and production. And when they do, the result will be a rise in income back toward the equilibrium-intersection level.[4] Thus ends our digression.

■ THE SIMPLIFIED THEORY OF INCOME DETERMINATION RESTATED

Figure 12-6 pulls together in a simplified way the main elements of income determination. Without saving and investment, there would be a circular flow of income between business and the public; above, business pays out wages, interest, rents, and profits to the public in return for the services of labor and property; and below, the public pays consumption funds to business in return for goods and services.

Realistically, we must recognize that the public will wish to save some of its income, as shown at the spigot Z. Hence, businesses cannot expect their consumption sales to be as large as the total of wages, interest, rents, and profits. Why not? Because dollars saved do not come back *as consumption sales.*

Some monetary cranks think that this saving necessarily means unemployment and depression. Such a view is simply incorrect. If there happen to be

---

[4] The recorded income statistics never show the gap depicted in JK and by Column (6) minus Column (5). Why not? Because these are gaps in people's *scheduled* quantities. They show levels that cannot continue to persist. On the other hand, the *measurable* statistics of saving and investment are definitionally equal no matter what income is doing: thus, when inventory is *involuntarily* piling up, the DBS statistician cares not that its identity of investment and saving is the result of *unintended investment.* Why should it? It need never go beyond the anatomy of the problem. But we—interested in dynamic physiology of income determination—are vitally interested in schedules. (NOTE: In the last few pages, words such as "voluntary," "scheduled," and "maintainable" were repeated and stressed to call attention to the difference between a magnitude permanently persisting as a schedule and the actual amounts measured after the fact in any disturbed short run. In the supply and demand schedules of Part Three, the same problem will recur; Chapter 4 showed that the wheat bought is always numerically identical with the wheat sold; but only at equilibrium market price do the *scheduled* amounts intersect.)

4th, A graph reinforces table's story of restoring equilibrium:

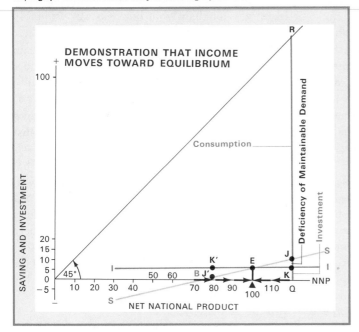

FIG. 12-5. Only at E is there no gap between scheduled saving and investment. A gap like that shown at JK will soon cause firms to cut their production, which explains the westward black arrow pushing NNP back to E's equilibrium level.

Show that the opposite gap at J'K' will mean that firms find their sales so great as to deplete their inventories; interpret the eastward black arrow showing that firms expand production to push NNP back to E.

sufficiently profitable investment opportunities, business firms will be paying out wages, interest, and other costs *in part for new-investment goods* rather than 100 per cent for consumption goods. Hence, to continue to be happy, business needs to receive back in consumption sales only *part* of the total income paid out to the public—only that part which involves the cost of current

Dynamic investment pumps national income up and down:

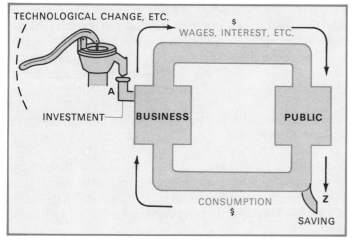

FIG. 12-6. Technological change, population growth, and other dynamic factors keep the investment pump handle going. Income rises and falls with changes in investment, its maintainable equilibrium level being realized only when intended saving at Z continues to match intended investment at A.

consumption goods. The saving that the public wants to make will do no harm to national income so long as it is not greater than what business can profitably continue to invest.

In Fig. 12-6, investment is shown being pumped into the income stream at A. The handle of the pump is being moved by (1) technological invention, (2) population growth, and (3) other dynamic factors that affect the profitability of investment (such as the opening of new regions to development).

When the investment pump is going at a rapid, steady pace, NNP is high and is at its maintainable equilibrium rate where scheduled saving at Z just balances scheduled investment at A.

This demonstrates that the pessimistic monetary cranks who thought that saving was always disastrous were plain wrong. Early members of the Social Credit Party, too, were obsessed with the leak in the system at Z; they stood for a steady inflow of new money at A to keep the circular flow from running dry, regardless of how strongly the pump handle was going anyway. But there is also a second misconception: some go to the opposite extreme and insist that saving and investment can never, in our modern mixed economy with all its frictions and rigidities, cause income to be too high or too low. They make the fatal error of automatically, and without regard to banking policy and fiscal policy, connecting the pipe at Z with the inflow at A.

Many books have been written on this subject of equilibrium income determination, and it is only in the last few decades that economists have learned how to separate the truth and falsity of both extremes. The next one-hundred or so pages will deal with this important question, in its relation to income, "inflationary or deflationary gaps," exports and imports, banking, and business-cycle policy. An essential step in the exposition is the next section's "multiplier" analysis.

B. INVESTMENT AND INCOME: THE "MULTIPLIER"

Now that we have seen how the intersection of saving and investment determines the level of national income, we realize that an increase in investment will increase the level of income and employment. Thus, an investment boom may bring a nation out of a deep or mild depression—by having a higher II schedule cut the SS schedule at a higher equilibrium level for NNP.

> An increase in private investment will cause income to expand; a decrease in investment will cause it to contract.

This is not a very surprising result. After all, we have learned that investment is one part of net national product; when one of the parts increases in value, we should naturally expect the whole to increase in value. That is only part of the story. Our theory of income determination gives us a much more striking result.

Modern income analysis shows that an increase in net investment will increase national income by a *multiplied* amount—by an amount greater than itself! Investment spending—like any independent shifts in governmental, foreign, or family spending—is high-powered, double-duty spending, so to speak.

This amplified effect of investment[5] on income is called the "multiplier" doctrine; the word multiplier itself is used for the *numerical coefficient showing how great an increase in income results from each increase in such investment spending.*

Some examples will make this terminology clear. Let there be an increase of investment of 5 billion dollars. If this causes an increase of income of 15 billion dollars, then the multiplier is 3. If instead the resulting increase in income were 20 billion dollars, then the multiplier would be 4.

Definition: The multiplier is the number by which the change in investment must be multiplied in order to present us with the resulting change in income.

No proof has yet been presented to show that the multiplier will be greater than 1. But using ordinary common sense one can see why, when I hire unemployed resources to build a $1,000 garage, there will be a *secondary* expansion of national income and production, over and above my primary investment. Here is why.

My carpenters and lumber producers will get an extra $1,000 in income. But that is not the end of the story. If they all have a marginal propensity to consume of 2⁄3, they will now spend $666.67 on new consumption goods. The producers of these goods will now have an extra income of $666.67. If their MPC is also 2⁄3, they in turn will spend $444.44, or 2⁄3 of $666.67 (or 2⁄3 of 2⁄3 of $1,000). So the process will go on, with each new round of spending being 2⁄3 of the previous round.

Thus a whole endless chain of secondary consumption respending is set up by my primary $1,000 of investment spending. But it is a dwindling chain, and it all adds up to a finite amount. By either grade-school arithmetic or high-school geometric progression,[6] we get

---

[5] Our later analysis will show that the multiplier can apply also to government and other shifts in spending; but first we stick to the simplifying assumption of shifts up and down of a horizontal investment schedule.

[6] High-school algebra says the formula for an infinite geometric progression is $1 + r + r^2 + r^3 + \ldots r^n + \ldots = \dfrac{1}{1-r}$ as long as r is less than 1 absolute value. This progression is central to the various "multipliers" in these two chapters and to Chapter 15's deposit-expansion process.

In this case, MPC = r. If the MPC were changing along a curved schedule, in the multiplier progression we should have to use an MPC at an income level somewhere between the original and the final level. Footnote 7 in the next chapter handles a non-horizontal *II* case.

$$
\left.\begin{array}{c}
\$1,000.00 \\
+ \\
666.67 \\
+ \\
444.44 \\
+ \\
296.30 \\
+ \\
197.53 \\
+ \\
\cdots
\end{array}\right\} = \left\{\begin{array}{l}
1 \quad \times \$1,000 \\
+ \\
2/3 \quad \times \$1,000 \\
+ \\
(2/3)^2 \times \$1,000 \\
+ \\
(2/3)^3 \times \$1,000 \\
+ \\
(2/3)^4 \times \$1,000 \\
+ \\
\cdots
\end{array}\right.
$$

$$
\begin{array}{cc}
\$2,999.999 & \\
\text{or} & \dfrac{1}{1 - 2/3} \times \$1,000, \text{ or } 3 \times \$1,000 \\
\$3,000 &
\end{array}
$$

This shows that, with an MPC of $2/3$, the multiplier is 3, consisting of the 1 of primary investment plus 2 extra of secondary consumption respending.

The same arithmetic would give a multiplier of 4 if the MPC were $3/4$, for the reason that $1 + 3/4 + (3/4)^2 + (3/4)^3 + \ldots$ finally adds up to 4. If the MPC were $1/2$, the multiplier would be 2. The size of the multiplier thus depends upon how large the MPC is; or it can be expressed in terms of the twin concept, the MPS. If the MPS were $1/4$, the MPC would be $3/4$, and the multiplier would be 4. If the MPS were $1/3$, the multiplier would be 3. If the MPS were $1/X$, the multiplier would be X.

By this time it is plain that the simple multiplier is always the upside-down or "reciprocal," of the marginal propensity to save. Our general multiplier formula (taxation and corporation saving being negligible) is always

$$
\text{Change in income} = \frac{1}{\text{MPS}} \times \text{change in investment}
$$

$$
= \frac{1}{1 - \text{MPC}} \times \text{change in investment}
$$

In other words, the greater the extra consumption respending, the greater the multiplier. The greater the MPS "leakage" into extra saving at each round of spending, the smaller the final multiplier.

■ GRAPHICAL PICTURE OF THE MULTIPLIER

Up to this point, we have discussed the multiplier in terms of common sense and arithmetic. Will our saving-investment analysis of income give us the same result? The answer must of course be, Yes.

Suppose, as back in Table 12-1, the MPS is $1/3$ and a new series of inventions comes along and gives rise to an extra 3 billion dollars of continuing investment opportunities, over and above our previous 6 billion dollars. Then the increase in investment should raise equilibrium NNP from 100 billion to what? To 109 billion dollars if the multiplier is correctly given as 3 by our previous analysis.

Figure 12-7, on the following page, confirms this result. Our old investment schedule II is shifted upward by 3 billion dollars to the new level $I'I'$. The new intersection point is E'. And lo, the increase in income is exactly three times as much as the increase in investment. This is because an MPS of only $\frac{1}{3}$ means a relatively flat SS saving schedule. As the arrows show, the horizontal income distance is three times as great as the "primary" vertical saving-investment distance, the discrepancy being equal to the secondary "consumption responding."

In short, income must rise enough to bring out a volume of voluntary saving equal to the new investment. With an MPS of $\frac{1}{3}$, income has to rise by how much in order to bring out 3 billion dollars of new saving to match exactly the new investment? By exactly 9 billion dollars.[7]

---

[7] Table 12-1 will also verify this answer. In Column (4), we now put in 9 billion dollars instead of 6 billion dollars of investment. The new equilibrium level of income now shifts one row up from the previous equilibrium row. The multiplier works downward also; thus a decline of 1 billion dollars in investment spending will induce an endless chain of negative items, leading ultimately to a 3-billion-dollar *reduction* in equilibrium income. (Check by cutting I from 6 to 3.)

We can also derive algebraically the simple investment multiplier formula used in the example above.

We know that in equilibrium of this simple economy

(1) $$NNP = Y = C + \overline{I}$$

(Bar over symbol means that it is constant.)

Now suppose scheduled consumption is given by the following simple linear equation:

(2) $$C = \overline{C} + b\,Y$$

where $\overline{C}$ is a constant amount of consumption, even when $Y = 0$. This consumption equation is also called a *consumption function* because it says that consumption depends upon, or *is a function of*, NNP. b, the marginal propensity to consume MPC, is represented here and in Fig. 11-2 as the steepness of the slope of CC. Footnote 5 of Chapter 11 showed that the steepness is the amount by which consumption increases, ΔC, for any increase in income, ΔY. That is,

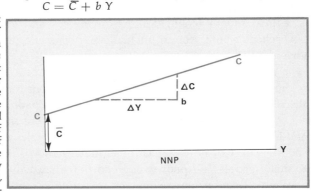

$$MPC = b = \Delta C / \Delta Y$$

Where CC is curved, b is not a constant, but becomes smaller with higher incomes.

Scheduled investment is assumed to remain constant at some given level, written as $\overline{I}$:

(3) $$I = \overline{I}$$

Now we simply substitute (2) and (3) into the NNP equation, so that

$$Y = \overline{C} + b\,Y + \overline{I}$$

or

$$Y - b\,Y = Y\,(1 - b) = \overline{C} + \overline{I}$$

Hence

(4) $$Y = \frac{1}{1-b}\,(\overline{C} + \overline{I})$$

Here, then, the multiplier is $1/(1 - b)$, or, in the terminology of the text, $1/(1 - MPC)$.

As shown in Chapter 11, Fig. 11-3, $1/(1 - b)$ is also equal to $1/MPS$. The multiplier expression $1/(1 - b)$ applies not only to unchanged total $\overline{I}$ but also to *changes* in investment ΔI. It will be shown below that this multiplier can be applied to autonomous schedule shifts in consumption ΔC (Fig. 13-2); and, in the next chapter, to changes in government purchases ΔG, or in exports ΔE.

**The saving-and-investment diagram has many applications.
It shows how:**

1st, Each dollar of investment can be "multiplied" into three dollars of income:

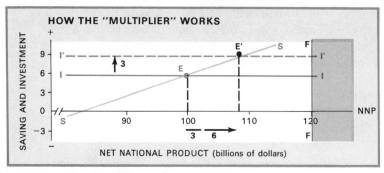

FIG. 12-7. New investment shifts *II* up to *I'I'*. *E'* gives the new
equilibrium income, with income increasing 3 for each 1 increase
in investment. (Note that the broken horizontal black arrow is 3
times the length of the vertical black arrow that shows the shift in
investment, and is broken to show 2 of consumption responding for
each 1 of investment.)

■ HOW SHIFTS IN THE CONSUMPTION SCHEDULE OR THRIFTINESS AFFECT INCOME

We have seen that investment affects incomes. Let us now consider *shifts* in
scheduled *saving* (changes in "thriftiness") and *consumption*. Won't the new
S'S' schedule intersect an unchanged *II* schedule in a new equilibrium *E'*? At a
lower NNP?

Yes, and yes. Figure 12-8 shows that an upward shift in saving—and, what
is the same thing, a downward shift in the consumption schedule—will tend in
the absence of any change in the investment schedule to *lower* equilibrium NNP.

Common sense tells us why. If people consume less out of their incomes
and if business will not willingly invest more, sales will fall and production must
soon be cut. Cut how far? Until so much national income has been destroyed as
to make people feel poor enough so that they will finally end up not trying to
save more than business will go on investing.

Perhaps this point seems obvious. But Fig. 12-8 tells us something more
surprising. It shows that a $1 upward shift in the saving schedule will kill off
$3 of income. Contrariwise, a $1 downward shift in the saving schedule, which
means a $1 upward shift in the consumption schedule, will produce a similar
multiplier $3 increase in income. (Note in Fig. 12-8 that the horizontal arrow
is 3 times the vertical arrow.)

> In short, just as investment spending is "high-powered spending," with
> multiplier effects on income, consumption spending that represents a genuine
> shift in the propensity to consume and save will also be "high-powered"!

We shall meet many examples of this. Thus, the next chapter shows how
reducing taxes can increase consumption—and thereby expand income by more

2d, Changes in thriftiness, or a shift in *CC*, will change income in a multiplied way:

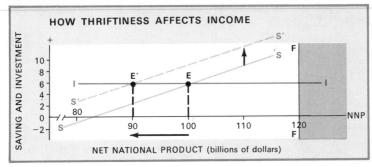

FIG. 12-8. A desire to consume less at every income level will shift the saving schedule upward. With *II* unchanged, equilibrium drops to the *E'* intersection. Why? Because income has to fall until people feel poor enough to again want to save what the system can invest.

than that consumption shift. Or, for a second example, take the spending prophets of the Great Depression. A famous Harvard economist, Frank Taussig, went on the radio to urge everyone to save less: to spend more on consumption. What had he in mind? He spoke before the modern theory of income determination was known; but he presumably meant that such spending would on the first round give jobs and incomes to people; that their respending on consumption would create second-round jobs and income; and that it would continue thus in a multiplier chain. (Major Douglas, the inventor of Social Credit, also sometimes argued that saving was excessive. More consumption was needed, he urged, in promoting his monetary schemes for bringing this about. But his intuitive analysis lacked the multiplier.)

A last example will arise in connection with the next sections' "paradox of thrift." The following summary paves the way for it.

> If scheduled investment holds constant, an upward shift in the saving schedule—which means an equal downward shift in the consumption schedule—will kill off national income in a multiplier way until income falls low enough to bring people's new desired saving again into equality with investment opportunities. Thus an *attempt* to save may not lead to more saving in some situations, but instead may then simply reduce national income.

■ INDUCED INVESTMENT

Until now we have always treated net investment as an autonomous element, absolutely independent of national income. All our investment schedules have been drawn as horizontal lines, their level being always the same regardless of NNP. This simplification can now be relaxed.

Any practical businessman will tell you that he is more likely to add to his plant or equipment if his sales are high relative to his plant capacity. In the short run (before businessmen have had time to adjust their capital stock to a changed plateau of income), it is reasonable for us to draw the *II* schedule in Fig. 12-9 as a rising curve. *An increase in employment and national product may induce a higher level of net investment.*

3d, Higher income will induce businessmen to want higher investment:

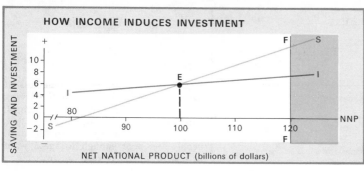

FIG. 12-9. Now we drop the assumption of a horizontal *II* schedule. Now *II* slopes upward, showing intended investment less than 6 billion dollars at low NNP and more than 6 billion dollars at high NNP. Equilibrium is still at *E*, where *SS* intersects *II* from below.

As before, the equilibrium level of (maintainable) national income is given by the intersection of the investment and saving schedules, or by *E* in Fig. 12-9. So long as the *SS* curve always cuts the *II* curve from below, businessmen's action must finally bring the economy back to the equilibrium level.[8]

Induced investment means that anything which increases national income is likely to be good for the capital-goods industries; anything hurting national income is likely to be bad for them.[9]

■ THE PARADOX OF THRIFT

This throws new light on the age-old question of thrift versus consumption.

An increased desire to consume—which is another way of looking at a decreased desire to save—is likely to boost business sales and thus increase investment. On the other hand, a decreased desire to consume—i.e., an increase in thriftiness—is likely to reduce inflationary pressure in times of booming incomes; but in time of depression, it could make the depression

[8] If the two curves crossed in the opposite way, the little arrows in Fig. 12-5 would point out instead of in and we should have unstable equilibrium; then the economy would rush away—in either direction—from the intersection neighborhood. A physical analogy may help: An egg on its side is in "stable equilibrium"; given a slight disturbance, it returns to equilibrium. An egg on its tip is in "unstable equilibrium," a light touch topples it.

[9] Here is the algebra for an induced-investment multiplier. As before,

(1) $$Y = C + I$$

Because *I* is not fixed, but a simple function of *Y*, we write:

(2) $$Y = (\bar{C} + b\,Y) + (\bar{I} + d\,Y)$$

Following a procedure similar to that in footnote 7, we get

(3) $$Y = \frac{1}{1 - b - d}\,(\bar{C} + \bar{I})$$

The fraction $1/(1 - b - d)$ is the multiplier in a situation where $1/d$ new investment is induced by every \$1 of new income. Is this more elaborate multiplier bigger or smaller than the simple multiplier? Compare the two: $1/(1 - b)$ differs from $1/(1 - b - d)$ in that (when *b* and *d* are less than 1) the denominator of the latter is smaller. Therefore the new induced-investment multiplier, for a shift in *CC*, *SS*, or *II*, is larger than the simple multiplier.

Another way of thinking about this is in the $r + r^2 + \ldots r^n + \ldots$ secondary-consumption series. An additional secondary chain of *induced investment* spending $s + s^2 + \ldots s^n + \ldots$ will reinforce the original. (r = MPC and s = marginal propensity to invest.)

worse and reduce the actual amount of net capital formation in the community. *High consumption and high investment are then hand in hand rather than opposed to each other.*

This surprising result is sometimes called the "paradox of thrift." It is a paradox because most of us were taught that thrift is *always* a good thing. Ben Franklin's *Poor Richard's Almanac* never tired of preaching the doctrine of saving. And now along comes a new generation of financial experts who seem to say that the old virtues may be modern sins in depressed times.

Let us for the moment leave our cherished beliefs aside and try to disentangle the paradox in a dispassionate, scientific manner. Two considerations will help to clarify the whole matter.

The first is this. In economics, we must always be on guard against the logical fallacy of composition. That is to say, what is good for each person separately need not always be good for all; under some circumstances, private prudence may be social folly. Specifically, this means that the *attempt* of each and every person to increase his saving may—under the conditions to be described—result in a reduction in *actual* saving by all the people in the community. Note the italicized words "attempt" and "actual"; between them, in our imperfect mixed economy, there may be a world of difference when people find themselves thrown out of jobs and with lowered incomes.

The second clue to the paradox of thrift lies in the question of whether or not national income is at a depressed level. If we were at full employment, then obviously the more of our national product we devoted to current consumption, the less would be available for capital formation. If output could be assumed to be always at its maximum, then the old-fashioned doctrine of thrift would be absolutely correct—correct, be it noted, from both the individual and the social standpoints. In primitive agricultural communities, just as in the Ontario Scottish settlements of John Kenneth Galbraith's boyhood, there was truth in Franklin's prescription. The same was true during World Wars I and II, and it is true during periods of boom and inflation: if people will become more thrifty, then less consumption will mean more investment.

But according to statistical records, full employment and inflationary demand conditions have occurred only at intervals in our nation's history. Much of the time there were some wasting of resources, some unemployment, and some insufficiency of demand, investment, and purchasing power. When this is the case, everything can go into reverse. What once was a social virtue may then become a social vice. What is true for the individual—that extra thriftiness means increased saving and wealth—may then become completely untrue for the community as a whole.

Under conditions of unemployment, the *attempt to save* may result in *less*, not more, saving. The individual who saves cuts down on his consumption. He passes on less purchasing power than before; therefore someone else's income is reduced, for one man's outgo is another man's income. If one man succeeds in saving more, maybe it is because someone else is forced to dissave. If one man succeeds in hoarding more money, someone else must do without.

4th, An attempt to save more could result in less actual saving and investment:

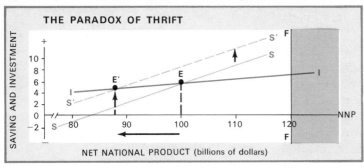

FIG. 12-10. The shift of *SS* upward to *S'S'* depresses income; and the drop of income kills off some investment, moving us southwest along the sloping *II* schedule. (If the system were straining at the full-employment level of *F*, the effect of increased thriftiness might be different.)

HIGH *C* INDUCING HIGH *I*　Thus, when there is stubborn unemployment, consumption and investment can be complementary, not competitive. What helps one helps the other. The attempt to cut down on consumption (to save) then only results in a reduction of income until everyone feels poor enough no longer to try to save more than can be invested. Moreover, at lower levels of income, less, and not more, capital goods will be needed. Therefore *investment will actually be less*. (As will be seen again and again, with prudent public and private policies, our system will be restored to proper operation, so that the paradox of thrift can be robbed of its applicability.)

Let us clinch our common-sense understanding of this paradox by combining Figs. 12-8 and 12-9 into Fig. 12-10. An increase in thriftiness or the desire to save will shift the *SS* curve upward to *S'S'*. Note that the new intersection *E'* is now at a lower level of income. Because of induced *disinvestment*, the drop in income will also mean lower investment. Thus both income and investment have actually decreased. The attempt to save more in depression times has resulted in less actual saving.

If true, this is an important lesson. It will never again be a satisfactory measure to urge men in time of depression to tighten their belts, to save more in order to restore prosperity. The result will all too likely be the reverse—a worsening of the vicious deflationary spiral. At such a time, many of the usual arguments go into reverse. An economic lobbyist of the capital-goods industries would, if he has their selfish interests at heart, advocate less thriftiness in depressed times, so that the consumption schedule will be pushed upward, and so that attempts to save—which then really lead only to decreases in income—will be discouraged. For only then will investment and sales of heavy capital goods flourish.[10]

---

[10] We have seen that this line of argument does not apply in conditions of full employment. It also requires some slight modifications to allow for the fact that thriftiness, by lowering income, may also lower interest rates and promote investment, or it may depress wages and prices and thereby increase the real purchasing power of people's money holdings enough to destroy their initial thriftiness. These qualifications are discussed later; in our imperfect mixed economy they seem rather unimportant considerations during deep depression.

Later, we shall see how fiscal and monetary policies can rid the paradox of thrift of its terrors.

■ THE DEFLATIONARY GAP

The multiplier is a two-edged sword. It will cut for you or against you. It will amplify new investment, as we have seen. But it will also amplify negatively any *decrease* in investment. Thus, if investment opportunities drop by 3 billion dollars in our earlier examples, then national income will have to fall by three times as much—by 9 billion dollars. If net investment drops away to zero, income will have to fall to the break-even point where the community is made poor enough to stop all net saving.

This reminds us once again that there may be nothing particularly good about what we have called the equilibrium level of national income. If investment is low, the equilibrium level of income will involve much unemployment and waste of national resources. The only level of national income that we are entitled to regard as a desirable goal is that near to full employment; but we shall end up at such a level of high employment only if investment opportunities happen to be as large as full-employment saving.

> Unless this full-employment saving is "offset" by private investment (or by public policies), the nation cannot continue to enjoy full employment. There is then said to be a "deflationary gap," its size being measured by the deficiency of investment compared with full-employment saving.

We can picture the deflationary gap in Fig. 12-3 as the vertical distance between the saving and investment schedules at the full-employment level of income indicated by the vertical line *FF*. Or, as in Fig. 12-11, on the following page, we can picture the deflationary gap on a consumption-plus-investment graph. Suppose that 120 billion dollars represents the full-employment income. Suppose that, at this income level *G*, the scheduled total of *C* + *I* adds up to only 116 billion dollars, as shown at *H*. *This leaves a 4-billion dollar deflationary gap between H and G.* Since obviously we cannot then remain at full employment, what will happen? Will income drop by only 4 billion dollars? Clearly not. It must drop by some greater multiple of the original deflationary gap. If each dollar of reduced income results in a cut of $2/3 in consumption spending, income will have to fall until it has dropped three times as much as the original deflationary gap (see point *E* in Fig. 12-11).[11]

---

[11]What can be done about this? If we continue to leave the government and foreign trade out of the picture, we must have either an increase in investment or an increase in consumption. By how much must the level of investment or of the consumption shift upward if full employment is to be restored? If we include government spending, and exports, how great must they be to remove unemployment? By the full 12 billion dollars of lost income? Surely not. Because of the multiplier, to wipe out a deflationary gap, the *C* + *I* + *G* + *E* schedule need shift upward only by the amount of the gap itself, not by any multiple of the gap. (In a saving-investment diagram like Fig. 12-9 you measure the deflationary gap by the vertical distance between the *SS* and *II* schedules at the full-employment income *FF*.)

When $C + I$ **spending that would be generated at full
employment differs from the full-employment NNP, we call:**

1st, Any spending deficiency a "deflationary" gap:

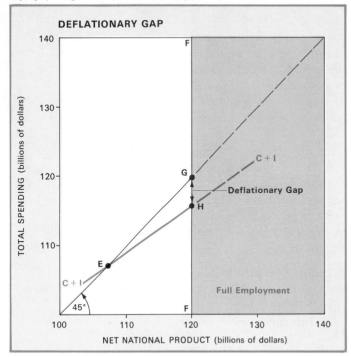

FIG. 12-11. The deflationary gap is always measured at the full-employment
NNP level. It is the vertical distance
there between the 45° line and the $C +
I$ schedule, that is, GH. Such a deflation-
ary gap will depress income in a multiplied way. (Later, after government is
introduced, we'll relabel $C + I$ as $C +
I + G$.)

■ THE PROCESS OF PRICE INFLATION

Instead of a deflationary gap, we may have an inflationary gap. If scheduled
investment tends to be greater than full-employment saving, then more goods
will be demanded of business than it can produce, and prices will begin to rise.
Figure 12-12 shows how we measure the inflationary gap as a vertical distance:
The new $C' + I'$ curve lies *above* the 45° line at the full-employment level by
the distance GH', giving us an inflationary gap of 3 billion dollars.

> If full-employment saving falls short of scheduled investment at full-em-
> ployment, there is said to be an "inflationary gap," its size being measured
> by the excess of the $C + I$ schedule above the 45° line's full-employment
> level (which is the same thing as the excess of full-employment scheduled
> II over SS).

Now what will result from the 3 billion-dollar gap? Can production rise by
9 billion dollars to give us a new equilibrium at E'? Plainly not. Everyone is already
fully employed, and factories are producing at their practical capacity points.
The region to the right of the vertical full-employment line through F is a never-
never land. It shows us what we should like to be able to produce, but not what
we are actually able to produce. Although an inflationary gap is the opposite of

2d, Any spending excess an "inflationary" gap:

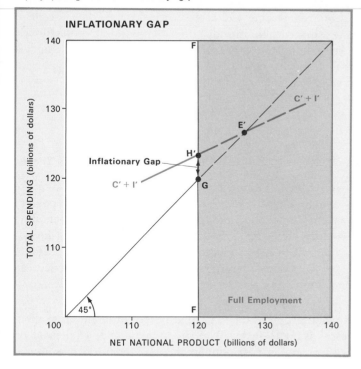

FIG. 12-12. *GH'* measures the inflationary gap. People are trying to buy more than can be produced, and thereby they are inflating the price level. (With all prices changing and no longer ignorable, the *EE* point and the spending schedules are likely to shift upward, so it would be a mistake to regard *E'* as an actually attainable equilibrium point of *real* income.)

a deflationary gap, its effects upon employment and production are of a slightly different qualitative nature. A deflationary gap can move production leftward, down to three-quarters or even one-half of a full-employment level; but an inflationary gap cannot possibly move employment rightward to 150 per cent of full or maximum employment. The economic system cannot move in *real terms* very far to the right of the black full-employment line.

The excess in purchasing power can result only in price increases and an inflationary spiral; *money* national income will rise because of "paper" price-tag changes, but *real* national product cannot go above its maximum full-employment level. Unfortunately, the upward movement of prices will continue for as long as there is an inflationary gap,[12] i.e., until we are lucky enough for investment or consumption demand to fall off or smart enough as a nation to adopt corrective policies that will wipe out the inflationary gap.

Far from being "depression economics," modern income analysis has many

---

[12] The process does not end with higher prices. The new higher price level will not equilibrate total supply and demand once and for all. On the contrary, since the higher prices received by businesses become in turn somebody's income—that of worker or property owner—demand again shifts upward and prices will continue to rise. Attempts of labor to secure higher wages as compensation for the soaring cost of living may only cause the inflationary spiral to zoom at a dizzier speed. (Lord Keynes formulated this theory of inflation in 1939.)

of its most important applications in connection with the process of inflation and what can be done about it. During and after World War II, the concept of the inflationary gap was indispensable in indicating the quantitative magnitude of taxation needed to keep decontrolled prices from rising; and without understanding the rudiments of income analysis, we cannot follow the important economic issues discussed in Parliament and the public press.[13]

SUMMARY

A.   USING THE CONSUMPTION AND SAVING SCHEDULES TO DETERMINE INCOME

■ 1 Unlike ancient poverty due to famine in a pre-industrial society, and unlike modern poverty due to uneven and bad income distribution, "poverty midst plenty" was due to "production gaps" between what full-employment operations could produce and what actual *laissez-faire* saving-investment intersections caused to get produced. Here we study the appearance of this gap, and in the next chapter we shall study how fiscal policy can do something about improving the acceptability of macroeconomic equilibrium.

■ 2 The motives that make people want to save are often different from those that make businesses want to invest. Net investment tends to depend on such autonomous elements as new population, new territory, new inventions, new tastes, and other growth elements; consumption and saving tend to behave in accordance with passive schedules plotted against national income.

■ 3 People's wishes to save and the willingness of businesses to invest are brought into line with each other primarily by means of changes in income. The equilibrium level of national income must be at the *intersection* of the saving and investment schedules, SS and II, or what is exactly the same thing, at the *intersection* of the consumption-plus-investment schedule $C + I$ with the 45° line.

■ 4 If incomes were temporarily above the equilibrium level, business would find itself unable to sell all it was producing at prices that fully covered expected costs of production. For a short time inventories might pile up involuntarily, and sales at a loss or untenable profit margin might take place, but eventually employment and production would be cut back toward the equilibrium level. The only equilibrium path of income that can be maintained is at the income level where families will voluntarily continue to save exactly as much as business will voluntarily continue to invest.

■ 5 To sum up in the most simplified case: investment calls the tune; invest-

---

[13] See Chapter 40 for further discussion of inflation, which includes along with the present kind of "excess-demand," or "demand-pull," inflation the possibility of "creeping cost-push inflationary tendencies."

ment causes income to rise or fall until voluntary, scheduled saving has adjusted itself to the level of maintainable investment.[14]

B. INVESTMENT AND INCOME

■ 6 Investment (and any autonomous schedule shift) has a *multiplier* effect on income. When investment changes, there is an equal *primary* change in national income. But as these primary income receivers in the capital-goods industries get more earned income, they set into motion a whole chain of additional *secondary* consumption spending and employment.

If people always spend about ⅔ of each extra dollar of income upon consumption, the total of the multiplier chain will be

$$1 + \frac{2}{3} + \left(\frac{2}{3}\right)^2 + \ldots = \frac{1}{1 - \frac{2}{3}} = 3$$

The multiplier works forward or backward, amplifying either increases or decreases in investment. The simplest multiplier is numerically equal to the reciprocal of the MPS; this is because it always takes more than a dollar's change in income to bring forth a dollar's change in saving.

■ 7 The *attempt* to save more is quite different from the achievement of increased saving for society as a whole. The "paradox of thrift" shows that an increase in thriftiness may reduce already depressed income and, *through induced effects on investment*, may actually result in *less* net investment. Only when employment remains full or unchanged are consumption and investment necessarily competing; only then are private virtues always social virtues.

The moral is not for each individual to squander his money during a depression, trying to be patriotic. Instead, through proper national policies, we must recreate a high-employment environment in which private virtues are no longer social follies.

■ 8 In short, we must avoid both inflationary and deflationary gaps, so that full-employment saving and investment just match without inflation. We measure the size of the deflationary or inflationary gap as (*a*) the vertical discrepancy at full-employment income between the saving and investment schedules, or what is exactly the same thing, by (*b*) the vertical distance between the $C + I$ (or $C + I + G$ when government is in the picture) schedule and the 45° line.

QUESTIONS FOR DISCUSSION

1. Can you recall from the last chapter how the *CC* and *SS* schedules are in a Siamese-twins relationship, with MPC + MPS = 1 always? Why does the break-even

---

[14] The equality of the saving that people are willing to maintain with the investment that business firms are willing to maintain is the equilibrium condition that permits national income to remain steady. This equality should not be confused with the definitional identity of measured saving and investment at every income level discussed in Chapter 10 and its Appendix.

point come at the same level of income (which will be on the horizontal axis in the lower part of Fig. 12-2 and on the 45° line in the upper part)?

2. If net investment were always zero, show that equilibrium would take place at the break-even point. (HINT: Income must fall to that low permanent level at which the amount that people would want to go on saving was zero—namely the break-even point.)

3. If the SS schedule had been lower in the late 1950s, or the II schedule had been higher, show that Fig. 12-1's wasteful gap would have been much smaller.

4. The saving-and-investment diagram and the 45° line (or C + I) diagram are two different ways of showing how national income is determined. Describe each. Show that they are equivalent. Which do you prefer?

5. Reconstruct Table 12-1, assuming that net investment is equal to (a) 9 billion dollars, (b) 12 billion dollars. What is the resulting difference in national income? Is this greater or smaller than the change in investment? Why? When I drops below 6, how much must NNP drop?

6. Which side do you support in the following argument?

Pessimist: "Automation means that people will not have enough purchasing power to create jobs for all."

Optimist: "Provided society can shift down the SS schedule enough or shift up the II schedule enough, their equilibrium intersection can be made to take place at the full employment FF level no matter how fast science is improving technology."

7. Describe in a few paragraphs (a) the common sense, (b) the arithmetic and (c) the geometry of the multiplier. What are the various multipliers when MPC = 0.9? 0.8? 0.5? When MPS = 0.1? 0.8?

8. Work out the chain of spending and respending when MPC = 4. Explain the economics of the arithmetic.

9. If $C = a + bY = 200 + \frac{2}{3}Y$ and $I = \bar{I} = 100$, solve $Y = C + I = 200 + \frac{2}{3}Y + 100$ to get $Y^* = 900$. Increase I by 10 and verify that Y^* goes up by 30. What is the multiplier? Why? (NOTE: Y is NNP in hundreds of millions of dollars.)

10. In Fig. 12-3, how would you measure the deflationary gap? In Figs. 12-4 and 12-5? In Table 12-1? How might you change the figures to show an inflationary gap?

11. Give arguments for and against thriftiness. Contrast carefully (a) the individual and the community viewpoint and (b) boom and depression.

12. Review your understanding of the following concepts:

consumption schedule CC	intended, maintainable saving and
saving schedule SS	investment versus measurable identity
45° helping line	of saving and investment
break-even point	multiplier impact of primary I
C + I schedule	through secondary C spending
equivalent intersection of	$\dfrac{1}{1 - \text{MPC}} = \dfrac{1}{\text{MPS}}$
SS and II schedules, or	
C + I schedule and	$= 1 + (\text{MPC}) + (\text{MPC})^2 + \ldots$
45° line	multiplier effects on income of
equilibrium intersection and forces	consumption or saving shifts
moving NNP when not in	induced investment
equilibrium	paradox of thrift
	inflationary, deflationary gaps
	cumulative inflation
	underemployment equilibrium

13

INCOME DETERMINATION: FISCAL POLICY, THE FOREIGN-TRADE MULTIPLIER, AND THE ACCELERATOR

The only good budget is a balanced budget.   ADAM SMITH (Glasgow, 1776)
Short-term instabilities ... call for tactical departures from long-term fiscal policy stability.
ARTHUR SMITH, E.C.C. (Ottawa, 1969).

The last chapter set forth the essentials of the modern theory of income determination. Here we must go on to discuss three important applications.

First, in Section A, we stop being the detached observers of whatever it is that happens in the income-determining process. Like the doctor who puts to work the objective findings of physiological science, we put to work the theory of income determination to show how government fiscal policy—expenditure and taxation—can influence and stabilize the level of national income.

In Section B, we explore the workings of the process in an economy where there are also exports and imports. This not only adds greatly to the realism and urgency of fiscal-policy discussion, but acts as a curtain-raiser for a fuller coverage of international trade in later chapters.

Then, in Section C, we look at the existence of business cycles and consider one of the best-known explanations of cycles, the acceleration principle, which explains changes in all-important investment.

A. FISCAL POLICY IN INCOME DETERMINATION

When there is a large inflationary or deflationary gap, the government is called upon to do something about the price rise or the widespread unemployment. Tax and government expenditure policies—the general name for which is "fiscal policy"—will change the equilibrium level of income. So we must now explicitly

Government expenditures act like consumption and investment in determining national income:

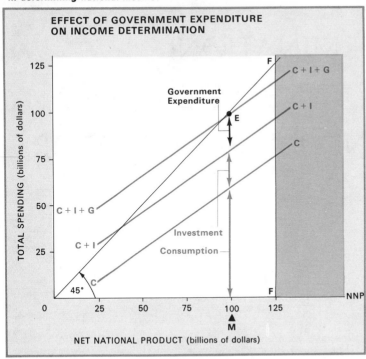

FIG. 13-1. On top of consumption spending and investment spending, we now add government spending on goods and services. This gives us the $C + I + G$ schedule. At E, where this intersects the 45° line, we find equilibrium. (What if G increases or decreases? Can you show the multiplied changes in income?)

introduce government fiscal policy into the picture to see exactly how income determination is affected. As you might guess, we now consider a $C + I + G$ spending schedule to show the equilibrium that results when government is in the picture.

It will simplify our task if in the beginning we analyze the effects of government expenditure with taxes held constant. With taxes in the picture, we can no longer ignore the distinction between disposable income and net national product. But with the tax revenue first held constant, they will differ always by the same amount; and taking account of such taxes, we can still plot the CC consumption schedule against NNP rather than against DI.

In Chapter 10 we learned that net national product consists of three rather than two parts; namely,

NNP = Consumption expenditure + private net Investment + Government
      expenditure on goods and services
    = $C + I + G$

Therefore, on our 45°-line diagram in Fig. 13-1, we must superimpose upon the consumption schedule not only private investment but also government expenditure G. This is because public road building is economically no different from private railroad building, and collective consumption expenditure involved in maintaining a free public library has the same effect upon jobs as private consumption expenditure for movies or rental libraries.

We end up with the three-layered $C + I + G$ schedule showing the amount of total spending forthcoming at each level of NNP. We now must go to the intersection with the 45° line to read off the equilibrium level of national product. At this equilibrium NNP level, the total the nation wants to spend on all goods is just equal in value to the full costs of production of these goods.

Figure 13-1 shows that government expenditure, taken by itself and disregarding taxes, has a multiplier effect upon income just like that of private investment. The reason is, of course, that a chain of *respending* is set into motion by the road builders, librarians, and other people who receive primary income from the government.[1]

To show the effects of an extra 2 billion dollars of G, shift $C + I + G$ in Fig. 13-1 up to $C + I + G'$ and show that the new E' will record a multiplier response of NNP to the government spending.

■ TAXATION AND DOWNWARD SHIFT OF CONSUMPTION SCHEDULE

Now let us turn to the depressing effects of taxes on the equilibrium NNP level. Without graphs, our common sense tells us what must happen when the government (1) takes away more from us in taxes while (2) at the same time holding its expenditure constant. Extra taxes will mean we have lower real disposable incomes, and lower disposable incomes mean we shall cut down on our consumption spending. Obviously, if investment and government expenditures remain the same, a reduction in consumption spending will then reduce net national product and employment; or if we already are having an inflationary gap, the new taxes will help close the gap and wipe out excessive inflationary price increases.

Our graphs can confirm this reasoning: the increase in taxes does *not* lower consumption directly, but reduces disposable income. $I + G$ is unchanged, but now with lower disposable income, the consumption schedule relating C to NNP can remain accurate only by *shifting* downward: less C for every level of NNP. So in all, the $C + I + G$ schedule must also shift downward. Pencil a new $C' + I + G$ schedule into Fig. 13-1 to confirm that its new intersection with the crucial 45° line must definitely be to the left—at a lower equilibrium level of NNP.

THE TAX MULTIPLIER   A change in T will have a multiplier effect, like shifts in I, C, or G, but the per-dollar effect of change is weaker. In Fig. 13-1, a rise of

---

[1] Our saving-investment diagram will give the same answer as the 45°-line diagram. The increase in government expenditure means an equivalent increase in the government deficit if taxes have not been increased. Net saving must always equal private investment + government deficit. Therefore we add the deficit on top of the II curve and get our new greater equilibrium level of national income at the intersection with the SS curve. Following Chapter 12's footnotes 7 and 9, we could employ Fig. 13-1 to show how induced investment or government expenditure (i.e., induced by a changed level of income) will enter into the multiplier. The final change in income resulting from a unit upward shift in the $C + I + G$ schedule will always turn out to be $\dfrac{1/(1 - k)}{k}$ where k is the slope of the $C + I + G$ schedule and might be called the "marginal propensity to spend (inclusive of induced C, I, and G effects)."

3 billion dollars in G shifts the $C + I + G$ schedule vertically upward by the same amount, but an increase of 3 billion dollars in taxes *lowers* $C + I + G$ vertically by less than 3 billion dollars.

Why? In Fig. 13-2, CC *is* shifted to the right by exactly the amount of the tax. This *rightward* shift measures the increase in the NNP necessary for consumption to remain at its former no-tax level. Figure 13-2 shows that the CC schedule shifts downward when it is moved to the right. The extent of the *downward* shift depends on the MPC. By experimentation, you can confirm that when MPC $= 0$, T does not shift CC downward at all, whereas when MPC $= 1$, the downward shift equals the rightward shift. For an intermediate MPC, $\frac{2}{3}$, if $T = 3$ billion dollars, any point on CC shifts right by 3 billion dollars, and down by only 2 billion dollars.

In common-sense terms, a change in taxation (and hence in disposable income) elicits not only a change in spending, but also a change in saving. The greater is MPC, the greater is the tax impact on spending rather than on saving, and so the greater is the downward shift in CC.

The "tax multiplier" measures the total (net) primary and secondary effects on total spending of a change in taxation. For example, an individual may find that a tax increase of $1,000 has reduced his disposable income by the same amount. If his MPC is $\frac{2}{3}$, this means that he will spend $666.67 less on consumption goods, and that, as a result, the producers of those goods will suffer a decrease of $666.67 in income. If their MPC is also $\frac{2}{3}$, they in turn will reduce their expenditures on consumption goods by $\frac{2}{3}$ of $666.67, or $444.44. Thus the primary effect on consumption, plus the secondary effect on the next person's consumption, and so on, will be *minus* ($666.67 + $444.44 + $296.30 + $\ldots$), or $-$2,000. This chain is identical to the series described in Chapter 12, on page 283, except that it starts out with $666.67 instead of $1,000. Thus it can also be expressed by the same geometrical progression used on page 284, $1 + \frac{2}{3} + (\frac{2}{3})^2 + (\frac{2}{3})^3 + \ldots$, that finally added up to 3. Three, multiplied by the initial drop in consumption of ($\frac{2}{3} \times -$1,000) gives you $-$2,000.

The final formula for the I or G multiplier was: change in Investment $\times \dfrac{1}{1 - \text{MPC}}$. For a change in tax the multiplier formula is nearly identical; the change in tax is first multiplied by MPC, then the old multiplier is applied:

$$\text{Change in income} = \frac{1}{1 - \text{MPC}} \times \text{MPC} \times \text{change in tax}$$

$$= \frac{\text{MPC}}{1 - \text{MPC}} \times \text{change in tax}^2$$

----

[2] More formally, the ordinary multiplier progression (footnote 6, page 283) is
$$1 + r + r^2 + r^3 + r^4 \ldots r^n = 1/(1 - r).$$
The taxation multiplier discussed above simply subtracts one from each side of the equation:
$$r + r^2 + r^3 \ldots r^n = 1/(1 - r) - 1.$$
The tax multiplier can be left in this form as $1/(1 - \text{MPC}) - 1$; or it can be converted to
$$1/(1 - \text{MPC}) - (1 - \text{MPC})/(1 - \text{MPC}) = \text{MPC}/(1 - \text{MPC}),$$
as in the text.

Higher taxes will cut disposable income and consumption:

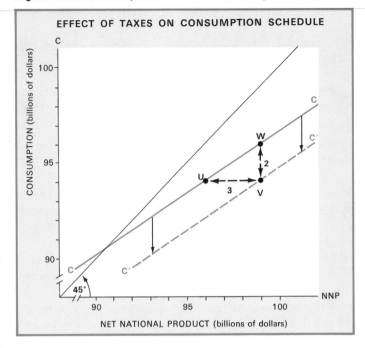

FIG. 13-2. Each dollar of tax lowers the CC schedule. Why? Because CC is shifted to the right by exactly the amount of the tax. (Example: First NNP =96 at U with zero tax; DI = 96 also. CC shows consumption at U of about 94. Now add tax of 3; NNP at V must equal 96 + 3 if DI is to remain 96 and consumption 94 there. So UV arrow shows C'C' is shifted rightward by exact amount of the tax.) A rightward CC shift means a downward CC shift. But the downward shift is only two-thirds of the rightward shift if CC's slope at MPC = ⅔. (Verify WV = ⅔ UV.)

With CC lowered, so will C + I + G in Fig. 13-1 be lowered. Show the drop in income there caused by such a tax increase.

Now we know something that common sense did not immediately tell us. To offset (cancel out) a 2-billion-dollar upward shift in $I + G$, we must increase tax collections by *more* than 2 billion dollars. Figure 13-2 shows needed taxes as 3 billion dollars when MPC = ⅔. This means that (1) when extra G is added to an already-balanced budget in a full-employment economy; then (2) if we are determined to avoid an inflationary gap we must raise tax collections by more than the extra G. We must "over-balance" the budget.[3] The 3 per cent tax surcharge of 1968-69 was an attempt by the Canadian government to close an inflationary gap by raising tax rates.

We can easily reverse the above analysis to explain why tax reductions help to fight a sluggish recession. Each dollar of tax reduction leads, through an upward and leftward shift in CC, to an increase in people's disposable income by a dollar and to almost a dollar increase in initial consumption spending.

[3] Advanced treatises call this phenomenon the "balanced budget multiplier theorem." New public works of G dollars raise NNP by $G \times 1/(1 - \text{MPC})$; while new balancing taxes of T dollars cause NNP to drop by $T \times \text{MPC}/(1 - \text{MPC})$. If $T = G$, the final effect on NNP is therefore $T \times (1 - \text{MPC})/(1 - \text{MPC})$, or T dollars. Hence a balanced fall or rise in G and T will move NNP by just the amount of the fall or rise. Note, contrary to footnote 1, that it is not merely the deficit or surplus $(G - T)$ that has NNP effects. Here is a fuller demonstration: Let

(1) $$\text{NNP} = Y = C + I + G$$

Hence, dollars of tax reduction are almost as powerful a weapon against mass unemployment as are increases in dollars of government expenditure.

Because tax potency is slightly less than expenditure potency, such a program may involve a larger deficit than an expenditure program would; but it also means that there is expansion of the private rather than of the government sector of the economic system. The United States, Japan, and the United Kingdom all used this tax-cut mechanism in the mid-sixties to increase their employment and income levels, a remarkable example of modern fiscal policy at work.

B.   FOREIGN TRADE AND INCOME DETERMINATION

In an "open" economy like Canada's, changes in national income can often be traced back to changes in exports or imports. The theory of income determination shows how foreigners buying more of our goods, or Canadians trying to buy more foreign-made goods, can change the Canadian NNP. Although one end of these transactions is outside the country, our end can be influenced and controlled by government action. For example, by setting high customs duties, the government dissuades Canadians from buying foreign-made wines, TV sets, and breakfast cereals. And, by reducing taxes on petroleum, it encourages foreigners to buy Canadian oil, which thus becomes cheaper measured in foreign moneys.

So we must first find where foreign transactions fit into our theory, and then survey the results of some typical policies. In a very complete treatment, we would stretch out our basic equations to read NNP $= C + I + G + (E - M)$, and show how changes in each of the parts of the equation would affect each other part, and so, finally, affect the NNP as a whole. But to keep our task

and following footnote 7 in the last chapter, let:

$$(2) \qquad DI = Y_d = Y - T$$
$$(3) \qquad C = \overline{C} + b\,Y_d$$
$$(4) \qquad I = \overline{I,}$$
$$(5) \qquad G = \overline{G}$$

and

$$(6) \qquad T = \overline{T}$$

Then, substituting in (1),

$$(7) \qquad NNP = Y = \overline{C} + b(Y - \overline{T}) + \overline{I} + \overline{G}$$
$$= \frac{1}{1-b}\,[\overline{C} - b\overline{T} + \overline{I} + \overline{G}]$$

This is the simple multiplier expanded to a world of government G and T. However, if $T = G$ in a balanced budget, then

$$(8) \qquad NNP = Y = \frac{1}{1-b}\,[\overline{C} + \overline{G}(1 - b) + \overline{I}]$$
$$= \frac{1}{1-b}\,[\overline{C} + \overline{I}] + \overline{G}$$

Notice that the multiplier for $\overline{C}$ and $\overline{I}$ is still $1/(1-b)$, but the multiplier for $\overline{G}$ is now 1. The absolute size of the budget (not the deficit alone) matters for the size of Y, even when taxes match G!

These multipliers, as shown in equations (7) and (8), apply as well to *changes* in C, I, G, or T.

simple, we initially omit government taxing and spending, and later bring them in only insofar as they influence the "foreign sector" of the economy.

In order to take the parts of the foreign sector one by one, we begin with exports, supposing that imports are zero. This allows us to delay tracing through the economy the desires of those exporters whose sales abroad have gone up or down to raise or lower the amount of imported goods that they and their suppliers want to buy.

Except in indirect ways we can safely neglect, national income does not influence exports. Sales to foreign customers are among those "autonomous" factors in a country's economic equilibrium. We may suppose, then, that export opportunities are such that foreigners would buy exactly $2 billion-worth every year, *regardless* of our NNP. This means that, if we now draw a schedule of exports against NNP, it will have to be a *horizontal* line—always the same distance above the axis. Look at Fig. 13-3, where this schedule is labeled *EE* to distinguish it from *II*, the investment schedule. *Both* are autonomous amounts of spending. (Indeed, most of the above paragraph is identical to the discussion of *II* on page 273.) So we add exports and investments to get the horizontal *I + E* schedule.

Suppose the economy is in equilibrium at *e*, with savings equal to domestic investment opportunities. Now the economy gets a chance to sell 2 billion dollars' worth of goods annually abroad. The old circular flow of consumption and investment is now joined by the output of restarted mills and factories, and the putting to work of unemployed loggers and factory hands. If these workers all have a marginal propensity to consume of ⅔, they will now spend this fraction of 2 billion dollars on new consumption goods. The makers of these foods, clothes, and so forth will get extra sales and will spend ⅔ of ⅔ of 2 billion dollars extra. So the process goes on.

Each extra dollar of exports can also be "multiplied" into three dollars of income:

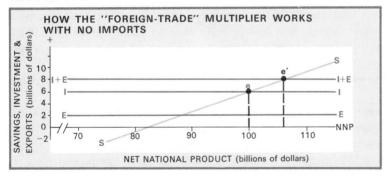

FIG. 13-3. New exports shift the "autonomous" spending schedule up from *II* to *I+E. e'* gives the new equilibrium NNP, with income increasing 3 for every 1 in exports. This diagram is almost the same as Fig. 12-7, showing that, when imports are zero, exports have the same effect as investment.

Just as on page 284, the final change in Canadian income can be worked out by the multiplier arithmetic:

$$\text{Change in income} = \frac{1}{\text{MPS}} \times \text{change in exports}$$

In this case, the change in Canada's NNP would be: $\frac{1}{1 - \frac{2}{3}} \times 2$ billion dollars, or 3×2 billion or 6 billion dollars. The multiplier, as on page 284, is 3. It follows from all that was said earlier about the multiplier, that if our exports had been previously 2.2 billion dollars and fell to 1.7 billion dollars, the Canadian income would fall by a multiplied amount. Here it is:

$$\text{Change in income} = \frac{1}{1 - \frac{2}{3}} \times (\$1.7 - 2.2 \text{ billion}) = 3 \times (-\$.5 \text{ billion})$$
$$= -\$1.5 \text{ billion}$$

This can be seen in Fig. 13-3. Before the export boom, NNP is in equilibrium at 100 billion dollars, with investment of 6 matched by savings of 6. After the boom has begun, investment is joined by exports of 2, making total "autonomous" spending of 8. But the increase in such spending is only the 2 billion dollars in exports. Thus the new equilibrium will be found where $(I + E)$ cuts the SS schedule at e'. Here the NNP has increased to 106. We have confirmed the arithmetic: an increase in exports of 2 billion dollars has yielded a multiplied increase in NNP of 6 billion dollars.

This is the main importance of exports in income-determination theory. They act *exactly* like government spending on goods and services, or investment, or any other "autonomous injection" of spending, in having a multiplied effect on the NNP.

If imports remain at zero, the effect of a change in exports (a shift in the EE schedule) is the same as the effect of a change in investment.

The thoughtful reader will say, "But how are these exports paid for? You have held imports unchanged, so the foreigners are not sending extra goods in return." The question points to a matter that can be clarified in Fig. 13-3. With imports at zero, foreigners can pay for these extra exports in one of two ways: they can in effect borrow from Canadians to pay the loggers and factory hands who produce the exports; or they can send money (not imports) to pay for the goods.

The first way of paying, borrowing from Canadians, is like using Canadian savings. This is seen in Fig. 13-3, where total savings at e' covers both investment and exports. So the NNP has expanded, with the export growth, until *the amount of saving that people want to do is matched by the amount of investment that businessmen are willing to maintain plus the amount of exports that foreigners want to take.* Clearly, by this way of paying, foreigners are going to go farther into debt to Canadian lenders every year. But this need not concern us until Chapter 32; all we need note here is that increased exports will raise NNP until they are matched by increased savings.

The second way of paying, sending money to Canada, is also the chief subject of Chapter 32. Briefly, it amounts to adding foreigners' funds to Canadian assets. These funds must be matched by Canadian saving, until again $S = I + E$. When these are equal, NNP again comes into equilibrium.[4]

We need not worry about the details of these two ways of paying, except to notice what surprises most students; if there is no change in imports, exports are just like investment, and must be matched, in final equilibrium at e', by intended saving.

■ IMPORTS ENTER THE PICTURE[5]

The simplicity of this addition of exports to our income-determination theory is due to our purposeful omission of imports. Including imports, however, is necessary, for we know that imports do not remain constant. Look at the lowest curve, below the axis, in Fig. 10-3. When Canadian incomes rise, Canadians buy more of all goods, including foreign-made goods. Thus the lumber-workers, and their suppliers who are now exporting more, will have higher incomes to buy not only more food and clothing but also more cars and TV sets, with their imported parts, more insurance from a foreign seller of actuarial services, and more gasoline from foreign service stations on the extra holidays they are now able to take outside Canada.

We know too that NNP $= C + I + G + (E - M)$, and we have learned how income determination works when each of these items changes, except the M at the end.

First we must examine what our symbols, C, I, and G mean. A review of Chapter 10 shows that they refer to Canadian spending on kinds of goods: consumer goods, government goods, and investment goods. But what happens when these three categories include both home-made and foreign-made goods? The propensity-to-consume schedule becomes, in part, a propensity-to-import schedule; and the government and investment spending schedules also reveal a demand for imports. Thus our theoretical tools are too dull to cut into the economic system to show what is happening to imports.

This difficulty, however, can be simply overcome by a once-for-all redefining of our terms. Let C^D be the consumption of goods of domestic origin, so that $C^D C^D$ is the propensity-to-consume home-made items of food, clothing, services, and so forth. Similarly, we redefine II to become $I^D I^D$, where I^D is investment expenditures on goods of domestic origin. Assume, however, as in

---

[4] Just how a foreign capital inflow can be added to Canadian saving is a question of how to "transfer" income or wealth from one country to another. It can be done most simply by moving gold, or some other good; that is, by importing something from abroad. But we have ruled out imports so far. The question now becomes one for advanced theory, where it is referred to as the "transfer problem."

[5] This section is more difficult and rigorous than the rest of this chapter. Bringing in M is a bit trickier than bringing in E. In Canada, imports amount to between 20 and 25 per cent of GNE. This is too big an item to slide over by merely looking at "net exports," $(E - M)$, as a single number.

Fig. 12-7 and Fig. 12-8, that all investment is constant, not induced. (From here on, we again ignore government, though similar modifications would have to be made for its purchases.) Then upper-loop NNP includes the sum of all goods and services *made in Canada*, including consumption, investment, and export goods, but not imported goods or services to be used in making, or used directly as, consumption, investment, and export goods. In symbols:

$$\text{NNP} = C^D + I^D + E$$

With these definitions, imports do not appear at all in the value-added or purchases loop of the circular flow of the economy.

But of course they must be taken into account in the income or production loop. In the *disposing* of NNP, people can buy consumer goods made in Canada, save, or buy imports.[6] In symbols:

$$\text{NNP} = C^D + S + M$$

This means that when persons' incomes rise, their spending and their suppliers' respending will not only go to consumption goods made by other Canadians (who can respend the income), but also may "leak" through *two* channels: saving or imports from abroad. Through the combination of these "leakages," our chain of induced domestic purchasing power will peter out faster than if domestic disposable income were saved or entirely spent on home-made goods. For there is no reason to believe that people's saving *intentions* will be different when they can buy both home-produced and foreign goods: the propensity-to-save will be as it was in a "closed" economy, and the import leakage will be added to it.

Our propensity to save, therefore, remains at $(1 - \frac{2}{3})$, or $\frac{1}{3}$. But let us say that for every 1 billion dollars of *extra* spending, Canada imports 1/6 billion dollars of foreign-made goods.[7] This means that the marginal propensity to import (MPM) is 1/6. With these two propensities, we can estimate the propensity to consume domestic products; arithmetically it must be the residual after saving and imports. If, out of every additional billion dollars in income

---

[6] We must be precise about M, imports. Recall that consumption spending is now divided between C^D and imported consumption goods, C^M; and similarly I now consists of I^D and I^M, imported machinery and other capital goods. Similarly, G consists of G^D and G^M. Then total M is defined as $C^M + I^M + G^M$. In the text, G is neglected for simplicity's sake.

[7] These pages on the foreign-trade multiplier avoid complexities which may occur to perceptive readers. Because little restriction has been placed on the marginal propensity to import (MPM), it might, therefore, cause consumption imports to increase with increasing NNP so fast that I and G, even though fixed in amount, must be spent on changing combinations of domestic and foreign goods (I^D and I^M, G^D and G^M). If so, the perceptive reader might well complain about the unlikelihood of government spending a larger fraction (of its fixed $G = G^D + G^M$) on imports G^M simply because NNP is higher. A more complete foreign-trade multiplier discussion which would show changing total G and I, each having changing import percentages, is quite possible but is algebraically complex. More advanced works do this. Here we wrap up increasing purchases of all types of foreign goods into one aggregative MPM, showing simply the ratio of the change in all imports to the change in NNP.

⅓ goes to saving and 1/6 to imports, then only ½ goes to buy home-made consumption goods.

$$\mathrm{MPC}^D = 1 - (\mathrm{MPS} + \mathrm{MPM})$$
$$= 1 - (1/3 + 1/6)$$
$$= ½$$

Now we can trace the effect of any additional outlays in the NNP, such as exports or investment. Suppose exports rise by 1 billion dollars. Then workers and owners of export plants (and their suppliers) will respend half of this on home-made goods, the other half being divided between their purchases of imported goods and their saving. And so it will go at every stage. The whole multiplier will now add up to only $1 + ½ + (½)^2 + \ldots$ or only $2 = \dfrac{1}{1 - ½}$, instead of 3, as was the case when there were no imports. (The reader now should go back to the paragraph above where exports rose by 2 billion dollars. With imports taking 1/6 of each autonomous increase in spending, what would be the final NNP?)[8]

If we look at our multiplier formulas, we find that this is a general rule:

So long as some fraction of income at every stage is leaking into domestic saving, a new dollar of exports will raise income, but can never lift it by enough to call forth a full dollar of new imports. That is, if the propensity-to-consume, -save, and -import add up to 1, the existence of a positive MPS means that MPM must be less than 1.

Figure 13-4 shows the whole process diagrammatically. SS is the same propensity-to-save schedule as earlier: ⅓ of every additional dollar of income is

[8] We can follow footnote 7 (page 285) of Chapter 12 to derive an algebraic formula for the multiplier in an open economy. We know:
(1) The equilibrium equation is
$$\mathrm{NNP} = Y = C^D + I^D + X + G$$
Then continue to distinguish between C^D and C^M and between I^D and I^M, so that $M = C^M + I^M$. We will continue to assume scheduled I is not induced, so that both I^D and I^M are constant (shown by a bar over the symbol) so that $\bar{I} = \bar{I}^D + \bar{I}^M$, and
(2) $$\bar{I}^D = \bar{I} - \bar{I}^M$$
Let the scheduled consumption of home-produced goods and services be
(3) $$C^D = \bar{C}^D + cY$$
where c is the domestic marginal propensity to consume, MPC^D. Taxes are neglected, for simplicity, and X and G are given and are independent of imports:
(4) $$X = \bar{X}^D$$
and
(5) $$G = \bar{G}^D$$
Substituting these expressions in the NNP equation given at the beginning of this footnote, we obtain
$$\mathrm{NNP} = Y = \bar{C}^D + cY + \bar{I}^D + \bar{X}^D + \bar{G}^D$$
whence
$$\mathrm{NNP} = Y = \frac{1}{1-c}[\bar{C}^D + \bar{I}^D + \bar{X}^D + \bar{G}^D]$$
Here the multiplier derived, $1/(1 - c)$ is, in the text above, $1/(1 - \mathrm{MPC}^D)$. The items in the square bracket are constant amounts of spending on home-produced goods; the multiplier would also apply to *changes* in C, I, X, or G: $\triangle$ C, $\triangle$ I, $\triangle$ X, or $\triangle$ G.

Increased spending on exports (or anything else) brings an increase in imports, but now each dollar of exports can be "multiplied" into only two additional dollars of income:

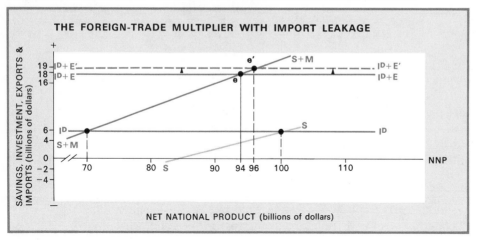

FIG. 13-4. The initial equilibrium is at 94, where home-produced exports and home-produced investment are balanced by imports and saving. When $I^D + E$ rises to $I^D + E'$, the NNP increases by twice as much, from 94 to 96. The diagram pictures an economy where imports are almost one-fifth of consumption. More important, while S increases 1 for every 3 in income, $S + M$ increases 1 for every 2. This larger "leakage" means that an I^D of 6 (and no exports), which in Fig. 12-7 had an equilibrium income of 100, here has an equilibrium NNP of only 70.

saved. Thus it has the same slope as before, rising one dollar for every three dollars it moves to the right.

To it is *added* the propensity-to-import schedule, so that the vertical distance between SS and $S + M$ shows the imports for every level of NNP. The total vertical distance from the horizontal axis up to $S + M$ shows the total "leakage" for every NNP on that axis.

When the NNP is in equilibrium at 94 billion dollars, it turns out that saving is less than investment and exports less than imports. However, $S + M = I^D + E$. This shows that *it is not necessary* for NNP equilibrium that $S = I^D$ and $E = M$. Only the sums need be equal.

See what happens when E increases by 1 billion dollars. $I^D + E$ moves up to $I^D + E'$, rising from 18 billion dollars to 19 billion dollars and cutting the $S + M$ schedule at e'. Along the horizontal axis, NNP moves from 94 billion dollars to 96 billion dollars. Notice that saving is now closer to investment. But the failure of exports to equal imports, or of investment to equal savings is unimportant. What really matters is that the extra saving-and-importing is equal to the extra exports; and that again $S + M = I^D + E$. The NNP is again in equilibrium. The multiplier is obviously at work.

$$\text{Change in income} = \frac{1}{\text{MPS} + \text{MPM}} \times \text{change in exports}$$

$$= \frac{1}{1 - \text{MPC}^D} \times \text{change in exports}$$

In this case, the effect on NNP is $\dfrac{1}{1/3 + 1/6} = \dfrac{1}{1/2} = 2 \times$ change in exports, or 2 billion dollars. This change can be read along the bottom axis between 94 and 96 billion dollars.

The point of all this is that when the economy is "open" to foreign trade, a rise in income and employment may be hindered by a rise in imports. Extra spending, autonomous schedule shifts of C, I, or G, may be largely (but not completely) siphoned off through two leakages: savings and imports.

Note that the import leakage is *always* with us. It is an error to associate the "foreign-trade multiplier" and the "import leakage" solely with changes in exports, arising abroad. The process of respending *any* injection of private capital formation, increased personal consumption outlays, public projects, etc., will, like a respending of export proceeds, lead to a diversion into the buying of imported goods and services.[9]

This explains why fiscal policy in Canada must be weaker, dollar for dollar, than it would be if the economy were closed. It is weaker than in the United States, even though both countries have the same MPC; for the U.S. MPM is small.

Thus the simple multiplier of the last chapter, which applies only in an economy with no trade abroad, must give way to a more general formula:

$$\text{Change in income} = \frac{1}{\text{MPS} + \text{MPM}} \times \text{change in } I, E, \text{ and/or } G$$

$$= \frac{1}{1 - \text{MPC}^D} \times \text{change in } I, E, \text{ and/or } G$$

■ TRADE POLICY AND NATIONAL INCOME

We see now why economists try hard to calculate a country's MPM. In an open economy, a jump in exports can raise the NNP dramatically, and so increase employment. Indeed, the multiplied effects of exports and the dampening effect of imports tempt policy makers to manipulate them to close both inflationary and deflationary gaps.

In inflation, lowering the domestic price of foreign currency makes imports potentially cheaper. And bringing in more imports will reduce total domestic spending and thus cool the inflationary gap. The same policy, exchange-rate upward revaluation, will make some exports too costly for foreigners to buy, cut E, and again cool the inflationary fires. Short-run reduction of tariff barriers will have the same effect.

---

[9] More advanced treatments of the general multiplier will take account of the fact that there is a different MPM for each of I, G, and E. If I is induced, and has import content, then the total schedule ($I^D + E^D + G^D$) *may* increase with NNP. If so, and if the schedule is cut from below by the ($S + M$) schedule, the intersection will indicate a stable NNP, as discussed in footnote 8, Chapter 12.

Note that another "leakage," taxation, has been omitted from the text above. Assiduous footnote readers may see a rough synthesis of all three leakages in Chapter 18, footnote 5.

In a slump what can be done? First, imports are often cut, by raising tariffs, by imposing quotas, and through exchange-rate devaluation. Exports, too, can be promoted, though final action depends on foreign governments.

We shall see in Part Five that such policies, especially those used in recessions, are dangerous when rigidly followed. They are like cutting off our nose to spite our face in that they invite retaliation from abroad in the form of higher tariff walls against *our* exports. They also have wasteful long-run effects because they encourage each nation toward self-sufficiency instead of the more efficient international specialization and division of labor in production. But, looking at trade from the standpoint of domestic full employment alone, it must be admitted that exports do have a multiplier effect on NNP, and it must be agreed that imports are a serious leakage which dampen the effect of domestic attempts to achieve stability.[10] You can see this for yourself by showing on Fig. 13-4 the effect of an increase in tariffs. (HINT: At every income level, imports will now be lower. Thus the vertical distance between S and $S + M$ must become narrower. What is the effect on NNP?)

■ THE MULTIPLIER: QUALIFICATIONS TO SAVING AND INVESTMENT ANALYSIS

The theory of income determination sketched in the last two chapters is a powerful tool.[11] It helps us to understand the ups and downs of the business cycle. It helps us to understand how foreign lending (which is one part of total net investment) affects domestic employment and income. It helps us to understand how governmental fiscal policy can be used to fight inflation and unemployment. All these topics are developed in later chapters.

But it would be a mistake to think that an economist can be made out of a parrot, simply by teaching him the magic words "saving" and "investment." Behind the scenes of the schedules a great deal is taking place.

For example, it should be noted that an increase in the public's holding of government bonds and other wealth may shift the consumption schedule upward. Or rising living standards (resulting from advertising and the invention of new products) may shift the consumption and import schedules up, just as they have in the past.

In short, it is an oversimplification to regard investment, government spending, and exports as always autonomous factors, and consumption and imports as always passive factors depending upon income. True, this is a fruitful oversimplification. But as we have already seen, some of net investment may be "induced" by income changes in the short run; and, as we shall see, changes in

---

[10] There are many policies that have the "right" kind of effect. For example, depreciating the Canadian dollar will help to raise exports (how?) and, by putting up the prices of foreign-made goods, cut down the propensity-to-import. Boosting the level of customs tariffs will also cut down imports. Such policies, used to raise income and employment, have been called by Cambridge economist Joan Robinson "beggar-my-neighbor" policies; for they tend, in reducing the import of goods from other countries, to export unemployment to those countries instead.

[11] Advanced discussions show corporate saving can be handled graphically much like taxes.

interest costs, availability of credit, and stock of money can alter the swings in investment and total spending. Furthermore, consumption also will sometimes shift autonomously even though income has remained constant. And as the reader can verify by experimenting with the saving-investment and the 45°-line diagrams, such shifts in the consumption, saving, or import schedules do have multiplier effects upon national income—*exactly* like the multiplier effects of changes in I, G, and E.

To summarize, the simple multiplier $\dfrac{1}{\text{MPS}}$ applies only to a simple economy, having only C and I spending. With the addition of government and foreign sectors, "the" multiplier becomes more complicated, containing not only MPS but also MPC^D and the "propensity to invest." The effects of "injections" also increase in complexity, including not only I, but also *shifts* in C, I, G, and E.

C. FLUCTUATIONS IN NATIONAL INCOME AND THE ACCELERATION PRINCIPLE

We have examined the economic forces operating to determine the level of national income—the balance of saving and investment. We now turn to the problem of how the level of national income has fluctuated, and to an explanation of the period-by-period processes which propagate these fluctuations. Any serious science should try to test bold theoretical formulation against a careful description of the empirical facts of life.[12]

■ PROSPERITY AND DEPRESSION

Business conditions rarely stand still. Prosperity may be followed by a panic or a crash. National income, employment, and production fall. Prices and profits decline, and men are thrown out of work. Eventually the bottom is reached, and revival begins. The recovery may be slow or fast. It may be incomplete, or it may be so strong as to lead to a new boom. The new prosperity may represent a long, sustained plateau of brisk demand, plentiful jobs, buoyant prices, and increased living standards. Or it may represent a quick, inflationary flaring up of prices and speculation, to be followed by another disastrous slump.

Such, in brief, was the so-called "business cycle" that used to characterize the industrialized nations of the world for the last century and a half at least, ever since an elaborate, interdependent *money economy* began to replace a relatively self-sufficient precommercial society. Is the business cycle a thing of the past, a museum piece? This we must study.

---

[12] The first (1969) Nobel laureates in economics, Ragnar Frisch of Norway and Jan Tinbergen of Holland, made important contributions to both the theory and the measurement of the elements of business fluctuations. The accelerator-multiplier interaction has been analyzed particularly by Nobel laureate Paul A. Samuelson. (A.D.S.)

No two business cycles are quite the same. Yet they have much in common. They are not identical twins, but they are recognizable as belonging to the same family. No exact formula, such as might apply to the motions of the moon or of a simple pendulum, can be used to predict the timing of future (or past) business cycles. Rather, in their rough appearance and irregularities, business cycles more closely resemble the fluctuations of disease epidemics, the vagaries of the weather, or the variations in a child's temperature.

From these introductory remarks, it will be clear that business fluctuations are simply one further aspect of the economic problem of achieving and maintaining high levels of jobs, production, and progressive growth.

■ MEASURING AND FORECASTING THE BUSINESS CYCLE

Figure 13-5 shows how the American economy has been plagued by the uncertainties of the business cycle since 1900. The compilers of this well-known chart have carried it back to the 1860s, and the same sequence of peaks and troughs is to be seen, although with slightly greater regularity in the nineteenth century. Nothing can match the sustained and costly slump of the post-1929 Great Depression. Turning points in the Canadian economy are similar, and the same pattern is reflected in England, Germany, and other foreign nations, with surprisingly few variations.

But it is a strange fact that the North American countries, although they have grown faster since their establishment than most other countries, have always tended to have greater average amounts of unemployment and greater variation in unemployment than these other countries. Not only was this true

Are business cycles calming down?

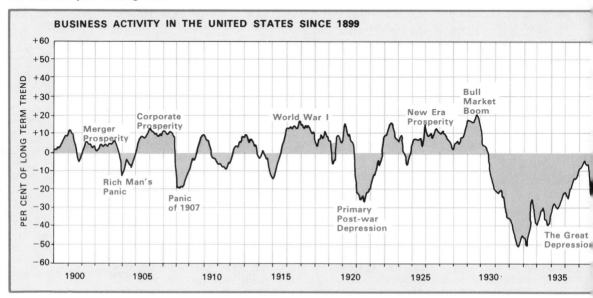

in 1933, when our percentage of unemployment rivaled even that of Germany, but it appears to have been the case for almost as far back as we have any records or indications. Only in the last 30 years have we avoided deep unemployment, but still our rates exceed those abroad.

Figure 13-6, on the following page, shows a number of diverse post-World War II economic "time series," presented for comparison. Note the all-pervasive common pulse of the business cycle: the recessions of 1953-1954, 1957-1958, and 1960-1961. These fluctuations show up in production, unemployment, incomes, and even in such particular series as stock-market prices and building. Moreover, if data had been included on such noneconomic matters as marriages, births, and malnutrition, we should also have been able to see in them the heavy hand of the business cycle. Even political elections follow the business cycle: in slumps, the ins go out.

Here we stick to the facts and statistics. Later, in the Appendix to this chapter, we will go into the history of cycles in more detail and attempt to devise hypotheses and explanatory theories to account for the complex facts.

■ THE ACCELERATION PRINCIPLE

One "economic law" closely associated with business cycle theory is the acceleration principle.

According to this law, society's needed stock of capital, whether inventory or equipment, depends primarily upon the level of income or production. Additions to the stock of capital, or what we customarily call *net* investment, will take place only when income is growing. As a result, a prosperity period may

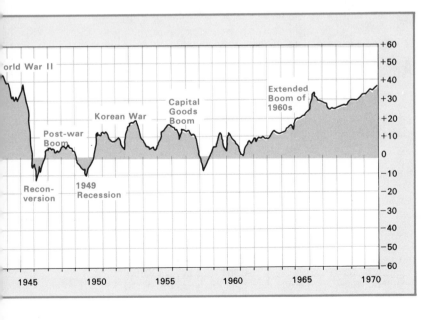

FIG. 13-5. For 25 years now North America has had no significant depressions. But it was not always so. (Source: Cleveland Trust Co.)

Most economic activities move up and down together:

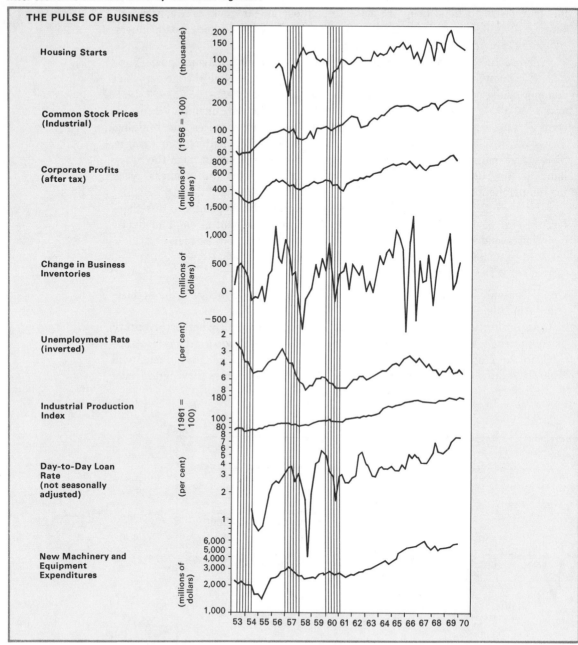

FIG. 13-6. The stretches composed of vertical black lines show recession contraction periods; the unshaded stretches show expansions. The upper curves are series that tend to turn before the others; but this tendency is variable. (Source: *Monthly business Analysis,* **by W. A. Beckett Associates Ltd., DBS** *National Accounts* **and** *Corporation Profits.***)**

The acceleration principle shows how variations in a system's growth rate will induce variations in its level of investment:

ILLUSTRATION OF THE ACCELERATION PRINCIPLE (in thousands of dollars)

TIME	YEARLY SALES	STOCK OF CAPITAL	NET IN-VESTMENT NI	GROSS INVESTMENT GI (NI + REPLACEMENT)
First phase				
First year	$1,000	$10,000	$ 0	1 machine at $500 = $500
Second year	1,000	10,000	0	1 machine at $500 = $500
Third year	1,000	10,000	0	1 machine at $500 = $500
Second phase				
Fourth year	$1,500	$15,000	$5,000	(1 + 10) machines at $500 = $5,500
Fifth year	2,000	20,000	5,000	(1 + 10) machines at $500 = $5,500
Sixth year	2,500	25,000	5,000	(1 + 10) machines at $500 = $5,500
Third phase				
Seventh year	$2,500	$25,000	$ 0	1 machine at $500 = $500
Fourth phase (to be filled in by reader)				
Eighth year	$2,450	$	–$ 500	....machines at $500 = $....

TABLE 13-1.

come to an end, not simply because consumption sales have gone down, but merely because sales have *leveled off* at a high level or have continued to grow, but at a lower rate than previously.

A simplified arithmetical example will make this clear. Imagine a typical textile-manufacturing firm whose stock of capital equipment is always kept equal to about ten times the value of its yearly sales of cloth.[13] Thus, when its sales have remained at 1 million dollars per year for some time, its balance sheet will show 10 million dollars of capital equipment, consisting of perhaps 20 machines of different ages, with one wearing out each year and being replaced. Because replacement just balances depreciation, there is no *net* investment or saving being done by the corporation. *Gross* investment takes place at the rate of 500 thousand dollars per year, representing the yearly replacement of 1 machine. (The other 500 thousand dollars of sales may be assumed to be wages and dividends.) The first phase of Table 13-1 shows this.

Now let us suppose that, in the fourth year, sales rise 50 per cent—from 1 to 1½ million dollars. Then the number of machines must also rise 50 per cent, or from 20 to 30 machines. In the fourth year, 11 machines must be bought—10 new ones in addition to the replacement of the worn-out one.

Sales rose 50 per cent. How much has machine production gone up? From 1 machine to 11; or by 1,000 per cent! This *accelerated* effect of a change in

[13] To keep the discussion simple, we use the exaggerated ratio 10:1 and ignore changes in interest rates or degree of utilization of capacity. The reader can include inventory change as well as equipment change in the analysis.

consumption or other final items on investment levels gives the acceleration principle its name.

If sales continue to rise in both the fifth and sixth years by 500 thousand dollars, then we shall continue to have 11 new machines ordered every year.

So far, the acceleration principle has given us no trouble. On the contrary, it has given us a tremendous increase in investment spending as a result of a moderate increase in consumption sales. As in this chapter's Part B, investment is "induced." But now it is a function not of simple income or consumption, but of the annual *increase* in consumption. Now we are riding a tiger.

> According to the acceleration principle, consumption has to continue to keep increasing in order for investment to stand still!

If consumption should stop growing at so rapid a rate—if it should level off in the seventh year even at the high level of 2½ million dollars per year—then net investment will fall away to zero, and gross investment will fall back to 1 machine (see Table 13-1). In other words, a drop of zero per cent in sales has resulted in a 90 per cent drop in gross investment and a 100 per cent drop in net investment. (See the third phase of Table 13-1, and fill in the fourth phase.)

The acceleration principle can work in both directions. Should sales drop below 2½ million dollars, gross investment would drop away to nothing; in fact, the firm would want to disinvest by selling some of its used machinery.

It is now clear that a depression can set in just because sales have stopped growing so rapidly, even if they have not dropped off absolutely but only leveled off at a high rate.

■ INTERACTIONS OF ACCELERATOR AND MULTIPLIER

Needless to say, the curtailment of production in the machine-producing industries will curtail income and spending on food and clothing and will lead to still further "multiplier" changes in spending. This might ultimately cause textile sales to stop growing altogether, or even to decline. This, in turn, will cause a further accelerated drop in net investment.

> Thus, we may be in a vicious circle where the acceleration principle and the multiplier interact to produce a cumulative deflationary (or inflationary) spiral.

Our example used machines. Does that mean the acceleration principle is not involved in the inventory "recessions" (such as 1920-1921, 1937-1938, 1948-1949, 1953-1954, 1957-1958, 1960-1961)? Not at all. The same principle—that stocks of capital goods try to hold in some proportion to sales per unit time—is valuable to help explain short inventory cycles.

This analysis can also explain how a downturn can result from the previous expansion itself. Suppose, in a situation of unemployment, we get income growing again. The rising income induces, via the accelerator, new investment. The new investment induces, via the multiplier, further rises in income. Hence, the rate of growth of output may be "self-warranting."

But how can a system grow forever at 6 or 7 per cent if its labor force grows only at 1 or 2 per cent and if workers' productivity grows at 2 or 3 per cent? It can't. The self-warranting expansion, even if we are lucky enough to get and keep it, must ultimately bump into the full-employment ceiling. Like a tennis ball (and unlike a wad of gum), it is likely to bounce back from the full-employment ceiling into a recession. Why? Because the minute the system stops its fast growth, the accelerator dictates the end of the high investment supporting the boom. Like an airplane that falls once it loses its motion, the economic system plummets downward.

Similar accelerator-multiplier analysis may explain the ultimate end of a recession and an upturn. When output plummets downward rapidly, the acceleration principle calls for negative investment (or disinvestment) greater than the rate at which machines can wear out. This wear-out rate puts a floor on how far it (the *SS-II* intersection) can push the economy below its break-even point.

Bumping along such a basement floor means that eventually firms will work down their capital stock to the level called for by that low level of income; and now the acceleration principle calls for a termination of disinvestment! Our image must shift from gum, ball, and airplane to that of an Olympic diver: once he stops moving downward under the water, he is buoyed up again. A new cycle can begin and repeat itself.

It is easy to see that, in the acceleration principle, we have a powerful factor making for economic instability. If business sales go up and down, the acceleration principle can intensify their fluctuation. It induces net investment on the upswing, but causes about the same amount of net *disinvestment* on the downswing.

In the long run, if the system is growing because of population increase and technical progress, then the acceleration principle works primarily as a stimulating factor: growing national income causes extensive growth of capital, which in turn means brisk investment demand and relatively low un-employment.[14]

We have seen that an economic system may well fluctuate and yet grow over the long run. The interested reader may wish to see the Appendix to this chapter, which discusses business cycle theory and the methods by which economists forecast the future. The following chapters will go on to discuss money and banking to show how the changes in credit, interest rates, and the supply of money may cause the spending schedules and their intersections to shift.

---

[14] The Appendix of Chapter 36 discusses warranted growth further, in connection with so-called "Harrod-Domar models of growth."

SUMMARY

A. FISCAL POLICY AND INCOME DETERMINATION

■ 1 An increase in government expenditure—taken by itself with taxes and investment unchanged—has expansionary effects on national product much like those of net investment. The schedule of $C + I + G$ shifts upward to a higher equilibrium intersection with the 45° line.

■ 2 An increase in taxes—taken by itself with investment and government expenditure unchanged—depresses the equilibrium level of national product. The schedule of consumption plotted against NNP is shifted downward and rightward by taxes; but since extra dollars go partly into saving, the dollar drop in consumption will not be quite so great as the dollars of new taxes. Therefore, to combat a given inflationary or deflationary gap, we may require an even larger change in taxation.

B. FOREIGN TRADE AND INCOME DETERMINATION

■ 3 An increase in exports—with imports unchanged—has the same impact on NNP as an increase in investment (leaving government and taxes out of the picture entirely). The II schedule in the saving-investment diagram shifts up to become $I + E$, and its intersection with the saving curve shows the new NNP.

■ 4 Imports are a leakage, much like savings. The greater the NNP, the greater are imports. The tendency of extra income to be spent on extra imports is called the MPM. This may be large, but never large enough to convert all extra domestic spending into extra imports, so long as the marginal propensity to save is above zero.

■ 5 In the final equilibrium, total investment and exports must be equal to total savings and imports. But exports need not be precisely equal to imports. Any difference is made up by foreign lending or borrowing, the NNP remaining in equilibrium.

■ 6 The multiplier that recognizes all leakages in the continued respending of consumption dollars from initial I, G, or E must include import leakage, MPM. In an open economy with imports and exports, this is "the" multiplier.

$$\text{Change in NNP} = \frac{1}{\text{MPS} + \text{MPM}} \times \text{change in } I, E, \text{ and/or } G$$

$$= \frac{1}{1 - \text{MPC}^D} \times \text{change in } I, E, \text{ and/or } G$$

■ 7 In the absence of foreign retaliation, policies that assist exports and inhibit imports tend to raise NNP and employment—and price levels. Correspondingly, policies that raise imports and reduce exports are deflationary, and may be helpful or harmful to stability. Such manipulation of foreign trade may have harmful long-run effects, however, which are discussed in Part Five.

C. FLUCTUATIONS IN NATIONAL INCOME AND THE ACCELERATION PRINCIPLE

■ 8 Fluctuations in national income are often called business cycles because they tend to take on a definite cyclical pattern. The West has known business cycles since before 1900. The Appendix to this chapter contains further discussion.

■ 9 One often-heard explanation of the business cycle is that changes in investment are linked to changes in final sales. The acceleration principle states that net investment depends upon *changes* in the level of income or consumption. The multiplier and the accelerator interact, bringing in dynamic rates of change, influencing levels of income and investment, and causing economic instability.

The art of economics consists in recognizing both the core of truth in the simple theory of income determination and also its needed qualifications. In later chapters we shall see how interest rates, exchange rates, and other factors may cause shifts in the *I, G,* and *E* schedules that determine levels of national income.

We leave to the final chapter of Part Two the analysis of government monetary and fiscal policy, and to Part Five the exploration of other aspects of international policy. In the next few chapters we turn to an analysis of money, banking policy, and interest policy.

QUESTIONS FOR DISCUSSION

1. "Even if the government spends a billion dollars on 'wasteful' armaments, during a depression this may help create jobs and several billions of new useful production." Discuss.

2. Describe briefly the effects upon income of (*a*) government expenditure, (*b*) taxes, (*c*) our sale of more goods and services to foreigners than we buy from them (i.e., positive net foreign investment).

3. "The purpose of fiscal policy is to help wipe out inflationary or deflationary gaps. Thus, if $C + I + G$ is too high, we have an inflationary gap; and we raise taxes to shift the new $C' + I' + G'$ schedule downward, thereby wiping out the inflationary gap." Explain. Show what you would do to taxes to fight a deflationary gap. To government expenditure.

4. Redraw Fig. 13-4 so that at an equilibrium point like *e'* exports are greater than imports. Now Canadians in effect lend to foreigners. Would you recommend a policy of increased foreign aid (giving, not lending) to raise Canadian employment? Can you construct a diagram in which the rise of exports from *E* to *E'* results in imports rising to exceed the new exports? Why not?

5. Write an explanation of the acceleration principle. Combine it with the multiplier.

6. Consider the impact of a "buy-Ontario" policy. Will Ontario's campaign, if successful, have a larger multiplier effect than a "buy-Canadian" policy?

7. Consider the effect of a tariff on Fig. 13-3. If the foreign countries retaliate and raise their tariffs, how will this be shown on the Figure?

8. Let NNP $= Y$, $DI = Y_d = Y - T$. Let $I = 100$, and $C = 100 + \frac{2}{3}Y_d$. When $G = 0$ and $\overline{I} = 100$, we use formula $Y = 200 + \frac{2}{3}(Y - T) + \overline{I} + \overline{G}$ to solve for

$Y^* = 900$. Likewise, verify the values in the following quadruplets of values for $(\overline{I}, \overline{G}, \overline{T}, Y^*)$: (101,0,0,903), (100,1,0,903), (100,0,1,898), (100,1,1,901).

9. Review your understanding of the following concepts:

$C + I + G$ schedule

fiscal policy (expenditure and taxes)

tax effect on CC and equilibrium

multiplier effects of an increase
  in exports

leakages

qualifications to the analysis

MPM and MPC^D

$I^D + E$ and $S + M$ schedules

accelerator-multiplier interaction

Appendix: Business Cycles and Forecasting

Economists, businessmen, investors, and the housewife glancing at the morning paper, all are concerned with business cycles and the future trend of the economy. Economists therefore have attempted to formulate a theoretical foundation against which empirical facts or statistics may be tested. We have, of course, not one but many theories of the business cycle. Similarly, we have many series of statistics. When these statistics are inserted into a theoretical framework, they will give us information about the present state of the economy and its possible future trends.

■ STATISTICAL CORRECTION FOR SEASONAL
   VARIATION AND FOR TRENDS

First, of course, we must remove from our statistical data irrelevant, disturbing factors, such as *seasonal* patterns, and also certain so-called long-term "trends." If Eaton's sales went up from November to December, 1960, we cannot conclude from this that the 1960 recession shown in Fig. 13-6 did not exist. Retail trade goes up every Christmas, just as Niagara Falls hotels tend to be crowded in summer. The statistician attempts to remove the "seasonal influence" by carefully studying previous yearly patterns. If he finds that every December tends to involve about 150 per cent as much business as the average month of the year, and every January only 90 per cent, then he will take the actual raw monthly data and divide all the December figures by 1.5, all the January figures by 0.9, and so forth for each month. After this has been done, the statisti-

cian will end up with a time series of monthly department-store sales which have been "seasonally adjusted." These will show what we expected all along, that business was really still declining throughout all the last months of 1960, because December's improvement was less than the seasonal norm.

Another kind of problem arises when we examine the fluctuations through time of such a rapidly growing time series as electric-power production or, in Fig. 13-6, page 314, industrial production. Such a growing series did not decline in any recession. But the recession is evident there, nevertheless. It rears its ugly head in the form of a *slowing down of the rate of growth* of the time series as compared with its normal or long-term "secular trend."

If we draw a smooth trend line or curve, either by eye or by some statistical formula, through the strongly growing components of NNP, we discover the business cycle in the twistings of the data above and below the trend line. If we measure the vertical deviations from the trend line and plot them on a separate diagram, we get a reasonably clear picture of the business cycle.[1] Let us take a look at it.

---

[1] The reader may be referred to any standard textbook on statistics for these technical procedures. However, cautious judgment must be exercised in using the mechanical tools of statistics. A beginner, carelessly "eliminating a trend," may throw out the baby along with the bath water if not careful, or at least distort the true appearance of the infant.

The business cycle, like the year, has its seasons:

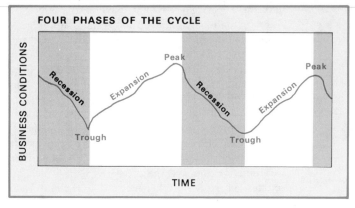

FOUR PHASES OF THE CYCLE

BUSINESS CONDITIONS

Recession

Expansion

Peak

Recession

Expansion

Peak

Trough

Trough

TIME

FIG. 13-7. Cyclical expansions follow contractions, with turning points in between. Following the leadership of the National Bureau of Economic Research of the United States, statisticians have dated these phases for the economic story of many countries. Not every peak reaches "prosperity" in the sense of low unemployment. Nor does every threatened recession materialize.

■ THE FOUR PHASES OF THE TRADITIONAL CYCLE

Early writers on the business cycle, possessing little quantitative information, tended to attach disproportionate attention to *panics* and *crises* such as the collapse of the South Sea Bubble in 1720, the severe credit panic of 1837 (which aggravated the political causes of the Canadian rebellions of that year), the world-wide slump of 1873 (which stopped the new Confederation, literally, in its railroad tracks), the brief downturn of 1893, the postwar crash of 1921, and, of course, the cataclysmic "Black Tuesday" on Wall Street, on October 29, 1929. Later writers soon began to speak of two phases of business: prosperity and depression, or boom and slump, with peaks and troughs marking the turning points in between.

Today, it is recognized that not every period of improving business need take us all the way to full employment. For example, throughout the decade of the 1930s there was a measure of recovery from the 1932-1933 trough levels, but we could by no means speak of the period as one of true prosperity. And from 1957 to 1965, unemployment never dropped even to a 4 per cent level.

The cycle used to be broken up by many economists into four phases, the two most important ones being called the periods of "expansion" and "contraction," or "recession." The expansion phase comes to an end and goes into the recession phase at the upper turning point, or so-called "peak." Similarly, the recession phase gives way to that of

expansion at the lower turning point, or so-called "trough," or "revival." Thus, the four phases are supposed to keep repeating themselves in the oversimplified picture as shown in Fig. 13-7. Note that the emphasis here is not so much on *high* or *low* business activity as on the dynamic aspects of *rising* or *falling* business activity. (But do not forget the unemployment gap and the importance of growth trends.)

Each phase of the cycle passes into the next. Each is characterized by different economic conditions[2] and requires special explanatory principles. But let us continue with more facts before attempting analysis and theorizing.

LENGTH OF CYCLE How long have the traditional economic cycles been? This depends upon how many minor cycles you wish to count. Most observers have no trouble in agreeing on the major cycles, which were about 8 to 10 years in length. Everyone agrees that the late 1920s represents a period of prosperity and the early 1930s one of depression, and similarly with other past major business cycles. Not all economists, however, attach importance to the shorter minor cycles that are to be seen in economic charts. In 1924 and 1927, there were small dips in business activity. Shall we call

[2] For example, during expansion we find that employment, production, prices, money, wages, interest rates, and profits are usually rising, with the reverse true in recession.

the 1920s, therefore, three different (minor) cycles or one major prosperity period? In 1948-1949, 1953-1954, 1957-1958, and again in 1960-1961, we suffered mild recessions. Should these count as cycles? And if so, why not the 'pauses' in 1951, 1962, and probably 1969-1970?

In an elementary introduction of this type, it is perhaps best to stick primarily to major business cycles. For our purposes we may accept the summary that Harvard's Alvin Hansen gave to pre-World War II economic history:[3]

> The American experience indicates that the major business cycle has had an average duration of a little over eight years. Thus, from 1795 to 1937 there were seventeen cycles of an average duration of 8.35 years. . . .
> Since one to two minor peaks regularly occur between the major peaks, it is clear that the minor cycle is something less than half the duration of the major cycle. In the one hundred and thirty-year period 1807 to 1937 there were thirty-seven minor cycles with an average duration of 3.51 years.
> . . . It appears that the building cycle averages somewhere between seventeen and eighteen years in length, or almost twice the length of the major business cycle. . . .
> . . . American experience indicates that with a high degree of regularity every other major business boom coincides roughly with a boom in building construction, while the succeeding major cycle recovery is forced to buck up against a building slump . . . the depressions which have fallen in the interval of the construction downswing are typically deep and long. And the succeeding recovery is held back and retarded by the unfavorable depressional influence from the slump in the building industry.

The long swings in building construction and other series, which average anywhere between 15 and 25 years in length, are often called Kuznets cycles, being named for the scholar who first noticed them in 1930.[4] Work by A. F. Burns, S. Kuznets,

and other U.S. National Bureau scholars suggests that these pervasive swings have been associated with fluctuations in immigration and natural rates of population growth, in railroad building and capital imports, and in the rate of growth of the money supply. Federal economist D. J. Daly has noted them for Canada too. They are of interest because they seem to involve three factors: variations in the supply trends of labor and other resources available to the economy; variations in productivity trends relating to the efficiency with which those supplies can be used; and, what is still provisional but important, variations in the average intensity with which resources get used—in other words, variations in rates of unemployment.

Was the notable sluggishness of the Canadian economy in the last part of the 1950s and early 1960s a reflection of our passing into a less favorable phase of the Kuznets cycle? Or, as some then thought, was it a forerunner of some more ominous trend? Or merely the natural relaxation after a postwar sprint?

In any case, remember that fiscal and monetary policies can compensate for adverse phases of the Kuznets cycle—which man does not regard as one of those disasters, like earthquakes and volcanoes, which science can do nothing about.

■ A FIRST CLUE TO BUSINESS FLUCTUATIONS: CAPITAL FORMATION

Hansen's emphasis on *construction* gives us our first clue to the causation of the business cycle. Certain economic variables always show greater fluctuations than others in the business cycle. Thus, if we plot pig-iron production and cigarette consumption side by side, we hardly notice the business cycle in the latter. But in the pig-iron series there is little else to see but the business cycle. Why? Because ciga-

[3] Alvin H. Hansen, *Fiscal Policy and Business Cycles* (Norton, New York, 1941), pp. 18-24.

[4] Kuznets cycles should not be confused with *alleged very long waves*, whose complete cycle length is about half a century. Thus, from the end of the Napoleonic Wars in 1815 to the middle of the nineteenth century, prices tended to fall and times tended to be unusually hard, on the average. After the Californian and Australian gold discoveries following 1850, and as a partial result of the Crimean War and the American Civil War,

prices tended to rise. A new long cycle of falling prices followed the 1873 depression and lasted until the 1890s, when there was a great increase in gold production following the African and Klondike gold discoveries. Whether these long waves are simply historical accidents due to chance gold discoveries, inventions, and political wars, it is still too soon to say. The interested reader may be referred to J. A. Schumpeter, *Business Cycles* (McGraw-Hill, New York, 1939), Chaps. 6 and 7, where long cycles are called "Kondratieffs."

rettes are nondurable consumers' goods, and in both good and bad times people are going to smoke the same amount. Pig iron, on the other hand, is one of the principal ingredients of capital and durable goods of all kinds: of plant equipment and durable machinery, of industrial and residential construction, and of automobiles, washing machines, and other durable consumers' goods.

> Check this by reexamining Fig. 13-6, page 314. Note how volatile are the housing starts series in contrast to the series on consumer credit. Note that production and profit fluctuations coincide with investment fluctuations.

By their nature, durable goods are subject to violently erratic patterns of demand. In bad times their new purchase can be indefinitely postponed; in a good year, everyone may suddenly decide to stock up on a 10-year supply of the services of durable goods.

Our first clue to the nature of the business cycle lies, then, in the fact that it is the durable- or capital-goods sector of the economy which shows by far the greatest cyclical fluctuations.

Their swings are wide compared with those of the economic time series which represent primarily consumption of services, of nondurables, and the *services* of durable goods. Except for a few short, choppy surface disturbances in such series, the latter tend to follow the general flow of income in a rather passive fashion. Ordinarily, consumption movements seem the effect rather than cause of the business cycle; however, there is good reason to believe that the movements of *durable* goods represent key causes in a more fundamental sense.

■ HOW SAVING AND INVESTMENT SCHEDULES APPLY

It is comforting to find that statistical analysis supports the emphasis in previous chapters on the crucial importance of the capital investment process. The income-determination theories of the last chapter do indeed help in understanding economic history. Here are but a few reminders:

1. *Wars* have always been great disrupters of an economy. How do they transmit their economic effects? Plainly, they lead to great swings in the G component of the $C + I + G$ schedule, and this causes even greater swings in the over-all level of production and incomes. Inflationary gaps appear at full-employment NNP, leading to price inflation.

2. In minor cycles of the postwar type, it is common for considerable fluctuations in the rate of *inventory investment* to occur. In the years of expansion, inventory accumulation is at a positive rate as merchants seek to rebuild their stocks and accommodate them to the growing level of sales. When merchants veer from a positive rate of inventory accumulation to a negative rate, the I component in the $C + I + G$ schedule goes down: then the production line is cut back, men are put on fewer average hours per week or are laid off, wages and profits fall, and all this gets registered in a multiplied drop in NNP or in its failure to grow along a normal trend.

3. When there are longer waves in construction and equipment, the I component in the $C + I + G$ schedule causes the whole schedule and its equilibrium to go through slow swings of considerable amplitude.

4. While it is an oversimplification to say that the consumption schedule never shifts over time, U.S. economists S. Kuznets and R. Goldsmith have made National Bureau of Economic Research studies indicating the over-all stability of saving behavior relative to income over a long period. Their general finding is that, aside from short-term cycles, the percentage saved out of income has been remarkably the same over the last century.

The one situation in which we cannot regard consumption purely as a passive and predictable force comes in those times when consumer demand for autos and other durable goods fluctuates. (E.g., the fact that Canadians and Americans liked the new 1962 and 1963 cars helped much to accelerate the recovery from the 1960-1961 recession.) Such *shifts* in the CC schedule also contribute to movements in the $C + I + G$ intersections, which, like any other shifts in autonomous factors, involve double-duty multiplier reactions.

■ A FEW THEORIES OF THE BUSINESS CYCLE

When it comes to explanations of why the income schedules shift, an industrious student could easily compile a list of separate theories of the business cycle that would run into the dozens.[5] Each theory seems to be quite different; but when we examine them closely and throw out those which obviously contradict the facts or the rules of logic, or which just appear to be conveying an explanation when really they are not saying anything at all—when we do all this, we are left with relatively few different explanations. Most of them differ from each other only in emphasis.

One man believes the cycle to be primarily the result of fluctuations in total net investment, while another prefers to attribute the cycle to fluctuations in the rate of technological inventions and innovations, which act on business *through* net investment. A third man says that the root of the cycle is to be found in the fact that the creation of deposit money by our banking system causes investment spending to expand and contract so as to create boom and bust.

These sound like three different theories, and in most advanced textbooks they might be given the names of three different writers, but from our standpoint they are but three different aspects of the same saving-investment process. As we shall see, this does not mean there is perfect agreement among all theories of the cycle or that there are not some important differences in emphasis among different writers.

■ EXTERNAL AND INTERNAL FACTORS

To classify the different theories, we may first

[5] We may mention just a few of the better-known theories: (1) the *monetary* theory—attributes the cycle to the expansion and contraction of bank credit, (Hawtrey, Friedman, et al.); (2) the *innovation* theory—attributes the cycle to the clustering of important inventions such as the railroad (Schumpeter, Hansen, et al.); (3) the *psychological* theory—treats the cycle as a case of people's infecting each other with pessimistic and optimistic expectations (Pigou, Bagehot, et al.); (4) the *underconsumption* theory—claims too much income goes to wealthy or thrifty people compared with what can be invested (Hobson, Sweezy, Foster and Catchings, et al.); (5) the *overinvestment* theory—claims too much rather than too little investment causes recessions (Hayek, Mises, et al.); (6) the *sunspot-weather-crop* theories (Jevons, H. L. Moore). The interested reader should consult G. Haberler, *Prosperity and Depression* (Harvard University Press, Cambridge, Mass., 1958, 4th ed.), or other business-cycle texts for further information.

divide them into the two categories of primarily *external* and primarily *internal* theories.

The external theories find the root of the business cycle in the fluctuations of something outside the economic system—in sunspot cycles, in wars, revolutions, and political events, in gold discoveries, in rates of growth of population and migrations, in discoveries of new lands and resources, and finally in scientific and technological discoveries and innovations.

The internal theories look for mechanisms within the economic system itself which will give rise to self-generating business cycles, so that every expansion will breed recession and contraction, and every contraction will in turn breed revival and expansion, in a quasi-regular, repeating, never-ending chain.

If you believe in the sunspot theory of the business cycle—and no respectable economists today do—then the distinction between external and internal is rather easy to draw; although even here, when you come to explain how and why disturbances on the surface of the sun give rise to the business cycle, you begin to get involved in the internal nature of the economic system. But at least no one can seriously argue that the direction of causation is in doubt, or that the economic system causes the sunspots to fluctuate, instead of vice versa. However, when it comes to such other external factors as wars and politics, or even births and gold discoveries, there is always some doubt as to whether the economic system does not at least react on the so-called "external" factors, thereby making the distinction between external and internal not such a hard and fast one. Still, no one will deny that any such "feedback" effects take us outside the traditional boundaries of economics, and this is our justification for distinguishing between external and internal theories.

■ THE BUSINESS CYCLE IN EACH ECONOMY

Another branch of business-cycle research is concerned with the transmission of fluctuations from one economy to another. The data indicate that each of the main recent contraction periods and expansion periods (shown in Fig. 13-6, page 314) is duplicated, almost to the day, in Canada and the United States. With some explainable lags, similarly parallel curves are found in Europe and elsewhere in the Western economy. Yet this was not always so: D. J. Daly has pointed out that while the U.S. GNP began to increase its rate of growth in 1911, the Canadian rate fell steadily from 1909 to 1919. But such divergences, which can be accounted for in part by Canada's previous immigration boom and her involvement in the war after 1914, are fairly rare. Most national statistical series are so coincident with one another that it is worth the time of researchers to try to explain the divergences that do occur.

This parallelism can be regarded in two ways, which overlap each other considerably. One group of economists says:

The Western group of nations is really all one economy. This entire system is experiencing the same external shocks (sunspots, innovations, wars, and changes in population growth) and is carrying out a single internal process of saving and investing. Thus there is no more reason to expect cycles to differ between countries than there is to expect England and Scotland to have different cyclical data.

The second group of economists says the first group claims too much:

You do not *know* that one Western economy actually exists. We propose to study the "transmission" of cycles from country to country, and then we shall understand better whether the United States and France are as strongly linked as England and Scotland.

Their research has used both theory and statistics.

The theorists have been studying how a drop in U.S. NNP will be accompanied (through the foreign-trade multiplier mechanism) by a drop in imports. This is the same as a drop in other countries' exports, and *their* multiplier mechanisms will result in a drop in their NNPs. But which will come first? In the example, the *cause* of the other countries' drop was the U.S. contraction. But all three contractions (the U.S. NNP, trade, and the other NNPs) may be simultaneous, or in any order. Thus, merely looking at the crude data will neither prove nor disprove the hypothesis that cycles start in the United States and are diffused to supplying countries.

The statisticians have given most attention to trying to find which series contract first in each country. One of their most interesting studies has been the relation between the Canadian and the U.S.

economies. Gideon Rosenbluth, for example, has suggested that export trade cannot explain the marked correspondence between the two countries: instead we must look to the vast network of foreign ownership, capital movements, cultural ties, inventions, and advertising to explain the coincidence. To a certain extent, therefore, his work (and that of other Canadian economists) tends to support the England-and-Scotland approach.

Much work remains to be done on the international transmission of cycles. But it is clear that the following discussion is applicable: for *either* business cycles originate in one country (with the mechanisms described below) and are communicated to other smaller countries; *or* the West is one big economy, in which case our discussion will apply to the entire area. In Chapter 33 we will return to some other aspects of the links between national economies. But here we consider the West as one big unspecified economic unit.[6]

■ PURELY INTERNAL THEORIES

As against the crude external sunspot theory, we may describe some simple examples of possible, crude internal theories.

"ECHO" WAVES OF REPLACEMENT   If machinery and other durable goods all had the same length of life (say, 8 or 10 years), then we might try to explain a business cycle of the same length by this fact. If a boom got started—never mind how—then there would be a bunching of new capital goods all of the same age. A few years later, before these goods had worn out, there would be little need for replacement. This would cause a depression. But after 8 or 10 years all the capital equipment would suddenly wear out and would all have to be replaced, giving rise to an inflationary boom. This in turn would give rise to another complete cycle, with new echoing cycles of depression and boom every decade. Thus, self-generating "replacement waves" provide a purely internal business-cycle theory.

---

[6] When we examine "long" cycles, such as the building cycle of 17 to 25 years, we note the research findings of Brinley Thomas and Simon Kuznets: that European and North American cycles have sometimes been directly out of phase with each other. When business and investment opportunities were up in North America, those in Europe were down, and migrants and capital tended to flow westward.

Actually, not all equipment has the same length of life; and identical automobiles produced on the same day will certainly not all be replaced at the same time. Consequently, any bunching of equipment expenditures will tend over time to spread itself out, at most giving rise to weaker and weaker replacement peaks. Twenty-five years after World War I one might have noted a deficit of births because of that conflict; another generation later, the dip would be hardly noticeable; and today it is just as if there had never been that particular violent disturbance of population. Replacement waves, therefore, are like the vibrations of a plucked violin string; they tend to dampen down and die away, unless there is a new disturbance.

PSYCHOLOGICAL SELF-GENERATING CYCLES   The laws of physics guarantee that friction will lessen any purely autonomous physical fluctuations. In social science, there is no law like the conservation of energy to prevent the creation of purchasing power. Therefore a much better example of a self-generating cycle than replacement waves would be the case where people become alternately optimistic and pessimistic, each stage leading as inevitably to the next as the manic stage of some people leads to the depressive stage. We cannot rule out such an internal theory. Nor can we be satisfied with it as it stands, for it says and explains little.

■ COMBINING EXTERNAL AND INTERNAL
   ELEMENTS INTO A SYNTHESIS

Everyone has observed how a window or a tuning fork may be activated into pronounced vibration when a certain note is sounded. Is this vibration externally or internally caused? The answer is, Both. The sounded note is certainly an external cause; but the window or tuning fork responds according to its own internal nature, coming into strong resonance, not with *any* sounded note, but only with one of a certain *definite* pitch. It takes the right kind of trumpets to bring down the walls of Jericho.

Similarly, we may look upon business cycles as not unlike a toy rocking horse that is subjected to occasional outside pushes. The pushes need not be regular; great technical innovations never are. But just as the wooden horse rocks with a frequency and amplitude that depend partly upon its internal nature (its size and weight), so too will the economic system respond to fluctuations in external

factors according to its *internal* nature. Both external and internal factors are important, then, in explaining the business cycle.

SYNTHESIS   Most economists today believe in a synthesis or combination of external and internal theories. In explaining the major cycles, they place crucial emphasis on fluctuations in *investment* or *capital* goods. Primary causes of these capricious and volatile investment fluctuations are to be found in such external factors as (1) technological innovation and (2) dynamic growth of population and of territory. With these external factors, we must combine the internal factors that cause any initial change in investment to be *amplified* in a cumulative, multiplied fashion—as people who are given work in the capital-goods industries respend part of their new income on consumption goods and as an air of optimism begins to pervade the business community, causing firms to go to the banks and the securities market for new credit accommodation.[7]

Also, it is necessary to point out that the general business situation definitely reacts in turn on investment. If high consumption sales make businessmen optimistic, they are more likely to embark upon venturesome investment programs. Inventions or scientific discoveries may occur independently of the business cycle, but their appreciable economic introduction will most certainly depend on business conditions. When NNP moved up in the 1960s year after year it was reasonable to expect that a considerable volume of capital formation (new machines, added inventories, construction) would be induced. Therefore, especially in the short run, investment movements are in part an *effect* as well as a cause of income movements.

In the longer run, no matter how high a plateau of income is maintained, the stock of capital goods

---

[7] With two dice you can manufacture something that looks a little like a business cycle. Record the results of successive tosses—as in the number sequence: 7, 4, 10, 3, 7, 11, 7, 2. . . . Then take 5-period moving averages—such as the successive numbers $(7 + 4 + 10 + 3 + 7)/5 \equiv 6\ 1/5$, $(4 + 10 + 3 + 7 + 11)/5 = 7, \ldots$ etc. A plot of these will look not too different from NNP or price fluctuations! Explanation: the random numbers are like exogenous investment shocks; the moving average is like the economic system's (or the wooden horse's) internal smoothing reactions of $C + I + G$ type.

will become adjusted at a higher level and new net investment will drop off to zero unless there is (1) a growth of income, (2) a continuing improvement of technology, or (3) a never-ending reduction in interest rates.

The first of these processes, showing how investment demand may be induced by growth of sales and income, has been given a rather high-sounding name—the "acceleration principle," which we met in Part C of Chapter 13. Most writers bring it in as one strand in their final business-cycle theories.

■ FORECASTING THE FUTURE OF BUSINESS ACTIVITY

Businessmen have to form guesses about the future in making their investment and production decisions. If they thought next year would bring a depression, they might want to reduce inventory now. If, on the contrary, they expected prices to rise greatly several months from now, they might hasten today to buy goods in advance and to add to equipment and plant. Similarly, speculators would like to know the future in order to be able to buy or sell common stock and make a profit. And more important, policy makers in Ottawa would like to have a peek at next year's national-income accounts to be able to take remedial fiscal and monetary actions now.

Statisticians and economists cannot yet make accurate forecasts. Their guesses occasionally turn out to be quite wrong. Nonetheless, people insist that they do their best. Why? Because lack of any forecast usually itself involves an *implicit* forecast and noneconomists have an even worse long-run average score at making forecasts than do trained statistical economists.

FORECASTING THE ECONOMIC FUTURE What methods do the best forecastors use? No simple description can be given, but here are a few of the most common practices.

1. They follow the national-income accounts very closely: GNP every quarter; personal income every month; new construction; equipment spending; the important short-run behavior of inventory change; estimates of coming government expenditures and taxes. They also watch monthly data: price indexes, the DBS index of production, exports, changes in the rate of growth of the money supply, and reports on unemployment and job totals. In addition, they watch many diverse statistics as they become available: department-store sales each week; chain-store sales and automobile dealer sales each month; new orders and inventory changes of manufacturing and trade each month.

2. In recent years, the forecaster can study various *surveys* of future events: the DBS-Department of Trade and Commerce questionnaire of business intentions to invest and the Department of Labour forecast. The attitudes reported by purchasing agents are important for inventories. For consumers, random sampling by public and private survey groups gives information on whether or not the consumer is in a buying mood and what his spending intentions are. For businessmen generally, *The Financial Post* and *Fortune* take frequent polls of opinions about future and present intentions. In Europe the technique of polling heads of businesses has also made great progress.

3. Many forecasters then try to draw up "$C + I + G + (E - M)$-type models" to make *approximate guesses* about future changes. They try to come out with a range of probable answers, not with a single answer accurate to two decimals.

4. Some reinforce these guesses by considering whether most diverse time series—such as those in Fig. 13-6—are going up or down. Are certain so-called "leading-indicator series," such as average hours worked per week, stock prices, construction awards, and new orders, predominantly signaling a turn now?

Men long looked for a statistical series (or group of series) that would manifest a turn a *fixed* number of months before business turned generally. Such a "leading indicator" would be invaluable for forecasting purposes; however, no such perfect guide has been discovered. Geoffrey Moore and Arthur F. Burns at the U.S. National Bureau of Economic Research, and Julius Shiskin at the U.S. Census Bureau, have found that certain series, such as have already been mentioned, can give some help in identifying turning points in advance and in confirming that they have just occurred. Forecasters cannot yet rely on indicators alone, for the reason that (as in periods like 1951 and 1962) they may give misleading signals; in expansions, the indicators often turn down too many months before the true peak; in recessions, they turn up only a month or two before the upturn—by the time the data become available for smoothing, their main (important) purpose is to tell us we have indeed already turned the corner. The Canadian government and private forecaster W. A. Beckett have made use of similar information. Economists look forward with

Leading indicators call the business-cycle turns:

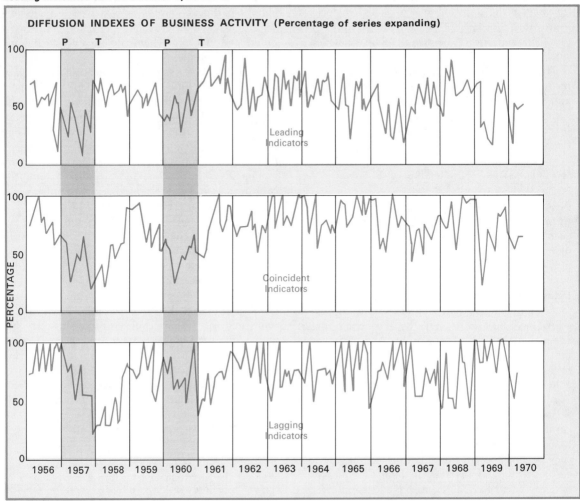

FIG. 13-8. The coincident indicators in the center panel cross the 50 per cent line in agree-ment with the shading of peak-to-trough or recession periods (PT). The leading series cross perhaps six months earlier, and the lagging indicators cross later. Note that the leading series seemed to promise a recession in 1965-1966; but this did not materialize. (Source: W. A. Beckett Associates Ltd.)

interest to further improvements in these techniques, and practical forecasters do supplement this kind of information. See Fig. 13-8 for some efforts in this direction.[8]

[8] Found among the useful leaders are new orders for durables, housing starts, and inventory changes; stock prices, corporate profits, and industrial materials prices; average workweek hours; rate of growth of the money supply, etc.

Experience shows that economic forecasts are in-dispensable for public and business decisions. Econ-omists' forecasts, although not infallible, average out to be more accurate than those of readers of tea leaves, hunch players, computer robots, or simple extrapolaters of present levels and trends. Although not perfect, economists' forecasts are the best science can produce.

■ REQUIEM FOR THE BUSINESS CYCLE?

Is the business cycle dead? Has the New Economics ended once and for all this curse of historic capitalism, in the same way that modern medicine has ended such scourges as polio and smallpox?

Many people do believe that the business cycle has finally been tamed. And indeed, study of Figs. 13-6 and 13-8 shows that the economy has reduced recessions in the post-World War II period to brief and infrequent punctuations in the progress of sustained growth. It used to be the case, under historic capitalism, that the charts showed the shadings of recession half the time.

Yet, to paraphrase Mark Twain's comment on the report of his demise, "It is *premature* to speak of the death of the business cycle." Back in 1929, just before the great stock-market crash, experts spoke of the country as being in a "new era" of perpetual prosperity. The gods take their revenge on those who are too proud.

What can be said scientifically about the outlook for business fluctuations? Most economists would pretty much agree with the following formulation:

Although nothing is impossible in an inexact science like economics, the probability of a great depression—a prolonged, cumulative, and chronic slump like that of the 1930s, the 1890s, or the 1870s—has been reduced to a negligible figure. No one should pay any appreciable insurance premium to be protected against the risk of a total breakdown in our banking system and of massive unemployment in which 25 per cent of the workers can find no jobs.

The reason for virtual disappearance of great depressions is the new attitude of the electorate. By the $C + I + G + (E - M)$ analysis of this and earlier chapters, economic science knows how to use monetary and fiscal policy to keep any recessions that break out from snowballing into lasting chronic slumps. The electorate in a mixed economy insists that any political party which is in power will take the expansionary actions that can prevent depressions.

Suppose we grant that great depressions are virtually a thing of the past. Does this mean that we must have perpetual prosperity—that recessions will never happen again, being replaced by what are euphemistically called "rolling readjustments" or mere "pauses"? Most scientists take a more cautious attitude, summarizing thus:

A mixed economy may still be subject to occasional *recessions:* inventory fluctuations can still occur; changes in cold-war spending can have initially destabilizing effects upon general business activity; attempts to bring inflation under control may sometimes result in downturns.

Nevertheless, now that the tools of income analysis are more widely understood and their use becoming mandatory, the probability of recession in any one year is less in the mixed economy than it used to be. Expansion periods tend to be frequent and longer.

Lest we close on an overoptimistic note, let us take warning that the forces of democracy are not so strongly balanced in the direction of controlling creeping inflation—as we shall see. And future scientists may have to redefine the phases of the business cycle, so that in economies like Germany or the United States we count as unsatisfactory those years in which the economy actually *grows less than its potential grows*, thereby wasting its true productivity in mounting "gaps."

SUMMARY

■ 1 The business cycle is a pulse common to most sectors of economic life and to various countries. Movements in national income, unemployment, production, prices, and profits are not so regular and predictable as the orbits of the planets or the oscillations of a pendulum, and there is no magical method of forecasting the turns of business activity.

■ 2 The four phases of expansion, peak, recession, and trough can be separated for analysis and can be distinguished from seasonal or long-term trends. The resulting pattern of 8- to

10-year major cycles, shorter minor cycles, and longer Kuznets construction cycles has been carefully described by economists, statisticians, and historians and found to be roughly coincident in Western economies.

■ 3 To explain the cycle, our first clue is to be found in the greater amplitude of fluctuations of investment or durable-capital-goods formation. Although most economists agree on this fact, they differ in their emphasis upon *external* or *internal* factors. Increasingly, however, the experts are tending toward a *synthesis* of external and internal factors. On the one hand, importance is attached to fluctuations in inventions, in population and territorial growth, and in gold discoveries and political warfare. On the other hand, economists stress too the way that these external changes in investment opportunities are modified by the reactions of the economic system; the credit practices of banks and the monetary policies of the Bank of Canada; waves of optimism and pessimism; replacement cycles; the multiplier and the acceleration principle, which bring in dynamic rates of change as well as levels; and other feedback effects of growth on investment.

■ 4 Forecasting is still inexact. Those with the best long-run batting averages follow national-income and related statistics very closely. They rely heavily on surveys of government, consumer, and business intentions. They reinforce their $C + I + G + (E - M)$ and money-supply guesses with the study of leading, coincident, and lagging indicators.

QUESTIONS FOR DISCUSSION

1. Describe the history of various cycles in this country.

2. Describe the different phases of the cycle. In what one are you now? How do you know?

3. Which theory or theories of the cycle do you like best? Why?

4. "The ups-and-downs of the traditional business cycle are less important objects of study today than the level of unemployment and the trends in real output growth and in the general price level." Explain and appraise.

5. Why is it important to be able to forecast the future of business activity? Give business and government examples. How would *you* forecast?

6. In the light of recent years' experience, reappraise the outlook for the business cycle.

7. Review your understanding of the following concepts:

business cycle, turning point, phase
peak, trough, expansion, recession
seasonal and trend corrections
internal and external theories
international transmission
acceleration principle
replacement waves, sunspots
forecasting methods
leading, coincident, and lagging indicators

14

PRICES

AND MONEY

Only one fellow in ten thousand understands the currency question, and we meet him every day.   KIN HUBBARD

Earlier chapters showed how the modern economist finds it convenient to analyze the forces making for expanding or contracting money income in terms of saving and investment schedules, or what is the same thing, in terms of the components of consumption, investment, and government spending. For the most part, except in the inflationary-gap section, it was assumed that price levels would not change much until an approach to high employment was reached. Or alternatively, it was tacitly assumed earlier that all the schedules were expressed in terms of dollars which had been corrected for changes in the measuring rod of the price level. Accordingly, until now, a shift in the schedule of consumption-plus-investment-plus-government spending could be thought of as expanding employment and production.

Now we want to focus on changes in the *price levels*. Why do prices rise swiftly in major wars? Why do prices increase millionsfold in galloping inflation when a disorganized nation is printing new currency by the bale? Why do prices begin to creep upward even before an expansion of $C + I + G$ spending restores the system to full or high employment? Why in a modern mixed economy might prices and wages rise even at a time of apparent excess plant capacity and slack labor markets?

These vital, and difficult, questions can be most fruitfully approached by the following program. This chapter will first give the facts about price-level changes and some of their effects. Then it will discuss the concept of the money supply M and the way M has generally moved in relation to long-term prices. Finally, the important "quantity theory of money," in its crude and sophisticated forms, will provide an initial glimpse into the importance of banking and Bank of Canada monetary policies, as discussed in subsequent chapters.

We shall discover that changes in the money supply have an important role in causing the $C + I + G$ spending schedule to shift upward and downward.

A.   PRICES AND THE MONEY SUPPLY

Figure 14-1 shows the historical ups and downs of wholesale prices. Each war is marked by high prices. At first glance there seem to be no general upward or downward trends. But the chart of consumer prices in Fig. 14-2, page 342, pinpoints the general trend of prices in this century. The trend of prices has been generally *upward*; the value of the dollar—as measured by what it can buy—has been cut almost in half since today's college student was born.

Do Wars Cause Price Rises?

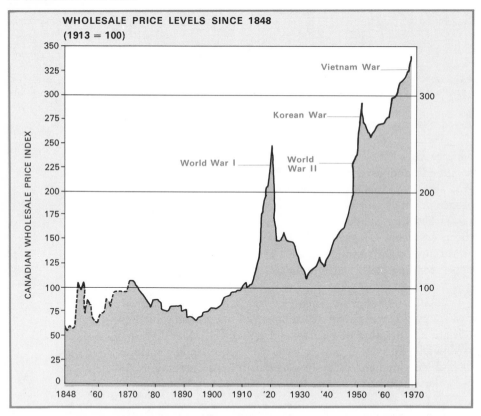

FIG. 14-1. Canadian prices do seem to have spurted upward after recent wars, though they failed to match the U.S. inflation in the aftermath of the American Civil War. After each such period, prices have dropped again: note the long "Great Depression" in the 1880s. The Great Depression of the 1930s was much deeper, but shorter. Since the 1890s the price trend has seemed definitely upward. After World War II there was no drop. (Before 1867, the prices are for foodstuffs only.) (Source: DBS and Michell, in Urquhart and Buckley, *Historical Statistics of Canada*, Cambridge University Press, 1965.)

As an omen for the future, note one very significant fact: After World War II there was no decline in prices at all comparable with what had followed previous wars. Wages and prices seem to have become "sticky" as far as *downward* movements are concerned; also, government has become quick to stem any depression of prices or output that threatens. Recent government targets for price stability have not been to reverse price increases—to restore former price levels—but simply to *slow* further increase. Naturally, if prices rise in good times and scarcely fall at all in bad times, what is the indicated long-term direction for prices?

■ INFLATION, DEFLATION, AND REDISTRIBUTION OF INCOME AMONG GROUPS

First, some definitions will be useful.

> By *inflation* we mean *a time of generally rising prices* for commodities and factors of production—rising prices for bread, cars, haircuts; rising wages, rents, etc.
>
> By *deflation* we mean a time when most prices and costs are falling.[1]

Neither in inflation nor in deflation do prices all move in the same direction or in exactly the same proportion. As a result of changes in *relative* prices and in total spending, the two processes of inflation and deflation cause definite and characteristic changes in (1) the distribution of income among economic classes and in (2) total output.

> Unforeseen inflation tends to favor debtors and profit receivers at the expense of creditors and fixed-income receivers. Deflation has the opposite effect.

Suppose you lend $1,000 today and are paid back one year from now. If in the meantime prices have doubled, then your debtor will be paying back only one-half as much real purchasing power as you gave him. If prices were to increase a trillionfold, as they did in the German inflation of 1920-1923, then the wealth of creditors would be completely wiped out. This actually happened to German university endowments and life-insurance assets.

Economists call the rate of return, adjusted for declining purchasing power in this way, the *real* rate of return (i.e., the market interest rate minus the annual rate of increase in the price level).[2] A Canadian security bought for $75

---

[1] "Deflation" sometimes has a secondary meaning too, namely a *drop in real output and an increase in unemployment* regardless of price behavior. And even our simple definition of inflation as rising prices will occasionally need modifying: thus in 1947 when wartime price controls were removed, prices shot upwards. Did stability of prices mean no inflation before 1947? Hardly. As scarcities of goods increased from 1939 to 1947, we were having "suppressed inflation." The 1947 price rise was primarily a "symptom" of the disease we were already experiencing.

[2] More precisely, if an inflation goes on for a long time and is "foreseen," these expectations may get built into the market interest rate an as allowance for a price rise. Thus, if we all expect prices to rise at 4 per cent per year, my pension funds invested in bonds and mortgages may pay me 8 per cent rather than 4 per cent. This adjustment of market interest rates to strong inflation may be widely observed; not only in Brazil and Chile, but also in North America and Western Europe.

in 1970 will pay off about $100 in 1975. But will the real rate of return be as high as zero per cent—will $100 in 1975 have as much purchasing power as $75 had in 1970? A Canadian who bought a long-term Government of Canada bond in 1939 and who kept it while reinvesting the interest payments at the going yields would scarcely have held his own in terms of the real purchasing power of the dollar. Admittedly, after 1954 he would have made some progress: a hundred dollars invested then would become $140 a decade later (by compounding the interest payments), whereas the *real purchasing power* would have slipped only so far that an item sold for $100 in the mid-fifties would have cost $120 in 1964. That is, over the entire period 1939-1970, the depreciation of purchasing power roughly equalled the rate of return; only in the shorter sub-period 1954-1964 was it somewhat less.

On the other hand, one who invests his money in real estate, in common stocks, or in sacks of flour makes a great money profit during unforeseen inflation. The volume of business sales shoots up. Prices rise between the time that businessmen buy and sell their merchandise. Fixed or overhead costs remain the same; other costs rise, but not so rapidly as prices. For all these reasons profits increase—often faster than does the cost of living. In periods of great inflation, every reckless fool can—must—become a great financier.

In time of *deflation*, the shoe is on the other foot. Creditors and fixed-income receivers tend to gain at the expense of debtors and profit receivers. If prices fall between the time that a creditor lends money and is repaid, then he gets back more purchasing power than he lent. Between the time that a merchant buys and sells goods, he will have to take a loss.

The school teacher who keeps her job and whose pay is not cut too sizably finds that her real income has increased. The widow who withstood the temptation to buy common stock during the boom and instead put all her money into gilt-edge government bonds finds herself better off. At the same time the government finds that the real burden of its public debt goes up relative to tax collections and national income. A hoarder who earns no money interest on his mattress cache nevertheless finds the real value of his wealth increasing every day as prices fall. If prices fall at the rate of 10 per cent each year, he is being rewarded for his antisocial act of hoarding at a 10 per cent rate of interest in real terms, while the businessman who is foolish enough to give someone a job may find that he cannot even get back his original outlay, much less earn a profit.

Modern research suggests that the greatest redistribution of income resulting from inflation is from older people to younger people. The dollars one puts aside at 25 for retirement at 70 often shrink in purchasing power: if prices rise at an average rate of about 3 per cent per year, the real purchasing power of a dollar held for 45 years will halve and halve again in that period.

■ EFFECTS OF CHANGING PRICES ON OUTPUT AND EMPLOYMENT

Aside from redistributing incomes, inflation may affect the total real income of the community.

An increase in prices is usually associated with high employment. In mild inflation the wheels of industry are well lubricated, and output is near capacity. Private investment is brisk, and jobs are plentiful. Such has been the historical pattern.

Thus, many businessmen and union spokesmen, in appraising a little deflation and a little inflation, speak of the latter as the lesser of two evils. The losses to fixed-income groups are usually less than the gains to the rest of the community. Even workers with relatively fixed wages are often better off because of improved employment opportunities and greater take-home pay; a rise in interest rates on new securities may partly make up any losses to creditors; and increases in pensions and transfers may partly make up losses to the retired. The ultimate sufferers are those who have least market power and least political power; conceivably, an inflationary, full-employment society could also arrange for their welfare by a transfer system.

In deflation, on the other hand, the growing decline in output causes the community's total well-being to be less; so the gainers get less than the losers lose. As a matter of fact, in deep depression, almost everyone—including the creditor who is left with uncollectible debts—suffers.

The above remarks show why an increase in consumption or investment spending is thought a good thing in times of unemployment, even if there is some upward pressure on prices. When the economic system is suffering from acute depression, few will criticize private or public spending on the ground that this might be inflationary. Actually, most of the increased spending will then go to increase production and create jobs.

But the same reasoning shows that once full employment and full plant capacity have been reached, any further increases in spending are likely to be completely wasted in price-tag increases. (Recall Chapter 12's discussion of "inflationary gaps.")

■ GALLOPING INFLATION

Slow price increases are one thing. But when each increase in prices becomes the signal for an increase in wages and costs, which again sends prices up still further, we may be in the midst of a malignant, galloping hyperinflation. Nothing good can be said for a rapid rise of prices such as took place in Germany in 1920-1923 and more recently in China and Hungary. Production and even the social order are then disorganized. The total wealth of large groups of the population is wiped out as money becomes worthless. Debtors ruthlessly pursue creditors in order to pay off their obligations in valueless money. Speculators profiteer. Housewives rush to spend their husbands' pay cheques before prices rise still further, but in doing so they only bid prices up even faster. As one Southerner said during the Confederate inflation of the American Civil War:

We used to go to the stores with money in our pockets and come back with food in our baskets. Now we go with money in baskets and return with food in our pockets. Everything is scarce except money! Prices are chaotic and production disorganized. A meal that used to cost the same amount as an opera ticket now costs twenty times as much. Business is often at a standstill because no one knows how much to charge. (We'll settle after the war, some say.) As a result, everybody tends to hoard "things" and to try to get rid of the "bad" paper money, which drives the "good" metal money out of circulation. A partial return to barter—with all its inconveniences—is the result.

Aside from hyperinflations of the German 1920-1923 type, we do see in countries like Chile and Brazil chronic inflation—say at the rate of 20 to 50 per cent per year—that goes on decade after decade. Somehow the people learn to live on such a merry-go-round. They hoard goods; buy homes; never, never lend money at ordinary interest rates; etc. Sometimes, as in Brazil, the economy manages to show real growth; too often, as in Chile, growth suffers.

Fortunately, there are few cases of hyperinflation except during war or in the backwash of war and revolution. The primary fear today for our mixed economy is about our steady upward *creep* in prices. Will such a creep inevitably become a trot? A trot become a canter? A canter become a gallop? Few economic experts would regard such a development as inevitable. But they are still concerned with too fast and steady a creep of prices.

In the first years after World War II, the rapid rise in prices drove some economists to the gloomy view: "We can never get near full employment without having rising wages and prices; only a price-fixing board can make full employment and price stability compatible." The 1936-1937, 1946-1948, 1956-1958, and 1965-1970 experiences did give this view some plausibility. On the other hand, 1951-1955 were mostly years of low unemployment and also years of falling wholesale prices and steady living costs. Price creep was fairly mild from 1958 to 1963. Still, as we shall see repeatedly in later chapters, every mixed economy must face the problem of a tendency for full employment to result in creeping inflation. Chapter 40 discusses the fact that each has yet to find a so-called "incomes policy" to help this performance.

■ THE CHOICE OF GOALS OF LONG-TERM PRICE BEHAVIOR

Ideally, we all want a progressive full-employment economy in which the excesses of the business cycle are moderated. We want to control the "mad dance of the dollar" as the business cycle passes from boom to crisis and slump. But as far as the *long-run trend* of prices is concerned, there are three possible programs that different economists sponsor as the soundest modern compromise:

1. *Prices—on the average—are to be stable.* As output increases over time because of population increase, capital formation, and technological progress, the total dollar spending rises. Money wages, and real wages also, rise as a result of increases in productivity over time.

2. *Prices are to be gently rising.* As high-employment output increases with productivity and growth, total dollar spending rises even faster than prices. Money wages also rise steadily; but the increase in real wages is not quite so great, because of the upward trend in the cost of living.

3. *Prices are to be falling steadily.* The total of money wages and property income remains almost constant. But the increase in output resulting from improved technological productivity is passed on to *all* consumers in lower prices. Real wages rise even though money wages may remain constant. Such a fall in prices need not depress business activity unduly, provided that it results from previous reductions in cost.

All three solutions are tolerable if unemployment is kept at a low figure. And in some ideal frictionless system, it would not matter much which pattern were followed, as long as the trend in prices was foreseeable and all adjustments were made to it. However, economic history and analysis suggest that we do not live in an ideal frictionless system. In a modern mixed economy, high employment is *least* likely to be maintained under the third possibility of falling price levels.

Most vigorous periods of healthy capitalist development without political unrest have come during periods of stable or gently rising prices. Capitalism itself developed during the centuries when Spanish New World gold flowed in— not because anyone planned it that way, but because the resultant general price increase eased the transition into the exchange economy with widespread use of coins and money.

B.   THE DEMAND FOR MONEY AND THE QUANTITY THEORY

We saw in Chapter 3 that a specialized economy uses money rather than barter:

> Money is the modern medium of exchange and the standard unit in which prices and debts are expressed. By controlling the behavior of money and credit, the government and its central bank can hope to affect the balance of saving and investment expenditure.

By quickening or moderating the growth in the money supply, the Bank of Canada can hope to raise or lower the $C + I + G$ intersections of earlier chapters. Here lies the vital importance of monetary theory.

■ THE THREE KINDS OF MONEY: COINS, CURRENCY, AND BANK DEPOSITS

Let us list the main kinds of money in daily use: small coins, paper currency, and chequing-account bank-deposit money.

COINAGE   First, there are the coins we use for small change: copper pennies, nickel five-cent pieces, and silvery dimes, quarters, half-dollars, and dollars. These constitute our so-called "fractional currency." Children think them important; but in total they do not add up to very much—in fact, to about one-seventh of the community's cash. Because the metal in all these coins is worth far *less* than their face value, they are termed "token money."[3] These coins are valued far beyond their metallic worth only because they can be readily converted into other money—20 nickels to the dollar, and so forth. Coins with negligible metallic value are not forced upon us; their quantity is limited by our demand for them to buy gum and newspapers.

CURRENCY Far more significant is the second kind of money: paper currency. Most of us know little more about a one-dollar or five-dollar bill than that each is inscribed with the picture of the Queen, that each bears the signature of one or another Bank of Canada official, and—most important of all—that each has a number showing its face value.

Examine a dollar bill or some other paper bill. You will find it says (ungrammatically) "One dollar / Bank of Canada / will pay to the bearer on demand / (two signatures of Bank of Canada officials)." This promise is, of course, nonsensical because, apart from giving the bearer small change, the Bank of Canada can make payment "on demand" with nothing but a similar bill. In denominations of 1, 2, 5, 10, 20, 50, and 100 dollars, the Bank's bills are full legal tender in Canada.

It was not always thus. Paper currency issued by the Crown or the government has at various times represented the willingness of the Treasury to exchange that note for silver or gold. For example, the British pound sterling has its name because it once stood for one pound of sterling silver. And the U.S. one dollar bill had printed on it "Silver Certificate" because Congress (until 1963) required that each bill be backed by an appropriate weight of silver. On demand, the government would give the bearer a silver dollar or silver metal! And in 1853, when the Canadian currency was established, its dollar was based on the British pound, a gold coin, with $4.86⅔ (Canadian) to the pound, or $10.00 to the eagle, the American gold coin. Small coins, including American decimal coins and British shillings and pennies, were then almost the only hand-to-hand currency. But when, decades later, "Dominion notes" were issued by the Department of Finance, they had this old relationship to the pound and eagle coins.

Until the 1930s, most bills in Canada were either these "Dominion notes" or true "bank notes." The latter were issued by the chartered banks, bore pictures of the banks' presidents or premises instead of the sovereign, and were fully accepted as a substitute for legal tender by everyone as long as the issuing bank was known to be able to exchange them, on demand, for legal tender. Since 1935 these private bank notes (of which a very few are still in existence) and Dominion bills have been replaced by today's Bank of Canada bills. All they will get you is more Bank of Canada bills!

[3] If a dictator insisted on supplementing the paper currency with coins whose metallic value equaled or came near their face values, he would show what an amateur he was at finance. Thus, as soon as platinum or silver rose enough in price on the auction markets of the world, the dictator would find his coins were being melted down for their metallic content for teeth, electronics, jewels, and photography. It is because coins and currency are made of cheap materials that they avoid this fate. Do facts bear out this theory? They do. When the price of silver rose in 1963 most governments had to stop using silver in coins; the Canadian mint stopped using silver in 1968. To keep new coins from being melted down and hoarded, they substituted cheaper cupronickel materials.

Today, and for many decades, all Canadian currency and coinage has been essentially "fiat" money. It is money because it is decreed to be so, and because we all accept it. Metallic backing has no real meaning any more (except, as will be seen later, when it serves to limit the total supply of fiat money).

Many middle-aged people today can remember from their childhood receiving five- or ten-dollar gold pieces for their birthdays. Because most of these pieces have been called in, they are now valuable for their weight in gold, or for their scarcity as coinage, whichever is greater. The U.S. buying price for gold, which has dominated world values since World War I, jumped from $21 to $35 per ounce in 1933-4, as part of the Roosevelt anti-depression program. In many places (especially in the United States) the holding of gold coins has become illegal, to support the calling-in of coins by the Treasury. However, Canada, with enough other places to make a world market, still permits dealing in and owning of coins and bullion bars. But few people bother: a country's paper money is accepted in all its regions. Only when people fear that the *international* value of paper money is in peril, do they rush to trade it for gold or a preferred currency.[4]

From the standpoint of understanding the nature of money, it is perhaps simpler that gold certificates and coins no longer exist. The modern student need not be misled, as were earlier generations of students, by some mystical belief that "gold backing" is what gives money its value. Certainly gold, as such, has little to do with the problem. In the late 1960s most experts ridiculed the claim that "money has more value if it can be exchanged into gold," asserting that without its monetary uses metallic gold would fall in price.[5] They argued that industrial gold, dental inlays, and wedding rings would be cheaper, and gold miners poorer, when the United States stopped guaranteeing the gold price.[6] By 1970, however, experts were less sure: the 1968 runs on the London gold

---

[4] As part of the gold-control system, all gold mined in Canada must be shipped to the Royal Canadian Mint for refining into bullion. The bullion is either bought by the Mint or turned back to those companies licensed to deal in bars. In recent years about 3.5 million troy ounces, in 400-ounce and one-kilo (32-ounce) bars, have been produced annually.

[5] That gold affects prices only through its ability to *limit or to expand the volume of paper money and total spending* was overlooked by foolish European chancellors of the exchequer who, after World War I, tried to stop inflation by *accumulating* new gold reserves through the purchase of gold on the open market with newly *printed* money! Of course, the effect was just the opposite. Only after they had reversed the process and used their gold to buy up and burn outstanding paper money did they enjoy any success.

[6] The Canadian gold industry is an *enigma* anyway. The *value* of gold bullion is more or less fixed at around $35 (U.S.) to the troy ounce, but the *cost* of mining has risen so much with inflation that it is not worth recovering gold ore from most Canadian properties. To help mining communities phase out, Canada has given cost-aid subsidies, by a complicated formula, since 1948. Aided mines have recently (1969) been getting about $11 per ounce. Miners used to be keen to see the U.S. price freed, but they now need a complete revaluation of the U.S. official price to get above $45 per ounce, the highest cost of production the scheme (under the Emergency Gold Mining Assistance Act) will support. Freeing the Canadian dollar in 1970 cost the few unsubsidized mines about $2 per ounce.

market, following some nervousness about holding U.S. dollars or British pounds, did reveal a *non-monetary* gold demand strong enough to pull the price above $35 (U.S.) to the ounce even when the U.S. guarantee to buy private gold at that price was revoked. This variation in view, of course, is not about basic principles. It simply reflects the different experts' slow acquisition of knowledge about supply and demand in what is now gradually becoming a competitive world gold market.

The sensible reason why conservatives today want to go back to gold-coin money is not that they think gold is needed to give money its value. Rather, they know that governmental actions can today strongly affect the value of money, and they are convinced that *governments cannot be trusted to refrain from abusing this power*; so they favor taking away from the U.S. government its power in these matters and prefer to put their trust in the vicissitudes of mine discoveries rather than in the actions of fallible or allegedly corrupt representative governments.

As we shall see in subsequent chapters and in the international discussions of Part Five, gold still does have a limited role to play in financial international transactions and in determining the world-wide trends of reserves held by the various central banks. Herein lies its true role in twentieth-century economics.

> Limitation in the supply of money is the necessary condition if it is to have value. If currency is so unlimited in amount as to become practically a free good, people would have so much of it to spend as to bid up all prices, wages, and incomes sky-high. That is why constitutional powers over money and banking are never given to private groups but are always vested in government.

BANK DEPOSITS   There is also a third category of what economists call money. This involves so-called "demand deposits"—made up of bank deposits subject to chequing on demand.

If I have $1,000 in my chequing account at the Bank of Montreal, that deposit can be regarded as money. Why? Because I can pay for purchases with cheques drawn on it. The deposit is like any other medium of exchange, and being payable on demand, it serves as a *"standard of value,"* or *"unit of account,"* in the same sense as $1,000 worth of silver quarters; i.e., both the deposit and the quarters are convertible into standard money or cash at fixed terms, dollar for dollar and penny for penny.

> Possessing the essential properties of money, bank demand deposits might just as well be counted as money. And they are.[7]

Actually, as was noted in the discussion of money in Chapter 3, bank money is quantitatively more important than currency because most transactions are made by cheque. The convenience of cheques for mailing, for paying the exact sum of money due, for providing a receipt in the form of the canceled

---

[7] My balance on deposit in the bank is usually called money—not the cheques I write.

Chartered bank deposits form over two-thirds of our money supply:

MONEY SUPPLY OF CANADA (millions of dollars)

KINDS OF MONEY	1963 (March)	1967 (March)	1970 (estimated)
Coins	$ 175	$ 295	$ 430
Paper Currency	1,720	2,160	2,700
Bank Deposits:			
Demand	3,830	5,145	5,600
Personal Savings	8,140	10,560	15,200
TOTAL M_1	$13,865	$18,160	$23,930
Other Deposits:			
Bank non-personal, notice and term deposits	$ 1,156	$ 2,824	$ 3,600
Deposits in credit unions, mortgage and trust companies, Quebec savings banks, government institutions, and post offices	2,394	3,661	4,500
TOTAL M_2	$17,415	$26,645	$32,030
General public's holdings of federal bills, bonds, and savings bonds	$13,000	$13,000	$14,000
TOTAL "near-money" and "money"	$30,415	$39,645	$46,030

TABLE 14-1. If to coinage, currency, and chequable bank deposits, we also add not only bank time and term deposits but also various types of savings-institution deposits, we get a broader and more rapidly growing concept of money—often called M_2, in contrast with M_1. (Canadian personal savings deposits actually belong to both categories, but are all included here with M_1.) (Source: Bank of Canada *Statistical Summary*.)

cheque voucher, for protecting against loss when stolen or misplaced (while un-endorsed or, for that matter, endorsed)—all these advantages are obvious and explain the widespread use of bank money.

Table 14-1 illustrates the quantitative importance of the three kinds of money: coin, currency, and demand deposits. The total of these is called M_1, money as narrowly defined.

■ LIQUID ASSETS, OR "NEAR-MONEY"

Along with the total of money M_1, Table 14-1 also shows the total of money broadly defined, M_2. What is meant by this broader concept? Different econom-ists define the term differently. Table 14-1 includes in money the total interest-bearing savings and time deposits which any person could quickly cash in, but excludes the total of government bonds which anyone could present for redemp-tion or sell for cash in the open market.[8]

[8] Some Canadian chartered-bank personal-savings deposits (unlike those in the United States) are widely chequable and withdrawable although they are legally subject to notice. So most Canadian economists include them in M_1, rather than merely in M_2.

Money and prices wind upward:

Fig. 14-2. Total money supply has risen faster than the consumer price level. But important turning points have similar timing. (Source: Urquhart and Buckley, *Historical Statistics of Canada*, **Cambridge University Press, 1965; Bank of Canada** *Statistical Supplement*.)

Suppose you have $10,000 on demand deposit and your brother has $5,000 on demand deposit plus $5,000 in a credit union; will your spending habits be very different? Probably not, and that is why M_2 is important. Time and savings deposits in chartered banks and "near banks" have gained mightily on demand deposits in recent decades.

Because it is difficult to draw a hard-and-fast line at any point in the chain of things that do have a direct bearing on spending, the exact definition of M, the money supply, is partly a matter of taste rather than of scientific necessity.

A century ago, demand deposits would not have been included in M. Today all economists would include demand deposits, since even the most stubborn adherent of the old narrow concept has to admit that the existence of chequing accounts does economize on the use of currency and thus acts much like an increase in the effective amount of currency. And most Canadian economists would argue along the same lines for inclusion of personal interest-bearing bank savings deposits in the measurement of the money supply.[9]

Economists are not all agreed on nomenclature in this field. Many would go so far as to append to M_1 and M_2 a further category of "liquid" assets (those that are easy to trade or redeem at fixed or predictable prices) called "near-money."[10] In the total, they would now include government bonds that anyone can present for redemption or sell at some price (perhaps not predictable long in advance). These near-money items have many of the properties of money. True, you don't pay your monthly expenses directly with bonds, and so we hesitate to call such items "money." Still, the fact that you have an asset so easy to cash means that your current spending habits are probably affected in much the same way as they would be if you owned a larger bank deposit instead of government bonds.

For the most part, this book will follow the most common practice and define the total money supply thus:

M is the sum of coin and currency in circulation outside the banks, plus *chequable* demand and personal time and savings deposits (after various routine adjustments are made in this magnitude). Along with this narrow definition of *M* (which we may call M_1), it is sometimes useful to work with a broader definition (called M_2) which includes time and savings deposits in addition to coin, currency, and demand deposits.

Figure 14-2 shows that the part of the money supply defined as M_1 is now ten times as great as it was just before World War II. For a further comparison of the growth of M_1, of M_2, and of price levels, examine Fig. 14-2.

---

[9] Some scholars, in attempting to include government bonds in money, prefer to give them some fractional weight and add them into a total called "effective" money supply, M_3.

[10] It would not be illogical to subtract out from people's liquid assets their current liabilities (charge accounts, installment loans, etc.). Along with income, perhaps their resulting "net worth" would be the single most important determinant of their spending.

■ THE DEMAND FOR MONEY

What are the functions of money? Here are some old and new ones:

1. Money is a *medium of exchange* enabling us to transact our national income and product without recourse to hopelessly inefficient barter.

2. Money is the *unit of account* in which we express prices for current transactions, and also for future or deferred transactions (such as when I borrow $1,000 today and agree to pay back $1,200 three years from now).

3. Money is a safe *way of holding* at least part of one's *wealth*—safe against the ups and downs inherent in stocks, land, homes, and bonds. When all these are going down in price, the canny hoarder of money is the most successful speculator in the community. (When prices rise, however, many holders suffer.)

4. Money holding is a necessary *precaution* against having a sudden expense occur or an unexpected delay in a receipt due from someone else. Similarly, the "liquidity" of money enables one to take advantage of a bargain in goods or in securities that might suddenly come up.

All these functions are worth paying for. And we each do incur a cost in holding a coin, a bill, or a demand deposit—namely, *the sacrificed interest and profit yield* that might be obtained from other assets.

> Massey Ferguson works just as hard to keep down its unnecessary cash as it does to keep down its unnecessary steel inventory and wastage. The business manager of a famous cartoonist was aghast to find that he had kept $120,000 idle in a demand deposit, earning no interest for years, merely because he never read his mail!

It is clear from the above that there are two main motives for *holding* money (for remaining "liquid"): (1) for the convenience of ordinary *transactions* needed at each level of income, and (2) to fill a prudent *precautionary* need arising from the uncertainties of safety and return from other forms of wealth, and the uncertainties of timing of expense outpayments and receipt inpayments.

At the turn of the century Alfred Marshall in Cambridge, England, and Irving Fisher in Yale summarized the factors determining the amount of money demanded thus:

> *Transaction and Precautionary Demands:* The higher their annual incomes, the more dollars of business people will want to transact: with various allowances for economies of scale, men hold M at any time about in proportion to their *income* rate per year or month. This *transaction demand* for money will be shifted downward a little when the interest rates offered on good bonds, savings deposits, and other close money substitutes rise. At higher interest you will economize on your cash balance, making each dollar turn over more rapidly.
>
> Men also hold M as a precautionary store of wealth, not wanting to put all their eggs in the basket of risky assets and wanting to be prepared for bargains or sudden expenses. This *precautionary* (or "asset") *demand*

for money will be much affected by factors other than income: total wealth; level of sacrificed interest and profit yields; optimism, pessimism, and plain uncertainty about the future; expected changes in prices of goods and assets and expected changes in interest rates—all the speculative elements that any investments depend on.

The elements in the second paragraph of this summary are in Marshall and Fisher, but were not much emphasized until the 1930s, when Keynes and practical bankers noted that transaction demand could not account for massive changes in cash holdings. Keynes dealt with both types of asset demand as people's "liquidity preference." Keynesian liquidity preference will be encountered next in Chapter 17, page 408.

Another school of thought, both pre-1930 and much more recent, emphasizes the M-and-income link by using the concept of "velocity of circulation of money," and to this we now turn.

■ VELOCITY OF CIRCULATION OF MONEY

It is a historical fact that as dollar NNP has grown, so has M. With M today six times as large as it was before World War II, dollar NNP is even more than six times as large as its earlier figure. Nor is this merely history. If NNP grows from its 1970 level of almost 80 billion dollars to reach 160 billion dollars in ten years, the betting odds are that M will also be nearly double its present amount then—a fair bet even before we know whether changes in M will be the "cause" of changes in NNP or the "effect" of them.

Why should there be any connection? M is a stock magnitude, something you can measure at an instant of time like any other balance-sheet asset. NNP is a flow of dollar income *per year*, something that you can measure only from income statements that refer to the passage of time between two dates.

A new concept can be introduced to describe the Fisher-Marshall ratios between two such different magnitudes: it is called the "velocity of circulation of money" per year and is written as V.

> *Definition of velocity:* The rate at which the stock of money is turning over per year to consummate income transactions is called the velocity of circulation of money (or more exactly, the *income* velocity).

If the stock of money is turning over very slowly, so that its rate of dollar income spending per year is low, V will be low. If people hold less money at each instant of time relative to the rate of NNP flow [(price of apples $\times$ apples) + (price of oranges $\times$ oranges) + ...], then V will be high.

The size of V will tend to rise with interest rates. Also, V can change over time with changes in financial institutions, habits, attitudes, expectations, and relative distributions of M among different kinds of institutions and income classes; but these changes in V need not be abrupt, volatile, or completely unpredictable.

In every case, this formal definition[11] of the velocity of circulation of money holds:

$$V \equiv \frac{\text{NNP}}{M} \equiv \frac{p_1 q_1 + p_2 q_2 + \ldots}{M} \equiv \frac{\text{sum } pq}{M} \equiv \frac{PQ}{M}$$

Here P stands for the average price level and goes up and down with an index of the price level, while Q stands for real (as distinct from current dollar) national product and has to be computed statistically by the previously mentioned process of "deflating" NNP with a price index.

Here is a helpful example. Table 14-1 shows that by late 1970 M_1 was about 25 billion dollars. NNP was then about 80 billion dollars per year. So 80 divided by 25 gives us an income velocity of about 3.2 per year. In view of the "near-money" quality of savings, suppose we decided that only half of personal savings deposits and the like should be defined to be part of M_1. M_1 would then be almost 18; so, with NNP of 80 billion dollars, V would be about 4.4 income velocity each year. (This rough figure happens to be close to the U.S. figure of recent years, 4.6.) This expression means that each unit of money was used for NNP transactions almost 4½ times a year; or putting this in an equivalent way, at any one time during the year people were holding money that amounted to over 11 weeks' average income.[12]

■ THE QUANTITY EQUATION OF EXCHANGE: AN IDENTITY

After economists have invented the concept of velocity of circulation of money, they can rearrange its formal definition to get a new identity called the "quantity equation of exchange":

$$MV \equiv PQ$$

This comes merely from shifting M from the denominator of our last definition's right-hand side over the numerator of the other side. By definition of V, the left-hand side in this new equation is identically equal to NNP, the rate of current national income or product per year. But the right-hand side, by virtue of what we have just defined P and Q to be, also is definitionally the same thing as NNP.

> EXAMPLE: If there were only a single good in the NNP, a billion baskets of bread selling at a price of $5 each, then NNP $\equiv PQ = 5$ billion dollars per year; when there is more than one commodity, we sum all such $p \times q$ products; and if all the

---

[11] More advanced discussions show that because NNP contains $(E - M)$ net exports, it is a less appropriate numerator for the definition of V than $C + I + G + (M - E)$. But NNP will serve as a rough approximation.

[12] In looking at the statements of particular banks, one does not know whether the "turnover" in chequable accounts is for NNP final transactions or for non-NNP transactions like transfers and intermediate goods. Such turnover figures tell us how often a dollar turns over in *all kinds* of transaction each year. They are much larger than income velocities. In 1963, current accounts in Canada turned over 68 times a year; savings accounts 1½ times. With its stock exchange, New York City turns its deposits over 140 times a year; but deposits in other U.S. cities turn over only 47 times.

q's stayed unchanged and all their p's doubled, then the average price level as denoted by P would double, naturally giving us a 10- rather than 5-billion-dollar NNP.[13]

All the definitional equations have been written with the three-bar identity symbol rather than with the more common two-bar equality symbol. This is to drive home the fact that they are what logicians call a "tautology"—statements which by themselves tell us nothing about reality but which would hold true by definition even if Canada reverted to barter or if its M halved while its NNP grew tenfold. Although it is important to remember that the equation of exchange is such a tautology, it is not legitimate to infer from this fact that it must thereby be useless. It may, or may not, be a useful way of separating out for individual analysis the factors apt to lead to empirical relations which do best describe actual economic life. Subsequent chapters will show that careful description of income determination by $C + I + G$ schedules and how they are interrelated by changes in banking policy can also be expressed in terms of the magnitudes in the equation of exchange, and vice versa.

■ THE QUANTITY THEORY OF MONEY AND PRICES: A HYPOTHESIS

THE CRUDE QUANTITY THEORY   If 1970 M is four times 1939 M, then an adherent of what can be called the "crude quantity theory of money and prices" would have to predict that the 1970 price level P should be almost exactly four times 1939 P. The fact that prices have only *doubled* in that period would be a refutation of this crude notion that the price level moves in direct proportion to the money supply.

> Arithmetically, the crude quantity theory might be written $P = kM$, where k is a positive proportionality constant that depends on units used; thus, if P and M are measured by index numbers which were 100 in the same base year, k could be replaced by 1.0 or omitted. Note that this is not intended to be an irrefutable definitional identity, but rather a useful empirical relationship about k's constancy.

The idea behind the crude quantity theory is simple. If the government effects a thousandfold increase in M, then one can predict that there will be a galloping inflation in which P rises a thousandfold. Or more cautiously, at least somewhere between five-hundredfold and two-thousandfold. Crude as this notion is, there is some usefulness to it. Thus when the head of the German central bank denied that its printing truckloads of currency had anything to do with the 1920-23 trillionfold increase in prices, his statement was nonsensical. If he had said, "I am just a civil servant, forced, by the clamor of the populace in a defeated nation with grave external and internal disorganization, to take part in an upward race between P and M"—if he had said this, we could feel

---

[13] Some find the following "explanation" of this necessary equality helpful. Every income transaction involves sale receipts equal to $p \times q$, which leads to the PQ totals on the right. But it is M that is used in such transactions. How much in a year? The stock M times its average velocity per year. Thus, value equals value, and the two sides must be the same.

sorry for him. But who can seriously deny the elementary theory that a vastly larger bidding of German marks for a limited supply of goods must have sent prices expressed in marks skyward?

Money differs basically from ordinary goods like wheat or steel. We want wheaten bread for its own sake. We want money only for the work it does in buying us wheat or steel. If in 1923, all German prices are a trillion times what they were in 1920, it is natural to want about a trillion times as much M as in 1920. Therein lies the valid case of the crude quantity theory. But we must be wary of extrapolating it to real-life cases where all P's have not changed in the same balanced proportions.

> Rudimentary as it is, then, the crude quantity theory linking P directly to M is useful to describe periods of hyperinflation and various long-term trends in prices, such as those in Spain and Europe after New World gold was discovered.

Since galloping inflation can put an intolerable strain on a democratic society, it is well to preach the crude quantity theory in season and out of season —not because in its crudest form it is in season very often, but because it is so urgently needed in those disorganized times when its message is in season.

A SOPHISTICATED QUANTITY THEORY   Few people still subscribe to the crude quantity theory. Yet we should not use its inadequacies to damn the whole idea that money can have important effects on macroeconomic magnitudes such as investment, employment, production, and prices.

The next few chapters will show how *monetary policy* does have an important influence on the *total of spending*—on the $C + I + G$ intersections of GNP. This analysis can be translated quite easily into the language of V and M, even though it was not fashionable to do so a couple of decades back. Since there has been something of a revival of interest in the quantity theory fostered in recent years by a number of competent economists, it is worth taking an eclectic approach here and reviewing the fundaments of a sophisticated quantity-theory approach, leaving until later a more extensive reconciliation of the various approaches.

The proof of the pudding is in the eating, and the test of all theories is their correspondence with the facts. Figure 14-2 shows that consumer prices and the supply of money have both generally grown, but by no means in perfect concordance.

Economists such as Chicago's Milton Friedman are not surprised to find M growing sixfold while P merely doubles; for they believe that only in time periods when real output remains roughly the same—say, at a high-employment level—can one expect M and P to be directly related. They expect M and GNP (or PQ) to be related. This belief is based upon the hypothesis that the velocity of circulation V can be predicted to be reasonably constant, or if not constant, at least subject to predictable changes.

While it is a fact that NNP has climbed somewhat faster than M since 1939, this rise in velocity has been a gradual one and perhaps one that might have been expected from the fact that 1939 was still a depressed year and still a time of very low interest rates and abnormally low V.

Historically, one observes that V has exhibited a downward trend since 1870, moving down somewhat as real income has grown. The short-run cyclical swings in V are quite the opposite: when production and real incomes have gone up, V has tended also to have a short-run rise; when output has fallen in the short run, V has fallen too.

A sophisticated quantity theorist cannot be accused of believing that V is a fundamental constant of nature. What he does believe is that controlling the behavior of M *will help much* to control NNP, for the reason that the resulting changes in V will either be so small or so predictable as to make one confident that dollar NNP will still move *in the same direction as M.* Qualitatively, this is in agreement with almost any modern theory of income determination, and the only possible argument concerns the confidence with which one can predict the quantitative potency of effects on NNP of changes in M, in comparison with other stimuli, such as fiscal policy and external investment swings.[14]

So, from all of the points of view, the discussions in the ensuing chapters—how chartered banks can create demand-deposit M as the Bank of Canada authorities affect their reserve positions, how a central bank such as the Bank of Canada itself operates, how monetary policy fits with income determination and with stabilizing fiscal policies—are of tremendous importance. Chapter 17, in particular, deals further with the sophisticated quantity theory approach.

[14] There is general agreement, too, that whenever the dollar NNP gets pushed too high, there will be a strong tendency for P to rise. Also there is some agreement that inflexibilities in our mixed economy can keep wages and prices up in slack times; if so, *employment* and *production* will drop with the total of dollar NNP rather than having the drop in dollar PQ simply transmit its effects to lower wages and lower prices. There is still controversy concerning the importance of a *cost-push* mechanism making for a price creep, as against inflationary effects of *excess dollar demand* alone. Later we shall attempt to appraise the measure of truth in both views. [It may be mentioned here that the *crude* quantity theory would be correct, if in the following rearrangement of the tautological equation of exchange $P \equiv (V/Q)M$, the expression in parentheses were a strict constant. Thus, if both V and Q changed little, or if their changes were always largely self-canceling, the crude theory would be correct. But once scholars agree that V may change appreciably when the economy goes from a 1929 high-interest prosperity to a 1939 low-interest depression, and that Q may fall from a full-employment 1929 level to a level that is far below full employment in some later year, they realize that a more sophisticated theory of money, production, interest rates and prices must be studied. A rather crude form of rejection of the significance of M was provided by the Radcliffe Committee Report published in 1959 by the British government. After arguing (correctly) that PQ is affected by over-all "liquidity" and bears no *simple* proportionality to M, it incorrectly inferred that induced changes in V are as likely as not to offset fully any contrived changes in M. The presumption in *all* modern theories (like that implied in Canada's 1964 *Report on Banking and Finance*) is that a continued rise in M *will* definitely tend to expand PQ. Note the logical fallacy, or *non sequitur*, in Radcliffe's argument: " 'Money alone matters' is false; *ergo*, 'money doesn't matter.' "]

SUMMARY

A. PRICES AND THE MONEY SUPPLY

■ 1 It is unrealistic to expect that expansions in investment and other spending will have effects solely on employment and output. Changes in price levels must be expected as well. The effects and causes of a general rise in prices and wages (i.e., inflation) and a general fall in prices (ie., deflation) are vital.

■ 2 Historically, prices have shown their greatest swings in times of war. But in this century the trend in prices seems to have been more of a one-way climb: the absence of a drop in prices after World War II is perhaps a sign that modern mixed economies are no longer likely to tolerate lengthy periods of unemployment, soft business conditions, and falling prices.

■ 3 Inflations and deflations are never of the balanced type in which all prices and wages move in the same percentage relation, with no one helped and no one hurt by the process. In the past, inflations have typically favored debtors, profit seekers, and risk-taking speculators. Unseen inflation has hurt creditors, fixed-income classes, pensioners, and conservative and timid investors. The old rather than the young are its prime victims.

■ 4 Aside from redistributional effects of inflation out of a fixed level of production, mild inflations like those found throughout most of capitalism's history have been regarded as being a little more likely to keep employment high and business brisk than mild deflations do. But the cause of the inflation may make a difference, and the threat that a mild creep of prices could break into a trot or gallop shows that complacency about price rises could be harmful to those who cannot adjust.

 If the processes were *foreseen* and steady, there would not be much difference among the three possible long-term patterns that various economists favor: (1) steady prices, with money and real wages rising with productivity; (2) gently rising prices, with money wages rising even faster than real wages and productivity; (3) slowly falling prices, with money wages constant and real wages rising as every consumer's dollar buys more and more goods—a pattern perhaps not feasible in rigid mixed economies.

■ 5 In addition to coins, currency, demand deposits, and chequable personal savings deposits—whose sum is the money supply M_1—there are also very important near-money or liquid-asset items: time or savings deposits (which pay interest and are *de facto* withdrawable at short notice, and which many economists include in a broad definition of money, M_2), "near-money" such as government bonds (which anyone can quickly liquidate into cash, at a price that depends on market forces at the time). However defined, M has increased mightily over the decades.

B. THE DEMAND FOR MONEY AND THE QUANTITY THEORY

■ 6 The demand for money consists of a *transactions* demand primarily related to income, and a *precautionary* (or asset) demand much dependent on interest and profit rates, wealth, volatile expectations, risk aversion, and speculative price expectations. The sum of these two demands was called, by Keynes, "liquidity preference."

■ 7 The (income) velocity of circulation of money is defined as the ratio of dollar NNP to M. While V is definitely not a constant, its movements are subject to some regularity and predictability; and from its *definition*

$$V \equiv \frac{\text{NNP}}{M} \equiv \frac{PQ}{M}$$

comes the quantity-theory-of-exchange *identity*

$$MV \equiv PQ$$

■ 8 The crude quantity *theory* of money and prices regarded P as almost strictly proportional to M. Useful as this view is in hyperinflation and for certain long-term trends, few would today uphold it in this crude form. It is generally agreed that action by the government and banks to affect the supply of money, its availability to investor borrowers, and the interest cost of such borrowings can have important effects on the total of *consumption* + *investment* + *(net exports)* spending, and thus on prices and wage levels. Subscribers to a sophisticated quantity theory and national-income theorists will both attach importance to the next chapters on banking and fiscal policy. Chapter 17 resumes discussion of the sophisticated quantity theory.

QUESTIONS FOR DISCUSSION

1. If sure of inflation ahead, what might you do to protect yourself? List some of the happenings that accompany galloping and mild inflation.

2. Explain what is meant by "near-money" and how it got its name.

3. If we printed and spent 10 billion dollars in new Bank of Canada notes, what do you think would happen to prices? Is there some truth, then, to the crude quantity theory? Differentiate between the crude and sophisticated quantity theorists in terms of how they regard $MV \equiv PQ$.

4. Show that the Marshall-Fisher-Keynes summary implies nonconstant V.

5. Review your understanding of the following concepts:

fiat money	fractional coins, token money
sticky price levels	transactions demand
real rate of return	precautionary demand
inflation, hyperinflation	liquidity preference
deflation and technological	demand versus time deposits
cost-price reduction	M_1, M_2, near-money
redistribution and employment	velocity definition
effects of price-level trends	equation of exchange, $MV \equiv PQ$
real versus money wage	crude quantity theory, $P = kM$

15

THE CHARTERED BANKS
AND DEPOSIT CREATION

"Is it deposited?" I asked in a hollow, vibrating voice.
"It is," said the accountant.
"Then I want to draw a cheque ..." STEPHEN LEACOCK, My Financial Career

The importance of bank deposits as part of the community's money supply has been established. This chapter continues with two distinct topics. First, we examine briefly the important facts and functionings of the modern banking system, showing how the present-day commercial bank gradually began to keep only "fractional cash reserves" against its deposits. Second, we see just how the banking system "manufactures" banking deposits—the most important component of our money supply.

A. NATURE AND FUNCTIONING OF THE MODERN BANKING SYSTEM

■ THE PRESENT STATUS OF BANKING

Like most of the Western world, Canada has a *branch* banking system of large banks chartered by Parliament. (Since 1960, three new companies have gone through the process of applying to Parliament for Acts to become "chartered banks," and two have been successful.) They have among them 5,000 branches in Canada and 150 branches abroad, most of them in the West Indies.

This provides about one branch for every thousand families, a striking contrast to the United States where 13,400 independent *unit* banks, with their (relatively few) branches, provide one main office or branch for every three thousand U.S. families. The Canadian, British, and other banks are for all purposes under national government supervision, but about half the U.S. banks (the smaller banks) are for most purposes supervised by state governments. Canadians notice three results of their system in contrast to the American: (1) there are, obviously, many more offices giving full banking services; (2) the nine banks are more *concentrated*, offering almost identical services at almost identical prices, and maintaining through their head offices personal contact with one another and with officers of the Bank of Canada; and (3) the rate of bank failure is very low.[1]

A primary economic function of commercial banks is *to hold demand and personal savings deposits and honor cheques drawn upon them*—in short to provide the economy with the largest component of the money supply and the payments system itself.

A second important function is to lend money to merchants, homeowners, farmers, and industrialists.

Banks have a variety of competitors in the performance of these functions, such as trust and mortgage companies; all are able to make loans and to accept notice, or *savings*, deposits. In some countries, such as the United States, bank savings deposits cannot be withdrawn without notice, sometimes as long as 30 days. In Canada, the practice has been that personal savings deposits can be withdrawn immediately, upon presentation of a cheque. For all practical purposes, therefore, personal savings deposits function in the same way as *demand* deposits; both are chequable and hence "spendable," as explained in Chapter 14, footnote 8. Further, trust and mortgage company savings deposits, in Canada, are becoming increasingly chequable.

The chartered banks are by no means, therefore, our only "banking institutions." However, they do hold the vast bulk of both demand and personal savings deposits in Canada, thus providing most of the "bank money" that can be conveniently used as a medium of exchange. Therein lies their primary economic importance.

The second and related function of banks is their credit function: they help manufacture short-term credit for businesses and families; they make long-term mortgage loans; and (despite an older view that banks should only lend seasonally) they increasingly provide intermediate-term credit through "term loans" of more than a year's duration.

◼ CANADA'S CENTRAL BANK: THE BANK OF CANADA

Unlike Britain whose Bank of England was founded in 1694, and the United States where the Federal Reserve system was set up in 1913, Canada got along until the mid-1930s without a central bank. The Department of Finance acted rather like a central bank in administering a series of "Finance Acts." These em-

---

[1] The last failure when customers lost some of their deposits was that of the Home Bank in 1923. On other occasions, before and since then, banks experiencing losses have been aided, by merger or otherwise by the stronger banks. U.S. banks frequently failed until the 1930s: 659 in prosperous 1929 alone! But the power of each of the relatively large Canadian banks to spread its risks and losses over large reserves is now duplicated by the insurance of most American depositors with the Federal Deposit Insurance Corporation (FDIC), which fully covers each deposit up to $10,000. In 1967 the Canadian Deposit Insurance Corporation was created to provide a similar service for Canadian banks *and* near-banks.

powered the Department to buy government bonds from the banks with new Dominion Notes, under certain circumstances: in other words, to expand the money supply. This power was widely used in World War I.

But by 1934 the Great Depression's unemployment had convinced many persons that a discretionary (nonautomatic) mechanism was needed, to prevent the *contraction of bank deposits during deflationary periods*. The public was not sure what a central bank could do against a depression; many radicals overrated its potentialities to "reflate" the country out of low prices and incomes; but everyone felt that the near-automatic working of the banking system was not good enough.[2]

Following the advice of a Royal Commission under Lord Macmillan, the government set up a "private" central bank in 1934, with a government-appointed Governor and Deputy. This was partly a concession to the principle of private enterprise, but also partly a realization of the theory that in "preserving orderly conditions" in the money markets, and in attempting to control P by controlling M, central banks ought to have some independence from political pressures in Ottawa. This theory was not tested until the 1950s, for in 1938 the Bank of Canada was made a Crown corporation.

The structure of the Bank of Canada today is simple. At the top are twelve Directors, the Deputy Minister of Finance (without a vote), the Deputy Governor, and the Governor. The last two, who are appointed by the Directors, actually run the Bank, and hold office for eight years at a time. (The first Governor, Graham Towers, had two terms. J. M. Coyne had one. The present Governor, Louis Rasminsky, took office in 1961.) The Board of Directors meets only eight times a year; but an Executive Council (the Governor, Deputy, Deputy Minister of Finance, and only one Director) acts for the Board and has all its powers. Even a superficial examination of the Bank's constitution, therefore, suggests that the Governor with his officers and the government will have to make most decisions without the help of the scattered Board members.

The Bank has a staff of about 800, of whom over 200 are in nine "regional agencies" in the main cities. The rest are in Ottawa, many of them performing fiscal and financial functions for the government. But in the following paragraphs, we refer only to those functions which are *essentially* those of a central bank: not only to coordinate and control the chartered banks, but also to help *regulate the nation's money supply and credit conditions*.

To whom is the Bank responsible? In the long run, it must be the government: the government has a vote in the appointment of the Governor and

---

[2] However, unlike critics in other countries, Canadian advocates of a central bank could not say that Canada was, in the 1920s, tied to the international gold standard. In some countries, the outflow of gold to other countries meant that the losing economies would have to reduce their money supply in an even greater proportion. The Finance Acts, however, allowed the Department of Finance to maintain the supply of Dominion Notes (the reserves for the structure of bank money) and even to expand this supply, in periods when gold was flowing out of the country. A contraction of the money supply did take place, but not because there was no official mechanism to allow the banks to maintain their customers' deposits.

Deputy Governor; the Deputy Minister of Finance sits (without vote) on both the Board and the Executive; and the Cabinet can veto any decision of the Executive. But most of these powers take time to exercise, and the veto power must obviously be used in moderation if the Governor and Executive Committee are to have any incentive to take independent responsibility for actions within their jurisdiction.

Most of Graham Towers' term was during the Depression and the war when there was obviously no scope for independent Bank behavior. But during James Coyne's term it was clear that the government did not disapprove of the measure of independence revealed by Bank actions, until a fairly direct contradiction of aims and of means was revealed in 1959 and 1960. An unpleasant public dispute then arose, and Mr. Coyne was replaced eventually by Mr. Rasminsky. The latter, on assuming office in 1961, said:

> I do not suggest a precise formula but have in mind two main principles to be established: (1) in the ordinary course of events, the Bank has the responsibility for monetary policy; and (2) if the Government disapproves of the monetary policy being carried out by the Bank, it has the right and the responsibility to direct the Bank as to the policy which the Bank is to carry out.

There the matter rests. No open disagreement between the Bank and the government has since been mentioned. Being in the last analysis subservient to the Cabinet, the Bank now takes its place alongside the formerly-independent Bank of England, which has a right to protest publicly but must coordinate its policies with those of the government. The present status of the Federal Reserve Board in the United States is less clear. Not only has it claimed stronger allegiance to Congress than to the Executive (president), but in the absence of clear directives from Congress, it has acted, occasionally, very much like an independent arm of government. Since the middle 1950s, however, cooperation has prevailed with the executive branch (the Treasury, White House, and Council of Economic Advisers) and conflict has been minor. With the American system of checks and balances among branches of government, such differences are perhaps inevitable and healthy; but it is widely felt today that Canada's and Britain's parliamentary system cannot tolerate a central bank if it is more than a "semi-detached" wing of the national government.

■ BANKING AS A BUSINESS

Banking is a business much like any other business. The chartered bank is a relatively simple business concern. A bank provides certain services for its customers (depositors and borrowers) and in return receives payments from them in one form or another. It tries to earn a profit for its stock owners.

A chartered bank's balance sheet shows certain assets, certain liabilities, and certain capital ownership. Except for minor rearrangements, the bank's published balance sheet looks, on the whole, much like the balance sheet of any other business, and rather simpler than most.

A special feature of the balance sheet shown in Table 15-1 is that such a large portion of the banks' liabilities are subject to chequing: all demand and

Deposits are important bank liabilities:

CONSOLIDATED BALANCE SHEET OF ALL CHARTERED BANKS, SPRING, 1970 (millions of dollars)			
ASSETS		**LIABILITIES AND NET WORTH**	
Reserves (cash and central bank deposits)	$ 1,700	Capital and shareholders' equity	$ 1,500
Loans	18,000	Demand deposits	7,000
Government of Canada bills and bonds	5,000	Personal savings deposits	15,000
Other securities	1,800	Other liabilities	8,000
Other assets	5,000		
Total	$31,500	Total	$31,500

TABLE 15-1. Reserves and deposits are the two key items of interest to our later economic analysis. Reserves are this large primarily because of legal requirements and not to provide against expected withdrawals. (Source: Bank of Canada Statistical Summary.)

many personal savings deposits can be withdrawn "on demand." It is as well to repeat: Canadian banks *may* require warning (notice) before depositors withdraw savings. They rarely do. And their vital reserves are, as we shall see, created and controlled by the central bank.

This fact is intriguing to the economist because he chooses to call such demand liabilities money; but to the banker it is a familiar condition which has long since been taken for granted. He knows well that, although it would be possible for every depositor suddenly to decide to withdraw all his money from the bank on the same day, the probability of this is quite remote. Each day, as some people withdraw their money, others normally make deposits tending to cancel the withdrawals. In a growing community new deposits more than offset the withdrawals from an average bank.

This, however, need not be strictly true at any one moment, in any one day, or in any one week. By chance alone the amount of withdrawals might exceed deposits for some period of time—just as a coin may land with heads turned up rather than tails for a consecutive number of tosses. For this reason, the banker would voluntarily keep a little cash handy in his vaults and perhaps a "reserve deposit" at the central bank. *Normally, the cash in the bank's own vaults and its deposits at the central bank*—as far as prudent protection from withdrawals is concerned and disregarding involuntary *legal requirements* to be mentioned soon—*need be only a small fraction of the bank's total deposits*; and the same mathematical law of large numbers that makes life insurance possible assures the banker that the larger his bank and more numerous his independent depositors, the smaller this fraction need be.

■ HOW BANKS DEVELOPED OUT OF GOLDSMITH ESTABLISHMENTS

All these facts are so much taken for granted by every modern banker that he is hardly aware of them; but it was not always so. According to superficial but useful history, commercial banking began with the ancient goldsmiths who developed the practice of storing people's gold and valuables for safekeeping. At first such establishments were simply like parcel checkrooms or warehouses. The depositor left his gold for safekeeping, was given a receipt, later presented that receipt, paid a small fee for safekeeping, and got back his gold.

Quite obviously, however, money is wanted only for what it will buy, not for its own sake. Money has an anonymous quality, so that one dollar is just as good as another, and one piece of pure gold as good as another. The goldsmiths soon found it more convenient *not* to have to tag the gold belonging to any one individual so as to be able to give to him upon request exactly the same piece of gold that he had left. Instead, the customer was quite willing to accept a receipt for an amount of gold or money *of a given value*, even though it was not the identical particle of matter that he actually left.

This "anonymity" is important. Therein lies a significant difference between today's bank and a checkroom or warehouse. If I check my bag at the airport and later see someone walking down the street with that same suitcase, I call my lawyer and sue the Department of Transport. If I mark my initials on a $10 bill, deposit it in my bank account, and later notice it in the hands of a stranger, I have no grievance against the bank management. They have only agreed to pay me on demand *any* $10 of legal tender.

But let us return to the goldsmith establishments, which are supposed to typify the first embryonic chartered banks. What would balance sheets of a typical establishment look like? Perhaps like Table 15-2.

We assume the company has long since dropped its activities as a smith and is principally occupied with storing people's money for safekeeping. Over past time, 1 million dollars has been deposited in its vaults, and this whole sum it holds as a cash asset. To balance this asset, there is a current deposit liability of the same amount. Actually, such a business need have no other assets (except the negligible value of its office space and vaults). But its owners could have—on the side, so to speak—subscribed $50,000 of capital to be lent out at interest or to buy securities such as stocks or bonds. On the asset side this amount is shown under the heading Loans and Investments; this is balanced on the right-hand side by a similar sum in the Capital and Surplus account.

The first goldsmith bank held 100 per cent cash against its demand deposits:

BALANCE SHEET OF EARLY BANK

ASSETS		LIABILITIES AND NET WORTH	
Cash	$1,000,000	Capital and surplus	$ 50,000
Loans and investments	50,000	Demand deposit liability	1,000,000
Total	$1,050,000	Total	$1,050,000

TABLE 15-2.

At this primitive stage, the bank would be of no particular interest to the economist. These investment and capital items have nothing to do with the bank's deposits; if all the bank's loans and investments should go sour and become worthless, the loss would fall completely on the stockholders who have agreed to take that risk in the hope of making a profit. Every depositor could still be paid off in full *out of the 100 per cent cash reserves* held by the bank. The bank would still cover its overhead and clerical expenses by making its customers pay storage charges. These would presumably vary with the length of time the customer left his money for safekeeping, the average amount of his money that required safekeeping, and the number of times the turnover of his account made a clerk wait on him and keep records.

Economists could ignore such a bank's operations. The bank money[3]—the demand deposits created jointly by the bank's willingness to accept a demand obligation and the customer's willingness to hold a deposit—would *just offset* the amount of ordinary money (currency or coin) placed in the bank's safe and withdrawn from active circulation. The process would be of no more interest than if the public decided to convert some dollar bills into an equivalent amount of dimes. One might then say that the banking system has a *neutral* effect on spending and prices—not adding or subtracting from *total M* or its velocity.

■ MODERN FRACTIONAL RESERVE BANKING

Let us return to our early goldsmith-banker to see how modern banks gradually evolved. If he were an alert fellow, he would soon notice that, although his deposits are payable on demand, they are not all withdrawn together. He would soon learn that, although 100 per cent reserves are necessary if the bank is to be liquidated and all depositors are to be paid off in full, such reserves are not at all necessary if his bank is a "going concern." New deposits tend to balance withdrawals. Only a little till money, perhaps less than 2 per cent, normally seems needed in the form of vault cash.[4]

At first he probably thought this discovery too good to be true. Then perhaps he recalled the story of a rival bank whose dishonest clerk ran off with 95 per cent of its cash reserve—which was never discovered for 12 years. No one ever had occasion to go to the back rooms of the vault because all withdrawals were financed by recently deposited money held in the front vaults.

---

[3] The economist would consider the demand deposit as money as soon as the custom grew up for depositors to pay for the goods they bought by giving the storekeeper a little note to the bank saying, "Mr. Goldsmith, pay to the order of T. Eaton Co. $2.99, (signed) John Q. Doe." In other words, as soon as the use and acceptability of cheques became customary.

[4] If the bank could pay off its depositors with one of its own cheques (or as in former times with one of its paper bank notes), it might not have to keep any till money at all. By judiciously limiting the rate at which it was making loans and investments, the bank could ensure that the cheques it received from other banks plus cash deposited were just matched by its outpayments. An occasional temporary outward drain of funds could be met by permitting the bank to pay by cheque what it owed to other banks for the few hours or days until some part of its asset portfolio could be liquidated or until it contracted its operations so as to get a surplus of inpayments over outpayments.

We can imagine our intelligent banker—at first cautiously—beginning to acquire bonds and other earning assets with some of the cash entrusted to his care. Everything works out all right: depositors are still paid off on demand, and the bank has made some extra earnings. Gradually, the banker no longer feels it necessary to conceal from his depositors what he is doing. If a depositor complains, the banker retorts, "Your money is safe. If you don't like my way of doing business, you are at liberty to withdraw your funds. Besides, haven't you noticed that the new method of fractional cash reserves has enabled me to *lower my service charges to you?* Also, it has enabled me to give a helping hand to our local businessmen who need more capital to buy new tools, buildings, and inventories. Such capital formation benefits consumers because they get better goods for lower prices. It also creates jobs for workers."

Little wonder, therefore, that banks should want to maximize their profits by putting most of the money deposited with them in earning assets and keeping only fractional cash reserves against deposits.

Indeed, as long as business confidence remains high and bank managers are judicious in their choice of loans and investments, there is no reason why the bank should keep much more than 2 per cent cash reserves against deposits.

DIVERSIFICATION AND LIQUIDITY OF EARNING INVESTMENTS   But what if the banker makes a mistake in his investments? Since nobody's judgment is perfect and all investments involve some element of speculative risk, this is certainly a possibility to reckon with. To lessen the chance of extreme losses, the banker can try to *diversify* his investments, not putting all his eggs in one basket. Besides, a conservative bank will have a considerable amount of capital put up by the stockholders. For example, capital stock may have been issued equal to 10 per cent of demand deposits. Then, even if all the bank's assets are in earning investments rather than in nonearning cash, depositors are protected against all capital losses that do not exceed 10 per cent of the bank's investment portfolio. Ordinarily, this will be sufficient, as long as it keeps to high-grade bonds, government-insured mortgages, and conservative business loans.

There is one last requirement the bank must meet if we are to give it an A+. The management must watch the general trend in the size of its deposits to make sure that its locality is not becoming a "ghost town" and that it is not losing deposits steadily over time. Were that the case, the bank's investment portfolio would have to be arranged to hold securities and loans that could be gradually liquidated and converted into cash to meet depositors' withdrawals. (Or, it might establish a branch in the town where deposits are moving.)

Even if the bank is not a declining business, prudent managers must still protect themselves against a temporary surge of withdrawals. To hold cash against such a contingency would be costly, since cash earns no yield. They will usually decide, therefore, to hold in their portfolios as "secondary reserves" some "liquid" securities that always have a ready market and can be easily sold without much loss before maturity.

Short-term government bonds serve this purpose admirably. Called "bills," "notes," or "certificates," they fluctuate little in value. Many can be liquidated simply by not buying new ones as the old ones come due every 90 days or 12 months. Even long-term government bonds, with 30 years of life before they mature, provide liquidity in the sense that in normal times they can always be transferred[5] to some other buyer at some quoted market price—albeit a varying price.

The important thing for liquidity is not the *date of maturity* of the bond or loan, but rather how "shiftable" it is to some other investment institution. A 90-day loan to a local merchant, which is nonshiftable, is in this sense less liquid than a 90-year gilt-edge bond traded on a securities exchange.

■ LEGAL RESERVE REQUIREMENTS

The above precepts of sound banking practice are quite simple and understandable. They are a little harder to carry out in practice than to state in principle; but the same is true of most prescriptions for wise living.

CASH RESERVES If we compare a "going and growing" bank with any corporation, the surprising thing is not how little cash reserves the banks keep, but that they keep any at all (in excess of minimal till-money requirements). *As long as financial skies are sunny, the same profit-maximizing logic that compels the abandonment of a system of 100 per cent reserves argues in favor of negligible reserves!*

Yet, if we turn to the facts, we find that a prudent modern bank is expected —and required by law!—to keep a substantial portion of its assets in nonearning cash. About six per cent of all Canadian deposits must be kept as "cash reserves." Roughly two-thirds of these reserves are kept on deposit at the Bank of Canada, the other one-third in notes and coins.

> Actually there are two cash reserve percentages: 12 per cent of demand deposits and 4 per cent of notice (savings) deposits. The *weighted* average of these two is about the 6 per cent given in the text above. Prior to 1967, one cash ratio, 8 per cent, applied to both demand and savings deposits. For simplicity, the following pages are based on the assumption of the continuation of this single 8 per cent cash ratio, which is half-way between the two legal figures. [United States' ratios are 16½ per cent (in large cities) and 12 per cent (elsewhere) against demand deposits, and 6 per cent against time deposits (everywhere).]

It must be emphasized that these *cash ratios are required of chartered banks in order to control their behavior.* The many (though unimportant) American banks that are *not* members of the Federal Reserve system do not voluntarily keep such large amounts of nonearning cash as a precaution against withdrawals as the members are obliged to keep. The recent Report of Canada's Royal Commission on Banking and Finance (The Porter Report) showed that trust companies, many of which have deposit liabilities to customers that are chequable

---

[5] There is a saying, "You can sell governments bonds even on Sunday."

like the chartered banks' savings deposit accounts, maintain lower cash reserve ratios against deposits. Indeed many experts agree with the Porter Commission's recommendation that *all* institutions in competition with the banks for this kind of time-deposit business should be subject to similar cash-reserve ratios.

Other experts, and the banks themselves, argue that the legal ratios are too high. One line of argument is that, in Canada, the chartered banks are so few that a large proportion of the withdrawals from any one bank will very soon be redeposited *in the same bank* by other customers. This claim, of course, makes sense for the three largest banks—Royal, Montreal, and Commerce—but not for the other six smaller banks. A simpler argument is merely that money required as legal reserves doesn't earn the bank that owns it one red cent. Bankers think wistfully of the interest earnings they are missing:

> Twelve per cent of our demand deposits is more than is needed for safety. After all, our withdrawals never bunch up much; the spreading of our customers across the country, in many industries and kinds of business activity, and the laws of probability take care of that. Besides, if we ever need more, we could sell off some government bonds or bills, or turn to the Bank of Canada or to a stronger chartered bank for help. Probably 5 per cent is all that prudence requires with so many ways out of temporary trouble.

There is much in what they say. American ratios have come down with the years, and since 1967 Canadian ratios have again been lowered a few points. One of their arguments doesn't hold much water though: spreading risks of heavy unexpected withdrawals across the country means that if one bank should suffer a "run on the bank," the others would be doing so too, for they frequently have branches in the same place.

But all this controversy is not very serious anyway. The banks know, and the Porter Commission's recent discussion shows, that the main purpose of legal cash ratios is *not* to make deposits safe and liquid, payable on demand. What is it, then?

> The vital function of legal cash reserves is to enable the authorities in the Bank of Canada to be able to control the amounts of deposits—or bank money—that the chartered banks can create. By imposing fixed reserve requirements, Ottawa can limit the growth of bank deposits.

SECONDARY RESERVES   Further indication that the purpose of legal reserves is to provide a keyboard in each bank on which the monetary authorities can play is given by the Canadian requirement that the chartered banks keep an *additional* percentage of their reserves against deposits, chiefly in the form of interest-earning assets. Chief among these is the 90-day Treasury Bill, but the banks may also count as part of this "secondary reserve" day-to-day loans to money-market dealers and additional cash. By setting up a total requirement of, 8 per cent cash and, say, 7 per cent in other liquid assets, or 15 per cent altogether (the rates assumed in our examples), the Bank of Canada is enabled to affect the makeup of the whole portfolio of earning assets held by the chartered banks (as in Table 15-1). And controlling the assets the banks may acquire means controlling their lending operations. To repeat, the main aim of setting up a legal secondary-reserve requirement is not to protect customers by making sure the banks hold a safe quantity of reserves. It is to force the banks to hold things (cash and treasury bills), the value or supply of which Ottawa can change.

Just how all this works, we shall soon learn.

■ THE GOVERNMENT STANDS BEHIND THE BANKS

Banks are much safer now than they were in the nineteenth century. If this safety doesn't stem from legal cash reserves, to what is it due?

> Some Canadians will claim that Canadian bankers are the answer. The overwhelming number of bankers with Scottish names has given the public the idea that the Canadian branch system was brought here from Scotland, and is based on different principles than the failure-rife American system. But economic historians, beginning with the work of Adam Shortt of Queen's, have shown this is simply not true. The early Canadian banks picked up their charters (organization charts, in fact) from predecessors in New York State which in turn traced their ancestry to systems of banking pioneered in the early days of the United States. The early Scottish-Canadian bankers learned their banking arts in Canada. The branch system was popular with American bankers, but was prevented by state legislatures, largely for reasons irrelevant to banking theory. Canadian bankers (as opposed to their American colleagues) did not until recently make loans on uninsured mortgages, or loans depending heavily on collateral such as cars and other equipment; these were forbidden by Canadian banking law. No doubt there are national banking types: British, Swiss, and Chinese bankers all work in their distinctive ways. But differences between their opportunities, national economies, and banking laws are much better explanations of their different systems than are the men themselves.

Indeed, for many decades the small Canadian banks did have a poor nineteenth-century record, and many of their customers lost their deposits. The happier record of the twentieth century has two basic explanations. One of these we have already mentioned. The branch system means that risks of sudden withdrawal in one area, and the losses from them, are balanced by events in other areas. The few large banks are less vulnerable than many small banks to unexpected drains. Also, being large, they have more experienced managers and supervisors, who examine and approve the larger or riskier loan applications. Finally, being large, they are better able to prevent and absorb the occasional embezzlements that might shake small banks to their foundations.[6]

1. *Regulation of bank formation.* Since Confederation, Ottawa has had complete control over money and banking. Promoters wishing to start banks receive charters from Parliament, after their applications have been scrutinized by the Treasury Board (a committee of the Cabinet) and by Standing Committees of the House of Commons and of the Senate. These charters are granted under the Bank Act, a unique piece of legislation that must be reviewed, before

---

[6] Readers should not assume that the many small U.S. banks are hopelessly vulnerable to these dangers. Most U.S. banks, since 1935, have insured their depositors against losses, privately or through the large FDIC. The U.S. federal government and many states have bank inspectors and auditors who guard against unskilled or dishonest accounting and lending practices.

its renewal, every ten years. All bank charters expire every ten years, and are renewed, phoenixlike, with, and on the terms of, every new Bank Act. The 1967 Bank Act aimed to keep control of banks among Canadian residents; but this revision has more to do with Canadian attitudes to foreign ownership than with the conduct of banking.

2. *Bank Regulation.* The Act, added to over the years, states what banks may and may not do. Until recently, it prohibited lending at rates above 6 per cent, thus confining the banks to dealing with customers whose credit was very good. But this upper limit has now been swept away. The Act has also, over the decades, forced the bank to stick to "commercial banking"; that is, to the making of loans that make possible commercial transactions that promise to lead to the quick repayment of the loan. With several exceptions, it forbade the making of mortgage loans, loans against chattels, or for the acquisition of equipment.

These restrictions are now of historical importance, explaining the present characteristics of the chartered banks and their managers. Since 1966-1967, there has been almost no legal restriction on the type or term of a bank loan, or on the rate of interest that might be charged. Thus, in their *assets* (loans), the chartered banks are today in possession of the same freedom that they have long had in the creation of *liabilities:* they can invent new kinds of deposit accounts, or issue new kinds of cheques.

It follows that, while our chartered banks are, as we shall see, restrained or encouraged in their lending activities by the Bank of Canada, they are today relatively free to compete, to offer services, and to levy charges, as they wish.

3. *Formation of the Bank of Canada.* The third great step forward was the establishment of a central bank. In emergencies it is required to stand like a Rock of Gibraltar, ready not only to use the full monetary powers of the government to stem collapse of the banking system, but also to help particular banks whose weakening threatens the deposits of its customers. It can then truly act as a "lender of last resort." But in normal times, it controls money supply and credit conditions, and acts as a final lender or bankers' bank only as part of its general monetary role.

In these ways the government stands behind the supply of credit created by the banks. The fewness and largeness of Canada's nine banks does not call for anything more. If protection of depositors were the only problem, the banks could probably get along pretty well with no governmental supervision at all. As with legal reserve ratios, so with special government banking functions: their purpose is to provide a set of tools by which Ottawa can protect and control the money supply and credit conditions. We shall see in later chapters how this protection and control lead to stable prices and full employment.

B.   THE CREATION OF BANK DEPOSITS

■ CAN BANKS REALLY CREATE MONEY?

We now turn to one of the most interesting aspects of money and credit, the process called "multiple expansion of bank deposits." Most people have heard that in some mysterious manner banks can create money out of thin air, but few really understand how the process works. Few understand that all our money arises out of debt and IOU operations.

Actually, there is nothing magical or incomprehensible about the creation of bank deposits. At every step of the way, one can follow what is happening to the banks' accounts. The true explanation of deposit creation is simple. What is hard to grasp is that false explanations still circulate.

According to these false explanations, the managers of an ordinary bank are able, by some use of their fountain pens, to lend several dollars for each dollar deposited with them. No wonder practical bankers see red when such power is attributed to them. They only wish they could do so. As every banker knows, he cannot invest money that he does not have; and money that he invests in buying a security or making a loan soon leaves his bank.

Bankers, therefore, often go to the opposite extreme. They sometimes argue that the banking system cannot (and does not) create money. "After all," they say, "we can invest only what is left with us. We don't create anything. We only put the community's savings to work." Bankers who argue in this way are quite wrong. They have become enmeshed in our old friend the fallacy of composition: what is true for each is not thereby true for all.

> The banking system as a whole can do what a single bank cannot do: it *can* expand its loans and investments many times the new reserves of cash created for it, even though each small bank is lending out only a fraction of its deposits.

Our answer, then, to the basic question is in the affirmative: Yes, the banking system and the public do, between them, create about $12.50 of bank de-

All banks together do what one can't do alone!

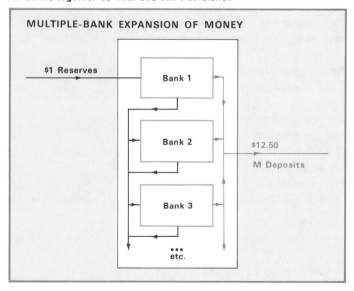

MULTIPLE-BANK EXPANSION OF MONEY

$1 Reserves

Bank 1

Bank 2

$12.50

M Deposits

Bank 3

• • •
etc.

FIG. 15-1. For each dollar of new reserves deposited at left into a bank, the system as a whole creates at right about $12.50 of cheque money. The black arrows in the box show that Bank 1 cannot do it alone. As we'll see, second, third, and other banks will get their share of the expansion.

Multiple-bank deposit creation is a story with many successive stages:

1st, A new deposit is added to the original bank's balance sheet:

ORIGINAL BANK IN INITIAL POSITION			
ASSETS		**LIABILITIES**	
Reserves	+$1,000	Deposits	+$1,000
Total	+$1,000	Total	+$1,000

TABLE 15-3(a).

posits for each new dollar of reserves that is created for the banks. Let us see how.

Figure 15-1 gives a preview of the process. The black box represents the banking system as a whole: Bank 1, which receives the initial new deposit, is at top; Bank 2, 3, ..., and all other banks (not shown) are listed below. We shall study how $1 of new reserves, deposited at the left as input into the box, produces $12.50 of total deposit money, shown at the right. But Bank 1 cannot do this in one single step; as the black arrows between the banks show, all banks get involved in the lengthy secondary chain of money creation. Though the chain has many links, each is a dwindling fraction and the whole effect does add up to the 12.5:1 total.

■ HOW DEPOSITS ARE CREATED: THE FIRST-BANK STAGE

We begin with a brand-new deposit of $1,000 brought to a bank. Where it came from is not important. It could have been from a widow's hoard, or from abroad, or more realistically, from someone's having just sold a bond to the Bank of Canada (which may have paid for it by printing off twenty 50-dollar bills). To avoid ambiguity, let us suppose it was merely a case of the government's having given a veteran $1,000 of newly printed money, which he deposited in his local bank. We shall see that *in the end* the banking system is going to manufacture $12,500 of new demand deposits out of this, thus taking in $1,000 of one kind of M (currency) and converting it into $12,500 of another kind of M (chequable) —for a net gain of $11,500!

FIRST-BANK STAGE   Now, if banks were to keep 100 per cent cash-reserve balances, like the old goldsmiths, they could not create any extra money out of a new deposit of $1,000 left with them. The depositor would simply be giving up $1,000 of currency for a $1,000 chequing deposit.

The change in the bank's balance sheet, as far as the new demand deposit is concerned, would be as shown in Table 15-3(*a*).[7]

---

[7] Important note: When bankers refer to their loans and investments as "investments" they mean their holdings of securities. They do not mean what we mean by I in $C + I + G$, namely, net capital formation for the community.

2d, Of course the bank cannot then loan out eleven times the amount of the deposit:

IMPOSSIBLE SITUATION FOR SINGLE SMALL BANK			
ASSETS		**LIABILITIES**	
Reserves	+$ 1,000	Deposits	+$12,500
Loans and			
investments	+ 11,500		
Total	+$12,500	Total	+$12,500

TABLE 15-3(b).

The bank has not created this deposit *alone*. The customer had to be willing to make the deposit. Once he took the initiative, the bank was also willing to accept his chequing account. Together the bank and the public "created" $1,000 of bank money, or deposit. But there is yet no multiple expansion, or 12.5 for 1, or anything else. So long as the banks keep 100 per cent reserves, the growth of bank M is just offset by the decline of currency-in-circulation M.

Suppose now that the bank does not have to keep 100 per cent reserves. Suppose that the law requires it to keep only 8 per cent legal reserves. (Remember that the actual legal cash reserves in Canada are 12 and 4 per cent against demand and notice deposits, respectively. In the discussion it is assumed that these two types of deposits are equal, so that the average rate is 8 per cent. Of course, a bank may always keep larger reserves if it wishes to; but if there are many outstanding alternatives such as relatively safe, interest-yielding government bonds or numerous profitable lending opportunities, the bank will not find it profitable to keep much more reserves than the law requires.)

What can the bank now do? Can it expand its loans and investments by $11,500 so that the change in its balance sheet looks as shown in Table 15-3(b). The answer is definitely, *No*. Why not? Total assets equal total liabilities. Cash reserves meet the legal requirement of being 8 per cent of total deposits.

True enough. But how did the bank pay for the investments or earning assets that it bought? Like everyone else, it had to write out a cheque to the man who sold the bond or signed the promissory note. If all such people would promise not to cash the bank's cheque—or what is the same thing, to hold all such money frozen on deposit in the bank—then, of course, the bank could buy all it wanted to without losing any cash.

But, in fact, no one will borrow money at 8 or 9 per cent just to hold it all in the bank. The borrower spends the money on labor, on materials, or perhaps on an automobile. The money will *very soon*,[8] therefore, have to be paid out of the bank. And if—as is likely—the bank is but one of several banks serving that

---

[8] If the bank made loans of $920 to its own customers, and they kept them on deposit, then for a brief period it would have deposits of $1,920. But as its borrowers spent their money, and unless the people who got that money were customers who put the money back on deposit in this original bank, it would soon find itself forced by the cash "drain" to other banks, toward the position of Table 15-3(c).

3rd, But what it can do is loan out eleven-twelfths of the deposit:

ORIGINAL BANK IN FINAL POSITION

ASSETS		LIABILITIES	
Reserves	+$ 80	Deposits	+$1,000
Loans and			
investments	+ 920		
Total	+$1,000	Total	+$1,000

TABLE 15-3(c).

city, county, province, and country, only a fraction of the sums withdrawn will ever come back to the original bank in another customer's deposit.

This loss of cash by a bank expanding its investments is even more clearly seen if the bank buys a bond rather than making a local loan. When my bank buys a government bond, what are the chances that the man who sells the bond will happen to have an account with it? The likelihood is as low as 1 in 9. Probably he lives in Montreal, or Vancouver, and deals with a rival bank. So my bank knows it will soon have to pay out *all* the money it placed in bonds. A bank cannot "eat its cake and have it, too." The bank cannot buy a bond and expect to keep its cash at the same time. Table 15-3(*b*) gives, therefore a completely false picture of what an individual bank can do.

Does this mean that Table 15-3(*a*) tells the end of the story? Must the bank, therefore, behave like the 100 per cent reserve goldsmith bankers?

Of course not. Although the bank cannot jack its deposits up to twelve and one half times its cash reserve, it certainly can *reduce its cash down* to 8 per cent of its deposits. Nothing is easier. For, as we have seen, all it has to do is acquire $920 worth of earning assets—bonds or loans. In a day or so it will lose practically all this cash as its cheques come back for payment. Now its balance sheet will be as shown in Table 15-3(*c*).

As far as this first bank is concerned, we are through. Its legal reserves are just enough to match its deposits. There is nothing more it can do until the public decides to bring in some more money for deposit.

Before leaving the single small bank, note this important fact: It has created money! How? Clearly *it* retains from the public only $80 of cash *M*; and it has added $1,000 of bank-deposit *M* to the public's total. Thus, its activity has created a net increase of $920 in money supply.

■ REPERCUSSIONS ON THE OTHER BANKS

But the banking system as a whole cannot settle down yet. The people who sold the bonds or borrowed from the bank will presumably deposit the proceeds in some other bank or pay them to someone else who will make such a deposit. Our original bank has thus lost $920 *to some other banks* in the system.

SECOND-GENERATION BANKS   If we lump these other banks all together and call them "second-generation banks," their balance sheets now appear as shown in

4th, The money loaned out by the original bank is soon deposited in other banks:

SECOND-GENERATION IN INITIAL POSITION			
ASSETS		**LIABILITIES**	
Reserves	+$920	Deposits	+$920
Total	+$920	Total	+$920

TABLE 15-3(d).

Table 15-3(*d*). (Our original bank might even constitute a part of the second generation as some of its cheques fell into the hands of its own depositors.) To these banks the dollars deposited are just like any other dollars, *just like our original deposit*; these banks do not know, and do not care, that they are second in a chain of deposits. They do know, and they do care, that they are now holding too much nonearning cash. Only 8 per cent of $920, or $73.60, is legally needed against $920 deposits. Therefore they can, and will, use the other 92 per cent to buy $846.40 worth of loans and investments, so that in a few days, their balance sheet will have reached equilibrium as shown in Table 15-3(*e*).

5th, Ninety-two per cent of this new deposit will be loaned out by the second-generation bank:

FINAL POSITION OF SECOND-GENERATION BANKS			
ASSETS		**LIABILITIES**	
Reserves	+$ 73.60	Deposits	+$920.00
Loans and investments	+ 846.40		
Total	+$920.00	Total	+$920.00

TABLE 15-3(e).

So much for the second-generation banks. They too have created money. Thus far, the original $1,000 taken out of hand-to-hand circulation and put into the banking system has given rise to $1,000 (first-generation deposits) plus $920 (second-generation deposits). The total of money has increased, and the end is not yet in sight. Here is the reason.

LATER-GENERATION BANKS   The $846.40 spent by the second-generation banks in acquiring loans and investments will go to a new set of banks called the "third-generation banks." The reader should by now be able to fill in their balance sheets as they look initially [see Table 15-3(*f*)]. Evidently, the third-generation banks will at first have *excess reserves* of an amount equal to 92 per cent of $846.40 or $778.69. After this has been spent on loans and investments—and only then—the third-generation banks will reach the equilibrium of Table 15-3(*g*).

6th, And similarly in third-generation banks:

INITIAL POSITION OF THIRD-GENERATION BANKS			
ASSETS		**LIABILITIES**	
Reserves	+	Deposits	+ ....
Loans and investments	....		
Total	+	Total	+$846.40

TABLE 15-3(f).

FINAL EQUILIBRIUM OF THIRD-GENERATION BANKS			
ASSETS		**LIABILITIES**	
Reserves	+$ 67.71	Deposits	+$846.40
Loans and investments	+ 778.69		
Total	+$846.40	Total	+$846.40

TABLE 15-3(g).

The total of bank-deposit M is now $1,000 plus $920 plus $846.40, or almost $2,767. This is already over 2.5:1 expansion of the original cash deposit. But a fourth generation of banks will clearly end up with 92 per cent of $846.40 in deposits, or $778.69; and the fifth generation will get 92 per cent of $778.69 or $716.39; and so on; until finally, we shall have all of the total sum of the infinitely many generations.

FINAL EQUILIBRIUM What will be the final sum: $1,000 + $920 + $846.40 + $778.69 + $716.39 + ...? If we patiently work out the sum by arithmetic, we shall find that it leads "finally" to $12,500. Table 15-3($h$) shows the complete effect of the chain of deposit creation, and we can also get the same answer in two other ways, by common sense and by elementary algebra.[9]

Common sense tells us the process of deposit creation must come to an end only when no bank *anywhere in the system* has reserves in excess of the 8 per cent reserve ratio to deposits. In all our previous examples no cash reserves have ever leaked out of the banking system, but have simply gone from one set of banks to another set of banks. Everyone will be at equilibrium only when a consolidated balance sheet for all the banks together—for the first, second, and

---

[9] This can be proved by algebra as follows:
$$\$1,000 + \$920 + \$846.40 + ... = \$1,000\ [1 + .92 + (.92)^2 + (.93)^3 + ...]$$
$$= \$1,000\ \left[\frac{1}{1-.92}\right] = \$1,000 \times \frac{1}{.08} = \$1,000 \times 12.5$$
$$= \$12,500$$
Just as the old multiplier (Chapter 12, page 284) made a flow of income rise threefold to generate the one-third of itself equal to the new dollar of I, here deposit M must rise twelve and one-half-fold so that 8 per cent of it will match the new dollars of reserves that started the chain.

7th, Through this chain process the banking system eventually creates total deposits equal to twelve and one half times the original reserves:

MULTIPLE EXPANSION OF BANK DEPOSITS THROUGH THE BANKING SYSTEM

POSITION OF BANK	NEW DEPOSITS	NEW LOANS AND INVESTMENTS	RESERVES
Original banks	$ 1,000.00	$ 920.00	$ 80.00
2nd-generation banks	920.00	846.40	73.60
3rd-generation banks	846.40	778.69	67.71
4th-generation banks	778.69	716.39	62.30
5th-generation banks	716.39	659.08	57.31
6th-generation banks	659.08	606.37	52.72
7th-generation banks	606.37	557.86	48.51
8th-generation banks	557.86	513.43	44.43
9th-generation banks	513.43	471.86	41.57
10th-generation banks	471.86	434.11	37.75
Sum of first 10 generation banks	$ 7,070.09	$ 6,504.19	$ 565.90
Sum of remaining generation banks	5,429.91	4,995.81	434.10
Total for banking system as a whole	$12,500.00	$11,500.00	$1,000.00

TABLE 15-3(h). Note that in every generation each *small* bank has "created" new money in the following sense: It ends up with final bank deposit twelve and one half times *the reserves it finally retains*. (From the second generation on, the data have been rounded off to two decimal places.)

hundredth generation—looks as shown in Table 15-3(*i*). For if total new deposits were less than $12,500, the 8 per cent ratio would not yet be reached and equilibrium would not yet have been everywhere attained.

If the reader will compare Table 15-3(*i*) with Table 15-3(*b*) previously judged "impossible," he will see this:

> The whole banking system *can* do what no one bank can do by itself. It can expand its deposits to 12.5 times the *initial* new deposit. *Bank money has been created 12.5 out of 1—and all the while each bank has invested and lent only a fraction of what it has received as deposits!*[10]

Who creates the multiple expansion[11] of deposits? Three parties do so jointly: the public by always keeping its money in the bank on deposit; the banks by keeping only a fraction of their deposits in the form of cash; the public and private borrowers who make it possible for the banks to find loans and

---

[10] In effect, each small bank creates 1M out of .08M but not 12.5M out of 1M. (NOTE: Whenever $1 of new reserves produces $12.50 of new demand-deposit money, the *net* creation of M is only $12.50 − $1 = $11.50. So when one writes a 12.5:1 expansion expression, it means that there is associated with this an 11.5:1 *net*-creation-of-M expansion.)

[11] There is nothing paradoxical in the fact that total bank deposits are several times greater than the amount of paper cash in existence anywhere; the same is true of the total of government bonds and real-estate values. Deposits are something that banks *owe* their customers; cash is *left* at a bank, but it does not *remain* in that bank. Throughout its lifetime a dollar may have been *left* at many banks, just as it may be used over a long period of time to buy hundreds of dollars of merchandise. The one thing to keep firmly in mind is that bank deposits are one of the three forms of modern money and, quantitatively, the most important.

8th, Now we can see that all banks together can do what is impossible for one alone:

CONSOLIDATED BALANCE SHEET SHOWING FINAL
POSITION OF ALL BANKS TOGETHER

ASSETS		LIABILITIES	
Reserves	+$ 1,000	Deposits	+$12,500
Loans and			
investments	+ 11,500		
Total	+$12,500	Total	+$12,500

TABLE 15-3(i).

attractive earning assets to buy with their excess cash. (There is also a fourth party, the central bank, which by its activities determines how much will be the new reserves to come to the banking system. It will be the task of the next chapters to survey and explain this process.)

Before leaving this section, test your knowledge of credit creation by tracing in detail what happens when the Bank of Canada permanently kills off $1,000 of reserves by selling a government bond to a widow who withdraws cash from her demand-deposit account to pay for it: (1) Her local bank loses $1,000 of reserves and $1,000 of deposits. But it previously held only 8 per cent cash reserves or $80 against her deposit. Clearly, it must have given up to her some of its legally necessary cash reserves held against its other demand deposits. Show that its total reserves are now below the legal minimum. (2) Therefore it must sell $920 worth of investments or call in that many loans. The first-generation bank will be in equilibrium only when its balance sheet finally looks as shown in a newly constructed Table 15-4(*a*).

But in selling its securities, our original bank has drained $920 from a second generation of banks: and they in turn, by liquidating securities and loans, drain reserves from a third. And so it goes—until the widow and Bank of Canada's withdrawal of $1,000 of reserves from the banking system have produced a chain "killing off" $12,500 worth of deposits throughout the whole system and $11,500 of bank-earning assets. The student should follow through each stage: Table 15-4(*b*), Table 15-4(*c*), . . .

You should also be able to show how an initial deposit of $7,000 can result in $100,000 of bank deposits if banks keep only 7 per cent reserve ratios.

■ A "MONOPOLY" BANK AND CHAIN BANKING

In all the above processes, it was assumed that no cash "drained" out of the banking system into someone's mattress; or, what is more important numerically,

9th, When a deposit is drawn out, a multiple contraction begins to take place:

EQUILIBRIUM POSITION OF ORIGINAL BANK LOSING
A DEPOSIT

ASSETS		LIABILITIES	
Reserves	−$ 80	Deposits	−$1,000
Loans and			
investments	− 920		
Total	−$1,000	Total	−$1,000

TABLE 15-4(a).

into permanent hand-to-hand circulation. (The latter used to be called "increased pocket-money needs.") In the absence of such drains, the banking system was then in the enviable position of finding that withdrawal cheques were always redeposited somewhere within itself.

In this condition, it is easy to see that a hypothetical single "monopoly bank" with many branches, which served the whole economy and took the place of the consolidate banking system outlined above, would be able to do *at once* what we have said each small bank cannot do. Its balance sheet could quickly go to the condition shown in Table 15-3(b) or 15-3(i). It could write cheques on itself freely to pay for securities or make loans, knowing that the people to whom they are paid would always redeposit their proceeds in the same one and only monopoly bank.

CHAIN BANKING It is now obvious that the Canadian system of chain banking belongs somewhere between the examples' system of many unit banks and the "monopoly bank." In this it is like the British, Swedish, and California systems. The cash drain from one branch now moves out into the banking system, probably to be redeposited in some other town. But the chances are now not so small that the redeposit will be in another branch of the same bank.

In Canada there are only nine chartered banks, all with branches. If they were all the same size, each bank would have one chance in nine that its loans and security payments would flow back into one of its own branches. Such odds are obviously infinitely better than those for an American bank: if all U.S. banks were the same size, a banker there would have only one chance in thirteen *thousand* that he would be the second generation depository for one of his own outpayments. With these odds, Canadian banks can clearly afford to have lower reserve ratios than American banks; and this is probably why *legal* cash ratios in Canada have always been, in fact, set lower than in the United States. (The U.S. reserve ratio for demand deposits in the main financial centers is about 17 per cent; for demand deposits elsewhere it is 12 per cent.)

Actually, for some Canadian banking business, the odds are better than one in nine. For the banks are not the same size. Roughly speaking the three largest banks (Canadian Imperial Bank of Commerce, Bank of Montreal, and Royal Bank of Canada) together operate one-half of all the branches in Canada and more than two-thirds of all their deposit liabilities. For any one of these banks, the odds are about one in five that their payments will be redeposited in their own branches. What is more important, any one of them can rely on nearly one-fifth of all their payments flowing back to them. If the legal cash ratio of one-twelfth happened to be right for the average Canadian payment from any bank, then these banks could lend out *more* than their excess reserves over the legal amount, knowing that almost one-fifth would be "self-returning." This temptation, of course, exists but it is barred by law.[12]

---

[12] The analytical reader should note that the real reason for the large self-returning flow is not the large number of branches but the small number of chartered banks. But of course he would have to admit that, in turn, the concentration in banking is probably caused by the branch system.

■ SIMULTANEOUS EXPANSION OR CONTRACTION BY ALL BANKS

In the previous section we have seen how the banking system can reach the limits of its expansion through many successive rounds or generations. If we allow half a week for cheques to clear at each stage and for decisions to be made, then 5 to 8 weeks might be required for the process substantially to work itself out through more than a dozen rounds.

As a practical matter, it is not necessary to follow the route of each dollar deposited through its successive rounds. Here is why. A rise in reserves will usually affect almost all the banks at the same time. They all receive some new deposits at about the same time. They all have excess reserves in the first instance, and all together make loans or buy securities.

If a single bank, all by itself, writes cheques to acquire securities, these cheques go to other banks and it loses cash. But when all are writing cheques simultaneously and in balance, there will tend to be a cancellation of new cheques deposited in each bank against those paid out. No one bank need lose cash reserves. Hence, without going through the successive generations of the previous section, all banks together can simply and blithely expand their loans and investments—so long as each does not jeopardize its reserve position—until deposits are finally brought into a 12.5:1 relation to reserves. Then the banking system has reached the limit of its ability to create money.

One could follow through the similar process by which all banks *simultaneously* contract money 12.5:1 for each dollar of reserve withdrawn from the banking system, and one could also show how a monopoly bank would contract. Figure 15-2, similar to Fig. 15-1, retells the multiple expansion story for a monopoly bank and for simultaneous multiple expansion.

■ TWO QUALIFICATIONS

Finally, two qualifications to the ideal condition must be made. We have shown that $1,000 of new reserves put into a bank can ultimately result in an increase

Other routes to multiple expansion:

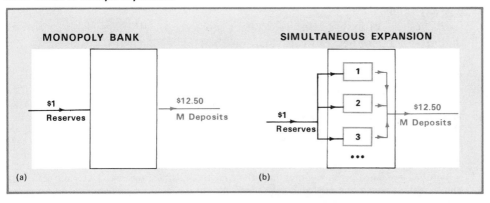

FIG. 15-2. In (a) there is no need for arrows within the box, because there is only one big bank. In (b), the arrows between the banks run in both directions and can be ignored.

of $12,500 of bank deposits. This assumed that all the new money remained somewhere in the banking system, in one bank or another at every stage, and that all banks could keep "loaned up" with no "excess reserves."

1. *Leakage into hand-to-hand circulation.* It is quite possible, however, and even likely, that somewhere along the chain of deposit expansion some individual who receives a cheque will not leave the proceeds in a bank but will withdraw it into circulation or into hoarding outside the banking system. As a matter of fact, in boom times when bank deposits are expanding, there is usually at the same time an increased need for pennies, dimes, and paper currency.

The effects of such withdrawals on our analysis are simple. When $1,000 stayed in the banking system, $12,500 of new deposits were created. If $100 were to leak into circulation outside the banks and only $900 of new reserves were to remain in the banking system, then the new deposits created would be $11,500 ($900 $\times$ 12.5). *The banking system can always amplify in a 12.5:1 ratio whatever amount of new reserves is permanently left with it,* given our assumed 8 per cent reserve ratio.

2. *Possible excess reserves.* Our description of multiple deposit creation has proceeded on the assumption that the banks stick fairly close to their legal reserve ratios. But there is no reason why a bank cannot choose to keep an *excess* over the required amount of reserves. Thus, suppose the original bank receiving a new $1,000 deposit had been satisfied to hold $920 of it in excess reserves. Then the whole process would have ended right there, with no multiple expansion of deposits. Or if banks were always to keep 17 per cent excess reserves, on top of the 8 per cent legal requirement, we would have a chain of expansion of deposits $[1 + \frac{3}{4} + (\frac{3}{4})^2 + \ldots]$, with only a 4:1 rather than a 12.5:1 expansion of deposits.

Back in the 1930s excess reserves—i.e., reserves over and above legally required reserves—were substantial, since bankers were then leery of loan opportunities and even of relatively safe government bills that were paying less than 1 per cent interest. Had the banking system then received $1,000 of new reserves, perhaps half might have gone into excess reserves. Nowadays excess reserves are less important, since large banks find attractive uses even for one-day funds.[13]

The level of excess reserves depends more on the attitudes of banks toward the interest rates they can earn than on their fears that withdrawals will catch

---

[13] A rather complex mechanism also exists, and flourishes, whereby banks can "lend" reserves to each other for a day or so at a time. The banks make day-to-day loans of large amounts to dealers in treasury bills and other short-term paper. These loans can be called back by any bank before noon on any day. Dealers whose loans are thus called back can turn to other banks, and thus the other banks indirectly "lend" reserves to those calling their loans. If no other banks have cash to spare, the dealers can turn to the Bank of Canada which always stands ready to accommodate them (at rather high rates of interest). The system has been in operation only since the mid-1950s, and is a special version of a "discount" market which has existed for decades between the Bank of England and the commercial banks in London. The system, which has many technical advantages, is too complex to go into here.

them unawares. When short-term interest rates become very low, and a banker finds that keeping an extra million dollars in idle reserves would not much change his earning position, he is not very anxious to get rid of all excess reserves. But as profit opportunities improve, he becomes more aggressive in putting his idle reserves to work earning a return for the stockholders.

The possibility that the excess reserves of banks can change over time is an important reminder that there is nothing mechanical and completely accurate about using a 12.5:1 or any other *fixed* ratio for money creation.

Accordingly, there is nothing automatic about deposit creation. Four factors are necessary: the banks must somehow receive new reserves; they must be willing to make loans or buy securities rather than hold new excess reserves; someone must be willing to borrow or to sell securities; and the public must choose to leave its money on deposit with the banks, not depleting them of reserves.

SUMMARY

A. THE MODERN BANKING SYSTEM

■ 1 The Canadian banking system consists of nine chain banks, chartered by the federal government. Three of them are quite large and have deposits equal to about 65 per cent of total deposits in Canadian banks.

■ 2 The functions of chartered banks are numerous and overlap with those of such other financial institutions as trust and mortgage companies, credit unions, finance companies, and insurance companies. But in their function of providing demand-deposit *M*, the commercial banks perform a unique and important economic role. Their demand deposits constitute the single most important component of our money supply or medium of exchange. And they are important sources for credit.

■ 3 The Bank of Canada is an arm of the government, run by a Governor, Deputy Governor, and Board of Directors. The government is represented at its meetings and participates in making appointments to it. Unlike the U.S. Federal Reserve System it is not in any sense a private enterprise.

Although it undertakes a wide variety of jobs for the government, connected with the currency and the selling and retiring of government bonds, its wide powers are applied for the public interest, not for banking profit. It works with the Department of Finance and Treasury Board, though in day-to-day matters it sometimes adopts independent attitudes that have led it into real conflict with the national government. As opposed to the multitude of aims of government, the Bank of Canada's single main goal is to control the supply of money and credit conditions, in this way helping to achieve full employment with stable prices. A natural but minor adjunct of this continuous job is to backstop the chartered banks, and other parts of the financial system, in time of crisis.

■ 4   Modern banks gradually evolved from the old goldsmith establishments in which money and valuables were stored. It finally became general practice to hold far less than 100 per cent reserves against deposits, the rest being put into securities and loans for an interest yield. Fractional-reserve banking had evolved.

■ 5   If the government did not stand ready to use its emergency powers to protect the banking system, an attempt by all depositors at the same time to withdraw their money would ruin any fractional-reserve banking system; but knowing the government is ready to act, people will never put it to the test.

The chartered banks are required to keep legal cash reserves (on deposit with the Bank of Canada or in till money) in proportion to their deposits, and they must also maintain secondary reserves. These legal reserve requirements are *not* primarily to protect deposits but to permit the Bank of Canada to control the total supply of M and keep credit conditions conducive to proper over-all spending.

B.   THE CREATION OF BANK DEPOSITS

■ 6   If banks kept 100 per cent cash reserves against all deposits, there would be no net creation of money when currency was taken out of circulation and deposited in the banking system. There would be only a 1:1 exchange of one kind of money for another kind of money.

■ 7   Modern banks in Canada are required to keep legal reserves of only 12 per cent against demand deposits and 4 per cent against notice (savings) deposits. Let 8 per cent, or 1/12.5, represent the average of these two rates. Then the banking system as a whole—together with public or private borrowers and the depositing public—does create deposit money almost 12.5:1 for each new dollar taken out of circulation and left on deposit somewhere in the system.

■ 8   Each bank is limited in its ability to expand its loans and investments. It cannot lend or invest more than it has received from depositors; it can lend only about 92 per cent as much. Its deposits are twelve and a half times its cash, only because its cash decreases, and not because its deposits increase; but it does create 1 unit of bank money for the 8 per cent of reserves it retains.

■ 9   The system as a whole can expand at once, as each bank cannot. This can be seen if we examine a monopoly bank in a closed community. The cheques written by such a bank always come back to it; therefore the only restriction upon its ability to expand its investments and deposits (its assets *and* its liabilities in double-entry bookkeeping) is the requirement that it keep 8 per cent cash-reserve ratios against deposits. When deposits have expanded until they are twelve and a half times the new reserves, the monopoly bank is "loaned up" and can create no further deposits until given more reserves.

■ 10 In present-day Canada, there is no monopoly bank. Nevertheless, the same 12.5:1 expansion of bank deposits takes place. The first chartered bank receiving a new $1,000 of deposits spends 92 per cent of its newly acquired cash on loans and investments. This gives a second group of banks 92 per cent of $1,000 in new deposits. They, in turn, keep 8 per cent in cash and spend the other 92 per cent for new earning assets; this causes them to lose cash to a third set of banks, whose deposits have gone up by 92 per cent of 92 per cent of $1,000. Obviously, if we follow through the successive groups of banks in the dwindling, never-ending chain, we find for the system as a whole new deposits of $1,000 + $920 + $846.40 + $778.69 + ...

$$= \$1,000 \times [1 + .92 + (.92)^2 + (.92)^3 + ...]$$

$$= \$1,000 \left[\frac{1}{1 - .92}\right] = \$1,000 \left[\frac{1}{.08}\right] = \$12,500$$

Only when each dollar of the $1,000 of new reserves supports $12.50 of deposits somewhere in the system will the limits to deposit expansion be reached. Then the system is loaned up; it can create no further deposits until it is given more reserves.

■ 11 In practice, it is not necessary to wait for the successive rounds on the route of $1,000, $920, $846.40, ... , to work themselves out. Usually, many banks tend to get new reserves at about the same time. If they all expand their loans and investments approximately in balance, their outpayments will tend to cancel each other. Thus, each will not lose cash; and all together can rather quickly expand their earning assets and deposits to the 12.5:1 limit.

■ 12 The Canadian system has only nine chartered banks, with many hundreds of branches. Thus each lending bank can expect that an appreciable proportion (as much as one-fifth) of its loans and security-purchase payments will flow back as deposits into its *own* branches. This places the actual Canadian (also British, Swedish, etc.) system between the many-small-banks system and the hypothetical monopoly or one-bank system of the examples. Large Canadian banks could safely keep less than the required legal cash reserve, but are forbidden to do so. The smaller Canadian banks are not in the same position of expecting to get a good share of their own cheques returning for deposits in their own branches; if there were no legal ratio, they would probably voluntarily keep about the same ratio anyway.

■ 13 As a minor qualification to the above discussion, we must note that there will be some leakage of the new cash reserves of the banking system into circulation *outside* the banks. Therefore, instead of $12,500 of new deposits created, as in the previous examples, we may have something less than that—the difference being due to what is withdrawn from the system.

A second qualification results from the fact that a bank may keep *excess reserves* above legally required reserves. While big banks do not hold much excess in prosperous times, others may hold varying amounts of excessive reserves, depending upon interest rates and precautionary expectations. So there is nothing automatic about a 12.5:1 or other fixed-gear ratio.

In this chapter we have seen how bank deposits are kept at about twelve times the legal reserves of the banking system. In Chapter 16 we shall learn how the Bank of Canada makes bank reserves go up when an expansion of the total money supply is desired. When a contraction of the quantity of money is in order, the authorities pull the brakes. Instead of pumping new reserves into the banking system, they draw off some of the reserves. We shall see that in so doing they are able to reduce the quantity of money, not 1 for 1, but (as just shown) 12.5 for 1.

QUESTIONS FOR DISCUSSION

1. Suppose that all banks kept 100 per cent reserves. How different would they be? What function do legal reserves perform? What are "excess reserves"?

2. Assume a 10 per cent reserve ratio. Trace the process of multiple bank expansion, duplicating Tables 15-3(*a*) to 15-3(*i*). Reverse the process.

3. Do bankers create deposits? Who does? If a banker receives a new deposit and new reserves, is he always able to find borrowers? Can he always expand his holdings of government securities? How does he go about it?

4. "Banks borrow from their depositors at zero or low interest rates and invest most of the proceeds in higher-yielding loans and investments. They use the difference to pay their expenses, to provide us with low-cost mediums for monetary transactions, and to reward their stockholders for taking on the risks of declines in earning-asset values. They constitute an efficient method of allocating the saving and newly created *M* of the community to worthy local enterprises. One can scarcely imagine a better system than this, particularly with the chain system that insures depositors from loss and makes psychological bank runs improbable." Discuss critically but fairly.

5. "My bank's books always balance. I merely *pass on* to investors the savings that money depositors bring to my bank. Who dares say a banker can create *M* or demand deposits?" Do you dare?

6. "The central bank should create new reserves indefinitely, as long as we bankers can find good productive loans to make, because then each new *M* will be balanced by new product *Q* and prices won't rise and the community will get a higher real NNP indefinitely". This view was widely supported by the founders of the U.S. Federal Reserve System in 1913. Can you see where the implied elasticity of *M* could be harmful in a world of fluctuating *C + I + G* schedules? (HINT: Banks would expand *M* in booms and contract *M* in recessions.)

7. Review your understanding of the following concepts:

Bank of Canada, Governor,
    Board of Directors,
    Department of Finance
bank balance sheet
goldsmiths and fractional-
    reserve banking
legal cash reserve ratio
    requirements
diversity and liquidity of
    earning assets

"generations" of banks
deposit creation for a monopoly
    bank versus a chain system
    of banks
excess reserves, leakage of
    reserves
qualifications to multiple
    deposit creation

16

THE
CENTRAL BANK
AND MONETARY POLICY

There have been three great inventions since the beginning of time: fire, the wheel, and central banking. WILL ROGERS

The Bank of Canada is our central bank, a bank for bankers and for the government. Every central bank has one prime function:

> *It operates to control the economy's supply of money and credit.* If business is getting worse and jobs are getting scarce, the Bank of Canada will try to expand money and credit. But if spending threatens to become excessive, so that prices are rising and there are many job vacancies, then the Bank of Canada will do all that is possible to step on the brakes and contract money and credit. The policy of the equivalent U.S. central bank, the Federal Reserve, has been aptly said to "lean against the wind" of prevailing deficient or excessive aggregate-demand spending, to promote optimal real growth and price-level stability. All mixed economies rely on such a central bank.

In a nutshell that is the function of central banking. In this chapter we shall survey the weapons that the Bank uses to expand or contract money and credit.

■ HOW MONETARY POLICY WORKS TO CONTROL SPENDING

What is the exact process by which the Bank affects general spending? Here are five steps of the process:

1. The last chapter showed that chartered banks must have reserves to support their assets and deposits. (So important are these "reserves" that we shall capitalize the word for the rest of this chapter.)

The first step of the Bank, therefore, when it wants to put on the monetary brakes, is to act to cut down on the Reserves available to the banks.

2. *Each dollar contraction in bank Reserves forces about a $12.50 contraction in total bank money, i.e., in total demand deposits.* (Recall the last chapter's analysis of multiple deposit creation in a fractional-reserve banking system.)

3. *The contraction in total money makes credit generally "tight;" that is, both dearer and less available.* We shall see that less *M* will raise interest rates. As important, less *M* will make credit less *available* to people.

Interest rates will also rise for mortgage borrowers; for local governments that want to build schools and roads; and for businessmen anxious to build plants, buy new equipment, or add to inventory.

Reinforcing higher interest cost will be credit's decreased availability. Thus, if you want to build a house, it matters to you that the interest rate has risen from 8 to 10 per cent. If you are like most families, it matters even more that you may now find it hard to get a mortgage with a low down payment. You may find your lender's manner a shade cooler; and he may discourage you from buying the $35,000 house that you really prefer to the $25,000 one you have been considering. When *M* is scarce, turndowns on loans become common.

4. *With credit expensive and hard to get, private and public investment will tend to fall.* Why this downward shift in the *I* and *G* schedules?[1] This is because people's decisions as to whether it is profitable to build a new house or plant, order a new machine, and hold more inventory usually depend upon how they can finance such investment spending. If they have to pay a high interest rate or find it very hard to get loans, they often scale down their investment plans. The same holds for provincial and municipal governments. The old road gets patched up and that new road postponed when the town finds it cannot float its bonds at any reasonable interest rate. The gymnasium and library are cut out of the new school plans when the citizens learn their tax rate is going up because it now costs 9 per cent to borrow, instead of 6 or 5 per cent.

5. *Finally, the pressure on credit and on investment spending will, through the downward shift in the I + G schedule, have downward effects on income spending, prices, and jobs.* The multiplier analysis of Chapter 12 showed how such a drop in investment will depress income spending sharply.

If the Bank of Canada has been right in its diagnosis of inflationary conditions the drop in money income will be just what the doctor ordered to help the situation. *M* contraction will have succeeded in reducing the inflationary gap.

■ RECAPITULATION

This five-step sequence—from the Bank of Canada's changing the chartered bank's Reserves, to 12.5:1 changes in total *M*, to changes in credit's interest cost

---

[1] Later chapters (particularly Chapter 29) show that higher interest rates tend to depress the market value of wealth items: land, bonds, buildings, equipment. With their total wealth less and installment credit hard to get, people's *CC* schedule may also drift down along with their *II* schedules.

and availability, to changes in private and public investment spending, and finally to multiplied changes in money income—is vital. By rereading the italicized parts of the previous section, you can consolidate your understanding of it. Better still, psychologists tell us we learn fastest by participating. The previous section was explained in terms of a time when the Bank wants to *contract* business activity. Tackle the problem of how things proceed when the Bank wants to *expand* business activity.

> Suppose you are Governor Rasminsky at a time when the economy is mildly depressed. Suppose you are called to testify before a Royal Commission—as Rasminsky was in 1963-1964—to explain just how your *expansionary* acts would operate. Retrace these detailed steps.
>
> The Bank acts to expand Reserves; chartered banks engineer something like a 12.5:1 expansion in demand deposits; increase in society's M is associated with "easier money conditions," i.e., lower interest rates on loans, bonds, and mortgages and, equally important, more easily available credit to would-be investors and government spenders. There results an increase in I, G, and perhaps even durable-goods C installment spending. And finally, there follow multiplier effects of the shift in the C + I + G schedule on income, employment, and possibly price levels.

■ BALANCE SHEET OF THE BANK OF CANADA

Now that we have surveyed the process of monetary policy with a telescope, let us study the mechanism in some detail. We shall not attempt to put Bank of Canada policy under a microscope, since that is the job of an intermediate course in money and banking; but we do want to get a general idea of exactly what weapons the Bank can use to affect bank Reserves.

Look at Table 16-1. This lists the balance sheet of the Bank of Canada. The Bank holds a negligible amount of gold. Canadian government securities make up most of the assets—the significance of this item will be explained soon. The foreign exchange assets are usually roughly balanced by foreign-exchange liabilities. Advances to chartered banks are very rare and usually zero. The interest rate the Bank of Canada charges banks for such loans is called the "Bank Rate," and it is varied by the Bank as part of its monetary policy.

The right-hand side lists the usual capital accounts: original capital subscribed plus "rest fund" or accumulated surplus. This would be much greater for so profitable a business were it not for the fact that the Bank gives back to the Treasury all its excess profits.

Notes in circulation are the Bank's principal liabilities. These are the one, two, five, and ten-dollar bills, etc., we all carry in our wallets. These IOUs cost the Bank no interest, and it is highly privileged to have been granted by Parliament this monopoly power to issue all of our currency except coinage.

Little comment is needed on several of its deposit liabilities: government deposits, foreign central bank deposits, and miscellaneous.

Of vital importance, though, are the chartered bank's reserve balances kept by them on deposit at the Bank of Canada. Along with small amounts of vault cash, these are the Reserves we have been talking about, which provide the basis for multiple deposit creation by the banks.

Central bank notes and deposits underlie the money system:

BALANCE SHEET OF BANK OF CANADA, SPRING, 1970 (in millions of dollars)

ASSETS		LIABILITIES	
Gold	$ —	Capital items	$ 30
Foreign exchange	170	Notes in circulation	3,300
Advances to chartered banks	10	Deposits:	
Government of Canada securities		Chartered bank reserves	1,200
and short-term bills	4,000	Government of Canada	50
All other assets	520	Foreign	30
		Other liabilities	90
Total assets	$4,700	Total liabilities	$4,700

TABLE 16-1. By (a) controlling its earning assets (government securities), the Bank of Canada (b) controls its liabilities (deposits and Bank of Canada notes in circulation), thereby (c) controlling the economy's money supply (currency and chartered bank deposits).

We shall see that the Bank, by altering its holding of government securities can create changes in the Reserves of the chartered banks—thereby starting off our earlier-mentioned five-step sequence. The total of the Government of Canada securities is watched carefully; its moves reflect the desires of the Bank of Canada to ease or restrain credit conditions. (Later, Fig. 16-2 will show how these important balance-sheet items have changed in recent years.)

■ DISCRETIONARY MONETARY POLICIES BY THE BANK OF CANADA: OPEN-MARKET OPERATIONS

To initiate the mentioned five-step stabilization sequence, the Bank of Canada has two main tools, which are listed in order of their present importance: (1) open-market operations, (2) bank-rate policy. (We shall review its five minor tools later in this chapter.)

> By selling or buying government bonds in the open market (mostly in Toronto and Montreal), the authorities can tighten chartered bank Reserves or loosen them. These so-called "open-market operations" are the Bank of Canada's most important stabilizing weapon.

At frequent intervals, even as you read this book, the officers of the Bank are meeting to decide whether to pump more Reserves into the banking system by buying treasury bills (i.e., short-term bonds) or longer bonds, or whether to tighten things up a little by selling government securities. It is a never-ending job.

To see how an open-market operation changes Reserves, let us suppose that the Bank of Canada thinks the economic winds are blowing up a little inflation. The Executive Committee holds its weekly meeting. The committee surveys the credit situation. This results in instructions to the securities department, one of which is to "sell 10 million dollars of government bonds from our portfolio to contract Reserves and over-all credit." To whom are the bonds sold? No one

Open-market sale cuts Reserves and cuts deposits 12.5:1:

(a) First, producing this change in the balance sheet of the Bank of Canada (millions of dollars)

ASSETS OF BANK OF CANADA		LIABILITIES OF BANK OF CANADA	
Government securities	−$10	Chartered bank deposits (Reserves)	−$10
Total	−$10	Total	−$10

(b) Finally, producing this change in the combined balance sheet of all chartered banks (millions of dollars)

ASSETS OF CHARTERED BANKS		LIABILITIES OF CHARTERED BANKS	
Reserves	−$ 10	Demand and savings deposits	−$125
Investments and loans	− 115		
Total	−$125	Total	−$125

TABLE 16-2(a) and (b). When an open-market sale of government securities kills off 10 million dollars of Reserves, it induces a drop of 125 million dollars in total deposits. The chartered banks must sell off their "investments" (i.e., securities they own) and cut new loans (or call in old loans) up to 115 million dollars.

knows: to the open market. The dealers in government bonds—there are about half a dozen big ones—will not reveal the names of the buyers. But you can guess that they are primarily insurance companies, commercial banks, and big business firms.

The buyer will most likely pay for the Bank of Canada bonds by a cheque drawn on his bank account. The Bank of Canada will present this cheque for payment to his bank. That bank will then lose an equivalent amount of its Reserve balances with the Bank of Canada. Table 16-2(*a*) shows the final effect on the central bank's balance sheet. The open-market sale has cut down on the Bank of Canada's assets and liabilities. (It has also initially cut down on bank Reserves and their demand deposits owed to the bond buyer.)

Actually, this shows only the *initial* potency of open-market sales. In all likelihood the 10 million-dollar sale of government bonds will result in a 125 million-dollar cut in the community's money supply. We've seen why before. Let us continue to assume that Reserves are kept at 8 per cent of demand and savings deposits.

Reserves go down by 10 million dollars, and that tends to set off a 125 million-dollar contraction of deposits. Table 16-2 shows the banks' position after Reserves have been extinguished by the open-market operation. In the end, the Bank of Canada's open-market sale has put 12.5:1 downward pressure on bank deposit *M*.

To test your understanding of open-market operations, consider the reverse process. Suppose incomes and jobs are at too low a level. What will the Bank of

Canada's Executive Committee want to do? Buy government bills on the open market and thereby create new Reserves for the chartered banks? Produce thereby a 12.5:1 expansion in M, thus making credit cheaper and more easily available to investors and consequently encouraging an upward shift in $C + I + G$ and a multiplier increase in NNP?

◼ BANK RATE POLICY: A SECOND WEAPON

The Bank of Canada also makes loans to the chartered banks. These we call "advances." They occur rarely and, when they do, are very small. Whenever the central bank is making advances, the banks are borrowing Reserves from the Bank of Canada. If advances are dropping or are made hard to get, the central bank is helping Reserves to contract.

Unfortunately, the Bank of Canada is not free to pursue an advance policy exactly the way it wants to. It cannot send salesmen out to drum up more loans to banks whenever it wants to expand them. All it can do is wait for banks to come to it. All it can do is name the "Bank Rate" which sets its interest charge for such advances.

In theory, the central bank could get more advances business by lowering Bank Rate, and could discourage banks from seeking this credit by raising it. But on the whole its role must be passive. It can sit and wait. It can say "No." It can set an attractive Bank Rate. But it certainly cannot *set* its amount of advances at any figure it wishes. Only in its open-market operations can it take an active role.

Two points of detail about advances and Bank Rate: (1) The U.S. Federal Reserve central bank, at its foundation in 1913, planned to make loans to commercial banks by "rediscounting" the promissory notes they had received from their customers. In effect, they could sell these loans and IOUs to the Federal Reserve bank for their face value minus interest at the rather high Bank Rate. This would protect bank borrowers against their local bank's ever running out of the power to lend for worthy investments. This is still possible in the United States and thus advances are called "discounts." But in fact today most U.S. banks sell government bills and bonds, not promissory notes to the Fed when they want help.

The whole idea is unpopular anyway today because the Fed does not want commercial banks to have the power to automatically increase their credit to customers, when they are short of Reserves, by rediscounting. Such power leads to an *elastic* money supply and to the aggravating of inflationary or depression problems.

(2) The Bank of Canada, for technical reasons, discourages the chartered banks from applying directly to the central bank for advances. It prefers to develop a system adapted from the Bank of England and now more or less common with central banks everywhere: forcing the banks to try to get cash for their Reserves from the money market before, as a last resort, they apply to the central bank for advances.

It works this way. A chartered bank, short of Reserves, calls in some of its very short-term loans to bond dealers and traders. (These are made on a day-today basis.) These money-market dealers have used the loans to finance their business inventories of securities. What are they to do now? First they try another chartered bank. If it can make a replacement day-to-day loan, everyone is happy and the first bank has in effect turned some of its earning assets (loans) into Reserves (cash), which were *indirectly* obtained from the second bank. Second, if the dealers cannot find a bank to make the loans, they apply to the Bank of Canada for a loan, pledging some of their inventory of bills and bonds (government securities). Thus the bank of Canada is practically "rediscounting" these bills. The dealer must pay Bank Rate for this advance. In this second case, the first chartered bank has indirectly obtained Reserves from the central bank. In the first case, the central bank was not involved at all.

CHANGING THE BANK RATE   In every economy, people in business and finance listen carefully for announcements of change in the central bank's interest rate. When, in 1964, the Bank of England raised the British rate from 5 to 7 per cent, it meant that loans and money-raising would be tighter and dearer to British borrowers. It also meant that North American lenders would find lending to British borrowers more profitable than to Canadian or U.S. business; so they began at once to sell their New York and Toronto securities and buy bonds in London. This "flight of capital" was stemmed the next day by raising the Federal Reserve discount rate and the Bank of Canada's Bank Rate. The example illustrates two things: (*a*) changes in the central bank's lending rate touch off many more events than mere changes in chartered bank advances—they often serve as an official signal of general policy intentions, visible to everyone concerned; (*b*) especially in the international economy, from which neither the large United States nor small Canada is insulated, Bank Rate changes often *follow* rather than lead market changes.

Even in a closed economy (one cut off from world capital flows), Bank Rate often follows the market. Even when the central bank doesn't have to protect the local money markets from winds of change blowing up elsewhere, they rarely rely on Bank Rate as their main monetary policy tool. Instead, they depend on open-market policy. What happens then? If the open-market policy is to tighten credit conditions, the chartered banks will find themselves steadily shorter of Reserves. The central bank wants them to reduce loans and investments—but they may attempt to obtain more Reserves instead, by seeking advances directly from the Bank of Canada or indirectly through the money market. If the profit on their investments is high, chartered banks will find it profitable to pay high Bank Rate for Reserves rather than cut down their investments (and loans). To prevent this (that is, to prevent the banks circumventing the aims of the original open-market operations), Bank Rate must now go up enough to make borrowing Reserves unprofitable.

For this reason, we usually find the Canadian Bank Rate fractionally higher than the rate banks can earn on short-term investments in the Toronto and Montreal money market. Indeed, for many years, Governor Coyne followed the policy of automatically, by formula, making Bank Rate depend on bill rates of the day; a policy fully understood by the money market. This formula procedure for setting Bank Rate has now been dropped, but the Bank of Canada still keeps close to the short-run market rate. (For example, in early 1971, day-to-day market loans by banks yielded 2.8 per cent, while the Bank Rate was 5.25 per cent.)

Because Bank Rate changes usually *reinforce* other policy measures (like a general having battalions in reserve that everyone knows about and that do not get into battle just because they exist), their chief role in all countries is to act as a *signal*. The mere announcement of a fall in official Bank Rate means that a high rate is no longer needed to reinforce open-market operations. That is, open-market operations must no longer be in effect to force monetary contraction. So the dealer, businessman, and borrower know at once that "credit is being eased"; and the local bank manager knows, even before his regional superintendent phones him, that he can be more helpful in meeting the loan requests of his customers. Further, other lenders outside the banking system know that they will have to cut their loan rates, or their customers will go to the banks instead. Thus, on the *signal* of the Bank Rate's cut, the whole money market begins to ease credit conditions. (The reader should check his understanding by rereading the effect of open-market operations, and working out what would happen if Bank Rate were not raised.[2])

■ AN ABANDONED WEAPON: CHANGING RESERVE REQUIREMENTS

The chartered banks must maintain a certain minimum cash ratio to deposits— 8 per cent in our examples. If the Bank of Canada were to raise this cash ratio, say by one percentage point a month, it would very quickly make credit conditions tight. The banks' existing holdings of cash (and Reserves at the Bank of Canada) would be less and less adequate for their deposits. They would have to reduce deposits in an effort to conform with the new legal cash requirements. If, on the other hand, the Bank of Canada wished to ease credit conditions, it could help by cutting legal cash reserve ratios.

Until May, 1967, the Bank of Canada had such powers to alter the reserve ratio. But it never used the powers, and abandoned them in the 1967 revision of the Bank Act.

Changing reserve requirements is a powerful tool that is used, occasionally, by the U.S. Federal Reserve system. It is not used every day, as in the case of open-market operations, which produce about the same effect. If we look at the working of this weapon in the United States, we can see why the Bank of Canada never used it even when it could.

---

[2] Note that both demand and supply come in here. A higher Bank Rate merely signals that supply is reduced. Lending interest rates go up, so that borrowers, together, want fewer or smaller loans. If loanable funds move in from abroad, as in our 1964 British example, supply at the higher interest rates may actually fall very little. This is because British open-market operations cut the supply of Reserves for British banks only. Foreign lenders are now in a position to replace British banks and lenders in London markets. But only as long as rates in London are higher than those in the United States or elsewhere. So the rate of interest must stay up, and this will dictate that total loans asked for by London borrowers will be smaller. Try drawing supply and demand curves to show these events.

Exactly how does an increase in required reserve ratios operate to tighten credit? Suppose the U.S. commercial banks had built up deposits in a 5:1 fashion as a result of the required ratio having been 20 per cent, with excess reserves being negligible. Now suppose the Federal Resrve Board wants to tighten credit and raises the required ratio to 25 per cent. Even if it does nothing by the way of open-market operations or discount policy to change bank Reserves, the commercial banks now have to contract greatly their loans and investments—and their deposits.

Why? Because in effect some of their previous Reserves have been impounded. Now the bank deposits can only be in a 4:1, not a 5:1, ratio. So there will have to be a drop by one-fifth in all deposits.

This painful cut will start to take place quickly. For as soon as the Federal Reserve Board signs the new fiat raising requirements to 25 per cent, banks will find themselves deficient with respect to Reserves. They will have to sell some of their bonds and call in some loans. The bond buyers will use up their demand deposits, and the borrowers whose loans are called will have to use up their demand deposits to pay back such loans. The process ends only after banks have brought down their deposits to four rather than five times their Reserves.

Table 16-3 shows how their combined balance sheets might look after the change. You may be sure that so great a change in so short a time would result in very high interest rates, in unavailable credit, in great cuts in I (and possibly in local G), and in great reductions in national income and employment. Hence, this powerful weapon of changing reserve requirements is rarely used, even in the United States.

■ AN AUXILIARY WEAPON: SECONDARY RESERVES

From 1955 to 1967 the Bank of Canada, by agreement, compelled the banks to keep a part of their assets in very liquid form; that is, it prevented them from selling these very liquid assets to gain cash Reserves. These informal powers were written into the Bank Act in 1966-1967. Today, the banks must maintain this *secondary reserve* at whatever percentage (between 6 and 12) of their

Raising Reserve requirements forces U.S. commercial banks to contract:

Before: when 1:5 prevails (billions of dollars)

MEMBER BANK ASSETS		MEMBER BANK LIABILITIES	
Reserves	$ 20	Demand deposits	$100
Loans and investments	80		
Total	$100	Total	$100

After: when 1:4 prevails (billions of dollars)

MEMBER BANK ASSETS		MEMBER BANK LIABILITIES	
Reserves	$20	Demand deposits	$80
Loans and investments	60		
Total	$80	Total	$80

TABLE 16-3. The same base of Reserves now supports only 4 : 1, not 5 : 1, of deposits. What will be happening on Main Street in the transition?

deposits the Bank of Canada shall dictate. The secondary reserve is made up of three types of assets: cash (additional to the cash that forms part of the primary legal cash reserve), treasury bills, and day-to-day money-market loans.

Hence, although it cannot now change the legal cash reserve ratio, the Bank of Canada has a new power to alter the secondary-reserve ratio. It set it at 7 per cent till 1969, then 8 per cent, then 9 per cent in June, 1970.

If the cash-reserve ratio were raised, the banks would try to convert their holdings of government securities into cash to meet the increasing cash requirement. Such selling would force down the price of securities, raise their yield, and so raise the market rate of interest even when the Bank of Canada did not want this interest-rate effect. Incidentally, it would also reduce the earnings of banks for reasons that had nothing to do with their performance or their competitive effectiveness.

But if instead the *secondary-reserve ratio* is raised, the banks need not all sell liquid assets such as treasury bills. The liquidity they have accumulated in slack times is simply immobilized and prevented from serving as the reserve basis of an expansion of bank lending or easing of credit conditions. Further, the banks do not lose the earnings from their liquid securities, as they would in responding to a rise in the cash reserve ratio.

It appears that the new power to change the secondary-reserve ratio will be more delicate than the former power to change the cash ratio.

◼ MORAL SUASION AND OTHER "QUALITATIVE" CONTROLS

The Bank of Canada and the monetary experts in the government are always concerned about the supply of credit and money. But they also take an interest in *who* is getting the credit available. This is partly because the credit availability to certain sectors of the economy (export industries, home builders, farmers) may be a special object of national social policy. It is also because changed credit conditions may have a magnified effect on national interest rates, prices, incomes, employment, and growth if they are allowed to concentrate on a particular sector. Thus, if the economy is progressing smoothly after a slump, with patches of unemployment still to be found, the central bank may want to restrain consumer credit (to prevent inflationary pressure on certain appliance industries) yet allow credit ease to other, slower-recovering sectors like building or forestry.

To do this it wants to exert an influence on the distribution of credit, not its total amount. In technical jargon, it wants to use "qualitative," not "quantitative," controls. The word quality in this use refers to the *kind* of bank customers to be favored or hindered rather than to their merit, the riskiness that they won't repay, or other aspects of their personal or financial "quality." It is just the opposite of "quantity" of credit. In Canada, except in national emergencies, moral suasion is the chief qualitative weapon available to the Bank of Canada.

"MORAL SUASION" This phrase is now part of official banking and economic jargon. Moral suasion is the opposite of the impersonal, mechanical weapons such as open-market operations and the two others. It involves personal contact between the Bank of Canada and the chartered bankers. On being questioned about moral suasion (which, being conducted in private meetings, is never fully known about except by rumor), Governor Rasminsky answered in 1964:

> The way moral suasion works in practice is that the Governor of the Bank of Canada meets with the executive officers of the chartered banks, expresses to them certain views regarding whatever it is he is trying morally to persuade them to, and asks for their cooperation in enforcing those views, which might relate on occasion to the distribution of credit. [That is, to the distribution of the banks' assets between extending loans to one kind of customer as against another, and between loans and securities.]. . . .
>
> The minimum liquid asset ratio agreement was of this type; it was in November and December of 1955. . . .
>
> From what I know of the matter, such suggestions [from the Bank of Canada] give rise to a good deal of give and take in discussion, but suggestions of this sort are not made unless there is a clear public interest in them being followed, and since the central bank by and large is somewhat reluctant to use these techniques, . . . the general experience is that the public interest is recognized by the chartered banks and after the discussion the cooperation of the chartered banks is forthcoming.

There is no doubt that in Canada moral suasion can be a powerful weapon. There are only nine banks; they all know the total national banking situation well, and are probably in sympathy with the central bank's problems. Just as important, the central bank is by law directly and indirectly in a position to "induce" their agreement—any bank that refuses to go along can have its business harmed by Bank of Canada operations later. But there is no record that threats of such harm actually occur in discussion; the evidence for their powerfulness is tangential: the installment finance companies, which are *not* responsible to the Bank of Canada, refused to change their policies in 1956 when Governor Coyne held a moral-suasion session with them. The nine banks recognize the latent power exercised over them by the Bank of Canada in a way that other financial companies do not.

Other evidence can be found abroad. The Bank of England, the birthplace of moral suasion, has a similarly small group of bankers to deal with, over whom it exerts immense moral power if it chooses. The Federal Reserve Banks in the United States also frequently call in their members for heart-to-heart talks. But there are so many banks, many of them very small, that maverick bank officers, who refuse to go along with moral suasion, will be found in every region. They prefer to take the risks rather than submit to suggestions that they change lending policies which are presently much in their interest. Consequently, moral suasion plays a weaker role than rules and laws in the United States. It is a technique that works best when there are few banks.

As the examples mentioned suggest, the usual aim of moral suasion in all countries is to influence the banks' asset or lending policies. The central bank may want them to favor certain kinds of borrowers, or to reduce their "margin" lending to stockbrokers, their "term" lending for up to five years, or their lending to domestic luxury trades rather than to export industries (a favorite of the Bank of England and the U.K. government). These are problems of *distribution* of credit rather than of total credit availability. If the latter is to be changed, the central bank can most easily act directly, by open-market operations.[3]

CONTROL OVER INSTALLMENT TERMS   In mid-1970, the federal government—*not* the Bank of Canada—claimed powers to set limits on installment contracts. Great Britain and the United States had done this, very effectively, for some years. Canada last did so during wartime emergency. Such powers may compel large down payments, large installment payments (short terms), and high charges—or the opposite, and thus shift the CC function. (In fact, the necessary legislation got lost in the events of May-June, 1970, and has not been proclaimed. But consumer finance control is likely to recur as a weapon of the central authorities).

OTHER GOVERNMENT INFLUENCES   Apart from central bank powers, the Ottawa government can make, and has made, laws about banking that affect the quality of bank credit. Sometimes the effect is negative or indirect.

> For example, commercial banks in this country could not until 1967 charge more than 6 per cent on loans, by law. (They did charge more, however, on consumer loans by asking 6 per cent per year on the *original* loan, while the amount already repaid by the borrower increased. Thus the interest payments were collected at a steadily higher rate on the unpaid balance of the loan. Mathematical tables show that the typical interest payment over the whole life of such bank consumer loans works out at about 10 per cent per annum.) The 6 per cent maximum meant that *commercial* borrowers whose projects were too risky to be given credit at this low price were forced to go elsewhere for credit. Royal commissions on banking gave attention to this matter, usually suggesting that there was no *economic* reason for holding commercial banks to business that is safe at 6 per cent. But members of Parliament were unwilling to change the law, which they believed protected voters against "usury" by the bankers. Actually, what it did was close the banks to many of them and force them to have recourse to more usurious financial firms than banks.
>
> Again, the law restrained the banks from going heartily into mortgage business. (There were also some ways around this.) The result was that the money market raised much of its mortgage money from specialized mortgage companies and from the government's Central Mortgage and Housing Corporation. There are other examples in farm lending, consumer credit against chattels, and term lending (up to five years). First the removal of the 6 per cent maximum interest rate and then the removal of any top NHA mortgage rate in 1969 changed the situation radically. The banks were permitted to enter the mortgage field, and they did so with gusto.
>
> All these regulations and new institutions had their virtues. They gave protection to some borrowers. And they left the chartered banks as very solid institu-

---

[3] The Bank of Canada has little or no legal power over mortgage and trust companies, which are "near-banks." Mostly, these institutions are under provincial jurisdiction, though there are other constitutional barriers too. In the United States, the Federal Reserve has power, at its discretion, to regulate how much of a stock or bond "margin" can be borrowed in stock exchange purchases; the minimum down payment on installment purchases by consumers; and the maximum interest rate that can be paid on time or savings deposits. In other countries such powers are not exercised at all; or if they are used, they are enforced directly by the government, not by the central bank. The central bank cannot vary them as part of its monetary policy.

tions by protecting their depositors against the banks' engaging in types of lending that might ultimately endanger their deposits.

But there were unintended results too. As competitive theory would predict, the regulations encouraged "near-banks" and other institutions to flourish. If these were owned by the government, they often worked in direct contradiction to central-bank policy. If they were private, their Reserves and policies would be under no control at all, except indirectly through the chartered banks with whom they deal. For this reason, many experts argued that the banking powers of the chartered banks should be broadened, if only to keep credit conditions directly under central-bank control. This broadening was achieved in 1966-1967, when the banks, apart from Reserve requirements, were essentially freed to compete with all other types of lenders. In particular, the cancellation of the proposed 1970 Bill to control consumer credit conditions served to permit banks to continue in the lucrative consumer loan market.

▮ FOREIGN EXCHANGE AND GOLD

Until now we have been speaking as if all changes in total M originate in deliberate actions by the Bank of Canada, aimed at changing bank Reserves in a desired direction. In all countries, and particularly in Canada, there is, however, an external force that may affect our M, namely foreign exchange movements and gold flows. These are primarily transactions in U.S. dollars or pounds-sterling to or from abroad. But it should be realized that while these flows can affect our M, the standard weapons of monetary policy can *offset* any such changes if they are thought to be against the national interest.

Part Five will deal with international trade in detail; here we need touch only upon its banking aspects. When Canadian exporters are selling more goods abroad than importers are buying, foreigners balance their books by sending us foreign exchange. (Actually, they rarely mail foreign currency; instead their payments result in Canadians owning deposits in foreign banks.) This is like new cash to Canada. People connected with exporting will make new deposits of their export earnings. The reader now may well ask, "Won't these deposits be a source of new chartered bank Reserves? And won't they make possible the familiar 12.5:1 expansion process—just as in our earlier examples where a widow, or a seller of bonds in a Bank of Canada open-market operation, or anyone else brought new Reserves to deposit in a chartered bank?" The answer is, Yes—*if* the export earnings have a form legally suitable for becoming Reserves. For example, when gold was still both a domestic and an international currency, and new export earnings always became a net addition to Canadian banks' Reserves, permitting a 12.5:1 expansion. Today, the effect of new foreign earnings depends on how we handle them. They may force a change in domestic M; alternatively we can offset (or "Sterilize") them, or adjust our rate of exchange.

THE OLD GOLD STANDARD Canadian currency was, until the Great Depression, convertible or redeemable in gold. Canadian banking and money markets were not very well developed, but in theory Canadians, Americans, and most Europeans used gold coins, gold certificates (a warehouse receipt for gold), or paper currency redeemable in gold.

In those days, when "America" sold more exports than she bought imports, the difference was received in gold bars. Whoever got the bars (the exporter, or a bank serving a group of exporters and importers) took them to the government and received gold coin or redeemable paper money. The exporter would take them to his bank, or the bank would put them to the credit of its exporting customers. Then would begin one of our familiar multiple expansions of credit. (The amount of expansion would depend upon the legal or customary reserve ratio of the day. In the United States it was lower than today's; in Canada it was higher.) The opposite effect, a *contraction* of M, would result if "America" exported gold bars to Europe, to pay for a surplus of imports over exports. This tended to occur when Canada, for example between 1900 and 1913, was growing very fast and badly needed supplies from abroad even when she had nothing new to sell. Chapter 32 gives more details—all we need know is that foreign transactions *automatically* changed the domestic M.

SINCE THE DEPRESSION   Since 1934 neither the Bank of Canada, nor the United States government, nor the United Kingdom has been prepared to redeem its currency in gold. Canada's gold stock did "stand behind" central bank notes till World War II, but in 1939 the government took over the gold stock and has held it in its Exchange Fund Account ever since. Today, neither Canada nor the United Kingdom stand ready to deliver gold, even to foreigners who have been selling more to Canada than they are buying from it.

> The United States, on the other hand, would until 1968 pay gold abroad to settle its excessive import bills and would sell U.S. currency to foreigners who offered gold. Furthermore, if U.S. exporters received gold in payment, they could sell it, receive Federal Reserve bank notes, deposit them in their own banks where they became new Reserves, and so touch off a new domestic monetary expansion. Thus in the United States, net foreign-trade surpluses or deficits, as in pre-Depression days, *automatically* changed the supply of money and credit.[4] In 1968, the United States altered its willingness to deal in gold; henceforth, it would buy or sell at $35 to the ounce only in trade with foreign central banks.
>
> The precise international importance of gold today is difficult to summarize. Some countries, especially the United States, have required a "gold backing" for their currency. And many countries tend to settle international debts in gold. But so far as Canada is concerned, gold has been officially just a handy export item, which could be sold to the U.S. government at $35 per ounce (U.S. funds) when foreign currency was needed.[5] Most of our stock was mined in Canada; but some is also received as payment for wheat exports to countries like Russia and China.

■ FOREIGN EXCHANGE AS A CONSTRAINT ON MONETARY POLICY

While our currency and Reserves are today independent of gold backing or the duty of gold redemption, our M is not yet independent of foreign transactions.

---

[4] The automatic change, however, may be simultaneously offset by the Federal Reserve Board. If an inflow of gold is swelling the money supply, as just discussed, a simultaneous open-market withdrawal of Reserves may tend to keep it where it was.

[5] Official statistics suggest that in December 1970 Canada held 23 million troy ounces of gold, worth about 791 million dollars. During the year she had exported about 2 million ounces.

Exports and imports still affect our credit conditions; and foreign considerations still influence our monetary policy. Much of this will come up again in Part Five, but the reader neglects it now at his peril. Today there is no country whose domestic economic health is free of balance of payment effects.

When an exporter gains foreign currency (or a deposit in a foreign bank) he sells it to his bank for Canadian dollars. He is then out of the transaction. If his bank has many such purchases, it sells them, through official brokers in Montreal and Toronto, to other banks who need them to supply foreign exchange to Canadian importers. Imagine now that exporters have more foreign money to sell than importers need. Their banks will still try to get rid of this foreign money, for they want Reserves in Canadian funds. Their efforts to dispose of it will drive down the price of foreign currency in Canadian terms; that is, tend to drive *up* the international value of Canadian money.

FREE EXCHANGE RATES   If official policy is to allow the exchange rate to find its own level, no intervention will occur when the Canadian dollar rises. What are the consequences?

The foreign customers of our exporters, like foreign buyers of Canadian land and securities, now have to pay more, and may decide to trade elsewhere. Foreign shares and goods bought by Canadian investors and importers are now cheaper, and will be brought in. Our tourists abroad get a windfall—unless their foreign currency was bought at the old rate!—but foreign tourists to Canada stay away in droves. Those who gain tend to buy more, and those who lose buy less: these are the familiar adjustments to a change in any price, including foreign exchange. These reactions, and adjustments, change demand and supply and prevent the rate from drifting upward (or downward) forever.

Our interest here lies in the connection between the exchange rate's level and freedom to conduct internal monetary policy. What must the monetary authorities do when the rate moves up? Nothing, unless they wish to push it back again. Normally, any rate is as good as any other. A change in the exchange rate, when it is unimpeded, will alter foreign-trade and other flows, but not in a way that need make credit conditions tighter, or easier.

Of course, the rate of exchange and monetary conditions are not independent. Open-market operations and other monetary weapons *will* change the exchange rate predictably, of course. For example, a policy of selling bonds will cut Reserves, reduce M, and tighten credit conditions. The five-step sequence presented on page 381 will then shift down $C + I + G$ schedules, including the *import content* of each of these types of spending. Such a fall in demand for imports will tend to reduce the Canadian demand for foreign currency, and produce a "strengthening"—an upward movement—in the value of our dollar. But this exchange-rate effect neither weakens nor strengthens the initial open-market operation, which can be continued until its domestic goal has been achieved.

Monetary policy may also influence exchange rates indirectly through capital movements. Stringent credit conditions, open-market selling, or a high Bank Rate may all lead to low prices and high yields on domestic bonds, attractive to foreign investors. In order to buy bonds, they may add to the demand for Canadian dollars, thus raising the exchange rate. Similarly easy-money conditions and low yields on government securities may cause a short-run capital exodus that depresses the exchange rate. Either way, however, this exchange-rate effect is not undesirable in itself.

FIXED EXCHANGE RATES   However, to allow such flexibility is frequently against government policy. The government, to enforce its decision to keep the world value of Canadian dollars at a certain level, must prevent export-earned foreign moneys from falling in price in Canadian terms. Since there is no money-market buyer who will take them *at the price the government wants to maintain*, the government's Exchange Fund Account must buy the foreign currency itself.[6]

It is at this stage that domestic M is affected. For the Exchange Fund Account (EFA) must have a supply of Canadian dollars with which to make quick offers for any foreign currency that threatens to fall in price below the predetermined limit acceptable to government exchange-rate policy. This Canadian cash must be advanced from the government's own chartered bank deposits. To acquire a chartered bank's foreign exchange for the EFA, the government writes a cheque on its own deposits in another bank. Thus one bank gains a deposit in selling foreign exchange, and another loses Reserves as the government's deposit is drawn upon. In effect, therefore, Reserves are shunted from one chartered bank to another, and total M is unchanged.

What if the government's deposits at chartered banks are insufficient to purchase all offered foreign exchange? Two alternatives present themselves. If the government borrows from the public or increases taxes to replenish its deposits, deposits are transferred from the public to government, but Reserves and therefore total M are unaffected. This transaction, in which the government raises money from the bond buyer or taxpayer to buy foreign exchange for the EFA, is similar to the government's raising money to buy an Old Master for the National Gallery: M does not change. Alternatively, the government may borrow from the Bank of Canada. Then the proceeds of the bonds will be new deposits in the Bank of Canada which the selling banks can add to their Reserves. It is in this type of case that the familiar 12.5:1 expansion process will begin. It turns out that foreign transactions have "caused" Canadian M to expand, just as would have happened if gold were still in use.

> To test his understanding, the reader should work out what happens when Canadian imports exceed exports. The EFA will now gain Canadian dollars and lose some of its stock of foreign money, as a result of an attempt to keep Canadian dollars from selling at below the desired price in, say, U.S. dollars. These Cana-

---

[6] All this is based on the assumption that Canada has a fixed exchange rate. Before 1961-1962, and since June 1, 1970, there has been no official value of the Canadian dollar. Its price in U.S. dollars is determined, each day, by supply and demand. Under a pure flexible exchange-rate system, the government does not interfere in the exchange market. (The Canadian government will stabilize the exchange market when it is deemed necessary, but no attempt is made to maintain a set rate.) As discussed on page 394, the government and the central bank allow the flexible rate to bear the impact of changes in trade or in capital flows.

dian dollars will be returned to the government, which may buy back some of its bonds from the public or lower taxes. If it buys bonds from the Bank of Canada, this will, as described in the section on open-market operations, reduce chartered bank Reserves and so contract the Canadian M.

It must be stressed, however, that neither of these operations now *automatically* changes Canadian M. The expansion of Reserves depends on whether the government decides to issue bonds to the Bank of Canada, or to run down its own funds instead. Even if it has no funds, the whole operation can be offset by a simultaneous Bank of Canada open-market operation to reduce chartered bank Reserves. In effect, it buys bonds from the government while selling bonds to the money market. M does not change.

FREEDOM TO CONDUCT MONETARY POLICY　But although the Bank of Canada may be able to offset or sterilize the flows of foreign currency, it is still unable to cut itself out of international financial influences. For the Bank must keep two goals in view; not only a nice control of Canadian M, but also a healthy rate of exchange and balance of international payments. If the first goal calls for credit ease, in order to encourage domestic I and G, the result observable to foreigners will be that Canadian interest rates will fall. This means that both Canadians and foreigners will prefer to move their funds to other countries, where they can get relatively higher interest rates on their deposits and loans. There will be a resulting "drain" of foreign currency. For example, the EFA will find that it is having to supply more and more of its stock of U.S. dollars to Canadian banks whose customers want to buy them. The result may eventually be that either (a) the EFA runs out of foreign currency and has to let the value of the Canadian dollar fall, or (b) the government has to persuade the Bank of Canada to let Canadian interest rates rise again. If (a) is an unacceptable policy, then the efforts of monetary policy to encourage the growth of NNP through credit ease must be abandoned.

The example is familiar to many countries. It is difficult, with a fixed rate of exchange, to achieve a healthy economy at home and to maintain a balance of international payments. We shall see in a later chapter that this fear of exchange-rate collapse has constrained the use of monetary policy, and has led either to the use of flexible rates, or to the suggestion that reliance be put upon fiscal policy instead.

■ THE PYRAMID OF CREDIT

We have seen that the public's M consists of the liabilities of the chartered banks and (as currency) of the Bank of Canada. The chartered banks' assets include loans, liabilities of the public; Reserves, liabilities of the Bank of Canada; and securities, liabilities of the government. The assets of the Bank of Canada are almost all liabilities of the government. Thus the supply of M used by the public is the broad top of an upside-down pyramid, which interlocks the assets and liabilities of three levels of credit, or lending, and narrows down to the credit of the government at the pointed end. Gold is not to be found in this structure, and foreign exchange affects it only indirectly.

Bank of Canada Reserves and Currency are central to our money supply:

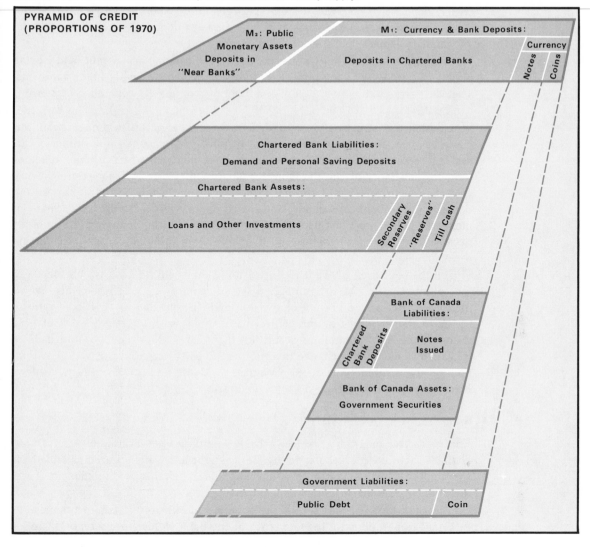

FIG. 16-1. The width of the "pyramid" is limited by Reserves; and these are controlled by Bank of Canada policies. In 1970, M_2 = 32 billion dollars, M_1 = 24 billion dollars, and Reserves = 1.9 billion dollars. "Near-money" is not effectively controlled.

The structure is shown, more or less to scale, in Fig. 16-1. At the bottom of the figure should be shown all the government's debts; but all that is pictured is the liabilities that are assets of the Bank of Canada, plus the supply of coinage. Moving upward in the figure, we see that to match these assets the central bank has liabilities: issued notes and deposits of the chartered banks. The latter are assets of the chartered banks, along with some currency, holdings of the government debt (bonds and bills), and a large amount of loans to bank customers, IOUs, and business securities.

Against these assets, the chartered banks have their own liabilities: significantly, deposits. These range from the very liquid and chequable demand deposits through personal savings and business term deposits. To their left are the very similar deposit liabilities of "near-banks."

All these bank liabilities are included in the monetary assets held by the public, M_2, along with the public's holdings of Bank of Canada notes and coins. The M_1 assets are the most liquid, and are most completely controlled by central-bank policy.

To call this structure a "pyramid" requires some graphical imagination. But it can be seen that a very large amount of public M is based on a slender point: the securities issued by the government and held as assets by the Bank of Canada. The taper of the pyramid depends upon two ratios that relate the size of one level to the size of the next: the legal reserve ratio of bank deposits to deposits in the Bank of Canada, and the secondary-reserve ratio. The armory of monetary-policy weapons uses these two ratios either by changing the amounts necessary to meet these ratios and available to maintain them, or by changing the compulsory ratios themselves.

In the countries where it is still required that gold be held as "backing" for the currency or for M, a box of gold would replace part of the box of government securities at the bottom of the pyramid. If gold had to be a fixed ratio to M, or to the liabilities of the central bank, then as the national stock of gold changed, the total amount of securities, loans, and other assets would have to be varied to eventually change the public's M. Until recently, this was the situation of the United States, but Congress in 1968 finally released the Federal Reserve system from keeping a fixed gold ratio.

■ FINANCIAL CHANGES WITHIN A YEAR

The preceding diagram gives us a fairly complete, but a still, picture. To see changes that take place, refer to Fig. 16-2. Important statistics are available from the Bank of Canada every month in the invaluable *Statistical Supplement*. These are published as charts and statistical tables.

In the following paragraphs the quoted remarks are the comments on Bank of Canada operations by the Governor of the Bank in his annual report covering 1969. It is worth taking time to compare his remarks with what the charts show (indicated in the square brackets).

"In an environment influenced by the continued strong demand for funds, entrenched inflationary expectations on the part of borrowers and lenders, and sharply rising interest rates abroad, monetary policy became increasingly restrictive during 1969. As a result, money became more difficult to obtain and its cost rose to very high levels. The Bank of Canada managed the cash reserves of the chartered banks in such a way as to oblige them to meet a considerable part of the strong demand for bank credit by running down their more liquid assets [Fig. 16-2(c)]. The Bank also supplemented its traditional techniques of monetary control through cash management by using its power to increase the minimum secondary reserve requirement and by a number of requests to the chartered banks." [Banks were *requested* to compete less aggressively through interest rates

During 1969, credit conditions tightened in Canada:

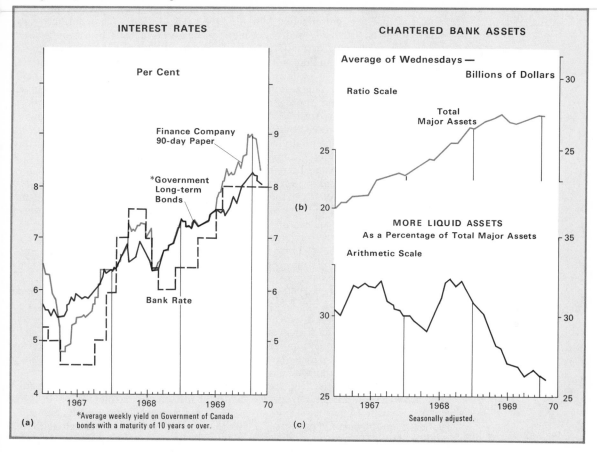

FIG. 16-2. (Source: Bank of Canada, Annual *Report* of the Governor to the Minister of Finance. 1969. Reproduced with the permission of Information Canada.)

for large blocks of Canadian dollar short-term deposits and to accept a temporary ceiling on foreign currency "swapped" deposits held in Canadian banks. "Moral suasion" was also applied in other areas—to soften tight credit's impact in less prosperous regions, to lend to small businesses with no alternative credit sources, to continue housing-mortgage lending, and to favor credit-worthy Canadian customers' loan demands above those from abroad.]

". . . The increase in total bank assets and in money supply, however defined, was much smaller in 1969 than in 1968 [Fig. 16-2(b)]. The implementation of monetary policy was facilitated by the improvement in the fiscal position of the Government of Canada. The elimination of the Government's need to add to the total volume of market issues outstanding made it possible for the supply arising from the reduction in the chartered banks' holdings to be absorbed by non-bank holders without putting even greater pressure on financial markets.

". . . Monetary policy again shifted towards severe restraint in the autumn of 1968. The Bank of Canada's cash reserve management was directed towards reducing the liquidity of the banking system. Short-term interest rates rose and the Bank Rate was increased from 6 per cent to 6½ per cent on December 18, 1968, and to 7 per cent effective March 3, 1969 [Fig. 16-2(a)]. The continued substantial demand for bank credit was met by the banks in part by running down their holdings of liquid assets [Fig. 16-2(c)]. By April 1969 the banks' more liquid assets were over 600 million dollars less than their peak level in the final quarter of 1968 and the ratio of such assets to total major assets was under 29 per cent, a low level by earlier standards [Fig. 16-2(c)]. Nonetheless, bank loans continued to increase strongly and in order to add to the pressure on the banks, the Bank of Canada announced on April 11 an increase from 7 per cent to 8 per cent in the minimum secondary reserve ratio required of the chartered banks, effective in June. The resources potentially available to the chartered banks for lending were thus reduced by a further 250 million dollars. Although the rate of growth in bank loans declined in May and June, the banks' more liquid asset ratio fell further to a new low of 27.6 per cent in June" [Fig. 16-2(c)].

[In June and July, 1969, the Bank Rate rose to 7½ per cent, then to 8 per cent in response to foreign upward pressure of Canadian short-term interest rates.]

"In response to requests of the Bank of Canada, the major banks agreed not to compete aggressively for large Canadian dollar term deposits, and the rate of interest paid on such deposits rose less than other short-term rates. It has remained at 7½ per cent since July and the volume of such deposits has declined considerably. By the end of July, typical short-term market yields had risen by about 1½ per cent from the end of 1968 and the rate on long-term Government of Canada securities had moved up by ¼ per cent over the same period.

"During the last six months of the year the tightness of credit conditions was very apparent. Short-term interest rates rose further. The chartered banks' more liquid asset ratio continued to decline and reached a level of 25.9 per cent at year-end [Fig. 16-2(c)]. Bank loans increased very little as the banks found it necessary to ration severely their available resources.

"Reflecting the persistent pressure on the banking system the chartered banks had advances outstanding from the central bank on 35 business days in 1969 compared with 14 business days in 1968. The average amount of advances outstanding on business days was 1.2 million dollars in 1969 compared with 0.2 million dollars in 1968. Over the same period securities held by the Bank under purchase and resale agreements with money market dealers were outstanding on 93 business days, compared with 35 business days in 1968 and averaged 9.4 million dollars on a daily basis in 1969 compared with 4.3 million dollars during the previous year."[7]

This brief examination of the data shows that the Bank of Canada is never idle. It is always restraining or encouraging the chartered banks. Of course, it cannot force the public to take more or fewer loans; it can only make it possible for the banks to relax credit conditions and offer loans on easier terms, or it can make the banks tighten credit conditions and offer loans on harder terms. The account is brief because it omits many activities. At the same time the central bank acts as "fiscal agent" for the government, that is as an investment dealer trying to see that the government gets good terms on its new issues of bonds and bills. In part, this means making sure that the prices of already-issued

---

[7] Bank of Canada, Annual *Report* of the Governor to the Minister of Finance, and statement of accounts. 1969. (Ottawa, 1970). Reproduced with the permission of Information Canada.

securities do not fall too far. Some experts claim that it is contradictory for the Bank to be simultaneously worried about the price of government bonds and about the health of the whole financial system—a conflict of interest.

Also simplified is the effect that foreign exchanges had during 1969. The central bank had either to permit or deny the effect of foreign-money flows, so that the effect in each case became eventually a part of the general policy of the day about credit conditions. But these foreign-exchange actions may also have an effect on the balance of payments, which it is the general policy of the government to keep from being in deficit. So part of the actions seen above may be in response to foreign, not domestic events. The matter will be revived in Part V. All that the reader should note here is that the Bank is not always free to influence domestic conditions by its weapons of monetary policy. Instead, it may be constrained by the fear of their effect on foreign balances and trade.

This difficulty about using monetary policy should be borne in mind when, in the next chapter, the monetary basis for the choice between fiscal and monetary methods of control is discussed.

■ ARE CENTRAL BANKS DOING THE RIGHT THING?

About the performance of any central bank, two questions can be asked: What is it trying to do?, and, Is it succeeding?

THE AIMS OF CENTRAL BANKS TODAY   First, although we do not discuss them till later, let us always remember that most central banks must be chiefly concerned with the foreign value of the currency and the state of international monetary reserves. This role naturally influences much of their domestic action, and they must get A's or E's on their report card for decisions most citizens never hear about.

The other aim is to help control price levels and employment trends by manipulating the money supply, as outlined in this chapter and the next. In this the central banks do have the support of Keynesian and post-Keynesian economists who in their various ways believe that the supply of M, "credit conditions," "availability," or "liquidity" does matter, and should be used to augment fiscal policy and international policy in adjusting the pitch of domestic business activity.

But this support, from academics at least, has never been whole-hearted. For in the first place, in the essential Keynesian system, "money matters" *only* through its effect on borrowing terms, the interest rate, and so, on new $C + I + G$. Because this linkage is loose and insensitive, many economists are more interested in fiscal than in monetary policy. The great Crash of 1929 and the following Depression punctured the illusion that the Bank of England or the U.S. Federal Reserve could tame the business cycle. Ever since, the majority of the experts think that monetary policy essentially *reinforces* stabilizing fiscal policies.

But, in the second place, the majority now is confronted by an important contending minority. A school we may call the "monetarists," led by the able economist Milton Friedman of the University of Chicago, and depending on a quasi-Keynesian tradition at Chicago and in Europe, is preaching that "only money matters." This group—the same group that has revived interest in the 1930-vintage Fisherian quantity theory (Chapter 14, page 345)—believes that essentially everything that can be done to control macroeconomic aggregates, i.e., inflationary gaps, epochs of depression, and slow growth, must be done by control of the money supply *alone*. Fiscal policy, Professor Friedman insists, should be confined only to helping to shape how much of the macroeconomic total is in the public sector as against the private sector, and in shaping the trend of interest rates and of the consumption share of GNE. On the basis of his superb studies of the history of money in the United States and of many other countries, he is convinced that fiscal policy in *itself* has no predictable effect on the prospects for inflation or deflation, for high employment or mass unemployment.[8]

Such negative, critical monetarism is extreme. But since it is proposed by economists with serious scientific interests, it should not be rejected just because it does not involve a mid-ground position. After all, scientific truth *could* turn out to be at one extreme rather than in the middle.

MONETARISTS VERSUS THE ECLECTIC MAJORITY   Where does the difference lie? A study and weighing of the evidence in favor of monetarism finds it—as a guide to policy—not only extreme but also essentially wrong. Recall what are the elements of the majority, eclectic view. Their neoclassical, post-Keynesian synthesis holds (1) that *both* fiscal and monetary policies and instruments matter much, (2) that the velocity of circulation is induced to increase systematically when interest rates rise, making it more economical for people to turn over their cash balances more rapidly (the "precautionary balances" of Chapter 14 are, as argued there, sensitive to the rate of interest), and (3) that open-market purchases which create new M for the community—and ease credit conditions—have their stimulating effects on I and other GNE spending dampened by the reduction in the liquid interest-bearing government bonds now held by the community, and the rise in the holding of essentially idle money.

Now examine some recent episodes. In both Canada and the United States, taxes were cut in 1964-1965. There was an increase in business spending thereafter. The Friedman view, for the United States, is that the stimulus was due to the extra M created to help finance the government deficit. In 1968-1969 taxes in the United States were raised, by a "surcharge." Friedman says that the only effect on inflation is that stemming from changes in the money supply in the period. Indeed, to a U.S. monetarist, the unprecedentedly long expansion of the 1960s would have taken place even if the budget had always been in balance at a low level—provided the Federal Reserve central bank had made M grow as it actually did during the decade.

---

[8] Reference can be made to M. Friedman and A. Schwartz, *A Monetary History of the United States* (Princeton University Press for the National Bureau of Economic Research, Princeton, N.J., 1963), and to articles pro and con monetarism by Friedman, Samuelson, and Walter Heller in P. A. Samuelson, ed., *Readings in Economics*, 6th Edition (McGraw-Hill, New York, 1970).

The majority of U.S. experts do not believe this, arguing that interest rates early in the decade would have been much lower and GNE spending lower because of the difference in the velocity of circulation that would have been induced. That is, M changes would have been chiefly differences in precautionary balances (defined in Chapter 14, p. 344) producing some fall in interest rates and rise in I, but not as much as the fiscal-policy-induced rises in GNE.

Economics is not an exact science. We cannot repeat the 1960s under controlled conditions to settle the debate. Therefore, an author should present in a textbook a framework of analysis that can be shaded in favor of either of these two scientifically proposed models. And this edition, particularly, has been written to make this possible.

For even if, in the end, monetarism should be deemed by the jury of science to have been one-sided, (1) it is based on evidence; (2) an increasing minority of important university economists embrace it, even outside Chicago; (3) it has an increasing following in government agencies (like the Joint Economic Committee) and even inside the central banks. More important, Friedman's evidence has been used by eclectic post-Keynesians like Yale's Tobin and MIT's Modigliani in their own insistence that *money does matter much*, and their opposition to the view of other post-Keynesians (especially those who prevailed in Britain's famous Radcliffe Report on banking in 1959) that money does not matter much or at all.

In the United States, these debates consider domestic policy and results alone. Britain and Canada must also compare monetarism with eclectic policy when capital inflows and exchange rates may be affected.

> For example eclectic economists may predict that a budget deficit will have most of its effect via $C + I + G$ spending, whereas monetarists may spotlight its effects (through selling bonds to the central bank) via increasing M. Open-economy economists however, must expect also that central-bank operations will lead to eventual M capital outflow, a downward international pressure on the fixed rate of exchange, and further central-bank action to sell foreign reserves and decrease M.

SELF-ADJUSTMENT, FINE TUNING, AND LEANING AGAINST THE WIND   These disputes are not academic or long-run. They shape day-to-day policy. You might think that a monetarist like Friedman, convinced that money matters exclusively or most, would want to use control over the money supply to fight against the ups and downs of business activity. But you would be wrong. Dr. Friedman insists that *no* "fine tuning" will work. Money does matter most, but *its* effects are not perfectly predictable, there being always uncertain lags and leads between cause and effect.

Reinforcing Dr. Friedman's skepticism about fine tuning is his philosophical position—really the "Chicago" position, echoing earlier individualist writers—that "rules" and not "discretionary authority by men or committees" should prevail. Hence his sole recommendation for monetary policy, his constructive advocacy, is elegantly simple.

Let the central bank stabilize the growth rate of the money supply—every year and every month—at some agreed-upon constant rate, say, between 4 and 5 per cent per year. Then, abandoning active fiscal policy, and all fine tuning, let the free market take care of the rest, including a floating rate of exchange. Let no man, no Governor, no committee try to manage interest rates, unemployment, price levels, or foreign balances.

To illustrate this important self-adjustment principle; consider the U.S. policy controversy of 1966 and 1969.

In 1966 when the U.S. Congress refused to raise taxes to prevent Vietnam inflation, the Federal Reserve slowed down the growth of M to a halt. There followed in early 1967 a pause or period of retardation but not a recession. Most experts think the Federal Reserve did pretty well in this period. But not the monetarists. They blame the Federal Reserve for not having made money grow at $4\frac{1}{2}$ per cent in 1966. Then in 1967 when it made money grow faster than $4\frac{1}{2}$ per cent to ensure that there would not be a recession (which the monetarists had said was "inevitable"), the Federal Reserve again gets a flunk from the monetarists. To the monetarists it is as if you compound the crime of running over a pedestrian, backing up your truck and running over him again; they get the Federal Reserve coming and going, for creating too much M at a time of threatened recession and too little at a time of battling inflation—rather than always creating a fixed amount.

To those who favor use of man's best intelligence to lean against the wind, one deviation tends to cancel out rather than aggravate the other. The helmsman tacks to the northeast and to the northwest to get north; he deserves a good mark for both decisions. Similarly in 1969, the monetarists espoused a gradual return toward their long-run growth number rather than the Federal Reserve's deliberate overshoot to below that number in order to make progress against the inflation. And, in power, the Nixon economists sided with the majority against the monetarists in this matter.

THE FUTURE   Economics is an exciting subject because there is always much to learn. Unquestionably the central banks in the future will give less weight than they did in the past to stabilizing interest rates even when that meant destabilizing the economy and the rate of growth of the monetary supply. Undoubtedly the control of "hot money" flows in search of higher interest rates must be better reconciled with monetarist closed-economy dogmas. The monetarists have made important contributions to economic knowledge. But turning over the steering of monetary policy to an autogyro-robot formula would represent, the authors believe, an inefficient retreat to coarse tuning that would jeopardize real growth, full employment, reasonable price stability, and desirable foreign balance.

SUMMARY

■ 1 The Bank of Canada is a central bank, a bank for bankers. Its duty is to control the community's supply of money, and its credit conditions. Its five-step mode of action goes thus: (1) it contracts Reserves, which (2) causes multiple contractions in total deposits, which (3) makes credit conditions tight (involving high interest rates), which (4) depresses private and public investment spending, which (5) puts a multiplied damper on both money income and prices.

■ 2 The powerful weapons the Bank uses are (*a*) open-market operations, (*b*) Bank-Rate policy, and (*c*) changes in secondary-reserve ratios. It depends heavily on (*d*) moral suasion. The government of Canada and the central banks of other countries (but not the Bank of Canada) can change legal cash ratios and exert selective controls over particular interest rates, margin borrowing, installment down payments, and mortgage finance terms.

■ 3 Sales by the Bank of Canada of government securities to the open-market represent a positive act which reduces its assets and liabilities and which reduces the Reserves of the chartered banks, and hence their base for deposits. Powerful day-to-day open-market operations should be understood by every student of monetary policy.

■ 4 Under a fixed exchange rate, foreign exchange outflows will reduce Reserves and M unless offset by other Bank of Canada open-market purchases of bonds. Under flexible exchanges, inflows don't affect M.

■ 5 The main facts of finance, as shown by the still picture of the credit pyramid or by the table of changing money and liquid assets, are to be understood in terms of this chapter's analysis. The view of monetarists—that the money supply dominates aggregate demand and that it should be set always at a fixed growth rate—clashes with the view of the majority's post-Keynesian synthesis—that, while M matters much, so also do tax, expenditure, and investment shifts in $C + I + G$, and that "leaning against the wind" will improve on automatic M rules.

QUESTIONS FOR DISCUSSION

1. Trace the effects of a 10-million-dollar open-market purchase. An open-market sale.

2. Trace the effects of a doubling of primary-reserve requirements; a halving. Which alters bank earnings more: open-market or primary-reserve-requirement action?

3. List the weapons of monetary control of the central bank. How powerful are they (*a*) to control M, (*b*) to control interest rates, (*c*) to control prices, and (*d*) to control employment and unemployment?

4. You patent a better mousetrap and sell the patent rights to a foreign manufacturer. Trace the resulting impact on Canadian M.

5. "In the heyday of the gold standard, gold movements affected prices only because our fathers used them as a barometer, signaling them to expand or contract the total of money supply. Of course, the gold standard was a stupid system; but they were wiser to tie themselves to such an imperfect system than to trust corrupt legislatures—whose tendency is always to print inflationary paper money." Discuss.

6. Discuss the following 1939 statement of the U.S. Reserve Board: "The Federal Reserve System can see to it that banks have enough reserves to make money available to commerce, industry, and agriculture at low rates; but it cannot make the people borrow, and it cannot make the public spend the deposits that result when the banks do make loans and investments.

7.   Some people say, "Measure monetary tightness by heights and rises in interest rates." Some say, "Measure tightness by general credit conditions." Others say, "Measure tightness only by what is happening to the growth rate of M." Eclectics say, "Use all three measures and more." What do you say?

8.   The Economic Council of Canada is often interpreted as agreeing with the Chicago position that the central bank's discretionary judgment should not be used on a month-to-month basis. Instead the Bank of Canada should only ensure that M grows at the right rate every year (e.g., 4 per cent). Give both sides of this debate between monetarists and the post-Keynesian mixed-economy majority. How have events since the revaluation of 1970 tilted the scientific issues?

9.   Review your understanding of the following concepts:

the five-step sequence	legal reserve ratio requirements
Reserves	moral suasion, interest ceiling
availability and cost of credit	Exchange Fund Account
liquid asset ratio requirements	selective credit controls
Bank of Canada notes	pyramid of credit
open-market purchases and sales	offsets to foreign exchange flows
Bank Rate, advances	monetarism, leaning against the wind
changing secondary reserve ratio	fine tuning

17

SYNTHESIS OF MONETARY ANALYSIS AND INCOME ANALYSIS

About this time there was a cry . . . for more paper-money. . . . I was on the side of an addition, being persuaded that the first small sum struck in 1723 had done much good, by increasing the trade, employment, and number of inhabitants in the province, since I now saw all the old houses inhabited, and many new ones building. . . . The utility of this currency became by time and experience so evident, as never afterwards to be much disputed. . . . Tho' . . . there are limits beyond which the quantity may be hurtful. BENJAMIN FRANKLIN

Chapters 12 and 13 showed how saving and investment schedules intersect to determine the level of national income. And the last chapters have shown how changes in Bank of Canada policy affect the community's stock of money.

In this chapter, we relate these two analyses. Monetary analysis is seen to fit in well with the modern theory of income determination; thus the stage is set for stabilization policy—(1) central bank monetary policies, and (2) government fiscal policies (public expenditure and taxation, with the implied budget deficit or surplus). These monetary and fiscal policies have to be coordinated to achieve the goal of a progressive economy that enjoys reasonable price stability and lives up to its production potentialities.

This chapter shows how stabilization policies work and interact. We leave more detailed study of fiscal policy issues for the remaining chapter of Part Two.

■ MONEY, LIQUIDITY PREFERENCE, MARGINAL EFFICIENCY, MULTIPLIER

The last chapters showed that M expansion by the central and commercial banks can shift upward the $C + I + G$ intersection point of Chapter 12. What is the same thing, an increase in M shifts upward the *SS-II* intersection point of Chapter 12, as follows:

When the central bank increases M, it primarily affects investment, shifting II upward. Its expansion of M bids up bond prices and thus bids down interest rates and makes credit loans more easily available to investors. Therefore, it has become more profitable to undertake new investment projects. In the simplest case, the sequence is this:

$$M \text{ up } \rightarrow i \text{ down } \rightarrow I \text{ up } \rightarrow \text{NNP up, up}$$

New graphs can illuminate this and also the process by which a shift in $C + I + G$ schedules—as, e.g., shifts due to increased exports, a technical investment boom, or a budget deficit—can increase the velocity of circulation (V), in the $MV = PQ$ relation of Chapter 14. The shift thereby increases GNP beyond any change originating in M itself.

Chapter 14 (page 344) showed that the demand for money, along with depending positively on the level of income transactions, also depends inversely on the interest and profit yields sacrificed in order to have the safety and convenience of holding M. To get more M held by the community, the Bank must, therefore, bid down interest rates enough to make people find it advantageous to economize less on their cash balances and hold more M. The so-called "liquidity-preference schedule" of Fig. 17-1(a) shows how an increase in M resulting from monetary policy (open-market purchases, etc.) leads initially to a reduced interest rate—from A's 6 per cent to B's 5 per cent.

Figure 17-1(b) picks up the story to show how reduced interest rates (and what does not show on the graph but is lurking in the background, namely, greater *availability* of credit) make more investment profitable. On Fig. 17-1(b)'s so-called "marginal efficiency of investment schedule," the drop in interest rate induces the rise in investment from A' to B'.

Figure 17-1(c) is merely Chapter 12's saving-investment diagram, page 275, turned on its side to line it up with Fig. 17-1(b)'s investment axis. Note that the interest drop from A to B led to the investment rise from A' to B', and this (through the multiplier) has led to the NNP rise from A'' to B''.

To clinch understanding of this vital sequence, consider the following *reverse* case where monetary policy is contracting to wipe out an inflationary gap:

Monetary contraction (open-market sales, increase cash- or secondary-reserve ratios, etc.) bids up interest rates[1] and decreases credit availability. This depresses investment spending, and via the multiplier depresses income even more. The basic sequence is now

$$M \text{ down } \rightarrow i \text{ up } \rightarrow I \text{ down } \rightarrow \text{NNP down, down}$$

Retrace the reverse BA, $B'A'$, and $B''A''$ sequence in Fig. 17-1 to see how money and income determination interact.

---

[1] Of course, if this monetary constriction is successful in ending rapid price inflation, interest rates in the longer run will not have to include a premium to cover depreciation of the dollar's real purchasing power. So the *initial* rise in interest rates from M restriction may well be reversed *in the end*. The real rate can converge on the market rate of interest.

Central bank affects money, interest, investment, and output:

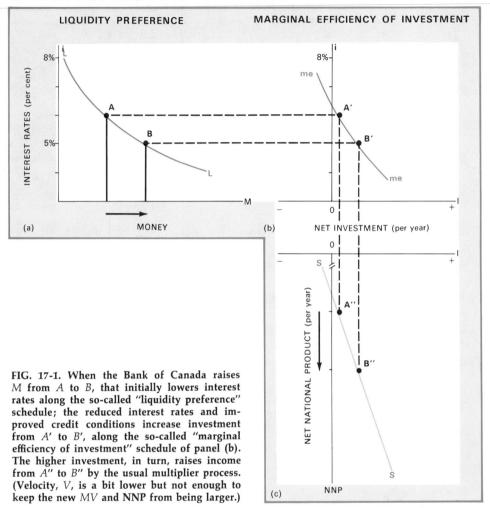

FIG. 17-1. When the Bank of Canada raises *M* from *A* to *B*, that initially lowers interest rates along the so-called "liquidity preference" schedule; the reduced interest rates and improved credit conditions increase investment from *A'* to *B'*, along the so-called "marginal efficiency of investment" schedule of panel (b). The higher investment, in turn, raises income from *A"* to *B"* by the usual multiplier process. (Velocity, *V*, is a bit lower but not enough to keep the new *MV* and NNP from being larger.)

Depression model. This reconciliation of the theories of money and of income determination is, of course, oversimplified and needs some qualifications. For example, it does not emphasize what can happen in *severe depression* when the liquidity-preference curve is practically *horizontal* because interest rates are already so low that people are quite indifferent whether they hold *M* or the near-*M* government treasury bills that the Bank wants to swap for *M*. In such a rare, but possible, case, the potency of monetary policy is at least temporarily very low. This is summarized in the aphorism "The central bank can pull on a string (to curb booms), but it can't *push on a string* (to reverse deep slumps)." Indeed, in such depressed times the profit expectations of businessmen are likely to be so low that they would not employ men and machines on new investment projects even if you let them borrow temporarily at a zero interest rate. In this case, the marginal-efficiency schedule of Fig. 17-1(*b*) is practically vertical; and again the chain of monetary action loses potency. (It is these "depression models" which are often, but wrongly, associated with the name of Keynes; and if they were his sole cases, his ideas would only rarely be of great interest in modern times.)

Classical case. The opposite "classical" or "monetarist" case, equally extreme, occurs when the liquidity schedule is practically vertical, so that each unit of M is under a strong compulsion to circulate at a constant velocity (with V a hard constant). (It can also occur when the marginal-efficiency schedule is so horizontal that the slightest reduction in interest rate is enough to wipe out any deflationary gap and the slightest rise in interest is enough to wipe out any inflationary gap. Appendix readers will find more on these polar cases there.)

As most economists interpret the history of the last few centuries, this extreme case is not deemed realistic. They cannot agree with the extreme classical view known as "Say's Law of Conservation of Purchasing Power." The Appendix to this chapter discusses this matter further. It is enough here to characterize Say's Law as alleging:

"There cannot be any such thing as a saving-and-investment problem. What is not consumed is surely destined to be spent on investment goods, without the possibility of any snag."

QUALIFICATIONS Eschewing polar cases, we must notice the point raised by experts in corporate finance. They point out that many firms, particularly large ones, finance their investments *out of retained earnings* and the cash flow generated by their own operations. Many avoid going to the banks or outside markets for borrowings or stock flotations. (EXAMPLE: The great Du Pont Company has not borrowed a cent for more than 40 years, yet has been an important source of progress in the chemical field.) In Canada, subsidiaries of American firms and other large firms simply borrow or lend in New York when the Bank of Canada makes the Canadian money market unattractive.

To the degree that investment does depend upon internal or foreign funds that are insulated from domestic market fluctuations in interest rate and credit availability, the potency of monetary policy is just that much less: it then takes greater action by the Bank to produce the same effect. One could go on to give other bits of evidence used to play down the importance of monetary policy (as, for example, the fact that when investors are uncertain about the future, small changes in safe-asset interest rates may have little effect upon the high profit rates investors require as inducement to undertake investment, and hence I may be insensitive to monetary policy).

Qualifications are not all in the direction of playing down the importance of M. We have noted in passing that credit policy does have some influence on G and C in $C + I + G$. Higher market evaluations of land, plant, and equipment, and of securities generally, may shift CC up. In the long run, if the increase in M comes, let us say, from gold mining or Treasury printing (and not merely from a swap by the Bank of Canada of M for near-M), the new M *adds directly to people's net worth*, and this does lead them, other things equal, to spend more on C, on I, and on G.[2]

---

[2] Some economists used to hope that higher interest rates would stimulate saving and kill consumption; i.e., they hoped an interest increase would shift up the SS schedule in Fig. 17-1(c), thereby reinforcing the effect of a downward shift in II. Experience, and the analysis of Chapter 30, suggest that, outside the area of installment-financed consumer durables, these

■ CONTRAST WITH FISCAL POLICY AND INCOME DETERMINATION

Let us now survey the fiscal policy powers of government. Aside from the central bank, the government has another major way of affecting current spending (as seen in Chapter 13). As part of its *fiscal policy* the government can expand its expenditures: build useful public roads and schools, hire more civil servants, increase defense expenditure, do a hundred and one useful (or foolish) things to expand total spending. This could be shown in a saving-investment diagram like Fig. 17-1(*b*), by shifting the *me* curve to the right.

But better still, we can show it as an *upward shift in the G component* of the $C + I + G$ schedule that was used as an alternative way to show income equilibrium. Figure 17-2(*a*) recapitulates the demonstration on page 298 of how an expansion of public expenditure G leads to an expansion of income, or how a Trudeau-type austerity in G spending can reduce $C + I + G$.

The same type of chart[3] can show, in Fig. 17-2(*b*), the other side of fiscal policy—changes in tax collections. To raise NNP the fiscal authorities cut taxes: this gives people higher disposable income, and since they have a propensity to consume out of extra income, this means they will consume more.

How can we show the increased consumption on Fig. 17-2(*b*)? We can show the effect of reduced taxes as an upward shift of the *CC* schedule, which is plotted against NNP and is a major component of the pictured $C + I + G$ schedule. With taxes lower, we subtract less from each level of NNP to get the corresponding level of disposable income. So, with higher disposable income corresponding to each NNP, we must show higher consumption—hence the higher *CC* curve.

We may summarize the effects of fiscal policy:

Increased G raises income by raising the GG component of $C + I + G$. Reduced taxes raise the CC component of the $C + I + G$ schedule. Both together—which also means deficit financing or a reduction in the budgetary surplus—result in an ever greater upward shift of the $C + I + G$ schedule and of equilibrium income. In the reverse case of contractionary fiscal policy, the final $C + I + G$ schedule shifts downward.

Here is a good test of one's understanding of the mechanics of fiscal policy:

Show what the effects on NNP of Mitchell Sharp's 1968 increase in personal income tax rates could be presumed to be (1) with no change in government expenditures and (2) with a simultaneous rise in G, as was expected.

effects are probably weak and cannot be much counted on. (WARNING: The B points in Fig. 17-1 are final equilibria only if the Bank of Canada now creates just enough further M to satisfy enhanced "active" or *income* needs; otherwise, we repeat the cycle with LL shifted by changed NNP level, finding final equilibria generally somewhere between the A and B points. See the Hicks-Hansen diagrams in the Appendix for a rigorous handling of this transactions-need feedback problem.)

[3] The treatment here recapitulates the treatment on page 299 of Chapter 13 and best handles the effects of personal income taxes. For more complicated analysis of sales and profit taxes, also taking account of tax effects on investment, see intermediate texts.

Fiscal policy means government expenditure and tax policy:

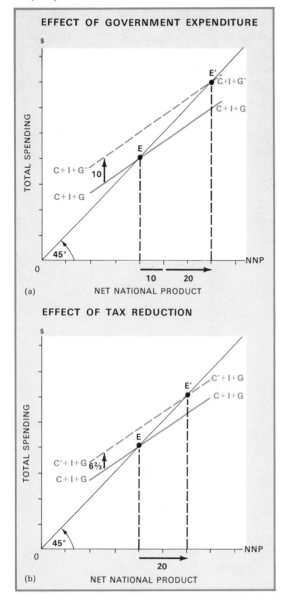

EFFECT OF GOVERNMENT EXPENDITURE

(a) NET NATIONAL PRODUCT

EFFECT OF TAX REDUCTION

(b) NET NATIONAL PRODUCT

FIG. 17-2(a). An increase of 10 in government expenditures on goods and services will shift $C + I + G$ up to $C + I + G'$, raising income to E'. Moreover, there is involved the usual multiplier effect of induced consumption spending (and, for that matter, induced private investment spending).

FIG. 17-2(b). Lowering taxes by 10 has similar expansionary effects on income. Lower tax collection gives you more disposable income out of NNP, and hence shifts the consumption schedule upward. We go from E to E' as a result of the new $C' + I + G$ schedule. (Dollar for dollar, tax reduction is a little weaker than G increase. Why? Because some tax rebate is saved rather than used to shift CC up. A cut in taxes of 10 shifts CC *leftward* that much, but *upward* only by $\frac{2}{3} \times 10 = 6\frac{2}{3}$ when the MPC is $\frac{2}{3}$.)

■ THE SYNTHESIS AT WORK: TECHNOLOGICAL UNEMPLOYMENT?

To appreciate how modern tools of income and monetary analysis really work, let us here apply them as a case study to one of the great long-run problems of our day.

A notable feature of our time is the development of "automation." Will this "new industrial revolution," in which machinery plays a new role, be a curse or a blessing to mankind? In particular, does it not confront the modern economy with the threat of mass unemployment?

Our tools enable us to give an optimistic answer; but our optimistic answer is quite different from the old-fashioned one, which simply *asserted that inventions would necessarily create new jobs just as fast as they killed off old ones.* Such a view was based upon an uninformed faith, and it was not persuasive. Sometimes experience accorded with it; sometimes experience went against it. In short, it made the outcome depend merely on *luck*. Our contemporary optimistic answer is truly more optimistic than that.

WHAT AUTOMATION IS   The word "automation" was coined in 1947 by Del Harder, vice-president of Ford Motor Company, to apply to "automatic handling of parts between progressive productive processes." At about the same time John Diebold, a management engineer, shortened the word "automization" into automation. Diebold stressed the use of control devices that operate by means of "feedback."

Automation has still other meanings. Giant electronic calculators, which are a millionfold faster than hand machines, have simplified data processing and record keeping. One pretty machine does the work of a hundred even prettier girls. Numbers recorded on magnetic tape can make a milling machine or lathe turn out intricate copies of a master pattern. Some modern digital computers can beat a good player at checkers, but none can yet beat a champion. None can yet play a really fine game of chess; at simple games such as ticktacktoe, the machine plays a perfect game.

DISPLACEMENT OF LABOR?   Whether one thinks automation is something absolutely new or represents a great postwar quickening of developments already known in principle, everyone admits it is a force to reckon with. Automation will presumably increase productivity; otherwise it would not be installed. Does this mean it will reduce the total need for labor and create mass unemployment? Back in the depression of the 1930s, long before we knew the term "automation," there was much fear of "technological unemployment." Should we again worry that modern man will become obsolete?

The late Norbert Wiener, MIT mathematician and one-time prodigy, who coined the name "cybernetics" (from the Greek word for "helmsman"), has pronounced on this subject in the following dramatic way[4]

> The industrial revolution has . . . displaced man and the beast as a source of power. . . . The factory of the future . . . will be controlled by something like a modern high-speed computing machine. . . . We can expect an abrupt and final cessation of the demand for the type of factory labor performing repetitive tasks . . . an intermediate transitional period of disastrous confusion. . . . Industry will be flooded with the new tools to the extent that they appear to yield immediate profits, irrespective of what long-time damage they can do. . . . It is perfectly clear

---

[4] Norbert Wiener, *The Human Use of Human Beings* (Houghton Mifflin, Boston, 1950), pp. 180, 181, 186, 188, 189.

that this will produce an unemployment situation, in comparison with which the present recession and even the depression of the thirties will seem a pleasant joke.

THE FORWARD LOOK   Any increase in productivity will indeed, *if output does not increase*, throw men out of work. In the Great Depression men readily believed total product would remain the same, that desired output would fail to grow with the growth of productivity. This view makes you look at unemployment in the following way: "Why did those unemployed workers over there lose their jobs? Which machines displaced them?" And so forth.

Modern students of income determination take a more fruitful tack. They say:

> Regardless of why these men lost their jobs, why aren't there enough *new* jobs for them? What fiscal and monetary policies are needed to create the new dollar purchasing power necessary for them to be hired anew?

"Satchel" Paige, a great American baseball player, once said: "Never look backward; someone may be gaining on you." This is good advice in economics, too. Do not look back to find what caused past layoffs; look forward to see what you have to do to restore high employment. This is much more efficient—and more helpful.

Better still, this approach means you do not have to decide whether the pessimists are right who argue that inventions will kill off more jobs than they create. Why care? *In every case we know that high employment without inflation will require monetary and fiscal policies of the correct magnitudes and mixed economies know what needs doing.*[5]

GRAPHICAL RESTORATION OF HIGH-EMPLOYMENT EQUILIBRIUM   To apply this fruitful approach, we can use our consumption + investment + government spending schedule and look for income equilibrium where the $C + I + G$ schedule just intersects the 45° helping line. Figure 17-3 illustrates this.

Suppose that automation makes labor 30 per cent more productive. This means that the same full-employment labor force could produce 30 per cent more real national product; hence, the FF full-employment line of Fig. 17-3(*a*) is now shifted rightward 30 per cent to $F'F'$. Let us make quite unfavorable assumptions: (1) that government leaves its expenditure G as it was; and that the new machines are so cheap and short-lived that they can be introduced just by using up the depreciation allowances of the wearing-out machines, so that (2) net investment I is no greater than before; finally, that automation gives people the same things for less but does not whet their appetites for new gadgets, which means that (3) the propensity-to-consume schedule (and propensity to save) will be exactly the same as before in terms of disposable income.

In short, we assume the $C + I + G$ schedule has none of its components shifted as a result of automation. Then the schedule must continue to intersect

---

[5] It is also necessary to seek exchange-rate policies consistent with the chosen monetary and fiscal policies. More will be said about them in Parts Five and Six.

The income-determination diagrams before and after automation:

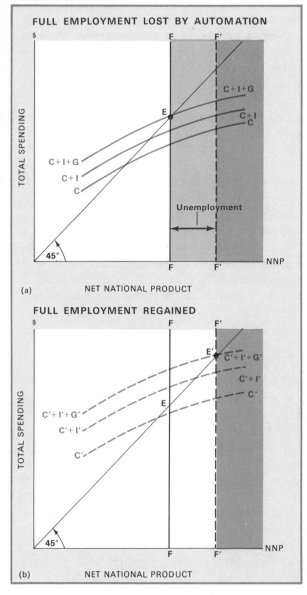

(a)

FULL EMPLOYMENT LOST BY AUTOMATION

(b)

FULL EMPLOYMENT REGAINED

FIG. 17-3(a). If inventions raise productivity 30 per cent, *FF* shifts 30 per cent rightward to *F'F'*. Were *C*, *I*, and *G* not to change, the intersection would still be at *E*, but now with mass unemployment. (Under *laissez-faire* no one can predict what the net final effect of such inventions on $C + I + G$ would be. They *might* tempt consumers to less thrift, and investors to more capital formation. But they might instead undermine $C + I + G$.)

FIG. 17-3(b). Regardless of inventions' effect on old spending schedules, expansionary monetary policy can raise *I* by the needed amount. Expansionary *fiscal* policy will lower taxes, raise disposable incomes, and shift up the consumption schedule to *C'C'*; and it can increase *G* to *G'*. Full-employment equilibrium will be restored at *E'*, where $C' + I' + G'$ has been shifted upward the needed amount by macroeconomic policy.

at the same *E* point as before. Whereas this *E* point was previously a full-employment equilibrium, it now represents a point of mass unemployment. A large fraction of the populace is now out of work completely, and many are working only part time. Were this the case, who can doubt that unions and the government would agitate to cut the length of the working week and sabotage new methods and machines? And who could blame them?

NEW ECONOMICS TO THE RESCUE Even this pessimistic case can be cured by proper therapy. Here is how. Let the central banks of the North Atlantic economy fight this slump by making credit much cheaper and much more freely available. (Recall open-market purchases, lowering of reserve requirements, and lowering the Bank Rate.) What will this do to the I schedule? Push it up. At the same time, let the government cut down on the heavy taxing it was doing in the previous full-employment situation. This will increase people's disposable incomes, will increase their consumption spending, and thus shift upward the C part of the $C + I + G$ schedule. (Maybe I will get further shifted, too.) Without increasing government expenditure directly, we can thus shift the $C + I + G$ schedule far enough upward until the new $C + I + G$ schedule intersects the 45° line at the new full-employment level E'. Alternatively, since there are always pressing needs in the public sector and overseas, expansion of G and E could be used to help shift $C + I + G + (E - M)$ up to the target level. Fig. 17-3(b) shows how these upward shifts have restored the full-employment equilibrium. By proper policy we have converted the machine from a curse to a blessing. *People now enjoy 30 per cent more output without being forced into bread lines.* They are not made to work short hours and do not have to take Mondays off because the limited work has to be shared. They do not have to throw their cigarette lighters into the works of the new machinery to protect their jobs and take-home pay.

DISARMAMENT AND OTHER "PROBLEMS" Figure 17-3 illustrates the approach of the New Economics to many issues: automation, regional decline, obsolescence of a city's main product, a new rage to buy imported products, and nation-wide or world-wide disarmament. Instead of being regarded as "problems," all these occurrences can now be hailed as opportunities to make use of the productive power of the labor force, factories, etc. released as a result of them.

You should be sure you know how to use Figure 17-3 to handle situations where the cause is an increase in I, resulting from a spontaneous increase in demand for new machines; an increase in C, G, or E; or a spontaneous decrease in any of C, I, G, or E. A change in M, either way, is also possible. You should be able to show how contractionary monetary and fiscal policy would be needed to wipe out the inflationary gaps created when C, I, G, or E had increased too far, as well as how expansionary policies could compensate for deflationary losses of employment suffered when these GNE components shrink.

Of course, the higher dollar demand engineered by fiscal and monetary policy cannot be expected to provide the same kind of jobs using exactly the same skills and paying exactly the same wage rates. Inevitably there will still be important transitional problems for particular workers, firms, and regions. Programs of retraining and of increasing labor mobility and flexibility are vital (as Chapters 28 and 38 both discuss), along with aggregate demand policies to ensure proper aggregate dollar demand. Regions that produce one or few "staple" products (wheat, fur, coal, wooden ships), or depend on depleted mines and forests particularly need these special manpower policies. But they must be fitted into a growing full-employment NNP.

■ THE NEW MIXED ECONOMY

Critics used to regard the classical principles of economics as out of date. Looking out the window at the long bread lines and the men selling apples on street corners, they said:

> Why speak of scarcity? Or efficiency? Or growth? Of fairness? Throw away your tools of supply and demand, your finespun theories of market pricing. Tear up the rule book. We live in a new era in which everything is upside down: attempts to save kill off investment: a hurricane or war is a blessing in that it creates jobs and gives food to the starving unemployed. Sanctions imposed by the United Nations on trade hasten a country's development. Capitalism is doomed to collapse in a crisis of underconsumption and overproduction.

What is the modern economist's answer to all this? He says:

> You are right to question the classical principles. All principles should be subjected to the closest examination with respect to both their logic and their factual relevance. The classical arguments were oversimple, and they admittedly did not allow for the facts of nineteenth- and twentieth-century life. But experience since 1932, and careful logical reasoning, suggest that money and aggregate $C + I + G + (E - M)$ spending *will not manage themselves*. A *laissez-faire* system is doomed to wasteful ups and downs of the business cycle and perhaps to long fits of stagnation.

Even among the economists of Eastern Europe there has developed a recognition of the new scientific knowledge about macroeconomic policy.

> Simple capitalism has been replaced virtually everywhere by the mixed economy ("the managed economy"). Everywhere in the Western world[6] governments and central banks have shown they can win the battle of the slump if people want them to. They have the weapons of fiscal policy (expenditure and taxes) and of monetary policy (open-market operations, discount-rate policy, legal reserve ratio policy) to shift the various schedules that determine national income and employment. Just as we no longer meekly accept disease, we no longer need accept mass unemployment.
>
> Under the managed macroeconomics of the mixed economy, many of the old classical principles of microeconomics will again apply; but now they apply because our macroeconomics has validated their premise of adequate demand—not because the world is lucky enough to have them apply automatically and at all times.

This is a brave answer, and essentially—most careful economists would today say—an accurate answer. But let us not be too boastful of our modern conquest of instability. There is no warrant for smugness. Let us quietly add the following qualifications:

> The worst consequences of the business cycle, which the Appendix to Chapter 13 showed plagued capitalism from its beginning, are probably a

---

[6] This, of course, includes Japan, India, and other Asian nations; Australia and New Zealand; Latin America; and the new African states.

thing of the past; but that does not mean that the cycle is gone. "Fine tuning" is not yet here. We still have minor inventory fluctuations, still shall have transitions from war to peace and from one kind of boom to another. The difference will be this: the age-old tendencies for the system to fluctuate will still be there, but no longer will the world let them snowball into vast depressions or into galloping inflations—no longer will we let our banking system falter and our nation go through the most painful debt deflation and bankruptcy.

▨ THREE QUALIFICATIONS

We should recognize that all Canadian political pressures do work to make a drastic slump unlikely. But can we be sure that the same pressures are strong enough to deal with three problems that are just as serious?

1. *International flow of unemployment.* Sceptics may smile at the thought of *Canadian* political pressures uniting to fight a slump: "Canadian employment and income determination obviously depend on exports and so on foreign (U.S. and Japanese) markets. Can Canadian monetary or fiscal policy hope to make up for crashes abroad?" For such doubters, the theory above is something for our customers abroad to use—it can never save us. They are right. Canada is only a small part of the Western economy. We can only hope that the modern mixed economies can, when a slump appears imminent, quickly focus the weapons of full employment on this crucial target.

At the same time, in milder crises, we must use the theory ourselves to resolve our "open-economy" problem of keeping a balance in international financial relations while dealing with domestic income and employment. This is the trick of keeping *both* internal and external balance.

For example, we have already seen that domestic monetary policies, changing interest rates, can attract or repel foreign capital. Capital-flow variations, in turn, can affect the value of our dollar. What then? *If* policy is to keep the exchange rate fixed, domestic policies will have to be altered to reverse the capital flow, or to arrange some compensating flow of other kinds of foreign money. On the other hand, *if* policy allows the dollar to float, exports and imports may have to adjust at the expense of important voting groups.

More on this in later chapters. The important contributions of Harry Johnson, Robert Mundell, Grant Reuber, and others have so far shown that certain combinations of domestic and foreign stabilization policy *are* compatible; but others rule each other out.

2. *Regional or "structural" unemployment.* In Canada's diverse economy, nation-wide "full employment" may actually represent over-full employment in Ontario and unemployment in Newfoundland. Inflation may have to be fought near Ottawa; but welfare and re-training may be the policies in some regions. In such circumstances, monetary and fiscal policy may not be widely accepted by all parties, especially when the slump is not yet cataclysmic enough to alarm all regions or industries.

Our aggregate demand weapons can do little about this disparate "structure" of the Canadian labor employment market. It can attempt to spread capital and jobs more evenly; and it can try moving the men to the work. These policies now exist. Furthermore, it is at least conceivable that "aggregate" monetary and fiscal weapons can be applied selectively: heavily in some regions and lightly elsewhere. A start on this approach was made in 1968-1969 and widened in 1970 in the application of anti-inflation policies.

3. *Inflation.* Can we be so sure that the same pressures that may unite against a slump will operate against mild inflation? Even if fiscal and monetary policies could prevent such chronic mild inflation as a couple of per cent per year, can we be sure they will be used to do so?

Chapter 40 returns to the vital problem of inflation, and the Appendix to the present chapter explores deeper the mechanisms of money and of income determination.

SUMMARY

■ 1 Monetary policy by the central bank is an important way of shifting the saving and investment schedules, or of shifting the total schedule of $C + I + G + (E - M)$ spending.

■ 2 Along the downward-sloping "liquidity-preference schedule," higher M induces a lower interest rate—enough lower to persuade people to hold all the new M. Along the downward-sloping "marginal efficiency of investment schedule," lower interest rate and more available credit make it profitable for new investment projects to get done. Along the familiar saving-investment multiplier-type diagram, the induced increase in I leads to higher production and income.[7]

■ 3 Fiscal policy means governmental tax and expenditure policy. It, too, affects income determination by shifting the spending schedules. Higher expenditure on goods and services directly raises the G component of $C + I + G$ schedule and thus raises its equilibrium intersection. Taxes work in reverse: *reduced* tax rates, by shifting the CC schedule leftward and upward, push *up* the $C + I + G$ schedule; increased tax rates have the opposite, contractionary effect; and in either case, tax changes are, dollar for dollar, a little less potent than government expenditure changes.

---

[7] If there is a deep-depression inelasticity of investment response to interest and/or a deep-depression horizontality of LL representing indifference to money holding, the effect of new M will fall to nil. In quantity-theory language, then and *only* then will the contrived rise in M be completely negated by a compensating fall in V, leaving $MV = PQ = NNP$ quite unchanged. Usually the induced drop in interest rates will cause V to decrease, but not by enough to offset the new M in the now higher MV. Only in the other extreme case of monetarism will V be a hard constant, responding in no systematic way to i, CC, II, and GG changes. The great neoclassical writers—Marshall, Wicksell, Pigou, Irving Fisher—never believed in such monetarism.

■ 4 The important case of technological invention shows how, by combination of fiscal and monetary policies, a modern economy can ensure the restoration of high-employment equilibrium even in the worst case where automation or disarmament is reducing the need for men to do any given amount of work and is not bringing in its train any spontaneous expansion of dollar demand elsewhere.

■ 5 Modern democracies have the fiscal and monetary tools, and the political will to use them, to end chronic slumps and galloping inflations. This makes obsolete the fear of overproduction and underconsumption, and obviates the need to bolster purchasing power by military or imperialistic programs. But it does not solve problems of income inequality or of monopolistic and other imperfections at the microeconomic level. Part Two's successful handling of macroeconomics merely sets up the stage for the again-relevant microeconomic problems of Parts Three and Four.

■ 6 Regional and foreign constraints reduce our freedom to use these neoclassical weapons, and reduce their power.

QUESTIONS FOR DISCUSSION

1. Redo Fig. 17-1(a), (b), and (c) to show tight monetary policies. Trace out the steps.

2. Wipe out a 1975 automation-created deflationary gap by (a) fiscal policy alone, (b) monetary policy alone, and (c) any blend of the two. Which path leads to full employment with slowest growth (i.e., least capital formation for the future)?

3. "Fiscal and monetary authority should be in one agency, or at least be coordinated. Otherwise they may conflict, one undoing what the other does." Discuss.

4. Use Fig. 17-2 to show that increasing G and taxes at the same time will tend to have canceling effects on income. Difficult question: Can you follow the intricate reasoning which has argued that, dollar for dollar, changes in G are a little more potent than changes in taxes—so that a balanced-budget decrease in G is likely to be somewhat deflationary?

5. The tools that handle automation problems can handle any threat of unemployment that might come from sudden peace and disarmament. Explain, anticipating Chapter 40's argument.

6. Explain critically the new look in macroeconomics.

7. Review your understanding of the following concepts:

M down $\rightarrow i$ up $\rightarrow I$ down
    $\rightarrow$ NNP down $= MV$ down
Shift of $C + I + G$: through
    monetary policy and through
    tax and expenditure changes
expenditure versus tax potency
liquidity-preference schedule

marginal-efficiency schedule
leftward CC shift from tax cut
automation and unemployment
mixed-economy "new look" macro-
    economics
foreign-balance constraints

APPENDIX: Mechanisms of Money and Income Determination

This is a brief discussion of how money, interest, investment, income, prices, and velocity of circulation are interrelated. Classical views that there can never be unemployment, and depression versions of the Keynesian system, will turn out to be alternative poles of such an analysis. And what most economists would consider to be the most realistic description of how our economy works and what are potencies of policy weapons will fall somewhere on the continuum between these extreme poles.

The topics will be covered in this order: velocity interrelations; classical and monetarist models; liquidity preference and income determination.

◼ BEHAVIOR OF VELOCITY

Instead of the chain $M \to i \to I \to$ NNP (or its even further elaboration to take account of wealth-capitalization effects and effects on G and C schedules), some proponents of monetarism prefer to short-circuit the process and use the concept of velocity. They write

$$M \to MV \equiv NNP$$

This asserts that an increase in M, unless *offset fully* by an induced shift in V of the type that neither they nor the believers in the four-link chain consider likely, will serve to increase dollar NNP with all the applied effects of the product of $P \times Q$.[1]

These different modes of language can formally represent the same facts, just as an account in English or an account in French can be given of any sequence of events. In a sense, therefore, reasonable

men will not argue about terminology and semantics.

At a deeper level, however, those who prefer one terminology usually think that certain hypotheses about the real world are more fruitful than others. Thus, those who like to use MV usually have more definite views about the probable behavior of V, and its invariance under a wide range of alternative conditions, than do those who like to use the $C + I + G$ and liquidity-preference approach explicitly. While the bulk of economists today incline toward the latter view, there is no need to be dogmatic about the matter. If the day ever arrives when the proponents of the velocity approach can prove by their researches that theirs is the more convenient tool, pragmatic scholars will welcome all its help. In any case, post-Keynesians and monetarists both agree that "money matters much."

◼ CLASSICAL PRICE FLEXIBILITY

More basic than the question of whether to use or not use the terminology of either school is the contrast between a *frictionless* system in which all market prices are *flexible* and the *realistic* world of a mixed economic system that exists here and elsewhere in the West. Many classical economists thought unemployment to be quite impossible because in their frictionless models whatever is not spent in one direction gets automatically spent in another.

SAY'S LAW   This view, called Say's Law, since its statement in 1803 by French writer J. B. Say, has been much debated because of the ambiguous form in which it was expressed: thus, Say and other classical writers felt that overproduction was impossible by its very nature, since all value relations were relative—shoes being comparable with spoons at some proper relative price; they felt that what a worker saves gets spent as truly on employing men in the machinery trades as what the worker spends on giving work in the food or other consumers' industries; they had at least a vague notion that the interest rate in a flexible capital market would always find a level at which (full-employment) saving and investment schedules would intersect; they, or their more sophisticated followers, had the notion that, if

---

[1] Some proponents would think V will stay constant after a sizable change in open-market operations; others would not think this a necessary assumption. Some, impressed by the empirical fact that in past short-term upswings, rises in M and V have tended to coincide, might choose to extrapolate this *post hoc* experience; others would set up more complicated hypotheses, depending upon the environment upon which the open-market operation impinged. Many will agree with our later liquidity-preference theory, whose Hicks-Hansen diagrams can be thought of as a theory of velocity—i.e., a theory in which V is an increasing function of the interest rate i.

only the money wage would fall flexibly far enough, it would always bring out job offers for every willing worker. So went their rather vague arguments.

In the years since 1800, there were often short periods of considerable unemployment, and on a few occasions there were longer periods of considerable unemployment or of *under*employment. So economists wanted to go beyond the simpler formulations of Say's Law: to deny some of its implicit presumptions about flexible prices and wages, or to abandon it and work from alternative hypotheses.

Today it is clear that the alternative approaches are fully capable of being reconciled, so that there is only a difference of degree and of realism between them, not a difference of kind. A. C. Pigou of Cambridge University showed in 1943 how his older cherished beliefs could be related to what he had first thought were Keynesian heresies; his reconciliation goes thus.

PIGOU EFFECTS   Let there be a certain M in the system that consists of coins or of imperishable paper currency. Suppose that initially there is unemployment because the SS and II schedules intersect to the left of the full-employment level. Suppose interest rates are in equilibrium on every bond and security market, with auctioneers finding matching supply and demand bids. And just to complete the simplified discussion, suppose there is no central banker or fiscal authority to do anything about the situation.

A sophisticated follower of Say would now assert: "There is just one flaw in this equilibrium. Men who want to work at going wages are not employed. To be fair, whether or not this is realistic, you should also imagine an auctioneer for the labor market. He makes the wage rate expressed in money fall whenever there is excessive labor supply."

Pigou agrees. He lets the wage rate fall. Money wages being an important cost of production, for all the reasons discussed in Parts Three and Four, this drop will result in considerable lowering of all prices. When prices and wages are low enough, what will happen to the SS and II intersection? Suppose I am a typical man who previously owned an acre of land, a machine, and $100 in cash. (I also may have owed on a mortgage or may have held someone's IOU stated in terms of money; but for the community as a whole, such interpersonal money liabilities and assets have to *cancel* out. Recall also that there are

no government bonds in the picture to worry about.)

For dramatic effect, suppose that wages fall to one-thousandth (0.001) of their previous level; suppose, although it is unnecessary except for simplicity of exposition to stick to the same number, that prices of all things also fall to 0.001 of their previous levels. This means that my acre of land and machine will fall to 0.001 of their previous value. Everything falls in value—except one item. My $100 bill is still a $100 bill. But now in terms of its real purchasing power, I own the equivalent of what was $100,000 before. I am rich!

Will I spend the same amount on consumption and on saving out of *income* levels that are the same as before either in money or in real terms? I will not. I am rich and can consume more before I die.

At some point, because of the enhanced real wealth effect of the increased purchasing power of the hard money in the economic system (induced by a large enough wage and price fall), CC schedules will shift up in real (not money) terms, and SS schedules shift equivalently downward. The new SS and II intersection can thus be moved to the right to the full-employment level. So, even if there were no favorable effects of the price-level or interest change on the II curves, by getting money wages and prices far enough down, the condition of "full employment" could theoretically be achieved. QED.

Pigou thus vindicated abstract classical principles by recourse to this "hard-money effect," which economists today call the "Pigou effect" in his honor.[2] But being a realistic observer of the difficulties of getting wages to move flexibly downward in a mixed capitalistic society, and having lived through eras in which the dynamic process of debt deflation led to bankruptcy, riots, slump, and even revolution, Pigou hastened to point out that he did not recommend such hyperdeflation to cure capitalism's unem-

---

[2] Mention may be made here of a non-Pigou, non-Say, non-Keynes version of full employment originated by Professor Nicholas Kaldor of Cambridge. He is widely interpreted to believe that, within wide limits, any change of I will induce just enough shift of the share of income accruing to thrifty profit receivers to produce a long-run *full-employment* intersection of SS and II always. If only it were valid such a view would be important. If only . . . .

ployment. He much preferred to accomplish the same thing by increasing dollar M; and actually, he adhered to the general notions of Part Two of this book. The fact that he often liked to use the word "velocity" in his Keynes-like theory shows that mere semantic matters are indeed of limited importance.

CRUDE QUANTITY THEORY IN THE CLASSICAL MODEL Recall now the crude quantity theory, which held prices must always be proportional to the amount of money—so that doubling M must exactly double P. For many situations in the realistic world—with its sticky prices, boom, depression, and thousands of changes always going on to confound the experiment —we saw that the crude quantity theory was not a good predicting device. But if we confine our attention to the perfectly frictionless model of the classical type used by Pigou and others in the above discussion, we can find an important nucleus of truth in the crude quantity theory; and we can understand better the reasons why it has some degree of predictive value during galloping inflations and over certain long time intervals.

Recall Pigou's fantastic but happy equilibrium which has made the representative man feel rich enough to save as little as society can invest at full employment. Now suppose his $100 bill had been a $10 bill. Do you see that merely by having all prices go down still another nine-tenths the equilibrium could be *exactly restored*, with every relative price and wage just the same as before and every physical commodity and input the same as before? *Cutting M to one-tenth has cut P to exactly one-tenth in this classical model.*

In this abstract model the crude quantity theory has come into its own. In the tautological equation of exchange $MV \equiv PQ$, there has not been the slightest reason for the Q or V to have changed (waiving all dynamic questions of how the system gets into the new equilibrium and "forgets" all its past price levels). So P does equal kM, where k is the ratio V/Q, whose numerator and denominator will have been constant in this abstract example, however much they may vary in reality.

This long-period full-employment frictionless classical model has the further property that *no change in interest rates can come from the balanced change in M*. As David Ricardo argued, if all prices and wages change in exactly the same proportion, so that what used to be called 4 pence is now 2 pence, then any asset that used to pay 5 per cent per annum in the form of 50 pence on 1,000 pence will now be paying 5 per cent in the form of 25 pence on 500 pence.

It should not be necessary to stress that the real world as we know it is a far cry from the abstract model. This is true especially in the short run; in the longer run, to the degree that all price adjustments get made and other disturbances are ruled out, the abstract model fits somewhat better. The art of economics is to know how to blend the elements of absurdity and of relevance of such a model in interpreting living events and policy.

PERMANENT PUBLIC DEBT   Even in the extreme classical model, all P's would not be proportional to M alone! Interest-bearing public bonds, which correspond to no government capital formation and which no taxpayer rationally expects to have to help retire *in his lifetime*, have effects similar to those of the noninterest *IOUs* we call M. Thus the Pigou effect from hyperdeflation involves an increase in the real value of such bonds *along with* an increase in the real value of hard-money M. Since a rational taxpayer will reckon that he *will* have to help pay taxes to keep up the interest payments (during his lifetime) on the public debt, $1 of such debt will not have the potency to produce as much spending as will $1 of M. Nevertheless, believers in a crude quantity theory in an extreme classical model *should* reformulate their theory to say:

Doubling M *and* permanent public debt will, other things equal, double all P's and leave all relative P's, physical quantities, and interest rates unchanged in the new long-term equilibrium. *Doubling M alone represents a nonneutral change* whose substantive effects are the greater the shorter is taxpayer life expectancy and the higher is the interest rate.[3]

■ LIQUIDITY PREFERENCE AND INCOME

We have seen that the amount of money people will hold depends upon the interest rate and is a declining function of interest in the sense that you must contrive lower yields on securities to coax people to

---

[3] Warning: Doubling M and PD (Permanent Debt) does not mean you can add $M + PD$ and treat that magnitude as if P's were proportional to it. Rather it is the case that $(2M, 2PD)$ implies $2P$.

be willing to hold more money. Figure 17-1(a) showed this liquidity-preference link between money and interest.

But, as already noted, there is a *transactions* motive for holding money along with the *store-of-wealth* or asset reason for holding money. So part of the money held can be said to depend upon the level of income: this so-called "active" component of the money holdings is a function of the level of NNP, rising as NNP rises. Indeed, if velocity were a strict constant for *all* money and not just for this idealized active-money component, there would be no room at all for the nonvertical liquidity-preference curve *LL* of Fig. 17-1(a).

Money-holdings' dependence on income was not depicted in the importance sequence of Fig. 17-1; it shows money dependence on interest only. The chapter's second footnote warned us that the diagram did not take into account the full feedback effect of the transactions demand for money induced by a successful expansion of NNP contrived by an increase in M. We can here make good this deficiency, and verify that the chapter's story is essentially correct, even if oversimplified in the telling; now we consider what is known as a Hicks-Hansen diagram, named for Sir John Hicks of Oxford and Alvin Hansen of Harvard who popularized it.

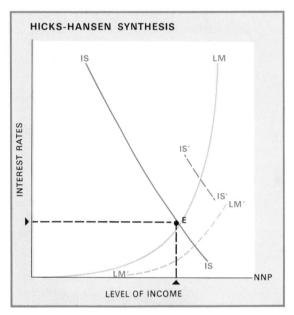

HICKS-HANSEN SYNTHESIS

Y-axis: INTEREST RATES
X-axis: LEVEL OF INCOME / NNP

FIG. 17-4.

The curve labeled *IS* in Fig. 17-4 recapitulates in a single income-interest-rate diagram the story told by Fig. 17-1(b) and (c), quite independently of (a). We see back on page 409 that when we change the interest rate we do end up changing the NNP level, as shown here on the curve. Back in Fig. 17-1, this took place in two steps: (1) the marginal-efficiency step of 17-1(b) in which changing interest rate changed investment in the opposite direction; and then (2) the old multiplier relation, inherited from our saving-investment analysis of Chapters 12 and 13, in which the change in investment resulted in an amplified change in income in the same direction due to primary spending and secondary respending. We call this result of the two steps the *IS* relation, because it shows the resulting correspondence—all the resulting combinations—of interest rate and income when scheduled saving and scheduled investment have been kept equal. (Recall this is the definition of maintainable equilibrium for NNP.)

The new element in Fig. 17-4 is the *LM* schedule. This relationship between the interest rate and the level of income is labeled *LM* because it is the complete liquidity-preference relationship between money and income after we have taken into account *both* the dependence of money holding on interest *and* on income. That is, we have recognized not only the *transaction* motive for holding "active money," which depends primarily on income; but also what Chapter 14 called the *precautionary* (or "asset") store-of-wealth motive for holding money, which depends upon the interest rates investors speculate will be earned on alternative stores of wealth (bonds, stocks, land, real capital goods—earning assets in general). Fig. 17-1(a) showed the effect of such speculation on "asset" demand for M.

It is important to emphasize that the *LM* schedule is drawn up on the proviso that the total amount of M is *fixed*. Why then does *LM* slope upward? Because an eastward increase in NNP will require more active M for transactions, leaving less M for people to hold as a wealth asset. The smaller amount of M for wealth holding can only be rationed out at a higher (or northward moving) interest rate, which coaxes people more into securities and more *out* of money.

We call the result of an NNP increase's tendency to increase the interest rate obtainable on the remaining precautionary assets, the *LM* curve. It shows all combinations of i and NNP that are possible, with a given supply of M, in the markets for earning financial assets.

Now we must combine the marginal-efficiency-multiplier curve IS with the liquidity-preference curve LM to show that their interaction does determine the equilibrium level of income and of interest rate for each given total of M. E shows the equilibrium intersection. There and only there has the existing amount of money created just low enough interest rate and just high enough investment to lead to a maintainable level of income: at this indicated NNP and i rate, the existing M supply just covers the transactions and holding demand for money. QED.

■ MONETARY AND FISCAL POLICY

What if the central bank in applying monetary policy engineers an increase in M? What will that do to the LM curve? Now with more money to be held at each level of income, the interest rate will have to be bid down. Hence, the LM curve clearly shifts downward (and hence *rightward*, as shown by the dashed line LM'). What about the IS curve? It does not have the money supply in it anywhere; IS stays unshifted by an M change. The rightward shift of LM increases the equilibrium NNP and the equilibrium interest rate moves downward. Pencil E' in.

By contrast to monetary policy, which shifts the LM curve, *fiscal policy* shifts the IS curve. How? An increase in government expenditure G (just like an increase in any component of a $C + I + G$ schedule) will shift the IS schedule *rightward*. Why? Because it leads to a higher income level at the same interest rate. Thus, you can show that expansionary fiscal policy leads to a new E higher on the unshifted LM curve, with equilibrium income and interest rate higher.[4] (The reader should test himself by penciling in on Fig. 17-4 a new LM curve for central bank contraction and a new IS curve for fiscal contraction. Contrast the new E intersections where the interest rate is concerned.)

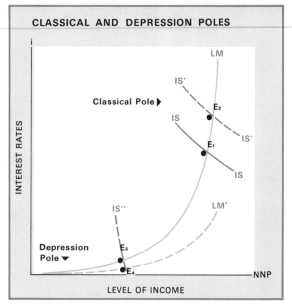

CLASSICAL AND DEPRESSION POLES

FIG. 17-5.

■ CLASSICAL AND DEPRESSION MODELS

Fig. 17-5 shows at the extremities of the LM curve the extreme "classical" pole and the extreme "depression" (or so-called "liquidity-trap") pole.[5] Where LM turns almost vertical, no shift in the IS curve can increase NNP: that is because money's velocity has reached its limit. (Note the constancy of NNP at E_1 and E_2.) At this classical pole, then, fiscal policy would accomplish little unless accompanied by central banking change in the money supply. Few modern economists think present-day mixed economies operate in such an extreme region. (In any case they would probably combine fiscal policy with monetary policy where such a threat became serious.)

At the other extreme, at vanishingly low interest rates such as prevailed in the late 1930s, the LM curve might turn horizontal. If the central bank engineered an increase in M by open-market purchases which involved swapping a near-money treasury bill

---

[4] Note that foreign-trade policy can easily be brought in. For example, a policy that increased net exports ($E - M$) by devaluation would be similar to the text's increasing of G, shifting IS rightward.

[5] Sometimes the "depression model" is called the "Keynesian model," but most authorities agree that this is bad terminology in that Keynes' *General Theory* covered all cases from the beginning and not merely that of the Great Depression.

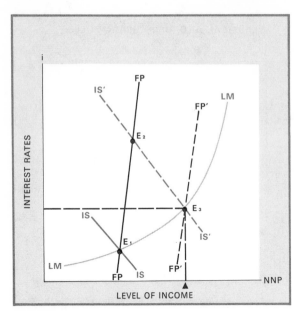

FIG. 17-6.

for M itself, the central bank would merely succeed in shifting the LM curve rightward, leaving its horizontal part virtually unchanged. In such a situation, and particularly where extreme inelasticity of the depression marginal-efficiency curve makes IS virtually a vertical line, monetary policy is practically impotent to affect NNP. (Note the virtual identity of NNP at the E_3 and E_4 intersections.)

■ INTERNAL AND EXTERNAL BALANCE

We can extend the Hicks-Hansen diagram to illustrate the problem of attaining full employment stability at home without losing financial respectability abroad. The extension requires a new curve, related this time to Chapter 16's discussion of the foreign-exchange market. Just as the IS curve shows combinations of i and NNP in which S = I; and just as the LM curve shows pairs of i and NNP at which a given M fully serves both transactions and assets motives for holding money; so the FP curve shows equality between Canada's sources of foreign currency (exports and capital inflows) and Canada's demand for foreign currency (imports and capital outflows). When these are equal, the foreign price of Canadian currency ($C) will tend neither to rise nor to fall.

If they stay on the FP curve, authorities main-

taining a fixed exchange rate need not have recourse to the Exchange Fund Account, or EFA (see page 395, above). Alternatively, if the rate of exchange is free, speculators will find that it remains at one particular level; currency dealers can rely on an unchanged value of $C.

What can we say about the shape of FP? It slopes upward and rightward. To see why, take one point, where annual inflows = outflows = 1 billion dollars. Moving northward from it, i rises and capital inflows increase total inflows to over 1 billion dollars and threaten to raise the value of the $C. This can be compensated, however, by a rise in money outflows, from imports. Imports rise, according to MPM (Chapter 13) only when NNP rises. So, to keep an international financial balance along the curve, when i rises, NNP must also rise. This gives the curve a slope to the northeast.

Another property of FP is that it divides Fig. 17-6 into two areas. All points to its left have an NNP that is too low (or an i that is too high). Currency inflows exceed outflows; so there the $C tends to rise indefinitely. Similarly, to the right of FP, i is too low and NNP too high—the $C is over-valued and sinking. Only along FP is the i-NNP combination just right to keep our dollar at a constant level overseas.

POLICY Fig. 17-6 introduces the policy problem. At E_1 the economy is at under-employment equilibrium, where IS and LM intersect, and foreign payments are in balance, as shown by the fact that an FP equilibrium line also passes through E_1. Now let us assume that fiscal-policy is used to move IS out to IS'. The new equilibrium would be at full-employment E_3, in the absence of foreign-payments constraints. But nothing happens to shift FP. If the government wishes to keep foreign balance, then i and NNP can both rise to E_2, but with domestic employment and NNP well below the desired E_3. Alternatively, the economy can move to E_3, but the $C will decline indefinitely: NNP-induced imports are too high and i too low. An exchange-rate crisis proceeds steadily, while employment remains high.

In such predicaments we find, from time to time, the authorities of every open economy. IS and LM curves have shown that there are often two policy routes to vitalizing the internal economy; but how to reconcile the desired intersection with external balance? Most of the discussion of foreign economic

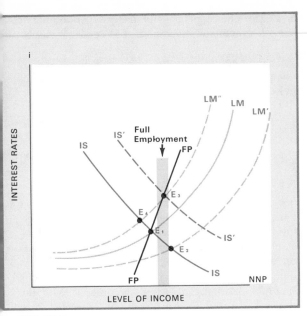

FIG. 17-7.

Of course, a steady fall in the $C may eventually increase exports, and this might push FP (farther than IS) to the right. Then no action need be taken. Furthermore, both IS and LM may shift upward, thus attracting foreign capital into the country to the higher i.

THE FOREIGN CONSTRAINT   That foreign balance can be a serious constraint on the choice of domestic policy is shown by Fig. 17-7. The economy is originally at E_1. This position is flawed by serious unemployment. One remedy is to increase M, thus shifting LM to LM'; intersecting IS at E_2. This position, however is not tenable; it is far from FP and hence suffers from steady currency depreciation. *Expansionary* monetary policy, therefore, will not work.

The correct mix is a *tight* monetary policy to raise i, offset internally by expansionary *fiscal* policy. Thus, M is reduced by open-market operations and LM shifts back to LM'', cutting FP at E_3. Now domestic equilibrium is far to the left at E_4 and unemployment is more serious than ever. This calls for fiscal policy. With reduced taxes or increased G and transfer payments, the government may shift IS up to IS', where all three curves meet in E_3. Internal and external balance are attained.

In other words, monetary policy could *not* be used to deal with unemployment in this case. Fiscal policy was called for; for reasons quite different from those that governed the choice in the closed-economy classical and depression cases.

policy is actually about how to do this by shifting FP to FP'. Part Five goes into this in depth. It is not difficult to see what must be done: either there must be fewer imports for each level of NNP (brought about by import controls, tariffs, and/or foreign-exchange regulations) or less capital outflow (brought about by tax concessions, loans from foreign governments and banks) at each domestic i.

SUMMARY TO APPENDIX

■ 1 The causal interrelations between M, i, I, and NNP could also be expressed in MV language. So long as one expects any induced changes to V to be such as not *fully* to offset the original change in M, then changing M can in one step be described as changing NNP. Semantics alone would be involved, were it not true that special hypotheses about the constancy of V may seem tenable to monetarists who use this concept.

■ 2 In a perfect classical world without frictions and with an inflexible hard-money public-debt base, Pigou proved in the 1940s that a sophisticated version of Say's Law could be asserted. For policy and realistic description, he preferred not to rely on hyperdeflation to produce such "Pigou effects." Pushing such a full-employment model to its logical limits, however, does enable one to reaffirm the crudest quantity theory in which P becomes strictly proportionate to M and public debt (the degree of the proportion varying only when extraneous *real* changes take place).

■ 3 Hicks-Hansen diagrams succeed in synthesizing fiscal and monetary policy, the theory of income determination and the theory of money; in addition they help synthesize the monetarist and Keynesian theories of macroeconomics by providing a definite and general theory of the velocity of money.

■ 4 The choice of policies depends on economic determinants shaping IS, LM, and FP curves.

Chapter 40 will discuss another policy problem of the 1970s—various types of inflation, possible solutions, and the "incomes policy" dilemma.

QUESTIONS FOR DISCUSSION

1. Is it reasonable for you to hold relatively less M and have a faster V when i is 9 rather than 1 per cent? When inflation is galloping? Use your answer to criticize simple monetarism.

2. Explain the Pigou-effect mechanism for restoring full employment when wages and prices are perfectly flexible. What is the role of public debt?

3. *Extra-credit problem:* Intermediate texts can use mathematical symbols to summarize a simple version of this Appendix. Let real saving, S, depend on real income, $Q = NNP/P$, namely: $S = S(Q) = .1Q$, say, much as in Fig. 17-1(c). Let real investment, I, depend inversely on the interest rate, as in Fig. 17-1(b)'s marginal-efficiency schedule, namely: $I = I(i) = 1/i$, for example. In the equation of exchange $MV = PQ$, let velocity, V, be an increasing function of the interest rate, namely: $V = V(i) = 4.4i/(1 + i)$, for example. Pick units so that full-employment output is $Q_F = 1$ (100 billion dollars, perhaps); and suppose that, prior to full employment, prices are constant (as determined by sticky wage-cost levels, etc.), so that by choice of units $P = 1$ until an inflationary gap lifts the price level. Finally, let the money supply, M, be set by the central bank at the level $\overline{M}$. Then to determine our two unknowns, Q and i, in Fig. 17-4 we have the two equations for the IS and LM schedules

$S(Q) = I(i)$ or $.1Q = 1/i$,
marginal efficiency and multiplier

$\overline{M} = PQ/V(i)$ or $\overline{M} = Q/[4.4i/(1 + i)]$,
liquidity-preference theory of V

Solving (by simple substitution or otherwise), we get Q as an increasing function of $\overline{M}$, and i as a decreasing function. After $\overline{M}$ has become so large that full-employment Q_F has been reached, along with its corresponding i_F and V_F, we put Q_F in both equations and solve for the price level P, with P now simply proportional to $\overline{M}$ (in accordance with the classical quantity theory of money), namely: $P = (V_F/Q_F)\,\overline{M}$.

NOTE: for the suggested special formulas above, substitution gives $i = 10/Q$, $V = 44/(Q + 10)$, $\overline{M} = Q(Q + 10)/44$, a quadratic equation for Q in terms of $\overline{M}$. To get full-employment $Q_F = 1$, evidently, $\overline{M} = 11/44 = \frac{1}{4}$ (i.e., 25 billion dollars, with $V_F = 4$ per year, or once every 3 months on the average); and $i_F = 10/Q_F = 10$ per cent per year. For underemployment equilibrium, the quadratic's relevant root is given by $Q = -5 + \sqrt{25 + 44\overline{M}}$. Verify that $\overline{M} = \frac{1}{4}$ does yield $Q = 1$.

4. Review your understanding of the following concepts:

Say's Law and classical models	liquidity preference: M dependence on both NNP and i
Pigou effects	
crude quantity theory	Hicks-Hansen LM and IS intersection
induced changes in V	
public-debt effects	depression and classical models
	internal and external balance

18

FISCAL POLICY
AND FULL EMPLOYMENT
WITHOUT INFLATION

I believe that all parties in this parliament and most Canadians share the view that the national budget is no longer a matter of the government accounts that should be balanced every twelve months on some financial rule of thumb. We view the national budget now as an integral part of the nation's business, influenced by and having an influence upon the state of employment, income, and prices.

MINISTER OF FINANCE, BUDGET SPEECH, 1948

We have seen in earlier chapters that the behavior of saving and investment determines the level of national income and employment. We have seen that investment and other spending often fluctuate widely from year to year. History shows how painful and wasteful the business cycle has been in the past. Today everyone is in agreement that, unless we succeed in laying to rest the ghost of instability, chronic slump, and snowballing inflation, our mixed economic system itself will be in jeopardy. Both the Economic Council of Canada and the federal Prices and Income Commission were set up with this in mind.

What prescription follows from our economic diagnosis? No single answer can be given; there is no single cure-all for the economic ills of society. Business, labor, the provincial governments, and agriculture must of course attempt to pursue price and wage policies aimed at maintaining a stable, high-employment economy. The Bank of Canada can also do much, by way of interest and monetary policy, to moderate instability. But while all these measures are being used, powerful help is still needed from the weapon of public *fiscal policy* (i.e., governmental tax and expenditure policies). Fiscal policy alone is not a cure-all, but it is an important part of any economic program.

Be warned that the subject matter of this chapter is still in a controversial stage. Even economic experts are not in full agreement on all the issues connected with budget deficits and the public debt. And yet it is fair to say that the differences in doctrine among economics scholars pale into insignificance in comparison with the wide gulf that persists between the ideological views on fiscal policy of the public and politicians in comparison with the views of experts on public finance. Gradually, however, informed lay opinion is becoming less archaic on such questions as the following:

> Must the budget be balanced every year? Should it be? Should it be balanced only over a complete business cycle rather than every year? Can it grow forever, as long as the Canadian economy grows?
>
> Is the growth of *debt, per se*, a good or bad thing? How different is public from private debt in this respect? If I as a private person overspend and incur debt, I invite disaster and bankruptcy. Is the same really true of a government that is financing a chronic debt by borrowing from its own citizens? Is a budget deficit necessarily inflationary? Or is it, in recession times, only antideflationary?

As will be seen in this chapter, experienced researchers into the facts and analytical principles of public finance have today, all over the world, quite different answers to these questions from those of the man in the street and of our forefathers. The problem for an introductory text is to explain the logic and experience underlying modern doctrines, not to indoctrinate the student into any one view. An objective analysis of the issues—both the pros and cons—should be helpful in giving each person the materials from which he can form his own opinion on these matters.

A. SHORT-RUN AND LONG-RUN FISCAL POLICY

By a positive fiscal policy, we mean the process of shaping public *taxation* and *public expenditure* in order (1) to help dampen down the swings of the business cycle and (2) to contribute toward the maintenance of a growing, high-employment economy free from excessive inflation or deflation.

Without fiscal and monetary policy, the economic system might in a particular year be threatened with a deflationary gap. Suppose private consumption and investment spending were too weak to provide adequate employment. What action would then be called for?

The Bank of Canada would use expansionary monetary policy to try to stimulate private investment. To the degree[1] that its efforts were not fully successful, the fiscal authorities would still be faced by a deflationary gap. This would be the signal for the Ottawa government to introduce tax and public-expenditure policies designed to help reachieve stable full employment.

Similar action would be called for in the case where private investment and consumption decisions were threatening the economy with an inflationary gap.

---

[1] How much of the stabilizing load is carried by monetary and how much by fiscal policy depends, as Chapters 35 and 40 will discuss, on public-growth targets and international-payments constraints. Also, the financing of deficits and surpluses can itself help shape the course of money-supply growth.

With prices rising and employers vying desperately for nonexistent workers, the Bank of Canada would initiate contractionary credit programs aimed to reduce the inflationary gap. But if the saving-investment or $C + I + G$ intersections still threatened the economy with a sustained inflationary gap, it would then be the duty of the Minister of Finance to initiate higher tax rates and/or lower-public-expenditure programs in the attempt to restore a high-employment equilibrium without inflation.

> In summary, fiscal policies dealing with taxes and public expenditure, in cooperation with stabilizing monetary policies, have for their goal a high-employment and growing economy—but one without price inflation. The fiscal and monetary authorities "lean against the prevailing economic winds," thereby helping provide a favorable economic environment within which the dynamic forces of private initiative can have the widest opportunity for achievement.

■ OUR IMPORTANT "BUILT-IN STABILIZERS"

One might get the impression from the above remarks that fiscal policy helps stabilize the economy only so long as government officials are carefully watching trends, are successfully anticipating future developments, and are meeting promptly to take decisive actions. Such "discretionary fiscal policies," involving the making and changing of explicit decisions, are indeed important; they are, fortunately, but part of the story.

The modern fiscal system has great inherent *automatic stabilizing* properties. All through the day and night, whether or not the government is in session, the fiscal system is helping to keep our economy stable. If a recession gets under way while a national crisis or an election is in progress, powerful automatic forces would go instantly into action to counteract it before there were Cabinet meetings or the exercise of special intelligence of any form.

What are these mysterious stabilizers? They are primarily the following:

1. *Automatic changes in tax receipts.* We saw in Chapters 8 and 9 that our federal tax system depends progressively on personal and corporate incomes. What does this mean for stability? It means that as soon as income begins to fall off, and even before Ottawa makes any changes in tax rates, the tax receipts of the government also fall off.

Now, reductions in tax receipts are just what the doctor prescribes in case of a dip in income. So our present tax system is a mighty and rapid built-in stabilizer.

> NOTE: Taxes stabilize against *upward* as well as downward movements. In times of inflation, this is a good thing; but when built-in rises in taxes stand in the way of healthy real growth, we call it "fiscal drag"—a subject discussed farther on in this chapter.

A century ago, writers thought that *stability* of tax revenue was a good thing, and they would have looked with disapproval on the present-day tendency for tax receipts to rise and fall with national income. Today, most economists believe that truth is just the reverse. Thus, to dampen a boom, a budgetary surplus is desirable. There are two ways to produce such a surplus: by a reduction in government expenditure, yes; but also by an increase in tax receipts. To fight a recession, there are likewise two ways open: raising expenditures, or cutting tax rates. Further, adjusting taxes interferes less with the private economy than altering the scale of public G. How lucky we are, therefore, that our present tax system has to some degree "automatic flexibility," with its receipts tending to rise in inflationary times and to fall in times of depression. This is a powerful factor stabilizing the economy and moderating the business cycle.[2]

2. *Unemployment compensation and other welfare transfers.* Since World War II, we have built up an elaborate system of unemployment compensation. Soon after men are laid off, they begin to receive benefits from the unemployment insurance fund. When they go back to work, the benefits cease; and their contributions to finance unemployment compensation rise when employment is high. During boom years, therefore, the unemployment reserves grow and exert stabilizing pressure against too great spending; conversely, during years of slack employment, the reserve funds are used to pay out income to sustain consumption and moderate the decline.

Other welfare programs—such as relief payments outside this social security system—also show an anticyclical automatic behavior of a stabilizing type.

3. *Price supports.* The various programs to aid agriculture, which we shall discuss later in Part Three, act like built-in stabilizers. When dollar spending drops off and farm prices fall, the federal government pays out dollars to farmers and absorbs surpluses. When inflation brews and prices soar, the government warehouses put forth goods and absorb dollars, thus cushioning any movement.[3]

4. *Federal finance.* Under the various tax-sharing and rental formulas used to pass tax collections from Ottawa to the provinces, the federal government has usually agreed to maintain payments even if NNP or local tax collections should go down. On the other hand, the provinces are among the most volatile and intemperate spenders when booms are on, thus destabilizing inflationary periods.

5. *Corporate savings and family savings.* Not all the applause goes to the government and its fiscal weapons. Our private institutions also have built-in stabilizers. Thus, the custom of corporations maintaining their dividends, even though their incomes change in the short run, does cause their retained savings to act like a shock absorber or built-in stabilizer.[4] And to the extent that families

---

[2] Many experts advocate increasing the stabilizers by having Parliament pass a law bringing in "formula flexibility," in which tax *rates* vary *automatically* with changes in various aggregative price and income indexes. But Parliament is traditionally unwilling to turn over to the Cabinet even discretionary power over taxes. In any case the Carter Commission *Report* (Volume 2, 1966) thought "formula flexibility" inadequate to deal with fluctuations and recommended discretionary policy.

[3] By pushing up the prices of raw materials, support formulas can also have an "escalating," or destabilizing effect; and to the extent that they simply limit supply at all times, they may redistribute and lower rather than stabilize income.

[4] To the extent that corporate investment is itself linked to corporate saving, this stabilizing influence is negated. A rise in the wages/profits ratio is a partial stabilizer on dips.

try to maintain previous living standards and are slow to adjust upward their living standards—to this extent, they too help stabilize. (To the extent that they rush out to spend extra income on down payments or hysterically cut down on consumption when economic clouds arise, they hinder stability.)

6. *Imports.* If firms and families spent a constant percentage of disposable income on imports, the tendency of foreign goods to siphon off part of total spending would be the same in inflationary times as in recession. However, luckily, the import percentage is usually highest when the economy is over-heated. What would otherwise be an inflationary gap is filled by foreign-produced goods. Correspondingly, in times of unemployment, the low price of Canadian goods and the inappropriately luxurious composition of the typical shipload of imports, tends to turn Canadian total spending toward home-produced goods and services. Hence the opportunity to import acts like an overflow pipe, used most when the demand level is too high.

Still other stabilizers are "built in" to the economy, but these are the main ones.

■ LIMITATIONS OF AUTOMATIC STABILIZERS

Before leaving the subject of automatic stabilizers, we should stress two things. First, the built-in stabilizers are our first line of defense, but are not by them-selves sufficient to maintain full stability. Second, reliance on them in preference to discretionary programs raises some philosophical and ethical questions. Let us look at these points.

The automatic tendency for taxes to take away a fraction of each extra dollar of NNP means that the size of the "multiplier" is cut down. Each dollar swing in investment—whether caused by sunspots, inventions, or anything else —will now have its destabilizing effect on the system reduced *but not wiped out completely.* Instead of such disturbances having their effects on NNP multiplied three or more times, there will now—because of the automatic stabilizing effect of taxes—be a multiplier effect of only 1.5 or 2 times.[5]

---

[5] We know from Chapter 13's footnotes 2 and 7 that MPC $= b$ as used in the simple multiplier formula must be cut down to allow for both imports and taxes. Here we evaluate this effect, on the rough assumptions that imports and taxes can both be identified with consumption.

First, imports: Let MPC $= 0.666$; MPS $= 0.333$; MPM $= 0.166$

Then $$\text{MPC}^D \equiv c = (1 - 0.666 + 0.166) = 0.5$$

Next, taxes that reduce disposable income below NNP:

Let $T = t\,Y = 0.35\,Y$

Because $$Y = \overline{C}^D + c(Y - T) + \overline{I}^D + \ldots,$$

then $$Y = c\,(Y - t\,Y) + \overline{K}$$

where $\overline{K}$ is the sum of constants $\overline{C}^D, \overline{I}^D, \overline{G}^D, \overline{E}$, etc.

Then $$Y = \left\{ \frac{1}{1 - c\,(1 - t)} \right\} \overline{K}$$

where the fraction is the multiplier modified for imports and taxes.

What is the numerical effect of the modification? The simple multiplier was

$$\frac{1}{1 - \text{MPC}} = \frac{1}{0.333} = 3$$

The modified multiplier is $$\frac{1}{1 - 0.5\,(1 - 0.35)} = 1.5$$

approximately, much weaker. The Report of the Carter Commission (Vol. 2) estimated that the attenuated multiplier for Canada was less than 2.

In short, a built-in stabilizer acts to reduce *part* of any fluctuation in the economy, but it does not serve to wipe out 100 per cent of the disturbance. It leaves the rest of the disturbance as a task for fiscal and monetary discretionary action.

Philosophically, some reformers dislike the need to have human beings decide policy. They speak of a "government of laws and not of men." They advocate setting up automatic rules and mechanisms that would go into action without ever depending on human decisions.

At the present time an automatic gyropilot can keep an airplane pretty stable while the pilot catches a nap; but when something unusual comes up, the human pilot must take over. No one has yet found a gadget with all the flexibility of man. Similarly in the social field: we have not yet arrived at a stage where any nation is likely to create for itself a set of constitutional procedures that will displace the need for discretionary policy formation and responsible human intelligence.

■ DISCRETIONARY FISCAL POLICY

The principal weapons of discretionary fiscal policy—programs which involve explicit public decision making—are (1) varying public works and other expenditure programs, (2) varying transfer expenditure programs, and (3) varying tax rates cyclically.

PUBLIC WORKS   When governments first began to do something active about depressions, they tended to initiate work on public investment projects for the unemployed. Often these were hastily devised, and in that they aimed primarily to create work for people, they often were rather inefficient; e.g., road building using as little machinery as possible to make the work stretch, leaf raking during the depression by relief workers, trumped-up pork-barrel projects of low utility and lacking careful planning. The extreme case is the mythical program in which men dig holes and then refill them.

The day is long past when a modern nation will let its economy collapse to the point where its only rescue must come from hastily contrived and wasteful public-works spending. The modern emphasis has, rightly, shifted away from such "make work" projects. Indeed, where a recession is expected to be a short one, economists today would wish to rely much more on a temporary reduction in tax rates than on an increase in public works.

Why this shift away from public works as a recession cure? Men now realize that it takes a long time to get a post office started or to put into effect programs for highway and airport construction, or for slum clearance. Plans must be made; blueprints drawn; land acquired by purchase and expropriation; existing buildings razed; and then new structures and roads constructed. All this may take five or more years; and, at the least, half of this time may elapse before any sizable amount of money will get spent on labor and materials. Suppose the recession turns out to last a year at most, followed by two years of steady advance. Then, just in the third year, when the economy may have gone all the way from too little demand to too much demand, there will suddenly come onto the market the government spending that was intended to help a recession. The lags may be even longer when provincial, rather than federal, public works are to be varied. Such timing would of course make fiscal policy an aggravator of instability rather than a reducer.

The above remarks should not be construed as an argument against public works. Slum clearance, urban rehabilitation, road building, and public construction might be deemed by Canadians to represent the most urgent use of their social resources. If that were the case, such programs should be pushed hard; but—and this is the point—they should not be pushed hard under guise of a program designed to achieve short-run stabilization. They should be carried out for their own sake and over that long period of time which is necessary if they are to be done well and efficiently.

Of course, the case will often arise where the economy is in a recession and where it may be possible to move ahead the date of carrying out a series of long-term public projects that the people had already agreed ought to get done anyway. An intelligently planned shelf of blueprints for desirable public-works projects, even though some costs would be involved in arranging them ahead of time and keeping them up to date, could much improve fiscal timing. Indeed, in the "reconstruction" discussions that followed World War II, Ottawa undertook to maintain an up-to-date shelf of projects in return for some of the provinces' powers over taxation. A favorite gibe of the parliamentary opposition was to ask Mr. Howe, the responsible minister, how the shelf was coming along. It soon became clear that the shelf was merely a figure of speech. Likewise, in 1970 Prime Minister Trudeau deemed some projects expendable and eliminated or "shelved" them in the interest of fighting inflation.

WELFARE EXPENDITURES　We saw that existing welfare programs, such as unemployment compensation and old-age retirement payments, do act as automatic stabilizers, rising automatically when incomes fall and needs increase.

In addition to such built-in stabilizers, it is possible for the federal or provincial government to institute various discretionary programs of transfer expenditures that will further stabilize. Thus, the government could refrain from giving some pending old-age bonus in inflationary times and push forward such disbursements in depressed times. If it intends to lower farm price support payments, the government might hope to time the change to coincide with boom times. Most important, in times of prolonged unemployment, the federal government has moderated the decline by prolonging the period for which the jobless can get paid unemployment compensation. It is precisely in times of sustained unemployment that the present system is most deficient, and it is in such times that there will be minimal harmful effects on job mobility and incentives from increasing unemployment disbursements.[6]

---

[6] Economists Cairns and Courchene have analyzed the expansionary and mobility-creating effects of the Canadian unemployment insurance. (See James P. Cairns, "Unemployment Insurance in Canada: The Problem of Conflicting Principles," *Canadian Journal of Economics and Political Science*, Vol. XXVIII, No. 2 (May, 1962), pp. 262-268; and J. J. Courchene, "Interprovincial Migration and Economic Adjustment," *Canadian Journal of Economics*, Vol. III, No. 4 (November, 1970), pp. 550-576. The 1970 *White Paper* proposals on unemployment insurance would make the scheme more expansionary, but might have perverse mobility effects, driving unemployed migrants back to regions where unemployment is worst.

A major drawback in using welfare transfer programs for short-run stabilizing purposes is the political fact that it may not be easy to terminate such emergency programs after times have become good again.

VARIATION OF TAX RATES   If there is good reason to think that a recession will be brief, a temporary cut in income tax rates can be a very good way of keeping disposable incomes from falling and of preventing a decline from snowballing. Under our payment-at-the-source system, the moment the federal government decides the economy needs stimulus through tax reduction, employers can begin to withhold less from salary paycheques at once. Some provincial tax collections are linked to the federal system. Varying tax *rates* can be used also to help control an inflationary gap and long-run sluggishness.

An obvious difficulty is that it takes Ottawa a long time to debate and act on tax changes, though the delay is probably less than in changing spending. A more psychological objection to temporary suspension of tax rates to counter a recession comes from the political fact of life that in our democracy it may be hard to get tax rates back up after the need for the emergency cut is over. Political sentiment to fight unemployment is often easier to mobilize than sentiment to fight inflationary gaps and more-than-full employment. (In long slumps this may be good.) Furthermore, if people know tax changes are temporary and will not be altering their permanent incomes much, they may not vary their consumption spending very much.

While advantages and disadvantages are claimed for various alternative fiscal programs, the observer should not let them blind him to the basic fact that in the last 30 years the proneness of the North American economic system to chronic slump and major instability has been drastically reduced. When Prime Ministers Bennett and King tried to fight the Great Depression, attitudes to government interference and to federal finance were more like those of 1867 than those of today! Yet even in 1970, we found Premiers Robarts and Bennett balking at blame for inflation pressures which the federal government had placed on the economies of Ontario and British Columbia.

■ SURPLUS AND DEFICIT FINANCING: STAGNATION, EXHILARATION, AND CONTRIVED GROWTH

So far we have been talking only about ironing out the business cycle. If the business cycle were around some "normal" level, most people would not worry too much so long as the boom-time budgetary surplus were always matched by the depression budgetary deficit. With such regularity, *the budget would be balanced over the business cycle* even though not balanced in every single year or month. There would be no secular trend upward in the public debt, nor downward.

But how can one be sure that the cycle will be so regular? What if our continental economy is in for what Harvard's Alvin Hansen called "secular stagnation"—which means a long period in which (1) slowing population increase, (2) passing of the frontier's free land, (3) high corporate saving, (4) the vast piling up of capital goods, and (5) a bias toward capital-saving inventions will imply depressed investment schedules relative to saving schedules? Will not an active fiscal policy designed to wipe out such deflationary gaps then result in running a deficit *most of the time*, leading to a secular growth in the public debt? The modern answer is "Under these conditions, yes; and over the decades the budget should not necessarily be balanced."

Contrariwise, suppose population is proliferating, new inventions are zooming, and investment is generally excessive relative to full-employment saving. If this threatens to go on most of the time, will not active fiscal policy require a budgetary surplus most of the time? Hence, will not such a condition of "secular exhilaration" lead to a secular decline in the public debt? Here the modern answer is, "Under these conditions, yes—and a good thing, too."

A new, third possibility looms for the 1970s. Suppose a democracy is concerned to accelerate its own rate of growth. Suppose its representative government wishes to increase the fraction of its full-employment income that gets devoted to capital formation rather than to consumption. If public policy succeeds in stepping up net investment by militant easy credit or other policies, how can consumption spending be cut down to prevent excessive dollar demands from precipitating inflation? Primarily by having the government pursue an

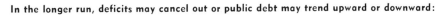

In the longer run, deficits may cancel out or public debt may trend upward or downward:

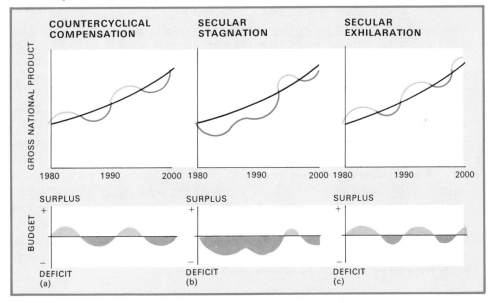

FIG. 18-1. In every case the trend line of policy-achieved full-employment output is shown in black. How the GNP would grow in absence of active fiscal policy is shown in brown. The indicated budget policy, of successful "leaning against the wind," is shown in gray below. In (a), the light areas of surplus cancel out the dark areas of deficit over the business cycle. In (b)'s case of secular stagnation, the dark deficits prevail over the surpluses and the debt trends upward. In (c), surpluses predominate on the average and debt declines.

austere fiscal policy: raising tax rates and cutting down on marginal expenditures, thereby contriving a *chronic* budget surplus to offset easy money.

In brief, one cannot set in advance the optimal trend of surplus or deficit. A diagram can summarize long-term budget alternatives. Figure 18-1 illustrates three variants of modern fiscal policy, all in contrast to a budget balanced in every single year.

In Fig. 18-1(a) we see *simple compensatory finance* to iron out the business cycle, with boom surpluses canceling out depression deficits.

In Fig. 18-1(b), under secular stagnation, surplus periods are rarer and do not suffice to keep the public debt from having a tendency to grow chronically. (In the Appendix to this chapter, we study the consequences and true burdens of public debt growth.)

In Fig. 18-1(c), with private $C + I$ spending either spontaneously strong or made strong by expansive Bank of Canada policy, the tendency for the system to run inflationary gaps much of the time is countered by budget surpluses most of the time, with the public debt tending to decline in the long run.

> In the longer run, deficits may cancel out, or public debt may trend upward or downward.

Canada illustrates all these general problems. In addition, her peculiar regional structure and external dependence create further questions to be solved. Suppose all the Canadian economy is zooming except a particular region. Should the whole economy be slowed down, or should special transfer payments be made to compensate or adapt that region? Suppose the problems of stagnation indicate that tax cuts are ineffective. How are the provinces to be induced *and* helped to step up the public works and welfare that are their own constitutional duties? Will political opinion support the economist who might then urge on Quebec or the prairies policies that the local people are opposed to?

Presumably time and statesmanship will settle these questions. But how are we to reconcile their solution with our *external* relationships? Public works nowadays have a high "import content" (refer back to Chapter 13). Thus expenditures to offset stagnation may "leak" out without having much or any multiplier effect on domestic employment. Conversely, in booms, decisions to delay federal public works may be nullified if private business and provinces borrow money in New York to speed up their own I and G. The impatient advocate of full-employment policies says, in effect, "Close the borders to these flows of money and goods." But if we do so, other nations will retaliate, cutting down our $E - M$ and driving us toward low-level self-sufficiency. We cannot escape easily from being a unit of the international economy.

■THE NEW ECONOMICS AT WORK

From 1945 till 1953, total demand in Canada and the United States was exuberant. Real growth of output was unusually rapid. After a Canadian slump in 1949, now seen as minor, unemployment levelled out at just above 3 per cent through 1953. But, though there have been cycles of three or four years ever since, in each successive cycle average unemployment was higher: 2.8 per cent till 1953, 4.3 per cent till 1957; and 6.7 per cent till 1962. Even in the post-1962 boom, it averaged about 5 to 5.5 per cent, never dropping below 5 per cent till 1965. (Between 1965 and 1969, however, the rate of unemployment was often below 5 per cent, dipping as low as 3.6 per cent in 1966.)

Moreover, the rates of growth of national output have been until recently very disappointing. Productivity or output per man-hour has grown at a somewhat slower rate since the late 1950s (4.2 per cent between 1949 and 1957 in contrast to 3.7 per cent for the 1958-1965 period). And, as shown in Chapter 13, what we have achieved has often fallen far short of the potential output of the economy. Although these omens do not add up to "secular stagnation," they have worried voters enough to win their support for heavy spending on regional transfers and other programs to melt the "structural" unemployment icebergs described in Chapter 40. As a result, the National Accounts show us that since 1959 government as a whole has been running a deficit. This is true of the Ottawa government in particular, which added about 6 billion dollars to its debt during the 1960s. By 1965, government deficits had won grudging political acceptance. The federal government's decision to reduce taxes came some months after the Kennedy-Johnson cuts in the United States, and, despite the growing government debt, Canadians gladly paid up to $300 less in their income tax bills in 1965.

To cut taxes when there was already a budget deficit was indeed "new" economics. Only after a long campaign of education did the man in the street generally become persuaded of the following precepts:

1. To the extent that a tax cut succeeds in stimulating business, our progressive tax system will collect extra revenues out of the higher income levels. Hence, a tax cut *may* in the long run imply little (or even no) loss in federal revenues, and hence no substantial increase in the long-run public debt.

2. There is no need to balance the budget, or try to balance it, in every year. In a growing economy prudent policy does not even require that the budget be balanced over a decade, or over a complete business cycle. So long as continuous deficits do not result in the public debt growing faster than GNP grows, good economic health can prevail. For the economy, "balance" means full employment and healthy growth with no wasteful gap between our potential and our actual real output, and also no inflationary gap.

At first the nonexpert public remained skeptical about these doctrines, though they have been central to recent monetary and fiscal surveys and reports. Recently, however, two influences have changed many people's thinking:

1. The American 10-billion-dollar tax cut of 1964 was able to change consumption, though of course it did not bring full employment overnight. Instead, it produced just about the gradual rise in consumer spending that the propensity-to-consume concept had predicted. It also stimulated investment. Finally, the multiplier doctrine worked much as textbooks had predicted.

2. The general view taken in the Carter Commission's *Report* and special studies was that federal discretionary fiscal policy contributed without question to the stability of the Canadian economy in the period 1945-1963.[7] Viewed over the shorter period since 1954, the fiscal policy was found to be pressing in the right direction more than half the time, and really wrong ("perverse") only in three years. This is strong support against the contrary view that (because of ignorance and long lags) fiscal policy may work so inefficiently and slowly as to *de*stabilize.

In economics, of course, controlled experiments are not possible. Other things will not remain constant. In the United States, by 1966 the unplanned increase in Vietnam expenditures caused the economy to overshoot the goal of full employment and to enter into a period of demand-pull inflationary gap. Canada too experienced some degree of over-full employment and inflationary pressures. Despite the advice of many economists to raise taxes, governments of both nations dragged their feet on the issue until 1968-1969, when they introduced increases in the form of a "surtax." By that time, prices had been rising for so long that stubborn inflationary *expectations* were aroused. The resulting rise in $C + I$ spending and in prices proved hard to quell by monetary and fiscal policy—hence, in Canada, the federal Prices and Incomes Commission was set up.

■ FISCAL DRAG[8]

In concluding this discussion of deficits and surpluses, and before taking up the issue of the public debt, we should notice some new principles which were developed in the 1960s. First, there is the important concept of fiscal, or revenue, drag. Second, there is the related concept of the "full-employment budgetary surplus (or deficit)" as contrasted with the actual surplus or deficit experienced at whatever NNP actually happens to be.

We have seen that a progressive income tax structure results in vast increases in tax revenues when incomes grow. Thus, every year that the economy shows 5 or 6 per cent growth in money NNP, the government collects about three-quarters of a billion dollars in extra revenue. Every year! Since existing government expenditures do not automatically grow by this amount, we are provided in effect with a "fiscal dividend" that can be used for public purposes.

If inflation is taking place, this built-in stabilizer is a great thing—just what the doctor ordered. But suppose the economy is in a normal healthy state of full employment without inflationary or deflationary gap? Then a collection of three-quarters of a billion new dollars of tax revenue can prove a *deflating* influence that may kill off full employment. And in this case we call it "fiscal drag," and know that we must get rid[9] of it either by cutting taxes, by raising

---

[7] See the Royal Commission on Taxation (the Carter Commission) *Report*, Volume 2, 1966, Chapter 3; and Study Number 17, *Canadian Fiscal Policy 1945-1963*, by R. M. Will, 1966, Chapter 5.

[8] The next two sections may be skipped in brief courses.

[9] As will be seen in Part Six, if there is no international constraint on expansionary monetary policy, fiscal drag can be offset by inducing higher investment to accelerate national growth.

**The new economics introduces new concepts:
full-employment budget and fiscal drag:**

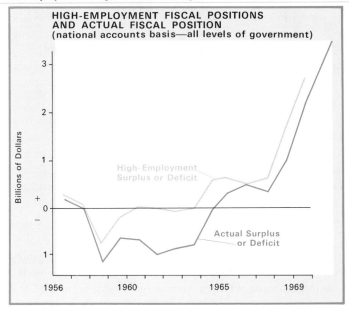

HIGH-EMPLOYMENT FISCAL POSITIONS
AND ACTUAL FISCAL POSITION
(national accounts basis—all levels of government)

High-Employment
Surplus or Deficit

Actual Surplus
or Deficit

FIG. 18-2. The dark brown line shows that the actual federal budget was in deficit steadily from 1958 to 1963. But the light brown line shows a surplus in every year except 1958, 1959, and 1962, in the full-employment budget (which gives the accounting if national output and employment were at the potential level). Growth of the economy enlarges this full-employment surplus every year and produces "fiscal drag" unless taxes are cut or expenditures raised. [Source: Economic Council of Canada, *Performance and Potential Mid 1950's to Mid 1970s.* (Ottawa: Information Canada, 1970.) Reproduced with the permission of Information Canada.]

federal expenditures, or by giving financial aid to the provinces, with their burgeoning social needs and inflexible tax systems.

> *Definition* "Fiscal drag or dividend" is the name for the automatic growth in tax revenues in an economy with a progressive tax structure and steady over-all growth. Unless needed to fight an inflationary gap, fiscal drag has to be offset by (1) federal expenditure increase on goods and services or on transfers deemed vital, (2) tax-rate cuts that increase people's disposable incomes and expenditures in the private sector, (3) coordination with provinces to increase their spending or to reduce their taxes, or (4) combinations of all of these.

■ THE FULL-EMPLOYMENT BUDGET SURPLUS

As a way of dramatizing this ever-recurring problem of fiscal drag, economists have learned not to look at the actual budget deficit. When, as in 1961, we had over 7 per cent unemployment and a large gap between our actual output and our full-employment potential, we were of course running a budget deficit.[10]

But modern economists make a new calculation, asking: "Suppose we were now at high or full employment, say with less than 4 per cent of the labor force unemployed and with firms at their desired 95 per cent of capacity. With all the

---

[10] This was true whether you used the official "administrative budget," or the so-called "cash budget," or the more informative "national accounts budget."

higher tax revenues that such an increase in NNP would bring, what then would our budget deficit be?"

The answer to this question—for all governments, and not just Ottawa— is indicated in Fig. 18-2. It shows that the long years in which governments were running at a deficit and adding to the total government debt would, even with the same spending programs and tax rates, have been years of breaking even or of debt reduction if there had been high employment. There has really been a "full-employment surplus" since 1963!

> To summarize, the "full-employment budget surplus or deficit" measures what *would* be the budget position *if* the economy were at full employment and the legislated tax and spending structures were in effect. Unless tax rates are cut or expenditures increased, there would be in every healthily growing economy an increase in the full-employment surplus and a resulting fiscal drag.

By now we have come a long way from the old-fashioned views of the man in the street. Economic emphasis has been put on the economy's healthy growth without inflation and not on the balancing of the budget. But is this sound economics? Can the economic system prudently bear the implied burden of the public debt? To that nagging question we turn for the remaining section of this chapter.

B. THE PUBLIC DEBT AND MODERN FISCAL POLICY

In Canada—as in Britain, Germany, Japan, and Holland—statesmen, editors, and the citizenry never know what their current budgetary deficits (or surpluses) are. (Test yourself!) In this they are like most economists who, if asked to make a list of important economic issues, will usually put the debt near the bottom. But they are unlike a small group of well-informed Canadians who, like most Americans, would put the debt at the top of the list.

Our task is not to explain this difference of attitude, but to survey the *economic* effects of debts, deficits, and surpluses. The facts agreed on by economic scholars are briefly summarized in this section. The Appendix then presents a survey of the analysis that underlies the economics of public debt, and of popular analogies.

No introduction can go into all the intricacies involved in a correct appraisal of the public debt. But modern economists give attention to the debt's true burden and diagnose its problems in a way significantly different from the approach the layman used to take.

■ BURDENS AND BENEFITS OF THE PUBLIC DEBT

As the Appendix shows,

> The main way that one generation can put a burden on a later generation is by using up currently the nation's stock of capital goods, or by failing to add the usual investment increment to the stock of capital.

Thus, the bulk of our 17 billion dollars of net federal debt came from World War II. The primary burden of that war came from the need *then* to eat up capital goods without replacing them in order to maximize our effectiveness against the enemy and shorten the conflict. (Hence, it was the prohibition against car manufacture or building construction and repair that produced this real burden, and not the happenstance that Parliament decided to finance part of the war effort on a loan-deficit basis rather than on a full tax-as-you-go basis.)

Looking to the future, we can say that *increases in public debt that are incurred in time of full employment* and involve no government capital formation, but *which do require that private investment be held down* (by monetary policy or by inflation itself), do represent a "burden." On the other hand, incurring debt when there is no other feasible way to move the $C + I + G + (E - M)$ equilibrium intersection up toward full employment actually represents a *negative* burden on the immediate future to the degree that it actually induces more current capital formation than would otherwise take place!

There is a second aspect of the public debt that needs stressing. An *external* debt (owed to foreigners) as the Appendix shows in detail, does involve a net subtraction from the goods and services available to the Canadian people to the extent that (*a*) we have to send goods abroad to pay interest on that debt, and (*b*) the incurring of the external debt was unproductive, failing to add to our capacity to turn out such goods and services.

An *internal* debt (owed by the government to its own citizens) is quite a different matter. Certainly one cannot blithely ignore an internal debt on the ground that "we owe it all to ourselves." There definitely are problems arising from the existence of an internal debt—but they do differ from those of an external debt.

TWO INTERNAL-DEBT EFFECTS   First, there are the *transfers* (of interest) that must be made to some people and the taxes that are levied upon all people for this purpose. To the degree that the people involved are different, and that the interest receivers are wealthier, more thrifty, or deemed less in need of income, there will be some—minor—*redistributional* effects to reckon with. But even if the same people are taxed to pay on the average the same amounts they receive in interest, there will still be the *distorting effects on incentives* that inescapably result from any tax. (The Appendix shows that taxing Peter to pay Paul bond interest may make Peter *work* less hard or harder, even if Peter and Paul are the same person—and either effect may be a distortion of efficiency and well-being. But keep all this in perspective: Interest payments are only about 13.78 per cent of total federal government revenue and less than 10 per cent of combined federal-provincial-municipal revenues.)

Second, there are the long-run saving and capital-formation effects. Because we do not live forever, we each tend to treat our holdings of the public debt as an addition to our net worth (added onto the value of the land, structures, and machinery we own). Each person tends to regard his government bond as an asset, but the future taxes to service these bonds he does not count in fully as a current personal liability, even though society will have to pay taxes equal to such debt service. This feeling of greater wealth may cause us to consume a bit more and save a bit less. Thus the existence of a large outstanding public debt may also have an influence on interest-rate levels. Some writers fear that channeling investment funds into the purchase of government bonds will raise the rate of interest to private borrowers. Many people meet this argument by pointing to the benefits of a safe place for the investment of funds so that widows, orphans, colleges, and other nonprofit institutions do not have to depend on public beneficence.

Both arguments need close scrutiny. A partial test is now being made in Canada. The expanding Canada Pension Plan requires that taxes (contributions for old age) rise, just as they must to support a large public debt. Does this mean that people will save less privately for their own wealth accumulation? Does it mean that there will therefore be a smaller market for private and municipal bonds and shares? This cannot be the *complete* effect, for the build-up of the Pension funds will provide cash for the purchase of federal and provincial bonds that would otherwise compete with private borrowers in tomorrow's money markets. So, even if people do save less and purchase fewer securities, there might still be as much or more market for private issues. So it cannot be concluded that private borrowers must meet worse credit conditions or higher interest rates. (The studies that have been made are mostly politically-colored guesses.) Nor can it be assumed that merely having a large public debt in existence makes private borrowing harder. Studies are needed.

■ EFFECTS ON PRIVATE INVESTMENT

There is much emotion involved in people's attitudes to the debt. Businessmen, in particular, refer to it continually. Many people used to predict the end of the world when the debt reached one-hundredth, one-tenth, and one-fifth of its present level; each year when the dire disaster had not appeared, they renewed their prediction for subsequent years.

Such attitudes may affect private investment. If, in times of unemployment, private investment could be assumed constant, then public expenditures would admittedly have favorable primary effects upon income and employment; more than that, the consumption respending of income would give rise to the familiar multiplier chain of favorable secondary effects. But what if private investment is frightened off by government expenditure or by the increase in debt involved?

A private utility company may curtail investment because it fears the threat of public dam projects. Or when the government spending gives people money to buy in retail stores, the effect in time of deep depression may simply be to permit the merchant to work off his inventory of surplus merchandise; if he does not reorder production goods, the public expenditure has been just neutralized by induced private *disinvestment* (in inventory), and the multiplier chain is stopped dead in its tracks.

On the other hand, there may be expansive effects on private investment that are just the opposite of these unfavorable repercussions of government finance. When current production is at a low ebb and there is excess plant capacity, no prudent businessman feels like undertaking new capital formation. If the government is able to boost retail sales and the production of consumption goods, then businessmen will have the financial ability and at least some motive to renew equipment and build new plants.[11] Sometimes purely psychological fears about the public debt and deficit could *accentuate* an inflation situation, even one with its origin outside the fiscal sphere.

Where there are two such opposing tendencies—expansive and contractionary effects upon private investment—facts rather than arguments must be our guide. Although economics does not permit us to make controlled experiments to settle the point conclusively, the bulk of the statistical data seems to suggest that private investment tends on the whole to move sympathetically with the level of national income.

■ THE QUANTITATIVE PROBLEM OF THE DEBT

To assess the importance of the present public debt, we must turn to the facts. Do interest payments on it swallow up most of the national income? How does the total of all interest payments, public and private, compare with past years and with the experience of other countries? What about the future?

To see how the present debt compares with the past and with some other countries, look at Table 18-1. It shows for selected times and places the size of national debts and their relationship to size of national income and interest payments. Thus, in 1970 our net national debt of about 17 billion dollars represented much less than one year of national income, and its interest payments represented only about 2 per cent of net national product. Note that Britain in 1818, 1923, and 1946 had an internal debt estimated at two or three times national income, and interest on the debt as a percentage of national income far exceeded anything that we need look forward to; yet the century before World War I was Britain's greatest century—greatest in power and material progress. Furthermore, as the table shows, her national debt was not substantially reduced; but with the steady growth of her national income, the debt and its charges shrank to almost nothing in relative magnitude!

In the light of these statistics and by careful qualitative analysis, the reader must form his own judgment as to whether the national debt can be rationally regarded as a problem of the first magnitude in comparison with the problems of national defense, the nuclear bomb, unemployment, and inflation. Whether productivity will continue to rise in the future, whether labor and management can learn to bargain collectively without strikes and inflation—to many observers these seem much more important than the debt itself.

■ CONCLUSION TO PART TWO: MACROECONOMICS OF THE MIXED ECONOMY

As the quotation beginning this chapter shows, the Canadian government assumed responsibility for stable employment, income, and prices in 1948. This claim is now regarded as a duty. Even if there were not such parliamentary

---

[11] An example of this was provided by the discussion in Chapter 13 of the acceleration principle relating induced investment to the upward change in sales.

Growing debt holds little peril for a dynamically growing economy:

NATIONAL DEBT AND INTEREST CHARGES RELATIVE TO NATIONAL INCOME

(1) YEAR	(2) NATIONAL DEBT	(3) INTEREST CHARGES ON DEBT	(4) NET NATIONAL INCOME	(5) SIZE OF DEBT IN YEARS OF NET NATIONAL INCOME (5) = (2) ÷ (4)	(6) INTEREST CHARGES AS A PERCENTAGE OF NET NATIONAL INCOME (6) = (3) ÷ (4) × 100
Canada (millions of dollars):					
1970	$16,880	$1,704	$63,770	.26	2.7
1969	17,326	1,442	59,436	.29	2.0
1966	15,543	1,077	43,054	.36	2.5
1965	15,504	1,012	38,819	.40	2.6
1960	12,089	736	27,433	.44	2.7
1950	11,645	440	14,161	.82	3.1
1940	3,271	129	5,063	.65	2.5
1935	2,846	138	3,099	.92	4.4
1930	3,178	122	4,399	.49	2.8
1920	2,249	107	4,865	.46	2.2
1910	336	13	1,830	.18	.7
1870	78	5	405	.19	1.2
United States (billions):					
1970	$360.0	$16.50	$815.0	.41	2.0
1965	321.4	11.43	559.0	0.6	2.0
1945	278.7	3.66	181.5	1.5	2.0
1939	47.6	0.95	72.6	0.7	1.3
1929	16.3	0.66	86.8	0.2	0.7
1920	24.3	1.02	79.1	0.3	1.3
1916	1.2	0.02	38.7	0.0+	0.0+
1868	2.6	0.13	6.8	0.4	1.9
Britain (millions):					
1970	£31,986	£1,198	£31,148	1.0	3.8
1964	30,250	620	26,500	1.1	2.3
1946	24,000	500	8,100	3.0	6.2
1923	7,700	325	3,950	1.9	8.2
1913	625	20	2,400	0.3	0.8
1818	840	31	400	2.1	7.7

TABLE 18-1. The countries' methods of measuring debt and income vary, but everywhere the burden is declining when the economy grows. (U.S., U.K.: gross national debt; Canada: net national debt.) (Sources: *Economic Almanac*, **U.S. Department of Commerce; U.S. Treasury; United Nations;** *Colwyn Report; Statistical Abstract of United Kingdom; Canada Year Book; Public Accounts of Canada*, **1966;** *The National Finances*, **1966-67, Canadian Tax Foundation; Urquhart and Buckley,** *Historical Statistics of Canada*, **Cambridge University Press, 1965; and Bank of Canada** *Statistical Summary*.)

proclamations, it is a fact all over the world that the populace of modern mixed economies require that their representative governments pursue economic policies that attempt to keep employment high, growth strong, and prices stable.

Part Two has presented the economic *tools of macroeconomics*: how the various schedules determine levels and movements in incomes and prices; and how monetary and fiscal policies can shift those schedules so as to avoid deflationary and inflationary gaps and promote growth. In Part Six certain special problems connected with the modern era—growth, demand and cost-push inflation, and so forth—will be discussed in greater detail.

The finding of our macroeconomic analysis rejects both the classical faith that *laissez-faire* must by itself lead to utopian stability and the pre-World War II pessimism that classical microeconomic principles have become inapplicable to the modern world. Instead we end up with the reasoned prospect that appropriate monetary and fiscal policies can ensure an economic environment which will *validate* the verities of microeconomics—that society has to choose among its alternative high-employment production possibilities, that paradoxes of thrift and the fallacies of composition will not be permitted to create cleavages between private and social virtues or private and public vices.

> By means of appropriately reinforcing monetary and fiscal policies, a mixed economy can avoid excesses of boom and slump and can look forward to healthy progressive growth. This being understood, the paradoxes that robbed the older classical principles dealing with small-scale "microeconomics" of much of their relevance and validity will now lose their sting. The broad cleavage between microeconomics and macroeconomics has been closed by active use of fiscal and monetary and exchange-rate policy.[12]

With good conscience we can turn to the analysis in Part Three of how the great social aggregates of national income and employment *get determined in their detailed parts* and to Part Four's analysis of *income distribution*.

SUMMARY

A. A SHORT- AND LONG-RUN FISCAL POLICY

■ 1 When private investment and consumption spending create an inflationary (or deflationary) gap, it is the task of fiscal and monetary policy to offset the gap in the attempt to preserve price stability, high employment, and growth.

■ 2 Fiscal weapons refer to taxation and expenditure policies. In this connection, the modern economy is blessed with important "built-in stabilizers." Requiring no discretionary action, tax receipts change *automatically* when income changes, thereby reducing the size of the multiplier and serving to wipe out part of any disturbance. (The same stabilizing effect is realized by unemployment compensation and other welfare transfers that automatically grow as income declines; by price supports for agriculture; by federal finance; by the propensity of corporations to pay out in dividends only

---

[12] Naturally, one can point out many needed qualifications to this optimistic formulation. But events of recent decades and the most painstaking economic research in universities, industry, and government justify our concentrating on the doughnut—not on its hole.

part of their current earnings; and by variations in the percentage of income spent on imports.)

■ 3 Because the automatic stabilizers never fully offset the instabilities of an economy, scope is left for discretionary programs. Public works and other expenditure on goods and services can involve such time lags in getting under way as to make their use to combat short recessions undesirable. Discretionary variations in transfer expenditures and in tax rates—politics aside—have greater short-run flexibility.

■ 4 When men began to drop the notion that the government's budget had to be balanced in every year or month, they first thought that it would be in balance over the business cycle—with the boom-time surpluses just matching the depression deficits. It is today realized that only by coincidence would the prosperity years just balance in their intensity the depression years, especially with the desired mix of consumption and capital formation.

If, as a few believe, we are in for "secular stagnation," with private saving and investment schedules tending much of the time to produce deflationary gaps, fiscal policy will probably succeed in maintaining stable high employment only by having a long-term increase in the public debt. If, as others believe, we are in for "chronic exhilaration," with demand so brisk as to lead much of the time to inflationary gaps, then active fiscal policy will probably mean a bias toward surplus financing and a secular downward trend in the public debt. Perhaps the majority of economists feel there is no need to try to predict what the distant future has in store, being prepared to advocate programs that the developing situation calls for. Actually, official predictions for Canada suggested that at the tax rates then current there would be a significant surplus for all governments taken together in 1970. It will be suggested later, in Chapter 40, that under such circumstances long-term surplus financing could be coupled with long-term easing of credit and special encouragements to capital formation. Such a policy would allow a mixed economy like ours to move its high-employment production in the direction of investment and rapid growth and away from current consumption.

Parliament met the sluggishness of the last decade by legislating a tax and expenditure structure which shows budget balance or surplus only when unemployment drops down close to a 4 per cent minimal level. In 1969 and 1970 it ran a budgetary surplus to meet inflationary pressures.

■ 5 To get a better measure of changes in discretionary fiscal policy, economists supplement knowledge of the *actual* budget surplus or deficit with hypothetical "full-employment budget surplus or deficit," which measures what the existing tax and spending structure *would* entail *if* NNP were at the full-employment level. In a growing economy, there would automatically be a steady growth in the size of the full-employment surplus and resulting "fiscal dividend" or "fiscal drag"—unless offset by expenditure increases, tax cuts, or coordination of spending and tax revenues with the provinces. In times of inflation, automatic fiscal drag is a good thing; and at all times a dividend from genuine growth provides resources for new public or private activities.

B.   THE PUBLIC DEBT AND MODERN FISCAL POLICY

■ 6 The public debt does not burden the shoulders of a nation as if each citizen were made to carry rocks on his back. There *are* real debt burdens, not only of *external* debt, but also from the transfers required by *internal* debt. However, the existence of the national debt may also have both "real" and possible psychological effects upon the minds of men. Through these effects a debt can make an important impact on the economy, even if they are not primarily those that editors preach about. They are discussed in the Appendix in detail.

■ 7 It is important, also, to know roughly the size of the post-World War II federal debt in relation to national income and interest charges, in order to assess the present, both in terms of the past and in terms of the future. In recent years the ratio of public debt to private debt and national product has been substantially declining.

■ 8 A full- (or high-) employment program has as its goal a level of total spending that is neither too little nor too great—so that the saving and investment schedules intersect in the region of full employment.

■ 9 To the extent that reinforcing monetary and fiscal policies are efficacious in stabilizing the worst excesses of boom and slump, we need no longer fear the clash between private and social virtues or the various paradoxes of a depressed economy. Mastery of the modern tools of income determination at the macroeconomic level will turn out to validate the basic truths in the classical doctrines of pricing and scarcity at the microeconomic level. This is the optimistic macroeconomics of the mixed economy or the "New Economics."

QUESTIONS FOR DISCUSSION

1. "No nation can avoid having a fiscal policy. With the government such an important part of the present-day economy, it is almost impossible even to define a 'neutral fiscal policy.' It is even harder to give rational reasons for preferring such a policy to an active program aimed at preventing inflation and deflation." Examine critically.

2. List various "built-in stabilizers." Show how they work in the 1970s.

3. What phase of the business cycle (if any) are you now in? What tax and expenditure policies would seem appropriate? Qualitatively, how would you vary the relative import-ance of different taxes (income-tax rates and exemptions, sales taxes, or property taxes) to fight unemployment or inflation?

4. From the early 1870s to the middle 1890s, depressions were deep and prolonged, booms were short-lived and relatively anemic, and the price level was declining. What long-run fiscal policy should have been followed in that quarter of a century? Would your answer be the same for the following 20 years leading up to World War I, a period of rising prices and comparative prosperity?

5. Formulate and evaluate the "New Economics."

6. Review your understanding of the following concepts:

inflationary and deflationary gap
tax receipts and tax rates
government expenditure on goods
  and transfer expenditures
built-in stabilizers and the reduced
  multiplier
discretionary fiscal programs
fiscal drag and fiscal dividend
the full employment budget surplus

internal versus external debt
present versus future generations
  and bequeathal of real capital
debt/income ratios here and abroad,
  today, yesterday, and tomorrow
chronic stagnation, exhilaration,
  and trends in the public debt
the New Economics.

APPENDIX: False and Genuine Burdens of the Public Debt

The popular image is that the public debt, prorated over the population, is like a load on each man's back. According to this same image, when Ottawa adds a dollar to the debt by running a current deficit of a dollar, that is like just one more rock added to the load our children or grandchildren will already have to carry on their backs.

This image is misleading in two ways. First it exaggerates the burdens that are truly involved. Second, by giving a mistaken view of the debt burden, it lays itself open to refutation and thereby to the mistaken conclusion that there are, after all, *no* burdens connected with the public debt. In other words, superficial and wrong analysis offers no genuine comfort to the conservatives, liberals, or radicals.

As a preview to a judicious appraisal, see how vulnerable the foregoing image is.

■ A DIALOGUE

Suppose all debt came from World War II. The war is over. Suppose all Canadian families (1) share equally in ideal nondistorting taxes, (2) hold equal shares of public-debt bonds, (3) all live forever (as individuals or as a cohesive family). With no debt held abroad, (4) "we all owe it to ourselves."

"Then such bonds are not rocks on our shoulders, nor even paper weights. If we unanimously voted to

abolish the bonds, there would be no real difference. If an enemy bombed our homes and factories, that would be a genuine personal and national burden. But if an enemy bombed our bond lock-boxes out of existence, that would merely save us the red tape of taxing ourselves to pay each of us back in bond interest just what the extra tax took away."

So goes the argument. Notice how simple the above refutation is. And how clever in taking the wind out of the sails of those who use the over-simplified rock-burden image. Moreover, the refutation is—granted its assumptions—logically rigorous.

Has the refutation proved the war involved no grievous burden? It has been cunningly silent on that matter. The Devil's Advocate who produced the refutation would, if pressed by a Tireless Truthseeker, have to concede much.

DEVIL'S ADVOCATE   Yes, the war involved a grievous economic burden at the time. We had to work hard and long hours. We had to cut wartime consumption to the bone: do with little meat, no cars, no travel—make do with few of the things that make life enjoyable rather than merely tolerable.

TIRELESS TRUTHSEEKER   With severe rationing controls, the contemporaneous wartime burden of sacrificed consumption would, according to your view, be much the same even if the war had been financed by pay-as-you-go wartime taxes instead of deficit?

D.A. Precisely. Postwar canceled tax receipts, instead of bonds, would make no difference.

T.T. But surely, we used up capital goods during the war by not replacing them. The enemy had to be fought with current 1939-1945 goods and not with 1970 goods. By using up capital goods *then*, we could throw more resources into the war effort. And that did put a real burden *on us in the postwar period* since we inherited less capital goods at war's end. In the postwar period we've had to consume less in order to rebuild those capital goods; and we've had to consume less than we should have if 1939-1945 had given us the normal peacetime increase in capital goods.

D.A. True. But wartime rationing produced that result. If no wartime deficits and bond indebtedness had been created, that *genuine burden* on the postwar group due to the war would still have had to take place.

T.T. I feel there must be a catch somewhere. Your argument sounds too facile.

1. I can't help feeling that the existence of the public debt leads (*a*) to tax distortions as we collect taxes to pay its interest, and (*b*) to a lower consumption schedule when poor people with higher MPC pay taxes for bond interest to wealthier people with a lower MPC.

2. Moreover, people don't live forever, and it is not irrational of them to feel wealthier because of the public debt (since they need count on paying taxes for debt interest *only through their remaining lifetime*). This increase in the CC propensity to consume could be at the expense of net capital formation in a full-employment postwar year, requiring contractionary M policy that hurts investment.

3. Besides, a fair part of our public debt is external and held abroad: sending them goods to cover the interest payments does constitute a definite subtraction from our NNP available for domestic consumption and investment.

4. While it may be true that transfers of purchasing power—between individuals living at one time, between individuals at different ages of their life spans, and between individuals alive today and yet unborn—can be engineered by the government without using the device of the public debt at all, yet I can't help believing that society is led by the presence of the debt to make some transfer decisions that it probably wouldn't otherwise have made.

5. If the decision to have a deficit in depression times (or in times when the international balance of payments made expansionary monetary policy infeasible) merely prevents unemployment, then I admit the implied deficit adds to, rather than subtracts from, the capital stock bequeathed to the post-depression times. But when a decision to have a deficit leads to a compensating cut in private capital formation through inducing more restrictive Bank of Canada monetary policy than would otherwise be the case, I say that such a way of increasing the public debt does *itself* put a real burden on the backs of later citizens.

6. Of course, I admit that floating a public debt to add to useful government capital is as legitimate as floating private debt to build useful private capital—because in each case the new paper assets are matched by real income-creating assets.

7. But in a well-run full-employment system, I have to regard loan finance for *current* public consumption as putting a kind of burden on the future through its effective cutting down on net capital formation at the time, and subsequently through its wealth stimulus on consumption that may be competitive with investment.

D.A. I've never denied anything you are saying. I merely assumed away most of your genuine burdens. If I may say so, you are now shifting over to the side of the angels and are beginning to analyze the true and false burdens of the public debt—and not merely using vivid analogies that obscure rather than illuminate the truth, the whole truth, and nothing but the truth.

▪ SUMMARY OF DEBT BURDENS AND BENEFITS

1. *Capital-bequeathed burden.* The principal way one generation puts a burden on itself later or on a later generation is by bequeathing it less real capital than would otherwise have been the case. Any growth of public debt that has this effect—as in the case of full-employment borrowing for current public consumption that has to be offset by contractionary monetary policy that will lower investment—most definitely does involve a genuine "burden."

2. *External-debt burden.* Any public debt that is externally held does involve a current burden on the citizens at home, since in the end they have to send goods abroad corresponding to the interest payments and debt service. (Of course, if the original borrow-

ing from abroad resulted in equivalent fruitful capital goods here, their fruits will cover the external-debt service; so the net effect of such external borrowing, taken as a complete package, would be favorable to our economy.)

3. *Transfer effects.* Taxing Peter to pay Paul bond interest, even if they are the same person, is certain to cause some harmful distortions of personal and business decisions. (EXAMPLE: Paul is taxed 10 per cent of his income to pay himself $1,000 of bond interest. He is under the illusion, and properly so as an individual, that he can work less and cut down on his tax, but if all do so, we simply have to increase the tax rate. Result: we all end up working less because taxes on each individual matched by exactly equal interest payments to him do not economically cancel out!)

Correlated with public-debt operations, but not always in an intrinsic way, are certain transfers that take place between different individuals, living at the same time, between the same individual at different periods of life, and between successive generations.[1]

4. *Wealth stimulus to consumption.* The existence of public debt, for reasons already seen, makes the average man feel wealthier. For good or evil, it raises his propensity-to-consume schedule: this may, in a poorly functioning system, be a great thing to reduce unemployment and increase both consumption and investment. Or in a system where employ-

---

[1] EXAMPLES: Twin Jane Day worked hard in World War II; twin Rose did not. Because our government used deficit financing, Jane ended up in 1945 with bonds rather than tax receipts. (Jane may have been motivated to work harder by the bribe of postwar command over goods.) Since 1945 Jane has been receiving a larger share of consumption than Rose; Rose is being taxed more than would otherwise have been the case in order to help pay interest and principal to Jane: Moral: A public debt can definitely involve *internal transfer effects* between individuals of the same or different ages.

Even if Jane Day had died in 1965, she could have consumed more in 1945-1965 by selling off her bonds.

The burden of *this* extra consumption could be imposed on those born after 1965 (1) by causing a reduced capital stock after 1965 due to lowered investment in 1945-1965, but also (2) by having an intermediate generation of young postwar workers (employed in 1945-1965 and who have bought Jane's bonds out of their personal saving) supported in their old age by the 1980 workers who will pay taxes on the public debt.

ment can be counted on to remain full by virtue of price flexibility, luck, or monetary management, the increase in C may be at the expense of I and reinforce the capital-bequeathed burden (paragraph 1).

5. *Effects on interest and money policy.* A large debt gives the Bank of Canada great leverage for massive open-market operations to achieve stabilization. Many experts believe that the existence of a broad market in government securities makes possible extensive open-market operations of a stabilizing type and tends to enhance the effectiveness of monetary policy. Debt management by the Bank by a proper policy of open-market operations in bonds of all maturities that was properly carried out could enhance the stability of a modern system.

6. *Effects on discipline and ideology.* It would be a tragedy if people, in giving up their irrational fears of deficit spending, were thereby led to call the sky the limit. Unlimited spending can produce inflation, chaos, and waste. It is to be hoped that the discipline of rationality can replace the discipline of superstition and misunderstanding. After the shibboleth of a balanced budget has lost its power to limit public spending, the good society will have to replace it by a calculus of cost and benefit.

GROWTH IN THE ECONOMY In dispassionately analyzing the growth of the debt, there is one error we must avoid: *We must not forget that the real national product of Canada is an ever-growing thing.*

Our population grows lustily. As to productivity, there is no indication that man-hour efficiency and new techniques have begun to slacken off. Upon this, "stagnationists" and "exhilarationists" both agree. What seemed like a big debt in 1867 would be nothing today. What our children will come to regard as a big debt, our great-grandchildren will deem relatively unimportant.

This explains why England and France, in the crucially formative years of the capitalistic system and the Industrial Revolution, were able to go on—not only decade after decade, but century after century—with their budgets in balance less than half the time. Figure 18-3 shows that growth since 1936 has drastically reduced the ratio of net national debt to net national income.

This fact of growth explains why, in Canada, where real national product grows at about 3 to 4 per cent per year, the public debt might increase by

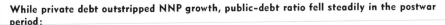

While private debt outstripped NNP growth, public-debt ratio fell steadily in the postwar period:

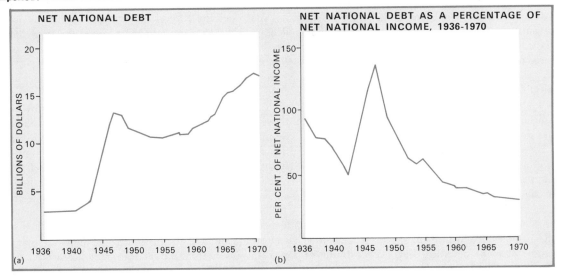

FIG. 18-3. Most of the federal debt held by the public came from wars. In the last 20 years, its ratio to the growing NNI has declined steadily. (Source: *Canada Yearbook*; *Public Accounts of Canada*, 1966; Urquhart and Buckley, *Historical Statistics of Canada*, **Cambridge University Press**, 1965; Bank of Canada *Statistical Summary*; and *Budget*, **1970.**)

more than 100 per cent in 25 years without its relative percentage burden growing at all.

This would give the wildest believer in government spending an average deficit of over 1 billion dollars per year before he would have to turn to such even more unorthodox financial expedients as printing money or selling interest-free bonds to the central bank.

Could a nation fanatically addicted to deficit spending pursue such a policy for the rest of our lives and beyond? Study of the mechanics of banking and income determination suggests that the barrier to this would not be financial. The barrier would have to be political; and the effects of such a policy depend crucially upon whether it impinges on an economy that is already inflationary or deflationary. And if the electorate learn the half-truth that expenditure is expansionary, while forgetting the fact that unpleasant taxes may be necessary to curb undue expansion, then the long-term outlook may be in the direction of rising prices.

Now we have looked carefully at the facts about the public debt here and abroad and have given the economic principles that underlie the burdens of a public debt. We have seen that there are certain definite problems involved, but that laymen often have mixed-up notions as to what are and are not genuine burdens.

There are many major problems ahead for our economy: inflation, slump, conservation and congestion, adequate growth, international balance of payments, and many others. Prudent fiscal and monetary policies impinge on them all; but in a sober man's list of grave problems, the present magnitude of the public debt does not come near the top.

■ PRIVATE AND PUBLIC ANALOGY

Undoubtedly the major reason for concern about the public debt does not involve sophisticated questions of whether or not it affects the stock of real capital goods. The major concern is our discomfort at the prospect of anything that may go on growing forever. We all are made uncomfortable by infinity; we are all frightened of the way things grow at compound interest. Some psychologists attribute this to the fact that every child is frightened of the prospect of dying, of *not* living forever.

"How can the government go on running up debt? If I or my wife lived beyond our means and ran a debt, we'd soon learn what trouble is." The person speaking has overlooked the fallacy of composition: what is true for each unit may not be at all true for the whole of society.

"Why do conservatives complain about the size of the public debt? Private debt has grown tremendously faster in the postwar period than public debt, and you don't hear complaints about that. All credit involves debt. The pyramid of credit could be called the pyramid of debt. If people are to have liquid assets, other people or institutions must have liabilities—d--t to the squeamish." The speaker here is also trying to use analogies with private finance, but this time to the advantage of a program for large deficits.

Both analogies are in principle suspect. Each contains some element of truth, but every strand of such arguments needs critical testing.

Thus, it is true that private debt is more than twice the public debt, and that it more than doubled in the last twenty years, while federal debt grew little at all. But it is also true that the private assets to back up that private debt have also gone up. And it is also true that one could imagine an economy—

not ours!—where everything was financed by *equity* issues without fixed debt.

What does the federal government use to pay its debt interest and refundings? Obviously, *it is the taxable capacity of the country's national product that any government can rely on.*

So long as the money NNP (or GNP) grows at 4 or 5 per cent from now until kingdom come, the public debt of the federal government can grow at those rates, ultimately passing one, two, or any number of trillion dollars. No inflation need result if the process takes place in balance. And no bankruptcy or increase in relative tax burden. And no embarrassment to the Treasury. Like life itself, there is no end to the process.

The above analogy is given only for those who feel a psychological need for reassuring analogies and as an antidote to misleading pessimistic analogies. It says nothing about the great harm governments can do if they spend their taxed or borrowed funds rashly and feed fuel to inflationary gaps when such exist. It says nothing about the proper scope and efficiency of government, because those issues were already clarified in Chapter 8. It says nothing about the proper rate of capital formation and rate of current consumption.

SUMMARY TO THE APPENDIX

1. Many of the most commonly heard arguments against the national debt are patently false. However some genuine burdens of national borrowing, and so of the national debt, do exist. To the degree that we now follow policies of reduced capital formation which will pass on to posterity less capital goods, we can directly affect the production possibilities open to them. To the degree that we now borrow *from abroad* for some transitory consumption purpose and pledge posterity to pay back the interest and principal on such *external debt*, we do place upon that posterity a net burden, which will be a subtraction from what they can later produce. To the degree that we now bequeath to posterity an *internal debt* but no change in capital stock beyond what would anyway have been given to them, there may be various internal transfer effects as one group in the community receives at the expense of another group a larger share of the goods then produced. At any one time there is no "net burden" of such internal transfers quite like the net subtraction involved in the external-debt payment, but there can

be important transfer effects between people of different ages then living and certain effects within the lifetime of each generation on how much its members will receive of such consumption and at what ages. And the process of taxing Peter to pay Paul, or taxing Peter to pay Peter, can have definite costs: these can involve various distortions of production and efficiency, but should not be confused with the actual sending of goods abroad.

2. The fact that Canada is a growing nation with ever increasing national income means that in real terms the burden of the debt has been decreasing over time and that the ratio of net national debt to net national income has fallen drastically since 1936.

3. The private and public analogy of the public debt contains only an element of the truth and needs critical testing. As long as the taxable capacity of the nation's national product grows over time, no serious threat is posed by a national debt that expands at a rate equal to or less than the rate of increase in national product.

QUESTIONS FOR DISCUSSION

1. Show briefly why "burden of the debt" is a complicated economic issue.

2. Comment on the 1840 views of the historian Macaulay:

> At every stage in the growth of that debt the nation has set up the same cry of anguish and despair. At every stage in the growth of that debt it has been seriously asserted by wise men that bankruptcy and ruin were at hand. Yet still the debt went on growing; and still bankruptcy and ruin were as remote as ever. . . .
>
> The prophets of evil were under a double delusion. They erroneously imagined that there was an exact analogy between the case of an individual who is in debt to another individual and the case of a society which is in debt to a part of itself. . . . They made no allowance for the effect produced by the incessant progress of every experimental science, and by the incessant efforts of every man to get on in life. They saw that the debt grew; and they forgot that other things grew as well. . . .

3. "Inflation has lifted the burden of the debt from the shoulders of future taxpayers." Is this correct? Who has assumed the burden?

4. Much of Canada's debt is held abroad, as are the securities and shares of Canadian business. In what sense is this debt a "burden"? Is it decreasing?

PART 3
THE COMPOSITION AND PRICING OF NATIONAL OUTPUT

19

DETERMINATION
OF PRICE BY SUPPLY
AND DEMAND

The end is easily foretold,
When every blessed thing you hold
Is made of silver, or of gold,
  You long for simple pewter.

When you have nothing else to wear
But cloth of gold and satins rare,
For cloth of gold you cease to care
  Up goes the price of shoddy.
                    GILBERT AND SULLIVAN, *The Gondoliers*

Part One of this book described the modern economic system and discussed the nature of national income. Part Two gave the modern theory of income determination: it showed why and how incomes, job opportunities, and levels of price fluctuate; it showed how money and banking fit in with income analysis; and most significantly, it showed how fiscal and monetary policy can keep the aggregate system working tolerably well. Today such analysis is called macroeconomics.

■ PREVIEW

Now Parts Three and Four analyze *micro*economics, which deals with the following important questions: What determines the relative prices of particular goods? What determines the quantitative breakdown of the national-income aggregates into various kinds of goods and services?

In order to understand the *system* of market prices which strikes an equilibrium among people's tastes for different goods and the scarcities of total resources that can produce them, Part Three studies in detail the tools of supply and demand that Chapter 4 introduced briefly.

Part Four follows with a closely related supply-and-demand analysis of what determines the prices of factors of production. Why are wages growing? Why does the share of land rent in the economy move in this way or that?

What determines interest? Why have unskilled wages been falling relative to white-collar wages? Such problems constitute the subject of "distribution of income" in Part Four.

We shall see that the concepts of supply and demand as they are developed further in this chapter are vital tools for mastering the analysis of varied branches of microeconomics. (As a matter of fact, the supply-and-demand tools are indispensable in explaining the international trade problems of Part Five and the current economic issues of Part Six.)

■ MICROECONOMICS VERSUS MACROECONOMICS?

Macroeconomics deals with the big picture—with the macroaggregates of income, employment, and price levels. But do not think that microeconomics deals with unimportant details. After all, the big picture is made up of its parts. Mere billions of dollars would be meaningless if they did not correspond to the thousand-and-one useful goods and services that people really need and want. And who would be impressed by a vast national income if its distribution among human beings was a matter of caprice and pointless inequality?

There is really no opposition between micro- and macroeconomics. Both are vital. You are less than half-educated if you understand one while being ignorant of the other. We cannot even say which comes first: some books begin with one; some with the other. And surveys show that even books like this one, which begin with macroeconomics, are used by about 40 per cent of the courses to teach microeconomics first.

Thirty years ago our society had such poor mastery over its macroeconomics as to make people naturally give less emphasis to microeconomics. With millions starving because of a slump, who could get excited about whether mutton or pork was in a proper relative-price configuration? Or who thought much about white-collar wage trends relative to unskilled wages, when the unemployed tramped the streets in shirts so faded you could not tell their color?

Today we hope all that is changed. Man has gained considerable mastery over his macroeconomic problems, and hence it is natural for the classical problems of microeconomics to move again to the forefront of his attention.

■ REVIEW OF FUNDAMENTALS OF SUPPLY AND DEMAND

Chapter 3 discussed how a system of pricing and of markets performs the task in any mixed economic system of determining WHAT shall be produced, How goods shall be produced, and FOR WHOM they are to be produced. Then Chapter 4 introduced the basic concepts of supply and demand: their description in terms of schedules of numbers and in terms of intersecting curves. It will be assumed that each reader has this material fresh in his mind, or has gone back to review what was learned earlier, or will stop and take time to master it now.

Our task here is to put the tools of supply and demand to work: to show how they help explain changes in price, in the short run and in the long run; to help predict what effect a tax will have on competitive price; to evaluate various policies that interfere with the laws of supply and demand.

We shall make repeated efforts to see what it is that market pricing is accomplishing in terms of the *efficiency* with which the economy fulfills its basic functions.

All through Part Three new tools of economic analysis will be introduced and the old tools will be gradually developed. But it would be a mistake for any reader to become enamored of tools for their own sake. It is the application of the tools to the richness of modern economic life that makes them exciting. Experience shows that one cannot understand the economic world of the present and the future without having at his command a systematic method of analyzing it. And the testimony of generations of students is that, however far away they later move from formal schooling and examinations, their understanding of the basic economic processes is forever keener, once they have mastered the elementary tools of economic analysis.

REVIEW Glancing back at the supply-and-demand diagram in Fig. 4-3 (page 87), we see how equilibrium P comes at the intersection of competitive dd and ss curves. We note that any departure above equilibrium creates an "over-supply" condition leading back to equilibrium, and that any fall in P below equilibrium creates an "excess demand" that bids P back up to restore the equilibrium.

The succeeding diagram, Fig. 4-4(a) on page 88, shows how a shift in supply, such as might be brought about by a bad harvest, will be likely to increase the equilibrium price P and decrease the equilibrium quantity Q. The new E' intersection point is found to be higher on the unshifted demand curve— just far enough up to cut consumption down to the depressed harvest level.

This illustrates well an important principle, the law of downward-sloping demand—the fact that the demand curve slopes down toward the southeast, in reflection of the observation that people will buy more at lower prices and buy less at higher ones. Likewise, Fig. 4-4(b) shows how an upward shift of the demand curve leads to a higher equilibrium price. So much for review.

A. ELASTICITY OF DEMAND AND SUPPLY

Second-graders, it is found, know that an increase in supply, whether because of an abundant harvest or for whatever reason, is likely to depress price. So it is no surprise that Gregory King, the English writer of the seventeenth century mentioned on page 88, should have remarked on this fact. But that same writer observed a fact perhaps less obvious: his studies convinced him that farmers as a whole received *less* total revenue when the harvest was good than when it was bad!

This fact, that high agricultural Q tends to be associated with low $P \times Q$, is one that every Minister of Agriculture has had to reckon with in facing the farm problem. To understand it and to lay the groundwork for the discussion of farm problems in Chapter 20, we must in this chapter consider and master a new and important economic concept, "elasticity of demand." Henry Ford, and any businessman tempted to cut his price in order to sell more goods and make more profit, is also interested in the concept of elasticity. And when the Canadian Transport Commission lets a railroad *raise* its prices in order to cut down on passenger-service losses, the elasticity concept is crucially involved.

■ ELASTICITY OF DEMAND

Various goods differ in the *degree* to which the Q bought will respond to changes in each respective P. Wheat Q may go up much less than 1 per cent for each 1 per cent cut in wheat P; Henry Ford's Q may rise far more than 1 per cent for each 1 per cent reduction in its P; in between is the borderline case of a good whose Q would just halve whenever its P doubled, where the percentage changes are just in balance.

Elasticity of demand is a concept devised to distinguish these three cases. Thus, the first case of weak percentage response of wheat Q is put into the category of "inelastic demand." The second case of a great percentage response is put in the category of "elastic demand." The borderline case is called "unitary elasticity of demand."

Here is how the economist goes about defining the three cases:

The crucial thing to concentrate on is the *total dollar revenue* that buyers pay to sellers. If consumers buy 5 units at $3 each, what is total revenue? It is not given by the $3 P alone; nor by the 5-unit Q. Total revenue is always, by definition, price times quantity, or the $15 product P × Q. By arithmetic multiplication, total revenue can always be calculated for each point in a demand schedule or diagram.

Elasticity of demand is important primarily as *an indicator of how total revenue changes* when a fall in P induces a rise in Q along the demand curve.

> *Definition of elasticity of demand*: This is a concept devised to indicate the degree of responsiveness of Q demanded to changes in market P. It depends primarily upon *percentage* changes and is independent of the units used to measure Q and P. Elasticity ends up qualitatively in one of three alternative categories:
>
> 1. When a cut in P raises Q so much as to *increase* total revenue P × Q, we speak of *elastic* demand—or of elasticity of demand *greater than unity*. The percentage change in Q exceeds the percentage change in P.
>
> 2. When a percentage cut in P results in an exactly compensating percentage rise in Q so as to leave total revenue P × Q exactly *unchanged*, we speak of *unitary elasticity of demand*—or of elasticity of demand that is numerically *exactly equal to unity*.
>
> 3. When a percentage cut in P evokes so small a percentage increase in Q as to make total revenue P × Q fall, we speak of *inelastic* demand— or of elasticity of demand that is *less than unity* (but not less than zero).

Figure 19-1 gives a graphic example of the three cases. In each case, P is halved from A to B, but it would be just as much in order to have used a very small percentage change in P. Perhaps at a first glance, it will be easiest to begin with the borderline case of unitary elasticity of demand.

Elasticity of demand comes in three cases, depending on how total revenue moves:

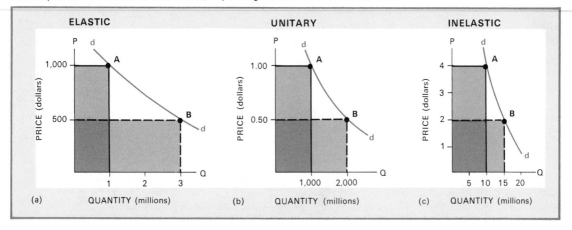

FIG. 19-1. In cutting *P* from *A* to *B*, we raise, leave unchanged, or lower the rectangle of total revenue, depending on whether demand is elastic, unitary elastic, or inelastic. That is, elasticity depends on percentage response of *Q* to each percentage change in *P*.

In Fig. 19-1(b), the doubling of *Q* exactly matches the halving of *P*, with the result that the total revenue collected remains unchanged at $1,000. This can be shown graphically by comparing certain rectangular areas. How? Price and quantity can be easily read off the curve at any point; but how do we read off total revenue, which is their arithmetic product $P \times Q$? When we recall that the area of a rectangle is always equal to the product of its base times its altitude, the answer is easy:

> Total revenue at any point is always as shown by the area of the rectangle which that point makes with the two axes. (Check that the shaded rectangle at *A* does have a base equal to *Q* and an altitude equal to *P*.) Hence, if our eye watches how the area of each point's rectangle changes as we cut price and move down the demand curve, we can know in which of the three categories of elasticity such a movement happens to fall.

Clearly, in the middle diagram, the areas are remaining exactly the same because of offsetting changes in their *Q* bases and *P* altitudes; consequently, this is the case neither of elastic nor of inelastic demand, but rather is the border-line case of unitary elasticity of demand.

The reader can now verify that Fig. 19-1(a) does correspond to *elastic* demand, with total revenue going up when *P* is cut and elasticity hence greater than unity. And Fig. 19-1(c) does correspond to the opposite case of *inelastic* demand, with total revenue falling off when *P* is cut and elasticity less than unity. [Which diagram best represents the Gregory King finding that smaller harvests meant higher total revenues for farmers? Which best represents the early belief of Henry Ford, that if only he could reduce his cars' *P*, he would encounter a tremendous increase in cars sold? Surely, 19-1(c) and 19-1(a), respectively.]

Dividing percentage price cut into percentage quantity rise gives numerical elasticity:

NUMERICAL CALCULATION OF ELASTICITY COEFFICIENT

P	$-\Delta P$	Q	ΔQ	$\dfrac{P_1 + P_2}{2}$	$\dfrac{Q_1 + Q_2}{2}$	$E = -\dfrac{\Delta Q}{(Q_1 + Q_2)/2} \div \dfrac{\Delta P}{(P_1 + P_2)/2}$
6		0				
	2		10	5	5	$^{10}\!/_5 \div ^2\!/_5 = 5 > 1$
4		10				
	2		10	3	15	$^{10}\!/_{15} \div ^2\!/_3 = 1$
2		20				
	2		10	1	25	$^{10}\!/_{25} \div ^2\!/_1 = .2 < 1$
0		30				

TABLE 19-1. Each P cut, $-\Delta P$, is related to the average P, $(P_1 + P_2)/2$; each Q rise, ΔQ, to the average Q, $(Q_1 + Q_2)/2$; the resulting ratio gives numerical E, a measure expressed in percentage (dimensionless) units, not in absolute slope units.

✗ ■ NUMERICAL MEASUREMENT OF ELASTICITY: A DIGRESSION[1]

The general notion of elastic, inelastic, and unitary elasticity as an indicator of the percentage responsiveness of quantity to price and as an indicator of how total revenue behaves is now clear. But some readers will be curious to know how these qualitative cases can be given exact numerical measurement by economists. What does it mean to say that the elasticity demand is 1.0? 2.3? 0.5? To answer this question, we give the following definition for a coefficient of elasticity E between two different price points on a demand curve:

$$\text{Elasticity coefficient } E = \frac{\text{per cent that } Q \text{ has risen}}{\text{per cent cut in } P}$$

Note that the movements along P and Q are in opposite directions because of the law of downward-sloping demand. Note, too, the use of *percentages*, which brings in the nice property that the units of a good or of money—bushels or pecks of wheat, dollars or pennies—do not affect elasticity.[2]

Do not get bogged down in numerical details of E calculation. Now that you have mastered the general idea of elastic, inelastic, and unitary demand, you can proceed to the following numerical examples.

Always there is a slight ambiguity about percentage changes. Suppose a grocer buys bread for 15 cents and sells for 25. Is that the 66⅔ per cent markup that comes from relating the change of 10 to the lower base 15? Or is it the 40 per

---

[1] In a short course the next two sections can be skipped.

[2] Units will affect the *slope* of the demand diagram, just as the draftsman can make a curve look steep or flat in slope by changing the scale of one of his axes. So the purpose of the next section is to help you avoid confusing *slope* and *elasticity*. As Fig. 19-1(b)'s curve with $E = 1$ shows, it is not a straight line with constant slope that corresponds to a curve of constant elasticity, but rather one whose slope varies in order to keep the percentage changes in the same ratio. (Mathematicians call the unitary-elastic curve a ["rectangular"] hyperbola.)

cent change that comes from relating 10 to the higher base 25? No one answer can be said to be right, and no one definitely wrong. Fortunately, when it comes to very small percentage changes, as from 100 to 99 or from 100 to 101, the difference between $\frac{1}{100}$ and $\frac{1}{99}$ becomes hardly worth talking about. For small changes, it does not matter much how you calculate the percentage changes; but for larger ones it may make quite a difference, and no single answer can be declared to be the right one.

What is a good rule to use? Long experience suggests this: As good a rule as any is to relate the price change to neither the higher nor the lower of the two P's, but to their average. Thus, is a cut from 101 to 99 a change of $\frac{2}{99}$ or $\frac{2}{101}$? By our convention, it is neither: we call it a change of $\frac{2}{100}$, because the average of 99 and 101 is $(99 + 101)/2 = \frac{200}{2} = 100$.

Table 19-1 is self-explanatory: it shows how to calculate E for three movements along a dd curve. We shall be seeing that most dd curves start out elastic at high P and end up inelastic at low P, passing through unitary elasticity at an intermediate position where total revenue $P \times Q$ is at its maximum. Table 19-1 illustrates this.

■ GRAPHICAL MEASUREMENT OF ELASTICITY: A DIGRESSION

Students tend to make a simple mistake: They often confuse the slope of a curve with its elasticity; they think a steep slope on dd must mean inelastic demand, and a flat slope must mean elastic demand. This is not quite true. Why not? Because slope of dd depends upon *absolute* change in P and Q, whereas elasticity was seen to depend upon *percentage* changes.

Absolute slope and percentage elasticity are not the same:

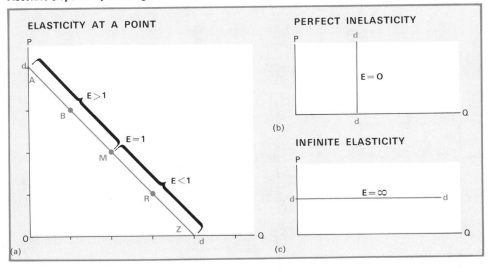

FIG. 19-2. All points on dd's straight-line demand in (a) have same absolute slope; but above the midpoint price, demand is elastic; below it demand is inelastic; at it demand is unitary. Only in the case of perfectly vertical or horizontal curves, as in (b) and (c), can you infer inelasticity and elasticity from slope alone.

The straight line *dd* in Fig. 19-2(a) illustrates the fallacy of confusing slope and elasticity. Everywhere it has the same absolute slope. But toward the top of the line, where (1) *P* is high and its percentage change low and (2) *Q* is very low and its percentage change therefore almost infinitely great, our numerical formula for *E* results in a very high elasticity.

Thus, above the midpoint *M* of any straight line, demand is elastic, with $E > 1$; at the midpoint, demand is of unitary elasticity, with $E = 1$; below the midpoint, demand is inelastic, with $E < 1$.[3]

When many people make the same mistake, there is usually a reason. The limiting cases of *completely vertical* and *completely horizontal* demand curves, shown in Fig. 19-2(b) and (c), do validly portray the limiting cases *completely inelastic* and *infinitely elastic* demands. But do not think that the in-between cases, where most of reality falls, can have their elasticities depicted by slope alone.

Now, we go back to the mainstream of demand and supply.

■ ELASTICITY OF SUPPLY

What we did for demand, we can also do for supply. Economists introduce the concept of "elasticity of supply" to give an indication of the percentage increase in the amount of *Q* supplied in response to a given percentage rise in competitive *P*. (Note that in the case of a *rising* supply curve, we now speak of an *increase* in *P*, rather than of a *decrease* in *P* as was done in the case of a downward-sloping demand curve.)

If the amount supplied is perfectly fixed, as in the case of perishable fish brought to today's market for sale at whatever price they will fetch, we face the

---

[3] Intermediate books tell how to calculate *E* at any one point on a straight line: *E* equals the length of the line segment below the point divided by the length of line segment above it. Since *M* is halfway, the formula there gives $E = 1$, unitary elasticity. At *B*, it gives $\frac{3}{1} = 3.0$; at *R*, $E = \frac{1}{3} = 0.33$. Knowing how to calculate *E* for a straight line enables you to calculate it for any point along a curved *dd*. (1) Draw with a ruler the straight line tangent

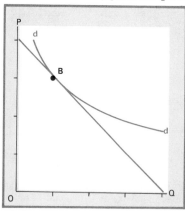

FIG. 19-3.

to the curve at your point (e.g., at *B* in Fig. 19-3); (2) calculate the *E* for the straight line at that point (e.g., *E* at $B = \frac{3}{1}$); (3) identify your resulting *E* as the correct elasticity for the *dd* curve at your chosen point. Question 7, page 483, proves the truth of the geometrical rule for calculating *E*.

NOTE: *E* at a point can be shown to be mathematically equivalent to the following limit:

$$\frac{-\Delta Q}{Q} \div \frac{\Delta P}{P} = -\frac{P}{Q}\frac{\Delta Q}{\Delta P} \to -\frac{P}{Q}\frac{dQ}{dP}$$

as ΔP goes to zero, taking ΔQ with it and making it immaterial which of the *P*'s and *Q*'s or their averages we use to compute percentage changes. Intermediate texts show that, when you plot *dd* on double-log paper, it becomes correct to identify slope with elasticity—because double-log paper does measure percentage changes. (See Question 7, page 483 for more on this.)

limiting case of *perfectly inelastic* or vertical supply. If we have a horizontal supply curve, so that the slightest cut in P will cause Q to become zero and the slightest rise in P will coax out an indefinitely large supply, we are at the extreme of *infinitely elastic* supply. Between such extremes, we call supply elastic or inelastic depending upon whether the percentage rise in Q is respectively greater than or less than the percentage rise in P bringing it about.[4]

Supply elasticity is a useful concept but not quite so useful a concept as demand elasticity, for the reason that elasticity of demand has the major additional function of telling us what is happening to total revenue.

There is, however, an important fact that supply elasticity can help describe. A given change in price will tend to have greater and greater effects on amount supplied as we move from the momentary situation to a short-run period of time and on to the long-run period. This means:

> Elasticity of supply tends to be greater in the long run, when all adjustments to the higher price have been made, than in shorter periods of time.

Let us see why.

■ MOMENTARY, SHORT-RUN, AND LONG-RUN EQUILIBRIUM

Alfred Marshall, Cambridge's great economist at the turn of the century, helped forge these tools of supply and demand. We can review our understanding of equilibrium and at the same time advance our knowledge if we survey Marshall's important emphasis on the *time element* of the problem.

He distinguishes at least three time periods: (1) *momentary* equilibrium, when the supply is fixed; (2) *short-run* equilibrium, when firms can produce more within given plants; and finally (3) *long-run* equilibrium (or "normal price"), when firms can abandon old plants or build new ones and when new firms can enter the industry or old ones leave it.

Let us imagine that the demand for a perishable good, such as fish that cannot be preserved, increases from dd to $d'd'$. With the amount of fish supplied unchanged, the stronger demand will sharply bid up the momentary price of fish. This is shown in Fig. 19-5(a), where the fixed supply curve $s_m s_m$ runs up to the

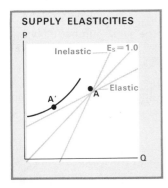

SUPPLY ELASTICITIES

FIG. 19-4.

[4] A numerical coefficient of supply elasticity E_s is defined thus: $E_s =$ (percentage change in Q)/(percentage change in P). Figure 19-4 shows three straight-line supply curves: at A the line going through the origin has elasticity of exactly 1.0; the steeper curve is inelastic, with elasticity coefficient less than 1; and the flatter curve is elastic, with elasticity coefficient greater than 1. (If—as we shall see can happen—the supply curve actually bends up backward, elasticity of supply as here defined could actually become negative.) Also, for a supply curve with curvature, one can reckon its elasticity at a point A' by drawing a straight line with a tangential ruler and seeing which curve of Fig. 19-4 it resembles; or plot it on double-log paper and study its slope at A'.

Effect of demand increase on price varies in the three time periods:

1st, The new momentary equilibrium raises P to ration out the unchanged supply:	2d, Short-run equilibrium coaxes out increased supply from existing plants:	3d, Normal long-run equilibrium comes when new plant, all resources, and costs get adjusted:

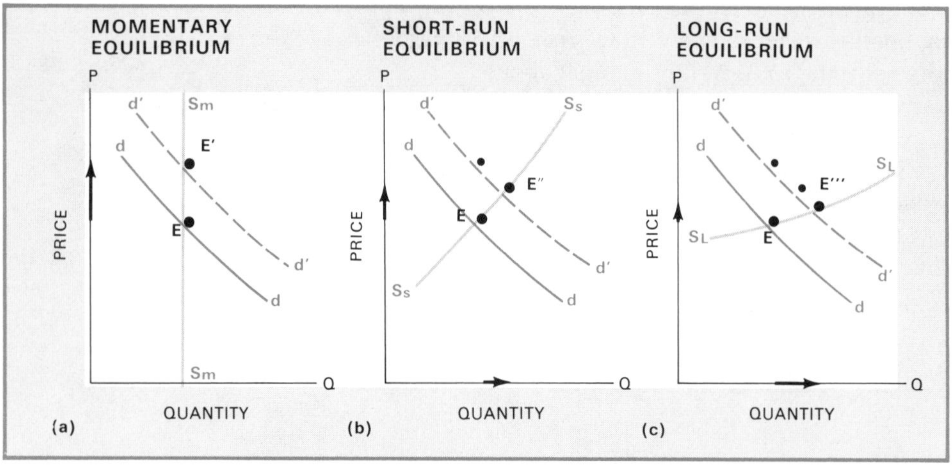

MOMENTARY EQUILIBRIUM

SHORT-RUN EQUILIBRIUM

LONG-RUN EQUILIBRIUM

P d' Sm d E' E d' d Sm PRICE QUANTITY Q

(a)

P d' Ss d E'' E d' Ss d PRICE QUANTITY Q

(b)

P d' d E''' SL SL E d' d PRICE QUANTITY Q

(c)

FIG. 19-5. Marshall distinguishes three different time periods, depending upon whether supply elements have time to make (a) no adjustments, (b) some adjustments of labor and variable factors, (c) full adjustment of all factors and all costs to price. (The upward slope of $s_L s_L$ puts this case in the "increasing cost" category discussed in the text. What would $s_L s_L$ be like in the "constant cost" case? Why might a very small industry have constant costs?)

new demand curve $d'd'$ to determine the new sharply higher momentary equilibrium price shown at E'. The price has had to rise so much in order to *ration* the limited supply of fish among the now eager demanders.

But with so high a price prevailing in the market, skippers of the fishing boats will be motivated to hire more men and to use more nets. Even if the period is so brief that they do not have the time to get new boats built, they will in the short run begin to bring to the market a greater supply of fish than they did at the old momentary equilibrium. Figure 19-5(b) shows the new $s_s s_s$ short-run supply schedule, and shows that it intersects the new demand curve at E'', the point of short-run equilibrium. Note that this equilibrium price is a little lower than the momentary E' price. Why? Because of the extra supply of fish induced in the short run by more intensive use of the same number of boats.

Figure 19-5(c) shows the final long-run equilibrium, or "normal," price. The higher prices that long prevailed have coaxed out more shipbuilding and attracted more trained sailors into the industry. Where the long-run supply curve, $s_L s_L$ intersects the demand curve $d'd'$ at E''' is the final equilibrium reached after *all* economic conditions (including number of ships and shipyards) have adjusted to the new level of demand.

Note that the long-run equilibrium price is not as high as the short-run equilibrium price, and not nearly as high as the momentary equilibrium price. Yet it is a little bit higher than the price that prevailed previously when demand was lower. Marshall would call this a case of "increasing cost" and would regard it as the normal one to be met in most sizable competitive industries. Why normal? For a variety of reasons. When a large industry (which has already achieved the economies of large-scale production) expands, it must coax men, ships, nets, and other productive factors away from other industries by bidding up their prices and thus its own cost. So the long-run supply curve $s_L s_L$ will usually be sloping gently upward as in Fig. 19-5(c). Only if the industry is small compared with the total of all other users of its factors will Marshall's $s_L s_L$ curve in Fig. 19-5(c) be horizontal—which is called the case of "constant cost."[5]

Another explanation for an upward sloping industry long-run supply curve and hence for increasing costs to the industry is found in the fact that all firms within the industry are not identical. Various firms have different degrees of technical and managerial know-how, different methods of production, different locations, etc. As greater and greater quantities of output are to be supplied, firms which are relatively less efficient are induced to enter the industry—to enter production. Thus this marginal firm enters at a higher cost per unit than do the "infra-marginal" firms already in production, although all firms supply the item only at the higher supply price of the marginal firm. At any lower price, the marginal firm would not be induced to enter production and hence the industry would not move to the right on its supply curve. So the long-run supply curve $s_L s_L$ will usually be gently sloping upward as in Fig. 19-5(c).

The reader can test his understanding of all the foregoing discussion by now assuming a downward shift in the demand curve back to *dd*. Show what happens in the new momentary run; in the short run; and in the long run. The Appendix to this chapter presents various cases of supply and demand. Chapter 22 will give in greater detail the factors underlying the various supply curves.

B.   APPLICATIONS AND QUALIFICATIONS OF SUPPLY AND DEMAND

Other things being equal, as economists are fond of saying, there is a unique schedule of supply or demand in any period of time. But other things will not remain equal. The demand for cotton is declining over the years because of reductions in the price of synthetics. The supply schedule of gasoline is shifting because technological progress permits more to be produced at the same cost. As costs and tastes change, as incomes vary, as the prices of rival products (coffee in relation to tea) or of cooperating products (sugar in relation to tea) change, our schedules will shift. What will be the effects on consumption, production, and price? That we must now study.

All beginners in the field of economics must beware of a common error. They must take care not to confuse an increase in *demand*—by which is meant a *shift* of the whole curve to the right and upward, as more is now bought at each same price—with an increase in the *quantity demanded* as a result of moving to a lower price *on the same demand curve*. By "demand" is meant the whole demand curve; by "supply" is meant the whole supply curve; by an "increase" in demand or supply is meant a *shift* of the whole curve in question to the right. To indicate a single point on a demand curve, we speak of the "quantity bought"

---

[5] See the cases in the Appendix.

Wheat tax falls both on consumer and producer:

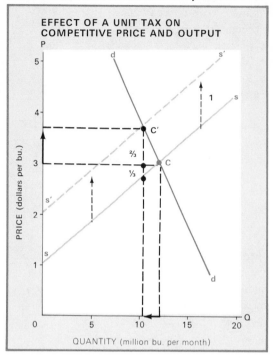

FIG. 19-6. A $1 tax shifts *ss* up $1 everwhere to give parallel *s's'*, shown as a dashed line. This intersects *dd* in new equilibrium at *C'*, where price to consumer has risen $2/3 above old *C* equilibrium and where price to producer has fallen by $1/3. The black arrows show change in *P* and *Q*. (Had *dd* been very elastic and flat relative to *ss*, most of the $1 tax would have fallen on the producer. Had *ss* been completely horizontal, the whole $1 tax would have been shifted forward onto the consumer.)

or the "quantity demanded" *at a particular price*. A movement *along* the same curve is "a change in the quantity demanded as a result of a price change." It does not represent any change in the demand schedule. The need for this warning will appear in a moment.

■ INCIDENCE OF A TAX[6]

We can illustrate the case of a shift in the entire curve by referring to supply and demand schedules for a good like wheat. Fig. 19-6 shows an equilibrium price at *C* of $3 per bushel before a tax is imposed.

Let us now introduce a new factor, which will disturb this equilibrium. In particular, assume that the government imposes a sales tax on wheat. On each and every sale, the producer is required to pay a tax of $1 per bushel of wheat.

What is the final effect, or what economists call the "incidence," of the tax? Is its burden shifted back completely onto the producer who must pay it in the first instance? Or may it be shifted forward in part to consumers? The answer can be derived only from our supply and demand curves.

There is no reason for the demand curve of the consumers to have changed at all. At $3, consumers will still be willing to buy only 12 (million) bushels; they neither know nor care that the producers must pay a tax.

But the whole supply curve is shifted upward and leftward: leftward

[6] For a brief review of the problems of tax incidence reread the final section of Chapter 9, page 220.

because at each market price the producers will now supply less as a result of the tax; upward because, to get the producers to bring any given quantity to market, say, 12 (million) units, we must give them a higher market price than before—$4 rather than $3, which is higher by the exact amount of the $1 tax the producer must pay.

The student should be able to fill in a new supply column, resembling Column (3) in Table 4-3, page 86, but with each price raised by $1. Here in Fig. 19-6, the demand curve *dd* is unchanged, but the supply curve *ss* has been shifted up everywhere by $1 to a vertically *parallel* supply curve *s's'*.

Where will the new equilibrium price be? The answer is found at the intersection of the new demand and supply curves, or at *C'*, where *s's'* and *dd* meet. Because supply has decreased, the price is higher. Also, the amount bought and the amount sold are less. If we read the graph carefully, we find that the new equilibrium price has risen from $3 to about $3⅔. The new equilibrium output, at which purchases and sales are in equilibrium, has fallen from 12 (million) per month to about 10.6 (million) bushels.

Who pays the tax? Well, the wheat farmers do in part, because now they receive only $2⅔, ($3⅔−$1), rather than $3. But the consumer also shares in the burden, because the price received by the producer has *not* fallen by as much as the tax. To the consumer, the wheat now costs $2⅔ plus the $1 tax, or $3⅔ in all. Because consumers want wheat so badly, they pay ⅔ of the tax, and producers pay ⅓ of the tax.[7]

[7] There is another and equivalent way to handle this tax problem, which is shown in Fig. 19-7. If the consumer were thought of as paying the tax in the first instance, you could subtract $1 everywhere from his *dd* curve. The new *d'd'* will intersect *ss* at the same new *Q*, and the same $2 ⅔ and $3 ⅔ prices will prevail. It goes without saying that all these figures are hypothetical.

This is the legalistic view of Canadian provincial sales taxes: They are levied "directly" on the consumer, not "indirectly" on farmers or producers.

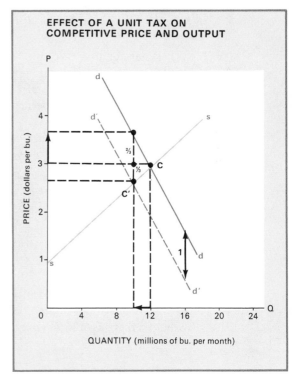

EFFECT OF A UNIT TAX ON COMPETITIVE PRICE AND OUTPUT

FIG. 19-7.

To check his understanding of the above reasoning, the student should consider the case of an opposite shift in supply. Let the government pay producers a subsidy of $1 per bushel of wheat instead of taxing them this amount. Shift ss down to the new curve $s''s''$. Where is C'', its intersection with dd? What is the new price? The new quantity? How much of the benefit goes to the producer? How much to the consumer?

> *Summary.* A sales tax on a good will raise its price most and reduce its quantity least when supply and demand curves are most *inelastic*. (When they are elastic, Q changes much and P changes little.)
>
> The tax is shifted forward onto the consumer when dd is very inelastic. It is shifted backward onto the producer when ss is relatively the more inelastic. Only with the apparatus of supply and demand can the economist analyze the incidence of various different taxes—import tariffs, cigarette and liquor excises, payroll and corporation taxes, etc.

■ A COMMON FALLACY

By now the student has mastered supply and demand. Or has he? He knows that a tax will have the effect of raising the price that the consumer will have to pay. Or does he know this? What about the following argument of a kind often seen in the press and heard from the platform:

> The effect of a tax on a commodity might seem at first sight to be an advance in price to the consumer. But an advance in price will diminish the demand. And a reduced demand will send the price down again. Therefore it is not certain, after all, that the tax will really raise the price.

What about it? Will the tax raise the price or not? According to the editor's written word and the parliamentarian's oratory, the answer is, No. Evidently, we have here an example of the treachery of words. One of the four sentences in the quotation is false because the word "demand" is being used in the wrong sense. The student has already been warned against confusing a movement *along* an unchanged curve with a shift in the curve. Actually, the correct answer[8] would be more or less as follows:

> A tax will raise the price to the consumer and will lower the price received by the producer, the difference going to the government. At the higher price a smaller quantity will be bought by consumers. This is at it should be, because producers are also supplying a smaller quantity at the lower price which they receive. Thus the amounts willingly bought and sold are in balance where the new supply and demand schedules intersect, and there will be no further change in price.

■ IS THE LAW OF SUPPLY AND DEMAND IMMUTABLE?

Competitive price and quantity are determined by supply and demand. But does not price depend on other factors, such as the amount of gold production or whether there is a war going on? Actually, price does depend on many such

---

[8] H. D. Henderson, *Supply and Demand* (Cambridge, London, 1922), p. 27, explains this.

factors. However, they are not *in addition* to supply and demand, but are included in the numerous forces which determine or *act through* supply and demand. Thus, if new gold production gives everyone higher incomes, it will shift demand curves and raise prices. But it is still true that competitive price is determined by supply and demand.

At this point a thoughtful reader should be moved to voice protest. Little has been said about price as being determined by cost of production. Should not this be listed as a third factor in addition to supply and demand? Our answer is a stubborn "No."

> Competitive price is affected by cost of production only to the extent that such cost affects supply.

If God sends nutritious manna from heaven without cost but in limited supply, then its price will not be zero but will be given by the intersection of the demand and supply curves. On the other hand, if it would cost $50,000 to print the national anthem on the head of a pin, but there is no demand for such a commodity, it simply will not be produced and would not command $50,000 if it were produced. (What the market price of something nonexistent should be called is left to the reader's pleasure.)

This does not mean that cost of production is unimportant for price determination. Under competition it is especially important. But its importance shows itself *through its effects upon supply*. Businessmen produce for profit. If they cannot get a price high enough to cover their past costs, then they will not like it. Nevertheless, once the crop is in, so to speak, there is not much they can do about it under competition. They have no choice but to minimize their short-term losses. But they will not continue *in the future* to supply goods at prices that fail to cover the *extra* costs incurred to produce these goods. Thus supply depends intimately on cost especially on what Chapter 22 and later chapters will call "extra" or "marginal" cost; and so too must price.

Moreover, to say that price equals cost does not in itself tell us which is the cause of which. In many cases where an industry uses a productive factor highly specialized to itself (e.g., baseball players, opera singers, vineyard land), *price determines cost rather than vice versa*. Grain land is dear because the price of grain is high. Apartment buildings sell for little because rents are low. This type of relationship was overlooked by the dairy farmers in Massachusetts who petitioned during World War II for a higher milk price "because the price of cows is high." If their request had been granted, they would soon have observed the price of cows chasing the milk price upward.[9]

USEFUL CATEGORIES Thus, supply and demand are not ultimate explanations of price. They are simply useful catchall categories for analyzing and describing the multitude of forces, causes, and factors impinging on price. Rather than final

---

[9] Where a factor of production is inelastic in supply, as in all these cases, its cost is "price-determined" rather than "price-determining" and its return is called an "economic rent." See Case 3 in the Appendix and also footnote 1 of Chapter 27.

answers, supply and demand simply represent initial questions. Our work is not over but just begun.

This should help to debunk the tendency of neophytes to utter sagely, "You can't repeal the law of supply and demand. King Canute knew he could not command the ocean tide to retreat from his throne on the seashore. No more can government get around, or interfere with, the workings of supply and demand."

It would be better not to have learned any economics than be left with this opinion. Of course the government can affect price. It can do so by affecting supply or demand, or both. In Chapter 20 we shall examine how government programs for restricting farm production can raise price and income by cutting down on supply. Similar programs by government cartels have been pursued all over the world: Brazil has burned coffee to raise its price; Britain during the 1920s tried artificially controlling the price of rubber; sugar and cocoa are still under international control.

These governments have not violated the law of supply and demand. They have worked (not always to good purpose) through the law of supply and demand. The state has no secret economic weapons or tricks. What is true for the state is also true for individuals. Anyone can affect the price of wheat as long as he has money to throw on the market or wheat to hold off it.

Trade-unions often influence wages, or try to, by directly or indirectly affecting the supply of labor. Anyone with a somewhat distinctive commodity may try by advertising to increase the demand for his product and, by restricting supply, to raise price above his extra costs of production. It should be emphasized, however, that as soon as individual producers grow in size and become important enough to affect the price of the things they sell, they then cease to be perfect competitors in the strict sense, and their behavior has to be analyzed in terms of a blend of monopoly and competition, i.e., in terms of imperfect competition as described in Chapters 24 and 25.

■ PRICES FIXED BY LAW

There is one genuine interference with supply and demand whose effects we must analyze. The government sometimes sets by law a maximum price or a minimum wage. During World War II, ceilings were placed on items in the cost of living. Recently, a floor of $1.65 was put under hourly wages of many workers. These interferences by law are quite different from government actions, previously described, which work *through* supply and demand.

PRICE CEILINGS AND RATIONING   Consider, say, the market for sugar, which has ordinary curves of supply and demand such as we have repeatedly met in this chapter. Suppose that the government through a Price Stabilization Board establishes an order prohibiting sugar from rising above 7 cents a pound (retail). Now, because of prosperity or bad crops, let demand be so high and supply so small that the equilibrium price would have been 20 cents a pound if the government had not intervened. This high price would have contributed to "profiteering" in that industry, it would have represented a rather heavy "tax" on the poor who could least afford it, and it would only have added fuel to an inflationary spiral in the cost of living, with all sorts of inflationary reactions on workers' wage demands. So go the arguments of price fixers.[10]

Therefore the government, through the Price Stabilization Board, decides to hold the line on prices. It passes a law putting a maximum price on sugar at the old level of 7 cents a pound. The line JK in Fig. 19-8 represents the legal price ceiling. Now what will happen?

At the legal ceiling price, supply and demand do not match. Consumers want thousands of pounds of sugar in excess of what producers are willing to supply. This is shown by the gap between J and K. This gap is so large that there will not long be enough sugar on grocers' shelves or in the warehouse to make up the difference. Somebody will have to drink bitter coffee. If it were not for the maximum-price law, this somebody would gladly bid the price up to 8 or 9 cents or more, rather than do without sugar. As in our earlier discussion (Fig. 4-3, page 87), we could have shown this by putting an upward-pointing arrow perpendicular to JK. Such an arrow would not stop pointing upward until price had been bid up to the equilibrium level of 20 cents.

But it is against the law for the consumer to bid a higher price. Even if the consumer should be so unpatriotic, the seller could not legally take the higher price. There follows a period of frustration and shortage—a game of musical chairs in which somebody is left without a seat when the music stops playing. The inadequate supply of sugar must somehow be rationed. At first, this may be done by "first come, first served," with or without limited sales to each customer. Lines form, and women have to spend much of their time foraging for food. But this is no solution, since somebody must be left at the end of the line when the sugar is gone.

The price mechanism is stymied and blocked. Nonmonetary considerations must determine who is the lucky buyer and who the unlucky one: the warmth of the smile that the customer flashes on the grocer, her previous standing at the store in question, the amount of other things the customer is willing to buy, or the accident of being in the store when the sugar is put on the shelves.

Nobody is happy, least of all the harassed grocer. Were it not for the community's elementary sense of fair play, the situation would soon become intolerable. Patriotism is more effective in motivating people to brief acts of intense heroism than to putting up day after day with an uncomfortable situation. It is no wonder that black markets occasionally develop; the really surprising thing is how infrequently they do occur.

> If for political or social reasons market price is not to be permitted to rise high enough to bring quantity demanded down to the level of quantity supplied, the ultimate solution may require outright allocation of *ration* tickets.

---

[10] Most economists would, in normal peacetime, favor controlling inflation by the tools of macroeconomics—fiscal and monetary policies—rather than by simply legislating price ceilings that lead to chaotic rationing of the "shortages," and often to black markets and law evasion.

A legal maximum price, without rationing, leaves a gap between demand and supply:

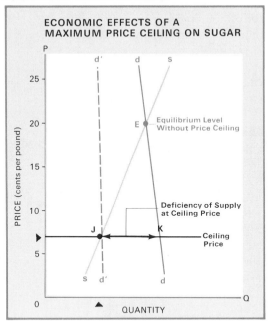

FIG. 19-8. Without a legal price ceiling, price would rise to *E*. At the artificial ceiling price, supply and demand do not balance and some method of rationing, formal or informal, is needed to allocate the short supply and bring the effective demand down to *d' d'*, shown as a dashed line.

Once rationing is adopted, most people heave a sigh of relief, because now sellers need not turn people away and buyers can count upon getting their fair quota of the limited supplies. Of course, there are always some cranky customers, longer on intuition than brains, who blame their troubles on the mechanism of rationing itself rather than on the shortage. "If only the government could print more ration tickets," they sigh. Such people are like the ignorant ancient kings who used to slay the messengers bringing them bad news. Their complaints need not be taken seriously; they only serve to add spice to the human comedy.

Just how do ration coupons work out in terms of supply and demand? Clearly, the Price Stabilization Board tries to issue just enough of them to lower the demand curve to *d'd'*, *where supply and the new demand balance at the ceiling price.* If too many coupons are issued, demand is still too far to the right and we encounter the old difficulties, but in lesser degree. If too few coupons are issued, stocks of sugar will pile up and *P* will fall below the ceiling price. This is the signal for liberalizing the sugar ration.

One goes to an insane asylum to learn to appreciate normal human behavior. So, too, the breakdown of the price mechanism during war gives us a new understanding of its remarkable efficiency in normal times.

Goods are always scarce, in the sense that there is never enough to give everyone all he wishes. Price itself is always rationing scarce supplies: rising to choke off excessive consumption and in order to expand production; falling to encourage consumption, discourage production, and work off excessive inventories.

MINIMUM FLOORS AND MAXIMUM CEILINGS   Even in peacetime, when there arises any kind of emergency or state of general shortage and inflation, political pressures for wage and price freezes develop. Experience has taught most economists, whether they be liberals or conservatives, that such emergency measures work very well in short emergencies but create more and more distortions the longer they are in effect. Economists therefore, in contrast to politicians, tend to recommend that such direct fiats be reserved for emergency periods and not squandered on minor peacetime situations.

Nevertheless, as Adam Smith well knew when he protested against the devices of the mercantilist advisers to the earlier kings, most economic systems are plagued by inefficiencies and inequities stemming from inexpert interferences with the mechanisms of supply and demand. Here is a brief list of such interferences (shown in Fig. 19-9).

1. *Minimum wage rates.* These often hurt those they are designed to help. What good does it do a youth to know that an employer must pay him $1.65 per hour, if the fact that he must be paid that amount is what keeps him from getting a job?[11]

2. *Rent ceilings.* Everyone hates a landlord and loves a farmer. To protect the poor from being gouged by landlords, maximum rentals are often fixed by law. These fiats may do good; but they may also do harm. Thus, France had practically no residential construction from 1914 to 1948 because of rent controls. If new construction had been subjected to such controls after World War II, the vigorous boom in French residential building since 1950 would never have taken place.

3. *Usury laws.* Interest rates have always been an object of suspicion. No longer is lending at interest a crime, but in many places a maximum rate is set by law.

Unfortunately, this ceiling is often far below what would be set by the competitive supply-and-demand market, after account is taken of riskiness and administrative expense connected with small loans. The result? Funds dry up completely. Cheap insured NHA housing mortgage loans were no use to those who could not get a loan in 1966-1968. And the "protection" of borrowers by Canada's 6 per cent ceiling on bank loans (till 1967) simply forced the public to borrow elsewhere at double this rate or more.

■ EFFICIENCY OF SUPPLY-DEMAND PRICING AND "EQUITY"

We do not study competitive pricing for the beauty of the subject. Nor for its realism alone, since often monopoly elements spoil the competitive picture. We study it for the light it throws on *efficient* organization of an economy's resources. The pathology of interference with supply and demand helps to bring out the remarkable efficiencies produced by perfect competition.

---

[11] See P. A. Samuelson, *Readings in Economics*, 6th Edition (McGraw-Hill, New York, 1970), for arguments pro and con minimum-wage legislation. See also Chapter 21's Appendix for graphical analysis of economic inefficiency of controls and rationing.

When government by fiat sets maximum or minimum prices, troublesome discrepancies between supply and demand may emerge:

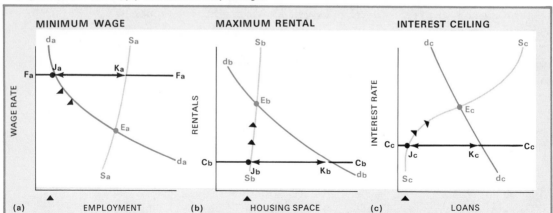

FIG. 19-9(a). Setting minimum-wage floor at $F_a F_a$, high above free-market equilibrium rate E_a, results in forced equilibrium at J_a. The too-high floor freezes workers into unemployment from J_a to K_a. Lowering the minimum wage will move us down along dd, as shown by black arrows, increasing employment. (If dd is elastic, total wage payrolls rise though hourly rate falls!)

FIG. 19-9(b). Setting maximum rental ceiling at $C_b C_b$, far below free-market equilibrium at E_b, causes fringe of unsatisfied renters between forced equilibrium at J_b and K_b. Raising the ceiling rate moves the system up $s_b s_b$, as shown by black arrows: new construction provides more living space, and old quarters are used more efficiently.

FIG. 19-9(c). Setting maximum interest rates at $C_c C_c$, far below free-market equilibrium rate E_c, results in drying up of available funds. Desperate borrowers at $J_c K_c$ turn to loan sharks. Raising interest ceiling moves system toward more loans, as shown by black arrows on $s_c s_c$.

Why then do politicians and the populace keep interfering with the mechanism? Because man does not live by efficiency alone. He is interested in the question: Efficiency for what? And for whom? Most of these floors and ceilings are set in the name of "equity"—to help some group deemed deserving at the expense of some other group deemed already affluent and amply well-off. Just as Robin Hood "robbed the rich to help the poor," these devices try to create or restore a distribution of real income considered more equitable. Their advocates are willing to pay some price in the form of lower efficiency and higher waste to bring about a "fairer" distribution of income. Economic science cannot pronounce that they are necessarily wrong, provided that they face the cost.

MONOPOLY INTERFERENCES WITH SUPPLY AND DEMAND

Aside from governmental interferences, there are serious monopolistic interferences with supply and demand. Competitive supply and demand is one way of organizing an economy. It is one way of getting the job done, but of course it is not the only way relied on in actual modern society. Certainly, when one or a few producers get monopoly control of an industry, they can move the final outcome away from the competitive equilibrium point. As we shall see later, a monopolist can reduce output and make the consumers travel up their demand curves to higher prices.

Is such an interference with supply and demand a "good thing"? If the monopolist were a more worthy soul than the rest of us, or if he were much poorer and had greater need for money than the rest of us, some might rise to defend his act of raising price. Or if he took our money and devoted it to better causes (charity, scientific research) than we should do, some might still defend him as a modern-day Robin Hood.

Chances are, however, that anyone in a position to contrive a monopoly will be at least as well off as his customers, and there is not much reason to think he would be of finer clay than anyone else. And though Robin Hood may have been all right in his day, in our day we tend to think it is the government that ought to do any subsidizing of worthy causes, not self-appointed monopolists; and we hope government can be more efficient in financing its good causes out of tax revenues than any monopolist could ever be. So what probably needs emphasis is this:

> Any *haphazard* interference with competitive supply and demand is likely —save in some exceptional circumstances—to be a bad rather than a good thing.

Thus, a monopolistic interference in Industry A reduces its output needlessly relative to Industry B. The fact that it produces such scarcity is reflected in the higher P_A/P_B ratio it creates, relative to the citizenry's desires for the goods and to their true relative costs as measured along the production-possibility frontier or by undistorted competitive costs. The monopoly may also lead to a bad distribution of income in that it may give extra income to one who already has as much income as he deserves.

> At this point monopoly's *restriction in output* relative to that of competitive industries perhaps needs more stressing than its distortion of the income distribution. For what if we taxed away the monopolist's ill-gotten gains?[12] We should then have rectified the income-distribution distortion of monopoly. But the community would still be left enjoying less of the (monopolized) consumption goods that it really does want in terms of what it really can produce.

Like sin, monopoly is one of those things most people are against. Therefore one need not labor the point that monopoly interferences with supply and demand are probably a bad thing. Still, it is better to know analytically why.

---

[12] Or what if many monopolists entered the industry, with all keeping their price too high but with total business so divided up among them that none ends up making any exorbitant monopoly profit? Then the evil effect on the income distribution would not exist, but the resulting wasteful pattern of inefficient production in the industry and too high price could persist until doomsday. More on this when Chapter 25 treats imperfect competition along the lines of Harvard's late E. H. Chamberlin.

■ GOVERNMENT INTERFERENCES WITH SUPPLY AND DEMAND EVALUATED

In conclusion let us appraise government interferences. Surely the government means well and its interferences are not to be as harshly judged as those of a monopolist?

Well, that all depends. If the government happens to know better than people what is really good and evil, its interferences may improve matters. An example might be opium. We do not treat the consumer as a sovereign who can decide how much opium he will spend his money votes on. Where opium is concerned we adopt a paternalistic attitude, treating the consumer a little the way we treat the insane, minors, and other "incompetents." Society is similarly beginning to move against cigarettes.

But where eight-cylinder cars or bubblegum are concerned, we usually are content to let the consumer spend his own dollars in his own way. We recognize that advertising has given us one set of tastes, which may not be intrinsically better than some other set, but in the interests of freedom we do treat the consumer as sovereign.

As we have seen, the matter becomes more complicated if the sellers or the buyers in a market happen to be especially rich, or especially poor, or especially "deserving," or especially "undeserving." For example, imagine an artificial case where 1 million very rich producers sell milk in competitive markets to 50 million very poor people. Some people would then be tempted to approve of any interference that lowered milk price. "That leads to what we call a fairer income distribution," they might say.

Without foisting his ethical judgments on others, the economist can remind us:

Interfering with the competitive supply-and-demand mechanism is an inefficient[13] way of correcting the income distribution. Whatever distribution

[13] The fact that buyers and sellers are different people who may have different incomes or worth hides the truth that the competitive equilibrium point has certain allocative efficiency properties in solving the WHAT and How economic problems. So consider a simplified case where I trade only with myself. I have 10 hours of leisure worth exactly $2.50 per hour to me. I can produce 1 Q unit with each hour of work or sacrificed leisure. Suppose the first Q unit is worth exactly $4 to me, and successive Q units are worth $3, $2, $1, and $0. Figure 19-10 shows *my* supply and demand for Q. Equilibrium is at E, where I consume exactly 2 of Q. I get $4 + $3 of "satisfaction" from them (as shown by light shading) and 8 times $2.50 from my 8 hours left of leisure (as shown by heavy shading), or $27 of satisfaction in all, as shown by the sum of the areas. You can show that any disturbance which makes me work 1 hour too much, or too little, kills off 50 cents of my satisfaction. Distortion of a second hour kills off $1.50 of satisfaction; each further distortion takes a heavier and heavier toll, as shown by the growing discrepancy between dd and ss. (See Figs. 21-4, 22-5, and 31-2, for more on "consumer's surplus," which can be used to demonstrate monopoly harm or price-control inefficiency.)

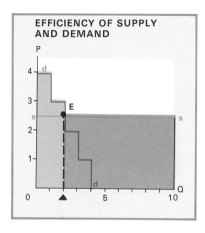

FIG. 19-10.

you want to end up with can often be more efficiently attained by using the tax system to redistribute income rather than using *ad hoc* Robin Hood interferences in a single market.

Indeed, if taxation always could be counted on to keep society's FOR WHOM problem optimally solved, then perfect competition (were it to prevail!) could be counted on to solve most WHAT and HOW problems efficiently.

Naturally, all this is a controversial area. There is no one answer, and any observer of the modern world can see that nations everywhere do interfere with the price system at many points. EXAMPLES: Blood for transfusions is not primarily obtained by commercial bidding, but rather through much voluntary effort. (Why?) Doctors often charge rich patients more than poor ones, in part subsidizing the latter from revenues of the former. (Why this private system of taxation?) Milk and other basic foods are often subsidized. To the degree that our demands reflect merely manipulated fads, engineered by profit-seeking advertisers, the merits of "consumer sovereignty" fade away.

The next chapter will deal with the extensive agricultural aid programs which the government has been following. And later chapters will discuss the effects of monopolistic imperfections of competition after competitive demand and the dependence of competitive supply on costs have been studied.

SUMMARY

A. ELASTICITY OF DEMAND AND SUPPLY

■ 1 A basic problem of microeconomics is the mechanism of market pricing: how it grapples with the economy's problems WHAT, HOW, FOR WHOM. The supply-and-demand curves in Chapter 4 explain what goes on in each particular competitive market.

■ 2 Elasticity of demand depends on what happens to total revenue as price is cut. Demand is elastic, inelastic, or unitary, according to whether a reduction in price increases, decreases, or does not change *total* revenue. The numerical coefficient of elasticity of demand is defined as "the percentage increase in quantity divided by the percentage cut in price." Depending upon whether the percentage rise in Q exceeds or falls short of the percentage fall in P, we have $E > 1$ or $E < 1$, with $E = 1$ in between. (Elasticity is dimensionless, involving percentages; it is not to be confused with absolute slope, as numerical tables and graphical measurements make clear.)

■ 3 Elasticity of supply measures percentage responsiveness of amount Q supplied by producers when market P is raised by a given percentage.

■ 4 Marshall stressed the time element: (*a*) *momentary* equilibrium of fixed supply; (*b*) *short-run* equilibrium with output varying within fixed plants and firms; (*c*) *long-run* equilibrium of normal price, when numbers of firms and plants, and all conditions, adjust to the new level of demand.

B.   APPLICATIONS AND QUALIFICATIONS OF SUPPLY AND DEMAND

■ 5   The apparatus of supply and demand enables us to analyze the effect of shifts in either curve, or in both simultaneously. Beginners must avoid the pitfall of confusing the expression "an increase in demand" (i.e., an outward *shift* of the whole demand curve) with "an increase in quantity demanded" as a result of a reduction in price (i.e., a movement *down* an unchanged demand curve).

■ 6   A tax of so many dollars per unit of a good will lead to a new equilibrium intersection and will be borne more largely by consumers rather than producers to the degree that the demand is inelastic relative to the supply. The more elastic *dd* and *ss* are, the less the P change and the greater the Q change.

■ 7   A thousand forces affect price; but in a free competitive market they do so only by acting through supply and demand. For example, cost of production affects competitive price only through affecting supply, not otherwise.

■ 8   Although the government usually affects price by operating on either supply or demand, occasionally it sets maximum ceilings or minimum floors that interfere with the workings of competitive markets. Under such circumstances, supply and demand need not be equal; some producer or consumer may *wish* to sell or buy more than he is able to do at the legal price. Distortions and inefficiencies result. Unless the discrepancies are parceled out by legislation (rationing, etc.), disorder and black markets may result.

■ 9   Haphazard, arbitrary interferences with supply and demand will often be harmful. Monopoly interference provides an obvious case, and here the evil is not so much that the distribution of income is distorted as that society has to put up unnecessarily with reduced relative output of a good that it really wants and really can afford.

Even in cases where government is interfering with supply and demand for the purpose of achieving some desired distribution of income or some other social goal, there may be hidden costs in the use of so inefficient a device—and often the same goal could be accomplished better by use of the tax system and preservation of the efficiency of market pricing.

QUESTIONS FOR DISCUSSION

1.   What factors might increase the demand for wheat? The supply?

2.   Which do you think has the most inelastic demand: perfume, salt, penicillin, cigarettes, ice cream, chocolate ice cream, Sealtest chocolate ice cream? Why?

3.   When demand is elastic (inelastic, or unitary), what will a rise in P do to total revenue? What will higher Q do in the three cases?

4.   "Elastic demand means elastic supply, since the curves meet." Refute.

5.   Explain Marshall's three time periods, their equilibria, the slope of $s_L s_L$.

6.   Examine the diagram below, which shows demand and supply curves for wheat for different years. Plot intersection points. Fill in the column at the right showing the price and quantity of wheat for each of the four years. (Note how hard it would be to estimate demand or supply curves from a plot of intersections.)

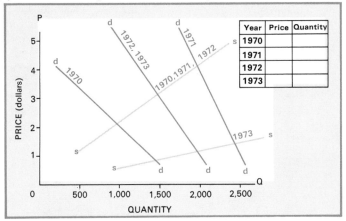

Year	Price	Quantity
1970		
1971		
1972		
1973		

7. As an extra-credit problem for those who like simple geometry and algebra,[14] try to justify the E rule given in footnote 3 (page 466) for a straight line. In the triangle below, the dd has the equation $Q = b - (b/a)P$, where b is the Q intercept and a the P intercept, and the absolute inverted slope of dd is $-(dQ/dP) = -\Delta Q/\Delta P = b/a$. Now apply the formula $E = -(dQ/dP)(P/Q)$ to get

$$E = \frac{b}{a}\frac{P}{b-(b/a)P} = \frac{P}{a-P}$$

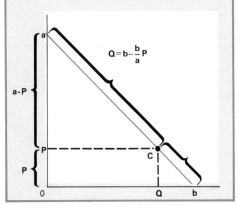

—the ratio of the lower vertical bracket to the upper. Can you show, by the property of similar triangles, that

$$E = \frac{P}{a-P} = \frac{bC}{aC}$$

equals "the length of the straight line below the point divided by its length above the point," as stated in footnote 3?

[14] As another extra-credit problem, try to relate Table 19-1's so-called "arc elasticity" formula for two different points on dd to the so-called "point elasticity" formula just given. First, draw an extended straight line through the two points on dd. Second, locate their average or midpoint on the line. Third, calculate E as the ratio of the extended line segment below this point to that above it. You will thus end up with a geometrical interpretation of

$$E = -\frac{\Delta Q\,(P_1 + P_2)/2}{\Delta P\,(Q_1 + Q_2)/2}$$

Those who tackled the mathematical question 10 of Chapter 4, page 99, can calculate E from the demand function $Q = f(P)$. Define

$$E = \frac{lim}{\Delta P \to O}\frac{-\Delta Q}{\Delta P}\frac{(P_1 + P_2)/2}{(Q_1 + Q_2)/2} = \frac{dQ}{dP}\frac{P}{Q} = \frac{-P\{df(P)/dP\}}{f(P)}$$

For $f(P) = b - (b/a)P$, calculate $E = P/(a - P)$. Show E to be respectively 1, 2, ⅓, k for $f(P)$ successively c/P, c/P^2, $c/P^{\frac{1}{3}}$, c/P^k. Taking logarithms (to any base) of the last expression, verify $\log Q = \log c - k \log P$ does give $E \equiv k$. [HINT: $(dQ/Q) \div (dP/P) = -d \log Q/d \log P \equiv -k$.]

8. Review your understanding of the following concepts:

microeconomics, macroeconomics
total revenue, $P \times Q$
elastic, inelastic, unitary elastic
elasticity of supply
Marshall's three time periods
demand versus amount demanded
shift versus movement along a curve
incidence of a tax
government actions to influence
   supply and demand curves

cost of production, supply, and price
rationing and price fixing
   maximum-price ceilings
   minimum-wage floors
monopoly reduction of relative outputs
   versus monopoly distortion of
   income distribution
possible efficiencies sacrificed when
   government interferes with supply and
   demand to achieve a worthy goal

APPENDIX: Cases on Supply and Demand[1]

Proposition 1. (a) As a general rule an increase in demand—supply being constant—will raise price.
(b) Probably also, but less certainly, increased demand will increase the quantity bought and sold. A decrease in demand has opposite effects.

Proposition 2. An increase in supply, demand being constant, will almost certainly lower price and increase the quantity bought and sold. A decrease in supply has opposite effects.

These two important propositions summarize the *qualitative* effects of shifts in supply and demand. But the exact *quantitative* degree of change in price and quantity depends upon the specific shapes of the curves in each instance. Here, then, are a number of possible cost and supply situations.

Case 1. Constant cost. Imagine a manufactured item, like pencils, whose production can be easily expanded by merely duplicating factories, machinery, and labor. To produce 100,000 pencils per day simply requires us to do the same thing as when we were manufacturing 1,000 per day, but on a hundredfold scale. In this case the supply curve *ss* in Fig. 19-11 is a horizontal line at the constant level of unit costs. A rise in demand will shift the new intersec-

tion point E' to the right, raising Q but leaving P the same.

What will be the effects of a sales tax of, say 5 cents per pencil, on output and price paid by the consumer? Fill in the diagram in the Fig. 19-6 manner.

Case 2. Increasing costs and diminishing returns. Suppose an industry like wine-grape growing re-

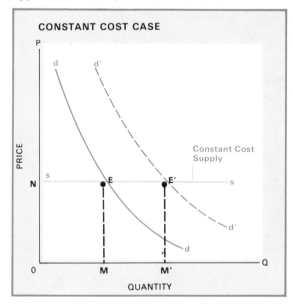

FIG. 19-11.

[1] Many courses may prefer to study this Appendix after Chapter 22 or 23.

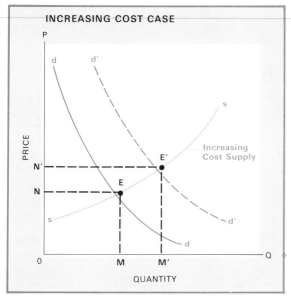

FIG. 19-12.

quires a certain kind of soil and location (sunny hillsides, etc.). Such sites are limited in number. The annual output of wine can be increased to some extent by adding more labor and fertilizer to each acre of land and by bidding away more hill sites from other uses. But as we saw in Chapter 2, the law of diminishing returns will begin to operate if variable factors of production, like labor and fertilizer, are added to fixed amounts of a factor like land. Why is that? Because each new *variable addition* of labor and fertilizer has a *smaller proportion* of land to work with. By the same token, each fixed unit of land has more labor and fertilizer cooperating with it. Therefore land's productivity and earnings are higher. The result: Getting extra amounts of wine sends total costs up more than proportionately. Therefore the cost per unit of wine is rising. The supply curve travels upward from southwest to northeast because at lower market prices, less will be supplied. At higher prices, more will be supplied.

Figure 19-12 shows the rising supply curve *ss*. What will be the effect on price of an increase in demand? Effect on quantity?

[Show by a diagram that a tax of so much per ounce of wine will raise price to the consumer by less than a similar tax on pencils did. Why? What will be the effect on the price received by the producer? If the original demand curves for wine and pencils are similar, show that the fall in output will be *greater* for pencils than for wine. Why?]

Case 3. Completely fixed or inelastic supply and economic rent. Some goods or productive factors are completely fixed in amount, regardless of price.

Thus there is only one *Mona Lisa* by Leonardo. Nature's original endowment of the "natural and indestructible" qualities of land can also often be taken as fixed in amount. Raising the price offered for water power cannot create more than Niagara Falls. High-paid artists and businessmen who love their work would continue to work at their jobs even at low pay. Once a toll bridge is built, it must earn "what the traffic will bear" regardless of past sunk costs.

In all such cases the supply curve goes vertically up and down, at least in the relevant region. Look at Fig. 19-13. A higher price cannot elicit an increase in Q; nor is the higher price necessary to bring out the existing Q, for even at lower prices the same amount will still be forthcoming. Because it is price-*determined* rather than price-*determining*, the return to such a factor of production is called a "pure economic rent," or "surplus," which need not be paid to call out the required supply.

If demand now shifts upward, the whole effect is to raise price. Quantity is unchanged. And the rise

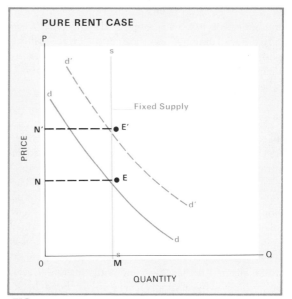

FIG. 19-13.

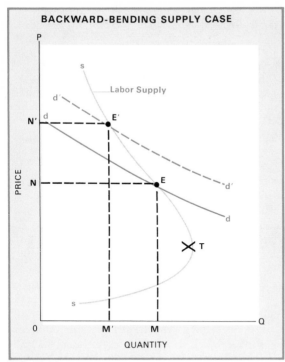

FIG. 19-14.

in price exactly equals the upward shift in demand. (More on this in Chapter 27.)

Likewise, if a tax is placed upon the commodity, its whole effect is to reduce the price received by the supplier by exactly the amount of the tax. The tax is shifted back completely to the supplier, who absorbs it all out of his economic rent or surplus. The consumer buys exactly as much of the good or service as before and at no extra cost.

Case 4. A backward-rising supply curve. Early explorers into new lands often noted that, when you raised the wages of natives, you received *less* rather than more labor. If wages were doubled, instead of working 6 days a week for their minimum of subsistence, the natives might go fishing for 3 days. The same has been observed among so-called "civilized" people. As improved technology raises real wages people feel that they ought to take part of their higher earnings in the form of more leisure, less work. (In Chapter 21, the discussion of the marginal utility theory, or income- and substitution-effects, will explain why a supply curve might bend backward.)

Figure 19-14 shows such a supply curve of labor.

At first it rises as higher wages coax out more labor, but beyond the point *T*, higher wages induce more leisure and less work. An increase in demand does increase the price of labor in agreement with Proposition 1(*a*). But note how lucky we were to have added the words "but less certainly" in 1(*b*)! For the increase in demand has *decreased* the quantity of labor.

A partial verification of such a possibility is found in the fact that a decrease in demand for farm products during a depression often causes farmers to work harder in order to restore their incomes. The result: More rather than less is produced in response to a decrease in demand.

Case 5. A possible exception: Decreasing cost. Heretofore our examples have agreed with Proposition 1(*a*), that an increase in demand raises price. But what about the often observed case where an increase in demand is followed by economies of mass production and decreasing costs?

A good theory must make room for all the facts. So we must frankly admit that our first proposition may break down and have exceptions. Of course, we can save some face by pointing out that many of the important reductions in cost following an increase in demand really represent *permanent downward shifts* in the supply curve rather than downward movements *along* a falling supply curve.

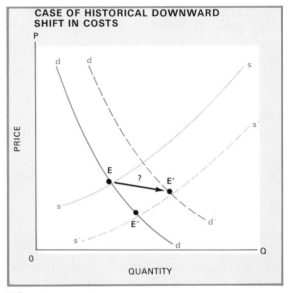

FIG. 19-15.

Let us illustrate this by the case where the government increases its demand for radar sets. The first few sets built must be constructed in the laboratory by experimental methods. They are tailor-made and very expensive per unit. But the know-how gained in the process makes possible the further production of sets for much less per unit. Even if demand went back again to its previous level, price would not return to its previous higher level. In traveling along the arrow EE' marked with a question mark in Fig. 19-15 we are not moving reversibly along the supply curve. Instead, the supply curve has shifted irreversibly downward from ss to s's', so that even when demand is back again at dd, the price is now lower at E'' than it was originally.

The case discussed really does not come under the heading of Proposition 1, but under Proposition 2 dealing with shifts in supply. The final result agrees with the latter's conclusion that an increase in supply will lower price and increase quantity. (Compare E and E''.) But the present case is still an unusual one because the shift of supply has been *induced* by a shift in demand.

In economic history, there have been important cases of reduced cost over time as a result of technological progress that was partly induced by the expansion of a mass market. Goods are constantly being improved in quality and cheapened in price.

What about the case of genuine *reversible* economies of large-scale production—cases where going back to small-scale production does send costs up again? The alert modern economist will not deny its importance; but he will suspect that some monopolistic imperfection of competition is present. He will point out that in a competitive industry each firm would have *already* expanded its output to where the *extra* cost of producing a unit of output has begun to turn up. This would be because each competitive producer has no fear of spoiling his own market and has every incentive to expand his production through and beyond the decreasing-cost stage.[2] (Later chapters analyze the imperfect competition that results when a few firms have decreasing cost and hence expand to capture much of the market.)

Case 6. Shifts in supply. All the above discussion, with the exception of part of Case 5, dealt with a

[2] There remains the possibility mentioned in Chapter 23: the case of an $s_L s_L$ curve that is downward-sloping because of Marshallian *external* economies.

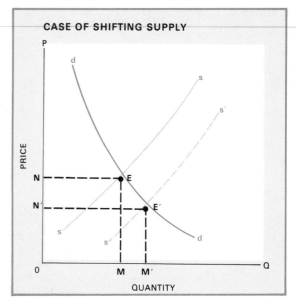

CASE OF SHIFTING SUPPLY

FIG. 19-16.

shift in demand and no shift in supply. To analyze Proposition 2, we must now shift supply, keeping demand constant. This is done in Fig. 19-16.

If the law of downward-sloping demand is valid,[3] then increased supply must send us *down* the demand curve, decreasing price and quantity. The student may verify, by drawing diagrams or by comparing automobiles and wheat, the following quantitative corollaries of Proposition 2:

(a) An increased supply will decrease price most when demand is inelastic, decrease it least when demand is relatively elastic.

(b) An increased supply will increase the quantity bought and sold least when demand is inelastic, most when demand is elastic.

[3] In Chapter 21 we shall meet the legitimate exception to the law of downward-sloping demand in the case of the Irish peasants who might be forced by higher potato P to consume *more* of such necessities. Another exception is provided by items such as diamonds or chic hats, which are valuable, not for their intrinsic qualities so much as for their "snob appeal" and expensiveness, and which may therefore fall off in demand if their price is cut. What appears to be another exception is the case in which a short-run rise in P may make people expect future P to be still higher, thus causing them to buy more rather than less now and thereby leading to unstabilizing speculation; but this is more properly to be interpreted as a case where the whole demand curve is shifting, rather than as a northeast move up dd.

What are common-sense reasons for these? Illustrate with elastic autos and inelastic wheat.

Case 7. A dynamic cobweb. There is a famous economic case which can be used to show that the tools of supply and demand are not restricted to handling static and unchanging situations, but can also be used fruitfully to analyze dynamic situations of change. (The next sections can be skipped by the time-pressed reader.)

Suppose that a competitive crop—let us take the conventional example of hogs for pork production—is auctioned off in the market in the usual way so as to fetch the P given by running up vertically from any given Q to the dd demand curve.

But now we want to make the supply side dynamic. Suppose farmers look at today's P and use it to determine the Q they will bring to market in the *next* period: specifically, if today's P is high, they begin to breed many new pigs, to feed and fatten them, and finally to bring them to market some months from now. The farmers do indeed have an ss supply curve, but it acts with a time lag and connects next period's Q with this period's P. (It is understood that we define a period as the time involved in producing hogs.)

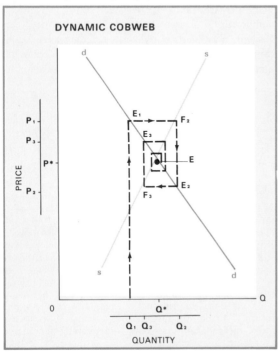

DYNAMIC COBWEB

FIG. 19-17.

If the market price were at the intersection of ss and dd in Fig. 19-17, this would represent an unchanging equilibrium in exactly the same way that it did in the nondynamic cases. Today, tomorrow, and in the period after that, the farmers would be on their ss curve producing the amount shown by E; and the amount consumers would gladly demand at that P would just match what farmers will gladly supply. As yet, then, no difference.

But suppose that, for some reason, such as hog cholera, the crop initially drops to Q_1, which is below the equilibrium amount Q^*. We run up to the demand curve to E_1 and see that we get the higher P_1 corresponding to the reduced crop. But that is not the end of the story. We are not at long-run equilibrium; because how much will the farmers produce tomorrow at this higher P_1? They will run over rightward to their supply curve and produce in the second period at the point marked F_2. We can see that this amount of Q is above the equilibrium Q^*. What will it sell for in the competitive market? We run down to the demand curve and see that P_2 will have to fall to the level shown at E_2. But we are not yet in final equilibrium. At this low price, farmers will plan to cut down tomorrow's production by going leftward to their ss curve, ending up at F_3. From there we move upward to the dd curve, to find the P_3 given at the E_3 point.

And thus it goes on and on. First Q is low and P is high. But high P makes next period's Q high and next period's P low. So—like a man on a tightrope who goes too far on one side, then corrects himself by going too far on the other—market price oscillates in successive periods above and below equilibrium, tracing out a spiderlike cobweb.

What is the final outcome? Figure 19-17 was drawn with the supply curve's slope at E *steeper* than the demand curve's falling slope. So, as can be seen from the diagram, the oscillations finally do dampen and die out: the cobweb winds inward to E. We are then back at equilibrium, where we can stay forever. Forever? Well, at least until the next outside disturbance comes to set off still another dying-out oscillation.

Not all equilibrium points are so dynamically stable. Figure 19-18 puts a microscope on the region around E in a number of other possible situations. Thus, in the first diagram, ss has been made *flatter* than dd, and the cobweb diverges outward in an explosive oscillation.

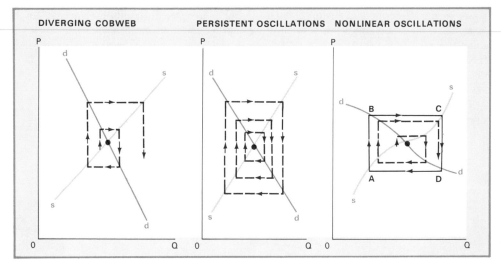

FIG. 19-18.

In the second diagram, the straight lines are of the *same slope* and we get a perfect cobweb: depending upon how severely it is disturbed, the market will oscillate endlessly around equilibrium, getting neither more nor less violent in its swings. (This is like the case of an ideal frictionless pendulum which would repeat its swings forever.)

The last diagram is designed to show that there is no need to stick with straight lines. Because its *ss* is flatter (more "elastic") than *dd* at the equilibrium point, any small disturbance will *at first* send the system into increasing oscillations. But no explosion can go on forever in real life; and the curvature of the schedules finally brings the system to the stable "box," indicated by the letters *ABCD*. Ultimately, then, the system oscillates repeatedly in an every-other-period box and the amplitude or degree of the oscillation will be determined by the curvatures of *dd* and *ss*. After any new disturbance, the system tends to come back to this box from within or without; and even if stationary equilibrium were restored at *E* by accident, the slightest new shock would send the market away from such an unstable equilibrium point. (The thoughtful student may ask at this point: Could prices swing forever in this every-other-period fashion without shrewd speculators beginning to notice the pattern? Would they not then tend to buy at low *P*, store, and resell at high *P*, thus tending to wipe out the price differentials? The Appendix to the next chapter deals with dynamic speculation and suggests that

just this might indeed happen.)

There was space here for only the briefest account of the cobweb model.[4] Statistics show that a corn-

[4] This cobweb model enabled Columbia's pioneering econometrician of half a century ago, H. L. Moore, to crack the problem of how to "identify" either the supply or the demand curve from historical data depicting (P, Q) intersections. Recall question 6, page 482, which illustrated the difficulty. Moore assumed that the points E_1, E_3, E_2 in Fig. 19-17 and *B, D* in Fig. 19-18, which depict *unlagged* (P_t, Q_t) values, defined the *dd* curve for him. Moore assumed that the points F_3, F_2, and *A, C*, which depict *lagged* variables (P_t, Q_{t+1}) defined his *ss* curve. Biological scientists, trying to "identify" the relation between cigarettes and longevity, can sympathize with the economist's difficulty in making controlled experiments. Here, briefly, are other methods econometricians use to "identify" *dd* and *ss* elasticities quantitatively: (1) If *ss* is very shifting (say, because of weather) and *dd* very stable, the resulting (P_t, Q_t) scatter traces out the points along the stable *dd* schedule, shown in dark brown. (Reverse the roles to get points along the *ss* schedule, shown in light brown.) (2) Or suppose Q_t of *dd* depends on another variable, say, GNP_t, as well as on P_t, and suppose Q_t of *ss* depends on a quite different other variable, say, fertilizer cost, F_t. Then by generalized multiple correlation techniques, separate dark brown and light brown relations between *P* and *Q* can be "identified." (DRAMATIC EXAMPLE: Suppose GNP_t changed only in odd years and F_t changed only in even years. Then odd-year (demand) changes would trace out light brown *ss* points; and even-year (supply) changes would trace out dark brown *dd* points.)

hog cycle like this has been part of modern history. And our simplified model throws some light on the business-cycle phenomena dealt with in Part Two, where a free enterprise system would tend to fluctuate if not moderated by public policy and equilibrating market mechanisms. Corporations, like pig farmers, can swing from one extreme to the other, thus causing instability.

20

SUPPLY AND DEMAND AS APPLIED TO AGRICULTURE

Though government subsidies to ease adjustment burdens and sustain incomes in the face of unfavorable prices have not, on the whole, been a major feature of government policy in Canada, nevertheless such policies may, and in some cases have, slowed down adjustment processes. . . . We continue to have too many farms, with many of the farmers earning low incomes. ECONOMIC COUNCIL OF CANADA, FIRST ANNUAL REVIEW

The economist's model of perfect competition, in which a homogeneous product is produced by many different people and auctioned off in a well-organized market, does not fit most of Canadian life at all closely. Therefore, in later chapters, we shall have to supplement it by the new tools of imperfect, or monopolistic, competition.

There is, however, one great area that does provide a valuable application of the basic tools of supply and demand. Agriculture is an important problem area. It makes the news. It shifts votes. No one can possibly understand the vital policy issues in this field without first understanding the basic economic concepts of supply and demand. This chapter puts them to work.

■ RELATIVE DECLINE OF AGRICULTURE

Farming is still our largest single industry. But the percentage of people engaged in it has been declining steadily for the last two centuries. We used to be a nation of farmers. That is no longer true. Though farmers still swing much political weight, today only 5.6 per cent of Canadian workers are in agriculture!

Why this relative shift away from farming? People seek the higher and more stable incomes of the city, shorter hours, and what many seem to regard as the better social life in town; they flee from ancient discrimination. (But as Chapter

Farm incomes rise slowly and are unstable:

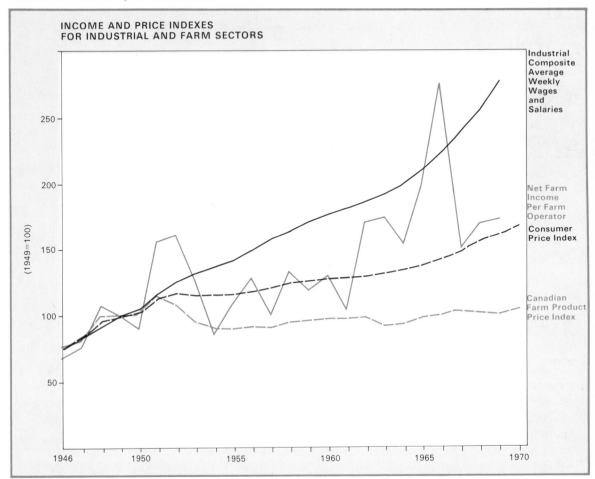

FIG. 20-1. The prices paid by farmers' wives at the grocery have risen faster than the price the farmer gets for his crops. Farm-operator income fluctuates with crops and with markets. (Source: Economic Council and estimates from DBS data.)

39's analysis of urban problems will show, the migrants to the city encounter new problems there.)

Figure 20-1 shows that, even in the short period since World War II, (*a*) unstable farm-operator incomes, fluctuating with crop successes and failures, have over most of the period risen more slowly than stable industrial wages; and (*b*) farm product prices have failed to rise with the general cost of living. Obviously, living on a farm is still precarious and generally less economically rewarding than working in the city.

DIFFERENTIAL BIRTH RATES   In a way, this out-migration from the country is lucky. For, as we saw in Chapter 2, birth rates are higher in rural areas than in cities. If it were not for this migration, cities might grow smaller and smaller; the rural share of total population would grow larger and larger. What does the law of diminishing returns tell us such an eventuality would mean? It would mean a great reduction in the productivity of each man-hour spent on the farm. The land would become crowded with many people, each producing little and each unable to buy many of the comforts of life with his produce.

Does this sound far-fetched? It is already a true picture of about two-thirds of the globe. In Asia especially, standards of living are pitifully poor. With three out of every four persons engaged in producing the food necessary for life, only one out of four can be producing the comforts of life. Contrast this with our near self-sufficiency, where each producer is today efficient enough to feed more than thirty other people as well. But Canada is not self-sufficient in food. Instead, we export large proportions of certain crops and import other foods from warmer climates.

TECHNOLOGY, TASTE, AND TRADE   Besides the differential in birth rates, there are two other reasons why agriculture is a problem area:

Technological progress has been greatly reducing the number of people needed to produce any given total of food and fiber. Use of the tractor, the combine, irrigation, fertilizer, experimental planting of varieties of wheat, and numerous other examples come to mind.

Coupled with the improvement in labor-saving technique is the unshakable fact that, *as we get richer, we do not want to expand our food consumption by as much as we want to expand our consumption of city products. Moreover, potential customers overseas do not want to use their scarce foreign exchange for our grains.* This has been shown by almost every statistical investigation here and abroad.

Birth rates, tastes, and technology dictate that agriculture must go on exporting people to industry, or increasing food exports abroad.

▪ AGRICULTURE'S LONG-RUN DECLINE: GRAPHICAL ANALYSIS

THE PRODUCTION-POSSIBILITY FRONTIER   This basic tool can illuminate the decline in agriculture. Turn back to Fig. 2-3 of Chapter 2, page 26. The figure shows that tremendous technological change has shifted out the *p-p frontier*; the even greater productivity in food production—from the use of tractors, fertilizers, hybrid seeds, and insecticides—is indicated by the strong eastward shift that flattens the whole curve. What does this flattening of the curve imply for the trend of farm prices relative to industrial prices? It means that a larger amount of food can be got from the same resources relative to nonfood. So food costs and prices must, in free markets, fall relative to nonfood. This is borne out by food price statistics. Both in Canada and the United States, farm prices have kept declining relative to the prices of industrial and other nonfarm goods. Even with

One diagram goes far to explain the farm problem:

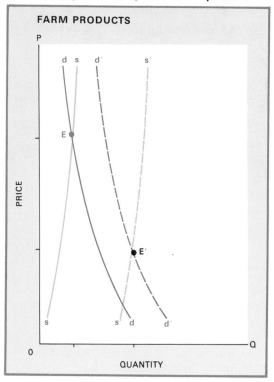

FARM PRODUCTS

FIG. 20-2. As the years go by, the increase in demand for farm products generated by population and income growth tends to be less than the vast increase in supply generated by technological productivity improvements. Thus free prices fall. With both schedules highly inelastic, prices fall hard; farm incomes deteriorate. And small shifts in inelastic curves generate large price fluctuations.

expanding export markets and rising world population, the ratio of food to non-food prices has been generally downward since World War I.[1]

A second reason for this price trend can also be seen back in Fig. 2-3. Food is a necessity whose expenditure drops relative to higher and higher incomes. As each nation grows richer, its move to B from A is not northeastward but almost due north, to an even flatter part of the technically flattened new p-p *frontier*. No wonder food prices drop in competitive markets (unless they are rescued by new export markets).

SUPPLY AND DEMAND CURVES   A single diagram is more useful in explaining the sagging trend of farm prices than libraries of orations and editorials.

In Fig. 20-2 let the point E represent the initial equilibrium of supply and demand at some earlier period. Now see what happens to these curves as the

---

[1] This ratio measures the extent to which farmers achieve "parity" in the pricing of their produce. In the United States, policy has resulted in giving the value of the ratio in 1913 a target value of 100. Whenever farm prices fall, the policy implication is that the government should support them until the ratio rises to the 1913 level. The value of the ratio since 1949 is indicated by the relationship of the two bottom lines in Fig. 20-1.

years go by. We know that *dd* will shift rightward as population grows and as higher real incomes make people want to consume more food at the same price; but we do know that basic foods are the kinds of necessities which do not grow in the family budget at all proportionately to increases in real income, and we realize that population no longer grows at the prodigious percentage rates of the nineteenth century. So the rightward demand shift to *d'd'* is of modest amount.

What about supply? Though many make the mistake of thinking of farming as a backward business, statistical records show that productivity in agriculture has increased at a pace even faster than productivity in industry. So each new improvement helps to shift the *ss* curve a great deal to the right.

What, then, must be happening to the new equilibrium *E'* that would prevail in the market if the government did not intervene? Certainly a shift in supply that outstrips the shift in demand must lead to a *downward trend of market prices* (relative, of course, to the general price level, so that effects of over-all inflation are disregarded). Naturally, this declining price trend means financial pressure and hardship on those farmers and rural workers whose efficiency has not undergone tremendous increase; and it means that there will be considerable pressure for people to leave the countryside for jobs in industry. It also means that consumers are paying lower prices for the raw-material component of their foods[2] and that the economy is reallocating its resources toward the things that are now most demanded in our growing society.

And, as we know, it means strong political pressures for government aid to agriculture.

■ INSTABILITY IN AGRICULTURE

Farming is an up-and-down industry. Oats, wheat, beef, pork, and other farm products are sold in highly competitive markets whose prices change yearly, daily, hourly, and by the minute. The farmer swings at the very end of our see-sawing economy. Good times bring him great percentage increases in income. Depressions cause his cash income to drop away to very little. The farmer particularly benefits from wartime demand conditions; and unlike most of the community, the farmer can ride out an inflationary period of skyrocketing prices. But since 1947 farm income has been sliding downward relative to other incomes, both in total and in per capita terms.

If we look closely at farm statistics, such as those in Fig. 20-1, we note a surprising fact.

---

[2] Even though the price the farmer gets for the food he sells will fall, the retail price need not fall so much or may even rise in the years ahead. Why? Agricultural experts claim this is not so much because railroads, packers, and supermarkets extort an undue share of the food dollar as that we consumers today want our food more and more fabricated (e.g., frozen, cut, cleaned, cooked, minutely packaged, premixed for baking, and so forth) and that greater technological progress may be taking place in producing raw food than in processing and marketing it. In the 1970s the farmer gets but one-third of the retail food dollar, as compared with about one-half in the years of high farm prices, right after World War II.

Farm *incomes* fluctuate between boom and bust to a greater degree than do nonfarm incomes, but farm *production* is remarkably more stable than industrial production. Stability of farm output contrasts with instability of farm prices!

Even the weather, which is a great threat to the stability of farm production in *any one* region, does not cause such sizable fluctuations in *total* farm crops over the whole nation. In the last quarter century, industrial production has fluctuated considerably more widely than has agricultural production.

The farmer's supply curves are relatively inelastic for many reasons. (1) When *P* falls, his own effort to increase output may increase, as he desperately tries to maintain family income. (2) Many of his costs go on anyway, whether he produces much or little, and he can save but little extra cost by cutting his *Q*; so he tends not to cut volume. (3) Once a farmer has planted a crop, he can do little to increase his output volume until the next crop season.

The amount of farm products demanded, in addition to growing little when income rises, is also quite inelastic in response to price changes.

What, then, is the result of (1) relatively inelastic demand coupled with (2) relatively inelastic supply when (3) both curves are quite shiftable?

To answer this, take a sheet of paper and construct price and quantity axes. Then draw on it a quite vertical supply curve intersecting a quite vertical demand curve, much as in Fig. 20-2. Now shift either curve a little bit. Do you see how great are the resulting shifts in *P*? Would anyone like having his standard of living dependent on a tiny shift of supply and demand, when inelastic curves produce a tremendous change in family income?

Figure 20-1 showed that fluctuations in the prices received by farmers are greater than the fluctuations in the prices of the things they must buy. In the Great Depression days of the early 1930s, prices received by farmers dropped about twice as far as did prices elsewhere. Even in the prosperous 1920s the farmer did badly; and, to make things worse, he then carried a heavy burden of mortgage debt left over from the war boom.

■ GOVERNMENT AID TO AGRICULTURE

From folk myths to cowboy films, the public seems always to have hated a landlord and loved a farmer, and perhaps this attitude has fostered the fairly widespread public support for farm aid. Even the skeptical 1969 Task Force on Agriculture, while asserting that agriculture should be "much as any other industry," proposes a complex list of boards and programs that is consistent with our history of politically inspired government assistance to farmers.[3]

Prior to the Great Depression of the 1930s, governments gave agriculture aid in almost every form except in the marketing or pricing of farm products. Even

---

[3] See the comprehensive *Canadian Agriculture in the Seventies*, Report of the Federal Task Force on Agriculture (Ottawa: Information Canada, December 1969).

Much of the historical and descriptive material in this section, and in the next, are background for the understanding of supply and demand, especially as applied to Canadian agriculture. Some readers may prefer to skip forward to the important price supports section on page 502.

this is not quite true: each province's department of agriculture, in company with the federal government, has long done what it could for rural areas. Three stages must be recognized: (1) There was a long period, up to the 1890s, when the government fought to get Canadian farm products, such as cheese and wheat, into the American and British markets, at the same time attempting to keep foreign foods out. (2) Then there was the western boom of 1896-1913, when government went all out to survey and open the prairie lands; to get settlers farming; to get railways built to deliver the crops; and to open schools, experimental farms, and other services to improve crop yields and incomes. (By the end of 1930 practically every part of the prairies on which farming was then feasible was *within ten miles* of a railway!) (3) From the late 1900s till 1930, there was a period of agricultural political dominance in many parts of Canada: Farmers had legislative majorities almost everywhere, and United Farmers and Progressive parties were forces to be reckoned with in Ottawa and the provinces.

But the net effect of all this was indirect. Mostly the farmer sold his grain, or fruit, or daily products on markets that (apart from slight sheltering of sales in Canada by tariffs) were exposed to the chill winds of international competition. Apart from tariff bargaining, to make sure that foreign markets were open to Canadian foodstuffs, the government left the food export industry on its own.

GRAIN AND THE WHEAT BOARD   The first steps away from individual selling were taken by the farmers themselves, through grain pools and marketing boards. (The setting up of these organizations was partly responsible for the emergence of farmers' political parties in the 1920s.) Cooperation was a way of life as well as a method of business, and pool-movement leaders like A. J. McPhail had prestige that is rarely found in industry.

Pools and marketing boards had similar beginnings. Grain growers marketed through private "line elevator" companies at least one of which had a country elevator at each railway point. Farmers therefore often had only one buyer for their grain, and were suspicious that the group of line companies either held down the price to farmers, or took too large a share of the Winnipeg price as payment for their marketing and storing services. Some farmers started the Grain Growers' Grain Company to market farmers' grain on the Winnipeg Wheat Exchange, and a short time later many districts started cooperative local elevators to ship to the GGG Co. This complex eventually grew into the "wheat pool" of each prairie province.[4]

At first, under the general heading of the principles of cooperation, they aspired to only two goals: to organize one central selling agency that would "even-up the bargaining power" between buyers and sellers; and to create a system of mass storage, the costs of which would be shared, to hold much of the crop off the market in bumper-crop, low-price years, and to sell this "carry-over" in leaner, high-price years. But this would work only if they had unusual foresight. They had to be able to identify unusually large crops and unusually

[4] During World War I the government moved in to market the entire prairie crop in the 1917, 1918, and 1919 crop years. But the subsequent Mackenzie King and Meighen governments declined to resume this intervention.

low prices and further, to be able to predict the crop and price in the following year. If they did not, they might carry over the stored crop into another low-price year, incur storage costs, forgo income from the unsold stored wheat, and have to either dump the carried-over wheat onto a market where it would push down the world price further, or to carry over an even larger amount to next year. This situation actually arose. The pools decided to carry over into 1930 an amount which was actually over 50 per cent of the 1929 crop. But the next year there was an even lower grain price.

The alternative to a carry-over was to sell all the crop for the best price it could earn that year. But even here there were difficulties. The pools offered their members an "initial" payment of about two-thirds the expected selling price, at the time when members delivered their grain to the country elevators. Being a democratic organization and having the best interests of their members perhaps too close to their heart, about 1929 they began to pay "initial" installments that were almost equal to the final selling price for the crop. When the pools made the "final" payment to each member, they overpaid. The prairie governments had to step in to protect the banks who had loaned much of the initial payment. The same thing happened the next year, when the total price to the farmer, which had been between 75 cents and one dollar for the last five years, fell to *less* than 50 cents. The federal government stepped in, taking over the pools' central selling agency, and the pools reverted to merely running their cooperative elevators.

Note two things. Even at its strongest, the pool complex was never a wheat monopolist. One reason for this was that many farmers still sold through the line companies, thus competing down the Canadian price. A more important reason was that Canadian wheat was never more than a large competitor in the world wheat market. Even if every prairie farmer had delivered his grain to the pools, such *monopsony* (single wheat-buyer) power in Canada would not have given the agency *monopoly* (single wheat-seller) power in the world market.

Note also that the government's role was very limited. It was by this time highly committed to backing the pools. The provinces had created laws that put the pools into business; had provided inspection and investigation services; and, together with Ottawa, had bailed the pools out more than once. But these aids still left the farmers on their own.

The government did not in peacetime resume the buying-agency role it had briefly played in the first war. In 1935 it set up the Wheat Board, which offered to buy grain at "emergency" prices, somewhat below the price that it thought would be ruling when the crop came in. Thus it provided a sort of minimum price. Mostly, in the Great Depression, equilibrium prices were above this floor, and the Wheat Board had little delivered to it. But in 1938-1939, the Wheat Board's floor price was 80 cents and the market price was lower, so that almost the whole prairie crop was delivered to the Wheat Board, which did not dispose of it until wartime shortages developed. We'll see below how such floor price mechanisms work.

Nowadays, the Wheat Board still acts as single selling agency. Most of its wheat is sold to Western world markets at prices set by an International Wheat

Agreement (IWA) between the main exporting countries and almost 40 importing countries. (Since 1967 a new world grain agreement has had a similar role.)
The Board has also sold direct to the USSR and China.

What, then, is the role of the government in setting the price received by
grain growers? It joins other countries in setting official world wheat prices, but
it certainly does not set the world *market* price. It exercises firm control over
railway and storage facilities for wheat, thus probably gaining some "economies
of scale" that small co-ops or line companies could not achieve (though this is
disputed by private members of the Winnipeg Grain Exchange, who are now
largely confined to managing wheat disposal for the Wheat Board and dealing in
feed grains). When the Wheat Board refuses to sell at low world prices (in every
year from 1957 to 1960, carry-over exceeded sales), the government may help
with the enormous storage costs, or it may advance (not give) payments to producers for grain on the farm that cannot be delivered to the choked public elevators. Thus the subsidy to the grain grower is relatively small and indirect. The
Wheat Board sells; deducts its expenses and those of the transport, storage, and
milling; and, after a complex series of payments and adjustments, returns all the
residue to the farmer.

> Only rarely has the government controlled total planted acreage; it did so in 1941
> and in 1970. The 1970 scheme ("Operation LIFT") pays operators of up to 20
> million acres $6 per acre for summer-fallowing—i.e., not producing anything.
> Furthermore and more valuable, the Wheat Board, in deciding which wheat pro-
> ducers are to be allowed to deliver (sell) their wheat to the glutted elevators,
> heavily favors those who have increased fallow (for forage) acreage on their farms.
> The scheme may be the most ambitious ever seen: The aim is to cut crop acreage
> by more than three-quarters in one year. However, if farmers actually withdraw
> their lowest-yielding acreage, and if they increase cultivation on their remaining
> land, production might fall, say, only 40 per cent. (See page 507 for more on this
> tendency to operate at cross-purposes.)
>
> Apart from LIFT, and for the small pre-delivery subsidies, the Board and the
> governments have confined their roles to those of super-broker, barker, and
> advisor—not principal participant.[5]

■ MARKETING BOARDS

Although the "wheat-board radicals" had thoughts about controlling the price of
wheat, they have had little success. Marketing boards for other crops on the

---

[5] The Wheat Board is not the only form of government intervention in the grain trade.
The Board of Grain Commissioners runs some public elevators and has an important inspect-
ing and grading role. The Prairie Farm Assistance Act takes one per cent of all farmers' grain
prices on the prairies and pays it out to farmers in regions of temporarily low yield. The
fund was supposed to be self-liquidating, but since 1939, the federal government has had to
add almost as much as the farmers have paid in. Ottawa and the provinces run Crop Insurance Acts, but these so far cover less than 10,000 farmers altogether, who have preferred
this approach to the one per cent fund approach. Finally, since 1929, Ottawa has backed the
Crown's Farm Credit Corporation. Its loans average about $12,000, at 5 per cent interest, to
about 8,000 borrowers a year on mortgage-type loans up to 30 years. This low rate involves
a considerable subsidy to the borrowers, but less than 30,000 borrowers are heavily involved
at any one time. There is also a farm improvement loan plan where small loans (about
$2,000) are guaranteed by Ottawa.

other hand have been able to operate on Q, the amount supplied, so as to make the price higher than it would be otherwise.

Marketing boards go back a long way; but because they are mostly under provincial jurisdiction and operate on prices of produce for local consumption, they are less well known or nationally important than the grain organizations.[6]

Like the grain pools, marketing boards grew out of cooperation. Farmers who produce fruit, poultry, tobacco, vegetables (such as sugar beets, soybeans, and potatoes), honey, and some dairy products have wanted to control the marketing of their crops. They hope to cut down the distribution, storage, and selling expenses, create a larger demand, and bargain on more even terms with buyers, instead of being forced to accept the posted price of a local produce dealer. For most of them the market is within the same region, and their farming area is the lowest-cost source for that market.

Short-circuiting the long historical and legal chronicle, imagine that you are a farmer in a fruit area. Crops are good, but your per-bushel price barely covers your costs. You know that retailers a hundred miles away are selling your fruit at twice the price you get. How can you get a larger farm price?

1. You are only one of many farmers. The final market is strictly competitive. If you advertise your fruit, to get city folk to demand more, most of the advantage will, arithmetically, flow to other farmers and to your dealer, who may not offer you enough to repay you for your advertising. Clearly you have to get together with other sellers.

2. So you form a co-op. This way you can run your own advertising, buying, selling to wholesalers in the city, storage, and packing. Maybe you can do it as cheaply as your former dealer; maybe you even hire him to manage your co-op. But now there is one more buying plant, all plants including yours will have slightly less business, and the industry as a whole has excess buying and packing capacity. So overhead (fixed) costs of the whole industry will go up a bit. In a study of producers' co-ops, conducted for the Gordon Commission, Drummond and Mackenzie point out the moral: the fruit business had better be in an expanding stage or everyone's marketing costs will go up.

3. How can you get a larger share of that final price? You and private dealers need a slightly higher price to cover the greater costs. Anyway, you now are a major seller and can deal on even terms with the big city wholesale buyer. He offers you $1 per bushel for your fruit. You refuse, demanding $1.25. Now

---

[6] For over forty years, the constitutional position of marketing boards has swung back and forward between Ottawa and province. Usually, either government has been willing to accept jurisdiction. But opponents of the boards have fought their controls and "fees" by claiming that they were *ultra vires* (beyond the constitutional jurisdiction of) whatever government set them up; and often these opponents have won their court cases. The status of the boards is ambiguous because agricultural jurisdiction is rather uncertainly shared by both levels of government; because the products controlled are sometimes purely local but sometimes move in interprovincial trade; and because the "fees" collected to run the boards are sometimes declared by the courts to be indirect taxes (see page 206) on produce and so beyond provincial jurisdiction. After more than forty years, the legal questions are by no means cleared up; the framers of the BNA Act failed miserably to leave a constitutional peg for these bodies.

comes the test. If you have succeeded in getting enough members so that your co-op controls a large fraction of the total supply, he (or a competing wholesaler) will have to pay the price.[7] But if your group is small, you'll be left with your fruit unsold.

4. The problem now is that, if you get the price up to $1.25, you can do so only by holding back some from the market—by reducing your Q. This means that each member gets a high price on some of his fruit, but the rest of it must be stored for next year, sold for low-value uses (juice, jam, animal feed), or destroyed. You can guess how the typical member will respond: he'll withdraw from the co-op, and take his fruit to the old dealer who will buy his whole crop at a price just below the $1.25 you've set. Other members will do this too and, unless you take action, the whole market will settle down, gradually, to the old $1.00 price; and your co-op will have few members.

5. How can you prevent this erosion of the monopoly price you've managed to set? Early organizers tried evangelism for voluntary cooperation. Everyone must stick by the cooperative selling agency. Growers must pledge, in writing, to deliver all their fruit to the co-op. When this failed, they turned to the government.

6. The government, usually provincial, is helpful. It has a Marketing Board Act designed to convert your group into a monopoly. The government will conduct a vote among all the producers in the area. If a specified majority agree, a board will be formed, made up mostly of farmers in the region. When set up, they have authority to control the marketing of *all* the produce in the region. They are not co-ops, and may allow the produce to flow through both co-ops and private-dealer channels. But they will at least conduct a sort of "collective bargaining" with city buyers on terms, prices, and grades of produce. If they are more ambitious, like the pioneering Okanagan apple growers, they will make vigorous attempts to control wholesale price, not only by bargaining, but by holding produce off the market in storage. And they will undertake retail advertising to broaden the market (shift the demand curve to the right).

7. You may even want to follow the Ontario tobacco growers, whose marketing board sets maximum production quotas for its members. If you can't get the farmers in your region to agree to go that far, you may at least follow some of the milk boards, who set quotas on the amount they'll accept from each member for the "fluid-milk" market. Many farmers in their regions have no quotas, and so can sell no fluid milk at all. (They can sell milk to cheese factories, skim-milk plants, and ice-cream dairies. But the price paid is much lower than the "fluid-milk" price.)

---

[7] Assuming you did not set the price so high that the wholesalers could import fruit cheaper than $1.25. If you are wise, you have got your MP to persuade the government to ban the import of fruit during your marketing season. Even then, the wholesaler may bring fruit from a distant region of Canada. Finally, your $1.25 may be so high that he refuses, knowing that customers will buy little fruit at retail after he has added his costs to your price. That is, he knows the final market demand is very elastic. (Try drawing a diagram, adding the wholesaler's $1.00 costs to the various wholesale prices.)

Marketing boards are more pervasive than people realize. There are some 80 of them now, controlling about one-quarter of the nongrain trade in Canada. Obviously, they are most successful when the producers for a certain commodity are grouped together in one region, within one province, so that they can organize themselves completely.

Note that, with the exception of tobacco and some dairy boards, they do not control the amount produced. They attempt instead to bring about "orderly marketing" of whatever Q their members deliver. Some boards store nonperishable produce, releasing it when the price is better. But the rest merely bargain for the best price on whatever they have to sell that season.

The role of the government is chiefly to set up the mechanism and declare it to be legal. Otherwise, it would be a "combination in restraint of trade," preventing individual producers from trading at whatever price, with whatever buyer, they choose.[8] For, if the final demand curve for produce has any elasticity at all, marketing-board success in keeping up price is bound to require holding some produce back from the market. Whenever this happens, farmers are tempted to sell privately, thus undercutting the monopolistic price and causing it to fall. In the previous section, it was seen that this individualistic tendency was stopped in the grain trade by compelling all growers to deliver to the Wheat Board. The same is true of marketing boards: instead of subsidizing them, the government issues them a permit to set their own price, eliminating price-cutting by farmers in their own regions by compelling all to deliver produce where and when the board decides.

■ PRICE SUPPORTS

When most people speak of government aid to farming, they either confuse the grain marketing boards with some sort of government financial subsidy, or talk about price-support programs. These are very prevalent in the United States, affecting an enormous number of farmers, especially wealthy and efficient farmers. The general philosophy is clear enough. The years 1909-1914 are looked back upon as the golden age of agriculture. So over the years the U.S. government has been pressed to somehow make prices as relatively favorable as they were then.

Figure 20-1 shows how Canadian farmers have sold their produce for prices that since 1949 have risen less rapidly than the prices farmers, and their wives, have had to pay. If one pays attention only to the ratio of these two price indexes, one can of course make a strong case that farmers are being ill-treated by the economic system. "Parity" in the treatment of farm and nonfarm prices requires that farm prices be boosted to a higher level.

---

[8] Actually, few members of marketing boards make large or any profits. Why? First, boards are rarely set up until market prices have fallen well below profitable levels for most producers in the regions. Second, if a monopoly profit is made and distributed, new producers flock in until it is dissipated in new capacity. The boards with quotas (tobacco and milk) try to prevent this by restricting the amount (Q) they will accept; their most efficient members do make some profit.

But deeper analysis shows that the attempt to peg farm prices at an arbitrary high level will result in an avalanche of surplus farm goods, and it has done so in every country that has supported prices. (Show the gap between the $s's'$ and $d'd'$ of Fig. 20-2 at prices kept higher than E', and show how that gap will grow over time.) The dollar costs of aid become astronomical. The distortions of production become cumulatively greater and greater. Thus the government storage bins are bursting, and policy-makers' time is spent working out new schemes to store the produce in emergency granaries, or on the farm, or give it away (preferably abroad, where it will not take some of the market and shift the demand curve to the left).

Compared to wasteful U.S. price-support programs, Canadian farm price-supports are pretty modest. But the same principles are involved, and occasionally, for certain products, the government has been caught in the same trap. So, although Canadian agriculture is *not* dominated by the U.S. parity system (nor by another U.K. price-escalation system), it is worth examining details of price-support programs.

We have already seen the real reason for the failure of farm prices to keep up with other prices.[9] Technical progress has simply been more rapid on the farm than in town. A recent study by L. Auer of the Economic Council of Canada has been summarized thus:[10]

> "Labour productivity in Canadian agriculture has advanced over the past two decades at nearly 6 per cent per year. . . . Over one-third of this gain has been associated with the movement of workers out of agriculture.[11] Another third is attributable to increased capital and materials inputs, and the balance to other productivity improvements [such as new varieties of crops and new farming techniques]."

City production of manufactured goods has also shown some improvements in efficiency, but nothing like this. So why in the world should city and farm items swap in a constant, "parity," ratio? If they did, the falling, relative real costs of farm products would create huge profits from increasing farm production, and the city would be swamped by extra food supplies. But, as Figure 20-1

---

[9] The discussion refers to the ability of Canadian farms to supply more and more food at the old real costs. In addition, it must always be remembered that Canada sells on international food markets. Each foreign competing supplier is also getting increases in productivity. And, for many products, there is an increasing number of competing countries.

[10] L. Auer, *Canadian Agricultural Productivity*, Staff Study No. 24, Economic Council of Canada, December 1969 (Queen's Printer, Ottawa, 1970), p. 39. Reproduced with the permission of Information Canada.

[11] The significance of this movement is explained on page 29 of the same publication from which the above quotation was taken. The explanation given is the following: "The most significant contribution to growth in labour productivity has come through adjustments in agricultural employment. Today, compared with two decades ago, a substantially greater output is produced by substantially fewer farmers. As older farmers have retired and many of the younger farm people have found employment in the nonagricultural sector, some of the marginal farm land has been abandoned or has reverted to forest land and some of the better farm land has been absorbed into larger farm units. Through further mechanization, the enlarged farm units could often be operated without additional farm labour."

shows, they didn't. The growing relative efficiency of farm production led to a fall in farm prices, which is what champions of farm price-support programs want to prevent.

The Agricultural Prices Support Act was passed in 1944, to help farmers adjust from the war to peace-time economies. In 1958 it was superseded by the act that established today's Agricultural Stabilization Board, or ASB.

For a list of nine commodities (three meats; three nonprairie grains; and butter, cheese, and eggs) the ASB is required to support the price. At what level? Not at the 1914 parity-ratio level, but at least at 80 per cent of the average price each has sold at over the previous ten years.

The ASB may also, on instruction, support other prices at any percentage of this ten-year base that the Cabinet decides. Over the years, fourteen commodities have appeared at one time or another on the ASB's noncompulsory, cabinet-decided list.

The ASB was given a fund of 250 million dollars to work with in 1958. In the early 1960s it was spending about 55 million dollars per year, mostly in two types of price support: government purchase of selected products, and government deficiency payments to producers of other products. These are explained below.

■ FORMS OF INTERVENTION IN FARM PRICING

What are the economic mechanisms by which the government can help, or seem to help, the farmer? We have seen that the marketing schemes now in effect require government permission, because they do what combinations of producers in other industries are forbidden to do: they join together to attempt to fix prices. We have also seen that price-support programs exist, in which the government makes a direct subsidy transfer to the growers of certain crops. Altogether, there are five types of cases:

1. Outright *gift* or relief payments, given to needy farmers who have established their need and misery.

2. Government programs that aim to increase the demand for farm products or cut their real costs of production.

3. Marketing-board programs that aim to cut the amount supplied and so raise price (i.e. to cut by the use of quotas or by limiting the acreage planted, the amount delivered to the board, or to cut the amount offered by the board to the market by getting rid of or storing part of what has been delivered to it).

4. Price supports that involve the government's buying, storing, and reselling the product.

5. Price supports that require the government to make up the "deficiency" in prices, but not to buy or hold the produce. In the United States, this type of action is named after Secretaries of Agriculture Benson and Brannan.

Case 1. Gifts and relief. There is nothing complicated about outright gifts or transfer payments, which might well be adjoined to our social security system or be part of Chapter 38's negative income tax. The organized farm pressure groups do not particularly want such aids, even though in strictest economic logic they may be the most defensible of all: If our nation wants to alleviate the burden on farmers (or the poor anywhere!) and provide minimum standards, outright gifts will clarify exactly what is involved and what it costs, thereby enabling the electorate to decide rationally what it wants to accomplish.

The dislike of farm pressure groups for gift or relief programs is not surprising, for the successful farmers who tend to constitute the pressure groups number less than one-eighth of all farmers but produce more than one-third of the value of farm output! On the other end of the ladder, almost one-half of the farmers sell less than $5,000 worth of produce a year and produce less than one-fifth of the amount of all crops sold each year. Most of them are in poverty; those who are not too old work much of the year off the farm at other jobs. A large number of programs (including the prairie farmers' own assistance act) reach out to help these people. But the current belief is that the long-run solution to the rural poverty problem is not in relief crop support programs. (The crops of poor farmers are too small to bring them much cash.) Rather, the solution lies in farm renewal and farmer resettlement (discussed later, see page 512).

Case 2. Demand promotion and research. After the post office and national defense departments, agriculture is the biggest employer in the federal government. In addition, each province has an agriculture department and one or more colleges of agriculture. Each of these institutions is searching for ways to make farming more profitable or more pleasant. Some of the employees are directly engaged in promoting markets, but most work in labs or directly with farmers, introducing new methods and varieties of produce. The success of the Department's science service in developing rust-resistant wheat is well-known; and similar services are provided for other crops. (At a recent count, slightly less than half the economists in government service were in the Department of Agriculture!)

Farms are still small business, and research and promotion for such firms can hardly be expected to be conducted by the farmers themselves. True, some new processes, fertilizers, and implements are developed for profit by manufacturers, and explained to the farmers. But the government does the rest. Some observers find it odd that much of government is encouraging reduced production or sales, and financing the evacuation of farms, while another branch is trying to increase productivity.

ECONOMICS OF THREE MAIN PRICE PROGRAMS　To understand the remaining three programs, our economic tools of supply and demand are absolutely necessary. Let us see how each case works.

Case 3. Sales or crop restriction. We have seen how marketing boards attempt to monopolize their local markets for vegetables or dairy products or fruit. The stronger ones, by the use of quotas, actually reduce (or prevent the increase of) production. The rest try to sell all that is delivered, but in a given year they may hold some off the market, storing it or consigning it to a low-price use (such as the milk that is delivered to factories and so does not enter the fluid-milk market).

In our diagrams, the hold-back of produce from the market is seen to be identical in effect to the restriction of production. If farmers sell (or produce) a smaller total Q, they will each receive a higher P. Because the demand for farm products is generally inelastic, limiting Q will actually *raise* the total revenues received by farmers—as the last chapter showed. Of course, consumers will be hurt by a scarcity of goods and by higher prices, just as they would be if a disaster such as a flood or a drought created a scarcity of foodstuffs. And it can be shown that many of the methods used to cut down on Q—such as holding wheat acres down to a quota, but leaving farmers free to use tremendous doses of fertilizer to expand production on the quota land—will lead to inefficient use of resources in producing the reduced Q.

To the extent that some of the benefits from the monopolistically contrived higher prices accrue to poverty-stricken farm families, there may be certain Robin Hood-like social gains to offset the social costs: current farm suffering may be alleviated; and some of the benefit may be used to get the young people out of low-productivity agriculture.

On the other hand, some of the desirable long-run shifts out of agriculture, and economic adjustments, may be slowed down by the sales-restricting boards and programs. Figure 20-3 tells its own story:

A cut in supply raises price and total revenue:

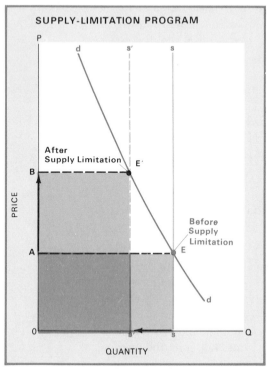

FIG. 20-3. Before government intervenes, the ss supply curve intersects the inelastic dd curve at the low price shown at E. As an individual competitor, each farmer has no motive to do anything to improve the situation. But if all together can form a marketing board to put monopolistic limits on their total Q, they can benefit.

When controls cut supply from ss to $s's'$, P rises to E'. Because demand is inelastic, total gross farm income is thereby increased. (Recall that $P \times Q$ revenues at E and E' are measured, respectively, by the $OsEA$ and $Os'E'B$ rectangular areas. Let your eye confirm that the gain in E' height over E outweighs the rectangle's loss in width; with elastic demand, the reverse would have been true.)

If a crop is sold on a market in which the demand is inelastic, reducing the amount offered on the market will bring not only a higher price, but also higher total receipts to farmers.

This is what we learn from supply-and-demand diagrams. What do such higher receipts mean to farming? Low-efficiency farms, which, at the lower price *E* would have had to turn to other crops or shut down altogether, are able to stay in production. If they had made the "adjustment" (of shutting down or turning to other crops), resources of labor, land, and capital would be reapplied to making or growing other things that society wants. But the higher farm receipts at *E'* frustrate this adjustment.

In terms of the production-possibility frontier of Fig. 2-3 (page 26), a sales-reduction program means that society is pushed *inside* the producible frontier. Not only is it getting less of the restricted-sales crop, but it is also not reallocating resources to produce something else.[12] Society is deliberately shifting economic resources away from places that produce the extra goods which people's dollar votes in the market place show they really want. Either those resources go into idleness, as occurs with land no longer cultivated, or they may go into secondary uses for which they are ill-fitted and which involve producing items that people do not much want.

Does the raising of farmers' receipts mean that sales restriction is bad? Not necessarily, since noneconomic ethical and political issues are also involved. But going *inside* the production frontier does mean that each bit of benefit to some farmers is bought at the price of a reduction in the output and income of *all* society. This sacrifice is more than economically and technically needed to raise farmers' receipts by a stated amount. It does suggest that society look around for *more efficient* methods.

Case 4.   Price support through government purchase.   This case, exemplified by our long experience with support of butter prices, is a little harder. Now the ASB guarantees the farmer a price higher than would have prevailed in the market. This "floor price" is shown by the black line *BB'* in Fig. 20-4. At so high a price, consumers will not buy all the butter supplied. Consumers will be on the demand curve at the point *C*. But farmers are supplying the full amount

---

[12] Of course, it is not uncommon in North America to restrict acreage and planting, rather than sales after production. When, in addition, farmers restrict supply because they are *paid* not to produce, they gain both ways. Under Operation LIFT, for example, revenue gained from output restriction is $6 per acre for all the acres that formerly yielded the supply between *Os* and *Os'* which have now been taken out of production.

Such schemes, whether subsidized or not, have side-effects that may be valuable: Soil conservation may be achieved if land gets a rest. They may also trigger some population exodus from rural regions. But prolonged study has shown that something different happens: the higher prices induce farmers to put the same amount, or even more, of labor or capital on the restricted acreages. Thus their *output does not fall*, though the cost of delivering a certain tonnage of crop usually goes up. They are now using more of society's resources than before, which means that there, too, society is pushed *inside* the production frontier by the acreage-restriction program. (LIFT is supposed to avoid these perils by running for only a year or so.)

Government purchases support price by acquiring unsold surplus:

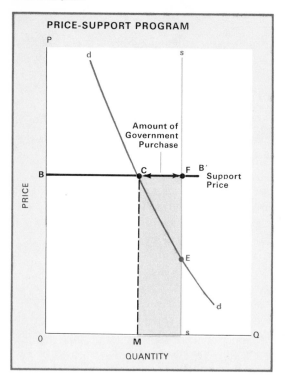

PRICE-SUPPORT PROGRAM

Amount of Government Purchase

FIG. 20-4. The government keeps price at indicated floor or support price *BB'* by acquiring for storage unsellable surplus shown by *CF.* The shaded area shows the total cost to the government of raising market price from *E* to *F.* Note that domestic consumers pay the higher price and get no current benefit from the *CF* part of the crop.

shown by the point *F.* If government does nothing, price must fall to *E,* which is below the support price (80 per cent of the average price in the last ten years).

So what must the ASB do? By outright purchase it must acquire the unsold portion between *C* and *F,* marked with an arrow. This will either go into cold storage, or be dumped abroad (as part of foreign aid perhaps), or (in the case of some types of perishable product) be left to rot. What, then, has been the final result?

The government has increased the price received by farmers from *E* to *F.* But unlike the sales-restriction case, the farmers can now sell as much as they want to; so the increased price is clear gravy to them, representing a clear increase in their incomes. The consumers are now paying a higher price and buying less; to them Case 4 is just as bad as Case 3.[13] Who then is footing the bill for the extra income now received by the farmers? Obviously the govern-

---

[13] The last two sentences need to be modified. In practice, the ASB can set quotas on the amount of output from each farm for which they will support the price (or make deficiency payments in Case 5). And, if farmers are allowed to sell as much as they want to at the supported price, they presumably do so efficiently. If so, society is not *inside* its production-possibility curve as it was in Case 3. It is merely too far east on it, producing more of the supported crop than dollar votes call for.

ment: The Treasury is having to shell out its tax receipts equal to the part of the butter output they must buy times the full market price. (In terms of area, the Treasury's expense is shown by the shaded area *CFsM*. Can you explain why?)

Of course, if the demand curve *dd* were in later years to shift upward so that it intersected the supply curve at *F* or above, then the treasury would not have to intervene to ensure the supported price. Indeed, it might in such a prosperous year exactly reverse the procedure; instead of buying part of the butter output to put it in cold storage, it might withdraw some from cold storage and sell it. The interested reader can draw a new *d'd'*, to see how stabilization works.

Case 5. "Deficiency" price supports. This is the hardest case of all; it is in all respects similar to the Benson-Brannan scheme in the United States. In Canada it has been used to support the prices of beets, potatoes, and eggs. Butter and other products, however, have been supported by the programs outlined in Case 4 above.

In a "deficiency-payment" program, the farmer is again guaranteed a support price *BB'*, just as in Case 4. But Fig. 20-5 must now show the new fact that

"Deficiency" plan pays farmers gap between actual consumer's price and producer's supported price:

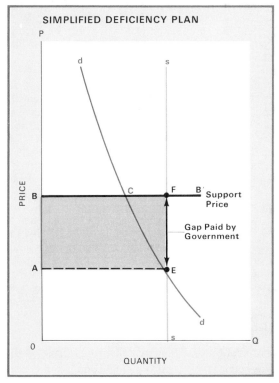

FIG. 20-5. The government lets price to consumer fall to *E*. It then makes up, by direct payments to farmers of *EF* per ton, the difference between the low market price and the desired support price. Farmers end up with total price return shown at *F*. The shaded area shows the cost to government of the direct payments involved in such a two-price system.

food, instead of being left in storage, is to be resold to the public for current consumption at whatever market price it will bring.

How is the farmer to receive the support price if market price proves to be below that figure? The ASB *simply writes him a cheque for the difference*. In effect, then, it is much as though the government had bought the crop at the support price—as in the support of Case 4—but had then sold it on the open market for whatever price it would bring.

Every bit produced, as shown by the *ss* supply curve, will now go to the consumer. Consumption will end up at the original point E. Why? Because the "law of supply and demand" tells us that, for consumers to buy the full crop, price must fall to the point where the demand curve intersects the market supply. But producers are promised the support price for their entire crop. So the price they are to receive is indicated by F (just as in Case 4). Who pays the difference? The government—by sending each primary producer a cheque, whose amount per ton is shown in Fig. 20-5 by the vertical arrow EF.

How much does this cost the government? The answer is clear, once we realize that the government must pay the difference between the producer's and consumer's price *on each and every unit produced!* (In terms of area, the expense to the government is the shaded rectangular area ABFE. Here the shaded rectangle goes all the way leftward to the price axis, whereas back in Case 4 the shaded rectangle of government expense went all the way downward to the quantity axis.)

> An important but tricky question is the following: Will the "deficiency" plan of Case 5 cost the Treasury more or less than would the plan of having the government withhold from the consumers part of the crop as outlined in Case 4? The answer to this complicated question turns out to depend upon our old friend the elasticity of demand and upon nothing else.
>
> Look at the problem this way: Under either plan the *producers* are equally well off, being at F in both cases and receiving the same total income. Remember, too, that under either plan the producer's revenue can come from only two sources: the total revenue paid by the consumers plus the government's contribution. Hence, to answer the question, "Which plan costs the government more dollars?" we need only to answer the much simpler question, "Which plan collects the greater total revenue from consumers: the plan where the consumers pay a high price and buy little or the plan where consumers pay a low price and buy much?"
>
> But note: this is nothing but the question we have met repeatedly in connection with the definition of elasticity. A point high upon the demand curve, such as C, will collect more total revenue than a point low down, such as E, provided the demand is *inelastic* in that interval. If demand were *elastic*, then the reverse would be true.
>
> So now we can answer the question of relative cost as follows: The "deficiency" plan of making more food available to consumers will currently cost the Treasury more money than will a purchase-for-storage-or-destruction program provided the demand curve is *inelastic*. If it had been *elastic*, the reverse would have been true. (Of course, wasteful storage costs militate against Case 4.)

From the standpoint of political economy, a plan which brings price to the consumer more nearly down to the social cost of producing food would have much to be said for it even if it should happen to result in costing the Treasury more money. If farmers are to get the same income by one way or the other, the important thing to us consumers is not so much how we divide our payments between market purchases and taxes as that food be produced and consumed up to the point where utilities and costs are more nearly in balance.[14]

■ ISSUES IN FARM AID

Roughly speaking, the history of Canadian farm policy has been a movement through these three cases. But not in exact sequence: at the present time much of the farm output is still under marketing boards (Case 3), while there is an increasing tendency to help farmers by "deficiency" payments (Case 5). The prolonged butter surplus (Case 4) made housewives aware that they paid more for this fat than for the competing margarine at a time when butter stocks were glutting the cold-storage warehouses, being dumped abroad, or being processed down into low-value butter oil, for sale to industry. This made the scheme unpopular. Once the subsidy was explicit, farmers also became critical. And foreign butter producers, sometimes observing that Canada was dumping subsidized butter in their markets, became very unfriendly.

Canada had, until February 1970, avoided acreage-limitation schemes of the type long favored in the United States. However, faced with a record wheat surplus, the government attempted to deal with it by offering western farmers some 140 million dollars to remove from production 22 million acres (which yielded most of the western wheat crop) during 1970. In effect, the farmers are paid *not* to produce. Like the sales-limitation scheme of Case 3, this scheme should tend to raise wheat prices. But, will the Canadian Government find, as its U.S. counterpart did, that acreage limitation does not necessarily reduce yields or harvests? Of course, the sheer magnitude of the plan should serve to limit the wheat crop—so few western acres are to remain in cultivation. In comparison, the marketing board approach is much less effective *potentially*, because most boards have not the power to reduce deliveries to them; but it is perhaps more workable, because the farmers themselves have the responsibility of setting the price and disposing of any unsold surpluses. The fact remains that, to the extent that either the acreage-limitation or the sales-limitation version of Case 3 is effective, it brings increased receipts to farmers by a hidden sales tax on food rather than by glaring subsidy items in the federal budget.

Farmers are active politically. They have had their own political parties; they have powerful organizations like the Canadian Federation of Agriculture, the pools, and the Farmers' Union to make their case in Ottawa; and they have long held the privilege of having the federal minister of agriculture appointed from a prairie constituency to the cabinet. (A notable exception was Ontario MP J. J. Greene who served as Minister of Agriculture between 1965 and 1969.) But

---

[14] If ss were drawn more realistically so as to be somewhat rightward-sloping, we should have the evil of too much Q being coaxed out by the too-high government subsidy; consumers would be getting too much farm Q at a P below true social costs of resources used.

they are not in complete agreement on which type of income-assistance they want. Nor do the main political parties present a coherent or lasting platform. As in the United States, each new government has tended to experiment with new types of farm aid, while maintaining much of the structure set up by earlier governments.

With this political power (now being mobilized in Eastern Canada, with aims different from those of the prairie blocs), farmers count on being able to get, one way or another, support from the politicians against the worst vicissitudes of free pricing. They apparently want handouts, but they do not like them to be obvious, preferring that they appear in the guise of market "earnings."

■ WHAT ECONOMIC ANALYSIS CAN SUGGEST

As other chapters in Part Three demonstrate, there is often a strong case for sticking to the competitive market's outcome. There are two main exceptions: (1) when the people who gain from government interference in the market are for some reason strongly preferred to those who lose; and (2) when it can be shown that there is no better way of helping them out of general taxes. How does this apply to the farm problem?

Are the gainers people whom we want to help? Many tough-minded economists would argue that much of the benefit of marketing boards, the Wheat Board, and price-support programs now goes to the most prosperous commercial farmers. Too little filters down to the really poor farmers, who have little production to support. Economists favor programs which extend to farmers in a more efficient way whatever aid it is decided they ought to have—so as to leave the rest of us with more than we now get. Such programs would involve more careful pinpointing of those who merit aid from the standpoint of need—as through a negative income tax.

In such a turnabout there would be three elements: the system of pricing farm produce; the "adjustment" of the agricultural part of society to changing demands; and the aid paid to those who could not adjust without hardship.

PRICING FARM PRODUCTS   There would be more reliance on market forces in determining food and fiber prices. As farm productivity increased or demand failed to grow fast enough, prices would be allowed to fall. Consumers generally would be able to afford more food, and especially more of the expensive protein foods such as milk and meat. Commercial farmers would feel pressure on them to become more efficient, and many of the remaining farm families would find their incomes below what they could earn in industry or in the service occupations.

HELPING FARM "ADJUSTMENT"   The price system would thus tend to drive people into new types of farming and off the farm altogether. This is a familiar process: farm boys have been migrating to the cities for decades. The labor force began to fall about 1930, though in the Depression it was easier to keep alive on the land than in the city. After the war, the migration began in earnest. By 1970 the farm labor force was just one-third of what it had been in 1941. Then it had made up one-quarter of the total national labor force, but this fraction has since been reduced to one-sixteenth, or about 450,000 workers. Those remaining on the land have tended to use it more intensively (putting in more machine hours and fertilizers per acre) and more extensively (doubling farm size). This is, of course, one reason why productivity has climbed so fast.

But many persons are unable to "adjust" to these new methods. They have not the youthful flexibility, nor the capital, nor the skill to become successful commercial farmers, no matter how hard they work. Neither have they the adaptability to move away into industry. This is the "adjustment" problem. Left alone, their income drops annually and rural slums develop.

Helping farmers to adjust has recently become a top-priority item on the government's agenda. Since World War I, the government has given advice on new crops and methods, has helped to pay for land clearing and improvement, and has acted as an increasingly liberal lender of farm-improvement capital. In 1961 the Diefenbaker government introduced ARDA (Agricultural Rehabilitation and Development Act), and the succeeding government expanded it, to study, promote, and subsidize better land use, and to strengthen the depopulated rural communities. Perhaps more important, other government programs are coming to grips with the retraining of farm youth and older farmers, some for continued work on the land, and many for the cities. Transport and removal expenses are sometimes offered by Ottawa, and the provinces are spending 30 to 40 million dollars each year on this approach. But much remains to be done, especially for older farm families, or those without education. "Adjustment" may be for them a process of going on the relief roll.

FARM AID   Noncommercial farmers who could not adjust would be left behind by a market-determined set of farm prices. In the turnabout of farm policy, they would have to be helped—not so much because they live on the farm, but for the same reason that government welfare aid is given to any families that are in poverty. Economists believe that most farm aid recipients would be over 45 or 50 years of age. In many parts of Canada, they would probably be encouraged to keep their homes and a little land, but to release most of their acreage to neighbors who could consolidate small holdings into workable farm enterprises.

The economists who stress these three elements say:

In terms of resource allocation, the Canadian consumer so little values an extra unit of food relative to other things, and our technology so easily permits us to produce an extra unit of food, that it is most worthwhile for us to equate supply and demand for food at low prices—at prices low enough to coax resources out of agriculture and into industry. There they will produce things for which there is a demand in the form of consumers' money votes unbuttressed by artificial government aids.[15] Resources should be forced out and attracted out of agriculture. The transitional distress should be alleviated by outright subsidies to aid "adjustment" and to

[15] Refer to page 480 for a graph of the argument that uninterfered-with pricing has a property of being "efficient," even if not necessarily "equitable."

relieve hardship. But these subsidies should not add to "inefficient distortion of production, and should (like aid to veterans) be designed to taper off after a number of years. Human suffering merits the same aid anywhere.

THE LONG-RUN SOLUTION?

Does all this sound cruel and heartless—hard-boiled? It is perhaps too extreme in giving too little weight to the argument that a civilization is happier when it seeks to protect any group in it from *sudden and drastic* changes in status.

But government cannot stand back and expect the farm-price problem to go away. Increasing technological capacity and stronger foreign competition continue to mean that fewer and fewer persons are needed as farmers. It has been a convenient thing that the inelasticity of consumer demand has lent itself to raising farm receipts, by holding back produce from consumers. But the "deficiency" approach is itself an admission that government cannot solve farm distress by holding up final prices. In the long run, farmers must turn to other crops or leave the land. When this is understood, the role of government will become at most one of stabilization of farm incomes.[16]

RURAL POVERTY

Looked at properly, Canada's real farm problem is that of rural poverty. Real incomes on the farm and in small towns average far below those elsewhere: 840,000 people fell below the poverty line in 1970. Although less than 30 per cent of the population is rural, approximately 40 per cent of the impoverished live in the country. Silently, invisibly, they lead miserable lives in the Maritimes and Quebec, where most of the rural poor are concentrated.

Solutions for them will not come from the mechanisms of supply and demand. The solutions must come—as Chapters 38 and 40 show—from transfer-payment programs, from education subsidies, from relocation and retraining, and from family-planning clinics. The mixed economy, and not *laissez-faire*, must provide the solutions.

SUMMARY

■ 1 Although the rural birth rate is higher than the urban, a persistent city-ward migration means that the percentage of the population engaged in agriculture is declining. Improvements in agricultural techniques mean that supply increases greatly and that the same total of food can be produced

---

[16] All this will remain for a long time a political issue. No one will begrudge the farmer his desire to be free from wildly fluctuating prices. In the Appendix we shall see how private speculators on an organized exchange are supposed in traditional theory to be able to iron out any *foreseeable* fluctuations. The question remains whether, gifts aside, we can expect the government to make better forecasts of the uncertain future than private speculative market can, and whether we can expect the government, through its various support programs, to be better than private markets in stabilizing prices.

with fewer workers; also, as incomes increase, the demand for food increases less than proportionately.

So free-equilibrium prices tend to fall. Farm income tends to be both low and unstable; as a result, government adopted a variety of programs to support farm-product prices and maintain farm incomes.

■ 2 Pegging prices at any ancient average ratio, despite its superficial plausibility and fairness, utterly disregards basic changes in demand and real costs of production. As time passes, such a ratio will produce prices differing sharply from "natural competitive" levels here and abroad. The results are huge surpluses, with the wrong goods being produced with growing distortions of efficiency.

■ 3 Aid programs involving (1) direct gifts or (2) promotion of demand and of cost research require no deep economic analysis. But the tools of supply and demand are needed to understand these three aid programs: (3) sales by marketing boards; (4) government price support by storage programs; (5) resale to consumers at competitive market prices of food bought at a pegged price, with the government footing the bill for the "deficiency." (Hybrids of all three are frequently legislated.) The resulting programs are colossally expensive, economically inefficient, and satisfactory to no groups.

■ 4 Because high and inflexible price support causes storage to grow astronomically and sends the government's aid costs skyward, Case 4 in practice leads to more and more of Case 3. (Farmers like 4 and accept 3 only as a necessary evil; consumers dislike 3 and 4, but like 5.)

■ 5 The long-run solution must involve maintenance of prosperity outside agriculture, so that people can continue to move to the lines of highest productivity and so that demand for agriculture will be optimally high. But mere prosperity in industry is not enough. The 1920s and 1970s show that the city and town can prosper while the country's economic position deteriorates.

In the long run, resources have to be helped to move out of low-efficiency rural uses and into more productive uses. That means a continuation of the trend toward fewer but more efficient farmers, and a need for short-run aids to help and speed the adjustment to this trend and to ease its human burdens. It also means flexible pricing practices that permit efficient Canadian farms to help feed the world. And, as Chapter 39 shows, the rural exodus creates urban problems elsewhere.

QUESTIONS FOR DISCUSSION

1. Contrast long-term and cyclical patterns of agriculture and industry.
2. Describe government indirect and direct farm aids.
3. Why might limiting a farm's acreage in one crop not reduce the total of it much? How would it affect noncontrolled crops? Fertilizer demand?
4. Use the p-p frontier concept to evaluate harm from farm aid.

5. "Major premise: Society should help poor people. Minor premise (of doubtful validity as stated): Farmers are poor people. (Dubious) Conclusion: Therefore society should help farmers. Actually, if society is to subsidize individuals, it should not be done on the basis of the occupations but because they are *poor—i.e.*, aid on an *income basis*." Does this argument by Professor Dudley Johnson fit with the 1969 Task Force on Agriculture's recommended income boosts that are restricted to the poorest and oldest *farmers*?

6. Review your understanding of the following concepts:

inelastic farm demand and supply
farm technology and declining
   percentage of income spent
   on food
free-farm-price trends
marketing boards
deficiency payments

Q limitation, P support, direct payments
   with consumer and producer P's
   different
pros and cons of free farm prices
long- and short-run solutions
adjustment problems
rural poverty

Appendix: Economics of Speculation, Risk, Insurance, and Conservation

Here we apply the tools of supply and demand to analyze price relations across space and time and the important problems involved in risk, speculation, and gambling. We deal not only with the purchase and sale of actual commodities such as corn or barley, but also with the purchase and sale of something more mysterious—of bits of paper.

These bits of paper are called "commodity futures": they are contracts that brokers deal with on organized commodity exchanges like the Chicago Board of Trade or the Winnipeg Grain Exchange. You and I may buy or sell such commodity futures even though we have never seen any real barley or corn. As speculators in such futures, the last thing in the world we should want to happen would be for a truck to roll up to our door seeking delivery of real honest-to-goodness commodities.

Yet, as we shall see, even though speculators never touch the real thing, they may under certain conditions be helping to even out the consumption of the crop between harvest times and be helping to carry over the proper amount of grain and fiber between seasons.

In his autobiography, the elder statesman Bernard Baruch said that ten years after he heard Professor George B. Newcomb lecture on supply and demand at City College of New York, he had made more than a million dollars from speculation—implying

that those lectures may have had something to do with it. Certainly, this Appendix is not designed to make you rich, and if you skip it, your knowledge of the rest of the book need not suffer much. But speculation is a fascinating topic and can serve as an example of important applications of supply and demand. Inevitably, it is a complicated subject which no elementary book can pretend to treat completely.

■ GEOGRAPHICAL PRICE PATTERNS

In a well-organized competitive market, there tends to be at any one time and place a single prevailing price. This is due to the action of professional speculators or "arbitragers" who keep their ear to the market and, as soon as they learn of any price differences, buy at the cheaper price and sell at the dearer price, thereby making a profit for themselves—at the same time tending to equalize the price.[1]

Two markets at a considerable distance from each other may have different prices. Wheat in Winnipeg

[1] On the floor of the Winnipeg Grain Exchange, the important market for grain, a number of important "pit brokers," or dealers, are said to make all their profits on price changes within each day, closing out all their transactions every night and sleeping peacefully until the next day. "Pit scalpers" on the floor of the Chicago Board of Trade, and specialists at the New York Stock Exchange act similarly.

may sell for a few cents more per bushel than identical wheat in Regina, because of shipping, insurance, and interest charges involved in transportation. If ever the price in Winnipeg should rise by more than the few cents of shipping costs, speculators will buy in Regina and ship to Winnipeg, thereby bringing the price up in Regina and down in Winnipeg to the normal maximum differential.

Nobody legislates these patterns. They follow from supply and demand.

■ SPECULATION AND PRICE CONTROL OVER TIME

In an ideal competitive market there tends to be a definite pattern of prices over time just as there is over space. But the difficulties of predicting the future make this pattern a less perfect one: we have an equilibrium that is constantly being disturbed but is always in the process of reforming itself—rather like the ocean's surface under the play of the winds.

STABILIZING SEASONAL PATTERNS Consider the simplest case of a grain, like barley, that is harvested at one period of the year. This crop must be made to last all the year if privation is to be avoided. Since no one passes a law regulating the storage of grain, how is this desirable state of affairs brought about? Through the attempts of speculators to make a profit.

A well-informed speculator who is a specialist in this grain realizes that, if all the grain is thrown on the market in the autumn, it will fetch a very low price because of the glutting of the market. On the other hand, months later, with almost no grain coming on the market, price will tend to skyrocket.

The above description tells what would tend to happen were it not for the action of speculators. Speculators realize that by (1) purchasing some of the autumn crop while it is cheap, (2) withholding it in storage; and (3) selling it later when the price has risen, they can make a profit. This they do. But in doing so, they increase the autumn demand for grain and raise its autumn price; and they increase the spring supply of grain and lower its spring price. At the same time that they are equalizing the price over the year, they are also equalizing the supply coming on the market in each month—which is as it should be.

Moreover, if there is brisk competition among speculators, none will make an excessive profit over the costs that he incurs (including of course the wages necessary to keep him in this line of activity). The speculator himself may never touch an ear of barley, nor need he know anything about storage, warehouses, or delivery. He merely buys and sells bits of paper. But the effect is exactly as described.

Now there is one and only one monthly price pattern that will result in neither profits nor losses. A little thought will show that it will not be a pattern of constant prices. Rather, the ideal price pattern will involve lowest prices in the autumn and then gradually rising prices until the peak is reached just before the new corn comes in. The price must rise from month to month to compensate for the storage and interest costs of carrying the crop in storage—in exactly the same way that the price must rise over space from one mile to the next to compensate for

For a good to be stored, expected price rise must match storing cost:

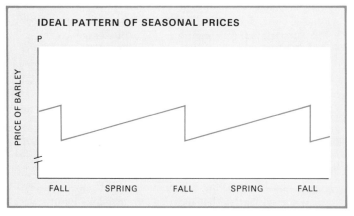

IDEAL PATTERN OF SEASONAL PRICES

P

PRICE OF BARLEY

FALL   SPRING   FALL   SPRING   FALL

FIG. 20-6. Ideally, P is lowest at harvest time, rising gently with accumulated storage costs until the next harvest. This flexible pattern tends to even out consumption over the seasons—as compared with a harvest glut with very low autumn price and summer scarcity with sky-high price.

the cost of transportation.[2] Figure 20-6 shows the behavior of prices over an idealized yearly cycle.

STABILIZING FORESEEABLE FLUCTUATIONS   Not all fluctuations in activity can be so accurately forecast as the seasonal harvesting of a crop. No one can predict with confidence next year's weather or the likelihood of a recession in the near future. But to the extent that speculators can form any accurate guesses today about the future *scarcity* of a commodity, they will tend to buy it now for *future* delivery, thereby causing (1) a withdrawal of present supply, (2) an increase of present price, (3) an increase in amount stored, (4) an increase in future supply, (5) a reduction in future price—or in all a relative stabilization of price and consumption over time.

The reader should try to visualize the opposite process by which speculators stabilize prices when they correctly foresee an exceptionally large future crop and a low future price: how they then begin to "sell short"[3] for future delivery, tending to depress current prices, raise consumption, and reduce carryover of stocks.

SPREADING OF RISKS   Aside from their possible influence toward stabilizing prices, speculators have another important function. By being willing to take risks on their own shoulders, they enable others to avoid risk.

---

[2] Do I, as a warehouse storer, need a crystal ball to tell me price will rise enough to pay me to store corn today? No. The market today will quote me a future price—for delivery of corn some months hence—and when this future price sufficiently exceeds the current spot price for physical corn, I get the signal to store corn.

[3] There is nothing mysterious about selling short. I simply put in an order to my broker in which I agree in return for a certain price *now*, to deliver *at some later date* an amount of grain. Usually, at the time of putting in the order, I do not have the grain on hand. But I legally fulfill my contract by later "covering," i.e., buying the grain and making delivery. If I later have to pay a higher price in covering than I now receive when selling short, then I take a loss. But if I have guessed right and prices do fall in the intervening period, then I "buy in" for less than I have sold and make a profit.

Selling short in the stock market works out similarly, except that I am free to cover and make future delivery of the stock at any time I please. Meanwhile the man who has bought the stock receives his stock shares. How? As a result of the fact that my broker, obligingly, lends me the stock certificates to make delivery. Later, when I cover, I buy in some stock and turn over the certificates to my obliging broker.

For example, a warehouse owner must carry large inventories of grain in the course of his business. If the price of grain goes up, he makes a windfall capital gain; if down, he incurs a windfall loss. But let us suppose that he is content to earn his living by storing grain and wishes to forgo all risk taking. This he can do by a process called "hedging." This complicated procedure is rather like a man who bets on the East to win the Grey Cup and then washes out this transaction, or covers it, by placing an equal bet on the West. Whichever side wins, he comes out the same, his left hand winning what his right hand loses.

To get a notion of how the complicated process of hedging works out, here is a highly simplified example. Suppose I am buying and storing barley in the late fall. I am a specialist in running a warehouse and wish to stick to my last rather than become involved in the risky business of taking speculative bets as to whether the price of barley will go up between now and the next spring when I expect to stop storing barley and to sell it. In effect, I should really like to sell it now for an agreed-upon price that will compensate me for my 9-cent-per-bushel storage expenses between now and later delivery time. If a speculative market exists, that is precisely what I can do by the device of hedging.

How do I hedge? For each 5,000 bushels of barley I buy in November to put into storage until next May, let us suppose I have to pay $1.24 a bushel to local Manitoba farmers. I look up the price quoted today, November 30, on the Winnipeg Grain Exchange for next May barley futures and see that this quotation is $1.33. I realize that this 9-cent excess over today's price will give me a fair return for my expenses of storage and that is why I am glad to store. I now hedge by *selling* a 5,000-bushel May-barley future contract. (The brokerage commission on this "short sale" transaction will be less than $1/2$ cent per bushel; my broker will require that I put up less than 10 cents per bushel as "margin" to ensure that I will fulfill my contractual obligation, and he will neither know or care whether I actually have some physical barley with which I might make later delivery.)

Now I am hedged. I happen to own 5,000 bushels of physical barley in storage. I also have sold 5,000 bushels of May barley futures. What will happen if slack barley demand and a tremendous winter wheat crop cause the price of barley to fall to $1.14 by next May?

My brother, who owns a warehouse and bought barley in the fall as I did *but did not hedge*, will now lose 10 cents per bushel. Indeed, he is worse off than that, because he is also out the 9 cents that it costs him to keep his warehouse going (watchmen's pay, and so forth). So he has really lost 19 cents per bushel *in toto*.

What about me, the cagy hedger? I do lose 10 cents a bushel *on my physical barley* because of the unforeseen change in price. But when, as May arrives, I look in the paper for the Grain Exchange quotation on my May future, I am relieved to see that it has fallen from $1.33 all the way down to $1.14—at which price I buy in, or "cover," my futures. Thus, *on short sale of my futures* I have gained 19 cents, or exactly as much as I (and my brother) have lost *in toto* on the sale of physical barley. *The hedge has protected me from all price fluctuations:* my left futures pocket has gained what my right physical-barley pocket lost. The speculator who made my hedge possible took price risks off my shoulders.[4]

To the extent that speculators forecast accurately, they provide a definite social service. To the extent that they forecast badly, they tend to aggravate the variability of prices. Were it not for the detailed statistical information provided by the Department of Agriculture and private agencies, the traders of the Winnipeg Grain Exchange would find themselves at the mercy of every idle rumor, hope, and fear. For

speculation is often a mass contagion, like the inexplicable dancing crazes that swept medieval villages, the Dutch tulip mania that sent the price of a single bulb higher than that of a house, the South Sea Bubble in which companies sold stock at fabulous prices for enterprises which would "later be revealed."

■ GAMBLING AND DIMINISHING MARGINAL UTILITY[5]

The defenders of speculation resent the charge that it represents simply another form of gambling, like betting on the horse races or buying a lottery ticket. They emphasize that an uncertain world necessarily involves risk and that *someone* must bear risks. They claim that the knowledge and the venturesomeness of the speculator are chained to a *socially useful purpose*, thereby reducing fluctuations and risks to others. (We have just seen that this is not always the case and that speculation may indeed be destabilizing; but certainly, no one can deny all validity to the above claims.)

Why is gambling considered such a bad thing? Part of the reason, perhaps the most important part, lies in the field of morals, ethics, and religion; upon these the economist is not qualified to pass exact judgment. There is, however, a substantial economic case to be made against gambling.

First, it involves simply *sterile transfers of money or goods* between individuals, creating no new money or goods.[6] Although it creates no output, gambling does nevertheless absorb time and resources. When pursued beyond the limits of recreation, where the main purpose after all is to "kill" time, gambling subtracts from the national income.

---

[4] To check your understanding, work through the case where a war sends up the price of physical barley in the May markets to, say, $1.43. Now my unhedged brother, in addition to his 9-cent return as a warehouseman, makes an additional windfall risk profit of 10 cents per bushel. What about me? On my physical barley which I bought at $1.24 and sell for $1.43, I gain; but I lose 10 cents on having to buy in my May futures at 10 cents more than I sold it for. So I end up making my 9-cent warehouse return and no more—regardless of what can happen to barley price fluctuations.

Actual hedging of millers, farmers, and storers can become more complicated. Also, it could happen that, in order to coax out speculators, the quotation in November of the May future would on the average have to sell for a little less than the $1.33 such physical barley can be expected to sell for in May; this means that the risk-bearing speculators require a premium for the insurance-like risk they are providing—a premium that, like any other cost, must be borne by producers and ultimate consumers.

[5] This discussion provides an alternative introduction to the theory of marginal utility which is picked up in orthodox fashion on page 528.

[6] Actually, in all professional gambling arrangements, the participants lose out on balance. The leakage comes from the fact that the odds are always rigged in favor of the "house," so that even an "honest" house will win in the long run. Moderate gambling among friends may be considered as a form of consumption or recreation activity whose cost to the group as a whole is zero. Oddly, some people who do not trust their ability to save do use steady purchase of "numbers" tickets as a way to cut down on current consumption and put themselves in the position of occasionally accumulating larger sums of money. In some past and present societies, the enhancement of inequality of income distribution by gambling may have made a roundabout contribution to social thrift and capital formation.

The second economic disadvantage of gambling is the fact that it tends to promote *inequality and instability of incomes*. People who sit down to the gambling table with the same amount of money go away with widely different amounts. A gambler (and his family) must expect to be on the top of the world one day, and when luck changes—which we have seen to be the only predictable thing about it—he may almost starve.

LAW OF DIMINISHING MARGINAL UTILITY AND CHANCE
But why is inequality of income over time and between persons considered such a bad thing? One answer is to be found in the widely held belief that the gain in utility achieved by an *extra* $1,000 of income is not so great as the loss in utility of forgoing $1,000 of income. Where that is the case, a bet at fair odds involves an economic loss: the money you stand to win balances the money you may lose; but the satisfaction you stand to win is *less* than the satisfaction you stand to lose.

Similarly, if it could be assumed that individuals are all "roughly the same" and are ethically comparable, so that their utilities can be added, then the dollars gained by the rich do not create as much "social welfare" or total utility as the dollars lost by the poor. This has been used not only as a criticism of gambling, but as a positive argument in favor of "progressive" taxation aimed at lowering the inequality of the distribution of income. The issue of incentives must also enter into forming any decision on policy, since discussions elsewhere show that redistributing the national pie may lessen its total.

Just as Malthus saw the law of diminishing returns as underlying his theory of population, so is the "law of diminishing marginal utility" used by many economists to condemn professional gambling. According to this theory, as money income increases, each new dollar adds something to utility, but less and less. Similarly, each extra unit of any good that can be bought with money contributes less and less satisfaction or utility. When we get as much of a good as we wish (e.g., air), it becomes a "free good" because still further units add nothing new to our utility.

■ WHY IDEAL STABILIZATION BY SPECULATORS IS OPTIMAL

We can now use the tools of marginal utility to show how ideal speculation would maximize total utility over time. Suppose every consumer has a utility schedule that holds for each year independently of any other year. Now suppose that in the first of two years there was a big crop—say, 3 units per person—and in the second a small crop of only 1 unit per person. If this crop deficiency could be foreseen, how should the consumption of the two-year 4-unit total be spread over the two years?

If we agree, for simplicity, to neglect all storage, interest, and insurance charges and all questions of utility commensurability over time, we can prove *that total utility for the two years together will be maximized only if consumption is equal in each year.*

Why is uniform consumption better than any other division of the available total? Because of the law of diminishing marginal utility. Here is the reasoning:

> Suppose I consume more in the first year than in the second. My last unit's marginal utility will then be low in the first year and high in the second. So if I carry some crop from the first to the second year, I shall be switching from low to high marginal utilities —and that will maximize my total utility.

But is not that exactly what the following ideal speculation pattern would accomplish?

If speculators can neglect interest, storage, and insurance charges and happen to forecast accurately next year's low crop, what will they do? They will figure it pays to carry goods over from this year's low price resulting from the high crop, hoping instead to sell at next year's scarcity price. But as each speculator subtracts from this year's supply and adds to next year's, what must finally happen? Equilibrium can be reached only when the two prices have been equalized! Then there will be no further incentive to carry over more crop.[7] (Of course, a

---

[7] A graph can illuminate this argument. If utility could be measured in dollars, with each dollar always denoting the same marginal utility, the demand curves would look just like the marginal utility schedule of page 529. The two curves of Fig. 20-7 show what would happen if there were no carryover—with price first determined at A_1, where $s_1 s_1$ intersects dd, and second at A_2, where the lower supply $s_2 s_2$ intersects dd. Total utility of the shaded areas would add up only to $(4 + 3 + 2) + 4$, or $13 per head. But with optimal carryover to the second year of 1 unit by speculators, P's and Q's will be equalized at E_1 and E_2, and now the total utility of the gray areas will add up to $(4 + 3) + (4 + 3)$, or $14 per head. (Show that the gain in utility of $1 is measured by the light block, which represents the excess of the second unit's marginal utility over the third unit's marginal utility; one can show that equality of marginal utilities is optimal.)

small payment for the speculator's effort might have to be included—but we have agreed to waive all costs just to keep the example simple.)

Do not for a moment get the impression that real flesh-and-blood speculators can guess the future correctly. They often make mistakes and often are prey to rumors and mass enthusiasms. So the process is not as ideal as here pictured. Still, to the degree that speculators can intelligently foresee the future—and those who have a terrible batting average may get eliminated fast as their capital is lost—they (and for that matter, *farsighted* government agencies, too) may help to provide a useful stabilizing function.

■ ECONOMICS OF CONSERVATION

These remarks on the social usefulness of speculation apply also to the market in natural resources. Commodity speculation rarely stretches into the future for more than a year, whereas decisions about whether to hold or use minerals, trees, and oil involve decades or centuries; but the theory is the same.

To simplify the idea of conservation, suppose many owners of potential iron mines are trying to decide whether to exploit their properties this year, or whether to hold back (either by mining slowly or simply by sitting on their undeveloped ores). The answer of the Conservation movement used to be: "Hold back. We are using up our resources too fast. None will be left for future generations. Society should restrain mineral owners from profiting today at the expense of the future."

This particular plea is rarely heard from Conservationists today, because it was based on a misunderstanding of how to make a maximum profit from holding a stock of anything, barley or ore. Leaving aside many complications (chiefly of the impact of the rate of interest, which we will encounter in Chapter 29), the Conservationists were not wrong about the ethics of considering the needs of later years, but in their belief that today's owner disregards them.

Imagine that you are an owner, and that you know what the Conservationists suggest: that other owners are profiting by selling today, and that there will be a serious scarcity in the future. How will you react? Just as the warehouseman did on page 518: hold your supply off today's market; allow today's price to rise; increase the amount of ore stored (in "reserves"); reduce the *future* scarcity of ore. Why? Because if you and the Conservationists are right about the future scarcity, mineral prices will be high then, and you can make a greater profit from your tons of ore reserves then than you can at today's prices. And other ore-property owners will also hold back (if their studies also suggest future scarcity). If all owners agree on the future scarcity, all will tend to hold back until present price rises and expected future price and scarcity fall sufficiently to (1) balance production and (2) equalize prices and profits, in the two periods.

Clearly, this is Conservation through the market. And just as clearly, it is an application of the theory of speculation and price behavior through time. And,

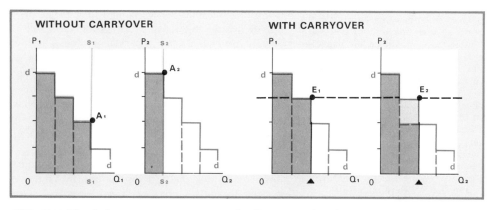

FIG. 20-7. The dark gray areas measure total utility enjoyed each year. Carrying one unit to the second year equalizes Q and also P, and increases total utility by the amount of the light gray block.

just as in speculation, gambling is likely to enter, resulting in either too much or too little being allocated to future use. Another similarity is in the uncertainty of future supplies: huge new discoveries of your mineral may be made before the future date arrives, thus depressing the price and wiping out your expected profit. Uncertainty about the likelihood of such discoveries affects different owners different ways: some like to take a chance, others like to make hay while the sun shines, even if it means forgoing a probable larger future profit.

Of course, Conservationists don't know any more about the future than owners in the industry. Society has to accept the future supplies based on a guess made by *someone*. In the price system, the guess is made by thousands of owners who, studying reported reserves and forecasts of consumption, stand to make the most profits from their own ores by making correct guesses.

■ ECONOMICS OF INSURANCE

We are now in a position to see why insurance, which appears to be just another form of gambling, actually has exactly opposite effects. For the same reasons that gambling is bad, insurance is economically advantageous.[8] Whereas gambling creates risks, insurance helps to lessen and spread risks.

In buying fire insurance on his house, the owner seems to be betting with the insurance company that his house will burn down. If it does not—and the odds are heavily in favor of its not burning—the

---

[8] The astute reader will note (1) that economics proves that those subject to diminishing marginal utility should not gamble and should insure, but that a man with *increasing* marginal utility will maximize his expected utility by gambling and by noninsuring; and (2) that any economist who uses observations on a person's reaction to situations involving probabilities as his test of how marginal utility varies for that person may end up with the following circular reasoning: those who gamble should gamble; those who insure should insure. So the case for prohibiting gambling must rest on extraneous ethical or religious grounds; or must be withdrawn; or must be based on the notion that society knows better than individuals what is truly good for them; or must be based on the notion that we are all imperfect beings who wish in the long run that we were not free to yield to short-run temptations. Some political economists feel that moderate gambling might be converted into socially useful channels.

owner forfeits the small premium charge. If it does burn down, the company must reimburse the owner to the tune of the agreed-upon loss. (For the obvious reason of removing temptation from hard-up home owners who like fire engines and excitement, the face value of the policy tends to be something less than the money value of the property insured.)

What is true of fire insurance is equally true of life, accident, automobile, or any other kind of insurance. Actually, at the famous Lloyd's of London, which is a place for insurance brokers to come together, you can arrange to insure a ball team or vacationer against rain, dancers against infantile paralysis, *and* a hotel keeper against a damage suit from the widow of a man killed in a fight with another man who bought a drink in the hotel's cocktail lounge; and you can get numerous other bizarre policies. But by the common law, Lloyd's may refuse to bet $10,000 with me that it will not snow on Christmas, since I do not have an "insurable interest" of that amount and the bet would be unenforceable in the courts. But a ski-resort owner, who stands to lose that much if it does not snow, would have such an insurable interest and could certainly buy such a policy. Economic theory shows that the difference between these two cases is that insuring the resort owner *stabilizes* income while insuring me *destabilizes* it.

The insurance company is not gambling, because what is unpredictable and subject to chance *for the individual* is highly predictable and uniform *in the mass*. Whether John C. Smith, age twenty and in good health, will live for 30 more years is a matter of chance, but the famous *law of large numbers* guarantees that out of 100,000-odd twenty-year-olds in good health, only a definite proportion will still be alive at the end of such a period of time. The life-insurance company can easily set a premium at which it will not lose money. Certainly, therefore, the company is not gambling.

What about the buyer of insurance? Is he gambling? The reverse can be shown to be true: the man who does not insure his house is doing the gambling. He is risking the whole value of his house against the small premium saved. If his house does not burn down in any year, he has won his bet; if it does, as occasionally must happen, he loses his bet and incurs a tremendous penalty.

At this point, a sporting man will say, "So what?

Of course, a man gambles when he doesn't buy insurance. But the odds on such a bet are not unfavorable. In fact, they are favorable, because we know that the insurance company is not in business for its health. It must keep records, it must support insurance salesmen, and so forth. All this costs money and must be 'loaded' onto the insurance premium, detracting from the perfect mathematical odds of the buyer and making the odds for the nonbuyer a little better."

To which a rational man will reply: "When I am among friends, I don't mind a small game of chance for relaxation even at slightly unfavorable odds. But when a big bet is involved, even if the odds are favorable, then I pass. I insure my house because I hardly miss the premium each year: but if it burned down without being covered, I'd feel the loss an awful lot. When I insure, my living standards over time and my income remain the same, come what may. When I don't insure, I may be up for a while, but I risk going way down."

Obviously, the law of diminishing marginal utility —which makes the satisfaction from wins less important than the privation from losses—is one way of justifying the above reasoning.[9] *This law of diminishing marginal utility tells us that a steady income, equitably divided among individuals instead of arbitrarily apportioned between the lucky and unlucky people whose house did or did not burn down, is economically advantageous.* (Also, when a family chooses to buy hospital and medical insurance, it may express the belief that this will be relatively painless forced "saving against a rainy day." This self-imposed "compulsory-saving" feature is another benefit of insurance.)

[9] Figure 20-7 of this Appendix can show all this. Change the titles "Without Carryover" and "With Carryover" to "Without Insurance" and "With Insurance" to see the gain in utility from insuring. Then, to prove the loss from gambling, relabel the left-hand figure "After Gambling" and the right-hand one "Before Gambling." To illustrate that equal incomes maximize the sum of utility of two ethically commensurable people relabel Fig. 20-7 again to read "Before Redistribution" and "After Redistribution."

■ WHAT CAN BE INSURED

Undoubtedly, insurance is a highly important way of spreading risks. Why, then, can we not insure ourselves against all the risks of life? The answer lies in the indisputable fact that certain definite mathematical conditions are necessary before sufficiently exact actuarial probabilities can be determined.

First, we must have a *large number of events.* Only then will a pooling of risks and a "cancellation" and "averaging of extremes" be possible. The bank at Monte Carlo knows there is safety in numbers. The lucky streak of an Arabian prince one night will be canceled by his next night's losings or by the losings of a fake Balkan countess. Once in a blue moon someone may "break the bank"; but in a few more lunar cycles the "house" will more than break even.

But large numbers are not enough. No prudent fire-insurance company would confine itself to the island of Montreal even though there are thousands of buildings there. *The uncertain events must be relatively independent.* Each throw of the dice, each chance loss by fire, should stand relatively by itself. Obviously, a disaster like the Halifax explosion in 1917, or the San Francisco earthquake, would subject all the buildings in the same locality to the same risk. The company would be making a bet on *one* event, not on thousands of independent events. Instead, it must diversify its risks. Private companies cannot, without government aid, bear the risks of nuclear-bomb insurance. Nor is it possible to buy unemployment insurance from a private company. Depressions are great plagues which hit all sections and all classes at one and the same time, with a probability that cannot be computed in advance with any precision. Therefore only the government, whose business it is to take losses, can assume the responsibility of providing unemployment compensation.

There still remain, and probably always will, numerous risks of personal and business life. No one can insure the success of a new beauty shop, a new mousetrap, or a hopeful opera singer. Without error there cannot be trial; and without trial there cannot be progress.

SUMMARY TO APPENDIX

■ **1** The intelligent profit-seeking action of speculators and arbitragers tends to create certain definite *equilibrium patterns of price over space and time.* To the extent that speculators moderate price and consumption instability, they perform a socially useful purpose. To the extent that they provide a market and permit others to hedge against risk, they perform a further useful function.

But to the extent that speculators pile onto price changes and cause great fluctuations in stock and commodity prices, and in foreign exchange rates and gold prices, they do social damage.

■ **2** Over a long period of time, property owners apply the theory of speculation to determine the amount of natural resources that will be available for the future. The Conservation movement used to argue the market took no account of future scarcities.

■ **3** The economic principle of diminishing marginal utility is one way of showing why consumption and price stability is good, and why gambling is economically unsound and insurance is sound. There are fundamental differences among what can be insured by private rather than social agencies and what can scarcely be insured at all.

QUESTIONS FOR DISCUSSION

1. How does ideal speculation work to stabilize seasonal prices? To spread risks?

2. "If all mineral owners were equally pessimistic about future ore discoveries, the price of ore would stay at a constant level." Why?

3. "Insurance reduces total risk; gambling increases the total. Therefore the former is good and the latter is bad." Explain.

4. "I love the thrill of gambling, of risking all on the turn of a card. What do I care for odds or economic principles?" Can economic science pass judgment on whether such a person should gamble or not?

5. Can you reverse the reasoning concerning the desirability of gambling and insurance so that it will apply to two individuals with increasing rather than decreasing marginal utility of income?

6. List some important differences between private and social insurance.

7. *Extra-credit problem* (for students of statistics): Suppose each of four cab companies faces accidents "normally distributed," with a standard deviation, $\sigma_i = \$3,000$, around a mean loss of $50,000. Let them now pool risks through mutual reinsurance. Show that this gives a total mean loss of $200,000 (or still $50,000 for each one's fair share; but now total variance is only $4 \times (3,000)^2$, or $\sigma^2 = 4\sigma_i^2 = \$36,000,000 = (6,000)^2$). So each ends up with a standard deviation of only $1,500 = \$6,000/4$—halving the risk through quadrupling the size! (Suppose at the beginning of Fig. 20-6, the harvest were many times the average crop. Then it would be rational to spread it over two crop years, not one. Can you show how P would drop so low in the first fall as to lead to a *steady* rise thereafter for two years, and with *no* drop in P at the time of the next intermediate autumn harvest?)

8. Review your understanding of the following concepts:

   spatial P equality but for transport costs
   ideal seasonal price pattern
   conservation through the market
   hedging, speculation, and short-sale
   law of diminishing marginal utility
   consumption stability versus instability
   gambling versus insurance
   social versus private insurance

21

THE
THEORY OF DEMAND
AND UTILITY

What is a cynic? A man who knows the price of everything,
and the value of nothing. OSCAR WILDE

In a competitive market, price is determined by the schedules of supply and demand. But what principles of economics lie behind the demand schedules? What principles behind the supply schedules?

In this chapter we shall investigate briefly the economic principles of *total utility* and *marginal utility* which underlie the market demand schedule, leaving to later chapters a survey of the cost concepts which underlie the competitive supply schedule and the behavior of monopolists.

■ SUMMING INDIVIDUAL DEMANDS TO GET MARKET DEMAND

The demand curve for a good such as tea is arrived at for the whole market by summing up the amounts of tea that will be demanded by each customer. Each consumer has a demand curve along which the quantity demanded can be plotted against the price of tea. It generally slopes downward and to the right, declining from northwest to southeast. If all consumers were exactly alike in their demands and there were 1 million consumers, then we could think of the market curve as a millionfold enlargement of each consumer's demand curve.

But people are not all exactly alike. Some have high incomes; some low. Some greatly desire tea; others prefer coffee or concerts. What must we do to the demand schedules or curves of each consumer to arrive at the total market demand *dd* curve?

All we have to do is calculate the sum total of what all the different consumers will consume at any given price; we then plot that total amount as a

To get market demand, we add all consumers' demand curves:

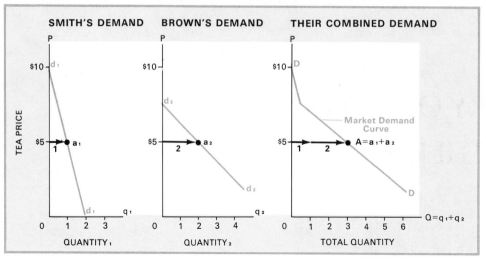

FIG. 21-1. At each price, such as $5, we *horizontally* add quantities demanded by each man to get market quantity demanded.

point on the market demand curve; or if we like, we may set the total down in a demand table like that first seen in Chapter 4.

> *Summary.* We sum individual amounts demanded at each price to end up finally with the market demand curve. (Figure 21-1 adds demand curves "horizontally.")

■ DEMAND SHIFTS FROM INCOME AND OTHER CHANGES

Factors other than changes in the price of tea can change the quantity demanded of tea. We know from budget studies, from historical experience, and from thinking about our own behavior that an increase in money income is a factor that will normally tend to increase the amount we are willing to buy of any good. Goods that are necessities tend to be less responsive to income changes, and goods that are luxuries tend to be more responsive; a very few abnormal goods, called "inferior" goods, may actually go down in quantity bought when we get enough income to be able to afford to replace them in the budget by other goods. (Potatoes, rye bread, bologna, soup bones and offal, lard, and oleomargarine might be examples of inferior goods, but the species is so rare that we can generally neglect it in our discussions.)

Let us now show what all this means in terms of the demand curve. This curve is, of course, simply the graphical picture of the response of quantity bought of a good to the change in its *own* price. But quantity bought may change also as a result of changes in the *price of other goods* or as a result of a change in the consumer's *income*. The demand curve is drawn on the assump-

Demand curve shifts with change in income or in another good's price:

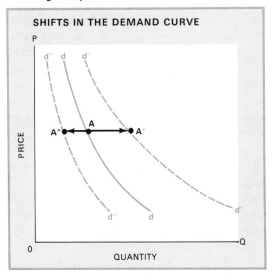

SHIFTS IN THE DEMAND CURVE

FIG. 21-2. Higher income will shift dd to $d'd'$. (Explain why; and why lowering income will shift dd to $d''d''$.) Similarly, a rise in price of coffee, which is a substitute for tea, might shift tea's dd out to $d'd'$. (What would a cut in coffee price do? Can you explain why a great rise in price of lemon, a complementary good used with tea, might shift dd leftward to $d''d''$?)

tion that these other things do not change. But what if they do? Then the whole demand curve will *shift* to the right or to the left.

Figure 21-2 illustrates such changes. Given a certain income and established prices for all other goods, we can draw the consumer's demand for tea dd. First, assume price and quantity are at point A. Suppose now that his income rises. Even though the price of tea is unchanged, he will in all probability buy more tea than before; hence the demand curve will have shifted to the right, say, to $d'd'$, with A' indicating his new total purchase of tea. If his income should fall, then we may expect a reduction in quantity bought—there *must* be a reduction if income falls far enough. This downward shift we illustrate by $d''d''$ and by A''.

Income is only one of many factors that the position of the demand curve depends upon. An increased taste or a fashion for tea would also shift the demand to the right, and a decreased taste would have the opposite effect. Advertisers seek to shift the dd curve. Even if each person consumed the same amount of a good, a growth in population would have the effect of increasing the total market demand for a product. If people think that a boom is about to get under way, they may increase their purchases now in order to beat the gun.[1] Still other factors operate all the time to shift demand.

---

[1] In fact, when I see in today's paper that the price of tea is going up, I may rush out to buy more: this may seem superficially to be an exception to the law of downward-sloping demand, but (as discussed on page 487, footnote 3) it can be reconciled with that law when we realize that I am buying more because of the *rising* price of tea and because I want to be able to buy less of it tomorrow when its price will have stabilized at a high level. Despite this *dynamic* effect of *changing* prices, it remains true that at a steady high price for tea, I shall consume less than at a steady low price (if other goods' prices do not change).

CROSS RELATIONS OF DEMAND: SUBSTITUTES AND COMPLEMENTS

Everyone knows that raising the price of tea will decrease the amount demanded of tea. We have seen that it will also affect the amounts demanded of other commodities. For example, a higher price for tea will lower the demand for a commodity such as lemon; i.e., it will shift the whole demand schedule of lemon downward. But it will also increase the amount demanded of coffee. Probably it will have little or no effect on the demand curve for salt.

We say, therefore, that tea and coffee are rival, or competing, products, or *substitutes*. Tea and lemon, on the other hand, are cooperating, or *complementary*, commodities, so-called *complements*. In-between pairs such as tea and salt are said to represent *independent* commodities. The reader will of course be able to classify such pairs as beef and pork, turkey and cranberry sauce, automobiles and gasoline, truck and railroad freight, oil and coal.

Besides showing effects of income changes, Fig. 21-2 also illustrates the effect of changed prices of other goods. A fall in the price of coffee may well cause our consumer to buy less tea; the demand curve shifts to, say, $d''d''$. But what if the price of lemon were to fall? The change may be small or nonexistent. But if there is any change, it will be in the direction of *increased* tea purchases—a rightward shift of dd. Why this difference in response? Because coffee is a rival, a *substitute* product for tea; lemon is a *complementary* commodity to tea.

THE LAW OF DIMINISHING MARGINAL UTILITY[2]

Return to the law of downward-sloping demand, which is so basic that we have to investigate the economic principles operating in the background to justify and explain it. A century ago economists hit upon the fundamental notion of "marginal utility," and it was from this analysis that they felt able for the first time to derive the demand curve and explain its properties. There is space here only to sketch the basic notions underlying such theories, leaving refinements and developments to specialized treatises on advanced economic theory.

As a customer you will buy a good because you feel it gives you satisfaction or "utility." A first unit of a good gives you a certain amount of psychological utility. Now imagine consuming a second unit. Your total utility goes up because the second unit of the good gives you some additional utility. What about adding a third and fourth unit of the same good?

A century ago economists proclaimed an important law that sounds like the law of diminishing returns; but instead of referring to the extra output added by successive doses of a factor input (as in Table 2-2 on page 29), this is a law about the behavior of psychological utility as you add more and more of a good. It can be described by words, by a table of numbers, and by two curves.

The law of diminishing marginal utility. As you consume more of the same good, your *total* (psychological) utility increases. However, let us use

---

[2] Recall that an alternative introduction to the idea of diminishing marginal utility was provided in the Appendix to Chapter 20, p. 519.

The law of decreasing marginal utility can be shown by numbers or curves:

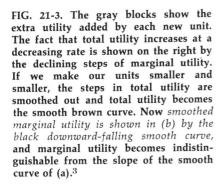

DECLINING RATE OF INCREASE
OF *TOTAL* UTILITY

(1) QUANTITY OF A GOOD CONSUMED	(2) TOTAL UTILITY	(3) MARGINAL UTILITY
0	0	
		4
1	4	
		3
2	7	
		2
3	9	
		1
4	10	
		0
5	10	

TABLE 21-1. Although *total* utility rises with consumption, it does so at a decreasing rate. This means that marginal utility—the extra utility added by each last extra unit of the good—will be decreasing. From this pyschological fact, older economists prepared their demonstration of the law of downward-sloping demand.

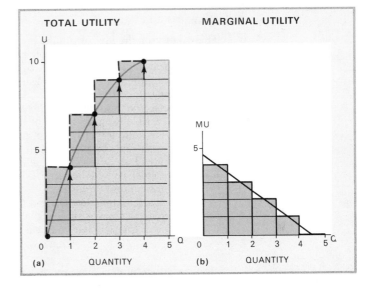

FIG. 21-3. The gray blocks show the extra utility added by each new unit. The fact that total utility increases at a decreasing rate is shown on the right by the declining steps of marginal utility. If we make our units smaller and smaller, the steps in total utility are smoothed out and total utility becomes the smooth brown curve. Now *smoothed marginal utility is shown in (b) by the black downward-falling smooth curve,* and marginal utility becomes indistinguishable from the slope of the smooth curve of (a).[3]

the term marginal utility to refer to "the extra utility added by one extra last unit of a good." Then, with successive new units of the good, your total

---

[3] NOTE: It will be found that the sum of all the marginal utilities in Table 21-1's Column (3), if reckoned above some point, must equal the amount of total utility in Column (2) at that point. [Thus, 4 + 3 + 2 does give us the 9 shown in Column (2). What does 4 + 3 give?] In terms of Fig. 21-3(b), the area under the marginal utility curve, as measured by blocks or by area under the smooth curve, must add up to equality with the numerical height of the total utility curve shown in (a)—it being understood that we make our comparison at a specified quantity level. All this portrays the fact that total utility is the sum of all the marginal (or extra) utilities added from the beginning.

utility will grow at a slower and slower rate because your psychological ability to appreciate more of the good tends to become less keen. This fact, that the increments in total utility fall off, economists describe as follows:

As the amount consumed of a good increases, the *marginal utility* of the good (or the extra utility added by its last unit) tends to decrease.

Column (2) of Table 21-1 shows that *total utility* enjoyed increases as Q grows, but at a decreasing rate. Column (3) measures *marginal utility* as the increment of total utility resulting when one last unit of the good is added; the fact that marginal utilities in the table are declining exemplifies the law of diminishing marginal utility.

Figure 21-3(a) pictures how total utility increases, but at a decreasing rate. Figure 21-3(b) depicts marginal utilities—increments of utility (not the total of utility itself). Whether we work with sizable units of the good and measure utilities by blocks and steps, or whether we smooth the drawings by use of the brown and black curves to reflect continuously divisible units, the law of diminishing marginal utility means that the relations in Fig. 21-3(b) must slope downward and—what is exactly the same thing—that the total utility relations in Fig. 21-3(a) must look concave from below, reflecting total utility's growth becoming less and less.

> The validity of the law of diminishing marginal utility seemed probable to econo-
> mists of an earlier generation as they looked into their own minds for their own
> psychological reactions to extra consumption. These findings of *introspection*
> seemed strengthened when they learned about numerous laboratory experiments
> by psychologists of the 1850s.
>
> Suppose you blindfold a man and ask him to hold out his hand, palm up.
> Now place a weight on his palm; he certainly will notice it. As you add more units
> of weight, he notices their addition too. But after his palm is carrying a good deal
> of weight, you can add just as big a weight as you did in the beginning, and yet
> this time he will reply that he is not conscious of any addition. In other words, the
> greater the *total* weight he is already carrying, the *less* will be the effect of an
> extra or *marginal* unit of weight.
>
> When older economists learned that perception of sound, light, and other sen-
> sations seemed to show a similar Weber-Fechner law of decreasing marginal effect,
> this gave them even greater confidence in the law of diminishing marginal utility.[4]

---

[4] The modern generation, however, has found that the exact way in which one measures utility is not particularly important to explain the price-quantity demand curve. Some economists would still use introspection. Others would want to observe whether you had to give a man 2 to 1 odds to get him to wager on the toss of a fair coin the loss of a new hat against the winning of a second new hat; and they would conclude from this that the marginal utility of the second hat decreases to half the marginal utility of the first hat. Such economists thus hope to measure his marginal utility "behavioristically" rather than intro-spectively. Probably the majority of economists in advanced graduate theory today would feel that what counts for consumer demand theory is whether certain situations have *more* total utility than others. These economists would not care to look for any numerical measure of utility beyond such "greater or less than" comparison; they would use the "indifference curves" of the Appendix to this chapter. By any of these methods, the general properties of the market demand curve can be securely established. (NOTE: Demand theory never has any need to make interpersonal comparisons of utility that involve adding or comparing utilities of different minds.)

■ THE PROCESS OF RATIONAL CHOICE

What is the fundamental equilibrium condition that has to be satisfied if a consumer is spending his income on the variously priced goods so as to make himself truly best off in terms of utility or well-being? Certainly he would not expect that the last egg he is buying brings him exactly the same marginal utility as the last lamb chop he is buying. For lamb chops cost much more apiece than eggs. On reflection, it would seem more reasonable that he should keep buying a good which costs twice as much per unit as another until it ends up in his equilibrium bringing him just twice as much in marginal utility.

In short, if he has arranged his consumption so that every single good is bringing him marginal utility just exactly *proportional* to its price, then it would seem that he could not better himself by departing from such an equilibrium. This same fundamental condition can be stated as follows:

> "Marginal utility proportional to respective price" means that there must be exact equality among the *ratios* of each good's marginal utility divided by its price. These *MU/P* ratios for each good are called the marginal utility *per dollar* that the consumer gets from spending his money on that good.
>
> So final equilibrium will require that there be *equality* of each and every good's *marginal utility per dollar.*

You maximize utility by choosing items with greatest marginal utility per dollar:

MARGINAL UTILITIES PER DOLLAR WHEN
EACH GOOD HAS $P = \$1$

(1) UNIT OF GOOD	(2) GOOD 1 CLOTHING MU_1/P_1	(3) GOOD 2 FOOD MU_2/P_2
0		10
1	4	9
2	3	1¾
3	2	¾
4	1	

TABLE 21-2. Food, being a necessity, has its MU_2 falling faster than MU_1 of clothing falls. In choosing how to spend each last dollar, the rule that gives you most total utility is this: Select any item whose MU/P is largest; if $MU_1/P_1 = MU_2/P_2$, you can be indifferent. (Hence, successive dollars of income go for food first, food second, clothing third, clothing fourth, . . .—because $10 > 9 > 4 > 3$. . . .)

TABLE 21-3. By choosing items in Table 21-2 with highest MU/P (i.e., marginal utility *per dollar*), you find your optimal equilibrium pattern of demand.

INCOME BUDGETARY PATTERN OF DEMAND								
INCOME (per day)	$1	$2	$3	$4	$5	$6	$7	$8
Clothing (demanded)	0	0	1	2	3	3	—	4
Food (demanded)	1	2	2	2	2	3	—	4

For those who like numerical examples, the next section digresses to work out a food and clothing case (and can be skipped at a first reading).

■ NUMERICAL EXAMPLE OF OPTIMAL CHOICE

Let's apply this MU/P reasoning to an actual two-good choice. Table 21-2 considers the case of clothing and food. Clothing price, P_1, is assumed to be \$1. Column (2) of Table 21-2 lists clothing's marginal utility per dollar, MU_1/P_1: thus, the first dollar spent on clothing brings you 1 clothing unit and $MU/P_1 = 4$. A second dollar spent on it brings in a marginal utility of only 3 utils. Why? Because of the law of diminishing marginal utility. Total utility has gone up from 4 to 7 (but not to 8!). What would a third and fourth dollar spent on clothing alone bring? Evidently they bring marginal utilities per dollar of 2 and 1, with total utility from 4 clothing units ending up at 10 utils.

To have a problem of choice, you must be confronted with at least two goods. So Column (3) brings into the picture a new good, food. It also is assumed to cost \$1; that is, $P_2 = \$1$. Being a necessity, food starts out with a very high MU_2 per dollar, namely 10. And at first its MU_2/P_2 drops very little, being 9 for the second unit. But once you are fed, your MU_2 and MU_2/P_2 drop very rapidly—to 1¾ for the third unit of food and to ¾ for the fourth unit.[5]

Now to choose. Start out with daily income of only \$1. Your best buy is food: 1 unit. Why? Because 10 utils from a dollar spent on food is better than 4 utils from a dollar spent on clothing.

Now consider \$2 of income. Again, all goes for food. The second food unit brings you 9 utils, which still beats the 4 utils that could come from the first clothing unit.

But now get \$3 of income. At last you have enough to buy a luxury: 1 unit of clothing along with your 2 of food. (Why a first unit of clothing rather than a third of food? Because $MU_1/P_1 = 4 > MU_2/P_2 = 1¾$. QED.)

Table 21-3 shows your budget pattern of food-clothing purchases at different income levels. How was it derived? Verify that you did maximize your total utility from all sources only if you always followed the rule of picking that unit of a good which gives you the larger MU/P. (Can you fill in the \$7 blanks as 3 food and 4 clothing? Why?)

So much for the important budgetary patterns of expenditure at different incomes with prices fixed. Can we derive the usual *demand curves with respect to price* from the utility data of Table 21-2? Yes, we can. Imagine that the price of food has halved, to $P_2 = 50$ cents. We want to show that, at unchanged income levels and with P_1 held at \$1, the cut in P_2 will indeed increase the quantity demanded of Q_2.

Clearly Table 21-2's clothing column of MU_1/P_1 remains unchanged at 4, 3, 2,

---

[5] WARNING: Goods 1 and 2 in Table 21-2 are assumed to have *independently* addable utilities. If they had been rival goods, like tea and coffee, the MU of the third tea unit would go down when you got one more coffee unit. If they had been complementary goods, like tea and lemon, the MU of the third tea unit would go up when you got one more lemon unit. The $MU_1/P_1 = MU_2/P_2$ rule would still hold in maximizing equilibrium; but you couldn't get these from *separate* columns. You would need the Appendix's indifference contours to handle such a case, or more complicated analysis.

1. But food's column now is $MU_2/\$\frac{1}{2}$ instead of $MU_2/\$1$; this means that the numbers 10, 9, 1¾, ... would have to be *doubled* to read 20, 18, 3½, ...

Now let us make our controlled experiment. Hold income constant at $1 per day and P_1 at $1, but cut P_2 to 50 cents. Now for each dollar we can buy 1 clothing unit, as before, or 2 food units. Because the new numbers 20 and 18 are both greater than 4, our first two half-dollars will both be spent on food. Consequently, comparing this 2-of-food result with the first entry in Table 21-3, which had shown only 1 of food bought, we see that *the price reduction of food has definitely caused its quantity bought to increase*—even though it is a necessity. (Actually, its price elasticity, as calculated by any of the formulas for Chapter 19, happens by accident to turn out to be unity, since the same total receipts are spent on it at both prices.)

We shall omit the calculations to show how any other level of income would be spent in the new situation,[6] and how any other cuts in the price of P_2 do tend to increase Q_2 bought.

▨ EQUILIBRIUM CONDITION: EQUAL MARGINAL UTILITIES PER DOLLAR FOR EVERY GOOD

After our digression for a numerical example, we restate the basic principle.

A consumer with a fixed income and facing given market prices of different goods can come into his equilibrium of maximum satisfaction or utility only when he acts thus:

Law of equal marginal utilities per dollar. Each good—such as sugar —is demanded up to the point where the marginal utility per dollar (or penny) spent on it is exactly the same as the marginal utility of a dollar (or penny) spent on any other good—such as salt. If any one good gave more marginal utility per dollar, the consumer would gain by taking money away from other goods and spending more on that good—up to the point where the law of diminishing marginal utility brought its marginal utility per dollar down to equality. If any good gave less marginal utility per dollar than the common level, the consumer would buy less of it until the marginal utility of the last dollar spent on it had risen back to the common level.[7]

This fundamental condition of consumer equilibrium can be written in terms of the marginal utilities and prices of the different goods as follows:

$$\frac{MU \text{ Good 1}}{P_1} = \frac{MU \text{ Good 2}}{P_2} = \frac{MU \text{ Good 3}}{P_3} = \cdots$$

$$= \text{common } MU \text{ per dollar of income}$$

[6] See Figs. 21-9 and 21-10 in the Appendix for a rigorous derivation of demand responses to income and price changes. Appendix footnote 6 discusses some problems due to lumpiness of units, as does footnote 7 below.

[7] At a few places in economics the indivisibility of units is important and cannot be glossed over. Thus, Cadillacs do not come like peas, and their indivisibility may matter. Suppose I buy one but definitely not two Cadillacs. Then the marginal utility of the first car is enough larger than the marginal utility of the same number of dollars spent elsewhere to induce me to buy this first unit. The marginal utility that the second Cadillac would bring is enough less to ensure I do *not* buy it. When indivisibility matters, our equality rule for equilibrium can be restated as an inequality rule. NOTE: As mentioned, the validity of the equilibrium condition can be made quite independent of how, or whether, we measure utility *numerically*. Only relative marginal utilities matter.

The logical meaning of this condition rather than the rote memorizing of a formula is, of course, what matters.

Nor need all this apply just to spending money. Suppose you have only a certain number of hours to spend on study for examinations. If you are so uncreative as to seek merely to maximize your grade average, how should you allocate your time? By spending equal hours on each course? Not necessarily. You have to shift from history to chemistry, from German to economics, until you are getting *the same marginal grade advantage from the last minute spent in each alternative use.*[8] The same marginal rule can show you how to allocate your time on a pleasant weekend. Our marginal equilibrium condition is not merely a law of economics; it is a law of logic itself.

A final remark may be in order at this point. A consumer is not expected to be a wizard at numbers or graphs, nor need he be, to approximate the demand behavior of this chapter. He can even make most of his decisions unconsciously or out of habit. As long as he is fairly consistent in his tastes and actions, all he has to do to make the present analysis relevant is to avoid repeating those mistakes which he found in the past did not give him the goods and services he most wanted and to avoid making wild and unpredictable changes in his buying behavior. If enough people act in this way, our scientific theory will provide a good measure of approximation to the facts.

SUBSTITUTION- AND INCOME-EFFECTS: A DIGRESSION

The concept of marginal utility has lent credence to the fundamental law of downward-sloping demand. A different way of looking at the same problem makes no mention of marginal utility explicitly; but it does lead rigorously to the desired result, and does provide an interesting insight into the factors that tend to make the response of quantity to price very great or very little.

SUBSTITUTION-EFFECT   The first factor explaining diminishing consumption when price rises is an obvious one. If the price of tea goes up while other prices do not, then tea has become relatively dearer. It pays, therefore, to *substitute* other goods for tea in order to maintain one's standard of living most cheaply. Thus tea becomes a relatively more costly source of stimulation than before, and less of it will be bought and more of coffee or cocoa. Similarly, a rise in price of movies relative to stage plays may cause the consumer to seek less of his amusement in the more expensive direction. The consumer is doing here only what every businessman does when rises in the price of one productive factor cause him to adjust his production methods so as to substitute cheap factor inputs for the costly factor inputs. By this process of substitution, he is able to produce the same output at least total cost. Similarly do consumers buy satisfaction at least cost.

---

[8] This does not mean that you study to get the same 89 grade in all classes. Your average may be maximized with grades of 93, 92, 90, and 81, but with each marginal hour of study adding one-tenth of a grade point to any subject.

INCOME-EFFECT   In the second place, when your money income is fixed, being forced to buy a good at a higher price is just like having a decrease in your *real* income or purchasing power, particularly if you have been buying a great deal of the raised commodity. With a lower real income you will now want to buy less tea. Thus, unless a good is an "inferior" good like bologna or oleo, the income-effect will *reinforce* the substitution-effect in making the demand curve downward-sloping.[9]

Of course, the quantitative importance of each of these effects varies with the good in question and with the consumer. Under some circumstances the resulting demand curve is very *elastic*: as where the consumer has been spending a good deal on the commodity and where ready substitutes are available—for example, a drunkard's demand for gin. But if a commodity, such as salt, involves only a small fraction of the consumer's budget, is not easily replaceable by other items, and is needed in small amounts to complement more important items, then demand will tend to be *inelastic*.

■ THE PARADOX OF VALUE

The preceding theories help to explain a famous question that troubled Adam Smith in *The Wealth of Nations*. He asked, How is it that water, which is so very useful that life is impossible without it, has such a low price—while diamonds, which are quite unnecessary, have such a high price?

Today even a beginning student can give a correct answer to this problem. "That's simply explained," he will write on an examination. "The supply and demand curves for water are such that they intersect at a very low price, while the supply and demand curves for diamonds are such that they intersect at a high price." (Today he could add that water is no longer all that cheap.)

This is not an incorrect answer. Adam Smith could not have given it because supply and demand curves as descriptive tools had not yet been invented, and were not to be for 75 years or more. But after he had mastered the lingo, old Adam Smith would naturally ask the question, "But *why* do supply and demand for water intersect at such a low price?"

The answer is by now easy to phrase. It consists of two parts:

Diamonds are very *scarce*, the cost of getting *extra* ones is high; and water is relatively *abundant*, with its cost low in many areas of the world. This first

---

[9] Income- and substitution-effects not only explain the downward slope of demand but also explain a possible, albeit extremely rare, exception to that law. When the 1845 Irish famine greatly raised the price of potatoes, families who consumed a lot of potatoes merely because they were too poor to consume much meat might have ended up consuming *more* rather than less of the high-P potatoes. Why? Because now they had to spend so much on potatoes, the necessity of life, as to make it quite impossible to afford any meat at all and hence were forced to become even more dependent than before on potatoes. In brief, the substitution-effect was here overcome by the perverse income-effect applicable to a peculiar "inferior" good, such as the potato, which tends to *decrease* in the poor man's budget when incomes *rise*. This *curiosum* is attributed to Sir Robert Giffen, a Victorian economist. (NOTE: In the case of ordinary inferior goods on which we spend little money, the perverse income-effects will not outweigh the substitution-effects to produce the odd Giffen case.)

part would have seemed reasonable to even the classical economists of more than a century ago, who would probably have let it go at that, and would not have known how to reconcile these facts about *cost* with the equally valid fact that the world's water is more *useful* than the world's supply of diamonds. In fact, Adam Smith never did quite resolve the paradox. He was content simply to point out that the "value in use" of a good—its total contribution to economic welfare—is not the same thing as its "value in exchange"—the total money value or revenue for which it will sell. Smith had not arrived at the point where he knew how to distinguish *marginal* utility from *total* utility!

Today, we should add to the above cost considerations a second truth:

The *total* utility of water does not determine its price or demand. Only the relative marginal utility and cost of the *last* little bit of water determine its price. Why? Because people are free to buy or not buy that last little bit. If water is priced higher than its marginal utility, then that last unit cannot be sold. Therefore the price must fall until it reaches the level of usefulness of the last little bit, no more and no less. Moreover, because every unit of water is exactly like any other unit and because there is only one price in a competitive market, *every unit must sell for what the last least useful unit sells for.* (As one student put the matter: The theory of economic value is easy to understand if you just remember that the tail wags the dog: concentrate on *marginal* and not on *total* utility.)

> Paradox resolved: The more there is of a commodity, the less the relative desirability of its *last* little unit becomes, even though its *total* usefulness always grows as we get more of the commodity. So, it is obvious why a large amount of water has a low price. Or why air is actually a free good despite its vast usefulness. The many *later* units pull down the market value of *all* units.

■ CONSUMER'S SURPLUS

The foregoing discussion emphasizes that the accounting system which records the "total economic value" or revenue of a good (price × quantity) differs from the measurement necessary to record "total welfare." The total economic value of air is zero; its contribution to welfare, very great.[10] Similarly, if we increase the quantity produced of a good, we increase the community's welfare; but if it is a good like wheat, whose demand is inelastic, we do at the same time destroy some economic value.

> Thus, there is always a sort of gap between total utility and total market value. This gap is in the nature of a *surplus*, which the consumer gets because he "receives more than he pays for."
>
> Nor does he benefit at the expense of the seller. In a swap, one party does not lose what the other gains. Unlike energy, which cannot be created or destroyed, the well-being of all participants is increased by trade.

---

[10] Or, as Smith would say, its value in use is very great; its value in exchange, negligible.

It is easy to see how this consumer's surplus arises. Each unit of a good that the consumer buys costs him only as much as the last unit is worth. But by our fundamental law of diminishing marginal utility, the *earlier* units are worth *more* to him than the last. Thus, he enjoys a surplus on each of these earlier units. When trade stops benefiting him and giving him a surplus, he stops buying.

As final clinching evidence that the consumer always receives a surplus, we may cite the fact that a ruthless seller could present the consumer with an ultimatum—what is called an "all-or-none" offer: "Either you pay me an extra amount of money for the whole block of the good that you are consuming, or you must go without all the units, from first to last. Take it or leave it!" The consumer would certainly be willing to pay extra rather than do altogether without the good of this discriminating monopolist.

How is the concept of consumer's surplus used? It is sometimes needed to help make correct social decisions. Suppose a new side road would cost the locality $100,000. Being free to all, it is expected to bring in no dollar revenues, and all the utility it gives to each user will represent his consumer's surplus. (To avoid extraneous interpersonal difficulties, let us assume there are 1,000 users all exactly alike in income and in their benefit from the road, and all equally worthy.) If each such similar man enjoys $100 (the road's *per capita* cost) or more of consumer's surplus from the road, they should all vote to build the road. If the consumer's surplus of each is less than $100, it is uneconomical for them to tax themselves for this public project.[11]

Many ingenious ways have been suggested for measuring consumer's surplus, but they are of no particular significance here.[12] The important thing is to see how lucky the citizens of modern efficient communities really are. The *privilege of being able to buy a vast array of goods at low prices cannot be over-estimated.*

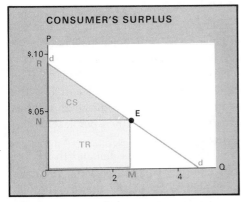

CONSUMER'S SURPLUS

FIG. 21-4.

[11] See Chapter 31 Appendix, Fig. 31-2, for a diagram illustrating this all-or-nothing social decision.

[12] In the special case where money provides a firm measuring rod of utility, consumer's surplus is easily measured and depicted. In Fig. 21-4, when the consumer buys *OM* sugar at *ON* price for each, he pays the total revenue indicated by the lighter rectangular area *OMEN*; but that much sugar gives him total utility (expressed in money) which is the whole area *OMER*; the darker triangular area *NER* left over is his consumer's surplus, and it obviously will be greater the lower the price becomes.

This geometrical concept is useful in illustrating how taxes, farm quotas, and monopolistic interferences create social inefficiency and loss.

This is a humbling thought. If ever a person becomes arrogantly proud of *his* economic productivity and *his* level of real earnings, let him pause and reflect. If he were transported with all his skills and energies intact to a primitive desert island, how much would his money earnings buy? Indeed, without capital machinery, without rich resources, without other labor, and above all without the technological knowledge which each generation inherits from the society's past, how much could *he* produce? It is only too clear that all of us reap the benefits of an economic world we never made. As L. T. Hobhouse said:

> The organizer of industry who thinks that he has "made" himself and his business has found a whole social system ready to his hand in skilled workers, machinery, a market, peace and order—a vast apparatus and a pervasive atmosphere, the joint creation of millions of men and scores of generations. Take away the whole social factor and we have not Robinson Crusoe, with his salvage from the wreck and his acquired knowledge, but the naked savage living on roots, berries, and vermin.

SUMMARY

1 The market demand curve for all consumers is derived by adding *horizontally* the separate demand curves of each consumer. A demand curve can shift for many reasons, such as the following: Normally, a rise in income will shift *dd* rightward, thus increasing demand; a rise in the price of a *substitute* good (coffee for tea, and so forth) will also create such an upward shift in demand; a rise in the price of a *complementary* good (such as lemon in its relation to tea) will represent a cross effect that shifts the *dd* curve downward and leftward. Still other factors—such as changing tastes, population, or expectations—can increase or decrease demand.

2 The concepts of total and marginal utility were introduced to explain the law of downward-sloping demand. The fact that *total utility* rises with each new marginal addition of a good but at a decreasing rate of growth can be expressed in a technical way. With equal additions to a good's quantity, its marginal utility (which is the increment of utility coming from adding a last extra unit of quantity) tends to decrease.

3 To get the most total utility, the consumer must achieve a fundamental marginal condition for demand equilibrium: A consumer has not maximized his well-being until he has succeeded in *making equal the respective marginal utilities per dollar spent on each and every good.* (Beware: The marginal utility of a $25-per-ounce bottle of perfume is not equal to the marginal utility of a 10-cent glass of cola; but their marginal utilities divided by price per unit—that is, their marginal utilities per last dollar, MU/P—are to be equalized in optimizing equilibrium.)

This is a fundamental rule of logic that transcends demand theory: If you want to allocate any limited resource among competing uses, whenever the marginal advantage in one use happened to be greater than in another, you can benefit by transferring from the low-marginal-advantage use to the high—until a final equilibrium is reached at which all have become equal.

4 Without using the marginal utility concept explicitly, we can gain new insight into the factors making for downward-sloping demand by analyzing the effect of a price rise into (1) its *substitution-effect* component and (2) its *income-effect* component. When P for a good rises, I tend to maintain the same level of well-being by *substituting* other goods for the good that has just become more costly. Reinforcing this decrease in a good's Q that arises out of substitution is the income-effect: Since I ordinarily buy less of the good in question when my family income is lower, the rise in its price—which has produced a *drop in my real income* or purchasing power —thus induces a further cut in consumption as the result of my now having a lower real income.

5 Adam Smith's paradox of value—that a commodity important for welfare may sell for less in the market than one less important—is clarified by the distinction between the concept of marginal and total utility. The scarcity of a good, as determined by its cost and supply conditions, interacts with the market demand for the good as determined by the usefulness of its *marginal* unit (not the usefulness of the *total* stock of the good).

6 The fact that market price is determined by marginal rather than total utility is dramatized by the concept of *consumer's surplus*. Since we pay in the market the same price for each unit that the marginal unit is worth to us, we reap a consumer's surplus on all the previous units. This consumer's surplus reflects the benefit we gain from being able to buy at low prices, rather than being confronted by a ruthless monopolist who insists we pay him for the whole of our consumption just what that total is worth to us. However difficult it may be to quantify consumer's surplus, advanced treatises show it is a concept relevant for many social decisions—such as deciding when the community should incur the heavy initial expenses of a road or bridge.[13]

Without reading the Appendix, we can go from the utility background of demand to the next chapter's cost background of supply.

QUESTIONS FOR DISCUSSION

1. As you add horizontally the demands of more and more people, the aggregate market curve begins to look flatter and flatter on the same scale. Show that this merely reflects the fact that the same cut in price induces more new sales from many buyers than from few. (NOTE: Elasticity need not change. Guess why. HINT: E is dimensionless, unaffected by scale changes.)

2. List several goods in order of their responsiveness to higher income.

[13] See Chapter 31 Appendix on this topic.

3. Which of the following goods do you think could be classified as *complementary*, *substitute*, and *independent* goods: beef, ketchup, lamb, applesauce, cigarettes, gum, pork, butter, paperbacks, taxis, and oleomargarine? Illustrate the resulting shift in the demand curve for one good when price of another good goes up. How would a change in income affect the demand curve for butter? The demand curve for oleomargarine?

4. Explain the difference between marginal and total utility. State the law of diminishing marginal utility. Be sure you understand what it means in terms of numbers and diagrams.

5. Why is it nonsensical to say, "In equilibrium, the marginal utilities of all goods must be exactly equal"? Reword to give a correct statement and explain.

6. If you wanted to avoid using the marginal utility concept, show that you can still justify the law of downward-sloping demand by reasoning that involves (1) substitution-effect and (2) income-effect.

7. How much would you be willing to pay rather than give up *all* movies? How much do you spend on movies? Estimate roughly your consumer's surplus.

8. Review your understanding of the following concepts:

market versus individual demand	law of diminishing marginal utility
demand shifts from income and other changes	equating marginal utility of last dollar spent on each good, $MU_1/P_1 = MU_2/P_2$
substitute, complementary, and independent goods	value in use versus value in exchange
income-effect and substitution-effect	paradox of marginal versus total utility
	consumer's surplus

Appendix: Geometrical Analysis of Consumer Equilibrium

It is instructive to show graphically, and without using the language of numerical utility, exactly what the consumer's equilibrium position looks like.

▨ THE INDIFFERENCE CURVE

We start out by considering a consumer who buys only two commodities, say, food and clothing, at definite quoted prices. We suppose the consumer can tell us whether (1) he prefers a given combination or batch of the two goods, say, 3 units of food and 2 of clothing, to some second combination or batch, say, 2 units of food and 3 of clothing, or (2) he is "indifferent" as between the two combinations.

Let us suppose that, actually, these two batches are equally good in the eyes of our consumer—that he is indifferent as to which of the two he receives. Let us go on to list in Table 21-4 some of the other combinations of goods between which he is likewise indifferent.

Figure 21-5 shows these combinations diagrammatically. We measure units of clothing upon one axis and units of food upon the other. Each of our four combinations or batches, A, B, C, D, is represented by its point. But these four are by no means the only combinations that would leave our consumer just indifferent as between them. Another batch, such as 1½ units of food and 4 of clothing, might be ranked as equal to any of A, B, C, or D above, and there are many others not shown.

The curved line of Fig. 21-5, linking up the four points, is an "indifference curve." *Every* point thereon represents a different combination of the two goods; and the indifference curve is so drawn that, if our consumer were given his choice of any

Food-clothing batches which give equal utility are "indifferent":

INDIFFERENCE COMBINATIONS		
	FOOD	CLOTHING
A	1	6
B	2	3
C	3	2
D	4	1½

TABLE 21-4. Getting more of one good compensates for giving up something of the other. The consumer likes situation A exactly as well as B, C, or D.

FIG. 21-5. The food-clothing combinations that yield equal satisfaction can be plotted as a smooth "indifference curve" (or so-called "equal-utility contour"). This is convex (from below) in accord with the law of substitution, which says: As you get more of a good, its "substitution ratio," or "indifference slope," diminishes.

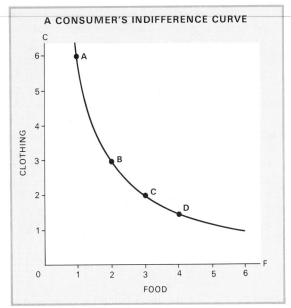

A CONSUMER'S INDIFFERENCE CURVE

point on it, he would not know which one to choose. All would be equally desirable to him, and he would be indifferent as to which batch he received.

It should be noted that this indifference curve is of convex curvature viewed from below. As we move downward and to the right along the curve—a movement which implies increasing the quantity of food and reducing that of clothing—the slope of the curve becomes flatter. The curve is drawn so because this illustrates a property which seems most often to hold true in real life and which we may call the "law of substitution":

The scarcer a good, the greater its relative sub-stitution value; its marginal utility rises relative to the marginal utility of the good that has become plentiful.

For example, the consumer who is at position A in Table 21-4 is willing to give up 3 units of clothing in order to get a second unit of food; thus, at A, he would swap 3 of his 6 clothing units in exchange for 1 extra food unit. But when he has moved to B, he would sacrifice only 1 of his remaining clothing supply in order to obtain a third food unit—a 1-for-1 swap. For a fourth unit of food, he would sacrifice only ½ unit from his dwindling supply of clothing.

If we join the points A and B of Fig. 21-5, we find that the slope of the resulting line (neglecting its negative sign) has a value of 3. Join B and C, and the slope is 1; join C and D, and the slope is ½. These figures—3, 1, ½—are simply the "swapping terms" that we noted just above.

But to move from A to B is to move a considerable distance along the curve. What about the swapping terms for smaller movements? If the consumer is at A and we consider a movement to the intermediate position (not shown in Table 21-4) of 1½ food and 4 clothing, the swapping ratio would be 4. And it is clear that, as the movement along the curve grows smaller, the closer the swapping terms come to the actual slope of the indifference curve.[1]

[1] By the arithmetic slope of the indifference curve, we mean this: To find the slope of the curve at, say, point B, take a ruler and place it so that it is just tangent to the curve at B—it touches the curve, but does not cross it either above or below B. Mark the points at which the ruler's edge crosses the two axes. The slope is the ratio of the distance cut off on the vertical axis to the distance cut off on the horizontal axis; e.g., at B, the slope is ⁶⁄₄, or 1½. Intermediate texts refer to the slope of the indifference curve at any point as the "substitution ratio," or "the marginal rate of substitution," or the *relative* marginal utility ratio" at that point.

So the slope of the indifference curve is the measure of the terms on which—for very small changes —the consumer would be willing to exchange a little of his supply of one good in return for a little more of the other.

And an indifference curve which is convex in the manner of Fig. 21-5 conforms to the law of substitution earlier noted. As the consumer's food goes up— and his clothing goes down—food must become relatively cheaper and cheaper in order for him to be persuaded to take a little extra food in exchange for a little sacrifice of clothing. The precise shape and slope of an indifference curve will, of course, vary from one consumer to the next; but for this introductory discussion, it seems reasonable to assume that the general convex shape of the curve in Fig. 21-5 is typical.

■ THE INDIFFERENCE MAP

Table 21-4 is but one of an infinite number of possible tables. We could have started out with a still higher level of satisfaction or indifference and listed some of the different combinations that belonged to it in the mind of our consumer. One such table might have begun with 2 food and 7 clothing; another with 3 food and 7 clothing. Each table could be portrayed graphically; each has its corresponding curve. Figure 21-6 shows four such curves; the old curve of Fig. 21-5 is now labeled U_3. This figure is analogous to a geographical contour map. A person who walks along the path indicated by a particular height contour on such a map will find that he is neither climbing nor descending; similarly, the consumer who moves from one position to another along a single indifference curve enjoys neither increasing nor decreasing satisfaction from the change in the flow of goods he is getting. Of course, only a few of the possible indifference curves or equal-utility contours are shown in Fig. 21-6.

Note that, as we increase both goods and hence move in a northeasterly direction across this "map," we are crossing successive indifference curves; we are reaching higher and higher levels of satisfaction. Unless the consumer is satiated, he would be enjoying increasing satisfaction from receiving increased quantities of *both* goods. Hence, curve U_3 stands for a higher level of satisfaction than U_2; U_4, for a higher level of satisfaction than U_3; etc.

Every point lies on one of the many indifference curves:

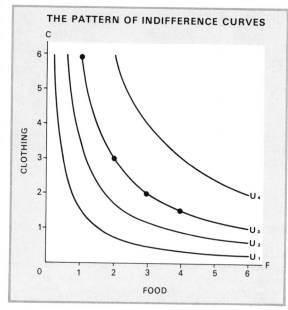

FIG. 21-6. The curves labeled, U_1, U_2, U_3, and U_4 represent indifference curves, or equal-utility contours. (Why is it better to be on a farther-out indifference curve?) U_3 is the indifference contour of Fig. 21-5.

■ THE CONSUMPTION-POSSIBILITY BUDGET LINE

Now let us set the consumer's indifference map aside for a moment and give him a fixed income. He has, say, $6 per day to spend, and he is confronted with fixed prices for each food and clothing unit—$1.50 for food, $1 for clothing. It is clear that he could spend his money on any one of a variety of alternative combinations of food and clothing. At one extreme, he could buy 4 food units and no clothing; at the other, 6 clothing units and no food. Table 21-5 illustrates some of the possible ways in which his $6 could be allocated.

Figure 21-7 shows these five possible positions on a diagram with axes similar to those of Fig. 21-5 and Fig. 21-6. Each position is indicated by a small dot, and it will be noted that they all lie on a straight line, which is labeled *NM*. Moreover, any other attainable point such as 3⅓ food units and 1 clothing unit, would lie upon *NM*. The straight line *NM* sums up all the possible positions that our consumer

Fixed income and market P's imply limited consumption possibilities:

ALTERNATIVE CONSUMPTION POSSIBILITIES		
	FOOD	CLOTHING
M	4	0
	3	1½
	2	3
	1	4½
N	0	6

TABLE 21-5. The costs of these budgets (reckoned as $1.50F + $1C) all add up to $6 income.

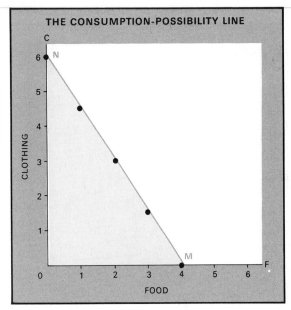

THE CONSUMPTION-POSSIBILITY LINE

FIG. 21-7. NM is the consumer's consumption-possibility budget line. When he spends just $6 daily, with food and clothing prices $1.50 and $1, he can choose any point on this line. Why is its slope $1.50/$1 = ³⁄₂?)

could occupy in spending his $6 of budget income.[2]

The slope of NM (neglecting its sign) is ³⁄₂, which is necessarily the ratio of food price to clothing price; and the common sense of line NM is clear enough. Given these prices, every time our consumer gives up 1½ clothing units (thereby dropping down 1½ vertical units on the diagram), he can gain 1 unit of food (i.e., move east 1 horizontal unit). Or what is the same thing, he can exchange 3 clothing units for 2 food units. We can call NM the consumer's "consumption-possibility" (or "budget") line.

▌ THE EQUILIBRIUM POSITION OF TANGENCY

Now we are ready to put our two parts together. The axes of Fig. 21-7 were the same as those of Fig. 21-5 and Fig. 21-6. We can superimpose the

consumption-possibility budget line NM upon the consumer's indifference map, as in Fig. 21-8. He is free to move anywhere along NM. Positions to the right and above NM are barred to him unless he has more than $6 of income to spend; and positions to the left and below NM are unimportant, since we assume that he will want to spend the full $6.

Where will the consumer move? Obviously, to that point which yields the greatest satisfaction; or, in other words, to the highest available indifference curve, which in this case must be at point B. At B, the consumption-possibility line just touches—but does not cross[3]—the indifference curve U_3; at this point of tangency is found the highest utility contour he can reach.

Geometrically, the consumer is at equilibrium where the slope of his consumption-possibility budget line is exactly equal to the slope of his indifference curve. And as already noted, the slope of the consumption-possibility line is the ratio of the price of food to the price of clothing.

[2] This is so because, if we designate quantities of food and clothing bought as F and C, respectively, total expenditure on food must be $1½F and total expenditure on clothing, $1C. If daily income and expenditure is $6, the following equation must hold: $6 = $1½F + $1C. This is a simple linear equation, the equation of the budget line NM. NOTE:

Arithmetic slope of NM = $1½ ÷ $1

= price of food ÷ price of clothing

[3] At any point on NM other than B, NM is crossing indifference curves. And as long as the consumer can keep crossing indifference curves, he can keep moving to higher ones.

Equilibrium is where consumer has reached highest satisfaction level:

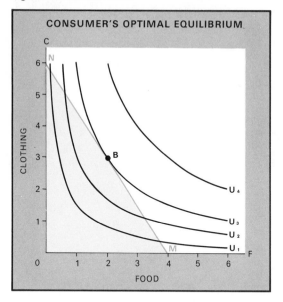

FIG. 21-8. At *B* the consumer reaches highest indifference curve attainable with his fixed income. *B* represents tangency of consumption-possibility budget line with highest indifference curve. (Why? If slopes were unequal, *NM* would *intersect* a *U* contour and he could cross over onto higher satisfaction levels.) At tangency point *B*, substitution ratio equals price ratio P_F/P_C. This means that all goods' marginal utilities are proportional to their prices, with marginal utility of the last dollar spent on every good being equalized—as demonstrated in the chapter's main text.

We may say, then, that equilibrium is attained when the consumer's *substitution* ratio is just equal to the ratio of food price to clothing price.[4]

■ CHANGES IN INCOME AND PRICE

Our understanding of the process will be furthered by considering the effects of (1) a change in money

---

income and (2) a change in the price of one of the two goods.

INCOME CHANGE   Assume, first, that the consumer's daily income is halved, the two prices remaining unchanged. We could prepare another table, similar to Table 21-4, showing the consumption possibilities that are now open to him. Plotting these points on a diagram such as Fig. 21-9, we should find that the new consumption-possibility budget line occupies the position *N'M'*. The line has made a *parallel* shift, toward the southwest.[5] The consumer is now free to move only along this new budget line. Again he will move to the highest attainable indifference curve, or to the point *B'*. A similar tangency condition for optimal equilibrium again applies.[6]

SINGLE-PRICE CHANGE   Now return our consumer to his previous daily income of $6, but assume that the price of food rises from $1.50 to $3. Again we must examine the change in the consumption-possibility budget line. This time we shall find that it has pivoted on the point *N* and is now *NM''*,[7] as in Fig. 21-10.

The common sense of such a shift is clear. Since the price of clothing is unchanged, the point *N* is just as available as it was before. But since the price of food has risen, point *M*, which meant 4 food units had been purchasable, is no longer attainable. With food costing $3 per unit, only 2 units can now be bought with a daily income of $6. So the new

---

[4] The substitution ratio, or slope of the indifference curve, can be shown to be nothing but the ratio of the marginal utility of food to the marginal utility of clothing. So our tangency condition is just another way of stating that a good's price and its marginal utility must be proportional in equilibrium—the consumer there getting the same marginal utility from his last penny spent on food as from his last penny spent on clothing (in agreement with page 533).

[5] The equation of the consumption-possibility line is now $3 = $1½ F + $1C.

[6] Join *B'* and *B* by a smooth curve to generate the important budgetary income-expenditure patterns of Fig. 11-1, page 258, or Table 21-3, page 531. The Appendix and most of the chapter assume goods come in minutely divisible units. If the student were to try to write down the new table like Table 21-2 for $P_2 = 50$ cents and derive from it a new budget-income table like Table 21-3, he would find that the lumpiness of the units presents a little problem. By working with pennies instead of dollars, and with hundredths of a unit of food instead of units, he could reduce this problem to a minimum. Or another trick might be used: To spend $1.50 per day, we might let him spend $2 on even days and $1 on odd days, averaging out to $1.50. Likewise, by having him buy 1 of clothing on every other day and 0 on the other day, he could manage to consume fractional amounts of clothing on the average.

[7] The equation of the consumption-possibility line is now $6 = $3F + $1C.

When income or a P changes we find new equilibrium:

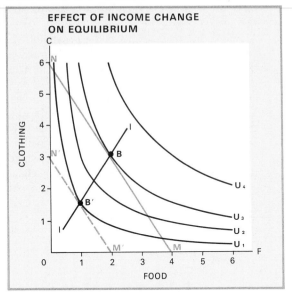

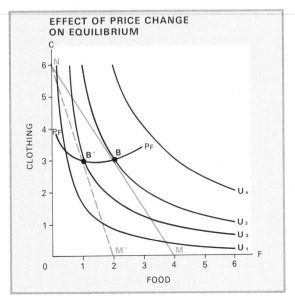

FIG. 21-9. An income change shifts the consumption-possibility budget line in a parallel way. Thus, halving income to $3 shifts NM to $N'M'$, moving equilibrium to B'. (Show what doubling income to $12 does to equilibrium. Pencil in a new tangency point.)

FIG. 21-10. A rise in the price of food makes the consumption-possibility budget line rotate from NM to NM''. New tangency equilibrium is at B'', with less food and either more or less clothing. (Can you handle a change in P_C?)

consumption-possibility line must still pass through N, but it must pivot around N and pass through M'', which is below M. (The new line has a slope of ¾. Why?)

Equilibrium is now at B''; we have a new tangency situation in that equilibrium. Higher food price has definitely reduced food consumption; higher P_F may change clothing consumption in either direction. (The dd demand curves of this chapter were derivable by plotting the P_F, Q_F data you can read off from the line passing through B and B''.)

To clinch his understanding, the interested reader should work out the cases of (1) an increase in income and (2) a fall in the price of clothing or food. (He should also connect all the tangency points

generated by income changes in order to get the Engel's budgetary patterns of Chapter 11.)

BALANCED-PRICE CHANGES   Suppose *all* prices exactly *double*. Then it is easy to see that this is exactly like a *halving* of income. Hence Fig. 21-9's halving of NM to get $N'M'$ will handle this case. This illustrates an important property of consumer demand.

Changing all prices and income in exactly the same proportion leaves equilibrium quantities demanded quite unchanged.

This provides the germ of truth underlying the quantity theory of money and prices (of Chapter 14 and Chapter 17 Appendix).

SUMMARY TO APPENDIX

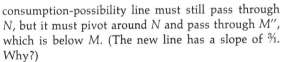 1 An "indifference curve" or "equal-utility contour" depicts the points of equally desirable consumption. The indifference contour is usu-

ally drawn convex from below, in accordance with the empirical law of diminishing relative marginal utilities (or of substitution ratios).

■ 2 If a consumer has a fixed money income, all of which he spends, and is confronted with market prices of two goods, the consumption-possibility budget line upon which he is free to move is a straight line. The steepness of the line's slope depends on the ratio of the two market prices; how far out it lies depends on the size of his income.

■ 3 The consumer will move along this consumption-possibility line until he reaches the highest indifference curve attainable. At this point, the consumption-possibility line will touch, but not cross, an indifference curve. Hence, equilibrium is at the point of *tangency*, where the *slope of the consumption-possibility line* (the ratio of the prices) exactly equals the

slope of the indifference curve (the substitution ratio or relative-marginal-utility ratio of the two goods).

■ 4 A fall in income will move the consumption-possibility line parallel inward, usually causing less of both goods to be bought. A change in the price of one good alone will, other things being equal, cause the consumption-possibility line to pivot so as to change its slope. In any case, whatever change has occurred, a new equilibrium point of highest satisfaction will be reached. It is a new point of tangency, where the marginal utility per dollar has become equal in every use. By comparing the new and old equilibrium points, we trace out the usual *dd* demand curve and income pattern.

QUESTIONS FOR DISCUSSION

1. Explain why one indifference curve will go through any point on an indifference map, and why two such curves never cross.

2. If the consumer is at a point on his consumption-possibility line where it *crosses* an indifference curve, explain why he cannot have reached equilibrium. How will he move?

3. Can *you* generate the ordinary *dd* food demand curve from Fig. 21-10? The *dd* for clothing?

4. Give Robinson Crusoe (or Utopia) a production-possibility curve between food and clothing like the curve of Chapter 2. Give him the indifference curves like those of this Appendix. Can you depict the basic equilibrium of any economy from the resulting tangency and interpret its price aspects?

5. *Extra-credit problem* (but only for the brave): Indifference maps can help solve the problem of calculating a "true cost-of-living index number." In Fig. 21-10, begin at B with original $1.50 and $1 prices for F and C. Now double F's price (as in moving from Montreal to New York, or from 1975 to 1980). By how much does ($3, $1) exceed ($1.50, $1)? Since clothing P has not gone up, it would be an exaggeration to say that the price level (i.e., the "average" price) has doubled to 200. Here is a better guess: Since we happen to be spending the same fraction of income on the two goods (by coincidence, both before and after in 21-10's example), we average a doubling with no change to get $\frac{1}{2}2 + \frac{1}{2}1$

= 1.50, or an index number of 150, representing a 50 per cent increase in the cost of living.

This is a good approximation. But actually, Fig. 21-10 can show 150 is a bit too high, as can be seen from two considerations. (1) Suppose your boss, in order to compensate you for the 150 index, does raise your income from $6 to $9. Now you can buy the 2 of F and 3 of C again as at old B. (Verify by arithmetic.) Geometrically, if your boss shifts your NM″ outward by 50 per cent, your new steep budget line will go right through B. (That's really how our averaging computed the number 1.50!) But note that given your choice on this new *steep* line, you will no longer find B to be an equilibrium *tangency*. You can do a bit better by moving northwest of B to a new higher tangency *above* the U_3 contour. So 150 was a bit too high.

(2) Now we have the hint on how to calculate the *exact* cost-of-living index. Define it as "the minimum ratio by which you must change money income so that the *same level of well-be*ing can be attained at the *new* prices as was obtained at the *old* prices." (Read and re-read.) By geometric exploration in Fig. 21-10 you will find that a parallel increase in NM″ of 41 per cent (giving "true" 141 < 150) will bring you to tangency with the U_3 contour at a point just northwest of B. (Mark it B‴ at about 4¼ for C and about 1⁷⁄₁₇ for F.) See an advanced text like R. G. D. Allen, *Mathematical Analysis for Economists* (Mac-

millan, London, 1936) for a thorough treatment of this topic. On reflection you will realize that a rich man's index may differ from a poor man's, if the latter's U_1 contour is of a quite different shape from the former's U_4. Actually, New York City has a higher rich-man's than poor-man's index. This shape-of-indifference curve factor, of course, just reflects tastes. It prevents us from swallowing the airy claim that "U.S. incomes are higher than Canadian, but their prices are also proportionately higher," as leading to the conclusion "Hence, they are no better off."

6. Geometry buffs can interpret the accompanying diagrams to show how the efficiency of rationing can be improved on. Before war, Man 2 at brown B_2 is richer than Man 1 at black B_1. With food scarce in wartime, both men are rationed to R_1 and R_2 points of equal *food* ($O_1f_1 = O_2f_2$) consumption. Because men have unequal substitution slopes there, shaded areas show how *both* can be made better off if the rich man can buy some of the poor man's food ration. They trade on parallel black arrows, ending at E points (of equal slopes!) where no further mutually beneficial moves are possible. (Can you show that pure competition equilibrium at B_1 and B_2 was "efficient" in the sense that *both* could *not* be made better off? HINT: Slope at B_1 equals slope at B_2 because of common tangency to common market-price ratio. NOTE: Final efficient E situation might also have been reached by a heavy money tax on the rich, with scarce goods being auctioned off to all men at common E_i price ratio. *Reference:* Question 4 of Chapter 26's Appendix uses a similar geometric technique of "box diagram" useful for more advanced "welfare economics" and you might reread the two together.)

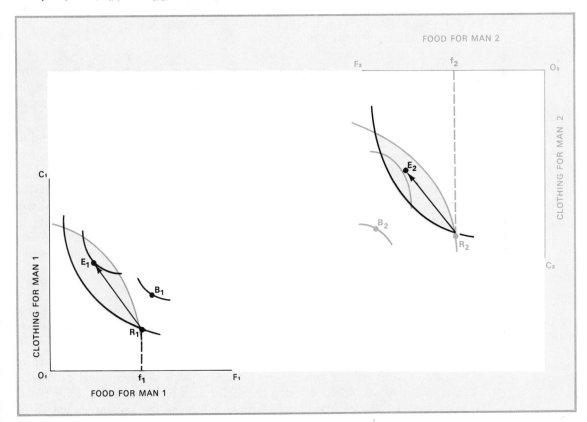

7. Review your understanding of the following concepts:
indifference curves or contours
slope or substitution ratio

consumption-possibility budget line
optimal tangency equilibrium:
P_F/P_C = substitution ratio = MU_F/MU_C
parallel and pivoted shifts

22

COMPETITIVE SUPPLY

Cost of production would have no effect on competitive price if it could have none on supply. JOHN STUART MILL

The last chapter looked behind the market demand curve for its base in terms of the marginal utilities of individuals. It showed how the demand curves of the different individuals in the market place can be summed to form the aggregate market demand schedule.

In this chapter we look behind the supply curve of the industry to find its base in the costs of the different competitive firms. A new concept—that of "marginal" or "extra" cost—is seen to be crucial.

We are interested in competitive supply not merely as a descriptive device. Here in this chapter, we are also interested in showing that the marginal cost concept has a crucially important role to play in allocating for any society its resources in the most efficient manner. (We leave to the following chapter a detailed view of the different kinds of costs that are important in economics.)

▪ SUMMING ALL FIRM SUPPLY CURVES TO GET MARKET SUPPLY

Figure 21-1 showed how we add horizontally all individual demand curves to get the aggregate market demand curve. The same horizontal addition applies to supply.

Suppose we are dealing with a competitive market for fish. How much of this commodity will be brought to market at each different level of market price? Firm A will bring so much to market at a particular price; Firm B will bring so much at this same price; Firm C will bring the amount shown on its supply curve; and so it goes. The total Q that will be brought to market at a given market P will be the sum of all the $q's$ which firms will want to supply at that price. And similarly at any other price.

To get market supply curve, we add all firms' supply curves:

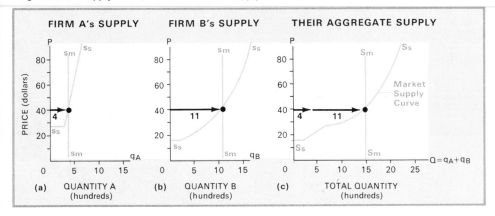

FIG. 22-1. At each price, such as $40, we add quantities supplied by each firm to get total market quantity supplied. This applies to any number of firms. In fact, if there were a thousand identical firms, the market supply curve could be made to look just like the supply curve of each firm by a careful thousandfold change of horizontal scale in the third diagram; if no horizontal scale change is made, aggregate supply must look flatter than each firm's.

Summary. To get the aggregate SS supply curve for a good, we must add horizontally the ss supply curves of the independent producers of that good.

This is illustrated for two firms by Fig. 22-1. Recall that the firms' momentary-run supply curves are defined as the inelastic supplies in a time period so short that no variability in output is possible:

To get the *industry's* vertical momentary supply curve S_mS_m, add horizontally, at the same P, *all firms'* vertical momentary supply curves.

Now recall from Chapter 19 (page 467) that Marshall's "intermediate" or "short run" is defined as that period of time in which the firm is stuck with certain fixed commitments, but in which some variable factors of production can be altered so as to produce more output along the various firms' supply curves:

Again, to get the industry's *short-run* supply curve S_sS_s, add horizontally at the same P the *short-run* supply curves of the fixed number of firms which exist in that short run.

Our problem is to see how a firm's supply curve is determinable from its costs.

■ DEFINITION OF MARGINAL COST NUMERICALLY AND GRAPHICALLY

Basic to industry supply is Marginal (or extra) Cost. Table 22-1 shows how we calculate Marginal Cost: By subtracting the $16,000 total cost of producing $q^* = 400$ units from the $16,040.05 total cost of producing $q = 401$, we find $MC = 40.05 for producing 1 more unit beyond q^*; to produce 1 less unit

Marginal or extra cost can be shown numerically by subtraction:

TYPICAL CALCULATION OF MARGINAL COST

(1) QUANTITY PRODUCED, q	(2) TOTAL COST TC	(3) MARGINAL COST MC
399	$15,960.05	
		$39.95
400	16,000.00	
		40.05
401	16,040.05	

TABLE 22-1. The difference in total dollar cost from producing an extra unit is found by subtracting adjacent items of total dollar cost in Column (2). At $q^* = 400$, $MC = \$40$ to a high degree of approximation.

involves a difference, $MC = \$39.95$, or $\$16,000 - 15,960.05$. So at q^* itself we may, by disregarding or averaging over the trifling differences caused by the trifling lumpiness of units, estimate $MC = \$40$.

> *Definition:* Marginal Cost at any production level q is the total cost of producing one extra unit more (or less);[1] it comes from subtracting total dollar costs of adjacent outputs.

Just as we can calculate MC for $q^* = 400$, we can calculate it for any and every q. Table 22-1 put a microscope on cost behavior around 400 and 401 units. To see the big picture,[2] let us stand off and see how the Marginal Cost curve behaves at *all* levels of output.

Figure 22-2 and Table 22-2 show that Marginal Cost is related to Total Cost in the same way that Fig. 21-3, page 529, related marginal utility to total utility. From Fig. 22-2(b), you will see this:

> MC tends to be U-shaped: ultimately it is rising, even though there may be an initial phase in which MC is falling.

Why can you expect Marginal Cost to be ultimately a rising curve? This takes us back to the law of diminishing returns of Chapter 2. Behind the dollar costs of the firm lies the production relationship between the firm's output and the labor and other factor inputs it hires. This will be discussed in depth in Chapter 26, but here we can indicate the general logic of the situation.

Suppose some factor is held fixed in the short run we are considering: it could be fixed land, or, in manufacturing, it could be fixed plant capacity. Sup-

---

[1] WARNING: MC is usually *not* the same as average cost per unit, which we get by dividing total cost by number of units produced: MC is extra cost, or incremental cost, or differential cost; or, as we have seen from the use of the word "marginal" in connection with *extra* utility, the appropriate name is indeed Marginal Cost.

[2] Figure 22-2 and Table 22-2 measure q in units of hundreds; hence, $q = 300, 400, 401, 500$ in Table 22-1 would show here as $q = 3, 4, 4.01, 5$, etc.

Marginal Cost is to Total Cost as marginal utility is to total utility:

CALCULATING MARGINAL COST

(1) OUTPUT (IN HUNDREDS) q	(2) TOTAL COST TC	(3) MARGINAL COST MC
0	$ 55	
		$30
1	85	
		25
2	110	
		20
3	130	
		30
4	160	
		50
5	210	

TABLE 22-2. To find the *MC* of producing the fifth unit, we subtract $160 from $210 to get $50. At *P* = $40, it will not pay to produce the fifth unit, but it will pay to produce the fourth unit. (Compare this table with marginal utility Table 21-1 on page 529.)

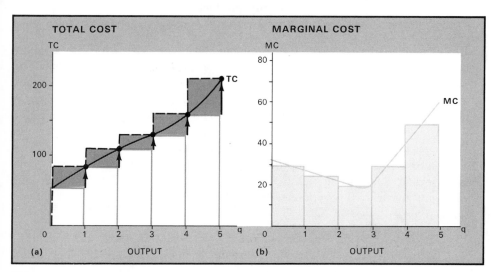

(a)   TOTAL COST   OUTPUT

(b)   MARGINAL COST   OUTPUT

FIG. 22-2. In (a) a smooth curve has been drawn through the points of *TC*. In (b) a smooth *MC* curve has been drawn through the steps of extra cost. Ultimately *MC* is rising, but it may at first fall, giving the curve a U-shaped contour.

pose that we get our varying amounts of *q* by hiring varying amounts of some factor input such as labor. If we can always buy labor at the same wage per unit, the only reason why our marginal or extra cost of getting more *q* should rise would be because the extra product added by each successive unit of labor is going down. Hence, if we do get diminishing returns to the varying labor factor, we shall certainly get increasing Marginal Cost.

Costs and productivity returns are merely opposite sides of the same relationship.

Why does MC often decline *at first*, as shown in Fig. 22-2(b)? Recall that the law of diminishing returns tends *ultimately* to hold: at the beginning, it might be negated by a strong tendency toward *increasing* returns, owing to the economies of large-scale production associated with indivisibility of the productive process and the chance to introduce more elaborate division of labor as scale expands. If at first we have strong *increasing* returns, we must at first have *declining* rather than increasing Marginal Cost.[3]

We can summarize the relationship between the productivity laws of returns and the laws of Marginal Cost:

A tendency for varying factors to show diminishing returns when applied to fixed factors implies a tendency for MC to be rising. If at first there is increasing returns, there will at first be declining MC—ultimately to be followed by diminishing returns and increasing MC.

▪ COMPETITIVE MAXIMUM PROFIT: DETERMINING THE QUANTITY TO SUPPLY

It is evident that costs are vital determinants of how much a firm will be willing to supply. It would supply nothing if market P were too low to cover its out-of-pocket expenses, and would supply much if P were very high. To decide how much to supply at each market P, the firm will want to know the *extra* or *marginal* cost to it of each extra unit of q. Thus, consider Firm A in Fig. 22-1, which is shown supplying 4 (hundred) units at a market price of $40 per unit. Why does $q = 400$ and not 401 or 399?

At first you might be tempted to reply: "Firm A has no choice but $q = 400$ because that is all it can sell at $40—no more, no less." What is wrong with such an answer? It overlooks the facts that this is a model of *perfect competition*.

Definition: A perfect competitor is too small and unimportant to affect the market price. Like a wheat farmer, he is a "price taker" who can sell

---

[3] Later we shall examine the behavior of Marginal Cost in the long run. Suppose we consider so extended a period of time that nothing can be regarded as fixed. Old plants can wear out and be replaced. New plants can be designed and built. Old land obligations can expire. New land contracts can be made. And so forth. In the long run, as a small firm, we may be able to buy *all* the factors of production in balance at unchanged prices. Now what will happen to long-run costs, particularly long-run MC, if the firm has no fixed factors and can enjoy "constant returns to scale"? (This is defined as a state where there is no reason for diminishing returns to operate, since *all* factors grow in balance, and where all economies of large-scale production have already been realized.) *Answer:* If long-run constant returns to scale holds, then doubling all inputs will exactly double their total dollar costs and will at the same time exactly double total output. Hence, there will be constant Marginal Cost, MC being *horizontal* rather than rising or falling. (See page 570 of Chapter 23 for the long-run envelope cost curves.)

all he wishes to at the ruling market price. In terms of elasticity of demand, a perfect competitor faces a (virtually) horizontal *dd* demand curve for *his* product—his elasticity of demand being infinite.[4]

Granted that a perfect competitor can sell any q he chooses at the going P, how does he pick his best q supply response? A perfect competitor picks the quantity he will supply by referring to his marginal cost curve, so that $P = MC$. Why? He will do this because he is interested in maximizing the total profit he can earn. Profit is the difference between the total revenue he receives from selling his output and the total cost incurred in producing that output. He increases his total profit so long as the *extra* revenue brought in from the last unit sold is greater than the *extra* cost which that last unit entailed. Total profit reaches its peak—is maximized—when there is no longer any extra profit to be earned by selling extra output. The last little unit he produces and sells is just in balance as far as extra revenue and extra cost are concerned. What is that extra revenue? It is price per unit. What is that extra cost? It is marginal cost.

Specifically, in Fig. 22-1(a), why might you choose to produce quantity $q^* = 400$ at $P = \$40$? Only one answer is correct: Because the 401*st* unit would involve you in extra (or so-called "marginal") cost of just over \$40; and the 399*th* unit involved you in extra cost of just under \$40; so that the 400*th* unit of q involves an *extra* or *marginal cost* just exactly equal to price P of \$40. (Reread Table 22-1 for an example.)

■ DERIVING THE FIRM'S SUPPLY CURVE FROM ITS *MC* CURVE

We say that a competitive firm is at its Maximum-profit position when it is definitely producing all units with MC less than P, and is not producing further units for which MC is definitely greater than P. Evidently, its Maximum-profit supply response comes when it follows the rule

$$\text{Price} = \text{Marginal Cost} \quad \text{or} \quad P = MC$$

This means that the firm's *supply curve* is given by its rising MC curve as shown in Fig. 22-4. Thus, at the indicated horizontal $d'd'$ level of \$50, the firm will find its Maximum-profit supply response at the intersection point A. (To check this, note that the loss of profit from producing a little less than at A is

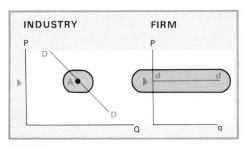

FIG. 22-3.

[4] Figure 22-3 shows the contrast between the industry demand curve DD, relating P to the sum of firm demands $Q = q_1 + q_2 \ldots$, and the dd curve facing any one small competitor. If there are thousands of firms in the industry, the draftsman will have to train a microscope on point A of the industry DD curve to show how this sloped curve will reappear as the horizontal dd curve to the Lilliputian eye of the firm.

**Profit-maximizing competitor has supply curve
determined by Marginal Cost:**

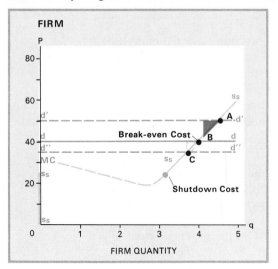

FIG. 22-4. If you can sell all you wish at P given by horizontal $d'd'$, your Maximum-profit equilibrium comes at its intersection with the MC curve at A: your maximum profit is positive; and the gray-shaded triangle shows you would lose some profit if you produced less than at A, since your extra revenue of P would exceed your extra cost, MC.

If P dropped to $d''d''$ level, you maximize profit at C: $P = MC$ there minimizes your unavoidable short-run loss. If P falls below Shutdown cost, your revenue fails to cover out-of-pocket expenses and you will shut down. If P is at Break-even cost B, your maximized profit (inclusive of normal return to your labor and capital) is just zero: new firms will not enter, and old ones will not leave.

shown by the shaded triangle, depicting the surplus of P over MC on the last little units.)

Alternatively, suppose the firm were faced by a horizontal dd at $40. Its Maximum-profit supply response is shown at the intersection point B. It happens, as our original cost Table 22-1 shows, that the firm just breaks even, covering all its long-run costs at this point (total cost = total revenue = $16,000).

Or suppose the firm faced $d''d''$. At this price below $40, the firm cannot break even; but it does *minimize its short-term losses* (or maximize its 'algebraic' profit) there at the C intersection with the MC curve (as you can show by penciling in a shaded triangle like that at A).

Thus, we see that the firm's competitive supply curve runs along its rising MC curve.

The next section establishes the lower end of the rising supply curve.

■ TOTAL COST AND SHORT-RUN SHUTDOWN CONDITIONS[5]

Recall that earlier the "short run" was defined as that period of time in which certain equipment, resources, and commitments of the firms are fixed; but it is

---

[5] This section may be skipped in a brief course.

a period long enough for the firm to vary its output by hiring more or fewer variable factors of production, such as labor, raw materials, and so forth. It is certainly not a precise period of time which will be the same for all industries. Even within an industry, we can be asking questions about "short-run" periods of different duration. At one ultra-short extreme, so many decisions have already been frozen as to make the resulting Marginal Cost curve practically a vertical and inelastic line. Or at the other extreme, we can permit so much time to pass as to let more and more of the equipment have a chance to wear away or be replaced, thereby making the resulting Marginal Cost curve almost as flat as it will be in the longest run, when *no* fixities are possible except those associated permanently with the management of the firm itself.

Now consider a firm making its short-run decisions. It has a certain "fixed cost": this is defined as the total of costs that will go on anyway because of its fixed commitments that are already frozen in the short run; examples would be bond interest, rentals, overhead salaries, franchise taxes, and so forth. The rest of its "total cost" is called "variable cost"; this is defined as the sum of all costs that vary with output; examples are cost of materials, wages for workers on the production line, and so forth. Chapter 23 will discuss all these in detail.

But now consider the firm facing lower and lower *P*. It always has the option of producing nothing at all. How much will it then lose? With its revenue zero and all its fixed cost going on anyway, its shutdown loss will exactly equal its fixed cost. When *P* falls so low as to recover *less revenue than the variable cost it incurs* to produce positive *q*, the firm will prefer to shut down completely: why should it produce if that means it incurs a loss greater than the fixed cost it incurs when shut down? So this rule holds:

Shutdown cost. At the critically low market price where the firm just recovers its *variable* cost by producing, it will be on the verge of shutting down. Below that point, it will produce nothing at all.

Above that *P*, it *will* produce along its short-run Marginal Cost curve. For, at such $MC = P$ points, the firm will be getting something toward covering its fixed cost; and .either it will be getting maximized positive profits, or at least will be minimizing its losses (and in that sense maximizing its algebraic profit).

The location of the Shutdown cost was shown in Fig. 22-4. The *MC* curve slopes up from below that point, but there the supply curve does not run along the *MC* curve.

We can summarize what has now been established. Just as marginal utility lies behind the demand curve, Marginal Cost lies behind the supply curve. *The supply curve of an industry is seen to be the summed rising MC curves of the firms in that industry.*[6]

---

[6] The next chapter will discuss the longest-run case in which new firms can come into the industry and old firms leave it.

Supply-demand intersection can help solve the Planner's welfare optimum of marginal utility and Marginal Cost:

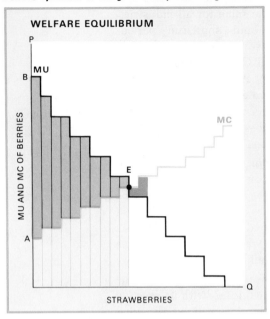

FIG. 22-5. Here Robinson Crusoe or a communal-state Planner utilizes apparatus of supply and demand to determine optimal well-being output. Black *MU* curve intersects light brown *MC* curve at *E*. Cost of picking strawberries is given by light brown area, measuring "utils" of forgone-leisure. Vertical slabs of light gray shaded area under *MU* give excess strawberry utils over utils of cost. Hence light gray shaded area of consumer's net surplus is maximized by producing at *E* intersection (dark gray shaded area to the right of *E* shows loss from producing too much).

▨ SYNTHESIS OF MARGINAL COST AND MARGINAL UTILITY

Having described market equilibrium, we are now in a position to understand *how important the MC concept is in helping society to organize its production efficiently and responsively.* We can now combine cost and utility, or more precisely Marginal Cost and marginal utility.

ROBINSON CRUSOE   Begin with the simplest case—that of Robinson Crusoe. A single man, so the story goes, works so many hours picking strawberries. (1) Each extra berry brings him *diminished* marginal utility. (2) Each extra hour of sweaty labor brings him *increasing marginal disutility.* (3) Working with fixed land, each extra minute of work, because of the law of *diminishing returns,* brings less and less extra berries.

It must follow from these assumptions that Crusoe will work up to the critical equilibrium intersection where a declining marginal-utility-of-berries curve (which looks like both an *MU* and a *dd* curve) intersects with a rising marginal curve of disutility involved in providing the effort needed for additional berries (which is like an *MC* and *ss* curve).

Figure 22-5 gives the Robinson Crusoe welfare equilibrium.[7] The light

---

[7] To keep matters at their simplest, suppose we can ignore (2) the increasing marginal disutility of sweaty labor, by continuing the measurement of all our welfare costs to fixed "disutils" of labor time; or better, what is the same thing, we consider each hour of forgone-

brown curve now rises because diminishing returns makes the MC of extra strawberries rise; the black curve falls because of diminishing MU. Welfare is maximized at E, where MU of berries is in balance with MC (measured, remember, in utils of forgone-leisure). The "triangular" area AEB represents the consumer's (net) surplus, and it is larger at E than anywhere else. (The shaded dark gray "triangle" beyond E shows the loss of well-being from producing that many berries. You can pencil in a similar "triangle" to the left of E reflecting what you would lose of consumer's (net) surplus if you did *not* produce the last units.)

COMMUNAL STATE   Economics is a science of *society*, not of a single isolated individual. Still, we can keep our story simple if we now apply it to a communal state, where all families are treated exactly alike or where some single benevolent or malevolent dictator provides the utility and disutility magnitudes that are to be maximized.

Figure 22-5 still serves to show optimal welfare for a monistic, communal state, just as it did for the one-man Crusoe world. Now a Planner, using computers or market devices, would want to realize the same MU and MC equality shown there.

Indeed, both Crusoe and a planning board might achieve the MU = MC equilibrium by introducing a price of strawberries, P.[8] Then by equating MU = P and MC = P, they would succeed in achieving their welfare optimum.

MANY GOODS   One last complication before considering the real world. Crusoe or a planning board would have to cope with many goods: strawberries versus tea versus cotton gloves, etc. Suppose labor is freely transferable among the different activities—tea, berries, etc. And, to keep the parable simple, suppose that *varying* labor is applied to different grades of *fixed* land, each land being completely specialized to its industry. Clearly, then, each good will have a rising MC curve in terms of labor (and hence leisure-utils) applied to it.

What about society's (or Crusoe's) marginal utility from berries, tea, gloves, etc.? For simplicity suppose each good *independently* has its own total utility and marginal-utility schedules like last chapter's Fig. 21-3. Now comes the vital question. How should Crusoe or the Planner most efficiently allocate labor among the different industries to effect the optimal-welfare pattern of berry production, tea production, etc.?

Obviously, to maximize welfare and allocation efficiency we must in each

---

leisure as having a constant marginal utility so that we can arithmetically reckon both disutilities and costs in these leisure-labor utils. This important notion of "forgone-*opportunity* cost" will be discussed again in the next chapter.

[8] This price could be in units-of-utility-of-forgone-leisure. Or, if we defined labor so that $1 equals the wage of 1 unit of work and 1 unit of forgone-leisure, then strawberry P could be expressed in dollars.

industry[9] get a balance of MU and of MC. If tea involves twice the MC of strawberries, its P must be twice as great. These $P_i = MC_i$ equivalences are vital in any society aiming to solve WHAT and HOW efficiently.

By now, the essential point should be obvious enough. But in leaving it, please notice that a simple "labor theory of value" will not properly solve the problem. Only if you reckon the *Marginal Cost* of a good can you get its proper price in terms of labor or of anything else! And setting prices merely proportional to labor used in an industry does not properly adjust for the scarcity of nonlabor inputs.

■ EFFICIENT MARKET ALLOCATION OF PRODUCTION

Now forget parables. Forget Robinson Crusoe. Forget a communal state. What about the anarchy of a million small competitors? Can a perfectly competitive market really achieve the same optimal MC equilibrium?

QUALIFICATIONS   The answer is, "Yes." Better still, "Yes, maybe." First, you must rule out monopoly: no one expects that an unbridled profiteer will achieve the social optimum. Second, you must not be considering cases where people's demand curves *deviate* from true utility. That is, don't try to apply the theory to heroin production. Or, if you believe that because of advertising and conformity consumers have let themselves demand worthless gadgets that don't deserve to have the word "utility" applied to them, don't try to apply the theory to that area. If there remains a group of goods and industries—say shoes, beef,

---

[9] For each new industry, we draw a new diagram like Fig. 22-5, and again maximize the area of "consumer's (net) surplus" where $P_i = MC_i$ and P_i reflects MU of the ith good as determined from consumer dd curves. (WARNING: if coffee is not *independent* of tea, you could not draw its diagram *independently* of that of tea. Also, if the transferable factor inputs in terms of which we measure the MC_i did not satisfy our simplifying axiom of strict constancy of forgone utils, the consumer's-surplus exposition here would have to be made more complicated; advanced economics handles the problem rigorously by the more complex tools of intermediate economic treatises. Fig. 22-6 here uses the methods of the Appendix to Chapter 21 to show the same welfare optimum as did Fig. 22-5. Robinson Crusoe maximizes welfare at E, where MC_{tea}/MC_{gloves} (as measured by the dark brown slope of his p-p frontier) and MU_{tea}/MU_{gloves} (as measured by the black slope of his indifference curves) are each equal to the market P_{tea}/P_{gloves} (as measured by the dark brown slope of the price-line through E). Verify that E does represent the highest well-being possible for this simplified society. The same holds if the black curve tangential to the p-p frontier at E depicts Planner's preference.

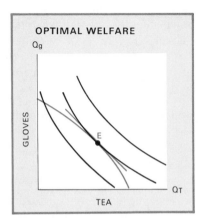

FIG. 22-6.

Competitive-industry market integrates consumer demands and producer's minimized cost:

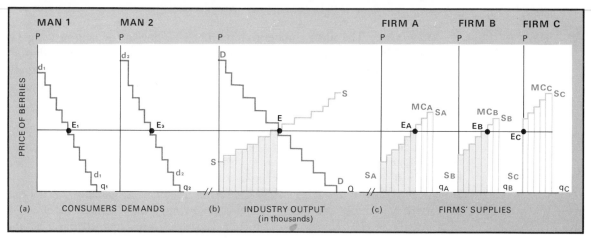

FIG. 22-7(a). Individual demands (as derived from Chapter 21's marginal utility considerations) are shown on the left. If there were 1,000 consumers like Man 1 and 1,000 like Man 2, we would add (horizontally) all their dd curves to get industry DD curve in the middle.

FIG. 22-7(b). The market brings together all consumer demands and firm supplies to reach equilibrium at E. The horizontal black line shows where each consumer on left and each firm on right reaches equilibrium. [Note: Light brown area under SS represents total cost (e.g., labor-leisure) of Q, and this area is at a minimum when all MC's are equal].

FIG. 22-7(c). For each of these competitive firms, profits are maximized when supply curve is given by rising MC curve. Light brown area represents firm's cost of producing. When $MC_A = P = MC_B$, we have Least-cost efficient allocation for industry!

MARKET SYNTHESIS   Now turn to Fig. 22-7 to see how a competitive system does bring out a balance between utility and cost. On the left, we add horizontally the demand curves for all consumers to get the market DD curve in the middle. (Recall Chapter 21, p. 526.) On the right, we add all the separate firms' MC curves to get industry SS curve in the middle. Note what the equilibrium price at the E intersection achieves: it gives people on the left what they are willing to pay for and buy of the good at the P reflecting efficient social MC. On the right, we see that the equilibrium market price does allocate production most

housing, etc.—where there are many reasonably informed consumers and many mutually competing competitive producers, then you may hope to achieve efficiency[10] by market pricing along MC lines.

---

[10] If the dollar votes of different consumers represented an "equitable" allocation, so that each person's dollar represented as ethically deserving a pull on the market as any other's, there would be no need to make the following important qualification: Efficient production and pricing does not mean that the FOR WHOM problem of society is being properly solved; it only means that the WHAT and How problems are being solved in the best way they can be solved consistent with the *existing distribution* of dollar-voting power and of sharing in national wealth and GNP. This qualification is vital.

efficiently. (That is, the light brown area under SS in the middle does represent the minimized sum of light brown cost areas on the right![11])

> *Summary:* **The ideal competitive market is a device for synthesizing (1) the willingness of people to pay for goods with (2) the actual (minimized) marginal costs of those goods. Without conscious planning, the competitive market does achieve the Robinson Crusoe or Planning most efficient allocation of resources to determine How to produce each good.**

Although Fig. 22-7 shows only one good, say, wheat, it can be duplicated to show how shoe production gets organized. Remember that labor and other resources are transferable not only between different wheat farms but also between the wheat and the shoe industries. Their respective MC_i reflect these social costs; and without the $P_i = MC_i$ conditions being satisfied, economic allocation would be "inefficient" in the following strong sense: "Unless *all* $P_i = MC_i$, one can reorganize production and make *everybody* better off—the poor, the rich,[12] wheat producers, shoe producers, etc!" Who pays for such an improvement? No one. It comes from cutting out deadweight waste and inefficiency in social allocation!

■ FINAL SUMMARY OF EFFICIENCY OF MARGINAL-COST PRICING

A coldly objective scientist, who wanted to know nothing beyond how to describe and analyze competitive supply behavior and who had not the slightest interest in society's welfare, would consider the Marginal Cost concept extremely important. But what about a person who was concerned also with human happiness and with the social efficiency of a pricing system? He would find the equating of price to Marginal Cost even more interesting. Our analysis has demonstrated the following remarkable truth:

> Only when prices of goods are equal to Marginal Costs is the economy squeezing from its scarce resources and limited technical knowledge the *maximum* of outputs. Only when each source of an industry's output has had its rising MC equated to *any* other source's MC—as will be the case when each MC has been set equal to the common P—can that industry be producing its total Q at *minimum Total Cost*. Only then will society be out on its production-possibility frontier and not inefficiently inside the frontier.

This equal-marginal-cost dictum is as applicable to a communist, socialist, or fascist society as it is to a capitalistic society. Unless wheat cultivation has

---

[11] Because dollar-voting power may not have been distributed so as to reflect ruling ethical notions of proper welfare and equity, the area under the market DD curve has not been shaded: for that would involve "adding" incommensurable utilities of different persons' dollars and an illegitimate leap from consumer's surplus to consumers' surplus.

[12] Of course, the gains from getting rid of inefficiency *could* be used to help only those deemed *most* in need of help.

been pushed in different parts of the Soviet Union so as to equalize Marginal Costs (including transportation), the Planners there will be failing to achieve the abundance of wheat and other goods that could be theirs with more efficient allocation of resources. (Perhaps it is not surprising to learn from reading the recent debates in their own economic journals that they are gradually becoming aware of this basic fact of logic and economics.)

Because Marginal Cost has this optimality property, it can with some care be used as a yardstick to detect inefficiency in any institutional setup. Thus, if perfectly competitive industries did not exist at all, or if they were rarer even than they are today, one would still derive great benefit from defining and studying the concept of Marginal Cost.

■ NONOPTIMALITY OF COMPETITIVE *LAISSEZ-FAIRE* PRICING

But we must not leave the subject of efficient pricing without a warning. We have not proved that *laissez-faire* with perfect competition maximizes the greatest good of the greatest number. We have not proved that it produces a maximum of social utility. We have not proved that it results in the best attainable level of social welfare. For people are not equally endowed with purchasing power: some are very poor through no fault of their own. Some are very rich, and not necessarily because of any virtue or effort that they or their ancestors have ever performed. So the weight of dollar votes, which lie behind the individual demand curves on the left side of Fig. 22-7, is not necessarily equitable or even tolerable as judged by many ethical systems (various forms of Christianity, Buddhism, "fair shares," etc.). In terms of many ethical systems, the social welfare might be improved by redistributive taxation, rather than letting the end result depend upon *laissez-faire* pricing by the property ownership that happens to prevail. All that marginal-cost pricing has been demonstrated to have in these discussions is the property of helping to lead to "efficiency"— efficiency in the sense that there is no "deadweight loss" in the system; i.e., *no possibility of making everybody better off* by moving from within to the edge or boundary of the production-possibility curve of Chapter 2. This type of falling short of full production possibilities will be referred to again in Chapter 25, footnote 10. When we depart from $P = MC$ pricing, along with inequities of distribution goes the inefficiency of deadweight loss. Marginal-cost pricing is part of the recipe for getting the good society: it is not alone a sufficient condition for having achieved it.

This completes our discussion of the relationship between Marginal Cost and industry supply, and of marginal-cost pricing in its relationship to efficient allocation of resources. The next chapter will go more deeply into the nature and variety of concepts of cost. And later chapters will examine the important cases that deviate from perfect competition—such as monopoly or oligopoly.

SUMMARY

■ 1 In a competitive market, aggregate supply of a group of independent firms comes from adding horizontally their separate supply curves.

■ 2 The short run is defined as that period of time in which some of the firm's productive factors and costs are fixed and some are variable.

■ 3 For a firm we can define Marginal Cost as its *extra* or incremental cost of producing an *extra* unit of output, and can compute the instantaneous rate of Marginal Cost at each output from a smoothed schedule or graph of costs.

■ 4 Behind cost relations lie production relationships and schedules. Thus upward or downward slopes of costs and of productivity-returns are reverse sides of the same coin: when the law of diminishing returns ultimately holds, the MC curve ultimately rises; when there is an initial stage of increasing returns, MC initially falls; if *all* factors of production could be brought in balance at unchanged prices, and if output were then to show constant returns to scale, long-run Marginal Costs could be horizontal forever.

■ 5 A perfectly competitive firm is defined as one which is able to sell all it wants to at the posted market price. To maximize its (algebraic) profit, it will move along its (horizontal) demand curve until it reaches its rising Marginal Cost curve. At this intersection, $MC = P$, and the firm is maximizing its profits or minimizing its losses. So the industry supply curve from a given number of firms will come from adding horizontally their relevant Marginal Cost curves.

■ 6 Out-of-pocket costs (or avoidable, variable costs) must be taken into consideration in determining a firm's short-run "Shutdown point." Below some critical P the firm will not even be recovering in price revenues the variable cost that could be saved completely if it shut down; so rather than end up losing more than its fixed cost, it will shut down and produce nothing at lower P's.

■ 7 Beyond its importance for describing and explaining *competitive supply*, the concept of Marginal Cost has great importance for *welfare economics*. The problem of How goods are to be produced is being solved most efficiently only if every source of production for a good is being utilized up to the same MC level—an optimal result that is guaranteed when $P = MC$ everywhere. The problem of WHAT goods are best to be produced and in what amounts is solved in a Robinson Crusoe or Planning world by equating marginal utilities and Marginal Costs. Just as MU lies behind dd, so does MC lie behind ss; the competitive market, despite its surface appearance of anarchy and chaos, does provide one method for achieving economic efficiency. (WARNING: By itself, competitive pricing cannot ensure that the FOR WHOM distribution of dollar voting power is ethically optimal: taxes and transfers might be needed for that, after which competitive pricing could do the rest of the job.)

QUESTIONS FOR DISCUSSION

1. Show that the differences between momentary, short-run, and long-run periods are a matter of degree and not of kind. In reality, there is a continuum of time periods in which there are fewer and fewer factors that are *fixed*.

2. "If a good can be stored, momentary supply will not be inelastic. When P gets very low, producers will *reserve* some product, storing it for future sale at a higher P." Justify. Can you show that this would make S_mS_m have a rising slope?

3. Give reasons why (positive) Marginal Cost might at first fall and later rise.

4. Why will you ever supply goods at a loss along a short-run MC curve?

5. "If I can get more than enough to cover my fixed costs, I will produce, forgetting my variable costs." Show that two words have been exactly reversed here.

6. Appraise this dialogue. *A:* "What does efficiency matter if the wrong people have all the money?" *B:* "Why risk making everybody worse off? Besides, use the tax system for redistribution rather than deviate from competitive pricing at $P = MC$ since the latter method of redistribution is an inefficient device." *A.* "But will the tax system be so used?"

7. Review your understanding of the following concepts:

summing ss curves to get SS

Marginal (or extra) Cost

$P = MC$, Maximum-profit condition

identity of firm ss supply curve and
   rising MC curve

diminishing returns and rising MC

Shutdown cost (or point)

Robinson Crusoe or Planner welfare
   optimum at $MU = MC$

industry efficiency of
   $MC_A = MC_B$

market efficiency of $P = MC$

23

ANALYSIS OF COSTS
AND LONG-RUN SUPPLY

A class in economics would be a real success if the students gained from it a real under-standing of the meaning of cost in all its many aspects.   J. M. CLARK

The last chapter introduced the definition of marginal cost, a fundamental concept that was seen to lie behind the supply curve of the competitive firm. Here in this chapter we shall go deeper into a variety of different cost concepts.

To understand the Maximum-profit equilibrium of any firm—whether it be the most perfect competitor, the most complete monopolist, or anywhere in the vast terrain of imperfect competition—we need to know how marginal and total costs are related to other cost concepts (such as average, or unit, costs) and to the breakdown between fixed costs and variable costs. Then we shall be ready in Chapter 24 to see how the marginal cost of *any* firm, whether competitive or not, has to be related to a similar concept on the demand side—namely, Chapter 24's *marginal* (or extra) *revenue*—in order to arrive at the Maximum-profit equilibrium of the firm.

■ TOTAL COST: FIXED AND VARIABLE

Consider a typical firm that produces the output q. At this stage, we do not care whether it is a perfect- or imperfect-competitor. At any one time, it has a certain state of technical knowledge, and it is confronted with the prices of the labor and other factor inputs it must buy. Now its accountants have been able to calculate what will be *its total dollar costs for producing each different level of q*.

Table 23-1 shows the simplified Total Cost[1] for each different level of output

---

[1] These data depend upon engineering technology *and* upon the market prices of labor, land, fertilizer, and other factor inputs that the firm needs to produce each output of the good in question. Before its accountants and production men were able to write down the numbers in Table 23-1, they had to make efficiency decisions in *engineering*, ensuring that the physical inputs cannot be combined to give more physical output. And what is not so obvious until we have studied production theory in Part Four, the firm must also have made minimizing decisions of an *economic* kind in arriving at its lowest expense for each q produced.

From schedule of firm's Total Cost, all other costs can be computed in a table:

VARIOUS COST CONCEPTS

(1) QUANTITY q	(2) FIXED COST FC	(3) VARIABLE COST VC	(4) TOTAL COST $TC = FC + VC$	(5) MARGINAL COST PER UNIT MC	(6) AVERAGE COST PER UNIT $AC = \dfrac{TC}{q}$	(7) AVERAGE FIXED COST PER UNIT $AFC = \dfrac{FC}{q}$	(8) AVERAGE VARIABLE COST PER UNIT $AVC = \dfrac{VC}{q}$
0	55	0	55	34 — (30)	Infinity	Infinity	
1	55	30	85	27 — (25)	85	55	30
2	55	55	110	22 — (20)	55	27½	27½
3	55	75	130	21 — (30)	43⅓	18⅓	25
4*	55	105	160	40 — (50)	40*	13¾	26¼
5	55	155	210	60 — (70)	42	11	—
6	55	225	280	80 — (90)	46⅚	9⅙	37⅚
7	55	3/5	370	100 — (110)	52⁶⁄₇	7⁶⁄₇	45
8	55	425	480	120 — (130)	60	6⅞	53⅛
9	55	555	610	140 — (150)	67⁷⁄₉	6⅑	61⁶⁄₉
10	55	705	760		76	5⁵⁄₁₀	70⁵⁄₁₀

*Minimum level of Average Cost.

TABLE 23-1. All the costs can be calculated from Column (4)'s rising TC. Columns (5) and (6) are the important ones to concentrate on: incremental Marginal Cost, calculated by subtraction of adjacent rows of TC and shown in bold brown; the light numbers of smoothed MC come from Fig. 23-1(b). In Column (6) note the point of minimum cost of $40 on the U-shaped AC curve. (Realize why the light $MC = AC$ at the minimum.)

q. Columns (1) and (4) are the crucial ones, showing that TC goes up as q goes up. This is natural because it takes more labor and factor inputs to produce more of a good, and these extra factors involve an extra money cost. It costs $110 in all to produce 2 units, $130 to produce 3 units, and so forth. (Figure 23-1(a), on page 566, verifies all this.)

FIXED COST Columns (2) and (3) break down Total Cost into two components: total Fixed Cost, FC; and total Variable Cost, VC. Figure 23-1(a) shows the breakdown.

Even when the firm produces zero output, it must honor its short-run commitments (contractual rentals, watchmen's pay) and continue to incur its total Fixed Cost of $55. By definition, FC is the amount of cost that goes on independently of output; so it remains constant at $55 in Column (2). Another name for Fixed Cost is overhead cost.

and also in diagrams:

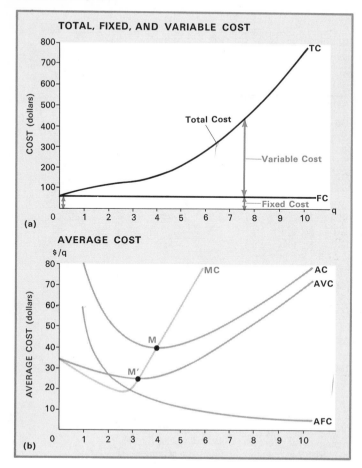

(a)

(b)

FIG. 23-1(a). The total Fixed Cost curve is horizontal by definition. Adding on top of it the rising total Variable Cost gives the rising Total Cost curve.

FIG. 23-1(b). The light-brown curve of Marginal Cost falls and ultimately rises, as in Chapter 22. MC is shown as a smooth curve after the steps of incremental cost are smoothed out; the numbers from the smooth MC curve are given in light brown in Column (5) of Table 23-1 (and correspond to the slope of Fig. 23-1(a)'s TC).

By dividing TC by q, we can plot Average Cost: $AC = TC/q$. Similarly AFC comes from FC/q, and AVC comes from VC/q. At any point, we can add these two gray curves, AFC and AVC, and also get the AC curve at that point.

Note that MC intersects the U-shaped AC at AC's minimum. This is no coincidence. To the left of M, MC is less than AC and hence is pulling AC down. To the right, $MC > AC$ and hence is pulling AC up. At the M minimum point, $MC = AC$; hence AC is horizontal there, being neither raised nor lowered by the equivalent MC. Also MC cuts the AVC curve at its bottom.

VARIABLE COST   Column (3) shows total Variable Cost. By definition, VC begins at zero when q is zero. It is the part of TC that grows with output; indeed, the jump in TC between any two outputs is the same as the jump in VC. Why? Because FC stays constant at \$55 throughout and cancels out in any such comparison. (By subtraction, fill in the blanks in the third column of Table 23-1 with the missing VC data.)

Definitions: "Total Cost" represents lowest aggregate dollar expense needed to produce each level of output q. TC rises as q rises.

"Fixed Cost" represents the total dollar expense that goes on even when a zero output is produced. It is often called "overhead cost" and usually includes contractual commitments for rental, maintenance, depreciation, overhead salaries and wages, etc. It is a sunk cost that is quite unaffected by any variation in q; in the time period for which it is sunk, the only rule is this: Disregard Fixed Cost because FC cancels completely out of every decision.

"Variable Cost" represents all items of TC except for FC—as, for example, raw materials, wages, fuel, etc. Always, by definition,

$$TC = FC + VC$$

(Note that TC and VC always show exactly the same increments $(=MC)$ as q changes, because FC is a strict constant.)

Figure 23-1(a) shows the rising TC curve, broken down into its constant FC and rising VC components.

■ MARGINAL COST REVIEW

We saw in Chapter 22 how Marginal Cost is defined as the increment of Total Cost that comes from producing an increment of one unit of q. (Recall that "marginal," whether applied to utility, cost, or anything else, always means "extra," "additional," or "incremental" in economics.)

The bold dark brown MC numbers in Column (5) of Table 23-1 come from subtracting the adjacent TC numbers in Column (4). Thus MC is $30 in going from 0 to 1 unit of q (i.e., $85 − $55 = $30).

MC is seen to be $110 − $85 = $25 in going from $q = 1$ to $q = 2$. MC is $20 for the third unit of q, $30 for the fourth, and thereafter rising steadily until it is shown as $150 in going from $q = 9$ to $q = 10$. (What is it in going from $q = 5$ to $q = 6$? Pencil in your answer.)

Instead of getting MC from the TC column, we could as easily get the MC number by subtracting each VC number of Column (4) from the row below it. Why? Because Variable Cost always *grows* exactly like Total Cost, the only difference being that it must—by definition—start out from 0 rather than from the constant FC level. (Check that $30 − 0 = 85 − 55$, and $55 − 30 = 110 − 85, \ldots$)

Figure 23-1(a) and (b) shows the behavior of Total Cost (in black) and Marginal Cost (in light brown). Note that the q axes of the graphs are just lined up so that the eye can see the correspondence between TC and MC.[2]

This example shows MC to be U-shaped—at first falling, but ultimately rising. We saw why on page 550: At first there may be great economies in using some or all of the productive factors on a larger scale; and so MC at first falls down to a minimum positive number before again rising. If we stick to the short run where some factors of production are fixed, ultimately the old law of diminishing returns will operate to reduce the extra product that comes from adding equal physical and dollar increments of the varying factors onto the fixed factors. So the cost of getting extra product will ultimately become more expensive, and the short-run curve of Marginal Cost will ultimately be rising.

---

[2] As in Fig. 22-2, we have assumed that units can be made indefinitely small, so that the smoothed-instantaneous MC values can be plotted and read off to give the brown numbers of Table 23-1, Column (5). To help understand the smoothed-instantaneous MC at point q, see Fig. 23-2. It helps to clarify the distinction already mentioned between MC as an

Marginal Cost has many uses. We saw in the last chapter that the rising *MC* curves of the firms provide us with the rising short-run *ss* supply curves which we sum horizontally to get the industry's short-run *SS* supply curve. In the next chapter we shall see that any firm—monopolistic or competitive—will find its Maximum-profit equilibrium by nicely balancing its extra cost against its extra revenue (i.e., by finding an intersection of its Marginal Cost curve and what will be defined as its "Marginal Revenue" curve).

■ AVERAGE, OR UNIT, COST

But first turn to Column (6) of Table 23-1. This gives Average Cost (per unit), which is simply the Total Cost divided by the number of *q* units produced.

$$\text{Average Cost} = \frac{\text{Total Cost}}{\text{output}} = \frac{TC}{q} = AC$$

In Column (6), when only 1 unit is produced, Average Cost has to be the same as Total Cost, or $85/1 = $85. But for $q = 2$, $AC = TC/2 = \$110/2 = \$55$, as shown. Note that Average Cost is, at first, falling lower and lower. (We shall see why in a moment.) But *AC* reaches a minimum of $40 at $q = 4$, and then slowly rises.

Figure 23-1(b) gives a careful plotting of U-shaped *AC*, nicely arranged below the *TC* it came from. We can now break down Average Cost into its two components, fixed and variable, just as earlier we had the breakdown of *TC* into *FC* and *VC*. By dividing each of the last two by *q*, we get Average Fixed Cost, $AFC = FC/q$ of Column (7); and Average Variable Cost, $AVC = VC/q$ of Column (8).

AVERAGE FIXED COST   Since total Fixed Cost is a constant, dividing it by *q* gives in Column (7) a steadily falling Average Fixed Cost curve. The *AFC* curve in

---

increment of cost for a finite step between two points of *q*, and *MC* as a smoothed-out instantaneous rate depicting the tangential slope at which *TC* is rising at one given *q* point. The distance from *a* to *b* represents one extra unit of output. The distance from *b* to *a'* represents the resulting increase in Total Cost, which is the first and simplest definition of incremental Marginal Cost. The second definition is given by the slope of the Total Cost curve at point *a*—and what mathematicians call $d(TC)/dq$—or what is the same thing numerically, by the distance from *b* to *c*. In the limit, as the size of the extra units becomes small and we reexamine the ratios in the new smaller triangle, the discrepancy between the two definitions becomes relatively negligible. (I.e., $ba' \div bc$ approaches one.)

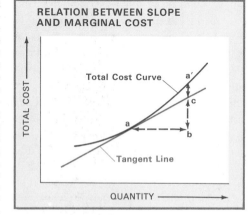

RELATION BETWEEN SLOPE AND MARGINAL COST

FIG. 23-2.

Fig. 23-1(b) looks like a unitary demand curve, or hyperbola that approaches both axes: it drops lower and lower, approaching the horizontal axis as the constant FC gets spread over more and more units. If we allow fractional and zero units of q, AC starts infinitely high, as the finite FC is spread over tinier and tinier units of q.

AVERAGE VARIABLE COST AVC of Column (8) and Fig. 23-1(b) at first falls and then ultimately rises. We could have predicted this U-shaped behavior of AVC from the U-shaped behavior of MC. When MC at first falls, each new q is pulling down the Average Variable Cost calculated over all the items.

THE POINTS OF MINIMUM AVERAGE COST   Figure 23-1(b) is an important economic diagram. Fix it on your eye's retina. Note particularly the typical U shape of the AC curve.

The AC curve is always pierced at its minimum point by the rising MC curve. This is no coincidence. And now we can explain why this has to be in the case.

Any average curve is pulled downward when MC is less than AC; if the last increment of cost is less than the average of all previous ones, it must pull the average down! But when MC gets as big as AC, AC no longer is pulled down; it now turns sideward or level. Then, if MC rises above the AC, it must of course pull AC up. So at the point where rising MC = AC, and only at that point, shall we find the point of Minimum AC.[3]

> *Summary.* So long as Marginal Cost is below Average Cost, it is pulling Average Cost down; when MC gets to be just equal to AC, AC is neither rising nor falling and is at Minimum AC; after MC is above AC, it is pulling AC up. Hence:
>   At bottom of U-shaped AC, $MC = AC = $ Minimum AC
> Likewise, the MC curve cuts the AVC curve at the bottom of its U, pulling it down before this point because $MC < AVC$ and pulling it up beyond that point because $MC > AVC$.

Now that we know how the MC curve intersects the AC and AVC curves where their U's bottom out, we can describe exactly how the firm's Shutdown cost and Break-even cost of Fig. 22-4, page 554, had been determined. The Break-even cost of long-run no-profit competitive equilibrium is seen here in Fig. 23-3 to be at the bottom of the U-shaped AC curve, in accordance with

$P = MC = $ Minimum AC, in long-run equilibrium of zero excess-profits.

---

[3] Here is an explanation of the MC and AC relationship in terms of college grade averages. With MC below AC, Average Cost keeps being pulled down by the lowered cost of the final unit—just as one's cumulative grade average is pulled down when one's incremental average in the junior year is less than one's cumulative average up to that time. Only when one's "marginal or current" grade average crosses above or below one's cumulative grade average will the latter reverse its direction.

Competitors are in long-run equilibrium where price equals minimum average cost:

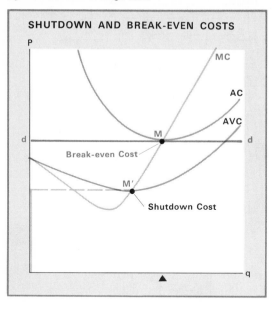

FIG. 23-3. The Break-even cost is at M where dd is tangent to AC and AC is at its minimum. The short-run Shutdown cost is similarly at the bottom of the AVC curve.

Likewise, the Shutdown cost would come at M', once the horizontal dd of the firm had fallen to a level of P so low as to just cover minimum AVC. A price below this level would cause the firm to produce zero output.

■ LONG-RUN-PLANNING ENVELOPE CURVE[4]

We now have all the technical apparatus of the various cost concepts needed to permit us to tackle the problem of how any firm will find its Maximum-profit equilibrium. But one last technicality is needed to explain how a firm may *in the longest run* be able to have lowest costs through adapting and varying the size of its plant.

Recall that, once the firm has a fixed plant, it has a short-run U-shaped AC curve (call it SAC to emphasize its short-run nature). If the firm builds a larger plant, the new SAC curve must be drawn to the right. Now, suppose the firm is still in the planning stage, still quite uncommitted by any fixed obligations. It can write down *all possible* different U-shaped SAC curves, and then choose to select for each prescribed output the SAC that gives it the lowest costs. As q changes permanently, the firm hops to a new SAC curve.

Figure 23-4(a) shows how, in the longest run, the firm selects SAC' for low q; for intermediate q, it does better to plan to use SAC''; for still larger q, SAC''' leads to lowest costs. The black curve of Long-run Average Cost (LAC) is composed of the three *lowest* branches. Figure 23-4(b) shows the same lower limit

---

[4] For more on this see the extra-credit problem, question 10, at the end of this chapter.

In the long run, a firm can choose its best plant sizes:

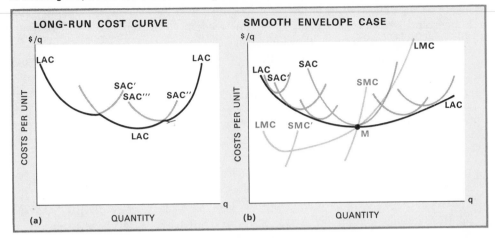

FIG. 23-4. In the long run, the firm can alter its plant size and number of plants. In (a) its *LAC* is the black "envelope" or lower frontier of the three possible choices of plant. In (b) there is an indefinite number of choices and we get *LAC* as a smooth black envelope. In the usual manner we can derive from the black *LAC* curve its light brown marginal curve, *LMC*.

in the case where the firm has choice of infinitely many smooth short-run *AC* curves (*SAC*, not *AVC*!): now *LAC* is the U-shaped smooth "lower-envelope" curve; and *its* well-behaved *LMC* provides the firm's long-run Marginal Cost curve, emerging from the *LAC* minimum point with a gentler slope than the short-run *SMC* curve there.

■ TASKS ACCOMPLISHED AND TASKS YET TO COME

The first half of this chapter is done. The important concepts of cost have been introduced: Total Cost, and its breakdown into total Fixed and total Variable Costs; Marginal Cost; all the different Average Costs (per unit), *AC*, *AFC*, and *AVC*; the interrelations between marginal and average concepts, including their intersection at the minimum point of the U-shaped average curve; finally, long-run envelope cost, *LAC*, when the number of plants and all elements can be adjusted to the level of production.

Since competitive firms must in the longest run realize a price equal to average cost—so that total dollar revenue equals total dollar cost, with no excess-profit—we are now equipped to carry on the analysis of longest-run competitive supply.

✗■ TOTAL COST AND LONG-RUN BREAK-EVEN CONDITIONS

Once I am stuck with certain fixed cost commitments, I will be willing to produce in the short run along my *MC* curve above the Shutdown cost—even though I am not earning enough to cover *all* my costs—as the last chapter showed. But only at some higher point on my MC curve will I be earning enough to cover *all* the costs that have to be met if I am to stay in business after the short run is over and I have regained my long-run freedom (1) to renew my old commitments or (2) to move to another industry.

There is, then, a critical "Break-even cost" below which *long-run P* cannot remain if I am to stay in this business. If every other firm were exactly like me, the long-run supply would dry up completely below this critical Break-even level which covers all costs of staying in business.

Now let us suppose further that entry into the industry is absolutely free in the long run, so that any number of firms can come into the industry and manage to produce in exactly the same way and at exactly the same costs as the firms already in my industry. Under such conditions of free "replication," it is obvious that long-run P cannot remain above this same critical Break-even cost at which they all cover their long-run total costs—including in these (1) all labor, materials, equipment, taxes, and other expenses; (2) all wages payable to the identical managers at the level determined competitively by the bidding in all industries for people of such talents and industriousness; and (3) the interest yield that any of them could get on the amounts of capital that they tie up in this industry instead of investing it elsewhere.

> Long-run Break-even condition: This comes at a critical P where the identical firms just cover their full competitive costs. At lower long-run P, firms would leave the industry until P had returned to the critical equilibrium level; at higher long-run P, new firms would enter the industry replicating what existing firms are doing and thereby forcing market price back down to the long-run equilibrium P where all competitive costs are just covered.[5] Thus, as shown back in page 570's Fig. 23-3,
>
> $P = MC$ = minimum competitive costs, the long-run Break-even equilibrium

■ IMPLICIT- AND OPPORTUNITY-COST ELEMENTS: A DIGRESSION

It is important to stress that the "full competitive minimum costs" which have to be just covered by normal price include more than accountants usually include in costs. Economists include a normal return to management services, as determined competitively in all industries; and a normal return to capital, as determined competitively elsewhere by industries of equal riskiness. In the above sense we may say that "normal profits" are included in costs and that "excess-profits" are competed away by entry of new firms, and "abnormal losses" are eliminated by long-run exit of firms.

IMPLICIT-COST ELEMENTS The return to a factor of production is economically important regardless of how it happens to be owned. To the economist, the

---

[5] If investors tend to be overoptimistic and repeatedly produce an oversupply in the industry so as to create permanent losses on the average, full competitive costs might be defined compatibly with such chronic losses resulting from repeated miscalculations.

returns that go to factors of production owned by the firm itself are so important as to deserve a new name: in contrast to wages that are *explicitly* paid to outside labor, we defined the concept of "implicit wages" as the return to the labor provided by the owner himself; and similarly, implicit rent and interest would be the returns to the land and capital provided by the owner himself rather than hired from outside owners.

Through miscalculation, a person may fail to receive his implicit wages in the short run; on the other hand, he may in the short run be getting more than the needed implicit return, the difference being a transient profit that has not yet been competed away. If he owns some special factors of production, like rich ore land, exceptional know-how, or fertile soil, his accounts may show a high return even in the long run; but we realize this is not so much profit as a return to that special factor of production he is lucky enough to own.[6]

OPPORTUNITY-COST ELEMENTS   Related to the above discussion is an even broader notion about cost. The man in the street can clearly recognize costs that are actual cash payments; the accountant must go well beyond that. But the economist goes even further. He realizes that some of the most important costs attributable to doing one thing rather than another stem from the *forgoing opportunities* that have to be sacrificed in doing this one thing. Thus, Robinson Crusoe pays no money to anyone, but realizes that the cost of picking strawberries can be thought of as the sacrificed amount of raspberries he might otherwise have picked with the same time and effort or the sacrificed amount of forgone-leisure. This sacrifice of doing something else is called "opportunity cost." (Note that opportunity cost would still exist even if he loves to spend that hour in doing both kinds of picking and recognizes not the slightest disutility or sweat in performing that type of work.)

How does all this apply to industry supply and the firm's Break-even costs? In this way: The long-run Break-even level of costs includes, in addition to *explicit* cost outlays, those *implicit* costs that accrue to factors which might otherwise be used in alternative ways. If my labor in wheat could have been used in rye or even in some other man's wheat patch, then its value in those uses has to be met[7] or I shall not continue to supply it to my own wheat patch. For these reasons, full competitive cost intimately involves *opportunity cost*. The latter is an important concept, which covers much more territory than does the

---

[6] If he happens to own very fertile land and persists in cultivating it by uneconomical methods, he will be paying for his folly or stubbornness by forgoing the high return such land is capable of yielding; in dollars, the land becomes worth more to others than to him, and if he refuses to rent or sell it, he is as surely spending his sustenance to please his own tastes as he would be doing if he sold the land and spent the proceeds on wine, song, or being a country squire. A young person with high IQ and versatile talents who stays in a dull dead-end job or dying industry is similarly squandering his economic potential.

[7] The *best* alternative use is of course the proper one to use in reckoning opportunity cost. If alternatives exist along an infinite and smooth continuum, such opportunity cost will set a tight limit on costs to this industry. If alternatives come in steps, then the next-best alternative may give us only a lower limit on factor-price, leaving a possible area in which it has to be determined by the "rent" analysis of Part Four.

Short-run and long-run industry supply depends on firms' costs:

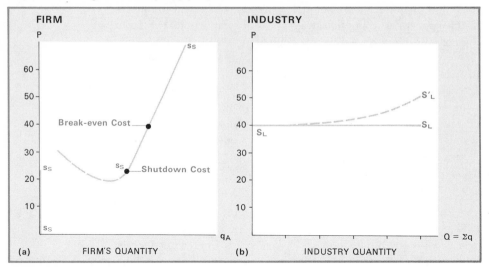

FIG. 23-5. With details omitted, Fig. 22-4 is shown again here in (a). In (b) the industry supply curve is shown. With entry and exit free and any number of firms able to produce on identical unchanged cost curves, the long-run SS curve will be horizontal at each firm's Break-even level. If industry cannot attract all the factors it uses at unchanged factor-prices, the $S_L \ S_L'$ supply curve will have to slope upward as each firm's cost curves are all shifted upward.

notion of implicit costs. The prices of labor and other factors that competitive farmers in an industry are forced to pay out explicitly depend importantly on the forgone opportunities for use in other industries or for leisure; and this means that all competitive costs involve opportunity costs in the background.

The terminology of economists is not uniform in this connection, but the concept of opportunity cost is important and we shall run into it again and again.

■ LONG-RUN INDUSTRY SUPPLY AND FIRMS' BREAK-EVEN COSTS

Now we can return to the behavior of industry supply as firms can enter or leave the industry. We resume the story begun in Fig. 22-1's short run and carried on up to Fig. 23-4.

Figure 23-5(b) pictures industry's long-run supply in relation to the supplies of firms—actual firms and *potential* firms. There are two (possibly three) cases.

HORIZONTAL LONG-RUN SUPPLY CURVE   It is easy to state the conditions that must exist if the industry is to expand or contract, in the long run, along a horizontal supply curve. Entry must be free; and the industry must be either an unimportant, or a typical, user of factors. If we can postulate conditions of absolutely free entry and complete replicability (no secret processes or ingredients!), firms will accumulate along $S_L S_L$ in Fig. 23-5(b) at precisely the original break-even cost level of $40 in Fig. 23-5(a). But duplication of earlier firms is not enough to assure horizontality. In addition horizontality—perfect elasticity—requires that prices of factor inputs do not rise. This postulate is easily satisfied if an expanding industry is unimportant or very small compared with the total of other industries—a very minor demander of all factors. Even if it is important, supply may be horizontal if our industry combines *all* the factors of production (land, capital, unskilled labor, professional workers, and so forth) in just the proportions they are used by the whole economy. Then contraction of other industries makes more factors available in the same mixture (proportions) as our expanding industry has already been employing them. It is a typical factor user. Either unimportance or typicality will assure that an industry's expansion (and contraction of other industries) will not significantly alter the demand for or price of any of the productive factors used in that industry. Hence even a vast replication of such an industry's identical (and potential) firms will leave all its cost curves, and its $S_L S_L$, at the same level.

RISING LONG-RUN SUPPLY CURVE   A second possibility is that the long-run expansion of this industry,—as more firms come into the market and as each firm expands its output—will produce an increase in the market prices of those factors of production that are particularly required by (i.e., are peculiar to) this industry. (EXAMPLE: If wine production were much expanded, those special hillsides suited for vineyard production could not be drawn away from other crops or uses at *constant* rental rates.) What would be the effect upon the $S_L S_L$ supply curve when an increase in industry Q raises the prices of those factors of production peculiarly important in this industry? It would certainly be *to shift upward* the marginal and other cost curves of the new and old firms. And the final result would be that the long-run supply curve of the industry will slope upward from the horizontal.

The law of diminishing returns is likely to become involved in the increasing-cost case.[8] As discussed in Chapter 2 and on page 468, if the sizable industry needs a specific factor—say, able seamen—more intensively than do the rest of industries, expanding its Q will put special upward pressure on that factor's relative price. To be sure, the scarcity of this factor can be partially compensated for by adding other factors to it. But remember what happens when the industry has to add variable factors to a relatively fixed one. They experience diminishing returns. The industry gets less from the new factor mixture, and that sends its long-run costs up. That this industry's $S_L S_L'$ curve is upward-sloping comes from the fact that expansion of its Q relative to other industries' outputs makes its factor-costs (and therefore its price) rise relative to theirs, fulfilling the expectation implied by the curvature of the production-possibility frontier of Chapter 2.

The relative rise in this industry's P and in its peculiar-factors' prices is a

---

[8] The discussion here concerns the *industry* level and does not merely repeat the earlier analysis relating the firm's rising MC to its short-run experience of diminishing returns. Even if each small firm had horizontal long-run MC, when *all* firms expand, the factor-prices faced by each firm will rise and thereby *shift up* each MC curve, thereby causing *the industry* to travel up the $S_L S_L'$ curve. (Chapter 26's Appendix extra-credit final question gives diagrams to show how the *p-p frontier* is attained.)

fact, but it also can be termed a desirable fact. Why? Not because the consumers who must pay more for this good are undeserving, nor because owners of the peculiarly scarce productive factors are especially deserving of higher incomes. Then why? Because any expansion of Q ought to be accomplished *efficiently* with least possible sacrifice of other Qs: the especially scarce factors have now to be severely rationed and be given more of other factors to work with; this will come about, not by a planning board's edict, but by a rise in the prices of this good and its peculiar factors, which will both signal the news of what must be done for efficiency and actually induce people to make the substitution needed if society is not to be inefficiently inside its *p-p frontier.*

If entry is really free, not only has perfect competition the nice property of ensuring that *each firm* ends up on an efficient curve and at the minimum point on it, but in addition the Invisible Hand ensures that *industry* gets its Q from the proper number of firms as some are squeezed out or attracted in.[9]

It will be noted that in industries where $S_L S_L'$ slopes upward, owners of mines, land, know-how, and any other productive factors peculiar to this industry will earn a higher income (or what will be called "rent") from those factors as the industry expands.

If you do not like their earning such an extra return, you might take some of this away from them by taxes or other devices. But any special price ceilings placed on them in order to keep them from reaping such a return will definitely interfere with the equality-of-marginal-cost condition that is needed for maximal social efficiency—and such egalitarian legislation should be passed only if no better way of achieving this purpose can be found and the game is deemed worth the candle it will cost.

DECREASING COSTS AND THE BREAKDOWN OF PERFECT COMPETITION   Economic textbooks of years ago used to supplement the cases of horizontal supply and upward-sloping supply by a third case in which Marginal Costs of the firms were falling rather than rising and in which this was thought to create an industry long-run supply curve that sloped gently downward. Actually, if we review our argument of page 553 telling us why a maximizing firm will want to produce where $MC = P$, we see that the argument *fails completely* in the case where the firm's MC curve is a downward-sloping one. For if you move to the right of a point on a falling MC curve, you find that your additional P per unit is in excess of the now lower MC; and so in the case of decreasing Marginal Cost, the firm will expand its output more and more beyond the MC curve to gain extra profit.

---

[9] If industry demand is large enough to permit numerous firms, then the optional quantity each firm should produce is at the bottom of its U. It can be proved that the no-profit no-loss condition of ruthless competition will then achieve the most efficient number of firms to *minimize* TC for the industry's Q. For why force more expensive extra output from an existing number of firms if it can be got cheaper by replication of firms? And why not be sure that each of the identical firms produces neither too much nor too little, instead producing that Break-even q where $P = MC$ and where likewise P equals the lowest Average Cost per unit that will keep the firm in business in the long run? (If market demand is not large enough to keep numerous competitors viable, there will arise problems connected with the discreteness of firm sizes that will be discussed in Fig. 24-2.) See final question 10 for more on this.

Under decreasing Marginal Cost, the first firm to get a head start will find its advantage increasing the greater it grows. As it forces other firms to contract their q's, their disadvantage will become aggravated as they are forced to travel back up their falling MC curves.

The result must be obvious:

Under persisting decreasing costs for the firms, one or a few of them will so expand their q's as to become a significant part of the market for the industry's total Q. We shall then end up with one of the following three cases:

(1) a single monopolist who dominates the industry

(2) a few large sellers who together dominate the industry and who will later be called "oligopolists"

(3) some kind of imperfection of competition that, in either a stable way or in connection with a series of intermittent price wars, represents an important departure from the economist's model of "perfect" competition where no firm has any control over industry price.

As the next section will show, when the firms in this industry all expand together, they could create what are called *external economies* (or *diseconomies*). Thus, a school for fishermen might become feasible only at high industry Q; and this training might cause a downward shift of every firm's cost curves as the industry total Q rises. The result could be an *industry $S_L S_L$* curve that slopes *downward* owing to *external* economies without the breakdown of perfect competition. But external economies do not alter our main conclusion. *Internally* decreasing cost for any firm destroys perfect competition, as Chapter 24 will discuss further.

■ EXTERNAL ECONOMIES AND DISECONOMIES[10]

Our discussion of decreasing costs has shown that it would be wrong to draw a curve of downward-sloping industry supply based upon costs falling *internally* within the firm. There is, however, a possible theoretical case in which the expansion of the industry's Q somehow causes each firm's cost curves as plotted against its q to *shift downward*. Alfred Marshall deemed this a case of downward-sloping industry supply based upon what he called *external* economies.

An "external economy" is defined as a favorable effect on one or more persons that emanates from the action of a different person or firm; it shifts the cost or utility curve of each person it helps, and such an *externally* caused shift should be distinguished from any *internal* movement along the affected individual's own cost curve.

An "external *dis*economy" is defined in the same way, except that it refers to external *harm* that is done to others. The case where expansion

---

[10] This section may be skipped at a first reading.

of fishing by others in limited waters serves to shift up each boat's cost curves would be an example of an external diseconomy; another case would be one where each man's haste to drill for oil near his neighbors' boundaries lowers the amount of oil each recovered. Smoke nuisance and water pollution are two other familiar instances.

External economies have a considerable importance in connection with government activities that provide benefits to many individuals (so-called "public goods"). They are important too in connection with growth, where the building of a public road or some kind of "social overhead capital" like a hospital or dam has favorable external repercussions on many families, firms, and industries. The kinds of favorable external economies that are peculiarly associated with expansions along an industry supply curve—our main subject here—are not so easy to find. But here are a few examples.

Because fishing Q is expanding, the number of trained fishermen that any firm might find to hire may go up. Or it may now pay the government, or some profit-seeking monopolist, to build a training school for fishermen, whereas previously such a school could not pay because of its high marginal cost at low scales of operation. A similar case would be one where specialized machinery for the fishing industry was producible by another industry only with excess capacity at decreasing marginal cost. Or if all of us in a neighborhood keep bees, I may find that I gain more wandering bees from your nearby acres when total Q of the honey industry rises; whereas when total honey Q is small, I find that some of my bees wander uselessly off to neighboring cornland and my neighboring corngrower has few bees that might in return wander back to me. Or one might conjure up the case where, when I drain my mine of water, I cannot help but make your neighboring mine somewhat drier and thereby confer an external economy on you.

It is easier to find examples of so-called "external diseconomies" resulting from larger-scale industry Q. Recall that these are defined as harmful effects upon other people that result from one man's production. Thus, expanding along a supply curve for steel will cause great belching forth of smoke. This external effect is not only a nuisance, it may actually be harmful to good health and costly in terms of needed cleaning bills. Smog in many cities comes from the external diseconomies of each man's auto and factory. The greatest external diseconomy of all results from one country's setting off nuclear bombs.

One does not need the case of the nuclear bomb to know that wherever there are externalities a strong case can be made for supplanting complete individualism by some kind of group action: consumers should be made to pay for the smoke damage that their purchases make inevitable, as would be the case if we supplemented *laissez-faire* by a tax or by coercive ordinances; a conservation subsidy to farmers, so that they will keep trees growing and thereby prevent disastrous floods hundreds of miles downstream, might represent rational social policy; regulations that prevent smallholders from digging oil wells frenziedly at the edge of their neighbors' property would be economically efficient. The reader can think of other limitations on individual freedom in the interest of all, arising from countless other externalities.[11]

No more need be said at this point about externalities. They can shift firm cost curves and thereby alter the slope of industry supply curves upward and downward. But even more important is their general role in connection with causing free pricing to be non-optimal, thereby creating a *prima facie* case for zoning laws, government controls, and alert planning.

The main concepts, and their relation to supply in the short and long run, have now been introduced. In the next chapter we can pit cost against revenue to learn how any firm finds its Maximum-profit equilibrium.

SUMMARY

■ 1 Total Cost can usefully be broken down into its Fixed and Variable Cost components. *FC* cancels out of all decisions relevant to the period for which it is truly fixed.

■ 2 Marginal Cost is the increment of extra Total Cost resulting from one increment of extra *q*. (If our units are divisible, *MC* can be defined as the slope of the smooth *TC* curve at any *q* point, and this slope will give a close approximation to the extra cost of producing one more small *q* increment.)

■ 3 Average (total) Cost, *AC*, is the sum of ever-declining Average Fixed Cost and of usually U-shaped Average Variable Cost. *AC* is U-shaped, being intersected at its bottom by the rising *MC* curve. Similarly, *AVC* is cut by *MC* at its bottom.[12]

■ 4 In the long run, when all fixed commitments expire and a firm is free to plan to operate any number of plants, the long-run cost curve *LAC* (and

---

[11] The late Professor A. C. Pigou, Marshall's prize pupil at Cambridge, was the economist who most emphasized the problem of externalities. There is a clear-cut economic case for a tax (or a subsidy) whenever an external diseconomy (or economy) creates a divergence between private pecuniary Marginal Cost as seen by a firm and true social Marginal Cost.

But this truth is quite independent of the supply slope of the *industry* in question. And Marshall and Pigou erred in thinking that a tax should be put on an industry whose supply curve rises in the fashion of Fig. 23-5(b); for they failed to recognize that the supply curve may rise because some *pecuniary* factor costs are raised to the firms externally by the expansion of industry Q—as Allyn Young pointed out half a century ago. We may add, they erred equally in thinking an industry should be subsidized if its *SS* curve slopes down, since the firms' curves may have been shifted down externally by pecuniary reductions in its factor input prices: so long as government assures that such a factor input is sold at *its* declining *MC* price, the pecuniary external economy it creates for our industry can be safely ignored. Young correctly emphasized that external *technological* economies and diseconomies merit interference. He showed that imposing a rent on private property in land succeeds in preventing it from becoming overcrowded by rugged individualists. Similarly, in the case of overcrowded fishing waters, subdividing the sea might somewhat reduce social inefficiencies; but certain government fees and rules of the road might well be devised which would do still better than would ordinary private ownership of the sea's acres.

[12] See no. 9 in the Questions for Discussion section for useful rules about *AC* and *MC* curves.

LTC) must be the lower-envelope frontier of best choice of plant for each level of output. This frontier will be a smooth envelope, containing at any point a tangential short-run cost curve, if potential plant sizes are smoothly continuous. Usually the long-run curve *LAC*, and its associated marginal curve, will be U-shaped: ultimately it will rise if not all factors of production (including management) are expandable at constant prices; and at very small outputs, indivisibilities in the inputs or the methods of combining them will cause costs initially to fall.

■ 5 An industry's long-run supply curve, $S_L S_L$, must take into account the entry of new firms and exodus of old ones. In the long run all the commitments of any firm will expire, and it will decide to stay in business only if price at least covers all its long-run costs—whether they be "explicit" out-of-pocket payments to labor, lenders, material suppliers, or landlords; or whether they be "implicit" wages (defined as the "opportunity costs" of its owners' labor which could be employed elsewhere in producing or in leisure) or implicit interest and rent on the property assets owned by the firm (and whose opportunity costs are measured by what they will fetch in other equally risky uses).

■ 6 Under conditions of free entry, where no one firm has any particular advantages of location, skill, or resources specialized to this industry, one can expect in the long run that free entry of would-be competitors will compete away any excess profits earned by existing firms in the industry. So, just as free exit means *P* cannot fall below the Break-even cost, free entry means it cannot persist above that point in the long-run equilibrium. Where an industry can expand by replication without pushing up the prices of any factors peculiar to it or used in peculiarly large proportions by it, the resulting long-run supply curve will be horizontal.

■ 7 More likely, any but the smallest industry will generally use some factors of production in large enough amounts to force up their prices slightly. As a result, its long-run supply curve will be sloping upward, at least gently.[13]

■ 8 It is not true that *downward*-sloping Marginal Cost curves of competitive firms can serve as their supply curves—for the very good reason that their profits will be at a minimum along such curves and they will rush away in either direction from such points. As a result, one or a few firms will tend to expand and the remaining firms will tend to contract. Thus lasting decreasing costs that are *internal* to firms implies the destruction of perfect competition. So it is wrong to talk of decreasing supply curves in such a case, or of competitive supply at all.

■ 9 There is, however, the possibility that *external economies* could prevail in an industry. In such cases expansion of *industry Q* could *shift* downward the cost curves of *single firms*; and in the complicated adding of the result-

---

[13] Or in extreme cases, where the labor it uses actually is supplied by families in reduced amounts when *Q* expansion bids up the wage, the industry $S_L S_L$ curve could even bend backward toward the northwest, as in Case 4 of the Appendix of Chapter 19.

ing supplies of all firms, the industry supply curve could end up as downward-sloping.

The concept of external economies or diseconomies is important beyond any such Marshallian application to industry supply. By definition, such externalities involve good and bad economic effects *upon others* resulting from one's own behavior. Since one person takes into account in the search for individual gain and well-being only private money benefits and costs as seen by him, there will then be a divergence between *social* costs and *pecuniary-private* costs. This means that there is a *prima facie* case in such instances for group action, by subsidy or public control, to expand situations fraught with external economies; and a similar case to contract, by tax or fiat, activities involving external diseconomies.

QUESTION FOR DISCUSSION

1. Make a list of cost elements: wages, salaries, fuel, rentals, etc. Divide them into the Fixed and Variable categories. (Your division will depend on your time periods.)
2. Explain the difference between Marginal Cost and Average Cost. Why should *AVC* always look much like *MC*? Why is *MC* the same when computed from *VC* as from *TC*?
3. To the $55 of Fixed Cost of Table 23-1, add $90 of additional *FC*. Now calculate a whole new table, with the same *VC* as before but new *FC* = $145. What happens to *MC*, *AVC*? To *TC*, *AC*, *AFC*? Can you verify that minimum *AC* is now at $q^* = 5$ with *AC* = $60 = *MC*? (You can check *MC* and *TC* of your table against Chapter 24's Table 24-3.)
4. Explain why *MC* cuts *AC* and *AVC* at the bottom of their U's. Recall, in connection with the last chapter, that minimum *AVC* can be shown to provide the short-run Shutdown cost, and minimum *AC* to provide the long-run Break-even cost.
5. Explain how the long-run envelope cost curve is defined as the lower frontier of all short-run curves. Illustrate with (a) the case of a few plant sizes, and (b) the case of infinitely-continuous plant sizes.
6. Relate the rising *MC* curve to the law of diminishing returns. Contrast the falling part of the curve with that law.
7. Interpret this dialogue. A: "How can competitive profits be zero in the long run? Who'll work for nothing?" B: "It is only *excess*-profits that are wiped out by competition. Managers get paid for their work; owners get a normal return on their capital in long-run equilibrium—no more and no less."
8. Give examples of external economies. External diseconomies. What public interferences do you suggest? What rights to sue in court? Distinguish from opportunity costs.
9. *Extra-credit problem:* With the help of the adjoining diagram, puzzle out the meaning of the following rules. *First rule:* If a Marginal Cost curve is below its associated Average Cost curve, it is pulling the *AC* curve down; if *MC* is above *AC*, it is pulling *AC* up; if *MC* = *AC*, *AC* must be horizontal. *Second rule:* If *AC* is a straight line, as in (a), (b), or (c), *MC* will be a straight line starting from the same vertical intercept point but with twice the slope of *AC*. (NOTE: This tells us how to find the *MC* point above or below the *AC* point on *any* non-straight-line *AC* curve. At a chosen *q* in (d), merely draw the tangent straight line to *AC*; from that line's vertical intercept, draw an *MC* line with twice the slope; read off from this last line the *MC* value at

your chosen q level. Of course, you must draw two new straight lines for every different q level.) Final query: Note horizontal brown line in (b); label it dd for perfect-
competitor's demand. Shade in triangle formed between dd and MC and note that you
gain by increasing your q indefinitely!

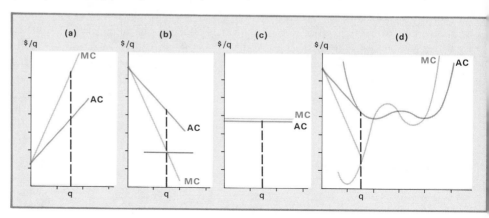

10. *Extra-credit problem:* Can you interpret the adjoining diagram to show that society
does get industry Q at lowest dollar and resource cost when each of many firms is at
bottom of its U-shaped *AC*? First U on left comes with 1 firm. Second U comes with
Q divided equally between 2 firms (so second U is merely the first with twice the
horizontal scale; and similarly for the $n = 3, 4, \ldots$ U's). Beyond the // break, n is
large—say, 100 firms. Naturally, industry Q is procured at least cost on *black lower
curve*, with lower and lower brown switch points at which it just pays to add one new
firm. Then to see how costs *for each typical firm* drop as Q and n grow, concentrate
on the markings on the left side of the first U. With $n = 1$, the sky is the limit. For
$n = 2$, the brown 2 shows highest that *AC* can ever be for any firm; for $n = 3$, brown

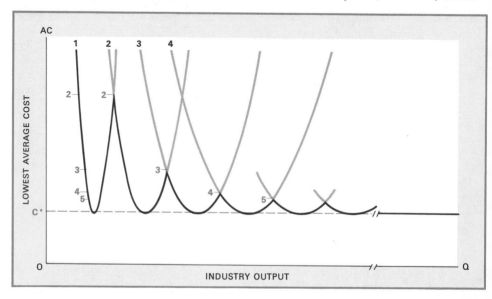

3 gives lower highest AC; and brown numbers (which are drawn at exact level corresponding to respective switch points) drop to minimum AC when DD is big enough for numerous competitive firms to survive. So beyond the // break, with many firms, the black industry curve looks smoothly horizontal.

11. Review your understanding of the following concepts:

Total Costs: Fixed and Variable	Break-even point at $P = MC = $ Min AC
$TC = FC + VC$	Shut-down point at $P = MC = $ Min AVC
$AC = TC/q = AFC + AVC$	horizontal and rising $S_L S_L$
Marginal Cost (incremental and smoothed)	implicit costs and opportunity costs
	decreasing costs and breakdown of competition
long-run envelope of cost, LAC and LMC	external economies and diseconomies

24

MAXIMUM PROFIT EQUILIBRIUM IMPERFECT COMPETITION

Both monopolistic and competitive forces combine in the determination of most prices. EDWARD H. CHAMBERLIN

In the last several chapters we have studied the workings of competitive supply and demand in considerable detail. For the most part, we have been studying the case called "perfect competition."

Perfect competition means something very definite to the economist. As we saw, the economist means by it something *much stronger* than the man in the street and the businessman do when they talk of "strong rivalry and keen competition among different business firms and industries."

The special case of perfect competition is very important. But it is only one case, and economists pay it so much attention because of the light it throws on the *efficiency* of resource use. Certainly, it cannot faithfully represent many of the facts about modern industries. The real world—as we know it in North America, Europe, or Asia—contains significant *mixtures of monopoly imperfections along with elements of competition*. The real world, then, is for the most part to be classified in the realm of "imperfect competition": it is neither perfectly competitive nor perfectly "monopolistic."

The remaining chapters of Part Three, therefore, will give us the tools to analyze imperfect as well as perfect competition. They will show what modifications have to be made in any conclusions that were based on an analysis of perfect competition. We shall see that the way a pricing system succeeds in solving the basic problems of WHAT, HOW, and FOR WHOM is affected to an important degree by any elements of monopolistic imperfection that may be involved in numerous modern industries.

Part A of this chapter gives an overview of *patterns of imperfect competition and of real-world market structure*. It also presents a new important tool—

the concept of Marginal Revenue. Part B portrays the equilibrium analysis of an idealized monopoly firm, to show how it *achieves maximization of profit by balancing its marginal cost and marginal revenue*. We then are ready to appraise at the end of this chapter the inefficiency inherent in imperfection of competition, and to develop in the Appendix the principles of public regulation.

A. OVERVIEW OF MARKET STRUCTURE AND THE CONCEPT OF MARGINAL REVENUE

■ PERFECT COMPETITION CONTRASTED WITH IMPERFECT COMPETITION

Figure 24-1(a) reminds us that, to an economist, a perfect competitor is defined as a firm that has no control over price—in the sense that it faces an essentially *horizontal dd* curve along which it can sell as much or as little output as it likes.

Remember how strict this definition of perfect competition is. Think of any commodity that comes to mind: razor blades, toothpaste, steel, aluminum, potatoes, wheat, cigarettes, tobacco, nylon, cotton. Which fit in with this strict definition? Certainly not razor blades or toothpaste, or cigarettes. Did you ever hear of an auction market for blades, or toothpaste, or cigarettes?

Neither aluminum nor steel meets the definition of perfect competition. For a long time there was only one aluminum company in North America, Alcoa (Aluminum Company of America); and even today there are only Alcoa, Alcan, Reynolds, Kaiser, and one or two others. Contrast this with the case of thousands, if not millions, of cotton and wheat farmers.

What about steel? It is true that one plant's steel output may be much like another's, but it is not true that most of the well-known firms (Bethlehem in the United States, or Stelco in Canada) are so weak that each could never depress the price of steel by throwing on the market as much as it could comfortably produce.

When you go down the list, you will find that only potatoes, tobacco, wheat, and cotton come within our strict definition of perfect competition. Nylon must compete with cotton; that is very true. But in the economist's strict sense, nylon is not a product supplied under "perfect competition," nor is each of its few producers a "perfect competitor" in the economist's sense of the term.[1]

---

[1] Sometimes economists use various synonyms for perfect competition: they often call it "pure competition," in contrast to "impure, or imperfect, or monopolistic competition"; or they occasionally call it "atomistic competition," to convey the notion of numerous small firms which combine like a multitude of tiny atoms to make up the industry. Occasionally, too, an economist will say: "By perfect, I mean really perfect. The wheat market isn't 'perfect competition' unless everyone in it is perfectly *informed* about all the future, there being nowhere any *uncertainty*." However, that is not the sense used here for perfect competition. The price of wheat will fluctuate in a way that no one can now foresee, but as long as *no seller can appreciably influence wheat price*, we shall agree to call the wheat market *perfect*. (Naturally, once you bring government buying programs into the wheat picture, as in Chapter 20, you are bringing monopolistic imperfections into this perfect-competition setup.)

The acid test for imperfect competition is slope of firm's demand:

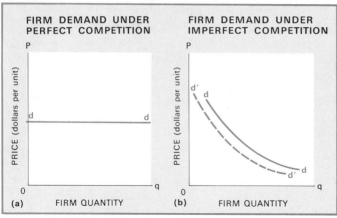

FIG. 24-1. The perfect-competitor firm can sell all it wants to along its horizontal *dd* curve, never depressing market price. But the imperfect-competitor firm will find that its demand curve slopes downward as its increased *q* forces down the *P* it can get. And unless it is a sheltered monopolist, a cut in its rivals' *P*'s will appreciably shift its own *dd* leftward to *d'd'*.

■ IMPERFECT COMPETITION DEFINED

But suppose the single firm finds itself facing a demand curve which slopes appreciably downward as in Fig. 24-1(b)—which means that when it insists on throwing more on the market, it definitely does depress price along its *dd* curve —then the firm is classified by the economist as an "imperfect competitor."

> *Definition:* "Imperfect competition" prevails in an industry or group of industries wherever the individual sellers are imperfect competitors, facing their own *nonhorizontal dd* curves and thereby having some measure of control over price.

This does not mean that a firm has absolute monopoly power over the price it can charge; as we shall see, there are varying degrees of monopolistic imperfection in different imperfectly competitive markets.[2]

Mind you, this does not mean that the owner of an imperfectly competitive firm is of poor character, that he beats his wife, or fails to pay his bills. Nor does the fact that a firm is an imperfect competitor mean that it is not keenly seeking to outsell and outadvertise its rivals. Intense commercial rivalry and "perfect competition" are not at all the same thing; indeed, Farmer Jones, perfect competitor, will do no advertising at all. Why should he? He can sell all the wheat he can produce without depressing market price. But Imperial Tobacco, producer of Buckingham cigarettes and an imperfect competitor, will spend

---

[2] The standard book on all this is E. H. Chamberlin, *Theory of Monopolistic Competition*, Eighth Edition (Harvard University Press, Cambridge, Mass., 1963), especially Chapters 1 and 4. Chamberlin prefers the term "monopolistic competition" for what is here called "imperfect competition," but that may give the impression to the layman that there is something especially nasty, or illegal, in not being a perfect competitor, which is not Chamberlin's view. Also, confusion can result from the fact that "monopolistic competition" is sometimes used by Chamberlin as a name for Fig. 25-3's special large-group case of symmetric sellers of differentiated products, a nomenclature avoided in this book.

much of its energies in trying to outsell Exports, the snuff industry, and even the candy industry.

■ COST PATTERNS AND STRUCTURE OF MARKET IMPERFECTION

At the end of Chapter 23 we saw that continuing decreasing cost is incompatible with perfect competition. If every, or even *any*, firm in an industry could always bring down its Marginal and Average Cost in the long run merely by expanding its output q, it would soon expand to become an important fraction of the industry. In short, it would expand to become some kind of monopolist, ceasing to be a price taker and now having some measure of control over the price it gets. As soon as it has control over price, it will cease to follow the $P = MC$ rule for profit maximization. Presently we shall see why. And as soon as somebody in the system raises Price above Marginal Cost, a critic is able to find a flaw of inefficiency in the economic organization of society.

Figure 24-2 illustrates some patterns of costs which lead to a breakdown of perfect competition. In Fig. 24-2(a) the firm is shown to have Average and Marginal Costs that fall forever. It displays "increasing returns to scale": as q grows, the firm finds more elaborate ways of specializing its equipment; it organizes its work gangs in larger and more efficient units; it can afford ever larger boilers and machines, which display greater net efficiency. All this without end. No matter how big is the demand for its product—no matter how far out the industry DD curve happens to lie, the most efficient operating size for this one

To avoid monopoly, costs must turn up soon:

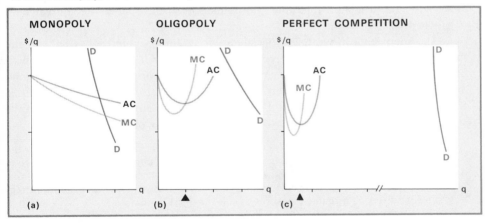

FIG. 24-2. When costs fall indefinitely, as in (a), any one firm can expand to monopolize the industry. In (b) costs eventually turn up, but not soon enough relative to total industry demand DD. Coexistence of numerous perfect competitors is impossible; some kind of few-seller oligopoly is likely. In (c) total industry demand DD is so vast relative to efficient scale of any one seller as to permit viable coexistence of numerous *perfect competitors*. [What if firms contrive to differentiate their product in (c), fragmenting the market and moving DD far to the left, ending up in some kind of Chamberlinian imperfect competition —like (b) or (a)?]

firm will be greater, and peaceful competitive coexistence of thousands of price takers will be quite impossible.

Perhaps the pattern of unlimited decreasing cost is unrealistic. Perhaps *ultimately* the economies of scale will all have been achieved, and the cost curves will level out or turn up. Figure 24-2(b) illustrates such a case: the firm's long-run MC and AC curves do finally turn up. But, alas, they do not turn up soon enough to avoid the breakdown of perfect competition. For note where the industry total demand curve DD now lies: it does not provide a big enough market to enable *numerous* firms to coexist at the efficient level of cooperation called for by the indicated cost curve. We shall still end up in some kind of monopoly or few-seller "oligopoly" situation. (*Oligos* means "few" in Greek.)

In Fig. 24-2(c), the outlook is more favorable for perfect competition. Why? Because the industry DD is so great compared with the optimum size of each firm, we can hope to replicate the large number of firms needed for truly perfect competition.

There is one encouraging feature of the modern industrial state. Large corporations find it pays them to produce many *different* products, not just the single q shown in these diagrams. Thus, Ford produces trucks, tractors, refrigerators, precision equipment, and not just automobiles. It is a big company—but it is not really big in the refrigerator or tractor or equipment markets. It must compete with other giants in these markets. As far as producing more refrigerators is concerned, its costs will not continue to fall, as in Fig. 24-2(a) or (b), until it has a dominant position. Actually, because of the competition of numerous other conglomerate giants, Ford's costs relative to each diverse market's demand might look more like that of Fig. 24-2(c). The result is encouraging because it may lead to a tolerable approximation to the P and MC equivalences of efficient, perfect competition.

As Adam Smith wrote, "Specialization is limited by the extent of the market." He meant by this that you often cannot use the most efficient known methods when serving a *small* market.[3] And this provided him with good ammunition for attacking the mercantilistic interferences by governments of his time that served to fragment the DD demands into many smaller DD demands —one for each country or county. He might have gone on to add this:

> If you are *still* in the stage where efficient specialization is being limited by the extent of the market, then you are not yet in the state appropriate for perfect competition; instead, not-yet-exhausted economies of scale leave you in some area of imperfect or monopolistic competition. In such a case there is all the more reason for society to promote measures that will extend the market.

One more important point. Suppose we begin in the Fig. 24-2(c) situation where DD is large enough relative to the efficient size of firm operation to permit coexistence of numerous viable competitors. But suppose something arises to

---

[3] Later chapters show that Canada—a *small* market—must either import products made in specialized plants elsewhere, or make do with the products of less efficient domestic methods.

fragment the aggregate *DD* demand into much smaller separate demands for the different firms. Then perfect competition will be dethroned. Since the new *DD* curve confronting any firm or segment of the market will be moved far to the left, we are really back in Fig. 24-2(b) or even 24-2(a).

Such a case arises when restrictive tariffs inhibit the international flow of goods and so fragment markets and encourage monopolistic situations. That even the man in the street understands this point is shown by the popular slogan "The tariff is the Mother of trusts [combines]." The aim of tariff-reduction programs, the European Common Market, and free trade in automobiles and parts is to place every *DD* curve far to the right, thereby promoting vigorous and effective competition.

■ DIFFERENTIATION OF PRODUCTS

What is not so obvious is that the *DD* demand curves for an industry can be *deliberately* fragmented into smaller segments by the profit-seeking activities of firms. This is what the late Edward Chamberlin called "differentiation of product."

CONTRIVED PRODUCT DIFFERENTIATION   Each seller tries to make his product a little different from that of any other sellers. He avoids the price competition of classical "perfect competition." Instead, he introduces brand quality competition, precisely because it is a profitable form of imperfect competition.

> EXAMPLE: He makes penicillin a little different chemically. He seeks patent protection. He advertises, or sends so-called "detail men" to call on doctors, to make them think his penicillin is different, whether or not it significantly is; or more important, he advertises so that you will attach significance to such differences as are there.

What is the result when everybody successfully differentiates his product? The result is that the *DD* curves of Fig. 24-2(c)'s model of perfect competition are moved so far to the left as to become like those of the models of monopoly or oligopoly shown in Fig. 24-2(a) and (b). Fortunately, each firm is not able at will to differentiate its product successfully to any degree that it wishes, even though Galbraithian converts do exaggerate the unilateral power of advertisers.

Chamberlin would agree with much that has been said here. But he would resent the implication that all product differentiation is an artificial, contrived thing whose only purpose is to increase monopoly power and bilk the consumer. Rather, he would insist that people's tastes differ: different people want different degrees of supposed or real effectiveness of penicillin; and even the same person may not want all his units of penicillin to be of the same degree or area of effectiveness. Creating a great variety of differentiated products is often, Chamberlin insists, a genuine catering to basic human wants and needs. Chamberlin does not agree that we would be better off if we all agreed to wear a few basic styles of clothes, each of which is produced in long and efficient factory runs. He would stress that all tastes, including noble tastes for Bach and Rembrandt, are made by society rather than arising from the individual himself. The change of fashion, frivolous though it be, adds zest to life.

In effect, Chamberlin is *reemphasizing the importance of decreasing costs in making perfect competition unviable.* He is saying, "Once we replace a homogeneous output Q of the industry (or what is the same thing, the homogeneous output q of a typical firm) by a whole complex of somewhat different Q_1, Q_2, ... , then the demands will just not be big enough to permit you to have many different producers at the bottom of their efficient U-shaped cost curves." Chamberlin is arguing, "You think that as DD grows in Fig. 24-2(b), with population or for any other reason, society will move from the imperfect-competition model of (b) to the perfect-competition model of (c). But you are wrong. With the *bigger scale* of DD will come a bigger opportunity for making *more*, and more minute, *differentiations of product."*

NATURAL PRODUCT DIFFERENTIATION   Even if we do not agree with Chamberlin's implication that the world is perpetually assigned to the realm of imperfect competition regardless of increases in scale, we must concede that he does have a valid and important point. His general *Weltanschauung*—that the economic world cannot be properly understood in terms of the simple models of perfect competition or complete monopoly, but must be interpreted in terms of a richer theory that involves phenomena not to be described as mere blends of these polar cases—is made more convincing by the following considerations:

Products are often differentiated by natural as well as man-made causes. Space itself, and the transport costs associated with it, provide one important example.

Consider the steel industry. It involves very large-scale production. Yet this is a big continent. So you might argue that we can expect numerous replications of the most efficient-sized plant. But what follows? North America does not constitute one single market for steel. Because of transport costs, each region and each part of each region provide us with relevant DD curves to compare with the efficient large-scale U of cost.[4] It would be ridiculous to think that even New York City could have the dozens or hundreds of independent integrated steel producers needed for the market model of perfect competition. And if the lobbyists of the steel industry got the import quotas they crave, the departure from competitive MC pricing would become even worse.

Similarly with electric-power production. In order to reach minimum Average Cost, one might today want to build a generating plant of more than 2 million kilowatts of capacity. But that efficient size is already much too big for perfect competition to prevail. Any *compact region* that had ten such competing plants would be plagued with dreadful overcapacity.

---

[4] Tariff barriers, like transport costs, work to reduce the size of markets and push DD curves to the left. Thus even efficient firms, unable to reach the bottom of U-shaped cost curves, may experience higher actual levels of LAC than less efficient firms selling abroad in larger markets.

We may conclude as follows:

Patterns of returns in which costs still decline relative to the effective size of the market imperil the realism of perfect competition and of $P = MC$ efficient social pricing. This problem is accentuated by man-made or natural differentiations of product which lower the effective DD levels of demands relative to the bottom of the U levels of efficient production, making *competitive* coexistence of numerous *rival* units simply nonviable. On the other hand, if larger firms produce many, many different kinds of products, each firm may be checked in its monopoly power in any one market by the fact that it meets the competition of *many* other large firms in each separate line.

Let us now survey the principal patterns of imperfections of competition.

■ THREE KINDS OF IMPERFECT COMPETITION: MONOPOLY, OLIGOPOLY, AND DIFFERENTIATED PRODUCTS

MONOPOLY   How imperfect can imperfect competition get? The extreme case would be that of a *single* seller with practically complete monopoly power. (He is called a "monopolist," from the Greek word *mono* for "one" and *polist* for "*seller*.") He is the only one producing in his industry, and there is no industry producing a close substitute for his good. (In Fig. 24-1(b) a change in another firm's price would shift his *dd* curve negligibly.)

Exclusive monopolies, like public utilities or telephones, are usually regulated by the government; and even they must usually take account of the potential competition of alternative products—oil for gas, or cables for telephones. This shows how relatively unimportant complete monopolies are.

OLIGOPOLY   We have seen that this horrible-sounding word means "few sellers." Oligopolists are of two types.

First, an oligopolist may be one of a *few* sellers who produce an *identical* (or almost identical) product. Thus, if A's steel is much the same as B's steel, then the smallest price difference will drive the consumer from A to B or vice versa. Neither A nor B could be called a monopolist. Yet, if the number of sellers is few, each has a very appreciable effect on market price.

This first kind of oligopoly is thought to be common in a number of our basic industries where *product is fairly homogeneous* and size of enterprise large —as in the aluminum and iron industries. Another example would be that of moving freight from coast to coast by any of the three or four alternative rail and sea routes. In the old days when rail rates were unregulated, there would be periodic price wars in which each route undercut the other in an attempt to gain more of the business: sometimes it would become cheaper to move freight from Vancouver to Montreal than to move it from Vancouver to Chicago, and occasionally it might be cheaper to move freight from Vancouver to Chicago via Montreal, with all the implied wasteful cross-haulage.

The second kind of oligopoly is typified by the case where there are *few* sellers who sell *differentiated* (rather than identical) products. The Big Three in the auto industry are examples: three producers dominate the industry, but the

Fords, Chevrolets, and Plymouths that they make are *somewhat differentiated* products. In the cigarette industry, a few large sellers own the numerous brands and types (filter, king-size, and regular) that compete for and get the bulk of the business. In heavy machinery, such companies as General Electric, Massey-Ferguson, Allis-Chalmers, and others illustrate the case of an oligopoly that has few sellers and some differentiation of product.

MANY DIFFERENTIATED SELLERS   This is the last in our list of imperfect competitors. Here there are many sellers, but now they do *not* produce *identical* products as in the case of perfect competition. Instead, they produce "differentiated products," i.e., products which differ somewhat in real qualities or which the buyer thinks differ in real qualities. My toothpaste is a little different from yours; and if I raise my price above yours, I may still hope to sell a good deal to those consumers conditioned by my advertising or by past use of my product.

Advertising, brand names, trademarks, patents, and custom may explain why there is product differentiation. Or it may merely be that a given barber shop or grocery store is in a locality near to certain consumers: the fact of this

Most industries are imperfectly competitive—a blend of monopoly and competition:

TYPES OF COMPETITION

KIND OF COMPETITION	NUMBER OF PRODUCERS AND DEGREE OF PRODUCT DIFFERENTIATION	PART OF ECONOMY WHERE PREVALENT	DEGREE OF CONTROL OVER PRICE	METHODS OF MARKETING
Perfect competition	Many producers; identical products	A few agricultural industries	None	Market exchange or auction
Imperfect competition:				
Many differentiated sellers	Many producers; many real or fancied differences in product	Toothpaste, retail trade; conglomerates	Some	Advertising and quality rivalry; administered prices
Oligopoly	Few producers; little or no difference in product	Steel, aluminum, lumber, pulp		
	Few producers; some differentiation of products	Autos, machinery, wallboards		
Complete monopoly	Single producer; single product without close substitutes	A few utilities	Considerable	Promotional and "institutional" public-relations advertising

TABLE 24-1.

nearness may give it a measure of monopoly power; and yet, if its price gets too high, it will find itself losing trade to more distant competitors. (In Fig. 24-1(b) when your rivals cut their P, your dd curve shifts downward *appreciably*.)

All these categories of market structure overlap. They range in degree from perfect competition, to a large number of differentiated sellers, to the two kinds of oligopoly, and finally to the limiting case of monopoly.

■ BRIEF SUMMARY OF KINDS OF COMPETITION AND MARKET STRUCTURE

Table 24-1 presents a brief picture of the various possible categories of imperfect and perfect competition. It merits close study, for we shall later examine each of its cases.

The remainder of this chapter will analyze the principles of profit maximization, concentrating mostly on the limiting case of a complete monopoly. As has been mentioned, few firms in real life enjoy anything like a complete monopoly: usually some other products will be partially substitutable for the ones you sell. If for some unnatural reason you were in a position of practically unchecked monopoly, we can be sure that the modern mixed economy would make you subject to public regulation. The example of public regulation of such utilities as electricity, gas, and telephones comes immediately to mind; and by the end of the chapter we shall be in a position to understand the proper principle of monopoly regulation.

The tools useful to understand Maximum-profit equilibrium for the complete monopoly—namely Marginal Cost and Marginal Revenue—turn out to be the tools needed to understand Maximum-profit equilibrium in the more realistic cases of oligopoly and various forms of imperfect competition. They lay the groundwork for Chapter 25's study of the combines policy of government to prevent and control monopolies.

■ PRICE, QUANTITY, AND TOTAL REVENUE

What is the Maximum-profit output q that a monopolist will try to produce in any situation? What is the accompanying Maximum-profit price P that it should charge? It turns out that old and new *marginal* concepts provide the key to the common-sense trial-and-error procedure of maximizing profit. The final results will agree with common sense, after analysis discloses the good sense in common sense.

As far as costs are concerned, all the tools that we shall need have already been developed in Chapter 23's discussion of costs (MC, AC, TC, and so forth). Here, therefore, we can begin with the sales revenue side of things. From the firm's demand curve dd, we know the relation between P and the q it can sell. Table 24-2 on page 595, indicates this relationship for a hypothetical firm, in Column (2). And Fig. 24-3(a) depicts, in brown, the dd demand curve for this monopolist (who is given, for simplicity, a stright-line demand curve). Column (3) of Table 24-2 shows how to get the firm's Total Revenue by multiplying $P \times q$: thus 0 units bring in $TR = 0$; 1 unit brings in $TR = \$180 \times 1$; 2 units bring in $\$160 \times 2 = \$320$. The general rule is this: $TR = P \times q$.

Marginal Revenue curve comes from demand curve:

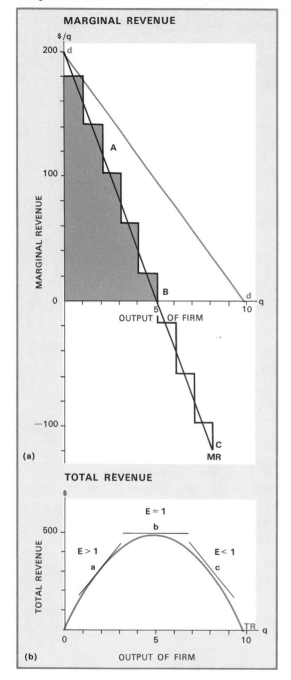

MARGINAL REVENUE

(a)

TOTAL REVENUE

(b)

FIG. 24-3(a). The black steps show the increments of Total Revenue from each new unit of output as calculated from Table 24-2 (or from the *TR* of Fig. 24-3(b) below). *MR* falls below *P* from the beginning, actually dropping twice as fast as the straight-line *dd* curve. *MR* becomes negative when *dd* turns inelastic. Smoothing the incremental steps of *MR* gives the black *MR* curve, which in the case of straightline *dd* will always have twice as steep a slope as *dd*.

FIG. 24-3(b). Total Revenue is dome-shaped, rising from zero (where $q = 0$) to a maximum (where *dd* has unitary elasticity) and then falling back to zero (where $P = 0$). *TR*'s slope gives instantaneous *MR*, just as its jumps give incremental *MR*.

Total Revenue at first rises with q, since the reduction in P needed to sell the extra q is moderate in this first *elastic* range of the demand curve. But when we get to some intermediate point on *dd*, *TR* reaches its maximum—at $q = 5$,

Marginal Revenue numbers come from demand schedule P and q data:

TOTAL AND MARGINAL REVENUE

(1) QUANTITY q	(2) PRICE $P = AR = \dfrac{TR}{q}$	(3) TOTAL REVENUE $TR = P \times q$	(4) MARGINAL REVENUE MR
0	$200	$ 0	+200
			+180
1	180	180	+160
			+140
2	160	320	+120
			+100
3	140	420	+ 80
			+ 60
4	120	480	+ 40
			+ 20
5	100	500	0
			− 20
6	80	480	− 40
			− 60
7	60	420	− 80
			−100
8	40	320	−120
			−140
9	20	180	−160
			−180
10	0	0	

TABLE 24-2. From demand curve data, Total Revenue is easily computed. To get dark brown Marginal Revenue, we increase q by a unit and calculate the difference in Total Revenue it brings. Note MR is at first positive, but after demand turns inelastic, MR becomes negative. Price never becomes negative, but MR lies below P because of loss owing to the necessity to lower price on previous units if the new unit of q is to get sold. (Light brown data of instantaneous Marginal Revenue come from smoothed MR curve of Fig. 24-3(a).)

$P = \$100$, and $TR = \$500$. Increasing q beyond this point brings you into *inelastic* demand regions, and now the percentage cut in P needed to sell 1 per cent more q is so much greater than 1 that it cuts down on TR. Figure 24-3(b) shows TR to be dome-shaped, rising from zero to a maximum of $500 and falling back to zero when P has become vanishingly small.

Already Table 24-2 illustrates an important fallacy: "A firm out to maximize its profits will always charge what the 'traffic will bear.' That means charging the highest possible price." This statement is wrong. A profit maximizer may not be an altruist; but that does not mean he is a fool. To charge the highest possible price is to sell no q at all and to get no TR at all! Even if we reinterpret this doctrine to mean charging the highest price at which anything at all can be sold, it is obvious that selling but one unit even at a high price is not the way to maximize your profit. Even if we neglect (for a moment) all costs, the correct interpretation of charging what the traffic will bear must mean that we find the best *compromise* between a high P and a high q if we are to get the best profit. In Table 24-2, it is at $q = 5$ that $P \times q = TR$ is at a maximum: this is the point where demand elasticity turns into demand inelasticity.

Before proceeding now to introduce the important concept of Marginal Revenue, we can note the fact that the *Price* at which each q is sold could be called *Average Revenue* to distinguish it from Total Revenue. Thus, we got $P \equiv AR$ by dividing TR by q (just as we earlier got AC by dividing TC by q). Verify that if Column (3) had been written down *before* Column (2), we could then have filled in Column (2) by division.

■ MARGINAL REVENUE AND PRICE

We need a test to determine whether Total Revenue is gaining or losing as we increase q. Marginal Revenue is the convenient concept for this purpose.

Definition: "Marginal Revenue" is defined as the increment of Total Revenue (plus or minus) that comes when we increase q by an increment of one unit. MR is plus when demand is still elastic, minus when demand is inelastic, and just crosses zero when demand turns from being elastic to being inelastic. (If units of q are divisible, the MR steps of Fig. 24-3(a) can be replaced by a smooth MR curve.)

The dark brown bold numbers of Marginal Revenue are shown in Column (4) of Table 24-2; they are calculated by subtracting the TR we get by selling q units from the TR we get by selling $q + 1$ units, the difference being our extra revenue or MR. Thus, from $q = 0$ to $q = 1$, we get $MR = \$180 - 0$. From 1 to 2, MR is $\$320 - 180 = \$140$.

MR is positive until we arrive at $q = 5$, and negative from then on. That does not mean you are giving goods away at a negative price. Actually, Average Revenue, which is P, continues to be positive. It is merely that, in order to sell the sixth unit of q, you must reduce the price so much on *all* the units as to end up getting less TR—which is what the negative MR is telling you.

This warns us: Do *not* confuse Marginal Revenue with Average Revenue or Price. The table shows they are different. Review Fig. 24-3(a) and note that the plotted black steps of MR definitely lie below the brown dd curve of AR. MR has already turned negative when dd is only partway down toward zero.

Just why is MR definitely less than P (or AR) for the imperfect competitor? True, I sell my last unit of q for P. But what did I have to do to coax out that last unit of sale? Clearly, I had to lower my P, since I didn't face a perfect competitor's horizontal dd. But in lowering my P for the last new buyer, I also had to *lower P for all the previous buyers.* So my extra revenue, my MR, is evidently less than P by this loss on previous units from the price drop. QED.

Summary: With dd demand sloping
$$P > MR \ (= P - \text{Loss on previous } q)$$

In Column (4) of Table 24-2, the brown numbers of the smoothed MR are also seen to be less than Column (2)'s P's.

Only under perfect competition, where the sale of extra units will never depress price at all, is the loss-in-revenue term zero. Only then will Price and Marginal Revenue be identical. Graphically, a straight-line MR curve always has twice the steepness of the dd curve. But if dd is horizontal, as in perfect competition, so then must MR be: thus, a perfect competitor's dd and MR coincide as the same horizontal line!

This completes our analysis of Marginal Revenue and equips us for the task of finding Maximum-profit equilibrium of the firm.

B.　MAXIMUM-PROFIT MONOPOLY EQUILIBRIUM: DIVERGENCE OF PRICE AND MARGINAL COST

Now suppose the firm wants to maximize its Total Profit. To do this it must bring in, along with the Total Revenue information it gets from its demand side, the Total Cost information described in Chapter 23.

Definition: Total Profit equals Total Revenue minus Total Cost:
$$TP = TR - TC = P \times q - TC$$

To maximize its profit the firm must seek out the equilibrium price and quantity, P^* and q^*, that gives it the largest difference, $TR - TC$. Common sense tells us this Maximum-profit will occur only where the firm's Marginal (or extra) Revenue has just come into balance with its Marginal (or extra) Cost.

We may now bring all our relevant facts together in a supertable, Table 24-3. Total Profit is, of course, the column of greatest interest in this table.

Equating Marginal Cost to Marginal Revenue gives the firm its Maximum-profit output and price:

SUMMARY OF FIRM'S REVENUE, COST, AND MAXIMUM PROFIT

(1) QUANTITY q	(2) PRICE P	(3) TOTAL REVENUE TR	(4) TOTAL COST TC	(5) TOTAL PROFIT TP	(6) MARGINAL REVENUE MR	(7) MARGINAL COST MC	
0	200	0	145	−145	+200	34	
					+180	30	$MR > MC$
1	180	180	175	+5	+160	27	
					+140	25	
2	160	320	200	+120	+120	22	
					+100	20	
3	140	420	220	+200	+80	21	
					+60	30	
4	120	480	250	+230	+40	40	$MR = MC$
					+20	50	
5	100	500	300	+200	0	60	
					−20	70	
6	80	480	370	+110	−40	80	
					−60	90	
7	60	420	460	−40	−80	100	
					−100	110	$MR < MC$
8	40	320					

TABLE 24-3. Total and Marginal Cost of production are now brought together with Total and Marginal Revenue. The Maximum-profit decision is where $MR = MC$, with $q^* = 4$, $P^* = \$120$, and maximum profit $TP = \$230 = \$120 \times 4 - \$250$. (NOTE: For convenience, the light brown MR and MC numbers are put in to give the smoothed instantaneous values at each q point itself: disregarding these, we could get the same result.)

What quantity q^* will maximize Total Profit, and at what price? The easiest way to solve this problem is to compute Column (5), Total Profit, which is simply the difference between Total Revenue and Total Cost. Running our eyes down this column tells us:

The optimal quantity is 4 units, with a price of $120 per unit. After taking account of Total Cost, we see that no other situation will give us as much profit as the $230 at $q^* = 4$ and $P^* = $120.

Another way of arriving at the same result is to compare Marginal Revenue, Column (6), and Marginal Cost, Column (7). (MR is computed from the TR column, as in Table 24-2. Recall from the last chapters that MC is similarly calculated from TC.)

As long as a step toward extra output gives us more Marginal Revenue than Marginal Cost, our profit is *increasing* and we continue to produce more output. But whenever Marginal Cost exceeds Marginal Revenue, we *contract* output. Where is equilibrium?

Maximum-profit equilibrium is where Marginal Revenue and Marginal Cost are equal.

$MR = MC$, the Maximum-profit point

This second way of finding the optimum point by comparing Marginal Cost and Marginal Revenue is neither better nor worse than the first method of simply examining Total Profits. They are essentially exactly the same method.

■ GRAPHICAL DEPICTION OF FIRM'S MAXIMUM-PROFIT POSITION

The curves of Fig. 24-4 illustrate these procedures. In Fig. 24-4(a), MC intersects MR at E, the Maximum-profit point, where $q^* = 4$. We run up vertically from E to the dd curve to G, where $P = $120. The fact that G lies *above* F, the point on the AC curve at $q^* = 4$, guarantees a positive profit. (We cannot read directly the amount of Total Profit unless we calculate the area of the shaded rectangle.)

The same story is told in Fig. 24-4(b) with total curves. Total Revenue is dome-shaped. Total Cost is ever-rising. The vertical difference between them is Total Profit, which begins negative and ends negative. In between, TP is positive, reaching its maximum of $230 at $q^* = 4$, where the black slopes of the TR and TC are equal and parallel: if these MR and MC slopes were pointing inward in a non-parallel fashion (as at $q = 2$), we should gain a little extra profit by contracting q. At $q^* = 4$, things are just right. This is verified by the Total Profit curve, whose black slope is horizontal at its peak: TP's slope is clearly the difference $MR - MC$, and this slope should definitely have a zero value at the maximum.[5]

[5] Those who know elementary calculus need not use the finite-step definitions of MR and MC as $\triangle TR$ and $\triangle TC$. Instead they can use the smoothed instantaneous slopes of the TR and TC functions of q: i.e., define $MR = d(TR)/dq$ and $MC = d(TC)/dq$ and note that maximizing $TR - TC$ of profit requires finding the q^* root of the equation: $d(profit)/dq = 0 = d(TC)/dq - d(TR)/dq = MR - MC$. QED. (See extra-credit problem, question 7, at the end of this chapter for more on this.)

**Graphs of marginal and total curves show
Maximum-profit equilibrium:**

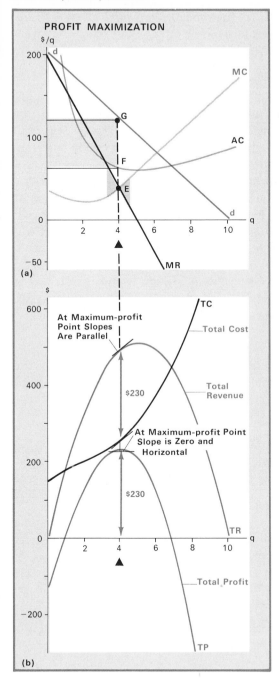

(a)

(b)

FIG. 24-4(a). At E, where MC intersects MR, equilibrium position of Maximum profit is found. Any move from E will lose some profit. Price is at G above E; and since P is above AC, the maximized profit is a positive profit. (Can you understand why the brown shaded rectangle measures Total Profit? And why the gray triangle of shading on either side of E shows the reduction in Total Profit that would come from a departure from $MR = MC$ — i.e., the greater loss of extra revenue in comparison with extra cost?)

FIG. 24-4(b). This tells the same story of maximizing profit as above, but uses total concepts rather than marginal concepts. Total Profit is given by vertical distance from TC up to TR. This is at a maximum where the two curves have equal and parallel slopes, $MR = MC$. This is necessary if brown TP curve is to be at a maximum, with its black slope horizontal as MR cancels out MC.

Excess of P above MC. For the firm with some monopoly power, maximizing profits by equating Marginal Revenue to Marginal Cost leads to a price that is *above* Marginal Cost. The canny seller *contrives an artificial scarcity of his product* so as not to spoil the price he can get on the earlier premarginal units.

■ PERFECT COMPETITION A SPECIAL CASE OF IMPERFECT COMPETITION

This completes our discussion of Marginal Revenue and Marginal Cost as tools to maximize profit. It will add to your confidence in the result if you find that the general $MR = MC$ rule is consistent, when applied to a *perfect competitor*, with Chapter 22's $P = MC$ rule for a profit-maximizing perfect competitor. It is? Yes, indeed. Here is why:

For a small perfect competitor, Marginal Revenue works out to be exactly the same thing as Price. With no need to cut your P to sell an extra unit of q, the incremental Marginal Revenue it brings you is precisely the P received for that last unit, with no loss on previous units being subtracted.[6] Hence, $MR = MC$ and $P \equiv MR$ do lead to the special rule for profit maximizing by a perfect competitor:

$P = MR = MC$ at a perfect competitor's Maximum-profit point

These tools to show how a rational firm will find its maximum-profit equilibrium will later apply to firms under monopoly, or anything else.

■ BYGONES AND MARGINS

While economic theory does not necessarily aim to make you a successful businessman, it does introduce you to some new ways of thinking. Here is one instance.

The economist always stresses the "extra," or "marginal," costs and advantages of any decision. He says:

Let bygones be bygones. Don't look backward. Don't moan about your sunk costs. Look forward. Make a hard-headed calculation of the *extra* costs you'll incur by any decision and weigh these against its *extra* advantages. Cancel out all the good things and bad things *that will go on anyway*, whether you make an affirmative or negative decision on the point under consideration.

This disregarding of bygones is extremely important, and most successful decision-makers practice it intuitively, even if they have not had a formal course in economics. Here is an application of this principle:

The King taxes a monopolist a flat sum for his match-monopoly franchise—say $100 per day, no matter what he does. How will this affect the new Maximum-profit P and q? If you have grasped the tools of this chapter, you will discover that a flat-sum tax will not shift either the MR or MC curve. If the monopolist successfully maximizes his profits before and after the tax and if nothing else changes and if he stays in business, *the flat-sum tax will have absolutely no effect on price or output*, but will be borne completely by the monopolist! (Can you

---

[6] If you redraw Fig. 24-4(a) for a perfect competitor, make dd horizontal and coinciding with MR. Then proceed to find the MR and MC intersection as usual (which gives the old MC supply story of Chapter 22). In the new Fig. 24-4(b), TR merely becomes a straight line, rising from the origin, but the slopes of TR and TC must still match at the Maximum-profit equilibrium point.

verify that adding $100 to every *TC* number in Table 24-3 merely subtracts $100 from every profit in Column (5), leaving you with the same Maximum-profit $q^* = 4$ and $P^* = \$120?$[7])

■ HOW IMPERFECTION OF COMPETITION AFFECTS RESOURCE ALLOCATION

In the next chapter we shall study some of the important cases of imperfect competition—oligopoly, and so forth. This will involve us in important public questions that lie in the field of "combines policy." As preparation, let us see again how deviations from perfect competition affect the efficiency with which a free-price system solves the important problems of WHAT, HOW, and FOR WHOM.

Suppose that, under free pricing, firms do definitely face a sloping demand curve so that their Marginal Revenue is below their Price. Then, to the degree that such imperfect competitors intelligently pursue their self-interest, they will *not* be led by Adam Smith's Invisible Hand to perform the acts needed to promote the general interest.

Let us recapitulate how this divergence between Price and Marginal Cost affect the goodness or badness of the way the economy is organizing its production and distribution. We have already met this complex question, and will do so again.

EXCESS PROFIT OF MONOPOLY   First, the imperfect competitor may be earning more than he would if the government somehow made him compete like a perfect competitor. If so, is that excess profit a good or a bad thing? Is he a more worthy man than most? Is he poorer than most, and more in need? (And will he use his gains to subsidize the arts, or to pay for vulgar display? Will he use any monopoly profits to sponsor new industrial research? Or to sponsor research in ways to convince consumers that his product is better than those of others?)

When the man in the street thinks of the monopoly problem, he gives most

[7] Suppose the King put a flat-sum of $230 on Fig. 24-4's monopolist to wipe out all his profit. The new Fig. 24-5 shows the story. *MR*, *MC*, and *dd* are exactly as before. (Why?) But now *AC* has been shifted up because of the added Fixed Cost. Only at the price of G, where the *dd* curve is *tangent* to the new *AC* curve, can the firm break even: everywhere else it makes a loss; maximizing profit by finding *MR* = *MC* now means avoiding loss. (But see the Appendix for a demonstration that taxing away monopoly profit does still leave society with a discrepancy between Price, or marginal utility, and Marginal Cost.)

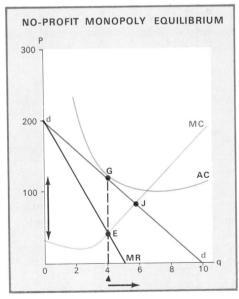

FIG. 24-5.

NO-PROFIT MONOPOLY EQUILIBRIUM

weight to the above type of questions—to the way it affects the FOR WHOM problem of distribution.[8] Yet, *even if it has no harmful effect on income distribution, imperfection of competition could still represent an important economic evil.*

DEFICIENT OUTPUT OF MONOPOLY   To see this, imagine that all money votes are distributed properly and that A is the only imperfect competitor in the system. Everyone else is a perfect competitor, who keeps his MC equal to his P. Price is the signal that consumers use to indicate how much they value various goods. Costs, and particularly Marginal Cost, are the indicators of how much of society's valuable resources each good's production utilizes: our scarce land, our sweaty labor, and other resources that could produce other goods. Everywhere else, competitive firms are giving people what they most want and are producing right up to the point of $P = MC$, where goods are shown to be worth what they cost.

But take the imperfect competitor A—the one deviant. What is he doing? A is not forcing people to buy from him. But the fact that A faces a sloping demand curve shows he does have some control over P. How is he using that power? Does he produce goods up to the point where their social cost—as measured by his MC—is equal to what the last unit of the good is worth to society—as measured by market P resulting from consumer money votes? No.

> The imperfect competitor is contriving to keep things a little scarce. He is contriving to keep P above MC because in that way he sets $MR = MC$ and thereby maximizes his profit. So society does not get quite as much of A's good as it really wants in terms of what that good really costs society to produce.[9]

Do not think A is a villain. If he did not intelligently try to maximize his firm's long-run profits, he might be displaced by the stockholders or be sued. Even if A owned the company and chose to lower P to MC, he would be shunting money from his wife and kids to the public at large. While there is no law against his being such an altruist, such as Santa Claus, the betting odds are against this. And in any case such an optimal solution to the problem *by*

---

[8] In Fig. 24-5 of the last footnote, the monopolist was stripped of his excess profit by taxes, but the vertical arrow showing the discrepancy between P (at G) and MC (at E) shows that monopoly q is still too small and should be expanded as shown by the lower horizontal arrow.

As the next chapter shows, imperfect competition might result in no one's making a profit if there is "free entry" into the Chamberlinian industry in question. Yet P might still stay above MC, and so the result might still be tremendous wastage of resources because we have too many corners with too many gasoline stations, each with too many idle attendants (who in the end are not even well rewarded for being imperfect competitors). To be sure, more gas stations could mean shorter walks for people out of gas and more consumer convenience generally; but who is to say that the optimal amount of such differentiation-of-product convenience is being provided under any particular regime of imperfect competition?

[9] As Fig. 19-9, page 478 showed, it is a social inefficiency when monopolists' outputs are too small and competitors' outputs get expanded beyond their optimal amounts. Chapter 22's Fig. 22-7 clinched the point with its comparison of competitive MC pricing with a Crusoe-Planner optimum of welfare. See this chapter's Appendix, pages 605-606, for more on this.

chivalry has nothing to do with Adam Smith's Invisible Hand—which insisted that *self*-interest (not altruism) would perform, under ruthless competition, the miracle of providing for the general interest.

The clue to the Invisible Hand paradox is this: Adam Smith would have to rely on strictly defined "perfect competition" to get his result. As soon as we have imperfect competition in the real world, we have left the Garden of Eden and there arises the problem of how to minimize the evil and wastes involved in such imperfections of competition. Chapter 25 analyzes the main forms of imperfect competition and surveys the antitrust policies of modern governments. And the brief Appendix to this chapter indicates the *economic* principles that should underlie public regulation of monopoly and imperfect competition and should underlie combines philosophy and law.

SUMMARY

A. OVERVIEW OF MARKET STRUCTURE AND THE CONCEPT OF MARGINAL REVENUE

■ 1 Most market situations in the real world can be thought of as falling on a line somewhere between the limiting extremes of perfect competition and complete monopoly. Imperfect competition involves some control by each of its firms over its own price, by virtue of the fact that there are not *a very large number of rivals* who sell *exactly the same product* as it does. (Note the italicized words.) Important cases are (1) *Oligopoly*—few sellers of similar or differentiated products—and (2) *many sellers of differentiated* products.

■ 2 Decreasing-cost tendencies are destructive of perfect competition, since one or a few corporations then kill off the numerous sellers needed for the competitive model. (However, big conglomerates, which produce many products and invade one another's markets, may each find themselves constitutional rather than absolute monarchs, unable to dominate their separate markets.)

■ 3 From the firm's demand curve, we can easily derive its Total Revenue curve. From the schedule or curve of Total Revenue we can easily derive its Marginal Revenue—the extra revenue resulting from the sale of an extra unit of output. Ordinarily, Marginal Revenue will fall short of Price because of the *loss on all previous units* of output that will result when we are forced to drop our price in order to sell an extra unit of output.

B. MAXIMUM-PROFIT MONOPOLY EQUILIBRIUM: DIVERGENCE OF PRICE AND MARGINAL COST

■ 4 A firm will find its Maximum-profit position where the last little unit it sells brings in extra revenue just equal to its extra cost. This same $MR = MC$ result can be shown graphically by intersecting MR and MC curves, or by equality of the slopes of the Total Revenue and Total Cost curves. In any case, *Marginal Revenue = Marginal Cost* must hold at the equilibrium position of Maximum profit.

■ 5 Economic reasoning leads to an emphasis upon *marginal* advantages and disadvantages—to a *cancellation of bygones* and factors that go on no matter how you make a decision.

■ 6 Imperfection of competition, by putting P above MC for some goods, acts as one extra deterrent to Adam Smith's Invisible Hand, which tried to convert mankind's selfish interest to a best solution of society's WHAT, HOW, and FOR WHOM problems.

QUESTIONS FOR DISCUSSION

1. List distinguishing features of perfect and imperfect competition. How might you characterize Stelco, Eaton's, Loblaws, Algoma Steel, Bell Telephone, Farmer Jones?

2. "A corporation charges what the traffic will bear." Interpret.

3. What is the numerical value of MR when dd has unitary elasticity and TR is constant?

4. Relate MR to P, at $q = 4$ or 5 in Tables 24-2 and 24-3, showing loss on previous units.

5. Figure 24-4(a) and (b) describes the Maximum-profit equilibrium position. Explain in detail that it really shows two different ways of describing exactly the same fact, namely, that a firm will stop when the extra cost of a further move just balances its extra revenue.

6. Here is a hard question. "If a monopolist is big enough to affect the P for the good he sells, he may also be big enough to affect the price of materials and the labor he buys. (He becomes what is called a 'monopsonist'—or 'single buyer.') In computing MC as it *looks to him*, he will debit against the last unit of q the *rise* in wage forced on all the *previous* units of labor by his need to hire more labor. Private pecuniary MC, so computed, is higher than the true MC society wants P equated to for efficiency." Interpret this if you can (but if you cannot, don't worry as Chapter 28's footnote 6, page 705, will return to this).

7. *Extra-credit problem:* Firm A has dd demand function, $P = 15 - .05q$, and hence $TR = qP = 15q - .05q^2$. Its $TC = q + .02q^2$. Verify: $MR = d(TR)/dq = 15 - .1q$, $MC = d(TC)/dq = 1 + .04q$. So $d(\text{profit})/dq = 0$ at $MR = MC$ or at $15 - .1q = 1 + .04q$ or at $q^* = 100$. Then $P^* = 15 - 5 = \$10 > MC^* = \$5$. Maximum-profit $= \$1,000 - (100 + 200) = \$700$. Can you show that a tax of $\$1$/unit will add $1q$ to TC, cutting q^* by $100/14$ units and raising P by $5/14$ units? Had the firm been competitive, with dd at the $\$5$ level, its Maximum-profit on $q^* = 100$ would have been $\$500 - \$300 = \$200$; and now a $\$1$/unit tax would cut competitor's q^* by much more than monopolist's—namely, by $100/4 = 25$ units. [HINT: Now maximize $\{5q - (q + .02q^2)\} - 1q$]

8. Review your understanding of the following concepts:

perfect versus imperfect competition

decreasing costs and monopolistic imperfection

monopoly, oligopoly, product differentiation

rivalry versus perfect competition

$MR = MC$ condition at Maximum profit

MR in relation to P (loss on previous units)

$MR = P, P = MC$, for perfect-competitor

bygones versus relevant alternatives

inefficiency of $P > MC$

imperfection of competition and Smith's Invisible Hand

Appendix: Monopoly Regulation and Exploitation; Game Theory

Figure 24-6 repeats a monopoly equilibrium like that of Fig. 24-4(a). The monopolist is seen to be (1) making a profit, as shown by the brown-shaded rectangle near G; and (2) charging a P above MC, as shown by the EG discrepancy.

Suppose a public-utility commission is set up to regulate the monopolist. Or suppose the government Combines Investigation Branch of the Department of Consumer Affairs threatens to arrest him. If the regulators decide to make him charge a price that will wipe out his excess-profits, they will move him to H, the intersection of his dd and AC curves. Here $P = AC$, and price covers only normal costs.

How good is this solution? Economically speaking, it probably does represent something of an improvement. First, the owner of the monopoly is probably no more deserving, or poorer, than the consumers. So there is no reason to let him extort monopoly profits from them. By wiping out monopolistic profit, we probably have a more "equitable distribution of income." (WARNING: Value judgments that go beyond technical economics are involved in such a conclusion.)

Second, the regulators have lowered the discrepancy between Price and Marginal Cost in making the monopolist cut his P from G to H. Why deem

this an improvement? Because (equity considerations aside and assuming that dollars truly reflect social utilities and social costs) the expanded q units are worth more to people in marginal utility than their extra or Marginal Cost. (PROOF: Between G and H, dd lies above the MC curve.)

■ IDEALLY REGULATED PRICING

If $P = MC$ is such a good thing, why shouldn't the regulators go all the way and make the monopolist lower P until he is at the intersection point of the dd and MC curves (at J)?

Actually, requiring $P = MC$ *is* the ideal target for optimal efficiency. But with a decreasing-cost situation like this one—and we saw in Fig. 24-2, page 587, that much of monopoly, oligopoly, and other forms of imperfect competition come from decreasing-cost cases—setting $P = MC$ while AC is still falling will involve the firm in a *chronic loss*. (REMEMBER: Falling AC means $MC < AC$; or $P = MC < AC$.)

How can society achieve its ideal of $P = MC$, where the marginal utility of output just matches its Marginal Cost at the equilibrium amount? The answer involves a *permanent government subsidy* to

Under unregulated monopoly, price is set too high:

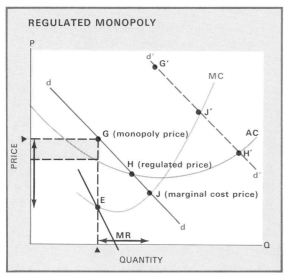

FIG. 24-6. Maximum-profit equilibrium for the unregulated monopolist is at G, directly above the intersection of MR and long-run MC, with P above MC and with monopoly profit shown by the shaded rectangle.

Public-utility regulation of the monopoly would set its price down to the H intersection of demand with long-run average cost; this wipes out excess profit; more important, it brings price down closer to the Marginal Cost level at J, where marginal social costs and benefits are appropriately balanced.

Ideally, P should be forced all the way down to MC at J, with the chronic loss being covered by permanent government (lump-sum) subsidy.

the decreasing-cost producer. Where does the subsidy come from? From the general budget (and ideally from taxes collected on a "lump-sum" basis so that people's marginal decisions are not distorted by attempts to minimize taxes).[1]

What if dd in Fig. 24-6 shifts to intersect MC at J', beyond the bottom of U-shaped AC? Then the regulators should insist on having P at the profitable J' point, not at the new H' Break-even point. But, as with profitable TV channels, the government should auction off licenses or tax away all their excess-profit.

HELPING ALL   We can now demonstrate that if $P_1 > MC_1$ in one monopolized industry and $P_i = MC_i$ in all other perfectly competitive industries, then it is possible to expand the monopoly Q_1 and contract the competitive outputs in such a way as to make any (and hence, if we wish, every) consumer or worker better off.[2]

Suppose we define units of goods so that monopoly P_1 equals competitive P_2 (i.e., we could use a dollar's worth of monopolized berries and of competitive wheat as our amounts). Since only the monopolist's P exceeds MC, this means that the ratio of MC in monopoly to MC in the competitive industries is less than 1. But recall from Chapter 21 that for each consumer $MU_1/P_1 = MU_2/P_2$. Hence, for any single consumer the ratio of marginal utili-

---

[1] Some qualifications are given in advanced treatises. (1) If lump-sum taxes are not politically feasible, the evil from $P = MC$ must be balanced against the distortion from taxation. (2) As Fig. 31-2 will show, a decision has to be made whether the money needed to subsidize the J point could not be used better elsewhere, with this q set equal to zero. (3) If the consumers of this good are especially "deserving"—or if this should be a good that society deems even more worthwhile than the valuations that consumers themselves act on—there may be a case for even greater subsidy. (Reverse the argument if the good is opium or is something bought only by those who already have too large a share of society's income.) (4) Recall Fig. 24-5 (and see Fig. 25-3), where it is shown that a flat-sum tax could wipe out the monopolist's profit but leave you with the socially inefficient $P - MC$ discrepancy. (5) If in many other industries $P > MC$, it may not be optimal to bring P all the way down to MC in this industry alone.

[2] When it is impossible to make everyone better off, advanced books speak of "Pareto optimality," named after Vilfredo Pareto. This concept does not come to grips with "interpersonal equities," but it does throw light on "efficiency."

---

ties is exactly one, and is thus greater than the ratios of Marginal Costs. This means that the monopoly good is being kept so scarce that it is still yielding more MU_1 than its true MC_1 cost.

Any one sovereign consumer could command: "Transfer a small amount of labor from competitive industry 2 to monopoly industry 1. This will give you more than 1 unit of new Q_1 for each lost unit of old Q_2, because $MC_1 < MC_2$, (that is, the resources in one extra unit of Q_1 are less than the resources in one extra unit of Q_2). Now freeze everyone in Canada except me at their old consumption levels. Then they are certainly as well off as before. But when you give me more than 1 new Q_1 for 1 sacrificed old Q_2, I am certainly now better off since previously each good has had the same MU to me. Hence, any one man like me can be made better off by removing monopoly imperfections without hurting anyone else! QED."

EXPLOITATION OF LABOR: A DIGRESSION   This sagacious consumer might even add: "Actually, if you had divided up the benefits more evenly, you could have made all people who consume the two goods better off.

"And furthermore, any worker who now chooses to work an extra new minute picking berries in the monopolized industry will find that the true amount of new berries he picks is greater than what he could buy at the monopolist's P_1 with his last minute's wage—because the monopolist is marking up P_1 over true Marginal Cost. (NOTE: the same improvement is not possible under competition.)

"Hence, the monopoly imperfection is indeed inefficient in the sense that there is seen to exist a way to depart from it and improve any worker while at the same time not hurting anyone else (i.e., have the worker spend an extra minute picking berries and eating them)! QED again."

Summary of Digression: Monopolistic deviation from $P = MC$, means "exploitation" of labor (and other transferable resources), in the sense that society's labor is misapplied as between goods and leisure or as between too-scarce monopolized goods in relation to too-plentiful competitive goods.

We shall have more to say about exploitation in Parts Four and Six. But one warning is in order here. Often monopolies can afford to pay workers *even more* than competitive industries can, sharing so to speak a mite of the monopoly swag with the workers. So raising wages in monopoly industries by trade-union action is *not* the way to get rid of *this* kind of exploitation.[3] It is *all* society that is being exploited, and it is a task for combines policy to reform the situation.

■ ECONOMIC WARFARE: THE THEORY OF GAMES

Oligopoly sometimes breaks out into intermittent warfare. Steinberg's, Loblaws, and Dominion cut and recut retail food prices, hoping to win a larger share of the consumer market—or even to drive the weakest out altogether. When Boeing and Douglas first brought jet planes to market, each had to wonder how high his rival would set his price, asking, "What do they think we think they will do?"

Such a situation, "where two (or more) *free wills* each choose strategies that will affect both *interdependently*," constitutes the essence of the philosophical problems involved in the theory of games. This theory, which sounds frivolous in its terminology borrowed from chess, bridge, and war, is fraught with significance and was largely developed by John von Neumann (1903-1957), Hungarian-born mathematical genius (and one of the three co-inventors of the United States hydrogen bomb).

Here we can only sketch the general notions involved in game theory.[4] Figure 24-7 shows a case of perpetual price cutting. Eaton's advertises, "We will not be undersold," but other stores, for example, Woolco, advertise, "We sell for less." Suppose, in Fig. 24-7, Woolco decides to sell for 10 per cent less. The vertical black arrows show Woolco's (or Black's) price cuts; the brown horizontal arrows show Eaton's (or Brown's) responding strategies of matching them.

It is just as if Black and Brown were playing a chess game: at Black's turn, he moves north-south; at Brown's turn, he moves east-west. Here the game

---

[3] See footnote 6, on page 705, for union actions that can offset "exploitation of labor" by employers who have monopoly-bargaining buying power in the labor, not the Q-good, market.

[4] Aside from the classic by von Neumann and Morgenstern cited in next chapter's footnote 2, the reader might study John McDonald, *Strategy in Poker, Business and War* (Norton, New York, 1950).

When irresistible force meets immovable object, something must give:

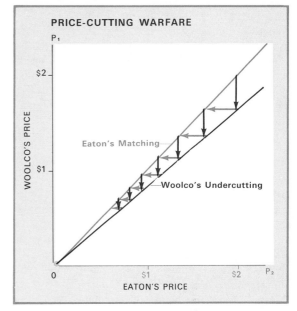

FIG. 24-7.

ends in mutual ruin, at zero price, where 90 per cent of nothing is compatible with equal (zero!) prices.

But finally Woolco gets wise and realizes that when it cuts P_1, the other P_2 will not stay constant but will follow it downward. Only if it is short-sighted does it think it can move south; actually as Brown reacts to match, both move southwestward together toward lower profits for both. If there were but two sellers and no combines laws to worry about, the two might collusively raise price to the monopoly level that maximized joint profits and represented $P > MC$.

Our joint-strategy diagram can be replaced by an equivalent two-way table (or "game-payoff matrix"). In Table 24-4 Black picks his P_1 strategy by selecting a row. Brown's P_2 strategy involves his choosing a column. Then in each of the four cells A, B, C, D the black number represents Black's profit-payoff at those prices and the brown number gives Brown's profit-payoff. Thus, in Cell A joint profits of 6 + 6 (thousand dollars) are maximized at the common monopoly price, $2 = P_1 = P_2$. But A is not "stable," in that if Black knew Brown would really stay in his first column, Black would gain by cutting P_1 down to C, getting the lion's share of the business there with payoff $9 > 6$. But, of course, Brown will now prefer to match Black's $1 P_1, taking us from Cell C to D.

Here at D (whose excess-profits just happen to be minimal), the competitive solution is stable. (That is, 0 is the largest black number in the *column* Brown has picked, and 0 is the largest brown number in the *row* Black has picked. Verify this light-brown-dot equilibrium.)

But we must be warned. The competitive solution is not stable as against a "collusive" move from D to A. This might come about by overt agreement or by tacit agreement. (If Black were reluctant to follow suit, Brown might in Hitler fashion blackmail him by threatening mutual ruin through cutting P far below any cost levels.) The only safe guarantee of competition is thus the potential pressure of really numerous sellers.

These game-theoretic considerations show the importance to oligopolists of finding some way to "agree." And they help explain, along with next chapter's "kinked" demand curve, why oligopoly prices tend to be administered in a "sticky" or rigid way. Were prices to change often, tacit agreements would be hard to identify and enforce.[5]

PRISONER'S DILEMMA AND LOVE   Game theory can throw light on one of the great needs of our age—

---

[5] Collusion is less worrisome in the simpler two-person games studied by von Neumann, the "constant-sum" games in which the brown and black payoffs add up to the *same* constant in *every* cell, as in the accompanying Table 25-5 (*a*) and (*b*).

In (*a*), cell D is a stable solution—representing what is called a "saddlepoint," i.e., a cell which gives maximum black numbers in *its* column and *minimum* black (and hence, maximum brown) numbers in its row.

But in (*b*), which can be given a penny-matching interpretation as Brown's "tails" matches Black's in Cell A, you will find no such minimax or light-brown-dot stable saddlepoint. (Thus, from A, Black moves to C; then Brown moves to D; then Black to B; then Brown back to A; and so we oscillate counter-clockwise forever!)

Von Neumann proves this remarkable theorem about (*b*); namely, each player should introduce *randomized* strategies: thus if each charges $1 or $2 with equal and independent probabilities, neither can then gain in *average* payoff by departing from this stable, minimax saddlepoint solution. Using probabilities, every constant-sum matrix has a saddle point. (Von Neumann proves

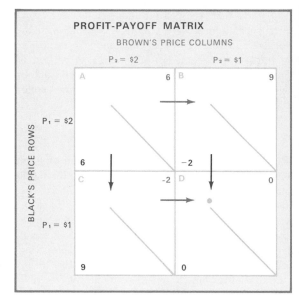

TABLE 24-4.

the need for altruism. (In a more sentimental time, love might be the word.)

In the game matrix of Table 24-4, self-interest (in a word, selfishness) was channeled by the mechanism of economic competition to bring the system to cell D, which happens in this context to be the optimum state. Thus, by a happy accident so to

---

many other fascinating theorems. For example, chess is as "trivial" as ticktacktoe. This means that when played "correctly," it must *always* end in the *same* one of the following: a draw, first man wins, second man wins—but what that outcome is for chess with its multiplicity of moves, no one knows, not even the electronic computer.)

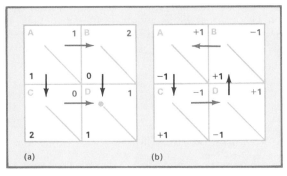

TABLE 24-5.

speak, there does exist a facet of social life—the perfectly-competitive market, when that is strictly applicable and viable—where Adam Smith's Invisible Hand does contrive the maximum of well-being out of the motivation of selfishness.

But that is a lucky accident, unlikely to be realized in other social situations. The following model, or fable, called "prisoner's dilemma," illustrates this basic truth in game-theoretic language. Table 24-6 is like Table 24-4, but reinterpret it in terms of prisoner's dilemma so that Black and Brown are two prisoners who have been caught in a joint crime. The Crown Prosecutor interviews each separately, saying "I have enough on both of you to send you to jail for a year. But if you *alone* will confess to the 10-year crime, I'll make a deal with you: You'll get off with a 3-month sentence, while your partner will serve 10 years. But if you *both* confess, you'll both get 5 years."

What should Black do? Confess and hope to get only a short sentence? That's better than the year from not confessing. But wait. There is an even better reason for confessing. For suppose Black doesn't confess and unknown to him, Brown does confess. Black stands to get 10 years! Better than *that* is to confess and get no worse than 5 years.

Brown is in the same dilemma: If only he knew what Black is thinking (or what Black thinks Brown thinks Black is thinking . . .).

Note that selfishness leads inevitably to long prison terms—5 years—in cell D of Table 24-6. Only by altruism—or social agreement (in this case, collusion)—can the best *common* state of the world, cell A, be realized.

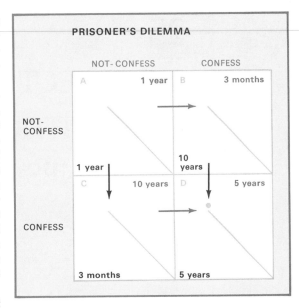

TABLE 24-6.

To see the need for altruism—or failing that, for collective decision making—apply Table 24-6 to the air pollution problem. (Replace not-confess by not-pollute, . . . , etc. And assume that when I pollute and you do not desist from polluting, I will be somewhat worse off if I alone decide to desist.) Then the same logic as in Table 24-6 proves that nationalistic pursuit of self-interest leads to all nations breathing the same foul and polluted air that shortens life expectancies.

Thus, game thory does point up the need for brotherhood and common rules of the road.

FOR REVIEW

1. Review your understanding of the following concepts:

$P = MC < AC$ regulation
improving all when $P_1 > MC_1$
monopoly exploitation of labor
profit-payoff game matrix
row and column strategy

stable point
collusion
prisoner's dilemma
constant-sum game
randomized strategies and necessarily-existent
    stable saddlepoint or minimax

25

IMPERFECT COMPETITION AND COMBINES POLICY

The French Colony of Canada was, during the greater part of the last century and some part of the present, under the government of an exclusive company. Under so unfavourable an administration its progress was necessarily very slow.... ADAM SMITH (1776)

The last chapter gave us the tools for analyzing the actual markets of the real world. Now we focus on the real world of the modern mixed economy in the last third of the twentieth century. We seek answers to questions like the following: How do firms actually go about setting their prices? What is the role of the theoretical tools developed to analyze profit maximization? What are some of the important patterns of imperfect competition? How does Galbraith's "new industrial state" change the conventional wisdom of the past? Part A deals with these subjects.

Part B then takes up the basic problem of the relevance of economics to improving the workings of the system. What are the important issues for public combines policy that patterns of imperfect competition raise?

A. ANALYTICAL PATTERNS OF IMPERFECT COMPETITION

■ DO FIRMS MAXIMIZE PROFITS?

To what degree do businessmen actually try to maximize their profits? To what extent do they succeed if they do try to? It is not easy to give precise answers to these questions. Certainly, this much is true:

If a firm is absolutely reckless in calculating costs and revenues, then the Darwinian law of survival of the fittest will probably eliminate it from the economic scene. Therefore those firms which actually do manage to survive cannot be completely oblivious to the maximization of profits.

But that does not necessarily mean that every oligopolist or monopolist is seeking desperately to squeeze the last ounce of profit from every transaction. As soon as the firm becomes of any considerable size and begins to enjoy some control over price, *it can often afford to relax a little* in its maximizing activities.

Moreover, it is probably good business to take the long view and not concentrate on purely immediate gains. Many acts of altruism and apparent generosity can be amply defended in terms of public relations and the maximization of *long-run* profits.

Consider a firm that is maximizing its profits in a fairly sensible manner. Does that mean that it is calculating elaborate geometrical curves of cost and revenue and from them deriving elaborate measures of marginal cost and revenue? Obviously not, as you will soon learn if you inquire about current business practices.

But even if the firm is not itself tackling the problem with conscious awareness of the particular marginal tools of the theoretical economists, *to the extent that it is truly making a pretty fair guess as to where its highest profits are realized*, it will be succeeding in making marginal revenue and marginal cost approximately equal. It does this without curves, just by feeling its way to the optimum by trial and error. And increasingly managerial economics is becoming a sophisticated art, utilizing giant computers and involving the statistical and mathematical techniques of operational research, linear programming, and probabilistic decision theory.

■ MARKUP PRICING

One of the reasons why business is a challenge is the fact that best guesses must be made on the basis of incomplete information. It is no small task for a large or small business to make an estimate of the shape of the demand curve for its products. The CNR can only guess whether a 20 per cent cut in fares will bring in many more customers. Because other things do not remain equal, a company has no exact way of judging the elasticity of demand for its many products.

Many observers claim that modern business firms—even the largest—cannot in real life accurately determine marginal revenue and marginal cost. They cannot determine their optimum price and output with neat exactitude. Yet the day's work must somehow get done. Prices must be set on their products. Here is where average, or unit, cost is often thought to play an important role. The argument goes as follows:

> Put yourself in the position of the president of a company producing many products. Prices are partly at your disposal. Your last year's sales are known to you, but your next period's sales can only be guessed even if you leave prices unchanged. Not knowing the extent or elasticity of demand for your products, you will be unable to determine marginal revenue. What will you do?

Probably, you call in your accountants and sales managers and ask, "What is our likely volume if we stay on our toes and keep our share of the market?" In answering, the sales force has to guess at the probable level of business activity, consumers' needs, results of market surveys, and much else.

After they have made their estimates, you turn to the cost experts and probably ask for the average cost of producing each product in question at those levels of output. There will be plenty of headaches in aiming at any sort of figure. For example, how should the administrative and plant overhead costs be allocated between different products? Or if a given process simultaneously creates joint products like meat and hides, how should the costs be allocated between them? Or if a building will last for many years, how much should be charged against current operations?

Headache or no headache, it is the practice of accountants to come out with some sort of answer as to average costs. Management must now decide by how much to mark up price over the cost figure. Depending upon its estimate of the consumers' reaction and the pricing policy of its competitors, the firm may perhaps decide on a 5, 10, 30, or 110 per cent markup.[1] Whether aware of it or not, the businessman is making some kind of implicit guess about his demand elasticity in setting his markup.

In bad times, when price competition is particularly keen, businessmen may even set prices at less than "full costs" because they realize that fixed expenses will go on whether or not production is at a low level. But price will never be set below average *variable* costs unless the item in question is being used as a "loss leader" to attract other business now and in the future, or unless the firm is willing to incur temporary losses in order to crush a rival and drive him out of business completely.

Many investigators of actual business pricing policies have testified that corporations often do follow the above-described practice of quoting administered prices on a "cost and markup" basis, hoping thereby not only to recover their "full cost outlays," but also to make a return on their investments. This theory therefore seems realistic, but it is not very informative. It stops tantalizingly short of telling *why* the average markup is 40 per cent in one industry and 5 per cent in another; it cannot tell why, before World War II, General Motors in the auto industry was able to earn 30 per cent on the book value of its invested capital while Ford, almost as large, could earn but $\frac{1}{2}$ of 1 per cent. Demand and cost just have to be regarded as lurking in the background of any business case.

Careful reading of the foregoing account suggests that it is compatible with the principles outlined in Chapter 24. So long as the percentage markup is subject to the pressures implicit in *MC* and *MR* analysis, markup pricing may hinge on the same conditions as in the simplified theory.

■ BREAK-EVEN COSTS AND "ADMINISTERED PRICES"

Businessmen often speak of their break-even costs. You will hear them complain that union wage demands during the long expansion of the 1960s have

---

[1] General Motors, one of the world's most successful enterprises, has used such markup methods for 40 years. Note that the average costs used prior to markup will for most firms *not already* include a return on the firm's own capital.

raised the level of their break-even costs to a dangerous degree, so that, if there is any slackening of the peak levels of sales, profits may soon turn into losses. What might I, a hypothetical businessman, mean by my "break-even cost"?

Suppose that I have already fixed upon the price to be charged. Probably I used some sort of markup rule to do so, guessing at the most profitable price range, but it does not much matter how I made the decision.

If I am like most firms, I shall not be changing my P every day. Probably I name a so-called "administered price" and—subject to varying discounts and other reflections of demand elasticity—I stick to it until further notice.

So long as my P is above MC and AVC, it is clear that my profits will grow with sales. As a matter of fact, at small outputs I shall not even be earning enough to cover fixed costs; but as sales increase, this loss will dwindle, and I shall reach a point where I just cover fixed and variable costs. My sales have now reached the break-even cost.

Beyond this break-even cost, my profits will begin to materialize. Anything I can do to increase sales will be all to the good. I am quite unlike a perfect competitor on a farm, he can always sell *all he wants to produce* at the market price. As an imperfect competitor, with $P > MC$, I am glad to sell more goods at the market price. That is why I advertise and hire salesmen. And that *willingness to sell more* marks me as no perfect competitor.

■ GALBRAITH'S NEW INDUSTRIAL STATE

Prior to John Kenneth Galbraith's 1958 masterwork, *The Affluent Society*, this versatile giant emphasized in his 1954 *American Capitalism* the notion of "countervailing power." Thus a mammoth corporation like General Electric produces, among many other things, refrigerators. It is, of course, checked somewhat in its market power in selling them by the competition of Westinghouse, Philco, General Motors, and many other selling rivals (particularly in this post-Galbraithian era of proliferating "conglomerates," which merge into one large corporation unrelated activities that cut across scores of industries).

Competition by selling rivals is old-fashioned competition, which may or may not suffice to prevent monopoly. Galbraith's emphasis is on something different.

COUNTERVAILING POWER   This is the check upon a giant corporation that comes from the organized competition among the units it buys from and among the units to which it sells. Countervailing power is the check on GE that comes from its being faced with a giant trade union in the market where it buys its labor; from its being faced with a government-led cartel of farmers and miners when it buys its raw materials; from its being faced by powerful chains of retail stores (Simpsons-Sears, Allied Stores, K-Mart Discount Stores), consumer co-operatives, and government purchasing agents to which it must sell, and which use their mass purchasing power to bargain down price and keep profits in check.

Essentially then, *countervailing* power adds, along with the conventional competition of rival sellers, the checks and balances of competition between giant buyers and sellers at every stage in the productive and distributive process.

To the degree that it does prevail, countervailing power will improve the performance of a mixed economy in comparison with the unlimited oligarchy of the giant trusts of 1900. But it does take us a long way from the world of simple *laissez-faire,* and inevitably it puts a great premium on lobbying and participation in politics to influence economic activity. (The whole concept of the "military-industrial complex" takes on a new potential in a world of countervailing power.)

THE TECHNOSTRUCTURE In his 1967 *New Industrial State,* Galbraith views the large corporation as the strategic economic unit of our time. Having much at stake, the corporation desires *stability,* not adventure or uncertainty. Desiring growth, growth, growth, it embraces rational *planning.* Needing *experts,* it increasingly uses, and *is increasingly taken over by,* a new breed of technicians. These bureaucrats are professional managers, who possess the esoteric skills of science, engineering, and social psychology. Members of this technostructure go back and forth between Ottawa and Toronto, or in Galbraith's United States, between New York and Washington. This year the graduate of the University of Toronto, Yale, and the Harvard Business School is merging seven companies; next year he is in Ottawa, helping draw up a trade agreement with Communist China, or in Washington, helping negotiate an arms treaty with the Russians.

It is Galbraith's contention that all over the world—in Vancouver or Vladivostok, in Peking or Poona—there is a *convergence* toward the same kind of society. On the other side of that bargaining table, the expert faces someone who is essentially his twin—the graduate of the top Moscow Institute, or the Inspecteur de Finance who led his class at the Ecole Polytechnique or the Ecole Supérieure. In what may be Galbraith's own Walter Mitty dream of glory, the new establishments everywhere are converging to the same pattern—to a "meritocracy" based on expert skills, in short, to a "technostructure."

PLUSES AND MINUSES Critically how are we to evaluate these new ideas? To say they are nonsense would itself be nonsense. To insist that they are not new— that Veblen had prophesied the triumph of the engineers 50 years ago, that James Burnham had stressed the role of the bureaucracy, that every tired radical of the 1930s took it for granted that consumer preferences were shaped by advertising efforts and did not well out of the spontaneous nature of man—is beside the point: those who live on in the history of thought and ideas are not those who first think of a notion, but rather those who synthesize its various meanings, who package it, and put it across.

Scholarly research is still going on to document quantitatively the merits and demerits of the Galbraithian vision. The results seem, all over the Western world, to be converging to a balance sheet something like the following.

1. Experts are increasingly in demand. But Galbraith exaggerates the unilateral power that they can exercise. Those who control the plurality of stockholders' votes—themselves usually a minority—still call the tune. The minute the company hits upon hard times and slow growth, the whiz-kid expert is

reminded of the layman's definition of the expert—"a bastard from out of town."

2. Large corporations do certainly have the elbow room for unilateral action denied to a small farmer or conventional family enterprise. They can give money to slum clearance. They can relax in their pursuit of profit. They can pursue growth even when it is more that of cancerous than of healthy cells. They can tempt consumers to buy the goods that the corporation would like to sell.

But the large corporation is not an absolute monarch. Ford could not sell Edsels. Lever Brothers could not, with all the wizardry of Madison Avenue, sell Swan soap. And no single company has been able to introduce unleaded gasoline. If one minority group of management lets profits languish so that the common-stock holders do not get capital gains, another ring of capitalists will stage a successful "take-over." The new crew may not be gentlemen from Upper Canada College, but this is the mixed economy's way of cutting its losses.

3. Having said all this, the objective scholar must assert that economics will never quite be the same as in the days before the Galbraith trilogy.

Most industries are imperfectly competitive—a blend of monopoly and competition:

TYPES OF COMPETITION

KIND OF COMPETITION	NUMBER OF PRODUCERS AND DEGREE OF PRODUCT DIFFERENTIATION	PART OF ECONOMY WHERE PREVALENT	DEGREE OF CONTROL OVER PRICE	METHODS OF MARKETING
Perfect competition	Many producers; identical products	A few agricultural industries	None	Market exchange or auction
Imperfect competition:				
Many differentiated sellers	Many producers; many real or fancied differences in product	Toothpaste, retail trade; conglomerates	Some	Advertising and quality rivalry; administered prices
Oligopoly	Few producers; little or no difference in product	Steel, aluminum, lumber, pulp		
	Few producers; some differentiation of products	Autos, machinery, wallboards		
Complete monopoly	Single producer; single product without close substitutes	A few utilities	Considerable	Promotional and "institutional" public-relations advertising

TABLE 25-1. (Source: Table 24-1, page 592.)

■ OLIGOPOLY: COMPETITION AMONG THE FEW

Table 24-1, page 592, gave a classification of different forms of market structure. It is important enough to warrant reproducing in this chapter as Table 25-1 (see page 615).

Monopoly (one seller) is a rare case. Duopoly (two sellers) happens occasionally, particularly in geographically distinct markets where a couple of steel makers or a couple of railroads or trucking companies dominate the market. More common still is the case of *oligopoly* (few sellers). We saw in Chapter 5, page 127, that most large-scale industries are dominated by a few giant firms. In the production of pig iron, matches, and soap, a few big firms predominate, and the same is true among the distilleries, tobacco processors, petroleum refineries, and breweries. Similar conditions prevail in other industries. In automobiles, the Big Three saturate most of the market; and so it goes in the aluminum, aircraft, meat-packing, and communications industries.

An economic theory of oligopoly has been developed to try to account for the facts of *administered* prices which change infrequently, and to account for the prevalence of markup pricing. Let us consider the case of three or four dominant firms. Already we know that the pattern of costs and returns is likely to be such that the *optimal size of efficient production*—at the bottom of Chapter 24's U-shaped long-run *AC* curve (see page 568)—will be *very large relative to the total market demand*. That is why the three or four firms do not become thirty or forty, or three hundred, or three thousand.

Thus, it probably costs a billion dollars to produce an integrated steel plant. Canada has only four integrated producers. If steel could be produced at the scale that wheat is produced, there would be thousands of Canadian steel companies, and the industry would have to fear much more competition than it now

Oligopoly means few sellers of the same or differentiated products:

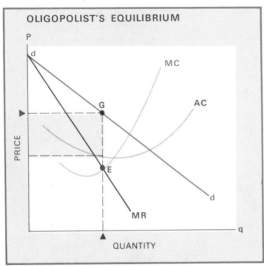

FIG. 25-1. After experience with disastrous price wars, each of the few rivals who dominate a given market is almost sure to recognize that price cutting begets canceling-out price cutting. So the typical oligopolist will estimate his demand curve *dd* by assuming others will be charging similar prices (and by taking into account the potential entry of new oligopolists). Since he gains little from cutting *P*, he will settle for sizeable markup of *P* over *AC* where *MC* = *MR*.

gets from European and Japanese imports and shipments from the eastern United States.

Figure 25-1 shows the large-scale operation of a typical oligopolist. The most acute case threatening instability of oligopolistic competition is that in which the different firms produce virtually *identical* or *homogeneous* products. If Firm A's sulphuric acid undersells Firm B's by even $1 a cartank, A will get practically all the business. In this case, we oligopolists are practically sure to recognize our "mutual interdependence"[2]—namely, that we must end up charging about the same prices, and that any initial advantage I get in undercutting your price will be lost when you are induced to cut your price in return. That is why the *dd* demand curve shown for Corporation A in Fig. 25-1 is *not* drawn up on the assumption of "other things (including rivals' prices) being held constant"; instead A's *dd* is just exactly as inelastic as the whole industry's *DD*, since it is A's prorated one-third or one-fourth of the shared market.

Where is the Maximum-profit equilibrium for the oligopolist? It is shown in Fig. 25-1 at *E*, the intersection of his *MC* and *MR* curves, with *P* at *G* on *dd* just above *E*. If you turn back to page 599, you see that this oligopoly equilibrium *looks* much like the simple monopoly equilibrium of Fig. 24-4(a). Only the assumption about rivals' prices differs.

INFLEXIBLE, ADMINISTERED PRICING   But there is an important difference under oligopoly. A monopolist might be expected to change his price every time his *dd* or *MC* curve shifts, which could be every year, every quarter, every month. We need an economic theory to explain the more inflexible price quotations administered typically by oligopolists. We deduce the needed theory of *P* inflexibility from the fact that rivals may behave one way when you *cut* your price—namely, matching your cuts and thwarting your hope for new business; and they behave another way when you *raise* your *P* above the customary level —namely, holding their prices constant in order to pick up some of your customers. In consequence, you have little motive to change your price in either direction. Instead you "administer" your own price in a rigid fashion, particularly since each oligopolist learns from experience that it is easier to agree— tacitly or explicitly—on a common *P* that is fixed rather than on one that is changing from month to month.[3]

---

[2] A century of theorizing by economists about what Mind A thinks Mind B will do if *he* thinks A will do such-and-such culminated in J. von Neumann and O. Morgenstern, *The Theory of Games and Economic Behavior* (Princeton University Press, Princeton, N.J., 1953, 3rd ed.). This mathematical theory, while it cannot clear up all the philosophical problems of how two omniscient minds will act against each other in an interdependent world, does offer many fine insights for political warfare as well as economics. (EXAMPLES: A teacher picks quiz questions *at random* from a book; a watchman makes his rounds at random, not in a discernible pattern. Facing you as a smart rival, I shall work hard to maximize my *most vulnerable* defence, knowing you will find out the weakest link in my chain. I bluff at poker, not simply, as some think, to win a pot with a *weak* hand, but rather to ensure that all players do *not* drop out when I bet high on a good hand.) The Appendix to the previous chapter surveys game theory.

[3] The remainder of this section can be skipped if desired.

A kinked or cornered demand curve can explain rigidity of oligopolists' administered price:

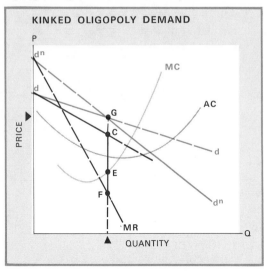

FIG. 25-2. The $d^n d^n$ curve through G, which corresponds to the dd curve in Fig. 25-1, is the demand curve when all sellers move prices *together* and share total market. However, dd is the more elastic demand curve when this firm *alone* changes its price and loses sales to its rivals. Below G, as others match your price cut, $d^n d^n$ prevails. Above G, when rivals do not match your price increase dd prevails. Geometrically, the different demand curves generate different MR curves, with the FC vertical discontinuity (or "kink") resulting from the corner at G. Considerably shifting MC curves will still lead to intersection on FC, and hence unchanged oligopoly price and quantity at G.

Figure 25-2 illustrates the "kinked" or "cornered" demand curve that economists postulate to explain rigid price behavior. The equilibrium price G is shown in Fig. 25-1 and Fig. 25-2 at about that markup level over costs which the oligopolists think will be best for them in the long run.[4]

But at G there is a kink in the effective demand and marginal revenue curves of Oligopolist A. Why? Because if he cuts his P below G, his rivals will follow him, and he moves down the $d^n d^n$ curve, which corresponds to the old steep dd curve in Fig. 25-1. But what if he *alone* raises his P above the tacit customary price at G? No rival will follow him, because they all hope to pick up some business at his expense. Most, but not all, of his customers are likely to leave him: hence, for *increases* in P, he is on the more elastic dd curve that reflects what he would sell when he *alone* changes P while all rivals *hold their prices constant* at the customary G level.

Geometrically, the corner on the demand curve implies the vertical discontinuity in the MR curve marked FC.[5] And now see that the MC level for the firm could shift considerably—anywhere between F and C—without changing the q^* intersection of MC and MR or the Maximum-profit P^* at G.

A "cornered" or "kinked" demand curve around an administered level of markup price—because P cuts are matched and P increases are not—can

---

[4] Actually, it would be realistic for them to draw up their $d^n d^n$ curves allowing for entry of *potential* rivals who might be tempted into the industry if they collude on so high a P as to make it profitable for new firms to come in. In consequence, each firm's $d^n d^n$ might be somewhat more elastic than that for the whole industry, but still more inelastic than the dd that results from no change in rival's P induced by your change in P.

[5] The straight-line geometry of page 582's diagram can demonstrate this. The flat dGd straight line generates the flat MR line; the steeper $d^n G d^n$ line generates the steeper MR line; between these MR lines comes the vertical "kink," FC.

help explain rigidity of oligopoly price compared with both perfect-competition and complete-monopoly flexible price. Also, this rigidity makes tacit agreement more easily possible.

COLLUSION, TACIT OR EXPLICIT   We see why combines policy should be greatly concerned with the problem of oligopoly collusion. Even where there is some differentiation of products, if there are but two, three, or a few sellers, they may come to realize that their prices are closely *interrelated*. Each will guess, or may soon learn from experience, that when it cuts its price, its rivals tend to meet or to exceed such a price cut. Economic warfare may result for a while, until the few sellers come to realize that they are in the same boat.

In the United States, before the antitrust laws were important, such oligopolists might have formed a "trust," or a tight little cartel or combine. Meeting at celebrated dinners, such as those that Judge Gary of the United States Steel Corporation held decades ago, the sellers would collusively set some kind of monopoly price. As high as a full-monopoly price? Sometimes, if they were sure they could keep newcomers out. But in the more realistic case where the oligopolists had to take account of the fact that setting a high price would tempt new rivals into their field, they would agree on a price higher than the purely competitive one but set with some moderation for fear of attracting new entry.

Today it would be illegal in both the United States and Canada for combines, cartels, or "trusts" to set prices collusively and shamelessly in order to maximize their mutual profits. On the other hand, if a few large firms encounter the same problem, experience suggests that they may—without ever meeting, phoning, winking, or corresponding—arrive at a *tacit* mode of behavior that avoids fierce price competition. With or without a price leader, the sellers may be quoting rather similar prices[6]—prices which come nowhere near the level of MC, as in the case of the perfectly competitive industry discussed in Chapter 22.

The richness of possible outcomes would exhaust a specialized book on the subject. The final equilibrium may end up much or little above the firm's marginal cost level. If fear of entry is great and if the number of existing sellers is considerable, then the $d''d''$ curve might be quite near to horizontal and give results not too different from perfect competition. But if sellers are few, and if they are large relative to the total demand, not very fearful of new entrants, and keenly conscious of the mutuality of their interest, the tacit price pattern may become a very high one relative to long-run or short-run marginal cost.

Also, oligopolists love to shift rivalry and competition into dimensions other than price: into advertising, into changing the wrapping of their product and the size of its replacement parts, into providing quick and reliable service.

---

[6] In 1946 the U.S. Supreme Court held that cigarette oligopolists could be guilty of price fixing even when there was no overt collusion!

Free entry of many imperfect competitors can wipe out profit but leave waste:

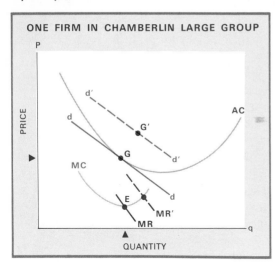

FIG. 25-3. The typical seller of one of many differentiated products can be forced by free entry into a long-run no-profit tangency at *G*. Such rivals split up the markets without depressing price to the marginal cost level as in perfect competition. He and all his rivals end up with *P* above *MC*; and producing *q* at which long-run average cost is still falling, because it is less than the particular *q** which is at the bottom of the U-shaped curve. Note: *MR'* is marginal to *d'd'*, and *MR* is marginal to the later *dd*.)

Some of this is undoubtedly valuable; some is definitely wasteful. What is the net balance of advantage over disadvantage? A priori reasoning alone cannot tell us; even study of the facts cannot lead to a conclusive answer independently of ethical value judgments. But what needs emphasizing by the economist is this:

Once the rules of perfect competition are left behind, there is no Invisible Hand principle which sets up a presumption that the working out of *laissez-faire* is likely to be in the direction of satisfying wants more efficiently.

■ MANY DIFFERENTIATED SELLERS: WASTE UNDER FREE ENTRY

Let us leave few-seller oligopoly and turn to the case of many sellers, but not of a homogeneous single product. This important case is the brainchild of the late E. H. Chamberlin.

In Fig. 25-3 a typical seller is briefly in short-run equilibrium at *G'*. His *d'd'* is sloped because his product is a little different from anyone else's. However, we assume that *entry is free* for new firms to produce their own differentiated products on as favorable terms as our typical seller can produce his.

Since he and all the other initial sellers are seen to be making good profits at the initial *G'*, new firms are tempted into the market. These new entrants cut into his demand and shift his *d'd'* curve leftward to *dd* until it just touches (and does not cross above) his *AC* curve.

Thus, final long-run equilibrium for the typical seller ends up at the *tangency* point *G*—the only point at which the seller can avoid losses. Note that downward-sloping *dd* means that tangential *AC* must be falling and that final output is smaller than the q^* corresponding to the bottom of the U-shaped AC curve.[7]

> *Chronic excess capacity and waste.* Free entry into the large group of sellers of *differentiated* products merely divides up markets, leading to excessive prices at the tangency points of downward-sloping demand curves with still-falling long-run AC curves. Minimum-cost scale of production is not attained. The imperfect competitors make no monopoly profits, but price does not get lowered to the bottom-of-the-U level. The consumer has to pay for chronic excess-capacity operation of too many sellers, each producing too little. These wastes are different from those of complete monopoly, and of course different from the efficiency of perfect competition.

If consumers were willing to sacrifice the differentiation of product, a lower equilibrium P would be possible as fewer firms were used more intensively to produce a more standardized output. But *laissez-faire* has no way of deciding how much extra people *ought* to pay in return for the extra variety of products they enjoy in Fig. 25-3.[8]

B. MODERN COMBINES PROBLEMS

■ SOME WASTES OF IMPERFECT COMPETITION RECAPITULATED

Before going into the legal, historical, and institutional aspects of combines legislation, we ought to remind ourselves what the economic evils are that are associated with various monopolistic and other imperfections of competition.

---

[7] The Chamberlin excess-capacity tangency of Fig. 25-3 should not be confused with the tangency under *perfect* competition shown here in Fig. 25-4. As discussed in earlier chapters, this typical perfect competitor is one of so many producers of an *identical* good that he faces a practically horizontal ("infinitely elastic") *dd* curve, even though the industry's very much larger *DD* curve can be very much more inelastic. If there is free entry and exit of well-informed firms that can replicate the cost conditions of any one firm, long-run equilibrium at E will involve no excess of profit over competitive costs (including properly computed implicit- and opportunity-cost returns). Society is getting its total output most efficiently, in recognition of the $P = MC$ condition of Chapter 22. It has neither excess capacity nor too few firms (forcing out of existing firms any output that could be obtained more cheaply by adding new firms).

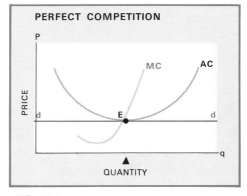

FIG. 25-4.

[8] Even if, as Chamberlain insists, people may want some of the extra variety of differentiated products that the tangency solution of Fig. 25-3 makes possible, that pattern cannot be ideally efficient. For it can be shown that wherever P exceeds MC anywhere, there definitely exists a new configuration (possibly involving subsidies, as in Chapter 24's Appendix) in which *everyone* can be made better off. This point is alluded to again on page 624, footnote 11.

MONOPOLY RESTRICTIONS   It is not the profit a monopoly (or an oligopoly, for that matter) makes that constitutes its greatest evil, but rather its tendency to set too high a price in relation to social marginal-cost pricing.[9] To see this, imagine our taxing away all the monopolist's profit by imposing on him a franchise tax of just the right size.

Clearly, the monopolist would end up with no profit. The state would get its profit, but the monopoly would not lower its P or raise its Q. Why not? Because the intersection of MR and MC would be unchanged by a lump-sum franchise tax: since such a tax is a fixed cost that varies not at all with Q, it will not affect MC; and MR depends only on the demand curve, not on costs or franchise taxes. So the consumer goes on getting too little of the product and paying too high a price. The state has now become the villainous recipient of monopoly profit and has failed to correct the misallocation of resources.

The moral: It is the contrived divergence between P and MC that constitutes the true additional burden of monopoly.[10]

OVERENTRY AND "SICK" INDUSTRIES   Many fields are characterized by an excessive number of firms. Most of these do a small volume of business and remain in the industry only until they have lost their capital. Grocery stores, taverns, funeral homes, restaurants, nightclubs, and gasoline stations are typical examples taken from retail trade. But much the same thing is true of the textile trade, the dress trade, and many others that require little initial capital.

Why don't such unprofitable concerns leave the industry? The answer is, They do. But as fast as they leave, new firms enter the industry, leaving the total number unchanged and even growing.

Why do new firms enter the industry in the face of the fact that most existing firms are incurring losses? Apparently, partly out of ignorance and

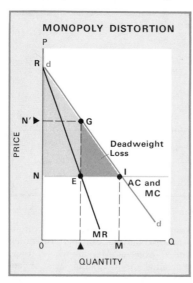

FIG. 25-5.

[9] Figure 19-10, page 480, and Chapter 24's Appendix have elaborated on this.

[10] Advanced treatises use the accompanying Fig. 25-5 to approximate the "deadweight loss" due to monopoly. At the competitive ideal I, each similar consumer enjoys Marshallian consumer's surplus given by the whole triangular area NIR. When monopoly raises P to the Maximum-profit point G, the consumer loses to the monopolist that part of his consumer's surplus represented by the profit rectangle $NEGN'$ and is left with but $N'GR$. What happens to the little triangle EIG? It is lost to everybody and represents "deadweight loss." Thus consumers lose more than the monopolist's profit; and even if they took back the $NEGN'$ profit by lump sum taxation, they would be losing to the devil of inefficiency the "deadweight triangle" which benefits *nobody*.

partly out of misplaced hope. An old couple putting their lifetime savings of a few thousand dollars into a little retail grocery store do so in the belief that *their* venture will be different, theirs will succeed—and anyway, in the grocery business no one need starve. But alas, with no special business aptitude and with less than the minimum amount of capital necessary for efficient operation, they last in business only until their original capital has gone.

Such chronically overcrowded industries need not be what the economist has called "perfectly competitive"—although in the case of agriculture or "cotton gray goods," they may happen to be approximately so. Having too many firms in a perfectly competitive industry is an undesirable condition, involving as it does wastes of resources and losses. But at least in such a *competitive* industry the consumer partly gains, through lower prices, what the overoptimistic producers are losing.

Unfortunately, in most chronically overcrowded sick industries, market competition is quite *imperfect*. Being inefficient producers, the small concerns do not sell very cheaply. Instead of competing on a price basis, they tend to charge fairly high prices and simply to *divide* the business.

> The resulting economic situation under this form of free-entry numerous-seller imperfect competition may be worse even than under complete monopoly: not only is price excessive, but in addition valuable resources are wasted because each firm has too much idle plant and manpower. The situation is triply bad: producers incur losses, resources are wasted, and the prices charged the consumer are too high.

Our earlier diagram from Chamberlin, Fig. 25-3, showed how imperfect competition may result in wastage of resources, too high price, and yet no profits for the imperfect competitors. It can show too how the spirit of Marshall's long-run analysis can be applied to the sector of imperfect competition characterized by free entry.

Imagine the diagram shows such a typical imperfect competitor, say, a local barbershop that can count on some customers' being unwilling to walk a long way to get a haircut. Its original demand $d'd'$ slopes downward; and hence it has been marking up P above MC. It is maximizing positive profit and charging more than full unit costs (AC).

But now other barbers see this profit opportunity. They move in. There is now one barbershop for every three blocks rather than for every four. What happens to the demand curve for our typical barber? Clearly, entry of new competitors divides up the existing business and causes demand to shift downward and leftward to dd, with each barber wasting more time in frustrating idleness. Now at the new maximum-profit point, each barber makes no profit, as can be seen from the fact that the new demand curve just touches tangentially the average cost curve. Marginal cost is equated to new marginal revenue —but that serves only to avoid losses, not to produce a positive profit.

The long-run equilibrium at G, which Marshall might shudder to call "normal," very clearly shows that price is higher than the most efficient cost level which prevails at the bottom of the U-shaped average-cost curve. The barbershop has excess capacity, with empty chairs much of the time. (Of course customers have to walk only three blocks now, not four, and may have to wait less. And that is worth something. But note that they have never, in most cities, really been given the choice of a slightly longer walk and haircuts at the lower prices that efficient capacity utilization would make possible.[11])

If there is lasting overentry of overoptimistic barbers, draw in a $d''d''$ curve still lower than dd and show wasteful social losses, and turnover of disappointed entrepreneurs. You can do the same in the case of perfect competition illustrated in Fig. 25-4 (see footnote 7, page 621).

EVILS OF OLIGOPOLY   Recall the already mentioned freight price wars of the past century. Customers shipping goods always pick the route that offers even a few pennies saving. Thus, each of the three or four carriers would intermittently undercut the existing rate schedules, until finally a disastrously low level of rates was reached. At the same time, for short hauls where shippers were at the mercy of one line, the railroads would jack up the rates, thus creating an anomalous, discriminatory pattern of charges.[12]

Even without government regulations, in industries characterized by heavy overhead costs and identical products, there is often a realization that competition is ruinous. Therefore, tacitly or explicitly, the firms try to agree on a price that maximizes the long-run profits of all. Trade associations, keeping one eye on the officers who enforce the Combines Act, may impose penalties on any chiseler in the industry who makes secret price concessions. Occasionally, as new conditions or firms upset the status quo in the industry, another price war may break out—to last until everyone has again learned his lesson and the morale of the industry is restored.

In appraising oligopoly we must note that the desire of corporations to earn a fair return on their *past* investments can at times be at variance with the well-being of the consumer. Too much plant capacity may have been built in the industry in the past; but that is not justification for continuing high prices and scarce output. Competition, which the businessman regards as destructive, cut-throat, and ruinous, may actually be the only way to get the redundant plant capacity into operation or to discourage its maintenance. (Having made the mistake of building the plants, society ought not to add the further error of

---

[11] Repeatedly, in our discussion of pricing "efficiency," we have seen what is proved rigorously in advanced texts: price in excess of marginal costs leads to a state from which it would be possible theoretically to make *everybody* better off—barbers, bald people, long-haired people who hate long walks and waits, and everybody else. But do not leap from this to the invalid inference that variety does not matter or that enforcing $P = MC$ everywhere would (in decreasing-cost situations with differential products) lead spontaneously to the "ideal" amount of variety. Here is a case where defining an optimum is actually a difficult social task.

[12] The Board of Transport Commissioners was established in 1904 to prevent such unstable price conditions, and to regulate rates where competition could not be relied on to keep them down.

failing to use them to best advantage.) Losses or subnormal profits is the free-enterprise way of discouraging excess capacity.

The pulp, steel, and other raw material industries are examples of this pattern of imperfect competition. How does all this work out these days in practice? In 1958-1960 we hit a lull. Pulp production went down to half its capacity. Some feared this would initiate a wave of price cuts which would reduce pulp companies' earnings to the break-even point or below. Did it work out that way? Not quite. The industry discovered it could make more money at levels far below capacity; price morale stayed high in the industry. It was not until 1964, when sales were up, profits were becoming large, and many new firms were threatening to enter pulp production, that West Coast firms began to cut prices—partly, at least, to discourage entry.

> In a perfectly competitive industry, when demand shifts leftward, P will fall. Profits will decline greatly. Yet competitive Q may not fall much at all, being sold for whatever it will fetch. The consumer does benefit from what the producer loses, and in time output will adjust to the new state of demand.
>
> By contrast, under oligopoly, price tends to stay firm with output taking up the great variation. Plants stand idle, and the product is not cheapened, in the hope of coaxing out new quantity demanded.

This downward inflexibility of "administered" (or named) prices, many economists fear, adds to the danger of creeping inflation. Why? Because if prices and costs rarely ever fall, there is but one way for the price index to go.

■ DYNAMIC RESEARCH AND MONOPOLY

All is not evil in any field. Some arguments concerning the virtues of imperfect competition can also be made. A common industrial pattern is that of a firm that has considerable control over price by virtue of its technological efficiency, its patents, its trademarks, and its slogans. Its "monopoly profits" are plowed back into further research and advertising, so that it is always able to keep abreast or ahead of its rivals. Alcan, CIL, and Massey-Ferguson are perhaps typical of such companies.

Because research and advertising are expensive and their results cumulative, success tends to breed success, and profits tend to breed more profits. Therefore small business claims that it cannot always effectively compete with such firms. In other words, industrial research may be subject to economies of large scale which small businesses cannot enjoy.[13] And yet, when Oxford's John Jewkes traced the source of the more important inventions of this century, he found that less than half came from laboratories of large corporations.

---

[13] Also, large firms are great "poolers of risks", being favored by the statistical fact that when you aggregate independent risks you cancel out much of the variation. (In fact, quadruple the size of the firm and you halve the average risk or variation per dollar—as probability books will show.)

Furthermore, instances of beer, cigarettes, and soap remind us that advertising and research are quite different things. O'Keefe beer sales may stay large because a national audience has been persuaded of its merits. Much soap advertising is aimed more to solidify the sales of one brand than to expand total soap use and cleanliness. Yet in many cases it will not be easy to decide whether a certain bit of applied industrial research is for the purpose of technical improvements or merely for market improvement.

Reread Schumpeter's eulogy of the dynamic innovational contribution of monopolists (page 130). Weigh this with the claims that many of our best discoveries come from small business, government, lone-wolf inventors, and university researchers. A sensible student realizes this is indeed a controversial matter.

While admitting the efficiency and progress of some of the firms described, some critics go on to argue that society would be *still* better off if the full advantages of efficiency were passed on to consumers or plowed back into research aimed at technological improvements and not simply at profits, and if fewer dollars were spent on "soap operas" and jingles and more dollars went into fundamental science rather than into patentable gadgets. Obviously, we are dealing here with moot issues, on which each citizen must form his own judgment. Obviously too, the giants of the new industrial state must be placed under ever-vigilant public scrutiny and surveillance.

■ WHAT TO DO ABOUT MONOPOLY IMPERFECTIONS

Is there no hope for limiting monopoly and oligopoly? Yes, there is.

For one thing, if we make sure that *barriers to entry are kept to a minimum*, the fear of potential competition and the actuality of it may help to keep the oligopoly prices down.

For a second thing, if we lower tariff barriers to imported goods, we both increase the sources of potential competition and lower the maximum to which Canadian prices can be raised.

For a third thing, if government combines policy bears down hard on the slightest sign of collusion to keep prices firm and to control supply, the oligopolists may find it harder to equate their marginal revenue and cost at a level high above society's true marginal cost.

For a fourth thing, some economists—such as Chicago's George J. Stigler—would argue that large firms should be broken up into many small pieces. He thinks the bottom of U-shaped cost curves comes early enough to make this a practical possibility that will not sacrifice any appreciable economies of large-scale production. With sellers now numerous, he hopes that competition can become much more like perfect competition than like oligopoly. (Needless to say, Stigler is against any mergers that might reduce numbers still further; and he believes that many of today's giants grew from mergers which had as their goal not *productive efficiency*, but rather *monopoly control over market price*.)

This is clearly a controversial area. Government regulation and government combines laws are the principal weapons the mixed economy uses to improve the workings of the price system. However, the courts' decisions, based on the interpretation of statutes, are of little help in making up our minds what a good policy *would* be. For example, the Supreme Court of Ontario found that a merger being carried out by Canadian Breweries Ltd. (Carling, O'Keefe, Dow, and other brands) with other breweries was acceptable because, with three large national breweries left, Canadian Breweries would still face competition. But the U.S. Supreme Court, a short time earlier, forbade Bethlehem Steel's planned merger with other firms, even though the resultant giant would have had no more than 20 per cent of the U.S. steel market. The two cases are very similar. Both firms argued in defence of their mergers that they would become more efficient in production as they grew—that is, that the bottom of their U-shaped cost curves would be far to the right. But although this argument was contested by the prosecution in both cases, the two courts' judgments were based chiefly on whether competition remained after the mergers, not on whether increased efficiency would result and should be encouraged. Thus the courts, especially in Canada, have not really dealt with the question of whether increase in size, per se, is a good thing.

■ PUBLIC-UTILITY REGULATION

To show what government can do about monopoly, let us consider in detail a monopoly under government regulation. Such "public utilities" include gas and light companies, telephone and communication services, railroads and public carriers, and so forth. Their importance is shown in Table 25-2. Since it seems uneconomical to have two local sets of telephone wires, an exclusive franchise is given to a single company. (Why not the same for milk delivery—another hard question.)

The government gives the utility company a complete monopoly, but then steps in to protect the consumer by setting maximum rates. Usually this is done by public regulating commissions, which specify the *maximum prices* that can be charged for each kind of service.

In setting such prices it has long been customary to pick prices that may give the company "a fair return on its capital." Rates such as 6, 7, or 8 per cent are often selected as representing a fair return. (Of course, any "guarantee" of a rate of return raises the problem of *motivating* the utility to keep efficient and cost-conscious.)

It is a complex problem, that of determining the *capital-value* base of the company to which this "fair rate" is to be applied. Three measures of fair capital value have been suggested at times: (1) *original cost* (minus depreciation)—or the sum of all past prudent investments; (2) *current reproduction or replacement cost* (minus depreciation)—or the cost of replacing the company's equipment *at present prices*, corrected for age and condition of the property; and (3) *capitalized market value* of the public utility's securities or assets.

ADVANTAGES AND DISADVANTAGES OF DIFFERENT METHODS OF REGULATION   Of these methods, the third is universally recognized to be nonsensical. As was shown in the earlier discussion of good will (Chapter 5), the market value of any income-

Most of GDP is subject to some pricing restrictions:

PERCENTAGE OF GDP SUBJECT TO PRICING OR COMBINES LAWS, 1967	PER CENT OF GDP
Subject to Combines Act (mostly commodity-producing)	53
Subject to Agricultural Marketing Boards, etc.	5
Subject to Public-Utility Regulation	12
Service industries under public ownership or jurisdiction	10
Not regulated (mostly services)	20

TABLE 25-2. The Combines Act covers only about half of Canadian production, but other regulations also exist. (Source: Economic Council of Canada, *Interim Report on Competition Policy*, **Queen's Printer, Ottawa, 1969;** adapted from Table 7-1 and other Tables.)

earning property is given by capitalizing its annual return by the interest rate.[14] For a regulating authority to use capitalized market value as a base for measuring capital would be tantamount to recognizing *any level of earnings*, high or low, as fair. (For example, let the earnings be high—excessively high. The stock market will then pay a lot for them.) Once capitalized into a new base, excessively high earnings will appear as only moderate interest returns, and the same is true of excessively low earnings. The method of capitalized earnings begs the question that the authorities must answer!

Canadian regulation has therefore vacillated between *original* cost and *reproduction* cost. So long as the general price level does not change, the two are not very different. But over a period of decades, when prices may greatly increase, reproduction cost will involve higher earnings and rates than original costs. In periods of declining prices, the reverse discrepancy is to be observed: original-cost capital-value (or rate base, as it is often called) tends to favor investors over customers. Canadian provincial authorities have preferred the more easily calculated original-cost base, and this appears also to be the implicit policy of the Canadian Transport Commission on railroad rates.[15] On the whole,

---

[14] The capitalization process is more fully discussed in Chapter 29.

[15] From the standpoint of the advanced discussions of "welfare economics," neither method is ideal as the last Appendix made clear. Some writers in this field have set up a perfectionist formula that would involve pricing of public-utility services at not more than the extra or marginal costs of services. (We have seen why $P = MC$ is "efficient" already many times.) However, marginal-cost pricing is a doctrine which, as a practical matter, few economists would endorse all the way. It could lead to excessive returns to the owners if demand was large in comparison with capacity. But with decreasing-cost situations so likely in the public-utility area, it would more likely give *inadequate* returns to original investors. Although the government could then, if it wished to, *by a subsidy* secure justice for investors without interfering with the desirable output or price, this would represent such a departure from present practice as to be unlikely to come about fully.

The great public projects like the South Saskatchewan dam and the Great Slave Lake railway are from one point of view partial approaches to such a system of pricing. But their multiple national and regional purposes make it difficult to compare them with the pricing policies of more routine public utilities.

however, reproduction cost leads to a more flexible price structure and gives less weight to the dead hand of past costs.

ECONOMIC LIMITS TO RATE-SETTING POWERS   But the freedom of the authorities to set rates always has economic limitations. It is obvious that a rate set too low will drive out investors, make utilities unable to maintain their equipment and lines, and bring public service to a halt. Fear of this has, in the opinion of Canadian writers on utilities, always kept authorities erring slightly on the side of generosity in deciding on a "fair return" on capital. But there is also a "competitive" limit preventing rates from being set too high. Even in the early days, railroad transport boards found that, if rail freight rates were set too high, traffic would be diverted via U.S. lines, or highway or steamship alternatives. That is, the fair return on capital could not be granted to utilities whose demand curves were made elastic by potential substitutes. Today this "competition between natural monopolies" is even keener. A gas utility has very limited scope for asking higher prices: if it gets them, it will lose its customers to the oil companies and other energy sellers. Even hydro utilities face competition: consumers can use oil or gas for many purposes, and industrial buyers can generate their own power if the utility's rate is set too high. Similarly, road carriers cannot easily set (or have set for them) high per-mile rates, or customer firms will run their own trucks.

PUBLIC OWNERSHIP VERSUS PUBLIC REGULATION

Where many utilities are publicly owned, the downward pressure on rates is also maintained by a rule that Crown corporations are not to be run for a profit. But often this rule is not followed, by government liquor stores, for example. Anyway, it is no substitute for close regulation both of allowable expenses in the rate base and of rates themselves. Many provincially and federally owned utilities run at no profit because they offer expensive services that private utilities would abandon. Rural electrical service is a good example. Another is telephone service: we are told that Bell Telephone kept away from small rural systems because they were unprofitable at rates acceptable to public utilities commissions. Yet in the provinces with publicly owned telephone systems, rural services are widely provided, and are in effect subsidized by city telephone users. Thus a "no-profit" *rule* cannot guarantee that costs will be kept down, or rates reasonable.

But *competition* still works to keep down rates, even in publicly owned services. Indeed, the CNR's rates over the years have been influenced chiefly by (1) parliamentary intervention to get low rates for regions like the maritimes and the prairie wheat belt, (2) the existence of competitive routes, such as the Panama Canal and inland waterways, and (3) the decisions of the Board of Transport Commissioners on the privately owned CPR's costs. And, where Canadians are frequently aware of prices in the United States, potential or demonstrable competition from new services already available in the United States may serve as well as actual competition.

The threat from competition today, however, is felt in a new way. Transportation and energy policies have been switched from regulation to keep customers from being exploited, to rather more explicit attempts to serve larger national goals. This is obviously true of the National Energy Board, which governs the export of energy to the United States from terms of reference that are only partly concerned with Canadian consumers, and are also concerned with Canadian taxpayers and Canada's future industrial prospects. This is also true of transportation. Utilities commissions, Parliament, and government royal commissions now seem to be struggling to free competitive carriers from regulation, and attempting instead to regulate their investment policy (and line-abandonment policy) so as to achieve explicit national and regional ends. The sanction from competition is only potential. New policy makers are saying, "Unless the railways or pipelines do so-and-so, the regions they serve will fail to develop as they should. This is bad in itself, and, incidentally, it will mean that there is no future traffic or business for the utilities." The McPherson Royal Commission on railroads was a good example of this planning approach to utility and railroad policy.

The reader who reflects on these examples may see a trend. Formerly, natural monopolies were regulated to prevent prices and rates being set too high. The utilities were free to decide on much of their capital investment and expansion policy, however, the utility commissions being there chiefly to determine what a "fair return" ought to be on both old and new outlays. Today the monopoly position of utilities is less strong. Each is becoming more like a firm in a small-numbers, differentiated-products industry. The gap between its P and MC depends on the vigor of competition and on the ease with which new competitors can enter the market. The trend seems to be to regulate the conditions under which this competition can take place, to make sure that it doesn't involve reckless commitments for labor or equipment; at the same time, being careful not to discourage competition or to entrench utilities in monopolistic positions. This trend is vague so far; all that can be observed is that regulatory policy is no longer concerned solely with setting or guaranteeing rates and prices.

■ CANADIAN COMBINES POLICY

The economics of Canada's particular policies to control "combinations in restraint of trade," or combines, have not been widely studied. At any given time, no more than a handful of academics have been fully informed on the laws and their administration. This situation is quite unlike that in Germany, Britain, or the United States, where economists, lawyers, and historians have long devoted their professional careers to one or another aspect of their monopoly laws.

American leadership stems chiefly from the fact that at the turn of the century trusts were becoming both the engine of further American economic development and the object of popular fear of their increased economic and political power. Small companies were merged into big; big and small companies combined collusively to limit supply and raise price. By retaliatory price-cutting, such trusts could and did brutally punish smaller firms that did not follow the trusts' price leadership. At the same time huge stock-market promotions of the securities and shares of the new mergers flourished. On a much smaller scale, similar events were taking place in Canada; but Canadian public opinion was really focused on other economic problems.

EARLY U.S. TRUSTBUSTING   Around 1889-1890, both countries took the first legal steps to go beyond the old common-law checks on combines. Canada added to its Criminal Code the famous Section 411, forbidding combinations that "unduly" lessen competition in production or sale of goods. (The federal government cannot easily regulate trade and commerce by civil law-making, because most trade and property matters are under provincial jurisdiction.) Soon after, the United States passed its Sherman Antitrust Act, making it illegal to monopolize trade or to combine in restraint of trade. There is no record of these Acts being vigorously enforced at the time; indeed, it is evident that few people had a clear idea of which actions were to be regarded as illegal.

Then in the early 1900s came the era of "trustbusting." The Roosevelt and Taft administrations dusted off the Sherman Act, and through the Supreme Court challenged the merging or monopolizing activities of J. P. Morgan, E. H. Harriman, and James J. Hill on railroads; of Duke on the American Tobacco Company; and of Rockefeller on the Standard Oil Co. The last two were broken up into independent companies. These were the great capitalists and the great firms of the day.

The tide of prosecution was stemmed by the view eventually taken by the U.S. Supreme Court that the Sherman Act could be applied only to *unreasonable* agreements, mergers, or predatory actions against competitors. With this doctrine, the Court eventually decided that United States Steel, a huge merger promoted by Morgan, Carnegie, Gary and others, was not an "unreasonable" project: "bigness" was not in itself to be a crime. In 1914, the Clayton Act and the Federal Trade Commission Act were also passed. The former exempted trade unions from being prosecuted as combines, but did not succeed in defining the practices to be forbidden more precisely. The latter set up a powerful body which polices industry, chiefly to prevent misleading advertising claims and other unfair methods of competition by particular firms.

The U.S. courts' insistence that mergers had to be "unreasonable" to be illegal was of course very similar to the Canadian law's insistence that only practices that "unduly" lessened competition were illegal. Both left the onus on the courts to decide what was unreasonable or undue. And in Canada because few companies were prosecuted, no body of case-law was set up to clarify what was "undue."

In both countries the vigor of public antipathy to combines was diverted to other subjects in the 1920s. Antitrust actions languished. Under Mackenzie King, however, Canada did make a start on combines legislation by passing the Combines Investigation Act. Like King's Industrial Disputes Investigation Act, which was discussed in Chapter 7, this measure relied on investigation and *publicity*. A small staff was appointed to investigate suspected infractions of the Criminal

Code section on combines, and of some sections that were inserted into the new act. The staff report was published, even if no legal prosecution was undertaken by the government. The staff was kept busy, but their reports and subsequent actions were directed mostly against small suppliers, contractors, and dealers. So inconspicuous was the Act that books published in the 1930s, criticizing what they called the trend to monopoly, sometimes failed even to mention the Combines Act!

During the Great Depression, antitrust and combines legislation had a mixed career. Left-wing politicians spoke with dislike of "monopoly power." Prime Minister R. B. Bennett launched a large "price spreads" investigation, because it was alleged that the prices paid to farmers, other suppliers, and "sweated labor" by larger industries were far below prices paid by consumers for their product. Indirectly, this was an allegation that monopoly power caused P to have a too-wide spread above MC. The commission uncovered some sensationally bad working conditions in certain industries, but little usable evidence of monopoly. In the United States, interest in trustbusting was for a while replaced by laws pointing in the other direction. The National Recovery Administration (later found unconstitutional) would have authorized firms and workers to form cartels to hold up prices. And "fair-trade" acts authorized or ordered retailers to sell only at prices set by the manufacturers of branded goods. Such policies are called "resale price maintenance."

Until Franklin Roosevelt's Attorney General Thurman Arnold reversed the trend in the late thirties, the mix of laws and administration in both countries was calculated to keep prices *up* rather than down. Indeed, economist Lloyd Reynolds wrote a treatise with the suggestive title "The Control of *Competition* in Canada," not "The Control of Combines."

During World War II, both countries were too concerned with production and fair allocation of food and clothing to be worried about inefficient mergers and combines. Economist John Kenneth Galbraith has shown that it was actually convenient for harassed war production directors to be able to get together a very few heads of very large firms to plan output and price policies.[16] In peace time this would have been called collusion.

■ SINCE WORLD WAR II

IN THE UNITED STATES   Under Presidents Truman and Eisenhower, the United States attacked trusts with renewed vigor but uncertain purpose. For example "bigness" itself was challenged: the A & P stores were prosecuted in the face of defence evidence that large-scale operations promoted efficiency and lower consumer prices; DuPont was forced to relinquish its controlling ownership of GM stock and to give up its joint ownership of CIL in Canada. A little earlier, antitrust pressure had forced a complete split between Aluminum Co. of America and Aluminium Ltd. of Canada (Alcoa and Alcan). Industries such as glass, cigarettes, cement, steel and many others came under attack.

[16] J. K. Galbraith, *American Capitalism* (Houghton Mifflin, Boston, 1952).

The justice department's antitrust division hired hundreds of lawyers; and in recent years, attorney generals have made their reputations as trustbusters.[17] In the 1960s, federal legal prosecutions and legislation tended to go beyond the original reasons for fearing size or collusion. Now any act or *horizontal merger* that tends to increase "market power" or to prevent increased entry, however minor, seems subject to legal restraint.

IN CANADA   After a 1950 investigation of combines policy, the government changed the set-up. Till then one Commissioner had been free to choose the industries he would investigate and publicly report upon. Investigated industries felt that (although an adverse report did not mean that a court must find a firm guilty) the single Commissioner had been both prosecutor and judge. Further the Commissioner had, since 1945, turned from small dealers and contractors to bigger industries: pulp and paper, rubber, tires, wire and cable, flat glass, and to the whole problem of international cartels (exporters preventing competition among one other).

The new set-up (formerly under the Department of Trade and Industry and now under the Department of Corporate and Consumer Affairs) provides two offices: (a) a Director of Investigation and Research, with a staff to collect evidence about certain firms' and industries' marketing practices and to put them before (b) a Restrictive Trade Practices Commission, for reviewing this evidence. The Commission's report is published; and it may (or may not) serve as the basis for a prosecution of the industries by the Department of Justice. The final decision, as before, is up to the courts: the quasijudicial procedure of the Commission results in a report, not in a legal decision. Since 1952, the small staffs of the two officers have been busy making investigations and turning out reports. But, until the early 1960s, the industries tackled (while much more significant than those investigated before the war) were still not the giants of Canadian industry. Rosenbluth has estimated that, until about 1960, less than 10 per cent of the GNP was produced by industries that had even been looked at by the "combines cops" as they are derisively called by the financial press. Rubber, flour-milling, and brewing were the biggest industries involved in cases of alleged price-fixing or anticompetitive mergers.

Under Justice Minister Fulton, the combines law was revised again in 1960. Though a number of changes were made, the most important was concerned with resale price maintenance. Many of the others provided greater guidance for the courts in determining whether a given monopoly, merger, or agreement was "against the public interest." (For example, the law now says that if firms agree to limit their advertising, to exchange statistics, or to conduct research

---

[17] Few of these cases involved old-style collusion. The usual government target was a merger or sheer bigness. Sometimes pricing practices (such as the basing-point system mentioned later) came under attack. In 1961 General Electric and Westinghouse were actually found guilty of surreptitious collusion in setting prices of heavy electrical goods. The cloak-and-dagger practices sent some of their executives to jail and made their companies liable for *treble* damages to over-charged companies. Of course, "attack" does not mean "guilty." Many government prosecutions have failed.

jointly, these activities shall not lead to a conviction as being against the public interest.)

■ RESALE PRICE MAINTENANCE (RPM)

As in most countries, Canadian dealers were long forced by one device or another to charge the same price for a branded product bought from a manufacturer. Prices were "maintained" at the same level everywhere in the market. Most retailers favored the practice because it exempted them from vigorous price competition and from cut-rate, discount, cash-and-carry, or other low-cost outlets. Instead, competition could lead only to rivalry on convenience of location, service, credit terms, or advertising. Manufacturers also favored the practice because it tended (so long as other manufacturers also maintained their prices) to widen the number of outlets carrying their goods—a form of advertising. Both were opposed to "loss leader selling": the practice, they said, was followed by bad retailers who sold well-known branded goods at a low price (or at a loss) in order to attract customers in to buy other things as well. Electric kettles and electric shavers were said to be often used as loss leaders.

Clearly, resale price maintenance is a practice that economists will oppose. It either reduces competition, denying to low-cost outlets the greater turnover and still lower costs they could pass on to consumers, or it forces all retailers to compete in one way: by accepting additional costs of advertising, services, etc. The Invisible Hand is not allowed to work; and more stores are kept in business than the public would patronize if goods could be sold both cheaply by no-service stores and more expensively by smaller and more convenient outlets.

In the United States, price maintenance (or "fair trade") is required or allowed in some states and forbidden in others. In the United Kingdom, it was forbidden, after a long parliamentary battle but few industries have yet been freed of maintained price.

A pioneer in this field, Canada has forbidden RPM since 1952. The consequences of this legislation have been studied several times, and it is concluded that although few businesses can be shown to have failed because RPM is now banned, prices are indeed somewhat more variable and flexible among competing outlets. Justice Minister Fulton's 1960 amendments have, however, weakened the legislation somewhat. It is observable that manufacturers are able to advertise "suggested" prices applicable in all outlets. And manufacturers now may refuse to sell to dealers who use their products as loss leaders or who mislead the public about them.

■ CONGLOMERATES AND BACKLASH

Conglomerate mergers, where a company in one industry takes on a company in another, were, like mutual funds, a difficult phenomenon in the 1960s. The firms are unrelated by technical or managerial overlap, and are linked together by the financial and speculative advantages they offer to ambitious and imaginative promoters and companies. Some firms are blocked from further expansion in their own industry, and wish to hedge against instability or decline by invest-ment and growth elsewhere.

In the 1950s, the courts had viewed mergers as a possible means of attain-ing monopolistic positions; a series of decisions in the United States, and a few in Canada, had made it clear that under certain circumstances the law preferred industrial growth to take place by methods other than the amalgamation of firms already dominant in their respective industries. For example, in 1957 the U.S. Supreme Court ruled that DuPont unduly dominated General Motors and made DuPont get rid of its GM stock.

But conglomerates, of course, need not have any effect on the degree of monopoly concentration existing in a particular market. Their attractiveness is elsewhere, following paths explored years ago by CPR, Argus Corporation, and utility holding companies, and by George Weston. Now Domtar, Imperial Tobacco, Noranda, and Seagram-Distillers Limited, like the U.S. Litton Indus-tries, Ling-Temco-Vought, and a host of imitators, each have taken over dozens of smaller firms in unrelated industries.

> Thus, Ling-Temco-Vought began with an airplane company but soon acquired scores of companies by clever offers of new varieties of Ling securities—preferred stock, convertible preferred, second convertible preferred, convertible bonds, bonds with attached (but detachable) warrant options to buy the common. One had to be an Einstein of finance to calculate the amount of dilution of ownership that would occur if all convertible securities were ultimately to be converted into common stock. (Professor Warren Law of the Harvard Business School admitted the Ling prospectus was beyond him!) Often, little conglomerates would take over giant cash-rich companies many times their own size, using in the end the cash of the company taken over to pay for the acquisition. Thirty-year-old whiz kids pyramided thousands of dollars into tens of millions almost overnight.
>
> Each new successful acquisition increased total sales and reported per share earnings, thereby enabling the conglomerates to acquire still more companies at lower and lower cash cost. (Often the reported gain in earnings was misleading, being merely the product of imaginative accounting, which ignored potential dilution by conversion, treated once-and-for-all paper gains on security sales as if they were recurring operating earnings, juggled the accounting treatment of good will, and reported as current income items for which payment would be received only in future installments. Franchise and land companies were some of the worst offenders.)

But what, after all, did the airplane business have in common with meat packing? Or typewriters with birth-control pills? Or computer leasing with passenger-bus operations? Good modern management, coupled with adequate finance, can of course help in any line of activity. And the history of the East India or Hudson's Bay companies does remind us that in underdeveloped coun-tries the only way to get the efficiencies associated with large-scale corporations may be through conglomerates. (Fancifully, if Harold Geneen has the genius to run scores of unrelated activities, mostly in Europe, under the headship of International Telephone & Telegraph, could he be the prototype and forerunner of Galbraith's expert-planner under socialism or some equivalent form of organi-zation of the future industrial state?)

By the late 1960s the bubble had burst on many U.S. conglomerates. It was a chain-letter form of growth which had to grow ever faster in order not to lead to disillusionment and collapse. When even the mighty Litton Industries had a pause in earnings growth, the jig was up for the Lings, Gulf & Westerns, and later imitators. Now "conglomerate" became a dirty word. Conglomerate stocks dropped. Acquisitions failed. Mergers were blocked in the United States by the Nixon Justice Department. A scapegoat was needed by the U.S. Congress and the public: conglomerates provided a convenient target. Bigness as such was held against them, on the *simpliste* theory that the unit with the "deeper pocket" can outbargain and destroy its competitors. There were threats to tax them, or take away from them the usual privilege of having bond interest tax-deductible. Fear of "reciprocity"—the practice of one big business to buy products from its own branches or from those other companies who reciprocate with purchases from it, even at unfavorable market terms—became rampant in the U.S. Antitrust Division and in the courts. Nonetheless, Professor Stigler, in a task-force investigation for President Nixon, concluded that reciprocity is quite trivial in economic importance and that much of the hostility to conglomerates is hysterically irrational. Often those seeking take-overs represented "outsiders," self-made newly arrived chaps who had not belonged to Yale's Skull and Bones (old school ties) or been vetted by the existing business establishment. Their crudities were thus specially to be resented. And yet, corporate oligarchies that had grown soft and arrogant under previous minority rule were often goaded into reform by fear of take-over or were even replaced by those better able to utilize the corporation's resources.

Take-overs, like bankruptcy, represent one of Nature's methods of eliminating deadwood in the struggle for survival. A more open—and more efficiently responsive—corporate society can result. But, without public surveillance and control, the opposite could also emerge. The Darwinian jungle is not guaranteed to produce a happy ending.

■ FOREIGN TRADE, TARIFFS, AND CONCENTRATION

Many of the industries prosecuted in Canada, the United Kingdom, or the United States have broad foreign ramifications. Some of them own subsidiaries abroad, some are world-wide oligopolists in certain products, and many of them have colluded with one another to share foreign markets. [For example, Britain's Imperial Chemical Industries (ICI) and the United States' DuPont divided up the world for the sales of certain chemicals. In Canada they shared the market by setting up CIL which, jointly owned, manufactured or sold both their products.] Finally, as in most countries, Canadian exporters are not forbidden to combine for the exploitation of foreign markets. (For example, Canadian newsprint suppliers have long been accused by American publishers of combining to maintain newsprint prices in the United States. The newsprint exporters are guilty of no crime even if this is true, for Canadian law does not prohibit such joint action. Similarly, American exporters are bound to submit only to a lightened version of their domestic antitrust rules.)

Volumes have been written about such "international cartels," which have denied consumers in less-developed countries the advantages of vigorous price competition.[18]

A less-studied aspect of foreign connections is the effect of a tariff on domestic competition and efficiency. Canada is a good test case. Many Canadian manufactured products are sold behind a tariff barrier. This barrier, (say 20 per cent) when added to the foreign selling price, provides the lowest level at which foreign competitors can sell in the Canadian market. Canadian firms can successfully undercut imported goods at any lower price. The result of this protection (in many but by no means all Canadian manufacturing industries) has been that prices tend to move swiftly to the protected level, regardless of costs of production in Canadian plants. There is in effect an "administered price," dictated by the government, as described on page 624.

Canadian economists like Stefan Stykolt, Harry Eastman, and H. E. English have studied the effect of this protection on the performance of industry. In general, their conclusion is that oligopoly tends to result, as in the earlier case of administered prices. Part of the reason is that the protection given is excessive; prices are set comfortably high enough to bring profits, and then to attract new industries. Because the Canadian market is small, the new firms and the old cannot expand, and tend to work with much of their productive capacity underused. This is the same inefficiency that emerges under ordinary oligopoly: prices are inflexible and the economy finds that it has allocated too many resources to the industry.

A further explanation is that a large number of near-competitive American and European firms, finding that they cannot export to Canada, tend to set up manufacturing subsidiaries within Canada. These small plants attempt to turn out the whole range of products and items made by the parent company for the larger markets abroad. This means that these plants cannot achieve full mass-production economies: their markets in Canada are too small. Thus their costs are higher than abroad, perhaps even up to the level of the tariff-protected price. The situation now is a little removed from oligopoly, for there may be *too many* firms—if the price were not protected the industry might become highly competitive. (However, if the tariff were removed, many U.S. plants would presumably shut their Canadian subsidiaries. There would be only one North American market for that product. More on this in Part Six.) But the resource-allocation effect remains—there are too many resources in Canada devoted to producing administered-price products.

To deal with oligopolies and other combines that are protected by tariffs in

---

[18] There are real resource-allocation effects too. If lack of competition between two chemical firms selling in a small country means that consumers must pay high prices, the result is not merely a redistribution of income from buyers to sellers in the same economy. The buying country must sell an extra amount abroad to pay for its high-price imports, or go without them, or a bit of both. These extra amounts are one measure of the real loss of a country when a monopoly uses too little capacity and competitive industries too much, within one country.

Canada, the combines authorities can recommend the removal of tariffs. This eventually requires parliamentary action, not a court decision. However this device is used infrequently, and economists who believe that economic efficiency is endangered by the high tariff wall have urged its consideration more often.

FOREIGN OWNERSHIP   To many Canadians in the seventies, the significance of the tariff lies in its encouragement of foreign ownership. [Up to twenty years ago, the most-debated effects of the tariff were, in addition to the previous section's discussion of oligopoly, as follows: (*a*) forcing Canadians to buy high-cost, homemade goods rather than low-cost imports; (*b*) creating jobs for Canadian workers; (*c*) encouraging industrialization of Canadian regions; and (*d*) diverting Canadian production away from specialization toward low-output self-sufficiency. Rarely was foreign ownership seriously discussed as a good or as an evil in itself.]

Whether foreign ownership is beneficial or not is a question that is too huge and too complicated to be easily answered here. The historians and the political scientists can bandy about the epithets "colonialism" and "imperialism," and, as descriptions of whole epochs, these terms are interesting and provocative. Certainly foreign ownership did characterize such manifestations of imperialism as Britain's dominion over India or Spain's rule over the New World. But, as practised by the economist, political economy must be more than mere approval or condemnation by classification. In order to criticize Canadian policy regarding foreign ownership, answers are needed to such questions as, "How much foreign ownership of particular industries, and in aggregate, is acceptable?" And to answer this question, Canadians must learn the extent to which varying the mix of domestic and foreign ownership will affect efficiency, occupational opportunities, export performance, and domestic and international powers of political and cultural self-determination. More of this topic appears in Chapter 34's Appendix.

The aim here is simply to point out that for foreign firms the processes of adjustment to tariff barriers may proceed either by the establishment of new plants and branches in Canada (as in the case of GM, Phillips, Datsun, or Volvo) or by the take-over of firms in the same industry which already exist in Canada. That this process must result in oligopolistic manufacturing industries is a *hypothesis* tested and so far confirmed in an increasing number of industry studies. That these oligopolies must have higher costs and prices than oligopolies abroad is a *theory* that is not necessarily the best explanation of Canadian industrial structure. But that this foreign investment has taken place mainly by take-overs of Canadian firms is a belief that has recently been disproved in a study by Reuber and Roseman.[19]

[19] G. L. Reuber and R. Roseman, *The Take-over of Canadian Firms, 1945-1961; An Empirical Study.* Economic Council of Canada, Special Study No. 10 (Queen's Printer, Ottawa, 1969). There was a slight difference between the types of Canadian and foreign take-overs. Canadian firms tended to acquire other firms for vertical or horizontal integration, but only about 8 per cent were interested in building "conglomerates" whereas almost 12 per cent of foreign take-overs were of the conglomerate type. Foreign interest in horizontal, or market-extension, mergers was much less than Canadian interest.

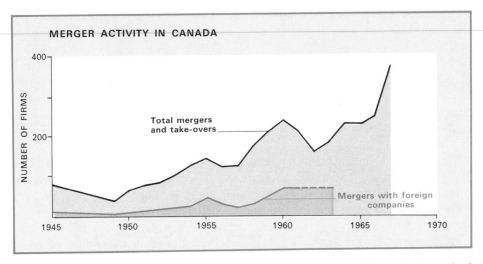

FIG. 25-6. **Foreign-takeover data is unavailable after 1961. (Source: Economic Council of Canada,** *Interim Report on Competition Policy.* **Queen's Printer, Ottawa, 1969; G. L. Reuber and F. Roseman,** *The Take-over of Canadian Firms, 1945-1961, An Empirical Study.* **Economic Council of Canada, Special Study No. 10. Queen's Printer, Ottawa, 1969.)**

Figure 25-6 shows that, at any rate for the period 1945-1961, the number of take-overs or mergers, especially of *foreign* take-overs, was relatively small (relative to the 100,000 firms available). And the foreign take-overs in this whole period after World War II rarely accounted for as much as 15 per cent of the total foreign ownership in any industry. Foreign investors, in other words, proceeded by investing in firms they already controlled or by establishing new firms, rather than by mergers and take-overs. Hence, foreign ownership is not best dealt with here, in a chapter on combines policy and mergers.

■ THE FUTURE OF COMBINES POLICY

Compared with the United States, or even with the United Kingdom, Canadian policy to prevent monopolistic inefficiency is unspectacular. The legal mind is not interested in relative prices, price flexibility, or resource allocation. Yet lawyers advocate, make, and administer the policies. The number of economists employed at any stage of an investigation or trial is very small, and frequently zero.

Some countries are even more lax than we are. For example, the governments of some Western European countries and of Japan seem actively to encourage mergers and cartels as a means of preventing the "wastes" of competition, encouraging exports, and exerting government controls for other purposes. Yet, except perhaps Japan, these countries (with the advent of the Common Market) have been strengthening their antitrust statutes, and groping toward what American economist J. M. Clark has called the concept of "workable competition."

Canadian policy and legislation are not a minor version of British or American concepts. But, like them, to the extent that they succeed they prevent practices that victimize consumers or waste national resources. And success is to be judged not only by successful court cases but also by the extent to which they keep sellers on the defensive, preventing them from adopting some of the flagrant practices of earlier generations or other countries. On the other hand, Stykolt and other economists have urged a change in Canadian combines procedures to limit new enquiries to those cases where "there is a good chance of applying corrective measures"—that is, measures to correct the economic situation, not to punish transgressors. This view implies that the goal should be to strengthen gradually industrial competitive performance, not to keep all business jittery in fear of prosecution. For although the government might win its case, such prosecution would not really improve effective competition in the whole Canadian market. But, at the present time, none of these policies is being pursued. Businessmen are certainly not jittery about immediate prosecution because of price practices or mergers: recent experience has shown that such cases may fail, bring very small fines, or even allow the continuation of the practice.

What is to be done?[20] Many critics, notably Rosenbluth and Thorburn, simply urge the government to get on with what it already has power to do: to show more nerve in tackling Canadian giants. Stykolt urged gunning for big industries in cases where success would really push the economy out towards its *p-p frontier*. The recent Report of the Economic Council of Canada, on competition policy is in partial agreement with the positive Stykolt approach; for it urged escape from criminal law and the use of an economic tribunal:

> ". . . most of the practices to be referred to the tribunal are capable in some circumstances of working to the public advantage, but the distinction between likely good and bad effects may require a difficult weighing of relevant economic circumstances and probabilities and therefore a kind of expertise that only a body of mixed professional disciplines could provide. The tribunal would be armed with injunctive remedies, the power to recommend other remedies, and with a power of general inquiry."[21]

But there is little sign that these proposals are being taken more seriously than were the proposals which preceded them, twenty years ago. Consumers are not interested in combines policy, and political parties find it embarassing, just as they do not like to think about the tariff wall. [Recently, the combines-investigation problem (and the mechanism discussed on page 633) was handed over to a new Department of Consumer and Corporate Affairs. In 1971-1972, a new combines law will come into effect, that may clearly apply to *services* like banking and even medicine.]

With its present obsessive rejection of simple and conglomerate mergers,

---

[20] See G. Rosenbluth and H. Thorburn, *Canadian Anti-combines Administration, 1952-1960* (University of Toronto Press, Toronto, 1963); Stefan Stykolt, *Efficiency in the Open Economy* (Oxford University Press, Toronto, 1969); and Economic Council of Canada, *Interim Report on Competition Policy* (Queen's Printer, Ottawa, 1969).

[21] Economic Council of Canada, *Interim Report on Competition Policy* (Queen's Printer, Ottawa, 1969). Reproduced with the permission of Information Canada.

no one would claim that American antitrust legislation and policy is completely logical or successful. But one has only to examine Canada, Europe, or Japan to realize how much better off the United States is because of its omnipotent threat of legal prosecution. American enterprise is kept on the defensive and would never dream of adopting the flagrant devices that are all too common in Canada and abroad.

Repeatedly, in Part Three, we have stressed the basic problem of how a pricing system solves society's questions WHAT, How, FOR WHOM. This frames the rational goal of combines policy.

We cannot expect competition to become everywhere "perfectly perfect," in the strict sense of the economist, but we can try to make it "workable." By public and private policies we can hope to improve the efficiency with which market prices reflect underlying needs, desires, and wants against the background of true costs of goods—costs in terms of alternative goods that could be produced and in terms of used-up scarce productive factors which involve sweat and disutility.

Part Four will be concerned with identical problems that arise in connection with the pricing of land, labor, and capital. Again, the function of such pricing in solving society's problems is the focal point of interest.

SUMMARY

A. ANALYTICAL PATTERNS OF IMPERFECT COMPETITION

1 Few business firms are able to develop exact curves of cost and revenue. This does not mean that they are oblivious to profit maximization. In terms of trial and error, they may be doing a tolerably good job of keeping alive as a business entity and of achieving long-run optimum profits.

2 Under imperfect competition, a firm may have to make rough guesses in setting its price. Often it will use some kind of *markup* over an estimate of unit cost. Nonetheless, it is often market conditions that determine how much of a markup any firm can safely count on getting; so in a sense the problem is merely re-posed. Only factual investigations of each situation can tell what the result is likely to be.

3 In Galbraith's vision of the new industrial state, bureaucrats of the technostructure exercise unilateral power to mold consumer tastes. They may be checked by the "countervailing power" of their large-scale suppliers or customers; and despite Galbraith's prose, even the largest corporations are subject to checks of numerous rival conglomerates, making collusion difficult and despotic rule shortsighted.

4 Various patterns of imperfect competition lend themselves to economic analysis: (1) monopoly, (2) oligopoly, in which few sellers compete with similar or differentiated products, (3) Chamberlinian models of many sellers of differentiated products, and finally (4) the case of perfect competition itself. The kinked demand curve of oligopoly helps to explain its rigid administered pricing. The no-profit tangency equilibrium of Cham-

berlin's large group leaves society with the wastes of excess capacity and overdifferentiated products.

B. MODERN COMBINES PROBLEMS

■ 5 The economic evils of such imperfections transcend the mere matter of monopolistic profits: entry may cut out excess profits *without* bringing prices down to marginal costs; overentry of imperfect competitors may waste resources without giving the consumer the benefit of lower prices; monopolistic and oligopolistic pricing above true marginal cost brings distortion of resource allocation (inefficiency and non responsiveness) even if the firms involved have their excess profits taxed away.

■ 6 Against the evils of monopoly and oligopoly must be weighed the possible Schumpeterian *dynamic* efficiencies that they may introduce. A large firm in a protected market may have the wherewithal to develop new inventions and also the assurance that it will not lose to competitors the advantages of its own research efforts. In strongly decreasing-cost industries, there is no hope for viable *perfect* competition, and substitute checks on the powers of few dominating firms have to come from either public control or tariff reduction.

■ 7 By public regulation of utilities and by various formal and informal combines activities of the state, some of the checks and balances that are not automatically enforceable by perfect competition can be achieved by governmental action.

■ 8 The history of Canadian combines legislation and enforcement has been an irregular one. Inaction has been followed by vigorous action; and sometimes by various backward steps, including laws which seem to reduce rather than enhance effective price competition. Although the legal mind of courts and legislators has not always concentrated on what economists consider the key pricing issue, some evolutionary progress toward "workable competition" has been made. After economists realize that perfect competition is not spontaneously attained or enforceable, the problem of defining and approaching "workable competition" becomes paramount. Here is the frontier for economic research and policy.

■ 9 The rapid and flashy growth of conglomerates was prominent in the 1960s but by the end of the decade the bubble had burst for many of them. Nevertheless, they provide a spectacular bit of history as well as a threat of take-over which may goad formerly complacent corporate management into making reforms.

■ 10 Tariffs have often resulted in a "protected-price level" (foreign selling price of import plus tariff imposed on it) toward which some prices of Canadian manufacturers tend to move—in effect an administered price with the consequent oligopoly inefficiencies. In other cases, foreign producers have set up Canadian subsidiaries to jump the tariff. In this case, too many producers of too many products, produced on too small a scale to be efficient, exist. Again, the result is an inefficient allocation of resources. Foreign ownership may also take the form of foreign take-over of existing

Canadian firms, though the majority of recent foreign investment has not, as it is often alleged, been through this type of take-over.

QUESTIONS FOR DISCUSSION

1. Give examples of behavior by business firms suggesting that they do seek to maximize their profits. Give some apparent exceptions.

2. Suppose you ran an electric company. How could you go about maximizing profits? How would you estimate elasticity of demand? Would an economics textbook be the source for learning how to be successful in this respect?

3. What is meant by administered pricing? Why is the *willingness to sell more* the sign of imperfect competition?

4. Describe the pattern of imperfect competition in the auto industry, cigarette industry, aluminum industry, mousetrap industry, women's-dress trade, retail grocery trade, barbershop trade, undertaking industry, pulp and paper industry, farm pulpwood industry.

5. "The tragedy of monopolistic competition often has nothing to do with excessive profits. Rather, there may be no profits at all, the high price being frittered away in small volume and inefficient production." Discuss.

6. U.S. decisions had the effect of breaking off the partnership of ICI and DuPont in Canadian Industries Ltd. (CIL). Now ICI owns CIL and DuPont has its own Canadian subsidiary. Do two such competitors duplicate perfect competition? Was there any advantage to Canada from this breakup? Did Canada lose the advantages of large-scale production in one big firm?

7. Canada now effectively permits export cartels. Is such collusion required to meet low-cost foreign competition? To meet foreign cartel competition? Why do Canadian exporters want to work together? Will their doing so affect the prices they must charge Canadian customers?

8. Consider the role of the tariff and of the degree of concentration in the rubber-tire industry. Why do tires cost more in Canada than in the United States?

9. Some Americans argue that "A & P is bad just because it is big." Do you agree? Consider the impact of A & P on the farmers and suppliers from whom it buys and on the other chains and stores with whom it competes. Do not neglect the consumers to whom it sells.

10. "Combinations of workers in unions must be forbidden if industrial combines are banned." Comment.

11. "Resale price maintenance should be encouraged because it protects customers from dealers who give no service and don't know their products." Consider this and other arguments for RPM.

12. Review your understanding of the following concepts:

fair return on original or reproduction cost or on market valuation	markup pricing, administered P
publicly owned utilities as measuring rods	Galbraithian countervailing power and technostructure
Combines Investigation Act, Sherman Antitrust Act	free entry
conglomerates	oligopoly, with or without tacit collusion
resale price maintenance	no-profit equilibrium of producers of differentiated products
Schumpeterian dynamic advantages	evils of imperfect competition
challenge of "workable competition"	utility rate regulation

PART 4
DISTRIBUTION OF INCOME: THE PRICING OF THE PRODUCTIVE FACTORS

26

THEORY OF PRODUCTION AND MARGINAL-PRODUCTS

Knowledge is the only instrument of production that is not subject to diminishing returns. J. M. CLARK

In the next few chapters of Part Four we shall be primarily concerned with how factors of production get priced in the market place—with the determination of (1) *rents* of land and other resources (Chapter 27), (2) *wages* of various kinds of labor (Chapter 28), (3) *interest* rates on capital assets (Chapter 29), and (4) *profit* (Chapter 30); there follows a grand summary (Chapter 31).

Economists call this the problem of "distribution." They do not mean by this term what the man in the street means when he refers to distribution as the marketing of goods and the carrying of goods to the final consumer. Instead Part Four distribution deals with the problem of For Whom goods are to be produced. It is pricing of factors of production by supply and demand that is helping determine For Whom. This same factor pricing also operates to solve the problem of How society is to produce.

Why are wages some three-quarters of the total national product? To understand this we must study the forces that determine market wage rates, market land rentals, market interest rates. Thus, if technological changes, reflecting automation in industry, lowered market wage rates relative to the returns to property, the wage share might fall. Because the number of owners of property is so much smaller than the number of owners of labor, the result would be to shift the Lorenz-curve measure of inequality toward greater income inequality. We can understand the economic forces affecting income distribution best by examining the markets where factors of production get priced. This will give us insight into optimality equilibria and into "exploitation."

The key to such factor pricing will turn out to be provided by the economic *theory of production.* So, as a prelude to our general discussion of distribution of income, this chapter will investigate the theory of production. It will define the important economic concept of "marginal-product" and relate this to the familiar law of diminishing returns. Finally, the chapter will show that the demand curves for the various factors of production—the demands for labor, land, and so forth—are to be expressed in terms of their marginal-products.

■ DEMAND FOR FACTORS A DERIVED DEMAND

We begin with some elementary observations about factor demand.

Why do consumers demand a finished good like a magazine or an overcoat? They do so because of the satisfaction they hope to enjoy from its use. But why does a businessman demand a factor input such as fertilizer or sulfur or un-skilled labor? Surely not for the *direct* satisfaction he hopes to receive. He wants the productive factors because of the production and revenue that he hopes to secure *indirectly* from them.

Satisfactions are in the picture, but at one stage removed. The satisfactions that consumers get from an overcoat help to determine how much a garment manufacturer can sell the coat for and how many coats it can sell. Therefore you would be right in insisting that consumer satisfactions do *ultimately* deter-mine the firm's demand for inputs. The firm's demand for labor is *derived indirectly* from the consumer demand for its final product. So economists speak of the demand for productive factors as a "derived demand."

> *Definition:* Derived demand refers to the fact that, when profit-seeking firms demand a factor of production, they do so because the factor input permits them to produce a good which consumers are willing to pay for now or in the future. The demand for the factor of production is thus derived ultimately from consumers' desires for final goods.

In short, effort involved in making coats, or sewing machines is of no interest to society for its own sake; we pay men and machines to sew because of the satisfaction believed to be gained from the finished product. Sometimes the derived demands go through many stages: Wool is wanted to spin yarn; yarn is wanted to weave cloth; cloth is wanted to make coats. All the previous demands are derived from the ultimate consumer demand for the satisfactions to be secured from the finished product.

■ DEMAND FOR FACTORS A JOINTLY INTERDEPENDENT DEMAND

Another peculiarity about the demand for inputs stems from this technological fact: Factors usually do not work alone. A shovel by itself is worthless to me if I wish a cellar; a man with his bare hands is equally worthless. Together the man and shovel can dig my cellar. In other words, the quantity of a good pro-duced depends *jointly* upon all the available factor inputs.

Sir William Petty, an early economist, put the matter in this striking way: Labor is the father and land the mother of product. One cannot say which is more important in producing a baby—a mother or a father. So, too, one cannot in most cases hope to demonstrate how much of the physical product has been *caused* by any one of the different factors *taken by itself*. The different factors *interact* with each other. Usually they reinforce each other's effectiveness, but sometimes they are substitutes for one another and they compete with, rather than complement, each other. There is an important consequence of this jointness, or interdependence among the productivities of the different factor inputs, namely: The amount of labor demanded will depend on its wage rate, but the labor demanded will depend also upon the price of machines. The same is true of the demand for machines. By raising miners' wages, John L. Lewis created good business for power tools.

> Thus, the demand for each input will depend upon the prices of *all* factor inputs, not on its own price alone. *Cross elasticities* between different factors are as important as regular *"own" elasticities.*

It is this interdependence of productivities of land, labor, and capital goods that makes the problem of distribution complex. For suppose we had to distribute at one harvest time the whole aggregate of output constituting the NNP. If land by itself had produced so much, and labor by itself had produced so much, and some third factor had by itself produced the rest, distribution might seem easy indeed. Crude notions of fairness might suggest that each factor share be simply set at what each has alone produced. Ethics aside, under free supply and demand if the separate factors could produce goods by themselves, they could jolly well make sure that they got the fruits of their activity; so, ethics aside, this would be a good description of the facts.

But reread the above paragraph and underline such words as *"by itself* produced" and *"has alone* produced." They refer to an *independence* of productivities which we know is simply lacking in the real world. If land and labor *together* produce the corn harvest, just how do you unscramble the separate contributions that supply and demand will parcel out to each?[1] A proud Canadian worker might reflect on what *he* would produce and get in India or in Canada as it was in 1900.

How is the problem resolved? It gets resolved by the process of supply and demand, operating in perfectly or imperfectly competitive markets and modified by government laws. A brief analysis of the economic theory of production provides the indispensable key.

---

[1] Labor leaders used to say, "Without labor there is zero product. So attribute to labor *all* the product." Spokesmen for capital used the same bad logic to produce the opposite result: "Take away all capital goods, and labor scratches a bare pittance from the earth; so practically all the product should go to capital." The trouble with such foolish proposals is that, taken together, they allocate 200 or 300 per cent of the total product to the two or three factors, whereas there is only 100 per cent of the harvest to be allocated. And it makes no sense to say, "There is some truth on both sides; so let us apply the Golden Mean and, by a rule of unreason, give each of the factors the largest equal shares that will use up the available 100 per cent of product." A real-world economy is not a courtroom where nimble legal minds illogically split hairs in order to solve society's problem of For Whom.

■ TECHNICAL LAW RELATING OUTPUT TO INPUTS: THE
  "PRODUCTION FUNCTION"

The theory of production begins with specific engineering or technological information. If you have a certain amount of labor, a certain amount of land, and
certain prescribed amounts of other inputs such as machines or raw materials,
how much output of a particular good can you get? The answer depends upon
the state of technology: if someone makes a new invention or discovers a new
industrial process, the obtainable output you can get from given factor inputs
will go up. *But at any time, there will be a maximum obtainable amount of
product for any given amounts of factor inputs.*

This technical law relating inputs to outputs is so important that economists have given it a name. They call it the "production function."

> *Definition:* The production function is the technical relationship telling the
> amount of output capable of being produced by each and every set of
> specified inputs (or factors of production). It is defined for a given state of
> technical knowledge.

Here is an example. An agricultural engineer lists in a thick book the various
combinations of land and labor that will produce various quantities of corn. On
one page of the book he lists the alternative combinations of land and labor
needed to produce 100 bushels of corn; on another page, the alternative factor
input combinations that will produce 200 bushels of corn; and so forth. Another
example of a production would be the chemical engineer's listing of the various
ways of producing gasoline of a given octane rating.

There are thousands of different production functions in the Canadian
economy: at least one for each of the innumerable firms or productive units. A
purpose of this chapter is to show how the firm's production function lies
behind its Total Cost curve discussed in Chapter 23 and to show how this provides the basis for the firm's derived demand for land, labor, capital, fertilizer,
and numerous other productive inputs that it goes out into the market to buy.

Thus, the firm is poised between two kinds of markets: (1) the commodity
market in which it appears as a supplier, selling its wares along the demand
curve *of its customers*; and (2) the markets for factors of production in which
it itself appears as a demander, buying inputs so as to minimize its total costs
of production and to produce its Maximum-profit output. It is these factor
markets that put prices upon the various productive inputs of the community,
and thus determine the distribution of income (wages, rent, interest, etc.).

■ THE AGGREGATE AMERICAN PRODUCTION FUNCTION

Suppose, first, we put away our microscope and train a telescope on the aggregate magnitudes of total labor, total capital, and total product for American
manufacturing. Such magnitudes must be measured with care and involve innumerable index-number problems of correct weighting; yet they are useful in
giving a broad description of society. Back in the late twenties, former U.S.
Senator Paul H. Douglas, then a University of Chicago professor of economics,

won an important prize for his pathbreaking statistical measurement of the United States' production function. His technique was widely adapted to the measurement of production functions elsewhere: manufacturing in Canada, for example. Later M.I.T.'s Robert Solow carried these studies a significant step further by showing how technological progress has been improving the productivity of American labor and capital.[2]

What have Douglas and Solow shown? Their statistics suggest that labor is the single most important factor of production in a certain subtle sense. Both labor and capital are needed in production: take away all capital, or alternatively all labor, and you will be left with negligible total product. But they find that a 1 per cent increase in labor seems to increase output about three times as much as would a 1 per cent increase in capital.[3] This largely corresponds with the widely known fact that wages are about three-fourths of the national product, while one-fourth (which is one-third of wages) is about the share of property incomes. There are numerous other findings from such studies, many of which have received important corroboration from similar undertakings in, or about, other countries. Here are a few of the most important empirical findings about the American economy:

1. The productivity of both labor and capital has been increasing throughout this century because of improved technology and skill. The average rate of improvement appears to be between 1 and 2 per cent per year.

2. The amount of capital has been growing at a faster rate than the labor supply because of thrift on the part of society as a whole and slower growth in man-hours worked. As a result, each laborer has more capital goods to work with, and his productivity wages have tended to rise even faster than the 1 to 2 per cent attributable to technological growth alone. Canadian data show a similar trend, although the capital has often been borrowed from abroad rather than being the result of local thrift.

3. The return per unit of capital might have been expected to encounter diminishing returns because each capital unit now has less labor to cooperate with it. Yet capital's return per unit has in fact remained about the same. Why? Because of the offsetting effect of technological progress. Technical improvements would probably have raised profits on capital had not the diminishing returns to increasing capital per laborer been taking place as an offset. In consequence of these simultaneous offsets, the sharing of the growing social pie

---

[2] P. H. Douglas, *Theory of Wages* (Macmillan, New York, 1934); R. M. Solow, "Technical Change and the Aggregate Production Function," *Review of Economics and Statistics*, vol. 39, 1957, pp. 312-320. Neither study measures land's separate contribution and share. In the 1970s this would probably be only about 5 per cent for the whole economy, and much less for manufacturing alone; but early in the century it was perhaps double that. Further work by E. Denison and D. Walters will be cited in Chapter 36, where modern growth models are discussed.

[3] Consistent with the law of diminishing returns, discussed in Chapter 2 and in the next sections of this chapter, a 1 per cent increase in either factor *alone* increases product by *less* than 1 per cent: actually by ¾ per cent in the case of labor and by ¼ per cent in the case of capital.

Diminishing returns restated as law of diminishing marginal–physical–product:

(1) UNITS OF LABOR	(2) TOTAL PRODUCT	(3) MARGINAL– PHYSICAL– PRODUCT
0	0	
		20
1	20	
		10
2	30	
		5
3	35	
		3
4	38	
		1
5	39	

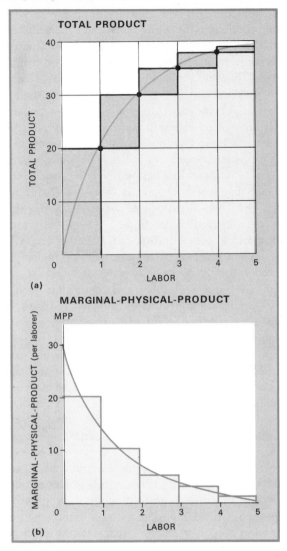

FIG. 26-1. In the lower diagram the rectangles of marginal-physical-product have been smoothed by a curve. The area under the marginal-physical-product curve (or of the rectangles) adds up to the total product shown above. (E.g., 20 + 10 + 5 = total product of 35 for three men. What gives total product for four men or five men?)

has remained not too far from the same three-fourths and one-fourth level—a remarkable fact in view of the growing union movement, the vast structural changes in the American economy since 1900, and the widespread notion that "automation" has downgraded the value of human brain power and skills.

Similar statistical measurements all over the globe help to put flesh on the bare bones of the economic theory of production and distribution, and serve as factual tests of the validity of economic principles—principles that Chapter 36 will use for growth theory. But now let us put the production function under a microscope.

■ MARGINAL-PRODUCTS DEFINED

In Chapter 2, the law of diminishing returns was defined. Figure 26-1 re-produces a table (like that shown earlier on page 29) of diminishing *extra product* for varying extra labor units added to fixed land. Back there, we were using the production-function concept without yet knowing the name.

Now we can introduce the economist's name for extra product. Recall that in economic theory the word "extra" is typically replaced by the word "marginal." It is natural, then, to define terms as follows:

Definition: The "marginal-product" of a productive factor is the extra product or output added by one extra unit of that factor, while other factors are being held constant. Labor's marginal-product is the extra output you get when you add one unit of labor, holding all other inputs constant. Similarly, land's marginal-product is the change in total product resulting from one additional unit of land, with all other inputs held constant—and so forth, for any factor.[4]

Note that the marginal-product of a factor is expressed in *physical* units of product per unit of extra input. So careful economists often speak of "marginal-physical-product" rather than plain marginal-product, particularly when they want to avoid any possible confusion with a later *dollar* concept called "marginal-revenue-product."

■ MARGINAL-PHYSICAL-PRODUCTS AND DIMINISHING RETURNS

Column (3) of the table in Fig. 26-1 can now be identified with the term "marginal-physical-product." Note the drop from 20 to 1, in accordance with diminishing returns. The same marginal-product is pictured in the lower diagram, which shows the steady drop of labor's marginal-physical-product. This reflects the fact that the upper chart shows total product rising in ever-smaller steps as we hold land constant and add equal extra units of labor. The law of diminishing returns could be renamed the "law of diminishing marginal-physical-product." For brevity, one often skips the word "physical" when no misunderstanding is possible and writes MP for MPP.

It is also important to note here that both the total product and the marginal-physical-product are directly related to Chapter 23's cost-of-production curves. The physical units of output are the same units (or q) found in Table 23-1 on page 565. But now we ask "given another unit of an input, how much output or additional output will be produced?" We will look more deeply into this relationship further on in this chapter.

What is true for one factor input is also true for another. We can inter-change land and labor, now holding labor constant and varying land. We can make up a new table, showing land's marginal (physical) product in its column. And this would also presumably obey the law of diminishing returns. Why?

---

[4] Chapter 29 will discuss some intricacies involved in defining "capital."

Because now each of the extra land units would have less and less of the fixed labor factor to work with.

■ DISTRIBUTION SOLVED BY MARGINAL-PRODUCTS

Now the riddle of the Sphinx—how to allocate among two (or more) cooperating factors the total product they *jointly* produce—can be solved by use of the marginal-product concept. John Bates Clark, a distinguished Columbia University economist, provided a simplified theory of distribution around 1890. It can be applied to competitive price-and-wage determination when there are any number of goods and factor inputs, but it is most easily grasped if we concentrate on one total harvest output—call it corn, or a basket of goods, or just Q. A production function tells how much Q is produced for each amount of man-hours, L, and number of acres of homogeneous land, A.

Although diminishing returns applies when one factor is added to the other fixed factor, perfect competition is best maintained when there are "constant returns to scale" when *all* factors are increased simultaneously in the same proportion. (Thus, when Clark doubles land *and* labor, he finds output has just doubled; when he increases L and A by any equal per cent, Q increases by that same per cent. For if Q were to grow by a greater per cent, there would be long-run decreasing costs for each firm, and the firm that grew largest first could reap so great an advantage as to create a monopoly.)

Now Clark reasons as follows. A first man produces great marginal-product because he has so much land to work with. Man 2 adds a large, but slightly smaller, marginal-product. But the two men are alike: they must get exactly the same wage. Which wage? The MP of Man 1? The lower MP of Man 2? The average of these? Under free competition, where landowners are free to employ as few or many L as they like, the answer is plain. Landlords will never freely hire that second man if the market wage they must pay him exceeds his marginal-product. So the dd demand curve for labor will ensure that *all* the men who get hired will receive *the lowest marginal-product of the last man.*

What happens to the excess of MP produced by the first man and all the earlier men up to the very last? That stays with the landlord. It is his rent. In free competitive markets, no one can take it away from him. Is he "profiteering"? Not in the usual sense of the word. Each landowner is but one of thousands: any acre of his is no better and no worse than the acres of the rest. Just as worker competes with worker for jobs, landowners compete with landowners for workers. There are no conspiracies, no employer associations, and no unions in Clark's competitive world.

Figure 26-2 shows that the marginal-product curve of labor gives the dd demand curve of all employers in terms of real wages (in corn, or market baskets of goods, or Q units). The population supply gives us ss, and the equilibrium wage comes at E. The total wage share of labor is given by $w \times L$ (for example, $w = 5$ and $L = 1$ million, total wages $= 5$ million); this is indicated by the light gray area of the rectangle at E.

Marginal-product principles determine factor shares of income:

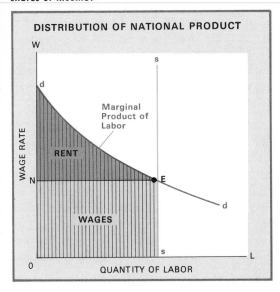

FIG. 26-2. Total wage is light gray rectangle's area: the wage-rate altitude times labor-quantity base. Rent gets what is left over, as shown by the dark gray residual triangle. Total product, the sum of wage-rectangle plus rent-triangle areas, is area under demand curve of society's marginal-product (the sum of all the vertical slabs — representing marginal products — added by each new worker).

We have determined not only the distributive share of labor, but also land rent. The indicated rent triangle simply measures all the "excesses over final marginal-product that the early workers brought and never got paid in wages." Whether fair or unfair, all the men are alike; all landlords are free competitors who can demand or not demand as they like; so it is inevitable that all workers get paid the *MP* of the last worker and, because of diminishing returns, that there be left the residual triangle of rent that goes to the landowners.

This completes the marginal-productivity theory of distribution. Note that labor wages get more than property rents in this example: the wage rectangle of *MP* is about three times as large as the residual rent triangle of property. That is realistic, but it depends on the facts of technology. If a new invention made the *dd* of *MP* decline very rapidly, land's triangle might swallow up 60 to 80 per cent of the total NNP!

If mass immigration or seven children per family increased *L* so much as to move society down the *dd* curve to a low wage, the rectangle share of labor *might* fall relative to the rent triangle of land. It might, but might not. Here is the explanation:

An increase in *L* along the *dd* curve of *MP must* always raise the absolute total of land's rent triangle. (Try it.) What about the absolute total of labor's rectangle? The elasticity discussion of Chapter 19 reminds us that labor's total wage rectangle will most certainly increase if *dd* has more-than-unitary elasticity. But can labor's rectangle grow *as great* in percentage as land's triangle, or even greater? Although not obvious until you experiment with drawing in *dd* curves, the answer is definite: Yes, the relative share of wage's rectangle can increase and the relative share of land's triangle decrease if the marginal-product curve slopes downward slowly enough. Senator Douglas' researches in the United States, corroborated for England and elsewhere by the late Sir Arthur Bowley, suggest that labor's relative share remains surprisingly constant over the decades, despite changing birth rates and technology!

GENERALIZATIONS Before summarizing the marginal-productivity theory of wages, let us appreciate J. B. Clark's advance over such classical economists as David Ricardo, a follower of Adam Smith, and a leader of economic thought in the early nineteenth century. Ricardo would have soon grasped, and agreed with, Clark's Fig. 26-2; it fits in well with Ricardian rent theory. But Clark said more than that. He also proved these remarkable facts:

> You can switch the roles of labor and land. Now hold labor constant. Add successive units of variable land to fixed labor. Calculate each successive acre's marginal-product. Draw a $d'd'$ curve showing how many acres labor-owners will demand of land at each rent rate. In the new version of Fig. 26-2 that you draw, find a new E' point of equilibrium. Identify land's *rectangle* of rent as determined by *its MP*. Identify labor's *residual* wage triangle. Ricardo would recognize the complete symmetry of the factors; that *all* factors can be thought of as having their distributive shares determined simultaneously by their respective interdependent marginal products.

That is not all. Instead of labor and land, suppose the only two factors were labor L and some versatile capital goods K. Suppose a smooth production function relates Q to L and K, with the same general properties as in Fig. 26-2. Then you can redraw Fig. 26-2 and get an identical picture of income distribution between L and K.[5]

SUMMARY Marginal productivities provide the clue to competitive pricing of factor inputs—of labor or of skilled and unskilled labor, of each grade of land, of capital goods (i.e., rentals for their use), of fertilizer, and of other inputs.

> Profit-maximizing employers in competitive factor markets will have their demand curves for inputs determined by what additions to their product successive units of a factor will bring, i.e., by marginal-products. In the simplified Clark case of a single Q output, firms' physical MP's are added horizontally—as dd and ss curves were added in Chapters 21 and 22—to get the market demand dd for labor or any other factor. At the level deter-

---

[5] That is still not all. Suppose we have three (or more) factors of production: L, A, and K. Again assume that a well-behaved production function gives Q output in terms of all three factor inputs. Again vary L alone; calculate its MP's. Then vary K alone; calculate its MP's. Vary A alone; calculate land's diminishing MP's. Now set up *three* simultaneous, interdependent demand curves of marginal-products. Set up three supply curves for the factors. It will follow that all Q, and no more, will get distributed by competition among the three factors according to equality of each factor-price to its marginal-product: $P_L = MP_L$, $P_A = MP_A$, $P_K =$ price charged for use of capital good $= MP_K$. All of any factor gets what its last unit produces of MP; the residual surplus, of early units' MP's over final MP, provides just enough Q to pay the other factors their final MP's (Some qualifications of this simple Clark model will occur in the Appendix to this chapter. Note here that monopoly bidding by employers would require alterations in the Clark model, as shown in page 705's footnote.)

mined by intersection of each dd with its factor-supply ss, we get

Wage = ~~Marginal-product of labor~~
Rent = Marginal-product of land
And so forth for any factor.

This distributes 100 per cent of Q, no more and no less, among all the factors of production.

■ COMPETITIVE EQUILIBRIUM A GOOD THING?

We have now completed a sketch of how the marginal-product theory "distributes" total product between two factors—land and labor—in a simplified world.

We have simply been observing how hard-boiled competition would work itself out under simple conditions. Just as the jungle has its laws without regard to right and wrong, so does the competitive market have its brute facts.

But did you notice one efficient thing that happened? Without a planning board, *society got its food produced in the most efficient way.* How did that happen? Well, efficiency certainly requires that the homogeneous land and labor be everywhere combined for food in exactly the same proportions. (PROOF: Suppose society were using much labor on half its land and little labor on the other half. The law of diminishing returns tells us that the marginal-product of the workers will be less on the dense than on the sparse half. So we can get some extra Q by shifting men to the sparse acres with higher MP. Maximum output comes when marginal-products are equal on both halves, i.e., when uniform labor and land are combined in the same proportions on both halves. QED.)

Ruthless competition with only the commercially fittest surviving did bring about the desirable equality everywhere of factor proportions and marginal-products. How did it do this? By landlords' seeking maximum rents; by workers' seeking maximum wages; by market prices being forced to lowest costs of production. These were the vital processes. (WARNING: A tendency toward "increasing returns to scale" would have killed off perfect competition and have brought in monopoly to spoil the whole story. Note also that if different acres were of different qualities, we would no longer use the same proportion of labor on each; instead the desirable equality of marginal-products of transferable labor would be achieved by competition's making sure that relatively more laborers get used on the better lands—a sensible result!)

We shall see again, in Chapter 31, that competitive pricing can help solve efficiently the How problem of any society. We shall see that charging a rent for God-given land is necessary if such scarce land is to be rightly allocated. But notice that we have not proved that the competitive result is "fair" or "equitable": efficiency by itself does not necessarily imply justice. To this issue we now turn.

■ THE CONCEPT OF EXPLOITATION

For two centuries socialist critics of the present order have asserted that labor has the right to the full product of society. What price the efficiency of marginal-product distribution if it gives a sizable fraction of the total product to property owners? This, they asserted, represents "exploitation" of labor.

It is naïve to think that if a word exists, there must always then exist some obvious real phenomenon corresponding to it. Thus, if I can say the name of a unicorn, need there be in some jungle somewhere such an animal? Or, if I can think of a perfect God-Being, *ergo* must He exist? Or, if the dictionary contains the word "exploitation," must there surely be some simple meaning to the concept that anyone can understand even *before* he has studied economics? To the scholar who studies economics and does research in the field, a naïve approach must be replaced by an attempt to analyze and isolate the meaningful and true concept of exploitation.

The late Oskar Lange, after spending a sojourn in the United States from 1934 to 1944 as a distinguished professor of both Marxian and non-Marxian economics, returned to his native Poland to become Ambassador to the United Nations and subsequently to serve as Vice President of Poland and a professor of economics. In his view, all that Marx wished to convey by the concept of "exploitation of labor" could be achieved without the trappings of the "labor theory of value" (which seemed to deny that scarce land and tools also contributed to competitive costs and to true social costs). Said Lange in effect, "The fact that people, who don't deserve to own the tools of production which work with labor and which are given their positive marginal-products out of the total product that might otherwise go to labor, receive a substantial fraction of the GNP, is ethically bad. The cure is to see that labor owns the tools of production and nature's gifts of land and other natural resources. Then labor, either in the form of wages or in the form of *its* share of property income, will indeed get all of the national product. Anything else is exploitation even in a prosperous capitalistic system where wages are very high (and much higher than are total incomes in egalitarian socialist societies)."

When we come to discuss land reform and increased education for labor, we shall see how laborers may come themselves to get a larger part of the property income of society. But before we leave the subject of exploitation, notice that the Lange (FOR WHOM) version of the concept does not depend upon monopoly or upon any imperfections of bargaining power between employer and employees.[6] What is involved here is a "value judgment" about the distribution of wealth ownership, not an alternative scientific finding.

---

[6] See page 704 of Chapter 28 for a discussion of a quite different concept of exploitation based on employer monopoly power in the buying of labor (so-called "monopsony"). Still a third concept of exploitation, explored on page 606 of Chapter 24's Appendix, of a factor like labor comes from what Cambridge's Joan Robinson calls "monopoly power of the firm in its product markets." As will be seen in the next sections, such a firm will be paying its factors less than the money value for which their marginal-products actually sell. Instead they get marginal revenue (which is less than price) times their marginal-products. Since the biggest and most monopolistic firms usually are the ones that actually pay the highest wages, such Robinsonian exploitation really means merely that monopolists are producing too little of their goods, that society at large is being exploited by this inefficiency, and that workers cannot from their wages buy for themselves the last extra product that an extra hour of work might actually produce.

■ MARGINAL-PRODUCT THEORY OF THE SINGLE FIRM[7]

Our main task is done. But there remains the need (1) to tie up these theories of production and distribution with Maximum-profit decisions of the firm, and (2) to show that the cost curves of Part Three were implicitly based on the marginal-productivity decisions of this chapter.

MARGINAL-REVENUE PRODUCT AND MAXIMIZING PROFIT   Exactly what does each last worker bring to my firm in cash dollar terms? He brings his marginal-physical-product; that we have seen. But he does not want his wage paid in toothpaste: the market wage is in *dollars*, not q units. And I, the employer, want to maximize dollars of profit.

Under perfect competition, the answer is easy. The marginal-physical product the worker brings me, MPP_L, can all be sold at the market price for my q output, P_q, which I as a perfect competitor cannot affect. If his MPP_L is 8 units of q and each sells for $P_q = \$5$, clearly, the dollar value of the last worker to me is $\$40$ ($= \$5 \times 8$). Generally, then, under perfect competition, each laborer is worth $P_q \times MPP_L$ to the firm. (For acres of land, this would be $P_q \times MPP_A$.)

But perfect competition is merely one limiting case of imperfect competition. It is the case of a horizontal dd schedule for my q. In the more common case of imperfect competition, dd is somewhat downward-sloping: Chapter 24 taught that the actual marginal revenue I then get from each extra physical q is less than market P_q (because of loss on previous units). With $MR_q < P_q$, the laborer's marginal-physical-product of 8 units will *not* be worth the market P_q = $\$5$ to me. How much, then? If $MR_q = \$3 < \$5 = P_q$, the answer is clear-cut: his final MPP_L is worth to me only $\$3 \times 8 = \$24$.

Generally, then, a firm's demand curve for a factor, such as labor, is given in dollar terms by "marginal revenue of q" times "marginal-physical-product of L." This important concept is given a name and defined as follows:

> *Definition:* "Marginal-revenue-product" is defined as marginal-physical-product multiplied by the marginal revenue the firm gets for its extra physical goods sold.
> Marginal-revenue-product of $L = MR_q \times$ marginal-physical-product of L
> Marginal-revenue-product of $A = MR_q \times$ marginal-physical-product of A
> And so forth.

Now we can put the new concept to work.

Rule: The firm's demand curve for any factor is given by its curve of marginal-revenue-product for that factor, a curve which declines because of (1) diminishing physical returns and (2) the downward slope of the MR_q curve which generally prevails under imperfect competition.

---

[7] Brief courses may skip the rest of this section without discontinuity.

In Maximum-profit equilibrium, every firm faced with competitive factor-prices—the money wage, the money rent rate per acre of land, and so forth—will aim to achieve

Marginal-revenue-product of L = Price of L
Marginal-revenue-product of A = Price of A
And so forth.

Maximum-profit equilibrium is attained when every factor is hired until its marginal benefit and costs are equated.[8]

MARGINAL-PRODUCTS AND LEAST-COST   Chapter 23 presented Total Cost data for each firm q. How did such minimal TC estimates get made? Marginal-productivity theory can now give the answer. Engineers told the firm it could produce $q = 9$ units with much land and little labor or with little land and much labor. Which is a more efficient choice: $A = 10$ and $L = 2$ or $A = 4$ and $L = 5$? Evidently, that must depend on the wage and rent rates the firm faces. If $P_L = \$5$ per hour and $P_A = \$2$ per acre, 10 acres and 2 hours give lower TC than do 4 acres and 5 hours. [Why? Because $(\$2 \times 10) + (\$5 \times 2) = \$30 < (\$2 \times 4) + (\$5 \times 5) = \$33$.]

What is the rule to follow to get lowest TC? The Least-cost position for producing each q comes from studying the marginal-physical-products of land and of labor. If labor and land each cost $\$1 = P_L = P_A$ and if I stopped where $6 = MPP_L > MPP_A = 4$, I should be foolish. Another dollar spent on labor and taken away from land would bring me a gain in product of $MPP_L - MPP_A = 6 - 4 = 2$ units, at *no* extra cost! So I should hire more L and drop A. But more L means diminishing returns for MPP_L, perhaps bringing it down to $MPP_L = 5$. And what is less obvious, the law of diminishing returns requires that, with *less* land, its MPP_A must *rise*. Say, MPP_A rises to 5.

Now am I at Least-cost equilibrium? Yes. Each last dollar allocated to labor gives me the same marginal-physical-product as does each last dollar devoted to land. My marginal-physical-return per dollar is now given by $MPP_L/P_L = 5/\$1$ and $MPP_A/P_A = 5/\$1$. I have found the cheapest TC to produce $q = 9$. (The reader could repeat the exposition for $q = 8$ or 10 or 1 or anything—ending up in each case with the Least-cost condition of equal marginal-product-per-dollar.)

We are now in a position to state the Least-cost rule for every case, not just the case where the factor-prices were equal. If an acre of land cost $P_A = \$200$, which was 100 times larger than an hour of labor's factor-price $P_L = \$2$, no one in his right mind would expect Least-cost to come from achieving equal *physical*-marginal-products of land and labor. Since land costs 100 times as much, it should give us 100 times the MPP of labor. It is evident that what has

---

[8] Repeatedly in Part Three, we saw that departures from the conditions of perfect competition led to inefficiencies and to nonresponsiveness to people's dollar-vote desires. It is to be understood here, therefore, that such aberrations will be ruled out *only* in the special case where $P_q = MR_q$, i.e. where the demand curve for q is perfectly horizontal so that $P_L = P_q \times MPP_L$, etc. This is actually what happened in the Clark model, where perfect competitors produced a homogeneous Q and had no "spoiling of the market problem" to bring MR_q below P_q and distort resource use.

to be equalized is the *MPP* per dollar spent on each factor. (Recall Chapter 21's similar equating of marginal-utilities-per-dollar.)

> *Least-cost rule:* To get the lowest Total Cost at each point on its TC curve, a rational firm will hire factors until it has equalized the marginal-physical-product per last dollar spent on each factor of production.

$$\frac{\text{Marginal-physical-product of } L}{\text{Price of } L} = \frac{\text{Marginal-physical-product of } A}{\text{Price of } A} = \ldots, \text{at Least-cost}$$

An obvious corollary of the above[9] can now be stated.

> *Substitution rule:* If the price of one factor, like labor, rises while other factor-prices remain fixed, it will generally pay the firm to produce its same *q* outputs by substituting, for the factor now become dearer, more of the remaining factors. (A rise in P_L will thus reduce MMP_L/P_L and cause L to be fired and A hired until equality is restored, thus lowering the amount of needed L and increasing the demand for land acres; a fall in P_L will do the reverse. A rise in P_A alone will, by the same logic, cause labor to be substituted for now dearer land.)

FINALE We have shown that the bird's-eye view of Clark's aggregate distribution is completely compatible with the realistic microeconomic pricing of any number of goods produced by any number of factor inputs. The triad of forces which determines competitive microeconomic distribution and value theory is seen to be (1) technology (the production function), (2) tastes and dollar-vote-power to demand various goods (the ultimate demand curves for goods, from which factor-price demands are derived), and (3) relative factor supplies (as determined by nature's abundance, inherited and acquired abilities, disutilities of different occupations).

The picture is oversimplified but important.

SUMMARY

■ 1 Distribution is concerned with the determination of different people's incomes, or with the basic question of FOR WHOM economic goods are to be produced. To understand what determines labor's and property's share in national product, and to understand forces acting on the degree of equality of income, distribution theory must study the problem of how the different factors of production—land, labor, capital, entrepreneurship, and risk-taking—get priced in the market. Thus it must study how supply and demand interact to determine all kinds of wages, rents, interest yields, and profits.

---

[9] The Least-cost rule involves no mention of marginal revenue, because it applies for *all q* on the *TC* curve even before the firm's demand curve has been mentioned. The Appendix will relate it to the marginal-revenue-product rule of Maximum-profit where $MR = MC$.

Market supply and demand forces setting these incomes also determine the distribution of the aggregate national income, unless society intervenes. *Ethically*, however, there is no reason to prefer market-determined income distributions from redistribution brought about by society's transfers. However, a socially desirable distribution of income may not be one of maximum efficiency. These chapters simply focus on the economic, rather than the governmental, forces at work.

■ 2 To understand why the demand curves for the factors of production are what they are, we must investigate the theory of production and cost within each firm. This is because the demand for factor inputs is a *derived demand*—derived indirectly from the final demand by the consumer. The problem is complicated by the fact that the demand for factors is a *joint demand*—joint because the factors interact in producing final product.

■ 3 The relationship between quantities of available factor inputs—land, labor, machines, fertilizer—and quantity of output is called the production function. By varying one factor in successive small increments, we define its marginal-physical-product. Diminishing returns implies falling *MPP* of any factor if other factors are held fixed. But when *all* factor inputs increase *in balanced proportion*, the J. B. Clark model of competition presupposes that there will be exactly *constant* returns (i.e., constant returns to scale).

■ 4 Competition of numerous free landowners and labor-owners will ensure that total product gets allocated among the factors by each having its factor-price equal to its marginal-product. That will allocate *exactly* 100 per cent of the product. Any factor, not just labor alone, can be the varying factor: because each of it gets paid only the *MP* of the last hired, there is enough of a residual surplus left (from the triangle of excess-of-early-over-last-*MP*'s) to pay the other factors their exact marginal-products. Hence, the Clark neoclassical theory of distribution, although simplified, is logically complete and a true picture of idealized competition.

■ 5 Ambitious attempts to measure an aggregate production function for the whole of American manufacturing seem to provide rough corroboration for the theories of production and marginal-products. In this century, technological progress has been shifting the productivities of both labor and capital upward. At the same time capital has been growing faster than the labor supply, with the following implications: (*a*) the increase of capital per worker has shifted his productivity wages up even faster than technological change would alone; (*b*) the tendency of each unit of capital to encounter diminishing returns has just about been canceled by technological innovations; (*c*) the relative shares of labor and property incomes have remained at about three-quarters and one-quarter despite the vast institutional changes in union organization and in automation of production. (Chapter 36's growth theory will return to this.)

■ 6 When the marginal-products of a factor in different uses are all equal to their common market wage, society's resources are being most efficiently allocated. (Any deviation from this inequality, whether under centralized

planning or under monopoly imperfections interfering with perfect competition, means that we are inside rather than out on Chapter 2's production-possibility frontier.) To socialists, like Poland's Oskar Lange, the
efficiency of the marginal-product method of distribution in enlarging the
size of the social pie was not an excuse for labor's not receiving all of the
product. If owners of scarce land and scarce tools could withhold them
from workers except when they command a fraction of the GNP through
their competitive marginal-product prices, then to Lange that represented
"exploitation" even if he had no particular use for Marx's labor theory of
value (and even if other kinds of exploitation associated with monopoly
power of firms in commodity or in labor markets were absent).

■ 7 If he is given ruling market prices of all factors and is given engineering,
technical information about the effects of factor changes on final product,
the businessman can simultaneously solve the two problems (*a*) of substituting the different factors for each other so as to realize the Least-cost
combination—at which he has *equalized the marginal-physical-product per
dollar spent on every factor used*—and (*b*) of finally determining which of
all possible outputs is his Maximum-profit position, where $MR = MC$.

■ 8 An exactly equivalent condition of factor equilibrium is the following
equality of marginal-*revenue*-products to factor-prices. Why must this hold
in the Maximum-profit equilibrium? Because any businessman with common sense will stop hiring any factor at the point where what its marginal-physical-product will bring in to his firm in actual dollars of marginal
revenue begins to fall short of the market price he must pay to hire as
much or little as he wants.

■ 9 Our analysis has shown why, when a factor-price rises, the quantity of it
that is demanded will tend to fall. Higher labor price will cause other factors to be substituted for it in producing each output; and higher labor cost
probably means that the Maximum-profit output will be at a lower level
where MR equals a now higher MC. What is the same, the marginal-
revenue-product demand curve for the factor tilts downward because of
technical diminishing returns, reinforced by spoiling of the monopolist's
market. (This last fact reminds us that monopolists produce too little and
hire too few factors.)

In the next few chapters we shall apply these principles to show how
supply and demand operate in the factor markets to determine rents,
wages, and other factor-prices. The Appendix to this chapter provides a
review of the theory of production for those interested in a more geometrical approach.

QUESTIONS FOR DISCUSSION

1. Give examples of derived demand and joint demand.
2. Explain the "production function concept" and various marginal-products.
3. Explain Clark's distribution theory, varying land in a new version of Fig. 26-2.

4. Define marginal-revenue-product, distinguishing it from marginal-physical product. Give a common-sense explanation to show that Maximum-profit is not attained unless each factor-price exactly equals its marginal-revenue-product.

5. Convince a skeptic of the truth of the rule that to reach a Least-cost point you must equalize the marginal-productivity-per-dollar spent on every factor. Show this to be true even when we have not yet decided on the Maximum-profit output.

6. Suppose NNP grows in a mixed economy faster than labor supply in every decade. If, contrary to Karl Marx's predictions, wage share stays about the same fraction of NNP, show that real wages rates must rise.

7. Review your understanding of the following concepts:

For Whom, How, factor pricing, distribution theory	MP rectangle, residual rent triangle
derived demand	exploitation as low competitive returns and as monopoly victimization
joint demand	marginal-product, marginal-physical-product, marginal-revenue-product, and factor-prices
production function	
diminishing returns	
aggregate production function	marginal-physical-product-per-last-dollar spent on each factor equalized
symmetry of land and labor	substitution rule of Least-cost
	$MR = MC$ and Maximum-profit q. . . .
	monopoly output and misallocated factors

Appendix: Graphical Depiction of Production Theory

The production theory of this chapter can be graphically presented. Table 26-1 is a numerical example of a simple production function relating output to two factor inputs, labor and land. It is the form of a two-way table, looking like a baseball schedule or a mileage chart of distances between cities.

Along the left-hand side are listed the varying amounts of land, going from 1 unit up through 6. Along the bottom are listed amounts of labor also happening to go from 1 through 6. Output corresponding to the specified land row and labor column is listed inside the table.

If we are interested in knowing exactly what output there will be when 5 units of land and 2 units of labor are available, we count up 5 units of land and then go over 2 units of labor. The answer is seen to be 448 units of product. Similarly, we find that 3 units of land and 6 of labor will produce 600 units of output. Thus, for any combination of labor and land, the production function tells us how much

product we shall have (using, of course, the best methods of the technical engineer).

■ THE LAW OF DIMINISHING MARGINAL-PHYSICAL-PRODUCT

The law of diminishing returns can be nicely illustrated by Table 26-1.

First recall that we have given the name "marginal-physical-product of labor" to the extra production resulting from *one* additional unit of labor, land being held constant. At any point in Table 26-1 the marginal-physical-product of labor can be derived by subtracting the given number (representing product at that point) from the number on its right lying in the same row. Thus, when there are 2 units of land and 4 units of labor, the marginal-physical-product of an additional laborer would be 48, or 448 minus 400 in the second row.

By the "marginal-physical-product of land" we mean, of course, the extra product resulting from one additional unit of land, labor being held constant. It involves a comparison of adjacent items in a given column. Thus, when there are 2 units of land and 4 units of labor, the marginal-physical-product of land is shown in the fourth column as 490 – 400, or 90. The reader should be able to compute the marginal-physical-product of labor or land at any point inside the table.

Having defined what we mean by the marginal-physical-product of an input, we are now in a position to restate the law of diminishing returns:

As we hold a fixed input constant and increase a variable input, the marginal-physical-product of the variable input will decline—at least after a point.

To illustrate this, hold land constant in Table 26-1 by sticking to a given row, say that corresponding to land equal to 2 units. Now let labor increase from 1 to 2 units, from 2 to 3 units, and so forth. What happens to product at each step?

As labor goes from 1 to 2 units, product increases from 200 to 282 units, or by 82 units. But the next dose of labor adds only 64 units, or 346 – 282. Diminishing returns has set in. Still further additions of a single unit of labor give us, respectively, only 54 extra units of output, 48 units, and finally 42 units. The reader should check some other row to verify that the law of diminishing returns holds there too. He should also verify that the same law holds true when labor is held constant and land is added in a number of steps. (Examine the changes in product in any *column*.)

At this point, it is well to recall the explanation given for diminishing returns. In Chapter 2, it was attributed to the fact that the fixed factor decreases *relative* to the variable factor. Each unit of the variable factor has less and less of the fixed factor to work with, and it is only natural that extra product should begin to fall off.

If this explanation is to hold water, there should be no diminishing returns when both factors are increased in proportion. When labor increases from 1 to 2 and land *simultaneously* increases from 1 to 2,

The production function summarizes technology:

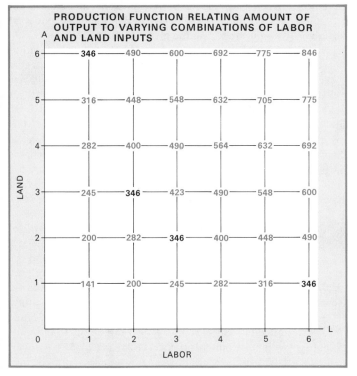

TABLE 26-1. When you have 3 land units and 2 labor units available, the engineer tells you your maximum obtainable output is 346 units. Note the different ways to produce 346 and to produce 490.

How we graphically find Least-cost point:

1st, Factors can be substituted to produce the same output:

EQUAL-OUTPUT FACTOR COMBINATIONS

	LABOR L	LAND A	TOTAL COST WHEN $P_L = \$2$ $P_A = \$3$	TOTAL COST WHEN $P_L = \$2$ $P_A = \$1$
A	1	6	$20	——
B	2	3	13	$7
C	3	2	12	——
D	6	1	15	——

TABLE 26-2. More labor can be substituted for less land to produce 346 units. When $P_L = \$2$ and $P_A = \$3$, calculate total of wage cost plus land cost to verify that their combination gives lowest cost $12 at C. Show that lowering P_A to $1 causes land to be substituted for labor as you move from C to B.

we should get the same increase in product as when both increase simultaneously from 2 to 3. This can be verified from Table 26-1.[1] In the first move we go from 141 to 282, and in the second move the product increases from 282 to 423, an equal jump of 141 units.

Also, this explanation of diminishing returns in terms of the proportions of the inputs would lead us to expect that increasing land will improve the marginal-physical-product of labor. Again this can be verified from our table: The fifth unit of labor adds 48 units of product when there are only 2 units of land; but at 3 units of land, a fifth unit of labor adds 58 units of product.

■ LEAST-COST FACTOR COMBINATION FOR A GIVEN OUTPUT

The numerical production function shows that the engineer is not able to tell us definitely how any given output is to be produced. There is more than one way to skin a cat. And there is more than one way to produce any given output. Thus, the black numbers in Table 26-1 show that the output $q = 346$ can be produced in any one of the ways shown in Table 26-2.[2]

As far as the engineer is concerned, each of these combinations is equally good at producing an output

of 346 units. But the accountant, interested in keeping profits of the firm at a maximum and costs at a minimum, knows that only one of these four combinations will give Least-cost. Just which one will depend, of course, on the respective prices of the two factors of production.

Let us suppose that the price of labor is $2 and the price of land $3. Then the sum of the labor and land costs in situation A will be $20 ($= 1 \times \$2 + 6 \times \$3$). And costs at B, C, and D will be, respectively, $13, $12, $15. At these stated factor input prices, there is no question but that C is the best way of producing the given output.

If either of the input prices changes, the equilibrium proportion of the inputs will always change so as to use *less* of the input that proportionately has gone up most in price. This is just like the substitution-effect of Chapter 21. Thus, if labor stays at $2 per unit but land falls to $1 per unit, the new optimal combination will be B, where more land is substituted for reduced labor and where total cost is only $7. The reader should verify this by computing the new total expense of all other combinations and seeing that they are higher. (Pencil in missing costs in Table 26-2.)

Exactly the same sort of thing can be done for any other output; as soon as all input prices are known, we can experiment until we have found the Least-cost input combination. (To guarantee your understanding of the principles involved, work out the optimum production decision and cost for output equal to 490 units when price of labor is $4 and price of land is $3. See that 3 labor and 4 land units will turn out to produce Least-cost of $24 for $q = 490$.)

[1] Not all production functions met within real economic life would have these special properties of so-called "constant returns to scale." Recall from Chapter 2 the discussion of increasing returns to scale, or economies of mass production.

[2] You can make up a similar table for output equal to 490.

2d, Equal-output factor combinations can also be graphed:

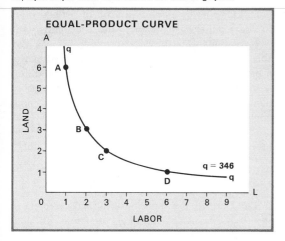

EQUAL-PRODUCT CURVE

FIG. 26-3. All the points on the curve represent the different combinations of land and labor that can be used to produce the same 346 units of output.

3d, Equal-cost contours are parallel lines:

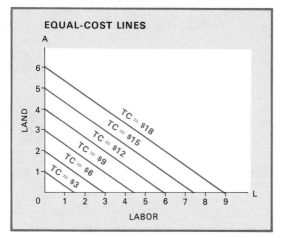

EQUAL-COST LINES

FIG. 26-4. Every point on a given line represents the same total cost. The lines are straight because of constant factor-prices, and they all have a numerical slope equal to the ratio of labor price to land price, \$2/\$3, and hence are parallel.

■ EQUAL-PRODUCT AND EQUAL-COST CONTOURS: GRAPH OF LEAST-COST POSITION

The common-sense numerical analysis of the way in which a firm will combine inputs to minimize costs can be made more vivid by the use of diagrams.

From the production schedule we can draw a picture of the different input combinations that will produce a given output. Figure 26-3 is the exact counterpart of Table 26-2. In it the smooth curve indicates the different combinations of labor and land that yield an output of 346 units. This could be called a "production-indifference curve" by analogy with the consumer's indifference curve of the Appendix to Chapter 21. But a more expressive name would be to call it an "equal-product" curve. (You should be able to draw in on Fig. 26-3, as a dotted curve, the corresponding equal-product curve for output equal to 490. You should realize that an infinite number of such equal-product contour lines could be drawn in, just as a topographical or weather map could be covered with an indefinitely large number of equal-altitude or equal-pressure contour lines.)

Given the price of labor and land, the firm can evaluate the total cost for points A, B, C, and D or for any other point on the equal-product curve. Obviously, it will be maximizing its profits only when it has found that optimum point on the equal-product curve at which it reaches Least-cost.

Purely as a graphical trick, the firm might try to save itself much tedious arithmetical computation by evaluating once and for all the total cost of every possible factor combination of land and labor. This is done in Fig. 26-4, where the family of parallel straight lines represents all possible equal-cost curves when the price of labor is \$2 and the price of land \$3.

To find the total cost for any point we have simply to read off the number appended to the equal cost line going through that point. The brown lines are all straight and parallel because the firm is assumed to be able to buy all it wishes of either factor input at constant prices. The lines are somewhat flatter than 45° because the price of labor P_L is somewhat less than the price of land P_A. More precisely, we can always say that the arithmetic value of the slope of each equal-cost line must equal the ratio of the price of labor to that of land[3]—in this case ⅔.

---

[3] The careful reader will notice the parallel between the geometry of this section and that of the analysis of consumer equilibrium in the Appendix to Chapter 21. Each equal-cost line indicates all the possible different quantities of labor and of land that the firm might buy

4th, We move on equal-product curve to Least-cost line:

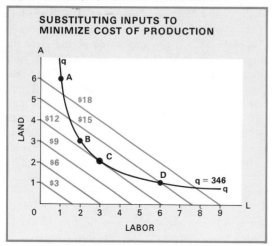

FIG. 26-5. Where the equal-product curve touches (but does not cross) the lowest total-cost contour is the Least-cost optimum position. This tangency means that factor-prices and marginal-physical-products (or "substitution ratios") are proportional.

It is now easy to recognize the optimum equilibrium input position of the firm at which total costs are minimized for the given output. The single black equal-product curve has superimposed upon it the family of brown equal-cost lines. This is shown in Fig. 26-5. The firm will always keep moving along the black convex curve of Fig. 26-5 as long as it is able to cross over to lower cost lines. Its equilibrium will therefore not be at A, B, or D. It will be at C, *where the equal-product curve touches (but does not cross) the lowest equal-cost line.* This is, of course, *a point of tangency,* where the slope of the equal-product curve just matches the slope of an equal-cost line and the curves are just kissing.

We already know that the slope of the equal-cost

for any given cost outlay. Each line is straight since its equation is $TC = \$2L + \$3A$. In the Appendix to Chapter 21, the consumer is buying goods, not factor services; otherwise his "consumption-possibility line" exactly parallels the equal-cost lines we are now discussing. We can explain, similarly, why the slope of an equal-cost line equals the ratio of the two prices involved.

But note this difference: The consumer was assumed to have a fixed budget; hence, he had but one consumption-possibility line. The firm is not limited to any particular level of costs; so it must consider many equal-cost lines before discovering its Least-cost equilibrium.

curve is P_L/P_A. But what is the slope of the equal-product curve? This slope is a kind of "substitution ratio" between the two factors, and it depends upon the *relative* marginal-physical-products of the two factors of production—just as the rate of substitution between two goods along a consumer's indifference curve was earlier shown to equal the ratio of the marginal, or extra, utilities of the two goods (Appendix to Chapter 21).

■ LEAST-COST CONDITIONS

Thus, our Least-cost equilibrium can be defined by any of the following equivalent relations:

1. The ratio of the marginal-physical-products of any two inputs must equal the ratio of their factor-prices.

That is, substitution ratio, or

$$\frac{\text{marginal-physical-product of labor}}{\text{marginal-physical-product of land}} = \frac{\text{price of labor}}{\text{price of land}}$$

2. The marginal-physical-product-per-dollar received from the (last) dollar of expenditure must be the same for every productive factor.

That is, $\dfrac{\text{marginal-physical-product of } L}{\text{price of } L}$

$= \dfrac{\text{marginal-physical-product of } A}{\text{price of } A} = \cdots$

Relation 2 is discussed in detail in the main body of the chapter. (It could also be derived from relation 1 by transposing terms from one numerator to the other denominator, i.e., by "interchanging means," as is always algebraically permissible.)

But the student should not be satisfied with any such abstract explanation. He should always remember the common-sense economic explanation which shows how a firm will redistribute its expenditure among inputs if any one factor offers a greater return for each last dollar spent on it. Finally, we may state the above Least-cost relations in the following form:

3. Input prices and their marginal-physical-products must be proportional, the factor of proportionality being marginal cost.[4]

[4] Why are these marginal-physical-products-per-dollar each equal to the reciprocal of marginal cost, or to $1/MC_q$? Because extra output per dollar is nothing but the upside-

MC of output $\times$ marginal-physical-product
$$\text{of labor} = \text{Price of labor}$$
MC of output $\times$ marginal-physical-product
$$\text{of land} = \text{Price of land}$$
And so on for any number of inputs.

The Least-cost relationships 1, 2, and 3 are all equivalent. Each holds at every point along the Total Cost curve, *whatever the output*. They do *not* tell the firm where it should finally produce.

■ MARGINAL-REVENUE-PRODUCT CONDITION OF MAXIMUM-PROFIT

But now we add the Maximum-profit condition that $MR = MC$; and we recall the definition of "marginal-revenue-product" as equal to "marginal-physical-product times marginal revenue." Then we can combine the Least-cost relations of item 3 just above and the Maximum-profit relationship to reach our final equilibrium condition:

Marginal-revenue-product of labor = Price of labor
Marginal-revenue-product of land = Price of land
And so on for any number of factors.

Thus, our graphical analysis has arrived at the same final result as our common-sense reasoning of this chapter—which tells us that we shall stop hiring more of a factor only at the point where the marginal-revenue-product it brings just matches its market price. This is what lies behind the firm's demand curve for a productive factor.

■ FIXITY OF PROPORTIONS

An important qualification must sometimes be made. We have calculated the marginal-physical-product of any one input by (1) holding all the other inputs constant and then (2) increasing the input in question by 1 unit. The resulting increase in physical product was then measured, and that was identified as the factor's marginal-physical-product. But in some technological processes the factor inputs work very intimately together, so that, when you increase only one of them, holding the others constant, you get *zero extra product*; and when you decrease one

down of extra dollars per unit of output, which is what we always have meant by MC.

factor alone, you lose *the whole product* produced by both together. Only when you change them both *in combination* do you seem to get a nice smooth curve of marginal-physical-product.

Certainly, such discontinuities can sometimes happen, but perhaps they do not occur quite so often as some critics have claimed. Thus, critics often point out examples where one man is always using one shovel or where it seems to take a certain amount of gold to produce a watchband and no amount of labor can substitute for this gold. But actually, in any digging operation, extra shovels must usually be kept on hand; and if shovel prices were very high and wages were low, workers on different shifts might use the same implements so that the shovel requirements could be kept to a minimum; also, we might in time change the size of the shovels or introduce bulldozers, thereby changing the proportions of the factors. Or in the above case of the gold watchband, there will almost certainly be some waste of metal in the form of shavings and dust; and if wages were low enough relative to the price of gold, it would pay us to hire more men to produce the same number of watchbands out of less gold— the labor being, in effect, a substitute for the use of more gold.

Numerous other arguments and examples could be given in reply to those who stress fixity of factor proportions and discontinuities in substitutability and marginal-products. Nonetheless, in some technical processes, there may not be continuous substitutability between the various inputs, and so the calculated marginal-physical-products may become very erratic and lumpy.

It was once thought that lack of substitutability would spoil the economic theory of production; but that is fortunately not necessarily so.

To see the case of fixed proportions, we would have to replace the smooth black contour of Figs. 26-3 and 26-5 by a black L-shaped equal-product contour. Regardless of how high or low the positive P_L/P_A ratio is, the Least-cost point of "tangency"— where the black contour touches but does not cross the minimal brown line of TC—comes always at the corner of the L. Hence, the Least-cost condition is even more easily found in the fixed-proportions case. (There now will be *no* substitution when one factor becomes dear relative to another, for the reason that no technical substitutability is possible.)

The derived demand of firms for factors is still

well determined, but with the difference that there may be inelastic stretches and some discontinuities in the factor-input demand curve. In Fig. 26-2, a vertical *dd* curve would spoil the simple Clark tale of rectangle and residual triangle.

Fortunately, dropping the one-good assumption of Clark and replacing a single Q by many goods (Q_1, Q_2, ...) can sometimes restore determinacy of distribution. Let's see why.

■ INTERCOMMODITY SUBSTITUTION AND QUALIFICATIONS

It is not hard to show what happens when we drop the simplified case of a single product. As any factor, such as unskilled labor, becomes more plentiful, its marginal-revenue-product and rental will tend to fall. Not only will more of it tend to be substituted for other factors in each line of production, but in addition, those special goods which happen to use much of this factor in their production will fall in price more than will prices generally. This relative price drop will tend to cause consumers to use more of such cheapened goods, and in this way the derived demand for the factor will become even more elastic.

Thus, *in addition to intracommodity technical substitutability between factors, there is also intercommodity substitutability resulting from differential price effects.* This suggests how distribution will be determined even when the continuous-substitutability assumptions of the marginal-product theory of production break down. If factors must be used in fixed proportions, their derived demands are still perfectly well determined. These demands, together with supply relations, help determine all prices. Intercommodity substitutions now become extremely important, as do the supply conditions for the factors.[5]

---

[5] An example illustrates how intercommodity substitutions can determine factor-prices even in the worst case of fixed-proportions, e.g., where 1 unit of land *and* 1 unit of labor are needed to produce a unit of wine and where 1 unit of land *and* 2 units of labor are needed to produce a unit of bread. Assume that wine sells for $10 per unit and bread for $12. Bread differs from wine by $2 in price and cost; and in terms of factor inputs, it differs by what? By 1 extra unit of labor. Hence wages must be exactly $2 per unit (= $12 − $10), and land use must be priced at $8

Finally, note this. To understand the different aspects of the problem of distribution is to begin to understand much of the history of the classical and modern theories of distribution and of competitive pricing. But it does not tell us much about the cases of imperfect competition: (1) where there may be economies of scale that lead to a few firms' gaining semi-monopoly power and (2) where consumers may develop a special preference for products that can be produced only by factors owned by a single firm. As Chapter 30 shows, in these cases the firms may earn "monopoly profits" or "monopoly rents" which the attempted competition of other firms may not take away from them. To "natural scarcity" is then being added artificial "contrived scarcity," brought about by someone's holding in his supply for fear of "spoiling the market."

---

per unit [= $10 − $2, or $12 − (2 × $2)]. So from commodity prices we can obtain factor-prices—even in this fixed-proportions case.

You will realize that the prices of wine and bread had also to be determined by supply and demand and will depend in part upon how much income goes to hungry laborers and thirsty machine owners and upon the initial supplies of the factors. For example, imagine that we started with a supply of 200 acres of land and 300 laborers, and let us summarize the resulting general equilibrium.

If we had started with factors in a 1:1 ratio—say, 200 of each—and *if* we required them to be fully employed, they would *all* have to go into wine production. We could not possibly produce any bread and still keep all our factors employed. Similarly, if our factor totals had been in a 1:2 proportion—say, 200 acres of land, 400 laborers—we should have to produce nothing but bread to preserve full employment.

But we start with a halfway ratio—200:300. Common sense and simple algebra tell us that we must then split our land half and half between the two industries, thereby using up the total of both factors in producing 100 wine units and 100 bread units. The prices of these supplies of goods would then be determined by the interplay of competitive supply and demand for the two goods and for the two factors, and thus we end up at the above equilibrium prices for goods and services.

[NOTE: A factor-price can be made zero by some demand and supply patterns, but this "free factor" possibility is neglected for simplicity. Neglected too is the case where one of the q's produced is *zero*. (If both goods used both factors in the same ratio that they are inelastically supplied, we would indeed be in a singular case where equilibrium would be indeterminate.)]

SUMMARY TO APPENDIX

■ 1 A production function lists, for each labor row and each land column, the output that is producible. Diminishing returns, to one variable factor applied to a fixed factor, can be shown by calculating the falloff of marginal-products in any row or column.

■ 2 An equal-product contour, usually drawn to be convex (from below), depicts the alternative input combinations that produce the same level of output. The slope, or substitution ratio, along such an "isoquant" equals relative marginal-products (e.g., MPP_L/MPP_A). Contours of equal Total Cost are parallel lines with slopes equal to factor-price ratios (P_L/P_A). Least-cost equilibrium comes at tangency point, where equal-product contour touches but does not cross the lowest TC contour. There marginal-products are proportional to factor-prices, with *equalized* marginal-product-per-dollar spent on all factors (e.g., equalized MPP_i/P_i).

■ 3 Of all points on TC curve, the Maximum-profit equilibrium comes where $MR = MC$; there each factor has marginal-revenue-product just equal to its price. (i.e., the Least-cost condition $P_i = MC \times MPP_i$ becomes at Maximum-profit $P_i = MR \times MPP_i$ as in main chapter.)

QUESTIONS FOR DISCUSSION

1. Show that raising labor wage while holding land rent constant will steepen the brown equal-cost lines and move tangency point C in Fig. 26-5 northwest toward B with now cheaper input substituted for now dearer one. Should union leaders take this into account?

2. (The remaining questions are not easy and can be skipped by those who have no interest or training in geometry and elementary calculus.) The famous statistical equation of Senator Douglas related Q output to L labor and C capital by the formula $Q = 1.01\ L^{.75}C^{.25}$. [Ignoring the 1.01 scale factor and identifying marginal-products with partial derivatives, show that labor's relative share is given by

$WL/PQ = L(W/P)/Q = L(\partial Q/\partial L)/Q = L(.75L^{.75-1}$ $C^{.25})/L^{.75}C^{.25} = .75$. Show also that capital's share is $C(\partial Q/\partial C)/Q = .25$.]

3. Let $P = P(q)$ be the declining demand curve for a monopolist firm, with $TR = qP(q) = R(q)$. Let its total costs be given by $TC = P_LL + P_AA$. Let its production function be written as $q = q(L,A)$, with marginal-products given by $MPP_L = \partial q/\partial L$, etc. Then Maximum profit requires the maximization of $R - C = R[q(L,A)] - P_LL - P_AA$. Such a maximum requires differentiating partially with respect to each input, giving us by the chain rule for the calculus the equality of marginal-revenue-products to factor prices. Verify

$$\partial \left\{ R[q(L,A)] - P_LL - P_AA \right\}/\partial L = R'[q] \times \partial q/\partial L - P_L = 0$$

and likewise for the $MR \times MPP_A$ equivalence. In the case of perfect competition, set $P(q) \equiv P$, a constant; then $R[q] \equiv Pq$, $R'[q] \equiv P$, and you derive the equivalence of factor-price and value of its marginal-product. Do it.

4. As a test of creative free association, use the following geometry to understand an important theorem in modern welfare economics: "Planners or markets are socially efficient, being out on and not inside society's production-possibility frontier for butter and guns (or, better, for food and clothing) only if the ratio of labor's marginal-physical-product to land's marginal-physical-product has been equated in every industry—equated to a common wage-free ratio."

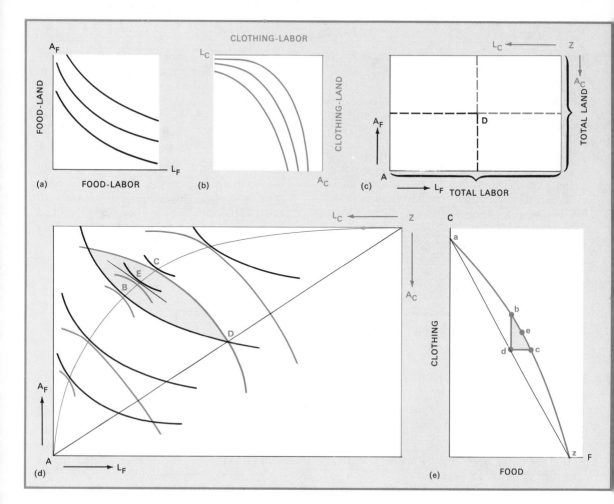

HINT: We superimpose (a) and (b) on (c) to get (d). At inefficient point like D, lack of tangency leads to shaded area of waste. At typical efficient frontier point on brown AZ curve, black and brown MPP ratios are equal to common wage-rent as shown by mutual tangency to fine black line through E.

5. Review your understanding of the following concepts:

> convex equal-product contours
> parallel equal-TC lines
> substitution slope $= MPP_L/MPP_A$
> Least-cost tangency, $MPP_L/MPP_A = P_L/P_A$
>   or $MPP_L/P_L = MPP_A/P_A$
> Maximum-profit condition,
> $MR \times MPP_L = P_L, \ldots$

27

PRICING OF FACTOR INPUTS: RENTS OF LAND AND OTHER RESOURCES

The price of pig,
Is something big;
Because its corn, you'll understand,
Is high-priced, too;
Because it grew
Upon the high-priced farming land.

If you'd know why
That land is high,
Consider this: its price is big
Because it pays
Thereon to raise
The costly corn, the high-priced pig.
H. J. DAVENPORT

The last chapter showed how each firm decides on its demand curve for any factor of production that it wants as an input for its production function. This chapter will show in detail how the demand curves of all firms and industries are added together to form the aggregate market demand for any factor of production. Such a demand curve, together with the supply curve for the factor, will be found to determine its market price; in this way a *market economy* determines the distribution of income to owners of the different factors of production.

The interesting special case of the rents to lands and other resources serves to illustrate these general principles. The following chapters will provide still other important applications to wages, interest, and profit.

■ AGGREGATE MARKET DEMAND CURVES FOR OUTPUT AND FOR EACH INPUT

Figure 27-1 shows how the demand for a given input, such as fertile cornland, must be regarded as derived from the consumers' demand curve for corn. This assumes, of course, that we hold constant the prices of such cooperating inputs as fertilizer, labor, and farm machinery. The last chapter showed this: At each land-rent price prevailing in the market place, any small farmer must decide on

Demand for factors is derived from demand for the goods they produce:

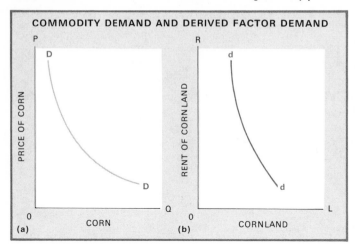

FIG. 27-1. The darker brown curve of derived demand for cornland, *dd*, comes from the lighter brown curve of commodity demand, *DD*, for corn. Shift *DD* up, and up goes *dd*. (Make the commodity curve *DD* more inelastic and vertical, and in part the same tends to happen to the factor curve *dd*.)

the Least-cost combination of the various inputs, and he must also decide on the Maximum-profit scale of his output to throw onto the market. Therefore each farmer will want to hire more and more of cornland up to the point where its marginal-revenue-product is equal to its market rental. At that point, the last unit just brings in an amount equal to its extra cost. That is why it is the equilibrium point at which the farmer ceases to demand more or less.

Recall that we are dealing with a competitive industry in which the single farmer is too small to affect the market price of corn. In such a competitive industry, no one need worry about spoiling the market for the previous units of corn being sold; consequently, marginal revenue and price are the same thing. It follows that marginal-revenue-product will be exactly the same thing as marginal-physical-product times corn price. For such a special perfectly competitive case, economists often use the special name "value of the marginal product" instead of marginal-revenue-product.

Five principles governing elasticity of this factor demand will perhaps seem reasonable. Demand for a factor tends to be the more inelastic (1) the more inelastic is the demand for the product; (2) the less important a fraction of total cost is this factor ("It is important to be unimportant"); (3) the less other factors can be technically substituted for this factor; (4) the more inelastic are the supplies of other factors; and (5) the more inflexible is the administered price at which the firm continues to sell its product. (Skilled electricians meet all the first four requirements: little is spent on them; they are indispensable; other labor, such as carpenters and masons, is inelastically supplied; and the demand for new structures is quite inelastic. See Chapter 28, page 705.)

■ FACTOR-PRICE DETERMINATION BY SUPPLY AND DEMAND

Until now we have worked only with the demand curve for a factor, taking its market price as given to the demanders. But obviously it is *all the firms together* that determine the factor's market price that each small firm faces. Let us now see how the total demand curve of all firms for the factor, together with its total supply curve, will interact to determine the equilibrium price tending to rule in the market place.

Figure 27-2 repeats the total derived demand curve for cornland *dd*; it was arrived at by adding together the demand curves of all the firms.

Now it is one of the peculiarities of land that, unlike most things, its total supply is relatively fixed by nature and in general cannot be augmented in response to a higher price for it or diminished in response to lower land rentals. (This is not strictly true. Land can sometimes be created by drainage, and the fertility of existing land can be depleted by overcropping.)

> Nonetheless, we can accept the complete fixity of land's supply as its characteristic feature. By tradition, we may confine our discussion to the "original and inexhaustible gift of nature" whose total supply is by definition *completely inelastic*. It was the price or return to such a factor that the classical economists of the last century called "rent."

This differs from ordinary usage in which rent or rental is the money paid for the use over a period of time of anything—of a house, truck, and so forth. (For the rest of Part Four we shall use the word "rent" to refer to the return to a factor whose supply is completely inelastic and "rental" to refer to money paid for the services, over a period of time, of any factor.)

In Figure 27-2, the supply curve for land *ss* is made to be completely inelastic because of the fixity of its supply. The demand and supply curves intersect at the equilibrium point E. It is toward this factor-price that the rent of land must tend. Why? Because if rent rose above the equilibrium price, the

Fixed land must work for what its demanders will bid:

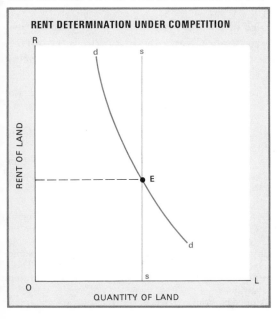

FIG. 27-2. Perfect inelasticity of supply characterizes the case of so-called "pure economic rent." We run up *ss* curve to factor demand curve to determine rent. (Aside from land, we can apply rent considerations to oil and mining properties, and anything in inelastic supply.)

amount of land demanded by all firms would be less than the existing amount that would be supplied; some property owners would be unable to rent their land at all; therefore they would offer their land for less and thus bid down its rent. By similar reasoning, the rent could not long remain below the equilibrium intersection. If it did, you should be able to show how the bidding of unsatisfied firms would force the factor-price back up toward the equilibrium level. Only at a competitive price where total amount demanded of land exactly equals the total supply will there be equilibrium. It is in this sense that supply and demand determine any factor-price.

Note that the man who owns land does not have to be a particularly deserving citizen in order to receive this rent. A virtuous and poor landowner will be given exactly the same rent by competition as will a wealthy wastrel. It is the productivity of the acre of land that is being paid for, and not the personal merits of the landowner.

Even this productivity of the land is not something absolute. For example, what would happen if the price of corn were to fall greatly because people began to desire other goods? Then the derived demand for cornland would shift drastically downward and to the left. What will happen to the rents received by landowners? After a time, rents must sink down to a new equilibrium intersection. The land is not less productive in a technical sense than it was before, and the landlords are neither more nor less virtuous than they were before. But factor demand-and-supply intersection has changed.

A factor of production like cornland is said to earn a "pure economic rent" (1) when its total supply is regarded as perfectly inelastic; and (2) when we can assume that the land *has no other uses*, such as in the production of sugar or rye. Adam Smith's great follower in England, David Ricardo, noted in 1815 that the case of such an inelastically supplied factor could be described as follows:

> It is not really true that the price of corn is high because the price of corn land is high. Actually the reverse is more nearly the truth; the price of corn land is high because the price of corn is high! Land's total supply being inelastic, it will always work for whatever is given to it by competition. Thus the value of the land is completely derived from the value of the product, and not vice versa.[1]

■ RENT AND COSTS[2]

Some economists went so far as to say: "Rent does not enter into the cost of production." As a digression let us see why.

---

[1] Land is not the only factor whose return may be considered as economic rent. For an example where most of a wage payment is a "pure rent," see page 696. And in the short run, the supply of a machine or plant may be entirely fixed; thus a hydroelectric plant takes a long time to build, still longer to wear out. The return to any factor in temporarily fixed supply is sometimes called a "quasi rent"—"quasi," because in the long run, its supply need not be fixed. Those farmers who petition for higher farm prices because of higher land and livestock prices, without knowing it, illustrate rent and quasi-rent doctrines.

[2] This theoretical digression may be skipped by brief courses.

The last section shows that there is a grain of truth in this. But still it is very dangerous terminology. If you were a farmer trying to go into the corn-raising business, you would certainly find that the landlord has to be paid like anybody else. You would certainly include rent in your costs of production; and if you could not pay your rent, you would go out of business.

IMPLICIT VERSUS EXPLICIT RETURNS   Even if you were a farmer who owned your own land, it would be a mistake to think that rent does not enter into your costs of production. After you had paid all your other bills, including wages to yourself at least as great as what you could earn elsewhere in the market, there would have to be left an amount at least equal to the market rental value of your land. For what if there were not? Then you would soon find that it would be better for you *to rent out your farm on the open market* and hire out your own labor to somebody else.

Sometimes economists call rent paid by a man to himself "implicit" rather than "explicit" rent. Very clearly, implicit rent is as much a part of long-run competitive firm costs as are any other costs, and the same can be said of the implicit wages or implicit interest earned on any other factors that you could sell rather than use personally. The reader is urged to refer to the discussion of opportunity cost in Chapter 23 (page 573), which bears on this point.

RELATIVITY OF VIEWPOINT   When some economists claim rent does not enter into society's cost of production, what are they driving at? As already noted, they are saying:

Since rent is the return to an inelastically supplied factor that would still be supplied to the community even at much lower prices, the direction of causation goes as follows: "The prices of goods really determine land rent—rather than land rent determining the prices of goods."

At this point we must avoid our old enemy "the fallacy of composition." What appears as a cost of production to each and every small firm using a particular kind of land may, as we have seen, be to the whole community merely a derived price-determined rent expense rather than a price-determining one. More than that, suppose the land is specialized and can be used only for the production of one industry. If a grade of land is inelastically supplied to one industry and, having no place else to go, will always work for whatever it can earn there, its return may appear to every small firm as a cost like any other. But as scientific observers of the whole industry, we still must recognize that the land return is a price-determined rent and not a price-determining cost.

Now let us move on to an alternative case. Suppose this land can be used for a variety of industries: for corn growing, rye growing, buckwheat growing, cattle grazing, and so forth. Then to each small industry (such as buckwheat growing), land's return will definitely appear as a necessary expense that the consumers of buckwheat will have to pay as cost before they can get their buckwheat. One small industry is just like any one small firm in this case: although the total of land is *inelastic* in supply for *all* uses, to any *one* small firm or industry it is in completely *elastic* supply.

To conclude: Whether rent is or is not a price-determining cost depends upon the viewpoint: that of a small firm, small industry, large and even exclusive-user industry, or whole economy. What is a price-determined rent return to a factor which is inelastic in supply to the whole community or dominant industry may, to each firm and to any small industry that is only one of many potential users, appear as a price-determining cost.[3]

■ HENRY GEORGE'S SINGLE-TAX MOVEMENT: TAXATION OF LAND "SURPLUS"

In the last part of the nineteenth century, settlers from the Old World were moving out to the frontiers of North America, Australia, and Africa, and even to newly reclaimed lands in Europe. As more and more people arrived, each acre had more people to work with. In a sense, therefore, the land became more productive. In any case its competitive rental value certainly tended to rise, and consequently its purchase price. This created handsome profits for some of those who were lucky or farsighted enough to get in on the ground floor and acquire land early. As the comedian Will Rogers put it, "Land is a good investment. They ain't making no more."

Nor was this true only in agriculture. All through the West men can remember when towns first began, and how they could have "picked up a quarter-section, where Main and Railway Avenues now cross, for $5 an acre. Now it's selling for $5 a front-foot." They would have been rich if they had bought before the site values soared with the growth in urban population. *Urban sites with good locations earn rents in the same sense that fertile areas or those rich in natural resources do.* Many people began to wonder why lucky landowners should be permitted to keep these "unearned land increments."

Henry George, a printer who thought much about economics, crystallized these sentiments in the single-tax movement. This movement had a considerable following a century ago, and there are still some adherents to it in New Zealand, Denmark, and western Canada. It is not likely, however, that anyone running for public office on a single-tax platform will again come so close to being elected as George did in 1886, when he was almost elected mayor of New York City. Nor is it likely that anyone will soon come along and write so persuasive a bible for the movement as Henry George did in his *Progress and Poverty*, a book which sold millions of copies. Anyone who recommends that the *government* establish an urban-land bank to stop speculation and/or to

---

[3] The Davenport verse opening this chapter hints at such a conclusion. To cover this case, economists use the technical expression "opportunity cost." (Recall Chapter 23's discussion around page 573.) To each owner of land, using it in his own business is wise only if its marginal product there will be sure to cover his "opportunity cost" or cost forgone in not selling it in the market for others to use. Similarly, a competitive industry can employ a factor only if its derived worth there measures at least up to the opportunity cost of using it elsewhere. In the terminology of Chapter 2's production-possibility frontier: The cost of guns is the forgone (or opportunity) cost of not producing butter even if every factor were in inelastic supply and earning price-determined or "residual" rents that are quite unnecessary to elicit their supply and effort.

capture the increase in land value is echoing George's platform. Britain may do it in the 1970s—she tried in 1945.

This is not the place to attempt any assessment of the merits and demerits of such a political movement. But one important principle of distribution and taxation can be illustrated by the valid central tenet of the movement:

> Pure land rent is in the nature of a "surplus" which can be taxed heavily *without distorting production incentives or efficiency.*

Let us see why. Suppose that supply and demand create an equilibrium land rent, as in Fig. 27-3 at E. Now what would happen if we were to introduce a 50 per cent tax on all land rents? Mind you, we are not taxing buildings or improvements; for that certainly would affect the volume of construction activity. All we are supposed to be taxing is the yield of the *naturally fixed supply* of agricultural and urban land sites, assuming that this can somehow be identified.

There has been no shift in the total demand curve for land; firms are still willing to pay the same amount as before for the same amount of land. Hence, with land fixed in supply, the market price that they pay must still be at the old intersection E. Why? Because supply has not changed and neither has demand. Because at any higher price than before, some land would have to go without any demanders. Hence, competitive rents could not permanently be raised to land users.

Tax on fixed land is shifted back on landlords, skimming off pure rent:

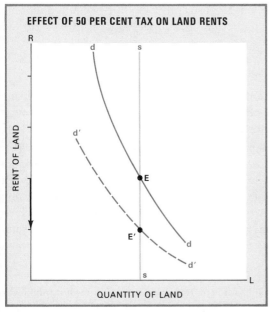

FIG. 27-3. A tax on fixed land leaves rentals paid by users unchanged at E but reduces rent retained by land-owners to E'. (What can the landowners do but accept less return?)

Of course, what the farmer pays and what the landlord receives are now two quite different things. As far as the landlords are concerned, once the government steps in to take its cut of 50 per cent, the effect is just the same as if the *net* demand *to the owners* had shifted down from *dd* to *d'd'*. Landowners' equilibrium return *after taxes* is now only as high as *E'*, or only half as high as *E*. *The whole of the tax has been shifted backward onto the owners of the factor in inelastic supply!* The landowners will not like this. But under competition there is nothing they can do about it, since they cannot alter the total supply and the land must work for whatever it can get. Half a loaf is better than none, or even than one-fourth of a loaf.

Whether or not it is a fair thing to take away part of the return of those who own land is quite another question. Perhaps many voters will feel that such owners are not less deserving than are investors who have put their money into other things; perhaps many will feel that no one should have the right to benefit from nature's windfall gifts of oil, minerals, or soil fertility.[4] But these are political questions that are not to be discussed at the present point. What is relevant is to point out that a similar 50 per cent tax put upon a factor of production whose total supply is *not* completely inelastic would certainly produce definite effects on the factor-prices charged in a competitive market. To some extent this tax would distort the pattern of production, and it would shift part of the burden *forward* onto the users of the factor and onto consumers. Thus, if the same acre of land were to be taxed differently when used for wheat rather than for corn production, this would certainly have distorting effects on the price of wheat relative to that of corn.

Since production studies show that pure land rent typically would be barely 5 per cent of the total GNP, if Henry George were alive today and facing the need of government for more than 25 per cent of GNP, he would undoubtedly change the name of his movement from "the single tax" to "the useful tax on unearned land surplus."

■ SUPPLY AND DEMAND FOR ANY FACTOR

The competitive determination of land rent by supply and demand is only one instance of the general analysis applicable to *any* factor of production. How is the rental value per week of a tractor to be determined in a competitive market?

We first sum up the derived demands of all business firms for tractors. (Of course, these derived demands have behind them marginal-revenue-product considerations of the last chapter; but this behind-the-scenes relation need not concern the observer of the aggregate market demand for this factor.) Along with the *dd* curve shown in Fig. 27-4, we must also have a supply curve such as *ss*. But there is now no reason why the supply curve should be perfectly vertical. It may now be positively elastic, rising upward toward the northeast.

---

[4] In most countries, the owner of land is not permitted to claim the full reward from lucky mineral discoveries on "his" terrain.

Factor supply and derived demand together determine income distribution:

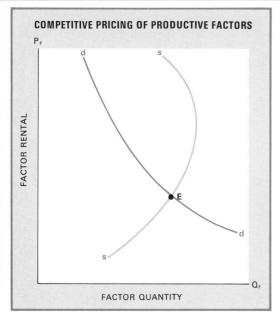

FIG. 27-4. Land's share in national income rises when its rent is bid up. Skilled and unskilled labor shares are determined, in competitive markets, by interplay of factor supply and demand. The same would hold for any factor.

(EXAMPLE: The case of tractor supply, dependent on rising marginal costs of production.) Alternatively, if the factor of production were labor, it might be that people would feel they could afford to work *fewer* hours when wages rise, so that the *ss* curve might eventually bend backward and northwestward from the vertical, rather than rising forward.

In any case, whether the supply curve is vertically inelastic, positively elastic, or negatively elastic, there will be an *ss* curve as in Fig. 27-4.

> Where the derived demand curve for a factor intersects its supply curve, the final equilibrium factor-price will be set. And if the demand curve for the factor shifts upward, its market price will tend to rise; on the other hand, if the supply offered of any factor increases, so that the supply curve shifts rightward, then the factor-price will tend to fall.

In a competitive market economy, therefore, factor-prices and the distribution of income are not determined at random. There are definite forces of supply and demand operating to create high returns to scarce factors that are very useful in producing the things wanted by people with purchasing power. But any factor's earnings will tend to drop if more of it becomes available, or if other close substitutes for it are found, or if people stop wanting the goods that this factor is best suited to make. Competition gives, and competition takes.

■ FACTOR PRICING AND EFFICIENCY: RENT AND FACTOR-PRICES AS DEVICES
TO RATION SCARCE RESOURCES

Competitive supply and demand helps determine the For Whom problem of
society. Whether or not we like its answer to this distribution question—and in
the case of rent, Henry George certainly did not—we have to admit that it does
contribute to an *efficient* solution of the How problem for society.

Thus, as a result of supply and demand in markets for goods and for
factors, in North America where land is plentiful and labor scarce, we find extensive agriculture. In Europe or Asia, where people are plentiful relative to
land, we find intensive agriculture.

Why? Because of government planning? No, not necessarily.

Rather it is the *signalling* of market pricing that results in efficient How.
Land has to be auctioned off at a low price here; labor auctioned off at a high
price here. So every farmer, seeking his Least-cost combination lest he go bankrupt, substitutes land for labor here. Contrariwise abroad, cheap labor gets
substituted for land. (More than that: with labor scarce here, we find that fussy
vegetables, which require much care, get priced relatively higher than those
which lend themselves to extensive methods. So the resulting high commodity
prices tend to make us *substitute the cheaper land-intensive goods* in our diet
for the more expensive labor-intensive ones. Abroad the opposite commodity
substitutions take place. Hence, the pricing system signals best commodity substitutions, as well as best factor substitutions!)

Thus, we see that charging rent has a function—even if you later tax part
of it away. And we can now appreciate examples showing how troubles in the
real world come from the fact that there is no way to charge the appropriate
rents.

Item: The sea is free to all. So everyone fishes in it until the fish are all
killed off or decimated. If society could somehow charge rents for commercial
fishing licenses, we might in the long run all be better off—including fishermen!
Refer to the discussion of external diseconomies in Chapter 23, and show that
letting workers overrun Ontario farmland at zero rents would lower society's
efficiency in using those acres.

Item: Our roads get very crowded on weekends and during rush hours.
We usually cannot charge tolls or rents. If we could, we might coax shoppers
and people who are on the margin of indifference to do their driving at some
less crowded time.

Item: Even if policemen can inspect and make collections from parking
meters at a cost which is a negligible fraction of the revenue collected by parking meters, it may be socially desirable to keep the tolls of such meters high
enough to create a rational use of limited curb space.

Other examples of how charging rent leads to efficient solutions for the
How question could be given. But this does not justify the status quo of
taxation or of unequal land ownership. That must be attacked or defended in
terms of ethical value judgments concerning the proper For Whom resolutions
in society.

■ CONSERVATION AND LAND TENURE

Ricardo and Henry George emphasized the original, unaugmentable, and indestructible gift of Nature. Actually, much of the land we use *has* been augmented by man: it has been drained, filled, and fertilized by investment effort
quite like that which builds machines and plants. Equally important, Nature's
gifts *can* be destroyed. There are now deserts where green acres once flourished.
There are used-up mines; deforested timber lands; eroded and depleted top-
soils. Part of the rental element in the sale of Alberta oil is a return of capital
for this exhaustible resource. More and more we must go to less accessible or
lower-grade deposits for raw materials to feed our machines.

Charging rents for use of resources may slow down their rate of depletion
and serve to ration out such scarce, exhaustible resources. But in a freely competitive system, the self-interest of owners may well lead to the rapid using up
of natural resources. The resulting depletion is not merely to the owner, who
is left with nothing more to sell or rent. Unsightly and unhealthy slag piles
may also be created. There may be short-term and long-term regional unemployment. There may be deforestation that causes floods and soil erosion
downstream. The existence of all these "external diseconomies" creates the following presumption: in making decisions involving the exploitation of resources, the owners have not been required to consider the costs or burdens
their decisions impose on other people. Consequently, governmental regulation
or intervention is advocated so that when decisions are taken, the claims of
present and future users of the scarce materials and the welfare of present and
future "bystanders" who might suffer are represented. To be effective, such
regulation must leave the property-owner free to adjust his operations to the
compulsory conservation standards in the way he sees fit; if he is also able to
profit by wise preservation and conservation measures, a further incentive would
be provided. Many economists advocate simply charging rentals and fees that
accurately reflect the costs of the damages suffered by others. Some of this has
already been discussed in Chapter 20's Appendix.

LAND- AND WATER-USE PROGRAMS   As Chapter 39 will discuss, civilization pollutes our environment: the atmosphere, rivers, lakes, and even seas. Urbanization and irrigation deplete water reservoirs and depress the level of the water
table below ground. The scarcity of fresh water becomes an urgent problem, and
the provinces and states around the Great Lakes fight over the allocation of
water for maintaining lake levels, supporting the fisheries, producing hydro
power, floating ships, and carrying away sewage. In a sense, by population
growth, industrialization, and urbanization, Nature's gift of free fresh water
has already been destroyed. In a similar sense, though, it is also augmentable.
Great dams store it for future use; canals and pipelines carry it to where its
value is maximized. Now the water-short U.S. cities and states are seriously
studying the purification of salt sea water, which would augment supplies at a
constant, though high, cost. The picture is similar everywhere: Britain is flood-
ing her dales and moors for reservoirs; Egypt now has her huge Aswan Dam
in use; Western Africa's Volta River will soon be harnessed; the waters of the

Ruhr are used over and over before they flow to the sea; even in troubled Vietnam and Kashmir, hostile neighbors sometimes pause to promote developments on their Mekong and Indus rivers.

With so many ways of killing off Nature and reviving her, "conservation" and "depletion" have become imprecise words. Economists are learning that it is no longer helpful to think of land as fixed in supply. Land, like machines and schools, is the source of many final products; like machines and schools, it can be protected, adapted, increased, or destroyed according to our demand.

As we shall see in Chapter 37's discussion of underdeveloped nations, at the village and farm level, inefficient systems of land tenancy may keep society inside its production-possibility frontier and even depress that frontier. Absentee landlords do not put money into the land; tenants on short and uncertain tenure have every incentive to mine the land and to refuse to make needed long-term improvements; credit is lacking for productive investment; and peasants who pay 40 per cent interest to moneylenders in order to tide them over until the new harvest alleviates starvation can hardly be expected to make capital investment in the land or even to maintain it.

Thus, the choice is not between ideal perfect competition and public regimentation. It is between imperfect *laissez-faire* and imperfect public coordination; between inefficient government fiats and rational democratic programming.

This is why most of the mixed economies put some limits on private freedom to use land. They make zoning restrictions and draw up regional and urban plans. They employ the right of expropriation, in which owners are made to sell their land at publicly determined prices. Parklands, owned by government, are used to create "external economies" and common consumption benefits. In Britain, Italy, France, Sweden, and elsewhere, limitations are put on the windfall capital gains that can be secured by those lucky enough to own farmland where a new city is to be located or those clever enough to speculate successfully on future developments.

■ CONCLUSIONS

The same general principles determining land rent also determine the prices of all inputs: capital goods, natural resources, or labor. Thus the rentals of threshing machines or of trucks are determined in essentially the same way. We might even go so far as to say that wages are the rentals paid for the use of a man's personal services for a day or a week or a year. This may seem a strange use of terms, but on second thought, one recognizes that every agreement to hire labor is really for some limited period of time. By outright purchase, you might avoid ever renting any kind of land. But in our society, labor is one of the few productive factors that cannot legally be bought outright. Labor can only be rented, and the wage rate is really a rental.

The next chapter deals with the peculiar problems of wages and labor markets. Chapter 29 will analyze the problems of capital and interest, which will be seen to be important in determining the supply of durable goods available for rental and use.

SUMMARY

■ 1 Factor demand curves are derived from commodity demand curves. An upward shift in the latter causes a similar upward shift in the former; and inelasticity in commodity demand makes for inelasticity of derived factor demand.

■ 2 We add up for all the firms their derived demands for a factor in order to get the aggregate demand curve. This, together with the specified supply curve of the factor, can be expected to determine an equilibrium intersection. At the equilibrium market price for the factor of production, the amounts demanded and supplied will be exactly equal—only there will factor-price have no tendency to change. Anywhere above the equilibrium price, suppliers will tend to undercut the market and to cause price to fall; anywhere below the equilibrium price, shortages will cause demanders to bid the price upward, restoring the equilibrium.

■ 3 The unchangeable quantity of natural land is an interesting special case where the supply curve happens to be perfectly vertical and *inelastic*. In such a so-called *pure* rent case, competition will still determine an equilibrium market rental. But in this case, we are faced with a cost element that is more price-*determined* than price-*determining*; the land rent is more the result of the market prices for the finished commodities than their cause. (Yet we must not forget that, to any small firm, or to any industry too small to affect appreciably the total demand for land, rent will still seem to enter explicitly or implicitly into the cost of production just like any other expense. To such a small industry, rent reflects the opportunity cost of using land elsewhere and appears to be as much price-determining as any other cost element.)

From the standpoint of the community as a whole, the rent of an inelastically supplied factor will be reckoned in the national income at its full dollar value, like anything else. But below the veil of money, it still remains true that this factor would be willing to work for less if it had to, and in that sense its return is in the nature of a "surplus" rather than in the nature of a reward necessary to coax out the factor supply. This provides the basis for Henry George's "single-tax" program, proposing to tax the unearned increment of land value—and without any shifting forward of the tax to the consumer or distorting effects on production.

■ 4 Whatever some may feel about the ethical nicety of its answers to the FOR WHOM problem, proper factor pricing does under perfect competition contribute to efficient solution of society's How problem. Indeed, *not charging rents*, or otherwise interfering with the *pricing* of factors of production may cause inefficient overcrowding and bad choice of use in many situations.

But market efficiency is only one of society's aims. Land use is so fraught with "neighborhood and externality effects," that society interferes with market processes by zoning and other land-use controls. Pollution, depletion of exhaustible resources, distorting forms of land tenure,

and destruction of the natural environment are also special problems calling for special examination. Furthermore, market efficiency may clash
with ethical ideals of distributional fairness; then each society must
choose its own mixture of efficiency and equity.

■ 5 The general principles of supply and demand can also be used to explain
the competitive price determination of all services other than those of
land. In common everyday usage, we speak of rent or rental as the price
paid for the use of any factor input, whether the factor's supply curve is inelastic or not. The rental of all inputs—including the wages that have to
be paid for the use of the services of human beings and the rentals of
durable machines—is determined in a competitive system by supply and
demand.

QUESTIONS FOR DISCUSSION

1.   Define the "pure rent" case. Explain the sense in which price of such a factor is
"price-*determined*" rather than "price-*determining*." Show that, nonetheless, an increase
in supply of the rent-earning factor will depress its return and lower prices of goods
that use it much.

2.   What was the Henry George single-tax movement all about? Use a diagram to
show the effect of taxing pure rent. Apply this to a ballplayer's inelastic supply.

3.   Discuss why it might avoid confusion if you reserved the word "rent" for the
strong case of inelastically supplied factors and used "rentals" for the more general
case.

4.   North America is now faced with problems of air and water pollution. The motorist
and industry are probably the prime causes. What interferences with freedom will
preventive measures require?

5.   Are rents always "unearned"? Discuss the case of gains made by the CPR and
others on land grants adjoining their railways.

6.   Revew your understanding of the following concepts:

derived demand	factor-price equilibrium
inelastic supply of God-given land,	price signaling of efficient factor and
pure rent	commodity substitutions
single tax, backward shifting of land	How, For Whom, and rents
tax, unearned increment	resource exhaustibility and conservation
price-*determined* expense versus	market versus ethical determination of
price-*determining* expense	land use and income distribution
supply-and-demand equilibrium	

28

COMPETITIVE WAGES AND COLLECTIVE BARGAINING

The laborer is worthy of his hire. NEW TESTAMENT

A man is much more than a commodity. Yet it is true that men do rent out their services for a price. This price is the wage rate, and of all prices it is by far the most important. For the vast majority of the population, the wage is the sole determinant of the family income. And when we remember that much of the income of farmers and of nonincorporated enterprises is in actuality a form of labor income, we realize that wages must constitute almost 80 per cent of the national income.

What is supposed to determine wages under competitive conditions? This is the first problem we shall tackle, in Section A below. Then, in Section B, we shall investigate the effect of deviations from competitive conditions. Developing further the problems introduced in Chapter 7, we shall analyze the economics of collective bargaining between trade-unions and employers.

A. WAGE DETERMINATION UNDER PERFECT COMPETITION

Wage rates differ enormously. The average wage is as hard to define as the average man. An auto executive may earn $500,000 a year at the same time that a clerk earns $7,000 and a farm hand $4,000. In the same factory, a skilled machinist may earn $150 a week, while an unskilled man gets $100. Experienced women may be paid $90 a week at the same time their younger brothers are starting at $110. Part of any theory of wages must explain these differentials.

Favorable resources and technology explain high Canadian wages:

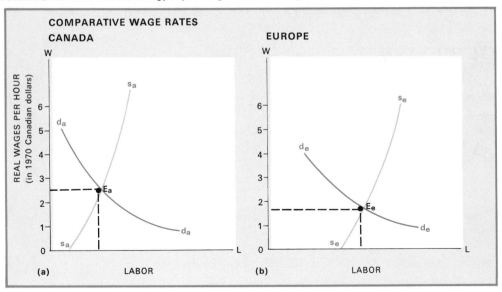

FIG. 28-1. Supply and demand determine a higher competitive wage in Canada than in Europe.

But important as these wage *differences* are, we must not overlook the general wage *level*. Wages of virtually every category of labor are higher than they used to be half a century ago. Wages are higher in North America than for similar categories in Europe, and they are higher in Europe than in Asia. Economics aims to provide understanding of such basic facts.

■ REAL WAGE DETERMINATION FOR A SINGLE GRADE

Let us begin by examining the simplified case of wages paid for similar jobs to laborers who are all exactly alike in skill, effort, and every other respect. Then competition will cause their wage rates per hour to be exactly equal. No employer would pay more for the work of one man than he would pay for his identical twin, and no worker would be able to ask more for his services.

How is this single market wage determined? If we know the supply and demand curves for these laborers—as in Fig. 28-1(a)—then the competitive equilibrium wage must be at E, the intersection point. If the wage rate were lower than E, spirited bidding by frustrated employers would restore the equilibrium.

We are interested in *real wages*—in what the wage will buy—and not just in the money wage. Therefore, in our illustrations, we express wages in money units whose purchasing power over goods is held constant at the level of some particular year and place, e.g., in terms of Canadian dollars of 1970 purchasing power. By definition, an index of the real wage represents an index of actual money wages deflated (or divided) by an index of the price level. [EXAMPLE: Money wage rates have more than doubled since 1953; however, since prices increased 50 per cent in that period, real wages increased by only 33 per cent (200/150 = 1.33).]

Imagine that, in comparison with Europe, Canada is typical of North America as a whole. Imagine further that Fig. 28-1(a) represents the state of affairs in North America and Fig. 28-1(b) that in Europe. Why are wages so much higher in North America than in Europe? Is it because we have unions and they do not? Or because we have passed higher minimum-wage laws than they? Experts doubt that these factors can explain the difference. In any case, such factors have been ruled out in our simplified competitive case. A true answer would be:

> Supply and demand are such in North America, compared with Europe, as to lead to a higher real wage here.

But *why* are supply and demand such as to lead to high North American wages? What lies behind these schedules? Why is labor's marginal product so high here?

■ RESOURCES, CAPITAL, AND TECHNOLOGY

In the first place we recall that the derived demand schedules for labor slope downward. Applied to page 650's *aggregate* production function for all of North America, the law of diminishing returns suggests that adding more and more labor to the same North American natural resources and land area will tend to diminish labor's marginal productivity, wages, and per capita (average) productivity. Suppose you let North American population increase so as to shift the supply curve *ss* far to the right in Fig. 28-1(a). Then the wage might fall to the European level or even lower.

One important explanation of high wages throughout North America, therefore, lies in the sphere of economic geography:

> Compared with the size of its working population, North America is generously supplied with land, fuels, forests, minerals, and water power.

The per capita supplies of these vital sinews of modern industrial production are less in Europe and still less in many other regions.

But economic geography does not tell the whole story. Two regions may be exactly alike in endowment of natural resources; but if one uses superior technological methods, its productivity and real wages may be much higher than the other's. In part, using superior technological methods involves better know-how, better applied science, better economic laws and customs, better management, more highly skilled and educated people, and better work methods; in part, it involves relative abundance of capital goods—of man-made machinery, materials, and plants.

Just why North America developed a superiority in know-how and capital availability is not well understood by economic historians. Our lead seems to be narrowing slightly, as all countries acquire the same know-how. But the truth of this superiority is not in doubt.

■ IMMIGRATION AND RESTRICTIONS OF LABOR SUPPLY

This raises the question, Why don't Europeans and Asians move from their low-wage area to our higher-wage area? People *did* migrate to this country in great numbers, especially between 1880 and 1890, and between 1900 and 1930. A few came to seek religious freedom, many came as political refugees, but by far the greatest number came to better their economic condition.

In Canada and the United States, laws have been passed limiting immigration. Some Europeans are welcome, but others, and colored people, are less so.[1] This is a first example of interference with free play of competition in the wage market. By keeping labor supply down, a restrictive immigration policy tends to keep wages high. Let us underline this basic principle:

Limitation of the supply of any grade of labor relative to all other productive factors can be expected to raise its wage rate; an increase in supply will, other things being equal, tend to depress wage rates.

The law of diminishing returns makes it easy to understand why doctors and trade-unions have favored restrictions on immigration. The same analysis helps to explain why unions have pressed for (1) a shorter and shorter working week and more days of vacation per year; (2) restrictions on child labor, encouragement of early old-age retirement; and exclusion of women from some areas of labor; and (3) restrictions on degree of effort and speed-ups. The old labor jingle

Whether you work by the week or the day,
The shorter the work the better the pay.

expresses the hope that workers can travel upward on the demand curve for labor.[2]

■ THEORY OF THE OPTIMUM POPULATION

At this point we must be careful not to overstate the law of aggregate diminishing marginal (and per capita) returns. Working against it, for a range at least,

---

[1] In 1967, Canada adopted the point or assessment system for potential immigrants. Under this system, admission of immigrants became based upon such factors as education and training, occupational skill, and occupational demand; rather than on race or color. However, it still has the effect of discriminating against certain nationalities and racial groups.

[2] Union policy today is by no means uniform in pressing for these restrictions upon supply. In recent years, many unions have revised their views on retirement age, now opposing compulsory retirement at sixty-five. Canadian unions have concurred in the 1967 reform of immigration laws described in footnote 1. Many unions still featherbed, but some others encourage increased productivity.

is a counterlaw: *the law of specialization, of increasing returns to scale, or of economies of mass production.*

One of the reasons the United States is so prosperous is that it is so *large* a free-trade area. Modern technology increasingly requires larger and larger plants: unless you can produce a thousand electric refrigerators per day, you will not realize the full economies of large-scale mass production. Before the Common Market brought down trade barriers in Europe, a small country found it difficult to have an efficient domestic industry unless it could use its colonies to augment its limited domestic market.

This raises a question: Would the huge American economy be better off in the 1970s if its population were cut by one-half? If you apply the law of diminishing returns uncritically, the answer is, Yes. But in view of the counterlaw of increasing returns, the answer is in doubt.

This discussion suggests a rather interesting theory of population. Why not have the best of both situations? Why not take advantage of increasing returns per capita as well as of diminishing returns? Specifically, why not aim at letting population grow up to the exact point where increasing returns end and decreasing returns begin? This point will give the highest level of real wages or real incomes, and is called the "optimum population." Figure 28-2 illustrates how the optimum is defined at the very top of the (average) productivity curve.

■ THE IRON LAW OF WAGES: MALTHUS AND MARX

In Chapter 2, we encountered the Malthusian theory of population, and we shall meet it again in Part Six. According to this theory, you should draw in on Fig.

Incomes reach a peak where population is not too large or small:

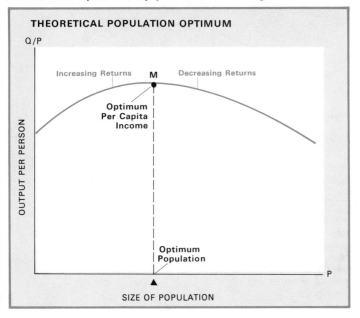

FIG. 28-2. At the point where decreasing per capita returns begins, output per person is at its very highest. Unfortunately, economists are unable to estimate just where the optimum is for a modern nation.

28-1(a) a *horizontal* long-run supply curve of labor. This should be drawn in at the wage level corresponding to the lowest standard of living at which people will just reproduce their numbers. A century and a half ago, economics was called "the dismal science" because many classical economists believed wages tended toward the bare minimum of subsistence. Our survey of rising living standards and growing populations showed how unrealistic for the West is the notion of a bare-minimum long-run supply curve of labor.

A quite different version of the iron law of wages was provided by Karl Marx. He put great emphasis upon the "reserve army of the unemployed." In effect, employers were supposed to lead their workers to the factory windows and point to the unemployed workers out at the factory gates, eager to work for less. This, Marx thought (or is interpreted as having thought), would depress wages to the subsistence level.

Let us try to show this on our diagrams. Figure 28-1(a) is redrawn as Fig.

Karl Marx exaggerated power of reserve army of the unemployed:

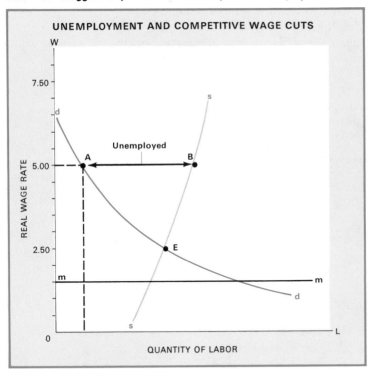

FIG. 28-3. Contrary to Marx, the "reserve army of the unemployed" —as shown by *AB*—need not depress real wages to the *mm* "minimum-subsistence" level. It can only depress competitive wages from *A* to *E*. If labor supply became so abundant that *ss* intersected *dd* at *mm*, the wage would be at a minimum level, as in many underdeveloped regions; but institutional or legal changes can do little when marginal productivity remains abysmally low.

28-3. Suppose that the wage is at $5 per hour in 1970 prices. Employment is at the level indicated by the point *A*. At this high wage, there would indeed be unemployment, as alleged. The amount of unemployment would be represented by the distance between the labor supplied and demanded *AB*. In our simple, idealized model of competition, such unemployment could certainly be expected to put downward pressure on wages.

But does the basic Marxian conclusion follow? Is there any tendency for real wage rates to fall to a *minimum subsistence level* such as *mm* in Fig. 28-3? None at all. There is absolutely no reason why in our simple model real wage rates should ever fall below the equilibrium level at *E*. In a country well endowed with capital and natural resources, this competitively determined equilibrium wage might be a very comfortable one indeed. In a less fortunate country, we should expect it to be lower. Thus we reach an important principle:

> If competition in the labor market were really perfect, there would be no necessary tendency in an advanced country for wages to fall to any minimum-subsistence level.
>
> Employers might prefer to pay low wages. But that would not matter. In a competitive market they are unable to set wage rates as they would *like*. As long as employers are numerous and do not act in collusion, their demands for any grade of labor will bid its wage up to equilibrium level at which the total forthcoming labor supply is absorbed. The workers may aspire to still higher wages, but under competition they do not get what they would *like* either; as long as they do not act collusively to limit the labor supply, their wishes will not serve to make wages rise above the competitive level.

■ LUMP-OF-LABOR FALLACY AND THE THIRTY-HOUR WEEK

It would be wrong to think that diminishing returns alone explains why unions pursue policies to restrict labor and effort. There is a related and still more powerful reason why workers fight for shorter hours. They fear unemployment; they tend to think the *total amount of work to be done is constant* in the short run. So what happens if a foreigner is put to work? Or a woman comes into the labor market? Or an old man refuses to retire? Or a fellow worker works too efficiently? Or a machine replaces a man? Or men work overtime? Each of these looms up as threat to a worker's job and livelihood.

This attitude, that there is only a fixed amount of work to be done, is sometimes called by economists the "lump-of-labor fallacy." We must give this notion its due. To a particular group of workers, with special skills and status and stuck in one region, the introduction of technological change may represent a real threat. Viewed from their personal standpoint, the lump-of-labor notion may not be so fallacious.

True enough, in a great depression, when there is mass and chronic unemployment, one can understand how workers generally may yield to lump-of-labor philosophy. But the lump-of-labor argument implies that there is only so much useful remunerative work to be done in any economic system, *and that is indeed a fallacy.*

> If proper monetary, fiscal, and pricing policies are being vigorously promulgated, we need not resign ourselves to mass unemployment. Although technological unemployment is not to be shrugged off lightly, its optimal solution lies in offsetting retraining policies that create adequate job opportunities and new skills, rather than in restrictions on production. Retraining is to be coupled at the macroeconomic level with expansionary fiscal and monetary policies.

There are, of course, still other arguments for or against cutting standard working hours from, say, 40 per week to 30. As our standards of living and productivity rise, it is only natural that we should feel we can afford more leisure. Historically, working hours have been progressively shortened, as we have already seen. Saturday work will no doubt become rare as it already is in Australia and New Zealand. Probably there will be a trend toward increased vacations with pay—not so much because the vacation will improve workers' productivity as that people get enjoyment from summer and winter vacations. Taking more time off will probably be one of the ways in which we shall choose to enjoy the fruits of technological progress. No doubt, too, our grandchildren will choose to work a still shorter week; but that should reflect choice, not necessity.

Still, at this stage of history would workers really wish to purchase 10 extra hours of leisure per week if this meant forgoing a sizable fraction of real and money income—say, 20 per cent of what potentially might be earned? One wonders. As our economy approached full employment in the 1960s, agitation for the 30-hour week declined. This suggests that the unemployment rather than the leisure argument really carried most weight. Moreover, when a union leader favors a shorter week, he at the same time asks that there be no cut in take-home pay. What worker could be against a free present of more leisure? A few pages later we shall investigate the degree to which unions can squeeze higher wages out of employers. But there is little doubt that drastic shortening of hours would imply lower real earnings than a full-employment economy is capable of providing.

■ GENERAL SUPPLY CURVE OF LABOR

Return now to the case of perfect competition. What is the supply curve of labor like? How does the wage rate affect population? Affect people's desire for a longer or shorter average working day? Influence the number of people *not* in the labor force (via age of retirement, years of schooling, and women workers)? Will higher wages motivate people to work more effectively or make them feel they can afford to relax?

These questions show that the supply of labor involves at least four dimensions: (1) population, (2) proportion of the population actually in the labor force, (3) average number of hours worked per week or year by workers, and (4) quality and quantity of effort and skill that workers provide.

These four labor-supply dimensions all depend on sociological as well as economic forces.[3] The third, though, is of particular economic interest.

"SUBSTITUTION-EFFECT" VERSUS "INCOME-EFFECT" What effect will wage rates have on the number of hours worked per year? We have already touched on this earlier. A diagram may help to make the issues clear. Figure 28-4 on the following page shows the supply curve of total hours that a group of people will want to work at each different wage. Note how the supply curve rises at first in a northeasterly direction; then at the critical point c, it begins to bend back in a northwesterly direction. How can we explain why higher wages may either *increase* or *decrease* the quantity of labor supplied?

Put yourself in the shoes of a worker who has just been offered higher hourly rates and is free to choose the number of hours worked. You are torn two different ways: On the one hand, you are tempted to work some extra hours because now *each hour of work is better paid.* Each hour of leisure has become more expensive—hence you are tempted to *substitute* extra work for leisure. But working against this so-called "substitution-effect" is an opposing "income-effect."[4] With the wage rate higher, you are, in effect, *a richer man.* Being richer, you will want to buy more clothes, more insurance, better food, and more of other consumer goods. But most important for the present problem, *you will tend also to buy more leisure!* Now you can afford to take Saturday off, have a week's vacation in the winter or an extra week in the summer.

Which will be more powerful, the substitution-effect or the income-effect? Or will they just balance each other and cancel each other out—so that the supply curve neither rises forward nor bends backward, but rises perfectly vertically and inelastically? There is no one answer. It depends upon the individual. In Fig. 28-4, from s' to c the substitution-effect outweighed the income-effect. But from c to s'', the income-effect was the more important.[5]

---

[3] The labor force sometimes tends to grow in deep depression: when a husband is thrown out of work, his wife and children may seek jobs. Tending to cancel this is the fact that women and others workers are, under prosperous conditions, attracted into jobs by plentiful employment opportunities. The labor force grew less from 1957 to 1967 than demographers had expected: apparently the high level of unemployment discouraged new entrants. When full employment finally reappeared, new entrants were coaxed back; U.S. experts estimate that every time aggregate demand policies create 10 new jobs, 3 additional persons will enter the labor market.

[4] See Chapter 21 for a discussion of "substitution-effects" and "income-effect" in connection with consumption, and Case 4 of the Appendix to Chapter 19. The income-effect of a wage increase is defined as its tendency to make you feel richer and able to afford more pleasurable leisure. Its substitution-effect is its tendency to make you want to react to the higher price of leisure—higher because of the higher hourly wage you now forgo to get each hour of leisure—by substituting for leisure the new goods your higher pay will buy. These two effects of a wage change oppose each other; when the income-effect wins, labor's supply curve bends back.

[5] On the hypothesis that the substitution-effect is most powerful, we would expect that taxes on wage income would cut labor supply. The verification of the hypothesis is important for tax, wage, and welfare assistance policies. What are the findings? Chaterjee and Robinson, surveying 369 Ontario taxpayers, found no important tax effects on work effort. (See A. Chaterjee and J. Robinson, "Effects of Personal Income Tax on Work Effort: A Sample Survey," *Canadian Tax Journal*, May-June, 1969.) Fields and Stanbury found that even many heavily taxed lawyers and accountants in England seem insensitive to tax burdens. (See D. Fields and W. Stanbury, "Incentives, Disincentives and the Income Tax: Further Empirical Evidence," *Public Finance*, No. 3, 1970. See this paper also for references to an extensive literature stemming from pioneering studies by G. F. Break.)

At a high enough wage we can afford to work less:

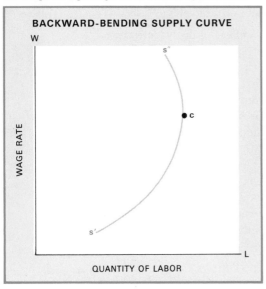

FIG. 28-4. Above the critical point *c*, raising the wage rate reduces amount of labor supplied. (Income-effect overcomes substitution-effect: at higher income, one feels he can afford more leisure even though each extra hour of leisure is costing him more than before.)

■ RENT ELEMENTS IN WAGES OF UNIQUE INDIVIDUALS

Generally, one could expect that, after people receive a comfortable margin over what they consider to be conventionally necessary, further increases in wage will not bring forth further hours of work. This was tested by a tax lawyer who studied his professional and business friends in New York City to learn the effect on them of heavy graduated taxes. Somewhat to his surprise, he discovered that taxes seemed to make them work harder so as to maintain their previous standards of living. Apparently, the short-run income-effect of reduced after-tax wages was more powerful than the substitution-effect. But probably most powerful were their nonmoney drives—desire for achievement and liking for their work. A Harvard Business School study gathered similar evidence, as did a study of English accountants and solicitors.

As we shall see in Chapter 30 on profits, the most harmful effects on incentives of our increasingly high tax rates seem to involve risk taking and venture capital rather than any connection with the supply of effort by gifted people. Most of the high earnings of outstanding individuals can probably be classified as "pure economic rent." Babe Ruth earned $100,000 a year playing baseball, something he liked to do anyway. Outside the field of sports it is doubtful if he could have counted on earning more than, say, $5,000 a year. Between these two limits his supply curve was almost completely *inelastic*, and so economists can term the excess of his income above the alternative wage he could have earned elsewhere *a pure rent*, logically like the rent to nature's fixed supply of land as discussed in the last chapter.

■ EQUALIZING DIFFERENCES IN WAGES

Let us now turn from the problem of supply of labor in general to investigate the vital problem of *differentials in competitive wages* among different categories of people and jobs. Supply conditions now become all-important in explaining the tremendous wage differentials observed in everyday life.

> When you look more closely at the differences among jobs, some of the observed pay differentials are easily explained. Jobs may differ in their unpleasantness; hence wages may have to be raised to coax people into the less attractive jobs. Such wage differentials that simply serve to *compensate for the nonmoney differences among jobs* are called "equalizing differences."

Steel erectors must be paid more than janitors because people do not like the risks of balancing aloft. Workers often receive 5 per cent extra pay on the 4 P.M. to 12 P.M. "swing shift" and 10 per cent extra pay for the 12 midnight to 8 A.M. "graveyard shift." For hours beyond 40 per week or for holiday and weekend work, 1½ times the base hourly pay is customary. And when you observe a doctor who earns $40,000 a year, you must remember that at least a part of this is an equalizing difference needed to induce people to incur tuition costs and endure the lack of pay for years. (And when you allow for the extra hours he puts in, you find that the doctor is not all that much ahead of people in other professions.) Similarly, a man who now earns more in Ontario than he did in Nova Scotia had to be induced to cut his home ties and to pay for the move to a different province.

Jobs that involve dirt, nerve strain, tiresome responsibility, tedium, low social prestige, irregular employment, seasonal layoff, short working life, and much dull training all tend to be less attractive to people. To recruit workers for such occupations you must raise the pay. On the other hand, jobs that are especially pleasant or attractive find many applicants, and remuneration is bid down. Many qualified people like white-collar jobs, and so clerical wages are often lower than blue-collar pay.

To test whether a given difference in pay is an equalizing one, ask people who are well qualified for both jobs: Would you take the higher-paying job in preference to the lower? If they are not eager to make such a choice, then it is fair to conclude that the higher-paid job is not really more attractive when due weight is given to all considerations, nonmonetary and monetary.

■ NONEQUALIZING DIFFERENTIALS: DIFFERENCES IN LABOR QUALITY

If all labor were homogeneous, we have seen that every observed competitive wage differential could be explained as an equalizing difference. But turn to the real world. True, some of the observed differentials can be regarded as equalizing. Yet everyone knows that the vast majority of higher-paid jobs are also *more pleasant*, rather than less pleasant. Most wage differentials cannot therefore be of the equalizing type. What, then causes them?

Are they perhaps due to the fact that competition is imperfect? Undoubtedly, some observed differentials are of this type. Studies show that workers do not have anything like perfect knowledge of job opportunities. Trade-unions or minimum-wage laws or a monopoly by the workers in a particular occupation can also explain part of the existing nonequalizing differentials. If you removed these obstructions due to monopolistic or imperfect competition, enough people would flow into some of the higher-paid jobs to bring pay in these jobs into equality with that prevailing elsewhere. We shall analyze these interferences with competition in a moment.

But never forget that many of the observed differentials in wages have little to do with the imperfections of competition; they would still persist if there were no monopoly elements. Even in a hypothetically perfect auction market, where all the different catgories of labor were priced by supply and demand, equilibrium would necessitate tremendous differentials in wages.

This is because of the tremendous *qualitative* differentials among people.

No one expects the competitive wage of a man to be the same as that of a horse. Then why expect one man to receive the same competitive wage as another man or woman? A zoologist may call us all members of the same *Homo sapiens* species, but any personnel officer who is trying to equalize the marginal-physical-product-per-dollar expended in every direction knows that people vary much in their abilities and contributions to his firm's dollar revenue.

There are more than 8 million people in our labor force. There is no single factor of production called labor; there are thousands of quite different kinds of labor. If you are hiring men to shovel railroad trains out of a blizzard, it will probably pay you to lump together as one indistinguishable factor of production all adult males of certain ages who appear to be reasonably healthy, muscular, and sober.

Thus, the labor market will always group people into certain general classifications for purposes of wage determination. But even after groupings are made, many distinguishable categories of labor remain, with wide dispersion of their wage rates.

■ "NONCOMPETING GROUPS IN THE LABOR MARKET"

A century ago, economists began to call these different categories of labor "noncompeting groups in the labor market." Instead of being a single factor of production, labor was recognized to be many different factors. Economists expected that as many different wage rates would result as there were noncompeting groups. Their instinct was sound, but there is some danger of misunderstanding their terminology.

In the first place, we must not think that in a perfectly competitive labor market the so-called "noncompeting groups" would disappear. We should still have different categories of labor—just as the near-perfect wheat market has winter wheat, spring wheat, grade 2 red wheat, etc. Second, no one can doubt that these different groups are in some sense competing with each other. Just as I decide between hiring a horse and a tractor, so must I decide between hiring a very skilled, fast-working, high-paid worker and a lower-paid, less skilled one.

The essential point, then, is this: The different categories compete with each other; yet they are not 100 per cent identical. They are *partial rather than perfect substitutes* for each other.

Workers can to some degree cross over from one category into another. If welders' wages were to become $100,000 a year, I might study the art and stop being a teacher. Or if I did not, others would. Therefore, even when the wages of the different categories of labor are different, quantitative wage differences are still subject to the laws of supply and demand. "Cross elasticity" of supply becomes very important: The wage you must pay to recruit foundrymen depends on what the nearby auto plant is paying men on the assembly line.

Or take the case of skilled surgeons. In all countries, they receive high pay compared with butchers. Why? Because their work is important? Only in part on this account. For suppose that (1) every year as many babies were born with the capacity necessary for a surgeon as with the capacity necessary for a butcher, (2) we knew how to train surgeons in no time at all, and (3) a surgeon's activities and responsibilities were not regarded as less pleasant or more taxing than those of a butcher. Then do you really think that surgeons would continue to receive higher earnings than butchers? And if you think the sanctity of human life is the key explanation, how do you account for the fact that the best plastic surgeons are higher-paid than the best heart surgeons?

A complete analysis of the economics of racial and other discrimination will emphasize that some of the differences in "quality" are in the eye of the beholder. If employers think that skin color, or ethnic background, denotes lower efficiency, that can become a stereotype built into the demand and supply schedules. All categories are dynamic, not static, being changeable by training, custom, and, indeed, legislation.

■ GENERAL EQUILIBRIUM OF LABOR MARKET

In real life as we know it, distinctions are not absolute. There is some mobility between different jobs; differences in wages will tend gradually over a long period of time to encourage greater and greater mobility; nor is it necessary for all workers to be mobile—a few movers are enough.

But there will still remain certain permanent barriers to mobility that depend upon the irreducible differences in biological and social inheritance. Hence, wage differentials will persist even in the long run.

How big will these differentials be? Suppose we made it easy for people to get the education they are fitted for and to travel from one region to another where their skills can be better used. And suppose we provided people with the best possible information about job opportunities and about their personal potentialities. Then differentials would be much reduced. But for such differen-

Competitive wage structure shows great variety of patterns:

COMPETITIVE WAGE DETERMINATION	
SITUATION	**RESULT**
1. People all alike—jobs all alike.	No differentials.
2. People all alike—some jobs differ in disutility.	Equalizing wage differentials.
3. People differ, but each type of labor is in unchangeable supply ("noncompeting groups").	Wage differentials that are "pure economic rents" or "surplus."
4. People differ, but there is some mobility between groups ("partially competing groups"; "cross elasticity" important).	General equilibrium pattern of wage differentials as determined by general demand and supply (includes 1-3 as special cases).

TABLE 28-1

tials as remain, how exactly are they determined? The answer is provided by supply and demand.

The market will tend toward that equilibrium pattern of wage differentials at which the total demand for each category of labor exactly matches its competitive supply. Then and only then will there be general equilibrium with no tendency for further widening or narrowing of wage differentials. Table 28-1 sums up our conclusions.

B. IMPERFECTIONS OF THE LABOR MARKET AND COLLECTIVE BARGAINING

Real-world labor markets are far removed from the ideal model of perfect competition. You can grade wheat into neat market categories, but you cannot do that with human beings. No auctioneer allocates workers to the highest bidders. Studies of areas such as Windsor, Ontario, show that workers often have only the most imperfect knowledge of nearby job opportunities and wage rates.

WAGE STICKINESS   Two tests indicate that the labor market is imperfect. When there is a considerable increase in unemployment—as in the sluggish 1950s—do wage rates drop as they would in a competitive market? History answers, No.

You may be every bit as capable as someone who has a job, and yet there is no way that you can take his job away by underbidding him. Just imagine going to Ford or any large corporation when the next depression comes, brandishing your degrees and certificates of IQ and excellence, and offering to work for less than they are paying. Could you get a job that way?

WAGE POLICY OF FIRMS   The fact that a firm of any size *must* have a wage policy is additional evidence of labor market imperfections. In a perfectly competitive market, a firm need not make decisions on its pay schedules; instead it would turn to the morning newspaper to learn what its wage policy would *have* to be. Any firm, by raising wages ever so little, could get all the extra help it wanted. If, on the other hand, it cut the wage ever so little, it would find no labor to hire at all in a perfectly competitive labor market.

But just because competition is not 100 per cent perfect does not mean that it must be zero. The world is a blend of (1) competition and (2) some degree of monopoly power over the wage to be paid. A firm that tries to set its wage too low will soon learn this. At first nothing much need happen; but eventually it will find its workers quitting a little more rapidly than would otherwise be the case. Recruitment of new people of the same quality will get harder and harder, and slackening off in the performance and productivity of those who remain on the job will become noticeable.

Availability of labor supply does, therefore, affect the wage you set under realistic conditions of imperfect competition. If you are a very small firm, you may even bargain and haggle with prospective workers so as not to pay more than you have to. But if you are any size at all, you will name a wage for each type of job, then decide how many of the applicants will be taken on; and in view of the number of applicants who respond, you may raise or lower your wage rate. Even in the absence of unions, you will find it a perplexing task to decide on an optimal wage policy.

EQUALITY OF BARGAINING POWER?   One of the reasons given in the past for starting trade-unions was the feeling that unorganized workers, facing financially strong employers, lacked "equality of bargaining power." By union organization it was hoped that a greater equality of bargaining power could be restored. But exactly how one goes about measuring equality or inequality of bargaining power remains a difficult research task for the economic theorist.

It is safe to say that prior to the formation of labor unions, the labor market was not a perfectly competitive one in the economist's sense of the term. And after the formation of unions it continues to differ from the perfectly competitive model. Moreover, a number of the features of labor markets usually associated with unions are also present even where there are no unions. Thus, large companies that have no union will typically introduce a standard trend-rate of pay and be slow to change it, even though the number of workers locally unemployed might go up or down. In years of labor market slack these firms raise their wage rates as much as unionized trades do, despite the fact that competitive theory would expect them then to be cutting rates.

■ FOUR WAYS UNIONS SEEK TO RAISE WAGES

Leaving the oversimplified picture of perfect competition behind, we can use economic theory to analyze how trade-unions operate. How might unions hope to raise wages in a particular industry?

There are four main methods of raising wages, all interrelated: (1) Unions can reduce the supply of labor. (2) They can use their collective bargaining power to raise standard wage rates directly. (3) They can cause the derived demand curve for labor to shift upward. (4) Unions can resist exploitation of laborers facing an employer with monopoly bargaining power. These four devices are much alike and often reinforce each other, but they also display significant differences.

1. Restriction of labor supply. We have already seen that a union may restrict the supply of labor in order to travel upward on the derived demand curve for labor. Immigration barriers, maximum-hour legislation, high initiation fees, long apprenticeships, refusal to admit new members into the union or to let nonunion members hold jobs—all these are obvious restrictive devices that have been used in the past. In addition, there are other, more subtle restrictions on labor supply: explicit union limits on work loads (artificial limits put on number of bricks per day, width of paintbrush, stand-by orchestras, number of looms attended, and similar "featherbedding" labor practices) and implicit understandings forcing a slowdown of the working pace.

2. Raising standard wage rates. Direct limitations on the labor supply are today no longer so necessary to unions, except to reinforce the ability of the union to secure a high standard wage rate and to maintain it. Union leaders have learned this important economic fact:

> If you can persuade or force employers always to pay a high standard wage—a wage rate that is publicly known and adhered to—then the supply of labor will take care of itself. At the standard rate, employers will hire the number of men they want, and any surplus job applicants will be *automatically excluded* from that labor market.

Figure 28-5(a) and (b) contrasts *direct* restriction of labor supply and *indirect* restriction via a high standard wage. In Fig. 28-5(a) the union cuts down supply from *ss* to *s's'* by insisting on long apprenticeships and high training fees. The wage consequently rises from E to E'. (Test your understanding of this: Explain the effects on doctors' earnings of a policy that reduced the number of students going through medical schools relative to the total population.)

Alternatively, in Fig. 28-5(b), the union gets all employers to agree to pay wages no lower than the minimum standard rate, as shown by the horizontal line *rr*. Note that here, too, the equilibrium is at E' where *rr* intersects the employer's demand curve. The workers from E' to F are as effectively excluded from jobs as if the union had directly limited entry. What now limits supply? It is the lack of job opportunities at the high standard wage rate.

This helps explain what used to puzzle many observers of modern unionism. At the same time that many unions were liberalizing restrictions on union membership, wage rates were often being pushed up by collective bargaining.

3. Shifting the derived demand curve upward. A union may hope to increase wages by any policy that improves the demand for labor. Thus, like the

To raise pay, unions restrict supply and enforce standard wage rate:

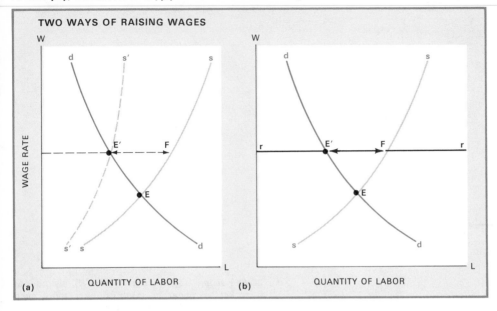

FIG. 28-5. Raising the standard wage to *rr* in (b) has exactly the same effect on wages as reducing the effective supply from *ss* to *s's'* in (a); the workers from *E'* to *F* are excluded from employment in either case.

International Ladies' Garment Workers Union, it may study ways of reducing garment prices by improving productivity of labor and management, or it may help the industry advertise its products. *Or,* in order to protect its industry, the union may press the government to maintain or increase an existing tariff, or to impose a new one, hoping thereby to raise the demand curve for domestic workers. *Or* it may persuade the government to pay higher rates on public contracts and to write make-work featherbedding restrictions into building codes. *Or* it may help the employers in an industry to maintain a high monopoly price, with some of the extra profits going into higher wages.

Moreover, if collective bargaining raises wages, and *if increased wages increase the marginal productivity of labor,* then labor will have shifted its own demand curve upward. Figure 28-6 on the following page depicts the case in which an increase in the wage from *rr* to *r'r'* itself results in an upward shift in the demand curve for labor—from *dd* to *d'd'*. Note that at the new equilibrium *E'*, both wage and employment have increased.

In the old days, the standard example of this was the case where workers were being paid so little that they were malnourished and hence inefficient; higher wages might then have made them more efficient and thus resulted in lower rather than higher production costs. Today, in this country, few workers are as physiologically undernourished. But psychological elements can be as

Some union policies try to shift the labor demand curve upward:

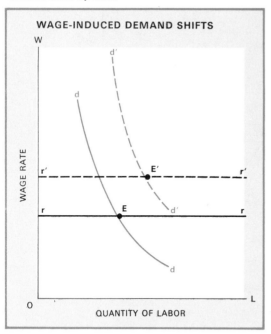

FIG. 28-6. Raising wages (from *rr* to *r'r'*), by making ill-fed workers stronger or resentful ones more energetic, in this case shifts the curve of demand productivity upward (from *dd* to *d'd'*), with employment actually increasing (from *E* to *E'*).

important as physiological. Many an employer has found that too-low wages are bad business even from a hardboiled dollars-and-cents standpoint.

It can be argued that high wages have a favorable "shock effect" on the employer's efficiency in using labor. One reason advanced for the high productivity of North American industry, even back in the nineteenth century when unions were unimportant, was the fact that high farm earnings made it necessary for industry to develop good machine methods in order to be able to pay high wages and still stay in business. Adversity, in the form of a kick in the pants from unions or from fate in general, can at times galvanize businessmen into finding improved ways of doing things. How much there is to this shock-effect argument, nobody knows. It should therefore be used with caution.

4. Removing exploitation by monopolist of labor (the "monopsonist"). Finally, there is the case where unions arise to offset monopoly power that employers may have in a labor market that has been far from competitive. Suppose there is a company town: unless you work for the dominant firm, you are unemployed; your alternatives are few or nonexistent, and you must take what the employer offers. In this case the employer does not think of himself as too small to affect appreciably the wage he pays; he does not hire factors up to the point where their marginal-revenue-products (as defined in the chapters just preceding) are equal to the wage he pays. Instead, the employer realizes that hiring an extra worker will raise the wage he must pay to all, and hence he had better not hire that worker unless the worker's marginal-product is much *greater* than the wage.

In this situation (which many modern economists call "monopsony," after the Greek words for the situation in which there is a "single buyer," just as "monopoly" means the situation in which there is a "single seller"), organizing a union can result in higher wages and without any decline in unemployment! Once the employer realizes the union is going to see to it that he must pay the standard wage, he will again be a "wage taker" who will hire men up to where their marginal-product fully equals that standard wage.

The lessening of exploitation by union organization is more important in isolated places, like the tin mines of Bolivia or the lumber camps of Canadian history, than it is in a modern economy where people are, in fact, mobile in moving to better job opportunities. There do still, however, remain areas of agriculture where employers hire workers below the market because of the workers' lack of other opportunities or their ignorance of such opportunities as do exist.[6]

■ WAGE INCREASES AND REDUCTIONS IN EMPLOYMENT

If raising wages means simply that you climb up the existing demand curve for labor, then employment will decrease in consequence. This is because demand curves almost always slope downward and to the right.[7] The amount of unemployment created in a particular occupation by wage increases would depend upon the elasticity of the demand curve for that particular category of labor. We saw in earlier chapters that a factor demand is a "derived demand," and we

[6] Intermediate economics texts show that, where an employer was previously possessed of monopoly-buying-power over labor, collective bargaining can—if not pushed to excess—right the balance, leading to both increased wages *and* increased employment. Before unionization, the employer monopsonist who is on his toes will set his equilibrium wage at *mm* in Fig. 28-7. This will be lower than the so-called "competitive wage" at *E*. Why will the monopsonist's equilibrium be at a point like *M*? The monopsonist will not want to travel upward from *M* to *E* because he realizes that any employment increase beyond *M* will raise the wages paid to *already hired workers* by more than the extra revenue resulting from hiring the new men. But now let the union raise the wages toward *E* by collective bargaining; the monopsonist employer now reluctantly travels up the *ss* curve, as shown by the black arrows. Note we do not travel up the marginal-revenue-product curve *dd*. Wages and employment both rise together. (QUERY: Suppose collective bargaining raises the standard wage to a level *r"r"* that lies *above* E. By drawing in the resulting arrows *above* E on *dd*, show that now unemployment will follow. What then will happen to employment? Draw in the resulting black arrows on the demand curve.)

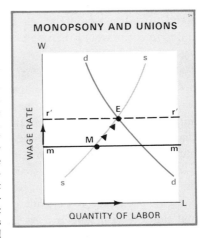

FIG. 28-7.

[7] Cases have been noted where short-run demand is virtually completely inelastic.

discussed on page 674 some of the conditions that determine how elastic or inelastic the derived demand might be. Here are two cases to help review those principles:

CASE OF INELASTIC DERIVED DEMAND   Suppose that a particular building-trades union, such as the electricians', raises wages. This case emphasizes the factors making for inelastic demand and a small resulting drop in employment of electricians. (1) Note that, in the short run, employers *cannot substitute* other factors—such as machines or plasterers—for electricians. (2) Do not forget *the importance of being unimportant:* The total cost of a house will be little affected by a change in the wage rate of electricians alone. This fact will tend to cause a mild reduction of employment as a result of an increase in their wages. (3) Suppose there is a great housing shortage so that people feel they need homes desperately. *In*elasticity of demand for the final product, housing, will lower the derived elasticity of demand for electricians. (4) Suppose that all practising electricians must be in the union so that an increase in wages is not followed by a great increase in the nonunion labor supplied. This inelasticity of supply of other complementary factors will tend to make the demand for union electricians inelastic. (5) Suppose finally, as in Fig. 25-2, that administered pricing or public regulation will not permit the prices at which houses are available to change much. This will make for an unchanged quantity of houses sold and hence inelastic demand for the factors that build houses.

CASE OF ELASTIC DEMAND   On the other hand, suppose you were a union leader in the glass-blowing industry. Suppose that labor costs are an important part of the total expense but that new mechanized processes exist which substitute machinery for men. Suppose, too, that a large part of the industry is not unionized, particularly those nonskilled workers who run the new machines. And finally, suppose that there are many commodity substitutes for glass, such as tin and paper. You can apply our principles to show qualitatively (1) that the demand for labor would then be quite elastic, and (2) how disastrous in terms of employment it would then be to raise wages.

■ THEORETICAL INDETERMINACY OF COLLECTIVE BARGAINING

Just as unions sometimes realize it would not be to their interest to get higher wages, managements sometimes take the view that an increase in wages would improve their long-run corporate earnings. But both these views are exceptional. Usually, at any collective bargaining conference, the workers are pressing for higher wages and fringe benefits than management wishes to pay.[8]

What will be the terms of the final agreement? Unfortunately, this is one important question that no economic theory can answer with precision. The game-theoretic result depends on psychology, politics, and countless intangible and unpredictable factors. As far as the economist is concerned, the final out-

---

[8] Part of the wage demand might take the form of a demand for pensions, a welfare-insurance fund, or a fund to soften automation's impact; but the same principles apply.

come is in principle indeterminate—as indeterminate as the haggling between two millionaires over a fine painting.

Eight main arguments will be appealed to during the bargaining:

1. If the cost of living is rising, the union economist will talk a great deal about the workers' *standard of living*; but if prices are falling, the employer brings this up.

2. If the company and industry have been prosperous, the union will stress *ability to pay*; but if the industry has had low profits, the employer will emphasize this fact.

3. If *productivity* has risen or fallen recently, this will be brought into the negotiations by one of the interested parties.

4. If other firms in the same area are paying *going wages* higher or lower than the firm in question, this fact will be brought out.

5. Labor will extol the philosophy of high wages as a means of bolstering *purchasing power* and national prosperity; management will emphasize the higher-cost aspects of wage increases.

6. If a *national pattern* of "fourth- or *n*th-round" wage increases of so much per hour has already been set by a few "key bargains" in large industries such as pulp, steel, or automobiles, that will have a great weight in the deliberations.

7. North American workers and employers have grown accustomed to steady money-wage increases. Almost as certainly as spring brings robins, it brings wage increases. So General Motors and many other firms build into their wage agreements a steady upward trend—the so-called "improvement factor." This may mean an average 3 to 4 per cent wage boost each year in addition to any cost-of-living escalator wage clauses.

8. The government may set forth *guideposts* for wages and prices as part of an "incomes policy," and these may be appealed to or ignored depending on the interests of the bargaining parties. As we shall see in Chapter 40, such guideposts broadly aim to have money wages increase with the *average* trend increase of *national* productivity: then if prices are lowered in industries of above-average productivity growth and raised in those of below-average, the general price level can be stable and customary wage-property shares be preserved.

Most often labor and management will arrive at a new yearly contract after some days of negotiation. But sometimes when they get stalled, a government conciliation officer may try to narrow down the few-cents disagreement. Then a conciliation board may be appointed to make a report to the government and to the two parties. Unfortunately, economic theory cannot tell us how such a board will arrive at its final decision. All the previously mentioned factors will be weighed, plus the all-important question, What decision is likely to be *acceptable* to both sides?

STRIKES AND COLLECTIVE BARGAINING   Both sides realize that failure to reach agreement will mean a costly strike. It may sometimes happen that management refuses to go above $3.75 an hour while labor refuses to take less than $3.80. A "work stoppage" will result. Should we call this an "employees' strike" or an "employer's lockout"? In popular speech, it will certainly be referred to as a strike. But since either party knows it can end the work stoppage by agreeing to the other party's terms, we could call it either.

Newsmen ask why workers go out on strike just because of a 5-cent disagreement; they point out that it might take two or three years for the workers to recover—at 5 cents an hour—their loss of earnings during the strike. But the workers look at it differently. To them the employer caused the strike by his stubbornness. They point out that the employer will lose more by the strike than refusing the extra 5 cents would save him in many years.

Actually, a strike is *not* over just the last 5 cents disagreement! The workers believe that the employer would not have been forced from $3.50 up even to $3.75 except for the threat of a strike, which hangs over the negotiation like a time bomb. To keep the bomb from going off, both sides must agree.

Threats become hollow unless occasionally carried out. Both parties must show that they are truly prepared to incur at some point the costs of a strike. Thus, suppose the employer was deprived, voluntarily or by law, of the right to refuse any wage demand if it would bring on a strike. Would this cost him only 5 cents an hour? Obviously not. There would then be no reason why the union might not hold out for a 50- rather than a 25-cent wage increase. Similarly, if the union could never exercise the right to strike, why should not the employer offer $2.75 rather than $3.75 per hour if he can get labor at that rate?

■ RESULTS FROM RECENT RESEARCH: QUALIFICATIONS

Patient research by labor economists has cast light on other aspects of the central importance of the union in the worker-market.

STRIKE PRONENESS   The outline of the factors influencing the elasticity of derived demand (on page 674) would suggest that certain kinds of industries would grant wage increases without much quarrel, while in others they would be achieved only reluctantly, and perhaps after frequent resort to strikes. Remember that wage increases tend to follow changes in the cost of living, profits of the employer, or higher wages elsewhere. Thus the demand curve does not stay still through time. Still, other things being the same, economists have tended to look to the elasticity of demand for a region or industry's final product as one source of explanation of different tendencies to strike or to lose days of work in disputes.

On the whole, this kind of explanation does not work. True, certain industries and regions do lead others broadly in strike proneness: Canada tends to lead the United States; British Columbia to lead Canada; mining to lead dry cleaning; and men to go on strike more than women. But these are only broad tendencies. Furthermore, economists have not been able to use elasticities of supply or demand to explain them, in particular cases.

Instead, labor economists like California's Clark Kerr and Abraham Siegel, and the University of British Columbia's Stuart Jamieson have found that *sociological* characteristics of the workers in an industry are the best explanation of why they strike more than men in other industries. One of the chief of these is "isolation": miners and workers in the woods are physically isolated from other contacts except with each other, the job, and the bosses; and city workers of certain ethnic origins or in certain occupations (like longshoremen) are also isolated from the rest of the urban labor force. Indeed, they suggest that a whole country's strike proneness may be better understood by examining the number of such "isolated" industries than by looking for special economic aspects of the country's industries or labor markets.

CAN UNIONS RAISE WAGE RATES?   The advocates of organized labor claim unions have raised real wages; the critics blame unions for having done just that and for having thereby distorted the efficient use-pattern of resources. Despite this agreement that unions raise real wages, the true facts are not all clear.

This finding raises the question: how would theory suggest unionism would make a difference? There are two kinds of answers. The first is to assert that a unionized industry should make greater wage gains than a nonunionized industry. (This is not a very convincing claim: would a unionized obsolescent farm-wagon industry make greater wage gains than a nonunionized computer industry? Still, if the unions are widely spread over many kinds of industry, the test has some interest.) Studies of the U.S. economy since the burst of union organization in the 1930s show a poor result for unions. Low-paid, unorganized workers like domestic servants and farm workers have made the greatest percentage and the greatest absolute wage gains. In fact, the *percentage* differentials between them and organized workers have been diminishing, as simple arithmetic would show they must. (For example, suppose you are a unionist earning $4 an hour, and I earn $2 in a nonunion trade. Now we both get a $1 increase; this leaves the absolute differential unchanged; but you no longer get twice my wage; instead you receive $5 to my $3.)

Ottawa's Sylvia Ostry found that, although in the decade 1945-1955 Canada's wage structure was not "compressed" (i.e., in the decade the differentials between wages paid to different occupations and industries did not narrow), unionism had no pronounced effect on maintaining the structure. In other countries, long-run trends do show a narrowing of differentials; but these trends are fairly independent of the growth of unions.

It is true that the average wage in unionized industries is about 20 per cent higher than the average wage in nonunionized industries. But that in itself does not prove that unions are responsible for the difference. The industries that are unionized tend also to be those dominated by large rather than small enterprise and by firms which use workers of higher-than-average skills. Even before they were unionized, these same industries paid higher-than-average wages.

On the other hand, well-known studies by Arthur Ross, Lloyd Reynolds, and others present U.S. data in which it appears that since the mid-1930s, *recently*-unionized industries have gained greater wage increases than nonunionized industries, and also greater than *long*-unionized industries. This suggests that the wage impact of the union may be only in its early years, not over its whole life.

ONE WARNING   Such statistics on the differential movements of union and nonunion wages cannot give the whole answer to the question whether unions have raised wages. Labor spokesmen claim that unions also help raise wages for the unorganized workers. Thus, a nonunion industry's policy may be to follow any changes in the wage scale hammered out in unionized plants nearby. If an industry raises wages in order to keep the union out, the figures will give the union no credit for its indirect influence. On the other hand, suppose the targets for union organizers are profitable, expanding, high-productivity, concentrated industries; then the union may be riding aboard a moving demand curve and be given credit for wage increases that would have occurred even in its absence. Which is cause and which effect?

PITFALLS IN THE CONCEPT OF A GENERAL DEMAND FOR LABOR   A second important warning must be given. It is legitimate to draw up a demand curve of the usual general shape for one *small* labor market: as long as *all other* prices and wages are more or less unaffected, it is indeed true that a higher money wage in one sector is the same as a higher real wage there; it is true also that employment there can be expected to fall off somewhat at the higher wage.

But remember the fallacy of composition. What is true for any *small* sector of the economy need not be true for the *whole aggregate*. If all wage rates rise, it is dangerous to suppose that commodity prices will remain constant. Thus, doubling all money wages *might* well result in a doubling of all prices. Were that the case, the real wage would not be changed at all. And hence, in a diagram such as Fig. 28-1, we should be moving neither upward nor downward on the demand curve. (Turn to Fig. 28-1 and note that the vertical axis represents real wages in dollars of *constant purchasing power*.)

Remember that wages are not simply costs: they also represent *incomes* of most of the population. Therefore the sales revenue of business enterprises is vastly affected by a substantial change in wage levels. Since the demand for labor is a demand derived from the demand for business products, it is clear that any change in general wages must shift the general demand curve for labor. Hence, it is dangerous to argue in terms of an unchanged demand curve for labor.

To illustrate this pitfall, ask the following question: In 1932 when there was widespread unemployment, would an all-round cut in money wages have *increased* employment? Or, as claimed by the trade-unionists, would such a decrease in general money wages have decreased "purchasing power" and *decreased* employment?

To the extent that a halving of wages would result in a halving of all prices, of all money incomes, and of all money spending, the answer must be obvious. Such a completely balanced deflation would neither help nor hurt the unemployment situation.[9] This serves as a warning against accepting the superficial claims of those critics of labor who argue in terms of simple *dd* curves, and of those friends of labor who argue in terms of "purchasing power."

SUMMING UP   We may cautiously conclude discussion of the economic effects of unions by quoting in turn from two leading students of labor economics, Princeton's Albert E. Rees and Yale's Lloyd G. Reynolds. According to Rees,[10]

> "We tend to overemphasize the role of the unions, both in . . . their own industries and . . . the economy as a whole. . . . The other two thirds may have their wages and salaries influenced by what the unions do, but I feel there are very strong independent forces on the demand side that govern their rates of pay. . . . Even in the . . . unionized [one third] there are some very weak or almost impotent unions that have had very little to do with the wages of their members. . . .
>
> "In a series of rough guesses, I would say perhaps a third of the trade unions have raised the wages of their members by 15 per cent to 20 per cent above what they might be in a nonunion situation; another third by perhaps 5 per cent to 10 per cent, and the remaining third not at all. . . . The high figures tend to be found, not in periods of inflation, but in periods of prosperity combined with stable prices. . . . In [an inflationary] period like 1946-1948, for example, the union people may even lag behind simply because of the rigidities involved in the collective bargaining process."

And Reynolds states the following conclusions of his researches:

> "Summing up these diverse consequences of collective bargaining, one can make a strong case that unionism has at any rate not worsened the wage structure. We are inclined to be more venturesome than this, and to say that its net effect has been beneficial. This conclusion will doubtless strike many economists as surprising. . . .
>
> "Fears that complete unionization will bring seismic disruption of the wage structure do not seem to be well founded. . . . The countries with the strongest

---

[9] Today most economic theorists believe that the favorable effects during recession of any overall general wage cut will depend upon how it affects the balance of saving and investment, or total real demand. If (1) lower wages cause prices to drop and (2) people's cash and holdings of government bonds do not drop in proportion, then the increase in people's real wealth may have expansionary effects on the real propensity to consume and on employment. But falling prices may aggravate debts and bankruptcy and, by making people pessimistic, may harm investment; consequently, most advanced treatises in economics seem to advocate expanding people's real wealth and real consumption schedule by means of expansionary bank and financial policy rather than by deflation. (Chapter 17's Appendix discusses this so-called "Pigou effect.")

[10] The Rees' quotation is from *Wage Inflation* (National Industrial Conference Board, New York, 1957), pp. 27-28; the Reynolds' quotation, from L. G. Reynolds and C. H. Taft, *The Evolution of Wage Structure* (Yale University Press, New Haven, 1956), pp. 194-195. Cf. the following quote from Sumner Slichter, J. Healy, E. R. Livernash, *The Impact of Collective Bargaining on Management* (Brookings Institution, Washington, 1960), p. 951: "Collective bargaining seems to have greatly encouraged the development of management . . . companies that have been relatively successful in union-management relations gave evidence of following wise basic policies, of negotiating balanced general policies, of developing good implementing and procedural arrangements to make policy effective at the operating level, and of having considerable initiative in labor relations administration. The challenge that unions presented to management has, if viewed broadly, created superior and better-balanced management, even though some exceptions must be recognized."

union movements appear to have a wage structure which is more orderly and defensible than the wage structure of countries where unionism has been weak."

In Part Six's Chapter 40 we shall face the important problem, as yet unsolved, of finding an "incomes" or "guidepost" policy that will make full employment compatible with reasonably stable price levels.

SUMMARY

A. WAGE DETERMINATION UNDER PERFECT COMPETITION

■ 1 In perfectly competitive equilibrium, if all men and jobs were exactly alike, there would be no wage differentials. The equilibrium wage rate would be determined by supply and demand. To the extent that Country A has (1) more natural resources per worker than Country B and (2) better productive methods (because of capital availability and technical knowledge), to that extent the competitive wage in A is likely to be higher than in B.

■ 2 The law of *diminishing returns* suggests that a reduction of labor relative to natural resources might be expected to raise real wages. While this principle lies behind labor's immigration policy and similar restrictions, historical examples of economies of mass production do point to the operation of a countertendency of *increasing returns*. In theory, the *"optimum* population" size is at the point where the two countertendencies have reached a balance of maximum per capita income.

■ 3 Though Malthusian overpopulation threatens many an underdeveloped country such as India, there is no tendency for population growth in Canada and developed nations to push real wages down to a minimum-subsistence level. Pressure exerted on real wages by the "reserve army of the unemployed" tends to depress real wages only to the *equilibrium* level. In the Western world, this equilibrium wage is much above the physiological *subsistence* level and increases with every decade.

■ 4 Fear of unemployment leads often to acceptance of the "lump-of-labor" fallacy. This belief that there is only a fixed amount of useful work to be done may result from experiencing technological unemployment or depression. It lies behind much of the agitation for a 30-hour week and featherbedding work rules. But the problem of unemployment calls for policies to furnish adequate job opportunities, not for defeatist restrictionism.

■ 5 The supply of labor has four dimensions: population size, percentage of people gainfully employed, average number of hours worked per week and per year, and quality of effort of workers.

■ 6 As wages rise, there are two opposite effects on the supply of labor: The "substitution-effect" tempts each worker to work longer because of the higher pay for each hour of work; the "income-effect" exerts influence in the opposite direction—in that higher wages mean that workers can now afford more leisure along with more commodities and other good things of life. At *some* critical wage, the supply curve may bend backward. The labor supply of very gifted, unique people is probably quite inelastic; their wages are likely to contain a large element of so-called "pure economic rent."

■ 7 Once we drop the unrealistic assumptions concerning the uniformity of people and jobs, we find that substantial wage differentials will characterize even a perfectly competitive labor market. "Equalizing wage differences," which compensate for nonmonetary *differences in disutility* between jobs, explain some of the differentials.

■ 8 But differences in the *quality* of various grades of labor are probably the most important cause of wage differences. Although it cannot be claimed that labor consists of wholly "noncompeting groups," it is nonetheless true that there are innumerable categories of partially competing groups. When the relative wage of one category rises, there are substantial cross-elasticity effects on labor supply as some people switch to the improved-pay occupation. The final pattern of wages would, in a perfectly competitive labor market, be determined by the general equilibrium of the interrelated schedules of supply and demand, as shown in the classification of general equilibrium in Table 28-1.

B. IMPERFECTIONS OF THE LABOR MARKET

■ 9 Labor markets are not perfectly competitive in real life. With unions or without them, employers usually have some control over wages, but their wage policy must be conditioned by the available supply of labor.

■ 10 Unions affect wages by (*a*) restricting labor supply, (*b*) bargaining for standard rates, (*c*) following policies designed to shift upward the derived demand schedule for labor, and (*d*) countering exploitation of labor by employers with monopoly bargaining power (i.e., by so-called "monopsonists").

■ 11 Relative increases in wages will in most industries result in less employment there. This is based on the assumption of a movement *along* a given demand schedule (i.e., no demand shifts from higher productivity).

■ 12 At the collective bargaining table the following are some of the determining factors around which argument is likely to center: (1) cost and standards of living, (2) ability to pay and profits, (3) productivity trends and improvement factors, (4) "going wages" paid elsewhere in the locality and in the industry, (5) the influence of higher wages on purchasing power and on the level of costs, (6) the "national pattern" as determined by "key bargains" in important industries, (7) continuous increases based upon improvement factors from long-term technical improvements, and (8) government guideposts designed to keep increases in money wages in line with *average* productivity increases of the economy, with prices coming down in industries of over-average productivity increase by enough to cancel out price increases in industries of below-average productivity increase. Economic theory cannot tell just what the final wage bargain will be, it being theoretically indeterminate.

■ 13   Usually a compromise settlement will be possible, without government intervention, formal arbitration, or a strike. But the *threat* of strike is ever-present and conditions the whole bargaining procedure. In vital industries, however, the interest of the public transcends the individual interests and rights of the disputing parties; consequently, voluntary collective bargaining is on trial in such strategic areas and is subject to government controls whenever damaging work stoppages occur.

■ 14   Historically, the extent to which unions have succeeded in raising wages is in doubt. Since the mid-1930s union membership has greatly increased, but in this same period wage differentials seem to have remained about the same in absolute terms. There seems to have been in North America and abroad a narrowing of percentage wage differentials. While it is true that *recently unionized* industries seem to show slightly greater wage increases since the mid-1930s, the quantitative difference is not great and it is not clear as to which is cause and which effect. Heavily concentrated and expanding industries may have been targets for unionization, and the high wages may have been the result of factors associated with or causing unionizing rather than of unionization as such.

■ 15   A final warning is in order: We must beware of the fallacy of composition in ascribing to the *demand curve for labor in general* the shape characteristic of the *demand curve for one small category of labor*. Wages are more than costs; they also constitute much of the income of consumers and heavily react back upon the demand for products of business. A general change in money wage rates can be expected to have important effects on prices. It is even possible that real wages will not change at all. To the extent that a general wage change is balanced by an equivalent percentage change in *all* prices, little substantive effect upon unemployment may result.

QUESTIONS FOR DISCUSSION

1.   Explain narrowing of wage differentials from competition of like people.

2.   What factors of technology, economic geography, and legislation help to determine the level of real wages? Show how diminishing returns and countertendencies are linked with the theory of optimum population.

3.   Define and contrast "equalizing and nonequalizing differences in wages." Which concept is exemplified by high wages that contained much "pure economic rent"? What about noncompeting groups?

4.   Give a list of imperfections in the labor market. Show that not all are related to monopoly power or to trade-union organization.

5.   Give three ways unions try to influence wages, as described in this chapter. Contrast the first two, and gauge their importance. Do the same for the third method.

6.   "Unions can raise real and money wages in a particular industry, but the result will be less employment." Evaluate, utilizing the elasticity of demand for labor.

7.   What is the public interest in voluntary collective bargaining?

8. Explain dangers involved in treating the general demand for labor like a particular group's demand. Show that wages are costs *and* sources of demand.

9. Prime Minister Trudeau tried in the 1970s to keep the government out of collective bargaining. Do you think this is possible; in a (*a*) rail strike, (*b*) steel strike, (*c*) long-shoreman or teamster strike, (*d*) one-town-newspaper strike, (*e*) auto strike, (*f*) postal strike? Where do you draw the line?

10. Review your understanding of the following concepts:

general equilibrium	noncompeting groups
optimum population	standard rate
subsistence wage level	monopoly-employer exploitation
backward-bending supply curve	elastic, inelastic derived demand
income- versus substitution-effect	collective bargaining
rent element in wages	strike, lockout, work stoppage
equalizing and nonequalizing wage	percentage and absolute differentials
differences	"incomes policy"

29

INTEREST
AND CAPITAL

How to have your cake and eat it too: lend it out at interest: ANONYMOUS

The last chapters have sketched the determination of the rents of resources and the wages of labor. Now in this chapter we turn to the third great category of productive factors, capital; and to the determination of its special price, which is called "interest."

Capital theory is one of the most difficult parts of economic theory. For this reason, an introductory treatment cannot hope to grapple with all the important issues. It seems best, therefore, to proceed as follows:

The main part of this chapter summarizes in an uncritical way the basic notions about capital and interest found in every standard treatment of the subject. Then, at the end are briefly given some of the key qualifications that ought to be made concerning the oversimplified traditional treatment. For the Appendix are reserved certain special topics of classical capital theory and reference to the modern doctrines of income determination.

■ LAND, LABOR, AND CAPITAL

Our traditional account of capital theory begins with a rather arbitrary division of all productive factors into three categories:

1. *Natural resources* provided by Nature in fixed supply, which cannot be augmented or used up. The return of this inelastic factor is called (pure economic) *rent*.

2. Human *labor* resources, not produced in response to economic conditions, but taken by the economist as determined by social and biological factors.

The return of this human factor is called *wages* (which includes the salaries for brain and managerial workers as well as wages for manual workers).

In the oversimplified traditional account, factors (1) and (2) are called "primary factors of production"—primary in the sense that their supplies are determined largely outside the economic system itself. To them we must now add an "intermediate" factor.

3. Capital goods, *produced by the economic system itself* to be used as productive inputs for further production of consumption and other goods and services. These capital goods can be long- or short-lived. They can be rented out in the competitive market just the way acres of land or hours of labor can be rented out. Their rents—or perhaps we might use the term "rentals," to avoid confusion with pure economic rent to natural resources in fixed supply—these rentals of capital goods are determined by the same demand conditions of marginal productivity discussed previously.

> However, in the traditional capital theory, the return or yield of capital is not taken to be the *rentals* of capital goods. What, then, is it? The yield of capital is the *interest rate per annum*, which is a pure percentage per unit time—independent of dollar or other value units. Of what is the interest rate 5 per cent per annum the yield? Obviously, it is the yield applied to the *dollar* value of capital goods.[1]

▪ CAPITALIZATION OF ASSETS

Now we can take a brief look at the important economic process by which capital goods get priced in the market at their "capitalized value." The interest rate plays a key role, and when this rate drops from a high to a low level, we shall see there must result a considerable rise in the capitalized value of machines, bonds, annuities, or any asset providing a stream of future property revenues.

To see how assets get capitalized, look at the simplest case of a piece of land or an annuity contract that is certain to pay you the *same* number of dollars each year from now until *eternity*. It turns out we can quite easily write down the formula for the present capitalized value V of any *permanent* income stream of $1 per year or $N per year. We ask, "How many dollars put out every

---

[1] In taking a census of total capital, we should not add to the 1-million-dollar value of a firm's plant, equipment, and inventory the 1-million-dollar value that its common-stock shares may sell for in Montreal. It is double counting to add the left side of a balance sheet to its right side. The value of all assets, or society's left side, should equal the *net* value of all individuals', rightside ownership: thus, if we reckon Crusoe's net worth by taking care to subtract from his gross assets his liabilities to Friday, the sum of their two net worths should equal the value of the island's goats, land, huts, and tools. If they are blessed with a government which has issued paper money and a public debt that cannot be expected to be retired during the lifetimes of Crusoe and Friday, they may very well include money and government bonds in their personal net worths; if they do, the sum of goat-and-other-real-assets will fall short of the sum of personal net worth by the amount of the ignored government liabilities and money.

year at the market rate of interest i per annum will give us exactly the same return of $1 per year or $N per year?" The answer is summarized in the rule

$$V = \frac{\$N}{i}$$

where V = present capital value (often called "present discounted value")

N = permanent annual receipts

i = interest rate expressed as a decimal (e.g., .05, or $\frac{5}{100}$, corresponding to 5 per cent)

Thus, if the interest rate will always be 5 per cent, any permanent income will sell for exactly 20 (= 1 ÷ $\frac{5}{100}$) times its annual income.[2] (To check our formula, realize that a principal of $20 at 5 per cent will yield $1 every year; so $20 must be the perpetual stream's capitalized value.)

■ NET PRODUCTIVITY OF CAPITAL

Now we ask ourselves this question: Why do people ever bother to transform the primary factors of labor and land into intermediate capital goods or into capital? The answer: It is a technological fact of life that you *can get more future consumption product by using indirect or roundabout methods.*

To see this, imagine two islands exactly alike. Each has exactly the same primary factors of labor and land. Island A uses these primary factors directly to produce consumption product; she uses no produced capital goods at all. Island B, on the other hand, for a preliminary period sacrifices current consumption; instead she uses some of her land and labor to produce intermediate capital goods such as plows, shovels, and synthesized chemicals. After this preliminary period of net capital formation, she ends up with a varied stock of capital goods, i.e., with a sizable amount of capital. Now let us measure the amount of consumption product she can go on permanently producing with her land, labor, and constantly replaced capital goods.

Careful measurement of Island B's "roundabout" product shows it to be greater than Island A's. Why is it greater? Why does B get *more* than 100 units of future consumption goods for her initial sacrifice of 100 units of present consumption? That is a technological engineering question. To sum up, the economist traditionally takes the following answer as a basic technical fact:

There exist roundabout processes, which take time to get started, that are more productive than direct processes.

---

[2] In the Middle Ages, they called this "20 years' purchase" and thus got around the taboo against interest. Show that 4 per cent interest means 25 years' purchase; 6 per cent, $16\frac{2}{3}$ years'. (See the Appendix for discussion of capitalization of nonpermanent income streams.)

NOTE: After land has been capitalized, its rent may appear as *interest* earned on its market value. In principle, *all* the nonwage part of NNP could be reported as interest on the value of property: if selling ourselves into slavery were not illegal, even wages might be reported as interest on the capital value of men! As is noted in Parts One and Six, investing in human capital by education and training is important: much of the wage of a high-income surgeon can be regarded as interest and return of principal on his father's or wife's investment in his training.

From this basic technological fact we can now draw an important economic conclusion:

> After allowing for all depreciation requirements, capital has a *net productivity* (or real interest yield) that can be expressed in the form of a percentage per annum; and the only reason you do not take further advantage of this opportunity to get more product by roundabout methods is that you must cut down on present consumption if you are to speed up capital's rate of growth and future consumption.

■ DEFINITION OF NET PRODUCTIVITY OF A CAPITAL GOOD OR INVESTMENT PROJECT

We need an exact definition of the net productivity of any capital project. We first calculate the original dollar cost of the factors you bought to begin each roundabout process. Then we calculate the total receipts that the roundabout methods give. We know very well that the receipts total must add up to more than the original cost total, else there is no net productivity. Having satisfied ourselves that there is indeed a positive net productivity, we need a way of measuring it quantitatively so as to make diverse projects comparable—projects involving apples and oranges, projects involving 50-year bridges and 5-month beer. Our final solution is to look for a measure that is a *percentage per annum*.

We end up defining the net productivity of a capital project thus:

> A capital or investment project's net productivity is that annual percentage yield which you could earn by tying up your money in it. What is the same thing, the project's net productivity is that market rate of interest at which it would just pay to undertake it.

EXAMPLE: I buy grape juice for $10, and a year later sell it as wine for $11. If there are no other expenses and no risk or effort to me, my interest yield (or "net productivity") is 10 per cent per annum—equal to $1/$10.[3]

As a community transfers part of its resources away from current consumption and toward capital accumulation, projects with lower and lower net productivity will be undertaken. Thus, this 50-year bridge with a net productivity of, say, 10 per cent will not be worth building if the market rate of interest is 11

---

[3] Here are two more examples. I plant a pine tree at labor cost of $50 plus 25 years' land rental cost—paid in advance—of $50, or $100 in all. At the end of 25 years the grown tree sells for $430. The net productivity of this capital project is then 330 per cent per quarter-century, which, interest tables tell us, is equivalent to a net productivity of 6 per cent per year. Or I buy a $10,000 truck. For 10 years it earns annual rentals of $5,000, but I pay $3,000 annually for fuel, driver, and maintenance. Its scrap value is zero. What is its net productivity or yield? The same as that of an annuity of $2,000 per year payable for 10 years and bought for $10,000. Compound interest tables for annuities show this truck's yield to be 15 per cent per year.

per cent. But when the market interest drops to 10 per cent or below, you will build the bridge.

The law of diminishing returns is invoked as more and more capital goods of all types become available to work with the limited supply of natural resources and land and with the more slowly growing number of workers. It implies that society and the private investors will run out of new projects with net productivities as high as the previous ones. And unless offset by technological innovations, this law of diminishing returns would work itself out in interest rates and investment yields falling through time. For without such a fall in interest, the low-yielding long-lived projects would not get undertaken.

■ A BIRD'S-EYE VIEW OF INTEREST DETERMINATION

We can now define the rate of interest and summarize the forces determining its competitive level.

> *Definition:* The market rate of interest is that percentage return per year which has to be paid on any safe loan of money, which has to be yielded by any safe bond or other type of security, and which has to be earned on the value of any capital asset (such as a machine, a hotel building, a patent right) in any competitive market where there are no risks or where all risk factors have already been taken care of by special premium payments to protect against risk.

> Thus, in an ideal capital market, the riskless rate of interest might be set by supply and demand at 6 per cent, just as the rent of fertile land is set at $20 an acre per year and the wage of skilled labor is set at $150 per 40-hour week.

That does not mean that I shall make a small loan at so low a rate to an applicant whom I do not know and who has lost three jobs in six months' time: I may have to charge him as much as 20 per cent per annum to compensate me for having to investigate him, dun him for collection, and cover the risk premium from default and costly litigation. Nor shall I buy risky mining stock that yields only 6 per cent. At any time there is a whole spread of interest rates for ventures of different riskiness, and this whole spread will move up or down when the pure, riskless rate of interest changes.

What are the changes in supply or demand that could move the pure interest rate up or down? Certainly, if scientists and engineers create new opportunities for capital investment, which have their *net productivities increased greatly* from the previous equilibrium, this will tend to bid up the market rate of interest. Contrariwise, if people become *less impatient* to consume now rather than in the future, their successful attempt to save—to shift resources from consumption-goods production to formation of capital goods—will bid down the interest rate, as more and more capital accumulation leads to diminishing returns and creates the need to take up capital projects with lower and lower net productivities.

As Yale's great expert Irving Fisher put the matter a half century ago:

> Supply-and-demand determination of the interest rate means that its level is determined by interaction between (1) people's *impatience* to consume now rather than accumulate more capital goods and (2) *investment opportunities* that exist to receive higher or lower net productivities from such capital accumulated.

The market rate of interest has two functions: it *rations out*, into the uses with highest net productivities, society's *existing scarce supply of capital goods*; and in the long run, it may (or may not[4]) induce people to *sacrifice current consumption and add to the stock of capital*.

■ GRAPHICAL DETERMINATION OF INTEREST

Supply and demand diagrams can amplify this survey of interest determination. But in the field of capital theory, they become rather complicated. At this point we can greatly simplify the exposition of the traditional theory if we agree to concentrate on the case where all physical capital goods are exactly alike. (Of course, in the real world, they are not all alike; and therefore advanced treatises have to go through a rather lengthy discussion to show how the diversity of capital goods is to be handled.[5])

Figure 29-1 on the following page illustrates how the interest rate is determined in traditional capital theory. Curve *dd* shows the demand curve for the stock of capital. Remember how the demand for labor was formed from the marginal productivity curve for labor. Similarly, the demand for capital is a "derived demand"—derived ultimately from the value of the extra consumption goods that extra capital makes possible. The demand for capital is made up of its *net productivity curve* (reckoned as a per cent per annum, as we have seen).

DIMINISHING RETURNS   We see the law of diminishing returns applying to capital as well as to other factors; that is shown by the *dd* curve's sloping downward; e.g., at levels where capital is very scarce, there are some very profitable roundabout projects that yield 12 or more per cent per annum. Gradually, through thrift, capital formation takes place and the community finds it has exploited all

---

[4] There is evidence that some people save *less* rather than more at higher interest rates; that many people save about the *same* amount regardless of the level of the interest rate; and that some people are induced to consume less only by the promise of higher interest returns. As we saw in the discussion of substitution- versus income-effects, in Chapters 21 and 28, economic principles alone cannot give us a decisive prediction. The bulk of the evidence suggests that the level of interest tends to cancel out of consumption and saving decisions, even though a rise in the rate paid by a trust company may bring it increased business because people will tend to transfer their assets from chartered banks or mutual funds (without their having altered consumption one bit). Some classical economists sought to justify interest as the reward for the pain of abstinence and waiting, just as they justified wages as the reward for sweat and psychic disutility. This gave rise to jests among Continental socialists concerning Baron Rothschild's painful sacrifices!

[5] See the Appendix's Fig. 29-3, page 732, for some further discussion of this problem and of the Fisher analysis.

Capital demand intersecting stock (supply) determines interest rate:

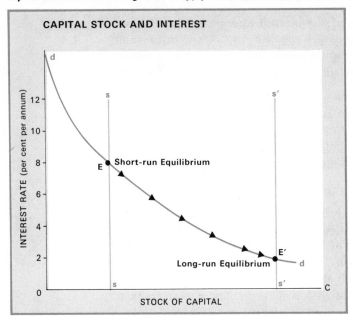

FIG. 29-1. Existing *stock* (supply) of capital intersects net productivity schedule to determine a moving equilibrium rate. Continued capital formation shifts *ss* sideward and leads to the indicated fall in interest rate along *dd*. Long-run equilibrium interest rate is at *E'*, where net saving ceases.

the 12 per cent projects; with total labor and land fixed, diminishing returns to the varying capital have set in. The community must then invest in 11 and 10 per cent projects as it moves down *dd*.

In Fig. 29-1, capital formation has taken place in the past until the existing supply of the stock of capital is given by the vertical supply curve *ss*. The equilibrium rate of interest must in the short run take place at the intersection of the *dd* demand curve and the *ss* short-run supply curve. Here's why. Below the equilibrium interest rate, there would exist too many investment projects; and the community's stock of capital is just big enough to take care of the projects yielding at least the shown equilibrium interest rate of 8 per cent.

SHORT-RUN EQUILIBRIUM   Why is the equilibrium at *E* only a short-run, moving equilibrium? Because 8 per cent is a rather high rate; and even though capital is currently scarce enough to keep us at *E*, people would probably want to go on saving part of their income there. This means the community will have capital formation continuously taking place; so as time passes, the community will be moving southeast on the *dd* curve as shown by the black arrows.

Specifically, (1) we move east because the accumulating amount of positive investment and capital formation means that the capital stock, and therefore the short-run supply curve, is being pushed more and more rightward. (In each new short run, the curve will again be vertical but farther to the right.) Now why does the interest rate move downward? (2) It moves downward because the law of diminishing returns tells us—other things such as labor, land, and knowledge of technology remaining unchanged!—that the net productivity of the increased stock of capital goods falls to ever lower percentages.[6]

LONG-TERM STEADY-STATE EQUILIBRIUM   The equilibrium at E is in the nature of a short-run equilibrium; short-run in the sense that people are still saving at the interest rate shown there. Capital is still growing, as is indicated by the black arrows; we are still moving down the dd curve. The interest rate at E is just big enough to keep us growing at the rate we are growing. But the interest rate at E is not yet low enough to choke off all desire to save, not yet low enough to make the community's average propensity to consume equal to 100 per cent of income.

It is at E' that *long-run equilibrium* is finally achieved. Again, the existing stock of capital is being auctioned off in the market for the highest short-run interest rate it can fetch. (You run vertically up the $s's'$ supply curve and read off the E' interest rate.) But now interest is so low that the net saving is zero; now capital stops growing, and the supply curve no longer shifts rightward. The arrows converge on E': at higher interest, capital would grow through positive saving and investment; at lower interest, it would decline through positive disinvestment and dissaving. So E' represents the stable long-run equilibrium that could prevail in the absence of technical change.

■ ANCIENT MISCONCEPTIONS ABOUT INTEREST

Before proceeding to criticize and qualify its oversimplifications, we can use the traditional theory of capital and interest to clear up some ancient debates.

FAIRNESS AND INEVITABILITY OF INTEREST   Pointing out that money is "barren," Aristotle said it was unfair to charge positive interest for loans. Many sophisticated medieval Schoolmen followed him in this view that interest represents unjustified usury. Indeed, throughout the Middle Ages, interest was forbidden by canon law; and many were the dodges to get around these restrictions.

How do we answer this view? First, we could point out what has been shown in earlier chapters—that holding a cash balance often does serve a useful function for which people will gladly pay up to a point. But let us meet the issue head on. Let us make the realistic assumption that when I borrow money from you, my purpose is not to hold onto the cash: instead I use the borrowed cash to buy capital goods; and, as we have seen, these intermediate capital goods are so scarce as to create a net product over and above their replacement cost. Therefore, if I did not pay you interest, I should really be cheating you out of the return that you could get by putting your own money directly into such productive investment projects!

[6] The process of accumulating capital goods faster than labor grows is important, and will be called "deepening of capital" in Chapter 36 (in contrast to mere duplication of capital goods to match a growing labor force, which is called "widening of capital"). The steady-state equilibrium shown at E' could, if population were growing at, say, 2 per cent per year, be a moving equilibrium in which capital is being accumulated *in balance* with labor, with no "deepening" but only "widening." See page 733, footnote 2.

CONSUMPTION LOANS   The Biblical utterances against interest and usury clearly refer to loans made for consumption rather than investment purposes. Suppose I, a poor man, borrow from you, a rich man, so that I can eat more today or pay a hospital bill. (1) Is it fair that I should have to pay you interest? (2) How do such consumption loans affect the short-run and long-run equilibrium interest rates?

The answer to the second question will help answer the first. Consumption lending is today less important than productive-investment lending; therefore productive investment primarily determines the behavior of interest rates.[7]

Now we can treat the fairness question. Are we assuming that there is effective competition in the money market for consumption loans so that no one —rich or poor—can take unfair *monopoly* advantage of anyone else by preventing him from borrowing at the cheapest available terms? If we explicitly assume effective competition *and* that people will not rashly sacrifice their future well-being just to consume more now, then it is hard to see why there is anything more unfair about *loan* transactions between rich and poor than there would be in *other* competitive transactions between rich and poor, e.g., when a rich butcher sells a poor consumer a pound of meat. Of course, the poor man would rather pay nothing for the meat than have to pay a positive price. But being a scarce good, the meat commands a positive price and one that changes with supply and demand. If the existing distribution of income seems unfair to the populace, the field of taxation would seem to offer the best remedies—not random interference with competitive loan or other market transactions.

IS A ZERO INTEREST RATE POSSIBLE?   In a world of perfect certainty, it is hard to see how people could ever save enough to bring the net productivity of capital all the way down to a zero interest rate. As long as there is a single hilly railroad track left, it would pay at a zero rate of interest to make it level. Why? Because over enough years, *any* saving in fuel would pay for the cost. As long as any increase in time-consuming processes could be counted on to produce any extra product and dollars of revenue, the yield of capital could not be zero. Also, as long as any land or other asset exists with a *sure perpetual net income*—and as long as people are willing to give only a *finite* amount of money today in exchange for a perpetual flow of income spread over the whole future—then we can hardly conceive of the rate of interest as falling to zero.[8]

---

[7] Nonetheless, to the extent that there is a desire to borrow now for present consumption purposes, we can take this into account in Fig. 29-1. If some people want to dissave, their consumption borrowing will make the community less thrifty as a whole than it would otherwise be. So we find the *ss* curve of the stock of capital shifting more slowly rightward; and we thereby progress more slowly downward on the *dd* curve from E toward E', with interest not falling so fast or far as otherwise.

[8] Under realistic conditions of uncertainty, we must qualify the above. Before you have recovered the costs of leveling the roadbed of the railway, airplanes might make railways obsolete—or earthquakes might undo your work. In 1932 people expected and experienced zero or negative returns from most capital projects. That is why investment ceased. Even today, if the profit rate (pure interest rate plus premium to cover risk) got forced down to 10 or 12 per cent before taxes, business as a whole might be unwilling to undertake an investment level equal to desired full-employment saving. See Appendix, page 733, for more on this.

A zero rate of interest is a little like an "absolute zero of temperature" in physics. We can imagine getting close to it, but we can hardly imagine actually reaching the limiting state of a zero equilibrium rate of interest. Thus, interest is a basic phenomenon that would not disappear even in the most ideal economic world.

INTEREST UNDER SOCIALISM?   Our economic analysis suggests that thinking is superficial if it concludes that interest is solely a monetary phenomenon of predatory capitalism. Students of planning in a centralized socialistic society have discovered that even such a society must introduce a concept like the interest rate into its plans. Every known society has, since Eden, had some limits on its supply of capital goods. Every society, therefore, has the important task of screening out investment projects, giving first priority to those that are most immediately productive of the things that society wants. Even in Utopia, you simply cannot do everything at once.

How, then, does the screening out among possible projects take place, so that definite priorities can be given? Clearly, there is no alternative but to choose (1) how much of present resources are to be used, and (2) how much of future useful products will be created. To reduce all the alternative patterns into a final single figure is not easy; but something like our earlier calculation of net productivities must be made. Unless you are satisfied to toss a coin or proceed by guess in your collectivist's society, *you have to introduce first those investment projects with the higher net productivity.* After much investment has gone into these in the past and diminishing returns has brought down the yield, you can go on to lower-net-productivity projects.

At some point, therefore, something like the interest rate necessarily comes into being. Recent studies show that the social engineers of the Soviet Union are anxious not to be denounced as capitalistic apologists, yet they need some form of interest rate (or "discount factor," or "pay-off period") for making efficient investment calculations. As a result, about a dozen different accounting methods are in vogue there for introducing a very thinly disguised interest-rate concept into Soviet planning procedures. But, of course no one necessarily receives interest *income* from them.

■ SUMMARY OF INTEREST DETERMINATION

We have now seen what determines interest rates over time. If Robinson Crusoe (or a Communist dictator or the average citizen in a free economy) cuts down on current consumption, then capital formation can be higher and capital goods can grow faster in number. The more capital goods there are, the lower their net productivities will tend to be. Why? Because of our old friend the law of diminishing returns: with population and natural resources unchanged, when you add more and more physical capital goods—or, what is closely related, when you make production more and more roundabout and time-consuming—you will add to total product, but generally at a decreasing rate.

When you have built the bridges, dams, factories, and production lines that yield a net productivity of 20 per cent, you have then to go on to investment projects with 19 per cent and still lower net productivities. The market rate of interest that can be earned on investments will thus fall, and this will be the signal for investors to undertake projects which were previously unprofitable at the earlier higher rates of interest.[9]

Two kinds of thrift are involved. First, people must resist the temptation to eat up some of the capital that was amassed in the past; they must "abstain" from consuming more than their current incomes, that is, continue to replace capital and abstain from making net saving become negative. Second, if there is to be positive capital formation, the community must usually be willing to undergo "waiting"—waiting in the sense of giving up consumption goods now in return for more such goods in the future.

All in all, consumption-saving decisions plus the technical net productivity of capital goods are needed to explain behavior of interest rates over time.[10]

■ SOME MAJOR QUALIFICATIONS

Now the main task of this chapter has been completed. But any traditional account of capital theory is in need of some important qualifications. This chapter concludes with only brief mention of the more important ones. The Appendix provides further discussion.

TECHNOLOGICAL DISTURBANCE In real life we cannot hold other things constant while the economy proceeds to accumulate capital and travel down the road of diminishing returns. In particular, new inventions and discoveries are constantly being made. Such technological changes will often raise the net productivity and the interest rates to be earned on the community's present capital stock and its future extensions. So, instead of there being a movement down an unchanged schedule, inventions may cause an upward shift of the net-productivity-of-capital schedule.[11] All this is not a fanciful possibility. Historical studies suggest that, for Europe and North America generally, the tendency toward falling interest rates via diminishing returns has been just about canceled out by technological progress: though real wage rates have been rising, the real interest return on capital has not been generally falling in this century, as would have been expected from the primitive classical analysis of capital accumulation of Fig. 29-1.

If technical change came to an end, the rate of interest might again march down toward zero or to the point where no saving took place. But, actually, new

---

[9] What is the same thing, a lowering of the interest rate at which we calculate present discounted values (as indicated on page 734) will raise more and more investment projects above their initial cost—and they will be undertaken to society's advantage.

[10] As we shall see, the government—through its monetary and fiscal policies that favor or retard the rate of capital formation and ensure against the paradox of aborted thrift—is also an important determinant of investment and interest rates. So two economies in which *private* individuals and corporations show the same thrift propensities may develop very differently over a decade or century, depending upon the policies being followed by government.

[11] Some inventions may be "capital saving" and twist the net productivity relationship downward, often tending to lower interest. (See Chapter 36.) Note that inventions may also destroy some capital by making it obsolete; and changes in consumer tastes can have similar disturbing effects.

inventions are constantly coming along to give interest rates an upward lift. Some economists (such as Schumpeter) have likened the process to a plucked violin string: other things being equal, the string will gradually come to rest as competitive capital formation undermines net yields; but before this can happen, some outside event or invention comes along to pluck it once more and to set it again into motion. (See Chapter 36 and its Appendix for more on this.)

UNCERTAINTY AND EXPECTATIONS   Our exposition of the traditional capital theory has assumed perfect foresight. This is a serious oversimplification. In real life no one has a crystal ball to read the future: all evaluations of capital and all investment decisions, resting as they do on estimates of future earnings, must necessarily be guesses—accurate guesses based on much thought and information in some cases, wild guesses in other cases, but in every case uncertain guesses. Each day we wake up to learn that our expectations were not quite accurate and have to be revalued; each night we go to bed realizing that the next morning will have some surprises for us.

The next chapter will show how significant uncertainty is for profit theory. Here, in connection with interest and capital theory, we must note an important effect of uncertainty:

Investors' optimism about future yields and risks can change markedly in a very short time; hence all relations will be very *shiftable*. They will shift with changes in opinion and rumor; with changes in population trends; with changes in technology and innovation; etc.[12]

SHIFTS IN SCHEDULES WITH INCOME   Even without disturbing outside factors, there is a serious drawback to traditional schedules. Changes in the level of *real income* profoundly *shift* classical saving and investment schedules at each rate of interest. (Only recall our long statistical and theoretical discussions of Part Two dealing with the propensity to consume and save at different levels of income. Also recall discussions of investment induced by increases in the level of income relative to fixed capacities of capital—or what is closely related, the "acceleration principle" of Chapter 13.)

Shifts of the basic schedules—as e.g., of *dd* in Fig. 29-1—represent serious weaknesses in the traditional theory. Many classical economists of a century ago were unaware of this problem because they had the comfortable view that chronic unemployment was impossible and income would not fluctuate. They did not always know why they believed full employment was inevitable. But they did believe that "supply always creates its own demand and general overproduction is an impossibility."[13]

---

[12] To illustrate this subjective volatility, Keynes once characterized the 1929 crash as "a sudden collapse in the [net productivity or] marginal efficiency of capital"—a true, but surface, explanation.

[13] For example, some believed in a miraculous law of conservation of market purchasing power: what was not spent in one direction they said *had* to be spent in another. A more defensible version of the theory claims that, if only wages and prices were never sticky, then flexible decreases in all prices and wages would ultimately so increase the real purchasing power of the coin and currency in each man's pocket as to reduce his thriftiness enough to restore full employment. The modern version of this hyper-deflation theory we have associated with A. C. Pigou, who did not recommend it for policy purposes. (See Appendix to Chapter 17 on Say's Law and Pigou effects.)

REAL VERSUS MONEY INTEREST RATE In Brazil interest rates often exceed 40 per cent a year. During the 1923 German inflation, they often were 1 million per cent per month! Canadians who bought government savings bonds a decade ago, with a nominal yield of $4\frac{1}{2}$ per cent, can actually buy less today with $100 than they could ten years ago with the $75 the bonds cost—entailing a "real interest return" of less than zero per cent.

These examples stress the need to define the "real interest rate" as the "money interest rate" minus "the percentage price rise." (Recall Chapter 14's discussion of the *real* rate of return, on page 333.) Thus, if the money rate is 8 per cent for Canadians and the annual price rise is 5 per cent, then the true real rate of interest is $8 - 5 = 3$ per cent. So to speak, 100 market baskets of goods lent today give you next year only 103 (not 108!) market baskets in return.

As people come to anticipate a steady rate of inflation, they build into their interest-rate supply and demand schedules an allowance for the inflation. They begin to prefer common stocks, shunning low-interest bonds. Thus in the post-1965 expansionary years, interest rates of 8 and 10 per cent became common. High rates? Yes, in money terms. But the calculated *real* interest rate held steady for 1965 to 1970 at the rather moderate level of 3 per cent.

■ PUBLIC AND PRIVATE POLICY IN DETERMINING CAPITAL FORMATION

Concretely, how does the modern *macro*analysis fit in with the valid elements of the traditional microeconomic theory? Here is its basic contribution:

Mix of monetary and fiscal policy determines rate of capital growth:

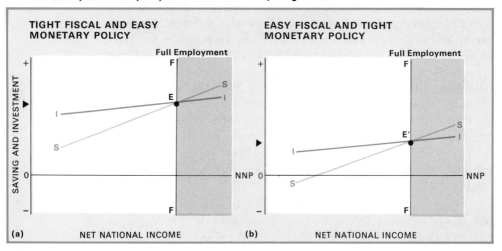

FIG. 29-2. (a) By tight fiscal and easy monetary policies, the first economy is causing full-employment saving and investment to reach equilibrium at E, with rapid rate of capital formation. (b) The second economy uses easy fiscal policy (low taxes and deficits) matched by tight monetary policy to create a low-saving-and-investment (high-consumption) full-employment equilibrium. Note that E' is much lower than E in investment.

Fiscal and monetary policies interact with private thrift to determine how fast society builds up its capital.

For example, consider a successful pattern of full-employment equilibrium without inflation. Recall that this requires the saving and investment curves of the theory of income determination in Chapters 12 and 13 to be intersecting at full employment, with no inflationary gap and no deflationary gap. Two instances are shown in Fig. 29-2.

The community's propensity-to-save-out-of-income curve will crucially depend upon budgetary fiscal policy. To see this, suppose tax rates are very high, so that revenues collected at full employment are very high relative to expenditure, the budget being overbalanced. Suppose, too, that the taxes fall most heavily on the relatively thriftless lower-income groups. Then the community's propensity-to-consume schedule will be a low one at every level of national income, including the full-employment level. The amount not consumed (equal to net personal saving *plus the government surplus*) will then be very great at every level and—what interests us here—SS will be great at the full-employment level of income shown in Fig. 29-2(a).

Would such a depressed consumption level cause unemployment? Not if macroeconomic management is working.[14] Aggressive easing of monetary policy (open-market purchases, reduced secondary-reserve requirements, lowered Bank Rate, and possibly aggressive selective credit programs) will push the community's investment schedule upward. Result: Tight fiscal policy plus very expansionary monetary policy have given us a full-employment income characterized by very high capital formation and relatively low consumption (see E in Fig. 29-2(a)).

We can work out the opposite mix of tight monetary and easy fiscal policies appropriate for a community that seeks a high-consumption low-investment full-employment income, as in Fig. 29-2(b). Looked at together, the two diagrams (a) and (b) show the alternative annual rates of capital formation in two societies, each characterized by the same degree of private thrift (as measured by family budget studies at each level of disposable income), but with alternative public policies. Note the resulting differences in capital formation, and remember that diminishing returns would be operating to bring down interest more rapidly in the high-investment society unless offset by special technological progress there.

A SOBERING PUBLIC RESPONSIBILITY   We conclude, then, with two reminders. Macroeconomic management can banish the paradoxical possibility of thrift becoming abortive and can in this sense validate the classical notions concerning capital formation and productivity. On the other hand, modern societies necessarily are engaging in monetary and fiscal policies—and it is these public policies that to an important degree do shape the resulting sharing of high-employment output (NNP) between consumption and investment.

This power over the community's rate of capital formation should constitute a sobering responsibility for the voters in any modern democracy.

[14] See pages 417-418 and page 736.

SUMMARY

■ 1   We can apply *primary* factors of production, land and labor, in indirect ways by introducing *intermediate* productive factors called *capital goods*. It is taken as a technological fact that this "roundaboutness" yields a *net productivity* over and above all replacement costs, expressible as an annual interest percentage and subject to the usual law of diminishing returns. (Read again the exact definition of net productivity.)

■ 2   To get the capitalized value of an asset, the interest rate is needed. It is also the device society uses to select investment projects that are most urgent and economical. When interest is high, only projects with highest net productivities can qualify. Gradually, after much past capital formation has invoked the law of diminishing returns, the interest rates will be falling. This provides the signal for introducing capital projects with lower net productivities.

■ 3   Thrift, in the sense of *abstaining* from consuming past capital accumulations and *waiting* for future consumption goods rather than consuming now, interacts with the technical net productivity of capital goods to determine the developing pattern of interest rates and capital formation. Even outside a collectivist world, government monetary and fiscal policies play an important role in this process.

■ 4   Even a planned state which is not run for private profit or gain would have to use some device like an interest rate as a sieve to determine which of the many possible investment projects represent the best use of the resources available today after present consumption needs have been determined. "Come the revolution"—come *laissez-faire*—Nature's law of diminishing returns is likely still to be in business.

■ 5   Consumption loans, while they are of minor importance today, do have some influence on the rate at which the community accumulates capital rather than consumes. Like the subjective factors of thrift, abstinence, waiting, foresight, impatience, and so forth, (1) personal borrowings do interact with (2) the technological fact of opportunity to invest in long-lived projects that yield a net productivity.

   Critics of interest had in mind the occurrence of consumption loan transactions in highly imperfectly competitive markets where the poor might be regarded as being at the mercy of the rich lender's bargaining power. Today no one would be in favor of usurious overcharges that take advantage of the poor man's inadequate access to competitive loan markets or his desperate neglect of his own future; but economists and philosophers recognize that the net productivity of capital is the technological fact most basic to modern-day interest: when you lend me money, you are giving up the opportunity to invest in land, machines, bonds, and stocks—forgone opportunities of which interest is the rough measure.

■ 6   Important qualifications of the oversimplified traditional capital theory include the following: Lack of perfect foresight means that the capital net productivity is very *shiftable* as expectations, technology, and income levels change. Also, a classical theory that ignores deviations from full-employment income does need modification. Finally, to get the real rate of interest, one must subtract from the money rate the anticipated percentage rate of price inflation.

■ 7 A great variety of compensating monetary and fiscal policies can succeed in maintaining reasonably full employment. Stable employment being assumed, Fig. 29-2 gives the needed qualification to the traditional theory; and it reveals that public policy has great responsibility for determining whether the composition of the full-employment national income will be heavily weighted toward investment or toward consumption; this means that the central bank and the legislature between them shape the environment within which private thriftiness provides one part of total social thriftiness.

QUESTIONS FOR DISCUSSION

1. Give some examples of efficient roundabout processes. Of "produced" or "intermediate" inputs.

2. Contrast three "prices" of capital: (*a*) rental of a capital good, (*b*) market price of the capital good, and (*c*) interest yield on the value of the good.

3. Irving Fisher wrote a book with the title *The Theory of Interest*. He gave it the subtitle *As Determined by Impatience to Spend and Opportunities to Invest*. Explain what these mean. Defend the following: "Fisher should have added 'and as affected by government monetary and fiscal policies.' "

4. "The interest rate was simply a bourgeois device for exploitation." Discuss.

5. Protestant, Catholic, and Jewish organizations today issue mortgages to build local places of worship, and they invest any surplus funds in bonds, or possibly, as in the case of the Church of England, in equity stocks. How might they ethically distinguish this from "taking usury"?

6. How do innovations and expectations affect traditional interest theory?

7. Interpret macroeconomic management in a modern mixed economy. Contrast full employment involving "tight money" and "easy fiscal policy" with an opposite full employment.

8. Explain the rule for calculating present discounted value of a perpetual income stream. At 5 per cent, what is the worth of a perpetuity paying $100 per year? Paying $200 per year? Paying $N per year? At 6 or 8 per cent, what is the worth of a perpetuity paying $96 per year? What does doubling of the interest rate do to the capitalized value of a perpetuity—say a perpetual bond?

9. Review your understanding of the following concepts:

net productivity of capital	abstinence and waiting
indirect, roundabout methods and diminishing returns	uncertainty and technological change
interest rate per annum	real versus money interest rate
capitalization by $V = \$N/i$	austere fiscal policy and easy monetary policy, or opposite
choosing among investment projects	public responsibility for rate of capital formation
zero interest under any ism	

Appendix: Theoretical Aspects of Interest, Money, and Policy

Here, very briefly, can be mentioned some elaborations and qualifications of this chapter's discussion.

■ PRODUCTIVITY OR IMPATIENCE?

Some people like to find a single cause for everything, and such people ask: "Is interest caused by the productivity of capital? Or by the fact that savers must be paid for the unpleasant task of 'abstinence' or 'waiting'? Which is more important: opportunity to invest or impatience to spend?"

Our previous argument shows this is a false antithesis. *Both* factors operate to determine the time path of interest: the impatience to spend, or the tendency to prefer the present to the future, limits the growth rate and attained size of capital; and the productivity factor tells us what is the interest or net productivity that can be earned as we have various amounts of diverse capital goods. Just as both blades of a scissors are needed to cut—so that you cannot say that one blade rather than the other is doing the actual work—similarly, both factors, impatience *and* productivity, interact to determine the behavior of interest rates.[1]

---

[1] Those who have mastered the indifference-curve graphs of the Appendix to Chapter 21 can use Fig. 29-3 to see that positive interest is caused by two factors: (1) a vertical bias of the AB production-possibility frontier between present and future consumption goods, and (2) a general vertical bias of the typical consumer's indifference contours between present and future consumption goods. Hence, the tangency-equilibrium at E has a slope steeper than 1.0, corresponding to positive interest. The experienced reader will recognize that these can be related to Böhm-Bawerk's three famous causes for interest. His third cause, technological superiority of roundabout processes, and his first cause, the expectation by the typical consumer that his future dollars will have lower marginal utility because his income will be higher in the future (as a result of technological progress or of the productivity of roundaboutness), relate to factor (1). Böhm's second cause—systematic time preference by consumers for present rather than future goods, for rational reasons of life's uncertainties and brevity or for irrational reasons—relates to (2). [Suppose we were to rule out factor (1) by making AB "symmetrical around the 45° line" and rule out factor (2) by making the indifference curves "symmetrical around the 45° line." Having thus ruled out net productivity and time preference, we should find that the equilibrium interest rate must then be zero. Leaving factor (1) in leaves interest positive.]

■ DETERMINATION OF THE INTEREST RATE

Can our account of interest determination avoid the use of Fig. 29-1's simplifying concept of a stock of homogeneous capital? Yes, in a number of ways, some of which are too complex to explain in an introductory work. Thus, we may work with a variety of different physical capital goods and processes, being careful never to add their heterogeneous units together, noting that the sum of their capitalized market values does depend (in a virtuously, and not viciously, circular way) on the market interest rate, and never forgetting that it is machines and not hunks of dollars which enter into physical production functions. If the realistic problem of uncertainty about the future and the risks thereby implied could be ignored, advanced treatises can show rigorously how an equilibrium interest-rate pattern can be\defined in such a heterogeneous model.

This is clearly not the place for such refinements. But it is desirable to mention that a theory of equilibrium interest rates can be given which avoids the homogeneous-capital assumptions of Fig. 29-1.

The key to a simple approach comes from Fisher's diagram, Fig. 29-3, in footnote 1, which states the following fundamental fact about the whole theory of interest:

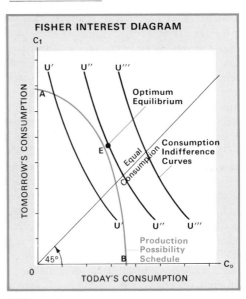

FIG. 29-3.

Society can exchange present consumption goods for future consumption goods at a trade-off rate depicted by the rate of interest.

LONG-RUN EQUILIBRIUM How long could this accumulation process of sacrificing current consumption go on? Just as Fig. 29-1 suggested, it can go on until the interest rate is zero, or until people want to do no net saving. At the zero rate of interest, if we could ever quite reach this point on the horizon, the plateau of consumption would be as high as is technically possible with the given labor, land, and primary resources. It would be a kind of "golden age."[2]

In real life three or more things keep us from reaching the golden age:

1. People may be so impatient that at some interest rate like 3 per cent, they won't want to do net saving.

2. Inventions will come along and offset diminishing returns by shifting upward all curves like dd in Fig. 29-1.

3. There is always riskiness in a dynamic society: long before the pure interest rate reaches zero, the profit-rate-inclusive-of-premium-for-risk may have hit a floor below which investment lags. We must examine this important matter.

■ AN UNCERTAINTY FLOOR TO RISKY RETURNS AND INVESTMENT?

It may be that under conditions of perfect certainty, persistent thrift can lead to no floor for interest except that of zero. But what about the real world where a measure of uncertainty must always be feared for any actual investment project? Can it not be the case that investors will dislike the task of taking risks on their shoulders? That they will insist on a rate of return on such investments which includes a certain definite positive percentage premium? Thus, even if the rate of interest to be earned on perfectly safe holdings were forced down to zero, might not people still insist on a 5 per cent after-tax return on a risky investment in a machine or in the purchase of land that produces an uncertain yearly rental?

This floor at 5 per cent, or at some positive level above zero, might be a realistic problem to contend with. And if it were to materialize, some serious problems for full-employment policy might one day arrive. Here is why: Suppose that Bank of Canada expansionary policies lowered the rate of interest on very safe short-term government bonds toward zero; this could be expected to bring the rates of return on risky enterprises down from, say, 12 per cent to 8 per cent. And since at the lower rate many new investment projects would now pay, an upswing in investment spending might result that, through the mechanism of the familiar multiplier process, would lift output, income, and employment.

But suppose all this were not enough to reestablish full employment. Then the Bank of Canada could do more of the same. *But by no amount of expansionary moves could it reduce the safe interest rate below the floor of zero.* And it might well be the case that a zero floor on safe holdings could pull the rates on risky investment down only to their floor of 5 per cent—and no further. Then it would be quite conceivable that the sticky 5 per cent floor would bar further reduction in rates needed to coax out a pace of current job-giving investment big enough to restore full employment.

Therefore it is conceivable that an impasse, a kind of Day of Judgment for our mixed system with its inflexible wage and price levels, might arrive when conventional measures to stimulate investment could not restore full employment and let our optimistic "managed money" work itself out smoothly and fully.[3]

---

[2] Advanced books show that this golden rule must be modified if primary resources such as labor are *all* growing at 3 or 5 per cent per year. Then the golden age of maximal per capita consumption comes when the interest rate has been brought down also to 3 or 5 per cent: then the young earners in society, who are saving for their old age, are just enough more numerous than the retired earners, who are eating up what they had earlier saved; and then there is just enough net saving and investing to keep all capital goods growing in full proportion to the growth in primary labor. Then we have an equilibrium, a nice moving equilibrium with balanced growth. (If land will not grow at all, Malthus reminds us that this Eden must, in the absence of inventions, come to an end with ultimate stationary population.)

[3] Without risk the problem of placing my assets is easy. I put all my wealth in Bank A if it offers me 5¾ per cent while Bank B offers only 5 per cent. I put all my wealth in building stores or tools if they offer more than Bank A's 5¾ per cent. So long as I know I can get any safe positive interest return, I hoard no money, keeping only minimal balances for transaction purposes. Without any risks, so long as interest yields remain positive, we should never run out of investment oppor-

While this pessimistic possibility may not now be at hand, a prudent society has to keep it in mind. And if that unhappy day should ever approach, more extensive remedial programs (such as insurance of loan risks or new institutions to provide venture capital) would have to be imaginatively explored.

■ MARKET CAPITALIZATION OF ASSETS EQUALS THEIR PRESENT DISCOUNTED VALUE

Here we can go beyond page 717's simple case of perpetual annuities to the general case. Under conditions of absolute certainty, anyone can borrow or lend as much as he wishes at the single competitive market rate of interest. Every asset must be yielding that same market rate of interest. This equality of yield results from the way competitors bid up or down the market price of any asset—whether it be a bond, stock, patent, going business, corner lot, or any earning stream of net rentals whatsoever.

What exactly is the formula for the capitalized market value of *any* asset?

Under absolute certainty, every asset will be capitalized *by the price bids of buyers and sellers* in the market place at the *present discounted value* of all its future net receipts. These dollar receipts cannot simply be added up regardless of the date when they are received. The farther off in the future a

given dollar receipt is, the less it is worth today. Why?

Because the positive market rate of interest means that all future payments must be *discounted*. A building far off looks tiny because of spatial perspective. The interest rate produces a similar shrinking of time perspective. Even if I knew you would pay $1 to my heirs 999 years from now, I should be foolish to advance you more than a cent today. To see why, let us review the arithmetic of this discounting process.

At 6 per cent interest I can set aside about 94 cents today, and it will grow to $1 within the year. Hence, the *present discounted value* of $1 payable a year from now is today only 94 cents (or to be exact $100/1.06 = 94\frac{36}{106}$ cents). The present discounted value of $1 payable in 2 years' time is only about 89 cents, or $\$1/(\$1.06)^2$. Similarly, any tables of compound interest will show how to compute present discounted values.[4]

The way to arrive at any asset's present discounted value is straightforward. Let each dollar stand on its own feet: evaluate the present worth of each part of the stream of future receipts, giving due allowance for the discounting required by its payment date. Then simply *add together* all these separate present discounted values. Thus we have arrived at the asset's capitalized market value, or what is called its "present discounted value."

Figure 29-4 shows this graphically for a machine that earns steady net annual rentals of $100 over a 20-year period and has no scrap value at the end. Its present value is not $2,000, but only $1,147. Note how much the later dollar earnings are scaled down or discounted because of the time perspective we have been talking about. The total area remaining *after* discounting (the light brown area) repre-

---

tunities and into unemployment problems on this account.

With risk, if I obey the law of diminishing marginal utility of Chapter 21, the Appendix of Chapter 20 showed that I shall avoid gambling and want insurance (since a gain in my wealth will be worth less to me than an equivalent *dollar* loss). Now I refuse to put all my eggs in one basket: I put some money in both banks in case one should fail; I prefer $5,000 in Canadian Pacific and $5,000 in Chemcell to $10,000 in either one alone; I buy many independent stocks for my portfolio; I particularly buy both war and peace stocks so as to be hedged against the worst that can happen. For safety's sake I always hold some idle cash even though it pays no interest. When the pure interest rate is below 2 per cent, I would just as soon hoard cash equal to a large fraction of my wealth or just as soon hold less. This is why Part Two's problem of great unemployment can persist—when a low investment schedule intersects the saving schedule at a point of low-employment NNP, and with profit and interest rates already at their bottom, there is relatively little that conventional banking policy can do in such unlucky times. Then we thank Providence for fiscal policy!

[4] The general rule for present discounted values is the following: To figure out the value today of $1 payable *t* years from now, ask yourself how much must be invested today at compound interest to grow into $1 at the end of *t* years. Now we know that at 6 per cent compound interest any principal grows in *t* years proportionally to $(1 + 0.06)^t$. Hence, we need only invert this expression to arrive at the final answer. Therefore the *present discounted value* of $1 payable *t* years from now is only $\$1/(1 + 0.06)^t$. What if the interest rate were 8 per cent per annum? Or *i* per cent?

Future dollar receipts are discounted to get their present value:

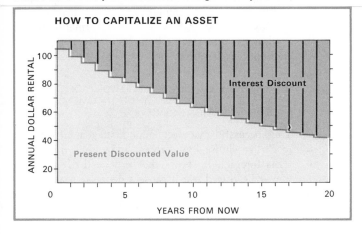

FIG. 29-4. The present value of a machine giving net annual rentals of $100 for 20 years (with interest rate prescribed at 6 per cent) is shown by the lower area. The upper area shows what has been discounted away. (Why does raising the interest rate depress the market price of an asset such as a machine or a bond? Note that the higher interest rate enlarges the discount area subtracted.)

sents the total of the machine's *present discounted value*—its capitalized market value.[5]

[5] Can you now verify our $V = \$N/i$ perpetuity formula? In high school algebra we learn to sum a convergent geometric progression

$$1 + K + K^2 + \ldots = \frac{1}{1 - K}$$

for K any fraction less than 1. If you set $K = \frac{1}{1 + i}$, you can with a little work verify our capitalization formula for a permanent income stream: write out *all* the discounted terms.

$$\frac{\$N}{1 + i} + \frac{\$N}{(1 + i)^2} + \ldots$$

$$= -\$N + \$N \left\{ 1 + \frac{1}{1 + i} + \left(\frac{1}{1 + i}\right)^2 + \ldots \right\}$$

$$= -\$N + \$N \frac{1}{1 - \dfrac{1}{1 + i}} = \frac{\$N}{i} \quad \text{[QED]}$$

But note that common-sense economics gives us an equally convincing proof: At interest i, $\$N/i$ is the only sum *whose earnings will exactly match the $N per year of income.*

(A FINE POINT: Sometimes you cannot be sure just which of two machines is the more "durable" one that will be brought into use at a lower interest rate. Suppose Machine A yields $100 of output one period from now and $132 of output three periods from now. Let Machine B yield $230 units of output two periods from now, and let it cost the same as A. Which is more durable? More capital-intensive? We can't say. At very low rates of interest, present discounted value or *PDV* of A

ACTING TO MAXIMIZE PRESENT DISCOUNTED VALUE   Our formula tells us how to write down in our balance sheets the value of any asset once we know how that asset will be used. But note that an asset's future receipts usually depend on our business decisions: Shall we use a truck 8 or 9 years? Shall we overhaul it once a month or once a year? Shall we replace it with a cheap nondurable truck or an expensive durable one?

There is one golden rule for giving correct answers to all investment decisions:

Calculate the present discounted value resulting from each possible decision. Then always act so as to achieve the maximum present discounted value. That way you will have more wealth, to spend whenever and however you like.[6]

exceeds *PDV* of B, since $100 + 132 > 230$. At very high rates of interest, *PDV* of A exceeds *PDV* of B, since the second and third periods' outputs are discounted away to almost nothing. But at intermediate interest rates, between 10 and 20 per cent per period, calculation shows *PDV* of B exceeds *PDV* of A, and B will be chosen. This "reswitching" phenomenon spoils any simple diminishing-returns story, as advanced treatises show.)

[6] This rule shows that business decisions in an ideal capital market would be independent of the decider's *personal* consumption-saving time preference. Why? Because it is always better to be able to sell out now for a larger money sum than for a small sum, no matter in what time pattern you decide to spend on consumption. In imperfect markets, personal time preference may matter.

■ MONEY, INTEREST, AND PUBLIC POLICY

Our final brief task is to suggest how the classical theory of interest fits in with the modern macroeconomic theory of effective demand and money.

Do changes in the amount of money affect the interest rate?

If you believed that employment was always full and that changes in money always resulted via a strict "quantity theory" in proportional changes in *all* prices, then interest rates would indeed be independent of monetary policy. This extreme classical version of neutral money is today believed by nobody to be applicable to short-run events. (Some economists would, as we saw earlier, grant it a measure of long-run validity, even today: refer back to Chapter 14's discussion of the "crude quantity theory.")

In Part Two we saw that an alternative to holding earning assets is holding money as an asset. Suppose people make no change in their current propensities to save and consume out of a given income when faced by a given interest-rate structure. But suppose they do decrease their desire to hold cash. Then they bid for existing stock, bonds, and titles to earning assets. This raises capital values and immediately *lowers interest rates*; it also may set capital to growing at a more rapid rate; but only after a time period of higher investment can the volume of real capital goods be appreciably increased. Unless offset by contractionary fiscal policy, all this will raise employment and/or expand wages and prices.

Note that the central bank can create exactly the same chain of events by engaging in expansionary monetary policies. (Recall from Chapter 16 the open-market operations, secondary-reserve rate, and Bank Rate changes, ...)

How do we reconcile this increase in investment that results from no change in personal thriftiness with classical notions? We do so by recognizing that moving interest downward and relaxing credit generally may raise employment and income and thereby increase achieved capital formation—thus sending us down capital's schedule of net productivity at a faster rate.

■ SYNTHESIS OF CLASSICAL THEORY OF INTEREST WITH THEORY OF INCOME DETERMINATION: REVIEW

The successful macroeconomic management referred to earlier shows how private and public thrift patterns interact. It shows that private thrift need no longer be feared lest it cause a depression and paradoxically abort itself. It deals with a well-running system that is kept near inflationless full employment by matching central bank and fiscal policies.

Thus, if we desire a high-investment full-employment condition, the central bank uses its "bag of tricks" to increase investment. Of course, given the community's private thrift patterns and technological-expectational investment patterns of the moment, we can stay at the full-employment level aimed at by the central bank only if Ottawa adopts a compensating fiscal policy.

What are the requirements of this compensating fiscal policy? Taxes and expenditure must be just contractionary enough to affect disposable incomes enough to cut the consumption propensity down to equality with full-employment product minus investment. (Describe what central bank and fiscal authorities must do to create full employment with high consumption, reversing all of the above steps.[7])

---

[7] See the Hicks-Hansen diagrams in the Appendix to Chapter 17. We can be, and stay, at full employment by having contractionary fiscal policy shift the *IS* curve rightward whilst expansionary central bank policy shifts the *LM* curve rightward. (Can you show how to engineer a high-consumption low-investment full employment by reversing this prescription?)

SUMMARY TO APPENDIX

■ **1** Technical opportunities to invest (to swap present consumption for future consumption goods) interact with people's subjective time preferences (about how much to consume or to add to the accumulated stocks of past capital formation) to determine the interest rate. As in all markets, *both* supply and demand factors interact.

■ 2 Avoiding the highly useful device of homogeneous stock of physical capital, we can still have a complete interest theory along Fisher lines. The interest rate equals terms of trade at which we can get next year's consumption goods for today's—106 chocolates next year for 100 today means a 6 cent cent interest rate per annum.

■ 3 The formula for capitalizing the asset value of a perpetual constant income can be extended when receipts are neither constant nor perpetual. Each dollar payable t years from now is worth only its "present discounted value" of $\$1/(1 + i)^t$. So for *any* net receipt stream $N_1, N_2, \ldots, N_t, \ldots)$,

$$PDV = \frac{N_1}{(1 + i)} + \frac{N_2}{(1 + i)^2} + \ldots + \frac{N_t}{(1 + i)^t} + \ldots$$

■ 4 Under conditions involving no uncertainty and no technical innovations, if the community insisted on accumulating more and more capital, diminishing returns might finally force capital's net productivity and the interest rate indefinitely down toward zero. Under real-life conditions of great uncertainty, there is the possibility that the floor on risky returns would be considerably higher than the floor of zero return on risk-free loans. So we cannot rule out the pessimistic possibility of a future Day of Judgment, where the authorities would have to supplement the orthodox methods by which the central bank eases interest rates if they are to succeed in coaxing out the volume of job-creating investment needed to keep employment high or full. But that day seems remote for mixed economies of the 1970s.

■ 5 The classical assumption that changes in the amount of money merely change the nominal price level and leave all relative prices, interest rates, and production and employment levels unchanged is in need of drastic modification in today's world, where wages and other prices are sticky in the short run, where wages may be hard to get down even in the long run, *and where the degree of unemployment may vary considerably.*

Increases in money (or decreases in people's desire to hold idle money) will often bid up security prices, lower interest rates, raise investment, and expand real and/or money incomes.

■ 6 But the classical analysis *can* be usefully applied if we make the New-economics assumption that central bank and fiscal policies will be so meshed as to preserve stable high-employment levels without undue inflation. (The central bank, so to speak, sets interest to achieve the desired investment level, and the fiscal authorities regulate taxes and expenditures to validate the needed thrift. Recall Fig. 29-2. Of course, both policies are to be *simultaneously* applied.)

QUESTIONS FOR DISCUSSION

1. After the H-bomb was discovered, my time preference for present over future consumption increased. After having learned that my uncle will bequeath me a fortune a decade from now, the same happened. Was this rational? Thinking of a lobster dinner tonight I offer you $6 on Saturday for $5 now. Is this irrational?

2. Two communities have the same technological production functions. Why might they show different interest-rate patterns in history?

3. Give reasons why lower interest rates might increase investment demand.

4. What might higher M do to interest? Why? What does higher income do? Explain why *independent* monetary and fiscal policies need not lead to full employment. Show that there is more than one investment rate compatible with full employment because of changing fiscal policies.

5. *Extra credit problem:* If a doubling of i halves the PDV of a perpetuity, can you show that the truck in Fig. 29-4 will *less* than halve in capitalized value? (HINT: The perpetuity has a rectangle that goes on forever, with its light brown area getting less and less. The truck lacks this infinite tail off to the right. Now the early year receipts get hardly changed in value at all, since (say) .96 is not much changed when it becomes .92. So the average change in all the truck's light brown area is less than that for the perpetuity. By similar reasoning establish the rule: Interest changes have their biggest effects on *long-term* bonds; their least effects on *short-term* bonds—whose principal will be repaid soon and is therefore hardly affected by any discounting.

6. Review your understanding of the following concepts:

abstinence, impatience, waiting
opportunity to invest
present discounted value
interest rate and planning
uncertainty
technical progress
public policy and capital growth

30

PROFITS AND
INCENTIVES

*The world will always be governed by self-interest. We should not try to stop
this, we should try to make the self-interest of cads a little more coincident
with that of decent people.* SAMUEL BUTLER

In addition to wages, interest, and rent, economists often talk about a fourth
category of income: profit. Wages are the return to labor; interest the return to
capital; rent the return to land. What is profit the return to?

The answer that economists give is a complex one. This chapter will show
that the word "profits" has many different meanings in everyday usage. From
these different possible meanings, the economist, after careful analysis, ends up
relating the concept of profit to dynamic innovation and uncertainty, and to the
problems of monopoly and incentives.

We shall first discuss the main notions of profit. The usual profit figures
bandied about will not check with any of these, as we shall see. Then, after
analyzing the main notions about profit, we shall conclude the chapter with a
summary of the role profit and loss play in the market pricing solution to
society's problems WHAT, HOW, and FOR WHOM.

▪ REPORTED PROFIT STATISTICS

When a United Nations or Dominion Bureau of Statistics statistician gives newspaper reporters a figure involving profits, what does he usually include?

First, he includes *corporation earnings*—whether they are paid out as dividends or retained as undistributed profits. (In some reports he includes and in
some he excludes corporate profit taxes, and sometimes he "adjusts" corporate
profits for changes in evaluation of inventories due to price-level changes. So
you must be careful in using published statistics.) He may also give a second
figure that has the flavor of profits about it, namely, *income of unincorporated
enterprises* (farmers, self-employed, doctors, partnerships, and so forth).

We understand how he arrived at such a statistical figure of profits for a corporation or unincorporated enterprise. From the sales revenue of the firm, he subtracted its costs: cost of materials, wage payments to employees, bond interest, depreciation, land rents, and the rest. What is left goes into the figures as profit.

■ FIRST VIEW: PROFIT AS "IMPLICIT" FACTOR RETURNS

To the economist, such statistical profits are a hodgepodge of different elements. Obviously, at least part of reported profits is merely the return to the owners of the firm for the factors supplied *by them*. Part may be the return to the personal work provided by the owners of the firm—by the farmer and his family, by the doctor, by the partners, or by corporate executives who also happen to be principal stockholders. Part may be the rent return on one's own natural resources; part the equivalent of interest on the owner's capital. (Recall Chapter 23's discussion, page 572.)

This shows us the first fact about profit:

> Much of what is ordinarily called profit is really nothing but interest, rents, and wages under a different name. *Implicit* interest, *implicit* rent, and *implicit* wages are the names economists give to this part of profit, i.e., to the earnings of *self-used* factors.

■ SECOND VIEW: PROFIT AS THE REWARD TO ENTERPRISE AND INNOVATION

Suppose we lived in a dreamworld of perfect competition, where we could read the future perfectly from the palms of our hands and where no innovations were permitted to disturb the settled routine of things. Then the economist says there would really be no profits at all! Here is what he means.

The statistician might still be reporting some profit figures to the press; but we know that, under these ideal equilibrium conditions, the *implicit returns* to the labor and property supplied by owners *would exactly swallow up all the profits reported*. Why? Because owners would hire out their factors on the market if they did not get equal rewards from using them in their own businesses. And because people who previously were hiring out their labor and property services would soon go into business for themselves if they knew they could earn more in that way.

Perfectly free entry of numerous competitors would, in a static world of perfect knowledge, bring price down to cost and squeeze out all profits above and beyond competitive wages, interest, and rent.[1]

We do not live in such a dreamworld. We never shall. In real life somebody must act as boss and decide how a business shall be run. Competition is never "perfectly perfect." Somebody must try to peer into the future to guess whether

---

[1] If people like running their own business, they may gladly take lower implicit wages. If, by contrast, people dislike having to boss other people and take responsibility for management decisions, then management wages may have to be higher.

there will be a demand for shoelaces or what will be the price of wheat. And in the world as we know it, there is a chance for a man with a brand-new idea to invent a revolutionary machine or a softer soft drink—to promote a new product or find a way to lower costs on an old one.

Let us call the man who does any of these things an *entrepreneur*, or *innovator*. Although it is hard to draw the line, let us distinguish him from the bureacratic executive or manager who simply keeps an established business running. Many economists—such as the late Joseph Schumpeter, Austrian-born economist who taught at Harvard—do not think of the wages of management as a profit: they think of the wages of management as wages—implicit or explicit, and high as they may be in the competitive market for gifted managers. But they think of *profit as the return to innovators, or entrepreneurs*.

Today it is easier for us to understand this distinction than it used to be half a century ago. We are all acquainted with huge corporations run by managers who own less than 1 per cent of the common stock. Even though these executives run the business, they are paid wages much like anybody else. Management of this type is a skill not different in kind from other skills, such as being able to keep books or supervise a production process. People who possess this skill are bid for in the market place, and like any other factor, they move into those jobs where they will receive the highest wages.

The innovator is different. Though he may not always succeed, he is trying to carry out new activities. He is the man with vision, originality, and daring. He may not be the scientist who invents the new process, but he is the one who successfully introduces it. Maxwell developed the scientific theory of radio waves; Hertz discovered them experimentally; but Marconi and Sarnoff made them commercially profitable. On the other hand, De Forest, who discovered the triode tube, also sought to put his inventions to commercial use; yet he went broke a number of times and on each occasion disappointed the hopes of investors who had put money into his enterprises. Many try; a few succeed.[2]

The dollars earned by the successful innovators are defined by some economists—like Schumpeter—as profit. Usually, these profit earnings are temporary and are finally competed out of existance by rivals and imitators. But as one source of innovational profits is disappearing, another is being born. So altogether, these profits will continue to exist.

■ THIRD VIEW: RISK, UNCERTAINTY, AND PROFIT

If the future were perfectly certain, there would be no opportunity for a bright young man to come along with a revolutionary innovation; everything would already be known. This shows that innovators' profits are closely tied up with

---

[2] Incidentally, the problem of innovation provides a partial defense of patents. Society deliberately gives a man a monopoly; this contrivance permits him artificially to keep something *partially* scarce. But society hopes that the offered bribe of temporary monopoly will encourage the invention of things that would otherwise be 100 per cent scarce.

risk and uncertainty. Frank Knight, a famous University of Chicago economist of the last 50 years, has an important theory that *all true profit is linked with uncertainty*.[3] Innovators' profits, discussed in the preceding section, represent one important category of uncertainty-induced profit.

> A factual examination of the great fortunes of the past shows a strong luck element in many of them. Oil discoveries, fortunate patents, marketing and speculative successes are examples of the chance elements in a profit-and-loss system.

In examining any profit figures, we must always keep uncertainty and risk in mind. We saw in earlier chapters that some low-grade risky bonds may appear to be yielding 10 per cent at the same time that high-grade safe bonds yield only 6 per cent. But if the chances are that 1 out of 20 low-grade issues will default on their principal in the coming year, then you are fooling yourself if you think that these bonds are a better buy. Actually, the extra 4 per cent may be no more than enough to cover the risk of default.

While people who buy lottery tickets face uncertainty, the promoter of the lottery faces no risk. He knows *he* will come out ahead. Similarly, a large insurance company may rely on mathematical laws of probability to reduce its relative riskiness. Why? Because the different risks tend to be canceled by each other if the numbers are large enough. To the extent that we can eliminate uncertainty by pooling and spreading risks, the problem of profits fails to arise. It arises only for the irreducible minimum of riskiness that remains.

In some years, the total losses may be greater than the total profits. Then risk bearers as a whole have paid out to labor, to capitalists, and to landowners more than those factors would have earned if the future had been certain. In another year, the algebraic total of Knight-defined profits may turn out to be positive—so that the factors of production have then received less than they would have if the future were certain. A big question is this:

Are risk bearers on the whole overly optimistic? As a class do they lose money and subsidize the other factors of production? Or are risk bearers as a class overly "pessimistic"—as claimed in most economics textbooks—so that profits represent a net positive payment for the service of risk bearing? Many economists think that businessmen on the whole act as if they dislike mere riskiness, and hence they must on the average be paid a positive premium or profit for shouldering risks.

RISK-PREMIA AS COSTS   All this means that for risky industries long-run costs of production must be high enough to include, along with wage and interest costs, *a positive profit premium* to compensate for aversion to risk and coax out the supply of risk bearing.

EXAMPLE: Wheat involves harvest risks due to weather. Production of syn-

---

[3] Frank H. Knight, *Risk, Uncertainty and Profit* (London School of Economics and Political Science, Series of Reprints of Scarce Tracts, No. 16, 1933).

thetic rubber does not. Suppose both involve the same wage costs per unit; suppose both involve the same capital outlay per unit. Suppose capital in rubber pays a sure return of 10 per cent, but that in wheat there are even odds that on each dollar invested you double your money or lose half of it. Your average return is then $\frac{1}{2}(2.00) + \frac{1}{2}(.50) = 1.25$, or 25 per cent per year. The 15 per cent premium, over and above the safe 10 per cent interest return, is competitively needed profit; and at the intersection of the long-run DD and SS schedules of the wheat industry, such profit will be included as a cost that must be covered.

We summarize the notion of profit as the reward of risk bearing thus:

If people generally act like risk averters, feeling that the marginal utility of the dollars they gain is less than that of the dollars they lose, they will prefer smaller steady incomes to erratic incomes even when those average out to a higher figure. Therefore *economic activities that involve much uncertainty and risk*, which will fall on the people who engage in them, *will be forced by competitive entry and exit of risk takers to pay*, over the long run, *a positive profit premium to compensate for aversion to risk*. The yield on capital invested in such industries will involve, in addition to pure interest corresponding to safe investments, an extra element corresponding to positive profit.[4]

■ FOURTH VIEW: PROFIT AS A "MONOPOLY RETURN"

We have noted three aspects of profit: (1) profit as *implicit* rents, wages, and interest; (2) profit as the temporary return to daring but unforeseen *innovations*; and (3) profit as the divergence—thrown up by the fact of *uncertainty*—between what people had *expected* to happen and what actually happened, tending to average out positive if people dislike risk and must be paid a positive premium to shoulder it.

If you point out the above to a person who feels vaguely critical toward profit, you may confuse him and make him uncertain as to what it is that he is against. His hazy notion of a capitalist as a fat man with a penchant for arithmetic, who somehow exploits the rest of the community, calls attention to a fourth possible meaning of profit, namely *profit as the earnings of monopoly.* Like most people, he may have an exaggerated notion of how much of each dollar spent on an automobile or a pork chop goes to profit receivers—according to any of our definitions. Most likely, he thinks that about 50 per cent of each dollar goes to wealthy monopolists; the prosaic truth is that, even in terms of the catchall statistical definition, corporate profits after taxes are less than *one-fifth* of corporations' wage payrolls (even after personal taxes).

PERFECT COMPETITION REDEFINED   Still, if we are to be objective, we must not close our eyes to this fact: In the world as we know it competition is not

---

[4] Other productive factors, such as labor in risky occupations, may also have profit premiums as bait necessary to keep them in the trade (e.g. fishermen on shares, miners on piece rates).

"perfect" as rigorously defined by the economist. Some elements of monopolistic imperfections do certainly exist. Perfect competition means that each seller has *absolutely no control* over price; it means that his demand curve is perfectly horizontal and *infinitely* elastic; it means that no person is able to control any significant fraction of the total of any category of productive resource.

We have seen in Chapter 24 and elsewhere that perfect competition is a far cry from the real world. Most firms, outside farming, can raise or lower their prices without losing or gaining *all* the customers in the market. Instead, their demand curves are somewhat sloped, and there is a discrepancy between price and marginal revenue. Most markets are imperfectly competitive—a blend of competition and monopoly. (So common a condition is by no means necessarily illegal or immoral but, as already seen, competitive imperfections have distorting effects on WHAT, HOW, and FOR WHOM.)

Now let us return to the fourth view of profits. When we examine the ownership of productive factors, we see that no two factors are quite alike. Your abilities as a worker and those of your neighbor differ somewhat. If we define your precise pattern of abilities as a separate factor of production, then we must admit that you do own and control an appreciable fraction of the total of that unique factor of production—100 per cent, in fact. Or you can be the sole owner of the patent to a particular process, or own the only site where the river narrows down to its most suitable place for a bridge. Or there may be no acre of Ontario land quite like yours.

Let us see how this ties in with imperfect competition. Your neighbors are a little different from you, certainly. But in all probability they are enough like you that the hourly wage rate for your services would not be appreciably higher even if you *withheld* some from the market. You really do not possess any appreciable monopoly power because the demand for the factor you own is for practical purposes infinitely elastic.

The same is true of your acre of good Ontario cornland. If you let half of it stand idle, the price of corn would not be affected; and the derived price for each acre of your land would be unchanged, even though you and your family know that there is no other farmstead quite like it.

And note this: If the land is sufficiently fertile, you will, of course, be making a fine living off your farm. Perhaps you may even be in the top 2 per cent of the income distribution. Even though competition is perfect, this rent return to the land you own *cannot* be competed away by rival farmers. As long as the Good Lord made only a limited amount of fertile Ontario farmland, it will earn a rent for its owner—regardless of how he originally acquired title to the land. *Competitively determined rents are the results of a natural scarcity.* They yield a "surplus" but not a pure profit.[5]

---

[5] If there is great inequality in the distribution of ownership of factors of production, then even under the most perfect competition (where pure profit is zero) there can still result a very rich, possibly idle, minority of plutocrats surrounded by masses of lower-income people. Recall Chapter 26's discussion of exploitation, pages 657-658.

■ "CONTRIVED SCARCITIES" VERSUS "NATURAL SCARCITIES"

It is quite a different matter if the demand for one of your factors of production is negatively inclined rather than infinitely elastic. (Let us review what this means: It means that, when you raise your price, you still can sell *some* of your factor; this is the sense in which you have monopoly control over price.) If you are the sole owner of an important patent, it will pay you to charge a price so as to limit its use. If audiences swoon to your singing as to nobody else's, then you will have to remember that, the more you sing, the lower will be the price the customers will pay for your singing. If you own the best site for a bridge, then you must be careful not to sell anyone else the lot next to it; otherwise he will be able to offer the bridge builders a site nearly as good as yours, and this will limit the dollars you can derive from yours. Part of the rent you earn on Nature's bridge site has a monopoly element in it by virtue of your withholding its use for fear of spoiling your dollar market.

What does all this add up to? It means that, *as soon as there is an appreciable deviation from perfect competition, it will pay you to take account of the fact that you will spoil the market the more you offer of your factor.*

Any prudent firm takes account of the loss on all previous units resulting when it sells an extra unit of product, and it is its marginal revenue—lower than price because of the loss on previous units—on which a prudent firm concentrates. Again with you as the owner of a factor: you are interested in the *marginal,* or *extra, revenue* that the factor brings you. You will not withhold all the factor from the market—that would bring you in *no* revenue at all. Nor will you provide so much of the factor that it becomes a free good and brings in no revenue. As a quasi-monopolist, or imperfect competitor, what should you do? You will withhold just as much of that service as will bring its marginal revenue down to zero.[6]

Our principle is this: *Under imperfect competition, it pays people to limit somewhat the supply of their factors.* By definition, natural scarcities are such that nothing can be done about them. But under imperfect competition, we encounter in addition so-called "contrived scarcities."

■ MONOPOLY EARNINGS AS THE RETURN TO "CONTRIVED SCARCITIES"

Hence, the fourth view of profits as a monopoly return is often reformulated in economics textbooks to read as follows:

Part of what is called profit is the return to a contrived or artificial scarcity. This return takes the form of rent, wages, or interest, depending

---

[6] Of course, there may be some discomfort to you in rendering the service, or you may have the opportunity of selling the service in some other market—as in the case where you could use your bridge site to grow corn. In these cases, you will obviously equate marginal revenue to some defined positive marginal *cost* rather than to zero. Toronto's Burton Keirstead has considered a theory of profit in which monopoly control over price reduces the risk of loss from innovation. Thus he combines three of the views discussed above. B. S. Keirstead, *Capital, Interest and Profits* (Oxford, Blackwell, 1959).

on the nature of the factor in question and on the contractual relations set up to handle the particular situation. (For example, an investor may buy the bridge-site land at the full capitalized value of its monopoly earning power. To him, the return will seem to be interest.) So monopoly profits are inextricably tied up with wages, interest, and rent.

Wherever contrived scarcities exist, they distort the optimum pattern of resource use. They may also create high earnings for the people involved. But high earnings do not always follow. Thus, under imperfect or monopolistic competition, there may be many taxicabs or grocery stores. Each owner may have a sloping demand curve and may be setting a price in excess of marginal cost. Yet there may be so many imperfect competitors that none of them is earning more than he could get in a perfectly competitive industry. Wiping out the imperfections and illegally contrived scarcities might improve the pattern of production, but it still might or might not have much effect on relative distribution of income. (See the Chamberlinian Fig. 25-3, page 620.)

■ ETHICAL ATTITUDES TOWARD PROFITS

Any sampling of public opinion shows some hostility toward profit. A statistician once asked a random sample of businessmen if they "tried to maximize their profit." To a man, they all denied this firmly, perhaps because they pictured a profit maximizer as some kind of chiseling extortionist or miser. But then the investigator asked the same businessmen whether they thought any change in their present price policies could be counted on to make them better off in the long run. To a man, they all replied that they were already doing as well as they could hope to do.

It is misleading to talk about "a profit system." Ours is a *profit-and-loss* system. Profits are the carrots held out as an incentive to efficiency, and losses are the kicks that penalize using inefficient methods or devoting resources to uses not desired by spending consumers. This metaphor of carrots and kicks is ancient, but apt.

Within the framework of law and custom—where it is both illegal and uncustomary to put sand in sugar—what does the pursuit of profit mean? It means that the businessman, like anybody else, is trying to get as much as he can for the resources at his disposal. (This is not different from what a worker is doing when he changes occupations or joins a union.) If competition is perfect, the businessman will end up with no *excess profits*. If competition worked perfectly, the attempt by all to reap excess profits would result in none succeeding. Competitors would have to run hard in order to stay in the same place! This is a paradox, but it is true nonetheless.

Would the competitive disappearance of profits mean that the businessman's land, acumen, sweat, and financing would go without reward? No, certainly not. Even under perfect competition, his factors would earn wages, interest, and rent. *Much of the hostility toward profit is really hostility toward the extremes of inequality in the distribution of money income that comes from unequal factor ownership*; this attitude to *wealth* should be kept distinct from hostility toward *profit* created by imperfections of the competitive process.

THE IMMEASURABILITY OF "PROFIT": TAX EFFECTS

How large are these four different categories of profit? We have no way of knowing. It would be nice if we could say that so many billion dollars of the reported total of profit is implicit wages, so many billions implicit interest, and so many billions implicit rents and, of the remainder, so much is innovator's profit and so much is the algebraic total due to uncertainty generally. It would be nice, too, if we could divide the total of all factor incomes into two separate parts: (1) the return to so-called "contrived scarcities" and (2) the competitive rent return to so-called "natural scarcities."

But probably we shall never be able to do this with precision. And what good would it do us if we could? Well, for one thing, some reformers believe that, if only Ottawa could easily identify every situation of an illegally contrived scarcity, it might act to bring about a more efficient use of resources. Or some citizens may think that, if Ottawa could identify the temporary profits due to innovation, it might try to tax them more heavily. And some may agitate for reversal of the present exemption (or light treatment under the 1970 White Paper) of capital gains and propose that the government tax the profits arising from luck or uncertainty more heavily than it taxes ordinary income.

TAXING PROFITS   Since many people think of profits as an unnecessary surplus not really needed as an incentive for production or as a deserved reward, governments often seek to tax profits particularly heavily. Thus, during war emergencies an excess-profits tax is often implemented and at rates much higher than the normal rate for corporate income or profits.

Chapter 27 showed that in some cases of inelastically supplied productive factors, such as Henry George's unearned Ricardian land rent, all the return is indeed a surplus. But in most cases of our multi-billion-dollar GNP, we are quite unable to identify, say, 2 billion dollars as a taxable surplus and 8 billion dollars as needed incentive payments. Only occasionally, as with mines and oil wells or with lucrative franchises to own TV stations or Cable TV systems, can the government appropriate by taxes a "monopoly" return.

As always, in seeking greater equality of wealth and/or income by redistributive taxation, some costs in the form of distortions must be borne.

A SERMON ON PROFIT AND WHAT, HOW, AND FOR WHOM

Back in Chapter 3 we surveyed how a price system helps solve society's basic problem of WHAT, HOW, and FOR WHOM. In Part Three we studied the tools of supply and demand that determine competitive market price. And we examined important effects of monopolistic imperfections of competition. The case for and against profit should be ruthlessly examined prior to the next chapter's complete review, in order to summarize the role of profit and loss in the over-all pricing process.

1. Each person seeks his own advantage. Workers seek highest wages; landlords, highest rents; capitalists, highest interest returns. Some of these factor returns will be implicit returns. Still other returns may arise from innovation and/or uncertainty, and for those reasons they may be called profit.

2. In the most general sense, profit seeking is simply seeking of self-advantage. Does this all lead to a jungle—"red in tooth and claw," and chaotic? Not if there are complete checks and balances. These checks and balances are most complete if competition is perfect; incomplete, if it is imperfect. Adam Smith's Invisible Hand cannot be counted on, alone, under monopolistically incomplete competition.

3. Where competition is perfect, or nearly so, there results a pattern of order, of efficiency. But not, mind you, any proven condition of utopia, with the poor become prosperous and the rich brought down near the mean.

Of course, shirkers get low incomes. And earnest people, born stupid and with weak muscles, also get low incomes for all their earnestness. Smart go-getters get high incomes. Highly intelligent altruists, who seek the well-being of other people, themselves get low incomes. Smart girls, born of smart and lucky fathers, get high incomes. Stupid girls, born of smart and lucky fathers, get high incomes. Those who get a good education from five to twenty, or four to twelve, stand to gain at the expense of those who do not. The Lorenz curves of income distribution will record persistent patterns of inequality subject only to slow (and unpredictable) drift. So it goes.

4. Profits and losses signal the advantages of activities. When a man is doing what some buyers in society want, he finds his wage or profit return rising. So he keeps on doing this. If he overdoes it, he gets penalized. Or, through no fault of his own, he gets penalized when someone better comes along. He may then get kicked into the next best thing for him to do.

PROFIT AS A COORDINATING DEVICE   Where knowledge is imperfect, a man may make money by correctly guessing the future. If he knows that oats will be scarce in Alberta, he ships oats there; or grows more oats there; or makes a bet about the scarcity of oats on the grain exchange; and by making this bet he may activate someone else to grow more oats, eat less, or ship more—or he may just gain from another bettor.

In a free pricing system, each man may use his initiative to create a new product or process. If his guess about the future is wrong, he stands to lose. And so do all the people who guessed that he was right—his workers who gave up other jobs, his capitalist backers, and so forth. If he turns out right, he strikes it rich; and his rival may go to the poorhouse. Any entrenched way of doing things can, under the freest competition, be bested and changed.

Profits and high factor returns are the bait; losses are our penalty kicks. Profits go to those who have been efficient in the past—efficient in making things, in selling things, in foreseeing things. Through profits, society is giving the command over new ventures to those who have piled up a record of success.

To understand this last point, imagine a bureaucratic board that awards money to people who apply to it for new projects. If a man was very successful in his last five projects, the board is likely to be favorable toward his new application. Well, profits that a man with high innovating abilities has piled up from the past automatically give him the go-ahead signal in his future enterprises. (But in life, and in the case of the bureaucratic board, how do you get your first start?) The apologist for profits sums up his case:

> Profits are the report card of the past, the incentive gold star for the future, and also the grubstake for new ventures.

5. Under perfect competition a man could get ahead only by doing things of value to himself or someone else. With knowledge perfect, he could not spread lies about fake uranium mines and make money that way or from false advertising claims. A perfect competitor would not cut down on his output in equating marginal revenue to marginal cost ($MR = MC$). Instead he would have no control over market price and would be doing what the utopian Invisible Hand says everyone has to do if the pricing system is to be 100 per cent efficient; namely, he would be equating price to marginal cost ($P = MC$). And he could not be making monopoly profits from contrived scarcity, because under perfect competition there are no monopoly positions.

And if a pricing system were really utopianly perfect in its working, no activity would be pouring smoke into the air without being made to share the cost that such smoke imposes on the rest of the community. No one would refuse to do basic research for fear that he could never tap its full advantage to society and thereby recover his own private research costs. All "external" benefits or costs connected with every activity would be correctly counted in. So when each maximized his own advantage, the checks and balances of perfect pricing would ensure that the benefit of all with money votes was being efficiently achieved.

6. The above remarks show that you would be wrong to say: The trouble with perfect competition is that it has never been tried. For could it ever be tried? Can we institute perfection? Monopoly aside, can we banish "external effects"? Obviously, no one can institute perfection. And obviously, no one can identify the existing world with perfect competition, or identify a government-do-nothing world of *laissez-faire* with perfect competition.

To the degree that public action can (1) lessen monopolistic imperfections, (2) increase imperfect knowledge, and (3) bring total social benefits and costs into closer alignment with private benefits and costs—to this degree will there be a creative economic role for the state worth the costs involved.

7. Where a democracy does not like the For Whom pattern that results from *laissez-faire*, it puts in tax changes, education and other expenditures, fiats, and subsidies to change the pattern. This helps some incomes, some property, and hurts others.

These redistributions are acquired at a cost. What cost? The cost of distortions of incentives, distortions which somewhat lessen the efficiency of the most efficient market system. There are costs, too, in tax collections and transfer payments. If the citizenry believes in notions of equity and greater equality of opportunity, wealth, and incomes, it will knowingly incur such costs up to a margin.

Our sermon on pricing is over. Taking into account the real world as we know it, students of the modern economy realize why, in the absence of a revolution, it has to be—from its very nature—a mixed economy. Competitive (market) pricing must carry most of the burden of solving society's WHAT, HOW, and FOR WHOM. But constructive public policies are needed to keep the system competitive and provide the favorable environment in which private initiative can achieve the common good.

SUMMARY

■ 1   Profit is a highly miscellaneous category. In national-income statistics, it is the total of lumped-together corporate earnings and the income of unincorporated enterprises. But economically we must distinguish four profit concepts.

■ 2   Much of what is called profit is really *implicit* interest, rent, and wages payable for the productive factors provided by the owners of the business.

■ 3   The special category of *high temporary earnings resulting from innovations* is often termed profit by many economists. Routine management earns wages, they say, but profit may accrue to genuine entrepreneurship.

■ 4   *Uncertainty* is the all-pervading fact of life. It makes innovation possible and also creates positive and negative divergencies between what factors expect to earn and what they actually end up earning. Knight and other economists define profit and loss as the *unforeseeable discrepancies created by uncertainty*. If people are generally averse to risk and erratic returns and resist being overoptimistic, a positive premium of profit will be required to coax out their limited supply of risk bearing. Goods involving risks in their production will have to be priced to cover sweat costs of labor, abstinence costs of capital, and risk-premium costs of uncertainty (i.e., will have to be priced to cover wages, interest, and "profits").

■ 5   Still another definition of profit is the return accruing as the result of some kind of monopoly position. This concept is sometimes varied to describe profit as part of the return resulting from a "contrived or artificial scarcity."

■ 6   The taxation of any of these categories of profit can be expected to have definite repercussions, some undesirable from any viewpoint. A fifth notion of profit as *an identifiable and taxable surplus rather than incentive payment* is oversimple. If the public wishes, it can use the tax system to modify the distribution of opportunity and living standards, facing up to the costs involved and deeming them worth the improvement gained.

■ 7   Profit or advantage seeking does, under perfectly competitive pricing conditions, lead to efficient HOW. If the distribution of initial wealth, abilities, and opportunities were made ethically optimal (and were continually adjusted to changing prices), and if there were no externalities or monopolistic imperfections of technology and markets, then the checks and balances of perfect competition could lead to a "best" solution of WHAT, How, and FOR WHOM.

In a mixed economy, public policies try to provide needed correctives and checks and balances and try to help align social and private benefits—in short, try to promote the best environment within which private initiative can function.

QUESTIONS FOR DISCUSSION

1. Define "implicit" factor earnings. Contrast with other profit concepts.

2. Give cases of innovation; of risk taking. How will taxes affect them?

3. What is meant by perfect competition? By imperfect competition? Can you specify a monopoly profit that all will think bad? Can you ever separate natural and contrived scarcities?

4. Cornflakes factories face riskless and steady demand; machine-tool demand is unpredictably volatile. Compare this pair of goods with the wheat and rubber example of the chapter. How will long-run competitive prices adjust to these risk patterns?

5. Discuss ethical and incentive aspects of taxing so-called "profits" or higher incomes generally. (For example, corporate income tax favors bond finance. So?)

6. "If the Lord gives a man strength, brains, and energy, then he's been given much. So he deserves lower material income—not higher." Contrast with "To each according to his ability—according to his marginal-product."

7. Review your understanding of the following concepts:

reported statistics of profits	imperfections of competition, monopoly
implicit versus explicit factor returns	contrived versus natural scarcity
wages of management	rent and surplus, incentive payments
reward for risk taking	initial and after-tax distribution of wealth
innovation, uncertainty	external effects, and divergence of private
probability, large-number of risks	and social benefit and cost
profit as premium for risk bearing	ethical questions and value judgments

31

EPILOGUE TO MICROECONOMIC PRICING

Truth can never be told so as to be understood and not be believed. WILLIAM BLAKE

Parts Three and Four are now completed. Let us review the broad principles of *value* and *distribution*.

■ SURVEY OF THE INTERDEPENDENT PRICING PROCESS

We have seen:

1. How competitive supply and demand operate in a *single* market, in both the short and long run.

2. How the relative marginal utility (or indifference) preferences of men lie behind their respective demand curves.

3. How total, marginal, and average costs all lie behind the competitive supply curves.

4. How the technical production function relating output to factor inputs lies behind the cost curves, which have been minimized by the firm's demanding inputs until their marginal-physical-products are proportional to factor-prices.

5. How these marginal-physical-products and marginal-revenue-products, summed for all firms, provide the "derived demands for the factors."

6. How these derived demands for land, labor, or capital goods interact with their market supplies to determine factor-prices such as rent, wages, rentals, and so forth.

7. How primary resources like labor and land are used to make produced capital goods, which are in turn used in roundabout ways to increase society's final output; that this "net productivity of capital" is reflected in the rate of interest, which, in the absence of technical change, is generally subject to diminishing returns much as labor and land are subject to that law; and that competitive markets evaluate all assets at their "present discounted values," using interest yields to screen out best investments.

8. Finally, how pursuit of profit and avoidance of loss furnish the motive force behind the whole competitive process—but that, paradoxically, under static conditions free of uncertainty and innovational change, competitive profits (other than implicit factor returns and wages of management) would tend to zero; but uncertainty brings income dispersion depending on luck; and how the persistence of risk coupled with a general aversion to risk taking, on the ground that dollar gains have less marginal utility than dollar losses, would lead to profit return as a systematic positive premium for risk bearing.

■ SIMULTANEOUS MUTUAL DETERMINATION

Notice that, in the listing of eight steps above, each follows from the preceding one—from step 1 to step 2 and then step 3, until finally we come to step 8. In the textbook chapters they follow in about the same order.

But in real life, which comes first? Is there any order and sequence, with prices being determined in single markets on Monday, consumers evaluating preferences on Tuesday, businessmen reckoning costs on Wednesday and mar-ginal-products on Thursday? Obviously not. All these processes are going on at one and the same time.

That is not all. These different processes do not go on independently side by side, each in its own little groove, careful not to get in the way of the other. All the processes of supply and demand, of cost and preference, of factor pro-ductivity and demand—all these are really different aspects of one vast simul-taneous *interdependent* process.

Thus, the supply curve for wheat given in the first chapter of Part Three is itself the resultant of the cost calculations given at the end of Part Three, of the production considerations given early in Part Four, and of the wage and rent and interest determinations given late in Part Four. Actually, you can take any one of the eight steps in the outline and draw arrows connecting it casually *with every other step.*

Figure 31-1 gives a summary picture of the interdependent system which economists call "general equilibrium." Recall the circular-flow diagram on national income (Fig. 10-1, page 225), showing plumbing pipes carrying dollars clockwise from business to families and from families to business. That gave what economists call the "aggregative," or "macroeconomic," picture of the nation's grand economic totals.

Now turn to Fig. 31-1. It also gives the circular flow of dollars. But this time we take a microscopic approach—what economists call the "micro-economic" picture. Now we do not talk about the grand total of factor incomes; instead we show derived demand by business for skilled labor, unskilled labor, good vineyard land, and for every other factor of production. Nor do we speak of total consumption: we specify; we show the consumer's demand for coffee, tea, shoes, and for each and every commodity or service.

Note that in the lower loop we have for each factor *both* a supply and a demand. (QUERY: Which of these schedules comes from business? Which from consumers?) And in the upper loop, you see *both* a business supply and consumer demand for each good. (Where?)

Thus, we can give an optimistic answer to the logical purist who poses the embarrassing question: "Your economic system isn't determinate until you have found conditions to determine a price *and* a quantity for *each* output and for

What, How, and For Whom is determined by general equilibrium pricing:

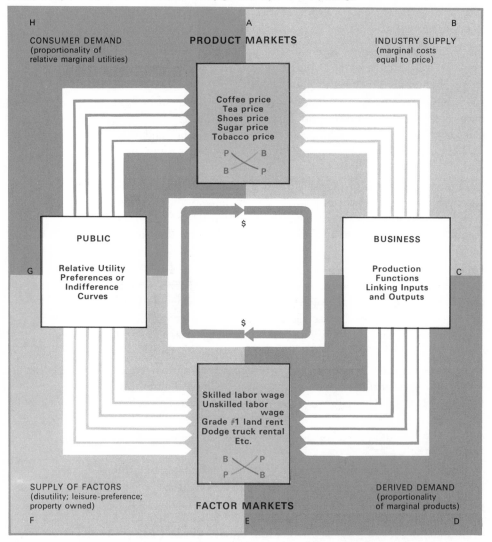

FIG. 31-1. The clockwise money flow is broken up to show consumer demand meeting industry supply at *A* to determine equilibrium price and quantity of each good. Similarly, derived factor demands of business meet public's supply of factors at *E* to determine equilibrium factor-prices and amounts. (Interpret what is going on behind *B, D, F,* and *H*—and inside *C* and *G*—and compare this with the What, How, and For Whom of Fig. 3-1, on page 58.)

each factor input. Do you have enough simultaneous conditions (or equations) to make your interdependent equilibrium system determinate?"

Fortunately, we can answer: "We do have for each output or input *both a supply and a demand condition*. So we can hope that the system will, by trial and error in the market place, finally settle down—if left undisturbed!—to a determinate competitive equilibrium.[1] And we can add: "The final competitive equilibrium is an 'efficient' one. Because prices equal marginal costs, output is being maximized, factor inputs minimized; and because prices reflect relative marginal utilities for each consumer, people who like apples are not being given oranges, etc. From so efficient a final point, you can no longer make everyone better off. You can help Joe only by hurting Tom."

Figure 31-1 here is the final development of Figure 3-1 on page 58 of Chapter 3, where we first asked how a price system goes about solving WHAT, How, and FOR WHOM. Only after mastering the tools of Parts Three and Four are we able to present this culmination of our original inquiry.

■ IMPERFECTIONS OF COMPETITION

This survey proceeded on the basis of some heroically abstract assumptions: no monopolies, no imperfections, no dynamic innovations or unforeseen disturbances, no governmental distortions, and so forth. Figure 31-1, therefore, is like the no-friction model of the physicist; it is not a picture of the real world as we know it when we step outside the library and rub elbows with real live breathing people on the street.

Yet, even though every engineer knows he must meet friction, he does find the frictionless model a valuable tool in throwing light on complicated reality. So it is with our ideal competitive model. In the long run, many imperfections turn out to be transient. *The competitive model, therefore, may suggest in its oversimple way some interesting hypotheses that turn out to have a measure of long-run validity!*

> EXAMPLE: An invention cuts cost of aluminum; the competitive model says price will fall and pressure will be put on use and price of steel. The sophisticated student of imperfect competition says the real world is not perfectly competitive, so no hard-and-fast conclusion can be drawn. Still, bet with him that the above result will happen *in the long run*—and probably you will win his money. A sure thing? No, but often a good bet.

Even if we agree that the perfect-competition model does give some approximate descriptions of reality, we cannot be satisfied with such crude approximations. Forty years ago an economics textbook would have had to confine itself to the case of perfect competition, and let it go at that. Thanks to the

---

[1] Léon Walras, a French economist of three-quarters of a century ago, is usually credited with the discovery of general equilibrium. But W. S. Jevons of England, C. Menger of Austria, Alfred Marshall of England, J. B. Clark of the United States, Vilfredo Pareto of Italy, and Knut Wicksell of Sweden all made significant contributions; and even in Adam Smith you can hunt out the germ of the idea of general equilibrium.

pioneering work in the theory of imperfect and monopolistic competition over the last generation, economists now have the tools (marginal revenue, etc.) to analyze oligopoly, monopoly, differentiation of products of numerous sellers, collective bargaining, and various intermediate cases. (Recall Chapter 25 and Table 24-1, page 592.)

We have seen that prices are often inflexibly administered, changing rarely and being subject only to minor hidden discounts, which is in contrast with the minute-to-minute volatility and year-to-year gyrations of competitive prices. We have seen that two union men may work in the same city or block at different wage rates for comparable work; that interference by a union with wage setting may correct a previous monopsony condition of unequal bargaining, or may increase the departure from the model of perfect competition. We have seen Chamberlinian cases where free entry may squeeze out profits while still leaving price above minimum average costs. We shall see, in Chapter 38, that prejudice under *laissez-faire* may lead to unequal employment opportunity and to both social inefficiency and inequity.

There is no need, therefore, to warn against overemphasis on the elegant model of perfect competition as an exact description of economic reality.

■ A WORD ON "WELFARE ECONOMICS"

Even if perfect competition were a poorer descriptive tool than it is, students of economics would still want to study it intensively and master its principles. This is so for a reason unconnected with mere description. The competitive model is extremely important in providing a bench mark for appraising the *efficiency* of an economic system. The Russians, the Chinese, the Indians, as well as the Swiss need to study its analytical principles.

For the most part in any science, scholars discuss what *is* and what will be under this or that situation. The task of positive description should be kept as free as is humanly possible from the taint of wishful thinking and ethical concern about what ought to be. Why? Because scientists are cold-blooded robots? No, rather because experience shows again and again that a more accurate job of positive description will be achieved if one tries to be objective. (Experience also shows that, try as we may, we humans never succeed in separating completely the objective and subjective aspects of a discipline. Indeed, the very choice of what scientists choose to measure, and the perspective from which they observe and measure it, and the reactions the observer produces in that which is observed—all these factors make the distinction between *is* and *ought*, between objective and subjective issues, at bottom a matter of degree rather than of kind. Recall, for example, Chapter 1's bird-antelope paradox.)

The citizenry, unlike the specialist, is in the end perhaps most interested in problems of "norms," of what *ought* to be done, of policy rather than mere description. That citizenry is best served by the scientists who can give it the most accurate description of what is relevant, and of what the consequences of different policy actions will be.

Very briefly then, in this epilogue, let us devote again a few lines to implications for economic welfare that have been developed in Parts Three and Four.

EFFICIENCY OPTIMALITY   First, we have seen repeatedly that a regime of perfectly competitive pricing would have certain efficiency properties if conditions were really present for the maintenance of perfect competition. Therefore Adam Smith, in his talk about an Invisible Hand, which led the selfish actions of individuals toward so harmonious a final result, did have some point. Smith never could state or prove exactly what that point was, but modern economics can state this property of ideal competitive pricing:

> Under perfectly perfect competition, where all prices end up equal to all marginal costs, where all factor-prices end up equal to values of marginal-products and all total costs are minimized, where the genuine desires and well-being of individuals are all represented by their marginal utilities as expressed in their dollar voting—*then* the resulting equilibrium has the efficiency property that "you can't make any one man better off without hurting some other man."

What does this mean exactly? It means that a planner could not come along with a slide rule and find a solution different from the *laissez-faire* one, which could improve the welfare of *everyone*.[2]

ARBITRARY DISTRIBUTION OF DOLLAR VOTES   What does it not mean? It does not mean that actual *laissez-faire*, with the imperfections of competition that will go with it, leads to efficiency, or necessarily even to a close approximation of efficiency.

And inefficiency aside, it does not mean that the people who are deemed by various religious or ethical observers to be most worthy, most deserving, or most needy will necessarily get their ethically best share of goods and services. *Laissez-faire* perfect competition *could* lead to starving cripples; to malnourished children who grow up to produce malnourished children; to perpetuation of Lorenz curves of great inequality of incomes and wealth for generations or forever. Or, if the initial distribution of dollar-wealth votes, genetic abilities, conditioned motivations, and training happened to be appropriate, perfect competition might lead to a rather egalitarian society characterized by uniformity greater than might please many an aristocratic ethical tradition.

In short, Adam Smith, in the famous passage quoted on page 53, had no right to assert that an Invisible Hand channels individuals selfishly seeking their own interest into promoting the "public interest"—as these last two words might be defined by a variety of prominent ethical and religious notions of what

---

[2] If A is the competitive equilibrium, there is no point B the planner could devise which could be approved over A by a *unanimous vote*. Some would be hurt in going to B, some might gain; but the gainers could never find it worthwhile to give big enough bribes to win the losers over to approving the move to B. Graduate treatises call this a case of "Pareto optimality," named after Pareto's work at the turn of the century as elucidated in our time by Abram Bergson of Harvard.

constitutes the welfare of a nation. Smith has proved nothing of this kind, nor has any economist or philosopher since his time.

REDEFINING THE INVISIBLE HAND DOCTRINE   If Smith were alive today, he would agree with all this; and one ventures the guess, from his biography, that he would probably reword his doctrine pretty much along the following lines.

1. Only if abilities and *dollar-wealth votes were originally distributed in "an ethically optimal" manner*—and kept so distributed by nondistorting, non-market interventions—could even perfectly competitive pricing be counted on (*a*) to produce an efficient configuration of production out on society's production-possibility frontier (and not inside it), and (*b*) to give people what they really deem is best for them, in accordance with their dollar votes that now reflect equally significant social utility. If *laissez-faire* were abandoned in favor of an ethically proper distribution of wealth and opportunity, the perfect-competition equilibrium could be used to attain optimally efficient and equitable organization of society.

2. Admittedly, *the demands of people in the market place sometimes do not reflect their true well-being* as these would be interpreted by even the most tolerant and individualistic of ethical observers. (EXAMPLE: A dope addict's craving for opium even at the expense of his food or his children's food; a child's desire for a seventh lollipop; a diabetic's craving for sweets; a spendthrift's mortgaging his house for an advertised sports car.) As a pragmatist, were Smith alive today, he would say, "People are entitled to make their own mistakes in many matters, but it is arrogant to think that anyone who is not a minor or a lunatic is in every respect a sovereign will; as men conscious that we were born not perfect and as inhabitants of a post-Freudian world, we shall sparingly and for good cause want (with due process) democratically to place restrictions on our own behavior. So again, *laissez-faire* perfect competition would not inevitably be the ideal."

Then, after emphasizing the need for tolerance and the virtues of freedom, Smith might strike a more technical note.

3. Where there are monopolistic imperfections that produce deviations from ideal competitive marginal-cost pricing—and in situations of strong increasing returns and decreasing costs, such deviations are practically inevitable—of course there is a *prima facie* case that *laissez-faire* pricing is not efficient. Public scrutiny, to see whether democratic controls would make the situation better or worse, has to be presumed in such quasi-monopoly situations.

4. Finally, Smith would add that wherever there are "external economies and diseconomies" (such as were analyzed at the end of Chapter 23 and in the discussion of public versus private goods in Chapter 8), there is a *prima facie* case for study to see whether zoning laws, taxes or subsidies, and government expenditure and regulation should be initiated in some degree. Where the checks and balances of perfect competition are not operative, the Darwinian struggle for existence is not led by an Invisible Hand to any kind of optimum. The creative role of government in economic life is vast in an interdependent crowded world.

■ CONCLUSION

The reader is warned that all the above issues of welfare economics can be given varying interpretations and can lead to controversy or debate. Such debates cannot be resolved within the realm of positive science alone. Conservatives may legitimately interpret the above principles in terms of their version of the good society. Middle-of-the-roaders may do the same for theirs. And radicals may call for small or large reforms of the present structure of a mixed economy by giving their interpretation of these principles. That means the reader may do so, too. Economic science arms one for the great debate.

The following Appendix gives in greater depth a view of the efficiency aspect of the system of interdependent economic pricing under capitalism or socialism.

Appendix: Review of Commodity and Factor Pricing: General Equilibrium and the Parable of Ideal Welfare Pricing

■ PARABLE OF UTOPIAN PRICING

Economists used to be twitted that their books always harped on Robinson Crusoe. True enough: we do find that the economic decisions of a single man furnish a dramatic way of simplifying our basic principles. But these days we have an even more dramatic device for illustrating the fundamental facts of economic life: we use the example of a fully collectivized society. This retains the same simplicity of ultimate decision making, but at the same time it involves the social interactions between people that the Crusoe model lacks. The contrast between such a model and our realistic everyday world is, of course, enormous. And therein lies its value. By examining the logic of such a model, we get new insight into the nature of our own pricing system.

Let us, therefore, examine how our economic analysis of pricing can be applied to a completely artificial planned society of the kind never seen in Russia or anywhere else. Call it Utopia, call it Hades, it exists. In analyzing the problem of pricing in a planned socialist state, we kill two birds with one stone:

1. We get one of the best possible reviews of the over-all working of a perfect *capitalistic* price system.

2. We get an introduction to problems of "welfare economics," the study of what is considered right and wrong about any economic system. This depends, of course, upon ethical points of view, themselves necessarily a-scientific. But the economist, as a disinterested observer, may help to throw light on how successfully an economic system realizes any suggested ethical *goals*.[1]

■ A DILEMMA FOR CENTRALIZED PLANNING

The earlier chapters of this book have shown how a system of market prices operates so as to solve the basic economic problems of WHAT, HOW, and FOR WHOM. To drive home what all this really means, try a mental experiment. Suppose you were given the job of making the blueprints for a completely planned economic system. How might you begin?

---

[1] For example, he may be personally opposed to an equal distribution of income, but that does not prevent him from measuring the degree of success in reaching this common ethical goal or of the costs involved.

First, let us suppose you are interested in giving people what they want, not in telling them what they ought to want. Obviously, you cannot give them everything they want: land, labor, capital goods, and technological knowledge are limited in amount. So you must make compromises and choices.

You may say: This is merely a complicated mathematical problem, calling for the use of lots of high-powered electronic high-speed calculating machines. But remember that we shall have to deal with the millions of items that are to be found in department stores, with thousands of grades of productive factors, and with numerous individuals and families. The number of unknowns of the mathematical problem will be in the millions, and the number of steps to its solution in the billions of billions. No known set of calculating machines or computers can even begin to tackle such a problem.

You are stumped. And discouraged. Perhaps you will lower your sights and stop being a perfectionist. Instead of giving people exactly what they think they want, you may decide that there will be only a few types of, say, shoe styles and sizes, so that the calculation problem will be simplified. Or you may start to give people goods that *you* find it convenient to give them.

One thing is clear: If centralized planning means that one centralized person must have in his mind all the myriad intricacies of detail, then it is an impossible job to do with any efficiency. So you will naturally begin to experiment with various devices to *decentralize* the job. And quite probably you will end up by introducing a *pricing* system in many ways like that of capitalism. How might such a system work?

■ PRICING IN A UTOPIAN STATE: CONSUMPTION-GOODS PRICES

In your new society, the consumer will still have *freedom of choice* and will not have dictated to him the relative amounts of different commodities which he is to "enjoy." As in the capitalist system, each person will receive a sum of money or abstract purchasing power to spend among different commodities as he wishes. Thus, vegetarians will not have to eat meat, and those who most prefer meat will be able to satisfy their preference.

How will relative prices between salmon and ham or any other consumers' goods be set by the socialist state? Generally speaking, prices will be set with the same double purpose as in a capitalist society: (1) just high enough to ration out the existing supplies of consumers' goods, so none are left over and none are short; and also (2) just high enough to cover the socially necessary extra costs of producing the goods in question—or, in technical terms, prices are to be set equal to relative "marginal utilities" and "marginal costs."

■ THE DISTRIBUTION OF INCOME

So far the process has worked much like the capitalistic system. Almost by definition, however, socialism means a society in which most land and capital goods or nonhuman resources of all kinds are owned collectively by society and not individually by people. In our society, a man who owns 50 parcels of Toronto land, each of which produces $60,000 of net rents per year, will receive an income of 3 million dollars per year—which may be 1,000 times what a night watchman is able to earn, and 200 times what the average skilled engineer can earn. In a society where most property is owned collectively and not distributed with great inequality among different individuals, an important source of inequality of income would be absent.

Many people profess to hold the ethical and philosophical belief that different individuals' wants and needs are very much alike, and that the present market mechanism works inadequately because the rich are given so many more votes in the control of production than the poor—which makes the market demand for goods a faulty indicator of their true social worth. Such people with a relatively egalitarian philosophy will welcome a great reduction in the spread of incomes between the lowest 90 per cent of all families and the highest 10 per cent. They may argue that taking away $1,000 from a man with an income of $100,000 and giving it to a man with an income of $2,000 will add to social well-being (by taking dollars from a place deemed low in marginal social utility to a place deemed higher). After the distribution of income between families has been determined correctly, according to society's fundamental (a-scientific) value judgments, then and only then will it be true that the dollars coming on the market will be valid indicators of the value of goods and services; and only then will they be serving to direct production into the proper channels and goods into the right hands. Hence, *lump-sum taxes will be used in Utopia to give ethically proper income distribution.* So goes the argument.

How is what is considered the proper ethical distribution of income to be achieved aside from the negative act of wiping out unduly high property owning and the appropriate lump-sum taxing of individuals?

Perfectionists have two answers: (1) in part by letting people get some of their income in the form of wages; but (2) in part by having these wages supplemented by receipt of a lump-sum *social dividend payment* or negative income tax. This cash payment in an egalitarian society might involve differences to compensate for different numbers of children, age, health, and abilities acquired or inherited.

It is an ethical rather than a scientific question as to just how large, relatively, each person's final income ought to be. As a science, economics can concern itself only with the best means of attaining given ends; it cannot prescribe the ends themselves.

Indeed, if someone decided that he preferred a feudal-fascistic kind of society, in which all people with little black mustaches were to be given especially high incomes, a pathological economist could set up the pricing rules for him to follow to achieve his strange design best. He would be told to determine his social dividend payments to achieve the required optimal distribution of income, after which each dollar coming on the market could be regarded as correctly representing (that eccentric philosopher's) true social values.

The social dividend differs from a wage because it is to be given to every individual *regardless of his own efforts.* That is why it is called a "lump-sum" dividend or transfer.[2] (Any bonus based upon productivity or effort is to be treated as a wage.)

We have not yet seen how wages are to be determined, but before doing so, let us first turn to another important problem.

---

[2] If the state is providing public goods for the people which require the use of more resources than the state owns, most of the social dividends may have to be *negative*—lump-sum taxes, rather than transfers.

■ PRICING OF NONHUMAN PRODUCTIVE RESOURCES AND INTERMEDIATE GOODS

What should be the role of land and other nonhuman productive resources as an element of cost in such a utopia? Some people would say that such nonhuman resources should not enter into cost at all; that only human sweat and skill are the true source of all value; and that any extra charges based upon the cost of land or machinery represent a capitalistic surplus which the owners of property are able to squeeze out of the exploited laboring masses by virtue of the private monopoly of ownership of the means of production. We have seen that this view is the traditional "labor theory of value," of Karl Marx and John Locke. Learned scholars disagree about just what Marx meant by the "labor theory of value," and debate whether he intended it to apply to a socialist economy in the short or long run.

We need not enter into this dispute. However, it is important to note that, in its simple form, *the labor theory of value will lead to incorrect and inefficient use of both labor and nonlabor resources in even the most perfect socialist society.*

So long as any economic resource is limited in quantity—i.e., *scarce* rather than free—the socialist planners must give it a price and charge a rent for its use. This price need not, as in the case of the millionaire under the capitalistic system, determine any individual's income. It can be a purely bookkeeping or accounting price (or so-called "shadow price") set up by the planners, rather than a market price. But there must be a price put upon the use of every such resource.

Why? First, we must price nonhuman resources to ensure that society is deciding How goods shall be produced in the best way, so that we really end up on the true production-possibility frontier of society and not somewhere inside it.[3] It would be absurd to get rid of the capitalistic system with its alleged wastes due to unemployment, and then, by stupid planning, end up far inside society's true production potentialities.

Related to the above point is the second need for all resources to be given a value if correct prices are to be charged to consumers for those final goods

---

[3] See Exercise 4 of Chapter 26's Appendix for geometric proof.

that use up a great deal of scarce resources. In other words, for society to find itself in the best of all possible positions out on the production-possibility frontier, we must price such consumption goods as food and clothing so as to reflect their true relative (extra or marginal) costs of using up *all* scarce resources. Otherwise, the free choice exerted by consumers on their dollar spending will not truly maximize their own and society's preferences, with utilities and costs properly balanced at the margin.

■ THE EXAMPLE OF LAND RENT

The foregoing two reasons may be hard to grasp. However, let us try to make the necessity for non-labor pricing clear by considering a single land example. Suppose there are twins in a farming utopia. What if one were to produce wheat on an acre of good land, and the other were to produce less wheat by the same year's work on an acre of bad land. If they are identical twins, working equally hard, we would certainly have to agree that their wage rates ought to be the same.

Now, if wages were to be treated as the only cost, in accord with the labor theory of value, then the same price could not be charged for the two different outputs of wheat, even though the kernels of wheat were identical. The good-land wheat would have involved low labor costs and will have to sell for less than the poor-land wheat.

This, of course, is absurd. A well-wishing social planner might try to get around the dilemma by charging the same price for both, losing money on the poor-land wheat and gaining on the other. Or what is almost the same thing, he might say, "To keep the costs of the two wheats the same, let us pay the twin on bad land lower wages than his brother; but then let us make the richer brother share his wages with the poorer."

Such a solution is not absurd, but it falls short of achieving the desired best results: maximum production and equal pay for equal human effort. In particular, *it fails to shift more labor onto the more productive land.*

The only correct procedure is to put an accounting price or rent tag on each land, with the good land having the higher tag. The prices of both kinds of wheat will be equal, because the land cost ("Ricardian rent") of the good-land wheat will be just enough higher than that of the poor-land wheat to make up the difference.

Most important of all, the socialist production manager must try to minimize the combined labor and land cost of producing each kind of wheat. If he does so according to the marginal-product principles discussed in Part Four, he will accomplish something important, undreamed of by the simple believer in the labor theory of value.

He will find it pays to work the good land more intensively, perhaps with the time of $1\frac{1}{2}$ men until the extra product there has been lowered by the law of diminishing returns so as to be just equal to the extra product of the $\frac{1}{2}$ man's time on the poor land. Only by putting a price upon inert sweatless land are we using it, and sweating breathing labor, most productively! The price or rent of land rises so as to ration its limited supply among the *best* uses.

Note, too, that the most finicky humanitarian will have nothing to complain of in our solution. By transferring labor from one acre to the other until labor's marginal productivity has been made equal, we get the largest possible total production of wheat.[4]

The two brothers are paid the same wages because they have worked equally hard. But their wages are not high enough to buy all the wheat, since part of the cost of the wheat has come from (bookkeeping) land-rent charges. However, the people through their government own the land equally. The land's return does not go to any property owner but is available to be distributed as a lump-sum social dividend to both brothers and to others according to their ethical deserts.

By putting a proper accounting price or rent on land, society has more consumption than was otherwise possible!

If we turn now to the production of more than one consumer's good, it will be obvious that their cost prices must be made to reflect the amount of

---

[4] As earlier discussions of marginal productivity have shown, *total product will be at a maximum only when labor has been transferred from the land where its marginal-product is low to the good land where its marginal-product is high.* Every such transfer must necessarily yield us extra product, until finally no further increases in output can result when the marginal-products have been equalized in the two uses.

socially limited land and machinery which they each use up. Field crops such as wheat require little labor and much land compared with a garden crop such as tomatoes. If we price each good on the basis of labor costs alone, wheat will sell for too little, and too much land will be forced out of tomato production. Everyone will be worse off.

■ MARGINAL-COST PRICING

One last point concerning the final determination of a product's cost and price. After the costs of all necessary factors of production have been added together to arrive at total cost, the planning authorities must set their prices at the marginal cost of production. Or more accurately, the socialist managers of a plant must behave like a perfect competitor: they must disregard any influence that their own production might have on market price and must continue to produce extra units up to the point where the last little unit costs just as much as its selling price.

For many industries, such as railroads, where unit costs are constantly falling, setting marginal costs equal to price will imply that *full* average costs are not covered. In a noncapitalistic society the difference would be made up by an (accounting) lump-sum grant from the state; for if a railroad system is worth building, it is worth being utilized well.[5]

[5] The long-run question as to whether to build a railroad in the first place may involve an "all-or-none deci-

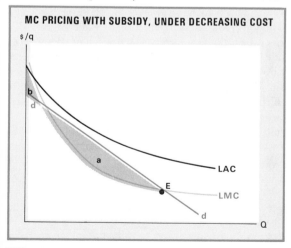

MC PRICING WITH SUBSIDY, UNDER DECREASING COST

FIG. 31-2.

■ SUMMARY OF RESOURCE PRICING

Correct social planning requires that all scarce resources, whether human labor or not, be given accounting prices at least. The final costs of consumers' goods should include the sum total of *all* extra costs necessary to produce each good, or in short, should equal *marginal cost.* The demand for consumers' goods is really an indirect demand for all productive resources, a demand which can be kept in proper check only by putting appropriate valuations on productive resources.

Otherwise, society's valuable nonhuman—and human!—resources will be incorrectly allocated and the market pricing of finished goods will not lead to maximum consumers' satisfaction. It is to be emphasized that the accounting prices of land and other nonhuman resources need not, in a socialist state, be part of the incomes of anyone. In the language of the visionary critic of private enterprise: no one is "exploited" by having a property owner skim off part of the final product. Instead, the contribution of capital and land to production is given

sion," which cannot be made step by step. In such a case, there must still be a balancing of the extra (or marginal) advantage and extra cost to society of the enterprise. But for such a big step, price is no longer a good indicator of total welfare, since—as we saw in Chapter 21—there is always an element of consumer's surplus in the total amount of goods a person consumes over what he has paid for them.

Figure 31-2 pictures a case where *dd*, which we assume reflects true marginal utilities to society, everywhere lies below decreasing long-run *AC.* So pricing at long-run *MC* can never recover full long-run social costs. Yet, with the *a* area a little larger than the *b* area, the total-utility area under *dd* is greater than the total-cost area under *LMC.* So society should produce at *E,* giving a lump-sum subsidy to cover the inevitable loss or somehow getting people to pay more for their earlier units that yielded great consumer surplus. (EXAMPLES: A railroad line to a country region; a monorail for urban commuters.) If *dd* shifted down enough to make *a < b,* the whole project should be abandoned. Even if *dd* shifted up a bit, so that part of it lay above *LAC* and price *could* cover all costs, *P* still should be kept down to *LMC* for efficient pricing. (All this needs qualifications if dollars do not represent true and constant marginal utility and true social costs, as in a world of many monopolies and in making big decisions.) Also, taxing to finance the subsidy may involve some distortions; so we may have to settle for a second-best solution with *P* between *LMC* and *LAC.*

to people in the form of government goods and the algebraic *social dividend.*

■ THE ROLE OF THE INTEREST RATE IN UTOPIA

We have seen that the interest rate has an important function in a capitalistic, socialistic, or any other kind of economic system. Capital goods have a "net productivity." As long as resources can be invested for the present or the future, it will be necessary to make important decisions with respect to capital. Shall we apply present land and labor to the production of a corn crop this year or to apples 15 years from now? Shall we have grape juice today or wine 10 years hence? Shall we replace a worn-out loom with a new expensive one which yields its services over a period of 20 years or buy a cheap one that will last only 14 years? Every one of these questions can be answered only by using an interest rate to relate future and present economic values. Without such an interest rate, the existing stock of fixed and circulating capital cannot be devoted to its best uses; and whatever amount of national income society has decided to invest in capital formation cannot be embodied in the best form without such an interest rate.

> The interest rate acts as a sieve or rationing device: all projects that can yield 10 per cent over time are undertaken before any projects that yield only 8 per cent.

It should be added that many economic writers on socialism do not think that the rate of interest should also determine—as it does in our economy, to some degree—the rate at which capital growth is to take place at the expense of current consumption. The decision as to how much should be saved would be determined by the state "in the light of national and social needs," and not by the "haphazard" notions of individuals with respect to the future. But the level of social saving and capital growth once having been determined, the interest rate must be used to allocate scarce "capital supplies" optimally and to determine the priority of alternative projects.[6]

[6] There is no logical reason why individuals who are willing to forgo present for future consumption should not be permitted to do such voluntary extra saving and receive an interest return equal to the net productivity of capital.

■ WAGE RATES AND INCENTIVE PRICING

We must now return to the problem of how the utopian planners would set wage rates, and then we are done. If the amounts of labor of all kinds and of all skills were perfectly fixed, there would be no reason why labor should not be given accounting prices just like any other productive factor. Workers would receive no wages at all. They would then receive all the national income in the form of an enlarged *social dividend.*

However, if heterogeneous people are to be free to choose their own occupations and given the choice of working a little harder and longer in return for extra consumption goods, then it will be necessary to set up a system of *actual market wages* at which people can sell their services.

Wages may differ depending upon how the irksomeness and unpleasantness of the job affects voluntary labor supplied; and unlike now, the pleasanter jobs may then be the lower-paid, and the ditchdiggers or garbage collectors may have to be higher-paid to attract people into these jobs. Occupations that require much training and skill will receive high pay, but much of that pay may be spent by the state in providing the education necessary to acquire those skills. Piece rates might be used, and a worker with a 20 per cent higher productivity will be receiving higher (pre-tax and pre-social-dividend) wages. Workers will in every case be offered wages equal to their marginal, or extra, productivity.

Therefore, it is not necessarily true that all incomes will be at a dead level in the utopian society. They will differ somewhat as a result of two distinct factors: (1) society's appraisal of the "needs and worth" of different individuals—as reflected primarily in the size of the individuals' lump-sum *social dividends*—and (2) the need for wages to differ to provide incentives and to compensate people for extra disutility and effort. Incomes need not differ, however, because of inequality in the ownership and inheritance of property and genetic talents. Wage rents (like Babe Ruth's) could be heavily lump-sum-taxed, exactly like Henry George's surplus land rents.

■ SUMMARY OF UTOPIAN PRICING

1. A utopian system could make use of four different kinds of pricing: (*a*) consumer-goods prices,

(b) wage and incentive rates, (c) accounting prices of intermediate goods or produced factor inputs, and (d) final lump-sum dividends (when positive, subsidies; when negative, taxes). The first three prices would be determined by supply and demand.

2. To give people free choice among consumers' goods, market prices would be set for such goods. Similarly, to provide freedom of choice of occupation, to give people incentives, and to provide compensation for differences between occupations, wage rates would have to be set to correspond to (marginal) productivities and disutilities.

3. Accounting prices would have to be set on all nonhuman productive resources to ration them in their best uses where their (relative) marginal productivities are equal and highest. Similarly, there would have to be a rate of interest to ration the existing and growing stock of capital among its best uses. Any consumption good would be produced up to the point where the full marginal cost of production (necessary to keep all resources from other uses and from leisure) is just equal to the price.[7]

4. Lastly, the final distribution of income would be made to correspond to what society regards as the ideal distribution pattern by means of payment of a lump-sum social dividend to people, depending upon "need, wants, and deservingness," but not—like a wage—on effort or performance. In Utopia, it might be felt that a much more nearly equal distribution of income will be necessary before the dollar votes of consumers can be expected to reflect true social preferences. However, this is an a-scientific, ethical question; and we could use the same economic principles to make blueprints for an inegalitarian utopia.

5. None of these processes except the last requires detailed *comprehensive planning by a central agency*. Mathematicians would not have to be called in to solve thousands and thousands of simultaneous equations. Instead, the *decentralized plan-*

ners would proceed by successive approximation, by trial and error—setting provisional market and accounting prices and cutting them or raising them, depending upon whether available supplies are piling up or running short.

It would be naïve to think that any actual society would succeed in reaching the ideal equilibrium positions described above. Errors of foresight would inevitably be made. Existing vested interests, anxious to preserve their security in a dynamic world of change, would resist and sabotage such change in the same qualitative fashion as they have done in historical societies. Even when politicians and the electorate do not pay much attention to the incentive mechanisms outlined in the preceding pages, the importance of this discussion is that it teaches us how to appraise the mechanical efficiency of pricing in a *non*socialist society.[8]

◼ WELFARE ECONOMICS IN A FREE ECONOMY

On the basis of the above principles of pricing, we are in a position to see what friendly and unfriendly critics think is wrong in our system, or not necessarily right from various ethical viewpoints. Critics list the following possible deviations from the social optimum:

---

[7] The decentralized managers of industries could generally achieve this result by seeking to maximize their net algebraic profits, measured by accounting points or actual dollars, but with *all* prices taken as given parameters. (NOTE: Under cost conditions suitable for viable *laissez-faire*, this type of behavior is actually policed by competition; but where bureaucrats "play the game of competition," there may be a hard administrative problem to make sure they do act in the prescribed pricetaker manner.)

[8] A brief history of welfare pricing doctrines may be of interest. From Smith's time at least, men saw beauty in the *laissez-faire* mechanism and inferred that it must have teleological significance in giving efficiency. But they were often uncritical, and often they overlooked the assumption that dollar votes were to be distributed in the ethically desired way; and they could not prove what they believed. Around 1900 Pareto showed that an ideal socialism would have to solve the same equations as competitive capitalism. Around 1920, Ludwig von Mises, perhaps unaware of Pareto's proof, set forth the challenging view that rational economic organization was *logically* impossible in the absence of free markets. Fred Taylor of Michigan, A. P. Lerner of England and California, and Oscar Lange of Poland answered Mises with the view that socialism could conceptually solve the problems of economic organization by a decentralized process of bureaucratic trial and error—"playing the game of competition" and "deliberately planning not to plan." F. A. Hayek has argued that this answer overlooks the problem of giving *each man the initiative* to better the existing order and that only with actual free enterprise do you efficiently utilize the dispersed information which each of us may possess. See the Appendix to Chapter 3 for the movement in Soviet Russia to depend more on prices and profitability.

1. The existing distribution of property, income, education, and economic opportunity is the result of past history and does not necessarily represent an optimum condition according to the ethical philosophies of Christianity, Buddhism, paganism, or other ideologies. Defenders of the capitalist system point out that such deviations from the optimum distribution can be corrected by appropriate tax policies, if that is desired. There are, however, some costs to be incurred in our capitalistic system from such policies because of taxation effects upon incentives, risk taking, effort, and productivity.

2. The widespread presence of monopoly elements in our system and the limited appearance of perfect competition mean that production is rarely being pushed to the optimum point of equality of marginal cost to price; because the elasticity of demand is not infinite to imperfect competitors, production is pushed only to the point of equality of marginal cost to marginal revenue. Because of the fear of "spoiling the market," monopoly price is then too high and monopoly output continues to be too low relative to competitive outputs.

This is related to a further Chamberlinian evil under imperfect competition when entry of new firms into an industry is very easy. There may then tend to be an inefficient division of production among too many firms; the P charged is too high, but through wasteful use of resources, no one need be making any profits.[9]

[9] Another evil, discussed in Chapter 23, is the fact that individual firms, in making their decisions, do not take

3. Finally, of course, as shown in Part Two, under a *laissez-faire* system, there may be great wastes due to unemployment and the business cycle. Consumers, labor, farmers, and business, together with public fiscal and monetary policy, must be mobilized in a never-ending war against this greatest of modern scourges—poverty, which has no real cause but stems only from an intricately misbehaving monetary society.

into account some possible effects of their production decisions on other firms or industries. In digging his oil well, Pat does not mind that he may be robbing Mike's oil pool; and the same with Mike—with the result that less oil is obtained in the end, and with more cost. Because of such so-called "external diseconomies or economies" apparent "private marginal costs" do not reflect true "social marginal costs"; and certain lines of activity deserve to be contracted and others to be expanded. Compare A. C. Pigou, *Economics of Welfare* (Macmillan, New York, 1932).

The paradox that really perfect competition would discourage people from inventing (since they would know their profits would disappear) can be understood in terms of external economies: my pecuniary reward from an invention may be much less than its social value after it has been widely imitated. Governmental activities are needed when "public goods" involve external benefits to more than one person at the same time, as shown in Chapter 8. See, too, Chapter 23's discussion of external economies, on page 578.

SUMMARY TO APPENDIX

■ 1 In a pure unmixed competitive society, the economic problems of WHAT shall be produced, How, and FOR WHOM are solved in an interdependent manner by the impersonal workings of profit-and-loss markets. Each variable depends upon every other, but all tend to be simultaneously determined at their general equilibrium values by a process of successive approximations and readjustments.

■ 2 Unless a utopian economy were uninterested in efficiency and economizing, or in freedom of choice of goods and jobs, it would have to institute a system of pricing. However, some prices would be purely accounting or bookkeeping figures; in addition, the final determination of the distribution of income would involve an outright social dividend or tax, in various lump-sum amounts to people as de-

termined by explicit a-scientifiic ethical decision of government and society designed to
make dollar votes properly reflective of society's value judgments.

■ 3 From the standpoint of welfare economics, it
is seen that any capitalistic system may depart

from what is considered a social optimum in
three main ways: through improper distribution of income, monopoly and externalities,
and unemployment.

Each of these evils can, in various degrees,
be ameliorated by appropriate policies, within
the framework of the mixed economy.

QUESTIONS FOR DISCUSSION

1. Summarize how a pricing system works to
solve the three fundamental economic problems.
Illustrate their interdependence.
2. Discuss the four kinds of prices in a planned,
utopian state.
3. What do you deem to be imperfections in our
economic order? Virtues? What defects would
plague a collectivist society?
4. Review your understanding of the following
concepts:

  interdependence, general equilibrium
  determinate final equilibrium

efficient final equilibrium
labor theory of value versus proper
  pricing of nonhuman resources
interest rate in capitalism and socialism
social dividend: lump-sum tax or transfer
wage rents, incentive wages
accounting prices versus actual prices
monopoly restrictions
"external" divergences between social
  and private benefits and costs
welfare economics, ethical distribution
  questions, value judgments

PART 5
INTERNATIONAL TRADE AND FINANCE

32

THE BALANCE
OF INTERNATIONAL
PAYMENTS AND FOREIGN EXCHANGE

MISS PRISM: *Cecily, you will read your political economy in my absence. The chapter on the Fall of the Rupee you may omit. It is somewhat too sensational. Even these metallic problems have their melodramatic side.*
OSCAR WILDE, The Importance of Being Earnest.

In the earlier chapters of this book, with the exception of Chapter 13, we took international trade more or less for granted. Here in Part Five we wish to analyze explicitly the interesting *international* economic problems arising as soon as an economy engages in foreign trade.

This chapter and its Appendix deal with the monetary mechanisms involved in international trade. Then the next two chapters concentrate on the basic real factors which underlie international trade and which are often obscured by the monetary veil that covers all international transactions. These basic real factors are involved in any rational appraisal of the problems raised by tariffs and other barriers to the international division of labor. In the final chapter all these principles are put to work to help us understand the contemporary international economic scene.

International trade is important for the following basic reason:

Foreign trade offers a "consumption-possibility frontier" that can give us more of all goods than can our own domestic production-possibility frontier!

EXAMPLE: Men in Malaysia give us rubber; we give the British wheat; the British give Malaysians cotton shirts. *Each of us ends up consuming more than he could produce alone.* The world is out on—and not inside—its true production-possibility frontier. That is the essence of foreign trade. So simple. And yet apparently so hard for members of parliament and voters to grasp and remember.

Our task in Part Five is to study the mechanics of international trade and finance: foreign exchange rates; balance of international payments; foreign lending and giving; tariff duties on imports, and import quotas; the so-called "principle of comparative advantage," which tells what kinds of trade will take place and why; and finally, the international economic problems of the 1970s, such as gold drains and hoardings, rigid versus flexible exchange rates, the European Common Market, the International Monetary Fund, long-term international liquidity problems, new ("paper-gold") Special Drawing Rights, problems of international capital flows, and foreign investment and ownership.

These are anything but abstract economic problems. They are the news that is being reported on the front page of tomorrow's newspapers. And they make the difference between fruitful international exchange and chaos.

A.   MECHANISMS OF FOREIGN EXCHANGE AND TRADE

▪ FOREIGN EXCHANGE RATES

First, how does trade take place? If I buy maple sugar from Quebec or pig iron from Hamilton, I naturally want to pay in dollars. Also, the farmer and steel producer expect to be paid in dollars, for the reason that their expenses and their living costs are all settled in dollars. Within a country, economic transactions seem simple.

If, however, I wish to buy a British racing car directly, matters are more complicated. I must ultimately pay in British money, or what is called "pounds sterling," rather than in dollars. Similarly, a man in Britain must somehow get dollars to a Canadian producer if he wants our merchandise. Many Canadians have never seen a British pound note. Certainly they would accept pounds only if they could be sure of converting them into Canadian dollars.

Clearly, therefore, exports and imports of goods between nations with different units of money introduce a new economic factor: the foreign exchange rate, giving the price of a foreigner's unit of money in terms of our own.

Thus the price of a British pound is $2.50 (Canadian). There is also a foreign exchange rate between our money and the currencies of each and every other country: 20 cents for the French franc; 30 cents for the Deutschemark; and so forth.[1] In early 1971 the price of a U.S. dollar hovered around $1.01.

Given the foreign exchange rate, it is now simple for me to buy my British car. Suppose its quoted price is £2,000. All I have to do is look in the newspaper for the foreign exchange rate for pounds. If this is $2.50 per pound, I simply go to a bank or post office with $5,000 and ask that the money be used

---

[1] There are also foreign exchange rates between the Deutschemark and the French franc. But these rates between other countries need not interest us much, particularly since, in a free competitive market, the mark-franc rate can be simply calculated from the mark-dollar and franc-dollar rate, because sharp-eyed international arbitragers see to it that relative "cross rates" do not get out of line: thus a mark must sell for a little less than 1.5 (= $.30/ $.20) francs. Of course, these examples have to be modified whenever official exchange rates are altered, as happened in 1969 and 1971 with revaluation of the mark.

to pay the British car exporter. Pay him what? Pounds, of course, the only kind of money he needs.

Whether I use the post office or a bank or a broker is of no particular importance. In fact, it is all the same if the British exporter sends me a bill requesting payment in dollars or if he deals with me through a Canadian dealer. In any case, he ultimately wants pounds, not dollars, and will soon trade the $5,000 for £2,000. (Needless to say, we are neglecting all commission charges and the cost of money orders.)

You should be able to show what a British importer of Canadian copper has to do if he wants to buy, say, a $25,000 shipment from a Canadian exporter. Here pounds must be converted into dollars. Why, when the foreign exchange rate is $2.50 per pound, will this cost him £10,000?

The businessman or tourist does not, as an individual, have to know anything more than this to get his imports or exports transacted. But the true economics of the problem cannot be grasped until we find out *why* the foreign exchange rate is at the level it is. What economic principles determine foreign exchange rates?

■ STABLE EXCHANGE RATE UNDER THE CLASSICAL GOLD STANDARD

There are three important cases to study:

1. The working of some kind of a pure or modified *gold standard*.

2. The case of *free foreign exchange rates*, available to every person in either country, but fluctuating from day to day according to *market demand and supply* (quite like the case of barley, which is available to all at a price that fluctuates from day to day, depending upon competitive supply and demand).

3. The case of *controlled* international trade, where each transaction requires a government license and where the foreign exchange rate may be different for different kinds of transactions, being set according to the will of the state.

The gold-standard case has been historically important; in severely modified form, it prevails in most countries today; in all likelihood, some vestige of it may be with us in the years ahead. It is also one of the easiest cases to master.

GOLD BARS   Suppose people everywhere insisted on being paid in bits of pure gold metal: weight alone would count, and its shape—whether round like a ball or a coin, or irregular like a sliver, or cylindrical like a broom handle—would not matter so long as there were a guarantee of its purity and weight. Then buying pig iron in Hamilton would require payment in gold at a price expressed in ounces of gold; and buying a bicycle in Britain would involve the same kind of payment. By definition, there would be no foreign-exchange-rate problem.

GOLD COINS   Since slivers and blobs of gold are inconvenient to carry and to assay for purity and for weight, it became customary for the state—in those days the prince—to stamp out in coin form a specified number of ounces of gold, carrying the seal of the state to guarantee purity and weight. (The edges were milled, so that removal of the edges would reveal light weight and fraud. Even so, since gold is soft and rubs off, merchants and banks weighed the coins.)

With gold coins as the exchange medium, would not foreign trade still be like domestic trade? Yes, essentially. But with some minor differences: If we used ounces and France used grams to measure weight, you would merely have to have a table of units' conversion. And the same problem would arise if Queen Victoria chose to make her coins about ¼ ounce of gold (the "sovereign") and U.S. President McKinley chose to make his ½₀ ounce of gold (the dollar). In that case, the pound sovereign, being five times as heavy as the dollar, would naturally have an exchange rate of $5 (American or Canadian) to £1.

Now that is essentially how the pre-1914 gold standard actually worked. Of course, local pride tended to keep the Americans and the British using their own coins. But anyone was free to melt down U.S. coins and get them converted into British coins (at very nominal costs). So except for the trifling costs of melting down, shipping across the ocean, and recoining, *all countries on the gold standard had essentially stable exchange rates whose par values, or parities, were determined by the gold content of their local money unit.*

> *Minor qualifications: "gold points."* Gold being quite inconvenient to carry around for spending purposes, inevitably governments issued paper certificates which were pledged to be redeemable in gold metal. People had the right to turn in gold for certificates and certificates for gold, and they often exercised that right. Also, in those days ocean transport was slow and costly: so there were "gold points" around the true mint parities within which the pound and (U.S.) dollar exchange rates could fluctuate. Thus, if it costs 2 cents to ship ¼ ounce of gold either way across the Atlantic Ocean (inclusive of insurance and interest costs), could the exchange rate depart a little from $5? Yes. In New York, the quoted price of a pound could rise to as much as $5.02 before it would pay to get gold bars and ship them to London to be exchanged for pounds; a price higher than $5.02 could not prevail because enough gold would be flowing to keep the price no higher than the upper gold point. It should be evident that the pound could fall below the mint parity of $5 by 2 cents to $4.98. When the exchange rate got down to this lower gold point, it would be cheaper for gold to be shipped from Britain to the United States. All this actually happened (except that $5 is substituted here for the correct pre-1914 parity of $4.87 (U.S.) to simplify the arithmetic, and the shipping costs are given only approximately). Before 1914, the foreign exchange rate of the pound and the U.S. dollar stayed essentially constant, varying but a trifle from these weight-determined mint parities when the gold points were touched and gold had to flow in the indicated direction.

THE HUME GOLD-FLOW EQUILIBRATING MECHANISM   Now that the mechanics of the problem are understood, we probe deeper to answer this question:

Under the gold standard, what kept the United States from buying more goods from Britain than Britain bought from her—which, after all, would have required Americans to keep shipping gold in final payment? Why would the United States not be drained of all her gold?

This is a good question, and the mercantilist writers, who preceded Adam Smith and his friend the noted philosopher David Hume, gave a plausible but superficial answer. The mercantilists said:

"A country will lose its gold unless the Prince introduces tariffs and quotas to cut down on imports of goods; and unless he gives subsidies to encourage exports; and unless he forbids skilled workmen to take their knowledge abroad and makes sure that all shipping takes place in our own boats, however dear they may be." As an afterthought, almost too obvious to require mention, they said: "Of course, losing gold is a terrible thing for a nation. Don't ask why. Everyone knows it to be one of the worst tragedies that can happen to a nation."

David Hume in 1752, and economists ever since, have given the refutation to this line of reasoning. First Hume noted that it could not be true that everyone would all the time be losing gold under free trade. Where would it go—into the sea? And he demonstrated that it is no tragedy at all if a country goes permanently from having 10 million ounces of gold to having 5 million, or even 1 million. *If having half the amount of gold means merely that all prices are exactly halved, no one in the country is the least bit better or worse off.* So, losing half or nine-tenths of a nation's gold is nothing to worry about, Hume pointed out, if it merely ends up with an equivalently reduced price level.

Here it is well to recall the crude quantity theory of money and prices discussed in Chapter 14. David Hume, along with John Locke and earlier writers, was one of the first to enunciate and hold to this theory concerning the proportionality of all prices to the stock of money (in this case M being gold).[2]

Now comes the second and important part of Hume's classical refutation of mercantilism and defense of free trade. He asserted that there was a four-pronged mechanism that tended always to keep in equilibrium the international balance of payments of countries on the gold standard. Briefly, the Hume mechanism is this.

Whenever one country imports too much and begins to lose gold, its loss of gold *reduces its price and cost level*, thereby (1) *decreasing its imports* of foreign goods that have become relatively expensive, and (2) *increasing exports* of its home-produced goods that have become relatively cheap.

The other country, which had been having a so-called "favorable balance of trade," in which it was sending more goods abroad than it was importing and merely receiving barren gold in exchange, now has (via the quantity theory) its price and cost levels of goods *raised*. This is a further reason (3) for its now-expensive *exports to go down* in physical amount and (4) for its citizens to import *more* of the now-cheap goods of the first country.

---

[2] He admitted that the equilibrium predicted by the quantity theory would not take place instantaneously; indeed, he was one of the first to recognize that a period of rising M and rising prices, when it was first happening and was not foreseen, would give profits to businessmen by causing their prices to rise more than their costs; he thought this would be good for full employment and capital formation in the short run.

The result of this four-pronged gold-flow price-level mechanism is to improve the balance of payments of the country that was losing gold and worsen that of the country with the favorable balance of trade—until equilibrium in international trade is established at relative prices that keep imports and exports in balance with no net gold flow. In theory the equilibrium is stable and self-correcting without tariffs and other state interference.

FLEXIBLE EXCHANGE RATES

Having seen how an idealized gold standard works, we turn now to the case where supply and demand are left free to determine the foreign exchange rate. In the absence of any tie to gold, the pound in the 1940s might have had an average price of $4 or $5, and in this decade, an average price of $2.50 (Canadian). Who knows, perhaps next decade it could be at $4.50, or $3, or $1.50, once floating exchange rates become the rule.

The forces of supply and demand will determine the answer. As we have seen, Canadians need pounds to buy British goods, and the British need Canadian dollars to buy our products. Suppose that Canadians want to buy so many British goods at the existing $2.50 level, but that the British want so few Canadian goods. Then we may be demanding more pounds as needed foreign exchange than they will be wanting to supply us with. If there is no longer a gold standard, one cannot get gold and ship it over so as to keep the foreign exchange rate within narrow gold points around the $2.50 parity. Instead, our urgent demand for pounds will bid up the foreign exchange rate—the price of a British pound in Canadian dollars. How far? Just far enough so that, at the new higher price of, say, $3.10 for the pound, our total demand for foreign exchange (in this case pounds) will be brought down into equality with the now larger amount of foreign exchange the British willingly supply.

Two main steps are involved: (1) With the higher price of pounds in Canadian dollars, it will cost more to import British bicycles and our physical demand for them will fall off in the usual fashion. (2) With our dollar now cheaper, our goods will cost less to the British and they will want to demand more of our export goods. (If we look at these two effects, from both their viewpoint and our own, we have something like the four-pronged action of Hume. But with certain important differences. Our *whole* domestic price level need not change, and neither need theirs. The change in the foreign exchange rate can *itself* bring about enhanced *relative* dearness and cheapness of export- and import-price levels.)

The familiar curves of supply and demand developed in Chapter 4 and Part Three are used in Fig. 32-1 to show equilibrium determination of flexible exchange rates. Canada's *dd* curve comes from our desire for foreign exchange to buy import goods, to make tourist visits, to hire shipping and insurance services, to finance our troops abroad and our foreign-aid grants, to pay the dividends and interest we owe to foreign owners of our securities and property; and also to finance long-term investment abroad by Canadian firms or stock

Demand bids up, supply bids down a free foreign exchange rate:

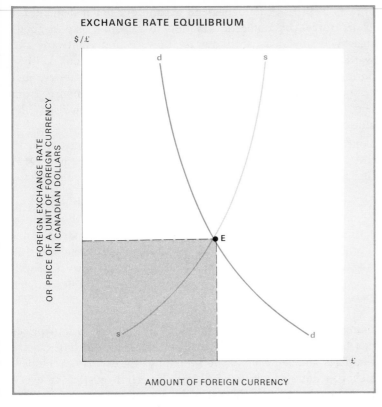

FIG. 32-1. Behind our *dd* is our desire to import British goods, buy British securities, visit the Bard's grave, and so forth. Behind their *ss* supply of pounds to be traded for Canadian dollars is their desire for our export goods and other items. If the rate were above *E*, there would be an excess of foreign currency that they would want to supply us over what we should want to demand. Such an excess of supply would bid the rate back down to *E*, where the market of foreign currency for dollars is just cleared. [Test yourself by replacing pounds (£) by 30-cent Deutschemarks (DM).]

buyers, and short-term investment in foreign near-term bonds or savings accounts.

What is behind the British demand for dollars—which shows up as the *ss* supply curve of the pound-foreign-exchange they offer us? The exactly similar items in *their* balance of payments: desire to import our export goods, need to pay us dividends, etc.

At the *dd* and *ss* intersection, the flexible foreign exchange rate will be established, having then no tendency to rise or fall from this equilibrium level.

What will happen if tomorrow we send more troops abroad, travel abroad more, find new bargains in British catalogues and expand our dollar demand for British goods, and are forced by domestic inflation to raise our export-goods prices? Such changes will obviously shift our *dd* upward and rightward and also their *ss* leftward and upward. With what resulting intersection? With a new higher equilibrium level of the exchange rate; as described above, just enough higher to coax out more Canadian exports and choke off imports from Britain. The exchange rate at which we buy foreign currencies has risen; the dollar's relative value has fallen.

A classical economist like Hume would understand all this very well. In fact, he (and Ricardo around 1817 and Sweden's Gustav Cassel around 1917) would offer this clue to the equilibrium level of a flexible exchange rate:

Purchasing-power parity. Let Canada and Britain be at equilibrium, say, at $2.50 per £1. Now let Canada double *all* her prices by domestically inflating her *M*; and let Britain keep her *M* limited enough to produce a steady price level. Then, other things being equal (such as employment remaining full and there being no inventions, crop failures, tariffs, or change in tastes), the new *dd* and *ss* intersection will come at twice the old $2.50 rate, namely, at $5.00 per £1.

Hume's reasoning would be classically simple. With all wages and prices here *exactly doubled* (and M doubled here to finance them), we can *buy exactly the same* physical imports and *sell exactly the same* physical exports at the new exchange rate which has doubled like everything else. (It is just as if every Canadian old dollar is now called two Canadian dollars, period.)[3]

DEPRECIATION, APPRECIATION, AND DEVALUATION   A doubling of the pound is a halving of the dollar. By definition, the fall in the price of one currency in terms of one or all others is called a "depreciation." A relative rise in the price of a currency in terms of another currency is called an "appreciation." Evidently, the pound has appreciated in our example, and the dollar has undergone a large depreciation.

The term "devaluation" is often confused with the term "depreciation." Devaluation usually is defined to mean a rise in the price of gold: thus, in 1933, President Roosevelt devalued the U.S. dollar, raising the price of gold from about $21 an ounce eventually to its present price of $35 an ounce. When the Swiss or French stayed on the gold standard at their previous parities, the devaluation of the U.S. dollar meant depreciation of the U.S. dollar relative to the undervalued French franc and Swiss franc; but in terms of the Canadian

---

[3] Cassel and other writers developed the doctrine of purchasing-power parity to predict how much World War I currencies would depreciate when internal inflation sent their price levels up by 100 per cent or more. His long-run predictions worked out better than his short-run predictions, but neither had perfect accuracy. In the real world, unlike the classical model, other things did not stay equal.

dollar, which devalued equally with the U.S. dollar, there was neither depreciation nor appreciation of the U.S. dollar.

Devaluation defined. When gold officially goes up in price relative to a
currency—as in 1934 from $21 (U.S.) an ounce to $35 (U.S.)—we say that
currency has been devalued.

Depreciation defined. When the price of a foreign currency rises relative
to a given currency—e.g., when the Canadian price of the U.S. dollar rose
10 per cent in 1949, from $1.00 to $1.10 per U.S. dollar—we say the
(domestic) currency has *depreciated*, and of course that the foreign
currency has had a relative *appreciation*.

If *all* countries *simultaneously* raised the price of gold by 100 per
cent, there would be no depreciation or appreciation but there would be a
devaluation.

If prices and wages lack the flexibility to make the needed trade adjustments under the gold standard, the deficit country may find itself forced into
a devaluation; this rise in the price at which it will buy and sell gold will imply
a depreciation of its currency relative to any currency that remains at the old
gold parities.[4] If all countries devalue together and in balance—to restore international liquidity or for any other reason—no appreciation or depreciation
of currencies relative to each other takes place.

Generally, a *depreciation* of the currency that has been running an international *deficit* can be expected[5] to help restore the equilibrium. Although this
alternative happens less frequently, equilibrium could also be restored by
having the *surplus* country *appreciate* its currency—examples would be the 5
per cent appreciation of the mark and the guilder engineered by the Germans
and the Dutch respectively in 1961 and the further 1969 appreciation of the
German mark, or the World War I appreciation of the Swedish krona.

EXAMPLES: Britain was forced by her international deficit into depreciating the
pound from $3.00 to $2.80 (Canadian) in 1967. Slowly, this did improve her export
competitiveness; but, if she had let wages and costs rise within the country by

---

[4] At the end of this chapter's Appendix, there is discussed a compromise proposal that
has some of the stability advantages of the gold standard's fixed exchange rates, and some of
the flexibility advantages of floating exchange rates set by market forces of supply and
demand. It is called the "crawling peg," and it permits limited changes in the exchange rate
each year; over several years an orderly change in parity can then be achieved.

[5] There is a theoretical possibility that the relative price changes brought about by
depreciation of the Canadian dollar could make the deficit worse rather than better if international demands turn out to be very inelastic rather than elastic. In such cases, lowering the
prices in pounds sterling of Canadian export goods will not expand our physical sales much;
therefore the British will actually offer fewer pounds for dollars rather than more pounds.
And this could outweigh the reduction of pounds we pay Britain for our reduced physical
imports. Thus, the price reaction to a depreciation of the dollar may be a perverse rather
than an equilibrating one: The dollar would have to depreciate still further until demands
ceased to be so inelastic; paradoxically, currency *appreciation* might in this perverse case
wipe out a country's import deficit. For more discussion on this, see Chapter 34's section
"The Foreigner Will Pay," page 841.

as much as the depreciation, she would have frittered away all its benefit. Again, in August, 1969, France devalued the franc by 11 to 12 per cent; unrest in 1968 had sent up French costs, and De Gaulle's stubborn refusal to depreciate had encouraged a speculative run on the franc.

CANADIAN EXPERIENCE   Canada is almost the only country that has allowed its exchange rate to float freely since the end of World War II. In 1951, despairing of finding a "pegged" rate that would be appropriate for the fluctuating foreign demands for Canadian exchange, the authorities turned the dollar loose on the world markets to find its own level. Within a year these foreign demands had increased, and the Canadian exchange rate for the U.S. dollar fell from $1.04 to 97 cents. [Or, what is the same, the price of the Canadian dollar rose from about $.95 to $1.03 (U.S.).]

Thereafter the Canadian dollar fluctuated, but remained at a "premium" until the exchange crisis of 1961-1962.

Before the exchange rate was pegged in 1962, what was the effect of being flexible? Whenever Canadian demand for foreign goods or money strengthened, the value of the Canadian dollar fell a little, imports became slightly more expensive for Canadian incomes, and people tended to import less. This happened in the boom year of 1956. And whenever foreign demand for Canadian goods became very strong, the value of the Canadian dollar was pulled up, Canadian lumber and wheat tended to rise in price to foreigners, and the demands slackened again. Indeed, exporters and importers grumbled about the unpredictability of the value of foreign currencies in Canadian terms, saying that it was hard to do business and that foreigners insisted on having prices quoted in foreign, "pegged-currency" terms.

The effect of being *flexible*, however, should not be confused with the effect of the appreciation of the Canadian dollar. Even if our dollar had not been free to fluctuate, even if our exchange rate had been fixed, it might well have "pegged" at a premium during the 1951-62 period. For if foreigners were willing to buy our goods at $1.05 (U.S.), they would have taken many more at $1.00 and our total exports would have been much greater. Economists today argue about whether that would have been a good thing, for it is true that both larger exports and smaller imports would have been a help during Canada's late-fifties' unemployment. But our foreign-payments accounts would have been in substantial surplus; all that we need note here is that the flexible rate, in floating to an appreciation, helped to keep this surplus down.[6]

---

[6] If countries are under a gold standard, flexible rates are out of the question. How then do they adjust to a deficit? First, Hume's mechanism should go to work, if prices and wages are sufficiently flexible to make the needed trade adjustments. If they are not, the country must devalue; this rise in the price at which it will buy or sell gold will imply a depreciation of the value of its currency relative to all others on the gold parities. This is what some experts advised the United States to do in struggling with her foreign deficits of the 1960s and 1970s. But if all countries devalue together, no depreciation of currencies relative to each other will result. Thus the U.S. deficit would remain, in real terms, as before; trade flows would not change. The only result would be that the world would have more gold, measured in the units of *any* currency. This may be defined as an increase in international liquidity, and has been claimed as a worth-while goal in itself.

The Canadian dollar has responded to capital movements, speculation:

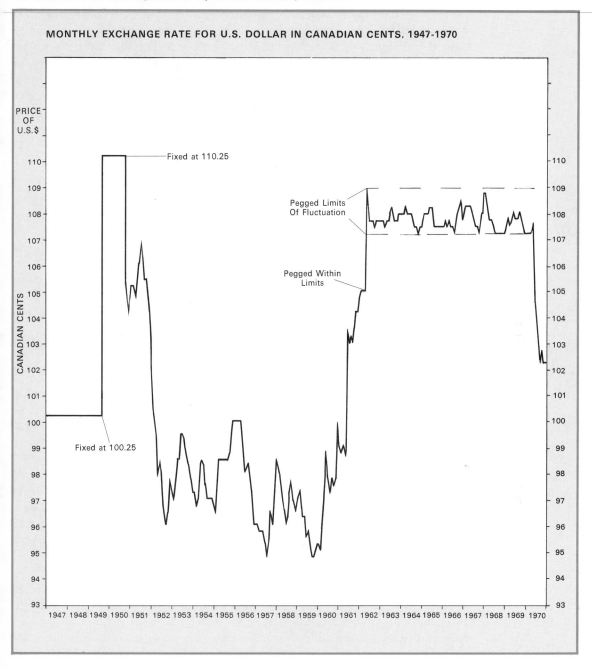

MONTHLY EXCHANGE RATE FOR U.S. DOLLAR IN CANADIAN CENTS, 1947-1970

FIG. 32-2. The freeing of the Canadian dollar from a pegged rate at the end of May, 1970, was a reversion to the system of the 1950s. The 1949-1950 rates were a response to Korean War transactions and speculation; the 1960-1961 rise was caused by capital inflows and government intervention.

On May 31, 1970, Finance Minister Edgar Benson announced that the Canadian dollar was again freed to find its own "market" level on world exchange markets. The move climaxed a period of continuing inflows of foreign exchange, primarily U.S. dollars, which placed strong upward pressure on the Canadian dollar at 92.5 cents (U.S.)—$1.08 (Canadian) per U.S. dollar—and forced the Exchange Fund Account (described on page 395) to spend unacceptably large amounts of Canadian dollars in purchasing the incoming foreign exchange. The results of freeing the dollar were still working themselves out in the summer of 1970, when the exchange rate fluctuated between the narrow bounds of $1.03 and $1.04 (Canadian) per $1.00 (U.S.). In early 1971, the exchange rate fluctuated around $1.01 and $1.02 per $1.00 (U.S.). Figure 32-2, on the preceding page, gives a graphic history of the Canadian/U.S. exchange rate.

EVOLUTION OF THE GOLD STANDARD   There is nothing sacred about gold. Silver, platinum, lead, or for that matter paper napkins would do, provided they had convenience for exchange, could not be falsified, and were enough limited in supply to keep the price level from soaring. Actually, the old gold standard was in its heyday only for a brief half-century prior to 1914. Before the nineteenth century, Britain had been more on a silver than on a gold standard, and had stumbled onto the gold standard as a result of market revaluations of the two precious metals without anyone's realizing it. Her great prestige caused France, the United States, and the rising empires of Germany and Japan to adopt the gold standard later.

Even in its brief heyday, several crises caused the gold standard to be "suspended"—to break down periodically (as, for example when the American Civil War forced the United States off gold for more than a decade). Only Britain's firm £4¼ to the ounce of gold kept the gold-standard idea alive. Moreover, the price level was at the mercy of the happenstance of gold discoveries. If world physical production was increasing in the years 1875 to 1895 at the rate of 5 per cent per year, the gold supply would—according to the quantity theory of money—have to increase by 5 per cent per year to keep prices stable. But mines, because of the ending of the Californian and Australian gold rushes, were not producing this much gold then; and as a result prices were sagging all over the world in the last third of the nineteenth century.

This "great depression" gave rise to much social unrest. In an ideal world of perfect price and wage flexibility, where the quantity theory worked smoothly both down and up, falling prices should not have mattered much. But as Hume himself insisted, prices and wages tend to be sticky downward; and falling price levels tend to lead to labor unrest, strikes, and unemployment, and radical movements generally. Precisely that happened in the United States and other countries during the period from 1875 to 1895. (Recall Chapter 7's account of the Knights of Labor.)

The most important radical movement formed in the United States during this time was the Popular Party, or Populists. It drew for its membership principally on debt-ridden farmers who were suffering from a persistent drop in farm prices, and on western silver miners who faced falling silver prices after the United States went on the single gold standard in 1873. Since a gold shortage seemed to be squeezing all prices downward, there was a clamor on the part of these people for the use of silver to supplement gold. This culminated in the historic speech by William Jennings Bryan at the 1896 Democratic Convention, in which he spoke in favor of 'bimetallism' and warned against crucifying mankind on a cross of gold.

FRACTIONAL RESERVES, BANKING, AND THE GOLD-EXCHANGE STANDARD   With Germany and Japan going on the gold standard, the deflationary pressure on prices would have been even worse had it not been for growing methods of economizing on gold. Modern banks, which hold only fractional reserves, began to develop: the demand-deposit M they created meant that not quite so much gold was needed to keep up with growing total output. Moreover, most of the countries on the gold standard did *not* keep 100 per cent gold reserves to back up the token coins and paper currency they issued. Thus, if the typical country held only one-fourth gold against its paper money, only a quarter as much gold would have to be mined to support the same world price level.

This process of domestic banking evolution to economize on the use of gold is important. For, as we shall see, it foreshadows the modern international development of economizing on and displacing gold by creating so-called "paper gold" (i.e., SDRs, or Special Drawing Rights). "Bimetallism," mentioned in the previous section, was also proposed as a means of economizing on the use of gold.

Bimetallism would mean that the nation's treasury would exchange its currency for *either* gold or silver, at some agreed-upon ratio. For example, the U.S. Treasury would exchange U.S. dollars for 16 ounces of silver *or* 1 ounce of gold. Unless all countries agreed upon the same 16/1 ratio, there would be a one-way movement of each metal to the place where it was most valued; and the place where gold was most valued would be on gold standard, while the place where silver was most valued would be on the silver standard. As a result, with every change in the relative supplies and demands for the two metals, there would be an ensuing fluctuation in the foreign exchange rates between the two countries. (The percentage size of the fluctuation could be only two-sixteenths if their respective bimetallic parities were 16/1 and 18/1. Even if all countries went on the same 16/1 ratio, any tendency for mines to pour out the two metals at substantially different rates would lead to the free market's bidding their price ratios to some figure other than 16/1; and in this case, by a form of what is known as Gresham's Law—"Cheap money drives out good"—the result would be that the cheapest metal in the market place would be given to the treasuries of the different countries, and in effect the world would be on a single standard again—that of the cheapest metal.)

Canada has never had official bimetallism, but in the early days, before she had her own coinage, she made official the coins of both the United States and Great Britain. In order for people to know how much to pay in taxes in either kind of coinage, she established an official parity ratio between the sterling and U.S. coins and notes. Because of the fractions involved, the rounded-off value of a British shilling was placed at 25 cents in gold instead of at the 24 cents ruling in London or New York. Shillings were thus overrated in Canada and appeared in large numbers, tending to drive out other coinage used in Canada.

The same phenomenon is noticed whenever Canada has changed the value of her currency. For example, when Canadian and U.S. dollars had an exchange rate of 1:1, Canadian housewives often paid for their groceries with U.S. bills. But when the Canadian dollar depreciated, that is, when the value of the U.S. dollar rose to $1.08 (Canadian), housewives held on to their U.S. bills to sell at the bank and bought their groceries with Canadian bills only. The dearer money was driven out of circulation at once, as Gresham's Law would predict.

Today no one favors two kinds of money.

Another development helped economize on gold. Many countries, particularly small ones (like the Philippines), kept their money exchangeable at fixed rates with respect to gold. But they held little or no gold. Instead, they would hold the money of some big countries (like Great Britain and the United States) which were on the gold standard. So long as the small country could stay on such a "gold-exchange standard," the effect would be much like the pure gold standard, but with great economizing on gold.

Fortunately for those who favored the gold standard, the deflationary pressures eased some when gold was discovered in the Klondike and South Africa in the mid-1890s and when the cyanide process greatly increased the output of gold mines. Together with the increasing leverage attained by having smaller and smaller fractional-reserve ratios and more and more gold-exchange standards, the increase in mining enabled the world to keep on the gold standard and stave off deflation up until the 1929 crash. Some experts actually attribute that slump to an increasing shortage of world liquidity.

THE DOLLAR STANDARD   During the Great Depression of the 1930s, political unrest and fear of Hitler's aggression caused an avalanche of gold to flow into the United States. After World II *the world was in fact on a dollar standard.* The pound sterling and the U.S. dollar were the "key currencies" in terms of which international trade and finance were carried on. Private and governmental reserves were kept largely in the form of dollar and sterling balances (i.e., in cash, bank deposits, and liquid short-term securities). Whereas before 1914 the pound had been king, by 1949 the U.S. dollar was established as *the* key currency.

> EXAMPLE: The Bretton Woods Conference of 1944, which set up the International Monetary Fund and the World Bank, defined in its Charter the parities of currencies not simply in terms of ounces of gold, but in terms of U.S. dollars (the equivalent of 1/35 ounce of gold).

The fact that the dollar served as a key currency gave the United States, in effect, something the same privilege of creating money out of thin air that the commercial banks enjoy domestically (as Chapter 15 discussed). To a degree, this key position gave the United States the right to get a certain amount of goods at no real cost. But it also put a special responsibility on the United States to keep its balance of payments in order.

In the 1970s the international standard is still undergoing evolution with the role of gold as a metal becoming less and less pivotal.[7]

■ EXCHANGE-RATE MECHANICS CONCLUDED

We have now surveyed the fundamentals of foreign exchange rates. Although money prices are quoted in international trade, in the longest run there must really be an international *barter* of goods and services against goods and services. Under a stable exchange-rate system like that of the modified gold standard, gold flows are supposed to lead to price-level adjustments big enough to restore equilibrium on the export and import side. Under flexible exchange rates, it is fluctuation in the foreign exchange rate that alters the relative costs and prices of foreign and home goods enough to restore an equilibrium balance in the international trade.

The remaining section of this chapter will go behind the demand and supply curves of international trade to examine each item involving foreign exchange payments and see how they all combine.

B. BALANCE OF INTERNATIONAL TRADE AND CAPITAL MOVEMENTS

■ THE BALANCE OF INTERNATIONAL PAYMENTS

Instead of referring to $E - M$ we now investigate exactly what is meant by a country's "balance of payments." This is a statement that takes into account the values of all goods, gifts, foreign aid, capital loans (IOUs), and gold and key-currency reserves coming in and going out, and the interconnections among all these items that lie behind Fig. 32-1's curves.

The balance of international payments summarizes these important relations. If you understand it, you have a fairly good grasp of foreign trade.

The Dominion Bureau of Statistics keeps records and makes estimates of all international transactions in a year. For example, from customs statistics it learns about merchandise imports and tourist spending. It must also record or guess at amounts of money lent abroad, gold movements, interest and dividends received or sent abroad, money sent home by emigrants, and so forth. They are all fitted into the "balance of international payments" for each year —simply a double-entry listing of all items, drawn up in such a way that it must always show a balance.[8]

---

[7] Chapter 35 will discuss the post-1968 creation of a "two-tier" gold system: within the official tier, a fixed total of gold exchanges at stable parities; but then in the unofficial tier, gold is bought and sold in the London, Zurich, and Paris markets at whatever price is determined by the shifting supply of mined gold and the shifting demand by jewelers, dentists, industrial users, and hoarders.

[8] Articles brought in by smuggling and some innocent items elude the record keepers; so it is necessary to introduce a miscellaneous category of omitted items, as in NNP's "residual error of estimate."

The Canadian balance has been prepared for many years; it was one of the first national statements to be officially presented. It is usually in two parts:

I. Current Account

    Merchandise (or the "balance of trade")

    Nonmerchandise (or "invisible" items)

        Travel

        Interest and dividend payments

        Freight and shipping outlays

        Inheritances and migrants' remittances home

        Other current transactions (including many by government and
            also the sale of insurance services)

II. Capital movements

    In long-term forms

        Government

        Private

    In short-term forms

        Government

        Private

        Other short-term (a residual, balancing item)

III. In addition, there is usually a final item that shows the change in the government's holdings of foreign exchange and gold, and in its net IMF position.

THE CURRENT-ACCOUNT BALANCE   The totality of items in Part I is usually referred to as the "balance on current account." This important magnitude summarizes the difference between our total exports of goods *and services* and our total imports of goods and services.

In a moment, we shall see how any surplus or deficit balance on current account is "financed"—or, more precisely, is offset—by capital movements under Section II and Section III. But before doing this, we shall describe briefly Section I's major current items.

Centuries ago, when *merchandise* items predominated, writers concentrated on this narrow category alone. If merchandise exports were greater in value than merchandise imports, they spoke of a "favorable balance of trade"; if imports exceeded exports, they spoke of an "unfavorable balance of trade." This is not a good choice of terms, for we shall see that a so-called "unfavorable" balance of trade may be a very good thing for a country.

In addition to such so-called "visible" merchandise items, we must not forget the important role played these days by the "invisibles." These consist of such nonmerchandise items as Canadian travel and tourist spending abroad, shipping and insurance services that we provide for foreigners or they provide for us, our interest earnings from abroad, and the gifts that immigrants send back home. On reflection, one realizes that an invisible item such as the expenditure of a Canadian for a drink in Paris has the same effect on the final balance of payments as does his import of French wine to be drunk here in

Canada. And when we provide shipping insurance service, that acts like an export.

DEBITS AND CREDITS   A good way to decide how any item should be treated is to ask the following question: Is the item like one of our merchandise exports, providing us with more foreign currencies? Such an export-type item is called a "credit item" and adds to our supply of foreign money. Or is the item like one of our merchandise imports, causing us to use up our stock of foreign currencies and making it necessary to make a payment of foreign currency? Such an import-type item is called a "debit item" and adds to our demand for foreign money.

To show how this rule works, ask the following question: How shall we treat interest and dividend income on investments received by Canadians from abroad? Clearly, they are receipt items like exports, in that they provide us with foreign currencies. The reader can reverse the argument to show that the interest and dividends which we mail out to foreigners must be treated like payment items—like imports, they use up our foreign currencies.

At this point a close look at Table 32-1 will be helpful. It presents official data on the Canadian balance of international payments for 1969. Note its division into sections: current and capital items. In addition, there is a short third section: changes in reserves. Each row is numbered for easy reference. Then, after each item has been listed by name in Column (a), we list in Column (b) the receipts (or "credits") we have earned from selling export-like items for foreign currencies. Next, in Column (c), are listed the payments (or "debits") that use up our holdings of foreign currencies when we buy import-like items. The second main division of the table is discussed later.

In the first division, it is shown that our merchandise exports in 1969 gave us receipts of 14,886 million dollars, but our merchandise imports cost us payments of 14,018 million dollars. Thus the difference (or "balance") between the two trade items was in that year 868 million dollars. It shows in the last Column (d). (A minus sign means that our "credits," or receipts, were smaller than our "debits," or payments; otherwise the balance is positive.) When the balance was positive, it used to be called "favorable"; even today our merchandise-trade export-surplus is called, misleadingly, a "favorable balance of trade." And when the balance is negative, it is called an "unfavorable balance of trade."

This term is deceptive because it suggests that only *visible* or merchandise trade is important, neglecting the next few items that also bring in current receipts or cause current payments, though they are "invisibles." The reader can interpret each line of these current items. Gold for export is placed here in the official statistics because the authorities want to separate this semimonetary item from ordinary merchandise, which is what it really is. The rest are routine. Foreigners travel in Canada, pay interest and dividends to Canadian owners of shares and bonds, pay rates for freight transported on Canadian carriers, send money "back home" to Canadians, buy insurance from Canadian companies, and in other minor ways make available to Canadians foreign

These figures summarize international transactions:

CANADIAN BALANCE OF INTERNATIONAL PAYMENTS, 1969 (in millions of dollars)

SECTION I: CURRENT ACCOUNT

NO.	ITEMS (a)	CURRENT RECEIPTS (b)	CURRENT PAYMENTS (c)	BALANCE ON CURRENT ACCOUNT (d)
1	**Merchandise** (adjusted)	$14,886	$14,018	$ 868
	Nonmerchandise:			
2	Gold production available for export	110	—	110
3	Travel	1,079	1,280	−201
4	Interest and dividends	406	1,364	−958
5	Freight and shipping	934	994	− 60
6	Inheritances and migrants' funds	363	190	173
7	Official contributions	—	143	−143
8	Other current transactions	1,109	1,620	−511
9	Total nonmerchandise trade	4,001	5,591	−1,590
10	Current account balance	$18,887	$19,609	−$ 722
11	With the United States			−710
12	With Great Britain			263
13	With all other countries			−275

money just as they would if they were buying Canadian goods. And Canadians make payments abroad on the same items.

The table shows that total current payments by Canadians are *larger* than their total current receipts. Thus the balance of *trade* (merchandise), though positive, is more than offset by the other items in the *balance on current account*, making it, in the older phraseology, "unfavorable." (Government's foreign transactions are not well shown in the Canadian official balance on current account. Mutual aid payments to NATO countries are not shown at all. "Official contributions" are amounts paid by Canada as its membership fees and quotas for the U.N., International Monetary Fund, etc., as shown in Chapter 35. Such payments as supplies for Canadian ships abroad are included among "merchandise imports." Obviously some official gifts *in kind* to foreign countries cannot be shown because they do not lead to Canadian receipts of foreign currencies, nor do we make payments abroad. For example, if we give locomotives to an underprivileged country, the payment is made at home, to our locomotive producers. There is no international financial transaction.)

In arriving at the "balance on current account" we have completed our survey of the *first* section of the table. We see that the balance is equal to −722 million dollars. Although every item has contributed to the final balance, it is clear that trade (exports) has had a positive influence, and interest and dividends (foreign earnings on funds lent to our industry and governments) a strong negative, or "unfavorable" influence.

As a matter of fact, we have run a negative balance on current account for most years since World War II, as may be seen in Fig. 32-3. How can we

CANADIAN BALANCE OF INTERNATIONAL PAYMENTS, 1969 (Continued)

SECTION II: CAPITAL ACCOUNT

NO.	ITEMS (a)	NET CAPITAL MOVEMENTS (b)	
	Capital Movements in Long-term Forms:		
	Direct Investment		
14	Direct investment in Canada	$ 625	
15	Direct investment abroad	−255	
	Canadian Stocks		
16	Trade in outstanding stocks	61	
17	New issues	197	
18	Retirements	−1	
	Canadian Bonds		
19	Trade in outstanding bonds	1	
	New issues minus retirements		
20	Government of Canada	−49	
21	Provincial and Municipal	1,087	
22	Corporate	449	
23	Other long-term capital	47	
24	Total Capital Movements in Long-term Forms		$2,162
	Capital Movements in Short-term Forms:		
25	Resident holdings of foreign bank balances	−1,609	
26	Nonresident holdings of Canadian assets	391	
27	Other short-term capital movements (*residual* item)	−157	
28	Total Capital Movements in Short-term Forms		−$1,375
29	Total Capital Movements		$ 787

CANADIAN BALANCE OF INTERNATIONAL PAYMENTS, 1969 (Continued)

SECTION III: CHANGE IN HOLDINGS OF FOREIGN EXCHANGE AND GOLD

30	To offset current balance	$ 722	
31	Increase in official holdings of gold and foreign reserves	65	
32	Total		$ 787
33	Over-all net balance of international payments		0

TABLE 32-1. (Source: DBS.)

do this? Indeed, because there must be some countries that typically run positive balances, how does *any* country offset its unbalanced current account? The answer is shown, for Canada, in Sections II and III of the table: either we borrow from abroad or we reduce our gold and reserve-asset holdings. The other countries, with positive current-account balances, must do the opposite: lend abroad or add to their holdings of gold and reserve assets. *For it is a tautology that what you get you must either pay for or owe for.* So, if Canada doesn't pay for all she imports with her exports, she must owe someone for the rest. In owing, she is *defined* to have borrowed. This fact of double-entry

Canada tends to deficits on current account and to surplus long-term capital inflows:

FIG. 32-3. Canada tends to positive inflows of capital in long-term form, and to negative balances on current account. Short-term capital movements tend to "accommodate" themselves to these two "independent" flows, being sometimes negative and sometimes positive. (Source: DBS.)

bookkeeping means that the whole table of the balance of international payments must show a final definitional balance. (Statistical errors and omissions, as in the case of GNP residual error of estimate discussed in Chapter 10, must of course be reckoned with if the double-entry bookkeeper is not given all the accurate facts; but this should not affect the *logic* of the perfect balance.)

CAPITAL ACCOUNT   Let us look at Section II of the table. It shows the long-term and short-term loans Canadian companies and persons make or receive from private foreign citizens. (E.g., Ford of Canada may receive funds from its parent in the United States; a Montreal trust company may make a loan in Latin America; you may make a deposit in a London bank or buy shares in a Texas oil company.) It also shows *government* capital transactions (foreigners may buy Canadian government bonds; Quebec may borrow in New York; Canada may repay Britons for bonds issued years ago; the United States makes a payment to Canada as part of the Columbia River Treaty).

It is easy to decide which capital transactions are payments by Canada and which are receipts, if you follow this rule: Always think of Canada as exporting and importing *capital securities*—or, for short, exporting and import-ing IOUs. Then you can treat these flows like any other exports or imports. When we lend abroad, is it a positive or negative item? Though our capital goes abroad, we are *importing* IOUs. Thus the sign is negative and the item is a payment, or a debit.

To avoid confusion, try another example. When we "import" capital heavily, as the table shows we do, we actually *export* securities and IOUs. Thus the borrowing is given a plus sign, just as if we were exporting newsprint. When we have a negative current account balance, we are importing more than we export. To offset this import balance we export IOUs, giving us a positive capital account balance. The positive cancels the negative.

Item 24 shows a total of 2,162 million dollars. This is positive: we were exporting long-term IOUs, or borrowing from abroad, chiefly by selling new issues of Canadian public and private securities to foreign lenders. This, too, has been typical of our post-World War II history—Canada has had more long-term investment opportunities than Canadian lenders could handle. But another big item is "direct investment in Canada," (Item 14) which is the measure of the amounts foreign companies have contributed directly to their subsidiaries and associates (like Esso in Imperial Oil, General Electric in Cana-dian General Electric, and so on). At the same time, Canadians have been in-vesting directly and in foreign securities abroad, but the totals are smaller. Over time, long-term investment inflows have been positive, as Fig. 32-3 illustrates.

The next group of items deals with short-term transactions. These are available in detail, and show mostly how we have drawn on or added to our holdings of bank deposits and other liquid assets abroad, and how foreigners have acted similarly. In the year 1969, a myriad of such individual, provincial, and municipal changes resulted in Canadians moving their wealth into foreign bank accounts to the extent of 1,609 million dollars, with a minus sign. This was, however, partially offset by foreigners tending to move their money to Canada to buy Canadian assets such as short-term bills: Item 26. Thus these two measured short-term amounts produced a net out-flow of $-1,218$ million dollars $(= -1,609$ million $+ 391$ million).

On most capital accounts, Item 27 is very large. This is because "other short-term capital movements" is the *residual* or balancing-figure which forces Sections I, II, and III into equality. In the case of Canada in 1969, we know that after taking account of all statistics showing current-account items, and all long- and short-term capital-movement and gold items, Canadians *must* have lent the rest of the world 157 million dollars. It would do so chiefly by IOUs and accounts payable by foreign merchants and importers. The reader should note that, although this is not the last item in the table, it is in fact that free or flexible item that the government statisticians add to or subtract from to make sure that the two parts of the table are in balance. (One result is that the item also includes amounts large enough to balance errors and omissions made in compiling other items in the table.)

After this residual item, the final items just tidy up the totals and provide a little more statistical information. Item 29 shows the total of all capital movements in long-term and short-term forms: a large net inflow of 787 million dollars. Taking the year as a whole, how was this capital inflow used? The answer is given in the last three lines. Because the current account balance was in deficit by 722 million dollars, that amount of the capital-inflow surplus had to be used to finance this deficit.

The amount left over in capital inflows was 65 million dollars. Since this amount was not used for any other purpose, it shows up as a net increase in Canada's holdings of gold, foreign exchange, and deposits with the International Monetary Fund. This total, the change in official holdings, is in fact a much-used indicator of the *over-all balance*, both in one year and over a run of years, of Canada's international payments. This balance is also referred to as the "official-settlements," "official-holdings," or "official-reserves" balance. These names stress that the items chosen for emphasis are changes in amounts that Canadian authorities owe (or are owed by) foreign central banks in their roles as those who must take responsibility for their countries' networks of private and public transactions in ways that do not affect their exchange rates. (See below).

> "*The basic balance*": There are other ways of adding to or deleting items in the final balance that have been proposed as useful single indicators of the outcome of a year's trade and payment. Some economists have advocated the "basic balance" (basic deficit or surplus), and it was stressed in earlier editions of this book. This is the total of the independent or autonomous traders' and investors' net demands for Canadian dollars. It is calculated by adding the current account balance −$722 (in millions) to long-run investment in Canada of +$2,162 (in millions), giving a basic surplus of $1,440 (in millions). The difference between this surplus and the official-settlements balance mentioned earlier is the $1,375 (Item 28) short-term outflow. Sometimes the basic concept differs from the official-settlements balance not only in amount (as it must) but also in sign. But, taking one year with another, we are likely to get the same message whichever concept we choose to measure and publish.

FLOATING EXCHANGE RATE   A reading of the balance of payments helps in understanding the difference between a floating and a fixed exchange rate. An increase in official Canadian holdings of reserves (Item 31, Table 32-1) is a manifestation of an increase in foreign demand for Canadian currency; or, to put it another way, it is a manifestation of an increase in the supply of foreign currency offered to Canada at the existing exchange rate. This can be shown on Fig. 32-1. *E*, the existing exchange rate, has already been set by the forces of supply and demand for the Canadian dollar, or, what is the same thing, for foreign currency, here the Pound Sterling. Now, with the rate remaining *temporarily* fixed, move the supply curve of pounds to the right. The British, perhaps, are buying more Canadian raw materials.

What happens? The new supply curve cuts our demand curve for pounds at a lower level than *E*, indicating that, with a freely floating exchange rate, the price of pounds in Canadian dollars would tend to fall (and that the price of Canadian dollars in pounds would tend to rise).

Imagine that this change had been permitted in 1969. Then Canadian exports would have been dearer abroad and fewer would have been bought. Foreigners might also have been encouraged to sell Canadian securities or to make fewer direct investments in Canada.[9] At the same time, Canadians would have found that imports were cheaper and therefore would have bought more foreign-made goods. Thus, in 1969, a floating exchange rate would have tended to wipe out the capital-account surplus, though it would have taken more than one year to make itself felt. A more serious factor for Canadian growth is that it would not have acted very effectively on the balance of capital movements in long-term forms, but rather would have pushed the current-account balance toward a larger deficit, tending automatically to offset any independent outflow of capital (i.e., an independent outflow of capital caused by the rise in the price of the Canadian dollar).

Actual experience in 1970 showed that, while the floating exchange rate did tend to cancel what might otherwise have been a current-account surplus, it had little effect on what were continuing capital *in*flows stemming from a variety of causes unrelated to the current account. What we should remember from the preceding discussion of a hypothetical floating exchange rate is that the surplus *tends* to be wiped out by a consequent fall in the price of foreign currency (i.e., a fall in the number of Canadian cents per pound, Deutschemark, or U.S. dollar). Similarly, a deficit tends to be wiped out by a rise in that price.

FIXED EXCHANGE RATE   In fact, in 1969, Canada kept its exchange rate fixed; the authorities held the rate at $1.081 (Canadian) per U.S. dollar. They did this just as a marketing board would hold the price of a farm product; they changed the stocks they commanded. If the fixed price of a vegetable threatens to fall, a marketing board can either withhold some of the stock or dig into cash reserves to buy up the supply offered at the existing price. Similarly, if the price of

---

[9] Actually this deterrent would not be very powerful unless potential foreign investors feared a later depreciation of the Canadian dollar (i.e. a reversal of the initial increased price of the Canadian dollar), which would make investments less valuable when measured in foreign money. The reader should try to explain to himself why anticipation of later appreciation is a strong spur to buying securities or equities in a foreign currency.

foreign currency in Canadian dollars threatens to fall, the authorities meet the extra supply by purchasing it with Canadian dollars from their own reserves, as they did in 1969 and in 1970. Or, if the price of foreign currency in Canadian dollars tends to rise, the authorities will supply foreign currency from their official reserve holdings and take into their reserves new amounts of Canadian dollars.[10] Thus, in 1969, our foreign exchange and gold rose by $1,440 - 1,375 = 65$ million dollars—that is, by the "basic surplus" minus short-term capital flows.

Remember that other countries must be in the opposite "basic" position. Among these was France in 1969. Her reserves of gold and foreign exchange decreased.

The United States had a small deficit on current account in 1968, as she imported more goods and services than she exported. But she also had a "basic deficit," as she has had since 1958. Over this long period the United States has experienced an increase in her debts to foreigners, in their holdings of U.S. dollar balances, and a drain of her gold. This was the great economic fact about which Presidents Kennedy, Johnson and Nixon worried: the American stocks of gold, built up in the 1930s, 1940s, and 1950s in the days of "dollar shortage" in foreign, import-hungry countries were drained in the days of "chronic deficit" in the current and long-term balance of the United States.

Canadians are well aware of two policies the United States adopted to prevent this drain of gold continuing.[11] First, they tried to build a current-account surplus by discouraging purchases for military purposes abroad and by restricting what American tourists could spend outside the country. (Both these policies hit Canadian merchants.) Second, they checked directly the flow of long-run capital abroad. Earlier they had tried "moral suasion" on some of the biggest firms planning capital investments in other countries. More significantly, they imposed an "interest-equalization tax" on Canadian and other securities that were offered to American lenders, to reduce the attractiveness of the high interest yields foreigners offered to Americans. Both the ban on lending and the tax were modified in their application to Canadian borrowing when Canadian diplomats pointed out that although Canada was indeed a net borrower from the United States, she was also a net importer on *current* account, as can be seen in Item 11 of Table 32-1. Their argument was that if Canada could not continue to get long-term U.S. capital, she would have to interfere with purchases from the United States. The total effect would leave the U.S. "basic balance" with Canada just about where it was already.)

---

[10] These reserves of foreign exchange will be depleted until the foreign demand for Canadian dollars is greater than the supply at the fixed exchange rate. Then the Canadian dollar can be kept from appreciating by buying foreign exchange and selling Canadian dollars —that is, adding to the supply of Canadian dollars to sustain the rate. In fact this latter situation was the "norm" in 1969 and 1970.

[11] Most of the actual U.S. gold exports were before March, 1968, when the two-tier system of gold markets was set up, after which the United States no longer fed official gold to free-market hoarders.

■ STAGES OF A COUNTRY'S BALANCE OF PAYMENTS

Historically, the United States has gone through four stages often said to be typical of the growth of a young agricultural nation into a well-developed industrialized one. A review of this history may be useful to consolidate understanding.[12]

1. *Young and growing debtor nation.* From the Revolutionary War era until just after the Civil War, the United States imported on current account more than she exported. Britain and Europe lent her the difference in order to build up her capital structure. The United States was a typical young and growing debtor nation.

2. *Mature debtor nation.* From about 1873 to 1914, the U.S. balance of trade appears to have become favorable. But growth of the dividends and interest that she had to pay abroad on past borrowing kept the balance on current account more or less in balance. Capital movements were also nearly in balance, new lending just about canceling borrowing.

3. *New creditor nation.* In World War I, the United States expanded her exports tremendously. At first, private U.S. citizens made loans to the warring Allied powers. After she got into the war, the government lent money to Britain and France for war equipment and postwar relief needs. The United States emerged from the war a creditor nation. But her psychological frame of mind had not adjusted itself to her new creditor position. She passed high tariff laws in the 1920s and in 1930. Because she refused to import, foreigners found it difficult to get the dollars to pay interest and dividends, much less repay principal.

So long as the United States remained in this third stage of being a new creditor country—so long, that is, as she kept making *new* private foreign loans all through the 1920s—everything momentarily appeared all right on the surface. Americans could continue to sell more than they were buying, by putting most of it "on the cuff." The rest of the world met this export surplus by sending gold and IOUs. As long as Wall Street bankers could interest Main Street investors in foreign bonds, everything seemed rosy. But by 1929 and later, when Americans would no longer lend abroad, the crash finally came. International trade broke down. Debts were defaulted. The United States, as much as the rest of the world, was to blame.

West Germany in the 1970s seems to be repeating many of the phases—and errors!—of the United States in the 1920s.

4. *Mature creditor nation.* Britain reached this stage some years ago, and as in all such cases, her imports exceeded her exports. Before we feel sorry for her because of her so-called "unfavorable" balance of trade, let us note what this really means.

Her citizens were living better because they were able to import much cheap food and in return did not have to part with much in the way of valuable export goods. The British were paying for their import surplus by the interest and dividend receipts they were receiving from past foreign lending.

Fine for the British. But what about the rest of the world? Were they not worse off for having to send exports to Britain in excess of imports? Not necessarily. Normally, the capital goods that Britain had previously lent them permitted them to add to their domestic production—to add *more* than had to be paid out

---

[12] This section may be skipped if desired, as the approach described is no longer found serviceable.

to Britain in interest and dividends. Both parties were better off. Nineteenth-century foreign lending was twice blessed: it blessed him who gave and him who received. Of course, international trade and finance did not always operate quite so smoothly. Some investments proved unwise. Political problems of colonies and nationalism complicated the situation. And the whole process went awry and broke down after World War I.

By virtue of her cold-war foreign-aid and defense commitments, the United States finally finds herself needing the income from previous investments to meet her current requirements from abroad.

At one time this system of "stages" of a country's balance of payments was widely used by economists and was interlocked with a classification of stages of the country's internal economic development (primary production, secondary manufacturing, services, and the production of luxuries, etc.). However, economists are no longer so keen about it. It does seem to fit the U.S. and British facts. But it no longer seems to offer useful predictions about other countries. For example, it suggests that Canada should soon move into Stage 3. Does this look likely? Will the British soon move back to Stage 1, 2 or 3? Or will they trim their imports to their receipts and stay in Stage 4?

■ INTERNATIONAL CAPITAL MOVEMENTS AND FOREIGN OWNERSHIP

Return now to the problem of capital movements. If political problems of nationalism and domestic problems of unemployment did not enter the picture, then the fundamentals of international lending would be easy to understand. We could easily cut through the fog of money and finance and concentrate on the real aspects in terms of goods and resources.

How does capital grow within a country? By our diverting labor, land, machinery, and other resources away from the production of current consumption goods. Instead, we plant trees, drain rivers, or build new machinery and buildings. All these add to our future income and consumption.

We are postponing present consumption for future consumption; in fact, for an even *greater* amount of future consumption. Where does the increase in future consumption come from? As Chapter 29 showed, *capital goods have a "net" productivity.* This constitutes the real aspect of the interest rate.

Different parts of the world have different amounts of resources: labor, minerals, climate, know-how. Were it not for ignorance or political boundaries, no one would push investment in North America down to the point of 5 per cent returns *if elsewhere there still existed 10 per cent opportunities.* Some capital would certainly be invested abroad. This would give foreign labor higher wages, because now the foreign worker has more and better tools to work with. It would increase foreign production. By how much? Not only by enough to pay for the constant replacement of used-up capital goods but, in addition, by enough to pay North Americans an interest or dividend return on their investment. This interest return would take the form of goods and services which North Americans receive from abroad and which add to their standard of living.

An all-wise scientist would probably approve of the process. It would make sense to him because capital is going into the regions where its productivity is highest.

When would North Americans be repaid their principal? So long as they are earning a good return, there is no reason why they should ever wish to have it repaid. However, the once-backward country may finally become rather prosperous. It may wish to pull in its belt as far as consumption is concerned and to use its savings to buy out North American ownership in its factories, farms, and mines. But suppose that North Americans are rich, with plenty of savings and with so much capital at home that their rate of interest is low. They might not particularly wish to sell out or be repaid. They might raise the selling price of their farm and factory holdings abroad. In other words, they might be content with a smaller percentage interest return. Thus, there is no necessary reason why a country should ever be paid off for its past lending, unless it has become relatively poorer.

When nationalism rears its head, matters change. Within one country, interest and dividends may stream from country to city and from West to Center, until doomsday. People do grumble about absentee owners, as Quebec grumbles about English-Canadian control and as Westerners attribute all misfortune to Toronto. But each province has courts and police to see that property rights are respected, and even the most radical Quebec nationalist has hesitated to suggest that his compatriots seize the T. Eaton stores in Quebec.

Not so between nations. When a country is capital-poor it is anxious to borrow, for schools, hydro systems, factories, and mines. After it becomes richer and more self-aware, it becomes unhappy to have to pay interest and dividends abroad. It smarts under the realization that much of its domestic trade is directed, at some levels, by foreigners. It gives little weight to the memory that its jobs were created and its prosperity sustained in part by past borrowing. More than an economic burden is involved: politically, countries do not like the principle of absentee ownership by foreigners. Such countries have taken a variety of courses. Canada has been unsure, sometimes discouraging foreign take-overs and investments, but usually passive politically and welcoming individually. Thirty years ago Mexico set a precedent by confiscating foreign-owned oil properties. Between these extremes are other ways of getting rid of foreign liabilities and control: buying off at fair or unfair prices, failing to make promised payments, interfering with business operations till harassment and losses lead to sale, etc. Chapter 34's Appendix discusses foreign ownership.

Economics and politics mix in ways too complicated to resolve. Some say "trade follows the flag." Others say the flag follows trade. Some say the pursuit of economic gain is the primary motive behind the imperialistic search for colonies. Others claim that national power (offensive and defensive) is an end in itself; that economic well-being is sacrificed to this end; and that economic resources are sought for their contribution to military strength (offensive and defensive) rather than for their contribution to economic well-being. According to this view, without wars and nationalism, anyone could invest and trade anywhere, and sensible people should prefer to live in small countries unhindered by costly military establishments and colonial administration. At the opposite extreme is the view that victory in battle, rather than comfortable living, is the only worthy end in life; that the foreigner is of no importance compared with the fatherland; that he can be stripped of his goods and land, and be made to work for the conquerors. The world of the last few centuries lies somewhere between these extreme cases.

■ FINANCIAL VERSUS REAL ASPECTS OF FOREIGN LENDING

Let us turn from politics back to economics. Consider the question first posed back in Chapter 13: What is the mechanism that turns financial borrowing into real foreign investment? There we saw that a country whose exports E exceed her imports M will be *lending* real goods and services abroad.

To follow this process, consider first the opposite case. To add to our capital stock of structures and equipment, we borrow from foreigners. We borrow *money*. We give an IOU in the form of a bond or stock certificate; we receive, say, U.S. dollars. If we simply hold them, or put them in a New York bank or buy a U.S. bond, there is as yet no capital movement. The United States has some form of our IOU and we have some form of hers. In the capital-movements section of each country's balance of payments, the items cancel out. (Try this on Table 32-1.)

Only when we use the receipts from the loan to import goods from the United States in excess of our exports to her do real (merchandise) and financial capital movements take place.

When the time comes to pay interest on our borrowing, we must export to the United States (and she must accept) more goods than we import in order to get the extra U.S. dollars to remit to her. Supposing that we had by now stopped borrowing, our transactions would all be shown on the current-accounts part of the statement. Thus, our exports would be up, and this increase would be equaled by a balancing increase in our interest and dividend payments. (Table 32-1's 1969 statistics do show something like this.)

(Now we can consider the original case from Chapter 13. A country with an export surplus in merchandise will originally accumulate foreign bonds and ship goods. Later, when lending has ceased, she will be entitled to interest and dividend payments, which she may take in the form of increased imports of goods. If she doesn't want the goods, she may reinvest the interest earnings abroad. If she accepts the goods, the original export surplus will now become an import surplus. If she reinvests the interest earnings, which item in Table 32-1 will balance the surplus in line 4?)

Should we feel glad or sorry about our trade balances? Originally, our borrowing will bring us extra imports; so financial journalists will bemoan our "unfavorable" merchandise balance. Later we will be repaying with extra exports, which our journalists will applaud as a "favorable" or healthy trade surplus. But there is little sense in these attitudes. We import to get goods which foreigners can produce better than we; we later export goods that might serve our own well-being in order to honor our obligations. Leaving aside the important consideration that exports create employment, and the altruistic satisfaction from sending our goods to other peoples, the beginning and the final balances are simply two ends of a swap that benefits us. (Otherwise we'd reject the whole deal.)

A century ago, John Stuart Mill properly stressed that *it is imports and not exports that add to a nation's well-being.* Before World War II, countries were handling the problem of maintaining full employment so badly that they began to revert back to mercantilism, putting the cart before the horse and treating exports as if they were an end for their own sake. This was the avowed motive of the Ottawa Agreements of 1932, a system of partial Commonwealth free trade. Every Commonwealth country in the system could export more to every other member. But no member really welcomed imports, for they were regarded as a threat to employment. Fortunately, nations are learning how proper monetary and fiscal policies can restore to validity the fundamental principles of classical economics. And to this degree Mill's sensible stress on imports comes back into its own.

SUMMARY

A. MECHANISMS OF FOREIGN EXCHANGE AND TRADE

■ 1 Buying or selling abroad presupposes a foreign exchange rate between home and foreign currencies. Two countries on a gold standard have a stable foreign exchange rate set by the stable, parity prices at which they each buy and sell gold—whether gold bars, coins, or fractional-reserve banking and gold-exchange standards, or any other variants are used.

■ 2 Classical economists (such as David Hume) relied on gold movements to alter relative price levels, (*a*) raising exports and (*b*) curbing imports of the deficit country, and (*c*) cutting exports and (*d*) raising imports of the surplus country.

■ 3 Once stable exchange rates under a gold standard were abandoned, flexible foreign rates would get set by interaction of supply and demand schedules for foreign exchange. The adjustment now involves changes in export and import prices and not necessarily absolute price levels.

■ 4 Gold coin and bullion evolved into gold-exchange standards internationally and fractional-reserve banking domestically. Gradually the U.S. dollar as a key currency gained over the British pound, and since World War II the world has been *de facto* on a dollar standard—which, as Chapter 35 will show, is badly in need of basic structural reform.

B. BALANCE OF INTERNATIONAL TRADE AND CAPITAL MOVEMENTS

■ 5 The balance of international payments refers to all transactions that use up foreign exchange or make foreign exchange available to us. It relates the total of our exports of goods and services to our imports. Our exports of goods, services, gold, or IOUs are receipt items, or "credits," making foreign currencies available to us. Our imports of those items are payments, or "debits," using up foreign currencies.

■ 6 Our net balance on current account comes from adjusting our merchandise trade balance for "invisible" service items. It and long– and short–term capital movements constitute the "over-all balance" which has to be offset by changes in holdings of foreign exchange and gold and by changes in our net IMF position.

■ 7 As a nation passes from the "young debtor" to the "mature creditor" stage, its payments go through a characteristic sequence of stages.

■ 8 No problem in international finance is more important than that of understanding the real and the monetary aspects of capital movements in their effect upon the industrial development of nations.

QUESTIONS FOR DISCUSSION

1. Contrast free and stable foreign exchange rates. Explain each.

2. What are the gold points exactly? Suppose transport costs diminish.

3. Draw up a list of items that belong on the credit or receipt side of the balance of international payments and another list of items that belong on the debit or payment side. What is meant by a "favorable balance of trade"? By the balance on current account? By an over-all balance? Why the term "invisible items"? What is the difference between short- and long-term capital movements?

4. If a young, developing country tends to be in debt to the rest of the world, what will be the signs of its balances on (*a*) merchandise, (*b*) current payments, and (*c*) long-term capital in its balance of payments statement? Contrast these balances with those of a "mature creditor," such as Great Britain was in 1913, living on the fruits of her property and loans overseas.

5. "Foreign lending causes war. Foreign giving postpones war. Free foreign trading prevents war." Comment.

6. Review your understanding of the following concepts:

gold standard versus free
   exchange rate
currency depreciation and
   devaluation
gold-exchange and dollar standard
debits and credits
balance of international payments,
   trade balance, invisibles, current
   account, government aid items

"favorable" balance
"gold points"
Canada's over-all balance,
   basic balance
gold movements
IOUs, capital movements
net foreign investment
historical capital movements, financial
   and real, in politics and economics

Appendix: Overvaluation and Productivity Growth

In the 1970s the United States is experiencing a serious "chronic deficit." Americans want to buy foreign goods and invest abroad to such an extent that the U.S. gold stocks have been in danger of running out. This is a shocking contrast to the situation ten years earlier, when the U.S. payments surplus was so great that the rest of the world, including Canada, experienced a "dollar shortage," making up the shortage by sending gold to the United States. The following pages suggest that this chronic deficit has the same essential cause as the earlier perpetual surplus: differences between the rates of productivity growth in Western countries. The problem is important to Canada and all the United States' trading partners because U.S. attempts to stem the outward flow of gold may take the form of barriers to trade, and of refusal to allow Americans to invest abroad.

■ OVERVALUATION OF CURRENCY AND
　UNEMPLOYMENT

Consider two countries. Call them A and E for America and Europe. Although Germany is not identical with Europe, let the respective currencies be called dollars and marks. Let A and E begin in long-run foreign exchange equilibrium with 4 marks to the U.S. dollar or $.25 per mark.

Now let productivity in Europe, even though it begins far below that in America, grow faster than in America. If all money wages and profits in E grew as quickly as productivity there, there need be no lasting disturbance to the equilibrium: thus doubling productivity and money wages and factor payments in E will leave her prices just as they were in relation to A's unchanged prices. The real income level in E has grown relative to that of A, perhaps closing some of the gap between them. But so long as Engel's laws imply that A's goods are as much in demand at higher income levels as E's, there need be no disturbance of the equilibrium. A is not hurt or helped by E's improved real income.

However, it is more realistic to assume that money wage and other factor costs do not *at once* grow abroad as fast as productivity does, even though they grow much faster than in relatively stagnant A. Now E's goods are bargains. Even if A has not had domestic wage or other inflation, A's goods are now relatively dear. What is the effect? E's exports expand physically and (probably) in

value; A's exports dwindle physically and (probably) in value. If international payments were in balance before, now A runs a chronic international deficit.

We can say: Before at the rate of 1 dollar per 4 marks, the U.S. dollar was neither undervalued nor overvalued; now at the rate of 1 to 4, the dollar is definitely an "overvalued currency," running a chronic deficit and having too high a cost level. This results from the more rapid technical change abroad, which partially closed the gap between E's technology and A's and lowered E's relative costs.

The deficit disequilibrium in A's balance on current account will probably be aggravated by a tendency for A's investors to want to invest in E, where profitability is likely to be very high as a result of (1) rapid growth in E; (2) rapid technical change in E; (3) great opportunity for A firms to profit from applying their "know-how" in E.

■ EFFECTS OF OVERVALUATION

1. If A previously had full employment, her loss of export production (and perhaps of domestic production displaced by cheap imports) implies a multiplier drop in employment and real NNP.

2. She cannot use easy money to stimulate domestic I, for fear that low interest yields will drive cool money to seek higher yields in E.

3. If A uses militant fiscal policy, as U.S. presidents Kennedy and Johnson did in the 1960s, expanding G expenditure and cutting tax rates to expand C and I, she can overcome her unemployment; but the resulting increase in NNP will wipe out the drop in A's imports from E that resulted from A's income drop (and which had *partially* relieved the international deficit).

4. If E previously had some slack, she is delighted with her good fortune to have become an *undervalued* currency nation, with the extra NNP and employment thereby implied. If E previously had full employment, she is now threatened with overemployment, with demand-push and cost-pull inflation. E will then complain bitterly that she is "importing inflation" from profligate A.

5. Actually, now that E is quoting prices low relative to those A is quoting, the disturbed-equilibrium terms of trade—the ratio of A's export to import prices—have moved against E and in favor of A. E is, so to speak, throwing away goods

to A. Not only is A getting cheap goods—the goal of rational nonmercantilistic nations—but she is also, for the moment, getting some goods in return simply for her shipping out barren gold or mere IOUs.

CORRECTING OVERVALUATION What can correct the situation? A can wait for inflation in E to raise E's prices and end the undervaluation of E's currency. If E's productivity continues to show miracles of growth, the wait may be a long and grueling one.

Or, in premodern times, A could try to deflate her own wage and cost level by 10 to 20 per cent. This seems not very practical in a mixed economy of rather rigid administered prices and wages: blood has often run in the streets of nations trying to adjust to an overvalued currency by internal cost deflation.

Or A might pray for a miracle that would increase her productivity. Exhortation by the American government and by each citizen to have everyone work harder and more skillfully will no doubt be forthcoming in abundance.

Or E might *ap*preciate the mark.[1] When the mark has risen from $.25 to $.27, European exports will be dear and imports from America cheap. Thus, there may again be equilibrium, with neither currency overvalued.[2] However, let us suppose that for the years in question appreciation is simply not politically feasible.

If A's gold is large enough to meet the chronic drain and E's willingness to take A's IOUs is sufficiently great, the disequilibrium situation may go

on for a long time. Perhaps in that time luck will shift the winds of demand in A's favor; or A's productivity might grow; or A may become a more profitable place for investors in either country to place their long-term funds; or the government in A may, reluctantly, cut down on its troop and aid expenditures abroad.

A country with an overvalued currency will be under great internal pressure to introduce government interference with free trade. Employers and workers will clamor for protective tariffs and quotas. The Parliament or Congress will reluctantly consider preventing costly tours abroad, curbing free flow of capital abroad, introducing comprehensive exchange controls, initiating export subsidies, tying up foreign aid, and requiring purchase of military equipment at home even at prices twice as high as they are abroad. The government will exhort or command businessmen to moderate profitable investment abroad by a "voluntary" and mandatory capital investment program, and will introduce "interest equalization taxes" which place perhaps a 10 to 20 per cent tax on long-term foreign loans.

Most chronically overvalued currencies in history have resulted in suspension of freely convertible currencies and in controlled international trade. Moreover, once the overvaluation of the currency has been handled in this way, there is no possibility of removing the controls: as soon as controls are ended, the international payments deficit reappears; history is replete with cases of premature dashes toward convertibility, which ended in fiascoes and return to controls.

THE ACHILLES' HEEL OF CLASSICISM What needs emphasis here is the economics of overvaluation. We shall discover that all the discredited notions of the mercantilists—fear of gold drain, insistence on import curbs and export subsidies, wish to export unemployment abroad, desire to give goods away cheaply rather than dearly, etc.—make some sense in the case of an overvalued currency. The skilled classical and neoclassical arguments of Hume, Smith, and Samuelson no longer carry the day because their major premise of equilibrium currency valuation is not realised in fact.

The next two chapters will elucidate the pro-and-con arguments for tariffs and will demonstrate the basic theory of comparative advantage that

---

[1] Or A might *de*preciate the dollar.

[2] If E's improved productivity has occurred across the board in all industries, she will be better off in the new equilibrium and A need not be hurt or helped. (For example, a relative 10 per cent improvement in E's productivity and costs relative to A's could be just offset by a 10 per cent appreciation. Americans import the same European goods at the same dollar costs as before; Europeans now can buy 10 per cent more of their domestic goods from an hour's work at home and 10 per cent more of imports from A at the 10-per-cent-cheapened dollar.) But suppose, as is more likely, that Europe's productivity is biased to rise more in goods that she had been on the borderline of importing from America. Then there is a presumption that in the new equilibrium A's export prices will fall relative to what she now pays for imports. Europe's progress has hurt A a bit, as A now loses "consumer's surplus" from no longer being able to trade at so "favorable terms of trade."

justifies mutually advantageous geographical division of labor and trade. If prices and wages were everywhere perfectly flexible and/or exchange rates could be counted on to be neither overvalued nor undervalued, the arguments of these chapters would be unanswerable. Here is an example:

Chapter 33 points out that the veil of money and foreign exchange merely covers the true barter nature of trade. It says, "One country cannot undersell the other in *all* goods, but only in those in which it has a comparative advantage, being undersold by the other country in those goods in which that country has a comparative advantage." That is absolutely true in a Ricardian model where the wage ratio between the two countries moves flexibly so that the resulting foreign exchange rate is neither overvalued nor undervalued.

But it is still quite obvious that if one country insists on pricing its goods sky high in money terms (because of sky-high wage rates *or* profit markups), it can certainly price itself out of the market, bringing upon itself an overvalued currency, unemployment, and international deficits. After all, any one of us can do that by insisting on $100,000 per hour; and any region, such as Ontario, could be undersold by the Maritimes in everything if it insisted on prices that cleared no markets. So this can certainly happen internationally as well as intranationally.

■ A CRAWLING (OR SLIDING) PEG

We have seen that stable exchange rates promote fruitful trade. We have also seen that a flexible, freely floating exchange rate, determined by monetary supply and demand as in Fig. 32-1, prevents long-term balance-of-payments disequilibrium of the kind that will be discussed in Chapter 35. A number of economists[3] have therefore suggested as a new reform measure an interesting compromise between exchange-rate stability and flexibility.

[3] J. M. Keynes proposed widening of the gold points in the 1920s. In the 1960s, A. W. Phillips, J. E. Meade, and J. Black of the United Kingdom proposed a sliding peg; and the Canadian 1964 Royal Commission on Money and Banking considered the subject. The scheme was endorsed by a large number of American experts in a 1965 petition. Chapter 35 will return to this subject.

1. The "gold points," which surround the parity exchange rate, are to be widened (and freed from any dependence on a fixed price of gold or the cost of shipping gold).

Thus instead of holding fluctuations of the £-$ rate within the range $2.50 ± .02, let it now freely move with supply and demand within the range of, say, $2.50 ± .20, That is, in any year the pound rate might fall from $2.70 to $2.30 if Britain's import debits were threatening to exceed her export credits.

Within the widened range, equilibrium would take place as a result of permitted, orderly rate adjustment (appreciation or depreciation).

2. Over a period of years, the midrange parity, around which the widened limits are drawn, would be permitted to rise or fall by, say, 1 or 1½ per cent per year.

Why? So that if Britain's cost structure were showing a long-term tendency to rise more than Canada's, the threatened fundamental disequilibrium could be averted. (Merely widening the upper and lower points would give only limited relief: for, if Britain's costs and prices rise chronically, the exchange rate would always be at the $2.30 floor; only by gradually lowering that floor could the growing dearness of Britain's exports be offset by long-term, orderly depreciation of the pound.)

The slowness of the long-term slide in the exchange-rate peg should go far to discourage speculators from "piling on" to a one-way movement, thereby aggravating it and making it even more disorderly.

Figure 32-4, on the following page, shows how the scheme might work in a hypothetical future period.

Note that in the early years, British prices (costs, wages, etc.) are rising faster than Canadian prices (these are shown above). By the "purchasing-power parity" doctrine of this chapter, that should depress the pound rate toward its floor. (Of course, monetary ups and downs of supply and demand change the exchange rate within the widened limits.)

Since Britain's relative price rise is chronic and not temporary, the gray tracks all move in one direction, at 1½ per cent per year. In a decade, an orderly 15 per cent exchange-rate adjustment has been made!

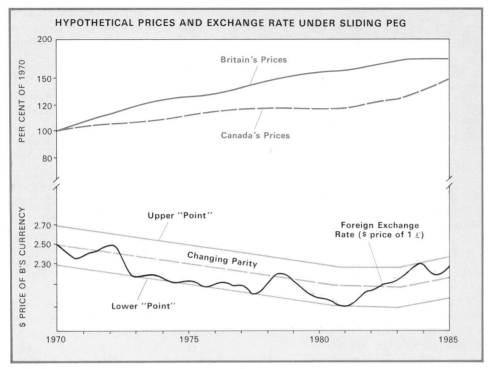

FIG. 32-4.

Best of all, the process can be a two-way street. If, much later, Canadian prices outsoar Britain's, it can be the Canadian dollar's turn to depreciate: now the pound appreciates toward the ceiling limit, and the tracks gradually rise.

So goes the experts' argument. Would it work this way? Much depends on whether speculation disequilibrium would in fact be avoided. The tracks, or sliding limits, moving at 1½ per cent per year would certainly dampen speculators' hopes of large fluctuations in one direction.

But only Canada has continuously maintained a flexible rate against the assaults of arbitragers and speculators. Over most of both "floating" periods (1952–1962 and 1970–?), fluctuations have been minor and acceptable to traders and tourists. In early 1971, Canadian economists were pleased with the performance of the foreign-currency market.

Hence Canadians have put the "adjustable peg" proposal on the shelf, though other Western countries are still discussing it. The conventional wisdom asserts:

1. A fixed rate must indeed be altered if the underlying trade and payments situation changes.

Otherwise either inflation or unemployment, or both, would arise at home, and exchange reserves would increase indefinitely or disappear.

2. "Frequent-changes," however, would create serious uncertainties in trade, capital flows, and domestic production. "If it came to be believed that changes were likely to occur, then at the slightest hint of difficulties in either direction, there would be widespread speculation on the Canadian dollar similar to that which took place in 1962."[4]

Much discussion of desirable exchange-rate policy stems from the 1950–1970 prolonged period of overvaluation of U.S. dollars. Recently, other countries' unemployment, inflation, and exchange rates have directed attention away from the "peg" scheme. Will this proposal, IMF drawing rights, or suggestions of one currency for the North Atlantic area be the next focal point?

[4] Royal Commission on Banking and Finance, *Report* (Ottawa: Queen's Printer, 1964), page 492. (Reproduced by permission of Information Canada.) See also A. F. W. Plumptre, *Exchange-Rate Policy: Experience with Canada's Floating Rate*. Essays in International Finance Series, No. 81 (Princeton: Princeton University Press, June 1970).

FOR REVIEW

Review your understanding of the following concepts:

overvaluation,
    undervaluation
unemployment and
    overvaluation

crawling peg of parity
widened "gold points"

33

INTERNATIONAL TRADE AND THE THEORY OF COMPARATIVE ADVANTAGE

The benefit of international trade—a more efficient employment of the productive forces of the world. JOHN STUART MILL.

Again and again we have seen how specialization increases productivity and standards of living. Now we must show exactly how this works out in the field of international trade, going behind the facade of international finance.

Why did North America specialize a century ago in the production of goods from the farm and forest, exchanging these for the manufactured output of Europe? Why is it able today to export highly complex mass-produced goods—and why does it also import highly complex goods? Why is the agriculture of Australia so different from that of Austria? How great would be the costs of complete self-sufficiency to a modern country? How do all countries benefit from trade?

The key to the correct answers to such questions, and many more, is provided by the theory of comparative advantage or comparative cost. Developed more than a century ago by David Ricardo, John Stuart Mill, and other English followers of Adam Smith, the theory of comparative advantage is a closely reasoned doctrine which, when properly stated, is unassailable. With it we can identify gross fallacies in the political propaganda for protective tariffs aimed at limiting imports. With it, we can identify the germs of truth that sometimes appear in the heated claims for tariff protection.

■ DIVERSITY OF CONDITIONS BETWEEN REGIONS OR COUNTRIES

For simplicity, begin by imagining two countries or continents, each endowed with certain quantities of natural resources, capital goods, kinds of labor, and technical knowledge or know-how. The first link in the comparative-cost chain of reasoning is the *diversity in conditions of production between different countries*. Specifically, this means that the production possibilities of the different countries are very different. Although people could try to produce something of every commodity in any region, it is obvious that they would not succeed; or if they did succeed, it would be only at a terrific cost. Smith pointed out that, with hothouse procedures and forcing methods, wine grapes could perhaps be grown in Scotland; but the cost in terms of economic resources would be exorbitant, and the resulting product would be scarcely fit to drink.

> Even if by chance two countries can both produce the same commodities, they generally find that it pays for each to concentrate its production especially on some goods and trade them for other goods.

If we consider trade between, say, the northern temperate zones and the southern tropics, the foregoing proposition will seem true. Of course, resources near the equator are more productive in the growing of bananas, and northern resources are better designed for wheat growing. Everyone can readily see that in this case specialization and trade will increase the amount of world production of goods, and also each country's ability to consume both goods.

It is not so immediately obvious, but it is no less true, that

> International trade is mutually profitable even when one of the two countries can produce *every commodity* more cheaply (in terms of labor hours or all resources) than the other country. Can Canada with $4 an hour wages benefit from trade with Japan where wages are $1 an hour? Yes, asserts the theory of comparative advantage.

One country may be *absolutely more efficient* in the production of *every* good than is the other country; and this means the other country has an absolute disadvantage in the production of every good. But so long as there are differences in the *relative* efficiencies of producing the different goods in the two countries, we can always be sure that even the poor country has a *comparative advantage* in the production of those commodities in which it is relatively most efficient; this same poor country will have a *comparative disadvantage* in those other commodities in which its inefficiency is more than average. Similarly, the rich, efficient country will find that it should specialize in those fields of production where it has a comparative advantage, planning to import those commodities in which it has a comparative disadvantage.

> A traditional example used to illustrate this paradox of comparative advantage is the case of the best lawyer in town who is also the best typist in town. Will he not specialize in law and leave typing to a secretary? How can he afford to give up precious time from the legal field, where his comparative advantage is very great, to perform typing activities in which he is efficient but in which he lacks *comparative* advantage? Or look at it from the secretary's point of view. She is less efficient than he in both activities; but her relative disadvantage compared with him is least in typing. Relatively speaking, she has a comparative advantage in typing.

So with countries. Suppose North America produces food with one-third the labor that Europe does, and produces clothing with one-half the labor. Then we shall see that North America has a comparative advantage in food and a comparative disadvantage in clothing—this, despite the fact that North America is absolutely most efficient in everything. By the same token, Europe has a comparative advantage in clothing.

■ "NORTH AMERICA" AND "EUROPE": A SIMPLE CASE

Let us illustrate these fundamental principles of international trade by a simplified example. Consider North America and Europe of a century ago, and concentrate on only two commodities, food and clothing. In both Canada and the United States, land and natural resources were then very plentiful relative to labor and capital; but in Great Britain, France, the low countries, and Germany, people and capital were plentiful relative to land.

This contrast is best seen if we look at the *intensive* agriculture of a country such as Belgium. There, in order to get the greatest possible output, small plots of land have to be cultivated assiduously by many people using much fertilizer. Compare this with the extensive agriculture of early North America: one family cultivated many acres, and national product was maximized by each man's "spreading himself thin" over the virtually free land. A Belgian farmer would have thought this wasteful. But in view of the relatively high cost of North American labor or capital and the low cost of land, it was prudent.

Of course, if surplus population could have all migrated from Belgium to North America, the law of diminishing returns would have caused real wages in North America to fall toward equality with rising wages in Belgium; and high land rents in Belgium would have fallen toward equality with rising rents in North America.[1]

But suppose that immigrants from abroad are to be kept out of North America in order to keep labor scarce and wages high. From this same selfish point of view, should Canada and the United States also impose a protective tariff designed to keep out imports from abroad? Or should they not? To answer this important social question we must measure carefully the amounts of food and clothing that will be produced and consumed in each country (1) if there is no international trade and (2) if trade, according to comparative advantage, is permitted to follow its own course.

■ THE LAW OF COMPARATIVE ADVANTAGE

David Ricardo, stockbroker and self-made millionaire, expert on the theory of land rent and of currency, came up in 1817 with the beautiful proof that international specialization pays for a nation. This is the famous theory of comparative advantage, or, as it is sometimes called, the "theory of comparative cost."

---

[1] Actually, this would have tended at the same time to increase *total world production.* Why? Because the transfer of workers from their poor Belgian farms to rich North American farms would increase their productivity and total world output.

**Comparative advantage depends only on
productivity ratios:**

LABOR REQUIREMENTS FOR PRODUCTION
IN EUROPE AND AMERICA

PRODUCT	IN AMERICA	IN EUROPE
1 unit of food	1 day's labor	3 days' labor
1 unit of clothing	2 days' labor	4 days' labor

TABLE 33-1. Even though America's 1 and 2 are, respectively, less than Europe's 3 and 4, America has *comparative* advantage in food and Europe has it in clothing. Why? Because A's 1 ÷ E's 3 is less than A's 2 ÷ E's 4 (or equivalently, because A's 1:2 is less than E's 3:4).

For simplicity Ricardo worked with only two countries; we shall call them *America* and *Europe*, and assume they are both about the same size. For simplicity he worked with only two goods; we shall call them food and clothing. For simplicity Ricardo chose to measure all costs in terms of hours of labor; we shall do the same, recognizing that more advanced treatises and the Appendix to this chapter can give some of the needed qualifications when our simple assumptions are relaxed. The germ of truth in the principle of comparative advantage will still remain.

UNCOMMON SENSE   Using common sense, people will probably agree that trade between America and Europe is likely to be mutually profitable in a first simple case where European labor has greater productivity in one good and American labor has greater productivity in another.

In this case, to produce a unit of food in America requires a smaller number of labor days than is needed in Europe to produce it, while to produce a unit of clothing takes a smaller number of labor days in Europe than in America. The man in the street needs no Ricardo to tell him that in such a case America will probably specialize in food production, exporting some food for Europe's clothing exports.

But Ricardo showed much more than this. He showed that even if American labor (or resources generally) were more productive than Europe's *in both* food *and* clothing, trade is still likely to be mutually advantageous.

Table 33-1 illustrates this principle of comparative advantage. In America a unit of food costs 1 day's labor and a unit of clothing costs 2 days' labor. In Europe the cost is 3 days' labor for food and 4 days' labor for clothing. By forming the proper two ratios of these four crucial numbers, Ricardo is able to prove conclusively that America and Europe will *both* benefit if America specializes in food and exports it for the clothing exports that Europe specializes in.

Before examining this, listen to the European in the street as he says:

> *Mon Dieu!* Trade could never be profitable for us with the American colossus. Her efficiency will enable her to undersell us in every line—food and clothing. We need import tariffs to protect the honest European worker.

Now listen to what is being said in America by the man in the street and the legislators who have not grasped the law of comparative advantage:

Since Europe is less prosperous (and less productive) than America, the European wage level most assuredly will be far below that enjoyed by Americans. If we subject the American workers to the unbridled competition of the European, who subsists on less per day than we do, the real wage of the American worker must fall drastically. A protective tariff against cheap imports is desperately needed to maintain the American standard of living.

What Ricardo shows is that both arguments are wrong. The European and American workers *both* can get higher real wages by international trade. Prohibitive tariffs on either or both sides will reduce real wages in both places. (And we may add in our day that there are better tools than protective tariffs to make sure that there are plenty of job opportunities and stable price levels in both places; namely, proper fiscal and central-bank monetary policies.)

BEFORE TRADE   If we start with a prohibitive tariff that has killed off all international trade, Table 33-1 shows that the real wage of the American worker for a day's work will be 1 unit of food or ½ unit of clothing. The European worker is even less well off and gets for a day's labor before trade only ⅓ unit of food or ¼ unit of clothing.

Evidently, under domestic competition alone in each isolated continent, the price ratios of food and clothing will be different in the two places because of the difference in relative labor cost ratios. In America clothing will be 2 times as dear as food because it takes twice as much labor. In Europe clothing will be only ¾ times as dear as food.

AFTER TRADE   Now we repeal the protective tariff and make trade free. The relative prices of clothing and food must now come to a common level, just as the water in two connecting pipes must come to a common intermediate level once you remove the barrier between them. Why?

Competitive merchants buy where things are cheap and sell where they are dear. With clothing relatively more expensive in America, merchants will soon ship clothing from Europe to America and ship food from America to the European markets, where it has been relatively dear. The American clothing industry will feel the keen price competition of imports, and if the values in Table 33-1 do not change, it will lose *all* its workers to the American food industry. The opposite will happen in Europe: workers will leave the food industry for the clothing industry, in which it has a comparative advantage.

America as a whole has benefited. Like any merchant who will buy electric power from another firm if he cannot produce it as cheaply himself, America has taken advantage of the fact that clothing does cost her less by barter than by domestic production. The same goes for Europe's benefit from specializing in clothing and getting her food more cheaply by barter.

> *Example of benefit.* Each unit of American labor still gets the 1 unit of food it produces there. But now 1 unit of American food trades for *more* than ½ unit of clothing. How much more? Certainly not more than the ¾ ratio set by Europe's costs. The common ratio after trade will be somewhere between ½ and ¾. American labor gains in clothing by any degree that it exceeds ½. Similarly, European labor gains in bartering clothing for food by any degree that the ratio falls short of ¾. (See footnote 2 and the Appendix for elaborations.)

Granted that Ricardo has proved that both countries have benefited from trade in accordance with comparative advantage, what about the workingman in each place? Table 33-1 can show that his real wages have improved in both places. Now the American worker's day of labor will buy him the same food as before, but he gets *more* imported clothing for a day of labor and can now afford to consume more of *both* goods. Likewise, the European worker can get more of the cheapened food for a day of his labor, and inasmuch as he gets the same real wage in clothing, his budget is also better off. It is the expanded *world* production of both goods, which specialization and trade created, that makes it possible for *everyone* to be better off.[2]

The principle of comparative advantage restated: Whether or not one of two regions is absolutely more efficient in the production of every good than is the other, if each specializes in the products in which it has a *comparative advantage* (greatest *relative* efficiency), trade will be mutually profitable to both regions. Real wages of productive factors will rise in both places.

---

[2] To see this graphically, look at Fig. 33-1(a), which shows America's brown domestic production-possibility frontier, with its slope depicting a ½ clothing-to-food price ratio.

Europe's black domestic production-possibility frontier has its ¾ slope. (Since Europe's population happens to be about equal that of America, why is the black curve this much "smaller" than the brown? Because America has double or more the productivity of Europe.) Ricardo says, "It is the difference in slopes that makes profitable trade possible." How profitable? The limits (as explained in the Appendix) are shown by the light gray areas between (*a*) each country's domestic curve and (*b*) a line drawn parallel to the other country's curve passed through each point of specialization. Thus the intermediate fine black arrows, with slopes intermediate between *A*'s ½ and *B*'s ¾, are one possible outcome: at posttrade equilibrium with food selling for two-thirds clothing (i.e., at ⅔), *A* gains by producing food alone and exporting it for clothing: *E* gains by producing clothing and exporting it in exchange for food.

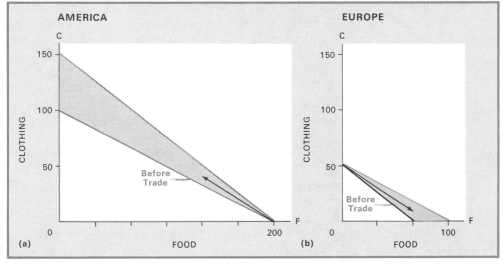

FIG. 33-1.

An ill-designed prohibitive tariff, far from helping the protected factor of production, will instead reduce its real wage by making imports expensive and by making the whole world less productive through eliminating the efficiency inherent in the best pattern of specialization and division of labor.

This simple principle provides the unshakable basis for international trade.

■ OTHER CAUSES OF INTERNATIONAL TRADE

DECREASING COSTS   If economies of mass production are overwhelmingly important, costs may decrease as output expands. This would strengthen the case for international exchange of goods. In fact, decreasing costs are a second great factor—in addition to differences in comparative costs—explaining why specialization and trade are profitable. For, as was discussed in Chapters 3 and 24, large-scale specialization is most fruitful when there is a widely expanded market.

In fact, even if there were no differences in comparative costs between two countries, it might pay for them to toss a coin to decide who was to produce each of two goods subject to increasing returns or decreasing costs. Complete specialization would increase world production of both goods. This may be illustrated by our example in Chapter 3 of the identical Indian twins who, despite their similarity, still find it advantageous to specialize to reap the efficiencies of "mass" production. The European Common Market (France, West Germany, Belgium, the Netherlands, Luxembourg, Italy) hopes to reap the advantages of such an extended division of labor.

These decreasing costs may rise not only from mass production inside an industry but also from the adaptation of the community to providing special skills, markets, transportation networks, and supplies. Such "external economies" were explored in Chapter 23. Mass production and external economies explain many puzzles in economic history, and are a technical way of expressing the idea: "It was a historical accident that the city of Nottingham in England started to make lace, but once it got started no other region could meet its quality and low costs." The most recent example of an economic *policy* depending on the appearance of decreasing costs is the Canadian-American automobile-tariff agreement. Canadian negotiators felt that the previous higher cost of automobile production was due to the lack of a Canadian home market for real mass production. Thus, when the U.S. market was opened to certain Canadian factories, Canada, too, experienced economies of mass production and decreasing costs over time.

Another very practical aspect of decreasing cost is the possibility that it may lead to the breakdown of perfect competition. Consider a Canadian manufacturing firm which produces small amounts at high costs. If it can begin to expand its sales, its costs will decrease, and it will undercut its competitors. If the process continues, it may even become a monopolist, its greater size enabling it to take over the whole domestic market. By excluding foreign competitors, a protective tariff would serve only to consolidate the position of the monopolist, whereas free trade may enlarge the market sufficiently to promote competition.

This is recognized in the old slogan, "The tariff is the mother of trusts." Freer international trade is often an effective and efficient way of *breaking up* monopoly positions and has been recognized as such in our Combines Act.[3]

DIFFERENCES IN TASTES OR DEMAND   Here is a third possible cause for trade. Even if costs were identical in the two countries and were increasing, trade might take place as the result of differences in *tastes*.

Thus, it might pay both Norway and Sweden to produce fish from the sea and meat from the land in about the same amounts. But if the Swedes have a relatively great fondness for meat and the Norwegians for fish, then a mutually profitable export of meat from Norway and fish from Sweden would take place. Both parties gain from this trade. The sum total of human happiness is increased, just as it is when Jack Spratt trades fat meat for his wife's lean. Both get some "consumer's surplus" from the swap.[4]

We have now gone beyond the financial facade of international trade to the real fundamentals. Now we can handle the remaining two chapters of Part Five.

■ FOREIGN-TRADE SUPPLY-AND-DEMAND CHARTS[5]

The foregoing theory of comparative advantage stripped international trade down to its barter essentials. It said nothing about dollars, pounds, or foreign exchange rates. How does the matter appear to the perfect competitors in one small food industry in America? Why does competitive P settle down so that America exports this item of wheat but not that item of cloth? How do the supply and demand curves look in the competitive market for a small clothing item exported by Europe—say, linen cloth?

Figure 33-2 first takes up the case of an American export good, wheat, in the simplest case where every European unit of money—call it a pound—is always worth exactly $3. Figure 33-2(a) shows the American demand and supply curves $d_a d_a$ and $s_a s_a$ for wheat expressed in dollars (which, by a 1/3 scale change, can also be read in pounds). Figure 33-2(b) shows the European supply and demand for wheat as $d_e d_e$ and $s_e s_e$ (in pounds, with vertical scales nicely aligned so as to be read in dollars or pounds).

Suppose trade in wheat were prohibited by quotas, tariffs, or sky-high transport costs. Where would *autarky* equilibrium be in each country? Under such an assumption of no trade, equilibrium would be at the separate inter-

---

[3] Still, one must admit that decreasing-cost situations might under free trade lead to bigger monopolies, and that decreasing-cost situations may have in them some of the valid elements of the "infant-industry" argument to be met in the next chapter.

[4] Even two individuals with identical amounts of two goods and the same tastes may in rare instances trade. Two sailors, each with a fifth of rye and a fifth of gin, might toss a coin to decide who is to have two fifths of gin and who two fifths of rye. You can reason out why the same might be true of herring and chocolate, but not of corned beef and cabbage. This fourth cause of trade is primarily of curiosity value.

[5] The next two sections are quite independent of the rest of this chapter, except for points 5 and 6 in the Summary. The next chapters do not require them or this chapter's Appendix.

Supply and demand here and abroad determine export P's

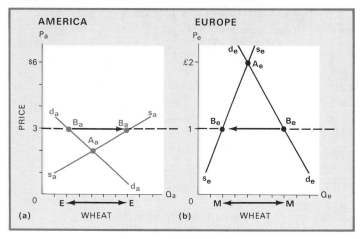

FIG. 33-2. With zero trade, American wheat price is at A_a, below European price at A_e. With free trade, goods flow from low- to high-price place, finally equalizing P's at that level where the export arrow just matches the import arrow.

section points A_a and A_e: Wheat's price (per bushel) in America would be $2, or £2/3; its price in Europe would be $6, or £2. Both markets are cleared; exports and imports are, of course, zero.

Now open up trade in wheat. If there are zero transport costs, quotas, and tariffs, both markets must have the same price. Why? Because sharp-eyed arbitragers could buy where wheat was cheap and send it for sale to where it was dear. With what result? Evidently, P_e would fall and P_a rise until equality was achieved. The amount of the price changes would depend on the slopes of each country's dd and ss curves.

> The condition for the new free-trade equilibrium is that the new common price should coax out an import demand abroad just equal to the export supply from home.

Free-trade equilibrium is at the $3 and £1 level, where America's export arrow EE or B_aB_a just matches (and opposes in direction) Europe's import arrow MM or B_eB_e. No other equilibrium can persist.

Figure 33-3 shows exactly the same phenomenon for the case of Europe's clothing export, linen. Who decides that linen will be Europe's export and wheat be America's? The levels of the no-trade equilibria intersections decide: goods flow uphill toward higher prices under free competition! (Because A_e is below A_a, Europe exports linen.)

The reader could draw a new figure where the no-trade P's happen to start out equal and where free trade leads to zero trade. This is a rare razor's-edge case of coincidental levels. However, in real life, there are always transport costs that impede trade. Thus, although bricks may seem to be cheaper in America, if the difference between the no-trade equilibrium intersections is less than the substantial *costs of shipping* heavy and bulky bricks, each country will produce its own bricks and there will be neither exports nor imports. Goods try to flow

Supply and demand here and abroad determine import P's

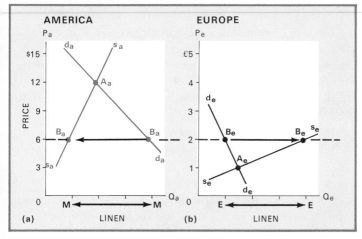

FIG. 33-3. Lower European P at zero trade means linen will be imported from Europe when trade is permitted. Common P is where imports and exports match. (Quotas, tariffs, or transport costs will make P's unequal.)

uphill toward higher prices, but transport-cost or tariff impediments can inhibit their flow.

This supply-and-demand analysis is a simple extension of that given in Chapter 4 (or Part Three). It is useful. But note that we should have to go to Ricardo's deeper analysis of comparative advantage to explain *why* the wheat prices will be such as to give America a money-cost advantage in exporting this food item. That same analysis of basic comparative advantage is needed to explain why the clothing item, linen, will have *dd* and *ss* intersections causing Europe to export it.[6]

■ EFFECTS OF TARIFFS AND QUOTAS

PROHIBITIVE TARIFF   Figure 33-3 can be used to illustrate the effect of an American tariff (or "customs tax") on the import of linen. If America taxes linen imports by more than the difference in price ($9 \equiv £3 = $12 - $3) shown between the no-trade A_a and A_e intersections, how much linen will get sent there? Absolutely none: the tariff of more than $9 will be a prohibitive one, shutting out all imports. Why? Because an importer who tries to buy linen at the European A_e price of $3 (or £1) can sell it for only $12 (or £4). But the tariff the importer has to pay would come to *more* than that difference! Hence, such a tariff kills off *all* the advantage of specialization and trade.

A smaller tariff will kill off some linen imports, in that sense partially "protecting" America's domestic linen industry.

SOCIAL COST OF TARIFFS   What happens to the American linen industry? The tariff gives it a higher price than it would have under free trade. The typical

---

[6] As economists put this matter: Marshall's supply and demand curves depict only "partial equilibrium." They have to be anchored on "general equilibrium" analysis, of which Ricardian comparative advantage is a simple but vital case.

effect, then, of any tariff that "protects" against imports is to raise the price to the domestic consumer.[7]

But does not the American government collect in tariff revenue about what the consumers now pay in extra prices? Our special example of a prohibitive tariff points up the negative answer that can be generally given. Here consumers pay more but the government collects nothing! This needs emphasis, and shows how foolish it is to try to measure a tariff's height and capacity for doing harm by the tax revenue it brings in.

Also, any tariff that limits imports makes American consumers pay a higher P for all the domestically supplied output, and *none* of this shows up in government revenue.

The higher P lowers the satisfaction and well-being of consumers. Whom does it benefit? The suppliers of this particular industry do benefit. If linen were a monopoly industry, the monopolist would benefit and could afford to lobby for tariffs. Some of the benefit would trickle down to his employees and to owners of resources especially fitted for linen production. Even if, as in Fig. 33-3(a), there is perfect competition rather than monopoly, the productive factors specialized for the protected industry will stand to get some benefit (higher P for linen, more jobs, high wage rates, higher economic rents on factors inelastically supplied to that industry).[8]

When the wife of one of these specialized employees complained about the high cost of linen and of living generally, resulting from a high-tariff government, her husband could reprimand her: "Stop complaining. *We* get more than *we* give as a result of the tariff. It's *the rest of the community* that experiences the net harm from the cessation of linen imports."

In wheat and other nonprotected industries, wives and husbands can both legitimately complain about this linen tariff. Indeed, let us consider (1) the harm done to consumers, (2) the revenue collected by government, and (3) the benefit received by suppliers. What is the net effect, on the supposition that both rich and poor, worthy and unworthy, are equally involved on all sides of the argument? It can be shown in the Appendix that the harm of a prohibitive tariff outweighs its gain, in this sense:

---

[7] The price rise need not be as great as the tariff itself; it will be that great only if, to continue our example, the European industry is so large compared with America's use of the product that one or both of their ss and dd schedules can be regarded as practically horizontal, America's imports being too small to affect their prices appreciably.

[8] Indeed, if $s_a s_a$ were completely vertical, all the money newly extorted from the consumer would be transferred to the producers in extra rent: this would presumably be a switch from not particularly unworthy consumers to not particularly worthy producers. But with $s_a s_a$ having some positive elasticity, the higher P will coax out extra domestic Q; this will represent a definite social inefficiency, to the degree that resources are drawn from fields where America has a comparative advantage into protected industries where she has a comparative disadvantage. In the extreme case of a horizontal $s_a s_a$, where factors are indifferent between this and other industries, *all* the tariff's benefits to producers are frittered away in inefficient resource allocation and not even do those in the industry derive a selfish benefit at the expense of the hard-hit consumers.

A system of prohibitive tariffs puts a society inefficiently *inside* the consumption-possibility-frontier that would be available if the efficiencies of international exchange and division of labor were utilized. This is absolutely true of the world as a whole, and absolutely true for a country that cuts off all imports and becomes self-sufficient.[9]

QUOTAS   The effect of a prohibitive tariff could be achieved by imposing a zero quota on all imports. The prices would find their A_a and A_e levels in both markets as before. Consumers in America will be hurt; and in the sense described above, they will be hurt more than producers are helped.

Suppose the quota is set, not at zero, but, say, at half the level of free-trade imports. The reader can verify that, in the special case of Fig. 33-3's straight-line curves, the American P will rise half the distance between the free-trade B_a price and the no-trade A_a price. (In Europe P will fall halfway.) Only at these new respective P's of $9 and £1½ will the arrow of Europe's physical linen exports match America's arrow of physical linen imports. (Verify.)

The quota has produced a price difference between America and Europe. As just said, that equilibrium difference is defined as just large enough to make exports and imports match. (Note: A tariff on each unit import of linen, which was exactly equal to this price difference, could have achieved the same equilibrium.[10])

There is thus no essential difference between tariffs and quotas. Except this: A nonprohibitive tariff at least gives revenue to the government, in part offsetting the net harm done to the importing country by the restriction on imports. A quota, on the other hand, puts the profit from the contrived price difference into the pocket of the importer lucky enough to get a quota license. He can afford to wine and dine the officials who give out import licenses; or if they are not already his kinfolk or political cronies, he can afford to bribe them.

This is why economists generally regard tariffs as a lesser evil than quotas. "At the least," they advise, "if you must introduce inefficient restrictive quotas,

---

[9] It is also true with rare (and unimportant) exceptions for a country that levies prohibitive tariffs on a subset of its goods. The exceptions apply to a country large enough to affect appreciably the relative prices of the goods it imports. By levying sufficiently small, shrewdly gauged tariffs, it might exploit its monopoly power to "make the foreigner pay" for its tariff. [This is an esoteric point, which could be illustrated by means of utility-disutility areas under the schedules in Fig. 33-3(a). But readers of Chapter 24's discussion of marginal revenue (and the loss taken on all earlier units when an extra unit of q is sold by a monopolist) can understand the point thus: The last little unit of import under free trade brings America zero marginal benefit; that is why it is the last unit. If America imposes a tiny tariff to keep it out, she does force a reduction in the P she pays on *all* previous units imported. So America could benefit a little from such a move (unless the $s_e s_e$ and/or $d_e d_e$ curves were horizontal). However, Europe could do the same to America's wheat, and when all play this game, there is some presumption that world inefficiency will make all (or most) worse off.]

[10] This gives the clue to how to compute the equilibrium prices for any tariff rate between the prohibitive and zero levels. In Fig. 33-3, shift the whole exporting country's diagram upward by the amount of the tariff (so that its vertical-scale prices now differ from the importing country's vertical scale by the amount of the duty). Then move a horizontal ruler up and down until you have located exactly equal export and import gaps between the respective schedules.

be sure that the government auctions off the scarce import-quota licenses so that the Treasury gains the swag and so that bureaucracy is not put under the strain of corruption and exercise of arbitrary power and caprice."

> The harmful effects of a nonprohibitive tariff or quota are seen to be of the same type as, but of lesser quantitative degree than, those of prohibitive tariffs or quotas. Generally, there is net harm done to the citizenry as it is forced to curb its consumption of the goods it desires most and to channel resources from lines of true comparative advantage to economically inefficient uses. Generally, real wages and average living standards are hurt by tariffs and quotas.

TRANSPORTATION COSTS   The economic costs of moving bulky and perishable goods also lessen the extent of profitable regional specialization.

The effects are like those produced by the passage of artificially restrictive tariff legislation. In the case of transportation costs, the evil is unavoidable, whereas protective tariffs or artificial barriers to interregional trade within a nation are squarely the responsibility of man.

This ends two sections of digression on particular markets' price equilibrium under trade and tariffs. We return again to basic comparative advantage.

■ QUALIFICATIONS AND CONCLUSIONS

Of course, comparative advantage holds for *any* two countries and goods, not just for America and Europe and food and clothing. (Ricardo used England and Portugal and cloth and wine in his examples.) The following Appendix shows how the principle of comparative advantage can be generalized to handle any number of goods; and more advanced books show how it can handle any number of countries or regions. Instead of using simple labor-cost examples, we could easily measure costs in terms of "doses" of labor, land, and capital goods of fixed proportions. We can also allow for changing factor proportions and diminishing returns. For all this and more, see the Appendix.

Perhaps a more serious defect of comparative advantage is its static assumptions. The theory is stated in terms of barter and relative price ratios. It disregards all stickiness of prices and wages, all transitional inflationary and overvaluation gaps, and all balance-of-payments problems. It supposes that when workers go out of one industry they always go into another more efficient industry—never into chronic unemployment. No wonder this abstract theory sold at a discount during the Great Depression. Recently its prestige has been coming back, although in 1970 it was challenged. To the extent that we can in the future count on successful macroeconomic management, which mobilizes modern theories of monetary and fiscal policy to banish chronic slumps and inflations— to that extent will the old classical theory of comparative advantage retain its vital social relevance.

If theories, like girls, could win beauty contests, comparative advantage would certainly rate high in that it is an elegantly logical structure. It is a highly simplified theory; an oversimplified one, as far as our rushing out to make immediate applications to real life is concerned. Yet, for all its oversimplification, the theory of comparative advantage provides a most important glimpse of truth. Political economy has found few more pregnant principles. A nation that neglects comparative advantage may pay a heavy price in terms of living standards and potential growth.

SUMMARY

■ 1 As soon as there are diversities of productivities within a country, specialization and exchange become profitable. The same holds for nations: international exchange is an efficient way for us to transform one good into another, more efficient than having to rely solely on domestic production.

■ 2 Without much study of economics, people see that trade is mutually beneficial between the tropics and the temperate zones—or between two countries, where one is more efficient in producing one good and the other is more efficient in producing the other good. But it takes the important Ricardian principle of *comparative* advantage to see that trade is no less mutually beneficial between two countries (or as in the case cited of the lawyer and stenographer, between any two units) even when one of the countries happens to be absolutely more efficient in every industry than is the other.

As long as there is a difference in *relative* efficiency, there will be powerful benefits to be derived from *specializing* in those goods in which there is a comparative advantage, *trading* them for the goods in which the other country has a comparative advantage.

■ 3 The law of comparative advantage not only predicts the geographical pattern of specialization and direction of trade; it also demonstrates that *both* countries are made better off and that the real wages (or returns to the factors of production taken as a whole) are improved by trade and the resulting *enlarged* totals of world production. Prohibitive tariffs that re-create *autarky* (i.e., national economic self-sufficiency, not to be confused with political *autarchy*) will hurt real wage and total factor returns—not help them.

■ 4 Decreasing costs (economies of scale) are an important cause of specialization and regional trade. Differences in tastes can also cause trade.

■ 5 In supply-demand markets for one small good, completely free trade will equalize prices, causing the good to be exported from the country with lowest zero-trade prices. The equilibrium uniform P is at the level which equates physical exports to physical imports.

■ 6 A tariff or quota, by lowering imports, will cause a rise in domestic P and a fall in foreign P. (So long as some imports continue, the P's will differ by the amount of the tariff.) The harm done to the domestic economy, from higher P and decreased home consumption, and from wastage of resources on goods lacking comparative advantage, will generally exceed the benefit to producers. Transport costs also cut down on trade and well-being.

■ 7 The important law of comparative advantage must be qualified to take into account certain interferences with it. Thus, if money wage rates are rigid in both countries or if fiscal and monetary policies are poorly run in both countries, then the blessing of cheap imports that international specialization gives might be turned into the curve of unemployment.[11] With proper public policies, modern nations can achieve a managed macroeconomics which need not sacrifice the great benefits from trade, but rather can recreate the environment in which the principle of comparative advantage will apply.

QUESTIONS FOR DISCUSSION

1. "Buying a good cheaper abroad than we can produce it at home is to our advantage." Is this consistent with comparative advantage? Show that it indeed is.

2. Are real wage levels, like water in connecting pipes, brought to the same level by completely free international trade? Why not? Are international prices? Why?

3. What happens if two countries are exactly alike in productivity and efficiency? Explain. Justify the slogan "Vive la différence!"

4. What if (1,2;3,4) in Table 33-1 became (1,2;1½,3)? Can you show that all trade is killed off? And that this certainly would be a worse position for America? (Footnote readers: redraw Fig. 33-1 with equal p-p slopes.) Show that if it now becomes (1,2; 1½,4,) Europe will export food.

5. Can a country once have a comparative advantage, say, in electric generating equipment, and then lose it? What then *will* happen? Should it?

6. Why might a new continent have a comparative advantage in food?

7. "If some goods continue to be imported after a new tariff the sum of the rise in domestic P and the fall in foreign P must equal the new tariff." Can you show why?

8. Review your understanding of the following concepts:

personal and regional diversity and specialization	barter versus home production
	international price equilibrium
absolute efficiencies versus comparative advantage	quota and tariff equilibrium
	prohibitive tariffs and real wages

---

[11] See the Appendix to the previous chapter for a demonstration that overvaluation of a country's currency can undercut these basic classical principles.

Appendix: Comparative Advantage Amplified and Qualified

Our discussion of comparative advantage has until now followed Ricardo and measured all costs in terms of labor. Modern economists know that the theory is still valid even if you do not want to assume a labor theory of value. The production-possibility, or transformation, frontier that we used in Chapter 2 to discuss guns and butter, or Agriculture (food) and Manufactures (clothing), is the tool that enables us to dispense with labor units: users of the production-possibility frontier choose to measure the cost of clothing in terms of the food we must sacrifice to get more clothing. (This is sometimes so-called "opportunity cost.")

The first part of this Appendix follows through in detail the America-Europe food-clothing case, showing the irrelevance of absolute labor costs.

■ AMERICA WITHOUT TRADE

In Chapter 2, we saw that every economy has a production-possibility (or transformation) schedule indicating how much of one commodity, food, can be produced if all resources are diverted to it; also how much of the other commodity, clothing, can be produced if all resources are diverted to its production; and how either good can be transformed into the other.

For simplicity, let us suppose food can always be transformed into units of clothing in America at the *constant ratio* of 10:3. For each 10 units of food sacrificed, we can always get 3 units of clothing. We further assume that, when all resources are diverted to food production, America will have altogether 100 (million) units of food.[1]

Then, clearly America can, if she chooses, have 90 units of food and 3 units of clothing, 80 and 6, . . . , or finally 0 of the food and 30 of clothing.

We may put this in the form of a schedule, as shown in Table 33-2. It may be plotted in Fig.

[1] Note that labor is never mentioned in the following discussion. But if you wanted to relate this discussion to Ricardo's labor treatment, you could merely change the numbers in Table 33-1 from (1,2: 3,4) to (3,10: 8,10), or more generally to (3a, 10a; 8b, 10b), where a and b are arbitrary positive numbers depending only on units and absolute efficiencies.

33-4, just as was done in Chapter 2, Fig. 2-2 (page 24). The solid line AK is America's production-possibility frontier. This new production-possibility frontier is a straight line, whereas the earlier one was rounded, being concave when looked at from below. The straight-line production-possibility schedule has been introduced in order to keep the argument simple—to relieve the student from having to remember many different cost ratios. As will be seen later, this will not seriously affect the validity of the argument. The few qualifications needed are made later.

So far we have been talking only about production. However, if America is isolated from all trade, what she produces is also what she consumes. Let us suppose, therefore, that the emphasized quantities for H in Table 33-2 and Fig. 33-4 represent the amounts produced and consumed by America in the absence of trade; or in numerical terms, America then produces and consumes 30 units of food and 21 units of clothing.

Why was this particular combination decided upon rather than one of the other possibilities? We know from earlier chapters that in a competitive system nobody "decides" upon this, but that the price mechanism, operating through supply and demand for goods and services, determines WHAT shall be produced, How, and FOR WHOM. Well, the indicated quantities are the WHAT. Very little need be said here about the How, except for the obvious remark that agricultural food production will require more land relative to labor than will more highly fabricated clothing output. As to the FOR WHOM, we need only remark parenthetically that scarcity of labor in America will mean rather high wages for workers, while superabundance of land here will mean low rents (per acre) for landlords.

TECHNICAL PROGRESS Let us proceed to introduce Europe into the picture. Before doing so, it will pave the way for the later argument to interject a question. What would happen if some American (like Eli Whitney, inventor of the cotton gin, for example) should make a clever invention, allowing each 10 units of food to be transformed into 6 rather than 3 units of clothing. Would America be potentially better off?

America can produce food or clothing, consuming before trade what she produces:

PRODUCTION-POSSIBILITY SCHEDULE OF
AMERICA (10/3 CONSTANT-COST RATIO)

| POSSIBILITIES | AMERICA | |
	FOOD, MILLIONS OF UNITS	CLOTHING, MILLIONS OF UNITS
A	100	0
B	90	3
C	80	6
D	70	9
E	60	12
F	50	15
G	40	18
H	30	21
I	20	24
J	10	27
K	0	30

TABLE 33-2.

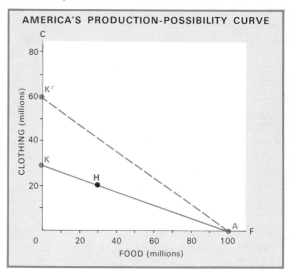

FIG. 33-4. The constant-cost line *AK* shows America's domestic production possibilities. The new line *AK'* indicates an increased ability to produce clothing and means that America can move northeast from *AK*, enjoying more of both goods.

The answer is, obviously, Yes. The production-possibility curve has shifted outward and upward and is now shown by the broken line *AK'* in Fig. 33-4. (Show that America could now go from *H* northeast to a new point *H'* and have *more of both* food and clothing.)

■ EUROPE WITHOUT TRADE

We can now do for Europe exactly what was done above for America, but with an important difference. Europe's plentiful endowment of labor relative to land would give her a different cost or transformation ratio between food and clothing. She might have a comparative advantage in clothing rather than in food. For her, each 10 units of foods may be transformable into, say, 8 units of clothing. She gets 5 more than was true of America because of her comparative advantage in clothing. However, in terms of food, America gets $^{10}\!/_3$, or 3.33 units, for each unit of clothing sacrificed, while Europe's comparative disadvantage in food production gives her only $^{10}\!/_8$, or 1.25 units of food, for each sacrificed unit of clothing. *The important*

thing to concentrate upon is the difference in the two cost ratios: $^{10}\!/_3$ for America and $^{10}\!/_8$ for Europe.

We shall still keep the two continents isolated from each other. What is Europe's exact production-possibility schedule? Let us suppose that Europe's population is so large and her land area such that before trade she was producing and consuming 50 units of food and 80 units of clothing. This fact, plus the constant-ratio $^{10}\!/_8$, tells us all we have to know in order to draw up Europe's complete production-possibility schedule as in Table 33-3. Check this against Fig. 33-5's production-possibility frontier.

■ THE OPENING UP OF TRADE

Now, for the first time, let us admit the possibility of trade between the two regions. Food can be bartered for clothing at some *terms of trade*, i.e., at some *price ratio*.[2] To dramatize the process, let us

---

[2] Terms of trade (or an exchange ratio) of, say, 10 food for 6 clothing means that clothing is more expensive than food, with the price ratio (clothing price)/ (food price) = $1^{2}\!/_3$ = $^{10}\!/_6$.

Europe's production possibilities favor clothing, in which she has comparative advantage:

PRODUCTION-POSSIBILITY SCHEDULE OF EUROPE (10/8 CONSTANT COST RATIO)		
	EUROPE	
POSSIBILITIES	FOOD, MILLIONS OF UNITS	CLOTHING, MILLIONS OF UNITS
A	150	0
B	100	40
C	50	80
D	0	120

TABLE 33-3.

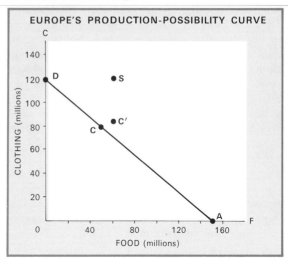

FIG. 33-5. Before international trade, Europe is on her domestic production-possibility curve at *C*, consuming just what she produces. (Disregard the points *C'* and *S* until later in the chapter.)

suppose that in mid-ocean there stands an impersonal auctioneer whose business it is to balance supply and demand—offers of clothing and offers of food. He does this by calling out to both countries an exchange rate or price ratio between food and clothing. Until supplies and demands are balanced, he keeps the bidding going. When he finally hits on the equilibrium price level *at which supply and demand balance*, he raps his gavel three times and says, "Going, going, *gone!*"

Probably, he will suspect in advance that Europe is going to specialize in clothing production, in which she has a comparative advantage, and that she will wish to export part of her clothing production in exchange for food imports. But he has no idea what the final exchange ratio, or terms of trade, between food and clothing will be—whether it will be $^{10}\!/_3$, $^{10}\!/_8$, $^{10}\!/_5$, $^{10}\!/_6$, or anything else. For that matter, if the auctioneer is very new at the game, or very stupid, he may think that the final equilibrium exchange level, or terms of trade, will be $^{10}\!/_1$ or $^{10}\!/_{12}$.

Actually, neither of these last two can be the final exchange ratio. He would soon learn this from

bitter experience. For let him tell America and Europe that they can get all the clothing they want in exchange for food at the rate of only 1 unit of clothing for every 10 units of food. What will America do? By producing at home, she can get 3 units of clothing for each 10 of food. Clearly, she will not be persuaded into trading food for clothing on those terms; she would rather remain self-sufficient.

That is only half the story. Why should not America go to the other extreme and export clothing in exchange for food imports? Each 1 unit of clothing gets her 10 units of food from the auctioneer. What will 1 unit of clothing get at home in domestic food production? Obviously, from the Table 33-2 and Fig. 33-4, only $^{10}\!/_3$, or 3.33, units of food. At $^{10}\!/_1$, therefore, America should certainly shift all her resources to clothing production; she should export some of her surplus clothing in return for food imports.

Now, what about Europe? At home she gets only $^{10}\!/_8$, or 1.25, units of food for each unit of clothing. At $^{10}\!/_1$, she too will want to trade clothing for food. We see, therefore, what a green hand the auctioneer was. By calling out $^{10}\!/_4$, he brings a flood supply of clothing on his head and only demands for food. Since he has no supplies of either good up his sleeve he must now change his tactics. He must raise the price of food relative to the price of clothing. He had better try the ratio $^{10}\!/_2$, or perhaps even $^{10}\!/_1$. You are now in a position to reason why neither of them will do: why $^{10}\!/_2$ will still induce a tidal wave of clothing and, on the other hand, why $^{10}\!/_1$ represents the opposite error, in which there is a tornado of food.

Clearly, *the final exchange ratio cannot be outside the original two-country limits of* $^{10}\!/_3$ *and* $^{10}\!/_8$! Anywhere between is a possibility—with America following her comparative advantage and specializing in food, and Europe following her comparative advantage and specializing in clothing.

■ EXACT DETERMINATION OF THE FINAL
    PRICE RATIO

Just where between the domestic cost ratios will the terms of trade settle down? Some of Ricardo's immediate followers were foolish enough to say, "Split the difference between the two countries' cost ratios, and pick 10/5½ as the equilibrium ratio."[3]

Actually, as John Stuart Mill, the third great classical economist (after Smith and Ricardo), showed a little later, *the exact final level of the terms of trade between the two cost ratios will depend upon the strength of world supply and demand for each of the two commodities.* If people have an intense desire for food relative to available supplies of food and clothing, the price ratio will settle near the upper limit of $^{10}\!/_8$; if clothing is much demanded by both countries, the final price ratio will settle nearer to $^{10}\!/_3$.[4]

[3] Or would they have said halfway between 10/3 and 10/8, giving us 110/48, which corresponds to 10/4$^4\!/_{11}$? Both answers are silly.

[4] Also, if America were very small relative to Europe, so that its supplies made hardly a "dent" on the market, then the price ratio might even stay at Europe's 10/8. America would then be specializing in food and importing clothing, but all America's food exports would amount to so little that Europe would still have to produce some food for herself. This is possible only at a price of 10/8. America would in this case get all the gains from international trade. It pays to have a large (different!) neighbor.

Mill did what our auctioneer would have to do. He drew up a schedule showing supply and demand at *each possible price ratio*:[5] how much food America would wish to export and how much food Europe would want to import; and at the same time, how much clothing Europe would be willing to export at each price ratio in comparison with the amount of clothing America expected to import. At one, and (usually) only one, intermediate price ratio, exports and imports will balance. At this equilibrium price, exports and imports will "mesh" (or match), quantitatively as well as qualitatively; the auctioneer and Mill will heave a sigh of relief, and trade will continue indefinitely until tastes or technology have changed.

For our numerical problem it has been assumed that the equilibrium terms-of-trade ratio is $^{10}\!/_6$, a little "nearer" to Europe's pre-trade ratio than to America's.

America concentrates her production completely on food. In Fig. 33-7, America is productionwise at

[5] The indifference curves in the Appendix to Chapter 21 can be used to summarize each country's tastes for food and clothing. Together with the *p-p* curves, these could derive the reciprocal demand curves of Mill, shown in Fig. 33-6. Unlike ordinary *dd* and *ss* curves, *C* is trading against *F*, not against money; hence, relative prices P_C/P_F, rather than money P_C, are plotted. (If tastes and incomes vary within each country, aggregate indifference curves would be replaced by more elaborate analysis.)

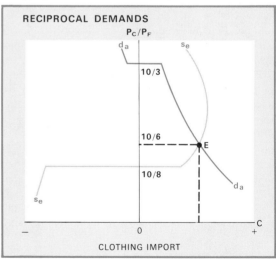

FIG. 33-6.

America specializes in food and imports clothing:

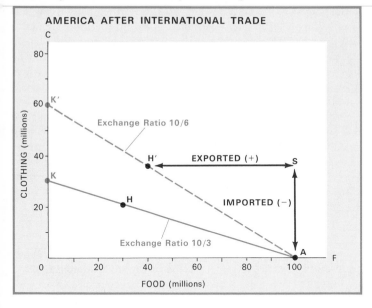

FIG. 33-7. The line *AK* represents America's domestic production-possibility curve; the line *AK'*, her new consumption-possibility curve when she is able to trade freely at the price ratio 10/6 and in consequence has decided to specialize completely in the production of food (at *A*). The black arrows from *S* to *H'* and *A* to *S* show the amounts exported (+) and imported (−) by America. As a result of free trade, she finally ends up at *H'* with more of both goods than before at *H*.

International trade makes larger world production possible:

SUMMARY SHOWING SPECIALIZATION AND GAIN FROM TRADE ACCORDING TO COMPARATIVE ADVANTAGE

AREA COMPARED	EXCHANGE RATIO OF FOOD FOR CLOTHING P_C/P_F	FOOD PRODUC- TION	FOOD CONSUMP- TION	FOOD EXPORTS (+) OR IMPORTS (−)	CLOTHING PRODUC- TION	CLOTHING CONSUMP- TION	CLOTHING EXPORTS (+) OR IMPORTS (−)
Situation before trade							
America	10/3	30	30	0	21	21	0
Europe	10/8	50	50	0	80	80	0
World	none	80	80	0	101	101	0
Situation after trade							
America	10/6	100	40	+60	0	36	−36
Europe	10/6	0	60	−60	120	84	+36
World	10/6	100	100	0	120	120	0
Gains from trade							
America	——	——	+10	——	——	+15	——
Europe	——	——	+10	——	——	+ 4	——
World	——	+20	+20	——	+19	+19	——

TABLE 33-4.

A. But since she can now trade freely at $^{10}\!/_{7}$, America is no longer limited to her old production-possibility curve. By trading, she can now move on the broken line AK' *just exactly as if a fruitful invention had been made.* Is America made potentially better off by trade? Indeed she is. Just where she will stop on this broken line, which we may call her new *consumption*-possibility curve, depends upon the workings of her internal price system. We assume that this causes her to stop at the point H', where 40 units of food and 36 units of clothing are consumed. The black arrows show America's exports ($+$) and imports ($-$).

All this is summarized in America's rows in Table 33-4, page 825. This table should be studied carefully. To understand it thoroughly is to understand the doctrine of comparative costs.

As a result of specialization and trade, America has become better off; she has more food and more clothing to consume. The same is true of Europe. What is the black magic by which something seems to have been got for nothing? In Table 33-4 the rows marked World, which represent the sum of the American and European rows, give the answer. *World production of both goods has been stepped up by specialization and trade.*

Actually, the sixth row gives the data the auctioneer would be most interested in. He is assured that equilibrium has been reached by two facts shown there: (1) World consumption of each product is identical with world production—no more, no less; and (2) the amounts that each country exports are just balanced by the amounts that the other country wishes to import. Thus the price ratio $^{10}\!/_{7}$ is the right one.[6]

This completes our explanation of comparative

advantage. You might test your full understanding by filling in on Fig. 33-5 for Europe everything that has already been filled in for America on Fig. 33-7. Europe's new consumption-possibility line, made possible by trade, pivots around the point D on the vertical axis and goes to C'. Draw in the arrows from D to S representing the amounts exported ($+$) and imported ($-$) as was done in Fig. 33-7. Note that Europe's arrows match America's but are opposite in sign. Why is this quantitative meshing of exports and imports necessary at equilibrium? The eager reader could add to the example labor measurements and wage data. Finally, note that comparative advantage, not absolute labor advantage, is the all-important condition.

■ MANY COMMODITIES

Very briefly, we must now show what happens when we remove some of the oversimplifications in the foregoing discussion. The conclusions are not essentially changed, and even the changes in details are usually not too difficult.

First note that until now we have simplified the discussion by considering only two commodities, food and clothing. Obviously, food stands for many different items (beef, milk, etc.), and similarly for clothing. Moreover, the advantages of exchange are equally great when we consider the thousand and one commodities that can and do enter into all phases of international trade.

As is shown in advanced treatises,[7] when there are many commodities producible in two countries at constant costs, they can be arranged in order according to their comparative advantage or cost. For example, the commodities automobiles, flax, perfumes, watches, wheat, and woolens might be arranged in the illustrated comparative-advantage sequence in Fig. 33-8. This means that wheat costs are lowest relative to all other commodities in America; Europe has its greatest comparative advantage in perfumes; its advantage in watches is not quite so great; and so forth.[8]

---

[6] To find this equilibrium, the auctioneer could have made up a whole book of such tables, each page corresponding to a different price ratio. Only one page is the right one, however, because at all other prices the algebraic total of exports and imports would not cancel out. Thus, at 10/7, America's desire for clothing imports would surpass Europe's willingness to export clothing. The world as a whole would be trying to consume more clothing than had been produced. Since the auctioneer has no inventories to draw upon, he would have to turn the pages toward a higher price for clothing and a lower price for food. On the right page the price ratio would be an equilibrium one: exports would balance imports, at the E intersection of Fig. 33-6.

[7] For example, G. Haberler, *Theory of International Trade* (Macmillan, New York, 1937). Haberler also pioneered the use of *p-p frontiers* in trade theory.

[8] This ordered array of goods might have arisen from the numerical data of Table 33-5, which are presented only for the curiosity of the more advanced reader and which are not essential for the above discussion. As

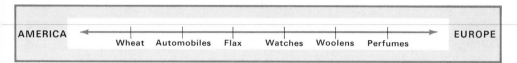

FIG. 33-8.

From the beginning we can be almost sure of one thing. The introduction of trade will cause America to produce wheat, and Europe perfume. But where will the dividing line fall? Between automobiles and flax? Or will America produce flax and Europe confine herself to watches, woolens, and perfumes? Or will the dividing line fall on one of the commodities rather than between them, so that, say, flax might be produced in both places at once?

You will not be surprised to find that the answer depends upon the comparative strength of international demand for the different goods. If we think of the commodities as beads arranged on a string according to their comparative advantage, the total demand-and-supply situation will determine where the dividing line between American and European production will fall. And an increased demand for automobiles and wheat, for

example, may tend to turn the terms of trade in the direction of America and make her so prosperous that it will no longer pay her to continue to produce her own flax. Also, there is the possibility that a new scientific discovery permitting America to grow flax on the desert might rearrange the order of the comparative advantages of the different commodities and alter the pattern of specialization and trade.

■ MANY COUNTRIES

So much for the complications introduced by many commodities. What about many countries? Europe and America are not the whole world, and even they include many separate so-called "sovereign nations."

Introducing many countries need not change our analysis. As far as any one country is concerned, all the other nations with whom she trades can be

before, it is not necessary to measure costs in terms of money or labor, but only in terms of the relative commodities into which any good can be "transformed." Suppose that we choose to measure the costs of every good in both countries in terms of woolens—selected arbitrarily because it comes last alphabetically. Then our data might be arranged alphabetically as in Table 33-5. This means that in America one must give up the production of 1,000 units of woolens to get 1 automobile, while in Europe the cost of 1 automobile is the sacrifice of 3,000 units of wool production. Therefore

(1) GOODS	(2) AMERICAN COST RATIO, IN TERMS OF WOOLENS	(3) EUROPEAN COST RATIO, IN TERMS OF WOOLENS	(4) COMPARATIVE EUROPEAN COSTS, IN TERMS OF AMERICAN COSTS (4)=(3)÷(2)
Automobiles	1,000	3,000	3.0
Flax	0.8	1.6	2.0
Perfumes	5.0	3.0	0.6
Watches	50	75	1.5
Wheat	0.2	0.8	4.0
Woolens	1.0	1.0	1.0

TABLE 33-5.

the comparative cost of automobiles relative to woolens is in Europe three times that in America, and so forth for the other goods.

Obviously, Europe's relative cost advantage is greatest in perfumes and least in wheat; in between, the commodities are arranged as shown in Fig. 33-8. The fact that the figures in the last column are predominantly greater than 1 in no way reflects on the efficiency of Europe; it merely results from the accidental fact that we chose woolens as our common denominator in which to express costs. Had we selected wheat or watches, the opposite would have been the case, and yet none of our results would be any different—except for a "scale factor" (such as converts inches to feet or yards).

TECHNICAL NOTE: Anyone who feels he must bring in labor productivities can write the respective American requirements in labor days as $A, B, C. . . .$, and Europe's as $a, b, c, . . .$ The whole analysis can then be worked out in terms of comparative ratios of the form A/B, $C/B, . . .$, and $a/b, c/b, . . .$; to explain trade patterns it is never necessary to compare absolute advantages between countries $A/a, B/b, . . .$ Of course, if he wants to compare money and real wages, these absolute advantages are necessary: by extending the analysis of Table 33-1, it can be shown that the ratio of European to American real wage must fall between the least and greatest of $A/a, B/b, . . .$; just *where* between depends on the working out of reciprocal demands.

lumped together into one group as "the rest of the world." The advantages of trade have no special relationship to state boundaries. The principles already developed apply between groups of countries and, indeed, between regions within the same country. In fact, but for historical accident, they would be more applicable to trade between the prairies and Ontario than to trade between the United States and Canada.

From the standpoint of pure economic welfare, the slogan "Buy Canadian" is as foolish as "Buy Ontario" would be, or "Buy Toronto," or "Buy Don Mills, Ontario." Part of our high per capita income and much of our economic activity come from the fortunate fact that there are no restrictive customs duties between our provinces, which thus form one great free-trade area.[9]

There is, however, one new aspect introduced by the existence of many countries. Consider merchandise trade, ignoring "invisible items" for the minute. Canada has long found it very profitable to trade indirectly with the United Kingdom. She has traditionally sold Britain raw materials, agricultural products, and some finished commodities. But Britain does not sell her manufactured goods to Canada; instead she exports manufactured goods, such as clothing, to the United States. Thus we have a very advantageous "North Atlantic triangle" of merchandise trade. Since the Great Depression this triangle has rounded out into a "world loop" of trade, with many spirals and diagonals. Part of it would look like this: Canada sells raw materials and wheat to Great Britain; she sells manufactured goods, such as clothing, to the countries of Africa and Southeast Asia; they sell rubber and other raw materials to the United States; the United States sells machines and other manufactured goods to Canada. Figure 33-9 shows the trade and the arrows indicate the direction of export surpluses.

What would happen if all countries tried to sign bilateral trade agreements, so that Canada could not and would not buy from the United States unless they bought an equal amount from us? And so forth, with every two nations? Clearly, trade

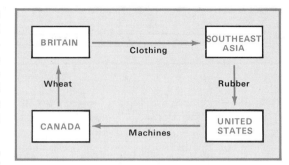

FIG. 33-9.

would be cut down severely. Imports would balance exports, but at the level of whichever is the lower. Each trading region would end up worse off.

■ INCREASING COSTS

Returning again to two countries and two commodities, we must now drop the assumption that costs are constant. The production-possibility frontiers of Figures 33-4, 33-5, and 33-7 should better have been bowed, as they were in Chapter 2. It is no longer possible to specify a single cost figure for each country.

On the whole, America is better endowed for food production than Europe; still, after a great amount of American food is produced, the cost of *extra* food will begin to exceed that of Europe. Even after American competition has drastically lowered the price of food relative to clothing, a little of the best land in Europe will be able to hold its own in food production. In the same way, that first little bit of American clothing production which can be achieved at low costs will continue even after international trade has reached an equilibrium level. However, any attempt to expand American clothing production further would entail higher extra costs and competitive losses.

We may summarize the modifications in international trade made necessary by increasing costs as follows:

As a result of international trade, each country will tend to specialize, as before, in the commodity in which it has the greatest comparative advantage; and it will export some of that commodity in exchange for the other country's surplus exports. But because of increasing relative costs, specialization need not be complete: something of both commodities may still be produced in either country, because even the less favored commodity may have low enough costs to compete when its production is small.[10]

[10] For the geometrically minded, Fig. 33-10 may be helpful. It shows America's condition before and after trade when increasing costs prevail. The production-possibility curve is now bowed out. Before international trade, America is consuming and producing at H. The domestic price ratio is 10/3, just equal to the ratio of extra costs of getting (at H) a little more clothing for a little sacrificed food. This is shown by the slope of the AK curve at H.

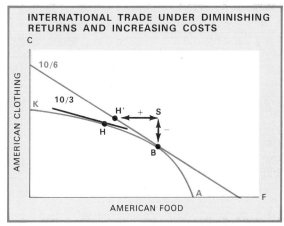

INTERNATIONAL TRADE UNDER DIMINISHING RETURNS AND INCREASING COSTS

FIG. 33-10.

After trade, when the common price ratio is 10/6, American production shifts to B, toward less clothing but not away from clothing altogether. The new production point B will be reached as a result of competition, because the slope of the curve there—i.e., the ratio of costs of extra clothing for extra food—is 10/6, or just equal to the common international price ratio. At B, and only there, will the value of America's national product (evaluated at the 10/6 price ratio) be at a maximum.

The straight line represents the new consumption-possibility curve America can achieve as a result of trade. It is straight and not bent because the auctioneer offers to trade freely, giving America at the 10/6 ratio as much or little clothing for food as she wishes. The final levels of consumption, determined by supply and demand, are given by the point H'. As before, arrows indicate exports and imports.

There are still gains from trade; but because of diminishing returns and increasing costs, there is not so much specialization as before and not quite such large gains. Note that at the equilibrium point, where no further

DETERIORATING TERMS OF TRADE Now that comparative advantage has been covered, we can tie in the last chapter's discussion of overvaluation. The Appendix to Chapter 32 showed that mercantilist fears of gold loss were rational when differences in productivity are not handled by changing exchange rates, or changing wage-price relations. But mercantilism needs improving with modern analysis. Combining that Appendix with the present one, here is an aspect of overvaluation that could be discovered only by analytical economics. Again, let A be America, using dollars, and E Europe, now using pounds.

Suppose that the productivity miracle in E involves a significant increase in her ability to produce the goods that A was previously exporting or producing for home consumption. Again A has an overvalued currency, just as in the previous case of across-the-board unbiased productivity advance in E. Again A has unemployment stagnation. Again equilibrium can be restored by depreciation of A's $1 relative to E's £1. But with this important difference:

Under unbiased technical change abroad, the new equilibrium terms of trade of A could be presumed to be about what they had been before. However, with technological change abroad biased toward improvements designed to narrow the gap between productivity *in those goods where A was enjoying comparative advantage*, there is a strong presumption that the new equilibrium will involve a permanent deterioration of A's terms of trade.

A is actually (somewhat) impoverished by the technical advance abroad, or at least slowed down in her rate of material progress by this event. How can she be hurt if her productivity has not deteriorated? Because worsened terms of trade cause A to lose some of the "consumer satisfaction" she enjoyed when she was gaining from international trade.

The universe was not made such that what helps one *must* help all; often what helps one thereby hurts another. In this case A, who is already quite rich, may find solace that E is becoming less poor and not regret too much the slight sacrifice implied

_____

trade is possible, relative (extra, or "marginal") production costs in the two countries are equal, each to the common price ratio 10/6.

for A. Chapter 35 shows that the foregoing analysis had relevance to the world of the late 1960s. It all did happen that way.

■ INTERNATIONAL GOODS MOVEMENTS AS A SUBSTITUTE FOR FACTOR MOVEMENTS

Having acknowledged the law of increasing costs described in Chapter 2 and elsewhere, we now examine implications of the related law of diminishing returns within each country.

After international trade takes place, resources in Europe flow from food to clothing production. Because clothing requires relatively much labor and little land, the pressure of population on the limited land of Europe is relieved. Land is no longer relatively so dear; rents fall compared with wages. In America the reverse happens after trade: concentration upon food production, in which labor is economized and land heavily utilized, tends to raise rents relative to wages.

In each case the free international movement of goods has effects which are partly like those following from free international movement of factors of production. Just as the movement of labor from Europe to America would relieve the scarcity of labor in America and of land in Europe, so the movement of clothing from Europe to America and of food from America to Europe tends to make the superabundant factor in each country less abundant and the scarce factor less scarce.

The person who has most clearly emphasized how commodity trade partially relieves the scarcity in all countries of the less abundant factors of production is the Swedish economist and statesman Ohlin (pronounced O'Leen).[11] He has made the following important addition to the classical doctrine of comparative cost:

Free movements of labor and capital between countries will tend to equalize wages and factor-prices. *However, even without any movements of productive factors across national boundaries, a tendency toward partial* (but not necessarily complete) *equalization of factor-prices will often result from the free movements of goods in international trade.*

It is clear, therefore, that although international trade increases national product in Europe, it may at the same time so reduce the share of particular groups that they are made worse off. Thus, the large British landowners who a century ago constituted the backbone of the Conservative party may have been selfish in opposing the famous repeal of the English corn-law tariffs in 1846, but they were not necessarily unintelligent in making their unsuccessful last-ditch fight to retain protective tariffs on imported grains.

---

[11] Bertil Ohlin, *Interregional and International Trade* (Harvard University Press, Cambridge, Mass., 1933).

SUMMARY TO APPENDIX

■ 1 If nature endows two regions unequally with factors of production, the *relative* cost of transforming one commodity into another domestically will probably be different for the two areas. (E.g., a land-rich area will have a comparative advantage in food and other land-intensive goods. A labor-rich area's comparative advantage will be in labor-intensive goods.)

■ 2 Under free trade, goods will exchange for each other at a price ratio somewhere *intermediate* between the original domestic cost ratios of the two countries (depending on reciprocal supply and demand).

■ 3 Each country will specialize in the commodity in which it has a comparative advantage and export its surplus of that product for imports from abroad.

■ 4 Each country is made better off by trade and specialization: America can get by trade more units of clothing than when she domestically transforms food into clothing; Europe does better when she trades clothing for food, doing better than when she domestically transforms clothing into food.

■ 5 Trade is *indirect* production. It is efficient production. Efficient production is always better than inefficient production. (Note that advantages of trade have nothing to do with *relative wage rates*. Under free trade, a country's wage tends to be pulled up to the higher levels of productivity of its export industry, not down to the low-efficiency level of its import industry.)

■ 6 Free movements of productive factors, can, without trade, equalize factor-prices. But even without migration of any factors, free movement of goods in trade can work to reduce or sometimes eliminate the differences in factor-prices that result from different geographical factor proportions.

QUESTIONS FOR DISCUSSION

1. Suppose two countries have the same-sloped *p-p frontiers* that are straight lines. Will self-sufficiency be different if one greatly exceeds the other in labor productivity all around?

2. Show that I benefit if your *p-p frontier* is as different from mine as possible.

3. Why would you expect land-rich Canada to export wheat to labor-rich China?

4. *Extra-credit problem:* Even where there are many goods and many countries, verify the correctness of the simple rule: For any two goods, say wheat and water, and any two countries, say France and Japan, we can calculate (from labor productivity data) which country has the comparative advantage in which good; and no country *can ever* export to the other country that good in which the latter has a comparative advantage. (WARNING: It may be that neither Japan nor France will produce any of either good; but that does not violate the stated rule!)

5. *Extra-credit problem:* Add to Table 33-5 the information that woolens happen to cost 1 day's labor in each country. Begin with $3 to £1. With wages in America $6 an hour and £1 in Europe, show that the cost-price of flax will be the same in both countries. Which goods will *A* produce cheapest? Which goods will *B*? Now let American wage rise relative to that in Europe, or let the dollar depreciate relative to the pound. Show that American exports will suffer and that American imports will rise.

6. Review your understanding of the following concepts:

straight-line and concave *p-p frontiers*
specialization point
pre- and post-trade equilibria
world loop of trade
matching trade arrows
many-good ordered array
deteriorating terms of trade

34

THE ECONOMICS OF
TARIFF PROTECTION
AND FREE TRADE

To the chamber of deputies: we are subjected to the intolerable competition of a foreign rival, who enjoys such superior facilities for the production of light that he can inundate *our* national market *at reduced price. This rival is no other than the sun. Our petition is to pass a law shutting up all windows, openings and fissures through which the light of the sun is used to penetrate our dwellings, to the prejudice of the profitable manufacture we have been enabled to bestow on the country. Signed: Candle Makers.*

F. BASTIAT

It would be absurd to try to decide whether God exists or not by counting on one hand all the arguments in the affirmative and on the other hand all the arguments in the negative, and then to award the decision to the side with the greater *number* of points. It is as absurd to evaluate the case for tariff protection by a mere count of unequally important pros and cons.

Indeed, as was shown in the previous chapter, there is essentially only one argument for free or freer trade, but it is an exceedingly powerful one, namely:

Unhampered trade promotes a mutually profitable international division of labor, greatly enhances the potential real national product of all countries, and makes possible higher standards of living all over the globe.

Recall that putting on a tariff duty (i.e., tax) discourages imports and raises prices to the domestic consumer. By killing off the fruitful international division of labor, it "protects" the relatively inefficient domestic producer. Import quotas do the same.

The arguments for high-tariff protection against the competition of foreign imports take many different forms. They may be divided into three categories:

1.   Those that are definitely economically false, some so obviously and

palpably as hardly to merit serious discussion, but some whose falsity can be detected only by subtle economic reasoning.

2.   A few arguments for protection that are without validity in a perfectly competitive "classical" static full-employment world, but that do contain some kernels of truth for a sizeable nation which monopolizes some crop, or for a nation undergoing economic development and subject to underemployment and balance of payment problems (an overvalued currency).

3.   Finally, certain noneconomic arguments that may make it desirable national policy to sacrifice economic welfare in order to subsidize certain activities admittedly not economically efficient.

■ NONECONOMIC GOALS

Let us begin with the last category of arguments, for they are most simply disposed of. If you ever are on a debating team and are given the assignment to defend free trade, you will strengthen your case at the beginning by conceding that economic welfare is not the sole goal of life. Political considerations are also important. Thus, it may be necessary to become partially self-sufficient in certain lines of activity, even at great cost, because of fear of future wars.

An example is petroleum production. If mineralogical know-how and capacity are considered necessary for national sovereignty and if the right amount of capacity is not able to survive under free trade, the economist cannot assert that national policy should be against protection of this industry. But he can suggest that a *subsidy* to domestic production might be preferable to a tariff: This would bring the domestic price down to the international price instead of raising the price to the consumer up to the domestic cost; also the subsidy would show clearly what the costs of national sovereignty are and would better enable the public to decide whether the flame is worth the candle.

The problem of whether to support our shipyards and merchant marine is similarly perplexing, when by doing so we both inspire retaliation by other countries and sacrifice the benefits to be gained from their comparative-advantage efficiencies. The economist can claim no special competence to advise on this problem. He can point out that selfish economic interests often conceal their true motives under a guise of nationalism and try to justify uneconomic projects in terms of national defense. He can ask suspiciously, "Was the increase in subsidies to Canadian shipyards justified by our defense needs for such capacity? Or was this merely a case of political pressure?" Finally the economist can also point out that mutually profitable international trade may help to promote international understanding and unity, and that political interferences with trade have in the past provided some of the frictions that led to war.

In conclusion, it is well to point out other noneconomic goals that may deserve consideration. Society may feel that there is some special sanctity about farm life, something worth preserving in the way of life of the "stout agricultural yeoman or happy peasant." (It is to be doubted that people who rhapsodize in this fashion typically come from farms.) Or some may agree with the Soviet

Union that rural living is worth fostering because the country has a higher birth rate than the cities.

Economist Harry Johnson has pointed out that many countries have a "preference for industrialization" and are willing (in international tariff-bargaining sessions) to disregard their comparatve advantage in raw-material production in order to keep a wall of tariff protection around their emerging manufacturing industries. Johnson argues that it is not for economists to say that this preference is irrational or that the new countries could get their manufactured goods cheaper if they imported them: a national aim is a national aim, even if it is "noneconomic."

In all such cases, subsidies rather than tariffs seem called for. A tariff is simply a rather indirect and clumsy form of subsidy that draws attention away from the problem.

Do not be left with the impression that the noneconomic arguments are generally favorable to tariffs. Any Member of Parliament who has gone on a foreign junket knows the serious harm done to Canada's reputation abroad by her capricious and discriminating barriers against the products of certain countries. And nothing is so detrimental to Canadian popularity abroad as our reputation for being a high-tariff country. Foreigners are convinced that as soon as they threaten domestic producers, we will clamp down with quotas and tariffs even though the consumer must pay higher prices at home. So it is to our political interest to resist many of the pressures that make for restrictions on international trade.

◼ GROSSLY FALLACIOUS ARGUMENTS FOR TARIFF

KEEPING MONEY IN THE COUNTRY   To Abraham Lincoln has been attributed the remark, "I don't know much about the tariff. But I do know that when I buy a coat from England, I have the coat and England has the money. But when I buy a coat in America, I have the coat and America has the money."

There is no evidence that he ever actually said this; but it does represent an age-old fallacy typical of the so-called "mercantilistic" writers of the seventeenth and eighteenth centuries who preceded Adam Smith. They considered a country lucky which *gave away* more goods than it received, because such a "favorable" (!) balance of trade meant that gold would flow into the country in question to pay for its export surplus.

In this day and age it should be unnecessary to labor the point that, while an increased amount of money in the hands of one person will make *him* better off, doubling the money in the hands of everybody in a full-employment economy will only serve to raise prices. Unless the single individual is a demented miser like King Midas, the money makes him better off, not for its own sake, but for what it will buy or bid away from other individuals. For society as a whole, once full employment is reached, new money cannot hope to buy any new goods.[1]

---

[1] Of course, the gold might be spent abroad. But this perfectly sensible way of improving welfare by importing was precisely what the mercantilist "bullionists" were arguing against.

A TARIFF FOR HIGHER MONEY WAGES   Today it is agreed that extreme protection can raise prices and attract gold into one country, if all other countries do not retaliate with tariffs. The tariff may even increase *money* wages; but it will tend to increase the cost of living by more than the increase in money wages, so that *real* wages will fall as labor becomes less productive. It is simply not the case that our general living standards can be raised by protecting every domestic industry threatened by cheaper imports.[2]

One could go on endlessly giving examples of protectionist fallacies that every thoughtful person can explode in a minute by subjecting them to analysis. This does not mean that such crude fallacies can be dismissed as unimportant. Actually, they are most important of all in shaping legislation, the other fancier arguments simply being used as window dressing.

TARIFFS FOR SPECIAL-INTEREST GROUPS   The single most important motivation for protective tariff is obvious to anyone who has watched delegations flock to Ottawa to press for a tariff revision. Powerful pressure groups and vested interests—both business and labor—know very well that a tariff on their products will help *them*, whatever its effect on total production and consumption. In the nineteenth century, Ottawa was very receptive to tariff suggestions. Today its resistance has stiffened somewhat, and lobbies are maintained in the capital to drum up enthusiasm for the good old cloth, chemical, or buttonhook industry.

Economically the case for freer trade may be strong, but politically the case for protection tends to exert undue pressure. Why? Because *freer trade helps everybody a little*, while *protection helps a few people a lot*. Does it matter politically that the bad points of protection outweigh the good? Not if those few who benefit from protection (or who are kept by protection from suffering harm) are politically active in pressing for their cause. It is much harder to organize the masses of consumers and producers to agitate for the even larger gains that they get from an efficient pattern of national specialization and trade. If political votes were in exact proportion to *total* economic benefit, every country would selfishly legislate most of its tariffs out of existence.

■ SOME LESS OBVIOUS FALLACIES

A TARIFF FOR REVENUE   First, there is the claim that the tariff should be used to raise government tax revenue. Actually, a customs duty on imports is only one form of regressive sales tax, and a rather bad one. A customs duty or tariff is especially bad because it draws economic resources away from their best uses. If the people who advance the revenue argument were really sincere, they would advocate an excise tax that would *also* fall on domestic production. (Canada has a few "excise duties" that do apply to both imported and home-produced goods, but they are supplemented by additional customs duties on imports.) Such a combined excise-and-tariff provides no protection at all.

For emerging countries with an ill-developed tax-collection machinery it is often argued that a customs duty is the only available source of revenue. Most

---

[2] See Chapter 33's discussion of comparative advantage and effects of a tariff.

of the Commonwealth countries made their start by depending on customs and even today Canada gets about 7 per cent of all public revenue from tariffs (10 per cent of federal revenue). This argument is obviously most relevant when a country has just one port of entry, where all the trade can be observed and taxed. But it has little to do with an argument for tariff protection, for a prohibitively high tariff that kept out all imports would collect no revenue at all! (In 1890, the U.S. Congress found itself with a surplus of tax revenue over expenditure. It met the problem of excessive tariff revenues, not by lowering tariff rates, but by *raising them high* enough to reduce the total of revenue collected.)

COMPETITION FROM CHEAP FOREIGN LABOR   A second argument has always carried immense weight in every industrialized country. In Canada it has been put forward both by industry and by trade unions. According to its usual version, "If we let in goods produced by cheap pauper foreign labor—by Chinese coolies who live on a few cents' worth of rice per day or by low-paid Japanese textile workers—then the higher standard of living of Canadian workers cannot be maintained." So stated, the argument cannot stand up.

We have seen that trade is mutually profitable even if one country can produce every good more cheaply in terms of resources than the other. The important thing is comparative advantage, not absolute advantage. In the last analysis, trade boils down to two-sided barter. One country cannot indefinitely undersell the other in every line of merchandise.

Earlier we showed that full employment at home need not depend in the long run on foreign trade. If, then, everyone in this country remains fully employed at his most suitable occupation, is it not to *our selfish advantage* for the workers of other countries to be willing to work for very little?

To put the matter another way: The comparative-cost doctrine shows that we benefit most by trading with countries of the Far East or the tropics which are *very different* from ours, rather than with countries such as England or Germany which have an industrial economy like our own![3] Against the pauper-labor argument, there is the clinching fact that the analysis of comparative advantage showed that absolute wage levels had nothing to do with the long-run increase in national income that resulted from trade.

So much from a theoretical point of view. If we turn to the real world, we find the arguments to be even more incorrect. Canadian workers beg for tariffs, saying, "protect us from the 'unfair competition' of high-paid efficient American workers who have skill and machinery far better than our own." The rest of the world lives in fear of competition from American mass-production industries.

---

[3] This argument must be qualified and amplified. Backward countries, so poor that they have little real purchasing power with which to import, at best can export little to us. Most trade today is between industrialized countries. As a backward country advances industrially, it buys more from industrial countries, not less; but perhaps not proportionately more, and perhaps there is *less consumer's surplus from trade* accruing to both parties.

The English protectionist claims that the American worker in Bridgeport, Connecticut, who is paid $4.50 per hour is more than three times as efficient as the English worker who gets paid $1.50 an hour. This is perhaps an overstatement, but it is close to the important truth.

> High North American real wages come from high efficiency, not from tariff protection. Such high wages do not handicap us in competing with foreign workers.

A TARIFF TO RAISE WAGE SHARE   Thus far we have had nothing but adverse criticism for the "cheap pauper foreign labor" tariff argument. To be objective —and without objectivity there can be no science—we must admit that it may have the following iota of possible truth. The Ohlin proposition in the Appendix to the preceding chapter suggested that free trade in goods may serve as a partial substitute for the movement of factors of production from countries where they are plentiful to countries where they are scarce. Thus North American importing of Europe's labor-intensive commodities, such as clothing, is a partial substitute for the immigration of European labor to North America. This implies that relative labor scarcity on this continent could be alleviated by our international specialization in labor-economizing products and that real wages here might actually *fall* under conditions of free trade. Real national product would go up, but the relative and absolute share of labor might go down.

Although admitting this as a possibility, most economists believe its grain of truth for a typical country is outweighed by more realistic considerations. No doubt immobile laborers such as textile or furniture workers might be hurt by removing a tariff. But since labor is such an important and flexible factor of production, it seems likely that other laborers would gain from expanded trade more than those hurt would lose. Labor as a whole would presumably in the long run share in the increased national product from trade.

Some Canadian economists have made serious investigations of the applicability of the Ohlin idea to Canada's tariff. Admitting that the tariff diverts Canadian capital and labor to low-productivity industries (compared to the comparatively advantageous export industries), they argue that Ontario and Quebec wage rates are higher than they would be if Canada specialized in low-labor industries such as pulp, mining, and wheat, and imported automobiles, furniture, and cloth.

Although admitting this as a theoretical possibility, most economists deny that it is actually true. Its validity depends upon the facts in each case. It is true that the pulp industry uses (creates a demand for) fewer workers than the protected automobile industry, per dollar of product. But it also demands *more* labor than the protected chemical, oil-refining, or smelting industries. Without finer measurement, no tariff policy conclusion can be reached. It seems likely that with labor such an important, flexible, and mobile factor of production, the losses from free trade suffered by some workers would be more than offset by the gains of others and of the same workers in new jobs.

In the mid-1950s, a new element was added to the debate. Pointing to Canada's easy-immigration policy, economists like Toronto's John Dales argued that tariffs do not raise wages but simply create more jobs that attract more immigrants. Thus the tariff maintains the cost of living above its international level,[4] but immigration prevents the Ohlin real-wage effect from emerging. The result is more industry and population than would exist if there were free trade: not higher per capita real incomes or real wages.[5]

The topic is still under discussion among economists, especially in Canada and Australia. The consensus so far is that while Ohlin may be correct that protection of labor-using industries may raise the percentage of the NNP going to wages, this rise may be cancelled out by the fall in the NNP per capita, in which labor shares.

A TARIFF FOR RETALIATION   Some people admit that a world of free trade would be preferable to a world of tariffs; but they say that so long as other countries are so foolish or so wicked as to pass restrictive tariff legislation, there is nothing that we can do but follow suit in self-defense.

Actually, however, a tariff is much like an increase in transportation costs. If other countries were foolish enough to let their roads go to ruin, would it pay us to chop holes in ours? The answer is, No. Analogously, if other countries hurt us and themselves by passing tariffs, we should not add to our own hurt by passing a tariff.

To make sure that you grasp the point that our tariff harms us as well as the foreigner, you should realize that there are four gains when a trade-agreements program succeeds in getting another country and ourselves to lower tariffs reciprocally. The other country's tariff reduction bestows gains (1) on us and (2) on them. Our tariff reduction adds two more gains: (3) for ourselves and (4) for them.

Therefore the only possible sense in the argument that we should retaliate when a foreign country raises tariffs is that our threat of retaliation may deter them from raising tariffs, and our promise to reduce tariffs may persuade them to reduce theirs. This would justify our passing an occasional tariff as a bluff, but if our bluffs do not work, we should give them up.

Most realistic students of political science infer from historical studies that retaliatory tariffs usually lead other nations to raise theirs still higher and are rarely an effective bargaining weapon for multilateral tariff reduction. And even in the smaller forum of Canadian-U.S. tariff bargaining, it is difficult to show that the occasional spiteful "retaliatory" tariffs had much to do with the subsequent hauling down of tariff barriers. On the other hand, many economists argue that the "Reciprocity" plea, the offer to cut tariffs in return for desired

---

[4] In 1956, John H. Young estimated for the Royal Commission on Canada's Economic Prospects that Canadians paid about 3½ to 4 per cent more for their gross private expenditure than they need have if they had bought goods at world price levels. This amounted to about 1 billion dollars at that time. (*Canadian Commercial Policy*, Ottawa, 1957.)

[5] John H. Dales' argument in *The Protective Tariff in Canada's Development*. It involves an extension of similar hypotheses by Queen's University Principal W. A. Mackintosh in the 1930s and by Manitoba's Clarence Barber in the *Canadian Journal of Economics and Political Science* in 1955.

cuts by the other country has usually met sympathetic (though not always effective) responses.

THE "SCIENTIFIC" TARIFF   This is one of the most insidious arguments for a tariff; insidious because it often sounds plausible and moderate but, if taken literally, would mean the end to all trade! According to its usual form, tariffs should be passed to "equalize the cost of production at home and abroad." The last chapter showed all the advantage from trade to rest on *differences* in cost or advantage. If tariffs were passed raising the costs of imports to that of the highest home producer, no goods would come in at all.[6]

There is nothing scientific about such a tariff. It is a grave reflection on the economic literacy of the Canadian people that this least defensible of all protectionist arguments is still sometimes pleaded. We are fortunate that it has not been taken as seriously by Canadian governments as it has by the U.S. Congress, which even wrote it into law upon occasion.

KEEPING AN INDUSTRY INTACT, AND DECLINING REGIONS   According to this view, a country should keep tariffs high enough to prevent an industry from having to go out of business entirely, though low enough to allow "some" imports in. It is therefore like some of the "noneconomic" arguments in favor of tariffs—those to do with keeping defense industries going as a matter of military preparedness. (The U.S. Congress for example has decided that when imports become so large that the survival of a home industry is in danger, it will be declared to be at the "peril point," and tariffs may be increased, or quotas tightened, to protect it from further decline.)

This argument sounds moderate. If home industries have many firms, some with high costs and some with lower costs, the tariff that keeps the industry intact may in fact only have to be high enough to protect one or two uneconomic plants; no more. The economist dislikes it, not for the relatively small cost that it may impose on consumers, but because its basic philosophy runs completely counter to the economic theory of comparative advantage. Our nation gains from trade by *specializing*, i.e., by giving up certain activities and moving their resources into other industries in which we have a greater comparative advantage. The industries in which we have strong comparative disadvantage should never have come into existence. And suppose an industry formerly had a comparative advantage but has lost it—because other industries have had greater technological improvements, because the domestic factors it uses have become more expensive through becoming more valuable elsewhere, because factors for that industry have become relatively cheaper abroad, or for any other reason. Then this industry *ought* to be killed off by the competition of our more productive industries. It ought to reach and pass the peril point.

---

[6] With nonconstant costs the scientific-tariff formula is indeterminate. A zero tariff may equalize foreign costs with those of our few most efficient producers; an almost prohibitive tariff equalize with our high-cost producers. Where can one scientifically draw the line?

This sounds ruthless indeed. No industry willingly dies; no region gladly undergoes conversion to new factor uses. In truth, any field that is imperiled is probably already a sick industry with a past history of suffering. So the already weak industry and region feels it is being singled out to carry the burden of getting the country into a more productive configuration.

The best plan, then, is to adopt policies that will aid the factors of production to be used efficiently (instead of being forced on consumers who would rather buy imports). In some regions this is easy enough. For several years Canada has had "designated areas," which, like Britain's development areas, consist of euphemistically named depressed regions. The government's policy is to attract new industries to these areas, so that they will fill the employment positions once occupied by the dying industries. To do this, it gives income-tax rebates, accelerated-depreciation tax allowances, or outright subsidies. For example, at the beginning of 1971, the federal government promised $30,000 for each new job created by industry in certain designated areas.

However, these rehabilitation or redevelopment programs have their drawbacks. Many communities and regions that formerly sold to the Canadian market (or were exporting regions) are ill-adapted to the location of new industries. Even if government subsidies tempt new factories, the fact remains that out-of-the-way locations will have permanently high costs. Thus subsidies may have to be perpetual (even if hidden in perpetual tax remissions or enforced low freight rates that are covered by high freight rates on other lines of the railways); or local workers may have to agree to perpetually low wages; or the new industries will soon become sick in their turn.

Official opinion now is beginning to accept the view that the best thing that can be done for some of these regions is to help them to close down, giving the vested factors time to move. On the one hand, if tariffs are to be removed immediately, government programs may be set up to retrain workers, lend or give them a moving allowance, help them to find new houses and jobs in active regions, and pay them well for their old properties.[7] On the other hand, the tariff reduction can take place gradually, in step with retraining and other policies designed to speed the transition and spread the burden more widely. (Canada has so far considered only the automobile tariff in this way; but the U.S. 1962 Trade Act specifically links general tariff reductions with location and mobility concessions.)

Much of what is said in the last two paragraphs applies to any declining industry or region, regardless of whether import competition is the source of the decline. Fortunately, full employment and rapid over-all growth help in the task of transferring factors to new industries and products. Although jobs and

---

[7] A few years ago, economists who urged mobility-creating programs were told that they were politically impossible; local politicians would always oppose measures that reduced their local electorate, even if each member of the departing labor force was benefited. This resistance still exists. But the federal Manpower, Industry, and Forestry departments now have in hand programs that make up a package of the kind mentioned in the text; and provincial governments are cooperating.

earnings falter in the buggy industry, the buoyant automobile industry clamors for skilled workers. Thus it is clear that policies that encourage strong export industries and high domestic demand (through the skillful use of monetary and fiscal weapons) will tend to clear up much of the depressed-region or sick-industry problem automatically. Having adopted such policies, the nation can with good conscience strive for the increase in real income made possible by specialization—and respecialization—according to the principles of comparative advantage. Striving to "keep industries intact" is a negation of this goal.

■ THE "FOREIGNER WILL PAY," OR TERMS-OF-TRADE-ARGUMENTS[8]

After dealing with fallacious tariff arguments, we find it refreshing to come now to a possibly valid one—which hopes tariff's will shift the terms of trade against the foreigner. Indeed, it is about the only argument that would be valid even under static competitive conditions, and it goes back 150 years to John Stuart Mill. Paradoxically, valid arguments for protection seem mostly to have come from free traders, not from protectionists!

If the United States puts a tariff on rubber, Mill would argue, that will raise the price in the States over its price abroad. But with U.S. demand now curtailed, and as the United States is an important demander of rubber, the price abroad will be bid down. So part of the tariff really falls on the foreigner. (Show that a smaller country, like Canada, could not use this argument, since it cannot budge world prices.)

In summary, a judicious tariff might improve an important country's terms of trade (defined as the ratio of her export to her import prices).

But here is a warning. *Prohibitive* tariffs, which suit the protectionist who really is against all trade, could never be justified by this terms-of-trade argument. Why? Because killing off *all* trade would kill off all the advantage you get from shifting the terms of trade in your favor. Mill and modern economists therefore insist that the "optimal tariff" is one just large enough to improve your terms of trade and just small enough to keep your physical exchange of imports and exports at the level most favorable to your own country.

Most economists think that all this would imply rather small tariff rates for most countries. And they hasten to point out that when all nations pursue such terms-of-trade tariff policies, the world pattern of production and exchange becomes less efficient. So most (if not all) nations tend to end up worse off under such beggar-my-neighbor policies.

■ ARGUMENTS FOR PROTECTION UNDER DYNAMIC CONDITIONS

At last we are arriving at a point in the protection versus free-trade debate where those in favor of tariffs can begin to score some weighty points. Three important arguments fall in this category: (1) that a tariff may help to reduce

---

[8] The argument is exactly like that of a domestic monopolist who raises his price above marginal cost but does not raise it sky-high, instead stopping where $MR = MC$. It was anticipated in Chapter 32, Chapter 33 (footnote 9), and Chapter 33's Appendix.

unemployment, (2) that tariffs may create diversified industries more immune to risk, and (3) that temporary tariff protection for an "infant industry" with growth potentialities may be desirable.

TARIFFS AND UNEMPLOYMENT Historically, one of the strongest arguments for protection has been the desire to make or preserve jobs. Earlier we discussed the favorable multiplier effects of exports and foreign investment on jobs and domestic spending, and also the unfavorable "leakage" effects of imports. So beggar-my-neighbor high-tariff policy might increase employment in the short run before other nations retaliated.

But can we accept such measures as a valid part of our national full-employment program? Is not freer trade much like a scientific discovery of new machinery and methods? Both represent increases in our *potentially producible* level of real national output; but either *might* in the short run tend to lower our actual *attained* level of output and employment. And yet, there is no need, in either the short or the long run, to tolerate a gap between actual and potentially producible product, for that represents an unnecessary frittering away of the gains from progress.

How, then, do we meet the arguments relating unemployment to too low tariffs? We refute these arguments just as we refute arguments concerning "technological unemployment." We point out the existence of domestic monetary, foreign-exchange-rate, and fiscal policies that can successfully *and efficiently* solve the problem of economic slump. (Recall our hundreds of pages on macroeconomics.)[9] If workers displaced by imports can find other jobs in a buoyant labor market, this protection plea loses its force.

Once again, we realize how vitally important it is to insist on rational macroeconomic management that employs the tools of monetary and fiscal analysis to create the favorable environment for stability and growth which is vitally necessary if the classical principles of economics are to be relevant and valid.

A further point needs emphasis. Today we include in a rational program the requirement that the foreign exchange rate not be a disequilibrium one. If the dollar parity represents "overvaluation," unemployment may result (as was shown in Chapter 32's Appendix). Of course, a tariff might work a little to offset such an overvaluation. But it is much more efficient—and equitable too—to lower the exchange rate rather than to rely on quotas, tariffs, and exchange controls.

DIVERSIFICATION TO REDUCE TERMS-OF-TRADE RISK Comparative advantage might tell a country to specialize completely on one good or a few goods. So she is to put all her eggs in one basket. But then what will happen if the prices of those goods drop? Or if her export prices oscillate? She will find such variations in

---

[9] If money wage rates are generally too high, the dollar may be "overvalued" (as defined in Chapter 32's Appendix). Chapter 35 shows this could call for a new exchange-rate parity.

her terms of trade very destabilizing to her real income; and she may be left with an industry which has become permanently unprofitable.

To avoid the perils of "monoculture," Latin American economists advise the introduction of tariffs. Just as an investor in securities will diversify to reduce risk rather than keeping all his eggs in one basket, so they tell a country to use tariffs to induce diversification.

This argument certainly deserves careful examination. Note though that it assumes private citizens are neglecting to take account of the riskiness in future prices of the industries they put their money and labor skills into. This argument has to assume that the government is better informed than private investors, or at least that the government is more farseeing than private investors in taking account of the future perils of price drops and price gyrations. If the future risks are genuine and are foreseen by private investors, those investors will not be misled by temporarily high profits into investing in these few industries; in truth, such industries will not then have a genuine long-run comparative advantage, and there will be no effective tendency to specialize in them.[10]

At this point a related argument for tariffs should be mentioned. Dr. Raúl Prebisch, long adviser to the U.N.'s Economic Commission for Latin America, argued that the *long-run terms of trade are always shifting against agricultural products*. So nations that specialize in them are betting on the wrong horse. He argued that their governments should instead impose tariffs aimed at building up manufacturing industries whose future terms of trade would be more favorable. [Against this argument is the following: If past and future reductions in food prices are matched by even greater drops in real food costs, because agriculture undergoes great technological improvements, then long-run comparative advantage might still validly tell a nation to specialize in food to improve its real income or, in other cases, to minimize its losses. (See Chapter 35.)]

This argument is really a debate about what the *future* comparative advantage of the countries in question will be. To the degree that governments are smarter than private investors in discerning trends threatening to the terms of trade, a valid case can be made for their interfering with free-market forces. But if government is wrong in its comparative-advantage forecasts, the loss in real income to the nation can become very considerable, and the nation may find its rate of development slowed down rather than speeded up.

TARIFFS FOR "INFANT INDUSTRIES"   Alexander Hamilton, in his famous "Report on Manufactures," raised this argument. It is also associated with the name of a nineteenth-century German economist, Friedrich List, and it has received the

---

[10] Suppose private employers do foresee the risk, but think they can fire workers when export prices drop, thereby throwing the burden of the unemployed on the state. Then we face a genuine so-called "external diseconomy," which might justify government intervention in the form of tariffs, quotas, or other programs. Also, recall the limited conditions under which the "foreigner will pay" argument has terms-of-trade validity.

cautious blessing of John Stuart Mill, Alfred Marshall, the late Professor Frank W. Taussig, and some orthodox economists.

According to this doctrine, there are activities in which a country would really have a comparative advantage, *if only it could get them started*. If confronted with foreign competition, such infant industries are not able to weather the initial period of experimentation and financial stress; but given a breathing space, they can be expected to develop economies of mass production and the technological efficiency typical of many modern processes. Although protection will at first raise prices to the consumer, once the industry grows up it will be so efficient that cost and price will actually have fallen. If the benefit to consumers at that late date would be enough to more than make up for the higher prices during the period of protection, a tariff is justified.

There is certainly something to this, at least as a possibility. Historical studies have turned up some genuine cases of infant industries that grew up to stand on their own feet; but history reveals even more cases of the contrary— of perpetual infants! Unfortunately for the practical importance of this argument, even promising infant industries cannot swing many votes. It is not they who tend to receive protection from tariffs, but rather the old and powerful vested interests who have never shed their diapers for these many years.

THE "YOUNG-ECONOMY" ARGUMENT   The infant-industry argument probably had more validity for Canada as it was in 1867-1897 than it has today.[11] Rather than lobbying for tariffs to protect it in its "infancy," any industry that now foresees eventual tariff-free low-cost mass production can more easily borrow from a receptive capital market to get the breathing space, working capital, and experience it needs. And the argument has more validity for present-day undeveloped nations than for those which have already experienced the transition from an agricultural to an industrial way of life. In a sense, such nations are still asleep; they cannot be said to be truly in equilibrium. All over the world, farmers seem to earn less than industrial workers. Consequently, there is everywhere a relative growth of industry and a decline of agriculture. Populations migrate cityward, but this movement is not rapid enough to achieve an equilibrium of earnings and productivity. A strong case can be made for using moderate protection to accelerate these economically desirable long-run trends. Such a defense of protection might better be called a "young-economy" rather than an infant-industry argument.

One final word: Please note that the infant-industry or young-economy arguments are not contradictory to the principle of comparative advantage. On the contrary, their validity rests upon the presumption of an induced, dynamic

---

[11] John H. Young, in his book on *Canadian Commercial Policy*, has reminded us that earlier Canadian politicians were usually in the habit of praising the tendency of a high-tariff policy to make a country self-sufficient; or as John A. Macdonald put it, "a union in interest, a union in trade, and a union in feeling." Although it was also hoped that the tariffs proposed in 1879 would help in "blasting a way into the markets of the world" (see Fig. 34-1), the Canadian "National Policy" associated with the Macdonald governments in fact rarely made use of any version of the infant-industry argument.

shift of the production-possibility frontier outward and in the direction of a *new* comparative advantage in the lines needing *temporary* protection.

■ CONCLUSION

While this chapter has usually spoken of tariffs, almost everything said would apply equally well to any other impediments to trade. Thus, quotas have all the bad effects of tariffs, and often quotas are even more restrictive.

Finally, we should mention the so-called "invisible tariff." In many countries—and Canada is no exception—the complicated administration of the customs can be as bad as the monetary duty that has to be paid. If an importer's shipments are unduly delayed or if a foreigner's exports to us are refused admittance for complicated reasons of health or of failure to comply with arbitrary regulations, then such red tape can be as harmful to trade as outright tariffs or quotas. Work toward simplification of customs administration still has a long way to go.

This completes our discussion of the tariff controversy. No fair-minded reader who takes the trouble to think the matter through can fail to see how shallow are most of the economic arguments for tariff protection. The only serious exception is the infant-industry or young-economy argument.

It is not surprising, therefore, that economists—who are supposed to agree on almost nothing—have been overwhelmingly in favor of steps to lower trade barriers. It has even been suggested that this enthusiasm alone is responsible for the disregard of their recommendations by Canadian statesmen, the "great Canadian noneconomists" as one writer has ruefully called them. In Canada, decisions have been particularly hard, for "noneconomic objectives" aimed at building a Canadian nation at almost any cost have been thought to run counter to free-trade principles. Economists are not agreed that the objectives are contradictory. (Is it a condition of nationhood that all Canadians drink Canadian apple juice? Is the United States less a nation now that it imports European transformers and Japanese transistors?) However, their stronger pleas have been unattractive to the politicians.

Thus the "National Policy" to protect Canadian manufacturing prevailed over the "Reciprocity" program to negotiate reciprocal tariff reductions, all the way to zero tariffs, with the United States and other countries. Sir Wilfrid Laurier tried Reciprocity with the United States on the electorate in 1911, and lost his majority to Sir Robert Borden. And in the 1920s and 1930s, tariff reduction moved backward as much as forward. But in the late 1930s Canada negotiated a reciprocal trade agreement with the United States; in the 1940s she eventually joined the General Agreement on Tariffs and Trade (GATT); and major Canadian political parties have from time to time proposed, very tentatively, free trade with the European Common Market, with the Commonwealth countries and the Common Market, with the United States and, recently, with the "North Atlantic" countries.

Meanwhile, progress is being made. First, we had free trade with the United

Tariffs reflect national policy and international attitudes:

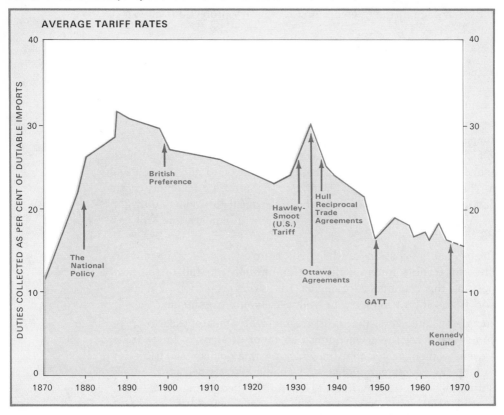

FIG. 34-1. After waves of tariff protection under the National Policy in the 1890s and in the Great Depression of the 1930s, Canada, like other Western nations, has now reduced the general level of her tariff rates. But many people still consider the present level, about 18 per cent, high. (Sources: John Young, *Canadian Commercial Policy*; *Canada Year Book*; *The National Finances*.)

States in farm equipment. Second, the more controversial automobile agreement has opened the U.S. market to some Canadian exports.[12]

In the 1960s, Canada participated in the "Kennedy Round" of tariff reductions at the GATT (General Agreement on Tariffs and Trade), which were

[12] In 1971, the government was still considering its response to a Royal Commission on the farm machinery situation.

The automobile agreement is too involved to be explained here. Roughly speaking, it encourages Canadian manufacturers to make parts for export by mass production, by allowing them to import for sale in Canada a high value of fully manufactured American cars or parts, duty-free. With some misgivings, the United States has agreed to remit duties on the imports of such Canadian-made parts. The chief popular criticism has been that although Canadian car manufacturers now pay less duty on imports, they have not been forced to cut their prices. The industry explains that it needs the extra earnings to cover the extra investment in facilities.

touched off by the Kennedy Trade Expansion Act of 1962. The U.S. administration was authorized to reduce existing U.S. tariffs by 50 per cent in reciprocal negotiations. From 1963 to 1967, almost 50 countries participated in the subsequent bargaining, and it is said that tariff cuts were made on a total of 45 billion dollars of trade.

The European Common Market, Britain, Japan, and the United States all made substantial reductions, thus assisting the entry of the products of Canada and other exporters into these markets. Most participants bargained about "linear" or equal percentage-point reduction on all tariffs. But Canada had little to gain from tariff reduction by countries that imported our raw materials on which tariffs were already low, and so instead she offered certain specific tariff reductions in return for specific concessions by our customers. This approach opened up some markets to Canadian exporters (and to their rivals in other exporting nations). On manufactured goods, Canada reduced percentage rates modestly by between 2½ to 5 per cent.[13]

Figure 34-1 indicates that, measured by the burden on dutiable imports, Canada has some way to go to achieve the standing of a low-tariff nation. But concessions and participation in the Kennedy Round all suggested that, perhaps in spite of the arguments given by economists, Canada was slowly moving in the general direction of tariff reduction. On the other hand, the early 1970s saw a return of pressure toward tariff increases and quotas, especially in textiles.

SUMMARY

■ 1 The case for freer trade rests upon the increased productivity that international specialization, according to the law of comparative advantage, makes possible. Higher world production is made possible, and all countries can have higher standards of living. Trade between countries with different standards of living is especially profitable.

■ 2 Most arguments for tariff protection are simply rationalizations for special benefits to particular pressure groups and do not stand up under analysis.

■ 3 An exception to the law of comparative advantage is provided by the need to favor certain uneconomical lines of activity for reasons of national defense. Perhaps outright government subsidies would be better in such cases.

■ 4 The only other exception of any practical importance in a full-employment economy[14] is provided by the case of infant industries or young economies that need temporary protection in order to realize their true long-run

---

[13] Canada completed those tariff cuts in 1969, ahead of schedule. By 1972, all participant nations should have completed scheduled reductions with European and U.S. tariffs at a lower percentage rate than those of Canada.

[14] The "foreigner will pay" argument, for all its theoretical attractiveness, is probably of limited actual importance for most countries. Chapter 32's Appendix shows how overvaluation of a currency gives comfort to the enemies of fruitful international trade.

comparative advantages. To the degree that public planning for development can discern long-run trends better than the free market can, trade interventions to spur industrialization might turn out to be beneficial.

QUESTIONS FOR DISCUSSION

1. What do you think is the single most favorable argument for a tariff or quota?

2. Make a list of fallacious tariff arguments. Weigh pros and cons. (Apply to, say, steel.)

3. Comment critically on the infant-industry and young-economy arguments. What is their relation to comparative advantage?

4. Mention some noneconomic considerations relevant to tariffs.

5. Relate the declining-region and "scientific tariff" arguments to comparative-advantage theory.

6. Suppose labor productivity grows mightily abroad, and Canadian goods start to be undersold in every line. Suppose that a mixed economy like ours has sticky wage rates. Suppose devaluation of the dollar is not feasible. Show that new tariffs might be a stopgap measure.

7. *Extra-credit problem:* To understand the fact that the foreigner can be made to pay part of a tariff, go back to linen imports in Fig. 33-3(b). Suppose a new tariff lowers the black arrows of imports shown there. Can you see that the new equilibrium position must involve lower price of linen there? So America is helped by the tariff to buy a bit more cheaply.

8. Review your understanding of the following concepts:

tariff protection, quota	terms of trade
scientific tariff, keeping an industry	specialization and risk
intact, and declining regions	infant industry and
national defense arguments	young economy

Appendix: Foreign Ownership and Control, or "Greed" versus "Nationalism"

Chapter 34 has dealt with tariffs as a restriction on the free movement of goods and services between countries, and hence as an instrument for insulating an economy from at least some foreign influences. It is clear that this "import substitution," by creating an incentive to invest within the tariff-protected economy, aggravates another problem: that of large-scale foreign ownership. This aspect of the tariff was discussed briefly on pages 638-639 of Chapter 25.

But, of course, the economics of the tariff are only a small part of the economics of foreign ownership and control; just as "import substitution" is only one of the reasons for increased foreign ownership and control. The purpose of this Appendix is to list briefly the forces leading to increased foreign ownership, and then to examine the pros and cons of it. Not much more can be done within a single chapter or appendix.

The economic pressures for integration with the world economy, and for international ownership and control, are steadily increasing; they include the prospect of material gains in the form of higher incomes, higher standards of living, more opportunities for employment, greater stability, and a greater choice of occupation and residence. Despite these pressures, a "preference for nationalism" has emerged in certain circles. Nationalists are opposed to yielding to the "greed," as they would put it, for material gains. They want restrictions imposed on foreign ownership, and advocate cutting the ties of trade and factor movements between their own country and the nation(s) on which their country has become economically dependent.

Many of the main tenets of those debating the issue of nationalism cannot be analyzed in economic terms. They are based on desires for a good society, sovereignty, and independence on the one hand, and the prospect of material gains for one's self and for one's fellow-citizens on the other. As a science, economics can be of help in this debate only when statements are made about the economic effects of more or less foreign ownership.

▪ WHY FOREIGN OWNERSHIP IS INCREASING

To attempt to explain the trend toward increasing foreign ownership is to open up the question of foreign investors' and lenders' behavior. Their incomes are rising with increased productivity at home, and their savings are being channelled automatically into a variety of pension and mutual funds. Probably these funds are under more flexible management than in the past: that is, a conscious decision is now taken to divide each person's contributions between secure government bonds and "go-go" stocks. Thus many small people are now indirectly financing industries, even through equities, that are in the high-risk categories. But why should any of this spill overseas, or across the Canadian border?

There are two reasons. The first is that new investment opportunities in the lending countries are probably less rapid and capital-absorbing than they appear to be abroad. At the same time knowledge—which brings security—about overseas borrowers and investing outlets is greater. Thus many wealthy persons and funds today do not hesitate to place a minor part of their wealth in investments in Europe, Australia, or Canada. A second reason is that foreign lenders, both individuals and businesses, are turning from indirect or portfolio lending abroad to *direct investment* or ownership. This trend makes the capital inflow more obvious; instead of being represented merely by IOUs and interest payments, it is constantly revealed by equity ownership of factories and services displaying well-known brands. Instead of going in for mortgages, bonds, and minority shareholdings, foreign investors now buy or build their own firms. Indeed, in Canada, between 1945 and the mid-1960s, direct investment increased from 40 per cent and approached 60 per cent of total long-term foreign indebtedness. The percentage is still climbing.

Once again, the reasons are fairly obvious. Modern communications make information about other countries easier to obtain than it was in the past; now investors can keep in daily touch with their investments abroad. Incorporation laws of Western nations are clearer and better understood. Tax laws are not merely neutral, but positively welcoming.

These are general reasons for increased foreign direct investment that "push" ownership and control out from the United States, Japan, Europe, and Britain. There are also special "pulls" in Canada and Australia, and (again) in Britain and Europe. Before we list them, however, note the following definitional aspects of our subject: not all foreign investment is direct investment; not all direct investment brings ownership or control; and not all direct investment is successful—foreigners fail too.

1. The multi-national corporation. There are almost 250 of these giant corporations in the Western world, having premises, staff, production facilities, and distributional networks so widely spread that almost one-tenth of them have more than one-third of their assets *outside* their home base: Royal Dutch Shell and Unilever would be good examples, though most of them are in fact American. Indeed, over 80 per cent of sales abroad by "American" corporations consist of goods that have been produced where they are sold, and less than 20 per cent are exports from the United States. Leaving the communist world aside, it is estimated that about one-fifth of the GNP of all countries outside the United States stems from plants in which there is a substantial U.S. interest.[1]

---

[1] Many of the statistics in these paragraphs are to be found in Roy A. Matthews, "The Multinational Corporation and the World of Tomorrow," *Behind the Headlines*, Vol. 29, CIIA Toronto, May 1970, pp. 11-16. A list of other recent references is appended to this article.

Whatever their origins, these corporations, having moved production and marketing abroad, have served as a channel or conduit not only for capital and skilled personnel, but, more important, for new technology, familiarity with certain management and production methods, and simple "know-how." Foreign investment by a national firm thus carried with it the parent firm's experience and factors of production. Indeed, the services of productive factors may soon be mostly bought abroad: labor hired, capital borrowed, management recruited, *and* products developed in the new country.

When this happens, the multi-national corporation tends to lose some of the coloration of its national origin and, soaking up men and ideas as it goes, becomes a global institution that could move its head office anywhere.

The ability of multi-national corporations to raise local funds, attract local skilled manpower, find products for the local market, etc. may raise apprehension and resentment. On the other hand, the possession of know-how and the ability to mobilize local capacities can be very welcome in developing countries. Furthermore they may also provide a large and critical market for the output of local suppliers, thus providing a welcome backward linkage into the host economy.

Truly, the multi-national corporation may be the instrument of technological dissemination of the future, and may capture an increasing part of world ownership and control—the embodiment indeed of Galbraith's "technostructure," in which skilled men and capital create and hold their own pre-eminence. On the other hand, like direct investment itself, the multi-national corporation is only a *form* of foreign investment and indebtedness. Why should this business form continue to supplant other forms of capital movement?

2. Technology and increasing returns to scale. These two advantages of the multi-national corporation have already been mentioned. The corporation brings foreign experience and know-how to undeveloped national industries and markets, more directly, flexibly, and relevantly than any other channel of innovation. Also, by its sheer size and market status it may have advantages of large-scale operation in financing, hiring, and developmental research or exploration.

3. Import substitution. As stated earlier, foreign producers are often prevented from exporting to a country by its tariff barriers. Naturally, many of these exporters accept the implied invitation to them: to manufacture locally the goods they would have preferred to ship from their home plants.

4. Oligopoly. Some economists claim that much foreign investment is simply a horizontal extension (to countries like Canada) of oligopolistic sales battles waged among the giants of the United States, Europe, or Japan. If true it is a bad reason for investment abroad. Much horizontal integration, and merging, would come in here; a less-than-satisfactory motive for moving abroad. (But a more traditional view would recall the opposite tendency in the bad old inter-war days. Oligopolists, combining internationally as cartels, would agree to *keep out* of certain foreign markets. Thus oil, chemical, and heavy electrical firms would divide up the world markets among themselves. Oligopoly theory is always a treacherous basis for prediction.)

5. Conglomerates. Unlike the multi-national firm which, as usually defined, sticks to one type of product, the conglomerate deliberately merges with or acquires firms in diverse industries. The diversity it requires to maintain its profit levels may take it abroad. (See pages 123 and 588.)

6. Integration for materials and energy. Americans seek Canadian and Venezuelan gas and oil; Japanese firms seek coal; Germany seeks Scandinavian iron; Poland seeks Russian energy. Attempting to get these materials as cheaply as possible and avoiding being tied to one source, firms are usually tempted to buy on a world-wide competitive market. But security from interruption or oligopolistic interference with their supplies often compels them to acquire mines, forests and so forth. Hence most of the world's sources of oil are tied to less than a score of enterprises in the industrialized countries.

CHARGES AGAINST FOREIGN OWNERSHIP

Listing these six reasons which, alone or in concert, may explain why most of Canada's automobile, appliance, forest-products, mining, food-products, publishing, hotel, and even oil companies are owned and/or controlled by foreign firms does *not* establish that anything is wrong. By now, the debate on the merits and evils of foreign investment, ownership, and control, which has grown from a few murmurs in the early 1950s, sprawls a very large literature. Not only left-wing philosophers like the NDP's Waffle group, but also middle-of-the-roaders like Walter Gordon and Lester Pearson and more right-wing groups like trade unions and the western branch of the Conservative Party, have complained about the "take-over" of Canadian industry and resources, the "sellout" or "give-away" of Canadian resources. Even to summarize their arguments is difficult. If you are disturbed about this question, read some of the pieces in footnote 2 below before you jump on a band wagon.[2]

The empirical and theoretical objections to foreign ownership are mostly based on the claim that local subsidiaries, having the welfare and profitability of the parent firm as objectives, cannot be expected to serve equally well the aims of the "host" country (e.g. Canada). The dispute about this claim of foreign subsidiaries is on two levels: theory and performance. At one level, there is argument about the acceptability or attractiveness of the *hypothesis* that firms owned abroad behave differently, or badly, just because of that foreign ownership. Such arguments, however, may be inconclusive because, as is generally admitted, other forces than foreign control influence the performance not only of these firms but also of their foreign parents and their Canadian-owned/controlled rivals with both of whom they're implicitly compared. (*NOTE: ownership and control are not identical. See below.*)

[2] In many respects, U.K. and Australian economists on the foreign ownership question are well ahead of their Canadian counterparts. The most recent of Professor A. E. Safarian's works on the *performance* of U.S. subsidiaries in Canada is the readable *The Performance of Foreign-Owned Subsidiaries in Canada* (Montreal, Canadian-American Committee, 1969), containing some useful references to other countries. Three more "official" studies are Irving Brecher and S. S. Reisman, *Canada-United States Economic Relations*, Royal Commission on Canada's Economic Prospects, 1957; *Foreign Ownership and the Structure of Canadian Industry* (Report of the Task Force on the Structure of Canadian Industry—the "Watkins Report"), 1968; and Herb Grey's forthcoming White Paper on Foreign Investment in Canada. Recently a number of symposium papers dealing with many countries, including the home countries of the investors, has appeared: C. P. Kindleberger, Editor, *International Corporation: A Symposium* (Cambridge, Massachusetts: M.I.T. Press, 1970).

EXPORTS   It is often said that foreign-owned firms restrict their Canadian subsidiaries by keeping export markets in third countries for the parent company. Thus Imperial Chemical Industries and DuPont were never enthusiastic about Canadian Industries Limited hunting for markets in Latin America. On the other hand, the Commonwealth preference—which meant lower tariffs on "British" goods—gave Canadian branches markets in other Commonwealth countries that were closed to their parent firms. That is, individual examples abound, pointing both ways.

Safarian's statistical evidence here is interesting but inconclusive. In Canada and Great Britain subsidiaries of foreign manufacturers tend to export *more* than domestic manufacturers as a whole, partly because they are concentrated in "export" industries. Such evidence does not reveal whether their exports are less than if their parent firms' hypothetical restraints on their exports were removed.

IMPORTS   "Foreign-owned firms tend to import parts and components more than native firms, especially if the subsidiary is a miniature version of a multiproduct foreign parent." This assertion accords with our observation of branches in Canada of such large manufacturers as Phillips, BMC, Westinghouse, McGraw-Hill, Hershey, Reckitt-Colman, and Mitsubishi. But note too that it conflicts with the widely accepted view that the Canadian tariff, in excluding imports, leads to the establishment of foreign subsidiaries. Which tendency is the more important?

Probably, both are significant. Foreign ownership is one important response to the tariff, making goods sold in Canada less expensive to consumers than if they were priced at foreign costs plus tariff. Consequently, only those brands and products which it does not pay to manufacture in Canada, even under shelter of the tariff, are imported. It is true, then, that foreign-owned subsidiaries tend to import more, both of components or parts to be assembled here, and of finished products. This tendency, however, can be seen chiefly as a preference of foreign exporters for selling directly through their own marketing and distributing outlets, usually connected with their subsidiary manufacturing plants, if any, rather than through Canadian importing agents or independent manufacturers in Canada who might wish to expand their lines. This preference for marketing through subsidiaries is strongest when the parent firm deals in one of Chapter 24's "differentiated" products, for then it becomes profitable to key distribution to advertising of the parent firm. Undifferentiated, unbranded, or standard trade items, on the other hand, might as well be sold through agents, jobbers, and wholesalers.

Thus it is possible that foreign-owned subsidiaries as a group are simultaneously avoiding the tariff on some goods by manufacturing them and importing others. That subsidiaries rather than Canadian-owned firms do the importing is of no great importance. Rather, the question to be investigated (for the benefit of those who dislike importing and exporting and the resulting division of labor) is whether, in the absence of foreign ownership, imports would be less. There is no evidence that they would.[3]

The "problem" of imports, indeed, is an object lesson for those who question the need for economic *analysis* of foreign ownership and investment. Those who promote tariff policies leading to Canadian self-sufficiency have been beguiled into using the evidence about imports as evidence of the harmfulness of foreign ownership, thus implicitly supporting the most feasible alternative to importing: the setting-up of foreign manufacturing in Canada. Whatever one's aims, honest partisans must thoroughly analyse so-called problems to avoid blindly citing both desired policies and their undesired side effects as "evils."

EXTRATERRITORIALITY This word has been re-defined to describe a particularly direct type of foreign influence: the obedience of a subsidiary to the same laws (on exports, blockades, sanctions, etc.) applying to the parent. For example, suppose that Ford (Canada) wants to export cars or parts to Cuba,

Russia, or China, and that it is prevented from doing so by the fear that if it violated U.S. law, its parent company could be prosecuted. Because such a law is in effect outside the United States, it is said to be operating extraterritorially.

Extraterritoriality is easy to understand. No foreign government wants its national corporations to escape national policy by establishing a nonconforming subsidiary elsewhere. Thus Canadians would not wish Massey-Ferguson to escape Canada's sanctions policy toward Rhodesia simply by operating through a subsidiary in Lisbon; nor would the United States wish her firms' subsidiaries either to trade with nations with whom she was more or less at war or to evade her comparatively strict antitrust, tax, and foreign-currency-conservation policies. Indeed Tax Treaties between pairs of countries contain many sections which in effect keep taxpayers under national laws even if they flee abroad.

But treaties are reciprocal whereas extraterritoriality is the naked application of foreign laws to domestic action, and therefore particularly offensive to those jealous of national independence. Even those politicians least concerned about nationalism are alert to prevent extraterritorial application of U.S. policies.

RESEARCH AND DEVELOPMENT Concerned with our country's technical development, many scientific and engineering observers fear that foreign ownership will prevent both basic and applied (technical) research in Canadian industry. Instead, they say, multi-national concerns tend (quite rationally) to centralize their research in large laboratories, or universities, nearer their home base.

This process, of course, is essential to the very transfer of technical information and skills outward from the parent company to its subsidiaries in other countries that has persuaded many writers (like Harry Johnson) that international direct investment is a swift vehicle for the world-wide transmission of new ideas, processes, and consumer desires for goods and services. Thus the fruits of scientific and technological advance achieved abroad are received at the price of stunting scientific and, especially, technological establishments at home and their educational offshoots in universities. "So be it" say many consumers who enjoy the power to buy foreign goods, even if their buying decisions remove the justification for more research and development in Canada. "Let science flourish," respond Canadians who de-

---

[3] Bruce Wilkinson and Kari Levitt both suggest that subsidiaries show a bias toward importing because their parent firms do not charge them the full price; something that anti-dumping laws prevent between exporter and independent importer. But if this practice exists, it seems rather merely to create an "unfair" advantage for integrated importers over independent importers. Their evidence does not indicate that this bias leads to imports being greater: only that imports tend to become concentrated in foreign-owned subsidiaries, at some gain to the consumer at the cost of the foreign exporter.

For a new survey of this and the other topics discussed in the Appendix, see Kari Levitt, *Silent Surrender*, (Toronto: Macmillan of Canada, 1970).

plore the branch-plantism that has deprived us of the harvesting of our plans for the *Arrow* airplane, a Canadian-made communications satellite or astronomical telescope, and that will soon witness the capture of all electronics activity by American, European, or Asian firms. So desperate have been Canadian scientists that many have espoused a more vigorous Canadian defense effort simply because of its scientific spin-off!

It is certainly true that Canada, Australia, France, and Great Britain are all low private spenders on R & D, while having high proportions of foreign ownership of industry. Perhaps as a response, Britain seems in the past decade to have turned major responsibility for technology over to government laboratories; France's Jean-Jacques Sevan-Schreiber in his *Le Défi Americain*, has urged his countrymen to use the European Common Market to set up firms with science establishments to rival these in the United States.

Safarian's research findings on Canadian R & D is consistent with the view that, even in research-oriented industries, much of the R & D is centralized in the parent's head office. However, he does not find that Canadian subsidiaries perform less research than their resident-owned counterparts—if anything, they seem to do more. It is obviously vain to expect that General Motors, General Electric, or Bell will ever perform 10 per cent of their basic or development research in Canada, even if Canadian scientific and taxation policies do make it attractive for them to expand their present efforts. Whether it is in our interest to get them to do much more awaits the economic study of science policy promised by Ottawa.

EMPLOYMENT   In less-developed countries, the chief aim of "nationalistic" policies is to hire, train, and promote local citizens, and the chief objection to foreign corporations, is their slowness to meet these aims.[4] This reminds us that, from a social point of view, the chief efficiency aim of producers should be

to make the best use of society's resources—instead of importing foreign resources (workers). But a difference of opinion may arise about how best to utilize local resources. The profit-maximizing corporation and the economic planner may agree that foreign talent is needed to complement local workers and to bring the best out in them. On the other hand, if such an outlook should be adopted as a policy, broader and less nationalistic than the aim described above, not only may it make an enclave or bridgehead of foreign professionals unpopular in the short run by frustrating nationalistic sentiment, but also it may in the long run inhibit on-the-job training of potential local recruits. Such recruits of course will support policies to open jobs to them. Indeed, Toronto's Albert Breton, in a well-known technical article on the economics of nationalism, has gone so far as to claim that nationalistic movements (such as Quebec's vis-à-vis Canada, or Canada's vis-à-vis the United States) are simply a means whereby a middle-income bourgeoisie (managers, professionals, authors, actors, professors) creates and protects a market for its own services. While this is a cynical and extreme view, its plausibility does illustrate that foreign control, even if it operates to make the best use of existing labor resources, may create diminished employment opportunities for members of the elite that, in identifying its own welfare with national interests, is most articulate and outspoken on matters of foreign ownership and control.

Studies of American owned firms in Canada, Australia, and Great Britain all suggest that, while these firms may have substantial autonomy or discretion, around one-third of their high-ranking executives and members of their boards are Americans; many of those who are on the boards of subsidiaries located in Canada do not live here.

CONSERVATION OF NATURAL RESOURCES   An increasingly important circumstance cited in debates about foreign ownership is the "take-over" of Canadian minerals, lands, waters, and energy by outsiders.

The *mining industry* has, of course, been extremely indifferent to national boundaries for centuries, and not only American, but also Canadian, British, German, Belgian, French, Japanese, firms are to be found in developments scattered around the world. Such businesses acquire specialized capacities and sources of capital, and move everywhere in search of sites or showings of deposits,

---

[4] Not always, however. In India and Pakistan foreign corporations are criticized because they hire the best local graduates, at high salaries (thus diverting them from lower-paid government work or teaching). Even in Canada, the practice of large foreign corporations in promoting Canadian executives up to leadership in the parent is much criticized as a "brain drain"; and so is the opposite practice of not promoting Canadians.

resources, etc., suitable for these special characteristics.

Most provinces owning their own *lands and forests* have at one time or another invoked nationalistic restrictions on the right to purchase or lease these lands. Most recently they have tended to restrict ownership of lakeshore cottage property, revealing a belief that Canadians, perhaps because they have lower incomes, cannot or will not outbid Americans, and some have limited the sale of Crown lands to Canadian residents. However, the latter regulation does not stop Canadian land speculators from buying property and selling it to those who can afford the highest prices. Thus the willingness of individuals and governments to sell a "public good" (see page 200 for this technical expression) when the price is high enough results in the subdivision of that good for private use and hence in its availability for purchase by foreigners. Other nationalistic restrictions on land or forest acquisition are usually designed to protect local processing mills, smelters, or refineries against the export of raw ore or wood.

The issue of the export of *water* is currently newsworthy and is undoubtedly an instance of the absence of even "accounting prices" (Ch. 31's Appendix, page 761) or other efficient or equitable devices to ration water use in either Canada or the United States. Consequently water for drinking, for receiving industrial effluents, or for irrigation is sought, held, and often wasted by rhetorical, legalistic, diplomatic, and political processes. Some enemies of water export believe that sales at *any* price will eventually place Canada at a competitive disadvantage to U.S. industry. Analytically, they are wrong: some price exists whereby both seller and buyer are better off trading *some* of a commodity than they would be if no transaction takes place. Their distrust may simply reflect the real difficulty of ensuring "arms-length" or impersonal pricing of raw materials and water at the border: very often buyers and sellers work in a "market" in which there are no competitors, and in which both are representing a common owner or political agreement. Most economists—not all—agree that it is worthwhile striving to achieve a rational price at which the buyer is willing to buy and the seller to sell (though the level decided on may result only in small sales), rather than taking the position that sales to the United States are by

definition undesirable. The export of electrical energy, gas, oil, and coal is now being seen as a single problem in which Canada attempts to obtain for these resources a price in excess of the value of the alternative use or need for energy in Canada. As with water, many critics argue that our *energy* endowment should in principle not be put at the disposal of foreign competitors. Less extreme thinkers agree with them on policy—the presence of massive government intervention in the United States (and Japan) and the absence of arm's-length pricing between parents and subsidiaries at the Canadian border does suggest the wisdom of a National Energy Board to police foreign commitments. It is additionally claimed that it is impossible to arrest or reverse energy flows once they are begun, so that sovereignty over even the future disposal of these resources is actually lost forever. (Loss of "sovereignty" is not necessarily a bad thing—the purpose of the debate is precisely to determine whether it is or not.) Some energy flows (of hydro power and of coal) *have* been altered or reversed. But the point is a matter of fact—if the seller reserves the right to cut off sales at a future date, will political realities preclude this action? If so, and if reversal will be sought, then sales now are more expensive in terms of *future* utility than the price obtained makes them appear to be. (See the "Economics of Conservation" pp. 521-522.)

■ POLICY ALTERNATIVES

It is clear that, except for the implementation of an extreme policy, foreign ownership and control are not one issue, but many. The extreme policy would be that further economic congress with the United States is increasingly undesirable. In that case the issue would merely be to decide on a program of increasingly severe restrictions on foreign investment and ownership, and possibly on migration, imports, and exports. (Recall Chapter 13's discussion of the relation between imports and exports and fiscal policy in an open economy such as Canada's.) The cost, in broad terms, would be the sum of the loss of the present specialization and division of labor that trade allows, the choice of occupation and location that labor mobility permits, and the reduction of capital and know-how that investment brings. Against these costs must be ranged the benefits of independence. This would be welcome *in itself* to many Canadians. It might also bring incentives to inventiveness, originality, and risk-taking that would make Canada in self-sufficiency a richer country than pessimistic economists usually predict.

In the absence of this all-enveloping, monolithic program, however, handling each of the "problems" listed in the sections above requires a complex of restrictions and requirements that threaten to assume mercantilistic, if not Byzantine, proportions. As the listing suggests, free foreign ownership or use of natural resources is already somewhat restricted, and many steps are proposed for both extending these policies to other fields of foreign entry (teaching in universities, banking, shipowning, publishing, or broadcasting) and intensifying the existing restrictions (e.g., uranium mines may not now be sold to U.S. interests).

Because the impact of each special policy instrument is likely to be relatively small (and evadable) it is not appropriate to devote much space to them here. Among the proposals are a national Development Corporation or agency which would either prevent the sale of businesses to foreigners or gradually recapture businesses already controlled abroad. The chief objections have been expense—i.e., the cost involved in using new capital, raised through taxes or saving, to acquire already existing assets rather than to finance further growth —and administrative difficulty—the problem of deciding who is to manage whatever is acquired. Both in Canada and in the less developed countries this task is sometimes addressed by having "partnerships" between a government agency and foreign owners; a substantial literature exists on the success of these consortia and joint ventures. Quebec and other provinces have also set up corporations to supplant the private sector in mineral exploration and industrial development; but it is not clear that their aim is to *prevent* foreign investment, or control. Other devices are that each foreign firm must not only report its Canadian operations in full to the Canadian authorities (even if they would not do so if they were Canadian-owned) but also meet certain minimum ratios of "Canadian content" in their blue-collar and management personnel. More negative, but perhaps more effective, are proposals to remove tax incentives and advantages for certain kinds of investment (for rural redevelopment, hiring Indians, removing pollution,

etc.) for foreign firms. Naturally, such policies would conflict with other social and economic goals.

The purpose of this discussion has not been to settle the extent to which nationalistic policies should interfere with unrestricted movement of people, capital, know-how and goods across the border, but to indicate that partial policy instruments are available. It remains only to summarise the spectrum of best-known positions on their choice, from extreme nationalism to extreme internationalism.

1. Foreign ownership which reduces sovereignty over resources, factors, and trade within Canada is undesirable, and therefore should be stopped. Such statements simply beg all the difficult questions about amount and quality of intervention and is undebatable in economist's terms.

2. Foreign ownership reduces the choices open to Canadians; narrows future development of the country into too few channels; and creates some of the more unattractive aspects of the "branch economy," with an uncommitted managerial elite, etc. Such statements, too, verge on being simply undebatable statements of tastes or preferences. However, they can be confronted with the cost of remedying these effects as measured by reduced incomes, wages, or choices of goods and services. Hence a choice between the economic isolation and self-sufficiency advocated by extreme nationalists and integration with the world economy can in principle be made, or the degree of independence which is desirable determined.

3. A third position concentrates on resources and energy. Trade in natural resources is in principle acceptable, but is actually undesirable because Canadians cannot trust themselves and their customers to strike a bargain that is sufficiently advantageous to present-day and future Canada. This position can be dealt with by advocating that institutions be set up to attempt to solve the pricing problems and to set all–or–nothing conditions of sale.

4. Foreign investment is highly desirable because it is the chief channel by which know-how is internationally transmitted.

5. Integration into the world economy is desirable because it promises the high personal incomes by which groups of people can afford

to set up any given set of national institutions. Only rich people, it is argued, can afford the luxuries of nationalism. (Nonsense, goes the reply, this argument is circular: if rich people do choose nationalism, you say they are then bound to become poorer. If so, why not opt for nationalistic policies immediately?)

6. Restrictions on freedom to invest, trade, or move factors or goods are illiberal and therefore undesirable. Furthermore, any nationalism at all simply impedes the arrival of a better world. Like the first statement, this sixth one is largely undebatable in economic terms, merely stating a preference for individualism and a certain version of *laissez-faire*.[5]

---

[5] An important Malthusian argument about nationalism is nowadays forgotten, even in the midst of concern about the environment. Some people argue that neither the world community in general nor the UN in particular can arrest world population growth soon enough to prevent serious overloading of the world's ability to produce food and energy. Accordingly they urge that individual large nations, as a temporary measure, take on the responsibility for world survival by keeping their populations down, preventing immigration, and endowing birth-control measures abroad. But an important counter-argument asserts that the earth's ecology, and its population, are each one and indivisible; no single nation can stem the tide of too many people. When the world is seen as a group of nations each with its own behavior and net rate of increase, according to Charles G. Darwin, ". . . the limitation of population is an unstable process, which cannot persist." He argues that, even if, over most of the world, there is severe population pressure and famine, the hope of civilization will be in a single universal culture, transcending nations. For the best investigation of this point of view, see Sir Charles Galton Darwin, *The Next Million Years* (New York: Dolphin Paperbacks, 1952).

■ GREED VERSUS NATIONALISM

This listing of causes, problems, positions and policies cannot help much to make decisions; but it should assist deciding what the issues are. Multinational corporations have decided advantages over local bodies, and it does not help much to dismiss them as simply catering to the "greed" of their supporters, especially when this "greed" is the desire of over-populated backward economies to take the next step in the process of development. In such a case, foreign direct investment provides a powerful and attractive means for importing the capacity to harness local resources and energies.

On the other hand, promoters should not dismiss the "nationalism" of those who fear direct investment. Subsidiaries may be kept dependent, if deprived of the autonomy to grow up and play their roles as entrepreneurs in the new economy; they may work against the development of competitive alternatives in the new economy; they may act as a channel for the power of the state in the home country of the multi-national corporation; and they may indeed not only disseminate technology and know-how but also alien culture and custom which are either international, or those of their home country, so as to weaken the social, literary, or political life of the host.

"Greed" and "nationalism" indeed are emotion-laden words that do little to clarify the problems. Foreign investment and national self-expression are already with us. Canada can hardly decide whether to opt entirely for one or the other. What it can do is examine the gains to be made or losses to be suffered from further applications of existing policies or the enacting of more stringent deterrents to foreign investment.

35

CURRENT
INTERNATIONAL
ECONOMIC PROBLEMS

Before I built a wall I'd ask to know what I was walling in or walling out,
and to whom I was like to give offence. ROBERT FROST

We must now turn to the main international economic problems facing Canada and the world in the years ahead. How can we understand the important facts? Which economic policies must we avoid? Which policies must we follow?

Economists have achieved more unanimous agreement about the principles of international trade than about any other aspect of their subject. Yet the gulf between the plain man's beliefs about international finance and those of the experts is almost as wide as elsewhere in economics, though that gulf has seemed to be narrowing slightly in recent decades.

Section A provides a survey of the main historical and contemporary trends in foreign trade. Section B analyzes the threatened breakdown in the international system—the United States' chronic gold drain, world shortage of international liquidity, and other trade problems which Canada and the world face. Against this background, Section C surveys the basic reforms in international finance that are now pending.

A. MODERN TRENDS AND INSTITUTIONS OF INTERNATIONAL FINANCE

■ TRENDS, 1914-1945

EXPORTS AND JOBS The first decade of the century was Canada's. Immigration and investment were very high, and exports of wheat, forest products, and minerals mounted. As in the 1950s, this had all been accompanied by an immense inward capital movement from Europe and the United States. But by 1913 Canada was entering a period of stagnation, which the early years of World War I did little to change. The smallness and weakness of the new economy was revealed when European capital ceased to flow in, and export markets were closed by the blockade. During the early years of the war, Canada borrowed heavily abroad—but later she reached full employment and borrowed at home.

In the United States, as the belligerents increased their imports from industrial America, the foreign-trade multiplier, explained in Part II, went to work to send her soaring out of her prewar depression to great prosperity. Gold and gilt-edge certificates flowed in. Then, when the United States entered the war in 1917 the demand for shot and shell took over, producing by a domestic multiplier all the trappings of a boom: high prices, plenty of jobs, and an expanding GNP.

Both economies wound up the war decade with a sharp recession, and a serious inflation.

After 1921, the North American economy prospered. Canada entered another investment boom, this time depending very heavily on U.S. long-term capital inflows. Canadian exports and imports both increased and international indebtedness in all forms became large. The United States steadily raised tariff levels, which were alleged to "protect the American workers' standard of living."

The United States became in truth a "young creditor" nation. Many wise and foolish, charitable and hard-nosed loans were made, not just to Canada, but to all the world. This lending contributed to the general U.S. prosperity, as the funds borrowed were eventually spent on U.S. goods. Such added *exports E*, like *I* and *G*, increased NNP and employment.

THE GREAT DEPRESSION   At the end of 1929, the stock market crashed. International lenders to European and Latin-American borrowers found their securities were worthless, and their attempts to recall their short-term funds made the monetary strain worse. Prices of primary products, like wheat, sagged. As aggregate demand fell, the political pressures for protection strengthened. Tariffs were raised, quotas imposed. The central European countries, alarmed by the flight of "hot" short-term capital, imposed foreign-exchange controls. Heavily involved in these exchange flights, Britain was forced off the gold standard in 1931, which led to a further fall in the export prices of the primary-producing countries.

In 1930, the United States raised the level of its tariffs to an all-time high with the introduction of the Hawley-Smoot tariff. Canada retaliated with tariff increases in 1930-1931 (see Fig. 34-1, page 846), and by 1932 she had raised her duties by an average of 50 per cent. H. L. Mencken, who never failed to call attention to the comedy of American life, rubbed his hands to see the farmers— who were net exporters and not importers of goods—being given import tariffs on their export products in return for their political support for tariffs on manufactured imports. Canada would have amused him just as much, though Canadian protection was unimportant abroad compared to the actions of the United States. Now the creditor of all the world, the United States was *trying to collect debts from abroad and at the same time shutting out the import goods that could alone have provided the payment for those debts.*

The fallacy of composition was at work. Every country believed that, if *it* could develop a favorable balance of trade, its employment would increase at the expense of its neighbors; in effect, it would be succeeding in exporting some of its unemployment. But for everybody to run a favorable trade balance simultaneously is a self-contradiction—as impossible as for everybody to be taller than anybody else.

Of course, the attempt to be taller—to generate a favorable surplus of exports over imports—could be predicted to cut down on the fruitful division of labor. And precisely that happened. As much as domestic and total world production declined, the volume of international trade declined still more. The situation reached the height of absurdity when countries traded with each other only on a *bilateral* basis: A bought from B only as much as B bought from A; under Hitler's economic adviser, Schacht, Latin American countries sent staples to Germany in return for aspirin, which piled up in warehouses.

The world was in a state of economic chaos. Inefficiency kept each nation well inside its production-possibility frontier. But since contractionary monetary and fiscal policies were being urged to promote "necessary" adjustment, destruction of goods seemed in order. Farmers poured milk into the gutters; coffee was burned to keep prices high; the United States government paid people to plow under the unripened corn; and the windows of empty factories became the targets for bored men who had been on relief for years. From 12 to 25 per cent of Canada's work force was unemployed.

Today, even schoolboys ask why people did not insist on deliberate programs of fiscal and monetary expansion. It is only too easy to remake history *after* the fact. But—and this is what concerns us here—one reason a single nation could not introduce expansion at home was the rational fear that if she increased her NNP while others kept theirs depressed, her imports would grow in the face of languishing exports. Thus, she would lose gold and, under the gold standard, she would either have to contract again or be forced into devaluation or bankruptcy.

As it happened, by 1931 England, Scandinavia, and the pound-sterling Commonwealth countries were forced off the gold standard. With the pound depreciated, these countries could afford to push their *internal* expansion; and if you look at the records, you see that Sweden and Britain were already recovering from the Depression when the United States, Germany, and France were experiencing the worst of it. Undoubtedly, some of the depreciating countries gained at the expense of those that stayed orthodoxly on gold. But the most authoritative studies suggest that the gain to the depreciating countries came *primarily from the freedom it gave them to expand domestically.*

Was old-fashioned virtue rewarded? Not in the 1930s. Belgium clung precariously to the old gold mint parities, even after Roosevelt deliberately devalued the United

States dollar and Canada followed part way. Political unrest and depression were Belgium's reward—until 1936, when she gave up the struggle and, instead of being smitten by thunderbolts for her apostasy, she immediately registered relief in her production and unemployment statistics. France, having been the wayward inflationist in the 1920s, practically tore herself apart politically by clinging to the old gold parity into the late 1930s. Only Switzerland seemed able to make gold work.

The Canadian depression was almost as deep as the American, and its recovery almost as slow, even though it cut itself off from gold earlier. It was not until World War II that full employment was approached. Toronto's A. E. Safarian has suggested three reasons for Canada's incomplete recovery.

1. The market for most Canadian exports was the United States. The failure of the United States to recover by 1937-1939 meant that the Canadian industrial capacity installed in the 1920s could not be used.

2. Trade restrictions, crop failures, and heavy overhead costs prevented the smooth adaptation of the Canadian economy to rising aggregate demand.

3. Depressed investment schedules, resulting from previous excessive private investment and pessimistic expectations of future markets, led to stagnant investment activity.[1]

In the down-swing, government policy was confined to raising the tariff. In the subsequent up-swing, high taxes and low government spending characterized domestic policy. Men felt that salvation could only come from an improvement in the international economic situation.

WAR   The Depression, which hit Germany and the United States especially hard, contributed to Hitler's rise to power. His preparations for war "solved" Germany's mass-unemployment problem and proved the potency of Keynes-like fiscal and monetary policies. When World War II came, the vast deficits in each country, financed with a new supply of money, brought about vast increases in the G of $C + I + G$ and had the predictable effect of, first, expanding production enough to get rid of unemployment, and second, swelling total demand so much as to create inflationary gaps and outright inflation. As in World War I, shipments of exports for the warring nations brought the United States full employment and enhanced real product.

War meant scarcity, not superabundance. So again the world became orderly. Mercantilistic notions, that it is good *to give away goods* abroad in return for as few imports as possible, were discarded. The emphasis again was on extending production-possibility frontiers outward and on making sure to be on those frontiers, and not inside. The classical theory of comparative advantage came into its own as the Allied powers allocated to each nation the tasks it could perform *relatively* most efficiently.

POSTWAR ADJUSTMENT AND THE "DOLLAR SHORTAGE"   When World War II was over, the scarcity of resources remained. The United States towered above its allies and former enemies in productive capacity. Most countries tried to produce and consume more than their war-modified or war-shattered economies would permit.

---

[1] A. E. Safarian, *The Canadian Economy in the Great Depression*, Canadian Studies in Economics No. 11 (Toronto, 1959), pp. 142-143.

Even Canada, which tried to maintain its exports to Europe on a loan or grants basis while importing consumer and capital goods from the United States, was forced to ration U.S. dollars and control imports. In Europe, the need to rebuild, develop, and make up for wartime scarcities led to pressure to import what was required as soon as possible; so dollars were carefully allocated to the most urgent needs. When American sources of supply were surveyed, it was found that the U.S. dollar was a seriously "undervalued currency" in the following sense.

> *Undervalued dollar and dollar shortage defined:* The total world demand for American dollars to buy needed imports from the United States was much greater than the total that private citizens in the United States would want to supply (to pay for trips to Paris and Rome, for goods and imports, direct investments, etc.). If the United States had not introduced a governmental policy of providing relief and reconstruction aid, of making loans and gifts, no country would have had the needed amount of gold or credit worthiness to finance its international deficit with America. In a free-exchange-rate world, the price of the U.S. dollar would have been bid sky-high; much of the rationing and control could have been abandoned.

Under the conditions of 1945-1950, in the absence of vast U.S. aid programs and other countries' tight regulation of imports and capital movements, when applied to the U.S. dollar the *dd* and *ss* schedules of Chapter 32, Fig. 32-1, page 777, would have shown a tremendous "dollar gap" at existing foreign exchange rates; this could have been met only by dropping to an equilibrium intersection where the U.S. dollar was much, much dearer in terms of foreign currencies—perhaps at $2 per £1 rather than $4, which was then prevailing, and likewise for the mark, franc, and yen.

That is the technical meaning of the term that used to be heard so widely then, namely, the "dollar shortage," or "dollar gap." (Reread the above brown paragraph.)

How was the gap handled? Not by immediate postwar depreciations (although later in 1949 Britain and most nations did have to depreciate, the pound dropping from $4 to $2.80). Instead, the so-called dollar gap was handled primarily by comprehensive exchange and imports controls on the part of the nations with "overvalued currencies" and, as we shall see, by vast U.S. aid and loan programs.

■ AID PROGRAMS

After the United Nations Relief and Rehabilitation Administration (UNRRA) had helped meet the immediate postwar aid needs, the United States introduced her dramatic Marshall Plan for European recovery. Subsequently, the United States shifted her grants to the North Atlantic Treaty Organization (NATO) and other military alliances. (Thus, the "Truman Doctrine" brought financial aid to Greece when that country was threatened by communism. Even Yugoslavia has received aid along with the Chinese Nationalists, the South Koreans, and the South Vietnamese.) United States aid to the neutral countries of Asia, Africa, and Latin America, for economic development, has been on a scale without precedent in all history.

Probably, the motive for many of those programs was U.S. fear of the spread of communism. Full stomachs may not save a democracy, it was argued, but empty ones can seal its doom. Putting modern guns into the hands of friends of the United States was intended both to help their defense and to save the lives of U.S. soldiers. Since other advanced nations—such as Britain, Germany, and the Soviet Union—have given foreign aid, an element of emulation and competition also entered U.S. motivations.

However, a close study of the postwar events leading up to the Marshall Plan and other foreign-aid programs shows that the United States in the postwar period has also had intermittent "do-good" motivations. Call this altruism if you wish, or call it long-run expediency: the United States' future existence depends upon a stable international order not overly hostile to Western economic and social ideas. Finally, close study of the facts does not well bear out the hypothesis that the United States embraced aid programs only because they would prevent a great depression at home. On the contrary, the United States gave most at times *when domestic inflation problems were most pressing*; and one of the gravest costs of aid was aggravation of U.S. concurrent domestic scarcities.

Aside from providing substantial material aid, there is one important thing that the United States and other donors do for other countries that costs them very little, namely, *helping them acquire the technical know-how to enable them to increase their levels of productivity and living standards*. This became known as "Point Four" assistance because it was first enunciated as the fourth point in the 1949 inaugural address of U.S. President Truman; he proposed "a bold new program for making the benefits of American scientific advances and industrial progress available for the improvement and growth of undeveloped areas," and invited other countries "to pool their technological resources in [a] . . . worldwide effort for the achievement of peace, plenty, and freedom."

CANADA AND OTHER COUNTRIES   Of course, the United States has not been the only country to give financial aid and other development assistance abroad, though it has been by far the biggest giver. The lion's share of *all* assistance given to the less developed countries has come from public and private sources in the 16 developed countries belonging to the Organization for European Cooperation and Development (OECD); in 1969, this aid came close to 15 billion dollars. Canadian aid, coming primarily from public sources, includes a smaller share of private investment and lending than that of the majority of other OECD countries; yet public sources usually account for more than one half of total aid extended by OECD nations. Nor has total Canadian aid been especially large in amount. It has represented about ½ of one per cent of our national income, in 1968 the lowest percentage of all OECD members! OECD donors are generally uninterested in military aid, mildly enthusiastic about aiding their own exports and farm surplus sales, lukewarm about helping the poorest countries simply because of poverty, and warmest about projects and proposals that promise real development (See pp. 946-947.)

■ THE INTERNATIONAL BANK AND FOREIGN LENDING

THE INTERNATIONAL BANK FOR RECONSTRUCTION AND DEVELOPMENT   There is no doubt that Asia, South America, and Africa could profitably use Western capital for their industrial development. But although the increase in production resulting from a loan would easily guarantee payment of generous interest and prompt repayment of the principal, private citizens have been reluctant to lend. Though corporations will build branch plants abroad and will invest in oil or mineral resources, substantial indirect private lending through buying risky foreign bonds or stocks disappeared sometime in 1929, seemingly forever. Yet Western citizens have savings which they would be glad to lend if such capital transactions could be guaranteed.

Therefore the leading nations of the world (except Soviet Russia) came together in 1944 to form the International Bank for Reconstruction and Development (IBRD) and its sister institution, the International Monetary Fund (IMF). As its name implies, the International Bank was formed to provide sound long-term loans for reconstruction and development. (The International Monetary Fund is concerned, as we shall see shortly, with short-term credit and the cooperative stabilization of foreign exchange rates.)

The International Bank system is easy to understand. The leading nations subscribe to its capital stock in proportion to their economic importance. (The United States' quota is about one-third of the total; Canada's, about 5 per cent.) The bank can use its capital to make sound international loans to people or countries whose projects seem economically sound but who cannot get private loans at acceptably low interest rates.

The International Bank's true importance arises not from the loans that it can make out of its own capital, but from the fact that it can float bonds and use the proceeds to make loans. (It has successfully floated bonds in the United States, Switzerland, Canada, and elsewhere.) The bonds are safe because they are backed by the credit of all the nations (up to 100 per cent of their quotas). Also, the International Bank can *insure* loans in return for a ½ or 1 per cent premium; private parties can then put up the money, knowing that the Bank's credit is behind the loan.

As a result of extending long-term credits, in the years ahead we can expect to see goods and services flowing out of the developed nations and aimed at international development. If sound, these loans will be repaid in full. If some go sour, the loss will be paid out of the Bank's interest or premium earnings. If still more go sour, the loss will be spread over all the member nations. While the loans are being made, jobs will increase in the lending countries (or if full employment exists, inflationary pressures will rise.) When the loans are being "serviced" or repaid, the lending countries should have an import surplus of useful goods. Production in the borrowing lands will rise by more than enough to pay interest on the loans, and domestic wage and other factor returns will be *greater*, not less, because of what foreign capital has added to the GNP of the borrowing country.

Has the Bank been a financial "success"? Decidedly. If anything, until Robert McNamara (formerly of Ford and the U.S. Pentagon) became its activist head in the late 1960s, the Bank may have been too conservative in its practice of lending only to self-liquidating projects. By 1970 an embarrassing volume of profits had accumulated. An increasing proportion of this now goes to the International Development Agency, set up by the Bank to make "soft loans" to nations for education, roads, hospitals, etc.; and to its International Finance Corporation, set up to make loans to foreign development banks for financing private investment projects.

■ THE INTERNATIONAL MONETARY FUND

The International Monetary Fund, like the International Bank, grew out of the 1944 international conferences held in Bretton Woods, New Hampshire. The IMF hopes to secure the advantages of the gold standard without its disadvantages; e.g., exchange rates were at first envisaged to be relatively stable, but with international cooperation to replace the previous automatic mechanism. Also, countries are to be spared the need for making adjustments that involve *deflating themselves into drastic unemployment.* It hopes to lessen need for import controls.

Ordinarily, a country will go along paying for its imports by means of its exports or long-term borrowing. Suppose a country, say, Britain, is in need of short-term credit from the Fund. How does the Fund enable such a debtor country to get hold of dollars, for instance? It does this by extending "purchasing rights." It simply permits the British to buy with British currency some of the Fund's own holdings of U.S. dollars. After the British balance of payments has improved, Britain is expected to buy back with gold (or with U.S. dollars or, as we'll see, with the new SDR's or "paper gold") the pounds she has sold to the Fund.

The Fund tries to set up rules and procedures to keep a country from going too deeply into debt, year after year. After a country has been piling up debts for a considerable period, certain financial penalties are applied. More important, the Fund's directors consult with the country and make recommendations for remedying the disequilibrium. However, they do not advise a country to create a depression in order to cut its national income down to such a low level that its imports will finally fall within its means. Instead, the country itself is permitted to depreciate (or appreciate) its currency by up to 10 per cent. This tends to restore equilibrium in its trade by expanding its exports and contracting imports.

If this is still not enough to correct the so-called "overvaluation" of the debtor country's currency, the Fund authorities may, after proper consultation, permit still further depreciation of the debtor country's exchange rate. But note this: All changes in rates are to take place in an orderly way. Most of the time, there is to be international stability. There is also provision for flexibility when needed, which is better by far than waiting for a great smash.

By the 1960s the IMF realized (what Keynes and others had urged at Bretton Woods) that it must shift onto the *surplus* countries some obligation to help restore basic equilibrium. Thus, Germany may be encouraged to appreciate the mark (as she did in 1961 and again in 1969). Such countries may be encouraged to lower import barriers and export subsidies; to lend abroad and increase their foreign aid; to reflate their domestic economies if stagnation exists.

At first the Fund was rather a disappointment. The postwar strains turned out to be much greater than anticipated in 1944; and the Fund's resources were inadequate to cope with those disequilibria. Since 1955 and the end of the dollar gap, however, the Fund has become increasingly important.

> For example, the United States reinforced its own international resources by drawing on the Fund. Canada's official holdings of gold and foreign exchange were supported by "stand-by credits" at the IMF in 1962, [when Finance Minister Fleming was trying to fix the Canadian dollar at $0.92 (U.S.) in the face of international speculators' bets that it would, eventually, fall farther]. Consider the sterling crisis faced by the British Labor Government in the years before the 1967 devaluation of the pound from $3.00 to $2.60 (Canadian) per pound. Britain borrowed several billion dollars from the IMF to support the pound, making her the greatest user of the Fund since its formation. In addition, the IMF helped coordinate the billions of dollars of support for the pound from the United States, Canada, and continental European countries (the other members of the "Club of Ten").

In any future major reforms of international liquidity or any future dollar problems, the International Monetary Fund will undoubtedly play a pivotal role, as we shall see.

■ THE EUROPEAN COMMON MARKET AND THE FREE-TRADE AREA

The last few chapters analyzed the economic gains from freer trade. One way of reducing trade impediments is for several countries to form a customs union. Within such a union, tariffs and quotas might be reduced or banished; but they might still persist with respect to external trade.

THE EUROPEAN ECONOMIC COMMUNITY (EEC)   One of the most exciting international developments of the century has been the formation of the six-nation European Economic Community, popularly known as the European Common Market. With vigorous U.S. encouragement, Belgium, France, Italy, Luxembourg, the Netherlands, and Western Germany signed the Treaty of Rome (March 1957) and other instruments to create the European Economic Community, which came into effect on January 1, 1958. Subject to exceptions, by 1973 each member-nation of "the Six" is to eliminate tariffs and import quotas on nonfarm goods produced *within* the area; to set up a common tariff against goods from countries outside the area; and to allow free movement of capital and labor. Although agricultural protection has, as with us, remained a conspicuous exception to policy reform, this liberalization timetable is otherwise being met.

THE EFTA   Anxious over the threat posed by the Common Market to their exports, seven other European countries formed the European Free Trade Association (EFTA); this consists of Austria, Denmark, Norway, Portugal, Sweden,

Switzerland, and Britain. The members are disparate in size and development; nevertheless they have achieved almost complete free trade in nonfarm products. EFTA's organization is very simple—unlike that of the Common Market, which is a community "not just in business but in politics" moving toward ever-greater integration of all trade, factor movements, and macroeconomic policy.

In 1971, when this book was going to press, it looked as if the applications of Britain and other EFTA members to join the Common Market would be accepted. The Community might then become the largest market area in the world. However, both in Britain and in France, the enthusiasm for "Europe" has been waning. Britons liked EFTA, minor as its influence was on British trade, because it left Britain substantially unhindered by international loyalties. Hence they dislike the Community. For this very reason, some French leaders distrust British entry, regarding it as a threat to the attainment of specifically French goals in agriculture.

ATLANTIC FREE TRADE Since France repulsed the first British application to join the EEC, Americans, Britons, and Canadians have discussed other means of achieving wider free trade. The Common Market looked as though it might shut out other exporters and so even *reduce* world trade. The General Agreement on Tariffs and Trade (GATT) could move no faster toward lower tariffs than the slowest negotiator.

Among the suggestions for new arrangements was not only the makeshift EFTA, but, more ambitiously, a North Atlantic Free Trade Area (NAFTA). In 1963, 1965, and 1967 there were advanced schemes whereby Canada, the United States, perhaps Great Britain, and also perhaps other developed countries, would virtually eliminate their trade barriers to one another over a fairly long transitional and adjustment period.

Would free north-south trade mean the end of industry in Canada? Actually, no. An outstanding series of studies of the impact of this program on Canadian industry has been made.[2] It has indicated that, with the type of transitional provisions made familiar by the smaller-scale Automobile Agreement, revamped Canadian industries could sell in the larger North American market competitively with U.S. industry (and, for that matter, with Japanese and European industry). But in 1970, the wave of nationalism in Canada, the U.S. withdrawal from foreign entanglements, and the renewed British application to the EEC may have caused interested policy-makers to shelve this idea, till, as with GATT, the nations can again establish a common cause.

> Some economists have worried whether the lowering of tariffs among the countries within a bloc is truly a movement toward a most efficient world pattern. They ask, "Won't there be a danger that the lower-than-average tariffs between the countries inside the union will distort the 'normal' pattern of trade (and each country's specialization in certain products) even more than it is already being distorted by separate nations' tariffs? Won't the differences between the 'ins' and

---

[2] See the trade-liberalization studies by English, Wonnacott, Johnson, Singer, Bond, and others in the slim paperback series *Canada in the Atlantic Economy* (Toronto: University of Toronto Press, 1968-1970).

the 'outs' be magnified and represent a distortion as serious as the pre-bloc situation?"

Others have replied: "Two wrongs don't make a right. If you can't get rid of trade impediments everywhere, at least get rid of them where you can. Then maybe a few great customs unions can ultimately merge into a worldwide free-trade area."

No definite answer will cover every case. Perhaps most economists would venture the guess that the lowering of tariffs in Europe did create much new production and trade among the new partners. Its effects on the division of labor would be beneficial to them, and they would ultimately be beneficial to other countries, if trade is later opened up to them. Readers can try for themselves another version of this problem by asking, "If Canada and the United States reach free trade, so that appliances and machinery are produced indifferently, and more economically in both countries, do their consequent improved efficiency and improved real incomes fully balance the loss of the chance for such specialization suffered by excluded Japanese or German exporters?"

■ FREER MULTILATERAL TRADE: GATT

During the 1930s, as remarked above, tariff levels went sky-high. Under the Ottawa agreements, the British countries seriously thought of Commonwealth self-sufficiency. Germany, Italy, France, and the USSR were keen to export but stubbornly reduced their imports. But readers should note that since World War II (in fact, since the round of bilateral treaties for reciprocal tariff reduction between the United States and other countries negotiated by Cordell Hull after 1935—see Fig. 34-1) most countries have been steadily whittling down their protective barriers. Economists properly stress that the barriers are still high; but they should not exaggerate the situation.

All stand to gain if fruitful multilateral trade can be restored. As mentioned in Chapter 34, the General Agreement on Tariffs and Trade (GATT) is a most important development toward international cooperation.

The so-called "Kennedy Round" for multilateral (nondiscriminating) tariff reductions is a good example of the gradual progress being made towards trade liberalization. Actually the late 1960s effort was the sixth round of tariff reduction under the auspices of GATT, earlier efforts having taken place in 1947, 1949, 1951, 1956, and 1961. Agreement was made difficult by the wish of certain members of the Common Market, most notably France, to increase protective tariffs on agriculture following a U.S. precedent of the 1950s. Thus, although France's comparative advantage in agricultural products is less than that of overseas suppliers, she has always insisted that her higher-cost producers be protected, even if this would entail higher prices to consumers in the other countries belonging to the Common Market. Indeed, the difficulties in the way of Britain's entrance into the Common Market have been related to the unwillingness of the British public to agree to France's insistence that Britain shift from cheap overseas sources to dear European sources for buying food.

B.   THREATENED BREAKDOWN OF THE INTERNATIONAL SYSTEM

Now that we have surveyed the post-World War II institutions of international finance, we can face up to the burning issues that confront Canada and the world.

■ FROM DOLLAR SHORTAGE TO DOLLAR GLUT

The Marshall Plan and other aid programs soon began to have very favorable effects on the less-than-most-affluent countries—Japan, Germany, the Netherlands, France, and Italy. Primarily on their own, by a process no one had predicted, they began a miraculous sprint of productivity growth in the 1950s. This miracle persists into the 1970s.

This growth in the *competitiveness* of foreign economies, plus the expensiveness of United States' *cold-war programs* (the Korean conflict, the Vietnam war, the NATO alliance, etc.), plus U.S. *civilian foreign-aid programs* (in Asia, Latin America, and elsewhere), plus the burgeoning outflow of *direct foreign investment by U.S. corporations* facing juicy profit opportunities abroad—all these factors led to a gradual cessation of the dollar shortage and an actual swing toward a shortage of foreign currencies.

> The "dollar shortage" of the 1950s turned into the "dollar glut" (i.e., draining of gold from the United States with chronic U.S. balance-of-payments deficits) of the 1960s and the early 1970s. Relatively high costs in the United States meant "overvaluation" of the dollar.

At first the drain on the U.S. gold supply went unnoticed. But after 1958, everybody could see that a new trend was in the making.

Figure 35-1(a) shows that in 1959 the United States' balance of payments deficit was as large as her surplus had been in 1947. This deficit was financed in part by a dramatic gold outflow: between 1949 and 1970 the United States' gold stock fell from its peak of 24 billion dollars to about 10 billion dollars. But to an even greater extent it was financed by foreigners accepting U.S. short-term IOUs. Figure 35-1(b) shows how liquid claims on the United States have grown to exceed her gold holdings.

Since the United States probably had a disproportionate share of the world's gold supply in 1950, U.S. experts rather welcomed the first part of the gold drain; for she was getting something back for all the gold she had accepted since the 1930s. However, with no equilibrium in clear sight, their attitude may be changing.

For the 25 years from 1933 to 1958, thanks in part to Hitler and the political uncertainties that sent gold to the United States for safekeeping, U.S. economic policy was *emancipated completely* from any concern for her international balance of payments. Now the United States has rejoined the human race: she too has a balance of payments deficit, and she has been forced to consider fiscal, monetary, and balance-of-payments problems together. Hence she had to take her balance-of-payments problem into account when, as in 1960-1965, she wished to lower interest rates in order to help achieve full-employment levels of investment and stimulate the capital formation that leads to a faster growth rate of her producible NNP. Since 1960, every U.S. official decision about foreign aid or about military action has been constrained by the threat of an adverse effect on the balance of payments.

Chronic foreign deficits weaken the U.S. dollar, cause hemorrhage of gold:

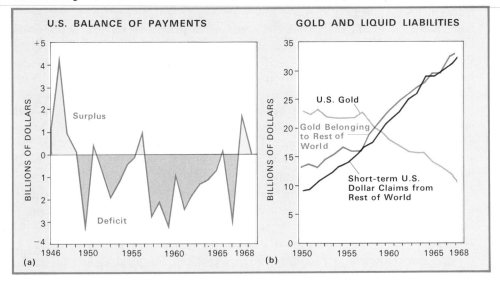

FIG. 35-1. The United States' continued international deficit shows the swing from the world-wide dollar shortage to the dollar glut. Her gold stock has dropped steadily. The rest of the world has steadily accumulated gold and liquid U.S. dollar claims. The deficit shown here is the over-all, or official settlements, balance referred to in Chapter 32, page 792. (Source: U.S. Department of Commerce.)

■ REASONS FOR CHRONIC U.S. INTERNATIONAL DEFICIT, 1955-1970

Many reasons are given for the United States' chronic international deficit. Most have an element of truth in them, but we shall see that the crucial cause for the 1955-1970 period is probably to be found in the vast improvement of technical productivity in other countries in recent years. Below are the causes commonly named for the deficit:

1. *Too much U.S. inflation.* If a country has more rapid wage increases than its neighbor, and if these are not matched by compensating differentials in worker productivity gains, then it is indeed likely to find itself running into a deficit in the balance of international payments.[3]

If we turn from conjecture to fact, an examination of any of the usual over-all index numbers of money prices and wages will show that up to 1965 there had not been more inflation in the United States than in other countries, such as the European nations and Japan. On the contrary, a list of the 20 principal countries of the world shows that the United States came almost at the bottom in terms of price-level increase in the last decade. The same is true of index numbers of money wage rates. Only after 1965 did U.S. price indices begin to soar.

---

[3] For further analysis, see Chapter 32's Appendix discussion on overvaluation of a currency.

There is this grain of truth, however, in the overpricing allegation. If one leaves over-all indices and turns to certain important *sectoral* price indices, it will indeed be found that American steel prices long rose relative to those of other countries. No wonder that Japanese steel invades the U.S. Pacific Coast; that foreign producers of such U.S. staples as *barbed wire, cars,* and *TV sets* have almost insolently captured traditional U.S. home markets; that steel from England and Belgium, helped by lengthy domestic strikes and fears of strikes, has got a foothold in U.S. markets. Similar occurrences are found in several machinery industries, where the great burst of demand in the equipment boom of 1956-1957 sent prices soaring. (The price rise in steel was thought by the Joint Economic Committee of the U.S. Congress to be more the result of "cost-push" by wages and maintained profit margins.)

We shall see that full employment, incident to the post-1965 Vietnam escalation, created a price-level escalation that caused deterioration of the United States' private current balance of exports over imports. Hence, from 1965 to 1970, the United States' basic deficit problems worsened.[4]

2. *Excessive aid and military programs.* When aiming to reduce her trade deficit by a billion dollars, the United States might think of simply cutting out that much foreign aid and military spending. However, many of her export credit items are present in the balance of payments *only because U.S. government programs have lent or given foreigners the "tied" funds to pay for them.* Cutting such programs by 1 billion dollars will cut into U.S. private exports E and in turn reduce her deficit by something less than 1 billion dollars. Thus only the failure of U.S. lending to create a larger demand for U.S. goods can be blamed.

Until Vietnam, U.S. governmental foreign-aid and military programs had not grown much in relative size; rather, it was more the case that, with the growth in private long-term investment, the United States' surplus on current *private* account was no longer large enough to let her aid programs be as extensive as they had been previously.[5] After 1965, Vietnam did become an important aggravator of her payments deficit.

3. *Lack of trust in the U.S. dollar.* From 1933 to 1955, the U.S. dollar

---

[4] If you plot (1) the United States' declining share of world exports against (2) the post-World War II rise in the ratio of her export prices to those abroad, the result does look a little like a downward-sloping *dd* curve, with the rise in relative P explaining the loss of relative Q.

[5] Even some experts do not realize how high the United States' surplus on current private account must be if she is to stay in healthy equilibrium with free long-term investment and to carry on aid and military operations abroad. Equilibrium might then require the expansion of U.S. exports of goods and services, in comparison with her imports, by enough to create a current private surplus of as much as 8 to 10 billion dollars! Would such a sizable surplus harm her trading partners? Some fear so. Others, concerned by financial disequilibrium and equilibrium of comparative advantage, urge that this be achieved. The United States is already supplying the rest of the world with the means to finance her enlarged surplus; hence they cannot be harmed. The private surplus must be large enough, however large that is, to fit in with over-all international equilibrium.

was considered everywhere to be a holding even better than gold. It was *the* key international reserve currency. But what happens when people and governments begin to believe that the United States is in international disequilibrium? And when they become apprehensive that the dollar *might* be devalued relative to gold? It is natural enough that, under these circumstances, some governments and private persons should, before the 1968 two-tier gold system made official gold unavailable for private persons, want to take out gold from the United States rather than continue to hold dollar currency or dollar IOUs. This so-called "shift in international liquidity preference" can help explain some of the chronic gold drain from the United States that led to the London gold panic of 1968.[6]

4. *Discriminations abroad against U.S. goods.* While the dollar was in short supply abroad, it was understandable why barriers against U.S. exports would have been common in other countries. Now, with the dollar weak not strong, Americans have good reason to argue that remaining discriminations against U.S. goods be removed or reduced. The Common Market did lessen some of the impediments to intra-European trade, and some progress has been made. However, during the 1970s, the Common Market may reverse its policy, and become more restrictive toward exports from non-member countries.

5. *The rapid growth of productivity abroad.* From a long-run viewpoint, the fundamental cause of the change in the United States' international position would seem to be the remarkable speeding up of productivity increase in Western Europe and Japan. Their production technology is still lagging, but the gap, particularly in the goods which the United States customarily exports and specializes in, has been narrowing. Even with real wages abroad rising more rapidly, foreigners can produce for themselves more cheaply than the United States has been producing for them; hence they can outsell her increasingly in third markets, and can even begin to outsell her in North America.

6. *High investment abroad by U.S. firms.* The miraculous productivity spurt abroad created tremendous profit opportunities for U.S. corporations. In the last decade, instead of wishing to invest in underdeveloped countries, they hastened to build branch factories in Canada, Europe, and Japan.

By 1965 the outflow of direct investments by U.S. firms had become so large that the government introduced a *voluntary* capital control program

---

[6] On the other hand, some experts—such as MIT's C. P. Kindleberger, Stanford's Emile Despres, and Princeton's Fritz Machlup—think the distrust of the dollar is a foolish state of mind that could be easily changed by a bold policy in which the United States makes the following kind of announcement: "Come exchange your dollars for gold right now at $35 per ounce—if you are foolish enough to want to do so. But don't think you can count on the United States to buy back that gold from you at a guaranteed price of $35 once again. Instead the United States may, at *her* pleasure, reduce its buying price of gold—perhaps abandoning gold altogether!" Given such an ultimatum, gold hoarders will realize the error of their ways and, so the argument goes, will swing over in liquidity preference to the dollar. Under the two-tier system, the Kindleberger-Despres doctrine takes a slightly modified form, as we shall see.

applied to commercial bank loans and to corporation-retained earnings and bond issues. In 1968, the voluntary program became mandatory, and quotas were tightened. The Nixon administration eased these quotas in 1970. Like all such programs, the control program tends to decrease in effectiveness with the passage of time.

Another measure adopted was an "interest-rate equalization tax." The United States would want low interest rates in order to keep prosperity at home. But such low rates would induce U.S. capitalists to lend abroad and foreign borrowers (including Canadian provinces and corporations) to float security issues cheaply in the United States. The tax, amounting to 11½ per cent or more, is levied on purchases by Americans from non-Americans of foreign stocks or long-term bonds, and thus it acts as a deterrent to U.S. investment abroad. (Canada and some other countries in the Western hemisphere which are closely tied to the U.S. capital market are exempted from the tax.)

Not unnaturally, U.S. measures to restrict lending and investment abroad are alarming to Canada and to other countries, especially when they are combined with the tendency of the United States to cut tourist allowances abroad, to procure her military supplies from domestic suppliers instead of in the countries where they are to be used, and to require underdeveloped countries to spend in the United States the dollars provided by U.S. aid. Our earlier examination of the Canadian balance of payments showed (1) that much of our current-account deficit is the result of our inability to sell as much to the United States as our tourists, consumers, and businesses buy there, and (2) that we have been able to finance this deficit—and to grow—by drawing on long-run American capital. The U.S. deficit-curing measures have luckily had a fairly small impact on Canada so far. But if they have to be extended to include higher tariffs and smaller quotas on raw materials such as oil, zinc, and lead, Canada and all the United States' other trading partners will begin to agree that the ultimate and least efficient stabilizing weapon is the export of unemployment.

■ EQUILIBRIUM IN THE 1970s?

Is the world moving toward international equilibrium in the 1970s? Here are the salient facts to show that fundamental structural reform cannot long be delayed.

1.   Certainly the decade of the 1960s began with the U.S. dollar and the British pound in fairly serious *disequilibrium* relative to the surplus countries of the Common Market.

> North American patterns of comparative advantage were changing, and a transition period is rarely comfortable. Moreover, it was not simply a question of shifting factors from one industry to another. So long as U.S. dollar costs tended to be high *all around*, the United States' currency could be called an "overvalued currency." A country with an overvalued currency tends to incur international deficits, to be undersold in most goods, to have capital outflow, and to be threatened with high unemployment and excess capacity. What may be needed is for her money prices and wages to fall relative to those in other countries, either falling absolutely or rising less rapidly than theirs. Even if no *real wage* change

were needed, we know that it is very far from easy in a modern democratic mixed society to have a deflation in money wages and prices.[7]

2. For the first half of the decade there were definite signs of improvement for the U.S. dollar. Perhaps the principal reason for this was the over-full employment on the Continent, which sent its wage and other money costs rising faster than costs in the more sluggish North American economy.

3. After 1965, North America also had full employment. This, combined with the Vietnam war, tended to increase the United States' imports relative to her exports. Costs no longer grew more slowly than in many of the surplus countries. By 1970, the experts were no longer sure that the U.S.-dollar disequilibrium was about to cure itself. Far from permitting the United States to remove the *ad hoc* measures she had used to defend her dollar ("tying of aid," interest-rate equalization tax, voluntary and mandatory capital-export control programs, etc.) the status of the U.S. dollar was jolted by speculation on the mark in 1971.

■ THERAPY FOR A CHRONIC DEFICIT

Economists know what are the programs generally needed to reverse a chronic international deficit. These have long been preached by the IMF to European deficit countries. They are difficult to follow.

1. Workers and industry in the United States can be urged to *increase domestic technical productivity*. Urging does not accomplish much. More important in the long run are supports for scientific research and investment.

2. Exporters in the United States can be urged to *improve selling practices* abroad. Since foreign salesmen are also similarly urged, mere exhortation accomplishes little.

3. The United States can press for further *reductions in discriminations against the U.S. dollar*. There are still trade impediments, and the Common Market threatens more.

4. She can ask that the prospering nations of the free world take up a *larger share of the aid, development, and defense burdens*.

5. She could *keep her economy depressed* at home, eschewing low interest rates needed for employment and growth, diminishing her demand for imports, and putting pressure on profit margins in export industries to make them hungry to drum up export business.[8] During the 1960s, the Kennedy-Johnson administration rejected a policy of deliberate creation of unemployment and sluggish growth in order to lessen international deficits. But in 1966-1970, the

---

[7] A rise in productivity in Canada, Europe, or Japan might increase U.S. real wages by cheapening imports. But (1) if it took the form of improvement in productivity in goods the United States had been specializing in and (2) if it reflected the discovery by U.S. corporations that their know-how could be applied to non-American workers, then the whole process might actually slow up the rate of real wage growth in the United States and could result in a *loss* of her gain (i.e., her consumer's surplus) from international trade. Cf. Chapter 32's Appendix.

[8] To the degree that unemployment domestically means low profit opportunities, it might worsen the U.S. balance by encouraging more foreign investment outflow.

British Labour Government had to introduce a deliberate domestic slowdown in order to strengthen the balance of payments, as did President Nixon in 1969-1970. In 1971, moderate fiscal and monetary expansion have been attempted.

6.   There could be a *depreciation of the U.S. dollar* relative to other currencies, with or without a unilateral *devaluation* relative to gold (in the official tier), or by some other move.

SECOND-BEST MEASURES   Any or all of the above measures are designed to get rid of any overvaluation of the U.S. dollar relative to other currencies. But suppose that they are not feasible in the needed amount, and that the United States will have to live with an overvalued dollar for some time. A host of new, and somewhat distasteful, measures can combat overvaluation. They are already in use elsewhere.

7.   She can *"tie" foreign-aid grants and loans further*, requiring that their proceeds be spent directly in the United States even if the cost is greater to recipient nations. She has already tied her own military expenditures in the sense that an item must be bought at home, no matter how much more expensive it is there than abroad.

8.   She can *limit tourism*, by cutting down on the goods that travelers can bring home free of duty or the fares they may pay for.

9.   She can put *restrictions or tax penalties on investment abroad*. Attracted by the high profits that growth and productivity improvements abroad make possible, there has been a vast outpouring of U.S. private investment to other countries. Except for the obviously special case of oil development in the Near East and Latin America, the bulk of this investment has gone to the developed nations. Some have blamed this single trend for most of the basic deficit.[9]

Congress did impose the "interest equalization tax", and a compulsory foreign investment control on commercial bank lending abroad and direct corporate foreign investment. Tax rebates on exports have been used elsewhere, and could help.

10.   She could revert to *protectionism* generally. Tariffs and quotas will not raise *real wages*, for the reasons seen in the previous chapters, but they can compensate a little for sticky money wages and an overvalued currency. Such a solution will be deplored by all who value the advantages that come from specialization according to comparative advantage and by all who think it is to the United States' political advantage to live down her old reputation as an unreliable customer.

11.   Finally, to bring the list to a close, she could hope that *the surplus countries of Europe and Japan would again experience an acceleration of inflation in their cost and price-levels*. Money wages on the Continent in 1959-1965 did grow faster than productivity there, and this fact probably did more to promote an ultimate solution of the United States' basic balance than anything else.

---

[9] In the long run, earnings from these investments would begin to help her deficit.

12. Alternatively, if surplus nations would undertake the politically unpopular task of *appreciating* their currencies (as West Germany and Holland did in 1961 and Germany did in 1969 and 1971), the overvalued dollar could be cured without any depreciation on the part of the U.S., or inflation abroad.

INTERNAL AND EXTERNAL BALANCE: THE CANADIAN CONCERN   The reader familiar with events in Canada in the past few years can readily identify Canada's concern over changes in long-run capital flows and point to the following causes: (1) Capital may be "pushed" from abroad by unfavorable political conditions, high savings rates, and especially by low yields and lack of investment opportunities. (2) Capital may be "pulled" into an economy by resource discoveries, new markets, general prosperity, tariff protection of particular industries, and generally, by high yields and investment opportunities. Thus capital flows in long-run form are more likely to be the result of comparisons of conditions *inside* two economies than of the exchange rates between them.[10]

This conclusion indicates one aspect of a very old problem: how is a country to achieve both internal full employment (often called "internal balance") and external payments balance? For generations the authorities of England and the United States gave external balance a higher priority. Thus, if capital inflows were too great for external balance, they would attempt to lower investment yields at home, even if this policy would produce internal stagnation or unemployment. The reader will note this attitude was similar to the gold-standard approach to the balance of trade: when imports are too great the outflow of gold would be corrected by effects causing internal deflation and unemployment.

Nowadays countries are less prepared to give external balance such a high priority. For example, in the early 1960s, the Kennedy administration's easy-credit-conditions policy, which helped to return the country to full employment, also caused an outflow of long-run capital seeking higher yields on loans elsewhere. As we have seen, the United States decided that internal prosperity was more important than seeking an instant stop to the capital outflow; so instead of raising interest rates at home she imposed the interest equalization tax and tried by moral suasion to stem the outflow.

All through the depressed years 1958-1962, Canada maintained relatively tight credit conditions. The external result was a fairly high capital inflow, and an exchange rate that placed the Canadian dollar at a premium, discouraged exports, and encouraged imports. The internal result of such comparatively tight credit conditions was that business expansion was discouraged and unemployment was high. Externally, Canada's financial position looked healthy, but output and growth were arrested.

---

[10] Of course, investment opportunities inside Canada may be the result of its exchange rate. A high rate may discourage imports and so attract capital into the country to build up import-competing industries. But it also discourages exports and so dries up the flow of funds to the raw-material-shipping sectors. Advanced texts stress that whether an exchange rate shift increases or decreases long-run capital inflows depends on whether the export or the import industries are the more capital-intensive.

In the early 1970s, substantial upward pressure on Canada's exchange rate resulted from large and rapid inflows of short-term capital combined with a more favorable movement (reduction in the deficit) in the current account. Canadian interest rates remained above their counterparts in the U.S., which augmented and accelerated the capital inflow. The Exchange Fund Account, in attempting to maintain the $0.92 pegged rate, was forced to purchase the foreign exchange. This in itself would have *expanded* the domestic money supply. (See page 395.) The monetary authorities, faced with this situation, used open-market operations to counteract this expansion of the money supply and limit its growth. This policy put more upward pressure on domestic interest rates and so stimulated *further* short-term capital inflows. The Government's solution eventually was to alter the exchange rate. This was done in June, 1970, by allowing it to be determined by the demand and supply forces in the market, i.e., by allowing it to "float."

Earlier, in the inflation-policy discussions of 1968-1969, many economists deplored attempts to use monetary policy. Why? The exchange rate was then fixed. So tighter credit conditions, raising interest rates, *attracted* foreign capital thus providing alternative lenders, or as mentioned above, forcing the government to expand the domestic money supply (to replenish the Exchange Fund Account).

These examples of the apparent incompatibility of internal and external balance have recently been intensively studied by economists. They have asked: what combinations of internal and external policies can produce certain outcomes, such as full employment, a stable price level, and foreign balance?

The nature of the analysis is too advanced to explore here. But an example will show how the reasoning runs.

Assume capital is perfectly mobile, running into a country when interest rates rise, and out when they fall. Many questions can be asked, but consider this one: will monetary or fiscal policy be a more effective stabilizer when exchange rates are flexible?[11]

If the country uses monetary policy to counter a domestic slump, credit conditions will ease and interest rates fall. Capital will then tend to leave the country. This will cause the flexible exchange rate to fall. In turn, this will cause exports to rise and imports to fall. Thus, with mobile capital and flexible rates, both domestic investment *and* exports will rise when monetary policy is used. Both will have a multiplied effect on the home economy.

In contrast, if the country uses fiscal policy, say deficit spending financed by government borrowing, interest rates will tend to rise—they will not fall, anyway. Thus capital will tend to enter the country. Exchange rates will tend to rise, and the balance on current account will show a fall in exports and a rise in imports. These effects will cancel out the employment-creating effect of the fiscal policy.

Thus, with mobile capital and flexible exchange rates, monetary policy is more effective than fiscal policy for fighting stagnation and unemployment. This is why, during the period of flexible exchange rates, economists urged Mr. Coyne to get

[11] See Chapter 32's discussion of flexible exchange rates, pages 776-782.

easier credit conditions for Canada, rather than urging the government to undertake fiscal policy.[12]

Each country is faced with these choices among levels of internal and external balance. It is usually impossible to be in ideal equilibrium in both. In the mid-1960s, for example, Germany suffered an excessive gold and capital inflow while coping with potential internal inflation and serious labor shortage. Britain, meanwhile, had full employment and a fair external balance; but persistently her internal price level got out of hand, and her current account floundered into increasing deficit—finally, to deal with the last problem, she revalued the pound sterling. Canada, like the United States, had full employment and rising prices, but Canada had a heavy capital inflow and the United States a chronic drain of gold and capital. When the pound was revalued; the shock led to brief worrying flights from both Canadian and American dollars; so that internal policies had to be adjusted to meet these external challenges.

Each country sought sets of policies that benefited both their internal and external economies; how were they to set about compromising between internal and external balance? Economists came to governments' aid by classifying the combinations, or "trade-offs," that *were possible* with certain sets of policies.

C. STRUCTURAL REFORM OF INTERNATIONAL FINANCE

Is the gold drain from the United States merely symptomatic of a more widespread malaise? Growing world production requires growing money supplies; but can gold mining keep up with this need? Growing international trade, and freer trade in a world more susceptible to political and economic irregularities, require larger liquid reserves for countries to hold as protection against swings in their balance of payments—particularly in mixed economies that will not let the rules of the gold standard dictate internal inflation or depression to achieve Hume's classical equilibrium. Will world gold supplies be adequate for this need, particularly in an environment where key currencies like the pound and dollar no longer command the respect that enabled them once to serve as a substitute for gold reserves?

Many economists, remembering the sobering experience of 1929, strongly believe that the whole world is in need of some basic *structural* reforms to provide needed elasticity in international reserves.

■ FOUR MAJOR PROBLEMS REQUIRING STRUCTURAL REFORM

By 1970, what was already evident to experts became unmistakably clear to government officials and financial men generally—namely, that the international

---

[12] Note that the analysis depends heavily on capital being perfectly mobile in response to credit conditions (interest rates). When capital movements are motivated by other things, the analysis has to be modified. The entire set of possibilities has been clearly worked out in a set of articles by R. A. Mundell. See for example his "Capital Mobility and Stabilization Policy Under Fixed and Flexible Exchange Rates," *Canadian Journal of Economics and Political Science* (November, 1963), pp. 475-9. Similar points have been made by Harry Johnson in his book *The Canadian Quandary* (Toronto: McGraw-Hill, 1965).

U.S.-dollar-and-gold standard was in serious trouble, and was probably not viable without fundamental reform. Four basic problems characterize the system and point to specific defects in need of repair.

INFLEXIBLE EXCHANGE RATES   A quarter of a century after Bretton Woods, experience has shown the system set up there to be flawed at the core by its reliance on exchange-rate parities that were to be *constant*. Economic theorists know that modern mixed economies are prone to drift apart through the years in their trends of price levels, wage costs, and productivities.

Hence, suppose the U.S. dollar and the German mark have exchange rates in equilibrium in 1949. Why should those rates still be suitable 20 years later? German productivity might outstrip the United States in an unpredictable way —and that is what happened. The United States might get involved in military programs necessitating vast offshore expenditures—and that too happened. Inventions may affect different regions differently in terms of their international competitiveness. Consumer tastes may change, causing what was an equilibrium parity to become a currency overvaluation or undervaluation. In a world where *everything changes*, where no price remains constant, why continue trying to build an international edifice on a foundation of *inflexible* exchange rates?[13]

DOLLAR DISEQUILIBRIUM   Compounding this basic flaw of inflexibility of exchange rates has been the fact that the United States dollar itself—the linchpin of the system—became progressively out of equilibrium in the 15 years following 1955.

"The dollar is even better than gold." Such a statement might have been true in the two decades following 1933, when there had been the dollar shortage and when U.S. currency was undervalued. But by the 1960s, after a decade of chronic United States balance-of-payments deficits, the attractiveness of U.S. dollars as a key international asset began to evaporate. Central bankers in Europe began to offer bets of champagne with former U.S. Federal Reserve Chairman Martin that the dollar would be depreciated, devalued, or both.

Increasingly in the 1960s central banks and foreign governments began to insist that the United States meet its deficit with gold; they would accept only a portion of the deficit in the form of dollar assets. (And undoubtedly if large official holders of U.S. dollars, such as Germany, Japan, and Italy, had not known very well that an attempt on their part to cash in those dollars for gold would be met by U.S. suspension of gold payments, they would have asked for still more gold. In other words, a good deal of the dollar holding was *involuntary* and not voluntary, and the loss of gold by the United States would have been even greater if it had reflected the spontaneous laws of supply and demand.)

---

[13] The architects of Bretton Woods did provide for *occasional* discontinuous exchange-rate adjustments by international agreement with the IMF. But what they did not sufficiently realize was the fact that such adjustments would be made only *after* the disequilibrium state had become apparent to all, and that this recognition would provide a field day for speculators who could sell the weak currency short, knowing that there was no risk of its moving against them and a great chance that it would move in their favor. Moreover, the speculators acting in concert could hope to precipitate the crisis which would make them their profit.

Private individuals and corporations, in France and other Continental countries where legal taboos on the holding of gold were not operative, felt free to hoard gold and did so increasingly. Speculators, scenting that the existing gold parities could only move upward and were not unlikely to do so, piled onto the bandwagon. And so private gold hoards mounted, depleting the gold reserves of central banks and official authorities.[14]

LONG-RUN GOLD AND LIQUIDITY SHORTAGE   This brings us to the third basic flaw in the international system. The long-run supply of gold cannot possibly keep up with the liquidity needs of growing international trade. Year in, year out, the volume of international trade increases annually at a 7 or 8 per cent rate. But dwindling world gold production from the mines of South Africa and Russia can increase at barely 2 per cent per year. And much of this new gold, hoarding quite aside, is preempted for normal *industrial* use. Hence any international system *dependent inflexibly* on gold for its reserve base is doomed to ultimate liquidity shortage and chronic emphysema.

As mentioned earlier, the replacement of gold coin by paper currency and the development of fractional-reserve banking systems served to economize domestically on gold in the last 75 years. Even then the system was being afflicted with sagging price levels until luck in the form of Alaskan and African gold rushes intervened. By 1929 luck had given out, and again by 1968 the gold-exchange and dollar-standard economizing and international devices for stretching out the use of gold had reached dangerous limits.

As long ago as 1955, Yale's Robert Triffin correctly prophesied the need for fundamental institutional reform to increase international liquidity.[15] Although the long-run liquidity shortage problem would have been inevitable quite independently of the dollar disequilibrium, the existence of the United States' chronic payments deficit in the years after 1950 led to her hemorrhaging gold. Since the U.S. gold outflows provided a gold infusion to the Common Market countries and the rest of the world generally, the problem of U.S. dollar disequilibrium served inadvertently to cover up and divert attention for a time from the long-run insufficiency of gold. Refer back to Fig. 35-1, page 869.)

DIRECT INVESTMENT AND "FOREIGN OWNERSHIP"   To these three technical problems and the politics of their solutions, we must add the problem of direct investment. At one time both long- and short-run capital movements took the form of IOUs and debts from portfolio lenders, with which borrowers could acquire foreign consumer and capital goods.

In this century, increased productivity, tariff barriers, and transport costs have led to equity purchases and *direct* investment by manufacturers and

[14] Continental hoarders could not *directly* get gold from the U.S. Treasury. But when they got gold from their central banks, those institutions acted as a conduit and exercised their official right to get gold from the U.S. Treasury.

[15] Indeed Lord Keynes at Bretton Woods in 1945 had already proposed a gold substitute —a new currency unit for international reserves called "Bancor." In addition to the Triffin Plan there have been a Bernstein Plan, a Stamp Plan, a Posthuma Plan, and a number of similar proposals for creating new reserve units, credits, or versions of "paper gold."

services of the main lending countries. The portfolio lenders and money market lend to the U.S. firm or investor, not abroad. The structural problems mentioned above led to (1) increased direct investment to avoid the instabilities of trade in goods and (2) U.S. borrowing in host countries (France, Canada, Australia) to finance foreign acquisitions, instead of borrowing at home (thus leading to complaints about those countries paying for the acquisition of control over their economies by firms in the United States, Japan, or Germany). Sometimes they borrowed "Eurodollars", actually supplied to European money markets by other U.S. lenders. In any case, the multi-national, technical, foreign owner tended to supply know-how and ambition rather than goods or finances. Obviously, foreign ownership is not *basically* due to the absence of flexibility in the structure of international finance. But it is clear that the overvaluation of the U.S. dollar should be seen as a result not only of U.S. payments weakness, but also of an unusual period of acquisition of direct control of foreign enterprises. See the Appendix to Chapter 34 for more on foreign ownership.

Unrealistic and inflexible dollar values tended to spawn U.S. investment abroad and some withdrawal from trade.

■ THE TWO-TIER GOLD SYSTEM

By 1968, time had run out on the precarious gold-and-dollar standard. When the rush for gold by hoarders became a stampede which would have stripped Fort Knox of all its gold within a matter of weeks, the ten leading nations of the world met during March, 1968, in Washington and Stockholm. They suspended all gold payments from official central banks to the free market. Henceforth there was to be a two-tier system.

THE OFFICIAL TIER   In the official tier, gold payments are made only between governments, and always at the official IMF parities. Thus, within the Club of Ten, if Germany has an export surplus with the United States that is to be partially paid for in gold, each $35 million payment will involve the United States sending Germany (or, more likely, merely earmarking in the vaults of the New York Federal Reserve Bank) a million ounces of gold. Since the IMF parity of the mark is 27+ cents, or about 3.6 marks to the U.S. dollar, the million ounces of gold represent 3.6 million marks to the Germans.

Essentially, all the gold in the official reserves as of March, 1968, was frozen forever into reserves. None can ever go outside the Club of Ten and the hundred other nations that belong to the IMF.[16] No government in the Club is to buy gold from any government that ever deals with the free market in gold.[17]

---

[16] At first General de Gaulle tried to block the new system. But the events of 1968 (student riots and the general strike) so depleted France's gold reserves as to make her return to the fold.

[17] Newly mined gold from South Africa provides an unresolved borderline case. South Africa would like to be able to sell part of her output in the free market at prices *above* $35 (U.S.) an ounce, and to sell the remainder to the Club at that official price—getting the best of both possible worlds. The others oppose this, and the constitutional question is still unresolved as to whether South Africa can *by right* sell to the IMF and Club at $35 (U.S.) an ounce, particularly when the free-market price *dips below* this level.

THE FREE-MARKET TIER   Outside the IMF Club, gold has finally been completely demonetized. Its price is freely set by supply and demand, just like the price of copper, wheat, silver, or salt. Thus, in 1970 the few American gold mines sold their output at a price near that set by auction in London or Zurich. When you buy a wedding ring, your jeweler pays the $40 an ounce, or $42 or $36, that happens to be quoted at the time.

Hoarders in the Near East and India can hoard to their heart's content. French merchants and international Mafia operators, out to evade taxes, can hide gold in their wine cellars and Swiss bank vaults. Speculators, in countries where citizens are allowed to deal in gold, can hope to make capital gains if they are able to sell gold at a higher price than they paid for it. But note this: with the price floating above any official floors, speculation and hoarding are now two-way streets. You can make a bundle if you buy at $40 and sell at $45, but you can lose your shirt if you buy at $43 and have to sell at $36—or $33!

EVALUATION   How has the two-tier system worked? Up until 1970 it has been working surprisingly well. The fear that some small central bank would buy gold at the $35 official price and surreptitiously feed it to the free market, making a neat profit of, say, $6 ($41 — $35) an ounce, has proved to be exaggerated. For the first time in 15 years the international financial structure has been able to be completely indifferent to the vagaries of hoarders and the ups and downs in free-market gold prices.

The two-tier system works well, but it is only a halfway house, a stopgap arrangement in structural reform. The frozen and limited total of official gold would soon put a throttle on the expansion of total world trade were it not for the new plan adopted by the IMF to create "paper gold" in the form of Special Drawing Rights.

■ ALTERNATIVE PROPOSALS FOR REFORM

Before looking into the new plan for creation of paper gold, we should explore the main reforms currently being debated. The most important are (1) "massively increasing the official price of gold"; (2) complete demonetization of gold, ejecting it even from the official tier and replacing the Hume gold-flow adjustment mechanism with its stable exchange rates by a new system of "freely floating, completely flexible exchange rates"; (3) adopting a system of a "sliding or crawling peg," in which stable exchange rates are abandoned but in which within any year the change in parity is limited to, say, 1 or 2 per cent.

INCREASING THE PRICE OF GOLD   This proposal was associated with De Gaulle and his economic adviser Jacques Rueff, and with Sir Roy Harrod of Oxford. Increase the price of gold from $35 to $70 or $100 per ounce. Similarly, increase gold's price in terms of *all* other currencies. This massive "devaluation" of all currencies, being in balance, will result in no "depreciation" or "appreciation" of any currency relative to another. But at the stroke of a pen, the shortage of international liquidity will have disappeared.

What are we to think of this plan? Naturally the South Africans love it. So does the Soviet Union, the other principal gold-mining nation. So do the gold hoarders. So do those nations that were least cooperative in the 1960s in resisting the temptation to hoard gold officially. So do the speculators, lusting after a quick capital gain.

Self-interest aside, what are the plan's merits and demerits? For Rueff, an archconservative, the price of gold is to be raised once and for all, *and then mankind is to go back onto a rigid gold standard.* Gold is to serve as a *discipline* for governments. The moment a nation inflates, it will lose gold and be forced back into deflation. If capitalists disapprove of their government, they can hoard gold coins and take their money abroad, creating a run on the currency and bringing down the ruling government. (This happened repeatedly in the history of France and other countries during the capitalist era.)

For Sir Roy Harrod, a Keynesian expansionist, doubling or tripling the price of gold is favored for reasons diametrically *opposed* to those of Rueff. With one stroke of the pen, governments everywhere will be given their freedom to pursue *expansionary* policies for another quarter of a century. After that time, another stroke of the pen. . . .

Most experts regard gold as an anachronism. How absurd to waste resources digging gold out of the bowels of the earth, only to inter it back again in the central banks' vaults! And why adopt a plan that gives a windfall profit to South Africa, Russia, speculators, and private or official hoarders? But the even more important objection to reliance on a rise in the price of gold is this:

> Modern mixed economies will not go through the agony of deflating themselves, running the risk of mass unemployment and stagnation, merely to obey the rules of the automatic gold-standard game. And if the gold-standard game is *not* played according to its rules, small disequilibria will not be prevented from accumulating into major disequilibria with ultimate crisis and breakdown.

Even though the world will not revert to the automatic gold standard, it is a fact that official gold does exist and is an important part of official international reserves. Hence the new IMF reforms are able, as we shall see, to *build around* gold and *supplement* it with new reserve assets.

FREELY FLEXIBLE EXCHANGE RATES   This reform is at the other extreme from that of restoring the automatic gold standard. In effect, it proposes:

1.   Turn all exchange rates completely over to the free market, avoiding all official interventions.

2.   Forget about the balance of payments. *Let supply and demand intersect to produce whatever pattern of exchange rates will clear the market.*

3.   Rely on the development of a speculative market in foreign exchange which will offer importers and exporters the opportunity—at a price, of course, but under vigorous competition not necessarily a very high price—to "hedge" their international merchandise and capital transactions.[18]

---

[18] To ensure against the risk that the foreign exchange rate for marks will rise 10 per cent between now and the time my import of German dyestuffs arrives, I turn today to the

For the mechanics of how freely floating exchange rates work, the reader can refer back to Chapter 32's pages 776-782. The main point to emphasize is that now a country can be free to do anything it wishes domestically, letting the exchange rate move to adjust in consequence. Thus, if the United States wilfully inflates its domestic prices to double or quadruple previous levels, there is nothing to stop it. (But, of course, as Chapter 32's discussion of purchasing-power parity shows on page 778, the foreign exchange rate for the U.S. dollar—in terms of the mark or the currency of any other country which has kept its prices stable—will automatically *depreciate* to about a half or a quarter of its previous level, going from, say, 4 marks to a dollar down to 2 marks, or even 1.

It is precisely this *autonomy* of domestic policy under floating exchange rates which opponents criticize in flexible exchange rates. They claim that healthy hedging possibilities and fruitful international trade will be possible only if exchange rates *do not move chronically in one direction*—i.e., only if a nation does not chronically induce or countenance inflation. "But," these critics point out, "if, after all, the country is going to have to *desist* from chronic inflation, there has been no true escape from the disciplines of the gold standard in the end; and one might as well have the advantages from the beginning that come with the traditional *fixed* exchange rates."

They go on to argue, "Within the 10 provinces, we do not have floating exchange rates. That would hurt the intranational volume of trade and division of labor. So why give up stability of exchange rates internationally?"

How do the advocates of flexible exchange rates reply? First, they stress that within a country like Canada there is one central government, one central bank and money system, and one labor market in the sense that workers can migrate from a region of serious unemployment to one with high employment. All these features are lacking internationally.

---

forward market and buy marks 90 days ahead. Who sells them to me? Possibly a Canadian exporter who wants to play safe and know exactly how many dollars he's going to get for the computer he is shipping today to Germany, and for which he will be paid marks in 90 days. But even if export and import transactions in both directions don't balance out, some speculators with sporting blood will sell marks forward hoping to be able to buy them cheaper later. If speculators are overoptimistic, they may end up providing this hedging service even at a loss to themselves; or if risk taking is so irksome as to require a positive premium for hedging, that cost will be added onto the price of international goods and, to a degree, will lessen the volume of and gains from trade. The analysis of hedging and speculation in a market for wheat, as described in the Appendix of Chapter 20, cannot be confidently applied to foreign exchange markets. Speculation in foreign exchange is more in danger of being destabilizing, since there is no natural par of supply and demand set by crop conditions and basic human demands for wheat. Instead, when our dollar is weak, all the speculators will pounce on it and make it weaker; they will force Canada into depreciation and into internal inflation, and thereby the new proper level for our dollar will be permanently lower, rewarding the speculators for their bear raid. Some critics go on to argue that if Canadian authorities resist such raids by keeping a tight rein on the domestic money supply, price level, and NNP level, they are as much restrained by the balance of payments as under a stable exchange standard: so why give up advantages of fixed exchange rates if you are going to have, in any case, their disadvantages? The answer of course is that a "tight rein" is a matter of degree. The restraint of a fixed rate is more chafing than that of a flexible rate.

Second, advocates say that flexible exchange rates were never intended as a panacea. What they can do is make the effects of unavoidable creeping inflation and price rigidities in the *mixed economy a little more tolerable*. Advocates of flexible exchange rates still insist that the economy will function best only if chronic inflationary and deflationary gaps are avoided by proper macroeconomic policy.

CANADA'S AMBIVALENT FLEXIBLE-RATE POLICY   Let us briefly review Canada's own experience with flexible exchange rates. Between 1951 and 1962 and in the early 1970s, Canada was almost the only IMF member nation not adhering to the prescribed "pegged" exchange rates. Rather, for most of both periods, the external value of the Canadian dollar was determined solely by supply and demand. When the dollar was "turned loose", its value was about $1.10 Canadian to one U.S. dollar. But in a year, the strong demand of foreign *investors* pushed it down to 100 cents, and then to a "premium" (one U.S. dollar to *less* than 100 Canadian cents) where it stayed in the early 1960s. The story is told in Figure 32-2, p. 781.

Yet, the first Canadian experiment was not an unqualified success if judged by the arguments in favor of a flexible exchange rate which we have just reviewed. Canadian critics of the system reply that during the 1951-1962 period, Canada experienced at least five years of deflation, with serious unemployment in the last four of them. How, they ask, can it be claimed that flexible rates insulated the economy from fluctuations?

This question is a fair one. It reveals what foreign champions of flexible rates seem to forget: that both in the earlier period and recently, Canada did not go on to a flexible system solely because of fluctuations in export and import supply and demand, but because of the combination of such fluctuations with very large swings in both short- and long-term capital movements to and from the United States. Such swings invite currency speculation which may be more destabilizing than when the exchange rate is allowed to float freely.

For example, consider the effects of an investment boom in Alberta oil. United States companies and individuals may rush to obtain Canadian dollars to participate. This pushes up the value of the floating Canadian dollar, tending to slow down the capital movement a little. At the same time speculators, seeing the new premium on Canadian dollars and judging it to be short-lived, take advantage of the premium to buy *American* dollars, thus making a profit if and when the premium disappears. This sequence of speculation is stabilizing, tending to reverse the upward push, because the speculators are now offering Canadian dollars as keenly as investors are trying to obtain them.

In contrast with this example, when Canada is on a fixed exchange rate, the currency authorities have to guess whether the oil boom is here to stay or is going to fade out fast. While the boom is on, their Exchange Fund Account must accept foreign currency and offer Canadian dollars. They get these Canadian dollars by drawing on the Government's dollar balances which may have to be replenished by fiscal means or by borrowing (see Chapter 16). Listing these sources shows it is difficult to insulate the home economy from an inflow of foreign currency while trying to hold a fixed exchange rate. Furthermore, if the authorities adopt a domestic policy which raises interest rates in Canada, the additional capital inflow that comes to take advantage of these higher rates and tighter credit conditions makes the whole foreign-balance situation worse. Thus both the capital inflow and the speculative flows accompanying it bring Canada (like others on fixed rates) under pressure to repeg the Canadian dollar at a higher value. (The reader can show that if the whole cycle were caused by a sudden capital outflow or new spate of imports, Canada would be losing its supply of foreign currency demanded by those trying to sell their Canadian dollars and would then be under great pressure to devalue our dollar.)

Speculation can be fatal to a fixed currency. It may also force a flexible currency to be too flexible, to bob around and make ordinary international business fraught with the possibility of loss on irrelevant currency depreciations. But when the Canadian authorities decided in either period to adopt the flexible system, they were not so much hopeful of insulating the Canadian economy from such supply-and-demand-of-exchange effects as they were despairing of maintaining any particular fixed rate in the face of shifting long-run investment changes combined with speculative pressures, encouraged by official periodic fixed-rate revaluations.

To summarize: one reason Canada is not everywhere regarded as a cogent example in controversies about the merits of a floating exchange rate for dealing with payments fluctuations is that Canada's fluctuations are frequently caused by rapid changes in long-run and short-run capital movements, not by trends in merchandise or in invisibles.

More positively, Canada's experience shows that fears about speculation being destabilizing (that is, justifying the hopes of bulls or bears by being pushed farther and farther in one direction) are not serious enough for countries like Canada to worry about. Both fixed and flexible rates can be attacked by speculators. Canada's experience was that, so long as the government is prepared to accept the market's judgment of the value of the Canadian dollar, the flexible rate will not fluctuate unduly. It is the determination of a government to fix its rate at a certain level that attracts speculative bets that it will fail to do so; and sometimes the speculators win their bets.

Evidently, the desirability of accepting floating exchange rates is a thorny question. Problems of day-to-day stability and speculation loom large. The Canadian experience throws light on some questions, but the debate continues. Even if other nations believe that Canada did the right thing in allowing her rate to be flexible, the ineptness of her internal monetary policy during the late 1950s and early 1960s makes her example unattractive. Perhaps the current experience will provide a better test. And, of course, policy advisors everywhere wish to avoid the fallacy of composition: the swift assumption that what was good for Canada would be good for the world as a whole. Consequently, even those who believe in flexible rates have proposed compromises, such as that described immediately below.

**Crawling peg provides compromise between
floating and rigid exchange rates:**

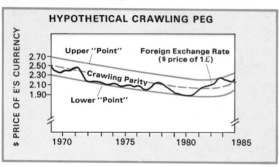

FIG. 35-2. Instead of fixed parity at $2.50, under this plan the parity can crawl downward or upward by 1 or 1½ per cent per year, achieving in a decade's time the 10 or 15 per cent needed to adjust for drifting apart of cost levels. Also at any one time the band between upper and lower "points," within which supply and demand can freely operate, are considerably widened. (Source: Figure 32-4, page 804.)

THE CRAWLING OR SLIDING PEG WITH WIDENED "GOLD POINTS"   This scheme, introduced in the Appendix to Chapter 32, provides a compromise between the inflexible exchange rates of the gold standard and Bretton Woods setup and a system of indefinitely floating exchange rates.

1. Within any one year the exchange-rate *parity* is to be permitted to move some maximum stipulated amount, say, 1 or 1½ per cent.

2. This slowly crawling parity level is to be surrounded by a *widened band,* within which supply and demand is free to set the actual exchange rate.

Even if foreseen, such a crawl in parity is not great enough to tempt an avalanche of speculation. But it produces enough flexibility to permit a 10 or 15 per cent adjustment of exchange rates over a decade! And that should be sufficient to compensate for the normal drifting apart of wage and price levels due to technological change, changing tastes, and differential degrees of wage-push inflation in the various mixed economies.

For the economics of the crawling peg, the reader can refer to Chapter 32's Appendix, particularly to Fig. 32-4, page 804. Part of that figure is reproduced here as Fig. 35-2. In this example, the dollar-pound parity begins at $2.50 in 1970. But now the exchange rate is no longer held within the $2.48–to–$2.52 band formerly set by the "gold points." Now the exchange rate can vary between $2.30 and $2.70 per pound. And next year, with parity moved[19] to, say, $2.45 by Britain's deficit, the range would be $2.25 to $2.65.

It is evident that academic opinion of the 1970s is virtually unanimous in favoring a move toward some measure of exchange-rate flexibility. And the practical men in government and the banks, impressed finally by the bitter experience with periodic international crises, have come privately to agree with this academic view.

---

[19] There are a variety of details proposed for the crawling peg. Thus, some would have the change be gradual within the year; some would permit the change to be determined by the governments involved; some would make the movement of the crawling peg to be determined by an automatic formula in terms of certain averages of previous months' deficits or surpluses in the balance of payments.

Thus the crawling peg seems to provide the most likely compromise that could be practically agreed upon for reform in the adjustment mechanisms of international trade.

However, "how to get from here (the old inflexible system) to there (a system with some flexibility)" is a conundrum no one has yet been able to solve.

■ SDRs AND PAPER GOLD

We conclude this discussion of current international problems with a description of the long-awaited plan for (1) augmenting official gold as international reserves by (2) the creation of a new reserve asset—the Special Drawing Rights, or SDRs, created by the International Monetary Fund. Because these SDRs will serve all the purposes of gold, they are usually called "paper gold."

The SDRs are set up by vote of the IMF members, subject to a veto by 15 per cent of the voting quotas. The exact amount newly created per year is determined by the Director General of the IMF, in consultation with the voting members. But the allocation of the new SDRs among the members is determined strictly in proportion to their quotas in the IMF. Thus, if in the years 1971-1973, $4 billion of new SDRs are to be created each year, the United States with its quota of 25 per cent will get $1,000 million annually of new paper gold to supplement its international reserves. Germany will get $240 million, the United Kingdom $480 million, Canada $150 million, and so forth.

> Thus, at long last the straitjacket of the happenstance of gold mining can be replaced by a rational international system whereby nations, through multilateral agreement, create the optimal amount of new international reserves—not too little so as to cause deflation, or too much so as to cause inflation.

Success of the system initiated in 1970 is not yet assured, but if it does evolve at all according to plan, the system of paper gold will represent a significant step forward.

It would be even more hopeful if the new SDR system could be combined with some degree of exchange-rate flexibility—e.g., the crawling peg. And, since the SDRs will not solve the problem of existing exchange-rate overvaluations and undervaluations, the new system should ideally be accompanied by an *initial realignment of major currency parities*—with the mark, the yen, and other *surplus* currencies *appreciating* relative to the *depreciation* of the dollar and other *overvalued currencies* subject to chronic balance-of-payments *deficits*. When all this is done, we can forget unofficial gold, letting it become the concern of dentists, jewelers, and smugglers.

SUMMARY

A. MODERN TRENDS AND INSTITUTIONS OF INTERNATIONAL FINANCE

■ 1 Expanded exports—as in World Wars I and II–will have multiplier expansionary effects on a country. If previously it had unemployment and excess capacity, the result will be more jobs and output. If previously it had inflationary pressures, the result will be an intensification of them. The beggar-my-neighbor policies of the depressed thirties, by which each nation vainly tries to export its unemployment abroad, are self-defeating.

■ 2 The International Bank, the International Monetary Fund, aid programs, Point Four assistance, the reciprocal-trade program for tariff reduction, the European Common Market—all these have been and are important factors in the postwar bid for more rational world trade.

■ 3 The first decade after World War II was the period of dollar shortage. The United States dollar was undervalued in the sense that the other countries of the world, disrupted by war and with high cost structures, were avid to buy from her more than she wanted to buy from them. The sizable devaluations abroad in 1949, plus the Marshall Plan and other U.S. aid programs, America's cold-war spending, and finally, the miraculous spurt of productivity in the Common Market and Japan—all brought dollar shortage to an end.

B. THREATENED BREAKDOWN OF THE INTERNATIONAL SYSTEM

■ 4 In the last decade a basic disequilibrium in America's balance of payments became evident: the United States' surplus on private current account simply was not large enough to offset (a) her substantial government defense and aid programs, and (b) the large volume of long-term foreign investment by United States firms seeking the high profits offered abroad in miracle-growth countries such as Canada. The testimony of this "basic deficit" was also shown by the more conventionally reported "official settlement" deficit shown in Fig. 35-1, which reveals growing distrust of the dollar.

■ 5 No single factor can account for the reversal of dollar shortage. Certainly a basic cause seems to be the more rapid rate of growth in productivity in Western Europe and Japan than in North America rather than any upswing in U.S. generosity or—until Vietnam!—domestic inflation. This "basic imbalance" in the annual international flows places important constraints on domestic growth and stabilization policies.

No single remedy for a chronic U.S. payment disequilibrium can be prescribed. Steps to improve the situation would include sharing by others of aid and military burdens, lessening of discriminations, programs designed to improve the United States' productivity and selling efficiency, better control over the cost-push pressures at home, and various other measures. Resort to protectionism and controls on foreign investment and trade would involve a sacrifice of economic and political advantage, and be inferior to a devaluation of her seemingly overvalued currency which would be a last desperate act of emergency. The recent increase in well-being abroad should be noted even if it means domestic adjustments (and even possibly a slight retardation in U.S. growth in real wages and consumer's surplus from international trade).

■ 6 These payment problems illustrate the task of all nations in devising a mix of reforms that will bring both internal and external balance.

C.   STRUCTURAL REFORM OF INTERNATIONAL FINANCE

■ 7 The gold drain of the United States long covered up (a) the basic weakness in a world of change (and in which mixed economies will not submit to deflation and inflation) of a dollar-and-gold standard system based on *fixed* exchange rates; (b) the growing disequilibrium of the (overvalued) U.S. dollar over 15 years, a fact of especial importance in view of the dollar's role as key currency; and (c) long-run liquidity shortage of reserves in a world where foreign trade grows at 7 or 8 per cent per year while gold from mines grows at barely 2 per cent (and part of this gold goes into non-monetary uses).

■ 8 The major structural reforms involve (a) a massive increase in gold price; (b) freely floating, flexible exchange rates set completely by supply and demand; and (c) some version of a "crawling peg," providing limited flexibility of parity in any year, but necessary long-run flexibility. (Usually widened "gold points" are proposed as part of the crawling peg.)

■ 9 The two-tier system of gold, plus the introduction of paper gold in the form of Special Drawing Rights by the IMF, provide transition reforms. Coupled with initial parity realignments and perhaps with some crawling peg, they would provide the world with a more rational and viable system.

QUESTIONS FOR DISCUSSION

1.   Describe analytically post-World War II changes in the position of the U.S. dollar.

2.   Contrast and compare the International Bank and the Monetary Fund.

3.   Draw up a list of what you consider our most important postwar economic problems. Which of them has external aspects?

4.   What effects can Canada expect from the European Common Market?

5.   "Not a single industry should be sacrificed in the name of the GATT program for realizing freer multilateral trade." Do you agree?

6.   Describe the extent of our postwar aid to the rest of the world compared to that of the United States and other countries. Should our "generosity" be as great as theirs?

7.   Contrast "dollar shortage" and "dollar glut." Diagnose and prescribe.

8.   Apply to an overvalued pound the reasonings used earlier for the U.S. dollar.

9.   Why would you expect an interest-rate equalization tax on all foreign long-term securities to help U.S. capital accounts and international deficit? As control programs on bank and corporate investing abroad begin to spring leaks, how might explicit taxing of foreign investment help the United States to buy the time needed to reattain equilibrium?

10.   Give pros and cons of flexible exchange rates, changing gold price, two-tier system.

11.   What do you understand the term "paper gold" to mean?

12. Review your understanding of the following concepts:

exports, foreign investment, and the multiplier

productivity growth abroad

International Bank and Fund aid programs

floating versus stable exchange rates

common market, customs union

overvaluation, undervaluation

GATT, the Kennedy Round

devaluation and gold's price

internal and external balance

international liquidity plans

dollar shortage and glut

crawling or sliding peg

chronic deficit

paper gold: SDRs

financial discipline

two-tier system

PART 6
CURRENT
ECONOMIC
PROBLEMS

36

THE THEORY OF GROWTH

. . . when you can measure what you are speaking about, and express it in numbers, you know something about it; when you cannot measure it, when you cannot express it in numbers, your knowledge is of a meager and unsatisfactory kind; it may be the beginning of knowledge, but you have scarcely, in your thoughts, advanced to the stage of science. . . . LORD KELVIN

In the final section of this book, we can mobilize the tools of economic analysis to show their relevance to the burning issues of our age. To theories of economic growth (Chapter 36). To the processes by which the less developed countries can better their economic well-being (Chapter 37). To the problems of growth and price stability in the advanced economies (Chapter 40).

As old problems get partially solved, new problems are forced into the social agenda. Chapter 38 deals with the stubborn problems of poverty and economic inequality. Chapter 39 faces up to the economic problems of cities, regions, and the polluted environment, phenomena of prime importance at home as well as abroad.

The key word in most economic discussions these days is "growth." Why did Germany and Japan grow faster than the other Western countries in the 1950s? Is the USSR growing as rapidly as it claims? Is it possible for it to grow as fast as a mixed enterprise system like ours? In overcrowded countries like India and Egypt, can the desperate effort to improve technology and to mechanize production overtake exploding population?

All the tools of economic analysis developed in this book are needed to shed light on such difficult and important social problems. This chapter will apply the *principles* of economic theory to the process of growth and development, in preparation for the next chapters' applications.[1]

STAGES OF HISTORY

Napoleon agreed with Voltaire that history is but "a fable agreed upon." It was long the fashion to regard economic development as a timetable. Dr. Spock can guess that a baby at so many weeks will begin to see things, and he can make predictions about when it will walk and talk. Often he may err, but *it is remarkable how predictable the stages of biological growth prove to be.* Scholars used to think economic history could be treated in the same way.

Friedrich List, in his 1841 *National System of Political Economy*, was one of the first to divide economic history into stages. Especially in Germany, this became a popular notion a century ago. A new group of scholars, called the Historical School, came near to saying: "Throw away fancy theories. Grub in the facts. Collect them. Sort and sift them. Let them tell their own story."

The first step for any scientist is indeed to maintain a respect for the facts. But alas, it is not the last. *The facts never tell their own story.* Truth, like beauty, is oft in the eye of the beholder. No two writers ever seem to be told the same fables of development by the accumulated almanacs of facts. Some, and they included Karl Marx (1818-1883), saw in history a one-way evolution:

PRIMITIVE CULTURE   First, there were marauding hunters and self-sufficient tribal families cultivating crops. (Supposedly, they still survive in some isolated jungles.)

FEUDALISM   Gradually, as elbow room began to be scarce, the primitive economy was succeeded by feudalism. In the Middle Ages, a settled chain of command from nobility down to serf governed all economic and social life.

CAPITALISM   Whether or not one thought the Middle Ages idyllic, feudalism in its turn was brought to an end when the periods of the Renaissance and Reformation ushered in the commercial and industrial revolutions. Peasants were alienated from the soil and forced into the cities as a proletariat. Rivers were dammed to harness water, and the invention of the steam engine enabled the energy of wood and coal to replace the energy of beast and man. The Calvinist ethic helped to create business-minded entrepreneurs. As if in a play, the curtain came down on feudalism, and mankind was supposedly ushered onto the stage of bourgeois, middle-class capitalism. (Of course, isolated countries like Japan were not expected to move from feudalism to capitalism in exactly the same time periods; but when their time came, the process could be expected to be qualitatively similar even if more compressed in duration.)

Self-satisfied historians of the Victorian age, like Macaulay or Herbert Spencer, looked upon the evolution of society as an ascent of man toward

---

[1] For a short course, this chapter can be skipped. Or skip the theoretical "Detailed Economic Analysis of Smith-Malthus" later in this chapter.

higher forms. But now that the more or less perfect state of Victorian capitalism had been reached, they thought evolution could have its final day of rest. All that remained was further progress toward removing tariffs and the few other governmental fiats still interfering with the *laissez-faire* market place. Spencer could contemplate with mathematical certainty the withering away of the state and the supremacy of free markets. Invention by science, better education of the masses, and individual initiative could be expected to produce steady gains in living standards in this best of all possible worlds. (In our time, Frederich Hayek in Freiburg and Milton Friedman in Chicago look back to the Victorian Whig society as a golden age, to be reattained by democratic dismantling of the welfare state.)

SOCIALISM AND COMMUNISM   Having eaten of the fruit of the tree of evolution, why should men think that the play of history has to be written in only three acts? In a country like Germany, which had never been imbued with the tradition of individual and business freedom, philosophers thought that capitalism, too, was but a passing stage, to be succeeded in its turn by state fascism or communism, just as it had succeeded dying feudalism. Marx and Engels wrote in *The Communist Manifesto*: "The modern bourgeois society has sprouted from the ruins of feudal society . . . The modern laborer . . . becomes a pauper . . . What the bourgeoisie therefore produces . . . are its own grave diggers. Its fall and the victory of the proletariat are equally inevitable."

■ FACT AND FICTION

Events rarely agree with fable.[2] Thus, the revolutions in France and Germany that Engels and Marx expected failed to materialize in the weeks, months, and years after their excited letters about them were written. And real wages, instead of falling or remaining constant in the decades since Marx's 1867 *Das Kapital*, turned out on statistical examination to have been rising dramatically under industrial capitalism. Even the rate of profit stubbornly refused to follow the rate of decline predicted for it and instead wanders without any strong trend.

It is true that *around the turn of the century there seemed to be a burgeoning of monopolies in advanced economies.* But it turned out that even the most capitalistic democracy, the United States, could and did produce antitrust legislation to limit this development; and study of the statistics of concentration of market shares among a few big oligopolists suggests that monopolistic concentration was less at mid-century than it was at the beginning. It is true that the Great Depression of the 1930s was one of the worst the capitalistic system has ever known; but it is also true that a mixed economic system subsequently re-

---

[2] M. I. Rostovtzeff, *Social and Economic History of the Roman Empire* (Oxford University Press, New York, 1926), showed that an elaborate system of international markets and trade in nonluxury goods existed long before the Middle Ages. Compound interest appears on Babylonian cuneiform tablets, and some nations are repeating in the 1970s the worst errors of historic mercantilism. Neither progress nor perpetual oscillation correctly portrays the richness of economic history.

placed rugged individualism and *laissez-faire*. The mixed economy introduced fiscal and monetary policies to moderate business cycles and control chronic slumps. We live in a world no prophet ever predicted! Mid-century miracle? What has been the single most surprising economic development of the mid-twentieth century?

Rapid progress under communism? No, in that few experts in 1950 expected the Soviet Union and the Eastern European planned economies to do much better or worse than they have since performed.

Reversion to beneficent *laissez-faire* and free private enterprise? Certainly not that, since except for the usual ebb and flow of political elections, there has been no trend back to the Victorian condition. When a Conservative party in Britain, Norway or Australia ousts a so-called "socialist" regime, most of the apparatus of a mixed economy is retained. When a Trudeau or Pearson succeeds a Diefenbaker or a Nixon succeeds a Johnson, only marginal changes in the national *Zeitgeist* emerge. The single most surprising development of our age has been the unpredicted vigor of the modern mixed economy. The miracles of sustained growth in production and living standards have taken place in the second level countries—Japan, Germany, Italy, France, Scandinavia, Western Europe generally—rather than in the most advanced countries like the United States and Canada or in the less developed countries of Latin America and Asia.

Social prophets of our day such as Schumpeter and Toynbee, to say nothing of the earlier Veblen or Spengler, thought of the mixed economy as "capitalism in an oxygen tent." But the growth experience of the years 1950-1970 revealed that a market economy enriched by government planning and macroeconomic control could perform favorably in comparison to past epochs of both capitalist and communist development.

We are thus warned to place limited confidence in the allegedly scientific proofs that one stage in history must inevitably be succeeded by a particular next stage. When Nikita Krushchev said to an American audience, "We will bury you . . . your grandchildren will be communists," he was repeating what is taught in elementary Russian economics textbooks. (WARNING: Critics of Russia should not make a similar mistake about immutable timetables of development. It may involve wishful thinking to argue, as some scholars have done: "True, the U.S.S.R. is now showing a faster percentage rate of growth than the United States or Canada. But wait until she becomes as mature as we; then she'll *have* to slow down!" Right-wing determinism is as poorly founded as left-wing.)

This sketch of the development of a mixed economy is all too brief, but it represents a fair summary of economic history as presented by Western historians. Because it is completely rejected by Communist writers, Voltaire and Napoleon were wrong: apparently "history is a fable *not* agreed upon." Let us now turn to various economic models which can help us to understand history rather than to compress it into neat explanations that pretend to predict the future with certainty. Our task is to understand the actual development of wages and profits, of labor and capital, and of national product.

■ THE "MAGNIFICENT DYNAMICS" OF SMITH AND MALTHUS

In *The Wealth of Nations* (1776), Adam Smith wrote a handbook of economic development. He preached the great efficiency that comes from specialization, division of labor, and exchange. He stressed the need to remove the blundering hand of mercantilistic governments; to cultivate attitudes of honesty, zeal, and thriftiness; to unleash the competitive profit motive, which would—as if led by an Invisible Hand—achieve the maximum well-being of all.

LABOR THEORY OF VALUE IN A GOLDEN AGE   Smith had also a theory of dynamic development. He and Malthus began with a hypothetical golden age—"that original state of things, which precedes both the appropriation of land and the accumulation of stock"—when labor alone counted, when land was freely available to all, and before the use of capital had begun. What determined pricing and distribution in this simple and timeless state? Answer: The labor theory of value.

To see this, consider Smith's famous case of deer and beaver. Suppose 2 hours of hunting yields 1 deer; or 4 hours yields 1 beaver. Then the price ratio between deer and beaver will be set by comparative labor time alone: the price of 1 beaver will equal 2 deer. Why 2 deer per beaver? Because the price ratio can be computed in necessary labor time as 4 hours (of sweaty work)/2 hours (of sweaty work). This determination of price by labor cost alone would apply no matter how many goods there were; and it would be enforced in any primitive market by having hunters shift from one good to the other if ever that other good's price got out of line and offered a profit advantage. It is still true that supply and demand is operating in this golden age; but the situation is so simple that we do not need elaborate *dd* and *ss* curves. The long-run *ss* curves for the different goods are simple horizontal lines at the stated labor costs; so long as there is enough demand to have the goods produced at all, labor costs will be determining. (NOTE: Demand is still there in the background; thus, if it would cost 10 hours to hunt a skunk, and yet nobody received any utility from skunks, skunks would not be hunted and would not be bought and sold at a price of 10 hours, or of 5 deer.)

POPULATION GROWTH   Now consider Smith-Malthus dynamics. Life is pleasant in the golden age. Babies are born, and the population doubles about every 25 years. Since there is plenty of land, people move west and spill over onto more acres. National output exactly doubles as population doubles. Price ratios of deer and beaver remain exactly as before. What about real wages? Real wages still get all the national income, there being as yet no subtractions for land rent or interest on capital. What is the real wage per hour? So long as land can expand proportionally to the expansion of labor, the law of diminishing returns cannot come into operation. The wage rate per hour remains at one-half deer or at one-fourth beaver, as determined by labor productivity.

That would be the end of the story, unless some clever inventor found a new way of doing in 1 hour what used to take 2 hours. This would raise the national product per capita. Such a balanced improvement would leave the price ratio of beaver to deer unchanged; but it would double the real wage rate.[3]

SCARCE LAND AND DIMINISHING RETURNS   Even had golden ages ever existed, they could not have lasted once all land became fully populated. As we saw in Chapter 2, Malthus pointed to this flaw in the happily expanding economy. Once the frontier of virgin land disappears, new laborers begin to crowd onto existing cultivated soils. For the first time, private property in land springs up; now land is scarce, and a rent is charged to ration it.

Growth does take place in this classical world of Smith-Malthus following on the golden age. Population grows, and so does national product. But product cannot grow proportionately to labor. Why? *Because with new laborers added to fixed land, each worker now has less land to work with.* Naturally, therefore, the law of diminishing returns (of Chapters 2 and 26) comes into operation. The increasing labor-land and decreasing output-land ratios mean a declining contribution of each last (or marginal) worker to product, and hence declining real wage rates.

As David Ricardo, a later classical economist, pointed out:

> A conflict of interests arises between classes. More babies mean lower per capita incomes and lower wage rates; lower wage rates mean higher rent rates per acre of land. Landlords gain as labor loses. This is why Carlyle criticized economics as the "dismal science."

To understand the brute fact of economic inequality, we have to jettison the simple labor theory of value and study the effects of scarcity in the productive factors that labor needs access to.

PARADISE LOST AND REGAINED   How bad can things get? Gloomy Malthus thought, at least in his first edition of 1798, that the end of economic development could be only an equilibrium down at *the minimum level of subsistence.* Above

---

[3] The graphical production-possibility frontier of Chapter 2 can show all this. For a society with 100 hours of labor, the *p-p frontier* must now be drawn as a straight line going from the intercept on the vertical axis of the 50 deer producible with that much labor to the intercept on the horizontal axis of 25 beaver. The absolute slope of this *p-p frontier* would give the 2/1 price ratio prevailing at any point where both goods were being produced and consumed. (The marginal-utility and indifference-curve analysis of Chapter 21 and its Appendix would still be needed to tell *where* society ends up on the *p-p frontier.*)

A doubling of labor productivity in all industries would move the *p-p frontier* out in a parallel position so as to depict an exact doubling of national product. The interested reader can show that an invention which tripled the productivity of beaver hunting, while only doubling that of deer hunting, would flatten the shifted-out curve, changing the price ratio from 2/1 (equals 4 hours per beaver ÷ 2 hours per deer) to 4/3 (equals 4/3 hours per beaver ÷ 1 hour per deer). Now the real wage rate has risen, but unequally when computed in terms of the different goods: the real wage has tripled in terms of beaver, but only doubled in terms of deer; lovers of fur coats have gained more than lovers of venison. (Note: Suppose laborers are not homogeneous. If men are *everywhere* twice as productive as women, Marx and Ricardo would redefine socially necessary labor units, treating 1 man as 2 basic labor units, etc. But if men are *unequally* superior to women in different jobs—being twice as productive in beaver, thrice as productive in deer, and half as productive in potatoes—the labor theory of value breaks down: now we must know the demand condition of non-Marxian economics to determine equilibrium prices.)

this subsistence wage, population would continue to grow; below it, population would die off; only at this level could there be lasting equilibrium (as we saw in earlier discussion of Malthus).

Biological fecundity was a fact of nature; diminishing returns was a fact of nature. Only sentimentalists could refuse to face the sad facts of life prevailing once man had left the golden Garden of Eden. It is for precisely these reasons that Adam Smith had earlier said: Lucky is a nation that is growing rapidly, for it has not yet made its sad rendezvous with its destined equilibrium at the minimum of subsistence. Sad is that nation which has reached the stationary equilibrium of the subsistence level, where deaths just cancel out births.

What did Malthus forget, or at least underestimate? He failed to realize how technical innovation could intervene—not to *repeal* the law of diminishing returns, but to *more than offset* it. He stood at the brink of a new century and failed to anticipate that the succeeding two centuries would show the greatest scientific gains history has ever recorded.

DETAILED ECONOMIC ANALYSIS OF SMITH-MALTHUS

To understand the world's population problem for the next centuries—and the problems of India, Indonesia, and China in the next two decades—we must master the above classical model, which may have more *future* relevance than it has had for us since Malthus' time. As a bonus, the same graphical tools will apply when we investigate the role of capital formation as a factor of growth for Germany, Japan, Canada, the United States, and the less developed countries of the world.

Table 36-1 and Fig. 36-1 show succinctly how the tendency of population to grow when the wage is above the level of minimum of subsistence will (1) end the golden age of abundant and free land, and (2) lead to an economic

Diminishing returns from population growth ends classical development:

RELATION OF OUTPUT TO LABOR AND LAND					
	(1) ACRES OF LAND	(2) MAN-DAYS OF LABOR	(3) OUTPUT OF FOOD	(4) WAGE IN FOOD PER DAY	(5) LABOR'S SHARE OF NNP, %	(6) RENT IN FOOD PER ACRE
A	1,000	500	4,000	8	100	0
		501	4,008			
A'	1,000	1,000	8,000	8	100	0
		1,001	8,008			
B	1,000	3,000	20,000	5	75	5
		3,001	20,005			
E	1,000	6,000	33,600	4.2	75	8.4
		6,001	33,604.2			
Z	1,000	8,000	39,000	0	0	39
		8,001	39,000			

TABLE 36-1. Higher labor-land density reduces output per man, lowers the marginal-product wage, and hence raises rent per acre.

growth path that approaches a stationary equilibrium at the minimum of subsistence.

Table 36-1 shows the decline in wage rate when the fixity of land keeps output from growing as fast as labor. Column (1) shows unchanged land. Column (2) shows growing labor. Column (3) shows the resulting growth in output, which, because of the fixity of land, is *less* than proportional to labor growth. All the remaining information can be computed from these production-function data alone.

To get the declining wage rate of Column (4), we have to repeat Chapter 26's calculation of what the *last* worker *adds* to total product. (Recall that this is termed the marginal-physical-product of each of the identical workers.) Let us add one worker to 1,000 existing workers at A'. Note that output rises from $Q = 8,000$ to $Q = 8,008$ units. This gives extra product per extra worker of 8; so the marginal-product and real wage rate must then be 8 units of output per worker. Check that the extra product and wage falls to 5.0 at B, to 4.2 at E, and finally to zero at Z, where land is so overcrowded as to be unable to produce any extra output regardless of added labor.

To get the relative share of labor in the net national product, we multiply the wage rate of each worker by the number of workers. Then we divide this total wage bill, wL, by total NNP, Q. Note that labor's share in Column (5) soon falls from 100 per cent of NNP to 75 per cent, and ultimately down to 0 per cent. Who gets the remaining share? By our assumption that there is no capital to clutter up the labor-and-land model, all other returns must go for land rent. With total acres unchanged, we simply divide up land's calculated share of total output by the fixed number of acres. Obviously, the rent per acre must therefore *rise* in Column (6) as the wage rate *falls* in Column (4), just as David Ricardo warned.

■ GRAPH OF MALTHUSIAN DEVELOPMENT

Figure 36-1 depicts all this. In Fig. 36-1(a), we see the wage rate declining as the law of diminishing returns pushes labor's marginal productivity downward. What keeps the wage from falling down to zero on this *dd* demand curve for labor? Actually, it stops falling where *dd* intersects the *ss* horizontal supply curve set by the minimum wage at which people can subsist and just barely reproduce their numbers. The Malthusian equilibrium at E is a gloomy one, anything but golden.

Gloomy or not, it does represent a *stable* equilibrium. Test it. Let a plague temporarily reduce numbers, moving us to the left at E. Real wages then become high (as they actually did after the Great Plague of 1665), standing at a point on the *dd* curve above E. But the system cannot stay there. With wages high enough to cause population to grow, we again move gradually back toward the equilibrium at E, as indicated by the converging arrows. (Show that a temporary growth of population beyond E, as used to result from an unusual run of good harvests, will mean a wage rate so much below subsistence as to kill people off until the arrow moves us up *dd* back to E.)

Figure 36-1(b) shows that the rent rate per acre rises as the wage rate per hour falls. On what may be called "the factor-price frontier" (shown as *ff*),

Population grows until Malthus subsistence state is reached:

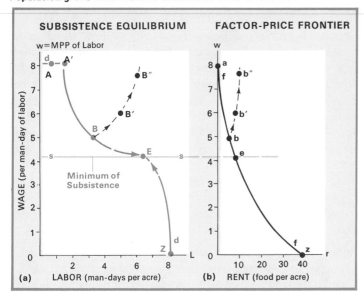

FIG. 36-1. Population growth moves us from the golden age of *A*, *A'*, and *a* down the diminishing-returns marginal-product curve *dd*, to the Malthusian equilibrium at intersection with *ss* supply curve of subsistence wage. The fall in real wage rate from *a* to *b* to *e* implies rising rent rates along the "factor-price frontier" *ff*. Because inventions shift *dd* and *ff* upward and rightward, historically the real wage rose from *B* to *B'* to *B"* levels, with rent rising from *b* to *b'* to *b"*.

landlords are seen to be better off at the high-rent Malthusian subsistence equilibrium *e* than they were in the earlier golden age at *a*. No wonder some landlords greeted with joy the introduction of the white potato, which enabled people to live on cheaper calories, and hence in effect lowered the old *ss* subsistence curve and raised equilibrium rents. And no wonder some few landlords regarded the spreading of birth-control information as a threat to their own standards of living. One man's slavery is another man's comfort.

The Ricardians actually exaggerated the conflict of class interest. While population growth might imply higher rent per acre, they were wrong to think it had to imply a larger *percentage share* of NNP going to land. Note in Column (5) of Table 36-1 that labor keeps getting 75 per cent of the total, although the wage rate drops from *B* to *E* and the rent rises from *b* to *e*.[4]

---

[4] Very little is known about what fraction of NNP is pure land rent. One reason is that statisticians are unable to disentangle rent from profit and interest in the accounts of the major land-using companies, or from any other incomes in the accounts of many farmers. Nor are we certain whether we would expect the fraction to rise or fall over time with economic growth, once we know that real wages are also rising in accordance with the development of new inventions and the rise in population. It is obvious that when the Canadian prairies were opened to settlement, rent incomes must have gone up—but did they rise as fast as the labor incomes of the new settlers? Colin Clark's estimates for various countries suggest that all were able to substitute capital and labor for scarce land; and important new estimates by Edward Denison imply that while land accounted for 9 per cent of American product in the 1900s, it accounts for only 3 per cent today. However, high scarcity rents of valuable lands, mines, and forests still exist, and still create incentives for man to "invent his way" to supplying final products from raw materials drawn from cheaper and more plentiful sources. Thus Canadian oilfields and forests yield nylon and rayon in place of the scarce mulberry-leaf and silkworm needed to grow silk in Japan. See the studies by D. Walters and E. Denison cited on page 1007, and the earlier, pioneering investigation by Colin Clark, *The Conditions of Economic Progress*, 3rd ed., (Macmillan, London, 1957).

■ END OF THE LABOR THEORY OF VALUE

The simple labor theory of value, which said that the price ratios of goods can be predicted from labor costs alone, independently of the utilities which bring out a demand for the goods, thus had to be dropped to account for the facts of land scarcity. Costs of production now include rent as well as wage payments. Two goods, like food and clothing, may now have equal labor costs per unit, but if food requires more land cost per unit than does clothing, they will no longer sell on a one-to-one basis.

Worse than that, from the standpoint of an advocate hankering for a labor theory of value, suppose that people in a capitalistic or socialistic state shift their demand toward producing more food and less clothing. This must make the price of food *rise* relative to that of clothing. Why? Because food requires more land per worker than does clothing. Hence, the fixed land becomes more scarce when people want more of the product that is "land-intensive," thus bidding up rent at the expense of wages.

> Under neither socialism nor capitalism can we succeed in predicting commodity prices from labor requirements alone, taking no account of the pattern of tastes and demand and its effects on scarcity of nonlabor factors.[5]

What about labor's right to *all* the product? Labor is the only input that is human and can sweat, laugh, cry, and pray. True. Yet, even though dirt cannot sweat or cry, it does contribute toward the growing of potatoes, and needs to be economized in the good society.

One who wants to make a logical case for labor's being "exploited" should not handicap himself by a simple labor theory of value. If his philosophy or that of the state he lives in dictates it, he may challenge the *title* to land of those who call themselves landlords and their special *right* to rents. He may claim that only the peasants have a valid title to the land and to rent, or that only the state does. Who receives rents is an ethical or legal problem. But whatever its solution, rational use of land does require that a rent cost be charged the consumers who buy its products and the factors that are best fitted to work with it. (Recall the Appendix to Chapter 31 on efficient socialist pricing.)

■ TECHNICAL ADVANCE AND CLASSICAL GROWTH THEORY

As mentioned, real wages have risen historically, not fallen. Population has not stabilized. Land rents per acre have risen surprisingly little and, relative to

---

[5] Footnote 3 pointed out that, in the golden age of free land, society's production-possibility schedule was a straight line with slope determined by labor productivities alone. Now with land scarce and more important in food than in clothing production, the production-possibility schedule is bowed out for the reasons explained in Chapter 2's discussion of the law of increasing (relative) cost. (Cf. also Appendix to Chapter 26, question 4.) The slope of the production-possibility frontier which determines the competitive price ratio now depends on where people's demand leaves us. (It can be shown that Ricardians erred in thinking they could "get rid of land as a complicating factor" by going out to "the external margin" of poor, no-rent land upon which production was so low that all its costs would have to go to labor alone.)

other factor-prices, have actually declined. It is evident that life has not consisted of a movement down an unchanged factor-price frontier or marginal-
product curve. Inventions of science, of engineering, and of managerial practice
have *shifted* the curves of Fig. 36-1 rightward and upward. The black lines of
progress—*BB′B″* and *bb′b″*—show the actual course of history; the reader may
draw on his copy of Fig. 36-1 the shifted *dd* and factor-price frontiers that
correspond to *B′* or *B″* and to *b′* or *bb″*. Such shifts have more than won the
race with diminishing returns, making the Malthusian equilibrium-point of
subsistence unrealistic in Western economies.

Not all inventions are *equally* favorable to labor and land. Thus, inventions which help to drain swamps or to grow more food on the same acres of
land might help wages more than they help rents. Some economists would call
these "land-saving inventions." In contrast, any inventions that tended to raise
rents more than wages, thereby tending to increase landlords' share of NNP,
might be called "labor-saving inventions." In between would be the case of
inventions that raised both factor returns by the same percentage, leaving
relative shares of NNP unchanged: these might be called "neutral inventions."
In the history of the West, inventions have appeared to be land-saving on
balance; but few inventions have been so land-saving as actually to lower rents
absolutely along with lowering them relative to wages.

The ghost of Carlyle should be relieved to know that economics, after all,
has not been a dismal science. It has been the impatient science of growth.

■ STAPLES, REGIONS, AND ECONOMIC GROWTH

So far we have stressed the classical preoccupation with scarce land. But classical economists based their theories chiefly on one-use land of varying qualities
on which either it paid to grow "corn" (wheat) or it paid to abandon it. This
was true even of classical authorities like Lord Durham's advisor and confi-
dant, Gibbon Wakefield, who was much involved in land settlement schemes
in the British colonies, or the earlier Colonel Torrens, an English monetary
expert who did much to devise the land-registry system now used in the Western provinces and Australia. They neglected the fact that some land may earn
a high rent under one use, but be valueless under another; Canadian forests,
for example, were valueless when early arrivals sought only fish, rose in value
under the fur trade, were declared a nuisance and avoided by those seeking
their fortune in agriculture, only to come back into their own again in the
lumber and pulp eras of recent history.

It was the particular contribution of Toronto's later economic historian
Harold A. Innis to point out that the course of Canadian economic development
depended on these successive demands for the harvest of Canadian resources.
Each of them in turn dominated the growth and expansion of the economy,
shaping the transportation network and pattern of settlement. Further, their
successive importance as "staples," as Innis called them, depended on technological change and tastes, usually in markets remote from Canada. The fur

trade, for example, depended partly on the existence in Europe of a felting process for using beaver fur in hats; the forest-products industry got its greatest boost from the growth of American literacy and the consequent demand for newsprint; waterpower development soared with the exploding world demand for aluminum, and so on.

EXPANSION VERSUS GROWTH   Recently a controversy has arisen about whether the undoubted successive emergence of "staples" had much to do with economic growth. Without going into the details of the criticisms of Innis and his followers (which, like all such arguments, is a dispute about what Innis "really meant"), it is now recognized that an important distinction must be made. The periods dominated by the production and export of a single staple all brought about "expansions" in the economy. They moved the marginal-product curve dd of Fig. 36-1 upward, when dd is interpreted as applying to the use of labor in a particular region. The workers in that region, if fixed in number, would now get a higher real wage. But if they were not fixed in number, the rise in real wages would draw in workers from other regions, *and immigrants from other countries* who previously earned less than the new real wage. Thus the region would "expand" as it produced the new staple. To the extent that the new workers came from abroad, the staple would cause the whole economy to "expand"; especially when it is remembered that the expansion would both require other workers to feed and clothe the new arrivals and motivate investment (with its multiplier effects) in new canals, railways, and schools.

The critics point out that such expansion is not the same as economic growth, because neither real wages nor NNP per person may be any higher after the staple is under full production than they were originally. All that may result is that the total population and work force will be larger. Professors Gordon and Chambers, for example, say that the wheat boom between 1901 and 1911 scarcely lifted the Canadian NNP per head but merely expanded the economy sideways across the continent. (Of course, the average immigrant was better off than he had been in Scotland or the Ukraine.)

On the other hand, all economists agree that, if the Canadian population remains mobile and immigration is small, the successive appearance of staples can set the stage for steady growth. As the value of the products of the various regions rises, Canadians move to wherever their marginal productivity is highest. The final effect is that the typical worker is "re-equipped" with more productive land; this is similar to re-equipping a worker, in a given location, with newly invented tools. Whether or not the appearance of a new staple product in the economy will lift the average output depends, therefore, on whether existing workers take the new jobs, thus raising their incomes, or whether new workers come in from abroad. In turn, this depends on whether Canadians are more mobile than potential immigrants. To the extent that a new staple product raises productivity, the staple approach to economic history in countries of numerous regions can be interpreted as a special kind of theory of economic growth. It is, however, very close analytically to more general theories that depend on giving a fixed number of workers an increased amount of capital to work with, such as the models next discussed.[6]

■ RICARDO-MARX-SOLOW MODELS OF CAPITAL ACCUMULATION

In the remainder of this chapter, we shall survey the more important model of capital and labor, pushing land and regional differences to the side as being less important for much of the developed part of the world. We can now use exactly the same tools.

> *Basic assumption of capital-labor model:* One factor grows relative to another. Now population will be regarded primarily as a noneconomic variable, being stationary (or growing slowly for sociological reasons). Accumulation will make capital the varying factor. In an oversimplified model where output is produced by a relatively fixed and a relatively varying factor, the law of diminishing returns sets in. The return of the augmented factor falls; the return of the relatively scarce labor factor rises. In the absence of technical change, a stationary state of equilibrium will be approached.

NOTIONS OF CAPITAL   It is now capital,[7] written as K, that is the factor growing relative to labor, L. Capital goods consist of a great variety of things: machines of various kinds, plants and houses, tools, raw materials and goods in process (seed grain, growing wheat plants, harvested wheat, flour, dough, warm loaves, wrapped and delivered bread), and canned and frozen edibles. Society can sum the market values of these physical goods to get total wealth or total capital value; but it cannot command a million dollars of electric generators to transmute themselves into a million dollars of oil-refining equipment.

It is true, however, that as generators wear out, the resources which could have gone to replacing them can be shifted to turn out extra refining equipment; the financial counterpart of this physical alchemy is to have investors in the generator industry take the money funds accruing on account of depreciation there and transfer them over to finance extra investment in the equipment industry. Result: although the total balance sheet of money capital may show a practically unchanged total and although the national-income statistician shows only a cancellation of one kind of disinvestment against another kind of investment, still society has managed to change the physical composition of its capital without undergoing any change in current consumption of goods.

EFFECTS OF CAPITAL DEEPENING   What happens to per capita output when capital grows relative to labor? Recall what happened to output per acre when labor grew relative to land. Output there grew less than proportionately to the growth

---

[6] The important difference is that new resources for new staples may be "free," not requiring much or any previous investment; whereas new capital goods invariably require previous saving and investment.

[7] Chapter 29 and Appendix discussed capital theory and problems of measuring it.

in the varying factor (labor), and its factor price (the wage) had to *fall*. A similar law of diminishing returns comes into operation in an over-simplified model whenever one factor (such as capital) grows faster than the other factor (such as labor) with all technical change absent:

1. Output will not grow in proportion to the growth in the capital stock.

2. The return to capital, the interest rate per annum—or what is the same thing if we rule out risk and technical change, the profit rate—will fall as capital deepens.

3. What happens to the wage rate now that each man works with more capital goods and with the more intricate capital goods the economy can now afford in the environment of a lower interest and profit rate? Just as the rent earned by relatively scarce land rose in Fig. 36-1, here the competitive wage return to relatively scarce labor will rise, as men become worth more to capitalists and meet with spirited bidding up of their market wage rates. (NOTE: Competition, not altruism, is at work.)

4. Higher wage rates and lower interest rates do *not* necessarily imply a higher percentage *share* for labor at the expense of the percentage share of capitalists. Why not? Because the increase in capital relative to labor might offset (or even more than offset) the decline in the interest rate and the rise in the real wage.[8]

5. Finally, since output (per capita or total) grew less than in proportion to the increase in capital (per capita or total), the capital-output ratio would rise in the absence of technical change (e.g., from capital value being 3 times annual NNP up to 3½ times).

Here is a final summary:

> Deepening of Capital (unchanged technology)
> Capital/labor up: interest or profit rate down: wage rate up: capital/output up

■ DEEPENING OF CAPITAL IN DIAGRAM FORM

Figure 36-2(a) and (b) needs no numerical table. It is like Fig. 36-1(a) and (b); but now capital is the relatively growing factor. Capital's amount per capita is given on the horizontal axis of (a), and its interest or profit return goes on the vertical axes. And now labor is the relatively fixed factor, and its wage goes on the horizontal axis of (b) just the way land rent did in Fig. 36-1(b).

In the absence of technical change, capital accumulation takes us down the *dd* curve from *A* to *B* and perhaps ultimately to the Ricardian equilibrium point *E* at which people feel it no longer pays them to save any per cent of their incomes for enhanced future consumption. On the factor-price frontier *ff* in

---

[8] Example: Let capital double from 1 million dollars to 2 million dollars, while labor stays at 30 men; let interest drop from 5 to 4 per cent, and the wage rise from $5,000 per year to $8,000. Total wage's return then continues to be 3 times that of capital's, each having risen by 60 per cent from their initial respective values of $150,000 and $50,000 per year.

Accumulation of capital raises output and wage, tends to depress interest rate:

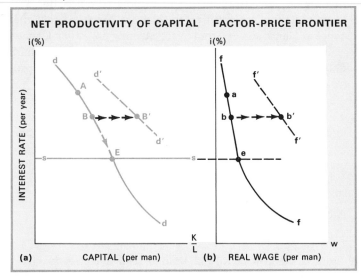

FIG. 36-2. Adding more and a greater variety of capital goods to fixed labor will, in the absence of technical change, add less and less to total product, causing interest rate earned to fall along dd from B to E, which is the Ricardian equilibrium point at which saving will cease. Along ff, fall in interest rate from b to e must raise the real wage earnable from labor's higher productivity.

Historically, technical innovation has shifted dd and ff rightward just about fast enough to offset diminishing returns and to keep the interest and profit rate almost unchanged, as shown by horizontal arrows from B to B' and b to b'.

Fig. 36-2(b), society can successively be at a; or at b with the higher wage rate and lower interest rate that are implied by an augmented capital stock (more machines available of every kind per man); or at e with a still higher capital-output and capital-labor ratio. The earlier literary summary of the effects of capital deepening is verified by these graphs.

TECHNICAL PROGRESS AND WAGES

Now let us reintroduce improving technology. This will shift the dd and ff curves outward, for example, to $d'd'$ and $f'f'$. Instead of moving from B down to E, society may find that diminishing returns are offset; and the economy might in actual historical fact move from B to B', negating or concealing the Ricardo-Marx law of the declining rate of profit. Note in Fig. 36-2(b) that the real wage rate must definitely rise, with or without technical improvements, so long as the profit rate stays the same or falls.[9]

An alternative theory would ascribe the rise of wages under capitalism to (1) trade-union pressure, (2) government regulation of monopoly, and (3) interventions of a welfare and regulatory kind by democratic governments reacting to militant political pressures from the masses. This cannot be rejected as without substance, for we have seen throughout this book that government actions do have consequences for both good and evil. But the magnitude and pattern of the rise in real wages in this last century have been such as to cast doubt on labor union or political action as an important part of the explanation. Thus,

---

[9] Indeed, we shall see later in the chapter that, unless an invention is so "labor-saving" as to raise the profit rate enormously, it must definitely boost the real wage rate.

real wages rose strongly in North America after World War I; yet unions were not strong, government intervention in production or income redistribution was minor, and monopoly was certainly not suppressed. Neither can it be said that *changes* in the importance of land and its rent were striking in either Canada or the United States. Similarly, Japan and West Germany have shown sharp growth in labor productivity, and this at times when government seemed pro-business rather than pro-labor.

With the advance of technology and the piling up of a larger stock of capital goods, it would take a veritable miracle (or tens of millions of immigrants) to keep real wages of men from being bid ever higher with each passing decade. Who fails to see that fails to understand economic history as it actually happened. Economic theories that do not fit these facts have had to be junked and replaced by others that do.

■ THE APPROXIMATE FACTS OF MODERN DEVELOPMENT

Let us summarize our theoretical researches.

> So far, we have studied the crucial role of limited land and growing labor in economic progress. Then we passed from the Smith-Malthus world to one that studied the role in economic growth of capital accumulation relative to labor. Last, but far from least, we stressed the factor of technological change and innovation. A look at the facts will show why present-day economists think that scientific and engineering progress has been quantitatively the single most important factor for growth in the advanced countries.

Thanks to two generations of economists and statisticians, we can formulate certain general uniformities of economic development. In Canada, data have emerged from national-accounts investigations for the prewar Rowell-Sirois Royal Commission; from postwar studies by Firestone, Buckley, and Urquhart—all then connected with the Department of Trade and Commerce; from the (Gordon) Royal Commission on Canada's Economic Prospects; from studies by the Economic Council of Canada; and from steady search and consolidation in the Dominion Bureau of Statistics.[10] These sources have more or less kept pace with pioneering efforts by Simon Kuznets and colleagues working at New York's National Bureau of Economics Research; and with Colin Clark and Alec Cairncross, and many others in the United Kingdom. Few of these have been content only to gather statistics: *what* data is needed, and *how* they are to be defined can be decided only by the researcher's question. However, much of the earlier material used here has been taken from its original application and fitted into the model developed by MIT's Robert Solow.[11] The ratio chart of Fig. 36-3 shows the strong trends of Canadian economic development. Similar trends

---

[10] Most Canadian material, with sources, is now available in M. C. Urquhart and K. A. H. Buckley, *Historical Statistics of Canada*, (Macmillan, Toronto, 1965).

[11] R. M. Solow, "Technical Change and the Aggregate Production Function," *Review of Economics and Statistics*, vol. 39, 1957, pp. 312-320.

Economic growth reveals long-run regulations:

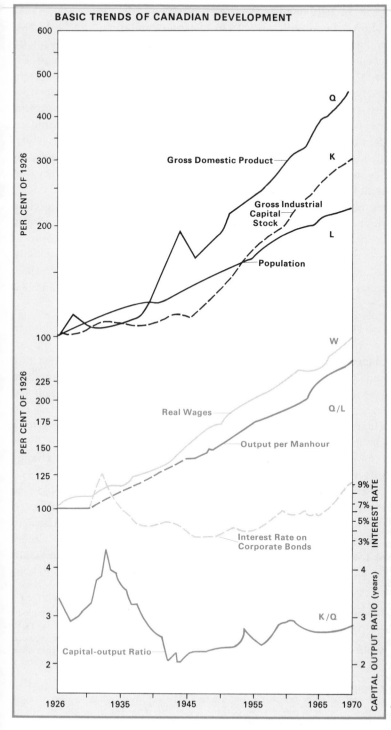

BASIC TRENDS OF CANADIAN DEVELOPMENT

FIG. 36-3. As output and capital growth outpace labor growth, the real wage and output per man-hour have risen together, leaving the relative shares of labor and capital about the same. The interest (or profit) rate displays no trend toward diminishing returns. Neither does the capital-output ratio show a steady rise. Hence the statical curves of Fig. 36-2 must have been shifted by technological advance and resource discovery. (Source: Hood and Scott, *Output, Labour and Capital in the Canadian Economy*; DBS; Economic Council of Canada, Staff Studies and *Annual Reviews*. See also J. E. La Tourette's article in the *Canadian Journal of Economics*, May 1970.)

have been found for the United States and for the advanced economies overseas. Figure 36-3 is crucially important. Linger over it.

The chart shows the growth since 1926 of labor, capital, and hence of output. Population has more than doubled in over 40 years of steady growth. (Taking into account shortening of the working week and changes in age distribution and in labor-force participation, the growth in total number of man-hours has been more modest.) While labor has about doubled, the stock of physical capital has increased to three times its 1926 size. Thus the substantial increase in capital per worker, the K/L ratio, does represent a significant amount of "capital deepening."

What about the growth in output? Has output grown less than in proportion to capital, as in the model that ignored technical change? No. The fact that the Q curve lies not between the two factor curves, but above the capital curve, shows that there must have been technical change in actual history. The close proximity of the output and capital curves shows that the capital-output ratio has not risen as in the simple deepening model; instead, as the K/Q curve in Fig. 36-3 shows, the capital-output ratio has remained remarkably constant, between 2.4 and 3.0 years since 1950 (i.e., a balance-sheet calculation of current value of all capital goods would show it to be equal to between 2.4 and 3.0 years of total product).[12]

RISING WAGES AND TRENDLESS PROFIT   The real wage has indeed risen steadily, in accordance with what one would expect from the growth in capital tools cooperating with labor, and from favorable technological trends. The interest rate —or, if we could get complete statistics, the rate of profit actually earned on more risky investments—does *not* show the decline that would be predicted from simple deepening of capital and diminishing returns. Interest rates and profit rates fluctuate much in the business cycle and war, but display no strong trend upward or downward for the whole period. Either by coincidence, or as the result of some economic mechanism that needs study, technological change has just about offset the effect of diminishing returns.[13]

As could be expected from the deepening of capital and from technological advance, output per manhour (Q/L) has risen steadily. Moreover—and this too represents a remarkable coincidence or the results of some economic mechanism needing study—the percentage growth in wage rates per hour has almost exactly matched the percentage growth in product per man-hour. This does not mean that labor has captured *all* the fruits of productivity advance. It means,

---

[12] This chart shows a tendency for the capital-output ratio to decline in the last part of the period. Much of such a decline in K/Q results from measuring the numerator so as to deflate out of it the relative rise that has taken place in capital-goods prices compared with other prices. It would be desirable for the present purpose to present a chart in which the components of K/Q are each measured in current dollars, or in current dollars deflated by a *common* price index, but Canadian data of this type are not available.

[13] Resist the temptation to think diminishing returns is not operating: if, instead of being hidden, it were actually not operating, the interest rate would have had to *rise* strongly as a result of technical change alone. (If we corrected interest rates for price changes—e.g., subtracting 1969's high percentage price rise from 1969's bond yields, as was done in earlier chapters—we would find the "real rate of interest or profit" to have been even steadier.)

rather, that labor must have kept about the *same share* of total product throughout the period, with property also earning approximately the same relative
share throughout the period. (A closer look at the chart suggests that there
might have been in the first half of the century a slow upward creep in the
share of labor in NNP, with property's share dropping accordingly; but part
of this might be the return to capital invested in human education and training.)

■ SIX BASIC TRENDS OF ECONOMIC DEVELOPMENT

These basic facts of economic history in the advanced nations can be summarized approximately by the following trends:

Trend 1 Population has grown, but at a much more modest rate than
has the capital stock, reflecting a "deepening of capital."

Trend 2 There has been a strong upward trend in real wage rates.

Trend 3 According to what is often called Bowley's Law, the share
of wages and salaries relative to the total return to property has shown
considerable constancy in the long run (but perhaps with slight signs of an
edging upward of labor's share).

Trend 4 Instead of observing a fall in the rate of interest or profit,
we actually observe their oscillation in the business cycle but no steady
upward or downward trend in this century (particularly if we deflate
interest and profit rates of their price-change components, and deal with
real rates).

Trend 5 Instead of observing a steady rise in the capital-output ratio
as the deepening of capital invokes the law of diminishing returns, we find
that the capital-output ratio has been approximately constant in this
century.

Trend 6 The ratio of saving to output has oscillated in the business
cycle—reaching about the same level at various high-employment phases of
the cycle. Or taking into account the approximate constancy of the capital-
output ratio, we can convert this approximate constancy of the ratio of
investment to income into the following: national product has generally
been growing at a roughly constant percentage rate per year.[14]

■ ANALYZING THE LAWS OF MOTION OF THE MIXED ECONOMY

While these are only approximate truths and not like the unrepealable laws of
physics, they portray fundamental facts about economic growth. How can we
explain them?

Trends 2 and 1—higher wage rates when capital deepens—fit nicely together with classical and neoclassical theories of production and distribution.

---

[14] Example: Although Fig. 36-3 shows K/Q about 2.7, hereafter it is assigned a convenient value of $3\frac{1}{3}$. Then Fig. 36-3's 3 per cent per annum growth of capital is possible
only if net capital formation is 10 per cent (equals $3\% \times 3\frac{1}{3}$) of output, as footnote 15
and the Appendix make clear.

Trend 3—Bowley's Law that the wage share is approximately constant—is an interesting coincidence that would be consistent with a *statical* neoclassical model only if it possessed a special kind of production function relating Q to L and K (what in advanced treatises is called the "Cobb-Douglas function," for which relative factor shares are constant).

Trends 4 and 5, however, warn us that neoclassical theory cannot hold in *static* form! A steady profit rate and a steady capital-output ratio are incompatible with the more basic law of diminishing returns under deepening of capital. We are forced, therefore, to introduce *technical innovations* into our statical neoclassical analysis to explain these dynamic facts. And a good thing it is that we are told to introduce technical change, since we have much independent evidence of the importance of science and engineering in the modern era.

> In terms of the analysis in Fig. 36-2, we are forced to introduce an outward shift in the *dd* and *ff* curves there to account for all five trends. Thus, the eastward move in Fig. 36-2(a) from B on *dd* to B' on *d'd'*, which corresponds to the eastward move in Fig. 36-2(b) from *b* to *b'*, will be consistent with trends 1 to 6. The tendency toward diminishing returns has just been offset by the technical shift, with interest remaining at the same horizontal level and the wage rate rising just as much as output per head. The capital-output ratio, which cannot easily be read in Fig. 36-2, must stay constant if the interest return on capital is to constitute the same relative share as before.[15]

Professor Solow, utilizing his own methods of analysis and corroborating the independent findings of numerous scholars at the U.S. National Bureau of Economic Research and elsewhere, has come up with the following remarkable conclusion for the United States:

> Less than half of the U.S. increase in productivity per capita and in real wages can be accounted for by the increase in capital itself. Considerably more than half of the increase in productivity seems to be attributable to technical change—to scientific and engineering advance, to industrial improvements, and to "know-how" of management methods and educational training of labor.

To a modified extent this finding also applies to Canada. But it needs careful interpretation.

First, although it is customary to measure and speak of the enhanced productivity of labor, there is no necessary implication that all of it (or most of it, or little of it) came from greater effort on the part of workers, or from more intensive conditions of sweat and strain; from more effort and education, or from more initiative and incentives of the human labor force. The facts do not point to any simple interpretation.

---

[15] As the Appendix shows, trends 3, 4, and 5 cannot be independent, since arithmetically the constancy of any two of the three magnitudes (iK/Q, i, K/Q) implies the constancy of the third.

Second, it is artificial to separate capital formation and technology completely. New techniques do tend to be *embodied* in new kinds of equipment. It is possible to imagine a stationary state—like the optimistic one of John Stuart Mill—in which there is no net saving and investment, but in which there is considerable technical progress as the depreciation charges of worn-out equipment finance their replacement by technically better equipment. Still, no one will deny that innovations can be introduced faster in a society which is performing *net* investment in addition to the gross investment corresponding to replacement. We all do learn from actually doing, and the society which gets to try out more new things will run that much ahead of the one which does little or no net saving.

■ ARE INVENTIONS LABOR-SAVING OR CAPITAL-SAVING?

Any invention that wins its way under competition must raise the real wage rate or the interest rate or both.[16]

However, some inventions will by their nature have a tendency to increase the relative share of labor; others to increase the relative share of capital and property generally; and others to affect both factors in about the same degree. This suggests the convenience of the following definition:

> *Definition:* An invention is called "labor-saving," "capital-saving," or "neutral," depending upon whether it tends to lower the relative share of labor, lower the relative share of property, or leave relative shares unchanged.

An extreme example of a labor-saving invention would be one that enabled unmanned machines to turn out robots that could do any of the manual and intellectual tasks of human labor. This would no doubt reduce the competitive wage drastically and could conceivably drop labor's share of NNP from its present level of about 75 to 80 per cent to below 50 per cent. An example of a capital-saving invention would be the case of a cheap computer that enabled firms to get along with much less inventory; or the invention of Kleenex tissue to replace durable handkerchiefs; or the invention of easily launched Telstar wave-reflecting satellites that made ocean cables unnecessary.[17] It is easy to

---

[16] In terms of Fig. 36-2's factor price frontier, *ff* must be shifted outward and upward or the invention will not succeed in the competitive market. Karl Marx erred in overlooking this. He promulgated the "law of the declining rate of profit [or interest rate]" alongside the "law of the immiserization of the working class [falling real wage rate]". Unless one invokes diminishing returns to land in the Malthus fashion—and Marx, who hated Malthus as an apologist for the rich and as a "plagiarist," paid insufficient attention to such phenomena—one has to give up at least one of the Marxian "laws."

[17] A capital-saving invention tends to tilt Fig. 36-2(a)'s productivity curve more toward the vertical and greater inelasticity, thereby tending to reduce the fruits of sacrificing current consumption and accumulating capital. A neutral technical change would be one that shifts Fig. 36-2's curves generally outward and upward. Advanced treatises deal with various distinct definitions of what is meant by labor-saving; the discussion here is left general so as not to be inconsistent with either the definition associated with J. R. Hicks or that different one associated with R. F. Harrod.

specify innumerable examples of capital-saving or labor-saving innovations and of neutral innovations in between.

The steady rise in wage rates is thought by many economists to *induce* employers to come up with labor-saving inventions. This tendency is often offered to help explain the failure of the profit-and-interest rate to fall as capital is accumulated. Marx more than a century ago had used such an explanation to account for the success of capitalists in resisting a rise in wages and in creating an industrial reserve army of the unemployed. Sir John Hicks of Oxford and Professor William Fellner of Yale have in our own day advanced similar arguments of an inherent bias toward labor-saving innovation.

Whatever the ultimate merits of such arguments, we must recognize that *any* invention which lowers cost of production can benefit the first competitor who introduces it. Furthermore, since the relative share of wages in total costs has been approximately constant for a century, any employer who is planning his research expenditures over the coming years will reasonably take this into account and will do well to spend now the same number of pennies on experimentation designed to save a dollar of future cost, whatever its source.[18]

We have seen that economic analysis can shed much light on the laws of motion of the mixed economy. Growth theory is still at the frontier of economics, and the experts are by no means in agreement on the mechanisms of explaining past and future paths of economic development. Some alternative theories are presented in the Appendix to this chapter. However, we are now armed to tackle in the next chapters the problems of growth in less developed economies and in advanced economies.

SUMMARY

■ 1 Many writers have tried to read into economic history a linear progression through inevitable stages, such as primitive economy, feudalism, capitalism, and some form of communism. The actual facts have not agreeably stuck to such timetables; in particular, the mixed economies that dominate the Western world came into being without the permission of social prophets.

---

[18] A theory of induced technical change can explain and unify all the six basic trends of economic development as follows: (1) Suppose any increase in capital relative to labor will raise labor's relative share. (2) Suppose that effort devoted to making each laborer the new equivalent of more than one laborer will go up when labor cost increases as the share of total costs. (3) Finally, assume that a constant fraction of income is always saved and invested and that labor population grows at a constant slow rate. Then it will follow that the system will ultimately grow in "golden-age balance": (a) Capital and output will grow at the same high rate with a constant K/Q ratio; (b) labor population will grow at a slower rate, but because of induced technological invention "labor in effective or efficiency units" will grow at precisely the same rate as capital and output; (c) now with Q, K, and "effective" L growing in balance, there will be no diminishing returns to capital and hence a constant interest rate and constant relative labor share; (d) finally, the real wage will grow because each worker is having his effectiveness raised by the induced technical change. QED: Rigorous proof of this was presented by several authors in the mid-1960s.

■ 2 The classical models of Smith and Malthus describe economic development in terms of fixed land and growing population. A simple labor theory of value prevails so long as land is superabundant; and output develops steadily with population in this golden age where labor gets all the national product.

■ 3 In the absence of technical change, increasing population ultimately exhausts the supply of free land. The resulting increase in population density invokes the law of diminishing returns: Fixity of land keeps output from growing proportionately to increased labor; with less and less of land to work with, each new man adds less and less extra product; the decline in labor's marginal-product means a decline in the competitively earned real wage. As each acre of land gets more and more labor to work with, its marginal-product and competitively earned rent go up. A fundamental factor-price frontier depicts how the rent rate must rise as the wage rate falls; but no one can predict what will happen to the *relative* shares of land and labor in national product.

■ 4 The Malthusian equilibrium comes when the wage has fallen to the subsistence level, below which the supply of labor will not reproduce itself. However, in realistic fact, technical change has kept economic development going by continually shifting the productivity curve of labor upward. How fast wages will rise must depend upon whether the technical changes are peculiarly labor-saving, or land-saving, or neutral.

■ 5 With land and resources and technology changing, either expansion or growth may follow from new staples becoming profitable in new regions. The result depends partly on factor mobility.

■ 6 The Ricardo-Marx-Solow model stresses the deepening of capital, i.e., the process of accumulating capital goods of varied types faster than the growth in population and labor hours. In the absence of technical change, an increase in capital per capita will not be matched by a proportional increase in output per capita because of diminishing returns. Hence, capital deepening lowers the interest rate (which is the same as the "profit rate" if risk is ignored), raises the real wage along the factor-price frontier, and raises the capital-output ratio.

■ 7 Historically, trends 1 and 2 on page 911—a rise in K/L and in w—are consistent with the *statical* model. Trend 3's approximate constancy of relative shares of labor and property—as measured by wL/Q and iK/Q, where $Q = wL + iK$—is not mandatory in the statical model, but is consistent with a special technical case of it (Cobb-Douglas). However, trends 4 and 5 —the failure of the interest and profit rate to fall and of the capital-output ratio to rise—show clearly that technical change must be brought into the analysis. Trend 6—approximate constancy of the investment/income ratio —taken together with the constancy of the capital-output ratio arithmetically implies a constant percentage growth of output per decade.

■ 8 The facts suggest the hypothesis that capital accumulation is second to technical change in explaining rising productivity. But innovation and investment interact, as new techniques get embodied in new equipment and people learn by trying new investments. Increasing productivity can be expressed conveniently in terms of labor productivity—i.e., Q/L—but this does not necessarily imply anything about the reasons for the rise.

■ 9 Inventions are defined as labor-saving, capital-saving, or neutral, depending upon whether they reduce labor's relative share of national product, reduce property's relative share, or leave shares unchanged. Experience with rising wage rates makes firms expect the trend to continue; whether or not they try for, and succeed in making, labor-saving inventions, firms will want to cut down on any cost items (labor, natural resources, capital costs).

Either by coincidence or by cancellation of offsetting trends, or as the result of economic mechanisms needing study,[19] the pace of invention has turned out to be just about enough to offset the effect of diminishing returns to capital on the interest and profit rate; and innovations have not turned out to be so labor-saving or capital-saving as to change much the relative shares of labor and property.

QUESTIONS FOR DISCUSSION

1. Does the mixed economy fit any of the timetables of history? Was it so hard to foresee?

2. "If the democratic state subsidizes science and invention, controls the business cycle, augments full-employment thrift by a budget surplus, and introduces sensible planning, we can expect growth that would astound the classical economists." Evaluate critically.

3. Draw the parallels between the models of Figs. 36-1 and 36-2: rising labor-output ratio and rising capital-output ratio; falling wage and falling interest rate; the two factor-price frontiers; technical shifts of dd and ff in both cases; land-saving or labor-saving and neutral innovations in both cases; relative factor shares; and other parallelisms.

4. "Saving helps capitalists today, workers tomorrow." Assess this filter-down view.

5. "Without technical change and unemployment, persistent capital accumulation would ultimately mean euthanasia (death) of the capitalists." Use Fig. 36-2 to explain this.

6. Since labor's share shows a slight uptrend and the capital-output ratio a slight downtrend, since the interest and profit rate fluctuate considerably, and since the ratio of private net investment to NNP shows fluctuation and in recent years signs of a downtrend—in view of these facts, would you be greatly surprised if the basic trends were to show future changes?

[19] Such as that of footnote 18.

7. Give examples of labor-saving and capital-saving inventions.

8. "Had America saved less but spent more on experimentation, she'd be richer." Comment. Does Canada gain most from U.S. dollars or U.S. know-how?

9. Review your understanding of the following concepts:

stages of history	capital deepening, K/L rise
Smithian golden age	capital-output ratio, K/Q
labor theory of value	interest rate and profit rate
Malthusian subsistence wage	technical progress
factor-price frontier ff	labor-saving
marginal-product dd	neutral
diminishing returns	capital-saving
relative factor shares	Q growth from inventions, from more K

Appendix: Modern Discussions of Development Theory

Economics, not being a settled subject, is itself still undergoing development. While the broad facts of historical development discussed in the chapter are not in dispute, different interpretations of them are given by different authors. Some of the ideas associated with the names of the late Joseph A. Schumpeter, Sir Roy Harrod of Oxford, W. W. Leontief of Harvard, Professors Joan Robinson and Nicholas Kaldor of Cambridge University, and various current American economists will be sketched briefly in this Appendix.

While an elementary textbook cannot pretend to resolve advanced topics, today one would consider an introduction to physics old-fashioned if it did not somewhere give the reader a glance at fundamental issues on the frontiers of knowledge: atomic theory, elementary particles, generalized relativity, and so forth.

Similarly many beginning students of economics will want to have a glimpse of the issues at the frontier of current economic analysis. Without mastering every intricacy of this Appendix, the interested reader can capture the flavor of developing economic thought from it. In particular, many readers who are not concerned with the rest of the theories discussed in this Appendix may still want to turn to its final discussion (pages 925 to 927) of the fascinating and useful subject of Leontief input-output analysis of interindustry flows.

■ SCHUMPETERIAN INNOVATION

Joseph Schumpeter (1883-1950) of Vienna and Harvard was author of two economic classics:[1] *The Theory of Economic Development* (English ed., Harvard University Press, Cambridge, 1934) and the posthumous *History of Economic Analysis* (Oxford University Press, Fair Lawn, N.J., 1954).

Schumpeter emphasized the role of the innovator —i.e., the inventor, the developer, the promoter, the man who initiates and recognizes technical improvements and who succeeds in getting them introduced. Like Carlyle's faith in the role of the great man in history, Schumpeter's theory regards the innovator

[1] As can be seen by readers of his stimulating *Capitalism, Socialism, and Democracy* (Harper, New York, 1942), Schumpeter was more than an economist. Believing the economic system to be itself essentially stable, Schumpeter advanced sociological and political reasons for his predicted decay of capitalism: he held that the very efficiency of capitalism will be its ruin, as intellectuals and the masses come to despise the market ideology and contrive to introduce hampering government interferences in the name of welfare. Unlike Marx, who thought capitalism would die of its own cancers, Schumpeter thought it would eventually commit suicide for psychosomatic reasons. The tremendous resurgence of *mixed economies* in the 25 years since Schumpeter cheerfully gave his gloomy prediction is, apparently, a deviation from *his* timetable of history, but the disaffection of affluent college activists may be a testimonial to his prophetic insight.

as the dynamic actor of capitalism, who rules profitably for a day only to have his profits nibbled away by imitating competitors.

Figure 36-2(a) well represents Schumpeter's notion of what would happen if all innovations ceased. Competition and capital accumulation would quickly push society down the diminishing-returns curve dd; indeed Schumpeter thought that the long-run ss horizontal line at which the supply of new saving will disappear would be at a zero rate of interest and profit, being properly drawn in Fig. 36-2(a) down on the horizontal axis itself. (His theory of a zero rate of interest in the innovationless stationary state can be replaced by a positive-interest-rate floor without appreciably altering his theory of cycles or development.)

But now Schumpeter plays his trump card. Innovation is periodically shifting the dd curve upward and outward. The violin string is plucked by innovation; without innovation it dies down to stationariness, but then along comes a new innovation to pluck it back into dynamic motion again. So it is with the profit rate in economic life.

The profits due to innovation, we have seen, will be competed away by imitators, with labor and consumers benefiting from price reductions. The innovation-induced rise in interest rates will soon coax out saving and capital formation, until the accumulation of the augmented capital stock leads to diminishing returns, a "profit squeeze," and minimal interest. But then along comes a new burst of innovations—railroads, electricity, automation—to pluck the system back into dynamic motion, and we are off on a new repetition of the process of development.

Ignoring Schumpeter's specific theories of the business cycle, we see that his theory of development is completely consistent with the first two trends of economic history: rising real wage rates, and capital increase outstripping population increase. Although his general theory does not specifically call for constant relative shares, a trendless profit rate, a constant capital-output ratio, a trendless average propensity-to-consume-and-save, still all or any of these could be quite consistent with his general schema.

■ UNEMPLOYMENT IN THE STATIONARY STATE?

Ricardo, Alfred Marshall, and Schumpeter had one thing in common with Lord Keynes of The General Theory of Employment, Interest, and Money. They all thought that profit rates would be pushed to minimal levels in the absence of technical change. But Ricardo and company all thought that when this day of judgment came, the economy would be voluntarily consuming 100 per cent of its full-employment income; although positive investment would cease, people would then be spending enough on consumption to maintain full employment. (In terms of the diagrams of Part Two, in the Ricardian stationary state the $C + I + G$ curve would be intersecting the 45° line at the FF full-employment level with $C + I + G$ actually equal there to $C + zero + G$, because net investment ceases in the stationary state.)

Keynes, on the other hand, feared that such minimal rates of interest and of profit on risky ventures might create a stationary state of stagnation with chronic unemployment:

People might still want to save at full employment, but no matching real investment would be forthcoming when the promised profit rate is too low to coax out risk taking; and when the interest to be earned on short-term gilt-edge government bonds has become so low as to make people indifferent between hoarding much or little safe, idle money,[2] central bank policy cannot do much to prevent stagnation.

This notion of a troublesome stationary state did not die with the 1930s. Prominent followers of Keynes at Cambridge University, such as Professors Joan Robinson, Lord Kahn, and Nicholas Kaldor, have grave doubts concerning the possibility of a successful deepening of capital accompanied by full employment in a mixed economy. At the least they would stress that it will never happen by itself in a country that confines itself to orthodox fiscal and monetary policies. At the most they would harbor grave doubts that "managed capitalism" could, or would, pursue the unorthodox policies of monetary and fiscal expansion implied by a successful synthesis of neoclassical and post-Keynesian analysis.

[2] This floor on the profit and interest rate could help account for the historical constancy of the profit rate named in trend 4 (page 911), particularly if someone could supply reasons for a profit ceiling. With the profit rate allegedly running between two channels, its constancy would be removed from the realm of coincidence. (Recall also the discussion of Say's Law on page 421; page 425's "liquidity trap" or "depression pole," when elevated by riskiness, might provide such a profit floor.)

Readers who go on to advanced economics can be referred to writings of these and other authors.[3] Here, briefly, will be presented some of the points that need to be considered in doing justice to both sides of the argument as it bears on long-term economic development: no attempt will be made to identify ideas and writers meticulously.

■ UNCHANGEABLE CAPITAL-OUTPUT RATIO?

The land-output and labor-output ratios were not constants in the first Smith-Malthus model of development. And the capital-output ratio in the Ricardo-Marx-Solow model of Fig. 36-2 was likewise not supposed to be a technical constant. In the absence of technical change, successful capital formation by society would enable output to grow; and the resulting phenomenon of diminishing returns would imply a *smoothly growing* capital-output ratio as capital deepening was taking place. On this view, dynamic technical change has seemed historically to provide about the extra productivity needed to offset statical diminishing returns, keeping the measured capital-output ratio constant.

Many modern economists—Professors Robert Eisner of Northwestern and Alvin Hansen of Harvard, Dr. Gerhard Colm of the National Planning Association, and others—are of the view that the capital-output ratio is very nearly a technical *constant*, and that any attempt to accumulate capital beyond the rate required by the annual growth in output will soon be unsuccessful. Profits or rents from equipment will fall off badly after any surge of capital investment like those of 1955-1957 and 1964-1970. Excess capacity will follow, and the resulting profit squeeze will kill off private investment, as it did in the sluggish years following 1957. Therefore, they argue, any long-term theory must utilize an *invariable* capital-output ratio like that shown in the historical data of Fig. 36-3.

■ HARROD-DOMAR GROWTH MODELS

These concepts can be illuminated by some interesting models of balanced compound-interest (or "exponential") growth developed by Sir Roy Harrod

in England and Professor E. Domar in America.[4] This theory has two aspects: the long-term "natural rate of growth" and the so-called "warranted rate of growth."

THE *natural* RATE OF GROWTH   The historical data of Fig. 36-3 can help explain Harrod's arithmetic; and, in turn, a simple Harrod-Domar model can give an oversimplified "explanation" of those historical trends.

Suppose hours of labor L grow steadily at about 1 per cent per year.[5] And for extreme simplicity, assume that technical change is in effect making every man's efficiency as a laborer grow at another 2 per cent per year. Either because of more scientific methods of production or better education, it is as if 98 men can this year do what it took 100 to do last year; and this is repeated indefinitely. To coin a phrase, while *actual L* in its human man-hour units is growing at but 1 per cent per year, the number of "efficiency units of labor" L^* is growing at 3 per cent per year because of the annual 2 per cent efficiency improvement. This leads to the concept of the natural rate of growth.

Definition: The *natural rate of growth* of a simplified Harrod system is the percentage growth per year of its labor supply expressed in "efficiency units" (which means natural labor units as augmented by the presumed increase in technical effectiveness of each man-hour); as a condition of *balanced* growth, output and capital must also be growing at this same natural rate per year.

With NNP (or Q) and with L^* growing steadily at this natural rate of 3 per cent per year, the stock of capital K must also grow at the same natural rate of 3 per cent per year so as to keep in balanced pace. How much investment is required each year to keep K growing at this natural rate of 3 per

[3] J. Robinson, *Economic Philosophy*, Chap. 5 (Macmillan, London, 1962); *Accumulation of Capital* (Macmillan, London, 1956); N. Kaldor, *Essays on Value and Distribution*; *On Economic Stability and Growth*; *On Economic Policy* (Duckworth, London, 1960).

[4] R. F. Harrod, *Towards a Dynamic Economics* (Macmillan, London, 1948); E. D. Domar, *Essays in the Theory of Economic Growth* (Oxford University Press, Fair Lawn, N.J., 1957). The discussion of interacting accelerator-multiplier models in Chapter 13 is here applied to the trend of economic development rather than to the business-cycle deviations from that trend.

[5] Expansion of an industrial sector through the utilization of an unlimited supply of rural labor is associated with the name of W. Arthur Lewis. Such diverse economists as the conservative Gustav Cassel of Sweden and the nonconservative Karl Marx had put forth similar Ricardian notions.

cent? Or, in other words, how much must people be steadily saving and investing out of their annual full-employment product to keep growth nicely balanced?

Evidently the needed saving-income ratio must depend on the numerical value of the capital-output ratio K/Q times the natural growth rate.[6]

We are now in a position to write down the arithmetic formula relating three historical things: the Harrod natural rate of growth of 0.03 per year, or in the general case g per year; the historical capital-output ratio of, say, $3\frac{1}{3}$ (to keep arithmetic simple, not 2.7 as in Fig. 36-3), or in the general case K/Q; the required saving-income ratio of 0.09, or in the general case s. We get

$$s = g \times \frac{K}{Q} \quad \text{or} \quad 0.10 = 0.03 \times 3\frac{1}{3}$$

This relationship determines the amount of voluntary saving *and* investment that is needed if the Harrod natural growth is to be an *equilibrium* situation.[7]

EXPLAINING THE TRENDS   Can this simplified Harrod-Domar model of balanced natural rate of growth account for all six of the basic trends listed on page 911? Yes. Let us check them off.

The model certainly gives a deepening of capital relative to man-hours of actual L, since K grows at 3 per cent and L only at 1 per cent. (In this simplified model, an observer who concentrates on L^*, labor in efficiency units, will see a constant K/L^* with no "deepening" going on but merely an ap-

parent "widening of capital" to keep K and L^* balanced.)

Trend 2 is verified also. The wage rate rises— actually at 2 per cent per year. Why? Because each actual man (L, not L^*) collects the marginal product of the increasing efficiency units *in him*, and these units work with their full quota of capital goods.

Trend 3 is verified and is no longer a coincidence. Because technical change was so nicely neutral as to make each man take on "the strength of ten," the balanced growth in K and L^* means we are *dividing shares between the factors in precisely the same way as before*. (Recall that an observer of L^* alone merely sees balanced widening of capital, not deepening.)

Trend 4's constancy of the interest rate is now precisely verified, being neither an approximation nor a coincidence. Each unit of K, being matched exactly by the same amount of L^* as before, experiences no diminishing returns and has imputed to it the same competitive interest rate. (If degree of risk is the same, constancy of the interest rate means constancy of the somewhat higher profit rate.)

Trend 5 is of course verified, since the Harrod natural rate of balanced growth assumes from the beginning an unchanged K/Q ratio. In terms of the Ricardo-Marx-Solow model, even if the capital-output ratio *could* smoothly change, it will not have to in a situation where widening of K to match L^* means no diminishing returns and entails Q growing in full proportion to K.

Trend 6's constancy of the saving-income ratio is verified from the basic Harrod formula for the natural rate of balanced growth at the same compound interest rate per year: s = constant g × constant K/Q.

INTERDEPENDENCE OF TRENDS   As mentioned in footnote 15, page 912, the six trends are not all logically independent. We could have saved time by checking any two of the three trends 3, 4, and 5, knowing that their correctness would arithmetically guarantee the correctness of the remaining trend. Here is why. If property always gets the same fraction of output, say one-fourth, and if the profit rate stays constant, then the process of capitalization of an income stream discussed in Chapter 29 shows that the value of the capital stock must be a determinate multiple of output. [I.e., K's fractional

---

[6] Thus, suppose Q is 900 billion dollars per year, and that the capital stock is about $3\frac{1}{3}$ times as great, being 3,000 billion dollars. Then to add 3 per cent to K this year we must have net investment of 90 billion dollars (equals 0.03 × 3,000 billion dollars), which means that people must be saving and investing exactly 10 per cent (equals 3% × $3\frac{1}{3}$) of their incomes. [Check your understanding by showing that a 4 per cent natural growth rate would in this case require a $13\frac{1}{3}$ per cent (equals 4% × $3\frac{1}{3}$) saving ratio out of income; and that a 3 per cent natural growth rate with a K/Q ratio of only 2 would require only a 6 per cent saving-income ratio.]

[7] This is really the $I = S$ schedule equality of Part Two. For in the case of the natural growth rate, g = I/K or $I = gK$; hence, $I/Q = S/Q = s = g(K/Q)$, the Harrod condition.

share of Q divided by the interest rate is equal to the capital-output ratio: $i(K/Q) \div i = K/Q$. Thus, if capital gets one-fourth of 900-billion-dollar Q, and this property return of 225 billion is capitalized by dividing it through by $i = 0.07\frac{1}{2} = \frac{3}{40}$, then the value of capital is seen to be determinate at 3,000 billion dollars, or $3\frac{1}{3}$ (as in footnote 14's example in the main chapter) times the value of output.]

HARROD'S WARRANTED RATE OF GROWTH   The natural rate of growth is designed to cope with long-term problems of economic development. A few words can be said about a related tool designed more to explain cyclical instability than trend.[8]

What if society's actual saving fraction differs from that needed to keep the natural growth rate in nice balance? That is, suppose actual desired S/Q at full employment is greater, or less, than s given by $g(K/Q)$. Too high a schedule of saving, we saw in Part Two, will tend to lead to unemployment. Too low a saving schedule, related to the investment schedule, was seen to produce an inflationary gap and a tendency toward price inflation.

Very well. No longer is the natural growth rate g the one that the system will realize. Growth in balance has now become rather irrelevant. Still Harrod can ask this rather odd question:

> Starting from enough unemployed resources so that the natural growth rate of labor and other resources provides no bottleneck or ceiling—starting from there, what rate of growth of output, W, if it could be achieved and maintained, would (through "the acceleration principle" of Chapter 13, page 313) lead to a large enough volume of investment to justify (via the multiplier analysis of Chapter 13) a continuance of its own growth rate W? The answering W is defined as the "warranted rate of growth."

In short, to get W, reinterpret the old Harrod relation $s = g(K/Q)$ and work it backward to solve for the growth rate of Q rather than for the needed saving ratio s. Follow these steps: (1) Replace s by the actual desired saving ratio S/Q. (2) Replace the g specified by labor force and technological growth by the unknown warranted rate of growth W. (3) Provided that the capital-output ratio K/Q is a

[8] These next two sections can be skipped.

hard constant, let it stand.[9] (4) Solve for W by removing K/Q to the denominator under S/Q.

We go from the natural rate to the warranted rate thus: $S/Q = W(K/Q)$ replaces $s = g(K/Q)$, and

$$W = \frac{S/Q}{K/Q}$$

An example will help. With $g = 0.03$ and $K/Q = 3\frac{1}{3}$, Harrod needs $s = 0.10$ for his natural-growth process. But suppose people want to save $S/Q = 0.13\frac{1}{3} > 0.10$. This overthrift would lead to unemployment. If somehow Harrod could start an expansion of W per cent per year in Q, which can always get the labor it needs from the ranks of the unemployed, how fast must it expand to generate enough I/Q to match $S/Q = 0.13\frac{1}{3}$? If every dollar of expanded Q always requires K to expand by $3\frac{1}{3}$ dollars, our answer is $W = 0.13\frac{1}{3} = 3\frac{1}{3}$. Any Q growth higher than 0.04 per year will generate $I/Q > 0.13\frac{1}{3}$, just as any Q growth less than $W = 0.04$ will generate $I/Q < 0.13\frac{1}{3}$.[10]

[9] If an extra amount of Q, written as ΔQ, calls for an amount of extra capital ΔK that gives a $\Delta K/\Delta Q$ *different* from K/Q then we would have to replace the latter in the Harrod formula by the former, which is called the *"incremental* capital-output ratio" or the "accelerator coefficient." Those who like symbols should read the next footnote.

[10] Suppose the capital-output ratio K/Q is not precisely equal to the incremental capital-output ratio $\Delta K/\Delta Q$ (where ΔQ means the annual change in Q or $Q_{t+1} - Q_t$, and $\Delta K = $ annual investment $= K_{t+1} - K_t$). Then we replace K/Q by $\Delta K/\Delta Q$ in the formula for the warranted rate. Economics aside, this can be seen from the obvious identity

$$\frac{\Delta K}{Q} = \frac{\Delta Q}{Q} \frac{\Delta K}{\Delta Q}$$

which comes from multiplying the left-hand side by $1 \equiv \Delta Q/\Delta Q$ and rearranging terms. If investment matches voluntary saving, this is seen to be the same as $S/Q = W(\Delta K/\Delta Q)$.

The natural growth rate stems from the slightly different identity

$$\frac{\Delta K}{Q} = \frac{\Delta K}{K} \frac{K}{Q}$$

where the left-hand side has merely been multiplied by $1 \equiv K/K$. Stipulating *balanced* natural growth, we require $g = \Delta K/K = \Delta Q/Q = \Delta L^*/L^*$. The last condition guarantees constancy of the K/Q ratio; and combining this last condition with the equilibrium requirement that maintained saving be equal to growth-induced investment, we convert the above identity into the already given natural-rate formula $s = g(K/Q)$.

The warranted rate is an odd concept. It does not tell you what will in fact happen, but only what would—if it came to happen by design or by luck —have certain self-warranting properties. Such a growth rate of output, W, if it could somehow be established and maintained, warrants a level of investment just big enough to match the voluntary saving that its own income growth entails.

CYCLES AND INSTABILITIES   Two observations should be made about cyclical instabilities involved in the warranted rate of growth.

1. Once all the unemployed are back at work, the natural rate of growth g must set a ceiling against which the faster warranted rate of growth must collide. Thus W of 4 or 5 per cent per year and g of only 3 per cent per year ultimately means the Harrod expansion will hit full employment. As was seen in the Appendix to Chapter 13 on business cycles, some writers[11] have constructed a theory of a collapse into recession based upon a bouncing back of the system from its collision with the natural-rate employment ceiling.

2. The warranted rate of growth, even if originally established, will not persist after being disturbed. In the Harrod model it is definitely unstable. To see this, note that if the actual growth rate temporarily exceeds $W = 4$ per cent, this new income will be generating in desired investment *more* than the $13\frac{1}{3}$ ($= 4\% \times 3\frac{1}{3}$) per cent ratio of desired saving—thereby *accelerating* its own growth still faster above W. (Show that a *less* than 4 per cent initial growth rate will similarly create a deficiency of intended investment relative to the $13\frac{1}{3}$ per cent intended saving, thereby *decelerating* its own growth still further below W.)

Just as an unmanned bicycle, which is unstable if disturbed from the vertical, can be converted into a stable system by a steadying and compensating human hand, so can a Harrod-Domar growth path that would be unstable under *laissez-faire* be made stable by compensating monetary and fiscal policies in a mixed economy.

[11] J. R. Hicks, *A Contribution to the Theory of the Trade Cycle* (Oxford University Press, Fair Lawn, N.J., 1950), gives a convenient summary of such nonlinear-cycle theories based on interacting accelerator-multiplier principles.

NEOCLASSICAL DYNAMICS

The Ricardo-Marx-Solow model of smooth substitutability of labor for capital (i.e., of labor for a great variety of alternatively producible capital goods) has less need to work with Harrod-Domar concepts than those models which regard the capital-output ratio as a hard constant. However, it is useful to interpret the Harrod-Domar concepts for a neoclassical model like Fig. 36-2.

By a simple "neoclassical growth model" is meant one in which the state uses monetary and fiscal policies to make sure that thriftiness does not lead to unemployment and abortive thrift: by making equity and loan funds available at lower interest and profit rates (and possibly by unorthodox credit policies that provide guarantees against risks and uncertainties) such a managed system can contrive deepening of capital as described earlier.[12] Alternatively, this neoclassical model can be interpreted as picturing the technology of an efficiently run collectivist society that never faces macroeconomic problems of unemployment or of inflation due to lack of proper effective demand.

In such a society, where whatever is withheld from consumption goes into capital formation, *any* rate of growth is essentially a "warranted rate of growth." This is because there is (1) no saving-investment problem, and (2) no hard constant for the capital-output ratio (or for the incremental capital-output ratio).

[12] This means that the variety of possible heterogeneous capital-goods processes is so great that any reduction of interest rate—even be it as little as from $i = 0.08$ to $i = 0.079$—will ultimately make it profitable to use some new pattern of known processes. E.g., at 0.079 the machine tools may be made a little more durable. In consequence, the factor-price frontier of Fig. 36-2(b) will look fairly smooth to the naked eye, even though a microscope will show that it contains little line segments that meet in corners. When we introduce realistic uncertainties into the model, one is first tempted to think that minute changes in interest rate will have negligible effects. Actually, however, replacing certainty by probabilities smooths the small steps in a demand function into a continuous curve: a small change in i, long maintained, pushes some investment projects on the borderline of doubt into actual operation. See J. E. Meade, *A Neoclassical Growth Model* (Oxford University Press, Fair Lawn, N.J., 1961), for alternative interpretations in terms of a flexible aggregate of capital.

Here is an idealized example. Add a new supply of L to a system that has a certain K and has previously been producing a certain Q. This new L can be put to work with the given K *as rapidly as* we like. There will result a growth rate of Q that can be *as high* as the growth in L can produce. People can consume and can invest out of the new output *as much or little* as they like. Depending on *whatever* amount of capital formation they decide on, there will result a gradual accumulation of K with the K/L ratio being able to move *in any way* without causing trouble.

All the above is in sharp contrast to a model with fixed capital-output ratio, which calls for a specific W growth rate of Q. Contrast the Harrod case with the italicized words in the above paragraph!

THREE SOURCES OF GROWTH   Neoclassical output growth can be decomposed into three separate sources: growth in labor or L, growth in capital or K, and technical innovation itself. Momentarily ignoring technical change, note that a 1 per cent per year growth rate in L together with a 1 per cent per year growth rate in K is assumed to cause output to grow also at a 1 per cent per year rate. (Resist the temptation to add 1 per cent to 1 per cent and come out with 2 per cent; L and K cooperate in production, each needing the other.)

Suppose L grows at 1 per cent per year and K at 5 per cent. It is tempting, but wrong, to guess that Q will then grow at 3 per cent, the simple average of 1 and 5. Why wrong? Because the two factors do not contribute equal shares to product: about three-fourths of all product goes to labor as wages and only one-fourth of Q goes to property as its interest-profit share. This means L's growth rate should get 3 times the weight of K's; hence, the correct answer is that Q will grow at 2 per cent per year ($= \frac{3}{4}$ of 1% $+ \frac{1}{4}$ of 5%).

Hence, output growth per year follows the law

$$\% \ Q \text{ growth} = \quad \frac{3}{4} \ (\% \ L \text{ growth})$$
$$+ \ \frac{1}{4} \ (\% \ K \text{ growth})$$
$$+ \ \text{T.C.}$$

where T.C. means technical changes that raise productivity by shifting the *dd* curve of Fig. 36-2; and where $\frac{3}{4}$ and $\frac{1}{4}$ would of course be replaced by new fractions if the relative shares of the factors had changed.

If we seek to explain *per capita* growth, matters are simpler still, since this enables us to get rid of L as a separate growth source. Now, using the fact that capital gets one-fourth share of output, we have simply

$$\% \ \frac{Q}{L} \text{ growth} = \frac{1}{4} \left(\% \ \frac{K}{L} \text{ growth} \right)$$
$$+ \ \text{t.c.}$$

This relation shows clearly how deepening of capital would raise the capital-output ratio if there were no technical improvements being made: output per capita grows only one-fourth as fast as capital per capita, reflecting one aspect of diminishing returns.

This relation now explains the meaning of Solow's conclusion—that more than half of the increased output recorded in historical statistics seems to be attributable to scientific advance rather than to thrift and capital formation. This means that the second term in the above relation—t.c. for per capita technical change—appears on statistical measurement to have been definitely bigger than the first term representing the investment contribution. When Solow tries to allow for the fact that new techniques get embodied in new capital goods, the relative importance of the first term rises; but apparently it still remains below 50 per cent. (While the primacy of technical change seems corroborated by German or Japanese statistics, the importance of the capital factor does seem greater in Britain, Canada, and Russia.)

■ ALTERNATIVE THEORIES

REPUDIATION OF AGGREGATE PRODUCTION FUNCTIONS Professors Joan Robinson and Nicholas Kaldor of Cambridge University are skeptical that "capital" can be usefully measured as an aggregate, which together with labor produces aggregate output. This is certainly a healthy skepticism. They are more skeptical that the marginal productivities calculated from such an alleged production function can be used to explain wage and profit rates and the relative shares in NNP of labor and property. They go even further and doubt that economists can work with a detailed breakdown of numerous heterogeneous capital goods—machines of type A, B, C, . . . —to get quantitative results at all like the neoclassical case, in an actual realistic mixed economy of uncertainty and uneven growth.[13]

DISSENTING VOICES Robinson and Kaldor by no means agree on what is to replace the aggregative analysis. Both incline, but in different degree, toward a macroeconomic theory of income distribution with the following property:

"Here is an economy with high-property share and high growth. How wrong to think that it is the thrift of the rich (or anyone) which *causes* that fast growth. The causation tends to run the other way: fast growth produces high profits, rather than vice versa."[14]

This seems to say something more than does the familiar assertion that when a country like Japan or Western Germany experiences a miracle of productivity growth, people find it easiest to be thrifty out of the increase in income and to be slow in renegotiating real wage rates commensurate with the recent rises in marginal productivities. It is beyond controversy that such induced thrift does further speed up capital formation and (in neoclassical fashion) speeds up growth still further.

LIFETIME SAVING AND THE WEALTH-INCOME RATIO Professor Franco Modigliani of MIT has put forward an alternative theory that is quite at variance with those just above. Modigliani does not consider the constancy of the capital-output ratio a mere coincidence. He tries to explain it, not in terms of technological production or by induced innovation as in page 914's footnote 18, but in terms of people's psychological decisions about wealth, consuming, saving, and dissaving. He puts the greatest stress on lifetime patterns of saving for old-age retirement.

Here is an example. An adult works for about 40 years and lives in retirement for 20. To keep his consumption standards somewhat equal all his life, he consumes less than his income during the working years; he gradually builds up his wealth to a maximum just before retirement; then he gradually uses up capital and pension rights by his retirement consumption; at death he leaves little wealth.

When population is growing at an even percentage rate, the age distribution remains constant over time. This steady increase in population, combined with confidently expected rising real income, causes the average level of wealth of the people as a whole to remain constant in ratio to total income. Except for the public-debt and land part of wealth, Modigliani has supplied a reason for K/Q to be constant!

A test of Modigliani's theory, as against that of someone like Kaldor who thinks that businessmen will somehow be led to make innovation and investment decisions in order to keep the K/Q ratio from changing much, would be to perform the hypothetical experiment of juggling the public debt up or down and seeing whether the K/Q ratio does change enough to keep the wealth-income ratio fairly constant. This experiment is not to be recommended, but it does remind us of the assertion of Chapter 18 that a public debt can make the present generation want to do more consuming and less saving for their old age.

■ COMPENSATING FISCAL POLICY

Suppose it were true that monetary policy—because of balance-of-payments constraints, Eisner-like cap-

---

[13] Their works cited earlier can be contrasted by the advanced student in economics with the general neo-neoclassical viewpoint exposited in an advanced work like R. Dorfman, P. A. Samuelson, R. M. Solow, *Linear Programming and Economic Analysis* (McGraw-Hill, New York, 1958). The latter makes the same supposition as was done here—that there are a great variety of alternative machines and processes known (or knowable) at any one time. If the interest rate changes even a little, say from 0.08 to 0.079 (as mentioned earlier), it will usually (but not inevitably!) pay to turn to a new blueprint that involves a slightly more durable machine. Hence, the ff curve of Fig. 36-2(b) will look almost smooth to the naked eye, even though a microscope reveals it to consist of many short line segments that meet in corners. The simplified K fable thus does give some useful insight into a more realistic model, be it the U.S.S.R., the United States, or India.

[14] In long-run balanced growth, Robinson and Kaldor identify i as g/s_p, where saving out of wages is negligible and s_p is the average propensity of property income to be saved. This comes from matching the bracketed terms in the following identities: $I = (I/K)K = [g]K = I = S = s_p(iK) = [s_p i]K$. With the interest or profit rate known, if you believe in a constant capital-output ratio, K/Q, you can calculate property share in income as $i(K/Q)$. Kaldor also has a short-run theory of distribution: when I drops exogenously in the short run, Kaldor denies that this produces multiplier drops in Q and employment (as in Chapters 12 and 13); instead this depresses business demands, causing business to cut prices (relative to wages) until total profit, iK, has dropped enough to equate $s_p(iK)$ with lowered I. Mrs. Robinson disagrees with this new version of Say's Law and inevitable full employment, and most statistical analyses of profits in the mixed economy do too.

ital-output fixity, or other impotency—could make no effective change in private investment spending I. Then compensating fiscal policy would lead to results quite different from those given by *laissez-faire* models of the simple Harrod and Kaldor type.

Whenever full-employment s was out of line with I/Q, the government would run a budgetary surplus or deficit just big enough to alter the effective s for society until it equaled I/Q. The effective "warranted rate of growth" could thereby be kept equal to any prescribed natural rate of full-employment growth.

Thus, in a year like 1969 when I/Q tended to exceed full-employment s, the rational thing for the government to do was to create a large budgetary surplus: to raise tax rates and lower people's disposable incomes and personal saving, to cut down on government use of resources and on transfers, or to do both. This surplus is, in effect, government saving: call it s_G and combine it with the private saving ratio s_{pr} to get s = average (s_G, s_{pr}) as big as is needed to equal I/Q without inflation.

During the sluggish years of the early 1960s, the opposite fiscal policies would be designed to compensate: With $I/Q < s_{pr}$, a budget deficit creates government dissaving (or negative saving); then at full employment $I/Q = s$, the average of s_{pr} and the government dissaving ratio.

In summary, *laissez-faire* Harrodian discrepancies can lose their terror and relevance in a mixed economy.

■ THE EXPANDING UNIVERSE: A DIGRESSION

The late John von Neumann, a brilliant mathematician who helped build the hydrogen bomb and who founded the theory of games, described an economic model in which everything could be produced out of everything. If land and/or labor are no longer scarce limiting factors, then the law of diminishing returns no longer applies. All the fruits of production, above and beyond the costs of subsistence for horses, rabbits, looms, and comfortably living men, are plowed back into the system for growth of more horses, rabbits, looms, men.

In this system, which is like Smith's golden age except that it definitely involves capital goods, there is a maximal rate of balanced growth. And it turns out that such a growth rate—call it g because of its resemblance to the Harrod natural rate of growth—is exactly equal to the interest rate i.

Because development theory, for countries like India and the United States, is preoccupied with the concept of "balanced growth," the Neumann model is of considerable interest. It is particularly relevant to the case where an industrial sector in a poor country finds it can get an unlimited supply of laborers from the rural sector at the same wage cost in terms of subsistence; needing little land, the industrial sector can "take off" and grow at a constant Neumann-percentage rate per year, provided it can produce the capital goods needed to match the new labor or can be helped by imports from foreign lenders, aiders, or exporters.

If there is technical change, the system can advance at a rate even faster than the Neumann rate, indeed, if the system can, so to speak, manufacture new inventions that make labor grow in efficiency at a steady percentage rate, it will then appear to an observer to be capable of even faster Neumann growth.

A simplest example of an expanding system would be the case of rabbits (or men) who produce 1.05 rabbits of output for each rabbit of input. The interest rate and the growth rate will obviously then be 5 per cent per period. Other examples are not quite so simple.

■ LEONTIEF'S INTERINDUSTRY INPUT-OUTPUT

The important interindustry tableau of Wassily Leontief is a modern-day realization of the eighteenth-century dream of a physiocratic economist, François Quesnay, who first envisaged the *Tableau Economique* or circular flow of economic life. A score of nations have computed input-output tables as an amplification of their national-income data and as a possible aid in development planning.[15]

---

[15] For additional discussion of theory and applications see Wassily Leontief, *The Structure of the American Economy, 1919-1929* (Harvard University Press, Cambridge, Mass., 1941) (2d ed.: *1919-1939*, Oxford University Press, Fair Lawn, N.J., 1951); or his *Input-Output Economics* (Oxford University Press, Fair Lawn, N.J., 1966). As part of the price that Leontief has to pay to make Walras's general equilibrium empirically measurable, he is forced to make the technical assumption that all factor proportions—to each other and to total output—are technologically *fixed* or constant. (Back in Chapter 26's Appendix, page 669, we found reason to doubt that such an engineering assumption can be strictly realistic; but Leontief's clever statistical use of fixed coefficients deserves notice. Canada's own DBS tables have been extensively applied by Matuszewski, Pitts, Sawyer, Rosenbluth, Wonnacott, and others.

Leontief's input-output tableau x-rays the economy:

EXAMPLE OF INTERINDUSTRY MONEY FLOWS
DURING HYPOTHETICAL COLD-WAR PERIOD
(in billions of dollars)

	AGRICULTURE	MANUFACTURING	HOUSEHOLD FINAL CONSUMPTIONS	GROSS TOTALS
Agriculture		400	200	600
Manufacturing	200		600	800
Household labor and other factors	400	400	——	——
Gross totals	600	800		1,400

TABLE 36-2. Each industry appears twice, in a row and column: its row lists allocation of its total gross output as inputs for other industries and for final consumption; its column shows inputs needed to produce it.

The bold black numbers show *gross* outputs, inclusive of amounts needed as intermediate inputs. To compute NNP without double counting, we add only the factor payments (or "value added") of the shaded row; or alternatively, only the final-consumption flows of the shaded column. (Fill in the proper NNP in the indicated blank, and check it two ways.)

Using agriculture and manufacturing as sample industries, Table 36-2 gives an oversimplified illustration of the table comprising several hundred industries that the government and Leontief have prepared for the U.S. economy. Here is its general idea. Each industry is listed twice: in a *row* as an *output*; in a *column* as a needed *input*. In addition, the final consumption of households is treated as an extra column and their *labor* (or other primary factors of production supplied by households) as an extra row. These household figures are the numbers that enter into national income or net national product and are on the shaded part of the table. (Actually Leontief also includes government, foreign trade, investment, and other detail.)

The *gross* value of agricultural output is shown by the black $600 (billion) twice; at its row's right as the sum of all the places where farm output went—$400 as input to manufacturing plus $200 directly consumed by households as food—and at its column's bottom as the sum of the $200 cost it paid for manufacturing inputs (chemical fertilizers, etc.) and the $400 cost it paid for labor input (and other household factors).

Give a similar interpretation of the $800 *gross* total for manufacturing.

The table also shows our old friend national income, or NNP. With no government or investment in the picture, NNP of 800 (billion, remember) equals the sum of the third (shaded) column's final products; or alternatively NNP equals the sum of

all factor-cost or values added shown in the shaded third row's wages. (NNP definitely doesn't include the intermediate purchases of one sector from another; the total in black of $1,400 unquestionably involves double counting.)

This input-output table is more than a record of past history. How does Leontief or a planner hope to use it? *He hopes to use it to forecast the effects of changing consumption requirements.*

Thus, suppose Table 36-2 refers to a current cold-war situation where manufacturing employment and output have been swollen by military needs. (For dramatic effect we may think of peacetime goods or "butter" as coming largely from the agricultural sector and military goods or "guns" as coming largely from the manufacturing sector.)

Now suppose "peace breaks out." What will have to be planned for the new deployment of labor and other inputs if full employment is still to be maintained? Suppose we now want to double agriculture's final consumption, from the old brown $200 to new $400, at the same time cutting the military manufacturing sector back from old brown $600 to new $400. On the basis of his assumption of fixed input-output coefficients, Leontief can solve linear equations for the new peacetime state and show that it *must* then be in the configuration given in Table 36-3. Ten per cent of the workers (i.e., $80/800$) must be shifted from war work to peace work. Similarly Leon-

Input-output tableau helps us plan:

NEW PEACETIME INPUT-OUTPUT FLOWS (in billions of dollars)				
	AGRICULTURE	MANUFACTURING	HOUSEHOLD FINAL CONSUMPTIONS	GROSS TOTALS
Agriculture		320	400	720
Manufacturing	240		400	640
Household labor and other factors	480	320	800	
Gross totals	720	640		1,360

TABLE 36-3. End of cold war causes shift from guns to butter: agricultural final consumption goes up by 200 billion dollars, manufacturing down by same. Using fixed input-output coefficients from Table 36-2, Leontief calculates needed change in gross outputs shown here and resulting needed labor shifts and intermediate input changes. Same techniques help in development planning.

tief's tableau scheme can help plan for any development change in final-consumption goods.[16]

[16] All details aside, his key assumption is that $200/600 = 1/3$ of agriculture receipts will always be spent on manufacturing input, with the remaining $400/600 = 2/3$ always spent on labor input. Similarly, $400/800 = 1/2$ is the fraction that manufacturing will always spend on its needed agricultural input, the remaining $1/2$ being spent on needed labor input.

$$
\begin{array}{cc}
0 & 400 \\
200 & 0 \\
\hline
400 & 400 \\
\hline
600 & 800
\end{array}
\longrightarrow
\begin{array}{cc}
0 & 1/2 \\
1/3 & 0 \\
\hline
2/3 & 1/2 \\
\hline
1 & 1
\end{array}
$$

Table 36-2 is repeated here in abbreviated form to show how one derives the brown fixed input-output coefficients needed for the transition to Table 36-3 or to any other situation envisaged by the planner. Now, if we call *gross outputs* of the two sectors X_A and X_M and their *final-consumption* amounts C_A and C_M, Leontief must finally allocate the total X's thus:

$$X_A = C_A + \tfrac{1}{2} X_M \qquad X_M = C_M + \tfrac{1}{3} X_A$$

For the peacetime tableau of Table 36-3, this means

$$X_A = 400 + \tfrac{1}{2} X_M \qquad X_M = 400 + \tfrac{1}{3} X_A$$

These can be solved simultaneously by simple algebra to give $X_A = 720$, $X_M = 640$, from which all of Table 36-3 can be filled in using the brown fractions.

REMARK: To avoid simultaneous equations, Leontief can use a "multiplier" method. Each manufacture requires $1/2$ of agriculture as input, and each of these in turn requires $1/3$ of manufacture as its input; so *indirectly* each manufacture requires $1/2 \times 1/3 = 1/6$ of extra manufactures to produce itself. So $[1 + 1/6 + (1/6)^2 + \ldots]$ adds up to 1.2, which is the needed expansion of new *gross* manufacture for each 1.0 expansion of *consumption* manufacture. Similarly Leontief can calculate a multiplier for agriculture, showing how each billion-dollar change in its final consumption requires its *own* gross output to go up (coincidentally!) by 1.2 billion dollars. To compute what the shift of 200 billion dollars from guns to butter entails, Leontief must know how much gross agriculture and how much labor is needed to accommodate the 1.2 of manufacture that its own consumption expansion generated. The answer is not hard: The second column's bold black manufacturing input requirements give the answers—$1/2$ of 1.2, or .6 in both cases. The reader should now be able to verify that when 1 new agriculture consumption entails 1.2 of its *own* gross output, the amounts needed for manufacturing and labor are $1/3(1.2) = .4$ and $2/3(1.2) = .8$. Given the knowledge of this paragraph's "own multipliers" and "cross multipliers"—the so-called "inverse matrix"—we perceive how Leontief is able to apply them to the $+200$ consumption shift to agriculture and -200 shift from manufacturing to get the changes needed to convert wartime Table 36-2 to peacetime Table 36-3.

SUMMARY TO APPENDIX

■ 1 Schumpeter's stress on innovation, followed by competitive erosion of profit, is an important process of economic development.

■ 2 If the capital-output ratio is an inflexible constant, neoclassical deepening of capital cannot be engineered by expansionist monetary policy.

■ 3 The Harrod-Domar concept of the "natural rate of growth" g is determined by population growth and technical change. If K and Q are to grow at this balanced rate, the required fraction of income that has to be voluntarily saved is given by the Harrod condition,

$$s = g(K/Q).$$

■ 4 The warranted rate of growth W will be higher than the natural rate g if the actual desired saving ratio S/Q exceeds the s needed by Harrod's condition. In the case where the K/Q is constant for previous and for new changes,

$$W = \frac{S/Q}{K/Q}$$

If this W rate persisted, it would be self-warranting in the sense of coaxing out investment just large enough to match desired saving.

It will not come of its own accord or be stable against upward or downward disturbances. When $W > g$, a self-warranting expansion from a low trough would ultimately bump into the ceiling set by population and other bottlenecks, possibly bouncing back into recession.

A stubborn divergence of S/Q from s, or of W from g, could be controlled by budget surpluses or deficits, which augmented (or subtracted from) private saving enough to keep $s = I/Q$ and $W = g$, and which by a steadying hand would overcome Harrodian instability of income growth.

■ 5 Where a neoclassical deepening of capital makes the K/Q ratio an accommodating variable, the Harrod conditions lose their terrors. Whatever people's thrift wants to make their private full-employment s be, a combination of monetary and fiscal policies can hope to induce the needed offsetting investment. Such fiscal and monetary policies can speed up capital formation and the technical changes embodied in, and stemming from, such new equipment. They can help the system grow faster than the natural growth of working population. They can stabilize the achievable rate of progress so that the system will be warranted in doing what comes naturally. But, even in a flexible neoclassical technology, *laissez-faire* will not—in the absence of appropriate public monetary and fiscal policies—be led by an Invisible Hand to these ideal conditions.

■ 6 The neoclassical model can parcel out the sources of Q growth into growth from more L, from more K, and from technical change. The last factor interacts with L through education and training and with K through embodiment in new machines. Still, technical change seems to have existed historically primarily in advanced nations.

■ 7 Robinson and Kaldor agree in their suspicion of aggregates of so-called capital and in their doubts about smooth deepening of capital under capitalism; both look to factors of dynamic growth for determination of profit shares. (All this is still controversial.)

■ 8 It is intellectually unsatisfying to explain some constancy trends by appeal to "coincidence" or to fortuitous canceling out of diverse tendencies of diminishing returns and technical change. So one can applaud the attempts to find mechanisms (induced invention, lifetime saving, etc.) that bring the constancies about. However if, like the present writer, you would not be much surprised to see K/Q fall in the future or drift in any direction, the wage share generally rise, or the rate of profit sag or soar, you must beware of "over-explanations." If a thing may actually be a coincidence, you are not saying much by calling it that. But to explain away a coincidence which truly is a coincidence is worse than a banality; it is a scientific sin.

■ 9 Leontief's tableau of interindustry flows gives a useful picture of the relations lying behind aggregate NNP data. By posting fixed input-output coefficients, a planner can use the Leontief technique to program a shift from war pattern of consumption to peace, or any other development target goal.

QUESTIONS FOR DISCUSSION

1. Add acres of land, A, to the neoclassical discussion along with L, K, and T.C.

2. Contrast unemployment notions of Keynes and Eisner-Hansen with those of Schumpeter and Ricardo.

3. Why is g important for long trends? W for business cycles? Reread Chapter 13's acceleration principle.

4. Explain to yourself the basic idea of the two-way Leontief tableau. Consider how it might be used to study the appearance of new markets (if tariff-free trade patterns emerge); disarmament; in-

dustrialization of northern Canada; and transmission of foreign inflation through imports.

5. Review your understanding of the following concepts:

innovation and deepening of capital
fixed versus variable K/Q ratio
natural versus warranted growth

$$s = g\,\frac{K}{Q} \text{ and } W = \frac{S/Q}{K/Q}$$

% Q growth = % L growth + ...
% Q/L growth = % K/L growth + t.c.
von Neumann model with $i = g$
input-output tableau

37

PROBLEMS OF
ECONOMIC GROWTH
AND DEVELOPMENT

I believe in materialism. I believe in all the proceeds of a healthy materialism,—good cooking, dry houses, dry feet, sewers, drain pipes, hot water, baths, electric lights, automobiles, good roads, bright streets, long vacations away from the village pump, new ideas, fast horses, swift conversation, theatres, operas, orchestras, bands,—I believe in them all for everybody. The man who dies without knowing these things may be as exquisite as a saint, and as rich as a poet; but it is in spite of, not because of, his deprivation.

FRANCIS HACKETT, IRELAND

All the economic principles we have learned can now be brought to bear on perhaps one of the most challenging problems of the next quarter century—the problem of underdeveloped economies.[1] There are about 3½ billion people in the world, and at this moment half of them are hungry—literally hungry. Only someone who has been pursuing beauty or health on a temporary diet of less than 1,500 calories per day will know how food can fill one's dreams and every waking thought.

For conscience's sake, we are impelled to help. Besides, history teaches us that men do not always starve quietly.

■ DEFINING UNDERDEVELOPMENT

Writers used to speak of "backward" nations, which naturally irritated the people of those lands. To avoid offense the United Nations sometimes used the roundabout expression "less developed" nation. Today most people adopt the expression "underdeveloped" nation. What is meant by the term? Alternative definitions are given; most seem to involve the following:

---

[1] Three useful anthologies on this subject are Theodore Morgan, George W. Betz, and N. K. Choudhry, *Readings in Economic Development* (Wadsworth Publishing Company, Belmont, Calif., 1963), A. N. Agarwala and S. P. Singh, *The Economics of Underdevelopment* (Oxford University Press, Fair Lawn, N.J., 1960), Bernard Okun and Richard W. Richardson, *Studies in Economic Development* (Holt, Rinehart and Winston, Inc., New York, 1961).

An underdeveloped nation is simply one with real per capita income that is low relative to the present-day per capita incomes of such nations as Canada, the United States, Great Britain, and Western Europe generally. Usually, an underdeveloped nation is one regarded as being capable of substantial improvement in its income level.

Of course, every country is underdeveloped in the sense that it is not yet perfect and hence is capable of being improved still further. Even the so-called "advanced" countries were once underdeveloped by our definition and had to go through the process of development. Table 37-1 on page 935 of this chapter gives a picture of the relative stages of development of different countries.

Less than one-seventh of the world's population live in the highly developed group A with more than $1,500 per capita; just over one-fifth live in the intermediate group B; about two-thirds live in the underdeveloped group C.

About one-third of the world's population lives behind the Iron Curtain. The Soviet Union and Czechoslovakia now fall in the highly developed A group, though only barely. As for the rest of the communist countries, how are their people divided among the groups? Recalling the vast population of China, we are not surprised to find two-thirds of the Iron Curtain peoples falling in the lowest group C. Little wonder, then, that economic development is a lively subject everywhere, in the East as well as in the West.

■ CHARACTERISTICS OF UNDERDEVELOPED ECONOMIES

To bring out the contrasts between advanced and underdeveloped economies, imagine that you are a typical twenty-one-year-old in one of the underdeveloped countries, be it Haiti, India, or Nigeria.

You are poor: even after making generous allowance for the goods that you both produce and consume, your annual income averages barely $100 per head, as against $3,500 per head of your fellow man in North America; perhaps you can find cold comfort in the thought that only 1 in 10 of the human race averages more than $1,200 per year. For each of your people who can read, there are three like you who are illiterate. Your life expectancy is only two-thirds that of the average man in advanced North America: already one or two of your brothers and sisters have died before reaching adulthood; and though your mother has had fewer children than your grandmother did, more of your brothers and sisters have lived to maturity, thanks to imported medical techniques—and you must compete with them for subsistence.

Most of your countrymen work on rural farms; few can be spared from food production for factories or service trades. You work with but one-fiftieth the horsepower of your prosperous North American fellow man. You know little of science, but much of folklore. Your methods and tools are primitive. Neither the discipline of markets nor the deliberations of planning commissions mean much to you. As a citizen in Asia, Africa, or Latin America, you and your fellows together constitute 70 per cent of the world population, but you must divide among you only 20 per cent of world income. You brood over the fact

Differentials of nations' living standards are great and still growing:

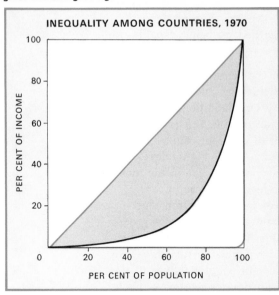

INEQUALITY AMONG COUNTRIES, 1970

PER CENT OF INCOME

PER CENT OF POPULATION

FIG. 37-1. The poorest half of the nations receive only 8 per cent of the total income. The richest 6 per cent (and guess who that is) receive one-third of the total. Contrast this degree of nation inequality with the Lorenz charts of Chapter 6 depicting intranation inequality. (Source: Center for International Studies, Massachusetts Institute of Technology.)

that North America, with 7 per cent of the people, enjoys more than 33 per cent of world income; and that Western Europe, with 10 per cent of the people, enjoys 25 per cent of world income.

■ URGENCY OF THE PROBLEM

There have always been differences between rich and poor. Why worry especially about the underdeveloped countries? Here are some reasons:

WIDENING DIFFERENTIALS   In contrast to the narrowing of income differentials within the advanced nations, the divergence between advanced and underdeveloped countries is probably now widening rather than narrowing. North America and Western Europe have almost doubled their production per head since 1940. Many authorities believe that living standards in India, Indonesia, and certain other underdeveloped countries have improved little since then and may even have deteriorated in some regions.

Figure 37-1 shows how unequal is the geographical distribution of real incomes. Contrast this Lorenz curve of inequality among nations with Figs. 6-2, 6-3, 6-4, and 9-1, which show less glaring inequality within a country.

IDEOLOGICAL STRUGGLE   In the modern ideological war between the free and the communist worlds, both sides regard the underdeveloped regions as being torn between following the pattern of the mixed economy or following the pattern of socialism. Revolutionaries ceaselessly agitate in such lands, never failing to point out the poverty there, never failing to contrast it with our wealth, never failing to remind the people there of real and fancied evils of "colonialism." Cuba is an example. Africa, Latin America, and Asia are cases in point.

Experience does not bear out the easy generalization, "Fill the stomachs of people, and they will refrain from going communistic." Men in utter misery often seem incapable of revolting; and the great revolutions of the past (such as the French and Russian) have often taken place at a time when some economic progress had already been achieved.

Nonetheless, to turn our backs on the problem of development is to court future disaster. Harvard's distinguished economic historian Alexander Gerschenkron has drawn the following important lesson from history:[2]

> "The Soviet government can be properly described as a product of the country's economic backwardness. Had serfdom been abolished by Catherine the Great or . . . in 1825, the peasant discontent, the driving force and the earnest of success of the Russian Revolution, would never have assumed disastrous proportions, while the economic development of the country would have proceeded in a much more gradual fashion. . . . The delayed industrial revolution was responsible for a political revolution in the course of which the power fell in the hands of a dictatorial government to which in the long run the vast majority of the population was opposed. . . . The paramount lesson of the twentieth century is that the problems of backward nations are not exclusively their own. They are just as much problems of the advanced countries. It is not only Russia but the whole world that pays the price for the failure to emancipate the Russian peasants and to embark upon industrialization policies at an early time. Advanced countries cannot afford to ignore economic backwardness."

To reinforce this, tick off the advanced countries in Table 37-1. You cannot find a single one that had a successful proletarian revolution when its economy was strong.

GREAT EXPECTATIONS AND "DEMONSTRATION EFFECTS"   Within the underdeveloped countries, people are today acutely aware of their poverty and its contrasts with rich lands. They do not like it. What is more, they insist on doing something about it.

This was not always so: a century ago the Emperor of China sent a message to the Queen of England saying that his country neither needed nor desired economic improvement. Look at today's frantic efforts in China and mark the contrast. In the ancient formula

$$\text{Happiness} = \frac{\text{material consumption}}{\text{desire}},$$

Thoreau's counsel to hold down the denominator now gives way to insistence on increasing the numerator of material real income.[3]

So nearly perfect are modern instruments of communication that people everywhere know about—and often envy—the comforts of modern Western life.

---

[2] Alexander Gerschenkron, *Economic Backwardness in Historical Perspective*, (The Belknap Press, Harvard University Press, Cambridge, Mass., 1962), pp. 28-30.

[3] In affluent North America or Sweden, particularly among high-income college students, there is a discernible trend away from materialism.

No longer do they shrug their shoulders and accept their relative poverty as the divine will of Allah. Most important, this increased awareness comes at a time when the role of government is highly developed.

Today, when people want something done, they are likely to turn to government and to insist that programs be adopted toward the desired goal. They want to foreshorten history and get now what developed lands got late.

They want better health; land reform, the breaking up of landowners' holdings; better methods of land cultivation; industrialization; political rights as individuals. It is easy to see that men want these things for natural individualistic reasons. But economic welfare is not the only reason why men desire development. Modern peoples desire development also for reasons of *nationalism*: people want their country to be powerful, to be respected, and—let us face it—to be feared. Thus, the British and Dutch may have brought sanitation to their former colonies; they may have thereby increased people's life spans and material well-being. But they did at the same time set up exclusive clubs whose front doors were barred to the native citizenry. "Freedom from contempt" is one Asian's way of describing his goal.

■ SUPERFICIAL THEORIES OF DEVELOPMENT

GEOGRAPHY A look at Table 37-1 shows that nearly all the advanced countries are in the temperate zones. Hence, so the argument used to go, it is all a matter of *climate*.

This sweeping explanation will not fit the facts. The first civilizations were in regions of the Mediterranean and Near East (or, if you will, in the Mayan regions of Central America). Greece was in her glory when Germans and Saxons were cowering over fireplaces in their caves.

Certainly, climate is an important factor, but it is not all-important. It does help not to have tropical heat and erosion from jungle floods. It does help not to have arctic snows. But one of the consequences of modern technology is that fevers can be checked by DDT. The bitter Oxford, Ottawa, or Oslo cold can be offset by heating; and the humid heat of Texas need no longer inhibit the pace of body and mind.

> The geographical distribution of *natural resources*—topsoil, rainfall, dammable water for irrigation and power, oil and ore deposits—all these are important. But in a world where trade is increasingly possible, grave deficiencies in this area can be at least partially offset, as the examples of Denmark, Japan, and Israel have shown.

RACE Throw a stone in the advanced countries and the skin you bruise is likely to be white. Ergo, the tale ran, prosperity is merely a matter of race.

No one has yet been able to find a causal link between a tendency toward albinism and productivity; the pioneers of Egyptian, Greek, Indian, and Roman cultures were generally not blond or tall. The most remarkable phenomenon of economic development in this last century and in this last decade has undoubt-

Most countries fall in the underdeveloped category:

COUNTRIES GROUPED BY LEVEL OF ECONOMIC DEVELOPMENT

A. Highly developed	C. Underdeveloped	
Australia	*Africa:*	*Americas* (continued):
Belgium	Algeria	Nicaragua
Canada	Angola	Paraguay
Czechoslovakia	Cameroon	Peru
Denmark	Chad	
Finland	Congo	
France	Dahomey	*Asia:*
Germany	Ethiopia	Afghanistan
Israel	Ghana	Burma
Japan	Guinea	Cambodia
Kuwait	Ivory Coast	Ceylon
Netherlands	Kenya	China
New Zealand	Liberia	Formosa
Norway	Malagasy Republic	India
Sweden	Malawi	Indonesia
Switzerland	Mali	Iran
U.S.S.R.	Morocco	Iraq
United Kingdom	Mozambique	Jordan
United States	Niger	Laos
	Nigeria	Malaysia
B. Intermediate	Rhodesia	Nepal
Argentina	Rwanda	North Korea
Austria	Senegal	Pakistan
Bulgaria	Sierra Leone	Philippines
Chile	Southern Rhodesia	Saudi Arabia
Costa Rica	Sudan	South Korea
Cuba	Tanzania	Syria
Greece	Togo	Thailand
Hungary	Tunisia	Turkey
Ireland	Uganda	Vietnam
Italy	United Arab Republic	Yemen
Jamaica	Upper Volta	
Lebanon	Zambia	
Libya		*Europe:*
Mexico		Albania
Panama	*Americas:*	
Poland	Bolivia	
Portugal	Brazil	
Puerto Rico	British West Indies	
Republic of South Africa	Colombia	
Rumania	Dominican Republic	
Singapore	Ecuador	
Spain	El Salvador	
Uruguay	Guatemala	
Venezuela	Haiti	
Yugoslavia	Honduras	

TABLE 37-1. (Sources: United Nations Statistical office; and Center for International Studies, MIT.)

edly been the Japanese. Anthropologists cannot completely agree in classifying *Homo sapiens* into the Mongolian, Caucasian, and other categories.

> A glance at history—at the Ethiopian and Berber cultures, at ancient China, primitive northwestern Europe, and flowering Near Eastern cultures— reveals that many factors have been dominant, and that the factor of race itself cannot be isolated as a discernible determinant of economic development.

CUSTOM AND CULTURE   Victorian England or Coolidge's America came as close as any culture ever has to being a business culture. In the 1920s a biography of Jesus in terms of accounting virtues could be a best-seller. Hence, some have leaped to the theory that people must behave like the *Homo economicus* of the classical textbooks if a nation is to prosper.

This is a caricature. It provides a truth, and hides a more important truth:

> Material progress does depend on replacement of a belief in magic and superstition by discernment of and belief in the cause-and-effect relations of engineering and science. If a nation's traditions abhor manual work or work in general, if they emphasize the hereafter as against this world, if they despise material prosperity, if they discourage ordinary honesty in contractual dealings with strangers; if its way of life puts a great premium on current consumption rather than provision for the future; if its government officials are corrupt and inefficient—all such cultural traits are not particularly conducive to economic development.

But putting stress on these noneconomic factors does not solve the problem of *explanation*. It poses new problems. Why did the brains that might have gone into business in many countries go into science, or the church, or the army? Why did the anthropologists who stressed the unchangeable inertia of custom in Mexico go wrong in their predictions that penetration of the money psychology would be slow there?

> We must not throw away seminal explanations merely because they turn out to be superficial and even wrong. But we must not overlook their superficialities and errors. Max Weber's celebrated emphasis on the "Protestant ethic" as both cause and effect of capitalistic development is a case in point. It did fit some facts: many of the advanced nations are Protestant. John Calvin and *some* Protestant theologians did break away from the Catholic Church's ancient edicts against interest. John D. Rockefeller, Sr., was both an avaricious profit maximizer and an ardent Baptist, who referred to his gains as "God's Gold." Yet the "buts" that have to be applied to the Weber thesis are many and serious.
>
> Northern Italy and Catholic Rhineland showed early development. You can find in eighteenth-century Japanese writings perfect passages of Weberian Protestantism. The Jews, Chinese, and Basques have in many places played the role of the alienated stranger who pioneers in economic entrepreneurship. And if Weber seriously regards Benjamin Franklin—who undoubtedly was a prototype of the scientist, innovator, and business go-getter—as an other-worldly Protestant, biographers of that cynical deist tell us the name has almost lost its meaning. Modern statistical research on the Protestant and Catholic neighborhoods in German cities,

upon which Weber originally rested part of his case, has found that correct statistical tabulation even belies Weber's own findings.

Whether or not Weber in some subtle sense was right, think how badly a crude belief in his theory would have served for prediction 20 years ago: The economies that have shown the greatest miracles of growth since 1950 have been Japan, Catholic France and Italy, largely Catholic West Germany, and atheistical Russia. Such predominantly Protestant countries as Canada, Britain, and the United States have done poorly in comparison.

All this proves nothing, because there is almost nothing to prove.

■ RECENT CONCEPTS TO DESCRIBE DEVELOPMENT

For three decades, economists have been intensely interested in economic development. While they have developed no unified theory that differs from the basic growth models introduced in the last chapter, they have added some special features to these models.

The following brief account represents a montage of the most important notions developed in the recent literature. It will pave the way for a systematic causal analysis in terms of the economic determinants of production: land and natural resources; labor (in quantity of man-hours and in quality of skills, training, and effort); capital formation; finally, technological knowledge and innovation. The chapter ends with a brief discussion of modern development planning.

PRECONDITIONS FOR GROWTH   Human history is long and economic development is exceptional, being primarily the outcome of the last few centuries of Western history. During most of history, life was nasty, brutish, and short. A cruel Malthusian equilibrium prevailed in which deaths kept in balance with births.

In a few lucky places, warfare diminished. Superior production methods were applied to ample resources. A surplus over subsistence became possible. And usually wealth was so unequally divided among the aristocratic landowners and the bulk of the populace that the rich were able to abstain from consumption and to funnel savings into capital formation. Economic development could now take place.

THE TAKE-OFF   The more historians study the facts, the more gradual and evolutionary seems the process of growth. But revolution is always better drama and journalism than evolution. So various economists like to use words such as "the take-off," "the spurt," and the "big push" to describe the period of accelerating growth. Thus, W. W. Rostow[4] develops stages of growth different from those of Marx and other writers described in the previous chapter. One of his stages is called the take-off, the obvious analogy being with an airplane, which can get off the ground only after it has attained a certain critical speed.

---

[4] W. W. Rostow, *The Stages of Economic Growth: A Non-Communist Manifesto* (Cambridge University Press, New York, 1960). See Paul A. Samuelson, J. R. Coleman, F. Skidmore, *Readings in Economics* (McGraw-Hill, New York, 1967, 5th ed.), for a strong critique of the Rostow thesis by Harvard's Simon Kuznets.

There is no purpose here in joining the search to find out when each country had or will have its take-off: England in the eighteenth century, Japan in the late nineteenth, the Congo in the 1990s. Nor shall we divide a country's development in stages the way Shakespeare divides a man's life into various ages. Instead, we abandon strict chronology to stress the important economic *principle* that the take-off serves to dramatize.

INCREASING RETURNS, SOCIAL OVERHEAD CAPITAL, AND EXTERNALITIES   The last chapter's models of production proceeded for the most part in terms of the conventional economic principle of diminishing returns—referring to statical variations in labor applied to relatively fixed land, or to variations in the stock of capital goods applied to less rapidly expanding labor supply. That conventional model of production assumed that doubling all the factors together would, typically, exactly double total product—a principle referred to as "constant returns to scale" and serving as a background to the law of diminishing returns to a varying factor.

In dynamic economic development, the phenomenon of *"increasing* returns" is to be expected. Smith's *Wealth of Nations* was in its day a manual of economic development: not for nothing did he encourage honesty and thrift. What Smith stressed was the advantage of *large-scale division of labor.* It is a case of the whole being bigger than the sum of its parts: if all factors together can be increased in size, product will grow *more* than proportionally. Each primitive region cannot develop the scale to achieve efficiency. A pile of enriched uranium suddenly goes active when it achieves a certain size. Similarly, the phenomenon of increasing returns can make it possible for dramatic spurts and accelerations to occur in economic development. (As we saw in Part Three, important areas of increasing returns cannot be left to the free play of competitive market forces; there is a case here for coordination, to prevent monopoly and to channel it into optimal patterns.)

Professor Paul Rosenstein-Rodan introduced, three decades ago, an important related phenomenon. He spoke of the crucial importance of "social overhead capital." To develop, a private economy must have public roads, a railroad, irrigation projects and dams, public health spraying against malarial mosquitoes. All these involve bulky *indivisibilities* of the increasing-returns type. No small firm or family can profitably undertake them; nor can pioneering private enterprise hope to make a profit from them before the markets have been developed. They spread their benefits *socially.* Hence, it is argued, public, as well as private, responsibility is intrinsically involved in economic development from the beginning.

Another way of putting this, as in Chapter 8, page 200, and in Chapter 23, pages 577-578, is thus:

Often there are strong *"external* economies" involved in development. A county agent adviser can simultaneously benefit all the farmers in his region. A railroad can benefit all industry. A multiple-purpose dam has similar externalities. It should be obvious that one can find examples of externalities that do not involve increasing returns, and examples of increasing returns that are unrelated to social overhead capital or externalities. But it should be evident that there is often a strong interrelationship between these three notions, which makes them worth being lumped together.

■ BALANCED GROWTH AND INDUSTRIALIZATION

In the development literature, there has often been a fascination with *balanced* growth. One would not want the skull to grow more rapidly than the head's skin. It is similarly argued that growth in a shoe factory should be accompanied by growth in a stocking factory and in a brewery, if what people want at a higher standard of living is shoes, socks, and beer.

For the world as a whole, the budgetary laws of Engel (which were reviewed on page 257) will impose some limited balance on consumption growth. Food will grow, but it will lag behind luxury items. Indeed, despite the emphasis on balanced growth, Colin Clark and other writers have long noted an apparent tendency for development to proceed in three stages: *agricultural* dominance first; then *manufacturing* dominance; and finally, as we all become affluent, a shift toward *services*. Supply and demand created these patterns in the old days of relatively free enterprise.

Is balanced growth inevitable or desirable for one region undergoing development? History suggests a negative answer:

> Canada, as we saw in Chapter 36, grew through *specialized* "staples": fish, furs, timber, and wheat. The United States first developed by *specializing* in agricultural exports. Belgium early developed by specializing in glass and woolen production. The whole theory of comparative advantage, presented in Chapters 33 and 34, suggested that growth within a region does *not* best take place in balance.

This does remind us of an important issue discussed on pages 843-844 as to whether there is not an "infant-industry" and "young-economy" argument that can validly be used to criticize extreme specialization of a country along a few vulnerable lines of comparative advantage. If coffee demand and supply are volatile, and if *future* comparative advantage may lie in certain nonagricultural industries, a country like Brazil may be well advised to interfere with the market tendency to specialize in coffee production. But diversification and truly balanced growth are by no means the same thing.

INDUSTRIALIZATION VERSUS AGRICULTURE   New Zealand, Denmark, Holland, western Ontario, and Argentina are all regions where productivity in agriculture does not compare too unfavorably with productivity in industry. They are the exceptions. In most parts of the world, incomes in urban cities are almost double those in rural agriculture. And in the affluent nations large fractions of total resources are devoted to urban manufacture. Hence, many nations jump to the conclusion that industrialization is a *cause* rather than an *effect* of affluence.

One must be wary of making such an inference. As the saying goes, "Rich men smoke expensive cigars; but going out to buy an expensive cigar will not make you rich." Vanity seems to make each country want (1) an airline and (2) a steel mill. Analysis of present and future comparative advantage suggests that for most nations these are ornamental luxuries.

It simply is not true that the greatest productivity advances of the last century have been in industry rather than agriculture. (Recall Chapter 20's discussion of agriculture.) If India's five-year plan could increase the productivity of farming by 20 per cent, that would do more to release resources for production of comforts than would exclusive reliance on promoting industry.

The points made here are obvious. Yet they are often overlooked in political debate. But before leaving the subject, we should point to the germ of truth in the argument for pushing industrialization in order to speed development.

> City and factory life tend to break up the cake of rural custom. People in close contact mutually stimulate each other. Hence, technical change is probably stimulated in the long run by subsidy to industrialization. Fortunately, there is often much "disguised unemployment" in rural areas, in the sense that several adult members of each family could move to the city or turn during off-harvest times to local industrial occupations without causing much loss of farm product.

■ CAPITAL NEEDS AND EFFICIENT RESOURCE ALLOCATION

To break out of a vicious circle of poverty and underdevelopment, capital formation is needed. But starving peasants cannot be expected to take much thought of the future. In past ages inequality of land ownership probably helped solve the problem of social thrift, but in a ruthless way. Collectivist economies like China and Russia can by fiat impose the same ruthless abstention from current consumption.

Why cannot free economies do the same? Why cannot they use the fiscal measures discussed throughout this book to curb consumption and stimulate investment? An important reason lies in the realm of political science. Some of the developed countries are able to impose progressive income taxes and find that the taxes do get paid. In most of the world, this is probably not possible. As well, tax administration is primitive and inefficient. People will not cooperate. The problem is made worse where poverty is so great that public officials become corrupt.

As a substitution for taxation and coercion, many writers (such as California's Professor Harvey Leibenstein) recommend that projects be favored which will produce incomes *for corporations and groups that can be counted on to do heavy investment.* They argue that this emphasis should be given even in some cases where there is an actual loss in current efficiency, not to mention the tendency to create a corporate oligarchy in a poor society.

PLANNING, WITH OR WITHOUT RESOURCE PRICING   After 1930 Soviet Russia established a first, second, and third Five-Year Plan. Most nations today, including those neutral between East and West, have similar development plans. These set up quantitative goals. Alternative goals are scrutinized for their realism and compatibility. Compromises are made, and finally a compromise set of aggregate targets is worked out.

These targets may be specified in general terms or in quite detailed terms. Thus, India will take into account her growth in labor force and food supply; her growth in capital resources from internal sources; the amount of capital she can import from America or the Soviet Union. She will canvass her need for dams and electric power; for steel mills and machinery; etc. In the end a system of priorities will have to be worked out lest the demands on the system become so great as to produce galloping inflation, or as to produce so much expenditure on imports that the country will run out of foreign exchange and have to either devalue or ration severely by a system of austere import licensing.

Much of this planning will be in on concrete physical terms. But much more has to be expressed in terms of rupees of *value*. More importantly, the planners will often find that the values quoted in the market place do not correspond to true national scarcities. Thus, in India people would starve if they were paid a zero wage; yet for many purposes labor is superabundant and ought to be regarded as almost a free factor of production. On the other hand, capital goods are truly scarce; charging fifty times as much for use of a tractor as use of a man may come nowhere near to doing justice to the tractor's scarcity and superior productivity. Hence, some sophisticated planners will actually apply corrected "shadow prices," or "accounting prices" to labor, capital, and imported goods for the purpose of getting a more rational valuation and allocation of scarce resources. That way growth can be maximized.

CAPITAL-OUTPUT RATIOS AND SCREENING OF INVESTMENT PROJECTS   Poor countries are long on labor, short on capital. They are advised, therefore, to economize on the use of heavily durable and intensely roundabout capital projects. Often they are advised to concentrate as much as they can on activities that have a low "capital-output ratio."

This advice is good. But it would be more accurate if expressed in terms of the investment concepts developed in Part Four. Each project should have calculated for it a percentage rate of return per annum: then a hydroelectric project that yields 20 per cent per annum ought to get done before a short-lived steam project that yields only 5 per cent per year—even if, to the superficial eye, the capital-output ratio of the steam plant seems smaller.[5]

We have described the general problem of underdevelopment, and surveyed the concepts used in this field. Now we can turn to the constructive task of analyzing the four economic fundamentals: (1) population, (2) natural resources, (3) capital formation, and (4) technology.

---

[5] When experts shift from the capital-output ratio to the "marginal capital-output ratio" they can come out with the economists' correct yield procedures. Also, if capital will be less scarce 20 years from now—so that the correct interest rate society ought to use for its projects is 30 per cent this decade and 18 per cent next decade—a proper planning calculation will take this into account.

■ POPULATION PROBLEMS

Mere growth in numbers does not necessarily mean development. Indeed, as writers since Malthus have warned, unbridled increase in numbers is likely to invoke the law of diminishing returns and to work against increases in per capita living standards. This can create problems. Thus we find many underdeveloped countries repeating the pattern of the eighteenth- and nineteenth-century economies: improved medical technology (e.g., sanitation and in our day cheap insecticides) first reduces the death rate; and with birth rates remaining high, population grows rapidly.

El Salvador, Java, and many other examples underline the twin lessons:

> First, much of the increase in output made possible by technological advance may be spent on duplication of numbers. And second, modern science, conquering disease faster than it operates on food supply, may in the future keep people from dying from germs—only to threaten them with death from famine as they vie for insufficient food.[6]

The grave question being asked by demographers is this:

Will birth rates fall in developing countries as they did in older countries? And before living standards actually deteriorate?

IMPROVING HUMAN RESOURCES Since labor is an important factor of production, there is much constructive programming to be done in this area. When planners draw up blueprints for hastening economic development, they write down the following specific manpower programs:

1. Control disease and increase health and nutrition programs—both to make people happier and to make them more productive workers. Accordingly, do not look on hospitals and sewerage projects as luxuries but as vitally needed social overhead capital.

2. Educated people make more productive workers. Therefore budget for schools and other programs to reduce illiteracy. Beyond reading and writing, train people in new techniques of agriculture and industry. Send your best minds abroad to bring back knowledge of engineering and business. (But beware lest they all get drained off to the advanced nations!)

DISGUISED UNEMPLOYMENT One important condition for promoting development is the better utilization of manpower. In poor countries, particularly rural ones, often a large part of the manpower pool does almost nothing because there is nothing for it to do. Such people may not be counted in the census of unemployment, but they can scarcely be called employed; they live with their kinfolk, and when a boom or a development plan comes along, sweeping them into productive city jobs, there is almost no reduction in the product back on the farm. The same phenomenon of disguised unemployment is met in advanced countries, both in the subsistence farming regions and in the city streets, where men eke

---

[6] Indians in northern Canada face this type of situation each winter.

out a bare existence doing door-to-door selling or begging whenever productive jobs are unavailable.

For a satisfactory solution to this underemployment and unemployment problem, governments sometimes find it desirable, along with manpower programs, to pursue expansionary fiscal and monetary policies—even though these methods raise problems of inflation and of deficit in the balance of international payments.

■ NATURAL RESOURCES

Presumably, most large poor countries were once rich in fertile land. But this endowment has been depleted, leaving large populations to divide inadequate resources. The romantic notion of overlooked geographical areas rich in resources has largely been exploded by geographers. Generally, people have *already* settled in the most productive regions.

True, geologists are still seeking and finding new hidden resources; and there are authenticated cases where control of malaria by DDT has reclaimed from the jungle hundreds of square miles of fertile Asian land. Balanced against these cheerful considerations is the fact that many underdeveloped countries are rapidly depleting their mines, their topsoil, and their irreplaceable natural resources.

Moreover, as was noted, many of the present-day resources of tropical countries are becoming obsolete in competition with scientific creation of *synthetic* substitutes from cheap substances found in abundance within the advanced countries. Thus nylon harmed the silk industry and impoverished millions; if synthetic rubber were to replace natural rubber completely, Eastern Asia would find itself unable to maintain its standard of living, low as that is.

Economic geographers are agreed that further development now largely comes from discovery and better use of existing resources. Gone are the opportunities of a Columbus; and half-closing is the open door beckoning the poor of the older regions, begging them to migrate to the fertile prairies of North and South America or to the empty regions of Australia and New Zealand.

Of course, the quip still holds: "There's nothing wrong with any poor country that discovery of oil can't cure." The fact that primitive Kuwait falls, in Fig. 37-1, in the most prosperous category illustrates the point. Venezuela, Iraq, Saudi Arabia, Libya, Iran, and Kuwait are cases where oil could help finance development.

LAND REFORM   Even without creating or finding new land, nations can make better use of the land they do have. The medieval village was divided into strips of land one could hardly turn around on, and each man might have to live off the produce of two or three such strips, frequently distant from each other. The same is still true in many parts of the world. It took from the thirteenth to the eighteenth century for the painful, and bitterly resented, *enclosure* movement in England to break up the common lands and to gather together into efficient larger-scale plots the land of the country. In the process many peasants were dispossessed and had to go to the city slums. The ruthless, and not altogether successful, "collectivization" of Russian agriculture in the 1920s provides an analogous case; China's collectivization program has encountered similar difficulties. The displacement of prairie and dust bowl farmers during the 1930s by the tractor, and by reversion to ranch-type cattle production, has, of course, been dramatically portrayed in John Steinbeck's best-seller *The Grapes of Wrath*. In many parts of the world, this same painful process of consolidating too-small holdings is yet to be carried out.

At the other extreme, we see in many underdeveloped countries feudal landholding of huge estates too large for efficiency.[7] The tenant farmer has no incentive to improve the property, knowing that he can be dispossessed at any time and having learned from bitter experience that little of the fruit of his initiative will ever accrue to him. The landlord in turn has no incentive to improve the property, never knowing whether an irresponsible tenant will dissipate the costly resources placed at his disposal.

The situation is explosive, and agitation for land reform signifies a ground swell of public sentiment not long to be denied. As more than one eminent agricultural economist has aptly said:

> Successful reform that puts land in the hands of owners who can count on the fruits of their own enterprise has again and again and in country after country literally "turned sand into gold."

The problems of natural-resource development merge with the problem of improved technology and with the problem of improved capital-goods capacity for utilizing and especially discovering natural resources.

■ CAPITAL FORMATION

The fingers and brains of men in the underdeveloped countries are much like the fingers and brains of their more prosperous brethren; but men in the advanced nations work with a plentiful supply of capital goods built up over the years. To pile up net capital formation requires, as we have earlier seen, a sacrifice of current consumption. But there's the rub; underdeveloped countries are already so poor as to be near the minimum of subsistence; they feel that they cannot—in fact, they do not—save a very large share of their current national incomes.

Thus, in the advanced nations, from 10 to 20 per cent of income may go into capital formation; but in the underdeveloped nations, the rate of saving and investment may be less than 5 per cent.[8] Merely to provide for rapidly growing

---

[7] We saw on page 684, Chapter 27, how inefficient systems of land tenancy can put society inside its production-possibility frontier.

[8] In countries going through civil disorders—like Malaysia or the Congo—net saving could be negative. When the shackles of colonialism are first thrown off, a decline in income often ensues.

population, the primitive tools and housing now enjoyed can use up most of this saving. What is left, then, for development?

> Until we learned how to prevent mass unemployment, many economists worried about *oversaving* in *advanced* countries. But for *underdeveloped* countries the problem is often the classical one of *undersaving:* more precisely, the problem is underinvestment in productive instruments capable of increasing the nation's rate of economic progress.

QUALITATIVE DISTORTION OF INVESTMENT   There is a further problem. Not only are saving and investment *quantitatively* low in these countries; equally serious is the fact that the *qualitative composition of investment* is often bad from the standpoint of national development. Thus, too much of the limited saving of India goes into hoarding of gold and jewelry, imported legally or illegally into the country and using up its scarce foreign exchange.

Many underdeveloped countries, like Brazil or Chile, suffer from chronic inflation; hence, there is a natural tendency for people to invest in real estate and in hoarding of inventory. When you can make 20 per cent on your money by hoarding goods, why seek an additional and problematical few per cent from manufacturing? Thus, no less than 55 per cent of Brazil's 1947 investment was in the form of construction. Observers are also struck with the fact that, in many of the poorest regions of the world, *luxury* apartment dwellings seem to mushroom, at the same time that industry is languishing for lack of new equipment.

Still another qualitative dissipation of the limited saving in an underdeveloped country comes from the frequent tendency of the wealthy to pile up their savings *abroad*, legally and illegally, thereby making them unavailable for internal development.

CAPITAL FROM ABROAD   If there are so many obstacles to domestic-financed capital formation, why not rely more heavily on foreign sources? After all, did not England in the nineteenth century invest heavily in the United States, Canada, Australia, and Latin America? Did not France before 1914 invest heavily in Czarist Russia and Egypt? And did not Germany invest heavily in Eastern Europe? Does not economic theory tell us that a rich country which has used up all its own high-interest investment projects can benefit itself and at the same time benefit a poor country if only it will shift investment to the high-interest projects not yet exploited abroad?

Actually, prior to 1914 economic development did proceed in this natural fashion. Britain in her heyday saved about 15 per cent of her national income and invested fully half this amount abroad! If the United States were to match these percentages today, *every year* she would have to lend and invest privately about 100 billion dollars, or many, many times the combined Marshall Plan and foreign-aid programs of her federal government, Export-Import Bank, and all the rest.

For many reasons, we moderns cannot expect such great amounts of foreign investment.[9] After all, was the pre-World War I pattern so natural, or was it perhaps the special result of fortuitous historical coincidences?

Thus, loans from Europe to the New World typically went together with migration of European peoples to those same new lands: Englishmen went along with their money, so to speak, to the American colonies, Canada, Australia, and other dominions; and notice that the same pattern of laws and customs prevailed in the capital-importing countries as in the capital-investing country.

Remember, too, that this antebellum world was an unbelievably cosmopolitan one. You could travel everywhere with no passport. You could migrate freely from country to country. You could expect low tariffs and no trade quotas. You knew the international gold standard would let you transfer capital from place to place at your slightest whim. You knew your property was safe abroad from government confiscation: back in those days few dreamed of questioning the sanctity of private property, and those nationalistic countries which did raise such questions could be easily intimidated by dispatching battleships for off-coast maneuvers. Finally, you could buy up—literally!—dictatorial governments in many backward countries and bribe them into giving you extremely favorable mining and other concessions.

If this sounds like an investor's paradise, be reminded that the historical facts were not really quite so rosy. Foreign investments often did go bankrupt, there being insufficient commercial demand for the railroads built across the plains of North America and elsewhere. Also, the people in the countries importing capital do not, from their historical utterances, seem to have been too happy over this investor's paradise. But the system did work. And it often did confer *mutual benefits* on both the advanced and backward areas. After dividends went abroad, a net increment of product due to the imported capital was left at home in the form of higher real wages.

Now all this is ancient history. This antebellum world is gone. Never was nationalism stronger than today. Never have borrower and lender been so in agreement: the underdeveloped countries are agreed not to sell to foreigners long-term rights in the development of their countries, no matter how advantageous the price; the developed countries are agreed it would be rash to buy bonds and stocks from backward countries in the old pattern.[10]

This does not mean we must rule out substantial foreign capital investment programs. Figure 37-2 shows that in 1968 private investments constituted a substantial proportion of the total capital flow to developing countries. But more and more, investments abroad must involve agreements between governments or various government guarantees of private ventures. Always foreign investment will have to take into account the rising tide of nationalism. Local

---

[9] The typical Canadian, for example, makes no contribution to foreign investment, either directly or through his bank, insurance, or pension plan.

[10] If any Canadian doubts this, he has only to recall that most Canadians now vote for policies that deter and harass U.S. investment in Canada. Consistently, they do not support platforms that propose government aid to investment in underdeveloped countries.

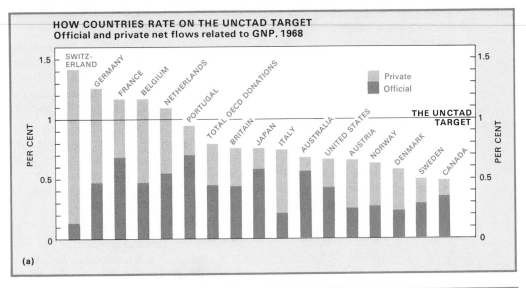

FIG. 37-2(a). The UNCTAD target is about the
same as that of the 1969 Pearson Commission
on economic aid. Canada does about as well as
the average OECD nation on official aid, but
falls short on private investment and lending.

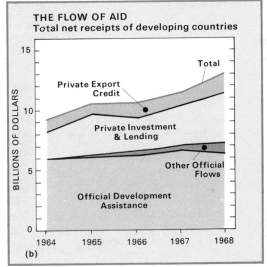

FIG. 37-2(b). This shows that *private* lending
is on the increase to all developing countries.
[Source: OECD, *Development Assistance—1969
Review* (Paris, 1969), Table 8.]

management must be trained to take over ultimately; local sharing in ownership
of branch plants is a modern necessity.

■ FOREIGN AID FROM OFFICIAL SOURCES

As outlined in Chapter 35, a large part of foreign investment flows through the
International Bank for Reconstruction and Development. An increasing propor-
tion of the IBRD's profits now go to the International Development Association
(IDA) set up by the Bank to make "soft" loans to nations for education, roads,

hospitals, etc. They also go into the International Finance Corporation to make loans to foreign development banks to finance private investment projects.

These are only two of what is now a long list of granting and lending agencies which receive contributions or loans, chiefly from the Western nations. Chief among these are United Nations' offshoots: the Special Fund, Children's Funds (UNICEF), relief and refugee organizations, and programs of technical assistance (UNTA); and regional agencies such as the Inter-American Development Bank and the Asian Development Bank.

Taken together, including the IBRD, these multilateral agencies now pay out well over a billion dollars a year, about one-tenth of which comes from repayments on loans. Their great advantage is that they do not usually tie the recipients to purchases from particular countries, though they do usually specify the projects or items to be bought.

Table 37-2 shows how Canada's official aid to developing countries was made up. Terms and categories are discussed below.

Technical assistance. Since 1949, when President Truman enunciated his "Point Four" program, technical assistance has increased to become about 12 per cent of all Western aid. There is a limit to the capacity of the Western world to supply capital goods and food. What it has done is to spread know-how by moving advisers, teachers, and volunteers overseas, and accepting students and trainees to learn, observe, and discuss. Today the OECD countries have about 110,000 experts and volunteers in less developed countries and about 80,000 student and trainee visitors. Other developed countries, in Eastern Europe, make an equivalent effort.

Terminology: (a) Commodity grants. This is a relatively recent form of aid—most gifts have gone to Asian nations. Very similar to this type of aid, which

Almost half of Canadian official aid is in bilateral grants:

CANADIAN AID	MILLIONS OF DOLLARS		PERCENTAGE OF TOTAL CANADIAN OFFICIAL AID	
Bilateral grants	$ 97.8		41.7%	
consisting of:				
Technical Assistance		$26.1		11.1%
Other Grants		71.7		30.6
Bilateral Loans, Gross	93.9		40.0	
Multilateral Contributions	42.6		18.1	
consisting of:				
I.D.A.		6.8		2.9
U.N. Agencies		24.5		10.4
Other		11.3		4.8
Total Payments, Gross	$234.3		100%	
Amortization	−20.3			
Total Payments, Net	$214.0			

TABLE 37-2. Official payments from Canada to less developed countries and international agencies, 1969. (Source: OECD.)

is usually tied to the agricultural exports of the donors, is financial noncapital aid chiefly from the former imperial countries (the United Kingdom, France, Holland, etc.) to former colonies. *(b) Capital projects.* The donor countries can give assistance either by loans or by grants. For all OECD countries, loans are the chief form of aid. *(c) Export credits and development loans.* The important aspect of loans is their "grant" or "subsidy" content. To what extent is the interest and maturity of loans for exports or capital projects more generous than what is available in the donor country's commercial money market? OECD has calculated that in 1968 about 50 per cent of loans could be regarded as grants. Canada's loans are unusually "soft" or generous, so that about 65 per cent of loans have a "grant element." *(d) Multilateral contributions.* About 18 per cent of all countries' official contributions take the form of subscriptions and grants to international (multilateral) agencies (see below). *(e) Amortization receipts.* Because loans play such a large part in developed countries' aid, it is to be expected that they will receive repayments. Such amortization has reduced Canada's aid cost by 10 per cent in recent years. Like bilateral aid and loans in general, most Canadian funds are *tied* both to Canadian exports and to specific projects or items approved by Canada.

▪ TECHNOLOGICAL CHANGE AND INNOVATIONS

In addition to the fundamental factors of population, natural resources, and capital formation, there is the vitally important fourth factor of technology. Here we can strike a cautiously optimistic note. Here the underdeveloped countries have one possible advantage. They can hope to benefit *by copying the more advanced technology of the developed nations.*

IMITATING TECHNOLOGY   The new lands do not have to develop still unborn Newtons to discover the law of gravity: they can read about it in any book. They do not have to go through the slow meandering climb of the Industrial Revolution: they can find in every machinery catalogue wonders undreamed of by the great inventors of the past.

Japan, Germany, and Russia clearly illustrate all this in their historical developments. Japan joined the industrial race late: at the end of the nineteenth century she sent her students abroad and began to copy Western technology. Her government took an active and creative role in stimulating the pace of development, building railroads and utilities, and taxing heavily the newly created increments of land value resulting from the improvements in agriculture. A few energetic, wealthy families were permitted to develop vast industrial empires, while at the same time the general population was made to work, and work hard, in order to earn its living. Without relying on net foreign capital imports, Japan in a few decades had moved into the front rank both as a military power and as an industrial nation.

Only after the Revolution of 1848 did Germany really accelerate her industrialization. Through government aid to her universities, German scientists soon became pre-eminent in mathematics, physics, chemistry, and engineering. Sixty years ago, most British and American professors of these subjects—and of history, economics and philology, too—went to Germany for their postgraduate degrees. German prowess in organic chemistry, optics, glass manufacture, and electrical equipment was unsurpassed until the two world wars set her back. Russia, too, illustrates the possibility of fast development through technological imitation, through study of Western techniques and practices.

Finally, the case of the United States itself provides an optimistic example to the rest of the world. Until Hitler made her a present in the 1930s of many of the best Continental scientists of all faiths, she could not honestly boast of having quite reached the very front rank in the field of pure science. Yet for a century American applied technology had admittedly been outstanding. Examine one by one the key inventions involving the automobile. Where did they originate? Mostly in Europe. Nevertheless, Henry Ford and General Motors long outproduced the rest of the world. "Yankee ingenuity" is a phrase that *explains* nothing; but it does refer to a real phenomenon.[11]

INTERPLAY OF TECHNOLOGY AND CAPITAL   It is all very well to speak of underdeveloped countries copying advanced technology. But have we not overlooked something important? Is not advanced technology embodied in the form of complex capital goods? And have we not already seen that those countries are short of capital? So how can we expect them to copy superior technology?

Certainly there is much truth in these suggestions. Technological change and capital investment do go hand in hand; often they are inseparable. All the same, we are right to treat them as analytically distinct—albeit related—processes. Here is one of many examples to show why:

> Farming is inefficient in many backward countries. You see peasants breaking up the soil by the same primitive methods their ancestors were using back in the time of David and Solomon. Perhaps an ingenious light plow—something simple that would cost no more than a dollar and would pay for itself in the first month —can be found that will both lessen the total amount of capital needed and greatly increase output. This shows how technological innovation can often be capital-*saving* rather than capital-*using*.

Moreover, even in the poorest countries, some gross capital formation is always going on as things are wearing out and are being replaced. Why replace them with the same thing? Why let much of the economy's capital go into mere *duplicative projects*? Surely, it is much better to embody the newly available investment funds in the form of more efficient technological implements. Thus we see how the interrelated factors of capital formation and technology can be mutually reinforcing.

ENTREPRENEURSHIP AND INNOVATIONS   Does it sound like an easy task for an underdeveloped economy? All that it must do to telescope into a few years the scores of years it took us to develop is this: Go abroad and copy more efficient methods; bring them back and put them into effect at home; then sit back and wait for the extra product to roll in.

---

[11] Indeed, Thomas Chandler Haliburton's *Sam Slick*, a Yankee clock salesman in the Maritime provinces, typified New England ingenuity in production and marketing almost three-quarters of a century before the rest of the world became aware of it.

Of course, it does not work quite this way. People in the underdeveloped countries know this from bitter experience. Yet the same illusion keeps cropping up among the people in the so-called "advanced" countries. Too often we think we can send a few technical experts on a short junket to a poor country; after surveying the field for a month or so, they can write up their recommendations for improvement, and then the neatly typed report they leave behind can be "implemented." In this way development will be solved.

Occasionally, in connection with particular technological processes, experts have indeed been able to work wonders in this facile way; thus, an American expert on tanning was sent out to Libya to advise on some of its difficulties, and in a short time he did diagnose the chemical troubles and come up with an effective cure.

> Technologists soon discover, however, that this sort of quick miracle is exactly what cannot be accomplished in connection with the *development of a whole economy*. Indeed, the typical pattern is one of complete disillusionment: after spending several months surveying an underdeveloped country, the expert is thoroughly impressed with the thousands of cultural and economic barriers to progress, so much so that he comes back with a hopeless feeling of defeat. This thoroughly pessimistic conclusion is probably just as wrong in its way as was the opposite optimistic illusion.

Experience shows development is truly a hard and slow process—but not an impossible one. To hasten its evolution, spontaneous entrepreneurship and innovation must develop among the peoples directly involved. Remember, many cultures begin with a contempt for dirty, hard work—a contempt they often inherit from the colonial elite who used to rule over them. Often, too, they have a contempt for business—for money-grubbing and production. Gradually, they must develop for themselves, *within their own mixed cultural pattern,* a creative group of producers alert to trying out new ways, alert to consumer wants, responsive to pecuniary risk-taking and rewards.

Why place the emphasis on creative innovation? Because it is by no means a cut-and-dried task to adapt advanced foreign technology to an underdeveloped country's own use. Remember, the advanced technology was itself developed to meet the special conditions of the advanced countries. What are these conditions? High money wage rates; laborers scarce in number but replete with industrial skills; plentiful capital inherited from the past; mass production; and so forth. These conditions do not prevail in underdeveloped lands.

> Time and time again, experience has shown us how easy it is to obtain a foreign loan to put up a model factory in Turkey or a fish-freezing plant in Malaya. Often it is imported piece by piece from abroad and embodies the latest wrinkles of Western technology. Yet, with what result? With high production and sales exceeding costs, so as to yield a comfortable profit which can be plowed back into further industrialization? Only too rarely. Often such grandiose imported projects turn out to be extremely unprofitable. The factory that is an optimal investment for New York may in Ankara be a fiasco, and the Canadian fish plant may never actually get into operation.

This task of creative innovation is not one for rugged individualism alone. The government can do much to set up extension services in every agricultural province for consulting with farmers on the best seeds, methods of cultivation, and implements. By sponsoring vocational schools and training courses in machine methods—and in bookkeeping, too—the government itself can innovate creatively.[12] Somewhere between complete *laissez-faire* and totalitarianism a developing nation must work out its destiny.

■ FIVE-YEAR PLANS

The advanced nations did not develop by means of a formal plan. Historically, England and the United States grew primarily in a spontaneous and unselfconscious fashion. Much the same is true of the nations late to become industrialized, such as Japan at the end of the nineteenth century. But Japan did concentrate on popular education in the late 1800s, and Canada did stake all on tariffs and the C.P.R. later. More explicitly, the Soviet Union introduced successive five-year plans from the 1920s onward.

Today all over the underdeveloped world, planning is a fashionable word. No country is too small or backward to have its five- or ten-year plan. Sometimes these are merely fancily worded documents that have little relationship to actual reality and performance. But sometimes they are carefully executed analyses which spell out in considerable detail programs for macroeconomic and microeconomic development. Here are some of the elements involved in a good plan.

1. The plan is based upon the *initial resources* of the country, presupposing a careful inventory of present and future availability of manpower and domestic resources.

2. The plan sets up feasible *targets* or *goals* for the terminal date.

3. The plan sets out the *feasible policies* that will permit achievement of the terminal goals from the initial resources, taking into account the intermediate economic resources that can be imported from abroad (through loans or gifts) and that can be produced at home out of the initial resources through the mechanism of investment or capital formation.

At the least, a plan will involve careful computation of the macroaggregates of gross national product: balance of saving and investment; allocation of resources between public and private sectors, between one region or another, between city and countryside. A good plan will not be so ambitious as to lead to inefficient galloping inflation, or so unambitious as to lead to stagnation and underemployment. Along with macroeconomic fiscal and monetary policies, it will take care that the resulting import demand does not exceed the available supply of foreign exchange, whether this is accomplished by the pricing system or by some method of central rationing. An ideal plan will provide for social

---

[12] In helping underdeveloped areas to set up extension courses and adult education services, and in promoting cooperation, Antigonish's St. Francis Xavier University may be making Canada's most important contribution to rural development.

overhead capital projects and be alert to the problems of externalities and indivisibilities.

Some plans will involve no more than "indicative planning" at the microeconomic levels, merely keeping diverse industries acquainted with what is going to happen to the aggregates and to their own share of the total, but leaving to their pursuit of profit the resulting net response. Other plans will involve detailed allocation of inputs among different output uses, taking care to check the balance between inputs and outputs. They may or may not use the input-output techniques of general equilibrium developed by Harvard's W. W. Leontief, which (as the last Appendix showed) gives a detailed view of inter-industry dollar and resource flows. The plan may or may not use the modern techniques of linear and nonlinear programming, in a form suitable for the giant electronic computer.

Often the plan will make mistakes. A crop failure due to bad weather may throw it out of kilter. Overambitious targets may produce foreign exchange shortages and rampant inflation. Sometimes the subsequent five-year plan will learn from the mistakes of its predecessors. Sometimes a situation goes from bad to worse. A cynic can find in the annals of the 1950s and 1960s countless examples of governmental and private bungling. But an optimist, looking at "miracles" of development in Thailand, Formosa, Korea, Puerto Rico, Israel, and El Salvador, can face the future with some confidence in the ability of nations to accelerate their own economic development.

SUMMARY

■ 1 Most of the world consists of underdeveloped countries: countries with low per capita incomes relative to the most advanced economies; countries capable of improvement but now lagging behind the growth rates of the advanced nations. The increasing political self-consciousness of such countries, plus the eagerness of the communist ideology to help them "skip the capitalistic stage of development," reinforces our own self-interest in finding new sources of mutually advantageous trade—not, mind you, new objects for imperialistic make-work programs. All this, and altruism too, make the development problem of major interest to us.

■ 2 Geography and climate, race and custom, religion and business attitudes—each factor conditions economic development, but none does so in a simple and invariable way.

■ 3 The phenomena of increasing returns, externalities, and social overhead capital provide some substance to notions of take-offs, spurts, and big pushes. They suggest a scope for supplementation of competitive market forces. But they do not lead at all necessarily to any simple concept of "balanced growth."

■ 4 The key to development lies in four fundamental factors: population, natural resources, capital formation, and technology. Population causes sociological problems of explosive growth in numbers as death rates fall before birth rates fall; the Malthusian devil of diminishing returns stalks the underdeveloped realms. On the constructive economic agenda, improving the population's health, education, and technical training has high priority. The pool of "disguised unemployment" in country and city provides an important manpower source for extra product; the "brain drain" of talented men to developed countries provides an important threat.

■ 5 Even in densely populated areas, discovery and better utilization of natural resources can help offset the law of diminishing returns. Land reform raises tremendous problems of transition. The process of capital formation—of investing in soil conservation, irrigation, drainage, and improvement—interacts with the natural-resource category, just as it does with population —through investing in people.

■ 6 Rates of productive capital formation in underdeveloped countries are low because of *(a)* poverty, *(b)* lack of a bourgeois ethic stressing frugality and acquisitiveness, *(c)* qualitative distortion of saving outlets toward unproductive hoarding of precious objects and idle inventory and toward luxurious real estate or money markets abroad, *(d)* emulation of consumption standards of advanced nations, and *(e)* nationalistic barriers to importing capital on terms acceptable to investors in the advanced countries, *(f)* lack of substantial volumes of foreign aid from developed regions.

■ 7 *Technological change* interacts with, and is embodied in, new capital goods. Nevertheless, it is a distinct process, and one which offers much hope to underdeveloped nations inasmuch as they can copy from advanced nations. The experience of Japan, Russia, Germany, and the United States shows that the process of adapting to one's own fruitful uses the methods developed elsewhere is not easy. It takes a degree of entrepreneurship and creative innovation. One of development's most pressing tasks is to hasten internal growth of the scarce entrepreneurial and commerical spirit.

■ 8 Five-year plans, involving feasible *targets* to be achieved out of *initial conditions* by suitable macroeconomic or microeconomic *intermediate programs*, occur widely.

QUESTIONS FOR DISCUSSION

1. Would you expect everyone to agree with the praise of material well-being expressed in the quotation at this chapter's beginning? A hippie? An affluent college senior?

2. Bertrand Russell was one of the greatest contemporary philosophers, logicians, and writers, yet the following words of his are agreed by all competent historians to be absolutely wrong in asserting that the Industrial Revolution worsened living standards: "The industrial revolution caused unspeakable misery both in England and in America. I do not think any student of economic history can doubt that the average happiness in England in the early nineteenth century was lower than it had been a hundred years earlier; and this was due almost entirely to scientific technique." Actually, real per capita incomes increased. Why the widespread contrary notions?

3. Formulate your views on geography, race, culture, and development.

4. Why should Canada accept the Pearson Commission's recommendations to give 1 per cent of her GNP to developing nations? If your share of GNP is now about $3,000, would you prefer to keep the marginal $30, give it to those in poverty in Canada, or send it abroad? Is 1 per cent enough?

5. Delineate factors important in development; fit each into the outline involving the four main factors: population, ...

6. Is it fair for the advanced countries, in the interest of conserving bird life, to deprive poor countries of the DDT that prevents early death from malaria?

7. Suggest some constructive policies to improve net capital formation and entrepreneurship in backward lands. Evaluate each.

8. Review your understanding of the following concepts:

characteristics of underdevelopment	capital and technology
take-off, spurt, etc.	inequality, poverty, emulation, foreign
increasing returns, externalities	lending, and capital formation
social overhead capital	entrepreneurship and planning
balanced growth, diversification	inflation and development
disguised unemployment	land reform
planning, accounting "shadow prices"	public and private responsibility
population and natural resources	plans: goals, programs, initial states
medical improvements without food	

38

ECONOMIC INEQUALITY: POVERTY, AFFLUENCE AND THE QUALITY OF LIFE

Ill fares the land, to hastening ills a prey, Where wealth accumulates, and men decay.
OLIVER GOLDSMITH, The Deserted Village

Man does not live by GNP alone. Better a smaller social pie divided *equitably* among the populace, many ethical observers will say, than a larger one devoted to the vulgar objects of material display. Why seek what William James called the Bitch-Goddess of success, if the price of that striving is despoliation of man's environment and in the end the nonattainment of happiness and serenity?

The issues raised in this chapter go beyond the technicalities of narrow economic analysis. Yet they are issues that have come to the forefront of debate all over the world: in the affluent society of North America; in the advanced countries of Europe; in the Soviet society, which has finally achieved a standard of living that goes beyond the utilitarian items of consumption and offers a little choice; and in the developing countries of the world, whose ancient cultural traditions of status—and in some cases even asceticism and otherworldliness—have been challenged by the temptations and promise of advanced technology.

■ ANALYSIS IN THE SERVICE OF CONTROVERSY

All of the present issues are controversial. Their analysis soon encounters value judgments, strong differences in tastes and convictions. But there is much that economic analysis can contribute to the elucidation of the issues. Thus, until you know the costs of alleviating inequality, how can you *rationally* determine how far to carry your campaign in that direction, away from abating pollution, repairing roads, or modernizing hospitals? And even if you believe that the end justifies the means, can you be sure, without economic analysis, that the means you advocate may not produce exactly the *opposite* effect?

Will a very high minimum wage add to the well-being of the poorer workers? Or will the poor be the prime victims of this well-intentioned measure?

Will putting a low interest ceiling on small loans to consumers—say, 8 per cent per annum, which to many will not seem very low—help the needy and unlucky? Or will it play right into the hands of the lobbyists for the loan sharks? What are the debits as well as credits of comprehensive rent ceilings long maintained—and this means debits and credits, not for landlords as opposed to tenants, but for the low-income families of our growing population?

Many a social revolution—in the Middle East, in Latin America, in Africa— has aimed to help the workers and peasants, but during the transition has resulted in a lower standard of life for all the population.

The problems of social reform are not easy. If they were, many reforms which gain a consensus among men of good will would have been made long ago. On the other hand, economic analysis can reveal how specious are many of the arguments for maintenance of the status quo. Despite what your grandfather's economic textbook used to say, a rich country can afford a large measure of redistributive taxation. The Roman Empire did not really fall, or even decline, because of unbalanced budgets, bungling bureaucratic planning, or free handouts and circuses.

In short, economic analysis is the indispensable handmaiden of those who wish to preserve and enhance the inherited order, no less than those who seek widespread social reforms.

■ SINCE EDEN

Chapter 6 has already summarized the important facts about poverty and income inequality. Under *laissez-faire*, income and wealth get distributed far from equally. A mixed economy can modify somewhat the inequality of distribution of a *laissez-faire* regime. But the Lorenz curves of Figs. 6-3 and 9-1 show how considerable are the variations in economic well-being that still remain.

Chapter 6 also demonstrated how, in a growing economy, everyone may become more affluent. The numbers below any fixed standard of living shrink. But affluence also causes the whole nation *to raise the standard of what it deems the minimum* needed for a decent life. We shall, therefore, always regret the poverty of the lowest 20 per cent, which we shall always have with us.

Recognizing the impossibility of abolishing poverty when it is defined as the bottom of the income pyramid actually sharpens our understanding of more attainable goals. Thus we seek to avoid another period like the 1920s, when rising NNP distracted attention from a probable worsening of income inequality. Ironically, it was probably in the war decade of the 1940s that we succeeded not only in raising average output but also narrowing dispersion around that average.

Some ask, "Why worry about our disparities of income when poverty here is nothing in comparison with that abroad? A family on relief lives infinitely better than a peasant in India. Hunger still exists here in rural and northern pockets; but it represents largely malnutrition and *isolated* hunger, not the widespread famine that has characterized all history and still characterizes large parts of the globe."

The answer usually given by humanitarians is something like the following: "An affluent society can afford to provide a decent minimum for all its members. The fact that India is too poor to ensure good food and housing for most of her people may be an argument for a larger measure of our foreign aid; but it is not a valid reason for our countenancing at home the glaring disparities that the market provides in solving the basic problems of WHAT, HOW, and FOR WHOM."

■ INEVITABLE LAWS OF THE DISMAL SCIENCE?

Vilfredo Pareto, the brilliant Italian economist and sociologist at the turn of the century, was one of the first to observe and describe statistically the extreme skewness of incomes. So impressed was he by the uniformity of inequality in diverse societies and times that he propounded an "inevitable" statistical law of inequality. To vulgarize his view, "Essentially nothing can be done about inequality. The basic forces determining inequality are apparently too strong and persistent to be affected by state intervention."

In this matter Pareto's "discovery" seemed in the tradition of most of the classical economists. The Reverend Malthus, Stockbroker Ricardo, and their popularizing disciples had all taught that economics was the dismal science of unalterable distribution of income. The wages of labor, the rent of land, the profit of capital were determined by Economic Law alone, not by Political Power. If labor unions or reform political parties tried to use the state to modify these facts of life, they would be ineffective in the end. All that they would accomplish in the attempt would be *to contrive a smaller social pie*, which would probably still get distributed in about the same way. Vexation and violence in trying to alter this would merely produce economic chaos and class warfare.

With some of this Karl Marx also would have agreed. Marx was an admirer of David Ricardo the analyst. Marx agreed that *under capitalism* things could *not* become better for the workers and the peasants. The proletariat was bound to be exploited. In the more vulgar form of the Marxist doctrines, the immiserization of the working classes was inevitable. Under capitalism the rich would get richer and the poor poorer. *Under capitalism*, that is! One logical corollary was to get rid of capitalism. In any case, the scientific doctrines of dynamic socialism predicted that capitalism would decay of its own contradictions—as the rich got richer and the poor poorer, as monopoly finance destroyed competition, and as the business cycle worsened and led to the ultimate capitalistic crisis and collapse. While waiting for the inevitable revolution into socialism to take place, one might as well hurry it along.

■ THE WELFARE STATE

Ricardo and Marx certainly failed to convince many that redistribution must be in vain. As every schoolboy knows, Bismarck in Germany and Gladstone and Disraeli in Britain began a century of increasing state intervention into the working of the price mechanism. This policy was accelerated by the Great Depression, emerging as the modern welfare state.

VOTING CLASS-INTERESTS   In retrospect there is nothing mysterious about this political process of using the state to change the distribution of income, and of wealth. Political thinkers everywhere believed in—and feared—the class struggle before Marx was born. In Europe, not only Tories but even Whigs like the historian Macaulay warned against the universal suffrage. Give votes to all and you must expect the instinct of self-interest—that same self-interest which Adam Smith counted on to work individualistically in the economic sphere— to lead to state interference with the inequality of incomes and property.

This debate had divided the French revolutionary philosophers and the founding fathers of the American constitution. Such Federalists as John Adams, James Madison, and Alexander Hamilton argued that the rights of property would be infringed if votes were given to all; under universal suffrage the poor would legislate against the established wealthy. Their point was accepted, and the U.S. Constitution eventually provided checks and balances to limit government. Furthermore, the suffrage was severely limited in the new republic's first fifty years.

Such a reaction led Victorian revolutionaries to prophesy that the privileged classes could *never* yield the right to vote to the proletariat. Yet in country after country, conscience and agitation led to widening of suffrage. And, less than a century after Bismarck and Gladstone introduced old-age pensions, social security has become a main function of the state. Parties win or lose particular elections, but the apparatus of the welfare state continues to grow: in conservative Alberta and radical Manitoba; in Protestant Norway and Catholic Italy; in remote New Zealand, or "home" in England.

A CENTURY'S PROGRESS   Figure 38-1 provides a simplified summary of the laws of motion of economic and political development of the last century. The point A on the low curve shows that the lowest half of the population got much less than half of the total social product in 1870. By 1970 the total of GNP had grown mightily. If Pareto were right about the inevitability of the same relative share of product, the new division would be at A'. Real wages would have risen mightily—along with real incomes from property. But if the cruder forms of Marxism had been right, the system would have deteriorated to Z, with the poor reaching complete immiserization (and with bloody revolution unavoidable).

Actually we have no accurate statistics of Lorenz curves for a century ago. What economic historians, such as Colin Clark and Simon Kuznets, do know is that there is some slight reduction of Lorenz-curve inequality in modern as compared with less-developed nations, and in welfare states such as Sweden or Israel as compared with free enterprise societies such as Switzerland. So their best guess is to suppose a country like the United States or Britain or Japan is now at a point just above A'. The welfare state, through redistributive taxation and through educational opportunity designed to lessen inequality of advantage, has moved the system somewhat toward greater equality. But note that the system is still a long way from the point E where both halves of the population get the same share of the total social product.

All classes have shared in century's progress:

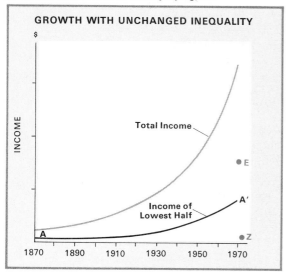

FIG. 38-1. Lower half of population has had rising real incomes, as shown by *AA'*. Immiserization of workers, at *Z*, has turned out to be bad prophecy. But utopian equality, as at *E*, has also not occurred.

Is this limited equalization a good or a bad thing? Apologists for the system say, "It is great; look at the doughnut and how it has grown." Critics of the system say: "It is not nearly enough; look at the hole in the doughnut." Displaced conservatives say, "It is a bad thing—it won't work, but it is working too well for the long-run health of the system."

In the 1970s there *is* available an agreed-upon record of facts about real wage trends in the last century. Real wages have risen steadily and strongly in the last century. These laws of motion of capitalism are, as Chapter 36's analysis of technical change delineates, in line with what we should expect from the dynamic forces of supply and demand. Auto workers get real wages ten times what their great-grandfathers got because their productivity enables that wage to be paid.

Even in the economic academies of Eastern Europe, it is now agreed that the mixed economies of Western Europe and North America are likely in 1999 to have real wages several times those prevailing in the 1970s.

But these days, good is not good enough. Why be satisfied with inequalities? Why permit any hunger in the affluent society? Why not an all-out war on poverty? So declare critics of the existing order in increasing numbers.

EQUITY VERSUS EFFICIENCY

Even without the gift of prophecy, one can bet that the welfare state will long be with us. Conservative politicians have consolidated rather than liquidated the economic reforms of their predecessors when progressive, welfarist or socialist governments in North America, Norway, Australia, or Britain were replaced by

Redistributing social pie may reduce its total:

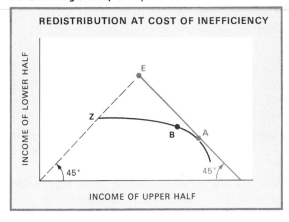

FIG. 38-2. If outcome at *A* (under relative *laissez-faire*) is to be shifted toward equality, deadweight loss or inefficiency may result. Instead of moving upward on the *p-p frontier* from *A* toward *E*, a shrinkage along *ABZ* (or even southwest!) may be the result. The challenge is to develop tax and other programs that more closely approximate *AE*.

more conservative parties. The question naturally arises, therefore, Why not go all or much of the way toward equality of incomes? Why wait until 1999 to do what can be done *today* by a determined electorate?

DEADWEIGHT BURDENS   Figure 38-2 illustrates the opportunities and difficulties. How can one go from the present point *A* to the equality point *E*? If we make income taxes more steeply progressive, decisions to invest in risky ventures and to work hard at one's profession will be profoundly affected. If we freeze prices and rents or put floors under wages, we alter production and employment. Conservatives no doubt exaggerate the problems of such "distortion," but only romantics deny their reality.

Schematically, the black *ABZ* curve bends inward as a result of the deadweight cost, or burden, that is inevitably associated with strong state interference with the workings of the market mechanism. Indeed, experience has shown that in some cases the distortions due to interference can become so great that the attempt to help one social class at the expense of another can end hurting them all. (Thus, before the 1948 decision by Ludwig Erhard to end rationing and stifling price controls, the West German economy lingered at *B* or inside *A* southwest of the *p-p frontier* at the expense of just about every income class.)

ARGUMENT AND COUNTERARGUMENT   Intentionally Fig. 38-2 presents a gloomy realistic picture of some of the difficulties. How might one react? First, some may say that the effort is still worth the cost, that greater equality is more important than greater affluence and is worth its cost. (And still others may demur, or reduce their aspirations.)

Second, one can mobilize the tools of economics to minimize the costs and distortions. Let the reader pencil in a new curve to lie between the black *ABZ* and brown *AE*. By skillful design of the programs against poverty and inequality, their deadweight burden can definitely be lessened and society may move on such a new and better curve. Thus,[1] the subsidy of low-income housing may be a more efficient long-run solution to our urban problems than freezing rents by direct controls. Some say that subsidising low-income *people* (not houses) would bring us closest to *AE*.

OUTRIGHT CONFISCATION So far the problem seems to have been phrased as if there must always be clash between equity and efficiency. Even if the trade-off is really there, the economist who keeps harping on the conflict may seem to act like an apologist for the status quo and an exponent of gradualism. But, actually, economic tools can cut both ways. A truly *revolutionary* policy—such as (1) confiscation of property of the wealthy, (2) a massive capital levy on the upper half of the income pyramid, or (3) steep wealth and inheritance taxation —might move one briskly yet durably from the status quo at *A* toward the equality point *E*. Under a less revolutionary system, which respects the right of private property and protects it from expropriation without due process and, what is more important to its owners, due compensation, complete efficiency of redistribution is indeed impossible. Paradoxically, it is a radical majority, which agrees with the 1848 definition of Proudhon that "all property is theft," that may have open to it a less distortive once-and-for-all redistribution from outright confiscation.

> EXAMPLE: Slavery was finally abolished in the British West Indies in 1838 and in the United States in 1863. Emancipation was a transfer of property from planters to workers—property in themselves. Earl Grey's government recompensed colonial slaveowners; Lincoln's emancipation simply dispossessed American planters. Under compensation, all the community, through taxation, had to work to pay off the indemnity, and the implied interest on it. Collecting these taxes and choosing the payees inevitably involved a great deal of deadweight loss, and friction. The end of Russian serfdom, under Nicholas, was similarly accomplished by compensation. In Fig. 38-2, the British and Russian cases may have approximated an *AB* movement, while the more drastic American abolition may have more nearly approximated an *AE* movement.

The example of confiscation illustrates that economic tools sometimes cut in the direction desired by conservatives, sometimes in the direction desired by revolutionaries. Experience and analysis also show that once-and-for-all confiscation can result in subsequent slower growth, unless the new order provides for efficient operation, maintenance, and growth of the capital which has changed ownership. *Capital will not automatically maintain itself, or be replaced, or be augmented along the most efficient lines without public or private entrepreneurship.*

---

[1] Chapter 39 deals further with urban problems. See also Chapter 21's theoretical demonstration of the dead-weight loss from price-fixing-plus-rationing (Question 6 in the Appendix). Canadian housing specialist Lawrence Smith has shrewdly commented that inferior housing and slum conditions are serious, but that they would ". . . . probably be better attacked within the context of an integrated poverty program." Bad housing is a symptom, not a cause. See Lawrence Smith, "The Housing Market, the Housing Problem, and Government Policy," in Officer and Smith, eds., *Canadian Economic Problems and Policies*, (McGraw-Hill, Toronto, 1970).

■ CAUSES OF INEQUALITY

To alleviate inequality one must first diagnose its principal causes. Here are some of the important factors involved.

DIFFERENCES IN PROPERTY WEALTH   The greatest disparities in income stem from differences in *wealth*. The Tudor monarchs became politically and economically independent when they appropriated the wealth of the monasteries. Windfall gains have helped too: Lord Durham came from a coal family; the Rhodes scholarships are based on diamonds and gold; the Hearst and Beaverbrook press empires were both based on resource *coups*. The special personal abilities of these men and of the Gettys and Rockefellers are dwarfed by the power stemming from their property.

Many of these differences in wealth were associated with plain luck *in discovery of natural resources*. Some were due in part to astuteness of exploration and perseverence in productive innovation. The *Wall Street Journal* and the London *Financial Times* are replete with stories of wealth in one generation due to innovational skill or luck. Since capital gains are not taxed, or only lightly taxed when they are realized by actual sale, it is not true that today's mixed economy prevents anyone from becoming a multimillionaire. Moreover, there are many loopholes in the tax laws that permit the retention and augmentation of initial wealth—special percentage depletion allowances for oil and other natural resources, stock options, capital-gains investments which escape all taxation at death, and so forth.

DIFFERENCES IN PERSONAL ABILITY   Some of these may be *inherited*: within every family there are evident differences in physical and mental abilities, and between families one expects from the Mendelian theory of genetics that there will be some dispersion. Students tend to think of intelligence or IQ as the important variable; but when it comes to making money, such traits as energy, ambition, canniness, and flair can be just as important. (As Mark Twain said: "You don't have to be smart to make money. But you *do* have to know how to make money!")

While differences in inherited ability play some role, the common man is inclined to overestimate them. The trained biologist and social psychologist point out that we all inherit from our environment as well as from our parents' genes. By the age of one, the affluent child of a serene and attentive mother already has a leg up in the race for economic status and success. By the time he is a six-year-old going to first grade in the suburbs, he already has an increased lead over the slum or rural six-year-old. And for the next 12 to 20 years, the scales are increasingly tipped toward those who already have.

DIFFERENCES IN EDUCATION AND TRAINING   The single most important factor working for reduced inequality in the last centuries has been the provision of public education. Here is the acid that has corroded the ancient order of privilege, in which there was infinite gulf between the educated upper classes and the illiterate masses.

As an educated man, John Stuart Mill could, in 1840, make the equivalent of 100,000 of today's dollars helping to run the East India Company (which in turn ran India). Perhaps it is not so remarkable that a man like Mill should receive an income twenty or thirty times that of the median man. But consider Charles Lamb, a lowborn cockney who also worked for the East India Company —as a clerk, and not a very hardworking one at that. Lamb too received several times the national average income. Why? Because he was *literate*: he could write, and add and subtract; scarcity of these skills made them command a handsome economic rent. The provision of schooling and the invention of the typewriter have done as much to emancipate women from the ancient domination of male chauvinists as all the hunger strikes of suffragettes or advanced plays of Ibsen and Shaw. (Indeed, Nora of Ibsen's *A Doll's House* could not have declared her independence if no careers were open to women.)

Modern economists have analyzed the problem of putting capital *into* people through education and training, in much the same way that one puts money capital into plant or equipment. To finish high school or medical school requires an investment that in the past those born poor simply could not afford. At the turn of this century only the affluent gentry went to Oxbridge and Yale; and attending even the more modest private and state-supported schools such as London, Toronto, and Michigan was reserved for a privileged few.

In a "meritocracy," opportunities to pursue advanced education and training are largely divorced from parental affluence. By fellowships and living allowances from the state and by partially repayable loans, those with the ability to benefit from education are granted the opportunity. Nor is this confined to professional training and advanced education: GNP is as much enhanced when high school dropouts are trained to program a computer or run a modern filing machine as when similar dollars are spent on a lawyer or a doctor. On-the-job training in welding, steam-fitting, plumbing, and other vocational pursuits involves great social payoff and also contributes toward the good society.

When higher education was scarce, the graduates of Eton, Upper Canada, and Groton, going on through Oxford, law school and the army staff school, reaped higher earnings than those who fought their way up. In part this was due to superior training and stringent selection standards. But much reflected differences in opportunity. Members of the elite were simply called to the boardroom, the professorships, and the Cabinet, though displaying no particular superiority over those from poorer schools.[2] As immigration, international competition, and more objective standards have become influential in staffing and promotion, we may expect to see more whose native tongue was not English, whose eyes are not blue, moving into high positions.

Although public expenditure on education has been an important historical influence making for a more open society, it is, alas, not the case that all such expenditures work toward reducing inequality. For there is a great deal of evidence that much public expenditure on higher education goes to *subsidize*

---

[2] The outstanding book on all this is John Porter, *The Vertical Mosaic* (Toronto: University of Toronto Press, 1965).

the middle classes rather than the urban and rural poor. Calculations made for California, where college attendance is more widespread than anywhere else in the world, show that the families of students at state universities (and at community colleges, too) have incomes well above the median of the population at large. The same relative scarcity of working-class families in public or state universities is found in Canada, in Britain, on the Continent, and in the developing world.

What can be done to prevent this outright subsidy to further inequality? First, more college students from the underprivileged classes can be actively recruited by revising entrance standards to seek promise, not grades. Second, funds can be diverted from higher education into vocational schooling. Third, if access to college education adds to earnings in later life—and statistics show this is indeed so—many argue that college students should be made to pay for the full costs of their extra education. I.e., fees should be tripled or quadrupled to cover more of tuition's true costs, and more repayable loans should replace scholarships (except in the case of the very poor). Does this seem inequitable? Adherents of equality reply that it is the present system, which taxes the poor as well as the rich to pay for state universities, which is inequitable. And certainly when we consider the high earnings of physicians, there is seen to be some merit in the argument.[3]

A strategy was recently outlined by the Economic Council of Canada. If society is to benefit from the potential abilities of family members, rather than support them in poverty, "the adults in the family must be enabled to participate in the labour force currently *and to prepare their children to do so in the future.* Thus *the concept of a minimum standard of living must be based on a definition of the family not merely as a consuming unit, but also as a producing [i.e. investing] unit.* . . . A substantial portion of the total investment in human capital is undertaken by family . . . initiatives. Public policies are needed to encourage this private investment process, and help protect it against the ravages of poverty."[4]

DISCRIMINATION AND NON-COMPETING GROUPS   Often however, equalization of education, training and even wealth does not produce equality of opportunity. Employers seem to disregard these productive aspects of workers and to show preference for male, white, young, English-speaking employees. Often this is, from their corporate point of view, a rational preference: employees, unions, and supervisors may make life easier if women, Indians, French Canadians, immigrants, and other "minorities" are excluded from the plant or office. Furthermore, of course, an ability to communicate easily with other workers, and to

---

[3] An article by E. J. Mishan of the London School of Economics, reprinted in P. A. Samuelson, *Readings in Economics* (McGraw-Hill, New York, 1970, 6th ed.), argues that full-cost tuition cum loans will get rid of radical student activists and troublemakers, replacing them with a docile, vocational-minded student body. It is debatable whether this would (or should) happen, but it can hardly be doubted that a cadre of perpetual students at Continental and Latin American universities does make for political activity.

[4] Economic Council of Canada, Sixth *Annual Review* (Queen's Printer, Ottawa, September 1969), p. 117. Reproduced by permission of Information Canada.

cooperate is an important part of what each worker contributes to an organization.

Notwithstanding these "real" disadvantages that women, non-whites or non-English-speakers (in English-speaking regions) have in comparison with typical English-speaking white male workers, it is widely admitted that Chapter 28's economic concept of "noncompeting groups" applies to them with a vengeance. Most well-paying jobs are simply not available. For example,

> "Even when Indians have the necessary educational or skill qualifications for employment, they face widespread discrimination from potential fellow workers as well as from employers. Many firms follow a definite policy (informally or unofficially, where such policies are illegal in terms of provincial legislation) of refusing to hire Indians at all, or in token numbers at best. Such discrimination is not against Indians as Indians, in most cases; it has developed as a result of unfortunate experiences with or observations of them as workers which tend to build up an unfavourable stereotype."[5]

Under these circumstances, Jamieson notes, Indians react defensively and aggressively, thus confirming white opinions. In this vicious circle, the supply of Indian or any "minority" labor offered is, in effect, simply auctioned off along the demand schedules for low-skilled hours.

Figure 38-3 shows how the economics of discriminatory exclusion works, here or abroad, against men or women. Supply and demand for some favored employments are shown in Fig. 38-3(a). The supply of white, male, English-speaking, "majority" hours is shown by SS. The demand curve for their labor, derived from their productive worth at the margin to the employers producing the important goods in industries from which the "minority" is excluded, is shown as DD. Equilibrium is at the high wage shown at E. Meantime, what is happening to casual labor or in the enforced ghetto is shown in Fig. 38-3(b). Working with inferior tools and being permitted to produce only certain limited goods that are not particularly desired by society, the demand curve for occupations open to the minority is shown as dd. Their supply ss intersects dd at the low equilibrium e, where *their* market is just cleared. Note the discrepancy between the two equilibria.

> *Exclusion has discriminated against the earning power of the minority workers.* They are much worse off than the favored workers. Such is the remorseless verdict of supply and demand if discrimination can be enforced by custom, law, or union collusion.

What would be the ideal situation in terms of both human equity and economic efficiency? If we let the ss supply of Fig. 38-3(b) be added to the SS supply of Fig. 38-3(a), we would have the new S + s curve of nondiscriminatory supply. Now at little expense to majority wages, we would see a near doubling of minority wages. Where would the extra wage income come from? It would *not* come primarily from an exaction by the minority on the majority (even though

[5] S. M. Jamieson, "Economic Development", in Canada Department of Indian Affairs and Northern Development, Indian Affairs Branch, *A Survey of the Contemporary Indians of Canada*, ed. H. B. Hawthorn, Vol. I (Ottawa, 1966). Reproduced by permission of Information Canada.

Exclusion exploits minority and lowers GNP:

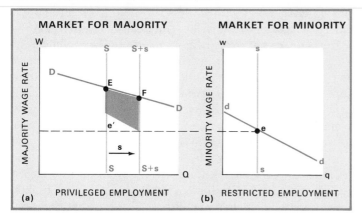

FIG. 38-3. Suppose a minority is excluded from good employment in (a) and ·must work in inferior employment in (b). Then majority *DD* and *SS* intersect at high-wage *E*; and minority *dd* and *ss* intersect in (b) at low-wage *e*. If all forms of discrimination and segregation were ended, all would go to highest-wage jobs, and members of the minority would go to (a), as shown by black arrow of shifted supply there. New equilibrium with equal wages for all would come at *F*, where *SS* + *ss* intersects demand. The great gain in minority wages would not be at the expense of an equal fall in majority wages (which would fall, but only a little, because of the gentle action of diminishing returns). Ending discrimination necessarily increases total of product; so gainers (including now-better-off capitalists belonging to the majority!) always get more than losers lose. The gray area under *EF* measures the gain in total GNP (because the area's lower boundary is drawn at the level of the productivity in (b) above and to the left of *e*).

justice might merit such a reparation if there were no other way to achieve equity). For these workers receive pretty much the same wage as before, their only diminution coming from the weak operation of the law of diminishing returns, as shown by the slight drop along *DD*. The extra income for the minority comes *from the extra GNP* that their higher productivity in their new employment brings as compared with their previous lower productivity enforced by discrimination. Instead of sweeping Milady's kitchen floor with an old broom, so to speak, now the black draws good pay working a modern computer-billing machine. Instead of existing on seasonal fur-trapping (and welfare) the Indian can work in the smelter or on the railway—or teaching French in the high school. That is the implication of Fig. 38-3 *after* discrimination has vanished and the educational disadvantages that went with it have disappeared.[6]

---

[6] For emphasis, Fig. 38-3 is drawn with *dd* shown as below *DD* from the beginning, implying that after discrimination is removed all inferior work disappears. It would be more realistic to redraw *dd* so that it rises upward on the left toward the vertical *W* axis. Then new equilibrium comes at intersection of vertically-added *SS* and *ss* with vertically added *DD* and *dd* at an equilibrium just above *F* (but at a common wage lower than *E*).

The day of nondiscrimination has not remotely arrived. Women writhe under exclusion from male preserves, or get paid less for equal work. Promotion is slow or rare for Indians, black immigrants, and orientals. Majority WASPs protest when minority workers are put over them as supervisors or foremen, or put alongside them on the bench or assembly line. Slowly, however, laws against discrimination, requiring equal pay for equal work, along with public education and militant protest are loosening up the pattern of segregation. The civil service started it, and industry and schools have followed, sometimes willingly, and sometimes in "tokenism" to advertise that the new vice-president, bank teller, or associate professor comes from a minority.

Of course, there is some improvement in employment status for some minorities. Most Indian families remain on welfare, but a few are in jobs closed to them a decade ago. Oriental and West-Indian workers have also broken through into many occupations with higher pay. Progress? Yes, slow progress. But note that much of the improvement came from the swing of the business cycle from the recessionary stagnation of the late 1950s to brisker growth. Further progress from this factor can hardly be expected once unemployment is brought down to minimum levels. To the contrary, every extra percentage of unemployment increases the likelihood that discrimination and exclusion will reappear, preserving jobs against non-whites and women. In particular, the non-discriminatory absorption of new immigrants and adjustment of Indians becomes almost impossible when the groups are conscious rivals for scarce jobs.

FRENCH-CANADIAN SEGREGATION   The above analysis of discrimination does not apply easily to the Province of Quebec. It is true that, near Montreal, some French-speaking workers are under disabilities similar to those suffered by non-English speakers elsewhere in Canada; this can only be treated as a variety of discrimination. But the phenomenon is better described as *segregation*: French employees work mostly for French employers. It results in part from discrimination against French workers by English-speaking employers, and leads to a parallel structure of trade and industry, duplicating some of the English-speaking structure. Of course, segregation may also arise from language barriers, educational differences, and cultural preferences, and not from discrimination.

It is not clear that segregation *in itself* is to be deplored, any more than the specialization that takes place as between French- and German-speakers in the European common market. What is a matter for worry is the outcome: higher rates of unemployment, lower-level occupations, smaller firms, and lower incomes in Quebec than in Ontario and western Canada (even after fully allowing for differences in education and rural-urban location). Racial or linguistic discrimination seems to be at least partly responsible, in the slowness of "foreign" (non-Quebec) corporations to hire or promote French-speakers and the unwillingness of English-speaking workers to cooperate in the plant with French-speakers.

The study and explanation of Quebec industry's lower incomes has been undertaken by Raynauld and others for the Bi and Bi Commission. It is clear that much of what they found can be removed if Quebec's headlong rush for higher levels of education is successful, and if Ottawa's language campaign creates a larger nucleus of bilingual workers. These two policies together may clean up much of the discrepancy, not only in Quebec but also wherever else French-speaking workers reside.

The residual "segregation" differences may be more lasting. What elements explain why Denmark has permanently lower income per capita than Sweden? Capital, natural resources, and geographic immobility of goods or factors. The same immobilities—the same reluctance of marginal units of capital to enter Quebec or of marginal members of the labor force to emigrate—may be the hard core that will maintain income differentials for a long period.[7]

The same comments (and the footnote) apply to the study of any segregated region with income out of step with the nation's; and to any country growing at a different rate from the Western economy's. But discrimination exists in enterprises that are not segregated, and is partly to blame for those of French origin having lower incomes than those of British origin of the same schooling, age, and occupation. The Bi and Bi investigators[8] found it impossible to measure the effect of discrimination on wages directly; instead they measured the effect of having French ethnic origins. In one approach this factor turned out to be trivial, accounting for perhaps 5 or 10 per cent of the discount French-speakers must accept. Another approach, however, suggested that it accounted for 35 per cent of the difference. But "ethnicity" covers both immobility of French Canadians (a supply factor) and discrimination against them (a demand factor). So although nothing conclusive may be said about the importance of *discrimination* against French Canadians in Montreal or Canada, it can be said that simply *being* a French-Canadian tends to explain low incomes, via some combination of immobility, discrimination, segregation, and education.

DIFFERENCE IN AGE AND HEALTH   Even if people were all born alike and subject to pretty much the same environment, some would suffer the vicissitudes of bad health. Cardiac disaster can strike anywhere. Neurosis and psychosis are not ailments that one can choose to have or not have. Alcohol and drugs take their toll in every stratum of society. And no one stays young and vigorous forever. Under *laissez-faire* it has always been the aged who have been most subject to economic want.[9]

---

[7] In the Appendix to Chapter 33 it was explained that commodity trade between regions can compensate for factor immobility. Thus goods moving between Quebec and elsewhere could under certain circumstances in the "Ohlin theorem" equalize wages, even if French-Canadians never move. But the conditions required are difficult to satisfy.

[8] For a full analysis of the economic position of French Canadians see "The Work World", Book III of the *Report of the Royal Commission on Bilingualism and Biculturalism*, Vol. 3A (Ottawa, 1969). For a study of the economic position of Canadian Indians see S. M. Jamieson, *op. cit.*

[9] In Montreal, Bi and Bi investigators found that *salaried men* of all ethnic origins did not reach the average for all men until age 30. Their highest income was attained about age 45, but they remained above average till age 65. Lowest incomes were for those under 19. A year of age increased earnings about $100 at age 45; maybe $150 in 1971. But it decreased earnings at age 65. The pattern of *incomes* is about the same, except that single persons, widows, and others suffer low incomes again at a younger age than salaried men.

A few years ago an English economist who was an enthusiast for the British Labour Party spent a year at an American university. He was fascinated at Christmas to read the histories of the 100 neediest cases described in the *New York Times*. He found among them anguishing cases of mental and physical illnesses but finally concluded, "There is scarcely an instance where better *macroeconomic* policy of the fiscal and monetary type could do much to touch the problem."

Actually, he was wrong and had fallen into the trap of those who say that good health doesn't matter to those who are lucky enough to enjoy it. If he had visited America in 1932, he would have learned how important good macroeconomic policy is. For at that time, people from every social stratum were in desperate economic need because of the Great Depression.

> The successful attainment of high employment has done more than any other single program to banish economic want and mitigate economic inequality. Differences in unemployment experienced have always been the single greatest cause of *economic variance within the working classes themselves*.

Moreover, if an observer were to follow a social welfare worker on her rounds in any typical week in the 1970s, he would find that every one of the health and personality problems encountered is exacerbated by the absence of money.

An alcoholic can be desperately unhappy. But if he is of independent means, his children need not go hungry on that account and his dependence upon a steady job is vitally lessened. In a lower-middle-class family, the onset of mental illness of a mother is a financial disaster in a way that is not true at the top of the income pyramid. Were it not for state-supported mental institutions, the vast bulk of the populace simply could not cope with the problem.

What inherited property has always provided for the privileged few, the modern welfare state in limited measure provides for the bulk of the populace. As we shall see, through *direct* public services and through *transfer*-payment programs, the modern mixed economy is in effect a gigantic *system of mutual insurance* against the worst economic disasters of life. "There but for the grace of God go I," each one of us thinks when he sees disaster strike some neighbor. And realizing we are all in the same boat, we troop to the polls at election time and vote upon ourselves the costs of the mutual-benefit programs that we call social insurance, health insurance, and welfare. And, as we are about to discuss, some kind of income-maintenance plan, in the form of a negative income tax or the like, has moved to the top of the agenda for modern debate in the years just ahead.

▪ DIRECT PROGRAMS FOR POVERTY AND INEQUALITY

Governments have always had some responsibility for the poor. Thus Elizabethan poor farms and Victorian orphanages have formed the targets of great novels of the past.

PRIVATE CHARITY   Years ago private charity had to play a significant if inadequate role: hand-me-downs for the poor, church missions and soup kitchens,
handouts for beggars, and free medical clinics were part of the conscience
money that the lucky paid to the unlucky.[10] Moreover, in an earlier time, the
extended family system meant that each working generation took care of its
parents in retirement: the institution of the baby-sitter was almost unknown
because there was always a resident maiden aunt or grandmother. After you
had settled in Toronto or Montreal, your cousins from Ireland, Poland, or Gaspé
could move in with you. Privacy is only a modern and middle-class privilege.

Private charity was never adequate (even though the situation would often
have been frightful without it). Today, it is quite eclipsed in relative importance
by the welfare functions of the state, of which the following are only a sample
list. The total expense is nearly 9 billion dollars per year, 5 billion dollars flowing
out of Ottawa.

HOSPITALS AND ASYLUMS   Help *in kind* was the primary form that public assistance originally took. Not very long ago it was said, "Only the very rich and
the very poor can afford adequate medical care." But that was of course an
exaggeration except as applied to those who happened to be near a teaching
hospital located in a slum, and who were not deterred by a demeaning means
test from providing their bodies for medical experimentation and demonstration.
As mentioned, poor farms and mental institutions are among the oldest of public
agencies.

FOOD COUPONS   In Canada, some cities and provinces give welfare recipients
tickets or coupons that can be redeemed for particular kinds of services or
merchandise. And after the United States rediscovered in the 1960s that there
were indeed still many subject to hunger in that most affluent of societies, Presidents Kennedy, Johnson, and Nixon instituted a vast expansion of the old food-
stamp program. Families that qualify by virtue of their low incomes receive
stamps that permit them to get allotments of food at fractional or even zero cost.

An argument continues in the modern welfare state. One school says, "Give
people money and let them buy health services and the foods they need." The
other school says, "If you give money for milk to the poor, they will spend it on
beer. Your dollar goes farther in alleviating the rickets of malnourishment and
the ravages of disease if you provide the services in kind. The dollar that a man
earns may be *his* to spend, but the dollar that society makes available to him to
meet particular deficiencies is a dollar that society has the right *paternalistically*
to channel directly to its targets."

Neither side wins the argument. Whether in Sweden or Canada, whether
at the national or local level of government, both forms of aid coexist.

WELFARE ASSISTANCE   In every country and city there exists some apparatus for
help to the destitute. These programs involve some element of direct aid at the

---

[10] See George Orwell, *Down and Out in Paris and London* (Penguin Books, London) and
James H. Gray, *The Winter Years* (Macmillan Co. of Canada, Toronto, 1967) for moving and
fascinating accounts of life among the derelicts of the 1930s.

same time that they often involve some element of transfer of abstract purchasing power. Thus a welfare mother with three young children may be receiving a check of $300 per month. Some of this she may be free to spend as she wishes; but some part of it will be under the close supervision of the welfare worker assigned to her case, who lays down guidelines of how much can go for clothing, house furnishings, and so forth.

Because the minimum standards insisted upon by modern society have risen significantly, the cost of welfare programs has burgeoned in recent decades. Consequently there is great unease among the tax-paying citizenry over such programs. A Gallup-like poll in 1971 would show that about half the public think that welfare assistance is shot through with gross abuses. Anecdotes are told of mothers who buy color television sets with funds that ought to go for the baby. Illegitimate births among mothers on relief are not greeted with the same tolerance as are similar blessed events among starlets and the jet set.

Among informed professionals in the area of welfare and social psychology, there is a similar feeling of disquiet with the present apparatus of welfare assistance. It is indeed costly. And often inefficient. It puts a heavy psychological tax upon the recipients, and in some cases helps to create a caste of poor who must be taken care of in the same way their parents were. A higher standard of sexual and other conduct is often demanded of those on relief than the critics themselves can, with all their advantages, live up to. The father of a family on relief may find that the noblest thing he can do to enhance the well-being of his loved ones is to leave home and disappear. Only then can his wife and children continue to get the aid they desperately need. (And lest he should return at night, the social-service caseworker is often supposed to initiate surprise bed checks—a practice that strikes sensitive observers as despicable.)

WELFARE PAYMENTS AND ECONOMIC DISINCENTIVES   If a relief father were to be offered a job that paid him several hundred dollars, taking that job might in some provinces or American states cost him several thousand dollars in the form of lost relief payments. Even a steady job at the minimum wage might represent a net loss to him in terms of what is left over after *deductions* from his relief allotments.

> Economically, the traditional system of welfare payments geared to need and earnings involves massive hidden costs in terms of *disincentive* effects. Literally billions of dollars of lost gross national product result from the disincentive structure of existing relief systems.

■ THE NEGATIVE INCOME TAX

Contemplating the great economic inefficiency of existing programs to mitigate inequality and poverty, economists of many persuasions have agreed on the need for a basic reform of the modern welfare state. The first gun was fired by Lady Juliet Rhys-Williams in Britain, in 1945. Later, both democratic advisor James Tobin of Yale and Republican brain-truster Milton Friedman published similar proposals for the United States. The basic idea is to cut through the

complexity and incentive-killing morass of welfarism by using the efficient apparatus of the *income-tax* structure to attune each person's income to his needs.

This is an idea whose time has come. True, like President Nixon's broad
"family-assistance" bill, which was given a frigid welcome by Congress, the
Munro 1970 White Paper on income security seems unlikely to achieve a negative income tax plan by 1972. Nevertheless, since 1967 Canada has utilized the
modest Guaranteed Income Supplement for pensioners, based on income-tax
computations. Almost everything is good about the negative income tax—except
its negative-sounding name. A better one might be the "incentive-guaranteed-
income" plan.

HOW IT WORKS   The basic notion of the broadest version is very simple. (Complexity comes only when narrower versions must be fitted into existing patterns
of welfare assistance and taxation.) When I make $10,000 a year, I pay positive
income taxes (as seen back in Chapter 9). When I earn an extra thousand dollars,
I do pay extra taxes, but only in fractional amounts so that I am strongly motivated to earn more in order to have more.

Now consider a family below some defined poverty level—say, $4,000, in a
typical year in the early 1970s, for a couple with two children. Below that level
they are deemed to have no capacity to pay any taxes; and indeed under current
philosophies of equity and ability to pay, our democracy feels that they should
receive government aids. In short, these aids constitute a tax in reverse—a *negative* income tax.

But here is where incentives come in. It is a common mistake to think that
only the unemployed are poor, or that only fatherless families are poor. Statistics
show that much of poverty is among the *working* poor—people who simply cannot earn in the marketplace what is today considered a minimum-needed income.
They, and their children, are deemed to merit government help.

Yet how can these aids be given them so as not to deter their efforts and
incentives? Here is where the negative income tax provides a great improvement
over those welfare programs which deprive people of all assistance the moment
they get even a poor job. (And, of course, those on assistance know this very
well and are thus deterred from trying to improve their position.) Just as the
positive income tax is geared between $10,000 and $11,000 to leave people with
an incentive to better themselves, the formula for the negative income tax is
gauged to leave the poor with more income after they have used their own
efforts to raise their private earnings by a thousand dollars, or even by a dollar.
Even when their total tax is negative, their marginal tax rate is always a positive
fraction less than unity.

POSSIBLE FORMULA   Table 38-1 illustrates how a typical negative income tax
might work. What is shown there for a family with two children could be easily
modified in the case of more or fewer family members. And of course, as the
country grows richer and can afford to be more generous, the formula could be
changed to begin at a higher level and to define a poverty level that is higher
both in dollar terms and perhaps in terms of constant-dollar purchasing power.

Negative income tax blends compassion with incentives:

POSSIBLE FORMULA FOR NEGATIVE INCOME TAX		
PRIVATE EARNINGS	ALGEBRAIC TAX (+ if tax; — if aid received)	AFTER-TAX INCOME
$ 0	—$2,000	$2,000
1,000	— 1,500	2,500
2,000	— 1,000	3,000
3,000	— 500	3,500
4,000	0	4,000
5,000	+500	4,500

TABLE 38-1. Here, a couple with two children is guaranteed at least $2,000 a year, but is left with incentive to work. (Verify this in last column.) The poverty line (shown in brown) could be raised as the nation gets wealthier, and, of course, the formula can be modified for families of varying sizes.

The paramount advantages of the negative income tax are the following:

1. It can replace much of present welfare assistance that destroys incentives for persons to work themselves off relief.

2. It is less demeaning to the poor, in treating taxpayers and welfare recipients exactly alike, under the same objective test.

3. It assigns administration simply to the tax-collecting departments in Ottawa or the provinces.

4. If desired, it simplifies a nation-wide drive to obtain one minimum level of well-being across our diverse regions. (It need not, however, be so centralized.)

That these advantages are valuable is obvious.[11] The negative income tax also has its critics.

1. Some say that it will be costly, and become a swollen monstrosity like health and hospital insurance; others, however, say that actual proposals are niggardly;

2. Some say that it will be too lavish in rural areas and too stingy in the high-cost cities, especially if administered on a nation-wide basis.

These are, however, criticisms of actual dollar proposals. More relevant are criticisms of the *idea* of a guaranteed minimum:

3. "People ought to have to work for their living, not be entitled to a guaranteed income handed to them on a silver platter."

---

[11] A recent, and tentative, study by Colin J. Hindle of poverty in Ontario is valuable evidence of the power of the negative income tax to eliminate poverty under Canadian circumstances. Focusing attention on the gap between a person's income and a poverty standard (equal to the level prescribed by Ontario welfare assistance rates), he measured how much of such poverty would be eliminated by the money now used in Ontario for today's welfare programs. He found that if the 1965 family allowance dollars were applied to a negative income tax, about 60 per cent of Ontario poverty would be eliminated. Better still, he found that if both family allowance *and* old age assistance were replaced by a negative income tax, more than 80 per cent of 1965 poverty would be eliminated. These are high percentages, attesting to the wasteful nature of today's universal assistance programs. [See Colin J. Hindle, "Negative Income Taxes and the Poverty Problem in Ontario," *Canadian Tax Journal*, Vol. XIX, No. 2 (March-April, 1971), pp. 116-123.]

4. The negative income tax can only supplement, not replace, existing welfare programs.[12]

TWO OTHER GUARANTEES FOR THE JOBLESS　The guaranteed income is the most general plan so far devised, putting the same secure floor under everyone regardless of job or need. It is at the opposite extreme from the social-assistance approach, with its complex system of special payments, each determined by the particular category into which the recipients' problems fall. *Between* these two extremes are two other policies that reflect the public's special concern for those of the disadvantaged and unemployed who are young enough and strong enough to work, if work can be found. One policy proposes to guarantee jobs for such people, while the other advocates supporting them while they look for work themselves.

1. Guaranteed jobs. Many people feel that the main duty of the state is to make it possible for *everyone* to work. They go farther than demanding the full use of fiscal and monetary policies to prevent unemployment and claim that the government itself should become the "employer of last resort." (Good examples of this approach working during times of *seasonal* unemployment were provided by the "winter-work" schemes of the 1960s, and by the Department of Manpower's 1971 and 1972 summer-job plans for high-school and college students. A guaranteed-employment scheme is a permanent, or recession-long, variant.)

Should the public sector be used as a sponge to soak up unwanted workers? Work for all is surely an attractive goal. But what if the government sector cannot devise useful, efficient, and satisfying work for the less employable part of the population? Digging holes and filling them up again, or standing around in pointless and transparent idleness, can be destructive to morale. Hence most economists recommend that fiscal and monetary policies be supplemented by manpower placement and training programs to achieve virtual full employment, rather than by expanding the civil service in make-work schemes.

2. Unemployment insurance. Originally based on private schemes like fire insurance, unemployment insurance became more widespread in the 1920s and the 1930s and eventually became public (governmental), compulsory, and national in scope. The latest (1971) revisions suggest that, apart from premium-like contributions, it has now lost all the usual trappings of insurance, and is primarily a pure transfer scheme to maintain worker morale and spending power during widespread cyclical unemployment. From the macroeconomic point of view, its near-automatic pay-out upon cessation of private income, and its close connection with central-government financing and funding, makes it a powerful employment weapon. From the point of view of a person who becomes unemployed and who may face poverty as a result, assistance begins much more quickly than a guaranteed *annual* income would. The only pity is that it works

---

[12] For more on the negative income tax, see the readings by James Tobin and Robert J. Lampman in P. A. Samuelson, *Readings, op. cit.*, and the article by Milton Friedman in Melvin Laird, ed., *The Republican Papers* (Anchor Books, Doubleday & Company, Inc., Garden City, N.Y., 1969).

best for those who are economically strongest—the previously well-employed, and neglects those who, because of their age or their health, are outside the labor force.

CASEWORK AND WELFARE PROGRAMS   Economists are vehement that most "case" poverty (physical or mental disability that bars people from the general economic advance) stems from the same causes as insular or regional poverty and unemployment: birth to low-income parents in low-income regions. Because poverty is both the cause and the result, the argument goes, the indicated treatment is to cut through the vicious circle and guarantee a decent minimum income.

The casework tradition of social work, which is interwound with *ad hoc* welfare payments for particular disabilities, sees the problem otherwise. Social workers will still have to advise and support broken families, neglected children, sufferers from addiction, dependents of those in jail, the feeble-minded, and so forth. In the best 19th century liberal tradition, they must help those who, even with funds, would not be fully able to cope with modern society. Obviously, a guaranteed income will help these casework "clients" as much as or more than it will help the "normal" poor. But the guaranteed income program will not render social workers unemployed, nor relieve the taxpayer of the need to help those who are physically or mentally weak.

To be fair, the attacks on social work and welfarism are not necessary to the guaranteed income proposal. Its unique attraction is that it allows people in poverty to continue to receive aid without the disincentives that now confine them in workless, aimless, endless idleness.

THE QUALITY OF LIFE

This chapter has discussed the problems of inequality and of poverty. The quantity of gross national product cannot be appraised independently of its distribution. But even if inequality could be considerably reduced and poverty largely alleviated, there still remain important and vexing questions about the quality of life.

In the nineteenth century, moralists like Thomas Carlyle and John Ruskin declaimed against the acquisitive society. The poet Wordsworth expressed a common sentiment in the lines

> Give all thou canst; high Heaven rejects the lore
> Of nicely-calculated less or more.

And as a society becomes more comfortably situated, the more it can afford to indulge this distaste for a purely pecuniary motivation based on self-interest.

WHEN SCARCITY ENDS   Indeed we do not face squarely the philosophical issue if we make an era of greater altruism wait on the disappearance of scarcity. Marxians early had the notion of the ultimate "withering away of the state," after a transitory period of state capitalism and dictatorship of the proletariat. But such pie in the sky cannot appease the legitimate desire in the here and now of a Soviet citizen for greater political freedom. Similarly, there is no great virtue in paying lip service to unselfishness *after* there is superabundance. The test of sincerity of belief in a cause is how much you will sacrifice for it.

Galbraith was premature in proclaiming the end of scarcity at mid-century. But actually John Maynard Keynes had anticipated Galbraith by almost 30 years. In 1930 Keynes made the following prophecy with respect to the future.[13]

> . . . suppose that a hundred years hence we are all of us . . . eight times better off . . . than we are today. . . . Assuming no important wars and no important increase in population, the *economic problem* may be solved. . . . This means that the economic problem is not—if we look into the future—*the permanent problem of the human race.*
>
> Why, you may ask, is this so startling? It is startling because—if instead of looking into the future, we look into the past—we find that the economic problem, the struggle for subsistence, always has been hitherto the primary, most pressing problem of the human race—not only of the human race, but of the whole of the biological kingdom from the beginnings of life in its most primitive forms.
>
> Thus we have been expressly evolved by nature—with all our impulses and deepest instincts—for the purpose of solving the economic problem. If the economic problem is solved, mankind will be deprived of its traditional purpose. . . . I think with dread of the readjustment of the habits and instincts of the ordinary man, bred into him for countless generations, which he may be asked to discard within a few decades.
>
> To use the language of today—must we not expect a general "nervous breakdown"? . . . Thus for the first time since his creation man will be faced with his real, his permanent problem—how to use his freedom from pressing economic cares, how to occupy the leisure, which science and compound interest will have won for him, to live wisely and agreeably and well. . . .
>
> There are changes in other spheres too which we must expect to come. When the accumulation of wealth is no longer of high social importance, there will be great changes in the code of morals. We shall be able to rid ourselves of many of the pseudo-moral principles which have hag-ridden us for two hundred years, by which we have exalted some of the most distasteful of human qualities into the position of the highest virtues. . . . The love of money as a possession—as distinguished from the love of money as a means to the enjoyments and realities of life —will be recognized for what it is, a somewhat disgusting morbidity, one of those semi-criminal, semi-pathological propensities which one hands over with a shudder to the specialists in mental disease.
>
> But beware! the time for all this is not yet. For at least another hundred years we must pretend to ourselves and to every one that fair is foul and foul is fair; for foul is useful and fair is not. Avarice and usury and precaution must be our gods for a little longer still.
>
> . . . in making preparations for our destiny . . . let us not overestimate the importance of the economic problem. . . . It should be a matter for specialists— like dentistry. If economists could manage to get themselves thought of as humble, competent people, on a level with dentists, that would be splendid!

This is indeed a passage of profound and prophetic insight. For one thing, despite the Great Depression, which had for a time set Keynes' time schedule

---

[13] J. M. Keynes, "Economic Possibilities for Our Grandchildren," reprinted in his *Essays in Persuasion* (Macmillan, London, 1933) and also in P. A. Samuelson, *Readings, op. cit.*

behind, we are now right on target. In the 40 years since Keynes wrote, real output per head has grown at almost precisely the 2 per cent per annum rate that Keynes had prophesied.

For another thing, has not Keynes perhaps given a clue to the nature of the generation gap that is so prominent a feature of our time? In college youth, among offspring of affluence particularly, we can perhaps see the change in moral code that Keynes predicted would be the outcome of affluence. In view of modern psychiatric opinion that many of the young in the advanced nations are plagued by the problem of "existential vacuum," one of whose symptoms is a disquieting search for meaning and purpose in life, there is an almost uncanny clinical precision in Keynes' diagnosis that hitherto economic necessity has shaped man's very biological nature and provided him with that purpose. For what is more purposeful than filling your belly when it is empty? Tigers in the jungle do not, Hamlet-like, debate the meaning of meaning.

■ ONE FOOT IN AFFLUENCE

But we are not yet arrived at Utopia. In the meantime, in the here and now, what is it that economists must economize? This was the title of a provocative address given by the late Sir Dennis Robertson of Trinity College, Cambridge, on the occasion of the two-hundredth anniversary of the founding of Columbia University. What economists economize, said Robertson, is "love," for that is the scarcest commodity in the universe. We must make what we have go a long way. We must not waste this precious resource on petty problems *which the mechanisms of the marketplace can handle.*[14]

If the time is not yet when we can dispense with the economic system, still the time is long past when we can permit it to be master rather than good servant. We do still need the efficiency of our large corporations. But that is no reason for permitting business and industry to be the arbiters of our national policy. We must be ungrateful recipients, and indeed bite the hand that helps to feed us. This is the privilege that the abundance of science and the Industrial Revolution have given us—to reverse the roles in the Emersonian plaint that

> Things are in the saddle
> And ride mankind.

---

[14] And yet, as was discussed in the Appendix to Chapter 24 dealing with game theory and with the problem of prisoners' dilemma, it is only in *special* social situations, where the checks and balances of competition happen to be available, that we can dispense with love and altruism if the good society is to be achieved.

SUMMARY

■ 1   Where economic inequality serves no economic purpose, ethical observers criticize its existence. And even where it does serve a function, such observers are willing to pay some price in terms of inefficiency for alleviating it. Now that a measure of affluence, above and beyond the minimum of subsistence, is available, the citizenry insists upon certain minimum living standards for all.

■ 2   The view, associated with Pareto, that inequality is a universal constant which cannot be much affected by policy, is not consonant with historical experience. In the advanced countries, Lorenz curves of inequality show less disparity of living standards than they do in the underdeveloped regions. Coupling Smithian self-interest with universal suffrage has led, as the founding fathers predicted, to the modern welfare state with its multifarious social security programs of *mutual reinsurance.*

■ 3   The laws of motion of capitalism, from Victorian *laissez-faire* to the modern mixed economy, follow no simple formulas. Without substantial redistributive transfer expenditure by government, inequality of standards of life would presumably persist. But, provided educational opportunities prevail and monopolization of markets is thwarted, there is not a valid iron law of ever-increasing polarization of wealth.

■ 4   The major causes of inequality involve differences in (*a*) property ownership, (*b*) personal ability (attributable to both environment and heredity), (*c*) education, training, and opportunity, (*d*) discrimination, and (*e*) age and health. Decaying, but still with us in some degree, is the belief that it is the fault of the poor themselves if they are poor; and that private charity should be relied on to handle the cases of greatest distress.

■ 5   For centuries public policy has provided asylums and hospitals, poor farms and old-people's homes, and various forms of *ad hoc* relief in times of famine and depression. But only in modern times has the positive role of government become dominant.

■ 6   Cradle-to-grave social security and medical care are common among the mixed economies abroad. Only since the 1930s have social insurance and federally financed relief and welfare programs developed here. And only since the 1960s has there been a determined battle at the national level against poverty. Some form of the negative income tax—i.e., minimum-guaranteed-income-cum-incentives—seems the next item on the social agenda, providing as it does fewer difficulties than a program of jobs for all in which the government is the employer of last resort for hard-core unemployables.

■ 7   As the problem of mere survival gradually recedes into the background (at least in the West), the problem of the quality of economic life begins to take precedence over the problem of mere quantity. How we shall use our new leisure and how we shall develop new codes of conduct are some problems the future will pose.

QUESTIONS FOR DISCUSSION

1. From 1945 to 1970 inequality of incomes in Canada or the United States has not changed much. Is this an indictment of the system in your view? Or a symptom of the difficulty of a program for changing matters quickly in this sphere?

2. Do colleges perpetuate inequality?

3. Why not jobs for all? What are next steps in your view (free higher education for all? . . .)?

4. Can you draw a graph of the tax structure both in the positive and the negative range of taxes? Is it the case that the more you earn the more you keep?

5. Was Keynes borrowing trouble in his worrying about the future? Cannot people be happy without working?

6. *Extra-credit problem:* Redraw Fig. 38-3 according to instructions of footnote 6. Better still, move (b) as follows: Line up w vertical axis to fall *on* (a)'s $S + s$ line, and flip-flop (b)'s horizontal axis so that it runs westward rather than eastward. As before, identify E and e (with e just below E). But contrast them with nondiscrimination intersection of DD and dd at F' just southeast of E and northeast of e. Shade the little triangle formed by e, E, and F'. Can you deduce that it measures gain in national product from eliminating discrimination?

7. Review your understanding of the following concepts:

Pareto's laws

Lorenz measures of inequality

negative income tax

discrimination and segregation

guaranteed jobs

end of scarcity

self-interest and altruism

39

ECONOMIC PROBLEMS
OF CITIES AND REGIONS,
AND THE POLLUTED ENVIRONMENT

*". . . what a community requires, as the word itself suggests, is common culture. . . .
But a common culture cannot be created merely by desiring it. It rests upon economic
foundations. It is incompatible with the existence of too violent a contrast between classes,
for such a contrast has as its result, not a common culture, but servility or resentment, on
the one hand, and patronage or arrogance, on the other. It involves, in short, a large
measure of economic equality."* R. H. TAWNEY, *Equality,* London, 1931.

Most readers of these pages will be urbanized. If we adopt as a minimum
definition of urban population at least 20,000 persons residing in one dense
built-up area, almost 66 per cent of today's Canadians would qualify, as compared to little more than 6.6 per cent in 1851; 40 per cent are now living in
"metropolitan areas" of at least 100,000. Fig. 39-1 tells some of the story.

Surprisingly, by international standards Canada has always been highly
urbanized. Even in 1825, with over 5 per cent of their people in Quebec and
Montreal, the Canadian colonies exceeded the world-wide urban population
proportion (those living in cities of 20,000 or over). The subsequent growth of
Toronto, Halifax, Saint John, Hamilton, Kitchener-Waterloo, London, Ottawa,
Windsor, Winnipeg, Calgary, Edmonton, Vancouver, and Victoria has also contributed to a clustering of total provincial population, including rural populations
in or near urban areas. Only Saskatchewan, Alberta, and the Atlantic Provinces
have kept some uniformity of population change between rural and urban areas.

Who does live in the cities? Mostly people born there or in other Canadian
urban centers. But more than one-third of city growth is direct immigration
(especially of young women) from the rural areas, and (mostly of young men)
from overseas. As migrants are usually already grown up, the cities are much
less "youthful" in their age composition than the rural fringes. Declining rural
job opportunities are particularly discouraging to females, and the growth of
urban service industries and marriage opportunities have drawn them to the
cities. Young married couples, too, move to the cities or their neighborhoods.

By 1980, 80 per cent of Canadians will be urbanized:

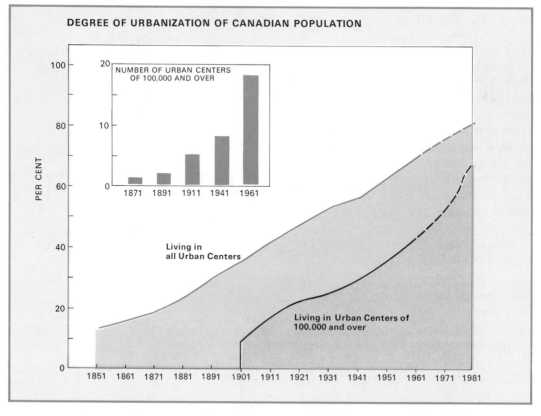

FIG. 39-1. Degree of urbanization is the percentage of total population living in urban centers of 1,000 persons and over. [Sources: Dominion Bureau of Statistics and L. O. Stone, *Urban Development in Canada* (Ottawa, Information Canada, 1968); and estimates by Economic Council of Canada: Fourth and Sixth *Annual Reviews*. Reproduced with the permission of Information Canada.]

Thus farm populations may now become less fertile, while the residential districts of the metropolitan areas will be characterized by high birthrates and demands for schools and skating rinks. The centers of the cities, however, will be populated by the retired, older couples, unskilled newcomers, and those in real poverty.

The inward movement is most pronounced in the Prairies, and least significant in the Maritimes; but evident everywhere. Furthermore, an increasing number of people are collecting in the suburbs, or even in deep rural areas; but not on the farm. Anywhere statistics indicate a nonurban population increase, investigation discloses an isolated suburb, a mining-forestry complex, or a tourist-recreation center. The "green revolution" is steadily reducing the number of farmers, exposing everyone to a productive and efficient, but congested and polluted, manmade urban environment.

■   WHAT ARE THE "PROBLEMS OF URBANIZATION?"

For the most part, they are the problems of population growth in general. For example, if Canadian natural increase and migration kept the same percentage of people on the farm and in the forests as at 1900, and allowed the towns and cities to grow only at the overall demographic rate, these towns and cities would still suffer urban growing pains. Additionally, a number of rural and foreign people *equal to the entire Canadian turn-of-the-century population* have migrated into the main cities. In a short chapter such as this, we can note only three of the many types of personal and policy problems that this massive reconcentration, superimposed on the general economic and population expansion of the nation, has produced. The first is the problem of the city center and the slum. The second is the problem of the urban-rural fringe and of land development generally. And the third is the related problem of widespread environmental pollution. [For all three aspects of urbanization, see the comprehensive new *Urban Canada: Problems and Prospects*, a report prepared by Norman Harvey Lithwick for the federal Cabinet (Central Mortgage and Housing Corporation, Ottawa, December 1970).]

Older urban development in Europe and North America typically took place slowly enough for the center to restyle itself as a location for such central activities as marketing, financial services, government, retailing, entertainment, and communications. Repeatedly, older buildings were razed and street patterns adapted to new requirements; landlords and burghers combined to see that central activities did not drift elsewhere. Thus the businesses of the City of London, Wall Street, and downtown Montreal are conducted within a stone's throw of where they were carried on many generations ago.

But landlords and great corporations have recently been less successful in fixing activities at the city center.

Traffic difficulties have pulled many retailers and services outward to neighborhood centers and plazas. Old business buildings, difficult to modernize, have been relegated to low-grade uses; financial and trading activity has moved to large structures in different neighborhoods; and older areas have been razed and left as parking or vacant lots. In turn this has speeded the accompanying migration from central houses and apartments to dwellings in the suburbs. Thus the stage has been set for modern North American cities: some partly empty at the core, others in the process of reoccupation by newcomers in search only of cheap, central accommodation. These slums and ghettos adjoin the surviving commercial district and supplant the former blocks of townhouses and middle-class apartments that clustered nearby.

ECONOMICS OF GHETTO HOUSING   The environmental disadvantages of slum living, as we saw in Chapter 38, can have a cumulative impact in handicapping the economic status of those in poverty, especially immigrants and non-white people. They do not choose to live in smog and congestion in preference to smart apartments or suburban greenlands. But race and language often restrict their choice. At one time racial clauses in real-estate covenants and local laws were used to keep neighborhoods unmixed with newer ethnic strains. After courts and votes had weakened such excluding devices, discrimination by land-lords, clubs, and real-estate agencies pretty much continued the same tendencies. In addition, foreign-language immigrants aggravated their isolation from English- and French-speaking majorities by choosing to live near other new arrivals, thus supporting their familiar institutions, churches, restaurants, and specialty stores while permitting the family elders to continue speaking their native language. This separateness also led to discrimination and bigotry against them.

In the beginning bigotry was shameless. Later it became somewhat shame-faced. More and more people began to say: "*I* am not bigoted. But *others* are. And it is a well-known fact that property values go to pieces when (blacks, Pakistanis, Chinese, Italians, Jews, etc.) get a toehold in a neighborhood."

This then threatens to become what sociologist Robert K. Merton calls a "self-fulfilling prophecy." If people believe in it and act on it, even if originally it were false, it may become true.

However, let us turn to the economic facts about race and real estate. Take the extreme case of blacks and whites. If you tabulate bills of sale in two similar communities, but where one has had blacks move into it and the other has not, what would such a controlled experiment show? That is, of course, the relevant question, because it is obvious that many slum neighborhoods which are in economic decay will have falling prices anyway even if there are no racial inter-mixtures; and it is also well known that the black community tends to be con-fined to those decaying neighborhoods that poor people can just afford.

> A careful study of *matched* city neighborhoods, carried out under the auspices of University of California[1] researchers and covering such diverse cities as Oakland and Detroit, Chicago and Portland, revealed that it was a complete myth of the real-estate fraternity that desegregation of a neigh-borhood harms real-estate values. "Block busting," so-called, in fact if anything raised property values (as the block buster who spreads false rumors knows very well).

And why not, when you come to think about it? Precisely because the black buyer and renter is discriminated against, his demand bids up the prices of those properties which may be available to him. Figure 39-2 illustrates the economics of housing discrimination in a fashion reminiscent of Fig. 38-3's demonstration of the economics of job discrimination. When the real-estate market is split into two parts, and if the blacks are allotted less than their per capita supply, the auction market bids up the rentals that can be exacted from them, limited only by their incomes. After the barriers have been eliminated, rentals for similar accommodations become equalized—resulting in both a more equitable and a more efficient equilibrium.

---

[1] L. Laurenti, *Property Value and Race: Studies in Seven Cities*, (University of California Press for Commission on Race and Housing, Berkeley and Los Angeles, 1960).

Discrimination raises rents to blacks:

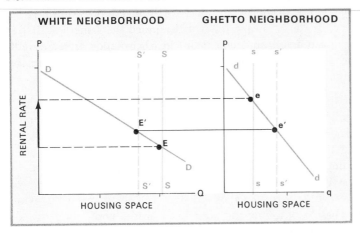

FIG. 39-2. Demand curves are drawn to be the same per capita. (That is, tastes and incomes are the same). Without discrimination, rents would be at the common level *E'* and *e'* with the same allocation of living space per capita. (In fact the markets could be combined in the absence of segregation, with everyone living at random.) But suppose under segregation blacks are given only half their per capita share of space. Then their *dd* intersects their allotted *ss* at high *e* rentals. Whites' *DD* intersects their unfairly swollen *SS* at low-level *E*. The black arrow on the left measures the gap due to discrimination. (Though slumlords gain, landlords as a class actually lose!) If blacks are poorer than whites, the gap will be smaller. Why?

■ ECONOMICS OF URBAN BLIGHT

Discussion of housing segregation brings us to the general problem of urban decay. This topic heavily overlaps the economics of races and minorities, since in regions with racial mixtures, the inner city is increasingly becoming the sole province of blacks, Chinese, North American Indians, and recent immigrant groups. Metropolitan areas continue to grow, but it is the suburban areas around the old city limits which show the most rapid growth. Half a century ago, urban sociologists such as Robert Park of the University of Chicago delineated *circular* patterns of city development. At the center is the downtown shopping district, the locale for luxury hotels, banks, and office buildings. Surrounding this nucleus is the tenderloin district of decay, where vice and vagrancy abound. Still farther out come workingmen's flats and homes; and then finally you arrive at middle-class country. Farthest out of all are the estates, polo fields, and hunting acres of the very rich.

The circles, however, fan out dynamically. As middle-class residents move farther out, their old neighborhoods change. Mansions are broken up into rooming houses, and apartments that once housed 4 people come to house 10 or more. A new tenderloin ghetto is born.

It is a mistake to think that this is an invariable pattern. A mountain or waterfront can modify the circular form, and also restrain the outward migration of the middle class. Or the ubiquity of the auto may destroy any real notion of a *center* to the city—which becomes, and perhaps should become nothing but a concrete switchboard for the rerouting of expressway traffic. As in Manhattan and London, so in Toronto and Vancouver, slum neighborhoods are repeatedly reclaimed by the gold-coast clientele through the force of dynamic competition. But still a general circular pattern can be discerned both here and abroad.

"TRICKLING DOWN"   Experts tell us that it is *not* the case that slum and ghetto dwellers are worse housed as a whole than in the past. A count of the number of persons per bathroom, the number of hot-water versus cold-water flats, of outdoor privies versus indoor toilets, reveals that, whatever middle-class visitors may think of the inner city, conditions there are actually better now, on the average, than they used to be. This improvement has not come about as the result of generosity or public programs so much as of the exodus of previous residents to the suburbs. At one time the poor lived on the fringes and walked to work; the rich lived at the center. Later the development of radial street railways brought the poor class to the core, near their jobs. Now the poor are diffused throughout the older inner city and aging suburbs, limited in their choices by the costliness of new buildings, transport availability, and social resistance to their arrival. Houses and streets "trickle down" from middle class to poorer occupants, who are the *temporary* beneficiaries of the previous residents' migration to modern or remote houses, perhaps as a result of the growth of commercial activity in the city that attracted the immigrants and the poor.

■ THE URBAN-RENEWAL BULLDOZER

Ironically, the efforts by government to redevelop the inner city have in some measure served to help the middle class and hurt the poor. When old buildings are torn down and new developments put in their place, to the eye there has been an aesthetic improvement and an increase in space per person. But for whose benefit? For those tenants who lived in crowded quarters before? Only too rarely. Often the occupants are hard put to find quarters anywhere near as good as those which had trickled down to them. And the new tenants who come in are young, professional and white-collar couples who are childless and (most often) white and English-speaking. If a black family can pay $300 a month it is free to live there. If . . . .

What can be done about this? Leave the slums to stew in their own juice, waiting for the Invisible Hand of perfect competition to rescue them? Deny governments the power to take land and buildings by expropriation? Some urbanists have suggested just this.

A more realistic approach, however, is to shape urban redevelopment along lines that will take account of the following concepts:

1. Rebuilding any neighborhood requires responsibility assumed *in advance* for those who will become the victims of the new program. This involves rehousing of those displaced, either within the new development, or through location in good housing elsewhere.

2. Residential *social capital*—utilities, transit, churches, water and sewers, recreation, trees, shopping centers, medical clinics, schools, and *social bonds and groupings*—are in just as much need of conservation or careful replacement as the private shelter of both new arrivals and the displaced.

3. Massive uniform low-income apartments can themselves become "urban blight" even before their paint and mortar are dry. These developments do not confirm the ancient canard "you can get people out of the slums, but you can't get the slums out of the people." But it is a sad fact of modern life that the frustration of such asphalt jungles can produce unhappiness and danger in urban open spaces after dark. More fragmented and meticulous (and more expensive) planning remedies much of this. Urban philosophers, however, have advocated two different approaches:

(*a*) Public purchase of land (one version of an urban "land bank"), later sold at reduced cost to smaller private builders charged with constructing houses and apartments without further subsidy. This would help produce varied but substantial buildings and neighborhoods. Some American and European renewal has proceeded along these lines.

(*b*) Rent subsidies to people, so that they can fix up their own houses or take over and improve existing structures. These have in many cases added more to the total of human happiness than have architectural cakeboxes on a grand scale.

■ THE PROCESS OF URBANIZATION

Before further examining the disadvantages and advantages of urbanization, we should ask why cities grow. It is relatively easy to describe the pains and problems of urban growth, but very difficult to make rigorous generalizations about the process that many living persons have witnessed: the agglomeration of people and enterprises into an urban unit with an apparent *inherent* ability to grow, almost biologically, without infusions or transfers from other urban places.

We cannot pause long to speculate on the very conception of cities. Geographers have been doing empirical work on the functions cities perform, the distances between them, and their size, for many years. Suffice it to say that sometimes it is not possible for economic activity to be spread out evenly, as over a featureless plain; and often it is not economic. Instead it pays regional-service industries to locate close together, thereby reducing transportation costs between them. Chicago and London, Ontario, are examples. As well, exporting regions gain by funneling their goods through a single railroad or port. In this way they reap gains similar to Marshall's *external economies* discussed in Chapters 23 and 37. This explanation *alone* will account for the existence of cities.

Whatever reason is most acceptable for the formation of cities, it is well known that even in the absence of stimulation from national population increase, urban growth tends to be self-sustaining because grouped industries create new demands and external economies in supply:

(1) specialized skills and knowledge which reduce labor costs for similar and competitive new arrivals,

(2) markets for specialized supplying firms and industries, that also reduce costs for everyone,

(3) by-products for other local exporters,

(4) markets for locally based business services,

(5) through increased employment, rising population and consumer expenditures, expanded retail and wholesale sectors,

(6) local manufacturing to replace outside consumer-goods suppliers, and

(7) suppliers to *these* manufacturers and

(8) users of *their* by-products, etc. . . .

The reader will recognize here yet another application of the "staple" model of expansion and economic growth. The demand for other industries, skills, and products are referred to as "linkages." The typical mass of consumer facilities and services appended to any new export feature is referred to as its regional, or urban, multiplier.

EXPORT BASE MULTIPLIER   This multiplier is, *algebraically*, very similar to our import-leakage multiplier of Chapter 13. Based on the growth of (the first three items in the above list of growth processes) new exporters, their direct suppliers, and by-product processors as the "export base," it summarizes the *local* respending of new incomes paid by the export-base industries, thus creating new incomes and new local industries and employment (items 4 to 8 in the above list). The multiplier that relates the income-dollar (or employment) growth of the export base to the income-dollar (or employment) growth of the whole city or region thus depends on the extent to which the city or region relies on "imported" goods and services rather than producing them locally. Obviously, in the short run, this multiplier merely summarizes spending in existing plants and stores. Its form is

$$\text{Change in urban income} = \frac{1}{\text{MPS} + \text{MPM}} \times \text{Change in export income,}$$

where MPS and MPM, the local propensities to save and import, are defined as in Chapter 13. Regional studies have shown that MPS + MPM may amount to about 0.55, so that the change in urban income for a million-dollar rise in local export incomes would be about 1.81; probably less than 2 for any North American city.

In the long run, however, the export-base multiplier is more than a simple employment-change number. It now relates the growth of *new* products and plants to the appearance of *new* local services and jobs to serve it, and serve its employees, and *their* employees.

Will the long-run multiplier be larger or smaller than the short-run? New marketing and transport services should improve the supply of imports, and expanded tastes and incomes should sharpen demand. Hence the import leakage MPM may increase and weaken the multiplier. This would explain why many cities no longer rely on local farmers, clothing industries, furniture factories, engineering works, or shipyards to the extent that abandoned farms and plants suggest they once did. More and more, the growing city goes to specialized regions for its goods.

But statistical studies show the opposite. It is true that expanding cities import proportionately more; the very diversity of their swollen requirements guarantees that. But there is an impressive countervailing force, a concentration process, in which the rate of growth is greater in already-large cities than in smaller ones. The larger the city, the greater its *percentage* rate of growth. The export base spawns more industries and firms. The input-output[2] matrix calls on a larger percentage of the capacity of a single plant (thus drawing a new branch or firm to this new city). Furthermore, the urban area tends to have a higher-than-average-for-cities specialization not only in such fabricating industries, but also in services to business management (accounting, computing services, personnel testing, actuarial services, engineering partnerships), financial and insurance head offices, and wholesale trade,[3] while smaller and slower-growing centers like St. John's, Halifax, Saint John, Hamilton, Quebec, Sudbury, and Victoria tend to specialize in provincial government activity, one or two local export industries, and health and welfare services. Thus size and growth beget growth and size, and the multiplier in the long run becomes merely a summary of the particular urbanizing forces in each region that have selected a community as its central place. With growth and size come diversity-complexity, culture and congestion.

SIX RESTRAINTS ON URBAN GROWTH

Will urban expansion continue indefinitely? Why not? The *attractions* are great: more people, more markets, more specialization, more culture, more scope for individuality (within rigid limits), more services—all these should induce national and regional natural and migratory population growth to concentrate in larger, and more, cities.

There are, of course, restraining factors as well. These can control urban growth, retarding or permitting it, depending chiefly on policy. "Policy" is not always *urban* policy, however; indeed, urban growth is often the result of national and provincial programs that are unmindful of the expenses and real costs of urbanization.

1. Immigration restrictions.   Apart from Indians and Eskimos, most Canadians are descended from immigrants who came to work in rural areas. Today's immigrants come from and, unless diverted, make for the city. A liberal immigration policy fills cities; when immigrants are excluded, city growth languishes.

---

[2] For the use of Leontief's Input-Output in forecasting the effects of a primary (export or government) change on related industries see Chapter 36's Appendix. See also "Urban Growth and Regional Contagion" in N. H. Lithwick and Gilles Paquet, *Urban Studies: A Canadian Perspective* (Methuen, Toronto, 1968).

[3] The numbers are mustered in L. O. Stone, *Urban Development in Canada* (Queen's Printer, Ottawa, 1967), Chapter 9. Geographers, sociologists and statisticians have detected national, or international, regularity in city sizes. Group cities in *logarithmic* categories of 3.3 (e.g. with boundaries of 10,000, 33,000, 100,000, 333 thousand, 1 million, 33 million, etc. . . .); then the number in each category will be about *twice* the number in the next-largest category. Thus, there are in Canada three metropolitan areas with over 1 million, and twice as many with a population between 333,000 and 1 million.

2. Rural development policies. Cities are also based on regional immigrants, pushed out by rural unemployment and monotony and pulled in by income opportunities and diversity. According to some people, then, rural redevelopment and rehabilitation should deter city growth.

There is logic in this theory. Regional growth policies that reduce the attractions of migration obviously must work, in part, against city growth. But the theory is based on a wrong view of total regional population, as a fixed group with a fixed birthrate, moving to and fro between city and farm until wages and incomes are the same in both places. The facts are that many rural people's incomes are, in general, so low that neither they nor their children even contemplate migration or self-betterment—without some initial rural improvement. Then, with more education, knowledge and skill, they can free themselves from rural bondage. The *remaining* farmers do become better endowed with personal capacity, land, and capital, and have no incentive to leave the land. Thus "rural development" often causes rural depopulation, by reducing the poverty and neglect that, paradoxically, hold down the number leaving the farm.

In addition, of course, rural growth leads to the flourishing of regional distribution and production centers. These, if they are still villages, are unlikely ever to rival metropolitan Montreal, or even Saint John. But as "growth points," "nodes," or "pôles de croissance,"[4] they may focus regional growth onto a single regional hamlet or collection point, lead to its dominance over its rivals, and so, as a part of rural revival, lead to urbanization (even with a *smaller* overall regional population, following earlier emigration). In any case, rural redevelopment will not necessarily restrain urban growth.

3. Congestion. As cities grow, they become more dependent on arteries that move goods and people among plants, offices, and homes. The sprawl into the suburbs is accomplished by capacious roads[5] and rails that converge on the central area, either nullifying its central role by occupying more and more of its space for traffic exchanges and parking, or leaving the center's old block patterns and narrow streets intact but impossibly congested and forbidding. Either way, further conventional single-centered growth is strangled. Either by the land market's abandoning the center to the slums discussed earlier in this chapter, or by official policy, some compromise between inner-city concentration and satellite-city decentralization is approached.

Congestion—which, like pollution, is discussed again below, is another example of "external diseconomies." In Chapter 27 it was suggested that tolls or rents be charged to ration scarce highway capacity. Another result might be to persuade commuters to travel by bus or train. Alternatively, travel might become

---

[4] Some regional specialists advocate a "growth point" approach to backward rural areas. This view, sometimes a matter of description rather than of deliberate policy, has been argued by T. W. Schultz (for a recent application see his "Some Economic Aspects of the Northland", p. 353 of Officer and Smith, eds., *Canadian Economic Problems and Policies* (McGraw-Hill, Toronto, 1970). The planning version owes much to France's François Perroux.

[5] For some strong opinions about expressways, see *The Bad Trip* by economists David and Nadine Nowlan (New Press, Toronto, 1970).

so dear that decentralization would flourish; moving the offices out to the people. Is this a good thing? Or is it "urban sprawl?"

4. *Land shortage.* How is urban growth affected by land scarcity? Does the impossibility of spreading out prevent the further rapid population growth of San Francisco, Manhattan, or Vancouver? Did their island locations account for the decline of Venice and Bruges?

The economics of this question are simple, though they do not take us far. We can picture families and firms, in successive decades, looking at costs and opportunities in other cities. The *costs* include land rents, building and maintenance costs, and taxes. If other places have disadvantages, but lower rents— owing to greater relative availability of land for development—people and industry will gradually migrate thence, until the "equalizing differences" (Chapter 28) between the rents make up for the disadvantages of the other locations. (Thus, rents were high in Venice, but protection against invaders was good too—the high rent level was an equalizing difference. As rents rose, it paid to drain more land, build more bridges, and build houses vertically. Similarly, residents of Manhattan, San Francisco, Vancouver, and the Thousand Islands attempt to mitigate space shortage and high rents by building vertically, reclaiming hillsides and swamps, or simply using less space per person.)

The upshot of this is that, like any other economic constraint, land scarcity sets economic men searching for substitutes: new cities, new urban designs, smaller homes and plants, etc. One "substitute" is migration elsewhere, thus restraining local urban growth.

This is a good place to review the question of land speculation first touched on in Chapter 20's Appendix. Urban development devours rural land, turning green pastures and rolling forests into suburbs, plazas, and industrial parks. As this juggernaut rolls on, far-sighted men and gamblers and fools *speculate* on a land-price rise. This has three well-known effects:

(a) it raises the assessed value of all nearby farm land, and thus the property tax burden, until farmers themselves go in for speculating or suburban land development;

(b) it creates a class of people, especially professional real-estate promoters, who have a vested interest in future development, and so tends to validate their gamble—makes it self-realizing; and

(c) it draws speculators to manipulate a price rise in an uninformed and non-competitive market, making price rises earlier or sharper than they would otherwise be.

On the other hand, speculators can perform a social function, holding land off the market until its price rise reveals that, in a competitive situation, demand has become acute; inappropriate developments are thus prevented. Indeed, faced with this resolute behavior by speculators, many municipal authorities have sought a public "land bank" to enable them to perform—for other, but not necessarily better, objectives—essentially the same role.

5. *Housing.* Urban growth means more people, more space and—especi-

ally in North America—more single-family dwellings. The cost and availability of new houses is thus a potential restraint upon urban development.

To analyze this, it is as well to start with a simple model of the supply and demand of new homes (both houses and apartments). *Demand* is clearly expanding. New families are appearing at x per cent per year, and the income of existing families is rising at y per cent per year. Consequently, the "income effects" (Chapter 21) dictate a rightward shift of demand and suggest also (a) "un-doubling" from parents' and in-laws' homes; and (b) at constant prices, a higher standard of housing. On the other hand substitution effects are also apparent. Many people now able to afford houses are increasingly attracted by travel, TV, cars, boats, and summer cottages. The price-elasticity of demand is increasing, at least for these people. Consequently these "affluent urban poor" appear to prefer less commodious or convenient housing, trailers, or remote suburbs, to buying the houses they could afford.

The demand for *new* housing is really a species of derived demand. Developers order the houses, depending on their estimation of the demand conditions above, and on the mortgage-market situation, which overshadows the whole new home market. Because of the high price of a home (relative to personal incomes) and its long useful life, a small change in the interest rate on the unpaid balance can dictate an alarmingly large change in monthly payments or in the number of months of payment.[6] Consequently, tightening credit conditions divert many prospective low-income new home buyers to (a) finding a larger down payment, or (b) buying a much smaller house, (c) "doubling up," or (d) renting empty space. Thus the elasticity of home demand in respect to interest rates and credit conditions may be greater, and more significant, than demand with respect to price or even income.

It is not surprising that the demand for all housing, even though it conforms perfectly well with theoretical expectations, fluctuates widely in response to credit conditions. Such fluctuations, whatever their macroeconomic value in stabilizing aggregate investment and GNE, are hardly encouraging to smooth urban planning or to an efficient, technically progressive house-building industry. As might be predicted, the urban literature is full of lamentations about stop-start conditions in construction.

On the *supply* side, the housing market is served by the land and the building industries. The scarcer land is, the higher will be both its rental (price) and the share of property taxes that it must bear. The building industries' costs are determined by its extremely high skilled-labor components ("medieval building methods") and the cost of lumber and fabricated building materials. On the whole, these latter prices keep pace with other economic real costs.

The final item to note is that most countries give special tax-and-subsidy treatment to dwellings. In Europe, public housing, for a favored minority, is

---

[6] For a 25-year amortization of a $20,000 house, a 10% interest rate carries a monthly payment of $180; a 7% rate only about $140. The term would have to be stretched to more than 45 years to get such a low monthly payment at 10%.

subsidized by local taxpayers. In Canada, home owners get a better break from the income tax than do renters, and also receive provincial "homeowner" grants, and NHA (insured private or public) loans. Some public housing adds to dwelling supplies. A few fiscal measures work the other way, but on the whole government policy encourages (subsidizes) housing supply rather than the opposite.

Urban expansion through the building of more houses, then, is restrained by a decline in the growth of population and of their incomes, and by the cost of alternatives. Less obviously, it is also seriously hindered by tight credit conditions and by the withdrawal of the various sources of subsidy that now swell housing supply.

Many people believe that urban population increase is autonomous, independent of housing. For example, immigration from overseas does not seem to be sensitive to or regulated by the availability of houses. If this is correct, then the restraints on housing supply may work against more spacious standards and urban sprawl, perhaps a good thing; but they also work to worsen doubling-up, delaying the replacement of older buildings, and overcrowding. Thus these restraints may simply produce urban slums.

6. *Cost of urban services.* Each city is a unit of government—a "municipality." As Chaper 8 made clear, it raises revenues to provide

  (a)   utility-like services (schools, sewage and garbage disposal)

  (b)   true "public goods" like police protection and public-health controls and outlays, and

  (c)   welfare transfers.

The divisions between these three categories are not watertight; the provision of most government services includes characteristics of private (voluntary-purchase) goods, social (automatically-for-all) goods, and welfare assistance in cash or in kind. Primary education, public housing, public transit, public parks, community centers, for example, embody all three characteristics.

The larger the city, the more of these services the municipality must provide. It finances them, to a very large extent, from property taxes of various kinds. It also has recourse to very large conditional and unconditional provincial (and federal) grants, and it can and does borrow heavily for public projects to be repaid over the projects' life out of tax revenues.

Does this municipal-service-and-property-tax mechanism inhibit urban growth? Does urban growth strain the system seriously? This question has many related questions and problems, too numerous even to list, involving actual research into the impact of various combinations of taxes, school finance, highway-and-street questions, federal-provincial-local finances, hospitals, relief systems, police coordination, pollution problems, and other standard items of local newspaper coverage. Table 39-1, on the following page, gives a recent forecast of the expected deficit.

We cannot even survey the political side of these questions. De Tocqueville rightly described local government as the "cornerstone of democracy," but it is not evident that local bureaucracies, municipal voters, or the forms, levels, or

Expected urban deficits will skyrocket:

ESTIMATED REVENUES AND EXPENDITURES OF
MUNICIPALITIES WITH POPULATIONS OF 100,000 AND
OVER (billions of dollars)

	1966	1980
Revenue from own tax sources	1.6	4.7
Transfers from senior governments	0.5	1.5
Total Revenue	2.1	6.2
Gross Expenditure*	2.6	8.6
Deficit—(Revenue less expenditures)	−0.5	−2.4

TABLE 39-1. Expenditure is rising about 30 per cent faster than revenue. The deficit can be covered by more borrowing, lower spending, or new tax sources. The revenue forecast is based on full employment and full use of property tax. The expenditure forecast is based upon some increase in per capita outlays as standards rise. (Source: Based on estimates by the Economic Council of Canada.)

* Expenditure on education and schools is omitted.

subdivisions of local participation are adequate for their tasks. Exhausted aldermen, venial councillors, super-governments, ignorant time-servers, frustrated planners, ward bosses, we know them all. But are they inevitable? Are they necessary? Are there better ways? Instead of analyzing *these* questions, we turn instead to some evidence on our economic question concerning the three kinds of municipal service.

We might expect the provision of municipal services to be a decreasing-cost industry, utilizing large capital-intensive plants to serve an increasing number of "customers", just as with railways or power companies. Recent evidence has suggested that unlimited "increasing returns to scale" *do* accrue in expanding waterworks and sewage systems. But costs of schools, police services, parks, and municipal government costs, as revealed by statistics, do not fall forever, or rise forever, with metropolitan size. There is some evidence that costs are lowest at about 100,000 population. But this evidence is so difficult to interpret as to be almost valueless, because (a) it is not clear that the *standards* of actual coverage or "courtesy" or service are the same in small and large cities, (b) in small towns, standards of public service may be poor because private alternatives are cheaply available, and (c) the studies treat fragmented many-municipality metropolises (like Montreal) sometimes as one city, sometimes as many cities. The surprising conclusion is that, while we know that some well-known large cities have bad standards of snow removal, police protection, garbage and litter collection, road repair, schools, health, welfare, water pressure, or whatever, we have *not* developed an acceptable way of comparing either the standards *or* the costs of these services over a cross-section of city sizes. It follows that we do not really know whether the cost of municipal services restrains city growth. Such statistical confusion, however may suggest that it does not.[7]

---

[7] Planners are very concerned with ideal city size, fragmentation, and decentralization. But they seem to give circulation, social intercourse, and economic activity as their criteria, not the cost of public services or of governments.

INTER-CITY RELATIONS   Even if a whole metropolitan area is able to expand at constant per-capita costs, the *distribution* of these costs is important to decisions about ideal size. Obviously, city-dwellers would like large provincial grants and low local taxes, and suburbanites would prefer separate towns and villages, leaving the central city with its high density and low income to cover its own costs. Such fragmentation, however fair or unfair, leads to predictable results: high property taxes and low standards of many services in the slums and industrial districts, coupled with lower taxes, suburban sprawl, and expensive education and police services, in the surrounding towns and villages. Such contrasts have chiefly political consequences—but one economic result is the migration of certain industries and trading establishments into the suburbs—for purely fiscal (not real) reasons.

The division of costs between property taxes and provincial grants is also chiefly of political, not economic, importance, especially if the real costs of services do not rise with urban expansion. However, in many cities an additional consideration is that the costs of *poverty*, not just in assistance but also in police, schools, housing, health and other services, get loaded onto property taxes until they become a positive disincentive to the use of taxable urban property. From this angle, city services do restrain urban *growth*. And this effect is important, for it means that highly taxable property may flee from organized municipalities, while the unemployed poor—and some workers—congregate in the cities. The company towns of the Canadian shield exemplify this behavior.

Many orthodox economists suggest service charges and user fees (prices) in place of taxes. These would both ration the use and finance the expansion of scarce municipal services. But, by the same token, they have three drawbacks: (a) expensive collection, (b) heavy impact on poor people, and (c) inapplicability to *pure* public goods like justice or smoothly flowing traffic. But in a few cases transfers or assistance to the poor, plus service charges, may deal with some financial and congestion problems of the expanding city.

In summary, we may ask whether the costs of urban growth can actually deter urbanization. We know they cannot, because they are not experienced by those who cause them, but *externally*, by the public at large, who cannot escape them. If cities are to be held to optimum size, political action is necessary.

■ THE POLLUTED ENVIRONMENT

One merely sees in the city in exaggerated degree a problem common to all modern life, namely contamination of the general environment. Smog is a sign in the skies of what is impending for industrial areas everywhere. Really clear days in Montreal or Hamilton, as in New York, Paris, or Tokyo, are almost completely a thing of the past.

Mark Twain said, "Man is the only species that feels shame—or has reason to." Certainly man is the only animal who has managed to pollute the atmosphere itself. Sulfur dioxide and particulates pollute the air of every industrial region. The climate of the world changes as a result of what industry and consumer opulence have done to the concentration of carbon dioxide in the air, far exceeding the smoke and fumes of the first Industrial Revolution. Some scientists now believe that the *irreversible* accumulation of lead—chiefly from automobile exhaust—in the air we breathe will soon become a problem everywhere in the world. Strontium 90 and radioactive trace elements have been the consequence of atomic testing; and the threat of the ultimate-doomsday cobalt bomb which will end all human life forever is more than an old-wives' bogey tale. Even noise pollutes the environment, both urban and rural.

Concern about water pollution, more local and visible, began sooner. Dissolved chemicals, from DDT to toxic mercury, have recently overshadowed the earlier bacteriological threats to health. And heat, oil spills, enriching phosphorus and disintegrating organic matter, distort or destroy normal ecological patterns, turning receiving waters into revolting, useless sumps. Table 39-2 shows that several Canadian cities still dump the bulk of their sewage untreated, while others dispose of most of their sewage through primary– or secondary–treatment plants.

Many metropolitan areas simply dump raw sewage:

SEWAGE TREATMENT IN SELECTED URBAN AREAS, 1969

METROPOLITAN AREA	WASTEWATER FLOW (MILLION GALLONS PER DAY)	PERCENTAGE OF WASTEWATER FLOW SUBJECT TO:		
		NO TREATMENT	PRIMARY	SECONDARY
St. John's	12.7	100.0		
Halifax-Dartmouth	9.9	99.0	1.0	
Saint John	5.4	99.8		0.2
Quebec	42.0	100.0		
Montreal	290.2	91.6	2.6	5.8
Ottawa	40.0		100.0	
Toronto	194.0			100.0
Hamilton	60.0		100.0	
Sudbury	11.0			100.0
London	28.0			100.0
Windsor	4.0	85.0		15.0
Winnipeg	46.3	4.0		96.0
Regina	12.0			100.0
Saskatoon	10.0	93.0		7.0
Edmonton	37.5		46.5	53.5
Calgary	38.8		100.0	
Vancouver	100.0	59.0	41.0	
Victoria	18.0	98.9		1.1

TABLE 39-2. Primary treatment removes 30–50 per cent of nonsuspended solids: secondary—or lagoon—treatment removes about 80–85 per cent of total solids and reduces the biological oxygen demand by about the same proportion. These are the largest urban centers. Smaller and poorer cities, outside Ontario, tend to dump *all* their sewage. Treatment plants are to be completed soon in many communities. [Source: Economic Council of Canada, Sixth *Annual Review* (September, 1969), Table 3-7, page 44. Reproduced by permission of Information Canada.]

EXTERNAL DISECONOMIES   Here is the most general case of what we have met earlier under the heading of "external diseconomy." The most pessimistic diagnosis of all is that ultimately the automobile is the prime cause of not only congestion and urban land sprawl, but also smog. Factories can be made to have high chimneys and to burn sulfur-free fuels. Strip-mining of coal, which despoils the scenery, can be forbidden unless the topography is restored. Electric power production, which threatens thermal contamination of rivers, can be controlled by zoning ordinances and costly cooling towers. But to deprive each commuter of his natural right of driving to work each day in a box full of air is apparently more than any modern electorate will stand.

If the consumer will not willingly pay for the extra devices needed to limit air pollution, how can one expect the auto manufacturers to solve the problem? That is like expecting the cigarette companies to commit suicide voluntarily.

Is reliance on spontaneous business efforts futile in the solution of a problem like this? Experience gives a pessimistic answer. There has been one case, though, that offers a glimmer of hope. Detergents poured into our sewage systems were found to be "non-degradable" and to continue as foam to contaminate the waters and water table into which rivers flow. Conservationists gave a great outcry. And, in this story with a happy ending, the trade association of the industry did under some official pressure sponsor chemical research that came up with a solution to that problem. By industry self-regulation, every firm in this relatively concentrated industry has adopted the new formulas, and we have heard nothing of the foam problem for many years. Would that the same vigor had been applied to the search for detergents that do not enrich plant growth in lakes and cause them to die for lack of oxygen. Or would that the contamination of wildlife by DDT, of which the late Rachel Carson wrote so eloquently, might as nicely disappear. Or that the perfect, profitable, electric battery, or more plausibly a steam engine, could be developed to eliminate the smog effects of the internal-combustion engine.

■ GOVERNMENT LAWS, TAXES AND PLANNING

Since no one profit-maker has the power, or, more important, the incentive, to solve problems involving "externalities," here is a clear case for some kind of public intervention. Thus the threat of California to ban all internal-combustion engines by 1975 may be an example of the action needed to galvanize Detroit into action. Or a heavy tax on fuming fuels, vehicles, or factories might be in order. Furthermore, the consumer has an important role to play. He must not curse his utility for burning fuel oil with a heavy sulfur content, and then complain if there is added onto his utilities bill an extra charge to cover the removal of sulfur or to finance the purchase of more expensive, sweeter fuels.

Regulations. Examples of the need for controls are endless. Lake Erie is dying, done in by the sewage, phosphate detergents, and fertilizers that have been allowed to pour into it. Not only must the cost of producing in the regions bordering on the lake be increased by the amount needed to remove industrial and other wastes, but in addition, each farmer cannot be allowed to use the chemical fertilizers *he* deems best nor each housewife the laundry soap *she* prefers—since the residue of them flows into Lake Erie.

Nor can farmers and firms elsewhere be allowed to dig all the artesian wells they please, since the water table underlying much of the country can become dangerously low from unrestrained use. Like the fisherman harvesting the fish stock, and the oil industry competitively pumping the petroleum field, they have no *incentive* to consider their externalities which raise the costs, or reduce the enjoyment, of others. Table 39-2 shows the progress made so far by municipalities forced by provinces (and bribed by Ottawa and the provinces) to treat their sewage. Regulations also attempt to control DDT, phosphates in detergent, mercury outflows, fishing catches, oil well spacing, defoliants, compulsory septic tanks, and exhaust-pipe mufflers. Others, similar in effect, are also in use—oil pumping pro-rating, some fisheries' quotas, and sprinkling regulations.

Effluent fees. Economists would like to improve on these shot-gun methods by introducing elements of the price system. For example a high "effluent fee" or tax on pollution discharges gives industries a choice: pollute and pay, or pay not to pollute.[8] Those wastes most expensive to purify will be discharged; those that are cheapest to eliminate will be purified out. The fee must then be set high enough that the total discharged is small enough to be acceptable. This system, used in Germany and contemplated under the 1970 Canada Water Act, achieves purification of a lake or river to any desired standard at the lowest social cost.[9]

Property Rights. A system long advocated for fisheries' rationalization has been recently suggested by Toronto economist John Dales[10] for water pollution: property rights. A simplified version, for a small lake, would be based on a single contaminant. The lake's total absorptive capacity, of $1,000x$ pounds, would be divided into, say, 1,000 property rights of x pounds each. These would be given or sold, or auctioned, to the 1,000 lakeshore municipalities, firms, hotels, and homes. Those who had less than x pounds to discharge could sell some or all their rights, at a price, to those who had more to discharge. The price of a right would rise until everyone had cut down their effluents to that level where it was just cheaper to purify x pounds than to buy another right. And total discharge would be held down to $1,000x$ pounds. This system would share the efficiency advantages of effluent taxes but would not require the extra knowledge that tax-collectors must have to set the right rate. Given a decision about the total acceptable discharge and the number of rights, the price of the rights is set by demand, based on the alternative costs of purification in each home and firm.

Ideally, these fees or prices would wind up equal to the marginal costs of purifying wastes and to the marginal utilities (expressed in dollar voting) of extra lake purity. This is Chapter 23's welfare condition for optimum pricing.

PROFITS AND POLLUTION Many conservationists and ecologists dislike these economists' techniques for rationing the environment's absorptive capacities. Some of them shrill that *any* pollution is immoral, and should not be validated by fees or rights. This is, of course, either an assertion of fact about "absorptive capacity" or an ethical dogma. It is capable of rational argument by scientists and concerned philosophers, but not on economic grounds.

---

[8] The British Columbia compulsory buy-back of beer containers gives no choice, so is more like a regulation than a fee.

[9] In addition to effluent fees, there can be effluent *subsidies*. Towns and firms are bribed to clear up their discharges. This system has the obvious drawback of all subsidies: people gain by lying about the amount of their performance.

[10] Dales' *Pollution, Property and Prices* (University of Toronto Press, Toronto, 1969), is highly recommended.

Another more interesting objection is that pricing the right to pollute is the wrong *economic* technique for dealing with the abuse of the environment. Polluters are imposing external diseconomies on other people, and enriching themselves by avoiding their total real (or social) costs of production. This diagnosis indicates that treatment should simply take the form of forcing the polluters to treat their wastes, paying for the facilities out of "profits." This proposal is not about the morality of pollution, but about *distribution*, or FOR WHOM the economic system and the environment are managed.

The proposal is not absurd. But for those who dislike profits and the unequal distribution of the GNP, it offers a too-easy solution to both injustice and pollution problems. Without full argument either way, note the following considerations:

1. Most pollution usually comes from old plants and poor municipalities. New profitable plants and towns waste less. Non-profit farmers, co-ops (and Soviet collective factories) are the worst offenders. Pollution and profit are not correlated as closely as would be convenient.

2. "Profitable" polluters are innovators or oligopolists. They will probably raise their selling prices to their customers if forced to treat their wastes. If they do not, it will be because their rivals have no similar treatment-cost liability— *i.e.* pollution continues elsewhere.

3. Treatment would be socially cheaper (i.e., it would use less labor and capital) if everyone were faced with an effluent tax or price than it would be if the burden were forced on to profits alone.

4. In general, *any* system that raises costs may drive the polluter to more tolerant regions. (Is this a good thing?)

5. It may be easier politically to get profitable firms to commence treatment first before towns have to raise their taxes or dig deeper into their pockets to build sewage plants.

■ HARD CHOICES AND THE ECOLOGY OF NATURE

Our 80 billion dollar GNE may be, in part, an illusion. When we finally pay our way in terms of conservation and in preserving the environment, perhaps we shall have left for ordinary consumption only nine-tenths as much. Nor is it a question of *affording* these expensive private and government programs to lessen pollution. In a real sense we cannot afford *not* to have them.

And, as in all cases of public interest, there will be conflicts of interest. Shall Ontario be allowed to get gas from Lake Erie wells if drilling threatens wildlife there? Shall developers be allowed to develop a skiing facility and ski village deep in the woods if that means disturbing the water table and spoiling the serenity of nature? Or to take a smaller example that points up the dilemma: Shall small towns be permitted to remain islands of rural peace if, as a result, the teeming masses of the cities have their recreational activities limited and are forced to huddle on the hot pavements and crowd a few adjacent beaches?

Modern economics teaches us that the curse of overpopulation is not simply that of Malthusian food shortage due to diminishing returns. Growth of population makes the ideal of a stable economy in a harmonious ecological environment impossible to attain. It results in the loss of privacy and quiet, uncrowded, clean living space. Modern technology has not solved all our economic problems nor repealed the laws of scarcity. On the contrary, for the rest of the century, the social agenda will be full of programs to deal with noise, congestion, overcrowding, and pollution, sometimes in conflict with programs for modern housing, economic growth, and reduction of poverty. Scarcity brings hard choices. Outraged advocacy does draw attention to abuses and pollution, but it does not resolve conflicts.

SUMMARY

■ 1   "Urbanization" problems are often just general problems, connected with city growth only because our whole economy is urbanized.

■ 2   The city center dies in many expanding cities. Slum housing leads to educational deprivation and isolation. The tools of supply and demand show that extreme segregation of racial minorities, however, leads to *higher* rents and real estate values, in contradiction to the common myths.

■ 3   Blight in the urban environment is strongly correlated with the adjustment problems of immigrant and racial minorities. Urban redevelopment measures, unless carefully planned, can harm those who are already the worst victims of city blight.

■ 4   The process of urbanization achieves *external economies* for new industrial arrivals and expanding markets for service industries. The *export base multiplier* forecasts the growth of service population as a result of stable export-industry growth.

■ 5   Urban growth is restrained, or influenced by, general population growth, rural development opportunities, congestion, land shortage, barriers to increases in housing, and the increasing costs, if any, of local government services. The evidence is not clear that there are serious *economic* barriers to urban growth.

■ 6   Finally, urban blight is merely a dramatic case of the more general blight of the environment produced by the modern technological economy and growth of population. Smog and air pollution can change the climate; water pollution by sewage, industrial wastes, fertilizers, and detergents, and even by the heat thrown off from nuclear and non-nuclear power plants, makes wasteland of our earthly inheritance. These "economic externalities and diseconomies" cannot be expected to be set aright by market competition and the pursuit of profit. They call for government zoning ordinances, fiats and prohibitions, planning and coordination, subsidies, and penalties of taxation. We are not so affluent as our statistics of GNE would indicate, and much remains on the future social agenda.

QUESTIONS FOR DISCUSSION

1. N. H. Lithwick's central chapter concludes (page 64): "The roots of the urban problem lie in the very process of urbanization itself." Is this gobbledygook? (HINT: "Urbanization" is a word that means *becoming* urban. Read the chapter. Reflect.)

2. Describe the overlap between segregated housing and economic opportunity. Between race and urban problems. Between urban blight and general environmental blight.

3. Look up "external economies" and "external diseconomies" in the Index and trace the pervasive influence in modern economics of this vital concept.

4. Can high mortgage rates actually *prevent* urban growth? How?

5. Compare civic services in a big city and a small town. Which cost most per capita? Which are best?

6. Design and discuss an effluent-fee system for a lake near you.

7. Can the price mechanism deal with pollution? Highway congestion? Could it, if incomes were divided equally?

8. Review your understanding of the following concepts:

"trickling down"	restraints on urban growth
rent differentials in divided markets	circles of urban decay
external economies of urban growth	external diseconomies of congestion, disturbed
export-base multiplier	ecology, and environmental pollution

40

THE POLITICAL ECONOMY
OF GROWTH VERSUS STABILITY

"Even when the experts all agree, they may well be mistaken."   BERTRAND RUSSELL

Economic development of backward countries has great popular interest. And so does the problem of how an advanced mixed economy can improve its growth performance without sacrificing stability and equity.

These are issues of intense public debate everywhere. In certain ways the problems of prospering nations are harder to analyse than those of a poor nation, which in the last analysis must primarily increase its productivity. Not even advanced treatises on economics are able to provide confident, conclusive answers to all the problems that impinge on an advanced economy.

Survey of contemporary history shows the predominant importance in the mixed economy of three related problems: economic growth; economic sluggishness and unemployment; and inflationary price creeps, of a "cost-push" type, different from older demand-pull inflation.

Accordingly, this chapter will not attempt to identify that one bold stroke of policy that will answer all our economic questions. When we have several goals we must use several policies, which may be both complementary and in conflict. In Section A we examine some of the more obvious routes to a satisfactory rate of growth. Section B is particularly concerned with some of the political and constitutional impediments to growth policies—the conflict with other goals. Section C then reviews the need to achieve simultaneously growth, full employment, and price stability.

A. THE NATURE OF ECONOMIC GROWTH

■ HOW TO KNOW WHETHER WE ARE GROWING

What is it we wish to grow? Population, output, personal incomes, leisure? A decision about desirable growth is meaningless until some indicator of our performance is accepted. And growth is obviously a many-sided process. Although no single number can portray the varied dimensions of overall growth, we've seen that the real national product (net or gross) is perhaps the best single indicator. Because GNP and NNP tell largely the same story and GNP data are more commonly met with, this chapter will concentrate on GNP or GNE. But certain cautions are in order.

1. *Per capita adjustment.* For some purposes, such as war and demonstrations of national sovereignty, the *absolute* magnitude of real (deflated) GNP may count. But generally, in thinking about welfare, one wants to insulate one's measurement from the mere increase in output due to high birth rates, low death rates, and high immigration. That is, one deflates GNP for population growth and concentrates on the growth of GNP *per capita.* Sometimes, however, population changes are insignificant; then one may rely simply on real GNP.

2. *Leisure* is one of the finest goods of life, but it is not registered in the GNP. To show that we are getting more out of life, separate allowance must be made for more holidays, shorter hours and earlier retirement. This can be done easily by showing GNP per year *per hour* of work, instead of *per capita.*

3. *Equity.* A mere increase in total GNP, if accompanied by a growing disparity between regions and by serious deterioration in its distribution among people, would be deemed by most people no improvement at all. Many will feel that the problem of WHAT should never be divorced from the problem of FOR WHOM, i.e., from the problem of "equity." The previous two chapters dealt with the important FOR WHOM questions.

4. *Quality improvements* in goods and services may not be registered accurately in GNP and price-level data, thereby tending to give them an overly pessimistic bias. Some rough allowance for this should be made. (The problem is peculiarly important if one compares a GNP made up of goods that people really want as compared with shoddy and undesired goods allocated to them in some kind of inefficiently run totalitarian society or advertising-dominated mobocracy.)

5. The measuring rod of money cannot gauge many of the important spiritual and other *noneconomic aspects of human welfare.* (We saw in the previous chapters that the money value of faddish material items in an "affluent society" may be indicators of nothing but money value; and that the denizens of smog-ridden cities are scarcely to be envied.)

▪ BRIEF HISTORY OF GROWTH

Economic growth has characterized the modern world. Nations have grown in population; in total production and employment; in real national product; in the standard of living that the typical family enjoys today, by comparison with what its grandparents enjoyed; in leisure hours off the job; in relief from the sweat and tedium that used to be man's lot in earning his subsistence. Any and all of these are aspects of economic growth. Each of these economic aspects can be loosely associated with the biological fact that people today live longer and enjoy more years free of sickness and pain.

The front flyleaf charts show the steady advancement in real GNP per capita of leading nations. While all such absolute comparisons are difficult, it will be noted that a century ago, Great Britain dropped from her position as the most opulent nation in the world because the United States' rate of growth carried her to the top. Today the United States, the U.S.S.R., and Japan are the three largest economies. Japan's recent sprint has been astounding. When one considers how different France and Germany have been in many of their governmental institutions, the similarity of their development is striking. The similar growth patterns of socialistic Sweden and individualistic Switzerland present the same paradox. (Space does not permit showing these or France on the flyleaf.)

Although the institutions of the mixed economy seem to have given citizens an advancing standard of living, the chart shows that the pace of growth has not been perfectly regular. World Wars I and II have left their mark. Moreover, just prior to World War I, in the veritable heyday of *laissez-faire*, so to speak, a number of historians thought they could detect a leveling off in growth rates generally for the advanced countries. The Great Depression of the thirties also left its mark, particularly in the North American case.

> Post-World War II growth in the mixed economies does outstrip the best performances of historic capitalism. When people speak nostalgically of the good old days, they should be reminded that the good old days were not so good.

■ WHY GROW?

For a decade or so, economic growth was a "motherhood" question; only a suicidal politician would speak out against it. But today, even motherhood is criticized. What are the alleged merits of growth?

1. The challenge of national power elsewhere. A larger GNP spells a greater ability to withstand the larger nations.

2. Impressiveness to smaller and neutral nations. Growth here may persuade others of the rightness of the Western nations' policies or the superiority of our system's mixed economy.

3. Galbraith's contention that we need more goods and services in the *public* sector (not for private consumption) can be most easily implemented if the necessary higher taxes come out of extra *growth* of GNP.

4. The belief that even if more material goods are not themselves most important, nevertheless, a society is happiest when it is moving forward and unhappiest when it is stagnating, beset by the protectionist and restrictive movements that thrive in such an environment.

These and other beliefs are often found in alliance: advocacy of more growth has attracted odd bedfellows. For many, it may be enough simply to know that in the public mind many policies are expansionist and growth-oriented, and it is these policies that attract the ballots. Growth seems to attract more support than would arise simply from private thrift, investment, and hard work.

But in the 1970s, this private and public acceptance is not enough. Thoughtful people see the litter and the waste in increased affluence, the pollution from increased production, the depletion of resources, the misuse of leisure; and say "why grow"? The answer must surely lie in two results of economic growth:

> Economic growth, like the development of poor countries, releases man from the bondage of perpetual work and saving for survival to the level where, for good or evil, he is able to *choose*, rationally and deliberately, how to use his time, his capacity, and his environment.
>
> Economic growth is also essential for those of us who are already above mankind's poverty level to assist those people, regions, and nations that swelter in stagnant unproductiveness.

GROWTHMANSHIP   "Growthmanship" is less concerned with the reasons for growing than with the public routes to be followed. Given that there are, in spite of the drawbacks, good reasons for further growth, skeptics may still argue that there is no scope for public intervention in favor of faster growth. In spite of official pronouncements and endorsement at the polls, not all citizens agree with the Economic Council of Canada's semi-official program of public interventions. Below are four samples from a wide spectrum of viewpoints:

Laissez-faire. This view is at the individualist extreme, as expressed in classical economics in expounding the following belief:

> *However fast* the citizenry want their economy to grow, as they determine themselves in their day-to-day decisions to save or consume, that is precisely how fast the economy ought to grow. Thus if in the late 1950s the annual rate of growth of the GNP fell off, then that primarily indicates the desire of the citizenry to live well now and not to grow fast.[1] The government should not do what in fact it did do: adopt a deliberate faster-growth policy.
>
> An even more controversial version of this view is that when the growth rate is dictated by foreign decisions (to buy our exports at different rates, ship less to us, invest less in our industry, hold fewer of our bonds or stop seeking to migrate here), we should continue, in the name of *laissez-faire,* to accept the checks or leaps in our growth rate.

This is not a popular view today. But the logic of its enemies is often distorted, and both approaches deserve a more scientific hearing than they usually receive.

POTENTIAL GROWTH   This modified version of the *laissez-faire* doctrine has been championed in the Reports of the Economic Council of Canada. (It is also implicit in the reports of the U.S. Council of Economic Advisers to the president). It is that the rates of population growth, voluntary capital accumulation, and technical advance all combine to spell out a rate at which Canada *can* grow. (For an example, see Fig. 12-1, page 272.) Any lower rate means either or both of (*a*) unemployed men and capacity, and (*b*) wasted productivity potential. In other words, a lower-than-potential rate of growth means that we are not

---

[1] To be fair, libertarians and classicists have an answer to the gibe, "I suppose our loss of GNP from 1929 to 1935 was evidence that the Canadian people did not *want* then to grow at all." They allege that, had the proper environment been provided for individualism by proper national and international monetary and other policies, there would have been no Great Depression, and growth would *then* truly have reflected basic desires.

keeping on our production-possibility curve. As population, capital, and technology expand, the production-possibility curve moves steadily outward, leaving us behind *inside* the curve. To avoid such waste, to remain on the frontier, we must adopt explicit growth-encouraging policies.

NO NEED FOR FURTHER GROWTH   Ideologically removed from the above view, but somewhat allied in terms of complacency about growth, would be the belief of some that we are *already* so affluent a society as to have no great need for further growth.

"Why have a third and fourth monstrous car in each garage?" would represent only a slight caricature of this position. Intellectual observers abroad, who regard North America as way out in front and as too materialistic anyway, are especially attracted to this view. Among youth, particularly children of the affluent, there are growing doubts about the importance of material things (as was observed at the end of Chapter 38).

FULL SPEED AHEAD   At the opposite extreme is the view of those who feel that growth is a good thing in itself. While some would be prepared to see the government take extraordinary powers to force the pace of economic growth, others, slightly more moderately, insist merely that public policy keep growth in mind in each and every action.

GROWTH AS ONE OF MANY GOALS   Most people feel that our mixed economy need not be satisfied by the spontaneous, unplanned growth rate. Growth is only one of many goals, but it is important and justifies additional positive measures to increase it. Moreover, growth itself may enable further fulfillment of other goals such as reduction of poverty.

■ HOW TO GROW

Let us assume that, from sources outside economics, faster growth is set as a major goal for Canada or any advanced nation. How does a mixed economy go about increasing its own rate of growth? The answers are by no means obvious. It is clear that a totalitarian society can by ruthless methods of coercion simply channel goods away from current consumption and into capital formation. But can a free society increase its own growth rate and still remain free?

Earlier chapters in Parts Two and Four show how, if at all, a mixed society can, in a democracy, hope to speed up the rate at which its real GNP rises. First, however, some ineffectual solutions ought to be noted.

Why not simply set up the target of 5 per cent growth rate per year? This is indeed easy to do and many have done so. But just as one cannot increase his own stature merely by thinking about it, mere assertion is not likely to accelerate growth. Only if a promotion campaign were really to change people's *fundamental propensities* to consume could much be hoped for here, and a careful scrutiny of exhortation campaigns suggests that they are more effective at selling one brand of soap than at making significant changes in people's *fundamental propensities*.

As we saw in our studies of production in Part Two and in the discussion of development of poorer countries in the last chapters, there are certain factors that have to be changed if the rate of growth is to be improved. These are the "Denison" inputs:

> The quantity of population and natural resources
> The quality of population and natural resources
> The stock of capital goods of all kinds
> The scientific and technical knowledge that compose
> > the technological efficiency with which the different
> > factor inputs combine to produce a larger output.

This list[2] provides the clues for an effective program to stimulate growth. In the remainder of the chapter we examine the conflicts and compatibilities of suggested measures.

▪ POPULATION AND RESOURCE ENDOWMENT

The quantity of land and natural resources available for use does not change easily in response to policy. Legally, Canada may alter slightly her fisheries' regions, but these changes have no significant effect on total growth rates. Much more important, the rate of spending on *discovering* resources may significantly increase our known stocks of minerals. Such outlays are included with "research" below.

Up to a few years ago, most economists would also accept the rate of population growth as given, and as not being significantly susceptible to growth-promoting policies. But today, in the less-developed countries birth control techniques are being vigorously distributed and in our own land, for environmental reasons, many people favor zero population growth. Population growth also varies according to our investment in reducing the death rate—chiefly the deaths of small children—and in permitting or attracting immigration.

But the Chamber-of-Commerce view that Canadian growth depends on more people is now widely rejected. Expansion does indeed cause a larger GNP, as well as regional development, urbanization, larger school enrollment, traffic congestion and highway building, resource extraction, air pollution, and ecological damage. But few people would follow Sir Clifford Sifton and other nation builders in deliberate attempts to build up the sheer size of the population. Instead there is increasing support for Professor John Dales:

> ". . . it should be noted that the United States consciously *reduced* the prospective levels of its GNP growth rate in the 1920s by its immigration restrictions. We on the other hand, to judge by our official policies, still hunger after higher and

---

[2] To serve as reminder, this list is based on the contributions to national income growth suggested in Chapter 36's Solow model and measured for the United States by Denison (see E. Denison, *The Sources of Economic Growth in the United States* (Committee for Economic Development [an American research organization], New York, 1962), and Paul A. Samuelson ed., *Readings in Economics*, No. 48) and for Canada by Dorothy Walters (see her *Canadian Income Levels and Growth: an International Perspective*, Economic Council of Canada Staff Study No. 23 (Queen's Printer, Ottawa, 1968), and her *Canadian Growth Revisited, 1950-1967*, Economic Council of Canada Staff Study No. 28 (Queen's Printer, Ottawa, 1970).)

higher population growth rates and GNP growth rates. The common claim that we do so *in order to increase our standard of living* at once gives the lie to the . . . claim that our immigration policy is based on high moral considerations and displays an utter disregard for the intricacies of the optimum population problem. In my opinion the pressure for a Big Canada that is exerted by politicians, big business, and a large segment of the general population, represents a vulgar wish for bigness for its own sake."[3]

There is a *possibility* that increased population alone can increase GNP per capita. If Canada could reap increasing returns to scale (Chapter 24) then having more people would make each of us better off. Social overhead capital (Chapter 37) is necessary for development to begin, yet its indivisibility makes it unprofitable and expensive for a small nation to install. Only a large nation can afford miles of railroad, pipelines, wharfage and so forth. The point was made decades ago by Canadian economic historians in considering the CPR and other nation-building investments—but Dales believes we have already passed the minimum size needed to reap important economies of scale. Beyond here, the matter becomes complicated, leading to consideration of the optimum size of markets for mass production of consumer goods, the optimum size of provinces for financing public works, and so forth.

In what follows, it will simply be assumed that economies of scale are important only to some Canadian *regions*, and that the diseconomies of having a smaller density of population than the most advanced nations is being made up by specialization and international trade. In other words,

> The measures for accelerating growth considered below can be considered as increases in per capita investment and spending in order to increase per capita GNP. These are often abbreviated as measures to increase *productivity*.

EXPANDED PUBLIC AND PRIVATE RESEARCH   We can begin with perhaps the least controversial measures in the Denison-Walters list. All agree that expanded research and investigation—in pure science, applied science, development and engineering, resource discovery and development, administration and management, city planning, communications, traffic control, and industrial location—can pay high social dividends in terms of per capita productivity. It has not been increased capital and labor so much as *increased technical productivity* that has been responsible for the historically achieved rates of growth. Having more people and more machines of the seventeenth-century variety would not be likely to take us far beyond the standards of living of the early settlers. Obviously better machines—not simply new machines—are needed for progress.

Business firms do much research and can be urged to do more. However, there is no reason to think that management is so stupid as not to see for itself how much research is likely to be profitable *to it*; so unless some new *public*

---

[3] J. H. Dales, *The Protective Tariff in Canada's Development* (Toronto: University of Toronto Press, 1966), pp. 165-166.

policies on research are added, we are unlikely to achieve greater progress here than is already the case.

This is where the government comes in. Since the 1930s the government has been directly and indirectly supporting much of the scientific research done in this country. It could expand the level of its support. But can this be justified as a legitimate function of government?

Recall from Chapter 8 that there is always a prima facie case for public intervention whenever there are such economic "externalities" present as to make it unlikely that each entrepreneur, as he reckons *his private benefit and costs* in money, will thereby be truly reflecting the non-money and money benefits and costs *to society* as a whole. Smoke nuisance was an example of an external diseconomy calling for public action. Similarly, research is an example of an "external economy" calling for public action, as the following soliloquy shows:

> When I, as a prudent businessman, balance the dollar cost to me of an extra unit of research with the benefit that it can bring me, I shall realize that most of the results of my research will soon—or in the case of patents, eventually—serve to benefit all other producers in my industry and in society generally. The benefit to society as a whole, then, is likely to be much greater than to me; so I shall not be motivated to do all the research that society needs. Because of this externality, the government has a reason to subsidize research—by direct grants to universities, firms, and its own laboratories and by favorable tax treatment of research.

We can therefore deduce this corollary.

The single least controversial measure for inducing greater growth is promotion and subsidy of more research and development, and of the search for unexploited natural resources.

EXPANDED EDUCATION AND TRAINING   We saw earlier that just as machinery is capital to society, so too are people. Investing in equipment might yield society an interest return of, say, 10 or 15 per cent per annum. If investing in people, by providing more in the way of education, can step up their economic productivity greatly—and the record suggests that this is indeed true—then society ought likewise to spend more for education to promote growth. (All this is *in addition* to the various noneconomic civic and humanistic reasons for devoting resources to education.)

Until the last decade, Canada put far fewer resources (relative to her labor force) into education than did either the United States or several European nations. As a result, the proportion of Canada's male labor force with some post-secondary education was, in 1961, only half of what it was in the United States.[4] To bridge this gap, education has been boosted to the largest single

---

[4] Over half of the United States male labor force had some education above the grade 12 level in 1961 while the Canadian figure was only 25 per cent! See Dorothy Walters, *Canadian Income Levels and Growth: An International Perspective*, Economic Council of Canada Staff Study No. 23 (Queen's Printer, Ottawa, 1968).

category of total Canadian governmental spending—over $6 billion in 1970! Enrolment in post-secondary institutions tripled in the same 1960-1970 period. Graduates of universities, colleges, and vocational institutions began to go into jobs toward the end of the decade, raising the labor force's average educational content perceptibly.

Has this *investment* paid off? Yes, to the degree that a more highly educated labor force (a more productive labor force) has contributed an additional amount to our national growth rate.[5] But a portion of our educational gains came not as the fruits of our own investment but rather through the immigration of people with above-average levels of education.[6]

Increasingly the government, rather than individual students or private donors, has paid the shot for expanded post-secondary facilities. Many people in Canada still feel that, after provision has been made for equality of opportunity in education, the nation can benefit from more resources spent on education. Partly their belief is based on confusion. They forget that the larger per capita income made possible by education will mostly be paid out to the students who got the cheapened schooling—a high-return gift from taxpayer to students. Partly, however, they reflect the fact that to *some* extent this upgrading will benefit *everyone* living in a highly skilled and educated society. Whatever the merits of outright gifts to enable students to obtain post-secondary education, the case is strong for enlarged funds to *lend* to students for training in lucrative callings, to be paid back by them out of the extra earnings their education makes possible. The seventh *Annual Report* of the Economic Council of Canada suggests that we continue to publicly subsidize education—but with an eye on efficiency and economy.[7]

B.   CONFLICTS BETWEEN GROWTH POLICIES AND OTHER AIMS

It is now time to recall that the economy is not single-mindedly intent on growth. Living in ten provinces in five great regions, the Canadian people rely on government policy to do a number of things, to each of which they give a very high priority. In this section we shall see that the regional nature of our economy and the federal nature of our polity create situations that slow down our growth potential but are acceptable in terms of other public demands.

---

[5] A sequel study by Dorothy Walters estimates that education contributed only one-tenth to the overall 2.2 per cent annual rate of growth of Net National Income per person employed in the 1955-62 period. In the next period, 1962-67, the contribution by education to the average annual growth rate of 2.6 per cent was found to have doubled. See Dorothy Walters, *Canadian Growth Revisited, 1950-1967*, Economic Council of Canada Staff Study No. 28 (Queen's Printer, Ottawa, 1970).

[6] In 1967, about 40 per cent of immigrant members of the labor force were high school graduates, whereas the national average was only 32 per cent. Similarly, some 9 per cent of immigrant workers had some university education versus about 5½ per cent of Canadian-born members of the labor force. Ibid., p. 16.

[7] The interested reader is referred to the Economic Council of Canada, *Annual Report for the Fiscal Year 1969-70* (Information Canada, Ottawa, 1970).

First we must examine the problem of structural unemployment and some of the reasons for its persistence. Then other obstacles to growth are considered. All are examples of the failure of the economy as a whole to stay on its production-possibility frontier.

■ STRUCTURAL UNEMPLOYMENT

There are many ways of raising the rate of growth of output per person. We might, for example, force every person to work longer hours and take shorter holidays.[8] But if the amount of leisure now enjoyed is the amount that everyone wants, there is little to be gained from more output (hence more growth) obtained at the sacrifice of leisure.

On the other hand, it was an unmitigated advantage in the mid-1960s to be able to increase our quantity of labor by being able to define full employment as a condition where 96 or 97 per cent of the labor force are employed, rather than as a condition where only 94 or 95 per cent are employed. This is an important point, because the upward drift of average unemployment rates from 1951-1961 was attributed by some to an increase in "structural unemployment." What does this term mean?

Structural unemployment is used in an allegedly contrasting sense to ordinary unemployment. The latter can be created by having too little $C + I + G + (E - M)$ aggregate dollar spending and can be reduced by expansionary fiscal and monetary policies that swell total spending. Unlike ordinary unemployment, structural unemployment is supposed to include people who are stranded in the wrong regions—in distressed areas like the mining country of West Virginia, Nova Scotia, or Wales. It includes *youths who have dropped out of school;* the *uneducated* and the *illiterate;* the *unskilled* or *semiskilled,* or the *highly skilled in obsolete arts* like glass-blowing or cigar-rolling. It includes the *neurotic* and *rebellious* (and possibly the radical malcontents), who demand unrealistically high wages and contribute little net marginal-product to the employer. It includes the congenitally low-IQ and poorly coordinated populace, who used to be capable of getting menial jobs at low pay in a rural society, but who increasingly are thrown out of employment by minimum union-, legislative-, and company-promulgated wage fiats. More doubtfully, it includes those who have quit one job and are taking their own sweet time in moving to a new one. More importantly, structural unemployment is supposed to include those who belong to various *minority groups:* the relatively aged, immigrants, and so forth.

DEFINING STRUCTURAL UNEMPLOYMENT   No one has been able to agree on the exact meaning of structural unemployment, but all are clear as to what it means in

---

[8] In an age where Saturday work has become rare and where summer and winter vacations are becoming more common, it is somewhat anomalous that youth from age 6 to 24 is being now urged to study and work harder than was ever before the case. Is one supposed to sprint while young in order to become rich enough to idle ever after?

extreme instances. Thus, if brisk over-all spending results in only 3 per cent unemployment and prices are not being pushed upward by wage increases induced in a tight labor market, all would agree that so-called structural unemployment is low.

On the other hand, if unemployment is at 6 per cent, and every increase in aggregate dollar spending (whether brought about by a private-investment boom, or by expansionary fiscal policy, or by monetary policy) seems merely to result in a fast bidding up of wages of those already employed, with little effect on job opportunities for those in the wrong regions, or those with apparently the wrong skills and talents in terms of what employers demand, then all will agree that structural unemployment appears to be high. This diagnosis will be confirmed if, with no concomitant change in aggregate demand, some mixture of retraining, transport improvements, a melting of minimum or union wage levels, and an increase in general wage flexibility leads to a marked reduction in unemployment.

In that case, the diagnosis is confirmed only after a treatment has been selected and tried over a period of years. First there must be a period of observation of the effects of national full employment policies on the pockets of unemployed; then a period of retraining, area-assistance, and relocation subsidies.

In practice, such ideal diagnostic conditions have not occurred in recent years. We have had periods of national full employment interrupted by years of heavy national unemployment. Over the long haul our observation has shown that the people of certain regions and of certain occupations and levels of skill are more frequently unemployed, and receive lower wages at work, than the national average. These groups have been the target of government policies in many countries. In Canada, for example, the Occupational Training for Adults program (OTA), the Area Development Act (ADA), the Agricultural Rehabilitation and Development Acts (ARDA), the Prairie Farm Rehabilitation and Development Act (PFRA), the Atlantic Development Board (ADB), the National Productivity Council, and a number of other policies have been enacted to tackle these problem groups "at the grass roots."

Can we be sure that the structural-unemployment target really exists? Some economists argue instead that what we observe is really a case like this: Aggregate demand has been fluctuating and sluggish on the average year after year. The long-term average rate of unemployment is high. Skills decay. Employers prefer keeping a few employees at work for long hours to spreading the jobs around. Average incomes drop. Children go to school for fewer years. Now, if government policy or a trade-cycle boom raises aggregate demand within a short time period, the probable result will again be rising wages and prices.

But now imagine that this high aggregate demand is sustained, instead of fading into a business downturn. As time passes, people get sucked out of the depressed areas into high-employment regions. Some low-wage regions attract new industries, seeking to reduce their manufacturing costs. Within the high-employment regions, workers switch gradually from blue-collar to supervisory and white-collar jobs, and many go into business for themselves. Employers find ways of using less-expensive low-I.Q. workers. With all these forces at work, the national unemployment average works its way down over the years to the 3 per cent goal the Economic Council of Canada thinks is our potential minimum.

> Economists who paint this picture say it shows that there is no hard and fast line between structural and nonstructural unemployment. The alleged hard core of the structurally unemployed is in fact a core made of ice and not of iron. The core of ice can be melted over a period of time by adequate effective demand, or it can be solidified by inadequate over-all demand.

■ DEPRESSED REGIONS

To examine the question further this section focuses attention on one type of structural problem that is very conspicuous in Canada: the large areas that have high rates of unemployment, low per capita incomes, and a rather low standard of government services. There are a number of home-made theories about these regions, some correct and some erroneous.

A SLOW RATE OF EXPANSION CREATES SLOW INCOME GROWTH   This theory is the basis for provincial development plans that try to get more employment and more industry. It neglects, however, the fact that the growth of income per person depends not only on the growth of local output, but also on the growth of the labor force. If output grows slowly but population grows even more slowly, the average income may rise faster than in a so-called expanding region. This has happened in Saskatchewan since World War II. In New Brunswick, on the other hand, a rapid rise in population has dissipated output gains so that average income has lagged behind the national growth rate.

REGIONAL POVERTY IS THE RESULT OF THE CONCENTRATION OF LOW-WAGE INDUSTRIES IN CERTAIN PROVINCES   This theory is the basis for provincial governments and local boards of trade inviting high-wage electronic and chemical industries to move into their regions. There is certainly something to the view: the low-income Atlantic provinces *are* heavily specialized in the low-paying fishing, farming, forestry, personal-service, and storekeeping industries. The prairie region is in a similar position.

But both economic theory and statistics work against this view as an explanation of regional disparities. The theory of comparative advantage discussed in Chapter 33 suggests that we would expect regional specialization (in mixed agriculture, for example) to be a result of the availability of excess labor, and not its cause. In general, we have to ask why wages are low and labor is plentiful so that low-paying industries settle in, not why the industries that are there pay low wages.

Statistics recently analyzed by the Economic Council of Canada confirm this criticism. For if the view were right we would expect "high-wage industries" to pay high wages even in the depressed regions, but to find few such industries there. In fact the statistics show that all industries give lower pay in the depressed regions than they do in Quebec, Ontario, or British Columbia. The Economic Council of Canada concludes that the low incomes are due to low productivity. In terms of Fig. 26-2 (page 655), this means that the industries that locate in the Atlantic provinces, finding labor plentiful and wages low, hire more labor and use less capital than they would in high-wage regions. (The Council's data also confirm this expected low amount of capital per man.)

Thus, policy aimed at improving the "mix" of industries in the poorer regions puts the cart before the horse.

THE POOR REGIONS ARE SHORT OF CAPITAL   This view is the basis of regional attempts to induce Ottawa and industry to invest more locally. The statistics mentioned above confirm that capital per man *is* lower in the poor regions than nationally. The stock of human capital (years of schooling per man) is similarly deficient.

Once again, the facts do not validate any particular theory of the need for subsidized investment. Capital is scarce just because industry chooses to invest elsewhere. This may be in part because the local population is unskilled and unschooled. But the willingness of industry to move capital *and* men to scarce-labor areas elsewhere suggests that skill-shortage cannot be a major explanation. The chief explanation must be that other geographical locations have advantages (close to North American markets, cheap energy, better natural resources) that attract investment.

Though the list can be extended to deal with other views that are frequently advanced to account for the stagnant areas of Canada and the United States, this important subject is too complex to be discussed fully here. Instead, we may assert the two following points. If structural unemployment and chronic low incomes are diagnosable anywhere in North America, the poorer Canadian regions are excellent candidates. In the United States the per capita incomes of various regions are *converging* on one another so that the difference between the average region and the poorest is being reduced. In Canada, however, as we saw in Chapter 6 (page 145), regional income disparities had remained unchanged for the four decades previous to 1961. Subsequently the disparities have narrowed somewhat.

Second, even if sustained high national aggregate demand has absorbed workers with the wrong skills and with no skills (with the help of retraining schemes), it has been less successful in reviving the stagnant regions.

As suggested above, a formidable array of government policies is being prepared to deal with these "low-income traps." The provinces themselves, with Ottawa's help, are attempting to attract industry, by subsidy if necessary. And they are taking long strides in raising the education and skill levels of their workers. Obviously a great deal can be done to raise the absolute income-level of the average family in these regions. The higher the national level of aggregate demand and the longer the program operates without interruption by business downturns, the greater will be its success.

Skeptical economists, however, point to the population factor mentioned in the first theory cited above. Recalling the "staple" approach mentioned in Chapter 36, they ask whether it is possible, in a world-trade economy like

Canada's, to satisfactorily narrow the gap between the poorest and the average region. Perhaps, they suggest, incomes are low because the people do not move to areas with greater natural advantages. If this is so, subsidies and education can never remedy a region's comparative scarcity of productive resources, locations, and sites. The poorer regions are trying to support too many people to achieve desired higher incomes.

▪ NATIONAL AND PROVINCIAL GROWTH

Unlike the geographer, the economist who is interested in policy cannot confine himself to "regions." He must look for policy-making governments and the areas for which they are responsible. In Canada and the United States he finds three categories: the central government, the provinces or states, and the local governments. For many long-run purposes this list can be whittled down to two types, for the local governments are legally the creatures of the provinces and must act in obedience to provincial statutes. Compared to the United States, Canada has a working constitution that gives very extensive powers and duties to its provinces, and strictly limits the rights of the central government.

> Carried to the extreme proposed by many people in Quebec, the Ottawa government would be responsible only for a very short list of activities. These would include national defense, most external relations, some forms of national transport and communications, money and banking, and perhaps criminal-law jurisdiction. Technically speaking, they propose that Canada be little more than a confederation, like a permanent alliance or like the European Common Market discussed in Chapter 35. This *can* work, as the examples of Switzerland and Benelux show. But it provides a much more modest role for Ottawa than the central government now plays.

The present debate about the relative powers to be exercised by the provinces and by Ottawa poses a threat to the growth measures discussed on the previous pages. These growth policies contemplate, among other things (*a*) fiscal and monetary policies to maintain high aggregate demand in the country as a whole which would gradually suck people out of low-income situations, and (*b*) the movement of people from poorer to richer regions. But such growth policies conflict with other aims.

FISCAL POLICY AND PROVINCIAL AUTONOMY   Fiscal policy to keep high aggregate demand requires variation of total taxes or total government spending to counterbalance dangerous variations in investment or in the balance of trade. Such variations can be carried out in the right amounts and at the right time only if one government has a budget big enough and flexible enough. This must be the central government. (There is no use in New Brunswick's trying to forestall a depression by varying *its* spending; even large Quebec and Ontario are too small to have a helpful effect by their unilateral actions.) But if the debate about switching spending power from Ottawa to the provinces continues to favor the provinces, some economists believe the central budget will be too small to permit it to undertake fiscal policy; all the variable taxes and spending will have been assigned to the provinces. (This argument continues, however, for other economists say that Ottawa is in fact assigned those types of welfare and other spending that are difficult to vary anyway.)[9]

MONETARY POLICY   Few champions of provincial autonomy wish to deprive Ottawa of its present control over money and banking. But they are quick to add that Ottawa should not vary credit conditions in such a way that provincial planning would be affected. That would be to infringe on the building of schools, roads, and other local-growth-producing outlays. Thus the conflict between the two types of government can be identified with a conflict of two approaches to the encouragement of growth. The central government would be favoring monetary stabilization and high employment as a means to the elimination of structural unemployment; the provinces would be favoring the use of such government measures as more training and more public capital goods.[10]

THE REGION VERSUS THE WHOLE   Actually we have two divisions, and the points discussed briefly just above arise from the division of types of power between the provinces and the federal government. The other type of division is that of the size of region that is to be benefited from government action. The provinces naturally worry about their own regions, while Ottawa is compelled to think about the country as a whole.

Thus Ottawa's politicians and civil servants are not very reluctant to encourage the greater efficiency of the country as a whole, and tend to discourage measures that reduce that efficiency. For example, they frown on barriers to interprovincial trade that would prevent the division of labor and specialization among regions. They favor, too, the nation-wide mobility of capital and labor, so that each factor may seek its use in work of the highest productivity.

The provinces, by their nature, cannot take this large view. Each province instead seeks to make laws that will encourage local expansion and development. Thus we have provincial ownership of industries, provincial trade barriers, provincial "buy-Quebec," or "buy-Saskatchewan" procurement laws, provincial support for the "exclusion" policies of professions that tend to bar from practice doctors, lawyers, or other specialists coming from "foreign" provinces, and some other hurdles to the free mobility of goods or factors.

Further we have little provincial support for educational schemes that will explicitly assist youths to find work in *other* regions, and no province offering its people subsidies to move to jobs elsewhere. Such measures, where they exist, help the persons involved and the national average income. But they reduce the size, votes, and tax revenues of the declining provinces. Thus it is not surprising that they are administered by Ottawa. In political-science terms, they work

---

[9] The Carter Commission's studies suggested that since World War II the increasing ". . . importance of provincial and municipal expenditures probably has not reduced and possibly has increased the built-in stability of the economy." Royal Commission on Taxation, *Report*, Vol. 2, 1966, p. 93.

[10] Another monetary policy difficulty, less related to growth aims, is that the provinces have jurisdiction over some near-banks, like trust companies and credit unions.

against the provinces' interests, even where it may be shown economically that they raise the remaining local factors' per capita incomes.

This is the final conflict in growth policies that can be mentioned here. The provinces see growth policy as a matter of raising the levels of all the provinces simultaneously. Even the Economic Council of Canada argues that it is in the national interest to "make the maximum contribution to improvements in productivity generally [within] the region." If this means holding labor and capital and maximizing their productivity *in situ*, it is of course very like the task that an isolated country sets itself. The essence of national potential growth policy, however, cannot be based on keeping *all* the regions going full speed ahead. Instead, it must accept the possibility that maximum potential growth depends upon the relative decline of some of the provinces. This view has also been well stated by the ECC,[11] when it asserts that national policy ought to avoid interfering with the "free flow of goods, capital, labor, and enterprise between all the provinces."

This conflict cannot be resolved by economic reasoning. It is not for the economist to say that the whole is more important than the parts. The Canadian federation is built on the idea of the political equality of the provinces. Canadians will have to decide whether they want national potential growth, or whether they want each province to maximize the return of which it is capable. Just as no nation wants to maximize over-all growth by sending its people and capital to another country, so no Canadian province is keen to preside over its own depopulation and capital exodus. Economists can point out the conflict, but economic analysis does not indicate the answer.

The upshot for growth is that the present debate about our federation is not simply a matter of taste about which legislatures shall make the laws. It is partly a matter of the conflict between aggregative fiscal and monetary policies and local structuralist policies. And it is also partly a matter of the conflict between those who favor national growth wherever it takes place, and those who favor "fair shares" in growth among the existing locations. In the next section we pay less attention to the regions and provinces, but develop further the idea that a country must "trade off" its growth aims for other desirable economic benefits.

C. NATIONAL STEADY GROWTH WITH PRICE STABILITY AND FULL EMPLOYMENT

In concentrating on the policies that can increase the rate of growth of our potential full-employment full-capacity GNP, we must not forget the less subtle contribution to growth that can come merely from *achieving a better approxi-*

---

[11] These two aims are taken from pages 176 and 177 of the 2nd *Annual Review* of the Economic Council of Canada. Though apparently contradictory, they can be reconciled by an application of theory. The "free flow of capital and labor" may reduce the factor-endowment of a province so that the *remaining* factors have their productivity maximized.

mation to full employment. Which decade showed by far the worst record of growth in Canadian history? It was the 1930s, when the Great Depression prevailed and there was no growth at all!

Those who speak most optimistically about 5.5 per cent targets for annual growth generally have in mind the improvements that would be possible if we could keep unemployment at minimal 3 per cent levels. This is a needed emphasis. It is not enough that the labor force grow at the predicted 2½ per cent and productivity per worker at 3 per cent. It is also crucial—for profit receivers as well as workers—that we maintain expansionary private and public policies to raise the $C + I + G + (E - M)$ equilibrium level of real NNP.

But a return to high employment is, in a sense, a once-for-all thing. From 1963 to 1966, with not only unprecedented growth in the labor force but also a reservoir of slack capacity in the economy to draw on, our economy hit a stride of over 6 per cent a year! But our *potential* output could not rise at this rate; only our *actual* performance could show that rapid growth, as for 3 years it narrowed the "gap," so that we rode up from low-employment to full-employment curves. After we close this *gap* our actual output must revert to the growth rate of potential GNP (which in the opinion of the Economic Council is around 5.5 per cent per year only if the measures discussed in this chapter are successfully applied). (Why is the U.S. potential rate presently a little lower than Canada's? Because, with the same potential growth in productivity, Canada has the higher growth in population and labor. But both countries must struggle to keep unemployment low—to have jobs for the new workers.)

Fortunately, our potential GNP grows like compound interest. If we realize it, the generous profits and labor incomes that it will make available for reinvestment will reinforce its own rate of growth. (I put 96 cents in the bank and you put in only 93. Even if our sums compound at the same 4 per cent interest rate, if our heirs live long enough, mine will have thousands of dollars more than yours. And if my 96 cents, which corresponds to full—rather than partial—employment, should generate a rate of 4½ per cent whereas your 93 cents generates only 3 per cent,[12] my heirs will eventually end up trillions of times as rich as yours.) These are elementary facts of compound interest applied to long-run growth.

■ EXPENDITURE AND PROSPERITY: AN IMPORTANT DIGRESSION

Before leaving the problem of getting to and staying at full employment, we should examine what would happen if the cold war were suddenly to fade out. Would a cut in world-wide defense spending confront us, in Canada, with a

---

[12] At high employment, attitudes of businessmen and labor toward increasing productivity may be better than in a soft-pressure economy with considerable idle manpower and capacity. If so, such favorable attitudes enhance the growth contribution of full-employment policies. On the other hand, if the whip of fear that results from unemployment in a slack economy makes workers and management more efficient, then there is the possibility that the low-pressure economy *might* after a lag overtake the high-employment one.

depression problem? Has our postwar level of employment avoided a Great Depression just because business activity depends on armament production?

The answer here is much like that given in Chapter 17 to the problem of some future acceleration of automation. If there is a political will, a mixed economy like ours can rather easily keep $C + I + G + (E - M)$ spending up to the level of full employment!

How does defense impinge on our aggregate demand? Like other countries, we have a high level of G, kept there in part by new and replacement orders for arms and supplies, and by the pay and allowances of the armed forces. In addition as a primary producer, we supply raw materials such as aluminum, cellulose, uranium, and energy sources which other countries, especially the United States and our other NATO allies, work up into armaments. Finally, in a small way we export finished war supplies such as aircraft, uniforms, and so on; though we import much more of these than we export. Thus a cooling-off of the cold war, uncompensated by other types of spending, would hit our economy through $(E - M)$ as much as or more than through $C + I + G$. As a small-to-middle power, Canada's economic role in Western defense is not in fielding an integrated and self-contained force, but in finding her comparative advantage in doing and producing certain things as part of a NATO-wide division of labor.

There is nothing special about spending on defense procurement of jets and guns—the multiplier effect is about the same as for roads and hospitals. The real problem is anticipating and forestalling the diffused and partially-unknown impacts of our own and U.S. cutbacks. To what extent are Canadian universities indirectly dependent on military research outlays?[13] To what extent are the Canadian wool and meat industries relying on demands from the U.S. army? No one really knows all the answers.[14] While the U.S. economy would welcome a curtailment of its foreign spending, the Canadian economy would experience the same sort of effect as has followed the recent closing-down of U.S. air force bases abroad.

On the other hand, a cutback of direct Canadian spending would enable us to cut taxes, thereby increasing disposable incomes and leading to enhanced C to meet family demands. Part of the budget surplus, instead of becoming tax reduction, could be reassigned to other government departments, and especially to the provinces, for spending on other social needs. Monetary policy could go

---

[13] Actually, expenditures on aerospace probably lead to fewer valuable research findings applicable to industry in general than did earlier military expenditure. It may cost 10 million dollars to find a reliable control device that can be put into a match box; but to produce ordinary civilian products, there is no need to keep parts as light, small, and dependable as in traveling to the moon. Recent defense programs may have used up as much high-powered scientific and engineering resources as they have contributed to fruitful civilian uses.

[14] It is not difficult to find some of the answers, however. UBC's Gideon Rosenbluth and other economists have already made estimates of the surprisingly small impact of certain assumed disarmament procedures. His and other economists' studies have suggested that the cutback in research and development (R&D) might be the kind of military outlay that a peacetime economy would be slowest to replace with other work for the engineers, scientists, and professors.

to. work to encourage private investment. (Home industry would be threatened by a lowering of the costs of U.S.-produced goods. Why? As the United States' military cutbacks would involve reduction of her government expenditures abroad, her international deficit would probably disappear and her dollar would no longer be so overvalued; consequently U.S. goods would now be *relatively* cheaper.) North America's potential and actual growth rate would be markedly increased: instead of so much being diverted to war production, more could be transferred to capital formation, research, and other growth-inducing areas.[15]

Is the story fully as optimistic as this? Yes. A *laissez-faire* economy might face a crisis of some duration; but a mixed economy that has been using the tools of macroeconomics developed in the last thirty years needs fear no such debacle.

There is but one possible flaw in the story. It lies inside the realm of politics, and not economics. An economically illiterate electorate may less reluctantly use the tools of the new economics for war than for peace purposes.

Any citizenry, any time and any place, that cannot ideologically stomach the political moves necessary to maintain healthy growth and high-capacity economic activity can create *for itself* a problem of mass unemployment. But the critic, Marxist or otherwise, should not blame such a depression on armament cuts—or on the dependence of our mixed economy on military spending and war.

■ PUBLICLY DETERMINED CAPITAL FORMATION

Now we take up again Section A's list of factors in growth. There remains capital formation as of significant importance for improving the steady growth rate. While the unemployment gap is being narrowed, capital investment and consumption expenditures may be mutually reinforcing in expanding growth. But once full employment were assured, a determination to accelerate growth at any cost would involve trying to change the full-employment mix of resource use *away* from current and private consumption and *toward* net capital formation.

There is a most important way that a mixed economy can hope to increase its own rate of growth. This is the mechanism referred to earlier in several places, chiefly in Chapter 17 of Part Two and Chapter 29 of Part Four.

> By properly blending its reliance on fiscal and monetary policy, the citizenry of a mixed economy can hope to shift the composition of its high-employment NNP more toward capital formation and away from current consumption.

By this device, it can hope to change its own growth rate.

What exactly is the control mechanism involved? First, recall from Part Two that Bank of Canada monetary policy can help to choke off investment spending and capital formation by making credit tight and very dear; alternatively, expansive monetary policy can hope to stimulate the rate of capital formation by making credit more easily available and interest rates lower. This whole process, by which

---

[15] How to determine how much to spend in various sectors was discussed back in the Appendix to Chapter 36. Tables 36-2 and 36-3 showed how the Leontief technique could program a shift from war to peace-time patterns of consumption and final spending.

a society undertakes more and more capital formation as interest rates become less and less and as credit becomes more widely available, was described in Chapter 36 under "deepening of capital." As we saw, the process of deepening capital may not always be a smooth one in a mixed economy; but let us review its operation in a managed mixed economy.

■ AUSTERE FISCAL POLICY COMBINED WITH EXPANSIONARY MONETARY POLICY

Assume that high employment is going to be maintained. (This could mean about 97 per cent of all workers employed, to allow for temporary switchings of jobs, or it could be any other agreed-upon percentage.) A fraction of such a high-employment output can be shifted away from consumption and toward capital formation by the following:

> On the one hand, *monetary policy is to be expansionary*, making for a deepening of capital and much capital formation.
>
> On the other hand, the tendency of such an increase in investment spending to create an inflationary gap is to be offset by an *austere fiscal policy* calling for high enough tax rates (and low enough government expenditure) to reduce people's disposable (after-tax) incomes enough to cause them to reduce their consumption enough to release resources for investment without causing any inflation.
>
> This pair of policies, by favoring investment, would be biased toward faster growth. The quantitative weight of taxes would have to be high in order to cut down on consumption. It might be accompanied by an increase in *imports* of consumption goods, to free our resources, gradually, for the production of capital goods, and for the extra exports that would pay for all imports. (If what we want is more growth, we can always call on the world market to supply those parts of final aggregate demand that we wish to minimize in our own production.)

The "open" nature of our economy always poses new monetary problems not so serious in more-or-less self-sufficient economies. For example, what happens to the rate of investment if the Bank of Canada does lower the rate of interest? The Porter Royal Commission reported that easier credit conditions in Canada do not have a *large* impact on our incentive to invest. Why not? First, they reduce the incentives of foreigners to invest in Canada. Second, tax and not credit conditions may be the most important conditions for investors, so that higher taxes would deter new *I* more than easier credit would encourage it. Third, if Canada opts for easier credit but the United States does not, Canadian lenders may decide to send their funds to New York. (This is another way of considering the first point.) Thus to encourage investment in Canada it may be necessary to "bribe" capital formation by special *tax* concessions similar to those already given for research, oil exploration, and investment in high-unemployment "designated areas." Allowing faster depreciation is now a favorite tax technique here and in other countries, but it is inferior to an outright subsidy because the latter is given only where extra investment actually takes place, while the former tax-reduction is "paid" to all investors. Finally, reducing the egalitarianism of income-taxes, and lightening the tax load on wealthy savers, will probably produce more lending and investing.

> What is the special virtue of this particular combination of policies? It is, to repeat, that by adopting it we can hope to keep full employment while altering upwards our effective rate of capital formation and potential for growth.

But this pair of policies will, for reasons given in the above paragraphs, be difficult to pursue in an open economy like ours. We are rarely free to determine our own course in isolation. Thus Canadian adoption of an austere fiscal policy plus easy credit as a route to higher capital formation[16] is easier if the United States adopts the same route. But if the United States' route is one that eases investment in the United States while impeding U.S. lending to Canada—as it easily may be until she gets the balance-of-payments deficit under control—Canada's success with her own growth policy might be very limited.

This open-economy qualification to the efficacy of combining fiscal and monetary policies so as to get faster growth without inflation is a serious one. However, for some Canadians it might be an advantage, for it suggests a way of reducing the balance-of-payments deficit and reducing our dependence on foreign capital.

Our present rate of growth is sustained by a large annual contribution of American and other foreign capital. This inflow reflects our long-term balance-of-payments deficit. Some have advocated maintaining our present growth rate without foreign capital by: (1) using currency depreciation to raise exports, reduce imports, and cut off capital imports; (2) tightening fiscal policy to reduce consumption out of a full-employment $C + I + G + (E - M)$ (as above); (3) reducing interest rates to encourage capital formation. It can be seen that this amounts to the previous, closed-economy policy, but now used not to raise the rate of growth but to prevent its decline if foreign capital is deliberately cut off.[17]

Whatever one thinks of the aims of reducing foreign ownership, this particular proposal illustrates one way of thinking about macroeconomic management: we need one policy weapon for every aim. In the present case, for example, we (1) adjust the exchange rate to hold the foreign deficit at the desired level; (2) adjust taxes and government spending to hold consumption at the desired level without inflation; and (3) adjust monetary policy to hold capital formation (and growth) at their desired rates. Except by accident, we can accomplish three desired objectives only by using three tools of economic policy.

---

[16] It is not clear that the government's economic advisers are pushing any particular pair of policies for growth or that such policies as were undertaken were aimed at growth. In early 1970, the Trudeau government, faced with unemployment plus inflationary pressures, seems to be opting for a tighter fiscal policy and a relatively tight monetary policy. They were forced to a flexible exchange rate (which allowed them to be more restrictive domestically without worry about a capital inflow).

[17] For a short discussion, see Royal Commission on Taxation, *Report*, Volume 2, 1966.

A second qualification was mentioned in the Appendix to Chapter 36. Some economists think that deepening of capital cannot be successfully achieved because the capital-output ratio is a stubborn constant. Here are their arguments:

> If you stimulate investment as was done in the plant-and-equipment boom of 1956-1957, 1965-1967, or 1968-1969, you will simply drive down to minimal levels the yield on further investment; and you will pay for it by reduced private capital formation in subsequent years. In the long run, investment will have to be held down to the requirements set by labor-force and technology growth. Be thankful for high consumption at full employment, because that is the *only* way you can maintain full employment.

A rebuttal might go along the following lines.

> In examining a planned economy like that of the Soviet Union, one certainly feels that their product could be enhanced by faster accumulation of capital goods. If that is a fact of technology, why does not the same hold for us? Current capital goods have a yield before taxes of as high as 15 per cent; therefore, goes this rebuttal, it is hard to believe that yields would drop to zero or below a minimal profit level (needed to offset risk) just because net capital formation is speeded up for a decade. Moreover, the advocates of enhanced investment for growth are willing, if it should prove necessary, to recommend nonconventional methods of credit expansion—guarantees and insurances against loss from risks, etc.—to engineer a deepening of capital.

There remains a final difficulty with an optimistic synthesis that keeps the mixed economic system at full employment and keeps it there with the desired mix of investment and consumption. This is the problem of possible cost-push, or "sellers' inflation."

■ A NEW COST-PUSH SELLERS' INFLATION?

No country in the world has been simultaneously enjoying (1) full employment, (2) free markets, and (3) stable price levels. Thus, from 1956 to 1958 our prices were generally rising: wholesale prices, farm prices, cost-of-living prices—in fact, all but staple prices. Everyone was disturbed about the month-after-month announcement of higher prices. But to what was it due? To excessive demand, like that of the 1960s' conventional $C + I + G + (E - M)$ inflationary gap?

Turning to look at each industry, one found it hard to perceive excessive demand in 1957-1958. Autos were not selling well; and farm-equipment salesmen sang the blues. TV manufacturers took out the red ink as sales slumped and as people began to buy the low-profit cheap models. The steel industry operated often far below 80 per cent of capacity. And so it went in industry after industry in Canada and the United States.

Still, the price index continued to advance. Therefore some experts began to wonder whether this was not the case of "wage-push" rather than "demand-pull." Money wages were raised each year, and often by more than the growth of productivity. Nor did it seem to take many strikes to accomplish this. The wage-push happened outside the unionized industries, too. In the unionized sectors some observers said: "In pushing for higher wages, labor is pushing against an open door. The employers do not fight the increases the way they used to. They act as if they think that the government will keep aggregate demand high enough to buy the higher-cost output; so they grant the wage increases, and this sends up costs of production, which sends up the prices firms charge for their goods. The result is a new kind of inflation. When and if the government tries to handle it by the usual weapons that affect demand, it creates unemployment and a recession as in 1957-1958. From 1958 to 1963, wholesale prices were stable, but it seemed to require unemployment of more than 5 per cent to make this so."

Explanatory emphasis has shifted away from exclusive reliance on wage-push to more general cost-push. Important research has suggested two additional elements: *first*, that in the United States, the increase in the price of steel was by itself responsible for a significant fraction of the increase in the U.S. wholesale price index; and *second*, that, in this administered-price industry, profit margins went up along with steelworkers' wage increases. Thus it was concluded that the pressure of nonlabor as well as labor costs was responsible.

The name, *sellers' inflation*, was given to the broadened concept by A. P. Lerner:

> If all sellers, whether of labor or of property services or of goods, negotiate and determine their prices so as to try to get them all more than 100 per cent of the total national product, then the result cannot help but be a frustrating upward push of the price level—a case of sellers' inflation.[18]

Figure 40-1 shows how low unemployment rates—as in the post-1965 boom, when the average rate dropped below 5.0 per cent, reaching 3.6 per cent by 1966 —are associated with a quickening of price inflation. This same incompatibility of full employment with price stability can be observed in mixed economies all over the world: in the United States; in Sweden and Switzerland; in Holland and France; in Britain and Belgium; and, to a lesser degree, in Japan, West Germany, and Italy. This important phenomenon calls for new analytical tools of description, interpretation, understanding, and prediction. The next section, which may be skipped in briefer courses, is a partial response to that need.

■ THE PHILLIPS-CURVE TRADE-OFF BETWEEN FULL EMPLOYMENT AND INFLATION

To understand conventional "demand-pull" inflation is easy in an idealized model where wages cannot rise so long as there is still one unemployed worker to keep down the wage rate. And in the same idealized model where goods are all auctioned off in perfectly competitive markets, there could be no general price rises so long as there is spare capacity available to produce more output at (marginal) costs no higher than the ruling prices.

---

[18] Experience with modern mixed economies suggests strongly there may be a current cost-push problem in this sense: our price level seems likely to creep up even when there is higher-than-desirable unemployment, e.g., even when more than 1 out of 30 men are without jobs.

Are full employment and price stability compatible?

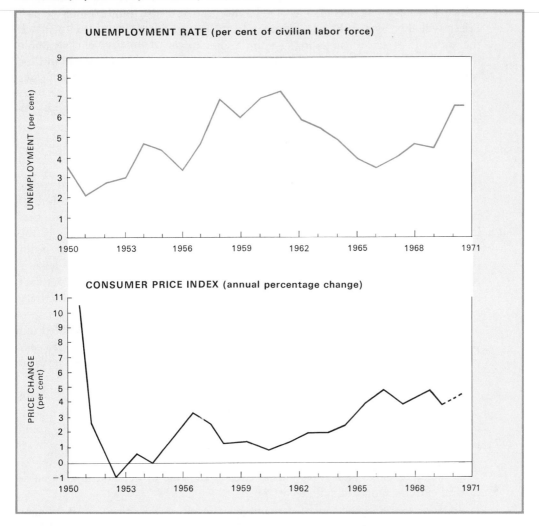

FIG. 40-1. From 1950 to 1960, each peak of the business cycle displayed higher unemployment, a disquieting trend. Fiscal and monetary policies were employed by the New Economics to end this stagnating. They could be used more extensively to raise employment, production, and real incomes were it not for the fear that the price level will be pushed up beyond a gentle creep. If an "incomes policy" could be found that would inhibit cost-push sellers' inflation, the ice block of structural unemployment could be melted by expanded aggregate demand, reinforced by retraining and relocation programs. This, in essence, is the *raison d'être* for Canada's Prices and Incomes Commission.

SIMPLE DEMAND-PULL   In such a model, begin with full employment, where the macroeconomic managers have created just enough $C + I + G = MV$ spending to absorb all the full-employment output. If the managers now raise total spending by, say, 10 per cent, there will be more dollars of spending coming on the demand markets than can be supplied with goods at the previous equilibrium prices. We have engineered one of Chapter 12's so-called "inflationary gaps." Prices will then generally rise—ultimately by the 10 per cent needed to match the added $C + I + G$ spending. At the higher prices, employers will scramble to get more workers, bidding up wages ultimately also by 10 per cent (and thus leaving profits also higher by 10 per cent, but with all real or deflated wages being exactly the same as before).

In this first simplified model, demand has pulled up prices and wages.[19] Hence the name "demand-pull."

SIMPLE COST-PUSH Now become more realistic. Drop the notion that labor gets auctioned off at a flexible wage rate. Go to the other extreme. Suppose that by union power or by the strong pressure of custom in the nonunionized areas, wage rates always rise by 5 per cent per year regardless of the amount of unemployment. And, since we are not trying to be entirely realistic, suppose that labor productivity always rises by exactly 3 per cent per year. Then if the employers can always administer their prices so as to keep the share of profit (or property return) unchanged—say, near the conventional one-fourth level—how will prices all rise? By arithmetic, we find that prices must rise by 2 per cent per year—which is the 5 per cent wage rise minus the 3 per cent productivity rise. The real wage rate also rises by only the 3 per cent productivity rise—since the 5 per cent money wage rise has the 2 per cent of price rise deflated out of it. The total *real* return to property owners has also risen by the 3 per cent change in average labor productivity—because the relative wage share stays at three-fourths.

Note that nothing at all has been said thus far about demand, about $C + I + G + (E - M)$ or MV total spending. In this extreme cost-push model, demand has nothing to do with prices—which get set exclusively by wages and productivity. Prices rise at 2 per cent per year whether there is peace or war, recession or prosperity, tight or loose monetary and fiscal policy, a Chapter 12 inflationary or deflationary gap. What then is the role of demand in this paradoxical extreme model of simple cost-push?

Under extreme cost-push, demand has *no* effect on prices, P. It became completely a theory of output, Q. Demand can still determine how total $PQ =$

---

[19] Note that money wage rates have risen by 10 per cent more than productivity (which in our simple example has actually not changed at all) is rising. But that fact tells us nothing about the direction of causation (which we know in this case definitely *not* to have been from wages as cause to prices as effect). Whenever prices are rising and the relative sharing of profits-to-wages is constant, as a matter of mere arithmetic money wage rates must be outstripping average labor productivity by the amount of the price rise, with real wages merely matching the productivity rise. But contrary to the confused arithmetic of conservative financial columnists, when real wages are thus advancing in line with average labor productivity, that does not mean that labor is "appropriating" or absorbing all the fruits of technological progress (which admittedly may have come from better machines and management methods as well as from greater worker effort or skill). It merely means that profit receivers and labor are *sharing* in progress on the same terms as before—say, at the historic fraction of about three-fourths for labor.

NNP behaves at all times; for these are simply other names for total $C + I + G + (E - M)$ or MV spending (as we saw in Chapter 14's tautological "equation of exchange"). Let us examine the problems now created for the macroeconomic managers of fiscal and monetary policy.

If we began at full employment and money wage rates go up by 5 per cent instead of the 3 per cent of productivity growth, unless the macro managers engineer an increase in aggregate demand of 5 per cent—big enough to match the wage increase, which means big enough to finance the 2 per cent increase in P and the 3 per cent increase in Q—full employment will ebb away. (Perhaps the union leaders and oligopolists were counting on the managers to create the needed increase in aggregate demand.)

Thus, suppose the macro managers wrongly think they are facing old-fashioned demand-pull inflation when actually they are facing simple cost-push. Logically, they might decide to hold down NNP demand constant. What will happen? Output and employment will drop by 5 per cent a year! First 1 man out of 20 will be unemployed; then 2; . . . ; and if the irresistible force of cost-push meets the immovable object of macroeconomic policy, in the end the system will run down to literally nothing, with the last starving man losing his job and dying out. This is not a very tenable outcome, and perhaps the macro managers will drop their stubbornness, with the result that they will create enough money spending to countenance the creeping inflation *indefinitely.*

PHILLIPS TRADE-OFF CURVE   It is too bad that the simple demand-pull model is not realistic, for under it the job of the macro managers would be the easy one of turning on or off the faucets of fiscal and monetary policy to keep employment just full but never overfull. Yet it is indeed fortunate that the nightmare of simple cost-push is also not realistic, for in simple cost-push there is no control of inflation or influence on it that the macro managers can contrive.

The real world is somewhere between the two extremes. The amount of unemployment does in some degree hold down the excess of money wage increase over productivity increase. Budget surpluses and open-market sales —all the weapons in Part Two's macro arsenal to control $C + I + G + (E - M)$ or MV total spending—can now have an effect on price and wage inflation.

Thus when relatively full employment coincided with the rise in spending caused by the Vietnam war, and this rise was not offset by determined tight monetary and fiscal policy, the United States experienced a quickening in the rate of price inflation, a quickening that soon gave rise to wage increases that both reflected and aggravated the rise in the general price level. In some ways, macro managers are thrown into the most perplexing of all possible worlds. They are neither in the easy world of simple demand-pull nor the hopeless world of simple cost-push where they can do nothing about the rate of inflation. They are in the difficult world where the attempt to bring a 6 per cent rate of inflation down to 3 per cent may, at least in the short run, necessitate a retardation of real growth like that of 1969-70, with rising unemployment, regional

**Real world falls between simple demand-pull
and cost-push:**

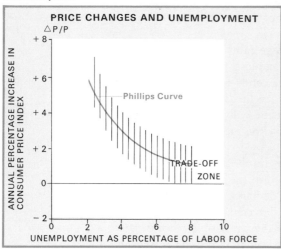

FIG. 40-2. If we move leftward toward full employment, before we get there, wages and prices may tend to rise and keep rising. Most mixed economies face this dilemma—a cruel one, for it would be a bitter cost to pay for price stability to have to move rightward where the poor and members of minority groups suffer high unemployment.

unrest, and all the wastes of a growing gap between their country's achieved and potential GNP.

Professor A. W. Phillips, of the London School of Economics and the Australian National University, made a pioneering attempt to quantify the tradeoff relationship between unemployment and price-wage rises. Figure 40-2 pictures the typical downward-sloping Phillips curve, in which as you move leftward to reduce unemployment, then the higher becomes the rate of price and wage creep along the curve. On the diagram's horizontal axis is the percentage of unemployment. On the vertical scale is the algebraic percentage change per annum in average prices.

The "Phillips Curve" in Fig. 40-2 reflects the experience of many countries that increasing the level of unemployment can moderate or wipe out the upward price creep. The rate of price rise tends to be high when the economy is buoyant and employment is full. In Canada, it also tends to be higher *whatever* the rate of unemployment when the rate of U.S. price increase, as reflected in our import prices, is higher. What we are presented with then is a complicated statistical relationship between unemployment and price increase, as in the 1953-1965 period, which cannot be displayed in a simple curve.[20] Consequently,

---

[20] The actual complex statistical relationship is taken from the Economic Council of Canada, *Price Stability and High Employment: the Options for Canadian Economic Policy*, an econometric study by Ronald G. Bodkin, Elizabeth P. Bond, Grant L. Reuber, and T. Russell Robinson (Queen's Printer, Ottawa, 1967). The study showed that the rate of Canadian price increase in the period 1953-1965 (second quarter) was statistically related to the rate of domestic unemployment, the rate of U.S. wage increase, the Canadian profit markup on output, and the rate of change in the implicit deflator for imports of goods and services in the National Accounts (a proxy for import prices).

It is not altogether clear that the statistical relationship for the period through 1965 is

the curve shown in Fig. 40-2 has been drawn halfway through an econome-
trically derived "trade-off zone," the range within which Canadian combinations
are likely to be found.

The zone shows a problem of choice. Policy makers or society as a whole,
cannot, in the present structure of the Canadian economy, have *both* price
stability and high employment. Instead, compromises must be accepted, "trading-
off" some departure from zero price change for some gain in employment. There
is no easy way to achieving both price stability and high employment. Moreover, in the face of large rates of U.S. inflation it would probably be very difficult to achieve a fully acceptable level of either target if a fixed exchange rate
(or one which is not allowed to fluctuate in line with market pressures—one
which remains controlled if not stable) were to prevail (as it did in the period
1962-1970).

> One can imagine a *right-hand* scale of percentage wage increases in Fig. 40-2, to
> complement the left-hand scale of annual price increases. The two scales would
> be much the same. The chief difference would be that the right-hand scale would
> be pushed down: the intercept on the line of zero price change would be 3 per
> cent; at 4 per cent change, the corresponding wage change would be 7 per cent,
> and so on. The difference of 3 per cent is the postulated amount of productivity
> increase. (A wage change of 5 per cent is partially absorbed by 3 per cent produc-
> tivity increase, leaving a 2 per cent price increase. This assumes that the fruits of
> the productivity change are shared in the same old proportions by labor and
> non-labor.)
>
> A jump in the rate of productivity increase would show itself by an equal
> downward shift of the Phillips curve and the imaginary right-hand scale. Thus,
> with productivity now growing at 4 per cent per year, a 5 per cent wage increase
> would correspond to only a 1 per cent price rise. A profit squeeze could be
> similarly shown. Thus it is possible that national "productivity drives" or national
> "incomes policies" could reduce the political strain of choosing a point on the
> curve by moving the curve itself to a more favorable set of alternatives.

Be it noted that the MV and $C + I + G + (E - M)$ approaches to aggregate
dollar spending are still applicable *offstage*, but one needs the information of
the Phillips curve to translate the resulting product $P \times Q$ into its separate
components. In simple demand pull, the Phillips curve would be a vertical line
at the minimal unemployment level: Q would then always correspond to full
employment, and P would float in free labor markets to whatever level total

---

applicable to a period of high economic activity such as we encountered in the late 1960s.
Students at the University of British Columbia sought, as a research project, to test the
stability of the Reuber, Bodkin, Bond, and Robinson relationship. Their results, while inconclusive because of the shortness of the period 1965 (third quarter) through 1969 (second
quarter), do strongly hint that the Philips curve may well shift: outward and upward
(resembling more closely the pure cost-push curve of footnote 21, page 1030) following periods
of low unemployment and increasing inflation, and downward and inward following periods
of decreasing inflation and high unemployment. Grauer, Ko, and Reid found that the importance of profits as an explanatory variable was open to some question in the earlier as well
as the later period. The importance of the rate of U.S. wage changes, on the other hand, was
apparently heightened in the later period.

money spending would determine. In the simple cost-push the Phillips curve is a horizontal line, with no level of unemployment leading to price stability.[21]

One can expect the Phillips curve for different mixed economies to be different, depending upon their institutional patterns and psychological outlooks. Thus, in the 1950s, the curve for Western Germany seemed more like the limiting cases mentioned earlier than did the United States, British, or Swedish curves. So in the latter countries you then heard more concern about cost-push creeps of inflation.

The Phillips curve is a dramatic way of describing the dilemma for macro-economic policy, even though it does not go much beyond description to give us "explanation." Thus, the problem is posed: how much can a mixed economy supplement macro policy so as to give itself a better Phillips curve? Better in what sense? Better because, without relying unduly on inefficient direct wage and price controls, it permits us to enjoy a lower minimum level of unemployment at which the system can avoid substantial price creep.

LONGER RUN   Before turning to the hard problems of policy, we should reemphasize that economics is not an exact science. The data will not really fit any one Phillips curve perfectly. More important still is the fact that the measured Phillips curves represent *short-term* relationships which will shift in the longer run. Thus, if Diefenbaker runs a slack economy for the late fifties and early sixties, that may kill off inflationary expectations and slow down wage demands. In short, much unemployment, long maintained, may gradually *shift* the short-term Phillips curve leftward. Then when a Pearson or a Trudeau comes along, he may

---

[21] Note the difference between the realistic Phillips curve and the way it would look in the cases of simple demand-pull and simple cost-push. In simple cost-push, Fig. 40-3(a) shows the curve to be completely horizontal with no trade-off possible. Figure 40-3(b) shows the curve becoming completely vertical in simple demand-pull, with no trade-off being necessary. (Actually, in Fig. 40-3(a), if the macro managers insisted on boosting demand faster than the indicated wage rise, they would push the system to such minimal unemployment as to cause a frantic bidding up by employers of the market wage rate *above* the wage administered by the unions; and this gives rise to what in Scandinavia has been called the "wage drift," in which wages always run ahead of the minima set by collective bargaining. This means the horizontal curve really ceases to be horizontal when you move near to the vertical axis.)

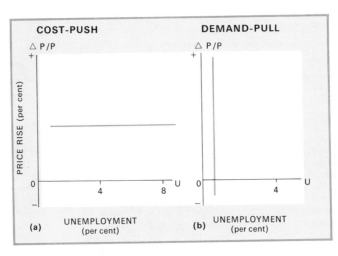

FIG. 40-3.

be lucky enough to cash in on the Diefenbaker "investment in sadism" by being able to engineer a long growth in $C + I + G + (E - M)$ before prices and wages misbehave badly. But by the same reasoning, after more than 100 months of uninterrupted expansion, and particularly with U.S. inflation, continued low unemployment may shift the short-term Phillips curve rightward, making the policy problems of the 1970s that much harder.[22]

ARE GROWTH AND PRICE STABILITY OPPOSING GOALS?

Let us return from our analytical excursions to the pressing Canadian problem of the modern mixed economy.

If consumer, wholesale, and general GNP prices all tend to creep upward when there is 4, 5, and even 6 per cent unemployment, what should the monetary and fiscal authorities do? Should they cut down on over-all demand (i.e., on $C + I + G + (E - M)$ or MV total spending), even though that means a further

---

[22] Some writers try to define a long-run curve from the systematic shiftings of the short-run curves (in much the same way that Fig. 19-5 was able to depict long-run Marshallian supply curves from systematically shifting short-run supply curves). The long-run Phillips curve tends to be twisted clockwise, as in Fig. 40-4(a). There is even one strong theory, suggested by W. Fellner and H. Wallich of Yale, M. Friedman of Chicago, and E. Phelps of Pennsylvania, which in effect says: "The Phillips trade-off is based only on the *illusion* of *unanticipated* price-wage inflation. Once the system settles down to any constant rate of price-wage inflation, people will come to learn the fact and to expect it in the future. So you will then have just as much excess wage pressure over that constant rate as you had when prices were stable. There is really a 'natural rate of unemployment,' defined by a vertical long-run Phillips curve as shown in Fig. 40-4(b). If you temporarily bring unemployment below the natural rate, your short-term curves will twist upward indefinitely and your price rise will accelerate; if you temporarily bring unemployment above the natural rate (the Eisenhower rather than Kennedy pattern), the short-term curves will then twist downward indefinitely and your price rise will decelerate. In order for people to be adjusted to the rate of price change so that it will not be accelerating or decelerating, you have to be *on the long-run vertical line*." These writers conclude: "Since you will be stuck with the natural rate of unemployment in the long run anyway, the macro managers should keep demand growing at only the rate of real growth of the system—say, 4 to 5 per cent per year so that P's will be steady. To reduce unemployment's natural rate, policies other than macro fiscal and monetary measures are needed—such as repealing minimum-wage laws or restrictive union practices." Critics of this view say that by the time *their* proposed equilibrium is reached, the system may well have been torn apart by voter revolt, urban riots, and unemployment-induced hardships and dissatisfactions. And besides the data of experience are not yet available to judge whether Fig. 40-4(a) or 40-4(b) is the more realistic.

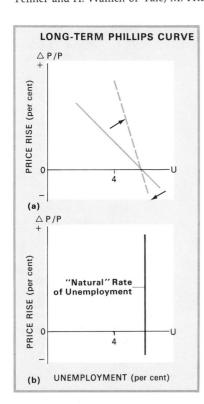

LONG-TERM PHILLIPS CURVE

$\Delta P / P$

PRICE RISE (per cent)

(a)

$\Delta P / P$

"Natural" Rate of Unemployment

PRICE RISE (per cent)

(b)   UNEMPLOYMENT (per cent)

FIG. 40-4.

lowering of production and employment? Or should they increase total spending, even though that means some further increase in prices?

There is no easy answer; nevertheless, here are four different viewpoints:

PRICE STABILITY AT ALL COSTS   Adherents of this view feel that a stable price level is itself so vital a social goal as to transcend other goals such as high employment and growth. Zealots would thus hold out for price stability if it were a question of having to choose among such goals.

Most adherents of this view, however, are not such zealots. They take the more hopeful view that *in the long run* there is really no clash between price stability and growth or high employment. They claim that inflation today means depression tomorrow. They claim that only in an environment of stable prices will efficient business decisions be made. They claim that countenancing a little inflation will result in the *creep* of inflation inevitably becoming a *trot*, the trot inevitably becoming a *gallop*, and the gallop inevitably becoming a *runaway*. Why then, let the whole process begin? Why not, so to speak, sacrifice a little of current output and employment as an investment in higher *future* growth and employment? So they argue.

GROWTH AT ALL COSTS   A contrary view is revealed by those who groan when central banks try to moderate the price increases of the 1970s. They apparently believe in full employment and growth as primary goals and would give them great emphasis in any case; but members of this camp generally do have the optimistic hope that, by insisting on achieving growth, society will in fact end up with better-behaved prices.

The argument that growth brings price stability, which is a kind of cousin to the earlier argument that price stability brings growth, runs thus:

> Higher output means downward pressure on prices, other things being equal.
>
> Since workers tend to get *money* wages that increase at a fixed rate, by achieving a faster rate of growth of productivity society can make this yield less price increases.
>
> At high levels of capacity, the unit costs of businessmen get lower; therefore they can charge lower prices and still make good profits.
>
> High employment and production make people efficient and venturesome.

Exponents of this view would, if necessary, make a short-run sacrifice of price stability as an investment in future growth and price stability.

SOME INFLATION WITH SOME GROWTH   If you read the recent *Reviews* of the Economic Council of Canada, the annual statements of the Governor of the Bank of Canada, the budget speeches of the Minister of Finance, or the full text of the report of the (Porter) Royal Commission on Banking and Finance, you will find an official view (roughly compatible with that in much of the financial press and with articles in learned journals) that rejects both the extremes just described.

You may not find it surprising that responsible officials are said to steer between extreme opinions. To understand why in this case it is surprising, consider the following: (*a*) It is believed to be the *duty* of officials of the Bank of

Canada to keep prices stable (the founders of the Bank would have added ". . . at all costs"). (b) Economists and financial writers, like insurance companies and pension experts, know better than most people how inflation erodes the value of past savings relied on by retired people, widows, and orphans. (c) Experts in fiscal and monetary policy have had little chance to demonstrate that they are able to dampen an inflationary spiral. (d) Only a few years ago, writers on economic policy asserted the desirability of growth *with* price stability. What has made the experts feel that some inflationary creep is quite acceptable?

Many economists believe that the effort to obtain absolute price stability may detract from high employment and growth in a modern mixed (and open) economy like ours. They believe that it would be necessary to introduce slackness into the economic structure if the gentle price creep were to be stopped entirely. They believe that a slow price creep, if matched by a similar creep in foreign mixed economies, need not cause any balance-of-payments difficulties. (Also, some of them argue that the price creep is illusory because the official price indices do not take into account the rising quality of the goods that annually show higher prices.)

Although the evidence tends to be a little contradictory, one study, by Western Ontario's Grant Reuber (prepared in 1963 for the Porter Commission on banking and finance) actually suggests that although it has been impossible in the conditions since 1945 to get full employment without some wage or consumer-price push, the same cannot be said of growth. Growth seems to have been "independent" or "not associated with" price movements.

Recently, Reuber's research has been extended in a wider examination of prices, productivity, and employment by the Economic Council of Canada. Little new has been said about the trade-offs with *growth*, mentioned above, but earlier studies have been confirmed on four points:

First. Upward changes in Canadian wages are affected (statistically "explained") by U.S. wage changes. This suggests that wage and cost stability may sometimes be beyond the reach of Canadian policy-makers.[23]

Second. The rate of change in average wages is positively influenced by the rate of unemployment. This influence is portrayed by the Phillips curve or price-level versus unemployment trade-off curve shown earlier. Statistical investigation of this curve for Canada since 1953 suggests that a wage creep of 2 to 3 per cent per year may be an inevitable companion to full employment. That is, some price stability must be traded off for fuller employment than has been present on the average since 1953.

---

[23] This complication raises the question of whether rising foreign prices (of imports to Canada) can be neutralized by a rise in the value of the Canadian dollar through official operations on our exchange rate. The topic has too many ramifications to go into here; anyway, the conclusions in the text above stand more or less independently of the source of the price rise. Assiduous footnote readers can turn to G. L. Reuber, "The Objectives of Canadian Monetary Policy, 1949-61: Empirical 'Trade-Offs' and the Reaction Function of the Authorities," *Journal of Political Economy*, Vol. LXXII, No. 2 (April, 1964), pp. 109-132.

Third. Past increases in wages and prices tend to produce present upward changes. This raises the question of whether a creep must turn to a trot, and a trot to an inflationary gallop. The evidence in Canada and the United States is scanty, some of it optimistic.[24] But it is not a question for which anyone wishes to seek an empirical answer.

Fourth. While one task of policy is to prevent the economy from moving either to the upper or to the lower extreme of the trade-off curve (by use of monetary, fiscal, and international policy), another task is to shift the curve downward. The task of policy is then not to bring about the optimum trade-off along the curve, but to improve the trade-off possibilities everywhere. This can be accomplished by melting structural unemployment (pages 1011-1012) and by "incomes policies" to which we now turn.

AN "INCOMES POLICY"?   Another group of specialists in effect urges that the state must stop inflation by keeping down all the personal incomes that ultimately make up costs. Thus the state, they argue, must intervene whenever the pricing of labor or capital services is being negotiated; e.g., through more vigorous enforcement of combines-legislation in the administered price area; changed legislation and attitudes toward trade-union attempts for higher money wages; parliamentary pressures in collective bargaining to uphold the consumer and national interest; a stronger and more permanent role for Canada's Prices and Incomes Commission; and other policies and vehicles yet unborn.

> Britain, looking longingly at what it thought were the successful mechanisms whereby the Netherlands and Sweden brought united employers and unions together and determined a satisfactory rate of advance of wage rates and other income items, tried in the 1960s to develop an "incomes policy" that would make full employment and price stability compatible. But in 1966, Harold Wilson's Labor Government felt it had to impose a legal wage and price freeze.

[24] Some writers have argued that the economy reallocates labor and capital between industries and regions *more* efficiently when wages and prices are rising. One variant of the argument comes from Britain, where long periods of near-full employment have taught employers to attempt to "stock-pile" skilled workers even when their skills are not fully needed. Some British writers argue that generally-rising wages enable other employers to attract these partly-wasted talents to factories and firms where they are really scarce. Other variants of the argument depend on the empirical observation that wages and prices are sticky, and because of unions, minimum-wage-laws, and other factors do not fall when particular demands slacken off. The argument runs that when price and wage levels are constant, stickiness inhibits those changes in relative prices which are necessary for the economy to adjust to changing tastes, techniques, and scarcities. Charles L. Schultze, Director of the Bureau of the Budget for President Johnson, has made this point. A third variant concerns workers in declining regions of Canada. With incomes that are sticky in a downward direction or with employment assistance money-payments that are fixed, these workers cannot be attracted to booming regions unless other wages go *much* higher—that is, unless the *general* wage level goes up. This variant is obviously a regional application of the second argument.

■ WANTED, AN "INCOMES POLICY": WAGE-PRICE GUIDEPOSTS?

It is harder in North America than in Europe to find united employers and unions who could come together to agree to permissible wage-rate increases. Indeed in Canada today there is almost no national wage bargaining. And the legal traditions of both Canada and the United States frown on combinations of firms that might agree on final prices. However, in the 1960s Presidents Kennedy and Johnson did suggest policies which were aimed at "holding the line." What principles are involved? They were worked out explicitly in Sweden in the early 1950s, and are now generally widely understood. Following Chapter 28, they may be summarized in the following terms:

> The average money-wage increase is to be no higher than the average increase in physical productivity; but the increase in each industry is to be divorced from the increase in physical productivity in that industry itself, the difference to be taken up in price reductions to consumers of items with unusually high productivity growth (wheat? autos?) and price increases to industries with unusually slow productivity growth (teaching?); departures from the common wage increase are to be permitted primarily where an industry needs to raise wage rates to attract new labor entrants and where a declining industry needs to lower wages in order to expedite labor exit.

These principles cannot be validly criticized as giving to labor all the fruits of technical progress; such a conclusion reflects merely bad arithmetic, which fails to recognize that an increase in wage rates in the same percentage as product means an increase of profits in that same percentage, not a zero increase in profits!

VOLUNTARY RESTRAINTS   These "guideposts," however, do not have the force of law; and scowls from the government, when an industry like steel raises its prices before excess capacity has been reduced to a low level, cannot solve the dilemmas of full employment and price stability.

How did these guideposts work out? As expected, employers grumbled that they were slanted only against price increases. Unions grumbled that they were slanted only against wage increases. Many observers said they had no effect at all; or that if they had any effect, it was to make the suggested guidepost wage increase the minimum raise that the unions asked for in beginning their bargaining.

The Economic Council of Canada reported in the mid-1960s against a wage-and-price restraint policy. It did not belittle the importance of guideposts or incomes policies elsewhere. But it did find that the absence of a broad *federal* labor jurisdiction under our constitution, the absence of strong *national* wage bargaining between centralized unions and employer groups, and various decentralised and international aspects of the Canadian economic structure, made the effort to mount an incomes policy unprofitable. It did not say that such policies would be unworkable, only that their introduction would absorb political attention and effort that ought to be going into other policy initiatives.

Yet by 1969, inflationary pressure became of such mounting national concern that the government announced the creation of a four-man Prices and

Incomes Commission (with UBC's Professor John Young at the helm). Charged with looking into the various causes of domestic inflation and suggesting possible courses of action, the Commission, in its various endeavors, attempted to set some guidelines—criteria for price and wage increases. Because of the federal problems noted earlier, the Commission's only real tool was strong admonition. Voluntary price restraint agreements (to make any price increase less than cost-wage increases) were negotiated between the Commission and Canadian management, but labor remained aloof—defiant.

By October 1970, the Commission's guideline and policing roles had been largely abandoned, its 6 per cent raise limit suffering, at the time of the postal settlement (August 1970), from what was termed a "credibility gap;" and the group was concentrating on studies of the inflationary process in an under-employed economy.

In a new perspective, four traditional problems loomed before the government and the economy: (1) inflation, continuing at a diminishing rate; (2) the trade-off of inflation for unemployment, with both exports and employment seriously low for the first time in 10 years; (3) large autonomous capital inflows, leading to an appreciated Canadian dollar and discouraging exports; (4) a delay in the reaction of each of these problems to Canadian policy weapons. Furthermore, the lags appeared to be changing capriciously. The long-run inflation rate, rate of growth and productivity are largely forgotten in the strain of equilibrating the 1971 economy. The extent to which the approach of the Commission to either restraint or investigation may yet bear fruit remains to be seen.[25] We are reminded that citizens of a modern mixed economy can find no shelters within which they can live with full security and without compromise.

■ CONCLUSION

Although economic growth presents challenges, it is essentially a cheerful subject. As Sir Arthur Lewis in particular has pointed out, the advantage of growth does not lie in the increasing utility or happiness that may result from it; for we are not agreed that the "haves" are in fact happier than the "have-nots." Rather, the advantage of economic growth consists of its capacity to broaden man's range of *choice*, to make man master of his environment instead of its slave. As long as man lives at a primitive level, he must devote all his time and energies to scratching out a bare subsistence, and is often subject to the ravages of poverty, starvation, and disease. At this point, man chooses to use his increasing production possibilities to gain control over his environment, and to wrest from nature food, fuel, shelter, and health. As the economy grows, and as man gains more control over it, he can also choose to have more leisure, to

[25] The Commission, in an April 1971 report, examining the 27-33 per cent increase in bank service charges, suggested that the banking industry has a large amount of discretion in setting its prices. The Minister for Corporate and Consumer Affairs announced after tabling the report that it was expected that the banks would be placed under the combines legislation.

travel more, and to enjoy more stability.[26] However, man's control over his environment may lead him to pollute it, and, after still more, or faster, economic growth, man will—many would say *must*—exercise his command over production possibilities to reduce this pollution. Such conservation will both minimize harmful external diseconomies (as discussed in Chapter 39) and satisfy man's growing esthetic desire to live in an ecologically balanced and flourishing milieu, to live in harmony with nature. The poorest societies have a very limited range of choice; only economic growth confers the power to select among alternative mixtures of work and leisure, of economic development (or increases in output) and environmental restoration. Moreover, only economic growth enables the multitude to learn how to choose wisely, as increased prosperity makes more opportunities to acquire an education available to more people.

Without doing much about it specifically, we can expect advanced economies to show a considerable measure of growth in the future, as they have in the past. The economy of North America, for example, can hardly help growing at the rate of $3\frac{1}{2}$ per cent or more, even if we do not rouse ourselves but merely keep our system working reasonably well.

If we do rouse ourselves and do the things which can speed up growth, a $4\frac{1}{2}$ per cent rate ought to be well within our grasp. Admittedly, this is not the 6 per cent rate which some proclaim, but that is no cause for despair.

Truly, it is a tremendous accomplishment if an economy can lift its annual growth rate by even $\frac{1}{2}$ per cent. That sounds small, but in terms of cumulative trends and absolute magnitudes, it would represent an important achievement. After carefully studying economics, one gradually perceives the importance of quantitative differences of degree, as opposed to journalistic alleged differences of kind.

SUMMARY

A. THE NATURE OF ECONOMIC GROWTH

■ 1 The best measure of growth is real GNP, modified by data on leisure, population size, distribution, quality, and noneconomic factors.

■ 2 Advanced nations have historically shown rather steady growth, and recent trends have been generally favorable. Attitudes toward the desirability of expediting growth vary, and in most places the citizenry by their frequent political decisions seem to indicate a desire to step up the rate of growth beyond that implied by their daily market decisions on saving and consuming.

■ 3 Expanded research and exploration for resources can accelerate growth. So can raising the educational quality of the labor force.

---

[26] W. A. Lewis, "Is Economic Growth Desirable?," *Theory of Economic Growth*, Appendix (London: Allen & Unwin Ltd., 1955), pp. 420-421.

B. CONFLICTS BETWEEN GROWTH POLICIES AND OTHER AIMS

■ 4 Economists differ on whether structural unemployment (the inability of high national aggregate demand to blot out pockets of unemployment) is a real, or permanent, phenomenon.

■ 5 In Canada, one of the most serious types of structural unemployment is revealed by the striking differences between employment rates and per capita incomes in the various regions. These differences do not seem to disappear.

■ 6 Some "grass roots" regional policies, aimed at helping these poorer regions, are apparently based on faulty understanding of the origins of low wages and low stocks of capital, per worker. It is possible that the poorer regions of the poorer provinces are incapable of supporting so many people.

■ 7 But if regional and provincial permanence and autonomy are national goals, the decentralizing of many powers and duties now in Ottawa's hands may weaken Canada's ability to soak up structural and regional unemployment through potent monetary and fiscal policies. Thus Canadians may have to "trade-off" desired provincial power against economic growth and full employment.

C. NATIONAL STEADY GROWTH WITH PRICE STABILITY AND FULL EMPLOYMENT

■ 8 To increase the rate of capital accumulation (investment) when there has been no change in personal, municipal, and corporate propensities to consume and save requires, according to the New Economics, the following combination: low interest rates (credit ease) designed to increase the net-capital-formation component of each year's high-employment national product, coupled with restrictive fiscal policy aimed at eliminating the resulting inflationary tendencies by cutting down on disposable incomes and consumption. If monetary policy (credit ease) does not succeed, as may be the case in Canada's "open" economy, it may be augmented by qualitative tax changes such as accelerated depreciation, which grant subsidies and loopholes to investment spenders.

By this paired program of easy monetary and tight fiscal policy we may hope to lift the economy's fraction of high-employment output going to net investment for the future, reducing consumption at high employment by the same amount. Our optimism however must be tempered by the realization not only that our international-payments position may prevent monetary policy from raising investment, but also that we may find investment of the capital-deepening variety does not emerge from credit ease. Then we must search for other means to stimulate investment.

■ 9 The presence of cost-push tendencies toward sellers' inflation, while it still permits us to get the proper mixture of consumption and investment for any degree of high employment we aim at, does limit our ability to aim for very high employment levels that are consistent with price-level stability.

■ 10 The essence of a cost-push mechanism is this: Is there a tendency for price levels to rise even when a sizable and undesirable level of unemployment persists. If there is such a modern tendency, then policy decision (along a Phillips-curve trade-off between full employment and inflation) becomes hard and compromises may be necessary. "Price stability is a prerequisite for growth." "Growth is a prerequisite for reasonable price stability." "New mechanisms for an incomes policy must coordinate free collective bargaining." "Some price creep may at times be the necessary compromise that must be made in the interest of growth and tolerably high employment." These are varying views, among which citizens and statesmen must today choose.

■ 11 Though growth presents conflicts, it is essentially a cheerful subject.

QUESTIONS FOR DISCUSSION

1. Evaluate the arguments that GNP growth is or is not a major goal.

2. "Cut down on consumption to promote growth? Are you mad? Only high C can give high I. I don't grasp this 'deepening of capital'." Explain.

3. Why are education, research, and high employment conducive to growth?

4. "Returning political and fiscal power to the provinces should encourage growth, because the provinces have stronger incentives than Ottawa to promote their local development." Have they? Compare the effects of the provincial and federal policy instruments for promoting growth.

5. "High aggregate demand, even to the point of over-full-employment, will do more for structural unemployment than will any device of policy aimed at further training, shortening hours, or relocation. How then can one speak of a clash between 'structural' and 'aggregate-demand' unemployment?" Appraise this man's facts and interpretations.

6. How does the international openness of our economy threaten the effectiveness of a combination of austere fiscal policy and credit ease as a means to growth?

7. Look up some recent statistics and size up the creeping inflation problem. How would your vote on the creeping inflation problem differ from that of the SDU?

8. What tax changes favor growth? Are they provincial or federal taxes?

9. *Extra-credit problem:* Write $PQ = WL + $ Profit. Assuming Profit$/WL = c$, a constant, rewrite this as $P = W(L/Q)[1 + c] = [k]W/(Q/L)$. Interpret this to say "Price is proportional to wage rate and inversely proportional to (average) labor productivity: real wage grows at same rate as productivity, and so do real profits; when prices grow *from any cause*, their percentage increase equals money-W increase minus productivity increase." Set up a guidepost rule from this. For industries $i = 1, 2, \ldots,$ write a like formula for P_i. If $(Q/L)_i$ grow at *different* rates, how will you modify your guidepost rules if (1) the *average* price level is to be constant, (2) interindustry wage structure remains about the same, and (3) relative profit shares do too?

10. Review your understanding of the following concepts:
real NNP or GNP, per capita
managed tight-fiscal and
  easy-monetary policies
structural unemployment

cost-push (sellers' inflation), demand-pull
Phillips-curve trade-off
"incomes policy"
dilemmas of goals

INDEX